Sociology

Visit the *Sociology: making sense of society, third edition*
Companion Website at **www.pearsoned.co.uk/marsh** to find
valuable **student** learning material including:

- Multiple choice questions to revise and test understanding
- Weblinks to take investigation further
- Flashcards to help you revise and check key concepts

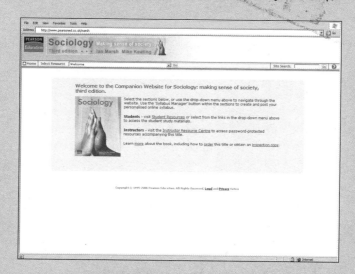

PEARSON
Education

We work with leading authors to develop the
strongest educational materials in sociology bringing
cutting-edge thinking and best learning practice
to a global market.

Under a range of well-known imprints, including
Prentice Hall, we craft high quality print and electronic
publications which help readers to understand and apply their
content, whether studying or at work.

To find out more about the complete range of our
publishing, please visit us on the World Wide Web at:
www.pearsoned.co.uk

Sociology
Making sense of society

Third Edition

Edited by

Ian Marsh

PEARSON

Prentice
Hall

Harlow, England • London • New York • Boston • San Francisco • Toronto • Sydney • Singapore • Hong Kong
Tokyo • Seoul • Taipei • New Delhi • Cape Town • Madrid • Mexico City • Amsterdam • Munich • Paris • Milan

Pearson Education Limited
Edinburgh Gate
Harlow
Essex CM20 2JE
England

and Associated Companies throughout the world

Visit us on the World Wide Web at:
www.pearsoned.co.uk

First published 1996
Second edition published 2000
Third edition published 2006

ISBN: 978-0-582-82312-9

British Library Cataloguing-in-Publication Data
A catalogue record for this book is available from the British Library

Library of Congress Cataloging-in-Publication Data
A catalog record for this book is available from the Library of Congress

10 9 8 7 6 5 4 3 2
10 09 08 07

Typeset in 9.75/13pt Minion by 35
Printed and bound by Mateu Cromo Artes Graficas, Madrid, Spain.

The publisher's policy is to use paper manufactured from sustainable forests.

short contents

contents

Contents

Supporting resources

Visit **www.pearsoned.co.uk/marsh** to find valuable online resources

Companion Website for students

- Multiple choice questions to revise and test understanding
- Weblinks to take investigation further
- Flashcards to help you revise and check key concepts

For instructors

- Instructor's Manual – including teaching notes highlighting key points and issues, sample essay questions and extra student activities for each chapter

Also: The Companion Website provides the following features:

- Search tool to help locate specific items of content
- E-mail results and profile tools to send results of quizzes to instructors
- Online help and support to assist with website usage and troubleshooting

For more information please contact your local Pearson Education sales representative or visit **www.pearsoned.co.uk/marsh**

case studies

world in focus

contributors

Rosie Campbell is a research associate in the Applied Research Centre of Liverpool Hope University, where she also co-ordinates the MA in applied women's studies. Her key areas of research are sexual health service provision and women's involvement in commercial sex. She is currently carrying out research on the health and welfare needs of women selling sex on the streets of Merseyside.

Anne Eyre specializes in disaster studies and lectures at the Centre for Disaster Management, Coventry University. She is a member of various international disaster research committees and is working to establish the subject of disasters as a more mainstream area of study within sociology.

Tony Finnegan is course leader for sociology at Liverpool Hope University. His main teaching and research interests are in social policy and welfare, globalization and popular culture. He has a particular interest in the development of autonomous learning using the World Wide Web.

Paul Graham lectures in political theory at Glasgow University. He is author (with John Hoffman) of *Introduction to Political Theory* (2006, Pearson Education).

Judith Green is senior lecturer in sociology at the London School of Hygiene and Tropical Medicine. Her main research interests are the sociology of accidents, primary care and health service organization. She is the author of *Risk and Misfortune: A Social Construction of Accidents* (1997, UCL Press) and co-author, with Nicki Thorogood, of *Analysing Health Policy: A Sociological Approach* (1998, Addison Wesley Longman).

Dawn Jones lectures in the Sociology Department at Liverpool Hope University. Her main teaching and research interests are in the areas of political sociology, economy and theories of the state and of 'race' and nation.

Mike Keating lectures in sociology at Liverpool Hope University, where he is course leader for the first-year course in sociology. His main teaching and research interests are in crime, deviance and the media. He is co-editor of *Classic and Contemporary Readings in Sociology* (1998, Addison Wesley Longman).

Mike Kilroe lectures in sociology and criminology at Liverpool Hope University. His main teaching and research interests are white-collar crime, police and policing.

Gayle Letherby is professor of sociology at the University of Plymouth. Her main teaching and research interests include methodology and epistemology, identities, working and learning in higher education and the sociology of travel.

Jen Marchbank is director of explorations, an interdisciplinary programme at Simon Fraser University in Canada. Her research interests include the politics of care, gender and education and conflict. She is author of *Women, Power and Politics: Comparative Studies of Childcare* (2000, Routledge) and co-editor of *States on Conflict: Gender, Violence and Resistance* (2000, Zed Books).

Ian Marsh lectures in sociology and criminology at Liverpool Hope University, where he is director of the MA in criminal justice. His main teaching and research interests are in crime, criminal justice and punishment. He has written, co-written and edited a number of texts, including *Criminal Justice: An Introduction to Philosophies, Theories and Practice* (2004, Routledge), *Sociology: Dealing with Data* (1999, Addison Wesley Longman), *Classic and Contemporary Readings in Sociology* (1998, Addison Wesley Longman) and *Sociology in Focus* (1995, Causeway Press).

Ian McIntosh lectures in Sociology in the Department of Applied Social Science at the University of Stirling. His research and teaching interests include the sociology of work and identities. He is co-author of *Get Set for Sociology* (2005, Edinburgh University Press) and editor of *Classical Sociological Theory* (1997, Edinburgh University Press).

Janet McKenzie lectures in the sociology of education at Anglia Polytechnic University. She also works as a therapeutic counsellor. Her research and teaching interests include the sociology and politics of education, the needs of families bereaved by homicide and other aspects of bereavement. She is author of *Changing Education: A Sociology of Education Since 1944* (2001, Prentice Hall).

Sam Pryke lectures in Sociology at Liverpool Hope University. His main teaching and research interests are in nationalism, race and ethnicity and globalization.

Samantha Punch lectures in Sociology in the Department of Applied Social Science at the University of Stirling. Her research and teaching interests include the sociology of childhood and development. She is co-author of *Get Set for Sociology* (2005, Edinburgh University Press) and co-editor of *Young Rural Lives* (2006, Routledge).

Nicki Thorogood is lecturer in sociology at the GKT Dental Institute, King's College London. Her main research interests are the sociology of public health and health promotion and of the body and identity. She is the co-author, with Judith Green, of *Analysing Health Policy: A Sociological Approach* (1998, Addison Wesley Longman).

preface

The third edition of *Sociology: Making sense of society* provides a general introduction to sociology. It is aimed at students following introductory sociology courses in higher education: in particular, first-year undergraduates following courses in sociology. It will also be useful for students on vocational and related courses where sociology forms an integral part of their studies – for instance, courses in the fields of nursing, social work, social policy and criminal justice. For some students such introductory courses provide their initial and only formal study of sociology; for others it serves as a basis for further study. Also, some students come to their first-year courses having studied A-level or access courses in sociology, while others have not studied the subject before. Indeed, one of the main objectives behind the development of this book has been to produce a text that meets and responds to the diversity of background knowledge of sociology among students starting their higher education courses.

While we would encourage students to read as widely and diversely as possible in sociology, the textbook is, we feel, a crucial tool for enabling students to get to grips with a new subject and for stimulating an interest and enthusiasm that will encourage them in further exploration of it. Although it is easy and sometimes fashionable to criticize large, all encompassing textbooks as presenting a formula-like approach, our feeling is that such texts play an important role in promoting their subjects; and, as far as sociology goes, we hope that this book will play a small part in that endeavour. (Indeed, it is often the textbooks that we had to buy and were told to use that remain in our memories long after we have finished the formal study of a subject.)

We have tried to produce a text that meets the needs of students and their tutors in contemporary higher education. Large numbers and ever-growing staff–student ratios are placing increasing pressure on teachers in higher education. In emphasizing an interactive approach to learning, we have tried to produce a book that will, in part at least, remove the burden of everything coming from the teacher and encourage students to become active participants in the learning process.

New to this edition

As a result of the very positive and encouraging responses to the first and second editions, the third edition has concentrated on refining and developing the content and features of its predecessors. In terms of the content, as well as general updating of research findings and data, each of the chapters in the original text has been reviewed by an expert in that particular area of sociology, which has led to substantial additional material being added to the text. Each chapter has been fully updated to include current data and issues – such as Islamaphobia, migration, 'lad' culture, global inequalities, third world debt and poverty. The third edition of *Sociology: Making sense of society* also includes two newly commissioned chapters – on Age (by Sam Punch) and Nationalism (by Sam Pryke).

Guided tour

'Key issues'
outline the main concepts and
themes at the start of each chapter

Web guided tour
- mutliple-choice questions to check your
  understanding
- flashcard definitions to check your knowledge
  of key terms
- links to the web for further investigation

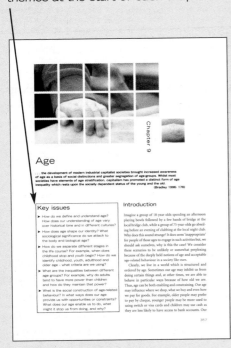

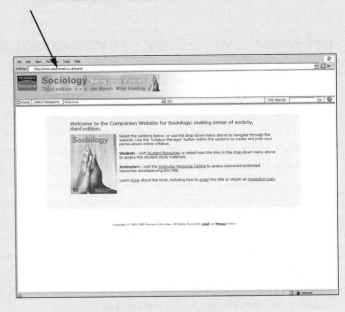

'Stop and think'
provide topical questions and
exercises to create discussion and
debate, and provide opportunity
for reflection

Case studies
focus in detail on a key topic. Follow-
up questions test understanding and
encourage reflection

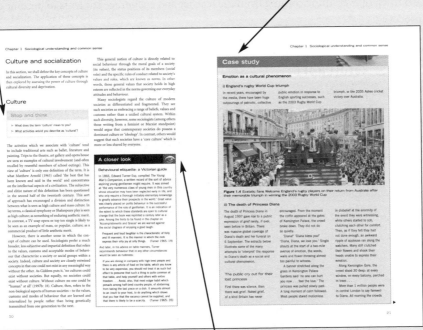

'A closer look'
highlight and expand on a key
concept, issue or individual

Guided tour

'World in focus'
provide stimulating case material with a global perspective

Primary Extracts
offer material from key texts, providing thorough coverage of theory and methodology

Links
highlight related sections and topic areas, at the end of each chapter

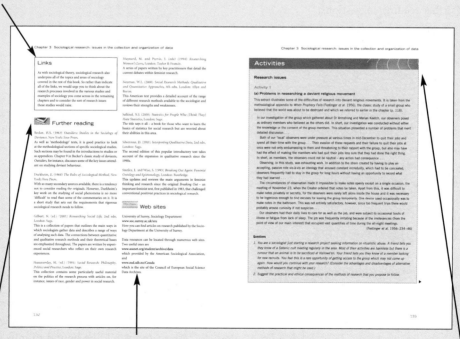

Annotated further reading and websites
provide an opportunity to investigate the topics further

Activities
provide opportunies to consolidate learning and apply understanding, as well as allowing deeper exploration of the ideas contained within the chapter

How to use the book

Each chapter consists of a number of features outlined below:

Chapter openers with specially commissioned cartoons, key issues and an opening quote to introduce the reader to the subject.

 Case studies, which contain specific examples of research, international perspectives and biographies of key writers.

 A closer look boxed sections, which highlight definitions and terminology and generally explain in more detail key themes mentioned in the text.

 Stop and think points to encourage reflection and discussion. These generally take the form of questions for students to consider either in a group/seminar situation or by themselves. In some cases they ask students to do things and may be developed for class exercises. Some ask for initial and gut reactions to an issue or to what they have just read; others require more thought and analysis.

 World in Focus boxes provide a global view of or perspective on a key issue.

Each chapter ends with:

 Summaries to remind students of the key themes, points and issues discussed in the chapter.

Links to show connections across chapters.

 Further reading suggestions.

 Web sites to encourage further investigation.

 Activities that enable a fuller exploration of some of the ideas or material looked at. These could form the basis for fuller classroom or seminar examination and discussion. In some instances, they could also be used as a basis for group or individual student projects.

A **Glossary** provides brief definitions of key terms and concepts used within the text.

Acknowledgements

As with the first and second editions, this book has been a collaborative endeavour between the team of writers and Pearson Education. We have had tremendous support from a number of people at Pearson Education – in particular Andrew Taylor, Emma Travis, Nicola Chilvers, Rhian McKay and Chris Shaw. It is conventional for writers to thank the various family members, friends, colleagues and academic influences who have helped and inspired them. With fifteen writers contributing to this book, such a list would be excessive and would be bound to miss out some key influence.

Publisher Acknowledgements

We are grateful to the following for permission to reproduce copyright material:

Figures 1.1, 17.12, 17.13 and Table 6.1 and 6.2 courtesy of Times Newspapers Ltd; Figure 1.3 courtesy of Photofusion Picture Library, © Brenda Prince/Photofusion; Figures 2.2; 5.1 and 10.10 images courtesy of Mary Evans Picture Library; Figure 2.5 Cartoon by Angela Martin; Figure 4.1 image courtesy of Explorer/Robert Harding, Robert Harding Picture Library Ltd; Figure 4.3 courtesy of the Institute for Employment Studies; Chapter 4 Table page 154 from HUMAN DEVELOPMENT REPORT website by United Nations Development Programme, copyright © 2004 by the United Nations Development Programme. Used by permission of Oxford University Press, Inc; Table 5.3 from *The British General Election of 2001*, Palgrave Macmillan (Butler, D. and Kavanagh, D.). Reproduced with permission of Palgrave Macmillan; Table 5.4 reproduced courtesy of MORI; Table 5.6 from *Contemporary British Society: A New Introduction to Sociology*, Cambridge: Polity Press (Abercrombie, N., Warde, A., Soothill, K., Urry, J. and Walby, S. 1988); Figure 5.3(a–c) from 'One-dimensional policy competition between 2 parties with voter preferences concentrated in the centre of the policy spectrum' in *Private Desires, Political Actions: An Invitation to the Politics of Rational Choice*, Sage Publications Ltd (Laver, M. 1997). Reprinted by permission of Sage Publications Ltd; Figure 5.4 Antoine Serra/in Visu/Carbis; Figures 5.5 and 5.7 from *Modernization and Postmodernization*, Princeton University Press (Inglehart, R. 1997) © Princeton University Press. Reprinted by permission of Princeton University Press; Figure 5.6 image courtesy of Empics, The Press Association; Table 5.7 from *Modernity and Self-Identity*, Cambridge: Polity Press (Giddens, A. 1991); Table 6.1 from 'How many classes are there in contemporary society?' in *Sociology* Vol 24 p. 389, Sage Publications Ltd (Runciman, W. G. 1990). Reprinted by permission of Sage Publications Ltd; Tables 6.1 and 6.2 NI Syndication; Figure 6.5 from *Income and Wealth; The latest evidence*, Joseph Rowntree Foundation (Hills, J. 1998). Reproduced by permission of the Joseph Rowntree Foundation; Figure 7.3 © *Men's Health*; Figure 7.4 © *Women's Health*; Figure 8.1 image courtesy of Getty Images; Figure 9.1 image courtesy of Grass Roots International; Figure 9.3 and Table 9.1 from *Growing Up and Growing Old* (Hockey, J. and James, A. 1993). Reprinted by permission of Sage Publications Ltd; Figure 10.7 from *The Sociology of Health and Healing* (Stacey, M. 1988). Reproduced courtesy of Taylor & Francis Group; Figure 10.9 from *Archives of Environmental Health* 12: 246–66 (Kaslm, S. V. and Cobb, S. 1966). Reprinted with permission of the Helen Dwight Reid Educational Foundation. Published by Heldref Publications, 1319 Eighteenth St., NW, Washington, DC 20036-1802. Copyright © (1996); Table 10.4 courtesy of The International Council of Nurses, Switzerland; Figure 10.11 courtesy of Guardian Newspapers Limited 2003 using data provided by the Royal College of Nursing; Table 10.5 from *OHE Compendium of Health Statistics, 17th Edition, 2005–2006, Radcliffe Publishing* (Yuen, P. 2001) courtesy of the Office of Health Economics. Table 10.7 from 'Childhood injuries: extent of the problem, epidemiological trends, and costs', *Injury Prevention 4* (Supplement): s10-16 (Roberts, I., DiGuiseppi, C. and Warde, H. 1998). Reproduced with permission from the BMJ Publishing Group; Figure 11.2 image courtesy of David Lomax/Robert Harding, Robert Harding Picture Library Ltd; Figures 11.3; 11.7; 11.9; 11.10; 11.11 and 11.12 from HUMAN DEVELOPMENT REPORT 2004: IDENTITY, DIVERSITY AND GLOBALIZATION by United Nations Development Programme, copyright © 2004 by the United Nations Development Programme. Used by permission of Oxford University Press, Inc; Figure 13.3a from *Sociology Update* p. 21 (Denscombe, M. 1998) Leicester: Olympus Books; Figure 13.3b © Jose Luis Pelaez, Inc./Corbis; Figure 13.5 from *Sociology Update* p. 19 (Denscombe, M. 1998) Leicester: Olympus Books; Figure 13.6 from *Sociology Update* p. 18 (Denscombe, M. 1998) Leicester: Olympus Books; Figure 14.11 from Eurostat Yearbook (2001) © European Communities, Source Eurostat; Figure 15.1 image courtesy of Luca Tettoni/Robert Harding, Robert Harding Picture Library Ltd; Figure 15.3 from *Sociology Update* p. 40 (Denscombe, M. 1998) Leicester: Olympus Books; Figure 15.4 image courtesy of Robert Harding Picture Library Ltd; Table 15.1 © The Archbishops' Council, 2005, and reproduced by permission; Figure 15.5 from *Sociology Update* p. 39 (Denscombe, M. 1998) Leicester: Olympus Books; Table 16.2 from *Sociology Update* p. 24 (Denscombe, M. 1998) Leicester: Olympus Books; Figure 16.1 courtesy of Jenny Pate/ Robert Harding Picture Library Ltd; Figure 16.3 copyright Guardian Newspapers Limited 2005; Figures 17.5 and 17.6 from *Mass Communications Theory: An introduction*, Sage Publications Ltd (McQuail, D. 1994). Reprinted by permission of Sage Publications Ltd; Table, Chapter 17 from *The Media: An Introduction*, Longman (Briggs, A. and

Cobley, P. 2002); Figure 17.11 image courtesy of Professor Dennis Galletta, University of Pittsburgh; Figure 17.14 © The Daily Telegraph 2005.

p. 4 Empics, p. 21 Empics, p. 29 Empics, p. 33 Empics, p. 44 Corbis/Bettmann, p. 58 Corbis/Hulton Archive, p. 68 Empics, p. 89 Scoop, France, p. 90 Getty/Gary M Prior, p. 107 Corbis/Pascal Parrot/Sygma, p. 119 Getty/Time & Life Pictures, p. 115 www.johnbirdsall.co.uk, p. 149 Getty/Sean Gallup, p. 159 Corbis/Sherwin Crasto/Reuters, p. 216 Empics, p. 264 Getty/Dave Benett, p. 275 Getty/AFP/Frederic J Brown, p. 297 Getty/John Chapple, p. 304 Getty/Time & Life Pictures, p. 349 Getty/AFP/Odd Anderson, p. 362 Corbis/Reuters, p. 367 Ulrike Preuss/Photofusion, p. 404, Corbis/Bob Krist, p. 420 Empics, p. 454 Alamy/Penny Tweedie, p. 455 (top) Alamy/Ambient Images Inc, p. 455 (bottom) Corbis/Liu Liqun, p. 499 Empics, p. 502 Empics, p. 504, Empics, p. 512 Getty/Scott Barbour, p. 513 BBC Photo Library, p. 520 Corbis/Neal Preston, p. 524 Ulrike Preuss/Photofusion, p. 534 Corbis/Michael Keller, p. 536 Corbis/Tom & Dee McCarthy, p. 549 Getty/AFP/Alessandro Abbonizio, p. 557 Corbis/Christine Osborne, p. 563 Jacky Chapman/Photofusion, p. 567 Getty/Catherine Ledner, p. 576 Jacky Chapman/Photofusion, p. 593 www.johnbirdsall.co.uk, p. 638 Empics, p. 672 Empics, p. 679 Empics.

Milo Books for an extract from *Cocky: The Rise and Fall of Curtis Warren Britain's Biggest Drug Baron* by Tony Barnes, Richard Elias and Peter Walsh; the *Independent* for extracts from 'Doctor Blames Parents for "Worse Case of Malnutrition" ' by Ian Herbert published in the *Independent* 24ᵗʰ November 2004, 'Why employ women when there are men out of work? It's better for women to do housework' by Helen Womack published in the *Independent* 21ˢᵗ March 1993, and 'Man loses fight to prove child is his' published in the *Independent* 6ᵗʰ February 1993; Guardian Newspapers Limited for extracts from 'Fly Away Peter' by Steve Mair published in the *Guardian* 18ᵗʰ October 1986, 'Full-time workers fall by 35 per cent' by Will Hutton published in the *Guardian* 3ʳᵈ April 1995, 'Rich and Excluded' by Richard Thomas published in the *Observer* 20ᵗʰ September 1998, 'Middle Class professionals are Britain's hidden poor' by David Ward published in the *Guardian* 26ᵗʰ July 2004, 'Third of children in the north-west live in poverty' by Helen Carter published in the *Guardian* 12ᵗʰ March 2005, 'Tebbit's cricket loyalty test hit for six' by John Carvel published in the *Guardian* 8ᵗʰ January 2004, 'Breakdown of family life can lead to crime' by Nikki Knewstub published in the *Guardian* 12ᵗʰ October 1991, 'You really can die of a broken heart' by John Illman published in the *Observer* 17ᵗʰ May 1998, 'The loutish lad is dead: Enter the caring lad in cashmere' by James Robinson published in the *Observer* 24ᵗʰ April 2005, and 'In the hood' by Gareth McLean published in the *Guardian* 13ᵗʰ May 2005; Philip Allan Updates for an extract from *Sociology Review* Vol 8 No 2 (1998) pp. 6–7; Pearson Education Limited for an extract from *Modern Social Theory* by Ian Craib; The British Society for Gerontology for an extract from 'Bedroom Abuse: the hidden work in a nursing home' by Geraldine Lee-Treweek published in *Generations Review* 4(1); HarperCollins Publishers Limited for an extract from *Refusing to be a Man* by John Stoltenberg © John Stoltenberg 1990; John Arlidge for his article 'Forget black, forget white: EA is what's hot' published in the *Observer* 4ᵗʰ January 2004; Jon Burnett for his article 'The South Asian Crime Unit: policing by ethnicity' published on the CARF website at www.carf.demon.co.uk/feat58.html; Taylor & Francis Group for an extract from 'Negotiating autonomy: Childhoods in rural Bolivia' by Samantha Punch from *Conceptualising Child-Adult Relations* edited by Berry Mayall and Leena Alanen published by Routledge 2001; Open University Press and McGraw-Hill Publishing Company for an extract from *Towards a Sociology for Childhood* by Berry Mayall published by Open University Press 2002; Cambridge University Press and Professor Tobias Hecht for an extract from *At Home in the Street: Street Children of Northeast Brazil* by Tobias Hecht published by Cambridge University Press 1998; Allyn and Bacon, a Pearson Education Company, for an extract from 'Changing Patterns of Family Life in India' by Pittu Laungani from *Families in Global Perspective* by Jaipaul L. Roopnarine and Uwe P. Gielen © Pearson Education Inc 2005; Times Educational Supplement for extracts from 'Unsung Success of Chinese pupils' by Dorothy Lepkowska published in *Times Educational Supplement* 27ᵗʰ August 2005, and 'Countries seek to close wealth gap' by Adi Bloom published in *Times Educational Supplement* 31ˢᵗ October 2003; Michael Fitzpatrick for his article 'Minister pulls plug on liberal policies' published in *Times Educational Supplement* 4ᵗʰ February 2005 © Michael Fitzpatrick 2005; Sage Publications for an extract from *Sociological Snapshots* by Jack Levin published by Pine Forge Press 1993; Blackwell Publishing Limited for an extract from *The British Press and Broadcasting Since 1945* by Colin Seymour-Ure; The Daily Telegraph for an extract from 'Children bombarded with junk food adverts' published in *The Daily Telegraph* 1st March 2004; and Reuters Limited for an extract from 'Iran parliament passes ban on satellite dishes' published in the *Guardian* 2nd January 1995 © Reuters Limited 1995.

The following are included courtesy of the United Kingdom Government:

Table 6.3 from Inland Revenue statistics; Figure 6.4 from Social Trends 35; Figure 6.6 from New Earnings Survey in Labour Market Trends; Figure 6.7 from Institute for Fiscal Studies; Figure 6.8 from European Community Household panel; Tables 8.1; 8.2 and 8.3 from Equal Opportunities Commission; Table 8.4 from Survey of English Housing; Tables 10.1 and 10.8 from *Living in Britain: Results from the 2001 General Household Survey*; Table 10.3 from DOH (1999) *Health and personal social services statistics for England, 1999*; Figure 10.13 from Longitudinal Study, Office for National Statistics; Table 10.10 from *Living in Britain: the Results of the 1996 General Household Survey* (1998); Figure 11.1 from the UK National Statistical Office (2005); Figures 14.1; 14.8 and 14.10 from www.dfes.gov.uk; Figures 14.6 and 14.9, and Tables 14.1; 14.2 and 14.3 from Social Trends 34 (2004); Figure 14.13 from *Minority Ethnic Attainment and Participation in Education and Training: The Evidence*, Department for Education and Skills: Research Topic Paper RTP01-03 (Bhattacharyya, G., Ison, L. and Blair, M. 2003); Tables 16.3 and 16.4 from Social Trends 33 (2003); Table 16.5 from Social Trends 24 (1994); Figure 17.1 from General Household Survey (2002); Figure 17.2 from National Statistics online.

Crown copyright material is reproduced with the permission of the Controller of HMSO and the Queen's Printer for Scotland.

We are grateful to the Financial Times Limited for permission to reprint the following material:

Table 17.2 Election 2005: 'What the papers said', FT.com, © *Financial Times*, 14 April 2005.

In some instances we have been unable to trace the owners of copyright material, and we would appreciate any information that would enable us to do so.

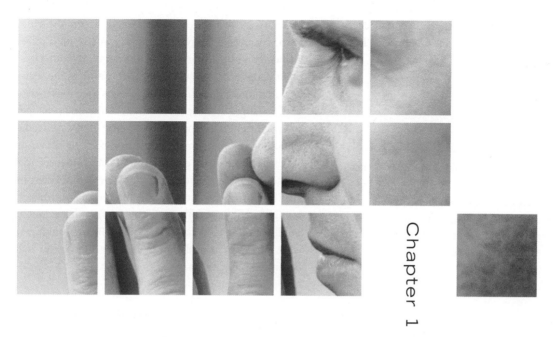

Chapter 1

Sociological understanding and common sense

I am always somewhat surprised when college students estimate that 30 per cent of the population of the United States is Jewish (actually, the figure is close to 1.9 per cent); that 40 per cent of all Americans are black (actually the figure for those who regard themselves as black or African American is more like 12 per cent); that 60 per cent of our population is Catholic (actually, the figure is 20 per cent maximum); that 40 per cent of our elders are in nursing homes (the figure is more like 4 per cent).

Where does this misinformation about our society come from? Why can't Americans get their social facts straight? Part of the answer is that all of us are socialised with unrepresentative samples of social reality. Inevitably, we learn to view the world from our own biased and limited slice of experience. We tend to apply what we see every day to what we don't see every day.

(Levin 1993: 44)

Key issues

➤ What is sociology?

➤ What are its origins as a discipline?

➤ What kinds of explanation does sociology offer for social and personal behaviour?

➤ What is culture and how does it affect social and personal behaviour?

Introduction

There is no reason to suppose that students (or non-students for that matter) in other countries would be any better informed about the 'social geography' of their own societies. Most of us were brought up in areas that could be characterized as predominantly middle or working class and that have predominantly white or ethnic minority populations. Most of us still mix mainly with people from similar class and ethnic backgrounds. Most of us grew up with people of a similar age and will still have as our closest friends people of a similar age. While there are many exceptions to these generalizations, modern, large-scale societies have almost invariably organized themselves by separating their schools and neighbourhoods by race, class, religion and age. It is not surprising that our knowledge of the social facts and geography of our own societies is so inaccurate.

Sociology provides us with a more accurate picture of the social geography of the society we live in. It offers particular and exciting ways of understanding ourselves, other people and the social world. It examines the social facts and forces that affect us all. It helps us to make sense of the changes that occur around us all the time; changes such as the effect of new technologies on everyday life; the variations in employment patterns as factories open or close; the influence on education, health and other services of economic and political philosophies and policies. In view of the insights into social life that sociology provides, it might seem strange that it is not a subject that is taught to all children as a matter of course. Before looking at what sociology is and how it has developed, we shall consider briefly its 'image'.

Case study

The Kray twins: local heroes?

The Krays were an old-fashioned East End family – tight, self-sufficient and devoted to each other. The name was Austrian, and the twins had Irish, Romany and Jewish blood. The centre of their world was to remain the tiny terrace house at 178 Vallance Road where they grew up and where their Aunt May and their maternal grandparents still lived. The area was badly bombed in the war; before that it was one of the poorest parts of the entire East End and a breeding ground for criminals. It was Bill Sykes' home ground, 'The Rookeries' of Dickens were once just down the road, and Jack the Ripper murdered one of his last victims around the corner in Hanbury Street.

The house, 178 Vallance Road, was tiny, the second in a row of four blank-faced Victorian terraced cottages. There was no bathroom,

the lavatory was in the yard at the back, and day and night the house shook as the Liverpool Street trains roared past the bedroom windows. For Violet none of this mattered. Her parents were just around the corner; so was her sister, Rose. Her other sister, May, was next door but one, and her brother, John Lee, kept the café across the street.

And old Grandfather Lee, who still kept his famous left hook in trim, punching a mattress hung up in the yard. He would sit with the twins for hours in his special chair by the fire . . . And sometimes the old man would talk about the other heroes of the old East End, its criminals. Spud Murphy of Hoxton, who killed two men in a spieler in Whitechapel and who shouted to the police that he'd bring a machine-gun and finish everyone off before he was caught; Martin and Baker, two Bethnal Green men who took the nine o'clock walk after shooting three policemen at Carlisle. And for the old man, Jack

the Ripper's murders were still a local happening.

(Adapted from Pearson 1972: 12–27)

Ronnie Kray's funeral, 1995

The East End of London accorded one of its most infamous sons the equivalent of a state funeral yesterday. Crowds big enough to gladden the heart of an emperor turned out to shower the last journey of Ronnie Kray with tribute, and to greet his handcuffed twin brother Reggie as though he were a conquering hero . . .

The Kray twins, who had long ago assumed the status of folk heroes, were each serving 30 years for different murders. Ronnie, the elder of the two by 45 minutes, died of a heart attack in Broadmoor two weeks ago aged 61; Reggie was let out of Maidstone for the day under heavy guard.

(*The Times* 30.3.95: 1)

Case study (continued)

Figure 1.1 The funeral of Ronnie Kray, from *The Times* 30.3.95
(Photograph by Adrian Brooks, courtesy of Times Newspapers Ltd)

Case study (continued)

Crowds gather for Kray's funeral

Large crowds are lining the streets in east London, as mourners prepare to say farewell to gangland killer Reggie Kray.

Six black plumed horses are leading the procession to St Matthews Church for the funeral, which Kray planned in the final days before his death from cancer.

Pavements along Bethnal Green Road have been cordoned off and there is a heavy police presence, as people gather outside the funeral directors where Kray's body was in a chapel of rest.

The last of three notorious brothers, Kray will be buried in the family plot at Chingford, alongside his twin, Ronnie, and older brother Charlie.

The procession is expected to bring the East End to a temporary standstill, with celebrity friends of the Krays among the mourners.

The cortege is scheduled to stop in Vallance Raod, where Kray and his twin brother Ronnie were brought up.

Outside the undertakers, the pavement was bedecked with wreaths – some in the shape of boxing gloves and others in the shape of an 'R'.

One wreath of roses was from the EastEnders actress, and Kray's friend, Barbara Windsor.

(BBC News 11.10.00)

Questions

1. *Does social background offer a 'complete explanation' for the Krays' criminal behaviour? What other factors might have played a part?*

2. *Why do you think the Krays have become 'folk heroes'?*

Case study

Cocky: Curtis Warren – Britain's biggest drug baron

Curtis Warren rose from being a street mugger to an international drug baron and one of the richest and most successful British criminals who has ever been caught. He is currently in prison in Holland. The extract below refers to his upbringing in the Toxteth district of Liverpool and is taken from the biography *Cocky: The Rise and Fall of Curtis Warren Britain's Biggest Drug Baron*

(Barnes, Elias and Walsh 2000)

Figure 1.2 Curtis Warren

On July 22, 1960, Curtis, then twenty-five, and Sylvia, twenty-one, were married at St Vincent of Paul's Roman Catholic Church. They took rooms in a Victorian townhouse at 238 Upper Parliament Street, the long, broad Toxteth thoroughfare that dissects the postal district of Liverpool 8 . . . Curtis Francis Warren was born at home on 31 May 1963 . . .

The Granby ward, where the Warrens lived . . . was a close-knit and self-supporting community where everyone knew everyone else. Down at

Case study (continued)

the seaward end of Parliament Street, the dockyards were still busy, the alehouses overflowed and prostitutes lolled under the lamplights, offering cheap sex . . . The streets were a bazaar. Granby Street had its Muslim butchers and its Arab, Pakistani and Bangladeshi food stores displaying strange fruits, vegetables and spices. Old West Indians in Panama hats smoked ganja on their doorsteps . . . At night it came alive. A clampdown on drinking dens in the city centre in 1957 to spruce up the city for an anniversary had pushed many shebeens into Toxteth . . .

Curtis junior followed his brother into the local Catholic primary school before enrolling at a comprehensive with a particularly tough reputation. Apparently he was rarely there beyond his early teens; though his mind was extremely acute, he did not take to the discipline of lessons. He was not alone: some schools regarded twenty per cent truancy as good . . . So Warren and others like him would 'sag' school. They had no money to go anywhere and no gardens to play in, so they spent the days hanging around . . .

Crime also beckoned. As unemployment began to rise from 1974, Toxteth was particularly hard hit. Jobs vanished; even casual work on the docks dried up. If you were black or mixed race, forget it . . . The area drew inwards, became alienated and bitter. By the later part of the decade Granby Street was littered with broken glass, its dwindling number of shops encased in wire grilles to deter burglars . . . In an increasingly tense environment, innocent child pastime paled. Nicking cars and joyriding became a fad . . .

Curtis Warren had just turned twelve when the police stopped him in a stolen car. Though barely big enough to see over the steering wheel, he was charged with the unauthorised taking of a motor vehicle . . . A year later he graduated to the magistrates court, this time for burglary. He was ordered to spend twenty-four hours at an attendance centre.

Young Curtis was caught on a spiral of petty offending. It seemed the thing to do. Youth crime was becoming a burning issue in the city. In 1975, a quarter of all people prosecuted in Liverpool were juveniles . . .

Young men of mixed race – like Warren – aroused particular unease in an almost exclusively white police force . . .

On 20 July 1978, the magistrates sent him to a detention centre for the first time, for three months. The centres, known as 'DCs', were schools for crime . . . Warren treated the place as a joke and came out worse than he went in.

(Adapted from Barnes, Elias and Walsh 2000: 14–21)

Questions

The Krays were brought up in the 1940s and 1950s and Curtis Warren in the 1970s and 1980s.

1. *Suggest the main similarities and differences between their respective upbringings.*

2. *What explanations can you offer – both for the similarities and the differences?*

The image of sociology

In the mid-1960s Peter Berger published a very readable introduction to the study of sociology which began by informing us that 'There are very few jokes about socio-logists'. He explained that this was probably due to their low profile in 'the popular imagination' (Berger 1967a). However, much has changed since then and sociology has a far higher public profile, largely due to its inclusion in the school curriculum, its status as a degree-bearing discipline and the regular appearance of its experts on television and radio documentaries. As a result the sociologist no longer escapes humorous mud-slinging at the professions. Whether it is at the hands of Malcolm Bradbury (*The History Man*), Ben Elton (*The Young Ones*) or simple throw-away comments about the number of sociologists it takes to change a lightbulb, the jokes have not been particularly flattering and have tended to rely on crude and predictable stereotypes.

Dr Christopher Pole made use of the BBC's *Punters* programme (Radio 4, 8 August 1991) to defend the professional and academic status of sociology and to broadcast his objections to the ridicule that sociology often attracts from the media. In the studio debate that followed, Roger Scruton (Professor of Aesthetics at Birkbeck College) castigated the study of sociology as 'an endless quest for knowledge about trivia'. Among other things, he complained that sociology was intellectually sloppy, politically biased and morally corrupting. 'This subject,' he said 'has concentrated on those areas of enquiry which are interesting to someone with a socialist agenda; obsessed with class, with domination, with hierarchy and exploitation . . . all those old ghastly nineteenth century ideas. All this amounts to a case to be answered by the sociological establishment.'

Dr Pole was joined in the studio by Professor of Sociology Jennifer Platt, who argued that such misconceptions informed much of the bad press received by sociology and the public ignorance and distrust surrounding it. Dr Pole advocated its continued study on the grounds that it encouraged inquiry, demanded intellectual precision and asked awkward questions:

> In any kind of sociology it is absolutely essential to question what we are doing and what we are being told . . . what we are studying and from which perspective. That is the very essence of the discipline; that is why I do sociology because I want to investigate, because I want to work at various different perspectives.

As this was precisely the reason for Professor Scruton's disenchantment it is hardly surprising that he remained unconvinced. He concluded by warning the audience:

> There are certain matters which should not be pried into . . . least of all by half-baked lefties from universities. . . . Because of this relentless questioning of human institutions and human realities it may be inappropriate for young people to study it.

Such views are no doubt shared by some politicians, journalists and members of the public but sociology is also an increasingly popular subject in schools and colleges throughout the Western world. Despite the attacks on its academic credentials, educational status and practical worth, sociology has survived to establish itself not only as a separate discipline but also as an integral part of education in general. As the Higginson Report (DES 1988) pointed out:

> A free society depends for its strength on the ability of individual members to make sense of their surroundings and to think for themselves.
>
> (quoted in McNeill 1990)

Sociology is regarded as an essential part of professional training courses for teachers, social workers and people who work within the National Health Service and the criminal justice system. In the United States and in continental Europe trained sociologists are employed as consultants in areas such as industrial relations; it is clear that having a degree in the subject is no barrier to future career prospects. Ministers in both Labour and Conservative Cabinets of recent times have held university degrees in the subject, while Ralph Dahrendorf, formerly Professor of Sociology and Director of the London School of Economics, was elevated to the House of Lords for his contribution to public life.

A review of university vice-chancellors in 1998 showed that the tradition of promoting classical academics from Oxbridge and public school backgrounds has changed and social scientists now account for over 30 per cent of these posts (the *Guardian* 14.7.98). In 1999 the *Guardian* could report that ten university chiefs are sociologists, with Anthony Giddens at the LSE the best known (19.1.99). This recognition of the value of 'sociological capital' in the labour market has led Sheila Miles (1997) to argue that skills learned on sociology courses can be a definite bonus in 'the process of job hunting'.

A closer look

A view from the girls

In this extract, three sociology graduates evaluate the usefulness of studying sociology.

Joanne

At university, the individual courses were of varying interest to me. Some in particular stand out as having helped to form my opinions and provide me with a much more tolerant and open view of society. At first, the issues tackled such as race, feminism and poverty gave me an unexpected cynicism about the world, but also made me more aware of different issues and the difficulties facing individuals within society. I feel that I learnt an awful lot about people and the structures within which we live. A focus on the workings of contemporary society has provided me with an insight which I feel has improved my understanding of the world.

Meeta

Learning about culture, race, class and sex has been invaluable during every step of my working life.

Although I have worked mostly in administration and computer support, what I have learned from sociology has taught me that there are so many inequalities. Recognizing and understanding how they arise does actually help to confront these challenges in a positive and constructive manner.

Jackie

When I did my teacher training, I realized how much sociology contributed to my understanding of education. It made me realize that people in societies do not behave the way they do by nature only, but they also *learn* behaviour. In my training, it was apparent that education was not just concerned with academic, but also with social learning. When teaching children about acceptable ways to behave, I could see that I was part of the socialization process.

As a social worker, I continue to be part of this process as I act *in loco parentis* to the children with whom I work. Some of these children are estranged from their families. Again, I have found that a sociological outlook has helped me to appreciate the various forces and pressures at work in society and this has helped me to be less judgemental in my work and more understanding of my clients' situations.

This view has also been useful in my general life. I would say that studying sociology has made me more open-minded, more accepting of difference, and more able to question societal norms.

(Adapted from 'Viewpoints from three sociology graduates' in Ballard *et al.* 1997: 372–4)

Stop and think

➤ What did you think sociology was about before you started to study the subject?

➤ What do other people think sociology is? (Carry out a brief survey of friends and family.)

➤ 'Sociology is nothing more than an endless quest for knowledge about trivia.' How would you respond to this attack on sociology from Roger Scruton?

➤ Why do you think some people – including politicians and journalists – might feel threatened by a subject which encourages the questioning of 'human institutions and human realities'?

The sociological perspective

We have already heard sociology dismissed as 'an endless quest for knowledge about trivia', and it is often criticized as being nothing more than 'common sense'. On the other hand, we find the subject being attacked as 'too theoretical' or obsessed with statistics. If aspects of social life such as poverty, child abuse, crime and educational failure can be regarded as 'trivia' then the first complaint must be true, but it is doubtful whether you would be reading this book if you agreed with it. The apparent contradictions between the view of sociology as common sense and the counter-objection (from many students) that it is too complex in its approach to everyday life can be resolved. Although sociology deals with everyday life and common sense, that does not mean that it limits itself to explanations which simply depend on feelings of what makes sense. Such opinions would rely on what Bauman (1990) has called 'a personalised world-view' and should be distinguished from a sociological perspective. Sociology and sociologists have a very strong relationship with common sense in that the object of study is often the common-sense view of social reality held by members of society. It is in the way that they study the experience of ordinary people's daily lives, the questions they ask and the concepts they use that distinguishes sociologists from other people and disciplines.

The theories and methods used by sociologists are the concern of Chapters 2 and 3, but we should note that in studying people going about their everyday lives, sociologists employ a scientific and theoretical perspective which seeks to establish some kind of factual picture of

Finally, it is worth asking whether the study of any subject should have to be justified in purely vocational terms. Sociology retains its popularity with young and old alike because it asks questions about the very things that directly affect our lives. It has an immediate relevance because it provides insights into the workings of the world we inhabit. Although he was writing in the 1960s, Peter Berger explained that sociology could be viewed as 'an individual pastime' because it transformed the meaning of those familiar things we all take for granted:

> The fascination of sociology lies in the fact that its perspective makes us see in a new light the very world in which we have lived all our lives. (Berger 1967a: 32–3)

For a more up-to-date and personal review of the importance of 'discovering sociology' see the recollections of Rex, Heidensohn and Kuvlesky in Ballard *et al.* (1997).

what is going on. This sociological perspective relies on rigorous procedures and is informed by rational argument, criticism and existing knowledge. In this sense sociology is a combination of common sense, statistical inquiry and social theory and provides a distinct, but partial, view of what is going on:

> Sociology as an approach to understanding the world, can be differentiated from other approaches in that it attempts to be scientific, that is to produce empirically warranted and verifiable statements about the social world and is basically distinguished by its distinctive assumptions, concepts, questions, methods and answers.
> (Cuff *et al.* 1990: 9)

The idea of 'the sociological perspective' as a way of interpreting and analyzing social life should not be taken to indicate that there is a universal agreement as to exactly how sociological investigation should proceed. As we highlight below, the discipline of sociology encourages creative debate, controversy and diversity.

Stop and think

- ➤ What common-sense assumptions do you have about (a) yourself; (b) your country and community; (c) your family?
- ➤ What evidence is there for these assumptions?
- ➤ Can you test them?
- ➤ How widely shared are they?

In the writings of Berger (1967a) and C.W. Mills (1970) and more recent contributions from Bauman (1990) and Kingdom (1991), we get a very strong notion of what sociology is, often as a result of stressing what it is not. They make clear that sociology is an antidote to personal and subjective observations and a complete rejection of explanations that are grounded in naturalistic or individualistic assumptions about 'human nature'. The emphasis is quite clearly on the individual as a social animal within the context of a social environment. As this emphasis challenges popular and sometimes deeply held notions of human nature and individual responsibility it is not surprising that sociology meets a certain amount of resistance. Anticipating what has become known as the 'structure versus agency debate', C.W. Mills pointed out in his introduction to *The Sociological Imagination* that the primary role of the sociologist is to

reveal the complex relationship between the individual and society:

> The sociological imagination enables us to grasp history and biography and the relations between the two within society. That is its task and its promise. To recognise this task and this promise is the mark of the classic social analyst . . . No social study that does not come back to the problem of biography, of history, and of their intersections within a society, has completed its intellectual journey.
> (Mills 1970: 12)

Mills demonstrates that by unifying biography and history we are forced to place our own individual experiences and attitudes in the context of social structure and that societies themselves are not unique but have to be placed within an historical context.

Thus we have to go beyond personal experience and common sense for answers to our questions. The most vivid example can be seen in Mills's distinction between 'personal troubles' and 'public issues'. Whether we are looking at unemployment, war, divorce or the problems of urban living, there are aspects of our lives over which we have some control – 'personal troubles' for which we bear some responsibility and to which we can offer some private solution. However, there are other conditions that offer no such remedy, because the troubles that we experience (no matter how personally) are beyond our control; they have historical and structural causes and as such represent 'public issues' which can be changed only by large-scale economic developments or social reform.

Writing twenty years later, Zygmunt Bauman reiterates the importance of Mills's early insights into the crucial relationship between history, society and biography:

> Deeply immersed in our daily routines, though, we hardly ever pause to think about the meaning of what we have gone through: even less often have we the opportunity to compare our private experience with the fate of others, to see the social in the individual, the general in the particular, this is precisely what sociologists can do for us. We would expect them to show us how our individual biographies intertwine with the history we share with fellow human beings.
> (Bauman 1990, quoted in Giddens 1997a: 14)

In Western societies, where the cult of the individual and the notion of voluntary action are crucial aspects of our cultural history, and the coverage of politics is often reduced to the antics of personalities rather than their policies, it is not surprising to hear prime ministers proclaiming that 'There is no such thing as society. There are individual men and women and there are families.' (Margaret Thatcher) or referring to 'the classless society' (John Major) as if it were a matter of agreed fact. In such a climate, sociology must struggle to assert the concepts on which its perspective is based; if it does not it will disappear among the clamour of those whom John Kingdom (1991) has called 'the new individualists'. As Burns reminds us, 'Sociology began as virtually a resistant movement against the trend towards individualism' (1992: 20).

Stop and think

> ➤ What do you think Margaret Thatcher meant when she proclaimed 'There is no such thing as society'? What are the broader (a) moral (b) political (c) sociological implications of such a statement?

The sociological perspective in practice

Sociology as an empirical enterprise

Sociology has had to fight to establish itself as a social science. Using the principles of the scientific method established by the natural sciences, sociologists have developed methods of data collection which enable them to claim that sociological knowledge is as reliable as that found in any other sphere of the social sciences. This does not mean that sociology can produce infallible laws of the human universe (many natural sciences have failed to do this) but it can endeavour to follow the rules of the scientific method to establish verifiable data and valid correlations which may be used to confirm or deny a hypothesis (or create a new one). In essence, sociologists demand that theoretical positions be tested against evidence and that this evidence be gathered by the most logical method in an objective manner and interpreted in an impartial way. The application of the scientific method to sociology is examined in Chapter 3. In general terms, the use of the scientific approach enables social researchers to establish two things.

First, through observation and measurement a statistical record of how things are can be compiled, much in the tradition of social accountancy discussed later in this chapter (pp. 17–18). Such statistics are based on and confirm the assumption that social life is largely routine,

predictable and unconscious. William James recognized the importance of this when writing about habitual behaviour over 100 years ago:

> Habit is . . . the enormous fly-wheel of society, its most precious conservative agent . . . It keeps the fisherman and the deck hand at sea through the winter; it holds the miner in the darkness, and nails the countryman to his log cabin and his lonely farm through all the months of snow. (James 1890: 143)

We normally take for granted the 'patterned regularity' of social life because we are steeped in the familiarity bred by habit. On a superficial level, these patterns may simply be descriptions of how people normally behave within their culture, perhaps dressing in an 'appropriate' manner for different occasions, such as interviews or funerals. On another level, it may be noticed that some forms of behaviour are exclusive, for example the majority of people do not enter higher education, while patterns may also emerge which change over time, such as the rise in the recorded levels of crime.

Second, the compilation of data allows us to identify possible correlations between the patterns of behaviour so that we begin to notice that certain patterns of behaviour are more commonly discovered among particular groups of people. Some social groups are less likely to pass exams than others, people who live in urban areas may be more prone to burglary than those who inhabit the suburbs or the countryside, and the children most likely to be found anywhere but school in term time come from backgrounds where education is not highly valued. This does not mean that sociology can predict exactly who will fail their exams, get burgled or bunk off from school, but it can make 'tendency statements' about the likelihood of the correlations reproducing themselves.

Sociology as explanation

Social correlations need to be explained, and the emphasis in sociology is on social conditions rather than biological, psychological or genetic factors. This is not to deny that we are, as a species, the product of millions of years of biological evolution or that individual differences call for psychological explanation. However, sociologists resist any generalization which suggests that behaviour can be reduced to biological explanations alone. Not only do such claims have very powerful ideological connotations, but they also fly in the face of the clear evidence linking behaviour to social circumstances and cultural experience.

The power of culture and the importance of the learning experience are examined later (pp. 20–24), but the areas we have used so far as examples are clear cases where social circumstances are an essential part of any explanation; educational failure, crime, truancy and mental breakdown are all issues that call for sociological illumination.

In the popular imagination, pure evil may still be the most appropriate explanation for senseless crime, madness may be conveniently dismissed as a disease of the mind, and some individuals are simply ineducatable. Sociology teaches us that educational success is related to gender and class, that recorded crime is largely committed by juveniles, that black people are more likely than whites to be diagnosed as schizophrenic by British and North American psychiatrists and that the number of British children truanting from school is currently running at about 30,000 per year – in some parts of inner-city London the rate is as high as 40 per cent. It is not surprising that when things happen to us which we were not expecting, we take it personally or blame it on chance. However, if we are aware of the way in which the odds are stacked the element of chance is drastically reduced: your failure to pass your exams is something you share with a lot of other people, your house was the third to be burgled in your street that week, and your children have discovered

YES – BUT IS IT NORMAL?

that their classmates who still attend the local community comprehensive school are now regarded as deviant.

Stop and think

➤ Think of some of the key events in your own life. To what extent was their outcome affected by (a) social factors (where you live, what school you went to); (b) biological factors (your gender, race); (c) psychological factors (your intelligence and personality)? How easy is it to distinguish between these different factors?

In this section we have talked of the sociological perspective as if it were a uniform and standardized body of concepts, theories and findings. This would give the impression of a discipline free from criticism and internal division and it would be wholly incorrect. One of the main difficulties that students of this subject experience is the failure of sociologists to agree with one another and the diversity of opinion that exists within it. Without exaggerating these differences, there are obvious disagreements over methodological procedures and theoretical perspectives which provide the conceptual backdrop to what sociology is all about and which are explored in Chapters 2 and 3.

Furthermore, there is political disagreement over the value and neutrality of sociology. Apart from the criticisms of philosophers who have argued that sociology cannot logically fit into the scientific frame of reference, there are complaints from within the discipline itself that sociology's claim to be an objective science is undone by its actual behaviour in the real world of research and theoretical activity. Radical and Marxist critics like Gouldner (1971, 1975) have complained that much sociology has developed into a tame form of social surveillance on behalf of the most powerful groups in society, into 'cow sociology' – a domesticated animal to be watered and fed in return for regular milking. On the other hand, Professor David Marsland has joined forces with Roger Scruton in his attack on the left-wing political bias which he claims is the overriding characteristic of current sociology.

Whatever its shortcomings, sociology is a rewarding area of study; it offers the opportunity to ask questions, to consider different perspectives, to evaluate evidence and to reflect on those attitudes previously thought of as 'common sense'. As a result, we begin to see ourselves and the social world we inhabit in a different way. As an echo of Berger's claim that the first wisdom of sociology is that 'things are not what they seem', Bauman has summarized the position brilliantly:

> When repeated often enough, things tend to become familiar, and familiar things are self-explanatory; they present no problems and arouse no curiosity ... Familiarity is the staunchest enemy of inquisitiveness and criticism – and thus also of innovation and the courage to change. In an encounter with that familiar world ruled by habits and reciprocally reasserting beliefs, sociology acts as a meddlesome and often irritating stranger. It disturbs the comfortingly quiet way of life by asking questions no one among the 'locals' remembers being asked, let alone answered. Such questions make evident things into puzzles: they defamiliarize the familiar. Suddenly, the daily way of life must come under scrutiny. It now appears to be just one of the possible ways, not the one and only, not the 'natural' way of life.
>
> (Bauman 1990, quoted in Giddens 1997: 17)

The origins of sociology

Sociology is generally regarded (by Western sociologists) as a Western academic pursuit. However, as Ritzer has acknowledged, 'scholars were doing sociology long ago and in other parts of the world' (Ritzer 1992: 8). Abdel Rahman ibn-Khaldun, for example, was engaged in what we would now call sociological research and teaching at Cairo University 500 years before its emergence as an academic discipline in Europe. This section, therefore, should be seen as an introduction to the foundations of Western sociology.

The intellectual roots of sociology stretch beyond the activists of the nineteenth century to the political and social philosophers of classical Greece, the social contract theories of Hobbes, Locke and Rousseau and the Enlightenment of eighteenth-century Europe. In their attempts to understand human nature and harness their insights to a vision of social improvement, the early writers discussed issues and employed concepts that were clearly sociological in nature:

> In the writings of Aristotle, Plato, Hobbes, Locke and Rousseau there are numerous sociological themes relating to problems of social differentiation, inequality, social conflict and social cohesion, the development of the division of labour and private property – but this does not make these theorists sociologists.
>
> (Swingewood 1991: 9–10)

Swingewood makes an important distinction between the early writers who focus attention on 'human nature as the basis of human society' and the writers of the Enlightenment, who emphasized the importance of social structure and social laws. He suggests that it was not until the Enlightenment of the eighteenth century that 'a peculiarly invigorating mixture of political philosophy, history, political economy and sociology' laid the basis for looking at the world in a new way.

The laws governing these historical and social processes were no longer deferred to as the hidden hand of God working mysteriously behind the scenes. Rather the dynamics of social order and historical change were seen as open to human inquiry – hidden truths that could be revealed by rational speculation and scientific study.

A closer look

Abdel Rahman ibn-Khaldun (1332–1406)

Ibn-Khaldun was born in Tunis, North Africa, in 1332. He was schooled in the Qur'an, mathematics and history and followed a career in politics, serving in a variety of positions in Tunis, Morocco, Spain and Algeria. After his 'political career', he undertook an intensive five-year period of study and writing and became a lecturer at the centre of Islamic study at the Al-Azhar Mosque University in Cairo. By his death in 1406, ibn-Khaldun had produced a number of studies that shared many ideas and themes with contemporary sociology. He believed in the scientific study of society, empirical research and the importance of locating the causes of social phenomena. He examined social institutions (in the political and economic spheres, for example) and was interested in comparing primitive and modern societies.

(Adapted from Ritzer 1992: 8)

Stop and think

➤ What differences might there be between a society in which historical and social processes are seen as the 'hand of God' and one in which they are open to rational human inquiry? Can you think of societies in which the two views coexist?

Social theory in Europe and America

European sociology has its recent origins in the intellectual aspirations and social upheavals of the nineteenth century; its foundation as a discipline is usually attributed to Auguste Comte (1798–1857). Comte invented the word 'sociology' and also the term 'positivism'. He established the Positivist Society in 1848 and saw positivism as the search for order and progress in the social world. He felt that a science based on experimentation and open to testing was the only valid form of human knowledge and, in the face of a great deal of academic prejudice, devoted himself to the establishing of sociology as the study of social facts. A year after Comte's death, Emile Durkheim (1858–1917) was born; he continued the fight for sociology to be recognized by the academic community as 'the science of institutions, their genesis and their functioning'.

At the same time, British sociology developed from the theoretical work of political economists like Adam Smith (1723–90) and the idea of social evolution advocated by Herbert Spencer (1820–1903). However, the major contribution of the early British sociologists was to be found in social research and the belief that social science could solve the social problems of industrial society through statistical analysis and social reform. Some early sociologists had to masquerade as anthropologists or botanists to achieve academic positions, but by 1903 the Sociological Society of London had been founded and in 1907 the London School of Economics and Political Science established the first department of sociology. Liverpool University created a new school of social science in the same year, although the emphasis was on social administration and social work training. Loss of direction, internal divisions and traditional academic resistance within the universities meant that the formal progress of sociology in Britain was very slow. While the USA could boast 169 institutions teaching sociology as early as 1901, British universities were tardy in recognizing the claim of sociology

and it was not until the 1950s that interest in the subject was revived. By the 1960s there were no more than forty sociologists in the whole of the UK and only twelve degree courses on offer (Abrams 1968; Kent 1981).

Meanwhile, in Germany the establishment of sociology as a discipline met similar opposition from academics who rejected Marxism as nothing more than a political philosophy but also refused to take seriously the efforts of Max Weber (1864–1920) and George Simmel (1858–1918), who founded the German Sociological Society in 1910. Both did achieve academic posts, but Weber was dogged by depression and poor health, while Simmel found that academic prejudice against his ideas was compounded by the anti-semitism that was so deeply rooted in German culture. Both writers probably achieved greater respect in the less prejudiced atmosphere of North American universities.

By contrast, in the USA sociology developed alongside the new universities of the late nineteenth century and as a result was treated with the same respect given to any other academic profession. The first sociology department was founded at the University of Kansas in 1889, and the famous centre of American sociology was established at Chicago in 1892.

Stop and think

➤ Why do you think sociology was more readily accepted in the USA than in Britain and continental Europe?

➤ Do you think these reasons are still applicable today?

The emergence of sociology

The emergence of sociology as a new discipline cannot simply be accounted for by identifying its intellectual ancestry. To understand why these ideas flourished in recent history it is necessary to place them within the context of the economic, social and political upheavals of the eighteenth and nineteenth centuries. In other words, the historical emergence of sociology needs to be treated sociologically. The work of the early sociologists has to be seen as a product of their direct experience, as middle-class intellectuals, of an age characterized by social change. We shall examine this age of transition to try to make sense of the social forces which shaped the interests, priorities and ideas of the major social theorists and researchers of early Western sociology.

Societies which had remained relatively static for centuries now found themselves embroiled in the dramatic transformation from feudalism to capitalism. Just as the religious and political certainties of absolutist monarchies were shaken by the critical attacks of the Enlightenment, so the traditional practices and social relationships of rural life gave way to the new demands of the industrial and political revolutions of the period. The shift from the traditional occupations of cottage industry and agricultural production to the new skills and practices of the factory system saw massive migrations of rural populations to the centres of industrial production and the rise of the 'industrial classes'. While the new middle classes were closely associated with the radical ideas of the Enlightenment and the French Revolution, the working classes were more clearly linked to the social crisis epitomized by urban poverty, crime and poor health and to the new forms of political unrest like chartism, trade unionism and socialism.

As Nisbet (1970) has pointed out, many of the terms that we now use in everyday discourse (e.g. industry, ideology, bureaucracy, capitalism, crisis) take their modern meaning from the attempts by nineteenth-century social commentators to make some sense of 'the collapse of the old regime under the blows of industrialism and revolutionary democracy'. The main features of these industrial and political upheavals can be summarized as the Industrial Revolution; the spirit of capitalism; mass society and urban life; political change; and the crisis of the modern mind. We shall look briefly at each of these features.

The Industrial Revolution

Through the Industrial Revolution, technology and the factory system transformed people's relationship to the work process, society and one another. Industrial production as a concept and a practice was not new; Colin Spencer (1986) tells us that the Romans were so keen on fish sauce that liquamen factories were to be found all over the Roman Empire where catches of sprats and anchovies were salted, fermented and bottled on a grand scale. What was new in the eighteenth and nineteenth centuries was the transformation of working methods to a system of factory production.

This new mode of production, linked to the individualism and enterprise of capitalism, not only uncorked 'productive energies' previously repressed and created wealth on a scale hitherto unimagined but also led to economic and social changes that were regretted by conservative and socialist thinkers alike. In particular, the shift

from the family to the factory as the unit of production and the 'degradation of labour' through the destruction of craft skills, the emergence of a specialized division of labour and an emphasis on a 'time-oriented' work discipline are seen at the root of a general decline in status and moral condition for the labourer. Such working practices and conditions not only encouraged feelings of alienation and exploitation but also provided an ideal environment for solidarity and resistance. Not surprisingly, the world of work is a crucial area of social investigation for all the early writers; this tradition was continued by empirical researchers in the field of industrial relations.

The spirit of capitalism

Despite being a contemporary phenomenon that has clear links with the Industrial Revolution, capitalism is not synonymous with it. The principles of enterprise and profit characterize early trading practices and money-lending as well as the agricultural revolution of eighteenth-century Britain. In 'post-industrial' societies the shift from manufacture towards service industries is still underpinned by the ethics of capitalism, while in socialist countries it has been claimed that industrialism is a necessary feature of any post-capitalist revolution and a force for public good.

Nevertheless, capitalism was inextricably bound up with the revolution in production and the industrialization of Western societies. Materialism, commercial enterprise and possessive individualism replaced what Nisbet (1970) calls 'the superior values of Christian-feudal society'. The economics of the free market and *laissez-faire* attitudes towards the obligations of employers and the rights of the workforce replaced romantic notions of *noblesse oblige* with the 'cash nexus'. The emphasis on money as the basis for relationships between people was mirrored in the relationship with the land. As the importance of landholding declined in the face of share ownership in large scale industrial enterprises, the allegiance that people had to their roots (in moral communities) was destroyed. While this idea of the link between people and the land might have been romanticized, it formed the backdrop to much of the writings about loss of community; it has been reflected in the feelings of isolation and loneliness that seem to be widely experienced in modern urban society.

Despite the characteristics of individualism and freedom, capitalism also contained contradictory elements that threatened its survival; these included the development of social classes, the intensification of class conflict and the irrational elements of a free-market economy.

In the view of Karl Marx, such a system was based on exploitation, alienated labour and political force.

Early sociological theorists differed widely over the nature, development and impact of capitalism (Chapter 2 looks at differing analyses of capitalism offered by the founding writers of sociology, in particular Max Weber's famous study *The Protestant Ethic and the Spirit of Capitalism*). They were, however, clearly aware that anyone trying to make sense of industrial society had to take account of the emergence of capitalism as the dominant Western economic system.

Stop and think

➤ Despite frequent predictions of the imminent demise of capitalism it is still the dominant political and economic paradigm in much of the Western world. Which of its characteristics do you think make it so attractive and so resilient as a system?

Mass society and urban life

Urbanism is also closely linked with the Industrial Revolution but, like capitalism, it is a separate social phenomenon. The concept of city living has a proud history that pre-dates the Industrial Revolution by centuries. The city states of Greece and Rome as well as the ancient civilizations of Africa, Asia and South America all celebrated their cultural and economic achievements in urban centres dedicated to art, politics and learning. Without over-romanticizing ancient and medieval city life, it was the Industrial Revolution that transformed the quality and meaning of urban living.

New cities dedicated to trade and industry emerged across Europe and North America in the nineteenth and twentieth centuries. Sprawling and unplanned, these new centres of economic activity and mass living grew at an alarming rate. They became battery farms for the production of labour for factory work and brought with them the social problems of poverty, overcrowding, poor health and political riot which have been associated with

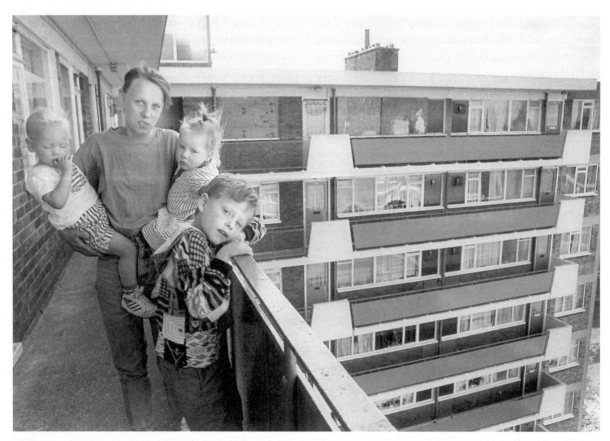

Figure 1.3 The social problems associated with inner-city living often have the biggest impact on children, with poor health and educational provision and a lack of leisure facilities
(Photograph by Brenda Price courtesy of Format Photographers)

inner-city living ever since. Nisbet highlights the concern with social issues created by modern urban life:

> It is ... the city that forms the context of most sociological propositions relating to disorganisation, alienation, and mental isolation – all stigmata of loss of community membership.   (Nisbet 1970: 28)

The 'mass society' thesis is closely associated with the work of the Frankfurt School and the elitist denunciation of popular culture, mass education and political democracy. This bleak view of modernity is often criticized for encouraging pessimism, exaggerating the homogeneity of the 'masses' and ignoring diversity (see pp. 82–3).

Political change

The new modes of thought, the changes in social relationships and the emphasis on individualism which have already been mentioned went hand in hand with the struggle for democracy. Nisbet (1970) has called this struggle 'the first great ideological revolution in Western history', and it started with the bloody and momentous events in France and North America at the end of the eighteenth century, continued throughout the nineteenth century and fuelled the civil rights movements of the mid-twentieth century. According to the concept of liberal democracy, the values of freedom and liberty were enshrined in the utilitarian principle of 'the greatest happiness of the greatest number', which along with the growth of the secular state became almost synonymous with mass society.

In this new world the rights of the individual and the power of the state challenged the traditional authority of the Christian Church, the monarchy and the guilds. Even the patriarchal family came under attack from those calling for equality in marriage, changes in divorce law and the protection of children. The traditional authority of the family and the Church was further undermined by the transfer of education to state control, where its provision rapidly became a sign of democratic civilization and a matter of legal obligation. The idea of equality (also bequeathed by the French Revolution) led to political aspirations of a different kind. Whereas liberty and freedom were the watchwords of liberal democracy, the egalitarianism of the French Revolution led directly to socialism as an expression of working-class political resistance. The growth of the trade union movement in Britain and syndicalism in France, the flourishing radical press and the writings of Marx and Engels, as well as the activities of the English chartists and Parisian Communards, all

indicate the extent to which revolution, once started, could not be contained by constitutional monarchs and electoral reform.

The crisis of the modern mind

The emergence of science and the decline of religion come together to create what Asa Briggs (1967) has called 'the crisis of the modern mind'. The one does not necessarily exclude the other, but the popularity and prestige of scientific discovery was clearly seen as a threat to religious authority. Science not only offered different types of explanations for the workings of the natural world but also provided the tools for its conquest and exploitation. The discoveries of archaeologists and astronomers had long since struck at the heart of biblical truth, while Darwin's view of the origins of the human race was at the centre of a growing conflict between science and religion. The emergence of this dual phenomenon is clearly reflected in the concern and attitudes of the early sociologists. The decline of religion attracted much attention, and examination of the social significance of religion permeates the theoretical work of Durkheim, Weber and, to a lesser extent, Marx. Meanwhile, the early theoretical models of Spencer and Comte attempt to mimic the mechanical, organic and evolutionary relationships discovered by physics and biology. Even the political manifesto of Marx and Engels was based on the principles of 'scientific socialism'. We have a curious mixture of overlapping themes here; some sociologists were clearly inspired by religion, others thought that sociology was a new religion based on the assumptions of scientific discovery, while a small group felt that sociological inquiry was a useful way of investigating religious belief and established the study of religion as a distinct area of sociology.

All these changes came together to create a dynamic and sometimes chaotic environment into which the early sociologists were born. Many of their ideas were products of the changes to which they were witness, and the major areas of sociological inquiry were more or less established during this period. The themes of religion, urbanism, capitalist development and political stability became essential areas of sociological speculation, while the issues of poverty, crime, industrial relations and family life have retained their place as objects of social inquiry ever since. This connection between the discipline and its historical origins was clearly reflected in both sociological theory and social research.

Confronted with a rapidly changing, fragmented and rootless mass society the early theorists developed their systematic critiques of the modern world. Whether it is Comte anguishing over the collapse of authority or Durkheim looking for a new moral order there is a strong conservative element in much sociological theory. This may be contrasted with Marx's celebration of social conflict as an inevitable consequence of class society and Weber's more pessimistic view of the eventual rationalization of society and the replacement of 'magic' with the 'iron cage' of bureaucratic order. Many of these perspectives are dealt with more fully later, but the crucial point is that without the momentous social and political events of the post-Enlightenment there would have been no great social crisis to observe, there would have been no middle-class intellectuals to recount it, and there would have been no social theory.

In Turner's review of the contribution of sociology's classic writers, he argues that despite their great differences in outlook they were united by an essential belief in the power of 'abstract and analytical thought to understand the social world'. This sense of purpose is as crucial to sociology's future as it was to its emergence in the ninteenth century;

Case study

The emergence of modern sociology

Many of the factors which led to the emergence of sociological enquiry can be found in Chicago at the beginning of the twentieth century. In a very short space of time 'Chicago had been transformed from a raucous western frontier town to a major city, the railroad and trade centre of the American plains and Midwest' (Lemert 1997: 69). Such intense transformation brought together the achievements and the social problems which accompany rapid economic and urban growth. In Schlosser's account, the application of the production line to meatpacking was Chicago's blessing and its curse.

> For more than a century . . . Chicago reigned as the meatpacking capital of the world. The Beef Trust was born there, the major meatpacking firms were headquartered there, and roughly forty thousand people were employed there in a square-mile meat district anchored by the Union Stockyards. Refrigerated sides of beef were shipped from Chicago not only throughout the United States, but also throughout Europe. At the dawn of the twentieth century, Upton Sinclair considered Chicago's Packingtown to be 'the greatest aggregation of labor and capital ever gathered in one place'. It was in his view the supreme achievement of American capitalism, as well as its greatest disgrace. The old Chicago slaughterhouses were usually brick buildings, four or five stories high. Cattle were herded up wooden ramps to the top floor, were they were struck on the head with a sledgehammer, slaughtered, then disassembled by skilled workers. The animals eventually left the building on the ground floor, coming out as sides of beef, cans of beef, or boxes of sausage ready to be loaded into railcars. The working conditions in these meatpacking plants were brutal. In *The Jungle* (1906) Upton Sinclair described a litany of horrors: severe back and shoulder injuries, lacerations, amputations, exposure to dangerous chemicals, and memorably, a workplace accident in which a man fell into a vat and got turned into lard. The plant kept running, and the lard was sold to unsuspecting consumers. Human beings, Sinclair argued, had been made 'cogs in the great packing machine', easily replaced and entirely disposable.
>
> (Schlosser 2002: 152)

Questions

1. *Why should the working processes and conditions described in Schlosser's account help to explain the emergence of American sociology at Chicago University at the turn of the century? To get a broader picture of the social conditions in Chicago in 1900 you might carry out a quick web search.*

2. *Conduct a brief enquiry into the origins of the Chicago School and find out;*
   a) *Who were its founders?*
   b) *What social problems did they investigate?*
   c) *What research methods did they use?*

Disciplines that have a theoretical canon make a difference in the world. The founders of sociology provided a vision of what was possible; and indeed, gave us many of the critical insights to forge a contemporary canon that can be used to make a real difference in the quality of human life at the close of the twentieth century. What those who begin to practice sociology in the twenty-first century must do is consolidate the canon, make it ever more coherent even in the face of specialization in the academic world, and, if one is still guided by the goals of the Enlightenment, to use sociology to inform public debate, political policy, and social action to reconstruct society.

(Turner 1997: 77)

Social research

If anything, social research was even more clearly linked to the social changes that were taking place than was social theorizing. The social problems which were related to urban living, particularly those that threatened the established order of society such as crime and political unrest, commanded the attention of early researchers. In the USA, Chicago had become an experimental laboratory in urban survival, while in Britain cities like London, Manchester and Liverpool attracted empirical social scientists like flies buzzing round a dung heap.

In Raymond Kent's (1981) history of empirical sociology, the British research movement is divided into two camps – the social accountants and the social explorers.

The social accountants

The purpose of collecting statistical data, according to McCulloch (1825), was 'to describe the condition of a particular country at a particular period'. Using survey techniques and official records a statistical history of Britain can be traced back to the 'Domesday Book' of 1086. Social surveys of Scotland (John Sinclair 1791–99) and England (Sir Frederick Eden 1797) as well as demographic compilations dating back to John Graunt's account of mortality in 1662 demonstrate that the desire for empirical information was nothing new.

In Bernstein's account, Graunt's study of the official records of births and deaths in London is described as a 'stunning breakthrough . . . [in] statistical and sociological research' (1998: 75). Not only did he develop the concepts of 'statistical inference' and 'market research' but created the means by which governments could collect data on health and crime along with the demographic

changes taking place. By building up a statistical picture of the rapidly expanding capital, Graunt provided invaluable information for those interested in trade, taxation and recruitment into the army. As Bernstein concluded, Graunt's work challenged contemporary common sense notions of social reality but also established the methodological basis for empirical social research:

The facts Graunt assembled changed people's perceptions of what the country they lived in was really like. In the process, he set forth the agenda for research into the country's social problems and what could be done to make things better . . . [His] pioneering work suggested the key theoretical concepts that are needed for making decisions under conditions of uncertainty. Sampling, averages and notions of what is normal make up the structure that would in time house the science of statistical analysis, putting information into the service of decision – making and influencing the degrees of belief we hold about the probabilities of future events'

(Bernstein 1998: 83–84)

In the nineteenth century, however, the demand for useful statistics was not only a consequence of the popularity of the social sciences but also the desire of the political elite to know what was going on in a rapidly changing world. The obsession with statistics developed in the USA and Germany but most obviously in Britain, where the government started its own ten-yearly census in 1801 and maintained an official statistical record of the state of the nation in the 'Blue Books' of the period. Statistical societies were established and attracted social reformers; the Statistical Society of London was, according to Kent (1981), 'almost . . . a branch of government' in its pursuit of politically useful 'state-istics'.

As a result, the emphasis of the social accountants was not simply on the state of society but on those areas of society that posed a political or moral threat to its survival. Studies of the condition of the working classes in general and social issues in particular dominate a twenty-year period after the founding of the first statistical societies in the early 1830s. Then, as now, much attention was paid to the phenomenon of rising crime and much effort was spent on teasing out the patterns of crime and their possible causes. Although the Reverend John Clay (1839) identified moral variables such as 'drunkenness, idleness, bad company, weak intellect and temptation' as the keys to understanding criminal behaviour, Plint's *Crime in England* (published in 1851) has a far more sociological feel to it as he played down the notion of urban decadence and emphasized economic inequality, class

Case study

Statistics held to account

Members of the various statistical societies were mostly middle-class men who were professionals, industrialists or members of the establishment, and they espoused policies of free trade and economic *laissez-faire*. They were suspicious of the factory reformers and preferred to see the towns rather than the factories as the major source of social ills. To them it was urbanization and the physical environment that it produced that determined the habits and character of the people; making surveys of their actual condition was the obvious first step to be taken towards its improvement. The goal, however, was not the formation of a welfare state, but the creation of an environment that would foster a thrifty and virtuous working class.

(Kent 1981: 31–2)

Question

1. *In what ways are social statistics still used today to justify particular economic and political views and interests? Give some examples.*

---

position and age as the crucial factors. Similar attention was given to politically sensitive areas such as education, strikes and health, all of which attracted the attention of political economists and social reformers.

By the 1850s 'social accountancy' was on the decline, but it had established the importance and usefulness of social statistics for those who felt threatened by movements they only dimly understood and needed to control. The early use of social statistics can therefore be seen as an attempt by those with economic and political power to chart those areas of the social world which were largely unknown to them, to identify potential trouble spots and to generate ideas for social reform that targeted the habits of the poor rather than the economic system of the day.

The social explorers

The accumulation of statistics was gradually overtaken by social anthropologists, who derived their inspiration and approach from the tradition of the industrial novel and who analyzed in depth the condition of the industrial working class. They were more concerned with identifying the structural context of social problems than simply blaming poverty on the fecklessness of the poor.

[Social exploration] is the discovery of the unknown and presupposes a rigid class structure in which a representative of a social class consciously sets out to explore, analyse and report upon the life of another class lower on the social scale. It tells the story of one person's journey into alien culture and offers the detailed results of his findings. . . . The data that emerges from social exploration are typically qualitative, often emotive, frequently narrative and utilise the imagery of exploration primarily to draw attention to the inequalities in society and to force upon the reader an awareness of his social blindness. (Kent 1981: 37)

One of the earliest examples of this approach was Engels' study of Manchester, which marks a reaction against the purely empirical collection of facts found in the work of the statistical societies. Engels' family were wealthy textile manufacturers who owned a factory in Manchester, where he was sent in 1842; while there he wrote his famous account of the *Condition of the Working Class in England* (1845). In it he attempted to describe the conditions of the working population of the day, although his accounts are very much based on personal observation. Mayhew's study of the London poor in the mid-nineteenth century (1949) may be seen as a more structured attempt to create a natural history of the urban underclass, because he was more concerned to record the attitudes and beliefs of the people he was studying in his endeavour 'to collect facts, and to register opinions'. As a result of such studies, the criminal and anti-social behaviour of the urban working class became more understandable as part of a subcultural reaction to harsh economic circumstances.

The journalistic and polemical approach of Engels and Mayhew was followed by the less critical but more thorough efforts of Charles Booth. The wealthy owner of a Liverpool shipping company and member of the London Statistical Society, Booth attempted to weld together the various techniques of social research used by his predecessors to study the problem of poverty. Observation, systematic interviews and official statistics were all employed in his survey of London poverty. Booth's (1889) massive survey was published in seventeen volumes and provides a detailed account of social conditions at the end of the nineteenth century. He used sampling techniques and preceded his twenty-year project with a 'pilot study' of London's East End. His investigations were based on a subsistence definition of poverty: if income fell below a certain level a family could be classified as 'poor' and if significantly below this level 'very poor'. Booth found that 35 per cent of people in East London were poor and 12.5 per cent very poor. His work attempted to examine poverty on a formal, impersonal level rather than on an anecdotal basis, which explains its importance as a pioneering piece of empirical sociological research.

Social explorers continued to use statistical analysis to probe 'darkest Britain' in the twentieth century. The Mass Observation studies of Tom Harrison and Charles Madge used another economic depression as an excuse to investigate the important events and hidden 'tribes' of England in the 1930s (Harrison and Madge 1986). The Mass Observation organization aimed to conduct surveys of the population and to report the results as widely as possible. The founders believed that social science should not be purely academic and attempted 'to marry social anthropology to journalism in the interests of revealing Britain to its inhabitants'. The movement involved a network of observers in different parts of the country making observations on how they and other people spent their daily lives. The results provided a very full picture of social change in Britain before and during the Second World War. Initially, Mass Observation tended to be associated with left-wing politics; however, it ended by stimulating the growth of 'market research and public opinion polling . . . rather than social investigation proper' (Mitchell 1968: 210).

the way that we might associate with traditional societies. Essentially, globalization refers to the interdependence of societies across the world – there is a constant flow of goods and information around the globe. Perhaps the most obvious changes have been in terms of economic globalization – illustrated by the activities of transnational corporations (TNCs) – and cultural globalization – apparent in the increasingly international flavour of the media and the worldwide interests and activities of particular media companies.

The massive changes associated with globalization (which are introduced and discussed more fully in Chapters 11 and 12) have meant that sociological analysis has had to move beyond the study of single societies.

Whether we are concerned about poverty, terrorism, crime or the formation of contemporary identities, we must recognize that whereas early sociological concerns tended to be bound by regional and national boundaries (as in the accounts of American and British sociology mentioned above), it is no longer possible to talk sensibly about social issues without considering the impact of global influences. For example, George Ritzer's concept of the McDonaldization of society began its life as an exploration of the ways in which the principles of the fast food industry were coming to dominate American everyday life but quickly moved on to examine the 'global existence and implications of McDonaldization'. In his more recent work, Ritzer has introduced the notions of *glocalization* to refer to the opportunities for cultural diversity, which stem from an interaction between local cultures and global systems of communication, and *grobalization*, which reveals the opposite tendency towards cultural imperialism and homogeneity. See Ritzer (2004: Chapter 8).

Stop and think

> Suggest how (a) social accountants and (b) social explorers would go about studying the following: changing family patterns; the role of religion in society; juvenile crime; and ethnic minority communities in contemporary Britain.

Stop and think

In what ways may the following be understood in terms of 'globalization'?
> Fast food
> Sport
> Pop music
> Nike sports wear
> The deaths of Chinese cockle pickers in Morecombe Bay in 2004
> The bombing of the Madrid express in 2004
> Hollywood movies
> The Bhopal Disaster in 1984

While the origins of the discipline of sociology are clearly linked with Western industrial societies, and the changes that took place within them, the increasing globalization of the modern world has taken contemporary sociology beyond the traditional 'nation-state' conception of society. No modern societies are self-contained in

Culture and socialization

In this section, we shall define the key concepts of culture and socialization. The application of these concepts is then explored by assessing the power of culture through cultural diversity and deprivation.

Culture

Stop and think

➤ What does the term 'culture' mean to you?

➤ What activities would you describe as 'cultural'?

The activities which we associate with 'culture' tend to include traditional arts such as ballet, literature and painting. Trips to the theatre, art gallery and opera house are seen as examples of cultural involvement (and often recalled by resentful members of school outings). This view of 'culture' is only one definition of the term. It is what Matthew Arnold (1963) called 'the best that has been known and said in the world' and concentrates on the intellectual aspects of a civilization. The subjective and elitist nature of this definition has been questioned in the second half of the twentieth century. This sort of approach has encouraged a division and distinction between what is seen as high culture and mass culture. In lay terms, a classical symphony or Shakespeare play is seen as high culture; as something of enduring aesthetic merit. In contrast, a TV soap opera or top ten single is likely to be seen as an example of mass, or popular, culture; as a commercial product of little aesthetic merit.

However, there is another sense in which the concept of culture can be used. Sociologists prefer a much broader, less subjective and impartial definition that refers to the values, customs and acceptable modes of behaviour that characterize a society or social groups within a society. Indeed, culture and society are closely entwined concepts in that one could not exist in any meaningful way without the other. As Giddens puts it, 'no cultures could exist without societies. But equally, no societies could exist without culture. Without culture no one could be "human" at all' (1997b: 18). Culture, then, refers to the non-biological aspects of human societies – to the values, customs and modes of behaviour that are learned and internalized by people rather than being genetically transmitted from one generation to the next.

This general notion of culture is directly related to social behaviour through the moral goals of a society (its *values*), the status positions of its members (*social roles*) and the specific rules of conduct related to society's values and roles, which are known as *norms.* In other words, those general values that society holds in high esteem are reflected in the norms governing our everyday attitudes and behaviour.

Many sociologists regard the culture of modern societies as differentiated and fragmented. They see such societies as embracing a range of beliefs, values and customs rather than a unified cultural system. Within such diversity, however, some sociologists (among others those writing from a feminist or Marxist standpoint) would argue that contemporary societies do possess a dominant culture or 'ideology'. In contrast, others would suggest that such societies have a 'core culture' which is more or less shared by everyone.

A closer look

Behavioural etiquette: a Victorian guide

In 1866, Edward Turner Esq. compiled *The Young Man's Companion*, a written record of the sort of advice aspiring young gentlemen might require. It was aimed at 'the very numerous class of young men in this country whose education may have been neglected early in life, and who only require a thorough initiatory elementary knowledge to greatly advance their prospects in the world.' Great value was clearly placed on polite behaviour in the successful performance of the role of gentleman. It is an indication of the extent to which these standards are open to cultural change that the book was reprinted a century later as a joke. Among the hints to be found in the chapter on 'Accomplishments and Graces' we are warned against the social disgrace of enjoying a good laugh:

> Frequent and loud laughter is the characteristic of folly and ill manners. It is the manner in which the mob express their silly joy at silly things.   (Turner 1965: 19)

And later, in his advice on table manners, Turner recommends behaviour that in any other circumstances would be seen as rudeness:

> If you are dining in company with high bred people and there is any article of food on the table, which you know to be very expensive, you should not treat it as such but effect to presume that such a thing is quite common at that table, and help yourself and others with entire freedom . . . Avoid, also, that most vulgar habit which prevails among half-bred country people, of abstaining from taking the last piece on a dish. It amounts almost to an insult to your host, to do anything which shows that you fear that the vacancy cannot be supplied, and that there is likely to be a scarcity.   (Turner 1965: 35)

Case study

Emotion as a cultural phenomenon

i) England's rugby World Cup triumph

In recent years, encouraged by the media, there have been huge outpourings of patriotic, collective public emotion in response to English sporting successes, such as the 2003 Rugby World Cup triumph, or the 2005 Ashes cricket victory over Australia.

Figure 1.4 Ecstatic fans Welcome England's rugby players on their return from Australia after their memorable triumph in winning the 2003 Rugby World Cup

ii) The death of Princess Diana

The death of Princess Diana in August 1997 gave rise to a public expression of grief rarely, if ever, seen before in Britain. There was massive global coverage of Diana's death and her funeral on 6 September. The extracts below illustrate some of the many attempts to 'interpret' the response to Diana's death as a social and cultural phenomenon.

The public cry out for their lost princess

First there was silence, then there was grief. Naked grief, of a kind Britain has never encouraged. From the moment the coffin appeared at the gates of Kensington Palace, the crowd broke down. They did not do so quietly.

'Diana!' 'Diana bless you!' 'Diana, Diana, we love you.' Single shouts at the start of a two-mile avenue of emotion, the words, wails and flower-throwing almost too painful to witness.

A banner stretched along the grass in Kensington Palace Gardens said 'no one can hurt you now . . . feel the love.' The princess was pulled slowly past. A long moment of calm followed. Most people stared motionless in disbelief at the enormity of the event they were witnessing, while others started to sob, clutching each other for comfort. Then, as if they felt they had not done enough, an awkward ripple of applause ran along the watchers. Many still clutched their flowers and shook their heads unable to express their emotion.

Along Kensington Gore, the crowd stood 30 deep: at every window, on every balcony, perched in trees . . .

More than 1 million people were in central London to say farewell to Diana. All morning the crowds

Case study (continued)

grew . . . Scotland Yard thought that 30,000 people had braved the cold overnight. At 6am the mourners were measured in hundreds of thousands; three hours later, when the gun carriage appeared out of Kensington Palace the crowds in Hyde Park were 20 deep. Some wanted to be at the princess's side as long as possible, following the coffin and not letting it out of sight.

They came from all corners of the country, from many other countries and from all walks of life. Those travelling on the Underground noted how the carriages were filled with the sweet smell of flowers, contrasting with the sombre faces of the mourners.

Why had they come? 'I came to say sorry,' said an elderly lady, hunting through her bag for a tissue. 'Sorry for what?' a reporter prompted gently. 'For wanting photos of her. For wanting to know what she was doing.' She twisted the tissue between her fingers. 'I bought all the papers and the magazines. She never had a moment to herself. I just didn't think. Now it's too late . . .'

The service was also relayed to the mourners in Whitehall, where skinheads and middle-aged men in suits sat together in sunlit silence. When Elton John sang, some lit candles. The opening bars of the ballad rolled over Hyde Park: the crowd rose and wept as Diana's friend sang of the nation's lost 'golden child.' At the end there was tumultuous applause.

(Tim Rayment,
Sunday Times 7.9.97)

Back to Blighty, and a vision of a ruling class on the run

On one level, the astonishing reaction to Diana's death can be seen simply as a great national catharsis, an outpouring of affection built up over the years for a troubled, but essentially decent young woman. On another level, however, the unprecedented display of people's power, which overwhelmed the palace, the politicians and the press, has demonstrated something much more profound: Britain is no longer the place it used to be. The empire, the Establishment and the old class system are dead. What will replace them is not yet clear, but it will be a society that is far more fluid, cosmopolitan and informal; in short the country will be more like America.

Many of the traits that we associate with the United States have been on display here during recent days: emotionalism, republicanism, multiculturalism, media overkill and celebrity worship . . .

Diana didn't create these changes – like all historical shifts, they are ultimately the product of great social and economic forces – but the manner of her death, and especially the initial reaction to her passing by the House of Windsor, has revealed how the tectonic plates have shifted for all to see. As the communist dictatorships in eastern Europe discovered to their cost, people power,

once unleashed, is difficult if not impossible to control.

What appears to be happening is not a mass outbreak of fully fledged republicanism – that remains the ideology of foreigners and middle-class radicals – but rather a general questioning among the British people of whether the Windsors are fit to be our royal family . . .

If the Windsors do not adapt to a newer, less stuffy Britain, they will not survive, and they won't deserve to . . .

Robbed of Diana's unique public appeal, the royals face an unpleasant future in which they are likely to be judged, like everybody else, by what they contribute to society. By the time Diana's son accedes to the throne, the Queen's family may well have become what some critics already claim they are: an antiquated tourist attraction in the British version of Disneyland.

(John Cassidy,
Sunday Times 7.9.97)

Questions

1. *How might a sociologist explain the reaction to Princess Diana's death?*

2. *What does this response tell us about British culture?*

3. *Do you agree with Cassidy's claim that the reaction to Diana's death shows that 'Britain is no longer the place it used to be. The empire, the establishment and the old class system are dead'? What evidence can you think of to support this claim? What evidence to dispute it?*

Stop and think

➤ The study of 'behavioural etiquette' on page 20 challenges our views about loud laughter and taking the last piece of food.

➤ What other examples can you think of where behaviour appropriate to one cultural context is seen as highly inappropriate in another? (Think of different historical and geographical cultural contexts.)

Socialization

The emphasis on culture, rather than biological instinct, as the key to understanding human behaviour implies that learning plays an essential part in creating social beings. In sociology, the term given to the process by which we learn the norms, values and roles approved by our society is 'socialization'. The survival of children into adulthood and the future of culture itself depend on a society's successful organization of this process.

Unless a society is to rely for its survival on the fear induced by the armed police forces or other agencies of control, socialization is the key to social cohesion and cultural endurance. The rules and customs governing normal social interaction must become internalized by the members of that society in such a way that they become part of the individual's view of the world and of themselves without the individual feeling brainwashed. As Berger makes clear, this balancing act can work only if it is achieved by stealth on the part of the society and through acceptance on behalf of the individual:

> Society not only controls our movements, but shapes our identity, our thought and our emotions. The structures of society become the structures of our own consciousness. Society does not stop on the surface of our skins. Society penetrates us as much as it envelops us. Our bondage to society is not so much established by conquest as by collusion.   (Berger 1967a: 140)

Gradually, as part of the process of 'growing up', individuals absorb the standards and expectations of a society so unconsciously that they become transformed into social beings almost without noticing it. The requirements, rules and standards of a society have become part of their own identity, motives and desires so imperceptibly that they are experienced as natural and unique although they are clearly social and uniform.

Individuals begin at an early age to become aware of the existence of others and to take this knowledge into account as they form their own identities. A society may not be capable of survival without its members' conformity, but equally individuals cannot develop clear ideas of who they are without some level of social interaction.

Stop and think

➤ Norms of conduct are often learned from an early age and unconsciously absorbed so that they become part of our 'taken-for-granted' assumptions about appropriate social behaviour.

➤ List as many norms of conduct as you can.

➤ How do these norms differ for different social groups – consider the differences between (a) young and old; (b) women and men; (c) poor and rich?

The cases which we mention later in this chapter of children who were deprived of such social interaction in their formative years are clear evidence of the crucial role played by the socialization process in the structuring of identity and the development of the individual.

Charles Cooley, one of the founders of the symbolic interactionist perspective in sociology (see pp. 65–9), examined the development of self-consciousness and maintained that consciousness in general and the self-concept in particular can be understood only in the context of an individual's interaction with society. He called this concept the 'looking-glass self' and argued that it developed on two levels of the socialization process involving primary and secondary groups.

Primary groups are based on intimate relationships and face-to-face interaction; they are crucial in establishing early codes of conduct as well as self-perception, both of which forge the link between an individual and society. The family is the clearest example of a primary group, and it is here that the most basic rules of culturally acceptable behaviour are established. Parents, says Erich Fromm (1960),

> in their own personalities . . . represent the social character of their society or class. They transmit to the child what we may call the psychological atmosphere or the spirit of a society just by being as they are – namely representatives of this very spirit. The family thus may be considered to be the psychological agent of society.
>
> (Fromm 1960, quoted in Meighan *et al.* 1979: 129)

Secondary groups are less intimate and more formal organizations, which do not provide the personal interaction of primary groups. These groups are often our first contact with society in general; as such, they not only reinforce the lessons learned within primary groups but also introduce us to new standards of behaviour which are universally agreed upon in society at large. These standards are often represented by individuals whose roles symbolize the wider values of society. The school is a good example of a secondary group, as here we begin to learn that we are not unique individuals at the centre of the universe but members of a wider society which will judge us by its rules and standards rather than our own. It has often been pointed out that after being the big fish in the little pond of family life children experience school as a microcosm of society within which they pick up the skills, values and tricks that will enable them to get by in the adult worlds of work, leisure and the social security system. In the view of Talcott Parsons (1959), the school classroom can be seen as a miniature social system:

> The school is an agency through which individual personalities are trained to be motivationally and technically adequate to the performance of adult roles . . . the socialisation function may be summed up as the development in individuals of the commitments and capacities which are essential prerequisites of their future role performance.
>
> (Parsons 1959, quoted in Miliband 1969: 215)

Culture and identity

The emergence of identity in modern society

According to some writers (e.g. Beck, Giddens, Foucault) the latter part of the twentieth century has seen people losing faith with the certainties of religion, social progress, class community and so on and turning instead to a contemplation of (and obsession with) the self. If the world 'out there' cannot offer security and becomes increasingly shaped by global forces, it is easy to see why people seek expression (and control) in their lives through local, regional and ethnic identities and become immersed in 'identity politics'. According to Martin Shaw, our response to this sense of powerlessness is to turn away from the big picture (public sphere) to the subjective and personal world of our individual existence (private sphere): 'Most people, most of the time, are concerned overwhelmingly with their private existence' (1995: 31).

However, as Baumeister (1986) points out the concern with identity is a fairly recent development which is strongly related to social change – notably the decline of religion and the perceived importance of the individual in social affairs. These changes have characterized historical change since the sixteenth century. Prior to (and during) this period of change people had pretty clear and stable ideas about who they were – if they thought about it at all – and saw themselves as almost indistinguishable from family, community and religion.

The notion of identity emerged alongside the ideology of individualism (see above) and the modern obsession with the *self*. However, the word identity comes from the Latin word meaning 'the same'. This occurs because personal identity draws upon two principles which are in a state of tension – if not outright conflict – with one another: on the one hand we experience ourselves as individual personalities open to constant fluctuation and different from everyone else, but on the other hand we remain largely unchanged over time and share many characteristics with other people. This combination of 'similarity' *and* 'difference' is what enables us to function in society but also retain some feeling that we are not the same as everyone else.

A closer look

Continuity and differentiation

So the whole idea of identity is premised on these contradictory principles:

The principle of continuity

Across time and social situations it is important that we remain recognizable as the same person and behave in more or less predictable ways.

The principle of differentiation

Just as we need some continuity over time to establish an identity of some substance, we also require a feeling that there is something unique or distinctive about this continuous self; something which distinguishes us from 'everyone else'. Some of these elements of differentiation are very broad, for example whether we are male or female, while others, such as our name, are very specific.

Both of these aspects of differentiation are important for establishing who we are to ourselves and to others.

A sense of identity can therefore be seen to function on three levels:

a) Personal – life is given a sense of purpose or direction especially through a clear set of values and priorities.

b) Social – successful interaction with others (essential in mass society) relies upon people understanding one another and fulfilling personal and social expectations. The successful accomplishment of such social interaction and 'people handling' skills involved not only contributes to social relationships (and social stability) but also reinforces positive feelings of self-worth/social value which are vital aspects of identity maintenance.

c) Potentiality – whereas a) and b) refer to those continuous and special aspects of identity which delineate who we *are*, individuals also need to have some idea of who they might become and whether they have the 'right stuff' to achieve it. Achievement is a self-confirming activity which provides personal fulfilment and increases positive feelings about the self. However, failure can undermine self-confidence and cause a crisis of identity.

Theories of identity formation

There are too many theories of identity to consider here but it is worth distinguishing between two general perspectives on identity before moving on.

➤ Essentialism – An essentialist perspective is one which emphasizes the fixed and usually biological basis of behaviour. According to this view, an individual's identity may be fixed by their genetic make up, personality traits or basic instincts/drives. It would be wrong to imply that all essentialist arguments are simply a matter of genetics as there are spiritual explanations which stress essential qualities (good/evil), psychological ones (aggression/sex) and even sociobiological and functionalist perspectives within sociology which stress the similarities between animal behaviour and that of humans. In all of these approaches identity is determined by some universal characteristics over which people have little control. Consequently essentialists are often criticized as 'reductionist'.

➤ Constructionism – At the other end of the spectrum are explanations which stress the social construction of identity, the cultural variety in identity formations and the opportunities for changing/choosing identities. The emphasis in this perspective is upon learning, culture and socialization; the social roles required by society and the influence upon the individual by the groups to which they belong are crucial. According to this view, the notion of individual identity cannot be separated from the idea of society – without one the other does not exist:

Baumeister (1986) has argued that the personal and the social aspects of identity are not two different points of view but different sides of the same coin (Baumeister's ideas are considered further in Activity 2, pp. 39–40). Whereas psychologists tend to talk of identity as being 'part of the personality' and sociologists stress identity as 'a set of roles or statutes . . . defined by society', Baumeister has suggested that it is possible to synthesize the 'inner' and the 'outer' aspects of identity particularly in modern societies which provide a loose context for action and a good deal of space within which the individual can 'shape identity by acts of personal choice and commitment' (1986: 252).

The processes involved in identity formation are a combination of the physical, the personal and the social. In this process of 'growing up' the individual does not simply assimilate the influences upon them but reflects, negotiates and incorporates (or rejects) them.

Stop and think

➤ Under the headings of 'Physical', 'Personal' and 'Social' identify the processes which have played the greatest role in the formation of your 'major' identity components.

In conclusion it is important to understand the distinction between the essentialist position which tends to suggest that identities are fixed by biology or culture or psychological trauma and the social constructionist perspective which emphasizes learning, choice and change. In the next section we consider issues around identity and socialization.

Identity and socialization

One of the growing areas of interest in sociology is the notion of the active subject. The emphasis is not on the deterministic forces of the social structure but on the conscious individual capable of self-awareness and reflection. These ideas stem from Cooley's idea of 'the looking glass self', Mead's work on the 'self-concept' and Goffman's 'presentation of self' (see pp. 66–9). These writers suggest that the identity of an individual is not the outcome of some essential personality but a more fluid creation which develops over time through the interrelationship between the self and those who comprise the outside world. In other words, our identities are a social construction and open to change. This does not mean, however, that we are completely free to choose whatever persona we fancy, and the role of culture in the formation of identities is a crucial one. The process of socialization helps us to become recognizable individuals, but it does so by providing us with options for group membership which shape our identity. The self-concept then is deeply embedded in the process of becoming social, and the resources from which our identity is created are found in key aspects of social life such as family, work and community. For this reason, social identity is not a simple outcome of upbringing but a combination of various and sometimes contradictory commitments that the individual self may have towards a range of identities; a Catholic male homosexual from a working-class background in Ireland who is the head of a suburban girls' comprehensive school in Yorkshire will have to juggle with a range of separate and competing claims on his self image which raise questions of gender, sexuality, region, nationality, class and ethnicity.

The major agencies of socialization are covered in detail in later chapters, where we look at the contribution of the family, the school, religion and the mass media to the reproduction of culture as it is handed on from one generation to the next. Here we shall look at the way in which the concept of culture has been applied by anthropologists, psychologists and sociologists in their attempts to identify its significance for individuals as well as society.

Stop and think

➤ Who are the key people involved in the socialization of children at the following ages: a) 0–4 years; b) 5–10 years; c) 11–15 years; d) 16–21 years?

➤ Consider the relative importance of primary and secondary groups at these different ages.

The power of culture

Cultural diversity

How would you feel about being offered dog meat for breakfast? What would be your reaction to a professor giving a lecture wearing nothing but a loin cloth? Would you be surprised to find people of your grandparents' generation using cocaine? Whether we look at fashion, food or leisure activities, anthropology and history reveal a wide range of cultural diversity over all forms of behaviour and belief, which suggests that human activity cannot be reduced to simple biological or social models which have been fixed for eternity. What is regarded as normal and acceptable behaviour by one society or cultural group may be punished as a crime elsewhere. As Matza (1969) reminds us, 'one man's deviation is another's custom', and it is clear that cultural standards are relative to time, place and social position.

Women's work and men's work

The diversity of sex roles is often used as an example of the power of cultural conditioning and is regularly quoted as evidence against conventional explanations for the differences between the sexes. In her analysis of women's work, Ann Oakley (1974a) argues that 'roles in traditional non-industrialised societies are often defined to some extent by sex status' but goes on to emphasize that there is no simple or universal rule for the division of labour by sex. Instead, we find that the rules regarding sex-appropriate tasks vary enormously from one culture to another. To demonstrate this argument she contrasts two African societies – the Mbuti pygmies of the northern Congo and the Lele from the south.

Love and marriage

The importance of culture is also obvious when we consider the relationship between men and women in their pursuit of one another. Courtship, marriage and sexual activity reveal patterns of normal behaviour which are anything but universal despite the fact that the desires and emotions involved are powerful natural drives genetically transmitted to ensure the survival of the species.

From a Western perspective, the notions of free choice, romantic love and jealousy may lead to the conclusion that monogamy is a natural response to the questions of courtship, marriage and sexual reproduction. However, the briefest review of other cultures or our own history demonstrates how relative such arrangements are.

Arranged marriages are often associated with the Hindu religion, but this practice is widespread, often touching on cultures where we would least expect to find it. Until the First World War (1914–18) the use of 'dynastic marriage' for political purposes was a crucial aspect of European history. For centuries it was regarded

World in focus

Two African societies: Mbuti and Lele

The Mbuti are a hunter-gatherer people who 'have no rules for the division of labour by sex'. Although there are some very loose practices of 'women's work' and 'men's work' these are not related to general types of activity but to specific tasks (men gather honey, women gather vegetables), while the most important task of hunting is carried out by men and women together. Child care is also shared but is carried out by the middle-aged men and women or by the older boys and girls. There is no division by sex between the worlds of domestic labour and economic production.

The Lele practise a very rigid division of labour by sex, although again it does not distinguish between the worlds of domestic activity and public production; nor do women have an unequal status to men because of the nature of the work they carry out. The division of labour and of life in general is geographical. The men inhabit the forest and cultivate raffia but are excluded from the grasslands, where the women cultivate groundnuts, collect firewood and tend the fishponds. Segregation also affects village life, where men and women keep to different parts of the village and enjoy segregated leisure and mealtimes. As Oakley points out, the main point here is not simply the massive cultural difference in sex-specific behaviour between two geographical neighbours but the general similarity between them when it comes to distinguishing between the domestic world and the economic:

> The situation among the Lele (and among the Mbuti) is the same as that in the majority of traditional African societies: the work done by the women is essential to the economic survival of the society. Despite the ritual allocation of some tasks to men and some to women, men's work and women's work are equal in status and importance . . . the separation between home and work is not a feature of human society as such but of industrialised society specifically.

(Oakley 1974a: 13)

as normal practice for royal marriages to act as a form of international diplomacy to maintain bonds of alliance and peace between states, nations and cultures (Baignent *et al.* 1986). Marriages were also arranged between wealthy families in order to increase their wealth, status or family honour.

Some marriages are still arranged in Japan, where the question of marriage partner is regarded as so important, especially for family honour, that it cannot be left to the romantic preferences of the daughter. A 'go-between' is employed to discover likely partners with good prospects from families of honourable status and background. This is as much an issue of parental concern for the daughter as it is a matter of family honour, because the bride changes family membership on her wedding day and belongs to her husband's family thereafter. To signify this 'death' in her parents' eyes on her wedding day, she wears white, the Japanese symbol of mourning. In Chinese communities, some arranged marriages are known as 'ghost weddings', which makes sense when placed in the context of a culture where a belief in the power of the spirit world still survives.

Recently, the *China Daily News* carried a report on July 14 1982. According to this Taiwanese newspaper, a 42-year-old man married his wife's sister who had died twenty years previously at the age of eight. The importunate spirit had visited her mother several times, saying that she wanted to marry her sister's husband. With the consent of the sister, a classical traditional wedding ceremony was held at which the living wife served as a maid of honour. On the night of the marriage ceremony, the man had to sleep alone so that the spirit of the dead woman could come to him and the marriage would be spiritually consummated. From that time onwards, the man had a double duty to his two wives and owed ritual duties to the ghost wife.

(Bloomfield 1983: 81–5)

Even if love and marriage do not necessarily go together, we might be tempted to assume that love and sex do. In 'dynastic marriages' it was not expected that the marriage would be fulfilling, but 'courtly love' provided the opportunity for satisfaction outside marriage. The well-publicized indiscretions of the British royal family in the 1990s suggest that such arrangements are still tolerated. However, in West Africa Nigel Barley's (1986) discussion of adultery with a Dowayo elder reveals that even simple rules regarding sexual attraction are by no means universal:

> All Dowayos, male and female, were to report on the appointed day and vote. It is the Chief's responsibility to ensure a good turn-out and Mayo humbly accepted this as his lot while Zuuldibo sat in the shade calling out instructions to those doing the work. I sat with him and we had a long discussion on the finer points of adultery. 'Take Mariyo,' he said. 'People always tried to say she was sleeping with my younger brother, but you saw how upset she was when he was ill. That showed there was nothing between them.' For Dowayos sex and affection were so separate that one disproved the other. I nodded wisely in agreement; there was no point in trying to explain that there was another way of looking at it.
> (Barley 1986: 135)

All this discussion has been based on the premise that sexual attraction, courtship and marriage are purely heterosexual activities. However, homosexuality has always been part of social life, even though the cultural and moral response to it varies enormously; while homosexual practice is an offence punishable by death in Iran, it is possible for gay couples to get married in Scandinavia. The issue of homosexual families is raised in Chapter 13.

Monogamy and polygamy

The practice of adultery has meaning only within societies that practise monogamous courtship and marriage. In such cultures the breaking of these rules can provide the grounds for divorce, justifiable homicide and punishment by the criminal justice system. However, in other cultures the practice of having more than one partner is not only tolerated but also institutionalized in polygamous marriage.

Among the Nyinba people of north-west Nepal the Western notion of romantic love is thought of as selfish and greedy and the inevitable cause of sorrow. Instead they practise fraternal polyandry, whereby the wife is shared by the brothers of the family she marries

Case study

Safe passage to the Celestial Kingdom

As Carys Bowen-Jones (1992) has described, girls in the Mormon community are 'turned in' to the priesthood leader once they reach 15 years of age and he 'places' them with an appropriate husband. It does not matter that the husband may already have a wife. Women are expected to share their husband and become 'wife sisters'. This arrangement has been sanctioned by the Mormon belief in 'plural marriage' and fear of social contamination.

Fundamentalist Mormons see polygamy as a sacred duty. They believe a polygamous lifestyle on earth will ensure their safe passage into a Celestial Kingdom after death, where every worthy male will be given a world of his own to people with his extended family . . . A woman's exaltation after death depends on the number of children she produces, and many women here remain in a state of almost constant pregnancy from their late teens to their late thirties . . . Contact with outsiders – or Gentiles as they're known here – is vigorously discouraged by the church elders, especially among the women . . .

The self-imposed social isolation of Colorado City, and of the neighbouring town of Hildale, which houses another 1,500 polygamists, is undoubtedly one of the main reasons why such a lifestyle has endured here for 60 years.

(Bowen-Jones 1992: 60)

Question

1. *Our discussion of cultural diversity has looked at sex roles and love and marriage. Describe the extent of cultural diversity in the areas of (a) fashion; (b) child-rearing; (c) recreational drug use. (In responding to this consider diversity over time and from place to place.)*

into. Such marriages are often arranged, but even when they are based on the sexual attraction of the bride for one particular brother she must still become the wife of the others, spending her wedding night with the eldest brother irrespective of her preference. For the purposes of family stability it is also important that the wife shows no favouritism to any individual brother and that she demonstrates this impartiality by bearing at least one child for each man. Strict penalties are maintained for anyone caught 'fooling around' outside the marriage.

A more commonly practised version of polygamy is polygamous marriage, which allows a man to have several wives. Despite this being against the teachings of the Bible and the laws of their societies, Mormon fundamentalists still believe that it is a sacred duty for a man to take several brides, even though the Mormon Church rejected the practice in 1890.

Culture and development

The importance of socialization and in particular the quality of the cultural experiences of children in the early years of the socialization process are crucial for physical, intellectual, emotional and social development.

This point is clearly demonstrated if we look at what happens when children are deprived of these cultural experiences. The cases that we shall look at illustrate different degrees of exclusion from culture and include examples where children have been partially deprived of what a culture has to offer as well as those extreme cases of children who have grown up beyond the frontiers of human civilization.

Feral children

Children who have been reared in 'the wild', outside of human society, are termed feral children. The legends of Romulus and Remus, Mowgli and Tarzan have etched into the minds of many of us distorted and romantic images of children reared in the wild by animals. According to legend these children come to little harm, retain their human characteristics and develop strong identities to become singing and dancing role models of the silver screen. The reality could not be more fantastic or further from the picture portrayed by *Greystoke* and *The Jungle Book*. Since the fourteenth century, more than fifty-three recorded cases have been found of feral children, including the Irish sheep-child, the Lithuanian bear-child and the Salzburg sow-girl. Other unlikely parents include wolves, baboons, leopards and an Indian panther (Malson and

Itard 1972: 80–2). Some of these cases may be 'the stuff of myth rather than experiences' (Maclean 1977), but Armen (1974) recorded the behaviour of a boy reared by gazelles in the Sahara and noted that the boy not only shared the physical characteristics of gazelles (sense of smell, speed, far-sightedness, etc.) but also seemed to participate in their social habits, rituals and games; as Armen made no attempt to capture and return the child to 'civilization' it is difficult to know how long the child managed to survive in the wild by reliance on those skills learned from gazelles.

In 1991 a six-year old boy, covered with body hair and running wild with a pack of monkeys, was captured in the Ugandan bush and placed with a local orphanage where he revealed that he had run away from home at the age of three and been reared by the monkeys. John Ssabunnya's story was doubted at the time but subsequent research established that he had learned the ways of monkeys and could communicate with them. He was raised with the other members of the Wasswa family and became a cherished member of the orphan community. In 1998 a similar story caught the attention of the world's press but this time it did not come from the African bush and it did not involve primate foster care: at the age of four Ivan Mishucov opted for a life on the streets of Moscow in

Figure 1.5 John Ssabunnya

World in focus

Kamala and Amala: the wolf-girls of Midnapore

In late September 1920, the Reverend Singh responded to appeals for help from local villagers in Bengal. They were being terrorized by ghosts in the form of 'man-beasts', and the Reverend Singh set up a hide from which to observe and destroy the creatures. At first, he tells us in his journal, he saw three wolves followed by two cubs but was then astonished by the apparition that followed:

Close after the cubs, came the 'ghost' – a hideous looking being, hand, foot and body like a human being; but the head was a big ball of something covering the shoulders and the upper portion of the bust leaving only a sharp contour of the face visible. Close at its heels there came another awful creature exactly like the first, but smaller in size. Their eyes were bright and piercing, unlike human eyes . . .

The first ghost appeared on the ground up to its bust, and placing its elbows on the edge of the hole, looked this side and that side and jumped out. It looked all round the place from the mouth of the hole before it leaped out to follow the cubs. It was followed by another tiny ghost of the same kind, behaving in the same manner. Both of them ran on all fours. (Maclean 1977: 60–1)

The children and wolf cubs were protected by the mother, who was quickly killed by the archers in the hunting party. The offspring were then trapped in sheets and taken into captivity, where the Reverend Singh hoped that he could return the feral children to the fold of God's love and human kindness in the safety of his orphanage.

His account of this struggle to civilize the wolf-children has been diligently researched by Charles Maclean, who reveals how far from recognizable human beings these children had become as a result of their bizarre upbringing. From the start both girls behaved more like wild animals than human children. They appeared frightened by daylight and slept naked on the floor during the middle of the day. They howled at night and shared the eating habits of dogs; they ate carrion as well as raw flesh and gobbled cockroaches, lizards and mice alive. They ran on all fours and relied heavily on sense of smell, showing a clear preference for the company of dogs over the friendship of other humans. They snarled and growled in fear when approached and even attacked the orphanage children who dared to get too close.

After three months the Reverend Singh had to record in his diary that the children had made no progress. They did not laugh or smile and continued in their nocturnal and antisocial habits. He was forced to conclude:

They had cultivated the animal nature and condition of life almost to perfection in the animal world . . . if they were to grow in humanity, they would have to fight with their fixed animal character, formed during those years with the wolves in their care and in the jungle i.e. the whole animal environment. Theirs was not a free growth as is the case of a human child of that age . . . it was hampered growth, consequently very, very slow in all its progress. (Maclean 1977: 60–1)

Gradually, however, the new environment began to work its changes. Over the next seven months, Mrs Singh's belief that 'love was the key' produced small signs of adaptation to human society. Amala, in particular, showed signs of intelligence and initiative and learned to recognize the names of food and drink. Vegetables were still refused but the children learned to use their hands when eating and drinking and began to play games when food was the reward. A year later they had mastered the skill of sleeping in a bed.

In September 1921, Amala died as the result of illness and the Reverend Singh claims that her 'sister' showed remorse and even cried over the body. Kamala now began to show signs of learning basic skills by copying other children. In June 1923, she stood for the first time and eventually learned to walk upright and moved into the girls' dormitory. By the time of her death in 1929, Kamala had showed the definite effects of her socialization in the orphanage. She had grown afraid of the dark, learned to sit at a table and came to prefer the friendship of other children. She understood language and developed a basic vocabulary of over thirty words, through her combinations of which she demonstrated a basic grasp of a self-concept. She proved to be pretty hopeless at household tasks but did show signs of recognizing the difference between right and wrong to the extent that the Reverend Singh decided that this 'sweet and obedient child' deserved to celebrate New Year's Day by being baptized.

preference to the alcoholic chaos of his family and became the adopted leader of a pack of dogs. In return for food, which Ivan begged from strangers, the dogs offered warmth and security. Eventually the police managed to separate the boy from his guardians and placed him with a foster family who coped with his canine behaviour and helped Ivan make slow progress with language and social skills.

In the case studies we can see not only how important early socialization is but also the extent to which it may be changed by later exposure to human contact.

Extreme deprivation

In the cases above, contact with human beings had been replaced by influences from other animals, so that the children had learned different survival skills through the processes of imprinting, identification and imitation. We now turn our attention to examples of human beings who have experienced extreme isolation and deprivation, usually as a result of being abandoned, and whose development is retarded rather than different. Again many

of these stories have excited the literary imagination. Alexander Selkirk, abandoned as a castaway on a desert island in 1704, became the inspiration for Defoe's Robinson Crusoe; Swift based Gulliver's meeting with the Yahoos on his own encounter with Peter of Hanover in 1726. The true story of John Merrick is now famous as the legend of the Elephant Man; Helen Keller's story has become widely known through her own books and the film of her life.

The most authentic account of such cases, however, remains Francois Truffaut's brilliant film of Dr Itard's attempts to educate Victor, the Wild Child of Aveyron. Identifying this film as the inspiration for his own research interest into wild children, Michael Newton described his first impressions of *L'Enfant Sauvage*:

> The film was elegant, beautiful, rationally delicate in its calm delineation of the central relationship between the young physician and the speechless wild child he sought to educate. It captivated me, agitated me: it woke me up.
> (Newton 2002: 9)

World in focus

Anna and Isabelle

In the USA in the 1940s two girls were separately discovered who had been living in almost total isolation from human contact. In both cases the girls were illegitimate and had been hidden away to protect the family's honour. They were discovered at around the same stage of development (6 years); both were provided with supplementary care and special education. In the more extreme case, Anna had survived with the barest minimum of human contact. Apart from being fed enough to keep her alive she was given no love or attention or any opportunity to develop physically through exploration or movement but left instead on filthy bedding in the attic in clothes that were rarely

changed. Not surprisingly, Anna had failed to develop physically and appeared to be deaf and blind. She was apathetic, expressionless and incapable of coordination and communication. In his report on the case, Kingsley Davis summarized the situation:

> Here, then, was a human organism which had missed nearly six years of socialisation. Her condition shows how little her purely biological resources, when acting alone, could contribute to making her a complete person.
> (Davis 1949: 205)

After four years of care and attention in a special school, Anna managed to learn to walk, to repeat words and try to carry on conversations, and to keep herself

and her clothes clean. She discovered the worlds of play and colour and had begun to develop intellectually and emotionally before she died at the age of 10.

Isabelle had the meagre advantage of being in regular contact with her mother, a deaf mute who had been incarcerated with her in a darkened room by Isabelle's grandfather. Although she had learned to communicate with her mother through a personal system of gesture, Isabelle was severely retarded physically and intellectually. She was fearful of strangers and reacted violently towards men. However, the specialist attention of doctors and psychologists enabled Isabelle to recapture the lost years of her early life through 'a systematic

World in focus (continued)

and skilful programme of training'. Isabelle's response to this intense socialization process was as rapid as it is remarkable and clearly demonstrates the essential role played by the environment and education in the stages of child development.

The task seemed hopeless at first, but gradually she began to respond. After the first few hurdles had at last been overcome, a curious thing happened. She went through the usual stages of learning characteristics of the years from one to six not only in proper succession but far more rapidly than normal. In a little over two months after her first vocalisation she was putting sentences together. Nine months after that she could identify words and sentences on the printed page, could write well, could add to ten and could retell a story after hearing it. Seven months beyond this point she had a vocabulary of 1500–2000 words and was asking complicated questions. Starting from an educational level of between one and three years, she had reached a normal level by the time she was eight and a half years old. In short, she covered in two years the stages of learning that ordinarily require six. She eventually entered school where she participated in all school activities as normally as other children.

(Davis 1949: 206–7)

Thirty years after the discovery of Anna and Isabelle, another well-known case came to light. For most of her 13 years Genie had been imprisoned in a darkened room of her father's house, where she was either tied up or caged. Her isolation appears to have been relieved only by interruptions for food and punishment. If she made a noise her father would respond with growls and barks and often beat her with a stick.

When she finally escaped with the help of her mother, Genie was found to be malnourished, incontinent and barely able to walk. She appeared to be almost blind, salivated constantly and could not speak. Like Isabelle she reacted violently to challenging situations and would urinate and masturbate in public. Under the guidance of a psychologist, Susan Curtiss, Genie learned to dress, eat correctly and use a toilet, but she had probably spent too many years of her bleak early life in isolation to ever catch up on her lost childhood; she never developed her ability with language beyond that of a 4-year-old, although her IQ score improved from 38 to 74 in the space of six years.

At the time Genie was seen as an opportunity to test out Chomsky and Lennenberg's new theories on language acquisition; while they both agreed that the origin of language, the ground rules of grammar and the capacity for speech are uniquely human characteristics which we are biologically programmed with, Lennenberg suggested that for language to develop it had to be learned during a 'critical period' between 2 and 13 years of age. In Newton's summary of the case, Genie made great progress in her acquisition of vocabulary but did not appear able to develop her natural linguistic potential despite being subjected to intense linguistic experimentation:

The results were disappointing in the end, for despite her wide vocabulary Genie failed to use grammatical structures. She had words, but could not make correct English sentences. Her failure appeared to prove Lennenberg's thesis of the critical period for language acquisition. Yet in one sense, Genie really did learn to communicate through words, if communication means simply making oneself understood, though her linguistic attainments were perhaps not sufficient to enable a fully fledged conversation . . . Nonetheless, she mastered the essential facets of language: she could produce novel sentences, play with words, listen, take turns in conversation, speak spontaneously and refer to people or events displaced in time.

(Newton 2002: 224)

The issue was further complicated by the evidence of damage to the part of Genie's brain which governs language; had Genie's brain not been physically impaired we cannot say how far she may have progressed. Such speculation and other important questions raised by this case remain unanswered due to Genie's father committing suicide and her mother bringing the support programme to an end with a court case in which she sued the children's hospital for damages (Pines 1981). In a more recent case, a 44-year-old woman called Lola Vina Costello was discovered in a pit in the basement of the family home in northern Spain. She had been there since 1957 and was suffering from severe photophobia (fear of light) and physical atrophy. Consequently, she had lost her powers of sight, hearing and speech and behaved more like an animal than a human being (*The Times* 10.2.97). Such cases are not just historic relics as the case study below, from Sheffield, reported in the *Independent* in November 2004, illustrates.

Case study

Doctor blames parents for 'worst case of malnutrition'

A doctor who treated twin babies rescued from a house of 'utter squalor' told a court yesterday that it was 'the worse case of malnutrition he had ever seen outside the developing world'.

The emaciated boys, one of them close to death, were among five children rescued from a terraced house in Sheffield, South Yorkshire, last June. The parents, David Askew and Sarah Whittaker, both 24, were each sentenced to seven years at Sheffield Crown Court after admitting five counts of cruelty.

Police officers involved in the rescue said they had difficulty not being physically sick in the filthy bedrooms and kitchen, but were astonished to find a neat living room, filled with state-of-the-art electrical appliances.

The Recorder of Sheffield, Alan Goldsack, told the couple: 'The reality is that behind the closed doors of your home your children were being slowly starved to death. Most members of the public will not begin to understand how in the twenty-first century children can slip through the net in the way yours

Figure 1.6 The house of 'utter squalor'

Case study (continued)

did.' The court heard how the horror at the three-bedroom house was discovered when, at his daughter's behest, Whittaker phoned for an ambulance because one of the twins was 'lifeless'. Paramedics found the boy skeletal and grey, suffering from hypothermia, hypoglycaemia (deficiency of glucose in the bloodstream) and severe malnourishment . . .

Both boys' growth was consistent with a four- to five-month-old baby, according to doctors. The other children in the house – now aged eight, four and three – were also living amid dog and human excrement, with urine-soaked mattresses and soiled clothes . . .

The judge heard that relatives who babysat for the couple had found the children in a terrible state and had told them to sort it out. Social services had never been involved with the family. Askew tried to distance himself from the cruelty, saying it was Whittaker's responsibility to look after the children. He told police that the house 'could do with tidying up'. Whittaker had become pregnant at 15 and had a number of miscarriages and terminations.

The children are now in local authority care. The court heard all five were thriving, although one of the twins may have permanent problems with his sight and hearing.

(Ian Herbert, *Independent*, 24.11.04)

Question

1. *Suggest both social and personal/psychological explanations for the actions of Askew and Whittaker. Which type of explanations do you find more convincing?*

As David Skuse has pointed out, the value of these studies is not simply that they demonstrate the importance of nurture over nature or of the environment over inheritance but that we can go too far in the direction of 'super environmentalism' and imagine that behaviour is fixed by experience as opposed to genetic blueprints.

> Extreme deprivation in early childhood is a condition of great theoretical and practical importance . . . Most human characteristics, with the possible exception of language . . . are virtually resistant to obliteration by even the most dire early environments. On removal to a favourable situation, the remarkable and rapid progress made by those with good potential seems allied to the total experience of living in a stimulating home and forming emotional bonds to a caring adult.
>
> (Skuse 1984: 571–2)

Stop and think

> ➤ The 'nature/nurture' debate as to how much we are influenced by our environment and how much we are the product of our biological and genetic inheritance has been long and fiercely argued. In what ways might a sociological perspective add to this debate? How could you use the case studies above to illustrate your argument?

Cultural deprivation and social opportunity

In the early studies of crime during the 1920s and 1930s and in the first attempts to understand educational failure, social scientists focused on the role played by cultural deprivation in the creation of deviance and under-achievement. The term was not restricted to intellectual and educational activity but referred to a broader concept which implied a culturally determined notion of desirable standards of material and social existence from which some individuals and families may be excluded. Such circumstances would be synonymous with poverty or poor housing, and the term is often used interchangeably with concepts such as 'underprivileged', 'disadvantaged', 'lower class' and, more recently, 'underclass' (Jencks 1993). 'Poor family conditions' have been offered since the end of the nineteenth century as a possible explanation for anti-social and criminal behaviour.

Crime and delinquency

During the early part of the twentieth century, the idea that delinquency could be related to deprivation took root. Juvenile courts began to require reports on the 'home surroundings' of young offenders, and in 1927 a Home Office committee accepted the view of many reformers that delinquent children were themselves victims:

There is little or no difference in character and needs between the neglected and the delinquent child. It is often mere accident whether he is brought before the court because he is wandering or beyond control or because he has committed some offence. Neglect leads to delinquency.

(Home Office 1927: 111, cited in Pachman 1981)

A series of reports between the 1940s and 1960s saw the emphasis shift away from evil and depravity towards the concept of deprivation and 'the lack of satisfactory family life' in the search for an understanding of rising juvenile crime. The social investigations of researchers such as J.B. Mays (1954) and Norman Tutt (1974) confirmed the relationship between delinquency and cultural deprivation.

In his summary of Sprott's (1954) work on lower-class families and 'Delinquent Subculture', Tutt paints a despairing picture of the criminal family type:

The ... families lived in an atmosphere of squalor, possessions were untidy and uncared for, and individual ownership was not prized. The families' leisure was largely taken up with gambling. Irregular sexual unions were frequent and openly discussed ... Minor acts of physical aggression – mothers clouting children, siblings fighting – were frequent. Parents tended to quarrel openly and violently; the father left the responsibility of bringing up the children entirely to the mother. Children were given pocket money at random to spend as they liked ... Neither were they encouraged to use their leisure time constructively.

(Tutt 1974: 25)

Educational failure

Alongside the concern with juvenile crime, and often overlapping with it, was the attempt by social researchers and politicians to understand educational failure in an age when educational opportunity was, in theory, a right for all children. Cyril Burt (1925) was one of the first researchers to confront the issue and, although his emphasis was on the inherited nature of intelligence, his ideas on selective education, which were used to support the development of the notorious '11 plus' examination, were partly justified as a device for rescuing able working-class children from homes blighted by poverty and educational deprivation.

In the 1950s and 1960s, the work of Riessman (1962) in the USA and Douglas (1964) in Britain firmly established the idea that the educational under-achievement of children from poor backgrounds was, in part, a result of cultural deprivation. Government investigations such as the Plowden Report in 1967 clearly identified parental attitudes towards education and the lack of educational resources in the home as the key to school performance.

During the 1980s the right of liberal reformers to monopolize the concept of cultural deprivation was challenged from the political right. Beneath the concern to identify the social causes of crime and failure there has always been a hint of moral superiority. It took only a change in the political climate for these feelings to manifest themselves in a way which seeks to 'blame the victims' rather than help them.

Charles Murray, a fellow of the American Enterprise Institute, has argued that welfare dependency and single motherhood have become part of a culture that threatens to destroy family life, social morality and the rule of law.

Children learn how to be responsible adults by watching what responsible adults do. The absence of such examples for boys seems especially dangerous. The violence and social chaos in America's inner cities tells us how a generation of males behave when about half of them grow to adolescence without a constraining sense of what it means to be an adult male.

(quoted in The Sunday Times 10.5.92)

According to Murray, unruly males may be the problem but it is their mothers who are to blame. If the subculture of deprivation is to be broken the answer is to stop tinkering with educational reform and eradicate the system of benefit that encourages such attitudes. Murray argued that by refusing benefits to single parents, the values surrounding marriage, family and proper child care will be resurrected. This less obvious aspect of the cultural deprivation argument is increasingly dominating the debates over moral decline, truancy and the rise in juvenile crime (see pp. 251–5 on the 'underclass debate').

Structure and agency

The idea that 'human nature' can be supplanted by the concepts of learning and socialization is often criticized for replacing biological reductionism with a form of cultural reductionism (see Skuse's comment on 'super environmentalism' on page 34). One of the first sociologists to raise this issue was Dennis Wrong. In his attack on functionalism, Wrong complains that macrosociology tends to exaggerate the power of social structures and processes and loses sight of the conscious and self-determining individual. This he referred to as an 'over-socialized conception of man' in which those individual forces resistant to the power of socialization and the restrictions of role playing are overlooked. If sociologists continued to ignore the unpredictable human element, he warned, 'we will end up imagining that man is the disembodied, conscience-driven, status-seeking phantom of current theory' (cited in Coser and Rosenberg 1969: 131) Wrong's warning anticipated a sociological controversy later known as 'the structure/agency debate'. Since the 1970s different sociologists have tried to accommodate the idea of the individual as an active agent within the powerful social and cultural influences which play upon them.

Summary

➤ Sociology helps us to make sense of the world we live in. It asks questions about and seeks answers for the things that directly affect our lives. In studying people and the societies that they live in, sociology relies on rigorous procedures and is informed by rational argument and existing knowledge.

➤ There is no uniform and all-embracing sociological perspective. Sociologists disagree over research procedures (methodologies) and theoretical perspectives; these different approaches and positions emerged as the subject of sociology developed.

➤ Modern (Western) sociology is generally seen as originating from the economic, social and political upheavals and revolutions of the nineteenth century, in particular as a result of developments such as the Industrial Revolution and the move to the factory system of production; urbanization; the growth of capitalism; and the wider acceptance of liberal democracy and the support for the rights of individuals.

➤ Culture and socialization are two key concepts used in sociology. Culture is used to refer to the values, customs and styles of behaviour of a society or social group and socialization to the process by which people learn the norms, values and roles approved in their society. Socialization depends on social interaction and without this individuals could not develop as social beings.

➤ The importance of these concepts is shown if we look at individuals who have been deprived of socialization and of cultural experiences – children brought up in the wild or shut away and ignored by their families and having no contact with other humans.

➤ Sociologists have utilized the concept of cultural deprivation to explain patterns of social behaviour such as differences in criminal behaviour or educational attainment between different social groups.

Links

The case study extracts referring to the criminal careers of the Krays and of Cocky Warren link with Chapter 16, particularly the section on theories of crime.

The information on capitalism, pages 13–14, links with Chapter 2.

The section on socialization, pages 23–6, links with Chapter 13.

The examination of cultural deprivation and opportunity links with both Chapters 14 and 16.

 ## Further reading

Ballard, C., Gubbay, J. and Middleton, C. (eds) (1997) *The Student's Companion to Sociology*, London: Blackwell.
This is a collection written by an international team (with an American editor, Ballard, and British editors, Gubbay and Middleton) that conveys the excitement of studying sociology. It provides plenty of practical advice for students new to the subject and for those hoping to use their sociological education to enhance their employment opportunities.

Bauman, Z. (1990) *Thinking Sociologically*, Oxford: Blackwell. An up-to-date and 'theoretical' introduction to sociology that discusses in some depth the relationship between sociology and common sense.

Bennett, T. and Watson, D. (eds) (2002) *Understanding Everyday Life*, Oxford: Blackwell.
This is the first book in a series of four that aims to provide an introduction to the sociological study of modern society. This book looks at how sociology can throw new light on familiar aspects of everyday life. The different chapters consider a range of sites, including the home, the street, the pub and the neighbourhood. The other books in the series are entitled *Social Differences and Divisions*, *Social Change* and *The Uses of Sociology*.

Levin, J. (1993) *Sociological Snapshots*, Newbury Park, Calif: Pine Forge.
This series of essays tries to relate the familiar, common-sense world of our everyday experiences to the more abstract sociological interpretation and theorizing. The first two sections, on culture and socialization, are particularly relevant to this introductory chapter.

Berger, P.L. (1967) *Invitation to Sociology: A Humanistic Perspective*, Harmondsworth: Penguin.

Mills, C.W. (1970) *The Sociological Imagination*, Harmondsworth: Penguin.
Given that this is an introductory chapter, there are no particular substantive studies that provide an overview of the area. However, the introductory books by Peter Berger and C. Wright Mills have had a tremendous impact and been an important influence on many people currently working in sociology. They are still well worth reading; perhaps more than any other introductory studies they capture the excitement and challenge of studying the human world.

Nisbet, R.A. (1970) *The Sociological Tradition*, London: Heinemann Educational.
In this classic introduction to the history of sociology, Nisbet focuses on the period between 1830 and 1900, which saw the emergence of modern sociology. He sets the development of sociology in its political and economic context, in particular highlighting the importance of the 'two revolutions' – the Industrial Revolution of the late eighteenth/early nineteenth century and the political revolution that started in France in 1789 – for nineteenth-century thought.

Web sites

British Sociological Association (BSA)
www.britsoc.org.uk
The web site for the British Sociological Association (BSA) provides information about sociology as a subject, including its history, where to study sociology and guidelines on good practice in doing sociology (such as appropriate language to use).

Sociological Research Online
www.socresonline.org.uk
The Sociological Research Online web site is a mine of useful information which provides details on sociology departments in this and other countries.

Activities

Activity 1

Sky burials

Steve Mair describes a burial ceremony in Tibet and demonstrates how the disposal of the dead is dealt with in a radically different manner from the way it is dealt with in contemporary Western society.

Fly away Peter

During a six-week visit to Tibet, Steve Mair set off from Llasa early one morning to attempt to witness one of the world's most startling spectacles. Photographs were forbidden. And unnecessary.

It was six-thirty on a cold Tibetan morning and still pitch black when, stumbling and yawning, we set off out of town towards the nearby hills . . .

Previously I'd had no intention of trying to see a sky burial since, although what I'd heard about this custom fascinated me, I thought that to intrude on other people's grief was obscene, to say the least. Joe had felt the same, and besides we had been told that we would not be welcome there and had even heard stories about rocks being thrown at Westerners who did try to go. This turned out to be true, but it was Westerners who had tried, stupidly, to take photographs of the burial after being warned not to do so.

Activities (continued)

However, two days before, we'd met a New Zealander who said she'd been to see a burial that morning, and that no hostility had been shown to her. Also, and most importantly, she said that there were no family of the deceased present during the ritual. So that was it, that there were no relatives present was the deciding factor (they apparently arrive later, after it's over, just to see that the job has been done and their loved ones properly dispatched). Joe and I both made up our minds to try to witness a burial before leaving Lhasa.

Now here we were, on a hill outside Lhasa, standing in the Tibetan pre-dawn chill with the man by the fire silently stropping his butcher's blade. For a few moments it was quite eerie as we stood gazing at the two covered bodies until finally, in sign language, we asked if we could stay. They asked if we had cameras. We assured them we didn't. They warned us again we should not take photographs, we said we understood, and then after a little discussion they motioned us to sit.

We sat for half an hour in almost total silence, trying to imagine the ceremony, while the Tibetans continued to smoke and drink tea and from time to time produce more large knives to be sharpened . . .

By now it was quite light and we'd been joined by three other Westerners, who had obviously had the same idea, and an old Buddhist monk carrying a large prayer flag, who had come down from the monastery on the opposite side of the hill to preside over the burial. First the monk made himself comfortable in a makeshift altar behind us, and then commenced a soft, rhythmic chanting while setting up a gentle staccato beat on a goatskin drum and blowing down a conch-like trumpet . . .

After he'd been praying for ten minutes or so and with the crisp morning air filled with these strange mystical sounds as well as the sweet smell of burning juniper bushes that one of the workmen had lit all around us, the sun suddenly appeared over the hills to the east instantly bathing the whole tableau in warmth and light. At this point seven of the workmen finished their tea, put out their cigarettes, donned grubby and bloodstained overalls, and set off towards the large rock that was thirty feet in front of us. At last the ceremony began.

Five of the workmen sat down behind the bodies, facing us, while the remaining two drew the large knives from their belts and threw the covers off the bodies. One of the bodies was of a plump female, perhaps in her forties, while the other was that of a skinny, old man. Mercifully they were lying face down so we couldn't see their faces. This was just as well since I think by now most of us had begun to feel a little queasy: I certainly had.

For most of the time we watched the 'butcher' who was working on the woman. He began by making a cut from the nape of the neck down to the buttocks and then on down the back of each leg up to the heel. He pulled off the skin from the back in two pieces and threw them to the ground with a loud slap. At this point the squeamishness left me as the red meat and white fat of the body was revealed: it was just like Smithfields, a side of beef waiting to be cut up. From then on, I watched in total fascination.

As he proceeded to cut up the torso, the knife pierced the gut, and the blood and juices flooded out over the rock and down its side. He chopped off the limbs and removed the bones, which he tossed in turn to the five men sitting down. They were crushers and, using large stone hammers, they began to reduce the bones to a fine powder . . .

Although we all sat and watched this strange spectacle in silence and awe, I came to realise they were just ordinary workmen doing a difficult and messy job. They could have been a gang of tarmac layers in the north of England . . .

After half an hour all that was left of the bodies were the heads. These were first scalped, cutting off all the hair, and then the skin peeled off to leave just the bare skulls. They placed the skulls in one of the shallow grooves that dotted the rock and smashed them open with a large stone. After tipping out the two halves of the brain they tossed the pieces to the crushers to do their job.

After 40 minutes the work was complete and both bodies had been reduced to a small, unrecognisable rubble-heap of flesh and powdered bone mixed with tsampa, the coarse flour made from barley that is the

Activities (continued)

Tibetans' staple diet. By that time a dozen or more vultures had gathered on the slope at the side of the rock and were silently waiting. As the two butchers wiped the blades on their overalls and made their way back to the fire one of the crushers picked up a piece of flesh and tossed it amongst the birds.

It was as if a dinner gong had sounded. A cacophony of screeches erupted from the previously silent birds and suddenly the sky overhead turned black as 60 to 70 of the largest vultures I've ever seen (I'd seen quite a few in India) descended on to the slope by the rock . . .

For a few seconds they milled around on the slope until one of the throng finally flew up on to the rock and began feeding. This seemed to be the signal as all at once the rest of the birds jumped, hopped, and flew on to the rock which became at once a brown, seething unidentifiable mass as, with wings folded and heads down, they began tearing at the food. The noise was terrible as they greedily devoured the remains, squawking and squabbling over the larger pieces, but after 10 minutes or so they had finished . . .

The 'burial' was over. It had taken less than one hour from beginning to end, and there was not a morsel of food left on the rock, just a few dark stains.

By now the men had removed their overalls and were smoking and drinking tea again as they cleaned and packed away their tools. Myself, Joe, and the three other Westerners rose stiffly to our feet (we had sat virtually without moving for over an hour), thanked the Tibetans, who now showed little interest in us, and started back down the hill, still in total silence, each of us trying to assess what we had just seen.

In a land where wood is scarce and at a premium, and the ground is as hard as rock, and where the Buddhist beliefs of the people proclaim the continuity of all life (birth, death, and rebirth) they had developed this unusual method of disposing of their dead. We had experienced no feelings of disgust or horror, merely a sense of wonderment, and also privilege, at having been allowed to witness this unique Tibetan custom.

On the way back to town I finally asked Joe what he had thought of it all. 'Bloody incredible,' he said, 'there's no need for photographs at all, it's something I'll remember for the rest of my life.' I totally agreed.

(The *Guardian* 18.10.86)

Questions

1. What aspects of the sky burials are very different from your own notions of a 'decent burial'?

2. What similarities are there between the Tibetan burial rituals and those practised in contemporary Britain?

3. What possible explanations might there be for the type of burial ceremony described by Mair?

4. How does Mair's account illustrate the relationship of culture to history and economic necessity?

Activity 2

Identity formation

Read the following extract from Baumeister on the role of the family and identity formation and then answer the questions below.

The infant is born into a mini-society, namely, the family. This little society provides the child with identity. The child's relation to that society is at first not problematic for the same reasons that the medieval adult's relationship to society was not problematic. That is, the society is narrow, inflexible and well defined, and the child holds the two basic attitudes that make the individual's relationship to society unproblematic. First, the child is equated with its place in the family. The infant's and small child's role in the family is not open to much redefinition, at least not from the child's perspective. The very young child has no private self or life apart from its role in the family. And if the child has an interesting experience during the parents' absence,

Activities (continued)

the child will probably tell them about it as soon as they return. Second, the child believes fulfilment to be contingent on performing its role in the family. The child trusts the family to love and care for it as long as the child does what it is supposed to do.

As the child grows, these two basic attitudes are undermined and the child's relationship with the family gradually becomes problematic. First, the child slowly ceases to equate itself with its role in the family as its social world expands through school, peer interactions, sports and so forth. The family may remain the most important society for the child, but it is not the only one, and therefore the child can conceptualise itself apart from the family. The second attitude is the belief that one will be fulfilled simply by doing what one's parents tell one to do. This attitude tends to die a complex and multifaceted death. By adolescence, the boy or girl is generally convinced of the necessity of becoming emotionally detached from the parents and seeking fulfilment elsewhere.

(Baumeister 1986: 254–5)

Questions

1. Why does Baumeister regard the family as such an important feature of identity formation?

2. How is this process undermined by 'growing up' and what impact might this have on identity formation?

3. What criticisms can you make of this view of family life and identity formation?

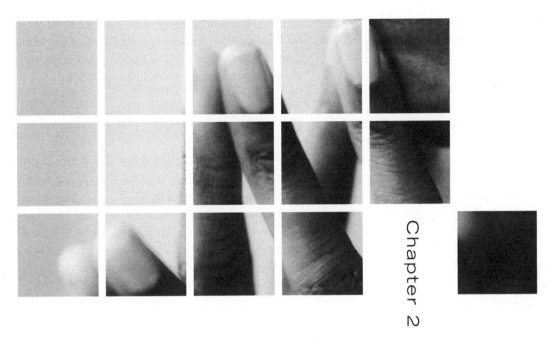

Sociological theories

To be sure, theory is useful. But without warmth of heart and without love it bruises the very ones it claims to save.

(Gide 1952)

Key issues

➤ What are the major theoretical perspectives in sociology?

➤ How have the writings of Durkheim, Marx and Weber influenced the development of sociological theories?

➤ How have the established sociological theories been criticized by feminism and other more recent theorizing?

Introduction

Sociological theory deals with the 'big questions' which we all ask ourselves from time to time. Questions such as: Who are we? Is there a reason for the way we are? How do our lives fit in with the wider society? Who has power and influence over us? Why do some people live in poverty?

Studying theory can and should be an exciting enterprise. However, many people, including students, are suspicious of theory and are keen to extol the virtues

of being 'down to earth' and practical. This distinction between practice and theory is not a clearcut one: most of our practical actions and decisions are influenced by the theoretical assumptions we hold. The decision to buy flowers for one's mother on Mother's Day, for instance, might be based on an assumption that males and females have different tastes that reflect their different personalities.

Stop and think

➤ List the kinds of 'theoretical assumption' that (a) teachers make about their pupils' attitudes to school work; (b) employers make about what motivates their employees; (c) influenced your decision to study sociology.

This chapter explains the development of the major theoretical approaches in sociology and looks at the work of some of the founders of modern sociology and at their continuing influence. The first section of the chapter will focus on the lives, ideas and work of the three thinkers who have had the greatest influence on modern sociology – Emile Durkheim, Karl Marx and Max Weber. While not exact contemporaries, all three were born in the nineteenth century and developed theories that responded to the economic, political and social changes of that century – the rapid industrialization of Europe and North America and the effects of capitalism on Western society. It is important to bear in mind that the origins of sociological theorizing were profoundly political. When Marx, Durkheim and Weber tried to understand nineteenth-century industrialization they did not do it just out of intellectual interest or academic indulgence, they aimed to explore the effects of these changes on the shape and quality of social life – and to consider how the changes might (or might not) improve this quality of life. Indeed the development of early, 'classical' sociology can be seen as an attempt to answer the question 'What is industrial society?' Durkheim, Marx, Weber and other early theorists tried to explain how industrial society had come about, what held it together and what kept pulling it apart.

However, this is not to imply that there was a general agreement or consensual approach among these early theorists. Marx's theorizing and analysis focused on capitalist society – on the workings of capitalism and the inevitability of its eventual collapse – rather than industrial society in general. In terms of their own beliefs, Marx was a political revolutionary, while Durkheim rejected the case for revolutionary politics; although attracted to socialism, Durkheim saw it as a protest against the disintegration of traditional social and moral values rather than as a means for promoting the abolition of private property. And although both Marx and Weber emphasized the importance of power and conflict in their social theorizing, Marx held as a general principle that economic relations had primacy over other aspects of the social structure, whereas Weber opposed this general theory of history and stressed the importance of culture and politics, as well as economics.

While sociological explanations and theories might be relatively recent, the questions that interest sociology have been considered by thinkers throughout history. What is new is the modern science of society. The roots of modern sociology can be found in the Enlightenment and the social revolutions of the eighteenth century. The scientific discoveries of the Enlightenment helped to transform the social order, with secular knowledge (based on reason and science) replacing sacred tradition. The revolutions in North America, France and England resulted from social movements based on notions of human rights; these revolutions advocated democracy rather than autocracy. As our account of the origins of sociology demonstrated (pp. 11–17), the world from which sociology emerged was characterized by rapid

and often frightening change. The Industrial Revolution, for instance, brought unprecedented productivity at the same time as increased poverty, congested cities, high unemployment and miserable living conditions.

Sociological perspectives

Although there are other, and earlier, writers whose work is important to sociology, Durkheim, Marx and Weber are generally reckoned to be the key figures in the development of sociological theory. Their work and ideas have been developed by later writers into particular schools of thought or perspectives with their own analytical styles and interpretations. While you may be puzzled by the diversity of theoretical approaches and perspectives, it is important to realize that there is no agreed theoretical standpoint in sociology. Giddens (1993) suggests that this lack of agreement is due to the nature of the subject itself: sociology is about people and their behaviour and it is a highly complex task to study this. The lack of one overall theoretical approach should not be taken as a sign of weakness but rather an indication of the vitality of sociology. Human behaviour is complicated, and it is unrealistic to expect a single unified theoretical perspective to cover all aspects of it. Although there is a diversity of theoretical approaches, there is also a good deal of overlap between them. All sociological theories have in common an emphasis on the ways in which human behaviour and belief are the products of social influences; indeed, this distinguishes sociology from other approaches to human behaviour.

Stop and think

➤ It is not just sociology that is characterized by theoretical disagreement. Consider the different subjects you have studied or are studying. What different and contradictory approaches or explanations have you come across in these subjects?

➤ Which subjects appear to have a unified theoretical stance? Why do you think this might be?

In introducing the sociological perspective in Chapter 1, alternative explanations of human behaviour were considered. Until relatively recently (the nineteenth century), interest in social aspects of behaviour had been very limited; non-social approaches to human behaviour were predominant. In reflecting on this lack of interest in the social aspects of human existence, Jones (2003) highlights two important non-sociological explanations of human behaviour – *naturalistic* explanations and *individualistic* explanations.

The naturalistic explanation suggests that human behaviour is the product of inherited disposition; humans, like animals, are programmed by nature. This style of explanation is common enough. For instance, it is sometimes argued that it is 'natural' for women and men to fall in love, marry and live in a small family unit (and, therefore, it is 'unnatural' not to want to do this). However, there are many variations to the supposedly 'natural' family practice in both Western, industrial societies and non-industrial societies.

The individualistic explanation sees human behaviour as a result of the psychological make-up of individuals. Criminals, for instance, are people with certain kinds of personality, maybe lacking a sense of right or wrong. Again, wider study casts doubt on these explanations. The bulk of people who are convicted of crime are male, young and from working-class backgrounds: is it feasible to believe that criminal personalities are concentrated in such groupings? And if class is important, why are working-class women under-represented among the criminal population?

These examples help to illustrate the importance of social influences on human behaviour. Where the particular sociological theories and approaches differ is in their emphasis on what these social influences are and how they can be explained.

Classical sociological theories

Durkheim and consensus

Although there is no definitive version of the history of Western sociology, there is a general agreement that it was developed in nineteenth-century France as a consequence of changes in French society brought about by the democratic revolution of 1789 (see p. 15). The two French writers who did most to 'create' the subject were Auguste Comte, who helped to establish the idea of the study of society as a project and who gave the subject its name, and Emile Durkheim, who gave sociology its academic credibility and influence. Durkheim devoted his life to establishing sociology as a distinctive and accepted field of study by building a profession of sociology in France. He established university departments to train students in the theories and methods of this new science and edited and directed the publication of a journal which was the leading light of the new sociological movement – *L'Année Sociologique*. As well as this organizing role, Durkheim is best known as an author. His four major studies have given him a key position in sociology:

➤ *The Division of Labour in Society*, 1893.

➤ *The Rules of Sociological Method*, 1895.

➤ *Suicide: A Study in Sociology*, 1897.

➤ *The Elementary Forms of the Religious Life*, 1912.

Durkheim's work

In attempting to answer the question 'What is industrial society?', Durkheim focused on the moral basis of social order and stability – the moral basis of what he termed social solidarity. He believed that social order was based on a core of shared values. This belief is a key aspect of the functionalist approach in sociology, which he helped to establish.

Durkheim argued that without the regulation of society, individuals would attempt to satisfy their own desires and wishes without regard to their fellows. This societal regulation or constraint had to be based on a shared set of values. Thus a working society necessitated the individuals within it accepting these common values. Durkheim called this common set of values the collective conscience. This term is a little ambiguous in that the French word 'conscience' means both 'consciousness' and 'conscience'. However, Durkheim defined the collective conscience as 'the totality of beliefs and sentiments common to average citizens of the same society'.

Stop and think

➤ What common, generally held values make up the 'collective conscience' of modern society?

➤ Which of these values do you use to guide your everyday life?

➤ Which of these values are used by (a) your family; (b) your friends; (c) your teachers?

Durkheim suggested that while we as individuals may think we choose to behave in certain ways, in reality the choices are made for us. The kinds of possibility of thought

A closer look

Emile Durkheim (1858–1917)

Durkheim's life spanned a period of great change in French and European history. He grew up in the aftermath of the French defeat by Prussia in the war of 1870–71, while the final years of his life were overshadowed by the outbreak of the First World War in 1914. Durkheim was the son of a rabbi and was brought up in an orthodox Jewish family. He was expected to follow in his father's footsteps and become a rabbi, but 'conversion' to Catholicism and then to agnosticism in his youth led him into an academic life. Durkheim was a brilliant student; he studied at the Ecole Normale Supérieure, Paris, where his interests in social and political philosophy developed. His political views matured while he was studying in Paris; he seems to have been pro-democracy and social reform in the face of the reactionary views of the monarchists and Catholic right. However, Durkheim tended to remain aloof from day-to-day political life, preferring to study and debate politics in terms of general theoretical principles. After graduating, Durkheim taught philosophy in several schools between 1882 and 1885. He then spent a year in Germany, where he was deeply impressed by German advances in social science and psychology. The articles he wrote on these developments helped him to get a post as lecturer in social science and education at the University of Bordeaux in 1887 – the first social science post at a French university. It was while at Bordeaux that Durkheim produced his major works; the first three books listed on page 43 were written during this period of his life. By 1902, Durkheim's academic reputation was established and he moved to Paris as professor of education and social science at the Sorbonne, where he remained until his death.

Figure 2.1 Emile Durkheim
© Bettman/Corbis

and experience available to us are not invented by us individually; they are learned. Durkheim uses religion to illustrate this point. Our religious beliefs and practices are learned; they were in existence before us and if we had been born in another society or age it is likely we would hold quite different beliefs and follow different religious practices. Although self-evident, this point is fundamental to the consensus approach in sociology and is illustrated by Durkheim's comment:

> When I fulfil my obligations as brother, husband or citizen I perform duties which are defined externally to myself and my acts, in law and custom. Even if they conform to my own sentiments and I feel their reality subjectively . . . I merely inherited them through my education. . . . The church member finds the beliefs and practices of his religious life made at birth, their existence prior to him implies their existence outside himself. (Durkheim 1964: 1–2)

For Durkheim, then, the achievement of social life among people, the existence of social order and social solidarity, is ensured by collective standards of behaviour and values. However, while social solidarity is crucial for the existence of society, the specific type or form it takes is not fixed and changes with the changing forms of society. In his first major work, *The Division of Labour in Society*, Durkheim examines the changes in the form of social solidarity from early, pre-modern societies to complex, modern ones.

The Division of Labour and forms of social solidarity

One of the major academic issues which Durkheim focused on was the significance of the rise of individualism in modern industrial society. *The Division of Labour in Society* attempts to demonstrate how the rise of individualism exemplifies the emergence of a new type of social order – an order that will increasingly transcend traditional forms of society.

Durkheim argues that the function of the division of labour in modern society is the social integration of individuals, which is achieved through their fulfilling a range of complementary roles and tasks. The theme of the study is the relationship between individuals and the collectivity. The question or problem that Durkheim tackles is 'How can a multiplicity of individuals make up a society?' or 'How can a consensus – the basic condition of social existence – be achieved?'

Durkheim addresses this question by distinguishing between two forms of social solidarity. He argues that the basis of social solidarity in pre-industrial, small-scale societies is different from that in modern industrial society; the former he termed *mechanical solidarity*, the latter *organic solidarity*.

A closer look

Mechanical solidarity

A solidarity of resemblance. Individuals are essentially alike: they feel the same emotions and hold the same things sacred. Individuals are not differentiated, in the sense that there is little job specialization. This type of solidarity has existed throughout most of human history; archaic, pre-literate societies were characterized by it. In such situations collective feelings predominate, property tends to be communally owned and the discipline of the small community and of tradition is dominant.

As societies became more complex, with increased division of labour, so mechanical solidarity becomes less evident and is superseded by organic solidarity.

Organic solidarity

Consensus comes, essentially, from differentiation between individuals. With the increasing range of functions and tasks in complex modern societies comes an increasing differentiation between individuals. Individuals are more interdependent: because people engage in different activities and ways of life they are very dependent on others, and this dependence leads to the development of networks of solidarity. In these situations, social order does not rest on uniformity but rather on individuals pursuing different but complementary functions. This differentiation releases and encourages individualism and individual talent. In the face of this, society needs a strong moral force and consensus to hold it together and to ensure interdependence. In spite of individuals being unlike one another (in terms of their occupations, for instance) they need to get on together in order for social life to work.

In defining and describing the different forms of solidarity, Durkheim is talking in general and abstract terms. He was not suggesting that there is a simplistic and rigid divide between mechanical and organic solidarity: societies do not necessarily exhibit either mechanical or organic solidarity. Societies with a highly developed organic solidarity will still need to have common beliefs; all societies have to have some common set of assumptions about the world. So the collective conscience is vital in all societies; without it there would just be disintegration into a collection of mutually antagonistic individuals. However, the collective conscience varies in extent and force from one society to another. Where mechanical solidarity is predominant it embraces virtually all of the individual conscience; in modern, differentiated societies characterized by organic solidarity the scope for individuality is greater – people have greater freedom to follow their own preferences.

Functionalism: Durkheim's approach developed

Emile Durkheim is generally regarded as the principal figure in the establishment of the sociological perspective of functionalism. In explaining social solidarity and the division of labour, Durkheim adapted the arguments of the Victorian sociologist Herbert Spencer that societies evolve according to the basic laws of natural selection, survival and adaptation. Thus they can be most easily understood and analyzed if they are compared to biological organisms. Durkheim suggested that societies or social systems work like organic systems: they are made up of structures of cultural rules (established practices and beliefs, for instance) and people are expected to conform to them. The organic analogy is used by Durkheim and

A closer look

Anomie

Durkheim also referred to 'abnormal' forms of the division of labour. In the context of modern societies, characterized by organic solidarity, the lack of a general and strong consensus that encouraged interdependence between people would lead to a situation of anomie. Durkheim felt that this was likely to be a particular problem in modern, developed societies that were experiencing rapid social upheaval, such as becoming industrialized. In small-scale societies, characterized by mechanical solidarity, it is easier for a general consensus to be upheld.

Anomie was initially used by Durkheim to refer to situations where there was substantial disagreement over the appropriate norms and values for governing social behaviour. It occurred when aspects of a society were inadequately regulated. However, anomie can be applied in an individual as well as a social context. Durkheim's analysis of suicide is the most famous illustration of this application of anomie. One of the four categories of suicide that Durkheim highlighted was 'anomic suicide': without the regulation of norms to define appropriate behaviour, life becomes aimless and the individual is more prone to commit suicide; as a society becomes more anomic in times of economic upheaval, such as periods of depression or boom, the suicide rate tends to increase.

Durkheim also found a link between divorce and suicide in that divorced men are particularly prone to suicide. He suggested that 'conjugal anomie' and the consequent greater likelihood of suicide occurred when the regulation of marriage was undermined. Here too anomie is a weakening of the established normative framework.

Questions

1. *How relevant do you think the concept of anomie is today?*

2. *Do you think it helps to explain the growing number of teenage male suicides?*

others as a way of getting to grips with the very abstract nature of sociological theory. The comparison of society to a living organism, such as a human being or a plant, provides a model for interpreting human behaviour.

Although by no means original, this analogy is central to Durkheim's work and to the functionalist perspective. From this perspective, the institutions of society – the kinds of educational arrangement and family forms it has, for instance – are analogous to the parts of an organism, such as the parts of a body. It is quite commonplace for the history of societies to be explained in terms of the human life cycle. Like individuals, societies tend to start as small units and get bigger and, sometimes, to wither away; the history of the Roman Empire, for instance, could be described by such a model. Thus the analogy

can be used in describing the development of societies: studies of the USA regularly refer to the 'birth of a nation'. In the development of sociological theory, this approach has been associated with the work of Herbert Spencer, who looked at the evolution of societies and compared them with individual organisms.

Another way in which the model of the organic analogy has been used is in comparing the structure of organisms with societies. As parts of the body, the heart or liver, for instance, are understood in terms of the function they perform, so social institutions, such as families or schools, have to be understood in terms of their functions for maintaining society. In order to understand how the body works, the various parts have to be examined in relation to one another. If one part was examined in isolation it would not tell us how life was maintained: scrutiny of the heart or liver by themselves would not tell us how the human body 'worked'. Similarly, any part of social life, any social institution, has to be understood in terms of the way it functions to maintain the whole social structure.

A closer look

The organic analogy and the functioning of society

The classic exponents of this application of the organic analogy have been anthropologists who have studied other societies 'in the field'. As the British anthropologist Radcliffe-Brown puts it:

> The life of an organism is conceived as the functioning of its structure . . . If we consider any recurrent part of the life process such as digestion, respiration, etc., its function is the part it plays in the contribution to the life of the organism as a whole.

Applying this analogy he goes on:

> The social life of a community is here defined as the functioning of the social structure. The function of any recurrent activity, such as the punishment of crime or a funeral ceremony, is the part it plays in the social life as a whole and therefore the contribution it makes to structural continuity.
>
> (Radcliffe-Brown 1952: 179–80)

The term 'function', then, is used to refer to the contribution an institution makes to the maintenance and survival of the wider social system. In determining the functions of the various institutions or parts of society, the functionalist approach assumes that there are certain basic requirements which must be met for the society to exist and survive; these requirements or needs are called *functional prerequisites*. Examples of these might include reproduction, systems of communication and agreed standards of behaviour.

Given that the parts of society are interconnected and interrelated, each part will affect all the other parts and for the system to survive there will have to be compatibility between the parts. Functionalists generally argue that this integration is based on value-consensus – essentially an agreement by members of society over values and standards. In Western society, for instance, materialism is widely valued. Hence the economic system is geared to producing a wide range of consumer goods; the economic system is backed up by the value placed on materialism by

the family, the mass media, the education system and so on. The rest of this section will look at how Durkheim's functionalist approach has been applied in the study of specific areas of society. In particular, we shall examine the functionalist approaches to the study of religion and crime.

Stop and think

> ➤ The functionalist analysis of any area or institution of society starts by asking what function does it perform for the maintenance of that society.

> ➤ What do you think are the functions of the following institutions: (a) the family; (b) the mass media; (c) the education system?

Functionalism and religion

The functionalist analysis of religion stresses how and to what extent religious beliefs and practices contribute to meeting the needs (or prerequisites) of society. Durkheim's study *The Elementary Forms of the Religious Life* (1912) describes how religion provides the basis of the collective conscience – the shared values and ideas – of a society. Religion, therefore, expresses and fulfils a social need and promotes social solidarity and cohesion: in other words, it binds people together.

Durkheim's ideas on the role of religion were based on anthropological material on the religion of the Australian aborigines, which he called 'totemism'. This term referred to the fact that each group of aborigines, each clan, had a sacred symbol or totem that they worshipped. The totem functioned as a symbol of both god and the society and in worshipping it the aborigines were, in effect, worshipping society.

Perhaps the most influential part of Durkheim's theory is the definition of religion by its functions, and the emphasis on religious rites, the collective acts of worship, rather than on what is actually believed. As Durkheim put it:

> The most barbarous and the most fantastic rites and the strangest myths translate some human need, some aspect of life . . . The reasons with which the faithful justify them may be, and generally are, erroneous . . . [but] In reality there are no religions which are false. All are true in their own fashion; all answer, though in different ways, to the given conditions of human existence. (Durkheim 1976: 14–15)

The religious rites of the aborigines were seen as a sort of ritual mechanism for reinforcing social integration. Although the aborigines who came together to perform a rain dance have, as far as they are concerned, come together with the purpose of producing rain, Durkheim suggests that this is largely irrelevant. The important point is that they have come together to perform a collective activity which binds them together and which reaffirms commitment to the group's values and norms.

Thus Durkheim is interested in how religion binds people to society; religion is seen as giving 'sacred authority to society's rules and values'. Functionalists writing since Durkheim have extended his analysis of primitive religions to all religion and have argued that religion of some form is a necessary integrating force in all societies. From this point of view the focus is not on the content of different religions – whether they be Protestant, Catholic or Hinduism, for instance – but the fact that they all form similar integrative functions.

The importance attached to religion as an integrating force raises the question of what happens when religion declines in importance in society. A response to this has been to emphasize that the functions of religion are still fulfilled by present-day equivalents of religion, such as nationalism or socialism, for example, where political figures become deified and 'worshipped'.

The functionalist approach suggests that religion, in one form or another, is a necessary feature of society. A major problem with this approach is that in modern societies several religions coexist, regulating and integrating their followers differently; thus religious pluralism will tend to work against social cohesion. This criticism implies that Durkheim's analysis of religion is perhaps more appropriate to small-scale, simpler societies. A second important problem is that functionalism focuses on the integrative functions of religion – the provision of shared values and so on – and tends to ignore the effect of religion as a force for division and disharmony in society. There are many societies divided over religious dogma and belief, and such divisions can be so deep-rooted as to lead to bitter and violent conflict, as a glance at both British and world news will soon reveal.

Functionalism and crime

> Crime is present . . . in all societies of all types. There is no society that is not confronted with the problem of criminality . . . To classify crime among the phenomena of normal sociology is not to say merely that it is an inevitable, although regrettable phenomenon . . . it is to affirm that it is a factor in public health, an integral part of all healthy societies.
>
> (Durkheim 1964: 65–7)

Case study

The role of religion

The role of religion in binding people together is regularly stressed by contemporary religious leaders. For example, the Archbishop of Canterbury, in response to criticisms about the Christian Church's lack of moral guidance to young people made after the trial of two 10-year-old boys found guilty of the murder of 2-year-old toddler James Bulger in 1993, commented that:

> Somehow we need to recover a sense of belonging to one society. Let us move away from the Do It Yourself morality that has been going on, with everyone doing what is right or wrong in their own eyes. It is not too late to return to a sense of purpose, to a sense of shared values based on the Christian tradition.
>
> (quoted in the *Guardian* 29.11.93)

Question

1. *Can you think of any other examples of how religion or religious leaders in the contemporary world have attempted to promote a sense of belonging to society?*

As with other areas of functionalist analysis, the importance of shared values and norms is central to the explanation of crime. Crime consists of behaviour that breaks or departs from the shared values and norms of society. The functionalist approach, as developed by Durkheim, focuses on the functions performed by the various institutions and parts of society – in particular, the function they perform in the promotion and maintenance of social unity and cohesion. This classic functionalist approach can be applied to crime as to other areas of society. Given that crime is behaviour that breaks rules, it might seem odd to talk about its functions. However, functionalists argue that crime is necessary and indeed useful for society; certainly it has to be controlled but it still has positive functions.

Put simply, the functionalist argument is that crime is universal, in that it exists, to some extent at least, in all known societies. Furthermore, as it is normal it must also be functional. And it is functional in that it helps to sustain conformity and stability. The fact that some individuals commit acts which break rules is accompanied by a sense of outrage which reinforces, for the majority, the support of those rules. When someone commits a particularly horrible crime, such as child murder, people often feel closer together through sharing their collective outrage. Through bringing people closer together crime can have the effect of contributing to social cohesion. Thus the presence of the criminal allows the rest of society to draw together and reaffirm their values: it strengthens the society or social group. The definition of behaviour as 'criminal' helps social cohesion by distinguishing between those who follow the laws and those who do not and by establishing a boundary between what is seen as acceptable and unacceptable behaviour.

Of course, it is not the criminal actions themselves that draw people together; rather it is the publicizing and punishing of crime that does this. The reaction to and punishment of crime is of central importance. The public trial of law breakers and the media obsession with publicizing crime and criminal trials help to clarify the boundaries of acceptable behaviour. The reaction to and the punishment of crime does not always correspond with the extent of social harm done by the particular criminal action. It does though, according to Durkheim, express the strength of common values and standards. The extent of harm done by an act of violence against a child, for instance, may be slight compared to the number of people harmed by a company ignoring pollution or industrial safety laws. However, the reaction against the child murderer will be far stronger than against the offending

company. The reaction to crime is essentially emotional rather than rational, and the demand for punishment seems to demonstrate a desire to see the offender suffer pain – evidenced by the angry crowds outside court-rooms at particularly horrific murder trials. These kinds of response can be best understood if crime is seen as an action that offends widely against strongly held norms and values. Durkheim argued that for there to be social cohesion and agreement people need to be able to react against those who depart from the shared rules and values and that crime creates this opportunity. (See pp. 644–6 for a fuller discussion of Durkheim's analysis of the punishment of crime.)

Marx and conflict

Karl Marx, like Durkheim, was concerned with broad questions about the dynamics of societies and how societies change over time. And, as with functionalism, Marxism is a structural theoretical perspective: it concentrates on the structure of society and explains individual actions in terms of the social structure in which they are located. Both functionalism and Marxism stress the crucial and pervasive influence of society. However, in contrast to functionalism, Marx's writings emphasized conflict in society.

Marx's work

For Marx, the way that people live is, in many ways, a consequence of the arrangements they make for survival, and the methods of producing and distributing food will to some extent determine lifestyle, religious belief, custom and so on. Marx starts his analysis of society and history at this point, that the most obvious and vital fact of life is the need to survive by finding food and shelter. The one constant universal factor in human existence is the system that people devise for maintaining existence, and this system will influence all else they do. Thus subsistence is basic to all societies, and how it is achieved affects their whole structure and organization.

Marx's analysis of society

For Marx, there are two essential components of a society: first, the *economic base* or *infastructure* (also called the *substructure* in some texts), which provides the material needs of life; and second, the *superstructure*, basically the

A closer look

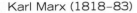

Karl Marx (1818–83)

Marx was born in Trier, Rhineland, where his father was a lawyer. He grew up in an atmosphere of sympathy for the ideas of the Enlightenment and the French Revolution. In 1835 he became a student at Berlin University, where his political ideas became more radical. As a student, Marx was influenced by the philosophy of Hegel and his followers, who were critical of the religion and politics of the Prussian state, of which Berlin was the capital. After university, Marx became a journalist (rather than his professed ambition of becoming a university lecturer), writing articles on social and political problems for the radical Cologne paper *Rheinische Zeitung*, which earned him some notoriety.

In 1843 Marx moved to Paris, where he was introduced to the ideas of socialism and communism and where he met Frederick Engels, who became his lifelong friend and co-writer. During this period Marx, studied economics and came across the theories of classical economists such as Adam Smith and David Ricardo. This interest in economics shaped Marx's belief that political power is closely linked to economic power; his political views cannot be separated from his historical analysis of the development of capitalist society.

After a brief spell in Germany, during the revolution of 1848, Marx moved to London and exile there in 1849. For the rest of his life Marx devoted his time to two major tasks: first, building a revolutionary workers' party; and second, producing a detailed analysis of the capitalist socio-economic system. These two tasks were connected in that Marx believed that an understanding of capitalism and its problems was a necessary prerequisite to its political overthrow. The quote on Marx's grave in Highgate

Figure 2.2 Dr Karl Marx, the German socialist writer, died 14 March 1883, aged 65

Cemetery, London, illustrates his commitment to political action: 'The philosophers have only interpreted the world in various ways; the point is to change it.' Marx never finished his analysis of capitalist society. *Das Kapital* (1867–95), perhaps his most famous work, was intended as only a part of this wider project.

rest of society including the family, the education system, ideas and beliefs, the legal system, and the political system. This division distinguishes between the material and the non-material world. The material world (the economic base) comes first and determines the non-material, because without it the non-material (the superstructure) would not be possible. The economic base is itself composed of the *forces* of production and the *relations* of production. The forces (or means) of production include factories, machinery, raw materials and technology. The relations of production refer to how people relate to one another at work, in particular to the relations that owners and employers have with those who work for them.

The superstructure is the non-material, but essentially it reflects the economic base. For example, the education

system and the legal system protect and support the basic values of the economic structure of society. In contemporary Western society, they support the capitalist economic system or base.

The development of capitalism: historical materialism

Marx was a prolific writer and in his work there are different emphases, hence the difficulty of interpreting Marx and the existence of various different interpretations. However, it is probably fair to say that the essence of Marx's work was to explain the nature and form of modern society, in particular to explain the evolution of capitalism and how it would lead eventually to a communist system.

Conflicts around the system of production, and especially in the relations of production, between workers and owners, were seen by Marx as the essential factors of modern society. These conflicts reveal the nature of capitalist societies and demonstrate how there will have to be a new system of social organization. Marx asserts that capitalism is a necessary stage prior to the establishment of communism in all modern societies (just as feudalism was a necessary forerunner to capitalism). This emphasis on conflict highlights the vital role of social classes in Marx's theory of social change. In all societies that have existed so far (apart from those characterized by early forms of communism – what Marx termed 'primitive' communism) there has been a broad division into two classes, one of which exploits the other. The struggle between these two class groupings (loosely the ruling and ruled classes) leads to societies moving from one form of economic system to another. Thus the role of social class and class struggle is a key element of Marx's analysis of society.

Marx's theory of social change, his theory of historical development, is called *historical materialism*. For Marx, social structures are not created randomly: there is a clear pattern to the way societies in different parts of the world and at different periods of history have organized the production of material goods. According to Marx, throughout history societies have exhibited one of five modes of production, which, in chronological order, are primitive communist, ancient, feudal, capitalist and communist. Each of these forms of society leads inevitably to the next. The importance of conflicts of production to Marx's historical analysis is demonstrated in his account of the ways in which societies move from one mode of production to another.

The emergence of capitalism from feudalism

Marx described the feudal relations of production as hierarchical and reciprocal. Hierarchical refers to the allegiance that peasants owed to their feudal lords, to whom they had to give their surplus produce; peasants farmed their own land, provided for themselves and gave the surplus they produced to their feudal masters. Reciprocal refers to the obligations of the lords to look after the peasants' interests by ensuring, for example, their physical security in 'exchange' for their allegiance.

A key development in the decline of feudalism was the enclosure of common land. This encouraged the development of commercial types of agriculture and the establishment of conditions where agriculture could produce a surplus. So early capitalists emerged from within the feudal system; commercial rather than subsistence agriculture led to people owning money rather than just land.

Marx argued that there were very clear differences between feudal and capitalist societies. In feudal societies, for instance, people were supposed to be paid on a fair, just basis rather than on economic calculations, and they were bound to one another by mutual obligations. The feudal lifestyle was in sharp contrast to the emerging capitalist mode of production. The concern that Marx and Engels felt at the destruction of these feudal relationships and ties is illustrated by their comments in the first section of the *Communist Manifesto* (1848):

The bourgeoisie, wherever it has got the upper hand, has put an end to all feudal, patriarchal, idyllic relations. It has pitilessly torn asunder the motley feudal ties that bound man to his 'natural superiors', and has left remaining no other nexus between man and man than naked self-interest, than callous 'cash payment'. It has drowned the most heavenly ecstasies of religious fervour, of chivalrous enthusiasm, of philistine sentimentalism, in the icy waters of egotistical calculation. It has resolved personal worth into exchange value . . . In one word, for exploitation, veiled by religious and political illusions, it has substituted naked, shameless, direct, brutal exploitation.

(Marx and Engels 1952: 44–5)

Marx emphasized the conflicts and contradictions in all societies, including feudal ones, and in contrasting feudal and capitalist economic systems, his portrayal of feudal relations as 'idyllic' is clearly somewhat idealized and exaggerated. The extract below is taken from an historical account of serfdom in medieval England.

Hereditary servile status in medieval Europe was the lot, by and large, of the bulk of the peasantry . . . The term normally employed by modern historians for unfree peasants is 'serfs' . . . The end of the thirteenth century and beginning of the fourteenth was the time when the situation of the customary tenant was most affected by the servile legal status which had been elaborated in the courts to his disadvantage for over a century . . . The villein (serf attached to a farm) could be made to pay for a licence fee before being allowed to sell any livestock; he would certainly have to pay for permission to marry off a daughter or even a son; his daughter would have to pay a fine if she became pregnant out of wedlock; his heir would have to hand over his best beast or chattel as *heriot* (as well as the second best beast as *mortuary* to the parson); he was not allowed to buy or sell land without permission; he was not allowed to leave the manor. These were the basic restrictions implicit in villeinage, and there might be more or less depending on the local custom . . .

In a peasant society the fundamental freedom, obviously enough, was the right of the peasant, if not to the full product of his labour, at any rate to enough to sustain a traditional standard of living. But any medieval peasant knew, of course, that his surplus product was going to be taken away bit by bit by landowner, by lord, by Church and by State.

(Hilton 1969: 9–30)

Stop and think

> ➤ To what extent does this account (a) support Marx's idealized picture of the feudal society; (b) refute it?

The capitalist mode of production: pursuit of profit

Marx stressed the importance of the system of production – of the economic base or substructure. In a capitalist society this system is based on the pursuit of profit. In this pursuit the capitalist, the owner of the means of production, must necessarily exploit the worker. For Marx, the essential element in the relationship between capitalist and worker is surplus value – basically the source of profit. Under capitalism the worker is paid a wage designed to enable him or her to survive, yet through the worker's labour power a product which has value over and above the cost of these wages is produced. As well as covering other costs that the capitalist might have – such as the buying of raw materials and renting premises – the surplus value also constitutes the capitalist's profit. For example, a person who works a forty-hour week may, in the first twenty hours of the week, produces all the value that will be received in wages; of the value produced in the remaining twenty hours, that person will receive nothing – it is stolen by the employers. Thus, the value produced by workers far exceeds the value of their wages.

Once a wage is fixed it is in the interests of the capitalist to get as much productivity as possible from the worker. Marx looked at the major ways of increasing exploitation used by capitalists; in *Das Kapital* he looked at how different forms of exploitation appeared and were used in different periods of history. Absolute exploitation would involve squeezing more output from the worker, by increasing the length of the working week perhaps. However, this is a very crude method and would be less likely to be used now. Nowadays the more usual way of raising productivity and therefore profit is to improve the efficiency of work without a commensurate rise in the labourer's wages rather than increase the time worked by the labourer. Marx saw this method of increasing profit as the dominant form of exploitation in the modern capitalist system.

The surplus value generated in modern capitalist societies has not only benefited the capitalists. The position of wage earners has improved in certain ways. However, the fact that the working population may get more – in terms of better living standards, ownership of consumer goods and so on – is seen by Marxist writers as necessary for the survival of the capitalist system. To explain this point briefly. As capitalism is a system based on profit it depends on continual growth and, therefore, it makes sense to give the mass of the population surplus wealth in order to enable them to buy goods: the more goods they buy the more the system can produce. Of course, the wealthy capitalists will also have plenty of money to spend on luxuries. However, one person can spend only so much, and it is more efficient to distribute surplus value around 20 million families rather than 20,000; then they can all buy televisions, washing machines, cars and cosmetics and thereby generate more production and profit. Personal wealth and savings are still heavily concentrated in a few hands, but most wages are now above subsistence levels and enable the mass of the population to buy a range of consumer goods.

The contradictions in capitalism

In their account of Marx's analysis of capitalism, Cuff *et al.* (1990) suggest that he saw capitalism as a system characterized by:

1 The exploitation of many people by a few.

2 Tensions, strains and contradictions between different social groups.

3 The certainty of drastic change via some form of social revolution.

Adopting this categorization, we shall examine each of these statements in turn.

First, Marx argued that there are basic contradictions within capitalist societies due to the conflict of interests between the various groups involved in the economic process: in particular, the conflict of interests between an exploiting and exploited group, between the owners of the means of production and the non-owners. Under capitalism the main link between people is an impersonal cash relationship. Most people have only one marketable asset – their labour. A small number of industrial capitalists own the means of production, such as factories, land and raw materials, and provide the main means of employment for the majority. It is unlikely that individual capitalists regard themselves as exploiters; they are in business to make profits. To do this they have to beat competitors by reducing prices, and a major way of reducing prices is to cut costs. The biggest recurring cost for most employers is likely to be labour, so capitalists, in trying to be competitive, have little option but to keep labour costs down. Essentially, the capitalist wants as much work as possible from as few workers for as little pay as possible: this exploitation is not due to the 'evil' nature of individual capitalists but is a necessary requirement of the whole capitalist system according to Marx.

Second, the capitalist system produces the very conflicts and tension that will eventually tear it apart: in particular, conflicts and tension over pay and conditions between capitalists and employees, but also conflicts and tension between different groups of wage earners and between capitalists themselves. Marx believed that the tensions inherent in capitalism would intensify, due to certain developments or trends that were inevitable in a capitalist system. These developments included polarization, homogenization and pauperization.

Third, Marx argued that the capitalist system was doomed: the contradictions would grow and a social revolution was inevitable. Capitalism would disintegrate as developments such as polarization, homogenization and pauperization intensified. This would open the way for the establishment of a new, alternative type of social system. However, for a new system to be created a new consciousness would have to develop among the exploited workers – a consciousness that would reflect the interests of the workers. Marx felt that this new consciousness could develop only if the exploited group actively opposed the capitalist system; only through struggle would the old, false consciousness be eradicated. The old consciousness is false because it reflects the

---

A closer look

Polarization

In modern industrial societies traditional skills were becoming redundant and there was a tendency for the working population to polarize into two distinct and hostile groups – the capitalists and the labourers.

Homogenization

Within these two groups, individuals were becoming increasing alike (or homogeneous). Among the capitalists, for example, competition was eliminating the smaller businesses and the successful ones were expanding, with the typical capitalist enterprise becoming a large and complex concern. Furthermore, workers would become increasingly homogeneous as a result of their dependence on work in these large factories and the decline of traditional skills.

Pauperization

In pursuing profit, capitalists need to keep their wage bills down. They need to ensure that the workers' wages do not rise in relation to those of capitalists, so that, in relation to capitalists, wage-workers are turned into paupers – they are 'pauperized'.

Question

1. *What contemporary evidence is there to support the argument that there is (a) a polarization of the working population; (b) homogenization among major groups of workers; (c) pauperization of workers in relation to capitalists?*

---

interests of the privileged ruling groups, not the interests of the bulk of the people. True consciousness for the mass of the population would come about only when they developed an ideology (a set of ideas and values) which supported their interests.

When this new consciousness develops and matures, the proletariat, according to Marx, would overturn the capitalist system. They would take over the means of production and the state – as the capitalists had done before them. This would lead to a fundamental shift in the relations of production and a new abundant society would emerge where everyone could work and live freely and enjoy equality of status:

It will be possible for me to do one thing today and another tomorrow, to hunt in the morning, fish in the afternoon, rear cattle in the evening, criticise after dinner, just as I have a mind to, without ever becoming a hunter, fisherman, shepherd or critic.

(Marx and Engels 1976 vol. 5: 47)

Only in this sort of liberated, communist society could humans fulfil their potential for creativity; in societies where one class group dominates the rest it is not possible.

This section has focused on the contradictions in the capitalist system: contradictions based on the exploitative relationship between owners and non-owners, between capitalists and workers. It is important to emphasize that we have looked at capitalism in a very general, simplistic manner. Contemporary capitalism differs considerably from early capitalism and from the model of capitalism that Marx wrote about. In the twenty-first century, instead of actually owning factories and industrial production, ownership usually takes the form of capital investment – stocks and shares. Marxists argue, however, that this does not alter the essentially exploitative features of capitalist society; the bourgeoisie may not make the goods but they still gain the benefit from the surplus value produced by workers. Although exploitation may not be as obvious as feudal masters extracting 'tithes' from their peasants (or as the exploitation of slaves), the relationship between capitalist and wage earner is essentially the same.

Alienation

Work is external to the worker, that is it is not part of his nature . . . consequently he does not fulfil himself in this work but denies himself, has a feeling of misery, not of well-being, does not develop freely a physical and mental energy, but is physically exhausted and mentally debased . . . [Work] is not the satisfaction of a need but only a means for satisfying other needs. Its alien character is clearly shown by the fact that as soon as there is no physical or other compulsion it is avoided like the plague.

(Marx, *Economic and Philosophical Manuscripts*, 1844, in Bottomore 1963: 124–5)

The antagonistic and unequal class structure characteristic of capitalist societies leads to what Marx termed alienation. Alienation refers to the separation, or estrangement, of individuals from themselves and from others. It is a complicated concept as it involves individuals' feelings. Alienation describes the sense of frustration, pointlessness and

lack of involvement felt by many working people. Marx saw alienation as a central feature of capitalism and one that could take different forms. As the quote above illustrates, workers became alienated from their work because what they produced was controlled by others. As well as work itself being an alienating activity, workers are alienated from each other. Relationships in a capitalist society are

A closer look

Alienation: Marxist interpretations

The notion of alienation has been given different emphases by the different versions of Marxism that have developed from Marx's work. These differing emphases can be seen in the two major divergent strands of Marxist theorizing – humanistic Marxism and structural Marxism.

The more orthodox, structural Marxism is concerned mainly with the economic laws of capitalism and the nature of the capitalist state; this approach formed the basis for the discussion of historical materialism and the contradictions in capitalism provided above.

In contrast, humanistic Marxism has tended to play down the importance of the economic base/superstructure division. The focus has been on Marx's analysis of the dehumanizing effects of the rise of capitalism and, in particular, Marx's writings on alienation. This approach developed from the early 1920s in the work of, among others, George Lukács, Antonio Gramsci and the Frankfurt School (see pp. 82–3). Humanist Marxism suggests that people are essentially cooperative but that the development of capitalism leads to their alienation. This alienation occurs not only in the economic context but also in other contexts due to the general influence of large bureaucracies, the mass media and oppressive forms of government. Alienation can be overcome only by abolishing capitalism.

Rather than stressing alienation, structural Marxism, exemplified in the work of the French Marxist philosopher Louis Althusser (1918–93), focuses on exploitation. The processes and structures of capitalism are seen as exploiting workers. This exploitation can be measured objectively; it is not based on speculative ideas about the 'human spirit'. Thus structural Marxism focuses on the economic base, where the exploitative mechanisms are located: 'the base/superstructure distinction is of paramount importance – it renders Marxism a scientifically valid method of analysis' (Lee and Newby 1983: 118).

those of competition (the 'dog eat dog' philosophy) rather than co-operation, even among the workers.

> ## Stop and think
>
> ➤ Give examples of 'alienating work' in modern society.
>
> ➤ Describe the extent and sort of alienation that might be found in the following occupations: nurse; shop assistant; car mechanic; taxi driver; food packager; teacher.
>
> ➤ In what areas of life other than work might alienation occur?

> ## Stop and think
>
> ➤ For a basically exploitative system such as modern capitalism to exist, either the inequalities (the fact that some people own Rolls Royces and yachts while others can barely afford household bills, for example) and exploitation must fail to be recognized by disadvantaged people or they must be persuaded that such a situation is acceptable and justified.
>
> ➤ Why do you think disadvantaged groups put up with their situation?
>
> ➤ What 'ideas, values and beliefs' might persuade people to accept their disadvantaged and exploited condition?

The role of ideology

The ideas of the ruling class are, in every age, the ruling ideas.　　　　(Marx and Engels 1976 vol. 5: 59)

The emphasis given to class exploitation and conflict raises the issue of why disadvantaged and exploited people accept their situation. Now, even in the modern, 'civilized' world a great deal of exploitation is exerted by pure force, particularly in states run by military and authoritarian regimes. However, that does not provide a complete explanation for the apparent acceptance of exploitation. In Marxist theory, ideas, values and beliefs perform a central function in maintaining inequalities and oppression. They act as ideologies supporting the (capitalist) system.

Although strictly speaking ideology means the science of ideas, it is generally taken to refer to a system of ideas that belong to a particular social group and is usually used in a negative and pejorative sense as implying false or mistaken ideas, values and beliefs. For Marx, an ideology was a system of ideas that misrepresent reality by serving the interests of the dominant social groups in society, particularly the ruling classes. The notion of ideology as a misrepresentation of reality is very close to Marx's description of false consciousness, and the two terms are, to a certain extent, almost interchangeable. In their discussion of the nature and functions of ideology in Marx's work, Cuff *et al.* suggest that ideologies:

Misrepresent reality in various ways: they conceal unacceptable aspects of it; they glorify things which are of themselves less than glorious; they make out things which are neither natural nor necessary as though they were both.　　　(Cuff *et al.* 1998: 27)

The importance of ideology highlights the crucial role of the superstructure – of society's cultural aspects and institutions – in ensuring that the economic system is considered legitimate. It also illustrates the importance of the notions of class consciousness and false consciousness to Marxist theory. Marx's theory of historical materialism is a good deal more complex than presented here. For instance, the relationship between the economic base and superstructure is not as rigid as we have perhaps implied. Marx was well aware that there was not a complete 'economic determinism' and that the superstructure had some influence on the economic system and could, indeed, influence the way in which the economic system developed. The variations in the capitalist system from one society to another demonstrate this: the different histories and cultures of Japan, the UK and the USA, for example, have affected the kind of capitalist economic system that prevails in those countries.

Marx and social class

According to Marx, there is a built-in antagonism and conflict between class groups in all societies; as his famous comment at the start of the *Communist Manifesto* puts it:

The history of all hitherto existing society is the history of class struggles.　　　(Marx and Engels 1952: 40)

Perhaps Marx's major intellectual aim was to discover the principle of change in society. However, he did not want just to describe divisions in society but to explain which groups had strong interests in maintaining the existing system and which in trying to change it. These groups, with differing interests, Marx saw as social classes.

Case study

Human nature as naturally selfish – a Marxist response

Cuff and colleagues examine the widely held idea that human beings are naturally selfish and competitive – that selfishness is in the nature of all living things – as an example of an ideological concept.

Such a view has two features which are common among ideologies: the suggestion that it is simply in our nature to be selfish and self-interested; and the implication that there is nothing we can do to change it because it is built into our natures. From the Marxist point of view, we are not innately competitive in this way. To talk about the natural, immutable competitiveness of the human species offers a false picture of our human natures. Such theories serve to justify a socio-economic system – competitive capitalism – which *is* based on unrelenting individual competition. These ideas justify that system by suggesting that, first, it gives full rein to our fundamental human natures and is therefore best suited to us and, second, there is little point in disapproving of or attempting to moderate the competitiveness of the system since it is our nature to be competitive . . . In one way or another, systems of ideas play this ideological role of convincing people that they cannot change their society, or that it is not worth their effort to try changing it.

(Cuff *et al.* 1998: 27)

Question

Suggest how the idea of natural human selfishness can be found in the following areas of popular cultural production:

1. *TV soap operas (consider the characters from your favourite soaps);*

2. *literature;*

3. *film;*

4. *sport (consider the behaviour/demands of sports personalities).*

How might a Marxist approach 'interpret' these examples?

Classes exist in all non-communist societies. In the ancient mode of production the two main classes were the slaves and the slave owners. In feudal society they were the servile peasantry and the landed nobility. Under capitalism, there are, similarly, two main classes – the *bourgeoisie*, who own the means of production, and the *proletariat*, who have only their labour to sell. In any class system, then, there are two main classes and, because one exploits the other, they are antagonistic to one another. This antagonism provides the driving force for social change (as we highlighted in discussing the contradiction in capitalism, pp. 52–3).

For Marx, class consciousness was of central importance in defining social class. Members of social classes could be distinguished by two criteria, both of which are necessary for a fully developed social class to exist:

1 *Objective criteria*   The sharing of a particular attribute, for example, a similar type of occupation or the same relationship to the means of production (being an owner or non-owner).

2 *Subjective criteria*   Grouping people in terms of a shared attribute does no more than create a category (all red-headed people could be lumped together in this way, for example); a category is only a possible or potential class and can be transformed into an active social class only when people become conscious of their position.

Marx summed up this distinction by stating that it was not enough for a class to be a class *in* itself, it had also to be a class *for* itself (with a full class consciousness and feelings of solidarity with others of that class). This distinction is central to Marx's theory of class and social change, and the notion of class consciousness is central to his theory of working-class revolution. Awareness and consciousness are necessary for the existence of an active social class; only when a class becomes a class for itself does it exist as a political force.

Marx believed that the working class was bound to develop this class consciousness once the appropriate conditions were present. These conditions would include the growing relative poverty of the proletariat and the increasing 'class polarization' between the proletariat and bourgeoisie. Members of the proletariat would become increasingly angered by bourgeois exploitation and would organize themselves – locally at first and then nationally – to improve their economic situation. As a consequence of this, they would eventually take control from the bourgeoisie and set up a new society. As this happened the proletariat, according to Marx, would transform themselves from a mere category of people who share the same conditions to a group of people who organize to change these conditions: they would move to become a class for themselves. Ultimately, Marx believed, then, that the proletariat would see through the bourgeois ideology and become revolutionary. He believed the bourgeoisie were incapable of developing a strong overall consciousness of their collective interests, due to the inevitable competition between individual capitalists chasing profit.

One of the major problems of the Marxist analysis is that the working classes in most capitalist countries have hardly ever come close to acquiring this class consciousness and becoming a class for itself. Most Western working-class groups have been content to squeeze the occasional reforms out of the ruling class rather than challenging the whole basis of class inequality. Linked with this failure to mobilize has been the growth of the middle classes. For Marx, all non-owners of the means of production are, objectively, members of the proletariat. However, what distinguishes the middle class is that they help to administer and perpetuate the capitalist system for the ruling class. They are not part of the ruling class but are its functionaries; lawyers, teachers, civil servants and so on are seen by Marxists as 'lackeys of the ruling class'. They enjoy more privileges than the exploited working classes but their power is no greater; without property to rely on for income the real interests of the middle classes are bound up with the working classes and in so far as they do not realize this they are victims of 'false consciousness'.

Stop and think

➤ How might groups of workers develop a sense of collective identity and class consciousness?

➤ What factors work against this in modern society?

➤ Where do you think the interests of 'professional' workers and manual workers coincide? Where do they diverge?

With the apparent demise of communism in the late 1980s, perhaps most symbolically represented with the dismantling of the Berlin Wall, it seemed that the work of Marx had little relevance to contemporary society. This judgement may prove to be somewhat premature in view of the economic crises in a number of societies (in South East Asia and Russia for example) in the late 1990s. Such developments have demonstrated how badly capitalism can go wrong and have led writers such as Eric Hobsbawn (1998) to say of Marx, 'What this man wrote 150 years ago about the nature and tendencies of global capitalism rings amazingly true today.' Echoing Marx's sentiments, Hobsbawm suggests that such crises make a compelling economic, social and moral case for reducing inequality and for promoting a more even distribution of incomes. He highlights the polarization between a concentration of high-income jobs in high-profit-making firms and low-wage, casual occupations, 'between the City dealers and the office cleaners and security staff'. Such polarization is economically and socially unhealthy; in contrast, social and economic equality improves 'a region's health, mortality, crime rates and "civic community". Hence, for those who need such arguments, the lower the financial cost to society'.

Weber and meaning

Max Weber is considered to be one of the 'trinity of founding thinkers' of sociology, along with Durkheim and Marx. Weber and Durkheim adopted quite distinct methods and theories in their sociological work. While Durkheim devoted himself to trying to establish sociology as an academic subject (founding journals and teaching departments), Weber was more a pure scholar, grappling with ideas. Like Marx, Weber was not 'just' a sociologist: his work extended into philosophy, economics, religion and history, for example. This work, however, has not led to the establishment of a coherent doctrine; there is not a 'Weberism' in the same way that there is a 'Marxism'. The focus of this introduction to Weber's work and its influence will be to examine some of the ideas and themes that he developed. His four major studies are:

➤ *The Protestant Ethic and the Spirit of Capitalism*, 1904/5.

➤ *The Sociology of Religion*, 1920.

➤ *The Theory of Social and Economic Organization*, 1922.

➤ *The Methodology of the Social Sciences*, 1949.

A closer look

Max Weber (1864–1920)

Weber was born in Germany and spent his academic career there. His first teaching job was in law at Berlin University. As his intellectual interests widened he was appointed to professorships in political economy and then economics at the universities of Freiberg and Heidelberg, respectively. However, mental illness and depression meant that he was unable to hold down full-time teaching positions throughout his whole life. In 1897 at Heidelberg, shortly after the death of his father, he suffered a nervous breakdown that cut short his career as it was beginning to develop. After that his academic life was spent writing and researching, with sociology becoming his main academic field.

Weber's lifetime spanned a period of massive change in German history. The unification of Germany led to the emergence of the modern German state and was accompanied by a phenomenal growth of industry; indeed, it was around this time that Germany challenged and overtook Britain as Europe's leading industrial power. The attempts to create a German empire culminated in the First World War and defeat towards the end of Weber's life.

Weber's work has been described as a debate with the 'ghost of Marx'. Weber was clearly influenced by Marx but was critical of some of his views. He criticized Marx's overemphasis on materialist explanations of historical development and argued that social divisions reflected more than solely economic or class conflict.

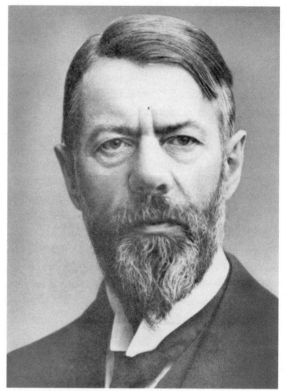

Figure 2.3 Max Weber
© Corbis/Hulton Archive

Weber's work

Weber wrote about the nature of sociology and how to go about studying society. He argued that people cannot be studied using the same procedures as those involved in investigating the physical world: people are thinking, reasoning beings who attach meanings to what they do, and sociology has to acknowledge this. Weber felt that sociology should adopt a sort of midway position between the 'hard' natural sciences and cultural studies such as literature, history and art.

For Weber, the basis of sociological analysis was the meaning that individuals give to the social world and their situation in it. This necessitated sociology following a different kind of method from that of the natural sciences. Sociology could not proceed in the same manner as the natural sciences, because individuals had a degree of free will which led to some unpredictability in their actions. Sociology had to aim to understand human action, and

to do this it had to acknowledge the particular and unique rather than always expect to be able to generalize.

In contrast to the other founding writers, Weber was interested in explaining individual social action and what motivates it. The basic unit of investigation should, therefore, be the individual, whereas Durkheim emphasized collectivity and Marx the social class groupings.

In particular, sociology had to adopt what Weber called *verstehen* – a German word meaning, roughly, empathetic or interpretative understanding – in order to show how people's beliefs and motives led to particular types of behaviour and action. Understanding and empathizing with the belief of others does not necessarily mean being sympathetic to or supportive of those beliefs. However, in order to gain a real appreciation of how others feel, we should try to think of ourselves as being in their situation and see things through their eyes.

While it might seem difficult to empathize with people from different cultures and periods of history, Weber saw *verstehen* as a method that could be applied to the understanding of events from different contexts: 'One need not have been Caesar in order to understand Caesar' (sense can be made of Caesar's actions by seeing them as an understandable sequence).

Stop and think

> How might *verstehen* help in the study of (a) religion; (b) poverty; (c) crime?

> What difficulties might face someone adopting such an approach?

Thus sociology, according to Weber, is the study of social action, and it is by placing meaning on and interpreting the behaviour of others that we are able to understand that behaviour. Of course, the meaning of an action requires an interpretation and the problem for sociology, as Weber sees it, is how to discover the meanings which other individuals and groups place on their behaviour. In interpreting behaviour, sociologists will inevitably be left with nagging doubts about their observations and analyses: 'How can I be sure that I have understood the subjective feelings of others? How would I know if I had totally misunderstood and misinterpreted them?'

These kinds of doubts and problems raise the issue of whether there is some standard of social action against which different types of behaviour can be related to and measured. Weber suggested there were four basic categories of action that could provide such a standard:

1 *Traditional action* The individual is driven by custom and habit, with behaviour often an automatic reaction. A great deal of everyday activity comes under this heading – eating, washing and so on.

2 *Affective action* The individual is guided by emotions. Such behaviour contains some distinctive and unconscious elements: it may involve seeking revenge or providing immediate sensual gratification, for instance.

3 *Value-rational action* The individual follows strongly held values and morals. Overall objectives or ends are seen as important, and behaviour is guided by ideals – doing the 'decent thing'.

4 *Technical-rational action* The individual chooses the objectives and means rationally, with a full account taken of the consequences. It is this sort of behaviour that is most open to sociological understanding and analysis.

Weber argued that technical-rational action was becoming more and more dominant in Western society and was driving out the other forms of action. This notion of rationality and the spread of it is a key principle of Weber's work.

A closer look

Ideal types

The categories of social action suggested by Weber are 'ideal types', a notion that is an important element of his work. Essentially, an ideal type is a way of classifying things; it is an abstraction that Weber employed in trying to get to grips with the complexities of the social world. Social phenomena cannot always be understood in their entirety, and it is often easier to emphasize certain key features. Thus, our ideal type of capitalism, democracy or whatever will not necessarily represent the 'real thing'; it will be a rather exaggerated and idealized version (a little like a cartoon characterization). Weber saw the ideal type as a sort of yardstick for comparing and evaluating other cases. It is quite possible for different ideal types to be constructed for the same phenomenon; there might be different ideal types of capitalism, for example.

Weber's work was wide-ranging and encompassed many topics. Here we shall focus on just two of his main concerns: the relationship between religion and the development of capitalism and the spread of bureaucratic administration in the modern world. As well as being extremely interesting and influential in their own right, both these areas of Weber's work give a good insight into the analytical methods he employed.

The Protestant Ethic and the Spirit of Capitalism

Weber's most famous study, *The Protestant Ethic and the Spirit of Capitalism* (1904/5), attempted to explain how a particular type of religious belief came to influence economic behaviour, thereby making it more rational; this is an application of his argument that technical-rational action was becoming the predominant form of social action in the modern Western world.

Weber studied a range of cultures and religions of the non-Western world in order to show that they had not developed a similar sort of rational capitalism to the

West due to religious and cultural factors. This approach can be contrasted with Marx's emphasis on the importance of economic, class factors in the rise of Western capitalism. Weber's work was critical of the Marxist view that religious ideas were always and inevitably shaped by economic factors. Weber did not deny that in certain situations religion may be shaped by economic factors, but he argued that this was not always the case. However, his main interest was in the ways in which religious ideas might affect and determine social change.

So, the 'Protestant ethic thesis' aimed to explain the development of capitalism in terms of the emergence of a particular form of Protestant religion. Weber tried to explain why capitalism had fully developed only in the Western world and had flourished in northern Europe. He argued that religion provided a clue. He suggested that the ideas and practices of Protestantism were particularly appropriate to capitalist development in a way that was not true of other religions, such as Islam, or of other forms of Christianity, such as Catholicism.

The capitalist spirit

Weber argued that there was a capitalist spirit which was based on a desire to be productive and accumulate. In Western society, hard work, investment and steady accumulation were seen as the 'proper' and correct attitudes, with idleness and overconsumption seen as wrong; elsewhere, production was more geared towards the production of goods for immediate use. The sort of Western attitudes that Weber identified with capitalist societies were, he felt, by no means natural. Why not, for instance, just produce enough for our needs and then stop working? Why not spend when we can, rather than save?

In looking at Weber's definition of capitalism, it is important to bear in mind that he was writing at the beginning of the twentieth century, and the attitudes and style of capitalism have changed since then. Also, his description is an 'ideal type': each capitalist society has its own peculiarities. Nonetheless, the essence of capitalism is seen as an 'enterprise whose aim is to make the maximum profit and whose means is the rational organisation of work and production'. This desire for profit in tandem with rational discipline constitutes the historically unique feature of Western capitalism. In all societies there have been merchants eager to make money, but what is unique is that this desire for profit should satisfy itself not by conquest and plunder but by discipline and science. Perhaps the term 'profit'

does not fully describe Weber's emphasis on the idea of unlimited accumulation. The capitalist, according to Weber, does not limit his appetite for gain in accordance with tradition or custom but is driven by a desire to keep accumulating.

With regard to the relationship between Western capitalism and religion, Weber suggested that a certain form of Protestantism provided conditions that were particularly favourable for the growth of the capitalist economic system. The key elements of his findings and argument can be summarized as:

1 In areas of mixed religions (such as his own society, Germany) particular groups of Protestants possessed a disproportionate amount of wealth and important positions.

2 This indicated a spiritual affinity – a link – between the Protestant religion and the spirit of capitalism.

3 The different styles of religion in different societies help to explain why Western capitalism did not develop elsewhere. Weber studied the religions of a number of areas of the world, including China, India and the Middle East. He argued that a particular attitude to work, determined by religious belief, was the crucial factor present in the West and absent elsewhere which helped to establish Western economic dominance.

A closer look

Capitalism according to Weber

Weber's definition of capitalism as an enterprise working towards unlimited acquisition of goods and functioning in a rational and disciplined way resembles Marx's definition but also presents various differences.

Similarities with Marx – The essence of capitalism is the pursuit of profit through the market; capitalism has utilized increasingly powerful technical means to achieve its ends – of extra profit.

Differences from Marx – The major characteristic of capitalism is rationalization, which would continue no matter who owned the means of production. The need for rational organization would persist beyond any revolution that might result in the state ownership of production; it would still exist in socialist or communist societies.

The Protestant ethic

What was the particular feature of this 'form of Protestantism' that Weber felt was so influential? The Protestant ethic was a sort of Puritanism that was based on Calvinism (John Calvin was one of the great religious reformers of the sixteenth century and the founder of the Presbyterian religion). The principal features of the Protestant ethic were:

1 The existence of an absolute, transcendent God who created the world and ruled over it.

2 This all-powerful God has predestined each person to salvation or damnation; this predestination cannot be altered.

3 God created the world for his glory, and everyone is obliged to work for the glory of God – whether they are to be saved or not.

4 Worldly things belong to the order of sin: salvation occurs only through divine grace.

Although each of these features exist separately in other religions, their combination in Calvinist Protestantism was, Weber argued, unique.

Weber saw a coincidence between certain requirements of this Protestantism and capitalist logic. The Protestant ethic asks the believer to beware of the things of this world and emphasizes the importance of self-denial. To work rationally in pursuit of profit which is not consumed but reinvested is the sort of conduct that was necessary to the development of capitalism. This demonstrates an aspect of what Weber called the spiritual affinity between the Protestant and capitalist attitudes. The Protestant ethic, according to Weber, provided an economic motivation for the 'strange' capitalist behaviour of accumulation for the sake of it – a behaviour which has no obvious parallel in non-Western societies.

Predestination

A central aspect of the Protestant ethic was the idea of predestination, which is a religious conviction based on the belief that God's decrees are ultimate, impenetrable and irrevocable. Grace is either bestowed on an individual or it is not, and there is little the individual can do to alter this. This belief helps to explain the rejection of the sacraments by Protestant religions. In some religions, people can find 'grace' through, for instance, confession and absolution from sins or from last rites. For Puritan Protestants these practices would make no difference to whether an individual was saved or not.

The belief in predestination leads to the elimination of many of the mystical elements of belief and, for Weber, highlighted the increasing rationalization of religion.

Believers in predestination are faced by crucial questions such as 'How does one know that one belongs to the elect?' and 'What is the sign that one is saved?' The early Protestants believed that the sign of election could be found in a personal life that followed religious teachings and in the social achievements of an individual. Social achievement would include success in the individual's professional activity – in their 'calling'. Effective and good work demonstrates the glory of God, so that a successful work career demonstrated a blessing on those activities and could, therefore, be interpreted as 'proof of election'. Individuals acquire the certainty of salvation through the strength of their faith, which would be reflected in success at work.

This notion of successful worldly achievement demonstrating spiritual salvation poses a dilemma. Growing business success will lead to greater affluence, which does not fit in with the rigour of a true Christian life, where worldly possessions would be seen as unimportant. However, Puritan Protestants believed that it was not the acquiring of wealth that was wrong but the enjoyment of the things that money can buy and the temptations it can bring. It was felt that individuals should take from their assets only what was needed for a life of personal sobriety and obedience to God's law and must follow an ascetic lifestyle.

The emphasis on hard work and productivity coupled with the rejection of luxuries led to a lifestyle that encouraged and influenced the spirit of capitalism.

The Protestant ethic thesis: discussion points

The Protestant ethic thesis is essentially a reaction to the Marxist assumption that all social events are reducible to a single factor – the economic context or substructure. Weber's argument is not the opposite of historical materialism; as he put it, 'It is not my aim to substitute for a one-sided materialistic an equally one-sided spiritualistic causal interpretation of history and culture' (Weber 1974: 183). What he demonstrated is that economic activity may be governed by systems of belief, just as at certain times systems of belief may be determined by the economic system. Thus Protestantism was not seen by Weber as the cause of capitalism but rather as one of the factors that led to its emergence and development. Weber's work has encouraged the recognition that there is no necessary determination of beliefs by economic and social reality, or rather that it is not justifiable to assume a determination of this kind to be the only and ultimate one.

A closer look

The Protestant ethic and asceticism

A lifestyle of asceticism was one based on self-denial and abstinence. In the context of the early Protestants, with their emphasis on the virtues of hard work, it was felt that wasting time was a sin: God's time should not be wasted by idle talk, by too much sleep or by sociability, for example. In addition, people should accept the position that God had assigned to them; whatever work one has to do, it should be done to God's greater glory. A person without a vocation was felt to lack the character demanded by asceticism; although irregular work might be unavoidable at times, it was not a good thing. If individuals did not try to be as productive as possible in their work then they were refusing to be a good steward of God's gifts and were not following a calling. Asceticism was hostile to leisure and cultural pursuits. The theatre was obnoxious to Puritans, as was ostentatious dress: thus the plain clothing worn by Puritans.

The link between this religious asceticism and capitalism was that industry was provided with sober and conscientious workers. Furthermore, it gave an assurance that inequality was part of God's plan and was not to be questioned. Asceticism, and particularly the notion that hard work was highly pleasing to God, was not a new phenomenon; nor was it unique to early Protestantism. However, the emphasis on work as a calling, and a sign of personal salvation, added an extra dimension to the ascetic idea. From a different perspective, it could be argued that the emphasis on work as a calling also provided a justification for employers' exploitation of their workforce, in that employers' business activities were also seen as callings, with profit making viewed positively.

Questions

1. Which particular stories or parables from the Bible could be used to 'support' the Protestant ethic's emphasis on asceticism?

2. How has the Protestant ethic influenced the way that people think about contemporary issues such as (a) unemployment and poverty; (b) divorce and changes in family structure?

Given its scope, it is not surprising that many doubts have been raised about the validity of Weber's thesis. First, although the early Protestant capitalists advocated an ascetic lifestyle and did not spend a great deal on luxuries, they did have power and status in their communities as well as financial security – and perhaps these things are enjoyments in themselves. Second, many of the early rich capitalists were not Protestants: there were also rich Catholic and Jewish business people. Third, while there probably was a link between capitalism and Protestantism, rather than Protestantism leading to capitalism the reverse occurred and Protestantism developed as a rationalization for capitalism. It justified the wealth of certain people by suggesting that this wealth would be viewed favourably by God. Fourth, some Calvinist communities did not develop along capitalist lines immediately. Scotland, for instance, although strongly Calvinist, had a slower capitalist development than other less obviously Protestant countries. Finally, the accumulation of investment capital in Britain, the Netherlands, New England in the USA and other early capitalist societies was arguably due as much to profiteering through trade with less developed countries as to careful saving by God-fearing Protestant business people.

Of course, Weber realized that capitalism was not solely the result of Protestantism: he was aware of the developments in trade and technology. He felt, however, that the age in which capitalism developed, which was also the age of the Reformation, was one where religion was a major force in society and social scientists should examine and explain the extent to which religious conduct could influence other activities. Weber did not believe he had exhausted the subject, as his comment in the last paragraph of *The Protestant Ethic and the Spirit of Capitalism* illustrates:

> Modern man [*sic*] is in general unable to give religious ideas a significance for cultural and national character which they deserve. (Weber 1974: 183)

Weber and bureaucracy

In the sociological study of organizations, Weber's work is generally taken as the starting-point. Weber examined, in particular, bureaucracy, the form of organization that he saw as becoming predominant in modern industrial society. In Britain, the word 'bureaucracy' tends to have negative connotations and to be seen as something of a 'problem'; indeed, the term 'bureaucrat' often doubles as a form of mild abuse. Nevertheless, the bureaucratic type of organizational structure would seem to be a fixed, permanent and perhaps even necessary feature of modern society.

Weber saw that as industrial societies developed they were characterized by the growth and spread of large-scale organizations – the civil service, the armed forces, churches, educational institutions, manufacturing companies and so on. Large-scale organizations were clearly having an increasing influence on all areas of social life.

Weber was particularly concerned with the problem of efficiency in organizations. The 'ideal type' blueprint for bureaucracy that he defined (see p. 64) was, he felt, the best way of ensuring efficiency in the administering of organizations. This 'ideal type' of Weber's was based on his analysis of alternative forms of power and authority. This analysis provides the context for an understanding of Weber's theorizing on bureaucracy.

Power was seen by Weber as the ability to get things done or to compel others to comply with one's commands. *Authority* also involves the ability to get things done but in situations where the particular order is seen as legitimate by those following it. Authority is, in essence, legitimized power, where legitimacy involves the acceptance of the rights of others to make decisions. So, power and authority are closely related concepts for Weber, but the notion of legitimacy is an important distinguishing feature. Weber then defined and distinguished three types of authority based on different 'types' of legitimacy. The three types were traditional, charismatic and rational-legal, and these were found, he argued, in one degree or another, in all forms of society.

In broad historical terms, Weber believed that the traditional and charismatic forms of authority existed in earlier, pre-industrial societies. In modern society, the rationalization process (by this Weber means the application of scientific thought and the influence of science in behaviour) has meant that authority has become increasingly rational-legal, based on formal rules. And, as suggested above, bureaucracy is the most typical form of rational-legal authority.

Weber's 'ideal type' bureaucracy

Bureaucracy was, for Weber, the characteristic form of administration in modern society. It was not just confined to the political arena but was common to all other forms of administration, including education, religion, the business world and so on. Essentially, Weber's explanation for the spread of bureaucracy was because of its efficiency in relation to other forms of organization.

A closer look

Weber's three types of authority

Traditional authority

This is based on the unquestioning acceptance of the distribution of power. Legitimacy is believed because it has 'always been so'; the leader has authority by virtue of the traditional status that the office of leader has.

Charismatic authority

This is based on the commitment and loyalty to a leader who is generally felt to possess very exceptional qualities. Charisma is a unique force that overrides tradition and law. In a system based on charismatic authority the word of the leader is seen as all-important; by its nature, this type of authority is very unstable. First, the particular leader has to keep the loyalty of the masses and, assuming this can be achieved, it is difficult to pass on charismatic authority after the leader's death. Second, the authority of charismatic leaders tends to become routinized over time; they will need to get a staff of assistants as the job of leader evolves. Weber argued that charismatic authority will eventually change its form and become routinized or bureaucratized; it will merge with the third and final type of authority he defined – the rational-legal.

Rational-legal authority

This is based on a legal framework which supports and maintains the distribution of power among individuals and groups in society. This form of authority is characterized by bureaucracy; the emphasis is on the rules rather than either the leader (charismatic authority) or the customs (traditional authority). The organization is supreme, with no one being 'above the law' (remember that Weber was talking in ideal terms!).

Questions

1. Give an example of (a) traditional; (b) charismatic; (c) rational-legal authority.

2. Give examples of people who illustrate or have illustrated each of these forms of authority.

It is important to note that Weber's belief in the efficiency of bureaucracy did not mean he saw bureaucracy as necessarily a 'good thing'. An overriding fear at the end of his life was that modern society would be subject to a deadening, dictatorial bureaucracy. This fear was tied in with Weber's work on rationalization; bureaucratic development was a logical consequence of increasing rationalization, which was undermining and removing spiritual influences from the world. Rationalization was, for Weber, a key feature of modern society and occurred in the fields of both religious belief and economic activity.

Weber's 'ideal type' model of bureaucracy contained six basic principles:

1 *Specialization*   Official tasks and positions are clearly divided; each covers a distinct and separate area of competence.

2 *Hierarchy*   There is an ordered system of superordination and subordination; every position or office is accountable to and supervised by a higher office.

3 *Rules*   There are clearly established, general rules which govern the management of the office.

4 *Impersonality*   Everyone within the organization is subject to formal equality of treatment.

5 *Officials*   They are (a) selected and appointed on the basis of technical qualifications (or some clearly recognized criteria); (b) full-time appointments, in that the particular post is the sole or major occupation of the individual; (c) subject to a formal career structure with a system of promotion according to either seniority or merit (in other words, there are objective criteria for promotions).

6 *Public–private division*   There is a clear separation between official activity and private life (the resources of the organization, for instance, are quite distinct from those of the officials as private individuals).

Essentially, then, Weber's 'ideal type' bureaucracy meant ordered administration by officials. Weber laid particular emphasis on the central importance of rules. Rules reduce tension between people; they allow people to feel that they are following a rule rather than a particular individual. Furthermore, rules apply to everyone (in the ideal situation, of course) and they legitimize punishments in that the rule and sanction for breaking it are known in advance. Weber felt that the impersonal quality of bureaucracy was also particularly important: it ensured that everyone received the same treatment and that they could calculate in advance what would happen in particular situations and circumstances.

The major reason for the development and spread of this form of administration has been its technical superiority over other forms of organization. Precision, discretion, continuity and speed are all achieved to a greater degree in a bureaucratic structure. For Weber, bureaucratization was simply the most efficient way of administering; there is a regular chain of command, always a higher authority to refer to.

Stop and think

➤ What organizations are you a part of or have regular contact with? Take each of the six elements of Weber's model of bureaucracy and describe briefly the extent to which they apply to these organizations.

➤ Following on from these descriptions, evaluate whether Weber's classification is a good basis for assessing the extent to which a particular organization is bureaucratized.

Weber and bureaucracy: criticisms

Weber's argument that bureaucracy is the most efficient form of organization has been criticized by a number of writers. Robert Merton, an American sociologist and a leading figure in functionalist sociology between the 1940s and 1970s, wrote a famous paper 'Bureaucratic Structure and Personality' (1952), which focused on the harmful consequences of bureaucracy. He highlighted a number of *dysfunctions* (things that hinder the workings of an institution or activity) of bureaucracy. He suggested that the 'virtues' of discipline and efficiency could become exaggerated in practice, to the extent that officials become obsessed with organizational rules. At the extreme, officials may become so enmeshed in the rules and 'doing things by the book' that they are unable to help their clients speedily or efficiently. Merton's argument is that bureaucracies create a bureaucratic personality – a personality that stresses conformity and, consequently, initiative and innovative behaviour are stifled and replaced with inflexibility and timidity. Merton also pointed out that strict conformity to rules can work against the achievement of organizational goals, particularly in circumstances of rapid change, when new ideas might be necessary. Thus the dysfunctions or problems of bureaucracy are seen by Merton as due to the stress on rules that become too rigid and cannot be altered to fit special circumstances.

Weber's description of the ideal type bureaucracy does not include concepts such as trust, cooperation and flexibility. Alvin Gouldner (1954), in a study of a gypsum plant in the USA, argued that while a bureaucratic structure might work well in stable, predictable situations, it was too rigid to cope with situations of rapid change, where trust, cooperation and flexibility are essential. In the context of industrial bureaucracies, a rule might be rational for achieving the ends of one group – management for instance – but might work against the interests of another group – the employees perhaps.

The importance that Weber attached to following rules was seen by Peter Blau (1963) as, on occasion, working against the efficiency of the organization. Some organizations function more effectively when workers gather into informal groups and disregard or break official rules. To illustrate his argument, Blau studied a federal law-enforcement agency in the USA. He found that officers who infringed rules regularly achieved a higher success rate in enforcing the law. Blau argues that bureaucratic structures can be too inflexible. No set of rules can anticipate all the potential problems, and it is important to study the informal workings of organizations as well as the formal structure.

Bureaucracy in practice is often quite distinct from the ideal type on paper. It must be emphasized that although Weber believed bureaucracies to be efficient, he was not an uncritical supporter of them. Indeed, Weber saw the growth of bureaucratic administration, which he felt was inevitable, as a grave threat to individual freedom (along with other aspects of the general process of rationalization in modern societies). He argued that bureaucracies have an inbuilt tendency to accumulate power and that once established they tend to take on a life of their own and become extremely hard to dismantle.

Weber's relevance in the twenty-first century

In 1989 Kaessler argued that if there was such a thing as the Sociological Hall of Fame, Max Weber would be honoured amongst its ranks. What he actually said was that according to a range of academic criteria Weber should be accepted as a 'classic' sociologist because his work and insights had stood the test of time.

More recently George Ritzer (1993) developed the concept of the McDonaldization of Society in which many of Weber's ideas on rationality were applied to the economic and social changes taking place in America 70 years after Weber's death. These ideas were later applied to other scenarios as Ritzer argued that the processes he was describing were not restricted to the American fast food industry but could be found in all walks of life

on a global scale. In the twenty-first century edition of his book and the Reader which accompanies it he demonstrates that far from being a 'dead white male' and a 'founding father' in sociology, Weber's ideas are probably more relevant today than when he was alive.

Contemporary sociological theories

This section discusses some important developments in sociological theory since the 1920s. Social theory did not come to an end with the deaths of the founding writers; rather their work has acted as a stimulus for a wide range of theoretical argument in sociology. This general introduction can provide only a flavour of the various complex developments in modern social theory; to capture the excitement and intricacies of these theoretical debates you will need to look at the original sources summarized here or, failing that, texts that focus on modern social theory (see Further Reading, p. 100).

Interpretative sociology

The title 'interpretative sociology' includes a number of more specific sociological theories, the best known of which are probably *symbolic interactionism* and *ethnomethodology*. As with other sociological theories, these approaches attempt to explain human behaviour and do this by examining the social influences on behaviour. However, rather than emphasizing the influence of the social structure and how it constrains people, interpretative theories argue that the most important influence on individuals' behaviour is the behaviour of others towards them.

Interpretative sociology concentrates on the micro-level of social life. Societies are the end-result of human interaction rather than the starting-point, and by looking at how this interaction occurs it is possible to understand how social order is created and maintained. In focusing on everyday life, this theoretical approach offers a clear contrast with those theories that examine 'grand' questions and issues, such as 'What is industrial society?', and provide a general explanation of society as a whole. Thus interpretative sociology offers a different approach and style of investigating society to the functionalist and conflict macro-theories and the work of the founding theorists looked at earlier in this chapter.

Meanings

These theories focus on the individual and the process of social interaction. They examine how people are able to understand one another; how they interpret what is going on around them and then choose to behave in particular ways. They emphasize the meanings that people give to actions and to things.

Human behaviour is seen as the product of conscious decisions and, in most cases, individuals have some choice as to how they act. Furthermore, actions are usually purposive: they are directed towards some goal. The particular goal or purpose that is followed is dependent on the way in which individuals interpret the world around them. People choose what to do in the light of their 'definition of the situation'. For instance, you might wake up on a wet morning and decide to work on an assignment or essay; if the weather brightens up you may decide to make the most of it and abandon the college work and go into town; in town you may meet a friend and decide to forget about any shopping plans and go to a café.

Theories that emphasize the meanings which individuals give to action clearly owe a great debt to Max Weber. The importance Weber attached to explaining individual social action and to the notion of *verstehen* (empathetic or interpretative understanding, see pp. 58–9) demonstrate his role as the founder of the interpretative approach in sociology. However, Weber applied the idea of *verstehen* to the analysis of large-scale social change and did not examine in detail the day-to-day interactions of individuals in specific situations. Interpretativist sociologists have adopted Weber's approach and applied it to small-scale and specific contexts.

Stop and think

➤ How can a greater understanding of social interaction on a micro-level aid our understanding of macro-sociological questions?

Symbolic interactionism

There are a number of related theoretical perspectives that fit under the broad heading of interpretative sociology. Symbolic interactionism is perhaps the most well established and will be the focus for this introductory discussion. It suggests that human behaviour is different from that of (other) animals because it uses symbols and attaches meanings to them. When people interact with one another they use symbols, especially in the form of language – hence the name 'symbolic interactionism'.

This theoretical perspective emerged from the writings of US sociologists and social psychologists in the 1920s and 1930s, in particular Charles Cooley, William Thomas and George Herbert Mead. Mead, who began his career as a philosopher, published little while he was alive, and his lectures form the basis for his key role as the founder of symbolic interactionism.

Mead's work emphasized the relationship between the individual and society. He called his approach 'social behaviourism' because it was closely linked with social psychology – the study of social groups. The basic idea behind Mead's approach was that the perceptions and the behaviour of individuals are influenced by the social groups of which they are members. The existence of social groups is essential for the development of what Mead termed the 'self'.

The self is perhaps the key concept of the symbolic interactionist perspective. It refers to how individuals see themselves. We all have a self-image, an identity and some conception of who we 'really' are – which we refer to as the self. This concept of the 'self' is only meaningful in relation to other 'selves'. We carry on a whole series of different interactions with different people; we are one thing to one person and another thing to another.

It is the ability to become self-conscious, to be able to stand outside our own situation and look at our behaviour retrospectively that provides the key to Mead's analysis. Questions such as 'What made me do that?' Mead saw as examples of reflexive questioning – of the individual 'taking the role of others'. So Mead's theory of self and socialization rests on the individual's ability to take the role of others and so of the wider community. This requires the organization of the individual's whole self in relation to the social groups and the community to which that individual belongs. The organized community or group which provides this unity of self for individuals was given the term the 'generalized other' by Mead. The attitude of the generalized other is the attitude of the whole community to which the individual belongs. It is through taking the attitude of the generalized other that individuals are able to see themselves as others do and to understand the attitudes of others towards the various aspects of social life.

The development of the self

The self develops or evolves through understanding the attitude and role of others. This development occurs through stages. Initially a young child adopts the role of particular individuals, for example through playing at being mummy, teacher, doctor and so on, and then gradually adopts the attitude of the whole community or society. The move from adopting individual to adopting general attitudes involves a change from copying behaviour to understanding behaviour. This development is exemplified in the change in a young child's reaction from 'Mummy says no' to 'One does not do this', where the child is relating to the generalized other.

Mead's theory of the development of self lays great stress on the individual's ability to interpret the behaviour of others. During social interaction the individual learns which behaviour is appropriate to particular situations. With experience the individual is able to generalize from specific instances and decide which types of behaviour are appropriate. Part of the process of socialization involves becoming aware of which particular role is applicable to a particular situation. So Mead regards the self as being made up of a series of roles, each of which relates to the social group of which the individual is a part. For a fully developed self, self-consciousness is necessary and is the core of the process of self-development.

> ## Stop and think
>
> ➤ List the different roles you play during the course of one day.
>
> ➤ Do any of these roles conflict with each other?
>
> ➤ If so, how is this conflict resolved?

All the world's a stage: the dramaturgical approach of Erving Goffman

Our discussion of the development of self looked at the ways in which individuals understand and adopt the role of others. The notion that in everyday life individuals play roles, negotiate situations and to a certain extent are forced to be 'actors' is the basis of the dramaturgical approach developed by Erving Goffman.

A closer look

Erving Goffman (1922–82)

The view of the 'world as a stage', with individuals performing and acting for their audiences in everyday life, has been particularly associated with the work of Goffman. Goffman wrote a number of widely read and influential books between 1956, the publication of *The Presentation of Self in Everyday Life*, and 1981, when *Forms of Talk*, his last book, was published. In this discussion we shall use Goffman's work, and particularly *The Presentation of Self in Everyday Life* and *Relations in Public* (1971), as a specific illustration of this interactionist approach. Goffman was primarily an observer of social interaction who 'possessed an extraordinary ability to appreciate the subtle importance of apparently insignificant aspects of everyday conduct' (Manning 1992). He argued that individual behaviour follows intricate patterns; in our everyday lives we follow a set of implicit instructions that influence and determine this behaviour.

Goffman's work

Goffman saw social encounters and interaction in theatrical terms, with his earlier work concentrating on how people present themselves and their activities to others. Using the theatre analogy, he talked about individuals' behaviour being 'performances' put on for audiences, with different parts or roles played on different occasions. As we mentioned earlier, all of us have many different roles, with different expectations attached to them. Each of you may have a role as a student, where you are expected to sit in classes, reasonably quietly, look interested and do the work set; but you will also have many different roles which will involve you acting in quite different ways – as brother/sister, friend or worker, for instance. Goffman's work provides many examples of how we play different roles and try to create different impressions for others. Bearing in mind that Goffman's research was undertaken in the late 1950s, the following example illustrates female students acting dumb to avoid creating the 'wrong' impression:

American college girls did, and no doubt do, play down their intelligence, skill, and determinativeness when in the presence of datable boys . . . These performers are reported to allow their boy friends to explain things to them tediously that they already know; they conceal proficiency in mathematics from their less able consorts; they lose ping-pong games just before the ending:

> 'One of the nicest techniques is to spell long words incorrectly once in a while. My boyfriend seems to get a great kick out of it and writes back, "Honey you certainly don't know how to spell."'

Through all of this the natural superiority of the male is demonstrated and the weaker role of the female affirmed. (Goffman 1969: 48)

As well as playing roles and creating impressions, Goffman highlighted other ways in which everyday behaviour can be compared to a theatrical performance. There is often a division into a back region, where a performance is prepared, and a front region, where it is presented. As the audience in a theatre does not see backstage, so access to certain aspects of everyday behaviour is controlled, to prevent outsiders seeing a performance that is not intended for them. Backstage is private, and it can be embarrassing if outsiders gain access to it; in hotels and cafés, for example, the differences between the front regions and back regions can be dramatic, and customers might be disappointed, or horrified, if they saw backstage. Also, the communication that occurs front and backstage can be quite different: customers who may be treated very respectfully to their faces may be caricatured, ridiculed or cursed as soon as they have gone.

When interacting with others most people want those others to reach a particular interpretation of their actions. It is possible to use dress, language, gestures and so on to organize and influence how others interpret behaviour and to ensure that they arrive at the desired interpretation. Although the police officer, businessperson or skinhead might make no apparent attempt to communicate with people who pass them on the street, they are creating an impression that will influence how others think about them. As a rule individuals will try to control or guide the impressions that others form of them, and there are common techniques that can be used to create and sustain these impressions. A fundamental point that underlies all social interaction is that when one individual interacts with others the person will want to discover as much about the situation as possible. To do that it is necessary to know as much as possible about others. Of course, such information is not usually available (we do not know the likes, dislikes, background and so on of everyone we interact with). So in the absence of this knowledge we have to make guesses or predictions about others.

Figure 2.4 A businessman and a skinhead: impression management at work and the outside world

The importance of giving a convincing impression to others, and the obligation to live up to that impression, often forces people to act a role. What people think of one another is dependent on the impression given (as a certain type of person), and this impression can be disrupted if others acquire information that they are not meant to have – as the regular revelations of scandals in the private lives of public figures demonstrate!

Stop and think

> What factors influence the first impressions you have of others?

> How can these first impressions be either supported or altered as you acquire more information?

> It is quite easy to think of examples from our own lives of instances where the 'wrong' person has seen or heard something that we would rather have kept hidden from them. Give examples of aspects of your own behaviour that you try to keep 'backstage' from others. What might happen if such behaviour were to exposed 'frontstage'?

Goffman was aware of the limitations of the theatrical analogy. In his later work he acknowledged the differences between face-to-face interaction in social life and on the stage. When watching a play the audience generally likes to see a complete performance and to hear all the lines of the actors, whereas in daily life this is often not the case, with interruptions a normal part of social interaction. However, while not offering a complete account of everyday life, the dramaturgical analogy does contribute to our understanding and analysis of aspects of everyday life. It is clear in our interaction with others that we play roles and display great skill in creating and managing impressions.

Normal appearances

Goffman applied the dramaturgical perspective on social interaction to how individuals behave in public, looking in particular at the expectations people hold of what is normal and acceptable behaviour. We have particular ideas about what is right and wrong. Goffman cites a story from the *New York Times* to illustrate this point.

> A hit-and-run driver fooled several witnesses who saw him hit another automobile. The driver got out of his car after an accident, went to the damaged car and left this note: 'I have just hit your car. People are watching me. They think I'm leaving my name. But I'm not.'
> The note was signed, 'the wrecker'.
> (Goffman 1971: 312)

This example illustrates the point that when people sense things are normal they will act in a normal manner. Acting normally or naturally is seen by Goffman as a key element in successful impression management. Indeed, it is relatively easy to 'con' people because of the expectations that are held as to what is normal behaviour. This is not to say that it is morally a good or decent thing to do, just that it is often much easier than we initially think to fabricate lies and to make them seem natural.

Perhaps the best examples of the use, or maybe misuse, of normal appearances and expectations occur in the context of criminal behaviour. Criminals have regularly used normal appearances to deceive.

> Tokyo – The bandit, about 22 years old, wearing the white helmet and black leather jacket of a traffic officer, rode a stolen motorbike up to a bank car carrying bonus money for employees of the Toshiba Electric Co., 20 miles west of Tokyo. He told the unarmed bank men, from the Nippon Trust and Banking Co., that he had information that dynamite had been planted in the car. When the four got out, the bandit got in and drove away with the car and three metal boxes full of unrecorded yen banknotes worth $816,667. 'He looked just like a policeman,' said Eiji Nakad, the driver of the auto. 'He said he had instructions from Koganei Police Station.'
> (Goffman 1971: 360)

Ethnomethodology and the rules of everyday life

The term 'ethnomethodology' means 'people's methods' and was used by Harold Garfinkel (1967) to describe a theoretical branch of sociology that he developed. Garfinkel felt that conventional sociology took social order for granted and assumed that the everyday social world we inhabit was a structured one. Ethnomethodology focuses on how people construct their social world; it investigates the background knowledge and assumptions that people hold and how they help to create and recreate social order. As with other interpretative approaches, there is an emphasis on how people give meanings to and interpret behaviour. However, ethnomethodology is particularly concerned with the processes by which this occurs, and specifically with the methods used by people to communicate with one another.

The importance of the meanings that we give to our actions can be clearly illustrated if we suspend the 'rules' of everyday life. Most of the time we, as individuals, live in a world that is taken for granted; we do not question what goes on. We do not think about the rules underlying everyday actions until something happens to interrupt the routine. During a college or school day it is a reasonably safe bet that nothing will happen to astound us. There is the possibility of a surprise – the building may catch fire, we might develop a passionate hatred or love for someone we meet. However, we all accept that what is going on is a routine, called college or school education. If this routine were not the case we would not get much done, we would constantly be being surprised by astounding happenings. Furthermore, even if a definite attempt were made to try something different this might soon become routine too. If a teacher went into the classroom and stood on a desk to teach, this would soon become routine if done regularly: there would be a change from 'Look what she's doing' to 'There she goes again'.

Case study

Rule-governed behaviour: Garfinkel's experiments

Various experiments have been carried out by interpretativist sociologists to demonstrate how rule-governed our everyday behaviour is. Garfinkel (1967) organized a number of experiments that involved the disruption of everyday life. In one case he asked a group of his students to take part in a new type of counselling. They were to put questions to an 'expert counsellor', who was to help them and give advice, but on the understanding that he would answer their questions only with a 'yes' or 'no' and no more. The 'counsellor' was, in fact, told to answer the questions by reading from a random list of 'yes's and 'no's which he had in front of him, paying no attention to the particular questions asked. Although the questions the students asked were meaningful, the answers given by the 'counsellor' were arbitrary and unrelated to the questions. However, because the students believed the answers came from an expert, they imposed meanings and relevance on them. Indeed, when asked by Garfinkel, the majority of the students said they felt the advice had been helpful. Garfinkel argued that this demonstrated how individuals construct meaning from chaos because of a need to fit things into underlying and understood patterns.

Questions

1. *What rules and routines do you follow in everyday activities such as (a) getting up; (b) eating; (c) travelling?*

2. *How do you feel when you are forced to change your regular routines?*

In focusing on how people go about constructing their social world, one of the key questions that Garfinkel considered was that of how people decide whether something is real or not, how they decide 'what really happened'. In some of his early research, Garfinkel studied how jurors made decisions about a defendant's guilt or innocence. This decision making necessitated jurors having to decide and act in a legal manner while not being trained lawyers, having to understand psychological motivations of people while not being psychologists, and so on. Similarly, in everyday life, decisions have to be made on a regular basis: we have to decide between fact and fiction, between the real and imagined, between right and wrong answers. Garfinkel's ethnomethodological approach involves examining the ways in which people go about responding to such questions or dilemmas and how these responses act as a basis for deciding what to do next. This detailed examination of how people go about defining and deciding on social reality in everyday situations offers a way of studying how daily life is organized.

The ethnomethodological focus on interpersonal communication and relationships has been criticized for ignoring the importance and complexity of social systems and the ways in which social factors constrain behaviour.

Indeed, it could be accused of denying the importance of real phenomena that clearly affect the face-to-face interactions studied by ethnomethodologists. As an illustration of this criticism, Cuff *et al.* (1998) comment that while ethnomethodology might be able to study communication among a group of software engineers meeting to discuss a software project, it would not be able to explain why software engineering had grown so phenomenally in the contemporary world. In other words, its analysis would not be informed by the broader picture. In defence, ethnomethodologists would see the criticism that they reject the wider social context as merely an attack on ethnomethodology for not being like other, conventional, sociology. However, as Cuff and colleagues say, 'the charge of rejecting the wider context refuses to go away' (1998: 177).

Feminist theories

Feminist theory and feminist sociological research have developed significantly since the 1960s in what has been described as a 'second wave' of feminism; the first wave is generally taken to refer to feminist struggles for the vote in the late nineteenth and early twentieth centuries. Feminism has a rich history: the breadth of ideas and theory can be only touched on in this introductory section.

Feminist sociologists have produced an extensive critique of conventional sociological theory. They have argued that sociological theories have been written from a male perspective, which has meant that women's experiences have been marginalized. Not only have feminist theorists criticized male-centred theory but they have also written new theories of society which place women's experiences centrally and attempt to explain divisions between men and women in society.

It is important to outline briefly feminist criticisms of the founders of sociology. A key problem with their work is that the founders either paid little or no attention to the issues of women's subordination or treated this as normal. Durkheim and Weber assumed that it was natural for women to be located in the private sphere of the home and men to be active in the public sphere of paid work. Both associated women with nature, biology and emotion and men with reason, culture and rationality. They treated the sexual division of labour and women's subordinate position within it as natural and inevitable (Sydie 1987). Weber's and Durkheim's analyses of social relations between men and women were shaped by assumptions that there were fundamental biological differences between women and men which suited the two sexes to distinctively different social roles. Sydie argues that for Durkheim and Weber,

> This belief in the significance of biological difference means that the hierarchies of power in society, which relegate women collectively to a subordinate status to men, are taken as givens that do not require sociological analysis. (Sydie 1987)

This sort of biological approach to gender relations has been identified as problematic by many feminists.

Although Marx acknowledged inequalities between men and women, he failed to treat gender as a crucial factor that shapes social experiences. His work focused on economic class relations and the exploitation of the working class, very much marginalizing gender relations and questions concerning the oppression of women. His theories were gender-blind: the working class were treated as an undifferentiated mass, yet much of his work was concerned with male members of the proletariat. This failure to treat gender as a crucial determining factor of our social experiences has been a fundamental weakness of much sociological theory according to

Figure 2.5 Feminist cartoon

feminist theorists (Maynard 1990). Many feminists have formulated theories which place the question of women's subordination and gender relations much more centrally.

Stop and think

> ➤ Durkheim, Marx and Weber are sometimes referred to as the 'founding fathers' of sociology. What does this suggest about the origins and development of the subject?
>
> ➤ Why are there no 'founding mothers' of sociology?

When we examine feminism it becomes clear that there are many different tendencies within feminism and that there is no one all-encompassing definition of feminism. Indeed, it is more appropriate to talk about feminisms than feminism (Humm 1992). Contrary to many common-sense interpretations of feminism, feminists do not always agree on ways in which we can explain gender differences and women's subordination. There are debates within feminism about the origins and causes of women's subordination and the strategies needed for change.

We shall outline here five of the different strands of feminism: liberal feminism, radical feminism, Marxist/socialist feminism, black feminism and postmodern feminism. Although any attempt at classification is likely to be incomplete and somewhat arbitrary, this approach provides a useful way of introducing feminist theorizing. However, it is important to note that some feminists cannot be assigned conveniently to a particular category, not all feminism is encompassed, and nor do these strands represent entirely distinct feminisms. So the five types of feminism introduced here represent key tendencies, but there are many other feminist perspectives – ecofeminism and psychoanalytical feminism are just two examples. Feminism is a diverse, constantly evolving body of thought.

Liberal feminism

Liberal feminism has its roots in the liberal tradition of the Enlightenment, which stressed the principles of justice, rationality, citizenship, human rights, equality and democracy. The treatment of women in society violates many of these values. From the days of Mary Wollstonecraft and the publication of her seminal book in 1792 *A Vindication of the Rights of Woman*, liberal feminists have stressed that as rational beings women should be entitled to full personhood and hence have the same legal, political, social and economic rights and opportunities as men. They recognize that women are on occasion unfairly discriminated against on the basis of their sex. Much of this discrimination is informal and based on custom, the product of sexist assumptions and prejudice which still endure in our culture and are the product of gender role conditioning. Liberal feminists advocate political action and reform, favouring educational strategies and formal and legislative changes in order to provide women with

opportunities and challenge stereotypes and prejudices. Yet many have recognized that formal equality is not enough and have supported legislation which outlaws sex discrimination against women and men.

Some contemporary liberal feminists believe that if the state is to enforce equal rights and ensure equal opportunities it must make it economically possible for women to exercise these rights. Hence the state should fund such things as child-care facilities and refuges for women who have experienced violence from their partners. Liberal feminists have historically put an emphasis on incorporating women into the mainstream, giving women the right to equal opportunities in the public sphere of education and employment. Some have suggested that having women in positions of power and influence will in itself have a knock-on effect, with such women in high-status positions acting as role models for others and taking account of women's interests in the formulation of policy.

Betty Friedan's influential liberal feminist text *The Feminine Mystique* was published in 1963. Friedan argued that North American women had been offered fulfilment through motherhood and wifehood only to find dissatisfaction: this was the feminine mystique. She criticized this notion that women should only be home-based carers and encouraged women to engage in paid work outside the home to provide more economic power and personal fulfilment. However, she has been criticized for not addressing how difficult it would be for women to combine motherhood and a career without challenging the notion of women as primary carers and considering the need for men to change. Black feminists pointed out that her theory was ethnocentric, i.e. based on the experiences of a particular ethnic group, in this case white middle-class women. Black women have historically had to work in the labour market and this has not brought them liberation.

Liberal feminists have been criticized for a range of reasons, many linked to what other feminists see as strategies that merely operate within the existing system rather than fundamentally changing social relations. While liberal feminism may bring opportunities and rewards for a few token women it brings little fundamental change in the lives of the large majority of women; despite some reform men still hold the majority of positions of power (Bryson 1992). Others argue that liberal feminism brings opportunities for women on men's terms, that women working within the *status quo* merely endorse the hierarchical and competitive structures of capitalism and patriarchy and indeed theoretically does not acknowledge these social relations.

Some feminists argue that liberal feminism encourages women to be male clones, i.e. successful women adopt 'male' strategies and values. It has been suggested, for example, that Margaret Thatcher became very successful because she conducted her politics in the traditional masculine style and also that she did little to improve the position of women in British society during her years as prime minister. These concerns reflect a debate within feminism concerning whether women should be struggling for equality with men, which suggests they are the same as men, or recognize the differences between women and men (whether innate or socially constructed) and attempt to shape societies based on 'feminine' values and strategies, which some feminists argue would create a more egalitarian, less competitive and less destructive world order. The liberal feminist emphasis on the public sphere is seen as reinforcing the notion of two separate spheres, the public and the private, and devaluing the private (Jaggar 1983; Pateman 1987).

> ### Stop and think
>
> ➤ How easy is it to think of women who have been successful in traditionally male-dominated areas such as business or politics?
>
> ➤ Would you describe the successful women you can think of as having adopted 'male' strategies and values?

Radical feminism

Contemporary radical feminism is associated with the women's liberation movement of the 1960s, yet although many of the ideas expressed by radical feminists were not new, in this period they began to be 'developed systematically as a self-conscious theory' (Bryson 1992). Some women within the movement argued that women's oppression was deeply rooted and that inequality between men and women was a primary source of oppression. This they felt was not being acknowledged in many existing social and political analyses and organizations, which they identified as androcentric (male-centred). As a result, the struggle for women's liberation was being marginalized and a new approach which prioritized women's oppression was needed. Radical feminists argued that gender inequalities are a central and primary form of social inequality and constructed theories which acknowledged this. Radical feminists explain gender inequalities and women's subordination as the outcome of an autonomous system of *patriarchy*.

A closer look

Patriarchy

Patriarchy is basically used to describe a structural system of male domination. It encapsulates the mechanisms, ideologies and social structures which have enabled men historically to gain and maintain their dominance and control over women. Stacey (1993) points out that radical feminists have found patriarchy to be useful theoretically as 'it has given some conceptual form to the nature of male domination in society' and has enabled radical feminists to describe 'how and why women are oppressed'.

Mies (1986) notes that it has provided a concept which captures the totality of women's oppression. Men dominate women in every sphere of life, all relationships between men and women are institutionalized relationships of power; this includes 'private', personal relationships, hence the feminists' slogan 'the personal is political'. Patriarchy is trans-historical, cross-cultural and universal; no area of society is free from male domination. Thus radical feminists are concerned to reveal how male power is exercised in all spheres of life and how patriarchy emerged historically.

Kate Millett's *Sexual Politics* (1970) has been identified as an important radical feminist text because it introduced the concept of patriarchy and contains many typical radical feminist concerns. Millett described all societies as patriarchal; men dominate and women are subordinate, hence all relations between men and women are political relations of power. Patriarchy is maintained via a process of sex role socialization which takes place in the male-headed family. The family is a patriarchal unit which reflects the rule of men in other areas of society. She documents how education, religion and literature reinforce the notion of female subordination and male superiority. She also argued that a whole range of strategies were utilized to control women if they did not conform; these included physical and sexual violence. Similar concerns are evident in the work of other radical feminists.

Radical feminism now constitutes a large and diverse body of thought, with radical feminists taking different positions on a range of issues. Abbott and Wallace (1990) identify three key issues of disagreement within radical feminism: the extent to which gender differences are the product of actual biological differences or are socially constructed; the relationship between feminist politics and personal sexual conduct; and the sort of political strategies that should be adopted to bring about change. An examination of the ideas of specific radical feminist theorists highlights these differences.

Unlike Millett, who stated that the differences between men and women are the product of socialization, the work of some radical feminists has been identified as proposing a biological basis for some differences between women and men. Rich (1977) argues that women's mothering capacity is at the core of men's oppression of women. Men are fearful of women's power to create life, and men sense that women's reproductive powers are somehow mysterious and uncontrollable. Rich and others have contended that as a result men have attempted to control women and even to control reproduction and birth itself. Feminists taking such a position are wary of developments in reproductive technology, which are seen as a means of enabling further male control of reproduction (O'Brien 1981). Rich (1977) stresses that motherhood itself is not inherently oppressive for women but has become oppressive under patriarchy. She celebrates female biology and the potential for motherhood and argues this is an important source of power that women should reclaim. She goes on to suggest that woman-centred cultures and societies in which children are raised in line with feminist values of care and nurture can provide the basis for an alternative non-patriarchal society. For other radical feminists this biological approach to gender differences is unacceptable and reinforces traditional divisions and roles.

Stop and think

> Some people who have fought for sexual equality or whose beliefs overlap with feminism have refused to be labelled as feminists. What might be their reasons for doing so?

Many feminists accept that women have had less power in sexual relationships than men, but some radical feminists such as Catherine MacKinnon identify sexuality as central to patriarchy. Sexual relations are seen not simply as a reflection of broader inequalities but as a source of power which men can exert over women. As MacKinnon (1982) puts it, 'Sexuality is the primary source of male power.'

For MacKinnon, sexuality is male-defined: in sexual relationships with men women are powerless and are merely objects to be used for male sexual pleasure.

Heterosexual sex is based on relations of dominance and submission. Some radical lesbian feminists such as Jeffreys also place sexuality at the heart of women's oppression, specifically heterosexuality. According to Jeffreys, the construction of heterosexuality as normal and natural and all other sexualities as deviant is the organizing principle of social relations of male supremacy; women are pressured into heterosexuality and this serves the interests of patriarchy:

> Without heterosexuality it would be difficult for individual men to extract unpaid sexual, reproductive, economic, domestic and emotional servicing from women. (Jeffreys 1994: 23)

In heterosexual relations with men, women invest their physical, emotional and sexual energies and leave themselves open to exploitation. The term 'hetero-patriarchy' has been used by some lesbian feminists to describe a patriarchal system which is not only male-dominated but also centred around heterosexuality (Penelope 1986; Wilton 1993). Within radical feminism, some feminists have suggested that as heterosexuality was central to oppression, to reclaim their selves it was necessary for women to reject heterosexuality and live a lesbian experience. This is sometimes referred to as political lesbianism.

Bunch (1981) argued that a lesbian existence in which women transferred their identity from men and put women first was an act of resistance in a world structured around the male. Part of the demand for a lesbian existence requires separatism, a strategy where women organize in a women-only context in order to create a space for women to develop an identification with other women and to regenerate women's energies and selves. This not only challenges patriarchy by withdrawing women's servicing of men but also provides a basis for developing alternative women-centred societies. Controversially, some radical lesbian feminists such as the Leeds Revolutionary Feminists Group (1981) accused heterosexual women of sleeping with the enemy. By contrast, other feminists have argued that the rejection of heterosexuality is unrealistic for those women who identify themselves as heterosexual. Segal (1994) also contends that radical feminists' analyses of heterosexuality have dismissed the pleasure found by some women in heterosexual sex and have focused on heterosexual women merely as victims of male exploitation. This has ignored the possibility of women being active agents of heterosexual desire, being able to make choices, take some control and experience pleasure in heterosexual relationships. Wilton (1993) has pointed out a dilemma for lesbian feminists: on the whole it has been left to lesbian feminists to produce a critique of what she calls the 'heterosexual imperative', yet in producing this they are criticized for being divisive.

A whole range of radical feminists have identified violence, both physical and sexual, as a key source of male control over women (Radford *et al.* 1995). The identification of violence against women as a political issue and social problem has been seen as an important achievement of feminism and has been associated particularly with radical feminism; Brownmiller (1976) argued that the act of rape lies at the origins of men's oppression of women. Although not all radical feminists would identify violence as the original source of women's subordination, many have seen it as an important mechanism for maintaining the subordination of women (Kelly 1988). This violence is an expression of power and hatred which controls, humiliates, objectifies and disempowers women.

This brief discussion shows that radical feminists' ideas have generated much debate and criticism from feminists and non-feminists alike. Some non-feminists have identified radical feminism as a misguided political ideology which by identifying men as oppressors and women as exploited has actually fuelled conflict between the sexes (Lyndon 1992). The concept of patriarchy has been identified as a static and rigid category that does not allow for changing and varied gender relations across cultures and across history (Rowbotham 1982). A key criticism of radical feminism is that it has tended to lump women together as a universal group; this is problematic because it masks women's 'varied and complex social reality' (hooks 1984). It ignores and denies the different experiences between women, differences based on such factors as class, race, nationality, age and sexual identity. The emphasis on women as a group with shared experiences and common interests has been identified as particularly problematic by black feminists, who have pointed out that this ignores the way that racism has impacted on the lives of black women creating different experiences for black and white women. They also stress that women exploit and oppress other women and that white women have often been in positions of dominance in relation to black women.

Black feminists have stressed that radical feminists have tended to treat all men as equally powerful, yet in systems such as slavery and imperialism black men have been denied positions in the white male hierarchy; patriarchy is racially demarcated (Murphy and Livingston 1985). Hence it is difficult to claim that black male dominance

over women always exists in the same forms as white male dominance. Black feminists have pointed out that black women have many common interests with black men: the strategy of separatism and the need to organize separately from men, proposed by some radical feminists, have been unacceptable because of the common struggle against racism that they share with black men. The identification within radical feminism of gender as the key source of inequality in society has been rejected by many. Marxist feminists, for instance, argue that gender inequalities are related to economic class relations.

Marxist/socialist feminism

Marxist feminists have attempted to develop Marxist concepts to understand the subordination of women in capitalist societies. They have argued that it is essential to recognize that the oppression of women is inextricably linked to the capitalist order and that although Marxist analyses of society may have marginalized women, they provide insights into the structure of capitalist society and the position of women within it.

Marxist feminism has been criticized by feminists within and outside the socialist tradition. In historical terms, Marxist feminism has been faulted for failing to account for the oppression of women prior to capitalism. It has also been pointed out that in revolutionary class struggles and supposedly socialist societies women have often found themselves occupying a secondary position, with relations between men and women fundamentally unchanged. Many individual socialist women have found a contradiction between socialist values of equality, solidarity and anti-exploitation and the treatment they receive from socialist men (Phillips 1987). Some socialist women have therefore questioned the adequacy of Marxism for explaining women's subordination, as it fails to acknowledge men's role in women's subordination and emphasizes economic class relations at the expense of gender relations. Yet these feminists have also rejected radical feminism as it does not place centrally economic relations of capitalism.

Some feminists working in the socialist tradition began to place greater emphasis on patriarchal gender relations in their theoretical analysis. These have been referred to as socialist feminists to indicate a shift away from orthodox Marxism. Michelle Barrett's *Women's Oppression Today* (1980) paid attention not only to the economic but also to the ideological conditions of women's oppression. She argued that women's oppression is the

A closer look

Marxist feminism

Many Marxist feminists have focused on how the economic class relations of capitalism produce women's continued subordination. They have argued that under capitalism a key cause of women's oppression is the sexual division of labour, which shapes gender relations in a way that reinforces the capitalist relations of production. In this sexual division of labour men are defined as breadwinners and women have been defined as primarily domestic labourers and excluded from wage labour. They have been allocated an exploitative and restrictive role in the household reproducing the relations of production. The traditional nuclear family and the role of women's domestic labour has been a central focus of the Marxist feminist position. Women's domestic and reproductive labour has been identified as a very cheap way of reproducing and maintaining the working class and reproducing the next generation of workers. The value that this labour has to capitalism was the subject of the domestic labour debate in the late 1970s. The family was seen as a useful means of social control, disciplining male workers, who must support their dependants, initiating children into restrictive gender roles and also acting as a useful unit of consumption. In terms of gaining liberation, Marxist feminists stressed the need to struggle for a communist society in which the social relations of the labour market and the family would be revolutionized, and child care and domestic labour would be socialized and the responsibility of the state. They also emphasized the need for women to enter productive labour and struggle alongside male workers. Marxist feminists have been very active in examining the exploitation of women in paid work.

product of not only the economic needs of capitalism but also patriarchal gender ideology, which existed prior to capitalism. The family–household system is crucial to women's oppression. This system controls women's access to paid labour by handicapping them as the reproducers of children and sexual objects for male pleasure. First, the family–household structure consists of a *social* structure, the household, which consists of a number of usually biologically related people who depend on the wages of adult members, primarily a husband or father, and also the unpaid labour of a wife and mother. Second, it consists of the *ideology* of the family, which defines family life as naturally organized in the above way with

a male breadwinner and financially dependent wife and children. So it defines the nuclear family and sexual division of labour as natural. Within this ideology are notions about 'natural' masculinity and femininity, while sexuality is defined as naturally heterosexual. With Mary McIntosh in *The Anti-Social Family* (1982), Barrett again emphasized the ideological significance of the family rather than the economic role. Barrett and McIntosh stressed that the ideological construct of the family as a haven not only masked the exploitation of women but also attracted attention away from social problems. They argued that the ideology of the family embodied principles that shore up the economic system – such as selfishness, looking after one's own or pursuing private property as opposed to altruism and community.

Some feminists went further, arguing that women's subordination is the outcome of two systems, patriarchy and capitalism. Exactly what effect these two systems have and how they work together has been the subject of much complex debate. These theorists have been referred to as dual-systems feminists. Walby (1986; 1990) argued that capitalism and patriarchy are separate systems that at times interact. Although there can be a conflict of interests between capitalism and patriarchy, for example over women's labour, these conflicts are generally resolved and some compromise is made between the interests of capital and the interests of patriarchy.

In *Patriarchy at Work* (1986), Walby outlined a range of struggles between male workers and capitalists to illustrate these patterns of conflict and compromise. In contemporary society women are excluded from certain areas of the labour market, which ensures men maintain economic and social privileges in the labour market and the household. Yet at the same time capitalism can utilize female labour in certain sectors of the labour market and pay lower wages by utilizing ideological notions of the male breadwinner, the secondary role of the female worker and women's suitability for certain types of work. Walby developed these ideas in *Theorizing Patriarchy* (1990), where she attempts to develop a theory of patriarchy which not only acknowledges how it interacts with capitalism but also acknowledges that gender and patriarchal relations can change. She also argues that in Western history in the nineteenth and twentieth centuries there have been two major forms of patriarchy. *Private* patriarchy is based on household production, in which a patriarch controls women individually in the household; this control is maintained through the exclusion of women from many aspects of the 'public' world. This reached its peak in the mid-nineteenth century, when violence against women was formally condoned, divorce was difficult to obtain and women were formally excluded from many areas of education and paid work. *Public* patriarchy involves less emphasis on control in the household; patriarchy is maintained through other structures, women can enter public arenas but are subordinated within them. The exploitation of women is performed more collectively: 'Women are no longer restricted to the domestic hearth, but have the whole society in which to roam and be exploited' (Walby 1990).

Most women enter paid work but have lower-paid, lower-status jobs; women have citizenship rights but form only a small percentage of elected representatives; divorce can be obtained, but women remain responsible for children; cultural institutions such as the arts and media allow women's participation but usually in an inferior way. In contemporary British society the public form of patriarchy predominates.

Although dual-systems approaches have tried to overcome some of the criticisms levelled at radical and Marxist feminism, they have been criticized by black feminists for failing to incorporate race into their theories (Anthias and Yuval-Davis 1993). Black feminists have argued that socialist feminism is ethnocentric; for example, its approach to the family does not consider women's varying experiences. Socialist feminists have tended to take the nuclear family as the only family, have neglected other family forms and have approached the family as simply a site of oppression. Yet Carby (1982a) points out that at certain points in history the family has provided a 'site of political and cultural resistance to racism'.

Black feminism

Black feminists have produced criticisms of each of the varying strands of feminism, and indeed have now developed an influential critique of what has been identified as white feminism. The key concerns about much of the theory and research produced by white feminists are that it has been ethnocentric and that it has failed to acknowledge differences between women and specifically the effects of race and racism on women's experiences.

Black feminists have not only criticized white feminists but have also proposed new directions for feminist theory. Some black feminists have pointed out that placing black women's experiences centrally, looking at the world from a black woman's standpoint, brings

new insights into social relations (Hill-Collins 1990). bell hooks (1984) has noted that the experiences of black women shows that oppression can be resisted, as black women have in very adverse circumstances struggled to survive and resist oppression. Feminists need to focus these strategies and resistances to counter the tendency to talk about women as victims and to develop alternative forms of empowerment. Another thing that is learned about oppression from the experience of black women is that it is complex. Many black feminists have stressed that race cannot be simply added on to existing feminist approaches: this would be mere tokenism (Bhavnani 1993). They have rejected what have been called additive approaches, which simply describe black women as being exposed to a triple oppression of race, class and gender. This approach suggests that you can add together these three factors to end up with the sum of black women's oppression: i.e. race + class + gender = black women's oppression. Yet black feminists argue that these factors interact to produce not necessarily a worse experience for black women but a qualitatively different experience. We can take women's experiences of contraception and abortion to illustrate this argument. In the 1970s and 1980s a key concern of white feminists around these issues was that white women's access to contraception and abortion had been restricted; struggles were focused on retaining legal access to abortion and increasing access to contraception and abortion. Yet black feminists pointed out that black women in Britain did not find it harder to get contraception and abortion but that they did experience concerted attempts to get their fertility restricted. They were more likely than white women to be encouraged to have abortions and also more likely to be offered forms of contraception with possible damaging side-effects, such as the injectable contraceptive Depo-Provera. This black feminist critique has led to the development of a broader reproductive rights movement which emphasizes the rights of women to have or not have children, which has relevance to all women.

Black feminists have stressed that any theoretical model that deals adequately with the experience of all women must recognize and explore the *interlocking* nature of class, race and gender:

> the realities of our daily lives make it imperative for us to consider the simultaneous nature of our oppression and exploitation. Only a synthesis of class, race, gender and sexuality can lead us forward, as these form the matrix of black women's oppression.
>
> (Amos and Parmar 1984)

In the same vein, some black feminists have pointed out that it is impossible to list a universal hierarchy of oppressions or to list which set of social relations is the most important and most oppressive. bell hooks (1984) makes reference to her own experience to make this point:

> I am often asked whether being black is more important than being a woman ... all such questions are rooted in competitive either/or thinking, the belief that the self is formed in opposition to an other. Most people are socialized to think in terms of opposition rather than compatibility. (hooks 1984: 29)

So she warns against theories that prioritize one form of oppression. Black feminists have proposed theories that begin to explore the *interconnectedness* of all forms of oppression, i.e. examine multiple systems of oppression.

Similarly, Hill-Collins (1990) proposes a theoretical model that she refers to as a matrix of oppression, which incorporates all relations of domination and subordination. Within this matrix race, class and gender must be viewed as axes that form part of a complex matrix which has other dimensions such as age, religion and sexual orientation. Feminism needs to explore the connections and interactions between women's oppression and other forms of oppression. In this model women's oppression is part of a more general system of domination; the liberation of women can be achieved only as part of a broader strategy which challenges all relations of domination and subordination. Similar issues have been raised by non-Western feminists, who have pointed out that the dominant voices of feminism have been white Western women, hence the experiences and voices of Third World women have been marginalized within feminism. They have stressed that Western feminism needs to incorporate the international relations of inequality if it is to be relevant to the lives of women in non-Western countries and again stressed the need to explore the interaction of gender relations with other social relations such as relations of colonialism (Mohanty *et al.* 1991).

Mirza (1997) argues that there is much that unifies black feminists and generates black feminist thought and activism in a variety of forms. She sees black feminism as providing a crucial space of identification for black women:

> In this 'place called home' named Black feminism, we as racialized, gendered subjects, can collectively mark our presence in a world where Black women have for so long been denied the privilege to speak; to have a 'valid' identity of our own, a space to 'name' ourselves (Mirza 1997: 4)

Postmodern feminism

In recent years, post-structuralism and postmodernism have had a significant impact on sociological theory, including feminist theory. Within feminism their influence has led to a questioning of what have been seen as some of the fundamental concepts of second-wave feminist theory and also to the creation of new feminist approaches and ideas. A more general introduction to post-structuralism and postmodernism is provided later in this chapter (pp. 91–7).

If you are new to postmodernism, do not worry if you find it difficult: like many theoretical tendencies it has its own language. You will not be alone in struggling with postmodernism, as the following comment from Caroline Ramazanoglu, a renowned feminist theorist, indicates:

> I arrived late at a women's studies meeting towards the end of the annual conference of the British Sociological Association a few years ago, to find some women expressing indignation at finding session after session of the conference dominated by men talking in terms of postmodernism. These women felt silenced, intimidated, excluded, put down and angry. They did not know whether 'postmodernism' was something they should take seriously, because they could not engage with a debate which made issues inaccessible to them. (Ramazanoglu 1993: 1)

It is not unusual to hear people saying that they do not understand postmodernism or that they find it elitist and exclusionary. For these reasons, some feminists have been wary of postmodernism, concerned that it has entrenched academic elitism and hence that it replicates the worst elements of masculinist social theory.

However, while some feminists have rejected postmodernism (Klein and Bell 1996), others have embraced it positively (Nicholson 1990) and some argue for the need to engage with it selectively and critically (Ramazanoglu 1993; McLaughlin 1997). Some commentators have noted that feminism and postmodernism share certain concerns (Assiter 1996; McLaughlin 1997). For instance, both have developed new forms of social criticism and have challenged 'universal' knowledge claims. In the 1970s and early 1980s, a number of feminists argued that many of the assertions that were put forward as universally true in social theory were only true for men; they were seen as examples of androcentric knowledge.

Postmodernism is a body of thought that has argued it is misleading to make universal claims about the world.

Yet postmodern feminists have argued that much feminist theory has in its own work replicated the universalizing assumptions which it criticized male-centred theory for producing. Hence postmodern feminism has produced a criticism of what have been called 'universalizing' feminisms (Flax 1990; Nicholson and Fraser 1990). It is argued that much of feminism has been part of grand theorizing, attempting to identify overarching structures which create gender inequality and women's subordination. A key proposition of postmodernism is that it is misguided to search for grand theories, to find one truth or explanation about complex social relations. Such totalizing theories or 'meta-narratives' are rejected within postmodern thought.

Marxist and radical feminist theories have been identified as and criticized for being meta-narratives which search for fundamental causes of women's oppression. As we have seen, many radical feminist theories of patriarchy identify male dominance as trans-historical and cross-cultural. Meta-narratives are 'large social theories' which claim, for example, to identify specific causes and features of sexism that operate across cultures and historical periods. For example, in the radical feminist work of Andrea Dworkin pornography is identified as a key cause of women's continued oppression. The Marxist feminist focus on the sexual division of labour has been similarly criticized. Such views, postmodern feminists argue, falsely universalize features of the theorists own 'era, society culture, class and sexual orientation and ethnic or radical group' (Nicholson and Fraser 1990).

These shifts in thinking have become more commonplace in much feminist thinking, particularly as a result of the criticisms voiced by black feminism. As outlined earlier in this chapter, black feminists have argued that in many feminist texts white feminists were making claims about women's experience but were implicitly referring to white women's experiences. Such points, which have brought to the fore differences between women, have led feminists to debate whether it is possible to make universal claims about women or to provide a universal theory of women's oppression. This debate is at the centre of postmodern feminism. Part of the debate concerns what has been central in much second-wave feminist theory – that it is based on women's experiences. Many feminist theorists have been explicit in stating that their work is based on women's experiences and have made claims and produced explanations about those experiences. For postmodern feminists this is problematic as they have argued that there are no universal features or experiences that all women share.

Problems with the category 'woman'

A number of feminists influenced by postmodernism have expressed scepticism about the category 'woman' and the concept of gender as it has been used by many feminists. In her book *Gender Trouble*, Judith Butler (1990) outlined the problems she identified with the category 'woman'. As other postmodern feminists have stressed, she proposed that there is no fixed identity of woman: a notion that has often been assumed in feminist theory and activism. She points out that the main subject of feminist theory, and this is the case for many of the strands of feminism outlined in this chapter, has been that of the category 'woman'. The goals of feminism have been concerned with making changes for the social group 'women'; feminist theory and activism has been about representing women and speaking on their behalf.

The problem with this, for Butler and others who share her theoretical analysis, is that a fixed identity of women does not actually exist. This has been a key proposition of postmodern feminism:

> Feminism has played an important role in showing that there are not now and never have been any generic 'men' at all – only gendered men and women. Once essential and universal man dissolves, so does his hidden companion, woman. We have instead myriads of women living in elaborate historical complexes of class, race and culture. (Harding 1987)

Some writers argue that this means that the notion of gender, which has been so important in feminist theory, is meaningless: '[It] is so thoroughly fragmented by race, class, historical particularity and individual difference, as to self-destruct as an analytical category' (Nicholson and Fraser 1990).

Butler argues that feminism has itself had a role in constructing the category of woman and has implicitly set women up as 'different' from men. In doing so it has constructed gender difference rather than challenged it. To talk about women as a category assumes that women share something, that they are 'all the same' and also that they are separate from men. For Butler, this is not far from the conceptualization of gender relations which feminism set out to challenge. She sets out to understand how the division between the sexes has come about and to deconstruct the idea that gender is an essential or indispensable category. The postmodern concerns that are visible in her work include the refusal to accept fixed categories or identities.

Butler's work demonstrates another central post-modern claim: that the individual self is a fiction. Within postmodernism and postmodern feminism the self or subjective identity is understood as an historically conditional construct. Butler explores how gender and gender identity are constructed and describes gender as 'performative, a masquerade, a complex role performance' (Butler 1993). Gender is not simply acted out in a robot-like manner but can involve resistance and mimicry. Like many postmodern feminists she demonstrates a preoccupation with exploring the varied ways in which many possible subjectivities are gendered.

Problems with postmodern and post-structuralist feminism

Some feminists continue to resist or reject postmodern influences on feminisms, including the argument that feminism is a meta-narrative and that the subject category of woman should be rejected. From this viewpoint, post-modernism is seen as denying the political and social influence of gender and perpetuating gender inequality. What is seen as the reality of male power or men's social advantage is dismissed or marginalized in postmodern theory. For example, it may be argued that if a woman is paid less than a male colleague, no matter what the theoretical problems are with the category 'woman,' she is still being denied certain rights or being treated in a particular way because of her gender. This argument seems to get lost in postmodern theorizing. Indeed, some have charged postmodern feminism with getting completely caught up in purely intellectual discussions and neglecting material realities and political activism (Bell and Klein 1996).

Linked to this, some theorists have felt that post-modern feminism is removed from the reality and daily conditions of women's lives. If you are struggling to maintain yourself and your children, have limited access to resources, income, health or welfare or are in a violent relationship it makes little difference how many identities you have. Hence some are sceptical of what they see as the anti-realism of postmodernism:

> Many recent advocates of postmodernism have been anti-realist, and the assertion that one cannot describe viewpoints as being true or false, or right or wrong, is becoming commonplace. It is sometimes said that all one can do is tell stories, and one chooses the story one likes best. I believe that in a world in which there are horrendous wars taking place, the environment is being destroyed, and there is mass starvation, this view is morally and politically reprehensible. It stems from claims that one cannot make claims about a world which is independentt of the speaker.
>
> (Assiter 1996)

Stop and think

➤ What sort of analysis might each of the five strands of feminism provide for (a) government policy on single parents; (b) prostitution?

➤ Would the different strands of feminism see an increase in the number of women in senior positions and top jobs as a positive step for women?

➤ In 1995 women in the British army (unlike the US military, for example) do not actually fight in war situations although they may be present in other roles on the front line. Do you think women should be entitled to a combatant role? What arguments can you propose for and against women entering combatant positions?

The pornography debate

Theoretical and strategic differences between feminists have manifested themselves in the ongoing debate about pornography. There are two general positions within feminism: the 'anti-pornography' approach and what has been called 'anti-censorship' feminism. A key anti-pornography feminist is North American radical feminist Andrea Dworkin, who has identified pornography as central to patriarchy, describing it as the 'nerve centre of patriarchy' and hence one of the main institutions of male supremacy.

> At the heart of the female condition is pornography: it is the ideology that is the source of all the rest.
>
> (Dworkin 1983: 34)

Many anti-pornography feminists share Dworkin's concerns about the effects of pornography. They feel that pornography objectifies women; it constructs an ideology of women as sexual objects to be used by men, hence women are dehumanized within pornography. Some anti-pornography feminists argue that pornography is actual male sexual violence against women. They argue that women used in the making of pornography often suffer actual physical harm and draw on the testimonies of women coerced, harmed or abused in making pornography and women whose lives have been damaged by their partners' use of pornography. They have argued that pornography encourages sexual violence against women. They have drawn on various social and psychological research which indicates the use by sexual offenders of pornography prior to their assaults and that pornography desensitizes men to rape and makes them more sexually violent. Pornography plays a role in shaping male sexuality and beliefs about female sexuality.

Itzin (1994) contends that it is always difficult to prove causation using scientific evidence but that it is possible to show correlation between two things. She argues that research on pornography shows that it contributes to a sexually violent culture which legitimizes violence against women. So pornography is a violation of women's civil rights that incites sexual hatred. It censors women by presenting them as one-dimensional sexual objects existing only to meet the sexual needs of men. Such representation plays an important role in reproducing sex discrimination and oppression. Anti-pornography feminists have campaigned for legislation which bans or censors pornography or enables women to seek compensation for pornography-related harm. This anti-pornography stance instigated by radical feminists was the dominant position within feminism and still has strong support, but another position has begun to gain ascendancy.

Anti-censorship feminists Elizabeth Wilson and Gillian Rodgerson (1991) contend that pornography merely reflects sexism in wider society; it did not create it. Rubin (1993) suggests that pornography is a modern phenomenon which women's subordination long predates; there are a whole range of social relations that are oppressive to women, and focusing on pornography as Dworkin does marginalizes these. Wilson and Rodgerson argue that feminism needs a broader cultural politics rather than a simple campaign against pornography. They say that pornography is not actual sexual violence; it is merely representational, and a distinction must be made. Rubin (1993) claims that anti-pornography feminists exaggerate the extent of violence depicted in pornography and argues there is a considerable amount of pornography in which women are portrayed as active participants who have their sexual needs met.

Anti-censorship feminists assert that despite the coercion of some women in the production of pornography, many women who work in the sex industry are not victims but choose to work in the sex industry. Feminists would be better struggling to improve working conditions for sex workers. Furthermore, they contend that the links between pornography and sexual violence are not proven. Many of the studies of the effects of pornography on men are inconclusive; some even show that many men do not express more hostile attitudes to women after viewing pornography (King 1993). They point out that in countries where pornography is widely available sex crimes are no higher than in countries where it is less readily available.

Anti-censorship feminists argue that censorship in any form curtails choice and freedom and is anti-democratic. Campaigning for censorship will only support the moral Right, which opposes sexual freedom and women's liberation. They point out that censorship would be and has been applied first and most strongly against lesbian and gay material rather than the material that feminist campaigners against pornography themselves identify to be most harmful.

This debate to a certain extent is linked to two different analyses of female sexuality. Radical feminists tend to see sexuality as male-centred and male-defined; pornography is a reflection of this male-centred model of sexuality, which shores up patriarchy and controls and disempowers women. Lynne Segal (1994) argues that some feminists have not moved beyond understanding female sexuality in terms of something that is male-defined and connected to sexual violation. In this analysis all women are defined as victims, and this has been reflected in the anti-pornography position. Anti-censorship feminists argue that radical feminism and the radical feminist analysis of pornography focuses on women only as sexual victims: women have gained some control over their sexuality and should have the right to the freedom of expression of their sexuality. Segal and Wilson, both socialist feminists, believe that women can be active agents of desire and can actively and willingly participate in a wide range of sexual practices and that some may enjoy the consumption of pornography. Anti-censorship feminists accept that much mainstream pornography is sexist and misrepresents female sexuality, yet they do not see censorship as the strategy to adopt: 'We believe feminism is about choice, about taking control of our lives and our bodies and this must include our sexual choices' (Wilson and Rodgerson 1991: 71).

A proliferation of voices

Clearly feminism is a diverse body of thought. In recent years, because of the arguments of many feminists, particularly black, non-Western and lesbian feminists, there has been an acknowledgement of the diverse experiences that women face. Also the influence of post-structuralism and postmodernism has led some feminists to suggest that although the concept and experience of being a 'woman' is important in feminist theory and politics it is misguided to assume one identity and experience and to search for one theory, one truth about women. Indeed, the diversity within feminism can be interpreted as a strength:

> No one method, form of writing, speaking position, mode of argument can act as a representative model or ideal for feminist theory. Instead of attempting to establish a new theoretical norm, feminist theory seeks a new discursive space, a space where women can write, read and think as women. This space will encourage a proliferation of voices, instead of a hierarchical structuring of them, a plurality of perspectives and interests instead of the monopoly of the one ... No one form would be privileged as the truth ... rather knowledges, methods, interpretations can be judged and used according to their appropriateness to a given context, a specific strategy and particular effects.
>
> (Gross 1992: 368)

The Frankfurt School and critical theory

In the 1920s, Georg Lukács and Antonio Gramsci criticized the mechanistic Marxist model of society that had become the dominant interpretation of Marxism after the Soviet Revolution of 1917. The mechanistic model, sometimes referred to as structural Marxism (see pp. 54–5), stressed the determining effect of the economic infrastructure: human action was fashioned by the inevitable laws of economic history. In contrast, this new interpretation, sometimes known as humanist Marxism, emphasized the concepts of alienation and ideology and highlighted the value of human struggle against impersonal systems. Lukács and Gramsci attempted to place the individual back at the centre of the stage and stressed the importance of winning the hearts and minds of people in the political struggle for socialism.

These ideas are closely linked to those of the Frankfurt School, which was established in 1923 to 'criticise and subvert domination in all its forms' (Bottomore 1983: 182) and which developed a critical approach to both capitalism and Soviet communism. Faced with the failure of working-class revolution after the First World War and the rise of fascism in Europe at the end of the 1920s, the Frankfurt School developed a very pessimistic view of society and culture which held out little hope of revolutionary change in a world increasingly dominated by bureaucracy, mass culture and authoritarianism. The leading members of the school, including Max Horkheimer, Theodor Adorno and Herbert Marcuse, were forced into exile in the USA by the triumph of Hitler in the 1930s.

In an attempt to explain the failure of the working-class revolution in the West, the critical theorists emphasized the power of culture and the declining importance of the individual. Instead of destroying capitalism the working class had become integrated into it by absorbing its culture and accepting its values and goals. In a pessimistic view of the postwar world, the Frankfurt School argues that as the working class finds its economic circumstances improved through wage increases and welfare reforms, it becomes increasingly impoverished in psychological, cultural and spiritual terms. The three most important features of this process of domination are instrumental reason; mass culture; and the establishment of the authoritarian personality.

Instrumental reason

Instrumental reason refers to the way in which rational thought had ceased to be a critical faculty and had become instead yet another instrument through which the powerful could exercise control and domination. During the Enlightenment and French Revolution of the eighteenth century reason had been celebrated as the source of liberation from tradition, superstition and religious bigotry. Under capitalism it had become 'domesticated' (Cuff *et al.* 1998: 194); according to Horkheimer, reason and science had become the tools of capitalism and bureaucracy. Instrumental reason is essentially the means by which we achieve the ends laid down by the system; it is the use of 'technocratic thinking' to achieve limited and practical ends or to solve immediate problems. This use of rational thought may produce short-term results and personal success, but it ignores long-term effects and moral questions about the ends themselves. Instrumental reason may tell us that certain qualifications will lead to more lucrative careers than others, but it does not consider 'ends' such as personal fulfilment. Similarly, cost–benefit analysis demonstrates the efficiency gained by introducing new technology into the workplace, but it takes no account of the resulting levels of unemployment. The laws of supply and demand reveal the economic necessity of committing more and more natural resources to the enterprise of industrial production, even though this may lead to global destruction and pollution.

Science, for so long the optimistic badge of reason, had become tarnished as a form of domination. Instead of fulfilling its promise of freedom and enlightenment, it had become an extension of capitalism and bureaucratic thinking. As society becomes more mechanized and social life more routinized, science and instrumental reason come to symbolize a modern world characterized by conformity and control; we become increasingly adept at servicing the bureaucratic machine but do not have the foggiest idea where it is going.

In *One Dimensional Man*, Herbert Marcuse (1964) argued that the subversive power of critical reason was being displaced by an all-embracing faith in the promise of 'positive science' and progress. Everyday life was becoming colonized by technological and pragmatic rationality as all forms of social and cultural life became dominated by 'mechanisms of conformity', and true individualism declined in the face of a 'totally administered society'. In the ultimate act of repression, our real needs had become transformed into false ones, which were then 'satisfied' by the pleasure industries in an orgy of contentment. In a technique known as 'repressive tolerance', Marcuse described how it was possible for a society to achieve total domination not through the suppression of sexual desire, aggression and criticism but by bringing them into the open and pretending to satisfy these instinctive aspects of the personality through a consumer culture apparently based on freedom of choice and containing its own self-justifying ideology.

In his exploration of the impact of technological rationality and the illusion of freedom, Marcuse argued that the passive consumption of superficial products leads to short-term contentment but in the long run creates an uncritical and one-dimensional society in which the working classes are incapable of revolt and only a handful of intellectuals present any challenge to the dominant culture. In this vision, the emergence of the authoritarian personality and the role of the culture industry are crucial.

The authoritarian personality

The authoritarian personality is largely associated with the work of Adorno. Using the psychoanalysis of Freud along with his own research, Adorno argued that the

forces of instrumental reason and mass culture required the members of technocratic societies to possess conformist personalities suited to the hierarchical structure of society and the routines of modern living:

> Domination is not simply built into the culture industry, it requires a particular character structure, one that is not only receptive to domination but actually seeks it. (Craib 1992: 219)

Whereas early capitalism relied on the repression of individualism and sexuality through strict upbringing and the development of strong personality, the modern age of mass culture and consumerism encouraged the abandonment of self-discipline and the expression of individualism through consumption. With a decline in parental control and the increasing influence of the culture industry, society was becoming inhabited by 'standardized' individuals who looked to the social system for approval. Instead of developing an independent personality based on a strong father figure, the child turns away from the family towards the role models and icons provided by the worlds of politics and popular culture. The weak and anxiety-ridden modern personality is seen as uncritical and incapable of independent judgement. It craves domination and strong leadership to allay the doubts and fears which beset it in an increasingly complex and ambiguous world.

The authoritarian personality relies on stereotypical and rigid thinking: racial prejudice and intolerance are characteristic symptoms, nationalism and fascism the potential outcomes.

> Rootless, lonely, directionless, 'mass man' thus constituted ready made fodder for totalitarian parties . . . [they] offered him a means by which he might overcome his puniness and isolation, the psychic pain of responsibility, by merging his will with that of a mass movement.
>
> (Hannah Arendt, in Bennett 1982: 36)

Mass culture

Mass culture attracted the critical attention of the Frankfurt School because of the emphasis it gave to the power of ideas in explaining human action. In its view, genuine art was seen as rising above the mundane and routine world of instrumental reason; indeed, the Frankfurt School would seem to share Picasso's belief in the critical power of art as 'the lie which tells the truth'. This subversive element of 'true' culture has been undermined and superseded by a new popular culture which is not spontaneous, genuine or critical. Popular culture is a false culture devised and packaged by capitalism to keep the masses content.

> The culture industry concerns itself with the predominance of the effect. It aims primarily at the creation of diversion and distractions, providing a temporary escape from the responsibilities and drudgery of everyday life. However the culture industry offers no genuine escape. For the relaxation it provides – free of demands and efforts – only serves to distract people from the basic pressures of their lives and to reproduce their will to work.
>
> (Bottomore 1983: 186)

In a fragmented 'mass society' populated by isolated and estranged individuals of weak personality and little substance, the role of the culture industry and its promotion of empty products to satisfy false needs holds a special interest for the Frankfurt School. Instead of being the expression of human potential and an affirmation of all we can achieve, culture is simply another commodity; robbed of its uplifting and inspirational qualities, artistic activity has no meaning other than the value placed on it by the marketplace. Works of art are mass-produced to satisfy general tastes, artists become famous and businessmen rich from the general 'dumbing down' of culture which results from giving people what they think they want in their pursuit of contentment and conformity. In a savage attack on the commodification of culture which some would criticize as elitist, Horkheimer and Adorno (1973) defend the achievements of serious art against the bland and predictable clichés of mass culture, which 'is uniform as a whole and in every part' and invades all aspects of life in a deliberate strategy of 'mass deception'.

The ideas of the Frankfurt School attracted a good deal of academic consideration and interest after the Second World War. It championed the cause of the individual in a world increasingly dominated by bureaucracy, strong state government and international capitalism. The critical approach to ideological control and mass culture seemed to focus on the concerns of the postwar period, and the student movement of the 1960s expressed many of its ideas. However, the Frankfurt School became the victim of its own pessimism. It had rejected traditional Marxism and its optimistic faith in the working class and had nowhere to go. As these critical theories lost their

influence, Marxist thought turned again to a consideration of its basic themes:

> the analysis of modes of production, structural contradictions and historical transformations, class structure and conflict, political power and the role of the state.   (Bottomore 1983: 76)

Attempts have been made to rehabilitate the ideas of the Frankfurt School. Jürgen Habermas (1971a), one-time research assistant to Adorno, developed a more optimistic approach which attempted to bring together the critical insights of Marx, Weber, Parsons and Mead. Utilizing Parsons' notion of 'system' and distinguishing it from the 'lifeworld' of everyday experience, Habermas highlighted the difference between the objective and constraining features of external society and our subjective and personal experience of it in an attempt to reconcile the age-old tensions between notions of 'structure' and 'agency'. While the world of work and the social system are dominated by the forces of instrumental reason, the lifeworld relies on our human ability to communicate with one another. This is at the root of understanding and interpretation (the 'hermaneutic sciences') and provides the basis for his optimistic belief in discussion and debate as a form of 'communicative action' which can resist 'instrumental reason' and encourage free and equal relationships between people. According to this view, the Enlightenment belief in the power of reason to unearth 'universal truths' is resurrected as an achievable ideal.

Habermas was aware, however, that the system will not tolerate attempts to subvert its domination and will seek to colonize the lifeworld and disrupt the practices of communicative action within it. Through its manipulation of the economic, political and sociocultural subsystems, the capitalist enterprise seeks to legitimate its authority as a system of control over people's lives. As long as there is some balance between what the system promises and our perceptions of what it delivers, society remains relatively stable. But once the contradictions within society and its inability to satisfy our lifeworld ambitions become apparent, the system faces a 'legitimation crisis'. Habermas believed that this would seriously challenge the value consensus and result in either a genuine transformation of society or political repression. Either way, the irrational and repressive nature of capitalism would have been exposed and the prospects for a free and rational society raised. As such, knowledge does not have to be a force for domination but can retain its critical and emancipatory power.

Case study

Mass culture as mass deception?

Movies and radio need no longer pretend to be art. The truth that they are just business is made into an ideology in order to justify the rubbish they deliberately produce . . . Not only are the hit songs, stars, and soap operas cyclically recurrent and rigidly invariable types, but the specific content of the entertainment itself is derived from them and only appears to change. The details are interchangeable. The short interval sequence which was effective in a hit song, the hero's momentary fall from grace (which he accepts as good sport), the rough treatment which the beloved gets from the male star, the latter's rugged defiance of the spoilt heiress, are, like all the other details, ready-made clichés to be slotted in anywhere; they never do anything more than fulfill the purpose allotted them in the overall plan. Their whole *raison d'être* is to confirm it by being constituent parts. As soon as the film begins, it is quite clear how it will end, and who will be rewarded, punished, or forgotten. In light music, once the trained ear has heard the first notes of the hit song, it can guess what is coming and feel flattered when it does come. The average length of the short story has to be rigidly adhered to. Even gags, effects, and jokes are calculated like the setting in which they are placed . . .

Real life is becoming indistinguishable from the movies. The sound film, far surpassing the theater of illusion, leaves no room for imagination or reflection on the part of the audience, who is unable to respond within the structure of the film, yet deviate from its precise detail without losing the thread of the story; hence the film forces its victims to equate it directly with reality. The stunting of the mass-media consumer's powers of imagination and spontaneity does not have to be traced back to any psychological mechanisms; he must ascribe the loss of those attributes to the objective nature of the products themselves, especially to the most characteristic of them, the sound film. They are so designed that quickness, powers of observation, and experience are undeniably needed to apprehend them at all; yet sustained thought is out of the question if the spectator is not to miss the relentless rush of facts. Even though the effort required for his response is semi-automatic, no scope is left for the imagination. Those who are so absorbed by the world of the movie – by its images, gestures, and words – that they are unable to supply what really makes it a world, do not have to dwell on particular points of its mechanics during a screening. All the other films and products of the entertainment industry which they have seen have taught them what to expect; they react automatically . . .

It is quite correct that the power of the culture industry resides in its identification with a manufactured need, and not in simple contrast to it, even if this contrast were one of complete power and complete powerlessness. Amusement under late capitalism is the prolongation of work. It is sought after as an escape from the mechanized work process, and to recruit strength in order to be able to cope with it again. But at the same time mechanization has such power over a man's leisure and happiness, and so profoundly determines the manufacture of amusement goods, that his experiences are inevitably afterimages of the work process itself. The ostensible content is merely a faded foreground; what sinks in is the automatic succession of standardized operations. What happens at work, in the factory, or in the office can only be escaped from by approximation to it in one's leisure time. All amusement suffers from this incurable malady. Pleasure hardens into boredom because, if it is to remain pleasure, it must not demand any effort and therefore moves rigorously in the worn grooves of association. No independent thinking must be expected from the audience: the product prescribes every reaction: not by its natural structure (which collapses under reflection), but by signals.

(Horkheimer and Adorno 1973 (original 1944): 121–37)

Questions

1. *Do you feel Horkheimer and Adorno's comments apply to contemporary film and music?*

2. *To what extent do you agree with them?*

Structuralism

Structuralist theories originated in the work of Durkheim and Marx and have since taken many forms both within and beyond sociology. Structuralism represents an attack on the importance of the individual 'subject' and advocates explanations of human consciousness and behaviour which refer to fixed and objective forces beyond our awareness and control. It implies that explanations for our thoughts, our actions and our culture are not to be found at the level of direct experience and personal awareness (surface structure) but rather in the hidden forces which construct our world and give it meaning (deep structure). In other words, 'being human involves living in a world which has already been determined' (Trigg 1985, cited in Jones 2003: 143). These ideas re-emerged in France at the end of the Second World War and represent a break with French humanism and, in particular, an alternative to the existentialism of Sartre, which laid so much stress on the role of the individual in history and the reponsibility of individuals for the consequences of their actions. In the view of this new breed of radical thinkers, individualism and subjectivism were a 'bourgeois' trait in philosophical thought which needed to be eradicated by the annihilation of the subject altogether.

These ideas have had a particular influence in three areas of the human sciences: linguistics, anthropology and sociology.

Linguistics

As with advocates of theories such as Marxism and functionalism, structuralists and post-structuralists believe that to explain social life it is necessary to look at structural influences beyond the individual. However, rather than focusing on institutional structures, they emphasize how systems of language provide us with our knowledge of the world: language defines our social reality. Linguistics is, then, clearly associated with the ideas of structuralism. In this context, the work of Ferdinand de Saussure (1857–1913) has particular importance. He made a crucial distinction between the everyday use of speech by individuals in their conscious communication with one another (parole) and the underlying system of collective language, which is governed by rules of conduct and meaning (langue). Words take their meaning from this language system and it is the system we unconsciously learn and use to impose sense and order on the world. We do this by learning to apply correct words to relevant concepts.

The importance of the rules governing grammar, sentence structure and sounds can be seen when we attempt to learn a new language. Nigel Barley reveals the importance of tone in changing the meaning of a word in the Dowayo language (from Cameroon, West Africa):

> My rather wobbly control of the language was also a grave danger. Obscenity is never very far away in Dowayo. One day I was summoned to the Chief's hut to be introduced to a rainmaker. This was a most valuable contact that I had nagged the Chief about for weeks. We chatted politely, very much sounding each other out . . . [and] agreed I would visit him. I rose and shook hands politely, 'Excuse me,' I said, 'I am cooking some meat.' At least that was what I had intended to say; owing to a tonal error I declared to an astonished audience, 'Excuse me, I am copulating with the blacksmith.' (Barley 1986: 57)

As this body of rules already exists and has to be learned, it is correct to say that language is not a reflection of reality but the definition and creation of it; it can be seen as the underlying structure which gives meaning to our experiences and enables us to share them with others. When a two-year-old child announces that she wishes to go to McDonald's even though she has never set foot in a fast-food restaurant she indicates the power of language to create conceptual categories that are independent of and prior to direct experience. The price we pay for this gift of communication is our enslavement by language through its power to constrain the way we think. As Doyal and Harris (1986) point out:

> You must learn from others the language you employ to describe even your most intimate and private feelings; thus even the way you describe yourself to yourself can only happen by using words publicly available, and learnt, by you.
>
> (cited in Jones 2003: 142)

The idea that words are only one form of communication has been applied by the science of signs known as semiotics. The work of Roland Barthes, for instance, has attempted to unearth the hidden messages of popular culture. Barthes (1972) has tried to illustrate how all forms of cultural phenomenon can be analysed as systems of signs that help us to understand our society. According to this approach a sign is made up of two elements – the actual object ('signifier') and that which it represents ('signified').

Case study

Signifiers and signifieds

Many of us have followed the adventure of a detective who was (like all the classical detectives) a first class semiologist. I am talking about Sherlock Holmes. Inevitably there is some situation that arises that puzzles everyone, which Holmes then 'solves'. He does this by reading signs which others ignore as trivial and inconsequential. In one story, 'The Blue Carbuncle',

Watson finds Holmes examining a hat that had been brought to him by a policeman. Watson describes the hat: it was old, its lining was discoloured, it was cracked, very dusty and spotted in places. Holmes asks Watson what he can deduce from the hat about its wearer. Watson examines the hat and says he can deduce nothing. Holmes then proceeds to describe, in remarkable detail, what the man who owned the hat is like. He is,

Holmes says: highly intellectual, has had a decline in fortune, his wife no longer loves him, he is sedentary, and probably doesn't have gas in his house. Watson exclaims, 'You are certainly joking, Holmes.' Holmes then shows Watson how he reached his conclusions. He examined the hat, noticed certain things about it (signifiers) and proceeded from there (described the implied signifieds).

Signifiers	Signifieds
Cubic capacity of hat (large brain)	Man is intellectual
Good quality of hat but three years old	Man hasn't a new hat, suggesting a decline in fortune
Hat hasn't been brushed in weeks	Man's wife no longer loves him
Dust on hat is brown housedust	Man seldom goes out
Wax stains from candles on hat	No gas in house

Holmes explains Watson's mistake. 'You fail . . . to reason from what you see. You are too timid in drawing your inferences.' Watson had failed to recognize the signifiers he examined for what they were . . . The meaning in signs, and texts (collections of signs) is not always (or even often) evident; it has to be elicited. And too many people are like Watson, I would suggest – not bold enough in drawing their inferences.

(Adapted from A. Berger 1991: 9–10)

Question

1. *Take three current adverts and describe the messages that they are conveying. (Choose adverts for different types of product – perhaps American jeans; cleaning material; a car; soft drinks.)*

In other words, we inhabit a world of signs, which exist on two levels. On the surface or 'connotive' level things have a purely empirical status as objects; but they also function at a deeper or 'denotive' level, where they act as symbols for something else – they convey meaning. The task of semiotics is to decode the signs of everyday life (body language, adverts, fashion and so on) in order to establish what they denote. A simple example of this, borrowed from Sherlock Holmes by Asa Berger, is shown above.

Anthropology

Regarded by many as the founder of French structuralism, Claude Lévi-Strauss applied structuralist ideas to the study of anthropology. He focused on the form rather than the content of particular cultures and attempted to explain all social phenomena as communication systems. He argued that myths and stories that might seem unintelligible to us made sense and could be shown to have a clear structure and order when studied as systems of signs and symbols. Lévi-Strauss adopted a similar approach in his examination of other aspects of human societies. His study of kinship structures, for example, revealed universal taboos of incest, which he argued were simply a means of ensuring that marriage took place outside the family. As a result, women became gifts between groups of men; gifts that expressed the value and respect which men had for one another. As with other forms of structuralism, what individuals themselves think or say they are doing is subjective and irrelevant. Ritzer points out that 'to engage in a science, the focus must shift from people to some sort of objective structure' (1992: 502). For Lévi-Strauss, social phenomena are the products of the mind and should be interpreted as reflections of 'the permanent and logical structures of the mind'. Whereas anthropology usually highlights examples of cross-cultural diversity in human behaviour, the structuralist model clearly suggests unconscious and universal similarities which unite human behaviour at a deeper level.

In a rejection of both ethnocentrism and cultural relativism, Lévi-Strauss argues that the distinction between so-called 'primitive' cultures and more rational ones is misleading as all cultures are based on logical thought, which is a universal human characteristic. This quality can be found underlying the construction of a totem pole, the invention of the traffic light and the development of computers.

In l968, Vladimir Propp published his attempt to apply the ideas of structuralism to the fairy tale. Despite the range and variety of fairy tales around the world, he argued that all such stories are simply myths created to communicate deeper meanings about ourselves. They display universal similarities in form irrespective of the differences in content. These shared characteristics can be reduced to a basic menu of 31 functions from which all myths and stories are created. Asa Berger (1991) applied Propp's ideas to various texts to show that the underlying themes can be applied as easily to Frankenstein and Sam Spade as they can to Little Red Riding Hood. He demonstrates that the basic elements in fairy tales recur in various genres:

Genre	Elements from fairy tales
Science fiction	Magical agents, magical powers, etc.; hero leaves home
Detective	Finding kidnapped heroines
Soap operas	Relationships between members of families
Spy stories	Finding false heroes; hero (unrecognized) arrives in a foreign country
Situation comedies	Reversal of problem stories about royal families; stories about tricksters
Western	Hero and villain fight, a chase (reversed, with villain pursued)

In Roland Barthes' work these ideas were applied to popular culture where he dispensed with the distinction between 'high' and 'low' culture, regarding all cultural artefacts as worthy of study. By analyzing the taken-for-granted aspects of everyday life, Barthes revealed the hidden ideological messages behind those things which we see as natural. Clearly influenced by Marxist notions of false consciousness, Barthes argued that all artefacts refer to meanings which are implicitly cultural but appear to be natural because the assumptions on which their meanings are based are so much part of our common-sense view of the world that we recognize them without having to make their cultural origins explicit. In the preface to *Mythologies* (1972), Barthes explains his project as an attempt to remind people of the historical (or cultural) origins of those things which they take for granted:

> The starting point of these reflections was usually a feeling of impatience at the sight of the 'naturalness' with which newspapers, art and common sense constantly dress up a reality which, even though it is the one we live in, is undoubtedly determined by history. In short, in the account given of our contemporary circumstances, I resented seeing Nature and History confused at every turn, and I wanted to track down, in the decorative display of what-goes-without-saying, the ideological abuse which, in my view, is hidden there.
>
> (Barthes 1972)

Food and drink, fashion, adverts and sport all contain messages which derive their meanings from underlying ideas of national identity, gender, status and so on which may appear to be natural but which have a cultural and political history which is disguised by the very natural-ness of their appearance. For this reason, Barthes uses the notion of 'myth' to describe how everyday cultural arte-facts operate to distort and disguise the social world by representing it as natural and fixed. A magazine photo-graph of a black soldier saluting the Tricolour emphasizes the inclusive nature of French citizenship but negates the colonial history of France in Africa. The drinking of coffee or wine calls up notions of 'Frenchness' and social status but disguises the conditions under which coffee beans or grapes are picked, while an advert for Italian groceries operates in a similar way to appeal to our sense of Italian culinary tradition without thinking too closely about who prepares the meals. The more natural a social practice appears the stronger its ideological power.

More recent attempts to apply these ideas to popular culture can be found in Williamson's (1978) work on advertising and Masterman's (1986) analysis of television programmes. Intended as a homage to Barthes, Masterman's edited series of essays concentrates on television partly because it was overlooked by Barthes in the 1950s but largely because of its power in contemporary

A closer look

Semiotics – then and now

In the 1950s France was still a colonial power using its military power to resist struggles for independence in North Africa and South – East Asia. In this extract from *Mythologies*, Barthes explains how he was struck by the connotive and denotive aspects of the front cover of *Paris Match*.

Figure 2.6 The *Paris Match* cover referred to by Barthes

A closer look (continued)

'I am at the barber's, and a copy of *Paris-Match* is offered to me. On the cover, a young Negro in a French uniform is saluting, with his eyes uplifted, probably fixed on a fold of the tricolour. All this is the *meaning* of the picture. But, whether naively or not, I see very well what it signifies to me: that France is a great Empire, that all her sons, without any colour discrimination, faithfully serve under her flag, and that there is no better answer to the detractors of an alleged colonialism than the zeal shown by this Negro in serving his so-called oppressors. I am therefore again faced with a greater semiological system: there is a signifier, itself already formed with a previous system (*a black soldier is giving the French salute*); there is a signified (it is here a purposeful mixture of Frenchness and militariness); finally, there is a presence of the signified through the signifier . . . In myth (and this is the chief peculiarity of the latter), the signifier is already formed by the signs of the language . . . Myth has in fact a double function: it points out and it notifies, it makes us understand something and it imposes it on us . . .'

Paraphrase (summarize in your own words) this extract to show that you understand what Barthes is saying.

In the Euro 2000 Football Championships, England were defeated 3 – 2 by Portugal in Eindhoven. The following photograph shows an England fan coping with defeat but what else does the image tell us?

Using Barthes's ideas on signification and myth, what sense can be made of such an image in a national newspaper on the day after the match?

Figure 2.7 An England fan in despair after his team's defeat in Euro 2000
© Getty/Gary M. Prior

society: 'Television, constantly denying its own mode of production, continually manufacturing for its audiences a seamless, plausible and authentic flow of "natural" images, easily outdoes all other media in its effortless production of cultural myths, "realities" which go-without-saying' (1986: 5).

Whether we are looking at the BBC's news coverage of 'the Battle of Orgreave' during the miners' strike, the trivialization of black history by *Blue Peter* or the hidden messages about national identity, gender and sexuality in the coverage of Torvill and Dean (Britain's Olympic ice-skating champions), these essays 'attempt to unearth some of the myths perpetuated by British television' in the early 1980s. *Tomorrow's World*, for example, is a popular programme which claims to glimpse the future through the inventions of today, but in Robins and Webster's 1986 account it is guilty of trivializing science, patronizing the audience and avoiding moral issues in a format which naturalizes technological progress and the superior authority of scientists:

Far more important, however, than all the image and hype of the *Tomorrow's World* rhetoric, is the way in which the programme mystifies our understanding of science and technology. Like a great deal of television output, *Tomorrow's World* connives in the myth of expertise and knowledge. It asks us to stand in awe at what scientists pull out of their top hats. It invites us to defer to a figure whose status and power (founded upon knowledge) is inverse to that of the viewer (founded upon ignorance). Significantly, however, the figure of the scientist is physically absent from the programme. Perhaps it is felt that his or her mandarin language will alienate the average peak-time viewer. Or perhaps it is assumed that he or she will be lacking in charisma. The consequence, though, is that the authority of the scientist (and of Science) is enhanced. Scientists become remote and revered deities above and beyond the daily run of things. Their expertise is safely protected from scrutiny and possible demystification.

(Robins and Webster 1986: 111)

Sociology

We have already acknowledged that the origins of structuralism can be found in the sociology of Marx and Durkheim and the emphasis they placed on the importance of social and economic structures for a deeper understanding of the causes of personal behaviour. In modern sociology these ideas have been developed by functionalists such as Robert Merton and the Marxism of Louis Althusser.

In common with other modern structuralists, Althusser (1965) attacked the idea of voluntaristic action and the notion of 'the subject', which he argued was simply an ideological condition whereby we are deluded into giving individualistic and personal accounts of social behaviour. However, he rejected the analyses of linguistic structuralists such as Saussure and Barthes and their attempt to explain social phenomena in terms of language and the structures of the human mind. He saw this as a form of 'psychological reductionism'. In Marxism the emphasis is on external structures which exist independently of the human mind and shape our ideas and which change over time (historical materialism).

For Althusser, the humanist Marxism of Lukács and Gramsci was unacceptable because it returned 'the subject' to the centre of the stage. However, he also rejected mechanistic Marxism for placing too much emphasis on the base/superstructure model and the overriding importance of the economy. Althusser agreed that in modern societies the economy might 'in the last instance' determine all other social phenomena, but he also stressed the importance of other structures which could enjoy 'relative autonomy' from the economic base. These included the political and ideological structures of society, which act to motivate and constrain the behaviour of individuals. He referred to these as 'structures in dominance' and classified them into two

broad types: *repressive state apparatus* (including the armed forces, police and mental hospitals) and *ideological state apparatus* (including religion, education and the media).

This model permits a certain amount of flexibility and allows societies the room to develop in different ways. You do not have to be a professor of history to see that across cultures and through time societies experience different types of domination by different structures, even though they may share the same economic modes of production. In some capitalist societies the dominant structure may be an ideological one such as religion, whereas others may be dominated by the political structure. Despite the relative flexibility of this model, its critics would point to the dehumanizing tendency of explaining action in terms of social structures. Craib has used the puppet theatre as a metaphor for this tendency in structural Marxism:

> Here we have the puppet theatre in full view: the strings originate at the economic level, the mode of production; they pass through the state and the ideological state apparatus, a second level of machinery that services the mode of production, keeping it in operation. And they finally work the puppets through an imaginary sense of being free, of choosing, of acting.
>
> (Craib 1992: 171)

Post-structuralism

Following the failure of the student revolt in Paris in May 1968, structuralist writers such as Roland Barthes, Jacques Derrida and Michel Foucault began to cast doubt on the promise of structuralist thought and the idea that there was a structural reality to be discovered behind the world of appearances through a scientific analysis of language and signs. To them the very language that the structuralists were forced to use made them as prone to ideological thought as anyone else; instead of revealing the true structures of the mind and the outside world, structuralism was simply another perspective and as such represented a dead end in the search for universal and unifying principles. Language was still seen as a powerful instrument for control, but it no longer offered the key to scientific analysis or social improvement, which were underlying elements of the Enlightenment, structuralism and the later work of Habermas (see p. 84).

In Foucault's (1977) work, the term 'discourse' is used to refer to the ways of talking and thinking which we use to make sense of the world and to communicate with one another. As we refine these tools of language, however, we become ensnared by them; it becomes almost impossible to separate our ideas from the language we use to express them. This implies that all attempts by intellectuals to speak on behalf of humanity in universal terms are corrupted by language and as such simply represent different discourses. This is as true for Marxism as it is for any other set of ideas; instead of providing a scientific analysis of social reality beyond false consciousness, Marxism represents one more ideology in the language of power. The failure of the student revolt in 1968 stands as a symbol of the 'decline [of Marxism] as a dogmatic framework' and led Foucault to consider its 'powerlessness . . . to confront a whole series of questions that were not traditionally a part of its statutory domain (questions about women, about relations between sexes, about medicine, about mental illness, about the environment, about minorities, about delinquency)' (in Kritzman 1988: x).

In breaking away from structuralism in general and Marxism in particular, Foucault suggests a far more relativist and accidental view of history and the development of knowledge/power. According to this perspective, familiar practices such as the treatment of disease in clinics, the care of the insane in asylums and the control of the criminals in prisons are the product of particular discourses which can be accounted for by unearthing the unconscious forces which shaped these ways of thinking and talking about the world at that time. This form of historicism is dramatically different from the Marxist notion of 'historical materialism' (see pp. 50–1) because it rejects the notion of a grand design, historical laws and the ultimate role of class conflict in the historical process. It also challenges the idea of a sovereign power centralized in the hands of a ruling class or elite group; rather, power is dispersed throughout the network of institutions, professions and bureaucracies which go to make up the 'carceral' society. These groups all use knowledge as a means of exercising their control over others, with the overall effect of producing a society characterized by surveillance and 'disciplinary control' in all places and at all levels.

Foucault's ideas have been influential not only as a critique of meta-narratives such as Christianity, Marxism and Freudian psychoanalysis but in their application to substantive areas of sociological inquiry such as crime, health and sexuality. In all these areas, the way in which knowledge is used in conjunction with power is crucial as Foucault strives to demonstrate that knowledge can be used as a form of domination. Instead of being progressive or civilizing influences, the discourses around medicine, prison reform and sexual difference become part of the processes of normalization and self-discipline. In serving the everyday interests of doctors, psychoanalysts and social reformers, the language of benevolence and improvement conceals the new barbarism of social control and disguises the overall social interest which is being served.

By studying the historical context within which these new discourses arose, Foucault attempted to take us beyond what the actors themselves thought they were doing to explain the specific historical circumstances which created the discourses in the first place. Indeed Foucault's historical accounts of madness, sexuality and punishment aimed to show how and why different discourses were established and accepted as defining such phenomena. With regard to madness, he argued that the origins of mental hospitals (initially called 'madhouses') could not be separated from the emergence of the power of reason (the opposite of madness), the medicalization of insanity and the vested interest of psychiatrists. The major explanation for this was institutional and almost accidental: the eradication of leprosy in post-Renaissance Europe had emptied the 'lazar houses' (which segregated lepers until the decline of leprosy in Europe) and provided the opportunity to segregate and incarcerate the mad.

Foucault rejected the idea that the provision of asylums for insane people was inspired by a genuine desire to provide the 'sick' with medical care; rather this represented a new age of incarceration in an increasingly rational world which sought to persecute the irrational and reinforce social control. In the new medical discourse, reason was the source of a healthy civilization, while madness was a sickness to be healed. Our resulting fear of madness ensures conformity and guarantees social control. Whether he was talking about medicine, punishment or sex, Foucault's unconventional ideas represent an attack on rational forms of knowledge as extensions of institutional control. They are not superior, they are simply dominant. This relativist approach to knowledge is shared by many postmodernist thinkers, who also reject the notion that history is determined by the civilizing forces of science and reason.

Stop and think

➤ Foucault and others have suggested that certain discourses represent a form of social control. How might this be applied to the way in which certain types of behaviour are defined as rational or insane?

➤ Give examples of behaviour which is generally seen as rational or insane. Why might society want to encourage the rational and control the insane behaviour?

Foucault, post-structuralism and feminism

The French theorist Michel Foucault is one of the key thinkers associated with post-structuralism. Although his work has been of enormous influence in sociology, it has been seen as problematic for feminists, in particular because of his lack of explicit interest in gender. However, some feminist theorists have argued that his ideas can be utilized to help to understand gender relations. Ramazanoglu (1993) argues that Foucault has 'much to offer in enhancing feminist understandings', particularly as regards how power is exercised and how women's bodies are controlled. One of the reasons that feminism should attend to Foucault is because his understanding of power relations can offer feminists new insights into women's relationships with men.

Central to Foucault's work was the concept of disciplinary regimes which exert power over people. He argued that during the nineteenth century there was a rise of a new and unprecedented style of discipline directed at the body. This discipline sought to invade and regulate the body and could be seen in the disciplinary practices in various social institutions, including schools, hospitals and prisons. Through these disciplinary practices docile bodies were produced through control exerted at the micro-level – control over the movement and space available to the body.

Bartky (1990) draws on Foucault's notion of disciplinary power to understand how women's behaviour and bodies are controlled. She argues that there are significant gender differences in posture, movement, gesture and general bodily comportment. Discursive practices surrounding the body are gendered, and women's bodies are subject to particular control. As Bartky puts it: 'Women are far more restricted than men in their manner of movement and in their lived spatiality, women's space is an enclosure in which she feels confined'.

These discursive practices produce concerns over notions of beauty, for instance, which impact on women: 'A woman's face must be made up, made over and so must her body . . . her lips must be made more kissable'.

She argues that these new forms of control of women are so powerful because women discipline themselves, thus they play a part in imposing such control. These disciplinary practices construct sexual difference and are part of the process through which the ideal body of femininity – and hence the feminine body subject – is constructed. The feminine body is, according to Bartky, inscribed with particular meaning and status which is seen as inferior to the masculine body.

Postmodernism

Since the Enlightenment the search for the truth has dominated philosophy, social theory and scientific research. This search for 'the truth' has resulted in all-encompassing theories of society and history known as *meta-narratives*. Meta-narratives claim to provide ever-improving and logical accounts of historical progress and destiny (and are an essential part of what Crook *et al.* (1992) have called the 'continuous qualitative progression of modernity'). Such accounts have dominated sociological thinking since its infancy, in the optimistic predictions of Marx and the pessimistic warnings of Weber. In the twentieth century, 'meta-narratives' surface in the theories of development put forward by Parsons (1966) and Rostow (1960) and in the post-capitalist theories of Dahrendorf (1959) and Bell (1973). A more recent exponent of the 'project of modernity' is Francis Fukuyama who has argued that history has been the evolution and final triumph of liberal democracy and global capitalism:

> What we may be witnessing is not just the end of the Cold War or the passing of a particular period of post-war history but the end of history as such; that is the end point of mankind's ideological evolution and the universalisation of western liberal democracy as the final form of human government.
>
> (Fukuyama 1989: 4)

This triumph of Western values may, however, produce 'soulless consumerism' and a world in which cultural and political differences disappear. This more critical view of modernity was summed up by Malcolm Muggeridge in *Things Past*.

> What they all want . . . is what the Americans have got – six lanes of large motor cars streaming powerfully into and out of gleaming cities; neon lights flashing, and juke boxes sounding and skyscrapers rising, storey upon storey into the sky. Driving at night into the town of Athens, Ohio (pop. 3,450), four bright coloured signs stood out in the darkness – 'Gas', 'Drugs', 'Beauty', 'Food'. These signs could have shone forth as clearly in Athens, Greece as in Athens, Ohio. They belonged as aptly to Turkestan, or Sind or Kamchatka . . . There are, properly speaking, no Communists, no capitalists, no Catholics, no Protestants, no black men. No Asians, no Europeans, no Right, no Left and no Center . . . There is only a vast and omnipresent longing for Gas, for Beauty, for Drugs and for Food.
>
> (Muggeridge 1978: 125, quoted in Dizard 1982: 18)

One of the most damning critiques of modernism is Bauman's analysis of the Holocaust in Nazi Germany (1989). In this work, he dismisses conventional explanations which suggest that the persecution of the Jews, Gypsies and other enemies of the Aryan ideal is an aberration in the 'march of progress' brought about by natural or unique aspects of the German character. Instead he argues that it is a predictable outcome of modernist thinking and behaviour, where man has replaced God and science supplanted morality; the growth of the modern bureaucratic state may not make such things inevitable, but modernity was a 'necessary condition' of the Holocaust. By applying the principles of technology, bureaucracy and the production line to 'the Jewish problem' we ended up with a 'final solution' symbolized by factories of death:

> The civil service infused the other hierarchies with its sure-footed planning and bureaucratic thoroughness. From the army the machinery of destruction acquired its military precision, discipline, and callousness. Industry's influence was felt in the great emphasis upon accounting, penny-saving, and salvage, as well as in factory-like efficiency of the killing centres. Finally, the party contributed to the entire apparatus an 'idealism', a sense of 'mission', and a notion of history-making ... It was indeed the organized society in one of its special roles. Though engaged in mass murder on a gigantic scale, this vast bureaucratic apparatus showed concern for correct bureaucratic procedure, for the niceties of precise definition, for the minutiae of bureaucratic regulation, and the compliance with the law.   (Bauman 1989: 13–14)

Such doubts about the modernist project have encouraged some writers to challenge the triumph of progress and the validity of scientific knowledge. Instead, it is argued we have entered a new age (the postmodern condition) which has generated a much more relativist view of the world (postmodernism). It is important to understand that it is possible to accept postmodern changes in social life without becoming a 'postmodernist', and as we shall see some sociologists manage to square the two while others reject both the idea of significant change and the postmodernist ideas associated with it.

In the work of writers like Lyotard (1985) and Baudrillard (1990) the end of modernism is celebrated and a postmodern world of disintegration, confusion and cultural choice opens up. The 'rational and rigid' guidelines of the meta-narratives of modernism have been swept away and replaced by the 'irrational and flexible' elements of a far more relativist position which says that 'anything goes'. This can be most clearly seen using examples from architecture, where the terms 'modernism' and 'postmodernism' are widely used. For example,

A closer look

Postmodernism and sociology: no special claim to the truth

First, the idea that social history is the rational and evolutionary progress of society towards some kind of end is rejected by postmodernists. The meta-narratives of Marx and Durkheim with their exclusive claims to truth have been replaced with a relativist perspective that treats their work as 'texts' rather than gospels. Postmodernism sees all points of view as valid with none able to claim superiority; they are simply different ways of looking at things. From this relativist position, all sociological accounts have equal validity. In a postmodern world, grand theoretical accounts such as Marxism and functionalism are obsolete. And sociology itself has no special claim to truth.

Second, postmodernists disdain the artificial classification of knowledge into separate disciplines; they emphasize the pluralistic character of knowledge. The boundaries between sociology, psychology, history, philosophy and so on are merely attempts to preserve one set of grand theories in opposition to all others. By dissolving such distinctions it is possible to become more eclectic in our approach – to 'pick and mix' from a range of disciplines and perspectives in order to create a more exciting blend of ideas. This can be seen in modern politics, where the old organizing principles of class and party are being replaced by issues such as famine, civil rights and the protection of the environment.

Third, in postmodernist writing the importance of popular culture is often stressed, especially in relation to the power of the media to create 'realities' – through advertising, popular music and television soap operas for instance. These new versions of historical reality have no respect for matters of fact or taste; they simply take what they need from the variety of characters, narratives and styles available and create new cultural forms – video games, adverts, comics. In Las Vegas there is a billion-dollar casino based on the Egyptian pyramids but it mixes together historical themes as diverse as Camelot and Henry VIII and characters from Charles Dickens. In this new pluralist culture, art is not the preserve of the elite but is available to all; there is no good or bad, there is simply choice.

housing officials in London decided to 'postmodernize' their high-rise flats with architectural features from earlier epochs and styles such as classical roof shapes, decorative façades and ornate balconies (Strinati 1992).

In sociological theory the shape and impact of postmodernism is less easy to describe, in part because it is not a unified theory but a collection of different positions and ideas. However, there are several identifying features of postmodernist thought which provide some kind of identity, if only because they tell us what postmodernism is not.

The confusion of time and space and the fragmentation of cultural traditions is the characteristic of postmodern consumer society in which we experience the erosion of 'collective and personal identities'. On the one hand, Strinati (1992) argues, we have lost the traditional sources of social identity once found in factors such as social class, religion, community and family life. On the other hand, popular culture has failed to create anything worth while enough to provide an alternative source of security. Television is the supreme example of this 'candy floss' culture, which 'speaks to everyone and no one in particular':

> TV is a constant flow which switches back and forth between different surface messages; it is not a genuine source of identity and belief. But . . . since there is nothing else, nowhere else, but the TV screen, people have no alternative (except perhaps to go to the shops) but to succumb to the TV image, to lose themselves in the blankness of the screen and the hollowness of its icons. (Strinati 1992: 7)

Stop and think

➤ *Shooting Stars* is a popular and irreverent TV show in Britain. The presenters have developed the ultimate postmodernist formula in which nothing is taken seriously. If you were the programme controller, would you interrupt the show to announce any of the following news items? If so, how would you 'present' them?

  ➤ the outbreak of war in central Europe;

  ➤ the election result;

  ➤ the break-up of a royal marriage;

  ➤ a TV personality involved in a sex scandal;

  ➤ the birth of kittens to your pet cat;

  ➤ a dramatic twist in a popular soap.

Many of these ideas emanate from French philosophy and in particular poststructuralism. However, while writers like Barthes and Foucault retained the notion that it was possible to go beyond the 'text' (and the discourses which produced the people who 'created' the texts) to uncover the structural elements responsible for the discourses which characterized specific periods in history, it seems as if the postmodernists have taken the next step to argue that there is no discernible reality beyond the text – there is only discourse. While positivism dismissed early forms of knowledge as myth and narrative (simple stories for simple people) which had been superseded by scientific accounts of the world, postmodernism suggests that *all* accounts of 'reality' are nothing more than stories; science is simply another narrative and sociology a branch of this tradition of story telling which refers to social life.

A closer look

Deconstruction refers to the movement, started by Derrida, which encourages us to think about the ways in which texts can be explained in terms of other texts rather than some external 'reality'. This confusing and sometimes incomprehensible position is captured by Harvey in his attempt to explain the relationship between meaning and intertextuality:

> 'Deconstructionism' is less a philosophical position than a way of thinking about and 'reading' texts. Writers who create texts or use words do so on the basis of all the other texts and words they have encountered, while readers deal with them in the same way. Cultural life is then viewed as a series of texts intersecting with other texts, producing more texts (including that of the literary critic, who aims to produce another piece of literature in which texts under consideration are intersecting freely with other texts that happen to have affected his or her thinking). This intertextual weaving has a life of its own. Whatever we write conveys meanings we do not or could not possibly intend, and our words cannot say what we mean. It is vain to try and master a text because the perpetual interweaving of texts and meanings is beyond our control. Language works through us. Recognizing that, the deconstructionist impulse is to look inside one text for another, dissolve one text into another, or build one text into another.
> (Harvey 1990: 49–51)

Chapter 2 Sociological theories

In this argument the work of Baudrillard is most significant, because he is not a philosopher but a Marxist
sociologist who demonstrates his roots to argue for the
'death of the social' and the triumph of popular culture.
In postmodernism, cultural images take on a life of
their own which is indistinguishable from what sociologists like to call 'real life'; they become one and the
same thing as the life of signs ('simulacrums') creates
a 'hyperreality' engulfing us all. People's lives are so
enmeshed with the daily diet of television that it
becomes almost impossible to discuss social reality as
an experience separated from our media apprehension
of it. Consequently, 'postmodernism (totally accepts)
the ephemerality, fragmentation, discontinuity and the
chaotic . . . half of . . . modernity. But . . . it does not try
to transcend it . . . Postmodernism swims, even wallows
in the fragmentary and the chaotic currents of change as
if that is all there is' (Harvey 1990: 44). In this new set
of arrangements, social reality and political struggle are
replaced by cultural candy floss and consumerism; the
promises of sociology and Marxism are dead.

Sociology has responded to this challenge in various
ways, with some writers 'rounding out' the discipline
to accommodate aspects of the postmodern critique and
others, particularly Marxists, rejecting it out of hand.
As Crooke et al. (1992) point out it is only those forms
of thinking which stress the scientific and structuralist
assumptions of positivist sociology which have much to
fear from the insights of postmodernism:

> Sociology is under threat from the 'end of the social'
> . . . no agenda for sociology is likely to succeed which
> is based on realist claims for the autonomy of and
> causal powers of the social. On the contrary, socio-
> logy needs to shift its attention to the boundaries
> between the once-autonomous spheres of modernity
> in order to gain some purchase on postmodernity.
> For this reason, if classical models for contemporary
> society are required, Simmel and Weber have more
> to offer a postmodernising sociology than do Marx
> and Durkheim.   (Crooke et al. 1992: 238)

By stressing the 'social action' approach, it is argued
that a postmodern sociology can develop which lays
emphasis on the major areas of 'uncertainty' which characterize post-modernism and the ways in which people
respond to these uncertainties in their interpretation
and negotiation of everyday life. They also argue that
sociology has a role to play in raising public awareness of
the ironic and playful aspects of postmodernism and in

encouraging policy makers to take these understandings
seriously when they make decisions or direct publicity
campaigns.

On the other hand, critics of postmodernism dismiss
it as an academic parlour game which plays about with
words and creates confusion. As such it is a dangerous
distraction which has little or no bearing on the lives of
most people and the enduring social constraints which
confront them; times may have changed, but the issues
of inequality, power, unemployment, alienation and so
on still shape the lives of people in a society which is 'late
modern' rather than postmodern. This has led Marxist
writers such as Callinicos to reject completely the notion
of a postmodern condition and the postmodernist
theorising which goes with it:

> Now I reject all this. I do not believe that we lived in
> 'New Times', in a 'post-industrial and postmodern
> age' fundamentally different from the capitalist mode
> of production globally dominant for the last two
> centuries.   (Callinicos 1990: 4)

In contrast to the modernist and postmodernist perspectives, there is also the argument that the world does
have a clear destiny but it is one that is doomed to failure
and collapse. In his pessimistic view of the future, Paul
Kennedy (1993) argues the case for a world divided by
crisis, domination and ecological decline. In the nineteenth century the predictions of Thomas Malthus that
British society would be destroyed by the ravages of
overpopulation and poverty were avoided through the
opportunities offered by colonialism and emigration.
In the twenty-first century the world will have no chance
for escape. According to this view, the world is destined
to face a crisis between the First World, based on a wealth
explosion, and the Third World, which cannot avoid a
massive explosion in population. In this unequal equation the values of the free market and liberal democracy
will evaporate in the face of world domination by multinational companies and global oligarchies.

The end-result will be disaster because the long-term
problems of ecological decline cannot be grasped by short-
term Western political culture, which is incapable of
confronting the crises of wealth creation. This view of the
future is an indictment of modernist writers and their naïve
belief in the inevitable progress of science and reason. It
is also a reminder of the limitations of postmodernist
thinking and its obsession with Western culture. Instead
of engineering a new period of history we may simply be
witnessing the disintegration of the old one.

A closer look

Sociologists' views on postmodernism

In pursuing their research, sociologists often canvas the opinions of the general public. In an interesting reversal of roles, A-level sociology student Daniel Morgan interviewed prominent sociologists over their views of postmodernism. These interviews were part of Daniel's coursework project in which he was examining 'How leading sociologists evaluate the contribution of postmodernism'. Some of Daniel's findings were included in an article on coursework in the journal *Sociology Review* and are included below. In the first extract, Professor Ken Thompson expresses an essentially positive view of postmodernism; in the second, John Westergaard is more critical. The two extracts demonstrate the divergence of opinion on the relevance of postmodernism among well-known and respected sociologists.

Ken Thompson

The concept of postmodernism has served a useful function for sociological theory in a number of ways. It has been useful in indicating a number of developments that do not seem to fit in with the ruling paradigm which sociology inherited from the Enlightenment meta-narratives of progress, rationalisation and secularisation. The underlying assumption in sociological theories of modernity and modernisation was that all societies were evolving in the same direction, characterised by increasing rationalisation and secularisation. Postmodernism, as related first of all to aesthetics, referred to an increased tendency towards pastiches of incongruent cultural codes, without any single articulating principle or theoretical foundation. This has been extremely useful in various fields of sociological interest for focusing attention on tendencies that are the reverse of those predicted in the paradigm of modernity and modernisation. To take just one example, the sociology of religion has had to take cognisance of religious revivals in various forms of 'fundamentalism',

especially those linked with ethnicity, nationalism and cultural identity.

John Westergaard

In my view, postmodernist approaches constitute neither a theoretical advance – on the contrary – nor even a backward step, but rather a declaration of intellectual bankruptcy. There is such bankruptcy involved when reasoned scepticism towards simplistic 'grand narrative' is extended into unreasoned rejection of all analysis of dominant socio-historical trends and shifts of societal configuration; when such rejection is itself at strident odds with postmodernist assumptions of a present transition from 'modernism' to a new era of postulated flux; when ever-observable complexities of social structure are misidentified, in their current forms, as signs of an absence of structure; when, correspondingly, ever-observable intricacies of social causation are taken to rule out significant scope for causal analysis at large; when speculative inferences about allegedly new and structure-freed modes of personal 'identity' are made from impressions unchecked by reference either to relevantly direct evidence or to demonstrable structural constraints on 'identity' formation; when, above all, the implications of such assertions and assumptions is to endorse a relativistic conception of knowledge impossible to square with that pursuit of knowledge in which, after all, even postmodernist enquiry itself purports to be engaged. I may add that the criticisms that I have so very summarily set out apply in my view not only to postmodernist theory – whose openly professed and fully-fledged adherents are few – but to those strands of postmodernist-inclined thinking which, under 'late modernist' or similar labels, tend in the directions I have outlined, albeit within broader and more flexible frameworks of interpretation.

(Extracts from an article on coursework in *Sociology Review*, November 1998: 6–7)

As Kennedy puts it:

What is clear is that as the Cold War fades away, we face not a 'new world order' but a troubled and fractured planet, whose problems deserve the serious attention of politicians and public alike ... The pace and complexity of the forces for change are

enormous and daunting; yet it may still be possible for intelligent men and women to lead their societies through the complex task of preparing for the century ahead. If these challenges are not met, however, humankind will have only itself to blame for the troubles, and the disasters, that could be lying ahead.

(1993: 349)

Case study

Giddens, Beck and the 'risk society'

Recent developments in social theorizing can be found in the arguments of Ulrich Beck and Anthony Giddens who suggest that at both the structural, macro, level and at the action, micro, level, contemporary life is becoming more uncertain and risky. This risk is felt in terms of the uncertainty at a global level of what the future holds and the supposed greater and more pervasive risks faced by individuals in their personal everyday lives. Giddens distinguished between different forms of risk that reflect different areas of contemporary life. External risk might involve concerns over what nature can do to us while manufactured risk relates to the impact humans have had on the world and nature (for instance threats to the environment through global warming).

Beck is most closely linked with the idea of the risk society (which was the title of his seminal 1992 text). He felt that the increased dangers of risk in modern society did not signal the end of modernity but rather the beginning of a new form of modernity – a phase of what he called 'reflexive modernization'. Awareness of the greater range of risks has led to doubts over the knowledge of 'experts' and to a questioning of science and scientists. It has also highlighted the importance of risk management – at both the individual and the wider levels.

So both Beck and Giddens see contemporary life as much more uncertain and risky than the past and their work in this area considers how a culture of risk and uncertainty affects individual and social life.

In looking at risk in the area of criminal justice, Kemshall (2003) cites an article in the *Daily Telegraph* which refers to 'a plethora of risks for the twenty-first century . . . from risks to newborn babies from their mothers' kisses, to vaccines, cot death, food risks and paedophile abductions en route to school' and suggests that 'being a mother in the twenty-first century is a fraught business' (2003: 3).

Questions

1. *What risks do we face nowadays that were not present in the past?*

2. *What risks did people face in the past which are no longer felt to be dangerous? (Consider life in the nineteenth century and in pre-industrial times.)*

3. *Do you agree that life is more risky today than in the past?*

Summary

➤ In reviewing different theoretical approaches it is important to stress that sociology is more than the sum of different theories. The sociological perspective is not tied to one theoretical point of view and sociologists should be able to use a range of different theories.

➤ Durkheim helped to establish sociology as a distinct academic subject. He outlined the scientific basis and methods that sociology should adopt. Durkheim's work emphasized the moral basis of social cohesion or solidarity, an approach that has developed in the functionalist perspective.

➤ Marx's analysis of society saw the economic base of society as affecting and determining all other aspects of social life. Marx argued that in all societies there are basic contradictions within this economic base, due to the conflict of interests between different social groups involved in the economic process – in particular

Summary (continued)

conflict between dominant and subordinate classes. Since Marx's death a number of strands of Marxism have emerged. In sociological theory, two major forms of Marxism can be identified: (a) structural Marxism, focusing on the importance of the economic base and class exploitation; and (b) humanist Marxism, stressing the alienation of the human spirit as a result of the rise of capitalism.

➤ Weber moved away from the structural theories of Durkheim and Marx and based his social analysis on the meanings that individuals give to the social world. He focused on social action and the motivations behind it. Weber developed this approach to suggest that structural Marxism, in particular, underplayed the role that non-economic factors might have in determining the development of society.

➤ There have been a number of important developments in sociological theory since the work of Durkheim, Marx and Weber.

➤ Interpretative sociology developed from the work of Weber and the importance attached to social action and includes a number of related theoretical perspectives. Symbolic interactionism focuses on the individual and the processes of social interaction. Ethnomethodology examines how people construct their social world. While emphasizing the importance of individuals' behaviour and of human interaction, interpretativists are aware that this cannot be divorced from the social situation in which behaviour and interaction occur.

➤ Feminist sociologists argued that sociological theory has been written from a male perspective. They have attempted to redress this state of affairs by placing women's experiences as central to the development of social theory and by trying to explain the divisions between women and men in society. There are various strands of feminist theory, including liberal feminism, radical feminism, Marxist feminism, black feminism and postmodern feminism.

➤ Critical theory, building on the work of Marx and Weber in particular, has emphasized the power of culture and the declining importance of the individual.

➤ Structuralism argues that the explanation for human behaviour cannot be found in the experience of the individual and that objective forces beyond our control have to be uncovered and examined. These forces can be found in systems of language and in the ideological and political structures of society. Poststructuralists look at how systems of language and ideological structures act as forms of power and control over people.

➤ Postmodernism suggests that the search for an ultimate explanation of and for human society is an enterprise doomed to failure. This perspective argues that all theoretical approaches are valid: none can claim to tell us the 'truth'.

Links

Sociological theories are applied throughout this book to the different areas of sociology being examined in specific chapters so theories are applied to education, religion, family and so on.

However, particular sections of this chapter which are expanded in later chapters include:

Functionalism and religion pp. 47–8 in Religion chapter p. 596–9

Functionalism and crime pp. 48–9 in Crime chapter pp. 617–8

Marx and class pp. 55–7 in Social Stratification chapter pp. 218–19

Mass culture pp. 83–5 in Media chapter pp. 700–01

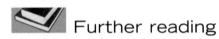 # Further reading

This chapter has introduced and reviewed a wide range of sociological theories and theoretical writing and it really goes without saying that to gain a fuller appreciation of this work you would need to read the original sources referred to. Indeed, it is often rewarding to read the 'real thing' and many of these sources are far more accessible and interesting than might be initially thought. Here, though, we highlight some more general texts that focus on sociological theorizing.

Craib, I. (1992) *Modern Social Theory*, London: Harvester Wheatsheaf.

Layder, D. (1994) *Understanding Social Theory*, London: Sage.

Ritzer, G. (2003) *Sociological Theory*, 6th edn, New York: McGraw-Hill.
These three studies provide thorough discussions of contemporary theories.

Cuff, E.C., Sharrock, W.W. and Francis, D.W. (1998) *Perspectives in Sociology*, 4th edn, London: Unwin Hyman.

Jones, P. (2003) *Introducing Social Theory*, London: Polity.

Marsh, I. (ed.) (2002) *Theory and Practice in Sociology*, London: Prentice Hall.
These texts offer clear general introductions to the different theoretical positions in sociology.

Andermahr, S., Lovell, T. and Wolkowitz, C. (1997) *A Concise Dictionary of Feminist Theory*, London: Arnold.

Humm, M. (ed.) (1992) *Feminisms: A Reader*, London: Harvester Wheatsheaf.

Nicholson, L. (ed.) (1997) *The Second Wave*, London: Routledge.

Whelehan, I. (1995) *Modern Feminist Thought: From Second Wave to Post-Feminism*, Edinburgh: Edinburgh University Press.
These four texts focus on feminist theory. The first provides an accessible and comprehensive dictionary of feminist thought; Whelehan is a detailed exposition of the various strands of feminist theory; and the two edited collections contain a range of extracts from key feminist theorists across the different strands of feminism.

Lemert, C. (ed.) (1993) *Social Theory: The Multicultural and Classic Readings*, Oxford: Westview.

Marsh, I., Campbell, R., Keating, M. (eds) (1998) *Classic and Contemporary Readings in Sociology*, Harlow: Addison Wesley Longman.
There are many readers on sociological theory and edited collections of theoretical writing. We particularly recommend these collections, which cover a range of 'classic' and contemporary writing.

http://www. Web sites

Sociosite
www.pscw.uva.nl/sociosite
This is a sociology web site run by the University of Amsterdam which provides details on important sociologists, including Weber, Marx and Foucault, plus information on courses, journals and university departments.

Details of web sites devoted to individual social theorists can be found in *Sociology on the Web: A Student Guide* by Stuart Stein (Harlow: Prentice Hall, 2002).

Activities

Activity 1

Sociological explanations of Christmas

How would the following sociological approaches interpret the rituals of Christmas?

1 Functionalism (consider the functions and dysfunctions of Christmas rituals).

2 Feminism (consider what women and men/girls and boys do at Christmas).

3 Interpretative sociology (consider the 'games' people play at Christmas and the impressions people create at family gatherings).

4 Marxism (consider who profits at Christmas and what ideological messages are conveyed by Christmas rituals).

5 Postmodernism (consider the role of popular culture at Christmas: the fragmentation of cultural traditions/confusion of time and space).

Activity 2

Why study sociological theory?

In the extract, Craib (1992) suggests that the problems which lead people to theoretical thinking are the problems that we all face in our everyday lives. It also provides an encouragement to those who 'don't like theory' because it shows that sociological theory can be applied to everyday events and can affect us as individuals.

I think the truth is that we all think theoretically but in a way which we are not often aware. What we are not used to is thinking theoretically in a systematic manner, with all the various constraints and rigours that involves . . .

What, then, are the problems in response to which we all think theoretically without realising it? Most of us are affected in some way by events over which we have no control and the causes of which are not immediately obvious . . . A member of the family might be made unemployed, for example, or fail to gain an expected place at university or college; some product or service might suddenly become unavailable because of a strike, or because of government or local authority economies . . . We can do things to alleviate the effects of all of these, but they happen whether we as individuals like it or not, and it is by no means clear why they happen. There are similar, more intimate events in our personal lives: The slow change in the relationship between parents and children or between lovers, which no one wills but which nonetheless happen. I might suddenly find a friend has turned hostile for no obvious reason . . .

In all these situations, we try to find some explanation. Often it takes the form of blaming somebody or thing, frequently unfairly – I lose my job because of all the blacks coming over here . . . Sometimes the blame is closer to the mark: I lose my job because of an economic situation largely created by government policy . . . Sometimes the explanations are more sophisticated, but my point is that as soon as we start thinking about and trying to explain something which happens to us, over which we have no control, we are beginning to think theoretically . . . Theory is an attempt to explain our everyday experience of the world, our 'closest' experience, in terms of something which is not so close – whether it be other people's actions, our past experience, our repressed emotions or whatever . . . every social theory makes some propositions which are counter to our immediate experiences and beliefs, and this is in fact the way in which we learn from theory. The punk might believe that she is in full rebellion against the culture of her parents and authority, yet for the functionalist theorist, she is setting in motion a series of adjustments by means of which that culture and society continue

Activities (continued)

to survive in a smoother-running way than before. The worker might believe she is getting a fair day's wage for a fair day's work but for the Marxist she is being systematically exploited. When I fail a student's exam paper, I might believe that I am applying a rule and upholding academic standards . . . The symbolic interactionist would say that I am creating a failure.

(Craib 1992: 5–10)

Questions

1. *What are the problems with social theory?*
2. *What is the purpose of social theory?*
3. *What are the dominant perspectives in sociological theory?*
4. *Who are the main contributors to these perspectives?*

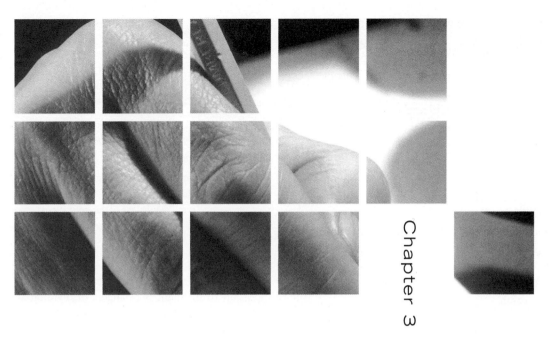

Sociological research: issues in the collection and organization of data

The sociologist [must] put himself [*sic*] in the same state of mind as the physicist, chemist or physiologist when he probes into a still unexplored region of the scientific domain. When he penetrates the social world, he must be aware that he is penetrating the unknown; he must feel himself in the presence of facts whose laws are as unsuspected as were those of life before the era of biology; he must be prepared for discoveries which will surprise and disturb him.

(Durkheim 1964: xlv)

Key issues

➤ What is sociological research?

➤ What different research methods are available to sociologists?

➤ What are the philosophies that underlie the collection and analysis of data?

➤ Why and in what ways have feminists criticized conventional sociological research?

Introduction

The Rules of Sociological Method was first published in 1895, and as Durkheim's comment illustrates, sociology had not then achieved the status of other academic disciplines (it also indicates the sexist language used by the early sociologists). The extent to which sociological research is accorded the same status as research in other disciplines is an issue that is still of concern to sociologists. Sociological research can provide explanations for issues that affect us both as individuals and as members of larger groups. It can help us to understand how our social background can affect our educational attainment and why people in some countries are dying from diseases that have long since been eradicated in other parts of the world.

People hold a vast range of views on social issues, such as why certain people become criminals, why women are massively under-represented in positions of power in the political and business world, or why fewer people attend religious services now than in the past. While the findings of sociological research might not help you to win arguments, they might lessen the misconceptions and prejudices that often accompany them.

Academic subjects require a 'methodology' to reach their conclusions; they must establish ways of obtaining relevant data and of analyzing those data. In this chapter we shall consider which research methods are most appropriate for sociology and discuss the strengths and problems associated with different methods. As with other areas of sociological inquiry, there is no general agreement as to what is the most effective method of sociological research.

A closer look

Method, methodology and epistemology

Method refers to a technique for gathering information, such as a questionnaire or interview.

Methodology refers to the theory of and analysis of how research should proceed. It suggests a commitment to a particular way of practising research. Feminists, for example, have been active in specifying the ethics of feminist practice and the principles that should underpin research.

Epistemology refers to the theory of the origins and nature of knowledge. It sets the rules for the validation of knowledge. It answers questions about who can be the 'knowers', who can say what truth is and what kinds of things constitute knowledge. Feminists argue that traditional epistemologies have excluded women as knowers and have seen men as the only authorized people able to decide what knowledge is.

A key question for sociology is whether it should adopt similar methods to those used in the natural sciences. At the risk of oversimplification, the basic issue is how far the study of human behaviour and social life is fundamentally different from the study of the natural world. There are two broad approaches in sociological research. The first advocates the application of scientific methods to sociological research – an approach that usually involves *quantitative* research. Second, the adoption of a more

humanistic approach to research involves the use of *qualitative* methods.

Stop and think

> Think back to lessons you have had in chemistry, physics or other sciences. How were you taught to find out about things?

> How might the methods you were taught in those subjects be used to find out about social issues, such as (a) why some groups get better educational qualifications than others; (b) why men commit more crime than women?

It is important to highlight the dangers of dividing all research into either quantitative or qualitative. There are various subdivisions within the two broad approaches, overlaps between quantitative and qualitative research, and many examples of sociological research that have adopted aspects of both approaches. Nonetheless, this broad division provides a structure for examining the various research methods used by sociologists.

A closer look

Quantitative and qualitative research

Quantitative research involves the collection and presentation of numerical data, which can be codified and subjected to detailed statistical testing. It follows the scientific method in so far as it attempts to discover and measure facts about society and social behaviour. Information is collected and analyzed in order to test a specific hypothesis (see p. 106). Methods of research include gathering social data through social surveys, questionnaires and structured interviews. These techniques usually involve studying large numbers of subjects so that the findings can be used as a basis for presenting general conclusions about social behaviour.

Qualitative research focuses on smaller units of society and on the understanding of social situations and the meanings that individuals attach to behaviour. It is a more subjective approach whereby the researcher aims to understand and interpret the experiences of the individuals involved by viewing the world through the eyes of the individuals being studied. Methods of research include various forms of observation and unstructured interviews.

Although it is not possible to establish hard and fast connections between styles of research and particular theoretical positions, quantitative methods are likely to be used by those who favour a 'macrosociological' perspective and qualitative methods by those favouring 'microsociology'. Many of the early, 'grand' social theorists adopted a macro- or large-scale approach in their writings. Karl Marx, for instance, set out to describe and explain the origins and development of modern industrial capitalist society. He examined different types of society – tribal, feudal, capitalist and communist – and explored how one type of system evolved from another. He was not concerned with why some people might join a particular religious group or become involved in football hooliganism. Marx and other classical sociologists who are regarded as the founders of the discipline, including Durkheim and Weber, based their analyses of society on evidence from second-hand, general and historical sources rather than on original, first-hand research. At a similar period to the writing of these early sociologists, around the turn of the century, social reformers such as Charles Booth and Seebohm Rowntree were engaged in quantitative research in the form of large-scale surveys.

The concern of qualitative research tends to be with the small scale; a close-up view of society is taken. Such sociological research might focus on one aspect of social behaviour, perhaps a religious group or a juvenile gang. While this form of research might consider broad issues, the emphasis is different; there is less concern with generalizing about whole societies from particular instances. The importance attached to interpreting behaviour is indicated by the use of the general term 'interpretativism'. Two other terms that are used in relation to the basic differences in approach to sociological research are 'positivism' and 'phenomenology'.

Many of the early sociological theorists adopted a positivist approach, but this does not indicate that quantitative research came first and has been superseded by qualitative research. McNeill (1990) emphasizes the cyclical nature of trends in sociological research. After the Second World War the importance of objective data and statistical proof was stressed, particularly in the sociological work pursued in the USA and UK. During the 1960s a reaction against this kind of sociological research developed, and qualitative methods and participant observation in particular became the vogue. The 'debate' between those sociologists who advocated the scientific approach and those who argued that sociological researchers need to get involved in the lives of those they

A closer look

Positivism and phenomenology

Positivism and positivist research is based on the logic and method of science and scientific inquiry. Positivism sees empirical science (science based on experiments that are testable) as the only valid form of human knowledge. Auguste Comte coined the term when arguing that the application of the methods of the natural sciences to sociology would produce a 'positive science of society'. In contrast, the phenomenological perspective maintains that there is a fundamental difference between the subject matter of the natural and the social sciences.

Phenomenology can be defined as the study of various forms of consciousness and the ways in which people understand and interpret the world in which they live. This perspective derives from the work of Max Weber. Although adopting a 'grand theoretical' approach, he argued that people cannot be studied in the same manner as the physical world. People attach meanings to what they do and sociology has to acknowledge this and attempt to interpret those meanings.

were studying has been described as a 'sociological war'. Using the same militaristic language, McNeill suggests that there has been an outbreak of peace in this methodological war and that it is now perfectly acceptable for sociologists to use a range of research techniques in their work (this development is discussed in the section on triangulation, pp. 130–1).

We shall consider the question of whether sociology is or should aim to be scientific prior to examining some of the specific methods of research favoured by sociologists.

The scientific method and sociology

Science is usually taken to refer to the natural sciences and (in the educational context) to subjects such as chemistry, physics and biology, which aim to explain the natural world in a logical manner by using specific techniques – the 'scientific method'. Science aims to produce knowledge that can be trusted because it is known to be true in all circumstances and at all times. It produces knowledge that has been empirically discovered and tested, rather than knowledge based on belief or faith.

Whether the scientific method can be applied to sociological research is a question that has excited considerable debate and divided opinion in sociology. Positivism supports the scientific method of research. Positivist research in sociology tries to discover 'scientific laws', which could explain the causes, functions and consequences of social phenomena, such as rates of crime or suicide. The term 'laws' reflects a fairly hard-line position; many positivists would aim to discover 'tendencies' rather than laws.

Karl Popper (b. 1902) has been one of the foremost supporters of the scientific approach to research. In his view, scientific knowledge is the only valid form of knowledge. The development of knowledge is dependent on mutual criticism in that we learn about the world only by testing ideas against reality. In a society without the freedom to criticize, knowledge would not be able to grow. The emphasis on criticism comes from Popper's concern with the 'problem of induction', whereby science proceeds through the gathering of facts based on observations of events. Popper suggested that if we observe swans and note that they are all white then we can deduce that all swans are white. However, as soon as one black swan is observed the generalization becomes invalid. Thus a generalization can never be proved just by observation, although a generalization can be shown to be false on the basis of one counter-example. Science proceeds by the disproving of generalizations, by refutation, according to Popper. Science should make generalizations or hypotheses that are open to testing. Popper's approach to scientific method was based on scepticism and questioning. Scientists should be detached observers, suspicious of common-sense ideas and intuitions and able to reject theories that they may hold when there is evidence against them.

Popper's idea of science as a process of refuting hypotheses has been criticized, most notably by Thomas Kuhn (b. 1922). Kuhn emphasizes the importance of social interests in shaping the things that are believed about the world. Scientific discovery does not just occur through open-minded inquiry; scientists are locked into particular theoretical positions that do not just depend on evidence but are influenced by the beliefs and interests of the scientific community. Kuhn suggests that 'social science' is almost a contradiction in terms.

Nevertheless, Popper's view has been widely accepted as an accurate account of what scientists do and has been instrumental in establishing the 'hypothetico-deductive' method: scientific knowledge and theory develop from the deducing and testing of hypotheses. The procedure is essentially a set of steps that describe how a particular piece of research is carried out. These steps are illustrated using the example of football hooliganism:

1 Identification of a specific social issue or phenomenon that it is to be investigated: football hooliganism.

2 Formulation of a hypothesis: football hooliganism is caused by young people in 'dead-end' jobs that have little future and allow no scope for creativity and self-expression.

3 Selection or design of a particular research method by which the hypothesis might be tested: checking of police records of people arrested at football matches, followed up by asking those arrested what they feel about their employment situation.

4 Collection of information: examine police records and interview or give questionnaires to known football hooligans.

5 Interpretation and analysis of the information gained: relating the data gathered to the hypothesis being investigated, how many football hooligans were in 'dead-end' jobs?

6 Formulation of a theory based on the tested hypothesis and the interpretation of the data collected: there is (or is not) a causal link between employment situation and football hooliganism.

7 Reporting the findings and conclusions, which must be open to discussion and retesting by others who may be interested. In some cases, the findings might be used in the formulation of policy, perhaps in deciding whether to introduce identity cards as a requirement for entry to football grounds or whether to segregate and fence groups of football supporters into self-contained areas of the grounds.

The steps need not be followed in the exact order indicated above. For instance, a scientist may observe something happening and examine it without having any clear hypothesis in mind as to why it occurred; the hypothesis may emerge later in the investigation, perhaps after some information has been collected. In reality, research is rarely as clearcut as a textbook suggests.

Figure 3.1 Should football hooligans be subjects for 'scientific' research?
© CORBIS

Stop and think

➤ Select another issue or phenomenon that sociologists might investigate and consider how steps 2 to 7 of the scientific method detailed above could be applied to it. Consider how this scientific method could be applied to an examination of (a) the extent to which the television portrayal of women influences children's attitudes towards the role of women; (b) the decline in attendance at religious services since the nineteenth century.

Consideration of the scientific method and its applicability to sociology highlights the relationship between sociological theory and method and the difficulty of looking at research methods in isolation. The formulation of a hypothesis and the type and style of questions asked will depend on the theoretical perspective favoured by the researcher. This theoretical perspective is also likely to guide the researcher towards certain 'facts'.

Hypotheses do not appear from nowhere: they might derive from beliefs and theories that are already held.

In our example of football hooliganism, the hypothesis emphasizing the employment situation could derive from a criticism of government economic policy as having caused an increase in the sense of frustration felt by certain groups of people or from a wider theory about the alienating nature of work under capitalism.

The link between the researcher's theoretical stance and the research methods adopted raises the issue of whether sociology can be *value-free*. The positivist argument that sociology should attempt to be as scientific as possible is based on the belief that only science can provide the 'truth'. Scientists discover this truth by being completely objective, by dealing with facts. In their research, sociologists must be objective and neutral, must not take sides and should adopt an approach based on a position of value-freedom. Weber, a famous advocate of this approach, argued that sociology was not simply the subjective interpretation of action and that sociologists had to avoid making personal value judgements on the social phenomena they investigated.

This idea of value-freedom in sociological research – or indeed in scientific research in general – has not been universally accepted by sociologists. The facts collected in

Case study

Value-freedom in sociology?

This extract is taken from Alvin Gouldner's attack on the model of objectivity promoted by positivist sociology.

Does the belief in a value-free sociology mean that sociology is a discipline actually free of values and that it successfully excludes all non-scientific assumptions in selecting, studying and reporting on a problem? Or does it mean that sociology *should* do so? Clearly, the first is untrue and I know of no one who even holds it possible for sociologists to exclude completely their non-scientific beliefs from their scientific work; and if this is so, on what grounds can this impossible task be held to be morally incumbent on sociologists?

Does the belief in a value-free sociology mean that sociologists are or should be indifferent to the moral implications of their work? Does it mean that sociologists can and should make value judgements so long as they are careful to point out that these are different from 'merely' factual statements? Does it mean that sociologists do not or should not have or express feelings for or against some of the things they study? Does it mean that sociologists should never take the initiative in asserting that some beliefs which laymen hold, such as the belief in the inherent inferiority of certain races, are false even when known to be contradicted by the facts of their discipline? Does it mean that sociologists should never speak out, or speak out only when invited, about the probable outcomes of a public course of action concerning which they are professionally knowledgeable? Does it mean that social scientists should never express values in their roles as teachers or in their roles as researchers, or in both? Does the belief in a value-free sociology mean that sociologists, either as teachers or researchers, have a right to covertly and unwittingly express their values but have no right to do so overtly and deliberately?

I fear that there are many sociologists today who, in conceiving social science to be value-free, mean widely different things, that many hold these beliefs dogmatically without having examined seriously the grounds upon which they are credible. Weber's own views on the relation between values and social science, and some current today are scarcely identical. If Weber insisted on the need to maintain scientific objectivity, he also warned that this was altogether different from moral indifference.

(Adapted from Gouldner 1973: 5–6)

Question

1. In what ways might the values of a researcher influence the following stages of research:
   (a) the choice of research issue;
   (b) the formulation of a hypothesis; (c) the choice of research method; (d) the choice of questions asked (if any);
   (e) the interpretation of results;
   (f) the presentation of findings?

research depend on the questions asked, and it has been argued that sociological research is inevitably directed by values – which are cultural products. From this perspective, knowledge is a cultural product. What a society defines as knowledge reflects the values of that society; another society and culture will accord other things the status of 'knowledge'.

Howard Becker is an advocate of the view that sociological research need not, and often cannot, be value-free. In his classic study of deviance, *Outsiders* (1963), he argues that it is difficult to study both 'sides' involved in deviance objectively – the rule breakers and rule enforcers – and that whichever group is chosen to study there will inevitably be some bias. Becker suggests that there is a strong case for sociologists representing the views and attitudes of the deviants as it is their views that will be least known about and therefore most open to misrepresentation. C. Wright Mills, in his renowned introduction to sociology, *The Sociological Imagination* (1970), also makes the point that social scientists cannot avoid choices of values influencing their work. Political and moral concerns are central to sociology and value-freedom is, therefore, impossible. In a similar vein to Becker and Wright Mills, Erving Goffman, in reflecting on his study of mental patients, *Asylums*, argued that it was unrealistic to aim to be value-neutral:

To describe the patient's situation faithfully is necessarily to present a partian view. For this bias I partly excuse myself by arguing that the imbalance is at least on the right side of the scale, since almost all professional literature on mental patients is written from the point of view of the psychiatrist.

(Goffman 1968: 8)

These arguments contrast with the positivist view that scientists must aim to produce value-neutral knowledge and that sociology should aim to be value-free. In her study of the 'Moonies', Eileen Barker's approach to her research was guided by her view that sociologists should simply seek facts and not pass opinions or make value judgements:

I do believe that passing value-judgements should be an enterprise that is separate from social science . . . There is little use in a research report that tells more about the researcher's personal values than the phenomenon studied.   (E. Barker 1984: 36)

The merits of these different positions can be considered when we look at the different methods of research.

Different methods of research

When investigating a particular issue or phenomenon, the sociologist is not limited to any one method; indeed using more than one method could provide a fuller and so more valid account. Thus it is important to be aware of the characteristics, strengths and weaknesses of the various methods of research commonly used by sociologists. Our review relates to steps 3 and 4 of the procedure followed by the scientific method detailed earlier (p. 106): the selection of the research method and the carrying out of the research.

All sociology textbooks contain descriptions of different methods of research and cover the same basic areas. The specific methods of research tend to be either quantitative or qualitative, but it is important to emphasize that they only 'tend' to; there are inevitably pitfalls in trying to pigeonhole and categorize, and the more sophisticated our understanding of sociology the more we come to recognize the overlap between different methods of research. Much sociological research uses aspects of both quantitative and qualitative research. Nonetheless, these broad headings provide a structure for reviewing a range of methods.

We referred earlier to the dispute or 'war' between the advocates of different approaches to sociological research. While various methodological approaches tend to be popular at different times, the extent of the division into an 'either one or the other' approach should not be overstated. Pawson (1989) suggests that the supposed war between positivists and interpretativists has led to certain methodological myths being propagated, in particular that the two traditions or approaches are mutually incompatible and in a state of permanent dispute. As he puts it, 'no good sociologist should get his or her hands dirty with the paradigm wars . . . both qualitative and quantitative approaches face identical problems and need to adopt common solutions' (1989: 31–2). Pawson argues that quantitative sociology can be

---

A closer look

Reliability and validity

Examination of the different methods of sociological research should consider the concepts of reliability and validity. The degree of reliability and validity acts as a sort of quality control indicator in the assessment of any particular research method.

Reliability occurs when repeated applications of the same technique of collecting or analyzing information produce the same results. The extent to which a technique is seen as unreliable will tend to depend on the general perspective of the researcher(s). From a positivist approach interviews should be highly structured so that any interviewer would collect the same types of data from the same respondent. Interviewer unreliability would be a human error that could be eliminated. A non-positivist approach, in contrast, would emphasize the importance of the social context of the interview and would see interviewer 'unreliability' as an inevitable aspect of attempting to understand the social world.

Validity refers to the extent to which a technique measures what the researcher intends it to measure. This is an obvious requirement for good research; however, the notion of validity applies differently to different approaches to research – to positivist and non-positivist approaches, for example. In general terms, it means the degree to which the findings of research can be relied on, and it involves an evaluation of all the methodological objections that can be made about the particular research.

based on non-positivist lines. Sociologists should not be afraid to admit that observation is influenced by theory: the fact that sociologists pick and choose the evidence they will examine according to their theoretical interests should not be seen as a failure of positivism. For example, in the sociological study of religion, one researcher might focus on the high proportions of people who believe in God and the growing numbers who express an interest in superstition and new forms of religious expression as evidence to demonstrate the continuing importance of religion in modern society. Another might emphasize declining attendance at mainstream churches as the key evidence on the importance of religion in society.

Pawson also points out that even in 'respected' sciences such as physics the data collected are influenced by theory; even the instruments used by physicists, such as thermometers, have been developed and constructed on the basis of complex theories.

Similarly, it is mythical to see qualitative research as a coherent and superior alternative that can get to grips with the special character of human meaning. Contemporary sociological research, according to Pawson, is essentially pluralistic: in many cases it is necessary to gather information by whatever means is practical and so to use both approaches. The combination of methods to gain a fuller picture of the area being investigated is now generally taken to be a sensible research strategy.

Quantitative research

Surveys

The survey is usually a large-scale method of research that involves collecting information from large numbers of people. While this information is typically gathered from questionnaires or interviews, a survey is not limited to any one technique of collecting information. In contrast to qualitative research, which provides a more indepth study of social life, surveys tend to produce information that is less detailed but which can form the basis for making statistical generalizations over broad areas.

There are many well-known examples of large-scale surveys that have been used in sociological research, including the studies of poverty in the early years of the twentieth century undertaken by Charles Booth and Seebohm Rowntree, the Oxford Mobility Studies of the 1970s and the British Crime Surveys of the last 20 plus

years. The British Crime Survey was set up in 1982 to investigate crime through a sample survey of 11,000 households that asked people about their experiences of crime. It was established to address the limitations of official crime statistics, particularly the fact that those statistics include only crimes that are known to the police. The British Crime Survey asked this large sample of people whether they had been victims of crime and whether they had themselves committed any crimes over the previous year. The British Crime Surveys have shown that there is a great deal of crime, including serious crime, that does not appear in the official statistics.

Stop and think

> ➤ What kinds of questions could be asked to find out whether people have been victims of crime?

> ➤ What do you think might be the problems with and limitations of surveys that ask about people's experiences of crime?

Surveys can be distinguished from other research methods by the forms of data collection and data analysis. Surveys produce structured or systematic sets of data, providing information on a number of variables or characteristics, such as age, sex or political affiliation. As questionnaires are the easiest way of getting such structured data they are the most common technique used in survey research. The analysis of data produced from a survey will provide standardized information on all the subjects being studied, for example how much television people watch a week or how people intend to vote. Surveys can also provide detail on the causes of phenomena, such as variations in age, and suggest the extent to which this influences television watching or voting behaviour.

Surveys are one method of collecting and analyzing data that usually involve large numbers of subjects. They are seen as highly reliable in that the data collected can be easily coded and analyzed and should not vary according to the person(s) collecting it. In conducting a large-scale survey it is clearly impossible to investigate every single case or person, which raises the issue of sampling, and whether a smaller number can be used to represent a larger population. However, the fact that the data gained from surveys are necessarily restricted can be seen as a strength, in that it enables the analysis of these data to focus on standardized questions.

Chapter 3 Sociological research: issues in the collection and organization of data

A closer look

Can surveys measure social change?

Surveys involving the collection of information at one point of time are referred to as **cross-sectional surveys;** they provide a snapshot picture. The data gathered provide information such as who would vote for a particular political party or who belongs to a particular occupational grouping. Cross-sectional surveys that are repeated at different times, such as the British Crime Survey or the General Household Survey, allow some analysis of change over time.

Longitudinal surveys provide data that enable the analysis of change at the individual or micro-level. One of the best-known longitudinal surveys in the UK is the cohort studies of the National Child Development Study, in which a sample of children born in April 1958 have been followed from birth and interviewed at various stages of their lives. More recently, the British Household Panel Survey has been established at the University of Essex. This is made up of 10,000 people who are to be interviewed annually throughout the 1990s. Such longitudinal surveys are concerned with the behaviour of people over time and are therefore well suited to the analysis of change.

(Adapted from Rose and Gershuny 1995: 11–12)

A closer look

Sampling methods

Random or probability sampling is where all the members of a population have a chance of selection – for instance, all schoolchildren of a particular age in a particular area – and perhaps one in every hundred is selected.

Quota or stratified sampling is the major form of non-probability sampling. Here the technique is to make the sample non-random deliberately by splitting it up beforehand, usually into categories such as sex, age or class, and then selecting a certain number for investigation from each category. For example, if we wanted to find out whether most people in a school or college would prefer to have a longer winter break rather than a longer summer one, then a quota sample might be the most appropriate to use. Rather than just asking the first hundred people what they felt, the total population of the institution could be broken down into quotas, for example 10 per cent administrators, 10 per cent teachers, 10 per cent canteen/cleaning staff and 70 per cent students. A quota sample of one hundred would then include ten administrators, ten teachers, ten canteen/cleaning staff and seventy students. Random sampling and quota sampling are the most commonly used methods of sampling.

Snowball or opportunity sampling is where one person selected and questioned recommends another person and so on.

Question

1. *What advantages and disadvantages can you think of for using a random sample, a quota sample and a snowball sample if you were conducting a survey of (a) religious attitudes of pupils in a comprehensive school; (b) the leisure activities of retired men.*

Surveys and sampling

Public opinion polls are an example of sampling for surveys that are particularly prevalent at election times. The key problem with taking a sample is making it representative; sampling is essentially the process of selecting people or information to represent a wider population. Different methods of sampling are available to the sociologist, including probability and non-probability sampling.

Criticisms of surveys

According to de Vaus (1986), the major criticisms of surveys can be classified as philosophical, technique-based and political. Philosophical criticisms suggest that surveys cannot uncover the meanings of social action: they neglect the role of human consciousness, goals and values as important sources of action. To some extent these kinds of criticisms are linked with more general criticisms of quantitative sociology as being too rigidly scientific, too focused on hypothesis testing and the collection of facts and statistics and as neglecting imaginative and creative thinking. Some surveys do, however, try to discover what people (say they) think: the British Crime Surveys ask respondents about their attitudes to crime.

Technique-based criticisms emphasize the restrictiveness of surveys due to their reliance on highly structured ways of collecting data. The statistical emphasis is seen as reducing interesting issues to sterile and incomprehensible numbers.

Political criticisms of surveys see them as being manipulative: the aura of science surrounding them gives power to those who commission and use the data. Survey data can be used to justify and further particular political interests. However, it is important to remember that surveys can provide unreliable information and are sometimes wrong. The surveys carried out before the 1992 general election in Britain predicted a very close-run election; however, the Conservatives were elected for a fourth term of office with an overall majority. The pre-election opinion poll surveys overestimated the Labour vote by 4 per cent and underestimated the Conservative vote by 4.5 per cent. Much of this difference was attributed by the Market Research Society to 'fundamental problems' in the way opinion polls are conducted. With regard to voting intentions there would seem to be a persistent and growing exaggeration of the Labour vote, which suggests that the sampling procedures used are missing a significant proportion of Conservative voters, or that some Conservatives lie about their voting intentions. Concern about the accuracy of survey polls has led to them being outlawed during election campaigns in some countries: in France, for example, they are banned for a period just prior to elections.

Collecting quantitative data: questionnaires and interviews

Although a number of techniques of collecting information are available to sociologists who conduct surveys, information is usually gathered from questionnaires and/or interviews. While there are clearly differences between questionnaires and interviews – in terms of the way they are administered and the issues and problems they raise – we shall focus here on some of the common elements. Respondents (the subjects from whom information is sought) can be asked questions which are either written down in a questionnaire or presented verbally in an interview.

Degree of structure

The questions used in survey research can be asked in a more or less structured form. Both questionnaires and interviews can be very standardized and structured – providing only a limited number of possible responses such as Yes, No and Don't Know or ticking one of a list of statements – or they can be more open-ended and less structured.

The degree of structure affects the extent to which data can be coded and analyzed. Using the example of the question on voting given overleaf, it would be straight-forward to code Conservative, Labour, Liberal Democrat and Other as 1, 2, 3, 4: such coding would make the statistical analysis of the data easier.

Reliability and validity

As they provide data that are both reliable and quantitative, the use of questionnaires and structured interviews is generally advocated by positivist research in an attempt to provide a scientific basis for sociology. However, these methods do raise some awkward questions concerning the reliability and validity of sociological research.

A closer look

Question styles

In a questionnaire that aimed to provide information on voting, a *closed-ended* question might be:

How did you vote in the 2005 general election? (please tick)

Conservative
Labour
Liberal Democrat
Other

An *open-ended* question might ask:

Why did you vote the way you did in the 2005 election?

with space left for a lengthy response.

In an interview the structure of the questions can vary similarly: in *structured* interviews the order and wording of the questions are predetermined, and each respondent is asked the same questions. In *semi-structured* (sometimes called focused) interviews the questions focus on certain predetermined topics but the interviewers have scope to choose words, to alter the order of questions and to develop points as the interview proceeds. Such interviews are essentially conversations between the interviewer and respondent; the interviewer can follow up points of interest and allow the respondent to talk freely. This style of interview is favoured in the more in-depth qualitative approach and particularly valued by ethnographic researchers. The more structured and formal style, for both questionnaires and interviews, fits in with the quantitative approach to research.

How can we be sure that the people we want to interview or question will agree? If they do, can we be sure that they are giving honest answers?

Not only will the researcher have little control over these problems – it is not feasible to force people to be interviewed – but there is also the difficulty of ensuring that the way in which the question is asked does not influence the way that it is answered. It is important to be aware of the danger of leading questions and loaded words in the design of questionnaires and interviews.

Order effect

Another factor that can influence people's responses to questionnaires and structured interviews is the way in which questions are ordered. In research into *order effect* in survey questionnaires, Schuman *et al.* (1985) noted a marked difference in the responses to the same question. They asked first: 'Do you think the United States should let Communist newspaper reporters from other countries in here and send back to their papers the news as they see it?' and followed this with 'Do you think a Communist country should let American newspaper reporters come in and send back to their papers the news as they see it?' In that order, 44 per cent of Americans asked said 'yes' to the first question. Using a split sample technique, where half the sample were asked the second question first, the numbers agreeing that communist reporters should be allowed to come to the United States rose markedly, to 70 per cent. It would seem that an initial antagonism to foreign, communist reporters was significantly modified once people considered how they would feel about limitations on access to other countries for their 'own' reporters.

Bias

Survey research, with the use of structured methods of collecting data, is seen as the most effective way to provide an objective science of society. As well as the doubts raised concerning the influence of the wording and ordering of questions on the objectivity of such research, the extent to which bias is eliminated from these methods has been challenged. The way in which people respond to questions may be influenced by *prestige bias*, in that answers which might be felt to undermine or threaten prestige may be avoided. People tend to claim that they read more than they do, for instance, or that they engage in more 'cultural' activities

> # A closer look
>
> ## Leading questions
>
> Leading questions are worded so that they are not neutral: they either suggest an answer or indicate the questioner's point of view.
>
> ## Loaded words
>
> Loaded words excite emotions in the respondent that will be likely to suggest automatic feelings of approval or disapproval: the respondent reacts to the particular word or phrase rather than the question itself.
>
> A classic and widely reported example of respondents reacting to a word concerns the different responses to the terms 'working class' and 'lower class'. A Gallup poll survey in the USA in 1933 found that 88 per cent of a sample of the population described themselves as middle class, while only 1 per cent said they were lower class. Members of the sample had been offered a choice of three alternatives – upper, middle or lower class. A similar survey was repeated shortly afterwards with the term 'lower class' replaced by 'working class'; this time, 51 per cent of the sample described themselves as working class.

than they do. Answers to certain questions can reflect unfavourably on an individual's lifestyle: negative answers to questions such as 'Are you satisfied with your job?' could be seen as being too self-critical, admitting one's life to be a bit of a failure.

Finally, there is also the danger of *interviewer bias*. Even with tightly structured questionnaires and interviews, the respondent might still react to the interviewer – to their age, background or race, for example – and provide answers that it is felt the interviewer is looking for. In his research into the failure of black children in the US educational system, Labov (1969) found that black children responded differently to white and black interviewers; with the white interviewer there seemed to be a sense of hostility that limited the responses from the children. Of course, race is not the only factor that influences interview responses. As Lawson (1986) puts it, 'the interviewee may be antagonistic towards interviewers for no other reason than a dislike of the clothes they are wearing.'

Stop and think

➤ You want to find out about attitudes to (a) unemployment and (b) juvenile delinquency. Give examples of 'loaded words' that you should avoid in framing your questions.

➤ Write down an example of a leading question for both areas of investigation.

➤ Write down a 'neutral' version of those questions.

➤ How might prestige bias and interviewer bias affect the findings from surveys?

➤ In addition to the points listed above, what other factors should sociologists take into account when designing surveys?

This discussion of survey research has not covered the range of research methods that could be put under the heading of 'quantitative', and we shall look at some of the other methods used by sociologists later in the chapter. In essence, quantitative research attempts to follow the scientific method of positivism. The research should be reliable and replicable: the data should be collected systematically and be standardized so that, regardless of who collects the data, the same findings will always emerge. These findings should be generalizable, allowing laws to be established on their basis.

In the next section, qualitative research is examined. Here the interest is in the smaller-scale research; the focus is on 'meanings' and 'experiences'. An attempt is made to understand the lives of those being studied, as well as the

Case study

Styles of interview

In his recent study *Deviant Knowledge: Criminology, Politics and Policy*, Reece Walters examined the politics of criminology and the ways in which criminological knowledge is generated. His study was based on 36 interviews with academics and administrators working in the field of criminology. Below is an extract from his account of the research methodology he followed.

The 36 semi-structured interviews for this book were conducted between 1998 and 2003 in Australia, New Zealand, the United States, England and Scotland. The average time for each interview was 1 hour and 20 minutes . . . The majority of interviewees were academic staff working in criminology, sociology and law departments . . . In addition the researcher interviewed a select number of government criminologists/researchers . . .

The interviewees for this book provided their informed consent for quotations to be used throughout this text. However, in accordance with codes of ethical practice expressed by criminological societies . . . every effort has been made to render the participants anonymous.

In trying to access and sift through the volume of opinion, I deployed a variety of interview and research techniques. While most of my interviews were semi-structured – adhering to a standard set of questions, as well as formulating new questions as and when required . . . they often combined with other well-known interviewing techniques. For example, I would often conduct a focused interviewing style (see Chadwick *et al.* 1984), a method which introduces scenarios or hypothetical situations in an attempt to elicit specific information about professional conduct, or ethical

principles, as well as to bring to life previous experiences.

There were also several occasions when I adopted a receptive interview style (Klenning 1988), allowing the interviewee to discuss issues at length without interruption, preferring to adopt the role of 'active listener'. I would often couple the receptive technique with the use of narrative interviews (see Schutz 1979), which involve less questioning and more narration, where the interviewee recounts or reconstructs a history of events describing specific themes . . . The researcher remains passive and allows the interviewee to recall, without prompting, how certain events unfolded.

(Walters 2003: 177–9)

Question

1. List the different interview techniques used by Walters. Suggest the advantages and disadvantages with each.

less structured, informal interviews such research has emphasized the importance of observation. At the risk of being overly repetitive, it should be stressed again that sociological research is not simply an either/or choice and that the trend in recent research has been to use a number of different methods, both quantitative and qualitative.

Qualitative research

This style of research is closely related to *ethnography*, an approach that has become increasingly popular since the 1960s. Hammersley (1992) highlights a basic disagreement over the definition of ethnography: some see it as a specific method of research and others as a more general approach to research. Here we adopt the latter usage advocated by Hammersley, ethnography being the in-depth study of a specific group or culture over a lengthy period. The emphasis of such study is usually on forms of social interaction (in, for example, a school, factory or juvenile gang) and the meanings that lie behind them. An ethnographic study would typically involve observing the behaviour of a social group and interpreting and describing that behaviour.

Observation

Observation can be either participant or not; however, in sociological research *participant observation* or *fieldwork* (the terms can be used interchangeably in introducing these methods) has been a widely and successfully used approach. Participant observation has its roots in anthropology and the studies of non-Western societies by anthropologists such as Bronislaw Malinowski, Edward Evans-Pritchard and Margaret Mead in the first half of the twentieth century. These researchers lived with the peoples they studied, learned their languages and cultures and provided fascinating accounts of such societies. More recently, this approach to sociological research has been used to study groups and cultures within Western societies. The work of sociologists at the University of Chicago in the 1930s (led by Robert Park) applied anthropological techniques to the lifestyles they found in the city of Chicago (Park *et al.* 1923). They promoted participant observation, with researchers observing the life of social groups while actually participating in them. Our introduction to participant observation will look at examples of sociological work that have used this method and will discuss some of the issues raised by it.

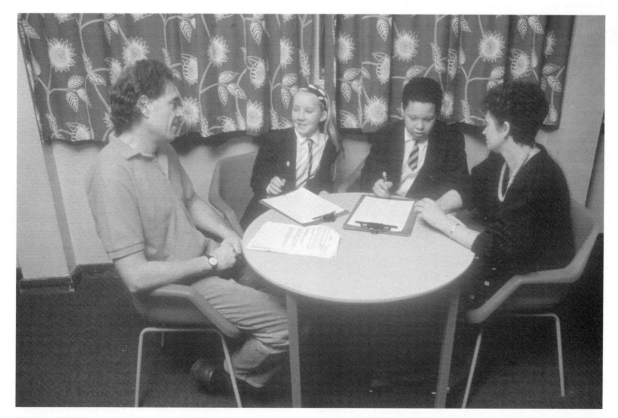

Figure 3.2 Research in a 'real life' setting

A closer look

Ethnography

Hammersley summarized the key assumptions that ethnography makes about the social world and how it should be studied:

1 An understanding of human behaviour has to be achieved by first-hand contact with it; thus ethnographers adopt a naturalistic focus and do their research in 'real life' settings.

2 Human actions do not consist of fixed or learned responses; to explain such actions it is necessary to understand the cultural perspectives on which they are based.

3 Research should aim to explore the nature of social phenomena rather than be limited to the testing of hypotheses; the emphasis should be on getting at the meanings and motivations that underlie behaviour.

These assumptions indicate why ethnography is linked with qualitative research and explain why ethnography uses methods of research that are less structured and do not follow the traditional scientific model discussed in the previous section.

Stop and think

➤ Participant observation has been used particularly in the study of unusual and deviant behaviour. One reason for this is the fact that such behaviour is by its very nature liable to be secretive and/or illegal and thus often difficult to study by more conventional means. Why might participant observation be particularly useful for the study of crime and deviance?

➤ Participant observation has also tended to be used when researching the less powerful groups in society. Why might this be?

While other research methods such as questionnaires and interviews can be, and are, used to gain a wider and more general picture of society, participant observation enables the researcher to gain insight into behaviour through direct experience. This does not mean that it is an easy method to use; the observer has to remain neutral while at the same time being closely involved with those being studied. Howard Becker (1963), in his studies of the sociology of deviance, attempted to understand such behaviour through observation and close contact with the people he was studying. He described the role of the participant observer as someone who 'watches the people he is studying to see what situations they ordinarily meet and how they behave in them. He enters into conversations with some or all of the participants in these situations and discovers their interpretations of the events he has observed' (Becker 1982: 247).

Gaining access

Participant observation involves the researcher becoming a part of a group or community in order to study it; initially, then, there is a need to gain access. Although this applies to all social research, it is particularly pertinent in qualitative, ethnographic study. For many researchers the issue of access is not usually problematic: the distribution of questionnaires, for example, does not usually raise this issue. However, getting permission to carry out research in a particular setting and with a particular group is not always straightforward. When Erving Goffman wanted to study a mental institution he took a job as a hospital orderly and in that role observed the day-to-day life of the hospital (which he recorded in his famous study, *Asylums*, 1968).

In reflecting on his research into child abuse, Steve Taylor (1992) highlighted the practical problems of gaining access to study a very sensitive topic. His research proposals were subjected to close scrutiny by a number of people, including the director of social services for the area where he was intending to conduct his research. As a result, he had to modify some of these proposals and guarantee absolute confidentiality. Once he had got access, Taylor still faced problems in making and keeping relationships with his subjects. He found that the social workers tended to feel scapegoated by the media – perhaps justifiably so, as their position in the 'front line' makes them particularly vulnerable to complaints. He argues that researchers need to be sensitive to these kinds of feelings and not look for and focus on cases that 'went wrong'. As well as the problems of being allowed access to investigate child abuse, Taylor also points out how he encountered examples of dreadful cruelty against children who were brought into care, and how amazed he was when these children were so openly and clearly affectionate to their abusing parents when they visited and tried to get them back.

Research into alternative religious movements raises similar problems of access. Roy Wallis's (1976) research into the Church of Scientology illustrates this. Scientology was founded by L. Ron Hubbard, a science fiction writer, who developed a religious doctrine based on the idea that humans can regain the spiritual powers they have lost through a process of training which would unlock the doors to these powers. The movement has attracted considerable controversy and following since the 1960s. Wallis's interest in studying scientology was hampered by its reluctance to be investigated. As a result he joined and followed an introductory course put on by scientologists and became a participant observer. As a secret or covert participant observer Wallis had difficulty in showing his support for and commitment to the beliefs of scientology and did not complete the course. Although he later requested, and was allowed, to speak to scientology leaders, the participant observation gave Wallis additional material and information on scientology from the perspective of a potential recruit.

Stop and think

➤ What problems of access would be faced by research into (a) inmate culture in prisons; (b) the division of household tasks between partners; (c) sexism and/or racism in the school playground; (d) the decision-making processes of business and companies?

The influence of the participant observer

Once access has been gained, the extent to which the participant observer might influence the group or activity being studied has to be considered. People are likely to behave differently when they are being observed, though this will depend to some extent on whether the subjects are aware of the fact that they are being observed. This raises the important distinction between open (overt) and secret (covert) observation. If the observation is going to be done overtly, the researcher will need to inform the subjects of the research of his or her identity. If it is to be done covertly, the researcher will need to observe under some sort of guise. Even if the researcher does not tell the subjects and they do not know that they are being investigated, the presence of another person may still, unwittingly, affect their behaviour. Covert participation observation, in particular, highlights ethical issues about observing people without informing them (although, incidentally, this is habitually done by journalists reporting on celebrities).

The points raised above about the influence of the participant observer and the ethics of such observation can be illustrated by looking at examples of sociological research.

Eileen Barker's (1984) study of the Reverend Moon's Unification Church adopted several research methods, including participant observation. Barker considered the argument that in researching religion more information would be gained if the researcher pretends to believe in the religion being studied – if observation is done covertly. This raised for her the ethical question as to whether it was morally permissible to get information through false pretences. In rejecting the covert style of observation, Barker pointed to the psychological difficulties of pretending to hold beliefs and performing actions that go against one's conscience.

Although this sort of dilemma is not confined to the sociology of religion, it does arise particularly in the examination of secretive religious movements unwilling to be studied. Barker argues that it is possible to carry out overt research even into fairly closed groups such as the 'Moonies'. Although suspicious of outsiders and of publicity, the Unification Church gave her access to a great deal of information and supported her research. Their media image was so bad that the 'Moonies' could not believe that someone who really tried to understand them and listen to them would come up with a worse account than that provided by the media. Barker also pointed out that covert observation can hamper the research by making it impossible to ask certain questions or to appear too curious. In contrast, the recognized, overt observer is expected to ask questions and exhibit curiosity; indeed, they might find themselves being sought out and told things that the believers want to share with a 'stranger' who is not part of the particular organization. Both overt and covert observers have to be careful of the extent to which they influence the behaviour they are meant to be observing.

Two well-known studies of deviant groups that used the method of participant observation and that illustrate the issues and problems attendant on this style of research are described in the following case studies.

As well as issues concerning access, influence and ethics, participant observation raises practical problems. Because of the difficulties involved in gaining access and trust, it is a time-consuming and therefore expensive method. Furthermore, it may well have significant effects on the lives of the researchers as well as the observed, as our second case study demonstrates.

These case studies illustrate that research by observation is by no means straightforward. Observers, particularly when working in a covert context, have to be detectives – listening, probing and ensuring that their 'cover' is not blown. Some of the practical and ethical considerations that need to be taken into account when

World in focus

When Prophecy Fails

When Prophecy Fails (Festinger *et al.* 1956) is a classic covert participant observation study of a small deviant religious movement that predicted the imminent end of the world. In Christian-based movements this has usually referred to the second coming of Jesus Christ and the establishment of a new Heaven and Earth, accompanied by the destruction of all sinners. Movements such as the Millerites in the 1840s and the Jehovah's Witnesses have prophesied that the world would end at a certain time (although the Jehovah's Witnesses have now abandoned these specific date-centred predictions).

Festinger and colleagues were fortunate to find a small group who appeared to believe in a prediction of catastrophe due to occur in the near future. The group was located as a result of a story in an American provincial paper, the *Lake City Herald*. This story detailed the prophecy of a Mrs Marian Keetch that Lake City would be destroyed

by a flood before dawn on 21 December; Mrs Keetch had received messages sent to her by superior beings from the planet 'Clarion' who had visited Earth and observed fault lines in its crust. The authors called on Mrs Keetch to discover whether there was a group of believers based around her. Their initial contact with her made it clear that any research could not be conducted openly. Given this, they described their basic research problem as 'obtaining entry for a sufficient number of observers to provide the needed coverage of members' activities, and keeping at a minimum any influence which these observers might have on the beliefs and actions of the members of the group' (Festinger *et al.* 1956: 234).

The bulk of the study describes how the group prepared for the end of the world and then how the followers came to terms with dis-confirmation of their beliefs. Fascinating though the whole study is, our interest is in the methodology of the research.

On the whole, the authors and the additional hired observers they used were welcomed into the group as new converts. It was clear, however, that the involvement of a number of new observers-cum-believers was having a definite influence on the group itself, as the following extract illustrates:

> One of the most obvious kinds of pressure on observers was to get them to take various kinds of responsibilities for recommending or taking action in the group. Most blatant was the situation that one of the authors encountered on November 23 when Marian Keetch asked him, in fact commanded him, to lead the meeting that night. His solution was to suggest that the group meditate silently and wait for inspiration. The agonising silence that followed was broken by Bertha's first plunge into mediamship . . . an act that was undoubtedly made possible by the silence and by the author's failure to act himself.
> (Festinger *et al.* 1956: 241)

Case study

Hell's Angels

Hunter Thompson's (1967) study of the notorious San Francisco Hell's Angels motorcycle gangs highlights the potential dangers of covert participant observation.

My dealings with the Angels lasted about a year, and never really ended. I came to know some of them well and most of them well enough to relax with . . .

By the middle of summer (1965) I became so involved in the outlaw scene that I was no longer sure whether I was doing research on the Hell's Angels or being slowly absorbed by them. I found myself spending two or three days each week in Angel bars, in their homes, and on runs and parties. In the beginning I kept them out of my own world, but after several months my friends grew accustomed to finding Hell's Angels in my apartment at any hour of the day or night. Their arrivals and departures caused periodic alarm in the neighbourhood and sometimes drew crowds . . . One morning I had Terry the Tramp answer the doorbell to fend off a rent collection, but this act was cut short by the arrival of a patrol car summoned by the woman next door. She was very polite while the Angels moved their bikes off her driveway, but the next day she asked me whether 'those boys' were my friends. I said yes and four days later received an eviction notice.

(Thompson 1967: 52–6)

As well as losing his accommodation, Thompson's research proved physically painful.

On Labour Day 1966 I pushed my luck a bit too far and got badly stomped by four or five Angels who seemed to feel I was taking advantage of them. A minor disagreement suddenly became very serious . . .

The first blow was launched without warning and I thought for a moment it was just one of those accidents that a man has to live with in this league. But within seconds I was clubbed from behind by the Angel I'd been talking to just a moment earlier. Then I was swamped in a general flail. As I went down I caught a glimpse of Tiny, standing on the rim of the action. His was the only familiar face I could see . . . and if there is any one person a non-Angel does not want to see among his attackers it is Tiny. I yelled to him for help but more out of desperation than hope.

(Thompson 1967: 283)

Questions

1. *How did being a participant observer influence Thompson's attitude towards the Hell's Angels and his relationships with people outside the group?*

2. *What other research methods could provide insights into the Hell's Angels? Give reasons for your answer.*

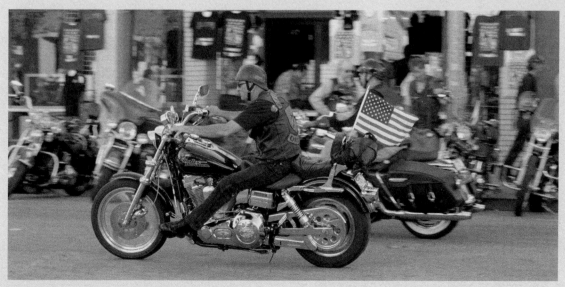

Figure 3.3 Hell's Angels
© Getty/Time & Life Pictures

pursuing sociological research are examined further in Activity 1 at the end of the chapter (see p. 133).

Theoretical problems in participant observation

In concluding this review of research by participant observation we shall refer to Howard Becker's (1982) reflections on the theoretical problems faced by those who adopt this method. Observational research typically produces vast quantities of descriptive material which the researcher has to analyze. This analysis, Becker suggests, needs to be carried out sequentially, while additional data are still being collected – and these additional data will take their direction from the provisional analysis. Becker distinguishes four stages involved in the analysis of data gathered from observational research:

1 The selection and definition stage. The observer looks for problems and issues that will help to provide an understanding of the topic or organization being studied. The researcher will be using available data and material to speculate about possibilities. The credibility of the informants will also have to be considered: do they have reason to lie about or conceal information? In assessing the reliability of evidence, the observer's role in the situation has to be examined: was observation overt or covert?

2 The frequency and distribution of the data have to be checked. Are the events typical? Does every member of the group respond in the same way?

3 The data have to be incorporated into a model which will help to explain it.

4 The presentation of the evidence and 'proof' of the results. Quantitative, statistical data are relatively easy to present in tables and charts. However, the qualitative data gained from observation are much more difficult to present adequately. Such data are less easy to count and categorize; the data are also generally too detailed to present in full, which raises the issue of selectivity of presentation.

Other methods of research

Our discussion of different methods of research has focused on those most often adopted in sociological investigations: questionnaires, interviews and observation. Other methods of sociological research include the

use of experiments and official statistics, most favoured by those who suggest that sociology should aim to be as 'scientific' as possible. Case studies and life histories are used most by sociologists adopting an interpretative approach. Some methods involve sociologists analyzing information that already exists and that has been gathered by other people and bodies: the use of official statistics and content analysis are examples of this sort of secondary analysis. By contrast, case studies and experiments are examples of methods that involve sociologists gathering fresh information and evidence in order to investigate social issues.

Official statistics

Statistics collected by or for the government are referred to as 'official statistics'; they come from surveys conducted or commissioned by the government. These include the census (a survey of the whole population of the United Kingdom every ten years) and smaller surveys based on samples of the population such as the General Household Survey. Official statistics are available to the public through a range of HMSO (Her Majesty's Stationery Office) publications, including the *Annual Abstract of Statistics* and *Social Trends* which provide summaries of statistical information under specific headings, such as Education, Employment or Crime.

Official statistics are a useful source of material for sociologists: they are already available and provide very full information that can be compared from one year to another. However, official statistics are collected by persons other than sociologists for purposes other than social scientific research. Official crime statistics, for example, are collected and published by the Home Office and are based on police records of crime; these statistics, then, omit many activities that break the criminal law but remain unknown to the police. There is a 'dark figure of unrecorded crime'. It is impossible to say what this figure may be, but common sense would suggest that for each crime the police know about there are likely to be many more that they are not aware of and so unable to record (problems with crime statistics are discussed in more detail in Chapter 16, pp. 625–6).

In addition to the amount of crime not recorded, the official statistics are also influenced by the way that the police enforce the law. Whether the police decide to arrest and recommend the prosecution of individuals or to 'warn' them will affect crime figures, as will the amount of police resources, including police officers. All the way through the process of dealing with crime, decisions are made about whether individuals are cautioned, arrested, charged and convicted, all of which affect the official crime statistics.

Stop and think

➤ What kinds of problems might the sociologist face in using official statistics on (a) unemployment; (b) religious beliefs; (c) child abuse; (d) homelessness?

Content analysis and discourse analysis

Content analysis concerns how people communicate and the messages conveyed when people talk or write. It is, essentially, the analysis of the content of communication and involves the classification of this content in order to understand the basic structure of communication. In practice it involves researchers creating categories that relate to the particular issues being studied and then classifying the content of the communication into these categories. Berger (1991) defines content analysis as:

> A research technique based upon measuring (counting) the amount of something (violence, percentage of Blacks, women, professional types, or whatever) in a random sampling of some forms of communication (such as comics, sitcoms, soap operas, news shows). The basic assumption implicit in content analysis is that an investigation of messages and communication gives insights into the people who receive these messages.

Content analysis has been widely used to investigate how the media transmit ideas and images. If examining the position of women in society, for example, a content analysis of school textbooks would probably find that the majority of characters are males and that women are portrayed in a more limited number of roles than men. A content analysis of television programmes would determine the percentage of leading characters that are male and female. Thus the content of books, television programmes and films can reveal aspects of the society and culture in which they are situated and so can be an important source of information for sociologists.

Content analysis produces quantitative data which can be measured and analyzed objectively, although the extent of this objectivity can be questioned in that subjective judgements have to be made in creating the categories which form the basis of the analysis.

Discourse analysis is a more sophisticated method that looks at and analyzes forms of communication or 'discourses' – in particular speech and writing. Discourse analysis has been utilized in a number of subject areas, including sociology, and these different subject disciplines (such as psychology, philosophy, history and literature) emphasize different aspects of discourse analysis. However, all approaches highlight the social nature of discourse: the fact that the meanings of words, for instance, depend on who uses them, to whom they are used and where they are used. So words and their meanings, and hence analyses of them, vary according to the social and institutional situations within which they are used. Thus a number of different discourses exist at any one time and these discourses can be, and often are, in competition and conflict with one another.

Discourse analysis does not aim to produce quantifiable data in the way that content analysis does, but rather it adopts a thematic approach, looking at areas and issues which are not (or are not so readily) quantifiable. For instance Foucault, a key figure in the development of discourse analysis, described and examined discourses of madness (ways of communicating and thinking about the concept of madness) in one of his early studies (Foucault 1967).

Jupp and Norris (1993) identify two broad theoretical strands of discourse analysis, each of which focuses on the relationship between power and discourse. First, the analysis of discourse and power at a macro, societal level; an approach emphasizing the role of the state in the production of ideologies and associated with structural Marxist analyses and the work of Althusser (see p. 54). Second, the work of Foucault and his concern with why different forms of discourse and knowledge emerge at different points of time. In *Discipline and Punish* (1977), for example, he discusses how different forms of punishment became dominant during different periods of history. Foucault sees discourses as mechanisms of power and control, but rather than highlighting the role of the state he argues that the state is only one of several points of control: power and control are pervasive throughout society.

Experiments

While experimentation is the standard method used in the natural sciences, and is regularly adopted in psychology, it has not been widely used in sociology. People are liable to act differently ('unnaturally') in an experimental situation compared with how they would in 'real life'; it is difficult to study people in a laboratory and expect them to act normally. This lack of realism might be resolved by not informing people that they are being experimented on, which is an ethical issue itself. However, there are some important and well-known examples of the use of experiments in research into areas of social life.

In the social sciences, controlled experiments allow the researcher to manipulate an independent variable so as to observe and measure changes in a dependent variable. *Variables* can be any measurable characteristic of individuals, groups or societies – income, educational attainment or rate of unemployment, for example. Experiments have been used, for example, to study the effects of violence in the mass media on children's behaviour. Some children were exposed to violent programmes and others to non-violent programmes, followed by comparisons of how each group behaved when provided with opportunities to act violently. The *independent variable* was the amount and type of programme viewed and the *dependent variable* the age or gender of the children. One experiment involved children watching different television sequences – some violent, others not – and then being told that they could hurt or help a child playing in another room by pressing either the 'hurt' or 'help' button (Liebert and Baron 1972). The results of this and many other studies have shown that viewing violence produces increased aggression in the young. However, such experiments are difficult to generalize from; it has been argued that violence on television can make people more tolerant and less likely to engage in real life violence.

The issue of the ethics of experimenting on people was highlighted in the now (in)famous experiments conducted by Milgram (1974). Milgram's hypothesis was that cruelty is not committed by cruel individuals but rather by ordinary women and men who are quite capable of behaving in a cruel manner when they feel it is required of them. Individuals will perform acts they would normally condemn if they are carrying out orders given by an authority they accept.

The volunteers in Milgram's experiments were asked to play the role of either 'teacher' or 'learner'; the teachers were then told to deliver electric shocks to the learners as punishments when they made errors. Although the 'teacher' volunteers did not know the experiment was set up so that no electric shock was transmitted, the majority of them were prepared to deliver what they felt to be severe shocks. When these teacher volunteers were told to force the victim's hands on to the plate through which the shock was supposedly delivered, 30 per cent continued to fulfil the command until the end of the experiment. When the victims were hidden and their 'screams' were not audible, the figure jumped to 65 per cent. Milgram argued that it is quite easy to be cruel towards a person we neither see nor hear.

Milgram's conclusion – that cruelty is social in its origin, rather than just being a personal characteristic – is supported by another 'sociological experiment' undertaken by Zimbardo (1972). This experiment involved volunteers playing the roles of prisoners and prison guards. The experiment was conducted in as realistic a manner as possible, the 'prisoners' and 'guards' dressed appropriately, neither group was allowed to call the other by name and the guards were expected to enforce a range of petty and humiliating regulations. The volunteers were supposed to play their roles for two weeks; however, they became so involved in them that the experiment was stopped after one week for fear that the volunteers might suffer irreparable damage if it ran for the planned length of time. The guards' superiority and the prisoners' submissiveness encouraged the guards to indulge in shows of power: they forced the prisoners to chant filthy songs and to clean toilets with bare hands, for example. It appeared that the apparently normal volunteers had changed into cruel and sadistic monsters. The extent of this cruelty took Zimbardo and his colleagues by surprise. However, it was clear that this stemmed from the social situation of prisoners and guards, not from any particular viciousness in the volunteers themselves. The experimenters concluded that many ordinary, generally law-abiding people will easily act in a cruel and even vicious way if such behaviour is required by a superior authority. They also found that a small number of the volunteers stood up to those in power and gave priority to their consciences.

Stop and think

> List the difficulties with the use of experiments in sociological research.

> What advantages might experiments have over other methods of research? What particular insight might they provide into social behaviour?

Due to the artificiality of laboratory-based experiments, researchers often conduct field experiments outside the laboratory. In a widely cited study examining the importance of teachers' attitudes to pupils' performance, Rosenthal and Jacobson (1968) tested how teachers responded to pupils of differing abilities. They randomly selected a number of pupils and told their teachers that they would improve significantly in the future. Although the children were chosen randomly, Rosenthal and Jacobson found that when they returned to the school the following year that these particular children had improved noticeably over their classmates. In this case it seemed that the teachers' expectations of those pupils influenced how they performed and progressed at school – or at least how they were seen by their teachers to have performed and progressed.

Case studies and life histories

Other qualitative approaches to sociological research include case studies and life histories. A case study investigates one or a few particular cases in some depth. Although case studies are only illustrative ('one offs'), they can be used as guides for further research. McNeill (1990) makes the point that, to a certain extent, any piece of qualitative research could be described as a case study given that all such research focuses on a relatively small group or on one particular institution. Case studies provide a different sort of data that can supplement other methods of research. As Walters puts it, 'the use of case studies aids the capturing of a process of events; they provide a sequence and structure that is often omitted in surveys or interviews . . . [they are] a useful means by which to chart ideas and develop themes for analysis' (2003: 179).

A life history consists of biographical material that has usually been gathered from a particular individual, perhaps from an interview or conversation. As well as relying on people's memories, other sources of information are used to build as detailed a picture as possible of the experiences, beliefs and attitudes of that individual; these sources might include letters or newspaper articles. As with qualitative research in general, the emphasis is on the individual's interpretation of behaviour and events. Like case studies, life histories are unreliable as a basis for generalizing about social behaviour, but they can be valuable sources of insight for the sociologist.

In particular, life histories can provide more detailed information than other methods of research about the development of beliefs and attitudes over time. And in general terms it could be argued that an historical outlook and analysis is important in many, if not all, areas of sociological research. In such cases, the life-history method can complement the examination of documents and written historical records.

Stop and think

> Reflect on your own life history. Consider the extent to which your personal development has been influenced by cultural factors.

Feminist research

Feminists have been concerned with the techniques used in carrying out research, the way research is practised and, more fundamentally, with the processes via which sociological knowledge is formulated. They have been concerned with methods, methodology and epistemology. Feminists have produced a scathing critique of orthodox sociological research methodology (Abbott and Wallace 1990).

As research generates the raw material of sociological theory and knowledge, feminists have in turn challenged how sociological knowledge is produced (Spender 1981). They have recognized that knowledge is socially constructed, the product of social and cultural relations. All human beings may generate explanations of the world; not all of them become legitimized and accepted explanations. Women have been excluded as producers of knowledge and as subjects of sociological knowledge. Sociological knowledge has been primarily androcentric, i.e. male-centred: 'The theories and methods of sociology, it seems, derive from the visions of the social world afforded to men' (Acker *et al.* 1983).

Feminists have aimed to produce research based on women's experiences which addresses women's oppression in society. They have moved beyond criticism and suggested principles that should underlie feminist research. Just as feminist theory is not a unified body of thought, similarly there is no one feminist methodology (Reinharz 1993).

Stop and think

> Name as many sociology books or studies as you can that have been written by (a) women; (b) men; (c) both.

> What topics were covered by the books and studies in your lists a, b and c?

> Is there a pattern in the topics researched and written about by female and male sociologists?

The feminist critique of conventional sociological research

Feminists have examined the sociological research community itself. This includes academic institutions, departments, funding bodies and publishing houses. Collectively these constitute what Liz Stanley (1990) has called the academic mode of production. She argues that the structure of this has contributed to the production of partial or limited knowledge. Certain individuals and groups have greater control over who can carry out research. Those individuals and groups with greater control include heads of department, professors, referees and editors; women are under-represented in these senior positions (Abbott 1991).

Abbott and Wallace (1990) have described orthodox sociological research as 'male stream'; they have described several levels on which sociological research has been male-centred.

Exclusion of women from research samples

Research has been androcentric because it has been based on male experiences. Women have often been absent from research samples. Conventional sociological research was carried out by male researchers and on male samples (Abbott and Wallace 1990). The majority of studies during the 1960s and 1970s in the sociology of work were of male paid labour. Findings and theories from these samples were often generalized to the whole population, including women. Goldthorpe and Lockwood's famous affluent worker study (Goldthorpe *et al.* 1968) suggested that manual workers were becoming increasingly affluent and were increasingly adopting the values and lifestyles of the middle class. Yet they were describing only the experiences of male workers; women have a different relationship to the labour market (see Chapter 7, pp. 294–300).

Deviant males

Although some researchers acknowledged the presence of the female sex, there was a tendency for researchers to present or interpret their behaviour in a distorted and sexist way (Abbott and Wallace 1990). Women were often compared with a normative masculine standard. Until the work of Angela McRobbie (1991), sociological studies of youth culture tended to be studies of male youth cultures. Gender relations were scarcely mentioned and the subordination of girls to boys was taken for granted rather than analyzed. Girls were portrayed as marginal or as playing out stereotypical roles.

> ## Stop and think
>
> ➤ Do girl 'punks' play out a stereotypical role? Do you think they are subordinate to the boys?
>
> ➤ Think of some other youth cultures. What are the gender relations within those cultures?

Areas and issues of concern to women

Men have set the research agenda and as a result areas and issues relevant to women have been neglected or marginalized. Topics such as sexual violence, domestic labour, childbirth and contraception received very little attention until the feminist impact on sociology. Feminists believe that there must be feminist research which addresses issues and social problems that affect women. A key aim of feminist research is to make women visible, to observe, listen and record the experiences of women and to write women back into sociological research.

Feminism has had an impact more broadly on sociology. Mary Maynard (1990) argues that feminism has begun to reshape sociology as many non-feminist sociologists are beginning to consider women and gender in their research and analysis. Feminists have stressed that men are influenced by gender relations, hence gender should be examined not only in research on women but also in all research.

Feminist principles

Stanley and Wise (among others) have argued that no one research method or set of methods should be seen as distinctively feminist: 'Feminists should use any and every means available for investigating the condition of women in sexist society' (Stanley and Wise 1983). Feminists have considered how the logistics of particular methods engage with feminist aims, yet it is the principles that underlie selected methods which distinguish a range of emerging feminist praxes (Stanley 1990). Feminist research involves a commitment to a particular way of practising research, and this may shape how the specific techniques are utilized. Liz Kelly (1988) has suggested that feminist 'practice' would be a more appropriate term than feminist methodology to avoid the assumption that particular methods are feminist.

Case study

Critique of positivism: male reason versus female emotion

Stanley and Wise (1983; 1993) have argued that positivism is problematic for feminists for several reasons. First, it is based on a series of dichotomies: science versus nature, objectivity versus subjectivity, reason versus emotion and male versus female. The problem is that positivism elevates science, objectivity, rationality and the masculine, hence denigrating nature, subjectivity, emotion and the feminine. Feminists have argued that in Western scientific thought and culture the masculine is associated with reason, science and objectivity, the feminine with nature, emotion and subjectivity.

Second, Stanley and Wise argue that the positivist emphasis on objectivity divorces sociological knowledge from the social conditions in which that knowledge is produced. Positivistic methodology produces 'hygienic'

research in which the researcher is absent (Stanley 1990). Feminists do not see research as orderly; they are suspicious of 'hygienic' research: 'hygienic research in which no problems occur, no emotions are involved, is "research as it is described" and not "research as it is experienced"' (Stanley and Wise 1983). Feminists argue that researchers are always part of the social relations which produce particular findings. Their beliefs and values will shape the research. The private and public spheres, the emotional and the rational, subjectivity and objectivity cannot be separated. Feminists have argued that personal subjective experience is political and important and should be recognized as such in research.

Third, feminists argue that the scientific approach produces a division and an imbalance of power between social science researchers and those people whose lives they research. Social scientists are seen

to have special knowledge and skills, they control the research process, they come along and do their research on people. Feminists have been keen to involve women in the research process itself in an attempt to reduce the imbalance of power and hierarchical relations.

In challenging the concept of objectivity, feminists have challenged the view that research should be value-free and apolitical. Indeed, they stress that feminist research not only must be of intellectual interest but also should further the political interests of women. Feminists argue that research should raise consciousness, empower women and bring about change.

(Harding 1987).

Questions

1. Do you agree that research cannot be value free?

2. How might a researcher's values influence the way s/he studied a) crime, b) poverty?

Not all feminists share a common view of research methodology: there is debate about what is and what should constitute a feminist methodology (Harding 1987). However, a set of recurring themes and principles does emerge, four of which have been selected here. They are of particular importance to feminist 'practice' (Kelly 1988):

➤ the centrality of women's experience;
➤ research for women;
➤ the rejection of hierarchy and empowerment;
➤ the critical reflexivity.

Centrality of women's experience

Feminists in their research draw on new empirical resources, the most significant being women's experiences. Feminism moves away from the androcentric position,

which sees male experiences as central, and places women's experiences as the foundation of social knowledge. The task of feminist research is to explore how women see themselves and the social world. McRobbie (1991) argues that the most important achievement of the growing body of feminist research is the revealing of women's hidden experiences both past and present. Underlying all feminist research is the goal of correcting both the invisibility and distortion of women's experiences by providing a vehicle for women to speak through. Women's experience must provide the raw material for theory construction.

Stanley (1990) argues that feminists should be committed to a belief that research and theorizing are not the result of the thinking of a group of experts different from those of 'mere people'. Stanley and Wise (1983) warn of the danger of the emergence of an academic elite of feminist researchers who distance their activities from the mass of women. They stress the need to ground theory in research and stress the two-way relationship between experience and theory. Indeed, many feminists reject any divide between theory and research.

Research for women

Ramazanoglu (1991a) notes that there has been a distinct shift in feminist methodology from an earlier position which defined feminist research as research of and by women to research that has a political commitment to be for women. Duelli-Klein (1983) differentiates between research on women, which merely records aspects of women's lives, and research for women, which 'tries to take women's needs, interests and experiences into account and aims at being instrumental in improving women's lives in one way or another' (Duelli-Klein 1983).

Feminist research is committed to improving women's position in society. Several feminists have stressed consciousness raising as a key role for feminist research in the emancipation process. Pollert (1981), in her participation observation of women factory workers, did not take a neutral stance but challenged both male managers and female workers about the sexist assumptions they made. She treated the situation as a consciousness-raising process for herself and the women in the factory.

Rejection of hierarchy and empowerment

A basic principle of feminist methodology has been not only to challenge relationships typical of traditional research based on hierarchy and power but also to aim to democratize the research process. Feminists have attempted to restore their subjects as active participants in the research process and to ensure that knowledge and skill are shared equally between researcher and subject. There has been a range of feminist research aimed at empowering and actively involving the women involved (Lather 1988). The aim to change as well as to understand the world means that some feminists build conscious empowerment into the research design.

Kelly (1988) wanted to ensure that all the women she spoke to had some involvement other than releasing information in the research process. She carried out follow-up interviews in which she discussed the themes and analysis that she was developing, asking for and noting the women's opinions. This enabled 'joint inter-

pretation of meaning', allowing the women to have an input into the findings.

The main objectives of the research by Hanmer and Saunders (1984) on violence against women were to feed their findings back into the community, to raise the profile of violence against women and to encourage women's groups in the community to undertake their own research into violence to women. They carried out community-based interviewing, using limited resources, in the Leeds area. This was at a time when Peter Sutcliffe (the so-called Yorkshire Ripper) was at large, and they were interested in how this had affected women's lives. They visited organizations in the area whose work in some way concerned violence against women and consulted neighbourhood groups. They fed the information gained back into the community in order to develop self-help among women. Research involvement led to a local support group for women being established.

Abbott and Wallace (1990) note that the logic of the feminist position on research seems to demand non-individual cooperative research, where the researcher helps the women involved to undertake their own research. The researcher acts as an enabler. Subject and researcher decide together how the findings are to be used, although in practice this is difficult to achieve.

> ## Stop and think
>
> ➤ Suggest how Abbott and Wallace's notion of cooperative research could be applied in the following areas: (a) male and female roles in the catering industry; (b) the sexual harassment of girls at school; (c) homelessness; (d) the role of women in the police force.
>
> ➤ What are the arguments for and against personal involvement in research?

Lather (1988) coordinated a group called the 'Women's Economic Development Project' in South Carolina. Low-income women were trained to research their own economic circumstances, in order to understand and change them. This participatory research design involved eleven low-income women working as community researchers on a one-year study of the economic circumstances of 3,000 low-income women. Information was gathered in order to bring action as a catalyst for change, to raise the consciousness of women regarding the sources of their economic circumstances, to promote community-based leadership, and to set up an active network of low-income rural women in the state to support new legislation concerning women's work and educational opportunities.

Critical reflexivity

Perhaps one of the most challenging developments in feminist practice has been the demand that the researcher must be located in the same critical plane as the researched; if it is accepted that researchers cannot be detached from the process but are part of it then their beliefs, motives and social position must be scrutinized. Researchers should create self-reflexive designs, scrutinizing their own role.

Harding argues that the most desirable feminist analysis not only researches women's experiences but also locates the researcher directly within the whole process:

> The best feminist analysis . . . insists that the inquirer her/himself be placed in the same critical plane as the overt subject matter, thereby recovering the entire research process for scrutiny in the results of research. That is, the class, race, culture, and gender assumptions, beliefs and behaviours of the researcher her/himself must be placed within the frame of the picture that s/he attempts to paint.   (Harding 1987: 9)

This is part of the attempt to restore subjectivity. It necessitates the researcher becoming visible and not the objective, detached, pretended object of orthodox research. This is a response to the recognition that the experiences, cultural beliefs and behaviours of feminist researchers shape the results of their analysis no less than do those of male researchers. Feminists must recognize that their role will always be central to the research product and be honest and explicit about this. The presence of the researcher as a human being cannot be avoided therefore; researchers must use this rather than pretend it does not exist.

Much of feminist research now shares this process of 'conscious reflexivity' (Kelly 1988). Feminists doing research examine their own roles and also use their own experiences to help make sense of the women they are researching. Kelly interviewed women about their experiences of sexual violence. She openly acknowledges that her research was the end-product of both the responses from the women she spoke to and her own interpretation of the experiences she was examining. It was a two-way process. In documenting her own involvement with the research, Kelly explains how while she had been involved in the women's refuge movement she had become aware of the extent of violence against women, which led her to

select violence against women as an area of research. She discusses how doing the research impacted on her life, how she became sensitized to instances of sexual violence in everyday life and herself recalled incidents of sexual violence while carrying out the research. This helped her to understand various aspects of her research, in this case how common it is to suppress painful experiences. She identified with women who did not have the words to tell or even understand what happened; this directly shaped her theorizing, leading her to explore in detail how sexual violence is defined by women.

Kelly stresses that the interaction of her experience with the women's experiences was crucial for understanding it and defends the feminist case for subjectivity:

> Moving between the interviews and my own experiences and reactions was an integral part of the research methodology. Had I 'turned out' these responses I would probably not have noticed or fully understood the importance of the aspects of women's experience of sexual violence.   (Kelly 1988: 19)

Mirza (1991), in her research on the experiences of young black women in a comprehensive school, also builds in reflexivity. She identifies herself as a black feminist who recognizes racism and sexism. She documents how she had experienced racism in school as a young woman. She argues that these experiences did not make her 'biased' but gave her a deeper understanding of the young women's experiences.

A research product is always filtered through the consciousness of the researcher, so it is argued that researchers must openly examine their beliefs, values and emotions. Feminists point out that researchers should not degrade or attempt to remove these but value and utilize them in their research.

Feminism and method

While researching certain experiences of women, feminist researchers have found existing techniques, or the conventional ways of using these techniques, inappropriate. In her research on the transition to motherhood, Oakley (1981) has exposed the limitations of conventional sociological criteria for interviewing. After six months as an observer on a maternity ward in London, Oakley interviewed sixty-six women on four occasions during their pregnancy. In this context she found that as a feminist she had to reassess how she had been trained as a sociologist to carry out interviewing. She argues that in many textbooks the interview is presented as distanced from normal social interaction. Interviewing is often presented as a clinical research tool: in order to maximize data collection the subject must be put at ease, yet at the same time the interviewer must remain detached to avoid 'interviewer bias'. In order to gain cooperation, interviewers must strike up 'rapport' but avoid involvement. Interviewing is presented as a one-way process in which the interviewer gathers information and does not emit any information. The relationship between interviewer and interviewee is hierarchical, and it is the body of knowledge possessed by the interviewer that allows the interview to proceed successfully. Oakley is critical of this model, which, she argues, is a product of the desire for scientific status.

Feminist researchers argue that bias is introduced when an interview is taken out of ordinary everyday relations and becomes a constructed and artificial relationship. Stanley and Wise (1983; 1993) also argue that the traditional (scientific/orthodox) model is 'unnatural': people in social interaction do not act as automatons, which creates an artificial interaction, likely to produce unauthentic responses. The orthodox model is highly problematic for feminists whose aim is to validate the subjective experiences of women. Oakley (1981) points out that so-called correct interviewing is associated with a set of values that in our patriarchal culture are more readily associated with the masculine, such as objectivity, detachment, science and hierarchy.

Oakley argues that interviewing, which relies on subjectivity and equality, is devalued as it does not meet the 'masculine' standards of social science, rationality and scientific objectivity and that it has been seen as potentially undermining the status of sociology as a science. In the social science model of interviewing, feeling, emotion and involvement are conventionally denigrated.

The traditional model of research derives from a set of attitudes that regards people as objects to be manipulated; this contradicts feminist principles (Ehrlich 1976). The hierarchical model of interviewing is not congruent with feminist principles, which challenge all relations of dominance and submission. Oakley suggests that when a feminist interviews women, it would be morally and ethically wrong to use prescribed interviewing practice.

In her research, Oakley (1981) discussed personal and intimate issues with women in repeated interviews, which inevitably meant that a personal relationship evolved. Oakley built up relationships and became close friends with some of these women; she answered all personal questions and questions about the research. As she herself was a mother the women would ask about her

opinion and experience of young babies and she would share her experience with them. Oakley argues that she could have taken no other direction than to treat the whole research relationship as a two-way process: the relationship cannot be left in the interview room but exists beyond the interview.

When interviewing women about their experiences of sexual violence, Kelly (1988) adopted an interviewing methodology similar to Oakley's. She rejected objective aloofness and a refusal to enter into dialogue. She stressed how artificial, unnatural and impossible the orthodox approach would have been considering that she was speaking to many of the women about very intimate and, for some, traumatic experiences: 'It is difficult for me to envisage being detached when I remember how shaken many women were during or after my interviews' (Kelly 1988: 11).

Feminist methodology therefore rejects any paradigm that does not place the subjective centrally, that denigrates personal experience and involvement rather than recognizing its value: 'personal involvement is more than dangerous bias – it is the condition under which people come to know each other and to admit others into their lives' (Oakley 1981: 58).

Oakley and Kelly argue that their approach meant that women provided much more detailed and rich information than the traditional model ever could. Interviewing does not have to be exploitative but if practised in a more democratic way it can provide a vehicle for women to document their own lives.

Stop and think

> Both Oakley and Kelly emphasize the importance of developing close personal relationships with the women they were researching. What difficulties might they have in doing this?

> How might this influence the information they gathered?

> Do you think this matters?

Quantitative or qualitative methods?

It is often assumed that feminist research involves only qualitative methods. Some feminist sociologists have been critical of quantitative methods. They have argued that questionnaires and structured interviews pre-code

Case study

Women's leisure, what leisure?

Green *et al.* (1990) used a social survey in combination with unstructured interviews and discussion groups in what is the most comprehensive study of women's leisure to date in Britain. They wanted to collect both general information about the types and levels of women's leisure participation and more detailed knowledge about women's perceptions and attitudes to leisure. They argued that as feminists are concerned both to understand patriarchal structures that oppress women and to seek to change them they must utilize the strengths of quantitative evidence. They argued that using a survey enabled them to generalize from their results to the larger female population and to exert greater political influence. They wanted to provide a statistical body of research that could actually form the basis for more informed policy decisions. They pointed out that policy-making bodies were more impressed with statistical data and it was crucial that such bodies examine and take note of their findings. They were fully aware of the limitations of the survey method in the context of women's lives and hence used qualitative research to complement the quantitative data. Hence the shift towards triangulation (see pp. 130–1) is also reflected in feminist research. Feminists will use any method appropriate to expose and oppose women's oppression.

Question

1. What 'limitations of the survey method' might there be in pursuing research into women's leisure activities?

experience, producing a false body of data which distorts the actors' meanings. Graham (1984b) claimed that survey methods and structured interviews 'fracture women experiences'. Surveys are seen to mask or misrepresent the position of women in male-dominated societies and fragment women's experiences.

Barbara Smith (1987) argues that there are aspects of women's lives which cannot be pre-known or predefined in such a way. Some feminists have stressed that the female subject gets lost in social science survey research. Oppression is such that it cannot be 'neatly encapsulated in the categories of survey research' (Graham 1984b). On many of these points feminist arguments overlap with ethnographic researchers.

Stop and think

➤ On the whole feminists have favoured qualitative methods, claiming that they fit more comfortably with feminist principles as well as being more appropriate and sensitive to women's experiences of oppression. Why do you think feminist research has 'favoured qualitative methods'?

Although feminist research has tended to be defined in terms of qualitative research, a growing body of feminists have attempted to break down the distinction between quantitative and qualitative research. They have stressed that there is nothing inherently sexist with quantitative research methods and techniques such as surveys (Epstein Jayaratne 1993; Kelly *et al.* 1992; Pugh 1990). If used sensitively they can be utilized to complement broader feminist research aims.

Many feminists have also proposed that the use of qualitative methods does not necessarily overcome some of the problems identified with quantitative methods. Stacey (1988) has pointed out that although ethnographic methods seem ideally suited to research in that they involve empathy and allow for an egalitarian, reciprocal relationship, they may expose the research subjects 'to greater risk of exploitation, betrayal and abandonment by the researcher than does much positivistic research' (Stacey 1988: 21).

Feminist research: an overview

Feminist research has involved discussion and criticism, primarily from feminists themselves, which reflects the diversity of feminism (see pp. 72–8) and the feminist concern constantly to challenge the *status quo*. Stanley and Wise (1983) argue that research inevitably involves power relations, and the question of exploitation has been raised by many feminists engaged in research: 'The researcher's goal is always to gather information, thus the danger always exists of manipulating friendships to that end' (Acker *et al.* 1983).

McRobbie (1991) argues that feminists must recognize that whatever methodology is used there is an unequal distribution of privilege. Feminist researchers often represent powerful educational establishments. They must acknowledge that this may be one reason why women are willing to participate in research. For example, she criticizes Oakley (whose work was considered earlier), who she claims fails to consider the imbalance of power between herself as a researcher and the young mothers:

> She does not concern herself with the fact that pregnant, in hospital . . . the women were delighted to find a friendly articulate knowledgeable woman to talk to [sic] their experiences about . . . their extreme involvement in the research could also be interpreted as yet another index of their powerlessness.
>
> (McRobbie 1991: 79)

There is always the danger that some women will use the experiences of women's oppression to further their careers, with women's suffering becoming a commodity. Angela McRobbie speaks honestly about the fact that doing research sometimes feels like 'holidaying on other people's misery'. She describes an interview with a 19-year-old woman who had been brought up in care:

> I was almost enjoying the interview, pleased it was going well and that Carol was relaxed and talkative. Yet there was Carol with her eyes filling up with tears as she recounted her life and how her mother had died.
>
> (McRobbie 1991: 77)

McRobbie also challenges the assumption that the feminist researcher will necessarily understand the women because of their 'shared' oppression. Women have a multiplicity of experiences. Feminists may have valuable personal experience, but they cannot assume that this will be the same as those they are researching. While feminism attempts to foster sisterhood, it cannot naïvely assume that women are bound together purely on the grounds of gender.

Although the principles enshrined in feminist research cannot eliminate the possibility of exploitation, they can serve as a check against it. As part of the conscious reflexivity feminists attempt to be explicit and open about power relations as they operate in the research process.

There is a great deal of debate about what a feminist methodology should contain. It is important to remember that there is not one easily identifiable feminist research methodology (Reinharz 1993). Yet there is some consensus about principles that feminists should consider when carrying out research. Kelly notes this ambivalent position:

> There is not, as yet, a distinctive 'feminist methodology'. Many of the methods used by feminist researchers are not original. What is new are the questions we have asked, the way we locate ourselves within our questions and the purposes of our work.   (Kelly 1988: 5–6)

Triangulation

In this chapter, we have introduced and discussed a range of methods by which sociologists gather new evidence and apply already existing information in order to address social issues and problems. We have tried to present these methods as complementary rather than mutually exclusive ways of pursuing research. The complementary nature of different research methods is shown when two or more methods are combined in one research project. The term given to the combining of research methods is triangulation. In these situations, the researcher does not have to rely on one method, so that the pitfalls of one particular methodological approach can be avoided or lessened by the use of another approach as well. Although sometimes described as a recent development, research that combines more than one technique for collecting information is by no means new. Most textbooks refer to examples of sociological research that have used triangulation, and we shall look briefly at a couple of examples here.

Roy Wallis's (1976) study of the scientology movement was mentioned earlier in the context of participant observation. Wallis not only followed an introductory course run by the movement as a participant observer but also interviewed and sent questionnaires to scientologists and ex-scientologists to provide him with a broader picture of the movement. In similar vein, Walters's (2003) use of different styles of interview in his research into the politics of criminology (see p. 114) was supplemented by a number of other research techniques. He used case studies so as to 'bring to life' research questions and themes identified through his interviews; he examined academic literature; and he conducted an extensive documentary analysis of official information, including records of parliamentary debates, the League of Nations, the United Nations and reports to the US congress.

Eileen Barker (1984) used a number of different research techniques in her work on the Unification Church of the Reverend Moon – the 'Moonies'. Barker adopted three main approaches – interviews, participant observation and questionnaires. About thirty in-depth interviews were carried out with a random sample of Moonies. These interviews extended over several hours and were fairly unstructured explorations of the attitudes and feelings of individual followers. Participant observation enabled Barker to examine the interaction and interrelationships between Moonies on a day-to-day basis. Finally, around 450 questionnaires were given to Moonies, along with another 100 to non-Moonies as a comparison, to provide statistical evidence of patterns and relationships within the movement and with the wider society. In reflecting on her research, Barker points out that each technique is interdependent. The questionnaire would not have been so thorough if she had not previously done a number of extended interviews with Moonies and actually lived with them and observed the so-called 'brainwashing' process at first hand; indeed, the participant observation familiarized Barker with the appropriate language to use in the questionnaire. As well as these three approaches to collecting first-hand information on the Moonies, Barker's research involved discovering and reviewing what others had written about the Unification Church and other new religious movements. The reviewing of secondary literature – library work – is an important first step in all sociological research.

Summary

➤ Sociological research involves the gathering of relevant material and data and interpreting and analyzing them.

➤ In undertaking research the sociologist can use a variety of techniques. The method chosen will be influenced by the nature of the issue being examined and by the theoretical approach favoured by the researcher.

➤ One issue that has been central to the style of research adopted has been the extent to which sociological research should follow the methodological approach of the natural sciences. A by-product of this issue has been the debate over whether sociology can and should be value-free and the extent to which the data gathered by sociologists are reliable and valid.

➤ Quantitative research is most closely associated with the conventional scientific methodology. Surveys involve collecting data from large numbers of people, usually from questionnaires or interviews that ask people about their behaviour and attitudes. Surveys are typically based on a sample of respondents drawn from a specific population. The use of official statistics and content analysis are other examples of quantitative research.

➤ Qualitative research gathers more detailed information from a smaller number of respondents. The focus is on the experiences of people and the meaning given to such experiences. Observation, in-depth interviews and case studies are qualitative methods.

➤ Feminist research has criticized orthodox sociological research methodology for being 'male stream', i.e. centred on men. Although feminist research is not a unified body of research, a major focus has been on women's experiences and how an understanding of them can help to explain and improve women's position in society.

➤ Throughout the chapter it has been stressed that sociological research is not confined to one or other specific method; indeed, a combination of methods is often the best strategy for the researcher to adopt.

Links

As with sociological theory, sociological research also underpins all of the topics and areas of sociology covered in the rest of this book. So rather than indicate all of the links, we would urge you to think about the research processes involved in the various studies and examples of sociology you come across in the remaining chapters and to consider the sort of research issues those studies would raise.

 ## Further reading

Becker, H.S. (1963) *Outsiders: Studies in the Sociology of Deviance*, New York: Free Press.

As well as 'methodology' texts, it is good practice to look at the methodological sections of specific sociological studies. Such sections may be found in the introductions to studies or as appendices. Chapter 9 in Becker's classic study of deviants, *Outsiders*, for instance, discusses some of the key issues attendant on studying deviant behaviour.

Durkheim, E. (1964) *The Rules of Sociological Method*, New York: Free Press.

With so many secondary sources available, there is a tendency not to consider reading the originals. However, Durkheim's key work on the studying of social phenomena is no more 'difficult' to read than some of the commentaries on it. It is a short study that sets out the requirements that rigorous sociological research needs to follow.

Gilbert, N. (ed.) (2001) *Researching Social Life*, 2nd edn, London: Sage.

This is a collection of papers that outlines the main ways in which sociologists gather data and describes a range of ways of analysing such data. The connections between quantitative and qualitative research methods and their theoretical bases are emphasized throughout. The papers are written by experienced social researchers who reflect on their own research experiences.

Hammersley, M. (ed.) (1993) *Social Research: Philosophy, Politics and Practice*, London: Sage.

This collection contains some particularly useful material on the politics of the research process with articles on, for instance, issues of race, gender and power in social research.

Maynard, M. and Purvis, J. (eds) (1994) *Researching Women's Lives*, London: Taylor & Francis.

A series of papers written by key practitioners that detail the current debates within feminist research.

Neuman, W.L. (2000) *Social Research Methods: Qualitative and Quantitative Approaches*, 4th edn, London: Allyn and Bacon.

This American text provides a detailed account of the range of different research methods available to the sociologist and reviews their strengths and weaknesses.

Salkind, N.J. (2000) *Statistics for People Who (Think They) Hate Statistics*, London: Sage.

The title says it all – a book for those who want to learn the basics of statistics for social research but are worried about their abilities in this area.

Silverman, D. (2001) *Interpreting Qualitative Data*, 2nd edn, London: Sage.

The second edition of this popular introductory text takes account of the expansion in qualitative research since the 1990s.

Stanley, L. and Wise, S. (1993) *Breaking Out Again: Feminist Ontology and Epistemology*, London: Routledge.

This updates and reviews the main arguments in feminist thinking and research since the original *Breaking Out* – an important feminist text, first published in 1983, that challenged conventional positivist practices in sociological research.

 ## Web sites

University of Surrey, Sociology Department
www.soc.surrey.ac.uk/sru
Here you can find articles on research published by the Sociology Department at the University of Surrey.

Data resources can be located through numerous web sites. Two useful ones are
www.asanet.org/student/archive/data
which provided by the American Sociological Association, and
www.nsd.uib.no/Cessda
which is the site of the Council of European Social Science Data Archives.

Activities

Research issues

Activity 1

(a) Problems in researching a deviant religious movement

This extract illustrates some of the difficulties of research into deviant religious movements. It is taken from the methodological appendix to *When Prophecy Fails* (Festinger *et al.* 1956), the classic study of a small group who believed that the world was about to be destroyed and which we referred to earlier in the chapter (p. 118).

> In our investigation of the group which gathered about Dr Armstrong and Marian Keetch, our observers posed as ordinary members who believed as the others did. In short, our investigation was conducted without either the knowledge or the consent of the group members. This situation presented a number of problems that merit detailed discussion . . .
>
> Both of our 'local' observers were under pressure at various times in mid-December to quit their jobs and spend all their time with the group . . . Their evasion of these requests and their failure to quit their jobs at once were not only embarrassing to them and threatening to their rapport with the group, but also may have had the effect of making the members who had quit their jobs less sure that they had done the right thing. In short, as members, the observers could not be neutral – any action had consequence . . .
>
> Observing, in this study, was exhausting work. In addition to the strain created by having to play an accepting, passive role vis-à-vis an ideology that aroused constant incredulity, which had to be concealed, observers frequently had to stay in the group for long hours without having an opportunity to record what they had learned . . .
>
> The circumstances of observation made it impossible to make notes openly except on a single occasion, the meeting of November 23, when the Creator ordered that notes be taken. Apart from this, it was difficult to make notes privately or secretly, for the observers were rarely left alone inside the house and it was necessary to be ingenious enough to find excuses for leaving the group temporarily. One device used occasionally was to make notes in the bathroom. This was not entirely satisfactory, however, since too frequent trips there would probably arouse curiosity if not suspicion . . .
>
> Our observers had their daily lives to care for as well as the job, and were subject to occasional bouts of illness or fatigue from lack of sleep. The job was frequently irritating because of the irrelevancies (from the point of view of our main interest) that occupied vast quantities of time during the all-night meetings.
>
> (Festinger *et al.* 1956: 234–46)

Questions

1. *You are a sociologist just starting a research project seeking information on ritualistic abuse. A friend tells you they know of a Satanic cult meeting regularly in the area. Most of their activities are harmless but there is a rumour that an animal is to be sacrificed at Hallowe'en. Your friend tells you they know of a member looking for new recruits. You feel this is a rare opportunity of getting access to the group which may not come up again. How would you continue with your research? (Consider the advantages and disadvantages of alternative methods of research that might be used.)*

2. *Suggest the practical and ethical consequences of the methods of research that you propose to follow.*

▶

Activities

(b) Problems in researching female factory workers

This extract is taken from a study of female workers in an electronics factory in Malaysia. It focuses on the problems faced by these workers, who were termed 'Minah Karan' (meaning, roughly, 'loose women'). Daud's research was carried out in a number of stages and involved several research methods: participant observation, in-depth interviews, official documents and surveys (based on questionnaires and including a follow-up survey five years after the initial research).

I started my fieldwork as a participant observer, by becoming a factory worker. It began in October 1976 and continued until June 1977. During the first five months I worked in the Variable Resistance Section (V.R.) and the Electrolytic Capacitor Section, working two-and-a-half months in each section. Then I carried out my in-depth interviews with 100 workers over a period of one month. At the end of the last two months of fieldwork I conducted a survey of 111 respondents to see the changes that had occurred between 1977 and 1982 . . .

Although work in the factory numbed the mind and tired the body, my research was strengthened by real knowledge of the long hours and tough working conditions. I discovered many advantages in becoming a worker in order to understand the real problems and situations of factory life. I could feel for myself the tiredness, depression, tension and other physical hazards; I discovered a lot of truth about the nature of a worker's life. For instance, cohabitation and illegitimate pregnancies were usually subjects for gossip. However, the workers talked about this only within their own groups. I believe that if I had not undertaken participant observation by becoming a factory worker, such private and personal matters would be very difficult to uncover . . .

During the first few days of my work I had asked them whether it was true, as people claimed, that factory workers cohabit. They replied that it was nonsense. But when they had accepted me as one of them, they told the truth . . .

There were drawbacks in becoming a worker and doing this 'undercover' work. Some of them are discussed below: The chief methodological problem was to keep my notes up to date while working normally with others. Each worker sat near another in the 'line' and I found there was a general interest in what I did and how I behaved since I was a newcomer. Only when there was a break could I write my notes in any detail. By becoming a worker I had to follow work regulations. Workers were not allowed to talk during work . . .

A few seniors especially the 'line leaders' became suspicious and were unhappy with me. They feared that I might be appointed to the supervision post after my 'training'. They viewed this as unfair since they were senior to me. They resented me and refused to be friendly. It is undeniable that becoming a factory worker was a very good method of carrying out my fieldwork. In not disclosing my real identity, I always had to be careful and be on the alert for rumours and suspicion among the workers . . .

The major advantage of using structured questionnaires is that it produces systematic data on information obtained during observation and in-depth interviews. But, there are also a few disavantages in using this method, namely: I noticed great differences in the quality of information obtained through the methods of participation and descriptive survey . . .

For example, when I asked about their attitudes towards the management, during my period of anonymity, almost all the workers condemned the management and said they hated it. But when questioned during the descriptive survey, half the sample said the managment was 'good'. I think this is because they were trying to be careful when answering the questionnaires administered by someone who was no longer their fellow-worker.

(Adapted from Daud 1985: 134–41)

Activities

Questions

1. *What sort of information on factory work would each of the methods adopted by Daud be likely to provide?*

2. *To what extent can these different methods be seen as (a) valid sources of information; (b) reliable sources of information?*

Activity 2

How sociological is your imagination?

Take out your notebook, sharpen your pencil, discard your most cherished cultural assumptions and suspend good old common sense. You are an outsider and your job is to observe and describe what you see around you.

Choose one type of activity (preferably one which you are not familiar with) and simply record your observations. This may be as simple as observing people in a café or pub (Who are they? Where do they sit? What do they do?) or it may involve you in an anthropological pursuit of the exotic and the bizarre: a night at the wrestling, an evening at the opera or an afternoon spent watching football or playing bingo (Who are the punters? What do they wear? How do they behave?).

Using your newly found sociological imagination, how do you interpret your observations? Do any patterns emerge? Do any hypotheses suggest themselves? What problems have you encountered in your search for new sociological truths?

Notes for students

This activity is intended to help you to understand the process all observers go through in making sense of the world around them. We all use information previously learned to make sense of situations, and we pick up clues from those we are watching or interacting with. No two people will therefore make sense in exactly the same way. The point of this exercise is to make you aware of what sociologists do when they 'explain behaviour', to raise the issues of subjectivity, value and interpretation. Whether or not you have studied sociology previously, it is hoped you will be stimulated into thinking differently about the world around you, questioning behaviour which might have been 'taken for granted'.

1 First you must select your observation. Think through some possible choices. Religious and cultural events lend themselves well to this activity, and you may find that local newspapers contain some helpful ideas.

2 You need to decide how you are going to record your observation. Will you keep notes in a book (obviously or unobtrusively)? Will you trust to your memory and write up your impression as soon as possible? Will you use a tape recorder/still camera/video? There is no right way in this activity: think about the pros and cons of each recording method.

3 After the observation, note the following. How long did the observation last? Did you know if the participants were typical? (How would you decide this?) Did anyone explain what they were doing? Were there written instructions (e.g. church prayer book – how much sense did that make?)? Did you make your own sense of what you saw?

4 Let your imagination generate explanations: you are allowed to present competing explanations for what you think you saw and should select the most likely account from your standpoint, explaining in terms of further logical arguments or theories.

Activities

Outline

A suggested outline for the written part of the assignment is as follows:

1 **Introduction** Observation chosen: Where? When? Why?

2 **Method** How the observation was recorded – pros and cons. Did you remain 'non-participant' or did you participate? What were the effects of this? In retrospect, would you change the way you did the activity?

3 **Explanations** This section should describe your observation – clues picked up both orally and visually from the participants should be highlighted. You should go beyond pure description and attempt imaginative explanations in order to generate hypotheses about the social behaviour you observed. Factors which may help you in considering explanations and gaining a sociological understanding of what you are observing might include the following: Does there appear to be a shared set of values and rules among the group? Is there a certain social etiquette that must be maintained? What social characteristics strike you about the group? Are they all male? All female? Predominantly older people? Why? What do the participants appear to get out of the interaction? Escape, pleasure, social contact, sense of identity, etc?

4 **Reflexive account** In this section you reflect on your own role in this observation: if you had been a different type of person would you have made another interpretation? It is in this section that you raise issues of objectivity/subjectivity, value and interpretation. You need to account for your own role in the process of under-standing, i.e. the interpretation you made of the situation. Are you male/female, white/black, disabled/able-bodied, young/mature, middle class/working class? Do you hold certain religious, moral or political beliefs? How did these factors shape your interpretation and also actually shape the behaviour of the people involved in the interaction?

5 **Conclusion** How useful did you find this exercise?

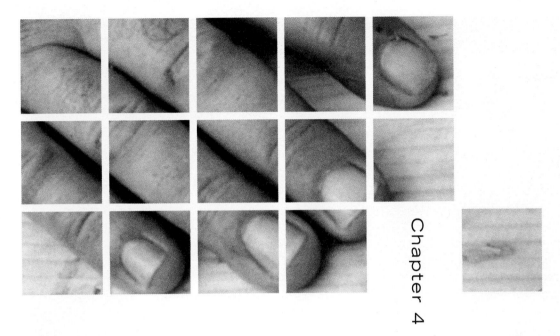

Chapter 4

Work

People who speak grandiosely of the 'meaning of work' should spend a year or two in a factory.
(quoted in Fraser 1968: 12)

Key issues

➤ What are the difficulties involved in defining 'work'?

➤ How has wage labour changed with the development of capitalist societies?

➤ Why have certain areas of employment expanded and others declined?

➤ What impact have these changes had on the structure of the labour market and on the role of trade unions?

➤ What effects has unemployment had on different groups in society?

➤ To what extent has capitalism become a global phenomenon?

Introduction

'So, what is it that you *do*?' This is a familiar question, one you will no doubt have been asked on many occasions. Although it is a question that seems obvious and commonplace it is worth some reflection as it makes huge assumptions about the way we live and how we categorize ourselves, our world and the knowledge we have of that world. The answer to this question, as we all instantly recognize, is to do with work. But what kind of work? Housework? The work we carry out as part of our hobbies or leisure activities? The work of caring for relatives or children? No, generally not. Almost always we tell people about our employment, the work that we are paid a regular income for, and those without such work might reply that they are currently without work or that they are 'not doing anything at the moment'.

Paid employment is, of course, by no means *all* that we do and people who are unemployed do not suddenly cease to exist – even if they may feel, and get treated, as though they do. Delineating the boundary between work and non-work is an extremely difficult thing to do. Imagine you come across someone sawing a piece of wood. They could be doing this as part of a hobby or doing it for a friend for a 'payment' of some kind. Perhaps the person involved is a joiner or maybe they are being forced to do it at gunpoint! The point is that simply observing a task will not serve as an accurate guide as to whether it will count as work or not. What is crucial is the context within which the activity takes place.

Figure 4.1 Teaching a child to read may be seen as work when done by a teacher and non-work when done by a parent
(SS, courtesy of Robert Harding Picture Library Ltd)

Stop and think

➤ Identify two activities that are conventionally seen as (a) work; (b) non-work.

➤ What are the characteristics that distinguish them?

➤ What activities are seen as both work and non-work within different contexts (consider, for example, Figure 4.1)?

In a society such as ours, paid labour is most often equated with work – in the above example only the person sawing the wood as a joiner would be seen to be 'at work'.

The contemporary centrality of wage-labour in many societies cannot be assumed and is in no sense a 'natural' or fixed state of affairs. That it often appears to us in this way is the outcome of a complex mix of social and economic changes, upheavals and struggles played out over a long period of time (Marx 1970). But in an 'advanced' capitalist society like the UK it is paid employment that has come to form a cornerstone of many people's lives, their sense of self and well-being, and the nucleus around which the bulk of wider social relationships gravitate. Given this, it is justifiable to begin with the classical analysis of wage-labour within capitalism, that of Karl Marx.

Marx and the labour process within capitalism

For Karl Marx (1818–83), *labour* was the quintessential human activity (see pp. 50–4), not in the narrow way in which we have come to understand labour today but labour in the broadest sense – a purposeful and sensuous interaction between people and nature. How people organized themselves in the act of production was the startingpoint for Marx's materialist method: 'Thus the first fact to be established is the physical organisation of these individuals and their consequent relation to the rest of nature' (Marx 1967: 42). Individuals, for Marx, 'begin to distinguish themselves from animals as soon as they begin to produce their means of subsistence' (Marx 1967: 42). The manner in which people 'produce their means of subsistence' forms the basis of Marx's basic unit of historical categorization, the *mode of production.*

A closer look

The mode of production

This has two key components:

➤ **a labour process** the manner in which purposeful human activity fashions objects and the tools (often referred to as the means of production) with which this is done;

➤ **the social relations of production** the relationships that form within and around the labour process.

It is only within the *capitalist mode of production* (CMP) that *wage-labour* comes to predominate. Essentially, within capitalism *labour power*, the mental and physical ability to labour, becomes all that a property-less working class has to sell to those who own the means of production – the ruling or capitalist class. Within the CMP, labour itself becomes a commodity. For an agreed period of time a worker relinquishes control of his or her labour power to the capitalist, who will then put it to use in an attempt to create surplus value and realize a profit in the marketplace. The CMP is thus an inherently exploitative, antagonistic and class-ridden socio-economic formation, and it is within CMP that *alienation* becomes endemic to wage labour and a perennial condition and experience for workers (see pp. 54–7 for an elaboration of these concepts). As Marx states, 'The whole system of capitalist production is based on the fact that the workman sells his [*sic*] labour power as a commodity' (Marx 1967: 571).

Braverman and *Labour and Monopoly Capital*

Harry Braverman (1974) attempted an extensive application of the Marxist analysis of the labour process for the twentieth century in *Labour and Monopoly Capital* (*LMC*). He argued that work in the twentieth century was undergoing a process of debasement and *deskilling* – hence the subtitle of the book, 'The Degradation of Work within the Twentieth Century'. In the era of 'monopoly capital' there was an intensification of the *division of labour* – the tendency towards a specialization of tasks – and the systematic, rational and 'scientific' application of managerial methods to work.

Taylorism

The most important catalyst and representative statement for such a management approach, according to Braverman, was to be found in F.W. Taylor's book *The Principles of Scientific Management* (1967; first published 1911). For Taylor, management's problem was essentially exerting total, or 'direct' (Friedman 1979), control over the workforce. Taylor reasoned that a workforce could not be trusted to maximize its output and efficiency on its own. 'Skill' represented something of an unknown to management and offered the workforce many opportunities to limit its output and subvert and deflect managerial authority. The following comment from Taylor is indicative of his perspective:

> hardly a competent workman can be found in a large establishment, whether he works by the day or on piece work, contract work or under any of the ordinary systems of compensating labour, who does not devote a considerable part of his time to studying just how slowly he can work and still convince his employer that he is going at a good pace.
>
> (quoted in Braverman 1974: 98)

Thus, Taylor believed that skilled tasks had to be broken down into simple and more 'manageable' operations and subjected to detailed and intensive timing – via time-and-motion study – and monitoring. An essential part of this was to ensure that 'All possible brain work should be removed from the shop and centred in the planning department' (Braverman 1974: 113). This was a process that Braverman laid great stress on and described as the 'separation of conception from execution'. He thought that this systematic 'deskilling' was inevitable within twentieth-century capitalism and would extend to all types of occupation throughout the economy. Thus the future for 'skilled' work and workers themselves within capitalism looked bleak.

Case study

Factory time

I work in a factory. For eight hours a day, five days a week, I'm the exception to the rule that life can't exist in a vacuum. Work to me is a void, and I begrudge every precious minute of my time that it takes. When writing about work I become bitter, bloody-minded and self-pitying, and I find difficulty in being objective. I can't tell you much about my job because I think it would be misleading to try to make something out of nothing; but as I write I am acutely aware of the effect that my working environment has upon my attitude towards work and leisure and life in general . . .

After clocking-in one starts work. Starts work, that is, if the lavatories are full. In an hourly paid job it pays to attend to the calls of nature in the firm's time. After the visit to the lavatory there is the tea-break to look forward to; after the tea-break the dinner-break; after the dinner-break the 'knocking-off' time. Work is done between the breaks, but it is done from habit and is given hardly a passing thought. Nothing is gained from the work itself – it has nothing to offer. The criterion is not to do a job well, but to get it over with quickly. Trouble is, one never does get it over with. Either one job is followed by another which is equally boring, or the same job goes on and on for ever: particles of production that stretch into an age of inconsequence. There is never a sense of fulfilment.

Time, rather than content, is the measure of factory life.

Time is what the factory worker sells: not labour, not skill, but time, dreary time. Desolate factory time that passes so slowly compared with the fleeting seconds of the weekend. Monday morning starts with a sigh, and the rest of the working-week is spent longing for Friday night. Everybody seems to be wishing his life away. And away it goes – sold to the man in the bowler hat.

People who speak grandiosely of the 'meaning of work' should spend a year or two in a factory.

(Fraser 1968: 11–12)

Questions

1. *Can we draw any parallels between this type of factory work and other forms of work?*

2. *What do you think are the social/personal/economic consequences of the types of feelings described in the passage?*

Braverman and the labour process debate

Braverman's book continues to be extremely influential and was the catalyst for what was to become known as the *labour process debate* (R. Brown 1992; Thompson 1989; Grint 1998). As a result of this debate, *LMC* has been subjected to an intense and prolonged critique. However, the subsequent elaboration and further discussion of *LMC*'s omissions and perceived shortcomings have greatly enhanced our understanding of work and employment. It is therefore worth while spending some time reviewing some of the more pertinent criticisms of *LMC*.

Braverman and skill

Given that Braverman's work has often been given the shorthand label of the 'deskilling thesis' and that the notion of skill obviously figures centrally within his investigations, it is somewhat surprising to find that nowhere in *LMC* does he systematically define, or even take to task, what 'skill' actually is or how it can be recognized. Braverman talks of 'skill' as though it were an axiomatic and unproblematic category which we all understand in a similar way. We should in no way dispense with the category of skill or portray it as being in some way false or illusory. However, it is important to bear in mind that the notion of skill is a socially and historically specific category which requires close sociological and empirical investigation.

Stop and think

➤ What do you think constitutes 'skill'?

➤ Why do you think the work that women do is often not seen to be skilled?

The creation of skill operates within relations of power and influence. Think of the ways that trade unions and professional bodies struggle to get their work defined as being 'skilful' in some way. We should reflect on why it is that the work women do (very often work that is extremely similar to that of men) is often not defined as being 'skilled', has less status and is consequently not so well rewarded financially. Much work away from the 'formal' sector of paid employment, especially domestic labour, is not regarded as being skilled or even 'proper' work. However, consider how much knowledge, physical effort and manual dexterity is involved in preparing, cooking and serving a meal for a group of people day after day. (If you doubt that there is any great skill involved in such a task then try it some time!) That most of the work done which is regarded as skilled and/or has a high status is generally carried out by white men, often from a middle-upper-class background, is not a mere coincidence and requires some explanation.

The implicit datum from which Braverman judges work in the twentieth century is a romanticized 'golden age' of skilled craft workers, a masculine world of artisans using a creative combination of hand and brain to fashion intricate goods and artifacts. This is an accusation Braverman refutes without any real conviction: 'I hope that no one draws . . . the conclusion that my views are shaped by nostalgia for an age that cannot be recaptured' (Braverman 1974: 6–7). This is not to say that such workers never existed, or do not exist now, and that we should not lament their 'deskilling', but Braverman offers little proof that this was ever the work experience for the vast majority. Braverman does not operate with the norm or average from the past, given that in the history of human toil it is probably fair to say that most people have been employed to pick things up and put them down again! Braverman also ignores the way that new 'skills' are created and have emerged throughout the twentieth century – for example, think of those people who work in the new telecommunications industries, with information technologies or computer programming and in the new service industries, to name but a few. Throughout the CMP the creation and

recomposition of skills has always provided something of a counterbalance to the destruction of skills – how ever we define skill!

Braverman and the influence of Taylorism

Braverman's assumption about the widespread influence of 'Taylorism' has also been cast in doubt (Burawoy 1985; Littler 1982; Wood 1982). It is by no means clear that Taylor and his writings had the profound impact on management practice that Braverman assumed to be the case. There was much resistance to Taylorist forms of management at all levels within many organizations. Leaving aside the huge amount of effort that a Taylorist 'direct control' strategy requires on the part of management, there is no reason why the same principles of 'scientific management' could not be turned on management themselves – especially middle management. Braverman's rigid and dogged use of 'Taylorism' as a coherent and dominant set of practices also greatly underestimates the variety and range of managerial methods employed in workplaces to best ensure efficient production and maintain 'acceptable' and 'realistic' levels of control over the workforce. As Grint says, 'Taylorism, at least in its total form, as a unique and discrete managerial strategy, rather than just one more form of an increasingly rationalized approach to management, had a very limited application anywhere' (Grint 1998: 177–9). In many ways, Taylorism can best be understood as a metaphor for the widespread intensification of the division of labour and the minute detailing of tasks in many workplaces in the twentieth century, part of Max Weber's all-pervasive rationalization of many areas of social and economic life in capitalist societies (Gerth and Mills 1991).

Braverman and workers' resistance

Another rather glaring omission from *LMC* revolves around Braverman's 'heroic' admission that 'no attempt will be made to deal with the modern working class on the level of its consciousness, organization or other activities' (Braverman 1974: 27). Braverman admits that this is a 'self-imposed limitation to the objective content of class and the omission of the subjective' (Braverman 1974: 27). Not to include an appreciation and discussion of workers' 'subjectivity' and 'agency' in his discussion of the development of the labour process greatly undermines the authenticity and power of Braverman's analysis. It is also something of a surprise, to say the least, for someone who was such a committed Marxist. The history of wage-labour within capitalism is fundamentally a history of struggle, resistance, subversion and sheer bloody-mindedness as well as being about domination, complicity and subordination. If we accept the Marxist understanding of the labour process outlined above, it could hardly be otherwise.

A closer look

Resistance

The women protested and resisted the target and grading system, individually and collectively, on a day-to-day basis. The work-study analysts were often marked out as the main enemy and were constantly discussed – at times, more vehemently than higher levels of management. These women were seen as the perpetrators of a system which presented to the shopfloor targets which could not be reached, let alone surpassed to allow for a bonus to be earned. It is the encounter between the work-study analyst and the shopfloor worker which encapsulates the collision between labour and capital, as this is the point at which the contract for the sale of labour power is realised and where labour power is turned into labour time and, thus, profits for the company . . .

[One] timed a woman and didn't ask if she could bring the clock out. It's against the rules. The girls are only timed if they agree to the clock coming out and it has to be visible to the girl. Well, this time it wasn't. She did it on the sly and when the girls found out they walked off the job. The nearest thing we've had to a strike here. We had to get John to sort it out. They have no idea what they are doing with their clocks and their minutes.

Outside the coffee bar, a row was developing which looked as though it might erupt into a walk-off. Gillian's unit had just been given minutes for making a baby garment – a tee-shirt which was edged, and had pants to match. Gillian was looking distraught and said: 'I hate this minutes thing; it's the worst part of my job. I feel sick, I've got a headache. Every time the minutes are given there is a row, every time.' Lisa, the assistant supervisor, was also looking very worried as the fury from the women grew. Some sat defiantly with arms folded while others talked together in small groups. The unit had disintegrated.   (Westwood 1983: 49–51)

Resistance from the workforce can materialize in a variety of ways. Strikes, walkouts, go-slows and works-to-rule are only the most visible, and organized, instances of workers' resistance. Less obvious, but at least as significant when taken in aggregate, are the countless occasions when workers deliberately, and often literally, 'put a spanner in the works' and subvert, renegotiate and reorder managerial authority through their own 'subcultures' (Roy 1954). Willis put it well when he wrote that people 'thread through the dead experience of work a living culture which isn't simply a reflex of defeat' (in Clarke *et al.* 1979: 188). Workers can sabotage machinery, limit their output, deceive the person from 'time and motion', hide in the toilets, go 'on the sick', jam the photocopier, break the drill, destroy the accounts, stop for a 'ciggy'. All these actions, and a million others, have to be coped with in some way by management. Therefore it is crucial that we take into account the subjectivity of the workforce to properly understand the development of the labour process within capitalism (Littler 1982; Jermier *et al.* 1994). Resistance is not only derivative but also determinative of the labour process (Burawoy 1985).

The organization of work

We have seen that maintaining control over a workforce is no easy task. Such a recognition has been the catalyst for a huge effort on the part of managers and a whole host of analysts, consultants and academics to devise ever more efficient methods to organize, control and increase the productivity of a workforce. Evidence of this can be seen in the seemingly never-ending stream of 'new' managerial methods and techniques, the impressive edifices of management and business schools seen in many large cities and the appearance on bestseller lists of 'management books' (Peters and Waterman 1982; Peters and Austin 1985). A former chairman of ICI, John Harvey-Jones, even fronted a popular TV series in the guise of a managerial 'troubleshooter'. In the space available we can only outline some of the more influential discussions, managerial strategies and techniques of work redesign (Thompson and McHugh 2003).

Bureaucratic control

R. Edwards (1979), in an influential study, offers a framework for understanding the development of managerial strategies in the twentieth century. This involves three stages (see box below).

A closer look

Managerial strategies

➤ **Simple control** management control via open displays of power and the personalized imposition of control and order.

➤ **Technical control** an intensive division of labour and the pacing of work via machinery (classically, the assembly line).

➤ **Bureaucratic control** managerial authority becomes increasingly depersonalized and diffused through a hierarchical system of impersonal rules and procedures. Companies use internal career ladders and labour markets to reward workers' commitment to the ideals and aims of the company. Control here is embedded in the social and organizational structure of the firm.

Although Edwards provides a useful shorthand account of attempts to exert control over the labour process, he has been taken to task over how prevalent such a system of bureaucratic control is (Grint 1998) and how successful it is in overcoming resistance and 'incorporating' the workforce. Rules and procedures, no matter how detailed, rarely cover every potentiality; control can never be that absolute. Further, rules can be subverted or they can be kept to rigidly – the basis of the long-established tactic of 'work-to-rule' – in such a way that the 'system breaks down'. The inflexible nature of bureaucratic and rigid systems can often be their Achilles' heel and when workers stop giving of themselves, organizations can often shudder to a halt (Gorz 1979).

Giving the workers some 'responsible autonomy'

Friedman (1979) points out the limitations, some of which were discussed above, of *direct control* (DC) methods (exemplified by Taylorism). He suggests that managerial strategies have emerged to overcome these limitations and increasingly involve giving the workforce a measure of what he terms '*responsible autonomy*' (RA); we can also understand these changes as being part of a move from 'low trust' to 'high trust' systems (Fox 1974). RA methods seek to empower workers by giving them some degree of control and decision making in the process of production and attempt to incorporate the 'subjectivity'

of the workers through aligning them more closely with the goals and aims of the company. This has been part of a long-standing interest in the '*humanization*' of work.

Work humanization and redesign

Two main techniques of work redesign are job rotation and job enlargement. *Job rotation* does nothing to change particular work tasks but entails moving workers around a number of jobs at regular intervals in order to reduce boredom and stimulate some interest through variety. *Job enlargement* involves merging a number of work tasks together to form a more complex and extended single operation. Obviously, these methods carry with them dangers of having the opposite effect of that intended, as both could lead to an intensification of tasks and a deterioration of working conditions.

Job enrichment revolves around an attempt to empower workers by giving them, in a way antithetical to the doctrines of Taylorism, not only a variety of work tasks but also an element of control and planning. Many repetitive and simplified production jobs could possibly be enriched 'by the inclusion of tasks such as machine maintenance, elements of inspection and quality control, or machine setting' (Fincham and Rhodes 1994: 207). Again, such methods have met with mixed success. As one worker memorably put it:

> You move from one boring, dirty monotonous job to another dirty, boring monotonous job and somehow you're supposed to come out of it all 'enriched'. But I never feel 'enriched' – I just feel knackered.
>
> (Beynon and Nichols 1977: 16)

Variants of *team working* have been tried within a wide range of organizations. *Quality circles* are the best-known method of team or group working and are most closely associated with work experiments in Japan.

In the mid-1980s, quality circles were found in at least 400 UK companies (Clarke *et al.* 1994: 366). Organizing workers into collaborative work groups obviously represents a major break from the assumptions about workers' behaviour implicit within Taylorist or DC methods. Workers themselves can decide how to overcome production problems and reach production targets instead of all such responsibility being delegated to management; in some cases workers even have the power to stop the production line. At a company level, there has been a move away from the classical bureaucratic and

World in focus

Quality circles

An aspect of the Japanese model that receives attention is *ringi seido* or bottom-up management, which is operationalized through the use of quality circles. Quality circles involve small groups of between five and ten employees who work together and volunteer to meet regularly to solve job-related problems. Usually meetings take place during company time, but the frequency varies; some are weekly while others are monthly. Normally though not always led by supervisors, circles aim to improve quality, reduce production costs, raise productivity and improve safety.

Specific characteristics distinguish quality circles from other managerial techniques such as project groups, joint problem solving and job laboratories. Firstly, quality circles have a permanent existence and meet regularly, and are not *ad hoc* creations to solve specific problems. Secondly, participants decide their own agenda of problems and priorities. Finally, all circle members are trained to use specialized tools of quality management which include elementary statistics.

Three important assumptions underlie quality circles: one, all employees, and not just managers or technical experts, are capable of improving quality and efficiency; two, among employees there exists a reservoir of relevant knowledge about work processes, which, under conventional work practices, is difficult to tap; three, quality is an integral part of the entire production process. It is not an adjunct but the responsibility of every employee.

(Clarke *et al.* 1994: 364)

---

hierarchical firm, characterized above by Edwards, towards much 'flatter' and less stratified organizations with fewer layers of middle management between the workforce and top-level management. US computer giants IBM and Compaq are examples of 'flat' organizations that also utilize team working.

Stop and think

➤ Consider the following occupations: shop assistant, waiter, teacher and cleaner. How might 'job enrichment' be applied to these jobs?

➤ What problems might arise from this?

Industrialism and de-industrialization

The march of industrialism halted?

For a long period, particularly after the Second World War, capitalism and 'industrialism' were increasingly seen as panaceas for the ills of all societies. *Convergence theory* explained how many previously diverse societies, particularly those from the Eastern bloc and the Western industrial societies, were travelling along a basically similar trajectory of social and economic development (Kumar 1978). The USA, in particular, was seen to be at the end of this long evolutionary path (Burns 1969; Kerr *et al.* 1962; Rostow 1960). The development of industrial societies in the postwar period was linked with powerful notions of 'progress' and 'modernity', and it seemed that most of the major social and economic problems in the industrialized world had either been solved or were about to be. Such extravagant claims were not solely down to the apologists for the capitalist system, as the advanced industrialized nations had indeed experienced some remarkable social changes. Unemployment had to a large extent been contained (especially when compared with the misery of mass unemployment in the 1920s and 1930s), economic growth had increased consistently, and wage levels and 'spending power' had reached unprecedented levels for many millions of people across the Western world. For the first time travel abroad became a realistic possibility for many, as did the purchase of, among many other things, cars, washing machines, television sets and record players.

To all intents and purposes capitalist industrialism, and the huge surpluses created by the manufacturing sector in particular, were seen to have solved most of the

World in focus

Japanization and 'lean production'

Japanese work organization and associated methods of *lean production* created a great deal of interest in the Western industrial world in the 1970s and early 1980s (Delbridge 1998; Sayer and Walker 1992; Thompson and McHugh 2003). At that time many envious corporate eyes were casting anxious glances to the 'East' and the spectacular growth of the Japanese economy and the success of companies such as Toyota and Nissan. Such was the impact of a fact-finding visit to Japan in 1980 on the head of Ford Europe (Bill Hayden) that it led to the company establishing a new calendar, replacing AD with AJ – 'After Japan'.

Japanization and lean production (the terms are often used interchangeably) defy precise definition being catch-all terms which describe a range of methods and production techniques, none of which are particularly original when taken in isolation. Essentially they involve a combination of the 'holy trinity' of flexibility, quality and teamwork. These elements are central to the work organization most closely associated with Japanization and lean production, also known as the *just-in-time* system (JIT). Put simply JIT 'is a system for delivering the exact quantity and defect-free quality of parts just in time for each stage of production' (Fincham and Rhodes 1994: 350). Such a system relies upon *total quality management* (TQM) whereby components must have 'zero defects' to ensure that production is not interrupted while faulty parts are being replaced. Systems of *kanban*, where components are instantly replenished when required, and of *zero stocks*, not holding 'buffer stocks' of components or partially completed assemblies, are also crucial to the smooth running of the JIT system. Work innovations such as quality circles (QCs) are used to help to ensure that production is closely monitored by workers and total quality can be maintained. Flexibility of labour is also a crucial requirement and JIT is a system that often entails the reworking of 'traditional' union practices (McIlroy 1995).

It is important, however, not to exaggerate the importance of Japanization within Western economies. In the UK (1996) there were 216 Japanese owned companies employing around 73,000 people (Delbridge 1998) compared with the half a million employed in 5,600 US companies. Also the take-up of a Japanese model by Western companies has been patchy and not enthusiastically embraced (Delbridge 1998; Thompson and McHugh 2003). Implementing QCs and JIT systems operate best within workplaces that are characterized by cultures of 'high trust' as opposed to cultures of 'low trust' – essentially the culture of 'us-and-them' – that are typical of many UK working environments. In many ways the rhetoric associated with Japanization and lean production systems operates most powerfully as a 'motivating' force for Western management and workers as companies strive to meet the challenges of a global economy. The terms also often serve as a summation of 'best practice' and a datum by which we should measure ourselves.

(Bradley *et al.* 2000)

---

pressing social and economic problems encountered in the 'Great Depression' of the 1920s. However, as the 1970s wore on, the industrial world appeared to be undergoing a series of far-reaching changes. Prime among them was the onset of *de-industrialization* – the reduction, in terms of employment and output, of the manufacturing and extractive industries. Such was the importance attached to successive developments that some thought that we were on the threshold of another 'Great Transformation' (Kumar 1978).

De-industrialization

Most advanced capitalist societies have apparently been undergoing some form and degree of de-industrialization. Although we have to be extremely careful how we measure de-industrialization (Allen and Massey 1988), for example employment can decline while output can actually increase in many industries, it seems to be the case that the composition of the workforce has changed dramatically in the postwar period. Certainly the statistics make for dramatic reading. In the UK in 1946 the manufacturing, construction and mining industries employed about 45 per cent of the labour force. By 1990 this had dwindled to around 20 per cent. The teaching profession now employs more people than mining, the steel industry and shipbuilding combined. To take the example of Scotland, one of the first industrialized nations, employment levels in a variety of occupational categories seem to show a marked shift away from the 'industrial sector'. In 1911, 183,000 people were employed in the metals, minerals and chemicals industries; by 1993 this had declined to 36,000.

During the same period employment in banking, finance, insurance and business services rose from 23,000 to an astonishing 204,000 (Lee 1995). A similar statistical profile can be shown for the UK as a whole and for other advanced industrial societies. The question arises, given the collapse of manufacturing employment and the general shrinking of industry (whatever definition we care to use), as to what extent we can continue to call a society like the UK 'industrial' in any meaningful sense? This is a question of great importance given that many of the occupations that are now disappearing were often the ones that were considered to be 'real' or 'proper' jobs. The trades, skills and work that made up these jobs – for example in mining, shipbuilding and engineering – were of course male-dominated and classic sites of masculine occupational cultures (Clarke *et al.* 1979; Morgan 1991). The iconography, meanings and powerful imagery of such occupations in many ways became synonymous, within industrial societies, with work generally and were often used erroneously as templates for all work, something, incidentally, which much 'sociology of work' – not long ago subsumed under the general heading of 'industrial sociology' – has done relatively little to counter. This is why 'de-industrialization' is about more than simply the demise of particular jobs but involves, among other things, the dismantling of social and cultural relations and a renegotiation of the meaning of work itself – particularly as a vehicle for masculinity.

At a broader level de-industrialization, given the spatial division of labour (Massey 1994), varies across geographical areas. This means that the social fabric and economies of certain regions can be particularly badly affected. This is evidenced, in the UK, in the huge pools of unemployed labour and industrial collapse of areas such as the northeast of England, Clydeside and South Wales as they deal with, often painfully felt, social and economic restructuring (Allen and Massey 1988; Massey and Allen 1988).

The coming of post-industrial society?

Some observed the changes that were taking place within many advanced industrial societies differently and in an altogether more positive and optimistic light. The collapse of employment in industry, or the manufacturing and the extractive industries to be more accurate, has been seen as symptomatic of the emergence of a new order. In particular the growth of employment in the *service sector* is seen to be a development of great significance. Some commentators argued that we are witnessing, and living through, the emergence of a new social formation – a break with previous societies that was as clear and revolutionary as the break between agricultural and industrial society.

The best-known and most influential statement of this *post-industrial* thesis or vision was put forward by Daniel Bell (1973) in *The Coming of Post-Industrial Society*. For Bell, the type of employment which is most common becomes a central and defining feature of society. Agricultural employment predominates in pre-industrial societies, factory work is the norm in industrial society and, Bell argues, employment in the service sector becomes the largest occupational category of post-industrial society.

In industrial society the rational pursuit of economic growth was the 'axial principle' around which large swathes of social and economic life were organized. People were now, according to Bell, less involved in the 'fabrication' of things and more involved in the manipulation, storing and processing of information and knowledge. For Bell, post-industrial society was also the 'information society'; information processing and knowledge generation have become the 'axial principle' of post-industrial society.

The huge advances in information technologies and global communications networks had provided the catalyst, and offered the opportunities, for a revolution in the workplace. The new types of work that people do will involve less capitalist rationalization and control and will be less alienating than the jobs associated with 'industrial society'. 'White collar' (as opposed to 'blue collar') and professional jobs would become the norm. Knowledge and 'professional elites' will hold power and influence in society and will replace the marginalized and anachronistic industrial ruling classes. Indeed, given that the old industrial working class would wither away, so too would class lose its importance as a major social divide and source of collective identity. Centres of information, knowledge, innovation and dynamism, such as universities and centres of research and development, will become the nerve centres of post-industrial society, not the factory or the industrial complexes of old. The new knowledge elites could utilize the available new technologies to plan and forecast the future more effectively, thus freeing society from the fluctuations and cyclical uncertainties of the old industry-based economy. Generally, post-industrial society would be a more stable and harmonious society in which there would be more time for creative and leisure pursuits. The drudgery of most people's work would be alleviated through the sensitive and systematic application of new technologies.

All versions of post-industrial theory (Touraine 1971) have been subjected to a sustained and thorough critique (Hall *et al.* 1992; Kumar 1978; 1995; Webster 1995), but they continue to display a remarkable longevity and resilience. Perhaps this is because they tap into widely held notions and fears about the pace of change of social and economic life and the ambiguous role of the bewildering range of new technologies. Post-industrial visions paint a generally positive and possibly comforting picture which many people find appealing and are wont to cling to. However, the shortcomings of 'post-industrial' theory are many and far-reaching.

The difficulty of defining services

The move to a service economy and the growth of people working in service occupations are central to discussions about post-industrial society and are used as incontrovertible evidence that we are undergoing a change of great significance. However, the definition of a service occupation or the service sector is notoriously difficult to achieve (Massey and Allen 1988). 'Services' are sometimes described as being 'anything that cannot be dropped on your foot', the absence of a physical product being crucial. However, we immediately run into problems, given that a wide variety of tasks which are generally included in most classifications of the service sector, such as catering, laundering and many financial services, very often do deal with a tangible product or 'thing'.

The problem of operating with a 'service sector' and 'manufacturing sector' distinction is that it blinds us to the interdependent and hugely complex nature of modern economies and the division of labour – something which Durkheim brought to our attention a long time ago. The use of labels such as 'services' and 'the service sector'

A closer look

Services

There are four different uses of the term 'services'.

➤ **Service industries** these make up the service sector.

➤ **Service occupations** these are present in all sectors of the economy and alert us to the fact that clerks, accountants, cleaners, catering staff, among others, are common and integral to many different industries and organizations, whether they be engineering plants or advertising agencies.

➤ **Service products** these refer to the fact that even manufacturing firms produce these in terms of 'follow-up services', service contracts, information services, etc.

➤ **Service functions** this category draws attention to the ways that many manufactured goods provide a 'service' to some degree, e.g. TVs and videos provide a 'home entertainment' service and washing machines and irons service people's laundry needs.

(Gershunny and Miles 1983)

tends to homogenize a heterogeneous group of activities. This is sociologically and empirically problematic as it glosses over a myriad of different labour processes, work environments and experiences. The term 'services' is a highly unsatisfactory social construction. However, it is probably unrealistic to expect people to dispense with the term completely, although we have to treat it with great caution. The 'service sector' is a 'rag-bag of industries as different as real-estate and massage parlours, transport and computer bureaux, public administration and public entertainment' (Jones, quoted in Webster 1995: 42). It is difficult to see how such a definite and crucial change as the move from industrial to post-industrial society could be based on such a flimsy and fractured foundation.

Post-industrialism: a radical change?

The extent of the change brought about by the developments discussed above is a matter of some controversy. Commentators such as Toffler (1970; 1980) maintain that we are witnessing nothing short of a revolution. However, as Kumar (1978; 1995) notes, service jobs have long been critical to any capitalist society; in fact, Scotland's 'service sector' was the major employer as long ago as 1900. No capitalist nation in fact has ever had the majority of its workforce employed in the manufacturing sector – with the exception, for a brief time, of the UK (Webster 1995). Also, post-industrial theorists give no compelling reasons as to why the decline in manufacturing jobs is such a cataclysmic change anyway. Why not, for instance, highlight the collapse of employment in agriculture and forestry? We have given some statistics which highlighted the decline of manufacturing in Scotland (p. 146). Over the same period, employment in agriculture and forestry plummeted from 238,000 in 1911 to only 27,000 in 1993 (Lee 1995). As Kumar suggests, if there has been a startling change in the structure of capitalist societies then it has been one from agricultural employment to service employment (Kumar 1978). However, we rarely hear of discussions about a 'post-agricultural society'.

Wage-labour (for Marx, the basis of the whole system of capitalist production) is still of course the predominant employment relationship. Many types of work often included within the service sector, such as work in the tourist industry, catering and cleaning, are poorly paid, casualized, characterized by insecurity and subject to the same kinds of rationalization and control that were supposed to be the preserve of industrial work.

Certainly 'fast food' restaurants, to take one example from a growing sector of employment, often display a level of control and systematization that Ford and Taylor would have been proud to have achieved. At McDonald's we are told that a 'quarter pounder is cooked for exactly 107

World in focus

McDonald's

The sheer number of fast-food restaurants has grown astronomically. For example, McDonald's, which first began franchising in 1955, opened its 12,000th outlet on March 22, 1991. By the end of 1991, McDonald's had 12,418 restaurants. The leading 100 restaurant chains operate more than 110,000 outlets in the United States alone. There is, therefore, 1 chain restaurant for every 2,250 Americans.

The McDonald's model has not only been adopted by other hamburger franchises but also by a wide array of other fast-food businesses, including those selling fried chicken and various ethnic foods (for example, Pizza Hut, Sbarro's, Taco Bell, Popeye's, and Charley Chan's) . . .

This American institution is making increasing inroads around the world as evidenced by the opening of American fast-food restaurants throughout Europe. (Not too many years ago scholars wrote about European resistance to fast-food restaurants.) Fast food has become a global phenomenon; consider the booming business at the brand-new McDonald's in Moscow where, as I write, almost 30,000 hamburgers a day are being sold by a staff of 1,200 young people working two to a cash register. There are plans to open 20 more McDonald's in the remnants of the Soviet Union in the next few years, and a vast new territory in Eastern Europe is now laid bare to an invasion of fast-food restaurants.

Already possessing a huge Kentucky Fried Chicken outlet, Beijing, China, witnessed the opening of the world's largest McDonald's, with 700 seats, 29 cash registers and nearly 1,000 employees, in April 1992. On its first day of business, it set a new one-day record for McDonald's by serving about 40,000 customers. In 1991, for the first time, McDonald's opened more restaurants abroad (427) than in the United States (188). The top 10 McDonald's outlets in terms of sales and profits are already overseas. By 1994, it is expected that more than 50 percent of McDonald's profits will come from its overseas operations. It has been announced that starting in 1992, McDonald's will start serving food on the Swiss railroad system. One presumes that the menu will include Big Macs and not cheese fondue.

(Ritzer 1993: 2–3)

Questions

1. How far do you think a society like the UK shows evidence of 'McDonaldization'? Give examples.

2. What spheres of work and employment do you think would be impossible to 'McDonaldize'?

Case study (continued)

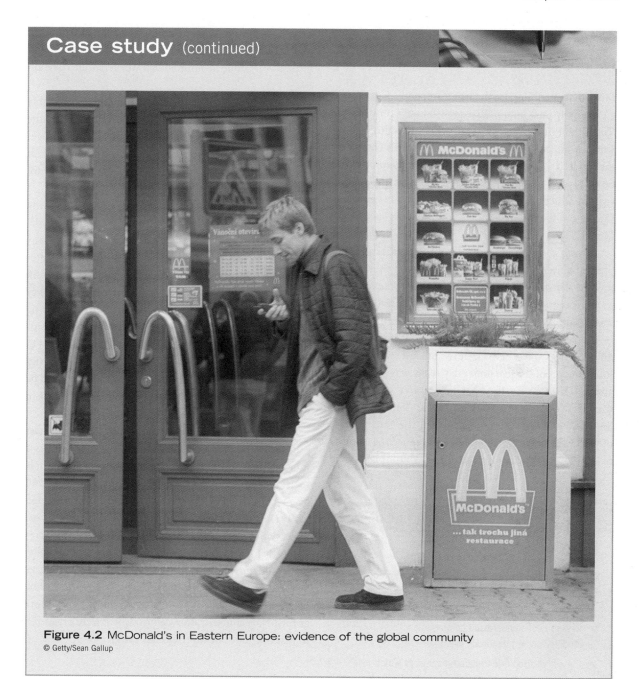

Figure 4.2 McDonald's in Eastern Europe: evidence of the global community
© Getty/Sean Gallup

seconds. Our fries are never more than 7 minutes old when sold . . . [we] aim to serve any order within 60 seconds' (quoted in Abercrombie and Warde 1992: 180).

As Beynon suggests,

If we take industrialisation to mean the production of commodities through the use of machinery aided with rational systems of organisation, the post war period can be seen as one in which areas of life hitherto un-affected by the march of capital were subjected to this process . . . Add to this the mechanisation of banking, transportation and the home and we have the bones of an on going industrialisation thesis and the *extended* rather than the *post*-industrial society.

(quoted in Abercrombie and Warde 1992: 180)

Certainly Beynon's analysis can be further supported if we look at the growth of industrialism as an international rather than a national phenomenon. Countries such as Taiwan, South Korea, Indonesia and Brazil are all experi-encing rapid economic growth which is based on an unbridled capitalist industrialism. So the case for post-industrialism becomes even more difficult to sustain if we look at the global picture (Webster 1995).

Fordism and mass production

More than anything else the image of people working on an assembly line (immortalized in Chaplin's film *Modern Times*) epitomizes the way that many of us think about work in the twentieth century. Henry Ford's creation – the Model T – has become the emblem of *mass production*. Ford pioneered the organization of mass production (within which the assembly line was only *one* element) for the production of complex commodities such as the Model T.

Of course the production of vast quantities of identical, or similar, commodities is pointless if they do not meet a demand in the marketplace. One answer was to increase the purchasing power of the workforce. This was done at Ford in 1914 through the introduction, in a qualified and partial way, of the (in)famous 'five dollar day' (Meyer 1981). It is unclear whether the introduction of the five dollar day really was a deliberate attempt to increase the spending power of the Ford workforce or, as seems more likely, was done in order to 'buy off' any organized resistance to the intense pace of work within the Detroit plant and reduce the number of employees leaving the company. Ford plants had exceptionally high levels of labour turnover: in 1913 Ford required around 13,000 workers to operate his plants and in that year alone around 50,000 workers quit (Beynon 1975: 19).

However, the growth of purchasing power for a large section of the working class during the Fordist era came to be seen as part of the Fordist 'bargain' – 'high' wages and spending power and 'continuous' employment in return for putting up with 'alienating' and repetitive work conditions.

Mass production thus required a corresponding *mass consumption*. Mass marketing and the mass media were used to 'create' demands for a bewildering array of products and commodities. Mass unionism, a state-regulated industrial relations framework and, in the realm of politics, general cross-party support over several key objectives – a commitment to 'full employment' being central – provided the essential regulatory mechanisms (often referred to in the UK as the 'postwar consensus') to keep the economy in dynamic equilibrium. Such a series of social and economic arrangements were thought to be particularly prevalent during the classic era of Fordism – roughly the postwar period up to the early 1970s.

'Fordism' has come to refer to more than the mass production of particular commodities and is used as a shorthand way to characterize the organization of a whole social system and a particular historical time period or epoch – the 'Fordist era' (Allen *et al.* 1992; Gramsci 1971; Harvey 1990). Many areas of social life and a host of activities are said to have been Fordized. Symbols of Fordism are not only automated factories, typing pools and people working 'on the line' but also large housing estates like Drumchapel in Glasgow or Hulme in Manchester, holiday camps, tower blocks and, more grimly, Nazi concentration camps, which were organized to mass-produce death (Bauman 1989).

The limits of Taylorism and Fordism: Fordism in crisis?

However, in the late 1960s and early 1970s it appeared that Fordism was showing signs of stress and breakdown. There were a series of shocks to the Fordist system, culminating in the 1973 'oil crisis'. Many Western economies were showing signs of a slowdown in economic growth and a falling away of levels of labour productivity and profits. The long and stable postwar boom was apparently coming to an end. Why? An important reason was to do with the apparent inability of the Fordist labour process

---

A closer look

Fordist mass production

Sabel describes this as 'the efficient production of one thing' (1982: 210); it operates along the following principles:

➤ long runs of standardized commodities, the Model T being the classic example;

➤ the use of fixed or dedicated machinery which is tooled up to produce many thousands of identical components;

➤ the widespread use of unskilled labour within the production process;

➤ an intensive and extensive division of labour.

With the systematic application of these fairly simple principles the Ford Motor Company was able to achieve incredible levels of relatively low-cost production, and Ford's plant in Detroit was quickly churning out vast quantities of cars; by 1913, Ford was producing around 180,000 vehicles a year, more than three times the output of all British companies (McIntosh 1991).

---

to secure further increases in productivity within the manufacturing sector and the inapplicability of Fordist methods to other sectors of the economy, especially the 'service sector'. The technical limits of Fordism had been reached. Waves of strikes across the Western world and apparently chronic and endemic problems with workforce resistance and unrest seemed to suggest that workers had also reached their limits within Fordized workplaces. The very inflexibility of the Fordist labour process was showing itself to be an unforeseen Achilles' heel. Consumers were increasingly making demands for individualized goods. Newly emerging social developments such as 'youth' and 'pop' cultures and styles, and shifting patterns of taste and demand, exposed the rigidity of Fordism. The stability of the Fordist global system, underwritten and maintained by the huge economic, financial and military might of the USA, was being challenged by the rise of other economies, especially in West Germany and Japan.

Post-Fordism and flexibility

Given the break-up of mass production, mass markets and mass consumption, some commentators have argued that we are witnessing a widespread move towards *post-Fordism* (Hall and Jacques 1989; Hall *et al.* 1992). The key term here is *flexibility*. As with the post-industrial discussion there is an important role for new technologies such as computer-integrated manufacturing systems and new social innovations at work, such as less hierarchical organizations, team working, flexi-time and a range of more flexible work practices – some of which were discussed above, particularly in relation to Japanization and lean production (see p. 145).

Some commentators see these tendencies coming together in the form of the *flexible firm*. The best-known and most influential discussion of the flexible firm is that of Atkinson (1984).

In the flexible firm, management is able to 'flex' production up and down to meet changes of demand in the marketplace. This is achieved through a reorganization of working practices, increased subcontracting and use of agency workers and employing workers on a range of different contracts of employment. This leads Atkinson to make a distinction between a group of '*core*' workers, who are multi-skilled and therefore have 'functional flexibility', and a '*peripheral*' group, who are employed variously on a part-time, seasonal or casual basis and can be hired and fired when required. This group Atkinson describes as having 'numerical flexibility'. Certainly at least one report has given some empirical support to this polarization, stating that the number of people in full-time permanent jobs has fallen dramatically from being 55.5 per cent of the workforce in 1979 to 35.9 per cent in 1993 (reported in the *Guardian* 3 April 1995).

Flexibility has become a buzzword for managers in a range of different workplaces and environments. Many areas of local government, for example, are seen to be reorganizing along more flexible and post-Fordist lines (Stewart and Stoker 1989; Burrows and Loader 1994). As a supervisor in a council cleansing department indicates, the 'new' world of flexible working practices can take its toll on workers and managers alike:

> We have had to become more 'business like' if you know what I mean, we have to price jobs up and be more careful in what we do . . . we have to respond more quickly and we have to be flexible and be able to respond immediately. Before you could leave things to the next day. Labour has to be far more flexible, work has to be done on the same day so it's important that they go out and do it and don't come back until it's finished. (McIntosh and Broderick 1996)

A closer look

Post-Fordist production

The following are the key elements of a post-Fordist labour process:

➤ flexible production systems;

➤ a move from economies of scale to economies of scope;

➤ flexible work organization – for example team working and JIT – and a concomitant restructuring of union practices and collective bargaining;

➤ a decentralization of production into more spatially diverse and smaller units;

➤ niche versus mass marketing.

Stop and think

➤ How might 'flexible' work practices benefit or disadvantage (a) management; (b) workers; (c) society as a whole?

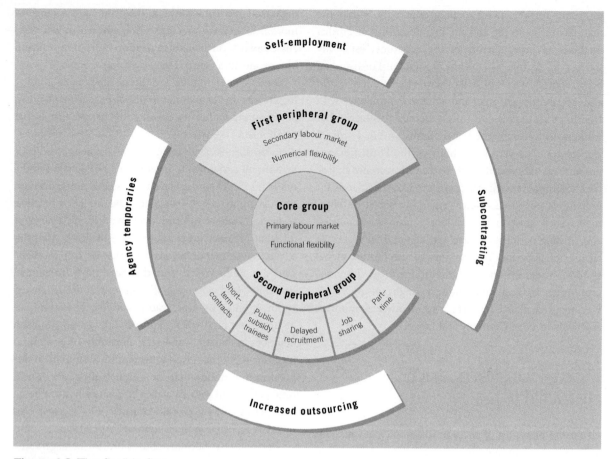

Figure 4.3 The flexible firm
Source: Atkinson 1984

The whole notion of 'flexible' working practices as a desirable, new and widespread phenomenon has come under much scrutiny (Pollert 1988a; 1988b). The bandying around of the terms 'flexibility' and 'flexible specialization' (Piore and Sabel 1984) often serves to give a gloss of sophistication to many changes that are taking place in UK workplaces. Basically, 'flexibility' often amounts to the very unsophisticated and long-established practices of shedding labour, increasing workloads and employing workers on a variety of seasonal and temporary contracts.

Similarly, the notion that post-Fordism represents a radical break from Fordism has been questioned (Hall *et al.* 1992; Kumar 1995; Sayer and Walker 1992; Webster 1995). To begin with, we have to question whether Fordism as it is often portrayed is a valid construction in the first place. Companies such as Ford have long been able to change production to meet changes in demand and have always hired and fired workers to maintain some flexibility in working arrangements. As one man who worked at Ford's Manchester plant in the 1920s says:

'If they got a bit slack they fired people and if they got a bit busy they took them on' (McIntosh 1995: 75).

Talk of Fordism's demise is also seen to be wide of the mark. Williams *et al.* (1987) point out that techniques of mass production are still very much in evidence. A whole range of 'new' commodities, such as compact disc players, dishwashers, flat-pack furniture, TVs and camcorders are still mass-produced and 'consumed' in their millions.

As with discussion of industrial and post-industrial society, debates around the move from Fordism to post-Fordism operate with sharply drawn 'binary histories' (Sayer and Walker 1992). Such a perspective can easily lead us to construct erroneous dichotomies into which we force 'relevant' bits of evidence. Underlying continuities get lost in the attempt to perceive dramatic change. The 'reality' is that Fordism and a range of flexible working practices can operate quite happily side by side – Japanese methods are a good example of this – and capitalism has long displayed an ability to adapt to changing socio-economic environments and pressures.

The labour market

When people look for employment they become involved in the *labour market*. It is through the labour market that people secure employment. We cannot understand this as a single market located at a particular place at a certain time. We have to think of the labour market in the abstract, a label attached to a hugely complex set of relationships.

A closer look

Labour market

Fevre (1992) has identified five 'functions' served by the labour market:

➤ **informing employers** about the availability of workers for employment;

➤ **informing workers** what jobs are available, through job centres, word of mouth, newspapers and other means;

➤ **screening workers** what skills and attributes workers have and how much or little they are prepared to work for;

➤ **screening employers** what the job pays and involves and how secure it is;

➤ **making an offer of employment,** which may or may not be bound up with a contract of employment.

An understanding of the workings of the labour market can have crucial implications for the way you come to view the world of work and paid labour. For some, generally on the right of the political spectrum, the labour market is seen to operate like any other: there will be a price (the wage) at which demand and supply will eventually meet. What is important for such people is that market forces should be left as far as possible to work themselves through in an unfettered manner. From this point of view there should be little or no 'interference' in the workings of the labour market from governments, trade unions and welfare systems. People should 'price themselves into a job', even if this means the driving down of wage levels. Essentially it is understood as a largely homogeneous single entity.

However, most would agree that this is a rather simplistic view of the world, although it may well have a powerful political influence. If you have looked for some paid employment you will quickly realize that the world is not so clearcut. The labour market is not a single entity but is fractured and divided and best understood as a whole series of labour markets which can operate at local, regional, national or international levels at different times and places and is always undergoing change and variation.

People enter the labour market (or a particular labour market to be more accurate) on different terms. They bring with them different resources and attributes, skills and abilities. The labour market does not operate in a vacuum but is inextricably interlinked within the society in which it operates. Thus if in society at large we see people divided and discriminated against along lines of class, gender, ethnicity or religion then it should come as no surprise to see such prejudices at work or emerging within the labour market. Sexism and racism limit the entry of women and black workers into the labour market and proscribe the kind of employment they can obtain. Similarly with people with disabilities. This is evidenced in terms of the jobs that people do and the rewards they can get. For example, women on average earn about 75 per cent of the wages that men get, even if they do similar types of work. The sexual division of work is extremely pronounced in the UK: women and men are segregated into occupations that are seen to be 'appropriate' for the genders; for example, the vast majority of clerical workers, nurses and canteen assistants are women (see pp. 294–308 for a fuller discussion of the gendered division of labour).

To take such factors into account, and to acknowledge people's differential access to the labour market, notions of the *dual* or *segmented labour market* have been put forward (Massey and Allen 1988). This corresponds closely to prior discussions of 'core' and 'peripheral' groups of workers and has similar consequences in that relatively powerless groups of workers find themselves trapped in disadvantaged 'segments' of the labour market characterized by low pay, insecurity and periods of unemployment.

More recently such apparent conditions in the labour market have led some commentators to talk of widespread insecurity and risk within the world of work and people's lives more generally (Beck 1992; Elliott and Atkinson 1999). As Heery and Salmon suggest, 'It is widely believed that jobs have become less secure, that the life-time career is disappearing and that an expanding proportion of employment contracts are temporary, part-time and contingent' (2000: xi). The evidence for, and the impact of, such changes and the growth of 'non-standard' employment is the subject of much scrutiny and debate (Bradley *et al.* 2000; Heery and Salmon 2000). The growth in part-time work, for example, may not

A closer look

International pay gap

2002	Female earnings as % male earned income	Female economic activity rate (as % of male rate), 15 plus
Argentina	37	48
Armenia	69	88
Australia	71	78
Bangladesh	56	76
Belgium	50	67
Brazil	42	52
Cambodia	77	97
Canada	63	83
Czech Republic	56	83
Ghana	75	98
Hungary	59	72
Ireland	40	53
Italy	45	59
Japan	46	68
Korea, Republic of	46	71
Lebanon	31	39
Malawi	68	90
Malaysia	40	62
Malta	37	38
Oman	22	26
Pakistan	33	44
Peru	27	44
Russian Federation	64	82
Saudi Arabia	21	29
Senegal	55	72
Singapore	50	64
Sweden	83	89
Uganda	66	88
UK	60	75
USA	62	82
Viet Nam	69	91
Zambia	55	74

Source: created from ILO & UN statistics at Human Development Reports, http://cfapp2.undp.org/statistics/data/rc_report.cfm, Aug

necessarily be a cause for insecurity for any particular individual. However, it seems clear that forms and types of paid employment we engage in have changed over the last 25 years or so and a lack of permanence and security has become a feature of many people's working lives (Heery and Salmon 2000).

Unemployment

Given previous discussion about what we actually count as being 'proper' work it follows that what 'unemployment' means is not as straightforward as we might first assume

(Whiteside 1991; Gallie 1989; Gallie *et al.* 1993). Unemployment is generally understood as referring to those out of paid employment, which as we know is a limited understanding of the notion of 'work'. Many people who are not directly involved in the formal economy often 'work' extremely hard – people (mainly women) who carry out the huge numbers of domestic tasks in the home, caring for children, elderly or sick relatives, people who might 'work' constantly on hobbies or who put in thousands of hours of voluntary work. Most of this work is generally ignored in discussions of unemployment.

However, not being part of the world of the formal economy and paid employment is most often for people a miserable state. Given the aforementioned centrality of work and the way that it can be a central source of our identity and sense of self, it should come as no surprise that to lose a job can be a devastating experience for many people (Gallie and Paugam 2000). Employment helps to provide a temporal structure without which many people become lost and stupefied. As one man says:

> I spend the odd hour or two walking up and down the stairs, counting each step. I still manage to read but my concentration is almost shot. In fact, half the time I am unable even to think. . . . I am six stones over-weight and pulling my brain and fat together isn't easy.
> (The *Independent* 9.2.94)

The loss of social contacts and being forced into a kind of semi-isolation is also a major problem for people who lose their jobs. Unemployment can also adversely affect peoples health and well-being and plunge them into a state of grinding poverty.

Official classifications of unemployment have shown a great deal of flexibility over the past 20 years. For example at least 14 changes were made to official definitions of unemployment in the period 1982–86. This had the effect of removing about 400,000 people from the total (Whiteside 1989; Gallie 1989; Gallie and Paugam 2000). Thus the current (September 2003) 'official' figure for unemployment of 1.48 million, or 5 per cent of the workforce (National Statistics Online: http://www.statistics.gov.uk/), has to be understood as just one of a variety of ways in which to measure unemployment in the UK (Centre for Economic and Social Inclusion: http://www.cesi.org.uk).

In addition unemployment levels display great regional disparities. This should come as no surprise given the variable nature of economic restructuring and processes of de-industrialization discussed above. So, in June 2003 Scotland had 5.8 per cent of its workforce unemployed, while the figure for the South-East was 4 per cent and 6.3 per cent for the North-East (National Statistics Online). These figures, which are still for big geographical areas and large populations, tend to average out the effect unemployment has on particular localities in the UK where almost no one works in full-time employment.

Unemployment also impacts differentially upon different groups within society. The unemployment rate in relation to ethnicity in the UK shows a wide variation, being 4.7 per cent for whites, 13.8 per cent for blacks and 22.9 per cent for Bangladeshis. Again this draws our attention to the way that discrimination can be structured into the workings of the labour market and

employers' strategies. Young people are often particularly affected by unemployment as the present (2003) unemployment rate of 14.6 per cent for the 16–24 age group indicates; nearly three times greater than the overall rate of 5 per cent.

We now face the very real prospect that, for the first time in the post-war period, a large number of people may never be in full-time and permanent employment. Thus whereas in the not so distant past 'full employment' was seen to be a key objective of all British governments now the very notion seems to have a rather utopian ring to it. Unemployment is in fact seen by many to be an unfortunate but unavoidable problem within modern societies. This, however, ignores the way that 'employment' and 'unemployment' are social and political categories, not timeless or immutable, and 'work' itself can be reorganized economically and reinterpreted socially and culturally in such a way that 'full employment' need not be such an unattainable goal (Dickens *et al.* 2004).

Stop and think

> ➤ How might employment be reorganized in order to reduce levels of unemployment?

> ➤ What would be the likely obstacles which would prevent such a reorganization taking place?

Trade unions

Millions of workers around the world are members of trade unions. Although the structure, size and power of unions show considerable variation, all unions attempt to provide workers with a degree of collective strength and to defend the interests of their members in relation to management and capital. In the UK, which has the world's oldest unions, they are a familiar part of the social, economic and political landscape. Unions and their activities are a constant source of copy for newspapers and the centre of endless discussions about their appropriate position and place within public life. Unions themselves often appear not to have a clearly defined role: are they defensive and sectional organizations concerned only to look after their members' pay and conditions, or can they have a more 'progressive' role in terms of being vehicles implementing partial, even revolutionary, social change? This is something of an ongoing dilemma for many unions that has never been satisfactorily resolved.

World in focus

Work and employment in the developing world

Unemployment in the developing world is frequently viewed as a symptom of unequal and inadequate development, but attempting to identify the 'unemployed' remains a highly controversial task . . . difficulties arise as attempts to measure categories of employment are generally constructed around Western concepts of work (Pahl 1988). Western theories of urban economic structure and labour force segregation have failed to adequately analyse and explain the structure of the urban labour force in developing countries. One issue which is widely agreed upon is the pressing need to work. A subject which is less clear centres on the definition of the boundary between work and employment in the developing world context.

Work undertaken outside the realms of officially accounted employment is prevalent in the urban economies of developing countries. Much productive work is undertaken outside the confines of the formal waged economy; indeed many household productive and reproductive activities are unremunerated. Informal activity, self-employment, casual work and home-based production have provided alternatives to formal employment for decades. It is important therefore to expand Western notions of work to include a wider range of social and economic activities which, due to their unregulated nature, often have most salience in urban areas.

There is also the problem of definition (Gilbert and Gugler 1992). The ILO defines the unemployed as those who are without work but who are actively seeking it. It is widely argued that the true unemployed are not amongst the urban poor. As far back as 1968 Myrdal argued that unemployment is a luxury few can afford in such circumstances . . . due to the absence of social security only educated professionals, such as white-collar workers or public sector executives, or possibly new entrants to the labour market who are able to rely on family support, contribute to the true 'unemployed' in most developing countries. As a result, Udall and Sinclair (1982) argue that the unemployment figures published by official agencies are meaningless and inappropriate, for they fail to provide a clear picture of the true structure of employment . . . Due to the inadequacy of the term 'unemployment', it is now widely recognized by researchers and academics that *underemployment* provides a better indication of the employment problem.

(Adapted from Potter and Lloyd-Evans 1998)

Questions

1. Consider the ways in which the categories of work, employment and unemployment are socially constructed and specific to particular societies.

2. In what way does considering the above passage make us question the relation and boundary between employment and unemployment?

3. Consider the relevance of using the term 'underemployment' within the context of Western economies.

Unions and social and economic change

As McIlroy says, 'Trade unions are inseparable from the society in which they are created and recreated' (1995: 1–2). Unions have been affected by, and have had to adapt to, contemporary changes to employment such as those outlined above. Membership of trade unions in the UK grew steadily through the post-war period, and union density (the proportion of employed workforce in unions) peaked in 1979 at 55 per cent – a total of just over 13 million people. In 2003, 7.3 million people were members of unions and union density has dropped to around 27 per cent. Such a figure means that the UK is still one of the most highly unionized countries in the world, although a long way behind Scandinavian countries such as Sweden, which has a union density of 80 per cent. Much of the fall in union membership can be accounted for by the impact of de-industrialization and the collapse of the manufacturing sector. Some of the UK's once largest and most powerful unions have fallen away drastically. The most dramatic example is that of the miners' union, the NUM, whose quarter-of-a-million membership in 1979 crumbled in 1998 to a mere 8,500 – a figure dwarfed by membership of the actors' union Equity, which is estimated at around 42,000.

Generally the industries that have contracted – such as mining, engineering and shipbuilding – were ones that had high union densities. A number of unions have maintained their membership at consistent levels – UNISON has a membership of 1.3 million. However, the restructuring of the economy and occupational changes have to a large extent altered the face of British trade unionism. The gender landscape of unions has changed as women are now as likely as men to be members of a trade union, with union density for both currently (2003) at 29 per cent (http://www.dti.gov.uk/er/emar/trade.htm). This challenges long-held notions that women are not 'interested' in union matters (Cockburn 1983). Women are still, however, under-represented at the top levels of union organization.

Unions themselves are having to adapt to the new labour market environment, given that the classic location for union organization was within the masculine work environments of the manufacturing industries. The post-war stability of the 'traditional' industries allowed for the development of powerful occupational cultures that provided the necessary social organization and networks and cultural resources that are crucial for the development of grassroots unionism. This form of unionism became the template for union organization in the UK, and unions are now faced with the difficult task of reorganizing and rethinking their practices to meet the demands of a post-industrial society, a fragmented workforce, the decline of full-time male employment, disparate working environments and the dispersal of plants away from the traditional urban base of British trade unionism. Lane (in Allen and Massey 1988) notes that a typical large company now has around a hundred plants dispersed around a number of 'greenfield' sites; the largest plant could employ up to a thousand workers and the smallest around fifteen. Many 'service' sector jobs (retailing, catering, tourism), all of which having been growing in employment terms, have proved difficult to unionize. Such 'industries' are characterized by high labour turnover, part-time work and short-term contracts and a lack of a 'union culture'. The Union of Shop, Distributive and Allied Workers (USDAW) has a membership of which

40 per cent are part-time, and around 30 per cent leave the union each year. The proportion of full-time employees belonging to a trade union stands at 32 per cent (2003) compared with 21 per cent for those working part-time (http://www.dti.gov.uk/er/emar/trade.htm).

Trade union power and ability to organize was also severely curtailed through the efforts of a Conservative government (1979–97) fundamentally hostile to unions. Unions in the UK have no direct or 'legitimate' role to play at a national level in terms of exerting an influence on government thinking or economic policy. Throughout the 1980s and 1990s, a range of sweeping legislation – for example, the Employment Acts of 1980, 1982 and 1988 and the Trade Union Act 1984 to mention a few – were passed with the aim of limiting the effectiveness of unions in defending their members' interests. What constitutes a 'proper' and 'lawful' trade union dispute has been limited, time off from work for union representatives has been reduced, all secondary action is now unlawful, seven days notice is now required for industrial action, and a host of other attacks (McIlroy 1995) on union power have severely limited their range of operation (Gospel and Wood 2003).

Unions have also had to face the might of giant 'transnational corporations', which can move production around the globe and set up plants in a number of different countries. Multinational companies can thus undermine national agreements and put immense pressure on unions to meet their demands for accepting no-strike deals, single-union agreements and flexible work practices. If unions do not accept such conditions, these giant enterprises can simply build their plant somewhere else. Ford did exactly this when it laid down a variety of conditions to unions before commencing building a factory in Dundee in 1987; when the unions involved failed to reach an agreement Ford built the proposed Dundee plant in Portugal.

Unions, then, face difficult times but their resolve and importance – at least as defensive organizations – should not be underestimated. There has been very little decline in union organization in workplaces where collective bargaining was already well established, and workplaces with over 200 employees largely continue to keep union recognition and organization (*Socialist Review* March 1995). According to numerous opinion polls and surveys, unions are regarded in an overwhelmingly positive manner. Eight out of ten people see unions as being essential for defending workers' rights, and only a minority of people think they have 'too much power' (McIlroy 1995). Thus despite the formidable challenges to unions it is clear that they will continue to play a crucial role in millions of people's working lives (Gospel and Wood 2003).

The globalization of economic life

The world, it is often said, is getting smaller, or as Harvey (1990) would have it, we are witnessing 'time–space compression'. This certainly seems to be the case in respect of the movement of capital around the world. Capitalism has long operated at an international level (Hirst and Thompson 1996). However, capitalist economies since the late 1960s have become increasingly integrated, encouraging talk of a 'global capitalist system' or a 'world economy' (Frobel *et al.* 1980). Production, trade and finance, with the aid of new information technologies, satellite and telecommunication systems, can now be organized at a global level rather than at a national or even international level. The most obvious protagonists of this capitalist world system are the multi-national or *transnational corporations* (TNCs). TNCs are the linchpins of what Frobel *et al.* (1980) call the 'new international division of labour'. Car firms such as Ford in the early 1970s began the production of their 'world car', the Fiesta, and reorganized production around the globe. Carburettors and distributors were built in Belfast, axles were built in Bordeaux and various bits of assembly were put together in plants in the UK, Spain and Germany. The world market allows TNCs such as Ford to distribute and sell products to all corners of the globe. Although it is important to note that most of the investment by TNCs is *within* the 'industrialized' nations, production can also be relocated in order to tap into cheap, and generally non-unionized, pools of labour in many 'developing' countries. The breakdown of production processes means that each operation can be done with minimal levels of skill, so labour need have few industrial skills.

Such a relocation and restructuring of capital has huge implications for work and employment in the 'old' centres of production and industry such as the UK. Increased competition from around the world and the movement of sites of production can accelerate the process of de-industrialization and decimate regional economies; we have only to think of the catastrophic impact that global competition in the shipbuilding industry had on regions in the UK such as Tyneside and Clydeside.

It is also increasingly difficult to think of these vast organizations as actually 'belonging' to a particular country in any meaningful way. One of the flagships of UK multinational capital, ICI, employs more people in its plants outside the UK than it does within the UK. Thus to what extent we can still apply a 'British' tag to a company like ICI, or BP for that matter, has to be cast in some doubt; indeed, firms such as ICI and BP *prefer* to be known as 'international companies'.

Some sectors of the UK economy, and thousands of jobs, are very dependent on and integrated into the global economic system. This is most obviously the case with the vast array of financial institutions and companies that comprise the City of London. London is one of the big three financial nerve centres of the global economy; New York and Tokyo are the others. It has more than 30 per cent of the world's foreign exchange business (nearly twice that of New York) and has more US banks than New York and more German banks than Frankfurt and 375 of the biggest 500 companies have offices there (*Europe: Magazine of the European Union* 1999 http://www.eurunion.org/magazine/home.htm).

Although not all parts of the UK economy are so globalized as the City of London, hundreds of thousands of jobs in the UK are closely linked to a global economy, a situation which brings both benefits and costs. The movement of UK Call Centres to Asia has highlighted the precarious nature of this connection. Over 10,000 jobs have been relocated to Asia (out of a UK total of 800,000) and this figure is expected to grow dramatically – in the USA half a million jobs in the financial sector have been 'offshored', mainly to the Philippines and India (*Sunday Herald* 30/11/03). The major reason given for this is cheaper costs due to the ability to pay lower wages in these countries.

TNCs are huge; financially relatively few countries are bigger than the largest TNCs. The revenues of the top 500 global companies (cf. *Fortune* Global 500 http://www.fortune.com/fortune/fortune500) amount

Figure 4.4 A call centre operative in India
© Sherwin Crasto/Reuters/Corbis

to over $11 trillion (a thousand billion), their assets exceed $32 trillion and they employ around 35 million people (Sklair 2001). By way of comparison the combined GDP of New Zealand, Greece, Egypt, South Africa, Czech Republic and Israel was $540 billion in 1998 (Held 2000). Indeed, of the largest 100 'economies' in the world 51 are global corporations and only 49 are countries. Their immense economic power means that they set the tone in terms of pricing, market innovation and leadership, and control of subsidiaries. Given the gargantuan size, huge resources and economic, political and financial power of TNCs it is debatable as to what extent we can still meaningfully talk about 'national economies'. The management of TNCs are not noted for paying too much attention to the dictates of 'national economic policy' – if nations do not want them to locate production on their territory (very unlikely given that most national governments actively compete with each other to offer the most attractive packages for TNCs to locate production within their borders) they can move to another, more amenable, part of the globe. Other supranational organisations such as the World Bank, the EC and the International Monetary Fund have all had the effect of eroding the sovereignty of nation states and limit their ability to withstand worldwide competitive pressures and offer protection to national industries and jobs.

However, it is important not to exaggerate the ability, or desire, of huge companies to move freely around the globe. Transnational corporations originate in a relatively limited number of wealthy countries (in particular Japan and the USA) and, although they account for about 25 per cent of world production, the vast bulk of their global trade, jobs and profits are shared between these already rich and powerful nations (Cohen and Kennedy 2000; Hirst and Thompson 1996). But there is little doubt that increasing processes of globalization will continue apace and the capitalist global economy looks set to wield its immense power over us for some time to come (Bauman 2000).

Summary

➤ Defining precisely what constitutes 'work' is problematic. 'Wage-labour', or 'paid employment', is often equated with work generally, but much unpaid and largely unacknowledged work gets done in contemporary societies.

➤ The classical and most influential discussion of wage-labour within capitalism is that of Karl Marx.

➤ Braverman (1974) utilized and extended Marx's analysis of the labour process and applied it to work in the twentieth century. Braverman thought that work had undergone a process of 'deskilling' and that the main catalyst for this was attempts by management to exert total control over the workforce. Taylorism exemplified this managerial strategy.

➤ Braverman has been strongly criticized on a number of points. The widespread influence of Taylorism has been questioned. Braverman's understanding of 'skill' was seen to be lacking and he failed to take adequate account of workers' resistance.

➤ A wide range of managerial strategies have been developed to control and maximize the productivity of a workforce. This has included giving the workforce some 'responsible autonomy', 'humanizing' work tasks and the reorganization of work through team working and 'Japanese' methods.

➤ Industrialization was seen by many to be an inevitable tendency for most countries of the world; however, this was put in doubt with the emergence of 'de-industrialization' and the decline of employment in a number of sectors of industry.

➤ Writers such as Bell (1973) foresaw the emergence of a 'post-industrial' society based on an economy where employment in the 'service sector' was dominant. Such ideas have been criticized as being overly optimistic, inaccurate and based on an erroneous interpretation of changes taking place within many capitalist societies.

➤ Fordism is a term used to describe a socio-economic system based on mass production and mass consumption, which was seen to be dominant during the post-war period. It is argued that Fordism reached its limits in the early 1970s and was increasingly replaced with more flexible methods of production and work organization. The term 'post-Fordism' is often used to describe these changes. The distinction between Fordism and post-Fordism has been criticized for being too polarized and based on an empirically weak foundation.

➤ Labour markets are where employers and prospective employees can 'meet' and/or gather information about each other. Labour markets can often display similar patterns of racism and sexism that are present within wider society to the extent that we can talk of dual or segmented labour markets.

➤ Unemployment is a feature of many modern societies and is generally experienced as a profoundly depressing and miserable state for most individuals. Rates of unemployment vary for different regions and for different 'groups' of people.

➤ Trade unions are a crucial part of our society. Unions have had to adapt to a changing socio-economic environment brought about by de-industrialization, falling membership, hostile legislation and transnational corporations, but they still provide an important function for millions of workers.

➤ Capitalism has to be understood as a world phenomenon. Production, trade and finance, with the aid of new information technologies, satellite and telecommunication systems, can now be organized at a global level, and massive transnational corporations wield enormous power and influence around the world.

Links

The section on Marx and the labour process within capitalism can be related to the discussion on Marx's analysis of capitalism in Chapter 2, pages 50–5.

The discussion of the globalization of economic life, pages 158–9, is developed in Chapter 11.

The section on unemployment, pages 154–5, links to the discussion on unemployment and ethnicity on pages 336–8.

 ## Further reading

Braverman, H. (1974) *Labour and Monopoly Capital: The Degradation of Work within the Twentieth Century*, New York: Monthly Review Press.
Regarded as a classic Marxist analysis of work in the twentieth century.

Brown, R.K. (ed.) (1997) *The Changing Shape of Work*, Basingstoke: Macmillan.
An excellent overview of the major issues and changes in the contemporary world of work.

Gallie, D. and Paugam, S. (eds) (2000) *Welfare Regimes and the Experience of Unemployment in Europe*, Oxford: Oxford University Press.
A detailed analysis of unemployment throughout Europe.

Gospel, H. and Wood, S. (eds) (2003) *Representing Workers: Trade Union Recognition and Membership in Britain*, London: Routledge.
A comprehensive look at contemporary trade unions in the UK.

Grint, K. (1998) *The Sociology of Work*, 2nd edn, Cambridge: Polity Press.
Concise introduction to the major issues in the sociology of work.

Kumar, K. (1995) *From Post-Industrial to Post-Modern Society*, Oxford: Blackwell.
Balanced discussion of post-Fordism, the 'information society' and postmodernism.

Thompson, P. and McHugh, D. (2003) *Work Organisations*, 3rd edn, London: Palgrave Macmillan.
The 3rd editon of a text that continues to provide a clear guide to major changes taking place in work organizations.

Webster, F. (1995) *Theories of the Information Society*, London: Routledge.
Contains critical discussions of post-industrialism and post-Fordism.

Webster, J. (1996) *Shaping Women's Work: Gender, Employment and Information Technology*, London: Longman.
Shows how gender relations in the workplace and the sexual division of labour affect the direction and pace of technological change. An innovative look at a major service sector which combines theory with empirical research.

 ## Web sites

Globalisation Guide
http://www.globalisationguide.org/09.html
A useful source of information on various issues to do with globalization. Also has numerous helpful links to other sites.

National Statistics Online
http://www.statistics.gov.uk/
An invaluable and huge source of information on many aspects of UK employment, unemployment, the labour market and much more.

Trades Union Congress
http://www.tuc.org.uk/
A good source of information on trade unions.

Activities

Activity 1

Full-time workers fall by 35 per cent

The proportion of the working population in full-time tenured employment has fallen by about 35 per cent over the last 20 years, says a new economic report released today, and 15 per cent of British homes now have no member in work.

Paul Gregg and Jonathan Wadsworth of the Centre for Economic Performance at the London School of Economics and the National Institute for Economic and Social Research say only 35.9 per cent of the working population held full-time tenured jobs in 1993, down from 55.5 per cent in 1975.

In a survey of the British labour market in the current edition of the Oxford Review of Economic Policy they report that jobs have become much more unstable with the typical duration of any individual's job falling by 20 per cent over the last 20 years.

However, while the average man's job now lasts 6.4 years compared to 7.9 years in 1975, women's employment patterns have become stabler – with the median job for a woman lasting 4.3 years in 1993 compared to 3.9 years in 1975, still lower than men's.

Labour turnover is rising especially for older workers and for unskilled men, they say. More and more older men are leaving the labour market altogether, and this has been driving the decline in full-time tenured jobs.

The jobs market is becoming two-tiered with a secondary sector 'characterised by higher labour turnover among the least skilled, young, and old and those in atypical employment'. A new insecurity has been concentrated on a minority for whom a job for life will be the 'stuff of legends'. But they dismiss government claims that this flexible labour market is necessary for employment.

They argue that 'current patterns of job creation are becoming less and less helpful in reducing the unemployment count'. The consequence will be 'long-run poverty among families systematically disenfranchised' from earning a living.

(Will Hutton, the *Guardian* 3.4.95)

Questions

The Guardian *report indicates that a series of dramatic changes may be taking place to the labour market and the nature of employment in the UK.*

1. What are these changes?

2. How might these developments be explained by someone adopting (a) a 'post-Fordist'; (b) a 'post-industrial'; (c) a Marxist perspective?

3. What impact do you think the tendencies noted in the report will have for trade union organization in UK workplaces?

Activity 2

Working in a nursing home

This article is drawn from ethnographic doctoral research undertaken in two homes for older people in the south-west of England.

The bedroom job

The bedroom was the main site of work for the auxiliaries and most of the patients' time in the home was spent there. Morning work was virtually all bedroom work and was officially begun by the auxiliaries entering patients' rooms on the tea round. This was a point of the day at which cups of tea were served and bottoms

Activities (continued)

were washed. It was customary to present the patients to the new shift intact, clean and quiet in their rooms for 8am. Presenting well-ordered bodies seemed to symbolise the job properly done. The next shift spent all the morning in the bedrooms, washing and dressing patients. The workers spent most of the morning getting patients ready, then taking them down to the lounge. By lunch time they were all down, but straight after lunch it was time to put them back to bed for a nap and later get them up again.

In the evenings work again revolved around the bedrooms as staff got patients ready for bed. By the time the night shift came on all patients were in bed. In this way the auxiliaries' work could be said to revolve around the bedroom. And it was in this private world that they were able to decide the rules and had total hidden control.

Making jokes at the patient's expense was seen as 'having some fun with the patients' (Vera) and workers argued it involved patients in some way with the work. For example, patients who could not walk properly were told to 'race' down the corridor, and jokes would be made about Nigel Mansell etc. Patients who were crying in pain would be told to buck up and smile. Mimicry was also common, with staff copying the words of confused residents. Most patients either could not hear, see or understand jokes that the workers made at their expense, while others became distressed at them. But 'joking' appeared to help auxiliaries get through the work; it broke up the stress and gave them some sort of control.

The hard culture

Auxiliary work in nursing homes is hard work: low paid, low status, dirty, physically back-breaking and tiring. However, far from complaining about the conditions of their work the nursing auxiliaries appeared to have elevated the notion of personal hardship with their subculture. Personal hardship and hard behaviour towards patients seemed central to auxiliaries' understanding of what they were supposed to do. They spoke about others, such as residential home workers, and trained staff, as too 'soft'. A strong emphasis was placed upon coping and getting on with the work, even avoiding the use of hoists and aides, despite a frequency of serious back problems.

Auxiliaries were not only trying to make sense of their work, given the poor working conditions, but also to make it easier and give themselves a clear role and place in relation to trained nursing workers. In response to this the auxiliaries at Cedar Court became the 'hardest' workers.

(Lee-Treweek 1994)

Questions

1. *The jobs discussed in the above extract are ones that are generally considered to be part of the 'service sector'. Do you think that they fit well into Bell's vision of 'service employment' in a 'post-industrial' society?*

2. *Can we draw any parallels between the work discussed by Lee-Treweek and work that takes place in other environments such as industry? You should have another look at the case study 'Factory Time' on p. 140.*

Chapter 5

Politics

[Politics is] the authoritative allocation of values in society.　　　**(David Easton)**

Politics is the process by which it is determined who gets what, when, and how.
　　　　　　　　　　　　　　　　　　　　　　　　　　　　　(Harold Laswell)

Key issues

➤ What is politics? To what extent are definitions of politics themselves 'political'?

➤ What are political *institutions*? What are the differences between national and international institutions?

➤ What are the main factors shaping political behaviour?

➤ Has there been a move away from an 'old politics' to a 'new politics' in the last forty years?

Introduction

In this chapter the emphasis is on how politics influences and is influenced by relationships between people, rather than on the finer details of how political systems are organized. Brief descriptions will be provided of some aspects of political systems, but these are intended to give a grounding to our principal analysis of people and

politics. The primary focus is on *political sociology*: the study of how human beings interact when they attempt to distribute the benefits and burdens of living together under authoritative institutions. Politics is about both conflict and co-operation. Without conflict there would be no need for institutions to allocate resources and determine the values of society, but without the possibility of co-operation – that is, the idea of politics as a 'non-zero-sum game', meaning that a gain for one person need not result in the loss for another – human beings would not readily submit to political institutions.

Definitions of 'politics' are problematic. The term is derived from the Greek word for 'polis', meaning a 'city', the central focus for public debate in ancient Greece.

But this is a narrow definition. A narrow definition is primarily concerned with descriptions of how formal institutions and systems function, evolve and adapt (as, for example, in the United Nations: see pp. 173–4). Wider definitions tend to encompass more than the formal, or institutional, aspects of social co-operation; they extend to class and gender relations. Politics, widely defined, is concerned with the subtle, as well as the obvious, exercise of power; as such, wider definitions tend to be more interesting to sociologists.

The concept of 'democracy' provides a focus for many of the themes encountered in political sociology, and again there are disagreements about how the term should be defined. Even the simple definition of 'rule by the people' (from the Greek words *demos*, meaning 'people', and *kratia*, meaning 'rule') tells us very little. In ancient Greece all 'citizens' were entitled to influence government – but women and slaves were excluded from citizenship. A simple definition of 'democracy' as 'rule by the people' therefore ignores important, and possibly 'concealed', power relationships. Wider definitions would include recognition of those who are excluded from influence. According to Riley (1988: 15–16) democracy is 'a variable concept, meaning popular control of those in power. It stresses certain basic rights: to assemble, to criticize, to vote unhindered by the authorities, to hold minority opinions and free elections.' This variable concept is rather more clearly defined when applied to 'liberal democracy', that is, a political system characterized by regular and free elections, representative institutions of government, and guarantees of individual rights.

We begin by looking at political institutions in Britain, and then widening the study out to international institutions, before considering the behavioural aspects of politics. It is important to make some distinctions regarding the academic study of politics (or political science). In, for example, universities, the study of politics is subdivided into: (a) comparative politics – the comparison of the political systems of different countries; (b) international politics (or, more specifically, international *relations*) – the analysis of global politics as a whole; (c) political behaviour – the study of individual and group behaviour, including the origin of political values. Our prime focus is on British politics, but we adopt a comparative approach to its study, because it is important to recognize that social and political change is part of a global process. We then briefly consider the international political system, and look in some detail at political behaviour, which includes such things as political activism and voting behaviour.

A closer look

Giddens on democratization

Giddens criticizes the 'fragile flower' theory of democratization, which assumes that although liberal democracy is spreading to many countries (because it is a superior system) it needs the fertile environment of a civic culture. This theory is challenged by the findings that some liberal democracies were established quickly, and apparently without a fertile environment (e.g. Germany and Japan after the war), yet are relatively stable.

Giddens prefers the 'sturdy plant' theory, which does not associate democracy simply with liberal democracy.

'Democracy is perhaps a sturdy plant that can in fact root in what was previously quite stony soil; it does not necessarily depend upon a long-established civic culture; but rather upon other structural conditions that on occasion can be put in place rather quickly. It is always probably vulnerable, but may have more inherent strengths than other competing types of political system or legitimation.' (Giddens 1996: 70)

He situates debates about democratization in the context of three major social developments:

1 *Globalization.* This 'is best understood as being about transformations of space and time, particularly the expansion of what I would call 'action at a distance' in our lives' (Giddens 1996: 70–1). These processes 'are complex, ambivalent and contradictory; they produce an accentuating of local identity, alter the conditions even of personal identity and transfigure many forms of localism. They also generate new institutions' (Giddens 1996: 71).

2 *De-traditionalization.* This is associated with the rise of new social movements (such as the women's movement) and 'newly visible worlds and ways of life' (Giddens 1996: 72). However, various forms of fundamentalism have emerged as a reaction and challenge to de-traditionalism.

3 *Higher levels of social reflexivity* in an environment in which 'Anatomy is no longer destiny and gender is no longer fate. In most areas of social life, whether they be affluent or less privileged, most people have to take a variety of life decisions that cannot be settled by appeal to past tradition' (Giddens 1996: 73).

'The outcome of these changes is that an increasingly active, reflective citizenry both demands democratisation and at the same time becomes disenchanted with politics. Political authoritarianism has scarcely disappeared and indeed this is all too evident in different parts of the world. Yet the counterpressures are also increasingly strong. Authoritarian regimes become vulnerable for much the same reason as bureaucratic organisations of the Weberian type become social dinosaurs.' (Giddens 1996: p. 74)

Having observed a growing disenchantment with politics, Giddens provides a more positive note by considering the possibility for the 'democratizing of democracy'. This would include various elements, for example:

➤ As the public domain has become more visible, influences such as patronage may be actively condemned.

➤ Power may also be devolved upwards and downwards; at global and local levels, to international organizations or to what Ulrich Beck (1992) calls the 'sub-politics' of everyday life.

➤ An effective 'dialogic democracy' would mean that more people may be able to have a say. Indeed (as global communications systems bring together people of different groups and cultures who are geographically distant) this is regarded as essential if communications are to thrive rather than degenerate.

➤ Efforts would be made to establish in political relationships those elements of a 'good relationship' that are promoted at a more personal level.

There is remarkable similarity between what a good relationship is like, as diagnosed in the literature of therapy and self-help, and the properties of formal democracy in the political sphere. A good relationship, in brief, is one in which each individual accepts that the other is independent and equal; problems in a relationship are settled through discussion, rather than coercion or violence; the relationship is an open and mobile one, corresponding to the changing needs of each partner, and negotiation and compromise are central. These traits could very well be taken as constitutive of a democratic polity, at least in the sense of deliberative democracy (Giddens 1996: 78).

Questions

1. *Is there really a process of globalization? Can you give everyday examples of globalization?*

2. *If there is a process of globalization, what are its good and bad consequences?*

3. *Do 'new social movements' undermine or reinforce democracy?*

Political structures in Britain: a comparative perspective

In this section we look at British political structures. Political systems differ, even where there are shared political values: all countries in the European Union can be described as liberal democracies, but there are significant institutional differences between, for example, the United Kingdom, Germany, France, Belgium and the Netherlands. Many of these differences can be accounted for in sociological terms as responses to cultural, ethnic, linguistic and religious 'cleavages'. But all political systems – or at least, all systems in advanced industrial countries – attempt to address fundamental social needs, among which are: (a) the necessity for reliable, public rules – that is, there must be institutions which issue laws; (b) the generation and maintenance of wealth – an effective economic system; (c) accommodation of different forms of diversity, such as religious diversity; (d) representation of the nation-state in the international arena.

With regard to (a), all European political systems make a distinction between three branches of the state: legislature, executive and judiciary (note the distinction between state and government: the *state* is an abstract, coercive power, which embraces all three branches, whereas the *government* is the executive branch of the state). Some political systems, such as the USA, maintain a strict separation of powers between the three branches, whereas others, such as the UK, allow for a degree of 'fusion' of powers – although the judiciary remains independent of the executive, some judges sit in Parliament (the Law Lords in the House of Lords) and certain government ministers have quasi-judicial powers.

Head of state

We have made a distinction between state and government, and in many political systems the head of state is not the head of government. This is the case in the UK, but not in France or the USA. The UK, however, among a minority of advanced industrial societies, is a 'constitutional monarchy' in which the head of state is selected by hereditary principle. Most other countries have an elected head of state; in some cases election is by the legislature – the German president is elected by the convention consisting of the federal and regional parliaments – or directly by the people, as in Ireland.

The British monarch, presently Queen Elizabeth II, retains considerable formal power but, in practice, she acts on the advice of her ministers, most of whom are elected members of parliament. These so-called 'prerogative powers' are effectively concentrated in the hands of the prime minister. The Queen does, however, have weekly 'audiences' with the prime minister and, given that the Queen has reigned for over fifty years, she has considerable reserves of experience, and quite possibly can influence the prime minister – we say 'quite possibly' because the audiences are confidential, one-to-one meetings, at which no minutes are taken. The powers of the British monarchy are often thought to be greater than those of other European monarchies, such as the Netherlands, Denmark and Spain. But, in fact, because the Netherlands has a multi-party political system, in which no one party ever has a parliamentary majority, the Dutch monarch (presently Queen Beatrix) appoints an 'informateur', who is often a party leader and potential new prime minister. The identity of that person is often an indication of the monarch's ideas about the political complexion of the new government. The norm in Britain is for single-party, majority government and so the role of the Queen in government formation is largely 'formal' – she invites the person whom she believes can command majority support in the House of Commons to form the government.

Much media attention in Britain focuses on the social life of the Royal Family, and from a sociological perspective the 'soap opera' dimension of the monarchy cannot be completely detached from the politics of the monarchy. The legitimacy of the monarchy depends on continued popular approval – as the present Queen once said, the prime minister and his government face an election every four or five years, but I must face public opinion every day. Some critics of the monarchy, such as Tom Nairn (Nairn 1988), maintain that the monarch stands atop, and reinforces, an apex below which is a rigid class structure. Others echo this comment by arguing that the continuation of the monarchy is a sign of social and political immaturity, and the hereditary principle is an anachronism.

Against these critics, there are distinct liberal democratic arguments for the monarchy: (a) the head of state has no party political history, unlike almost all successful candidates in Germany or Ireland; (b) relatedly, there are no divisive periodic elections – remember, that the head of state should stand above party politics; (c) loyalty is to the crown, rather than to the 'people'. This last point is particularly important. The concept of the 'people' seems democratic and inclusive, but it frequently is not, for it

implies distinct characteristics, which may be ethnic or linguistic. It is notable that the Queen goes out of her way to embrace cultural and ethnic diversity.

The constitution and sovereignty

The constitution is a set of rules which determine what is, or is not, legitimate 'law'. If you like, the constitution is like the rules of a game, such as football, or chess: it determines what are, or are not, valid 'moves'. The UK has a partially written, or 'uncodified', constitution, consisting of 'conventions' and entrenched Acts of Parliament. Almost all other countries have codified constitutions, and constitutional courts charged with interpreting the constitution. In theory, the British Parliament can pass any laws it wishes and one parliament cannot bind a future one; in practice, certain Acts have a special status – they are 'entrenched'. The Act which limits the lifetime of a parliament to five years, except when both Houses and the Monarch permit an extension – the parliament elected in 1935 was extended to 1945 because of the 1939–45 War – is entrenched. Sovereignty – the ultimate source of authority, or legality – is vested in the 'Queen (or King) in Parliament', meaning that parliament has three parts (elected commons, unelected lords, monarch), each of which must approve legislation according to a set of rules. The House of Lords cannot, however, block a 'Money Bill' (the government's budget, or taxation and spending proposals), and can only *delay* other legislation. Once approved by both Houses, the Queen must give her 'assent' to a Bill in order for it to become law – the last time assent was refused was 1707. Other countries express sovereignty in different ways; in the USA sovereignty is effectively located in the Constitution.

The legislature

The legislature in any state may do one, or all, of the following: (a) pass laws; (b) scrutinize the executive (government ministers); (c) supply personnel to the executive; (d) represent the views and interests of the voters of particular electoral districts. In the UK, the elected House of Commons does all four things; in the USA, the separation of powers means that the legislature (Congress, which consists of two houses: House of Representatives and the Senate) cannot supply members of the government, or administration.

Some states (New Zealand and various Scandinavian states) have a unicameral (one house) legislature. As in the USA and many other European countries, Britain has a bicameral parliament, which means that there are two chambers – the House of Commons (lower house) and the House of Lords (upper house) – although the word 'parliament' is often used to refer to only the House of Commons and its 646 members (in 2005) of parliament (MPs).

Although debates about the election of MPs will be considered later it is clear that the legitimacy of the House of Commons is rarely challenged. The nature and legitimacy of the 'upper house', however, has been subject to criticism for many years. Its traditional function has been to scrutinize and approve Bills from the House of Commons and it may suggest amendments to those Bills. If it fails to give approval, its decisions tend to be (eventually) overridden by the House of Commons. Members of the 'upper house' can introduce private members' Bills and raise and discuss issues that the 'lower house' is unwilling to raise (sometimes because elected MPs need to maintain popularity with voters). As the UK does not observe the doctrine of the separation of powers, the 'upper house' also includes experienced judges (Law Lords), who can act as a court of appeal. Some members of the 'upper house' are also government ministers, although not democratically elected and having attained that status because of past achievements (usually in some form of public service).

While fulfilling an important role, the House of Lords has never been able to claim to be a representative assembly, because some of its members inherited their position and the rest are appointed, largely on the recommendation of the political parties. A major reform took place in 1999, when most of the hereditary peers (Lords) were removed. The resulting House of Lords contained (as of 2005) 695 peers, of whom 88 were hereditary, 578 were life peers (appointed for life) 26 were 'Lords Spiritual' (Church of England Bishops) and 2 were royalty (they do not attend). This compared with a pre-1999 House of well over 1,000 peers – the largest upper chamber in the world – of whom a majority were hereditary. It is worth comparing the political balance of Lords and Commons. The Labour Party won the 2005 election with 356 seats, compared with 197 for the Conservatives, 62 for the Liberal Democrats and 31 others. In the Lords the composition (as of 2005) was: 203 Labour; 202 Conservative; 69 Liberal Democrat; 219 Cross-Benchers (really Independents, but tending towards the right), Independents (proper) and Lords Spiritual. The Conservative Party still enjoys a relative advantage in the Lords, but that advantage has been much reduced: in 1996, in a much larger Lords, 476 peers were Conservatives and 108 were Labour (and Cross-Benchers tend to vote with Conservatives). Lords reform has been a thorny issue for over one hundred years: the challenge is to create a second chamber which acts as a check on the elected chamber, but which has some legitimacy though not too much. A wholly *directly* elected second chamber would assert itself against the first chamber and there would be potential 'gridlock', especially if the two chambers were controlled by different parties. Britain is not unique in facing these problems; while other countries have the advantage of federalism, which allows for *indirect* elections by regional assemblies, they can still face gridlock. This has been especially the case in Germany, where there is a Social Democratic–Green (red–green) majority in the directly elected *Bundestag*, but a centre-right majority in the indirectly elected *Bundesrat*.

Head of Government

In Britain the electoral system means that the prime minister must be leader of the party with a majority in the House of Commons. Since the prime minister exercises prerogative powers, he often acts as if he were head of state, rather than merely head of government. It is a common criticism of the British prime minister that he is 'presidential', with the implication that he abuses his power. In popular discussions Margaret Thatcher (prime minister 1979–90) has been identified as the first 'Presidential' prime minister, and Tony Blair (prime minister since 1997), it is argued, is even more presidential. In fact, the nature of the post means that any effective prime minister will behave as more than *primus inter pares* (first among equals), and there were many presidential prime ministers before Thatcher.

The prime minister's role in various other European states has evolved in different ways to that of the British prime minister. In France the prime minister is subordinate to the president, who is head of state and has the greater control of government policy. Other countries are closer to Britain, but there are key differences: (a) multiparty systems, such as the Netherlands or the Scandinavian countries, tend to produce weaker, *primus inter pares* models; (b) in some systems the prime minister must be nominated as such prior to the election – this is the case in Germany where the chancellor must be a 'chancellor-candidate' (*Kanzlerkandidat*); other countries, such as Ireland, require a parliamentary vote.

Cabinet government

The British cabinet consists of ministers responsible for the main executive functions of the government. There are so many junior ministers that the cabinet would no longer be a small forum for debate if all were included; it therefore comprises senior ministers but can call other ministers to attend. All junior and senior ministers are appointed by the prime minister and are members of the party with a majority in the House of Commons, although they can come from either House (and, technically, from outside parliament, although this is very rare).

Throughout the twentieth century, and into the twenty-first, cabinets have been criticized for not including a representative social mix. Conservative cabinets, in particular, were criticized for being mostly (sometimes entirely) male, middle-class or upper-class, privately educated graduates and businessmen. The salaries of government ministers are high in relation to average wages, but considered relatively low compared with those of heads of industry or with their counterparts in other states. This means that their salaries are often cited as one of the reasons why former ministers engage in financial activities after leaving office, and often exploit the expertise and contacts acquired in government.

Before the 1970s there were two commonly recognized conventions affecting cabinet members but, since then, these conventions have been weakened. The convention of *collective responsibility* asserted that once a decision was taken in cabinet members would not refer in public to disagreements between government ministers. The convention of *ministerial responsibility* asserted that ministers would accept ultimate responsibility for any major problems in their department and would therefore resign.

Since the 1960s the convention of collective responsibility has fallen by the way and politicians have become increasingly prone to revealing their disagreements through 'leaks' to the media, or the publication of memoirs; the latter trend began after the 1964–70 Labour government left office, with the publication of diaries of former cabinet ministers Richard Crossman, Barbara Castle and, later, Tony Benn. Collective cabinet responsibility was formally suspended during the 1975 referendum to approve Britain's 'renegotiation' of the terms of the 1973 entry to the (then) European Economic Community (EEC). The referendum was, in effect, a vote on whether or not to stay in the EEC, and the cabinet was split two-thirds in favour of staying in, with one-third strongly supporting withdrawal.

Similarly, the convention of ministerial responsibility has often been disregarded. Resignations due to acceptance of ministerial responsibility for policy failure have been rare: the most cited cases are the resignation in 1954 of agriculture minister Sir Thomas Dugdale over the 'Crichel Down affair' and that of Foreign Secretary Lord Carrington in 1982 after the Argentinian invasion of the Falkland Islands. Arguably, the resignation of Education Secretary Estelle Morris in 2002 on grounds that she herself felt she was not good enough at her job might fit the convention, but there was no one event or action which triggered the resignation. In a complex society it is very difficult to maintain the convention – if a minister was held responsible for everything that happened in institutions for which he was 'responsible' there would be no ministers left. Michael Howard, who was Home Secretary (interior minister) in 1995, refused to resign over a prison breakout, and instead argued that the civil servant in charge of the prison service should be held responsible. Howard argued for a distinction between policy and operation; whether it was properly applied in this case, the distinction itself is valid. Other countries face issues of responsibility, and there is certainly a need for clear lines of responsibility. The Marc Dutroux case in Belgium, in which the pursuit and investigation into a notorious series of paedophile murders by Dutroux were negligently handled, with responsibility for that failure going right up into the highest echelons of the government, is a case of blurred lines of responsibility, possibly exacerbated by the linguistic politics of that country.

Stop and think

> Should ministers 'toe the line' once a decision has been made by the government?

> Should ministers be held responsible for failures in their departments?

In answering these questions feel free to discuss countries other than Britain.

Devolution

So far we have tended to use the term 'state' without explanation, but it is only possible to understand the introduction of regional assemblies in Britain if we appreciate that, whereas a 'state' consists of territories sharing a common government and administration, the word 'nation' relates to a sense of common identity and may even apply to people who do not share a common territory (for example, a diaspora nation such as the Kurds or Jews). Nationalistic conflicts have existed throughout history. At their most extreme they have been associated with conflicting ethnic identities, such as an imagined Aryan Reich in the mid-twentieth century and the rhetoric of 'ethnic cleansing' in some parts of Eastern Europe since the early 1990s.

Most of the larger countries of Europe employ some form of devolution; Britain has tended to operate on a 'unitary' model, although Northern Ireland was a devolved territory from its creation in 1920 to 1973, and Scotland had *administrative* devolution for most of the twentieth century. In 1979 referendums were held in Wales and Scotland with the proposal being to create regional assemblies – the vote was lost in Wales by a four-to-one margin, but carried narrowly in Scotland. However, the Act which would have established a Scottish Assembly required that 40 per cent of the electorate, and not just of those who voted, should approve it; in fact, 33 per cent approved it. The Conservative governments of 1979–97 rejected devolution in Wales and Scotland, although attempts were made to create a Northern Ireland Assembly. The Labour government elected in 1997 quickly called referendums – in fact, before the details had been approved by parliament – and Scotland voted 74 per cent in favour of a 'parliament' (note the change from 'assembly') and 63 per cent in favour of giving it tax-varying powers. The positive vote for a national assembly – with very many fewer powers than that enjoyed by a Scottish Parliament – for Wales was much closer: 50.3 per cent in favour. The Belfast Agreement (also known as the 'Good Friday Agreement') created a complex set of institutions which attempted to address the problem that politics in Northern Ireland is dominated by a single 'cleavage' – religion. We take a closer look at Northern Ireland (right).

Devolution is an attempt to: (a) create a counter-balance to central state power; (b) make the state more legitimate through allowing people to express local allegiances, including nationalist sentiments. In essence, it is part of a pluralistic state. The stresses from pluralism vary from one country to another, and not all have a geographical basis. Countries with high levels of cultural stress include many African and Asian states, Canada, Belgium, Bosnia-Herzegovina and, until relatively recently, the Netherlands. Writing about the Netherlands in the 1960s Dutch political scientist Arendt Lijphart (Lijphart 1975) coined the phrase 'consociational democracy' to

A closer look

The Belfast Agreement: consociational democracy?

In order to tackle traditional sectarian divides in Northern Ireland, three interconnected bodies of government were introduced through the Belfast Agreement: a Northern Ireland Assembly, a North/South Ministerial Council and a Council of the Isles:

The Northern Ireland Assembly This consists of 108 members, six from each of the 18 Westminster constituencies, elected by proportional representation. The assembly has legislative powers and its first duty was to set up the North/South Ministerial Council. Key decisions are made by a weighted majority system to ensure that the majority Unionist (mostly Protestant) community cannot dominate the minority Nationalist (overwhelmingly Catholic) community (parties must declare themselves as Unionist, Nationalist or non-aligned). The assembly has an executive committee of 12 ministers, comprising the first and deputy first ministers and heads of departments (including economic development, health, education, the environment, agriculture and finance). The first minister and deputy first minister must be elected with cross-community support, meaning they must win majorities in both communities.

The North/South Ministerial Council This provides a forum for ministers from Dublin and Belfast to promote joint policies. It can implement all-Ireland policies, but only with the approval of the Assembly and the Dublin Parliament. This was introduced to satisfy Nationalists who aspire to the reunification of Ireland.

The Council of the Isles This includes representatives from the Assembly, the Dublin government, the Westminster government, the Scottish Parliament and the Welsh Assembly. It meets twice each year but has no administrative or legislative powers. This was introduced to satisfy Unionists, who wanted a counterbalance to the North/South institutions.

The Assembly was suspended for short periods in 2001, and has been suspended since 2002. Elections held in 2003 resulted in a shift from the relatively moderate parties (nationalist SDLP and Ulster Unionist Party) to the more hardline Sinn Fein and the Democratic Unionist Party (DUP). The Agreement is currently under review. The DUP claims to be willing to govern with Sinn Fein so long as it breaks its ties with the paramilitary Provisional IRA (Irish Republican Army), and the IRA declares that the 'war is over' and is willing to decommission its weapons.

describe the 'pillarization' of Dutch society into Catholic, Protestant and secular. The chief characteristics of consociational democracy are: (a) grand coalition (or, at least, qualified majority voting); (b) proportional representation; (c) a veto by one 'pillar' on key issues; (d) segmental autonomy. This model is not applicable to Scotland or Wales, but it is important in understanding the Northern Irish settlement.

Civil service

All states require personnel and institutions capable of implementing legislation: a civil service. The term 'civil service' can be used quite narrowly to mean the higher echelons of central government ministries, such as, in Britain, the Ministry of Defence or Department for Education and Skills, but it can also be used in a wide sense to embrace any government employee, including, for example, clerks in employment offices. In some countries, such as Germany, teachers and university lecturers are classed as civil servants. If we restrict the discussion to the 'higher' civil service, then different models operate in different countries. In the USA the highest levels are political appointments, which changes with a new administration; in the UK there is a permanent civil service, although increasingly there are political appointees with civil service status. Alongside the political/non-political distinction lies a distinction between 'generalist' and 'specialist' – the British model is generalist, with the permanent secretaries (a permanent secretary is the chief civil servant in a department) shifting between departments. So, for example, the Permanent Secretary in the Treasury (the finance department) is rarely an economist. Of course, departments have specialists, but they are part of parallel and subordinate structure.

Some observers have argued that the British civil service is not as 'non-political' or 'neutral' as its advocates claim. Interestingly, this criticism has come from both the political left and right – in the 1970s left-wing cabinet minister Tony Benn complained that the civil service blocked the implementation of socialist policies, while in the 1980s Conservative ministers argued that the civil service stood in the way of free market policies. Less partisan commentators have expressed concern that when one party is in power for a long time, as were the Conservatives (1979–97), the distance between the civil service and that party narrows as civil servants begin to anticipate the wishes of their 'political masters'.

Defenders of the civil service argue that what civil servants want is a clear political direction and that the public service ethic is a strong counterweight to political manipulation. One worrying feature for defenders of the traditional civil service has been the breakdown of ministerial responsibility (discussed above). Although we argued that in a modern, complex society it is unrealistic to hold a minister responsible for everything which happens in his department, one of the justifications for the convention of ministerial responsibility is that civil servants must remain silent in public – they cannot defend themselves – and so to blame civil servants for failures, such as prison breakouts, is unfair. The increasing tendency to blame civil servants is linked by some observers to the privatization, or 'contracting out', of public services, a process which has continued under the Labour government (1997–); although privatization in itself may not be to blame, the structures which have been created have blurred the lines of responsibility. These changes in the nature of administration are not unique to Britain – all industrialized countries are faced with the challenge of increasing efficiency whilst at the same time guaranteeing democratic control. Britain has gone further than most European countries, but not as far as the USA, in privatizing the state's functions (see discussion below of the 'third way', p. 180).

International political institutions

It would be difficult today to find any state that is truly isolated from the complex web of international political, economic and cultural systems, communications networks, multinational companies and so on. A brief description of the activities of the United Nations and the European Union not only highlights the interdependence of national and international political structures and processes but also demonstrates the long-term impact of two world wars, fears of nuclear war and growing concerns about the environment.

The League of Nations was created after the First World War in an effort to keep peace between the nations of the world and maintain a sense of collective security. In the 1930s Japan, Germany and Italy withdrew from the league, and by the start of the Second World War the league had been totally undermined. The Second World War resulted in more debates about human rights at an international level and led to the creation of the United Nations.

The United Nations

Fifty countries signed the founding charter of the United Nations in 1945. Its stated aims were to

> save succeeding generations from the scourge of war, which twice in our lifetime has brought untold sorrow to mankind, and to reaffirm faith in fundamental human rights, in the dignity of the human person, in the equal rights of men and women and of nations large and small.   www.un.org/aboutun/charter

These aims appeal to common humanitarian instincts, and the UN has had some success in tackling conflict situations, but it is difficult to implement principles of equality and human rights when negotiating in the face of states' interests. Perhaps the greatest contribution the UN has made has been to create a discourse around human rights: even if states violate those rights, they are, at least forced to justify their actions. However, there is a problem right at the heart of that discourse: on the one hand, there is the Universal Declaration of Human Rights (created in 1947) which asserts the rights of *individual* human beings, but on the other hand there is also a right to *national self-determination* which prohibits other states intervening in a state's affairs, even if that state is violating the rights of its own citizens. The only ground for intervention would be if one state waged a war of aggression against another. So, there was wide support for military action against Iraq after it invaded Kuwait in 1990, but action against Serbia (technically, Yugoslavia) in 1999 on grounds that it was oppressing ethnic Albanians in Kosovo was, in *legal* terms, much more questionable. The action by Western states operating under NATO (North Atlantic Treaty Organization) auspices against Serbia was contrasted with the inaction of the UN and NATO against Russian violation of human rights in the province of Chechnya (since 1995), and the failure to stop the Rwandan genocide in 1995 (an estimated 800,000 mostly Tutsis were murdered in the space of one hundred days). This may reveal the mix of morality and *Realpolitik* (politics of realism), and often indifference, that characterizes international politics.

One of the greatest challenges to face the United Nations in the last quarter century has been the US-led invasion of Iraq in 2003, intended to bring down the regime of Saddam Hussein. The legality of this war has been disputed, but many in the USA argue that the United Nations is a flawed organization incapable of standing up to tyranny. The 'neo-conservatives' argue for a 'coalition of the willing' to take on what they perceive to be Islamic

A closer look

Institutions of the United Nations

International Court of Justice

States can refer their disputes to the International Court of Justice and abide by its decisions in an effort to avoid the resolution of conflict by force or war.

General Assembly

Each member state has one vote in the Assembly, and important resolutions must be passed with a two-thirds majority. However, these are only recommendations and cannot be enforced by law.

Security Council

The Council consists of fifteen members. Ten of these are elected for two years by the General Assembly. Five (China, France, the USA, Russia and the UK) are permanent. Each of the five permanent members can cancel a decision made by other members, i.e. it has a veto. The Security Council can respond to conflict by providing its own teams of negotiators, asking member countries to supply troops to form a peace-keeping force, sending unarmed observers to monitor a permanent ceasefire, instructing its members to impose trading sanctions on one or more warring parties, or intervening directly in extreme cases (UN resolutions could be enforced by multinational forces).

Humanitarian agencies

UN agencies include the World Health Organization (WHO), International Monetary Fund (IMF), United Nations International Children's Emergency Fund (UNICEF), United Nations Educational, Scientific and Cultural Organization (UNESCO) and United Nations High Commissioner for Refugees (UNHCR).

Questions

1. *In view of the aims stated in the founding charter, why do you think the UN has not intervened more forcefully to (a) stop the violation of human rights in Chechnya; (b) address poverty and starvation in large parts of the world, and especially sub-Saharan Africa?*

2. *Should the UN always be respected? Is intervention in the affairs of another state justified even if it has not received UN approval?*

extremism, which they liken to the threat from the Soviet Union in the period 1945–89 – just as the USA took uni-lateralist action under President Ronald Reagan (President 1981–89) to roll back Soviet power so it requires strong leadership from President George W. Bush (President since 2001) to defend what are perceived as Western values. The attack on the World Trade Center in 2001 has thrown into relief the difference between neo-conservative unilateralists and liberal multilaterialists.

Long-established international concerns about war-fare and human rights have been broadened by growing concerns about the global environment in general and an appreciation of the impact of 'action at a distance' (Giddens 1996). Politicians are increasingly drawn into the rhetoric of environmentalism but there are no easy solutions. In 1997 the Kyoto Agreement was drawn up, which committed industrialized nations to reduce the emissions of greenhouse gasses by around 5.2 per cent below their 1990 levels over the following decade. The agreement was dealt a blow in March 2001 when newly elected President Bush announced the United States would never sign it. A more modest version of the agreement was finalized at talks in Bonn (Germany) in 2002. The revised treaty is due to come into effect in 2008. The Bonn agreement created a complex emissions trading system: for example, a Western European country could buy 'credits' to emit carbon from an Eastern European country which could not afford the fuel that would have emitted the carbon in the first place. The United States, which generated 36 per cent of the world's emissions in 1990, has still not agreed to this watered down version of Kyoto.

The European Union

As in the case of the United Nations, the foundations of the European Union were laid after the Second World War. During the war the British prime minister, Winston Churchill, proposed that a European council should be created, which would include at least ten states and would have its own army and law courts. He called this 'a kind of United States of Europe'. However, during negotiations with France, Italy and Belgium in 1949 he refused to allow such a joint European body to take decisions over the head of the British government. He said that Britain was 'linked but not compromised' with Europe.

Churchill's reservations set the tone of political debate in Britain: politicians have often expressed mixed feelings about the relationship between Britain and the rest of

Europe. Many have wanted to see closer economic links but have been anxious to maintain national sovereignty – meaning that UK laws can only emanate from the British Parliament (see above for a discussion of sovereignty).

Some sort of economic co-operation has nevertheless been seen as a way of rebuilding the economic structures that had been damaged by the war and of enhancing long-term peace. Economic co-operation started on a relatively small scale with an emphasis on coal and steel in the 'Benelux' agreement of 1952 between Belgium, the Netherlands and Luxembourg. This economic co-operation was expanded in 1957 when the six original members of the 'European Economic Community' (Belgium, France, Germany, Italy, Luxembourg and the Netherlands) signed the Treaty of Rome. This was primarily a customs union in which members agreed not to put tariffs on goods imported from other member states. Gradually, the Union – renamed the European Community (EC) and then the European Union (EU) – has expanded in membership:

> 1952 (1957): The original six (as above).
> 1973: Denmark, Ireland, UK.
> 1981: Greece.
> 1986: Portugal, Spain.
> 1995: Austria, Finland, Sweden.
> 2004: Cyprus, Czech Republic, Estonia, Hungary. Latvia, Lithuania, Malta, Poland, Slovakia, Slovenia.
> Likely to join in 2007–8: Bulgaria, Romania.
> Under discussion: Turkey.

There have been various landmark treaties in the last twenty years: the Single European Act (1986) was an attempt to create a single market and give the EC (as it was then) a stronger identity. It provided for qualified majority voting (requiring more than a bare majority, but ruling out a veto by one country) in key areas of policy, and it laid down a timetable for the creation of single currency. The Maastricht Treaty (in force, 1993) gave legal form to the single currency (eventually named the 'euro'), although some countries, such as the UK, negotiated an 'opt-out'. The Amsterdam Treaty (1999) extended the areas of competence of the EU. The single currency technically came into force in 1999, when the existing national currencies of the participant states were 'locked' rather than floating against one another and dual pricing appeared on products, but for most people the currency became a reality in 2002 when national notes and coins were phased out and the euro phased in. As of 2005 the UK remains outside 'Euroland' and there seems no prospect of entry before 2010 at the earliest.

Critics of the EU argue that it is undemocratic because governments make decisions which are not scrutinized by national parliaments – qualified majority voting means laws can be imposed on states. From a sociological perspective, the EU, it is suggested, undermines the political culture of the national democracies because people feel alienated from such a huge, multilingual entity: demo-cracy, it is claimed, only works if people can develop a psychological identification with political institutions. Furthermore, despite shared liberal democratic values and a Christian heritage, the cultural differences in Europe are just too great for a European consciousness to evolve. The expansion of the EU to include a Muslim country, such as Turkey, would generate further economic and cultural strains. Against this, defenders of the EU argue that with globalization many areas of policy cannot be adequately addressed at a national level and the EU can be a great counterbalance to American power.

The latest development in EU policy is the signing of a Treaty to create a European constitution. This long, and complex, document requires approval from all 25 states, and in most cases that approval will take the form of a referendum. Spain has approved it by a large margin (but on a low turnout), whilst opinion polls in France and the Netherlands (May 2005) suggest it will be defeated. The Netherlands has been one of the most enthusiastic members of the EU and one Dutch journalist commented that if Britain were to reject the treaty then Britain would have a problem, but if the Dutch reject it then the EU would have a problem. Interestingly, in France the constitution was perceived as an 'Anglo-Saxon' plot to extend the free market across the EU at the expense of the French 'social model', whereas in Britain it was attacked as a Franco-German attempt to create a 'country called Europe' with a single president and army.

A closer look

Institutions of the European Union

The European Union functions through four main institutions.

European Commission

This institution is based in Brussels and has 25 members – one per member state. The Commission proposes new laws for the Council of Ministers to consider. It is also responsible for the implementation of decisions once they have been finalized.

Council of Ministers

This is the main decision-making body of the European Union. The Council discusses proposals from the Commission and aims to reach agreement. Each country has one seat on the council, although the occupants of those seats vary, as different specialists attend according to what is being discussed. On some issues all countries have to agree and the veto of one country can block a new law.

European Parliament

The European Parliament acts as a forum for discussion, scrutinizing proposals from the Commission and Council of Ministers and suggesting amendments. In 2005 there were 732 members of the European Parliament (MEPs). Each nation's contingent is roughly approximate to the population of the country, but the smaller states are 'over-represented'. Elections are fought on national lines but national political parties form groups in the Parliament. After the 2004 elections the centre-right had 268 members, the socialists 202 and the liberals 88 – the rest belonged to four groups and there were 28 non-attached.

European Court of Justice

This institution considers any infringement of European Union law and any queries about the interpretation of the law.

Stop and think

➤ What the arguments for and against the EU?

➤ What are the arguments for and against the *further expansion* of the EU?

➤ Do you think the EU gets a 'fair press' in Britain?

Political ideas

So far we have looked at institutions; we now turn to ideas. Various distinctions need to be made when exploring political ideas:

➤ *Social structure*: different social structures generate different sets of ideas. Political sociologists categorize societies into totalitarian, pluralist, oligarchic, corporatist and elitist.

➤ *Ideology*: an ideology is a relatively coherent set
of ideas encompassing large aspects of society.
The nature of a society's ideology is determined in
part by its social structure. As we argue there are
different ideological levels – confusion over the term
'liberalism' arises because it used to describe a whole
society (social structure) but also a movement within
that society.

The last point explains why many people in a liberal
democracy feel that 'all politicians are alike' or that political parties have so much in common that voting for
one of them is a waste of time. If you feel this way, then
you will find that some political scientists agree with
you to some extent. Most notably, the American political
scientist Daniel Bell (1973) pronounced 'the end of
ideology' in Western societies and, even before the fall
of the Berlin wall, another American, Francis Fukuyama
(1989) argued that Western liberal democratic (and
capitalist) ideas had triumphed over all other ideologies,
and as such 'history' – meaning ideological conflict –
was over. Yet political sociologists have also shown that
political cultures (the norms and values legitimizing a
political system) can, and do, vary considerably between
states. One of the most well-known comparative studies
is Almond and Verba's *The Civic Culture* (1963), which
provided a comparative analysis of political cultures in
five countries. Although rather dated, this study provided
a grounding for subsequent debates and further research,
and a general appreciation that not only do political
cultures vary but also they can arise in various ways.
Rather than developing naturally, some can be imposed
by force or threats, or otherwise introduced and accepted
quite quickly (see pp. 166–7 for Giddens' comments on
democratization). They may also react and adapt differently to key social developments such as globalization,
de-traditionalization and a more reflexive citizenship.

Totalitarianism

In a totalitarian state opposition to the dominant political group and its associated policies is not allowed;
a totalitarian state need not be one in which control is
'total' – that is impossible – but is one in which pluralism
is not formally recognized and respected. A totalitarian
state can be extremely left-wing or extremely right-wing
(see below) or have some other (often military) political
identity. We can therefore see a similarity between the
extremes of communism and fascism, discussed below.

Although based on radically different philosophies, neither leaves room for alternative theories and each has
been associated with an element of force. This could be
seen if we compared the atrocities of Hitler's concentration camps with the horrors of Stalin's gulags. In such
circumstances there is apparently no room for opposition, yet we have seen a process of gradual change from
fascism to 'pluralism' in Spain and from communism to
'pluralism' in the former Eastern bloc.

Fascism, Nazism and other forms of racism or extreme
xenophobia are normally categorized as the 'extreme
right' of totalitarianism. Fascist movements have historically arisen in situations of great economic and social
turmoil. The most obvious example would be the rise
of the Nazis in a Germany which had been devastated by
the First World War. In such situations fascist leaders
exploit the dire need for strong leadership by offering the
promise of order, security and prosperity. Common fears
and hatreds, nationalistic allegiances and, usually, racism
could be exploited in order to generate unquestioning
support. For those reasons, fascist states are inevitably
totalitarian and authoritarian.

It would, however, be wrong simply to describe fascists
as extremely right-wing. In some ways fascists have been
as suspicious of free-market capitalism as communists:
the economy of Franco's Spain was heavily regulated.
Fascist leaders try to achieve a populist image, which may
include appeal to working-class and left-wing supporters.
For example, Oswald Mosley (1896–1980), the leader
of the British Union of Fascists before the start of the
Second World War, was formerly a junior minister in
the Labour Party. Hitler's fascist party was the National
Socialist German Workers' Party (NSDAP). Even during
the mid-1990s, the warring factions within the former
Yugoslavia could be distinguished primarily by their
national and cultural identities, rather than by their
positions on a left- to right-wing polarity of perspectives.
Fascism therefore tends to draw on common fears and/or
the appeal of superiority and domination over others
and could still be seen in the late twentieth century with
the resurgence of Fascist parties in Europe.

On the 'extreme left' we have class-based socialist
movements – the key difference between fascism and
state-socialism (or communism) is that the latter makes
a claim to universalism – 'workers of the world unite'
– even if, in practice, as in Stalin's Russia, a policy of
building 'socialism in one country' was pursued. A distinction should be made between Marxism and communism:
Marxism is a body of social and philosophical reflection,
in which there is little discussion of communism, or the

Figure 5.1 Hitler at the Bükeberg party rally 1934
(courtesy of Mary Evans Pictures)

nature of a classless society. Marx argues that the ideas of a society are the ideas of the dominant class. It is possible to apply Marxist analysis, and believe in a classless society, without endorsing state socialism. This is not to say that the origins of totalitarianism cannot be found in Marx's thought, or that Eastern bloc socialism bore no relation to what Marx had 'intended' – Marx was hostile to liberal pluralism but offered no prescriptions for a classless society, thus leaving open a space for authoritarian forms of socialism. What developed in the Soviet Union and Eastern Europe had its roots in both Marxism and Leninism – Lenin developed a model of 'democratic centralism' for the Communist Party in which decisions were taken at the top of a pyramid and they had to be enforced lower down.

Pluralism

When trying to explain the meaning of pluralism, Woolf (1969) used the image of a weather vane (central and local government) responding to the wind (of public opinion). Government responses are portrayed as compromises between a plurality and fragmentation of influences. Efforts are made to avoid the alienation of any particular section of interests. Power is spread across a wide range of social locations, and organizations representing various interests and democracy exist because no one interest group is allowed to dominate. According to this view, individuals – by themselves as voters, in pressure groups, political parties, etc. – can genuinely influence those who hold power. As sociologists we can see how this relates to Durkheim's argument that social solidarity is based on an acceptance of diversity (see p. 45).

At least two types of pluralism have been identified by political scientists. First, conventional pluralism represents the government as a neutral umpire, balancing inputs (of influence) with outputs (policy) in such a way that influence is balanced among a plurality of groups. As this may seem to be impractical or a rather idealized conception of reality, a second type, neo-pluralism, observes the state negotiating with some groups (particularly influential pressure groups) and individuals (experts) more than others. Indeed, some theories about neo-pluralism are almost indistinguishable from theories about oligarchies, corporatism and elitism. The differences between them tend to relate to the types of people who are most regularly consulted by the state.

Oligarchy

Oligarchy describes a political structure in which an individual (oligarch) or small group (oligarchy) controls the decision-making processes. Michels (1959) studied trade unions, which were apparently examples of egalitarianism and pluralist ideals, and concluded (his Iron Law of Oligarchy) that, once elected or accepted, officials and leaders will systematically exclude others from the decision-making process. This could even be seen as a natural development because most members would not want to commit themselves to more demanding political activity.

Corporatism

In a corporatist state some large interest groups have become more powerful than others in the political and economic arena. Decision making is generally by compromise between representatives of labour (unions), capital (employers) and the state. They come together to co-ordinate the economy and provide a balance between private enterprise and state control. Again this may take place in an apparently pluralist state, and it may be argued that it is still a pluralist state because the government is responding to a plurality of views.

Elitism

Schattschneider (1969: 31) wrote that 'the flaw in the pluralist heaven is that the heavenly choir sings with a strongly upper-class accent'. Theories about elitism claim that elitist states systematically exclude the majority from political influence and rely on the deference of the masses, created by their socialization into an acceptance of elite domination. Power is held by an elite group of political experts and not just by an economically dominant group (as suggested by Marxist theories and Schattschneider's choir). Although an elitist government works in the elite's interests, this could be seen as enabling the system to run efficiently. The elite may

claim that a limited democracy exists, and full democracy is worth sacrificing in favour of rule by experts. Elite influence is cumulative and transferable between institutions, and the elite determines access to elite positions (an example being the role of elite public schools in providing personnel). Pareto labelled this process the 'circulation of elites' (1935), and C. Wright Mills (1956) argued that the USA was governed by a self-perpetuating network of affluent white men.

Dahl's elite model (1958) emphasizes the following conditions that must be met in order to identify elite rule:

1 The ruling elite is a well-defined group.

2 There are several instances of cases involving key political decisions when the preferences of the ruling elite group have run counter to those that might be suggested by any other likely group.

3 In the cases described in (2) the preferences of the elite group regularly prevail.

Most elite theorists do not see elite dominance as a matter of deliberate manipulation but of subscribing to an ideology in which elite domination is seen as natural. This ultimately means that some writers (such as Mosca 1939; Pareto 1935; Schumpeter 1976) take a very low view of the capabilities of the masses for self-government, or of their desire for it. Mosca said that the rulers' dominance of the ruled was the result of their superior organization.

Stop and think

➤ How would you characterize (a) Britain; (b) USA; (c) Russia, in terms of the above descriptions?

European political parties

We now move the discussion from social structures to ideologies. First, we need to make a distinction between large-scale ideologies which characterize an entire political system and political culture, and ideological streams within a political system. Fukuyama argued that liberalism (or liberal democracy) had triumphed. He is here describing a large-scale ideology which stresses individual freedom, representative democracy and a basically capitalist economic system. But within liberal democracies

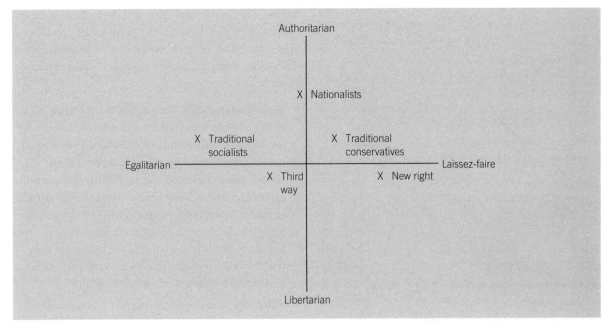

Figure 5.2 Political compass

there are parties calling themselves Liberal, as distinct from Conservative, Christian Democrat, Socialist, etc. Furthermore, there is small 'l' liberalism such as social liberalism and economic liberalism. The easiest way to make sense of this is to distinguish attitudes to the basic social and political institutions of a society, and more specific policy positions. As we argued earlier all societies have 'rules of the game' by which they operate, but the 'moves' within the 'game' can differ. For example, different political parties may favour different electoral systems (we discuss these different systems later), but no mainstream party would advocate abandoning the principle of one (adult) person, one vote. Likewise, there can be disagreements about how free speech should be, but most parties support some kind of basic freedom of speech or expression.

It is commonplace to line up parties along a left–right axis, and indeed we have used the language of left and right at several places in this chapter. A more sophisticated way to categorize parties is on a two-dimensional 'compass' (see Figure 5.2).

In a liberal democracy the parties will tend to be clustered in the middle. It is worth noting that if there is just one dimension those political parties intent on maximizing their support will move as close to the 'median voter' as possible. If we take the egalitarian–laissez-faire dimension, which arguably is concerned with the distribution of wealth, with the left supporting

high tax and a high degree of distribution, and the right supporting low taxes and a low degree of redistribution, then these represent the two extremes and there are various positions in between. Voters are ranged along this axis from left to right. Consider the three voter distributions in Figures 5.3a, b and c.

The point Laver makes is that if there are just two parties *and only one axis* then to maximize its vote a party has an incentive to adopt a policy position as close to the median voter as possible. This is the case even under distribution (b) where the median voter is in a tiny minority. This is, however, a very pure example: add other axes, or dimensions, and it becomes more complex. It does, however, explain, at least to some extent, why parties have traditionally converged in an attempt to win elections. In fact, in Britain getting your party's supporters out to vote has become as important, if not more important, than winning over the median voter; consequently, 'wedge issues' have become important, that is, parties emphasize divisive questions, combined with inculcating fear of the other parties in order to motivate their supporters to vote. Sometimes an appeal to the median vote is combined with an appeal to 'core supporters': to use a journalistic term from Australia there are 'dog whistle' issues – for example, a party may use immigration to mobilize their supporters to vote, but they 'code' it in such a way that they do not also mobilize opposition voters to vote.

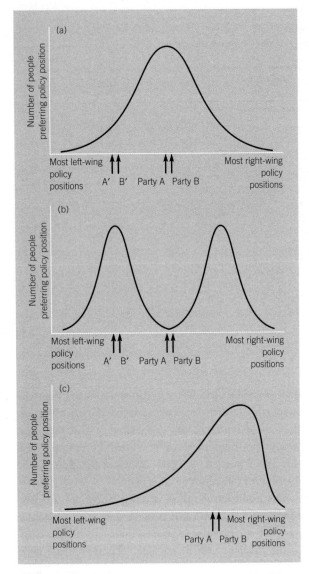

Figure 5.3 (a) One-dimensional policy competition between two parties with voter preferences concentrated in the centre of the policy spectrum. **(b)** One-dimensional policy competition between two parties with voter preferences concentrated towards the ends of the policy spectrum. **(c)** One dimensional policy competition between two parties with voter preferences skewed towards the right end of the policy spectrum

Source: Laver 1997

In Figure 5.2 we identified a number of political positions: traditional socialist; third way; traditional conservative; new right; nationalist. The categorization is based largely on the British political system, but it can be applied to (especially) other Western European countries, Canada, Australia, New Zealand and, to a much lesser extent, the USA. Note we do not use party names. This is because you will find these different political positions in the same party (after providing a brief description of each position we summarize their differences along a number of policy dimensions: see Table 5.1).

▶ **Traditional socialists** see politics in class terms, as a struggle between the buyers and sellers of labour. For traditional socialists the British Labour Party should indeed represent *labour*. The old clause 4 of the Labour Party talks about taking industry into public ownership; one of Tony Blair's first moves on election to the leadership of the party in 1994 was to seek to have this clause replaced with one which simply talked about the importance of the 'many not the few'. Many European social democratic parties can be described as largely 'traditional socialist'.

▶ **Third way** is, as the name suggests, a compromise between traditional socialism and capitalism. It is too crude to say that it 'splits the difference', but rather it tends to disaggregate issues: it does not see all issues in terms of a single ideological system. There is a strong element of 'pick and mix'. 'New Labour' in Britain is the most striking example of a third way party; critics argue that it is nothing more than a piece of political advertising, albeit a brilliant one in electoral terms. Other observers, such as Tony Giddens, have attempted to build something more substantial. New Labour was much influenced by (former American President) Bill Clinton's 'New Democrats'; a less successful attempt to develop a third way is the 'red–green' government of Gerhardt Schröder in Germany – for a time he used the label 'neue Mitte' (new centre).

▶ **Traditional conservatives** do not reject progress, but argue that we should see the past as a storehouse of wisdom and not assume that new is always better – progress should be tentative. Traditional conservatism has been in steep decline, mainly because of increasing secularization and a loss of respect for authority – the decline in deference. Conservatives believe that personal freedom is important and they are hostile to social engineering – that is, trying to change human nature – but freedom is only achieved gradually and must be balanced against other values, such as community. In mainland Europe conservatives tend to be found in parties calling themselves 'Christian Democrat', but the link with Christianity is fairly loose and in no way corresponds to the evangelical right in the United States.

Table 5.1 Policy differences of main political positions

Traditional socialist	Third way	Traditional conservative	New right (libertarian)	Nationalist
1. Redistribution: to what extent should the state redistribute resources from the rich to the poor? Is the creation of a more equal society an end-in-itself?				
High level of redistribution; equality is important.	Fairly high level of redistribution, but equality is not an end in itself.	Reasonable level of redistribution, but too much undermines voluntary giving.	A basic level of redistribution is justified, but in general people should keep what they earn.	Fairly high level of redistribution, but extreme nationalists argue that it should favour 'indigenous' people.
2. Should there be state ownership of industry and public services?				
Yes: both industry and public services.	Industry: no. Public services: if the market is more efficient it should be used. The state should *fund* services, but it does not have to *run* them.	Industry: no. Public services: important to encourage a public service ethic – markets may undermine it. The voluntary sector is important.	Strongly in favour of private ownership. More radical in the use of the market in delivering public services than the third way.	Supports some state industries and, for example, laments the foreign ownership of the British motor industry.
3. How much freedom should individuals have? What are the causes of crime?				
Crime is caused by the breakdown of traditional employment structures. Freedom is important, but the social good can override it.	The causes of crime are complex – individuals must to an extent be held responsible for their actions. It is important to build 'strong communities'. There should be rules but no prejudice against minority groups. Sometimes people should be protected against themselves, for example, we should reduce the number of smokers.	Loss of respect for authority is a major cause of crime. The state has a role in moulding human behaviour but it should not engage in social engineering.	People should be free to do whatever they want to do so long as they respect other people's freedom.	Crime is best tackled by inculcating national pride. Extreme nationalists tend to blame immigrants for high levels of crime.
4. How open should the state be to other peoples? What is a valid foreign policy?				
Socialists are internationalist, but they are suspicious of 'capitalist clubs', such as the EU and G8. More sympathetic to the UN. Socialists tend to favour protectionism rather than 'neo-liberal' free trade.	International organizations should work to the interests of the participant states. Human rights should be at the heart of foreign policy. It is better for the EU and US to work together. Globalization is to be welcomed; the challenge is to ensure *fair* trade. Writing off Third World debt is an important means to tackling world poverty.	States' interests are paramount – states should only go to war where their vital interests are at stake, or where there has been an act of aggression against another state.	Globalization and free trade are good things. The EU is treated with suspicion because it is seen as protectionist.	Nations must be protected against global forces which threaten national cultural identity. Protectionism can be justified. Extreme nationalists favour an end to immigration and 'repatriation'.

➤ **New right**: within the British Conservative Party the 'battle' has been between traditional conservatives and the 'new right'. New right policies include privatization of state industry, wider share and home ownership, tough fiscal policies and hostility to international organizations perceived as 'socialist' or 'protectionist'. Within the new right there can be discerned what might be termed a 'purer' variety of *libertarianism*: libertarians stress both economic and personal freedom, and so would argue for the decriminalization of sex between consenting adults and of recreational drug use.

➤ **Nationalists**: the nationalist spectrum stretches from a relatively 'benign' patriotism to racism and xenophobia. Much nationalist concern is focused on the perceived loss of sovereignty to such organizations as the EU and the 'threat' of immigration. Many observers condemn nationalists as irrational, but it is possible to understand nationalism as a rational response among relatively unskilled workers to the competition from immigrant labour. As globalization deepens there is a possibility that more extreme forms of nationalism will achieve popular appeal.

Political behaviour

We have discussed institutions and ideas and we now turn to political behaviour: how people interact with another in the political sphere. The focus is on groups and individuals. Those who study political behaviour typically focus on elections and public opinion; in many ways, political behaviour is, for sociologists, the most interesting aspect of politics. It cannot, however, be studied in isolation from institutions and ideology. Indeed, there is a relatively new body of theory – new institutionalism – which argues that institutions, ideology and behaviour act upon one another: people behave differently when

institutions change. A good example is voting behaviour in Scotland. In the second Scottish parliamentary election, held in 2003, support for 'minor parties', such as the Greens and the Scottish Socialist Party, was much higher than in the previous and subsequent Westminster elections (2001 and 2005), and support for the Scottish National Party (SNP) is consistently higher in Scottish parliamentary elections than in Westminster ones. Clearly, the operation of a form of 'proportional representation' and the perception that the Scottish Parliament is distinctly 'Scottish' affects behaviour. In short, institutions determine, to a significant extent, behaviour.

Elections

Martin Harrop and William Miller argue that elections serve two types of function: 'bottom up' and 'top down'. Put simply, the two types focus on the benefits to voters (bottom up) and politicians (top down) of elections. Bottom up functions of elections include: (a) providing representation; (b) offering choice; (c) making governments; (d) influencing policies; (e) influencing politicians. Top down functions include: (a) providing a mandate to govern; (b) adding legitimacy to government decisions; (c) educating voters about policies. How well each of these functions is fulfilled depends on the nature of the electoral system.

Electoral systems

There are many different electoral systems, and we will restrict our survey to the main ones. Often a distinction is made between 'first past the post' (plurality system) and 'proportional representation' (PR). However, many so-called PR systems, for example STV, are far from proportional. A simulation of the 1997 general election in the UK (excluding Northern Ireland) predicted the breakdown of seats under different systems: see Table 5.2.

Table 5.2 1997 general election: breakdown of seats under different systems						
Voting system	Conservative	Labour	Liberal Democrat	SNP/PC	Others	Deviation from proportionality
Party list (one list)	202	285	110	16	28	0%
STV (5-member seats)	144	342	131	24	0	13.5%
AMS (50/50)	203	303	115	20	0	2%
AV	110	436	84	10	1	23.5%
Plurality (actual result)	165	419	46	10	1	21%

Source: www.charter88.com/publications/demand/dall.html

Below is a brief discussion of the main electoral systems, with some reflections on the functional advantages, and likely *social* consequences, of each. Among the social consequences are: (a) the extent to which the electoral system in question produces a parliament which reflects the make-up of society, in terms of, say, gender or ethnicity; (b) the relationship between voter and representative, and the effect of that relationship on the sense of legitimacy of politicians; (c) the degree to which different electoral systems create, or exacerbate social fragmentation, such as religious differences.

➤ **List system** In its purest form the entire electorate votes on a single list – so, for example, if there are one hundred seats, a party presents the voters with a list of up to one hundred names (maybe more, in order to allow for mid-term replacement of MPs). List systems, even 'open ones' where voters can vote for individual candidates, tend to give parties enormous power and do not allow for a strong link between voter and representative. They do, however, tend to facilitate equal gender representation and representation of minority groups. If proportionality is important, then the list system is the most proportional; the price, however, is political fragmentation and the election of extremists.

➤ **Single Transferable Vote** STV operates with multi-member constituencies, which can vary in size from two to any number. The larger (in number of seats) the constituency the more complex counting votes becomes, but larger seats are more proportional. The main social effects are: (a) voters have enormous power – no MP can be considered 'safe'; (b) parties – typically centre parties – capable of winning lower level preferences along with a decent number of first preferences will do disproportionately well; (c) there is a tendency for STV to encourage 'parish pump' politics – that is, focusing on very local issues at the expense of national issues.

➤ **Additional Member System** AMS is a mix of 'first past the post' as used in British national elections and the list system, typically regional lists. Voters normally have two votes: a constituency vote and a regional vote. AMS is a compromise between proportionality and the perceived need for a direct link between voter and representative. It is used in Germany, where it is thought to function well (there is, however, a requirement to achieve 5 per cent of the list vote, or win three constituencies, in order to get list representation). However, in Scotland conflicts arise between constituency and list MSPs (Members of the Scottish Parliament).

➤ **Plurality and Alternative Vote** Plurality voting is simple: the country is divided into constituencies and the candidate who wins the most votes in a seat is elected. The alternative vote is a variant: candidates have to receive 50 per cent of the vote, so voters put the candidates in preference order. Both systems tend to be highly disproportional. There is also evidence that fewer women and ethnic minorities get elected under these systems. If decisive election results are important, then these systems are superior to others, but they can undermine legitimacy: in the 2005 UK election the Labour Party won a comfortable majority on just 36 per cent of the vote.

Representation of social groups in the political system

An important area of investigation for political sociologists is that of grouping in the social structure (especially gender, race and social class) and how these are represented in politics. Here we will start by considering the representation of some groups among British MPs and then appraise the monitoring of public opinion in general, theories about voting, and the relationships between gender, race and social class and voting behaviour.

Social backgrounds of Members of Parliament

Although the social mix among MPs is often criticized, it is difficult to change because many current MPs have been serving for a very long time and few are replaced at each election. The massive swing to Labour in 1997 brought in many new MPs, but more than 60 per cent of all MPs had served in the previous parliament. After the 2001 election the social class make-up of the House of Commons was as shown in Table 5.3.

MPs have traditionally been more middle-class, highly educated and affluent than the general public, and this is clear from the table that graduates are significantly over-represented, and the private school educated massively so. However, if we concentrate on those features in particular, we obscure the finer distinctions between political parties regarding social class and occupation. Labour has consistently had more working-class MPs than the Conservatives, but the percentage declined between 1951 and 2001. Labour has also consistently had fewer MPs from

Table 5.3 Social backgrounds of MPs

	Labour %	Conservative %	Liberal Democrat %
University educated	67	83	70
Independent (private) school educated	17	64	35
Professional occupation	43	39	52
Business	8	36	27
Miscellaneous	36	25	19
Manual workers	12	1	2

Source: Butler and Kavanagh 2001

the business community. In the Conservative Party many of the MPs classified as 'professional' are from the legal profession, while in the Labour Party teachers and lecturers are strongly represented in this category. One feature of occupation is the growing 'miscellaneous' category: many of these are 'professional' politicians – people who have worked as assistants to MPs or ministers.

Between 1945 and 1983 the number of female MPs was fairly stable but very low indeed. There was a dramatic rise in the number of female MPs in 1987 and 1992, but still few female MPs overall – just 9.2 per cent of all MPs after the 1992 general election. One of the problems was that, when a woman candidate was selected, it was often for an unwinnable seat. In 1993 the Labour Party tackled this by adopting a policy of all-women short lists in a number of constituencies. The policy was rejected by an employment tribunal in 1996 on the grounds that it breached sex discrimination legislation, but this decision was too late to affect seats where female candidates had already been selected, and the law itself was changed after the 1997 election in order to permit all-women shortlists. Other parties took a less pro-active approach, relying more on encouragement and training, rather than changing actual selection procedures. As a result, after the 1997 election, 35 per cent of Labour MPs (101 of the Labour MPs elected in 1997), 12 per cent of Conservative MPs and 7 per cent of Liberal Democrat MPs were female. After the 2001 election there was a small decline in the number of female MPs, but for the 2005 election more women were selected for 'safe' Labour seats than had been the case in previous elections, and 127 women were elected – nearly 20 per cent of the total.

The Labour Party includes a pressure group called 'Emily's List', which aims to have more women elected as Labour MPs. Members of the all-party 300 Group aim to encourage and enable more women to stand for Parliament and increase the number of women MPs to about 300. Yet divisions between feminists have been

particularly noticeable, as some feminists claim that just increasing the number of women MPs simply addresses electoral issues and does not deal with more fundamental issues regarding the role of women in politics. Many feminists argue that the way politics is conducted is 'masculinist' and alienates women. This is perhaps more the case in Britain than in other European countries because the model of party competition has traditionally been two-party and confrontational. This may be changing for several reasons: (a) the dominance of the two parties has declined in those elected bodies where 'proportional representation' is used; (b) even at Westminster the number of third party MPs has increased; (c) election campaigns, whilst still confrontational, are subtly changing, as public meetings have been replaced by one-to-one interaction with the voters – in general, women interact much better at a personal level than men, and there is evidence that women voters marginally prefer a female candidate while male voters are indifferent to the candidate's gender, thus giving female candidates an electoral advantage.

Similar concern has been expressed about the racial mix of MPs. 'Black' candidates have been more successful in local authority elections than in parliamentary elections. The first black MP was in office as long ago as 1922–29: Shapurji Saklatvala was the Communist and Labour MP representing North Battersea. However, for many years since then, all MPs could have been described as white. In the 1979 general election there were five black candidates and none was elected; in the 1983 general election, there were eighteen black candidates and, again, none was elected. This can at least partly be explained by the 'unwinnable' seats in which black candidates stood (Saggar 1992: 165–8) and the kinds of seats in which they tended to be most successful (generally inner city areas). In the 1987 general election there were thirty-two black candidates and four were elected; by the 1992 general election, there were even more black candidates but only six were elected, although that group included the first Asian Conservative for a hundred years. After the 1997 election there were nine MPs from ethnic minorities, and after the 2005 election there were thirteen ethnic minority MPs – twelve Labour and one Liberal Democrat (who entered Parliament in a by-election in 2004). There was a big jump in the number of ethnic minority candidates in the 2005 election (2001 election figures in brackets): Labour 29 (21); Conservative 39 (16); Liberal Democrat 41 (29). Of those 15 were elected (13 Labour and 2 Conservative).

Public opinion

Political sociology is perhaps best known for its interest in monitoring public opinion (usually shown in general attitude surveys). It would not be possible for us to analyze various survey findings in detail, but some general comments must be made about political research methods, theories about voting behaviour, and the relationships between gender, race, social class and voting behaviour.

Problems with opinion polls

At the 1992 general election the error in forecasting the gap between the Conservative Party and Labour was greater than ever before (an average of 8.9 per cent error in the final polls by the leading organizations, compared with 4.0 per cent in 1987, 3.6 per cent in 1983 and 2.4 per cent in 1979). The credibility of opinion polls was so badly damaged after 1992 that, during the 1997 general election campaign, the polls' predictions of a

---

A closer look

Butler and Kavanagh on polling methods

A committee set up by the Market Research Society reported, in 1994, that there had been four main sources of error in the 1992 polls.

1 *Unrepresentative selection of respondents.* All the pollsters were found to have set quotas that resulted in too few interviews with two-car owners and too many with council tenants.

2 *A late swing.* Plainly there was a small swing in the final hours between the interviews and the vote, partially linked to differential turnout.

3 *A 'spiral of silence'.* There was a refusal by some voters, disproportionately older and more Conservative, to admit to their voting preference or to be interviewed at all.

4 *Selective participation.* There was a small error due to under-registration, which mainly affected Labour voters and was partly attributable to the poll tax.

Crewe (1992) argued that: 'Had the campaign polls consistently shown the Conservatives to be ahead – as they probably were – the government might not have mobilised the anti-Labour vote so effectively and hence may not have survived in office.'

Up to 1992 there had been a consensus on method in the polling industry. There was general agreement on face-to-face interviews, on ignoring 'don't knows' and 'won't says', and on the quota selection of respondents.

In the aftermath of 1992 some or all of these were abandoned or modified by each of the pollsters, though in differing ways:

➤ ICM tried using secret ballots to reassure its respondents before turning to telephone polling (94 per cent of the population were approachable by telephone); it also introduced adjustments, based partly on reports of past voting and partly on answers to other questions, to allow for refusals and don't knows.

➤ Gallup also switched at the end of 1996 to telephone polls, using random-digit dialling to reach ex-directory numbers. Gallup, in addition, made a small adjustment to allow for the bias caused by refusals.

➤ NOP and Harris continued to use face-to-face quota polls, but they too made small adjustments for presumed non-response.

➤ MORI was alone in headlining its unadjusted figures; however, it used a larger number of smaller sampling points, giving tighter control over the characteristics of the sample.

(*Source*: Butler and Kavanagh 1997: 120–2)

Questions

1. *Do opinion polls still play an important role in British politics?*

2. *What arguments can you suggest for and against the banning of opinion polls in the last week of an election campaign?*

---

landslide victory for Labour were not taken seriously. Yet the companies carrying out opinion polls had investigated and improved their methods between 1992 and 1997. Butler and Kavanagh (1997) reported on their activities, which we have a closer look at on p. 185. The polls were fairly accurate in the 2005 election.

Theories about voting behaviour

Theories about voting behaviour have been continually refined since the 1960s, when Butler and Stokes developed their influential party identification (or expressive) model. This model included an emphasis on how family influenced voting behaviour.

A long-term allegiance to one particular party often developed from family circumstances and socialization and meant that in any election the main parties could be assured of support from strong identifiers (sometimes called core voters). They also described the four 'ages of political man' to explain the process of political socialization and how awareness and attitudes developed and changed over time. Furthermore, they identified three criteria by which an issue could be judged in terms of its impact on voting behaviour: the issue must be associated differently with the political parties in the voters' minds, there should be considerable strength of feeling about the issue, and opinion on the issue must be skewed (i.e. it must strongly favour one side of the argument).

Developments since the 1960s suggest that, although the largest proportion of voters are still strong identifiers, they have declined as a proportion of all voters (party dealignment) and that social class is no longer such a major influence on voting behaviour (class dealignment). Today political scientists are more likely to identify fluctuations in votes and emphasize instrumental motives. For example, it is estimated (Curtice and Steed 1997) that in 1997 the Conservative Party lost 25–35 seats due to tactical voting, i.e. voting for someone who is not the preferred candidate in order to prevent the least preferred candidate being elected. In the 2001 there was a 1.5 per cent swing from Labour to Conservative, which should have resulted in a gain for the Conservatives of twenty seats, but in fact they gained only six (because they lost seats to the Liberal Democrats the net gain was only one seat). A small number of seats may have had little effect when the winning party had a landslide victory but could be significant in other elections.

Instrumental interests are emphasized in Crewe et al.'s (1992) rational choice (or consumer) model, which argues that political issues and self-interest are particularly influential. According to this model party identification is conditional and parties must persuade voters that their policies are valid. David Denver (1989) developed a model which combined Butler and Stokes' emphasis on party identification with Crewe's emphasis on rational choice. He presented social location (party identification model), policy preferences (rational choice model) and party choice as points on a triangle and suggested three possible relationships between them:

➤ In one possible relationship social location determines both party choice and policy preferences, resulting in an indirect relationship between party choice and policy preference.

➤ In a second relationship social location determines policy preferences, which determines party choice. This results in an indirect relationship between social location and party choice.

➤ In a third relationship social location determines vote, and policy preferences are adjusted to accommodate party choice. This results in an indirect relationship between social location and policy preferences.

Since the 1980s, Crewe (Budge et al. 1998: 352) has refined his rational choice model, and his 'Essex model' was fairly accurate in predicting and explaining the result of general elections by evaluating factors affecting government popularity (e.g. the model predicted that in 1997 the Conservative vote would be 32.2 per cent, when the actual Conservative vote was 31.5 per cent). The model considers three main elements:

1 Opinion poll findings about recent voting support.

2 Two permanent underlying influences. These are both related to voters' economic self-interest: (a) optimism about personal economic circumstances (the 'feel good factor') increases support for the government, while pessimists tend to blame the government and withdraw their support; (b) raising taxation reduces support for the government.

3 Short-term political effects, some of which will have a longer-lasting impact than others. For example, the Conservative Party lost votes in 1997 due to its image as a divided party, while Labour benefited from its image as a more united party under the dynamic leadership of Tony Blair.

Table 5.4 How Britain voted in the 2001 general election

	Conservative	Labour	Liberal Democrat	Turnout
	%	%	%	%
RESULT:	33	42	19	59
Men	32	42	18	61
Women	33	42	19	58
18–24	27	41	24	39
25–34	24	51	19	46
35–44	28	45	19	59
45–54	32	41	20	65
55–64	39	37	17	69
65+	40	39	17	70
AB Class	39	30	25	68
C1	36	38	20	60
C2	29	49	15	56
DE	24	55	13	53

Source: MORI (www.mori.com)

Stop and think

➤ Which of these theories do you find most convincing as explanations of voting behaviour? Why?

➤ It is often said that there has been a decline in class voting in Britain – is this true?

Gender and voting behaviour

In Table 5.4 we can see that there was very little difference in the voting behaviour of men and women at the 2001 general election. However, for much of post-war British history there was a 'gender gap', whereby the Conservatives did much better among women than among men. This gap has disappeared. It is notable that in the USA the Democrats do much better among women; this may be due to the greater 'salience' of so-called cultural issues, such as abortion, where women are more supportive of, and feel more strongly about, the 'pro-choice' position.

A probing study of gender and voting behaviour is beyond the limits of this chapter and incorporates gender differences in levels of political participation and feminist critiques of political scientists. It is too easy to speculate about attitudes and generalize about women as a group without acknowledging their diverse experiences and views. Before proceeding to analyze gender differences in political behaviour it is important to bear in mind the following feminist criticisms of social scientists.

1 They sometimes 'fudge the footnotes', which includes producing misleading statements or statements that are unsupported by references.

2 They may assume that men influence women's political attitudes, but not *vice versa*.

3 Political attitudes that are characteristic of men are used to define mature political behaviour.

> Those characteristics and enthusiasms which supposedly sway men (wars, controversy, electoral manipulation) are defined as political, while those characteristics and enthusiasms which supposedly sway women (human need for food, clothing, shelter, adherence to consistent moral principles, a rejection of war as rational) are simply not considered political.
>
> (Bourque and Grossholtz 1984: 118)

4 The political contribution of women is equated with their role as mothers.

5 Feminists often claim that there has been a tendency among political scientists to separate the public world of politics and employment from the private world of the family and interpersonal relations. This idea is embodied in the notion of the private woman and the public man. For example, Siltanen and Stanworth (1984) argued that politics must intervene in private situations in order 'to protest against abuses of freedom and dignity. Intimacy and privacy are neither licences for, nor protection against, inhuman conduct' (1984: 207). They were concerned that the idealized image of the family 'offers no solace to battered women and children who suffer from the neglect of our political institutions in the name of personal freedom' (1984: 207).

Cynthia Cockburn (1987) presented a view that reflected item 3 on our list of feminist criticisms. She argued that the interests of women were not included within definitions of 'politics'. Furthermore, she suggested that behaviour that may be labelled 'naive' is actually a rejection of the terms of political debate (see Activity 1 at the end of this chapter, p. 201).

Ethnicity and voting behaviour

You can read elsewhere in this book about the problems researchers have in categorizing 'ethnicity'. As ethnic minority groups are heterogeneous, and include other significant social groupings (such as social classes, genders, religions, age groups, geographical areas, etc.), doubts may be cast on what limited research there has been into voting patterns amongst 'ethnic minorities'. However, with all the usual provisos about definitions, researchers in the 1980s and 1990s found strong and consistent support for the Labour Party from Indians, Pakistanis and Afro-Caribbeans (generally over 80 per cent but with a low of 72 per cent in 1987) and lack of support for the Con-servative Party from ethnic minorities (generally less than 10 per cent in general elections since 1974, but with a high of 18 per cent in 1987; Saggar 1997: 696). Since 2001, and especially since the 2003 war in Iraq, there has been a dramatic shift away from Labour among Muslims. An opinion poll in 2004 (ICM for the *Guardian*, November 2004) showed that support for Labour in the Muslim com-munity had fallen from 75 per cent at the 2001 Election to just 32 per cent, and most of that loss went to the Liberal Democrats (a survey in Scotland showed a similar collapse, but there it was to the benefit of the Scottish National Party). At the 2005 election there were significant swings away from Labour to the anti-war Liberal Democrats and to the newly formed Respect–Unity Coalition in seats with large Muslim communities. Respect, with its leader George Galloway as candidate, narrowly took Bethnal Green and Bow, one of the most ethnically diverse con-stituencies in the UK, from Labour.

Clearly international relations have a huge impact on political support among ethnic minorities, and there are historical precedents. Geoffrey Alderman (1983) has traced the political attitudes of the British Jewish community and has shown that support often shifted between parties depending on their foreign policy – since 1948 attitudes to the Israel–Palestine question have resulted in a shift of support from Labour to the Conservatives, although the rising prosperity of the community also explains that shift. In general, newly established immigrant communities favour parties of the left, unless they engage in foreign policy decisions which alienate those communities. The role of ethnicity is, however, more striking in the United States. Table 5.5 shows how the different groups voted in the 2004 presidential election.

Bush made significant advances among Latino and Asian (meaning here: east Asian) voters, and given that

Table 5.5 Voting in 2004 US presidential election

	Bush (Republican) %	Kerry (Democrat) %
Ethnic groups (as defined by the polling agency)		
White (77% of voters)	58	41
African-American (11%)	11	88
Latino (8%)	44	53
Asian (2%)	44	56
Religion (as defined by the polling agency)		
Protestant (54%)	59	40
Catholic (27%)	52	47
Jewish (3%)	25	74
RESULT	51	48

the former are the fastest expanding group the prospects for future Republican electoral success are very bright – indeed, this fact, much more than the emphasis on Bush's support among conservative evangelical Christians, was the most important characteristic of the 2004 election.

Social class and voting behaviour

Many political sociologists associate changes in the relationship between social class and voting behaviour with postmodernism. We will be referring to the work of Curtice (1994: 33–42) throughout this section because he acknowledges diversity within social classes (a feature of postmodernism) but argues that the effects of this on the British political system seem to have been exagger-ated by many analysts.

Curtice acknowledges the changing sizes and charac-teristics of social classes, with more white-collar workers now than blue-collar workers, more home ownership, more voters with a higher education, and a reduction in religious adherence. Yet he argues that our main interest is in the proportion of Conservative and Labour votes that come from different classes. If the proportions for each of these parties have become similar to each other we can claim that there has been a decline in relative class voting.

Although there have been some changes in social class allegiances, Table 5.4 still indicates a pattern of voting according to social class. However, what the table does not reveal is the shift over a number of elections between the parties. In general, middle-class (Class AB) support has shifted from the Conservatives to Labour and the Liberal Democrats. The Liberal Democrats' class profile has become less 'flat' – most of its growth in support has been among the AB group, and this explains its capture of some very affluent seats from the Conservatives.

Age (and turnout)

It is notable that younger voters tend to support parties of the left. This is a pattern repeated in many countries. However, there are two kinds of explanation: life cycle and cohort. The life-cycle view is that as voters get older their concerns shift – issues such as taxation and spending become more important – and consequently there is a shift to the right (the shift must always be measured by deviation from the average – for example, the Conservatives received 33 per cent of the vote in 2001 but only 27 per cent of the those aged 18–24, so consequently they had a deficit of 6 per cent – if the Conservative vote was, say, 40 per cent, but they got 29 per cent of the 18–24 age-group vote then the deficit would be bigger). The cohort view is that contemporary experience affects an age group for life – of course, there can be a weakening of the effect but personal experience is still the primary determinant. This means that if a party 'loses' an age group it is lost for ever.

An increasingly important factor – and one which applies especially to age, but is relevant to all social groups – is the propensity to vote. Indeed, this is one of the reasons why opinion polls have recently had a poor record in predicting election results – it is very difficult to calculate how likely a person is to vote. Interestingly, popular media coverage emphasizes the contempt which people have for politicians, and yet respondents to opinion polls tend to overestimate turnout: as a rule of thumb if 70 per cent say they are certain to vote, 60 per cent will, in fact, vote. This suggests that some voters are ashamed to admit they will not vote.

Turnout fell dramatically between 1997 and 2001 – from 71 per cent to 59 per cent (it had never fallen below 70 per cent in the post-1945 period), and picked up only slightly in 2005 to 61 per cent. Some political scientists explain the low turnout as the result of assuming a Labour victory, or in terms of a level of contentment, with the implication that we should not be worried about falling turnout – it is notable the turnout was very high in Northern Ireland, where three Sinn Fein MPs do not recognize the legitimacy of the parliament to which they have been elected! However, the contentment argument is unconvincing because turnout varies by social class – the poorest are least likely to vote (see Table 5.4: there was a turnout of 68 per cent among social class AB, but only 53 per cent among DE).

Theories of class dealignment

Many researchers have observed that, since the 1970s, there has been a fundamental decline in the relationship between social class and loyalty to one political party: a decline that has been confounded by difficulties in allocating individuals to class categories. The former 'working class' now includes workers who have shares in their companies and do not therefore conform to the proletariat of Marx's lifetime.

Divisions in the middle class can also be perceived, including the different political allegiances of many public and private employees. It was argued (Dunleavy 1980) that production and consumption sectoral cleavages may be better indicators of voting behaviour than simple definitions of social class based on occupational groupings (e.g. the revised and updated version of the Registrar-General's scale, Office for National Statistics 1998a). The claim is that production sectors can be significant because public employees are more likely to favour policies supporting a generously financed public sector, while those working in the private (commercial) sector are more likely to favour policies emphasizing unfettered market forces. Similarly, consumption sectoral cleavages denote levels of reliance on mainly public or private services (such as education, health care, transport and housing). In Leadbetter's analysis of the divided workforce (Riley 1988: 313) we can also see potential differences in workers' attitudes based on their level of job security.

Theories of partisan dealignment

Since the 1970s there has been a dilution of loyalty to the two major political parties' philosophies and policies. Voters are less likely to have a lifetime commitment to one political party. Their vote may change over time and according to the context of the election (e.g. voting differently at general elections and local authority elections).

'Floating voters' may be open to persuasion at election time and may, for example, be politically apathetic or primarily influenced by the issues of the day (see our earlier resumé of some 'Theories about voting behaviour', pp. 186–7).

Curtice (1994) argued that there was no real evidence of a pattern of partisan dealignment. He argued that the effects of social change and electoral volatility had been exaggerated, and that these theories underestimate the resistance of political systems to social change. An important part of this resistance is the first-past-the-post electoral system (see pp. 182–3) as it would not accurately reflect partisan dealignment. Even if social change had been responsible for a collapse in the strength of the two-party system at the popular level, we would have had to conclude that its impact on the way that Britain is governed had so far been muted. For the impact of social change on politics is mediated by the institutional rules as well as the actions of politicians (Curtice 1994: 42). Above all, social class remains an important cleavage at both elite and mass level. Rather than the helpless plaything of sociological forces, post-war British politics has been vitally shaped by political choices and developments (Curtice 1994: 41). Curtice argued that, rather than a straightforward pattern in the relationship between class and vote, there has been a 'trendless fluctuation' which could be explained by the particular circumstances of each election.

Who are the activists?

We have already considered political participation with regard to elections and voting behaviour. Here we ask how politically active people are and what is the nature of their activity. Before looking at some research findings, we ask you to assess your own political activity.

The British Political Participation Study (BPPS) carried out by Parry *et al.* (1989) comprised a national sample (1,578) survey of the population of England, Wales and Scotland (carried out in 1984/5 – this is quite a dated study but still valuable) together with a survey of citizens and leaders in local communities.

The researchers observed that an issue must be identified as susceptible to individual influence. They list four main reasons why people take action:

1 *Instrumentally* – to defend or promote their own interests.

2 *Communitarian* – for the good of the community at large.

A closer look

How politically active are you?

➤ Individually, and honestly, decide whether you fit any of the following categories. If you do not fit any, how do you define yourself?

➤ In a group, list the categories on a board, together with the numbers in the group who fit each category (or do not fit any).

➤ What problems have arisen?

➤ How would you describe your group's level of political activity?

➤ Are you, as students of political sociology, representative of the wider population?

1 Inactive: do not vote regularly or have any other involvement.

2 A voting specialist: only vote.

3 A group specialist: involvement only in a group context.

4 A party campaign specialist: have campaigned for a political party.

5 A contacting specialist: have contacted politicians (by letter, by telephone, by e-mail at the politician's surgery or in other ways).

6 A protesting specialist: participated in marches, demonstrations, sent protest letters.

7 A complete activist: active across the board from 2 to 6.

---

3 *Educative and developmental* – to increase understanding of society or politics.

4 *Expressive* – to state their position on a matter that may or may not affect them and on which they might not expect immediate return in terms of changed policy.

Parry *et al.* note that an individual may take action for more than one of the above reasons. Very little action was taken on issues that were considered to be beyond their respondents' sphere of influence. More action was taken on relatively local issues, such as housing, the environment, education and transport, which were perceived as both affecting the household directly and most amenable to influence.

Perhaps the most consistent claims about political activity relate to the social location of the particularly active or inactive. The British Political Participation Study found that professionals were 'massively over-represented' among complete activists, by about five times their relative size in the population. Some other non-manual grades were also over-represented:

> One can see very clearly that being part of the participatory elite corresponds very closely to being from the non-manual, and especially managerial, strata of society. Most members of the middle class are not political activists, but the reverse seems plainly to be the case. Conversely, those from manual occupations, and particularly those from households outside the economically active sector, are under represented. In the latter case, we may be observing some age-related effects. Whatever the case, however, in social terms, both they and the proletariat are conspicuous by their relative absence. The 'chorus' of complete activists clearly 'sings with an upper-class accent'.
>
> (Parry *et al.* 1989: 29)

Such claims have been generally accepted by political sociologists for many years, but when we look at a possible change from 'old' to 'new' politics we see that new political themes and activities may be bringing with them a broader range of activists. Below is a nice comment on the anti-poll tax demonstrations in Britain in 1989–90, but it could easily be applied to more recent anti-globalization protests:

> Some people were poorly dressed and looked worse fed than their mongrel dogs, some wore the fatigues and black leather that say 'anarchist!' to the media. But the crowd . . . was overwhelmingly a natural-looking bunch of people, and I only hope that they were Marxists and anarchists, because if they were, then they've infiltrated every walk of life in Britain. Every home has got one.
>
> (Anon., describing an anti-poll tax demonstration in Trafalgar Square, in Waddington *et al.* 1989: 9)

Figure 5.4 Anti-globalization protests are growing in number throughout the world
Source: Antoine Serra in Visu/CORBIS

Parry *et al.* categorized respondents according to level of political activity as follows (compare these findings with your group findings):

➤ 25.8 per cent were inactive: did not vote regularly or have any other involvement.

➤ 51.0 per cent were voting specialists: only voted.

➤ 8.7 per cent were group specialists: involvement only in a group context.

➤ 2.2 per cent were party campaign specialists.

➤ 7.7 per cent were contacting specialists: contacted politicians, etc.).

➤ 3.1 per cent were protesting specialists: marches, demonstrations, letters.

➤ 1.5 per cent were complete activists: active across the board.

The BPPS researchers supported their findings with more findings about action and assertiveness from the annual British Social Attitudes surveys (e.g. Jowell *et al.* 1992). Levels of local and national assertiveness were measured and an apparent increase in national assertiveness was found. Comparisons in local assertiveness were made over time, using the 1960 study (Almond and Verba 1963) and a survey carried out for the Redcliffe Maud Committee on local government during the early months of 1965. These are rather dated but useful for assessing changes in attitudes over time.

All three surveys (Almond and Verba, Redcliffe Maud and various BSA surveys) provide evidence of the greater willingness of individuals to act on their own account when roused by some proposed local action. They also found that the most highly educated and most affluent were more likely to act.

It has long been claimed that more men than women take action. Although more women are active in local politics, in 1998 a census of councillors by the Local Government Management Board had a response rate of nearly two-thirds of all councillors (almost 15,000 responses) and found that three-quarters were male. However, if you look back to our discussion of gender and voting (p. 187) you will see that there are criticisms of how action is defined and of sexism in political studies. It would be useful to consider these criticisms, together with the implications of the following:

1 More full-time employees and trade unionists are active.

2 Women may be more tied to the home.

3 The most highly educated tend to express feelings of political efficacy. Even at a time when girls are achieving more than boys in school-leaving examinations, more men than women in the older population have had a higher education.

4 Bourque and Grossholtz argued that women might simply be more realistic:

> One might offer the alternative hypothesis, that given the very limited number of issues that citizens can affect, the lower sense of political efficacy expressed by women is a perceptive assessment of the process. Men, on the other hand, express irrationally high rates of efficacy because of the limitations of their sex role which teaches them that they are masterful and capable of affecting the political process. In fact, few of us have any political influence in any case.
>
> (Bourque and Grossholtz 1984: 107)

One possible explanation for levels of political activity arises from Maslow's theory of a hierarchy of human motivations (1970). According to this theory, an individual's material needs and psychological safety need to be satisfied before more expressive needs can be satisfied. Expressive needs include such emotions as affection, esteem and self-actualization, and although there is some overlapping of the hierarchy – affection can, for example, be felt in the most dire circumstances – expressive needs are considered less important than physical and spiritual survival. Political activity could be assigned to Maslow's fifth, and lowest, tier of needs ('self-actualization').

Perhaps the ordinary person in the street is more inclined to take political action as a result of a shift from an 'old' style of politics to a 'new' style with a greater emphasis on self-actualization, new motivations and new forms of activity. This helps explain the rise of a 'new' pattern of political activity.

> Today's decision makers grew up in a post-colonial, post-global war world, where women and foreigners and racial minorities and homosexuals and the sick and the disabled and children and old people are known to have rights, even when those rights are deliberately thwarted. The big difference is that until our parents' generation people could be blinkered and still semi-legitimately excuse themselves for being blinkered. 'We didn't know. There wasn't anything we could do. They deserved it.' Having reached the end of a century of extremes we now live in an age where there is no excuse not to know and no excuse not to take a stand.
>
> (Button 1995: 44)

Button also claims that when he refers to 'radicalism' it can most closely be associated with empowerment and that 'a new fearlessness has emerged – a realisation that oppressive centralised power must be resisted and balanced by "people power"' (Button 1995: 12). New forms of political activity often appear as the sort of civil disobedience or 'direct action' now seen in a wide range of political protests.

> I will take the core notion of direct action as being the idea that a person or group of people act to achieve a particular social or political goal without primarily mediating that action through the formal processes and structures of the State and economic relations. Thus workers who strike unofficially, homeless people who squat in empty properties, campaigners who perform civil disobedience acts, and people who organise co-ops can all be said to have performed direct actions. Such a notion does not exclude the fact that violence may be part of some direct actions. Therefore it is also necessary to distinguish between direct action and nonviolent direct action (NVDA). (Hart 1997: 42–3)

Some individual activities may be loosely linked by a sense of common identity with others in a wider social movement, and the study of social movements is particularly important in political sociology.

> A social movement is a collective actor constituted by individuals who understand themselves to have common interests and, for at least some significant part of their social existence, a common identity. Social movements are distinguished from other collective actors, such as political parties and pressure groups, in that they have mass mobilisation, or the threat of mobilisation, as their prime source of social sanction, and hence of power. They are further distinguished from other collectivities, such as voluntary associations and clubs, in being chiefly concerned to defend or change society, or the relative position of the group in society. (Scott 1990: 6)

To Scott the study of new social movements is primarily political, while to Alain Touraine sociology *is* the study of social movements and

> The concept of social movement is all the more necessary to the extent to which it facilitates the trancendence of the present weakness and confusion of sociology by offering a direct critique of the model of analysis which is in crisis and by introducing a new general approach, new debates, and new fields of concrete research. (Touraine 1985: 787)

Stop and think

➤ Do you agree with Button's contention that 'we now live in an age where there is no excuse not to know and no excuse not to take a stand'?

➤ Would you be more likely to act on a local issue than a national issue? (You might consider what action, if any you would take if either your local council or Parliament was considering a law which you regarded as unjust or harmful.)

➤ List and discuss possible reasons for the lack of political activity.

Political change

Some political analysts claim that in Western democracies an 'old' style of political participation, involving social class alignment, class-based social movements, partisan alignment and formal pressure group activity, has been replaced, or is in transition towards, a 'new' style of political participation, involving class dealignment, partisan dealignment and new social movements with a greater emphasis on wider moral concerns. A summary of what Klaus Offe identified as the main features of 'old' and 'new' politics is provided in Table 5.6 below.

An additional dimension can be added by looking at Inglehart's materialist/post-materialist hypothesis (1997), which supports Maslow's theory (see p. 192) as well as distinctions between 'old' and 'new' political attitudes.

> Satisfaction of the survival needs, we hypothesised, leads to growing emphasis on nonphysiological or 'Post-materialist' goals. A large share of the public in Western societies have been socialised in an environment that provides an unprecedentedly secure prospect that one's physiological needs will be met. Consequently, Western public's responses should tend to polarise along a Materialist/Postmaterialist dimension, with some individuals consistently emphasising Materialist goals, while others tend to give priority to Post-materialist goals. (Inglehart 1997: 110)

Inglehart tested his hypothesis on data from two main sources: the Euro-Barometer surveys, carried out annually in all EU countries since 1970, and World Values surveys, which provided data from 22 countries in 1980 and 43 countries (including the original 22) in 1990–94. From factor analysis of a wide range of variables,

Table 5.6 The distinctiveness of 'old' and 'new' political action

	'Old' politics	'New' politics
Issues and values	Economic growth and management; social security; material distribution	Preservation of peace and the environment; establishment of equal human rights
	Security; equal opportunity; personal consumption and material improvement	Opposition to centralized, bureaucratic or state control. In search of personal autonomy and democratic self-management
Internal organization	Formal organization and large representative associations (e.g. parties, pressure groups)	Informal, spontaneous, egalitarian, impermanent groups of campaigners
The organization of action	Interest group bargaining; competitive party politics	Protest based on demands, formulated in negative terms about single issues, using unconventional tactics
Social bases of participants	Classes and occupational groups acting in their own group interests, especially with respect to material rewards	Certain socio-economic groups (especially the 'new middle class') acting not in own interests but on behalf of other ascriptive collectivities (e.g. women, youth, humankind)
Axis of politics	Class interest	Moral concern

Source: Adapted by Abercrombie *et al.* 1994: Fig. 12.12 p. 518, from Offe 1985: 832

Inglehart identified six key indicators of materialist values: these were 'strong defence forces', 'fight rising prices', 'fight against crime', 'maintain order', 'economic growth' and 'maintain stable economy'. Five other key indicators of post-materialist values were identified: these were 'less impersonal society', 'more say in job', 'more say in government', 'ideas count more than money' and 'freedom of speech'. Thus materialist interests are associated with 'old' politics, post-materialist interests with 'new' politics, and Figure 5.5 represents findings about the shift towards post-materialist values in some of the countries studied.

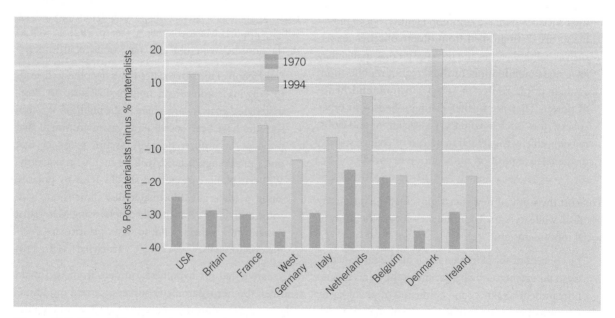

Figure 5.5 The shift towards post-materialist values among the publics of nine Western societies, 1970–94

Source: Inglehart 1997, Fig. 5.4, p. 140. European Community surveys, February 1970 and autumn 1994 and US national election surveys from 1972 and 1992
Copyright © 1997 by Princeton University Press. Reprinted by permission

A closer look

Table 5.7 The emergence of life politics

Emancipatory politics	Life politics
1 The freeing of social life from the fixities of tradition and custom.	1 Political decisions flowing from freedom of choice and generative power (power as transformative capacity).
2 The reduction or elimination of exploitation, inequality or oppression. Concerned with the divisive distribution of power/resources.	2 The creation of morally justifiable forms of life that will promote self-actualization in the context of global interdependence.
3 Obeys imperatives suggested by the ethics of justice, equality and participation.	3 Develops ethics concerning the issue 'How should we live?' in a post-traditional order and against the backdrop of existential questions.

Source: Giddens 1991: 215

Giddens on life politics

Life politics presumes (a certain level of) emancipation, in both the main senses noted above: emancipation from the fixities of tradition and from conditions of hierarchical domination. It would be too crude to say simply that life politics focuses on what happens once individuals have achieved a certain level of autonomy of action, because other factors are involved; but this provides at least an initial orientation. Life politics does not primarily concern the conditions which liberate us in order to make choices: it is a politics of choice. While emancipatory politics is a politics of life chances, life politics is a politics of lifestyle.

(Giddens 1991: 214)

Questions

1. *Do Giddens and Inglehart assume a narrow or a wide definition of politics?*

2. *Provide an illustration/example of 'emancipatory politics'.*

3. *Explain and discuss (with at least one example) what Giddens means by 'politics of lifestyle'.*

Giddens also identified changes of this sort. We have already seen his theories about a process of democratization and noted the influence of his theories on a 'third way' between left- and right-wing perspectives. He distinguished between a form of politics associated with emancipation – often from constraints of social class or gender – and a form of politics that goes further to raise issues of identity, self-actualization and reflexivity. Examples of this new political style can be seen in political activities by feminists, gays and disabled people, who are not simply protesting about discriminatory practices but also reflecting on how they really want to live their own lives.

Similar trends were identified when Seidler looked at *Recovering the Self* (1994: 159, 178) and associated modernism, the Enlightenment and industrialization with rationalism and, as a result, denial of emotions, the rejection of tradition, loss of sense of self and identity, and denial of feelings. Modernist ideas meant that science came to be regarded as superior to nature and people had become morally confused. Again there is an emphasis on the need for individuals to confront this moral confusion and develop new attitudes to life and to their own identities.

Roche (1995: 53) notes that such feeling are not new and that Durkheim saw capitalist society as particularly prone to anomie. Durkheim also associated anomie with the problems of adapting to rapid social change.

> Whether in terms of the classical or renewed conception of anomie, social phenomena distinctive of the twentieth century Western society such as consumerism (the mass cultivation of attitudes of envy and greed, instability and addiction towards objects and possessions) and ecological crisis, are usefully seen as anomic (unlimited, self-destructive, etc.).
>
> (Roche 1995: 55)

Roche rethinks theories about anomie using a rational humanist perspective and an emphasis on human obligation to perpetuate and support the human species. He says that ethics and moral obligation need to be restored and citizenship should be seen as relating to obligations as well as rights. By emphasizing obligations as well as rights, new social movements such as women's liberation and ecology are, he claims, 'counter anomic': feminist problems are anomie problems. In the past the discourse of citizenship was largely a 'rights discourse' but it now also includes a 'duties discourse', emphasizing social obligations.

'Old' political issues

The 'old' style of politics is often associated with modernist themes, such as industrialization, mass production, an emphasis on class conflict, Marxist critiques, the trade union movement and pressure group activity working within formal political systems. However, it is important not to accept too easily what may be a rather simple image of the past. For example, Button (1995) suggests that there are some remaining elements of 'old' politics.

First, Button claims that the gap between the haves and the have-nots has been widened by economic policies favouring a market economy. Second, he argues that those policies have promoted money as the only valid measure of value. In the second half of the twentieth century, commercial and relatively covert political tactics helped to disempower the silent majority and increasingly replaced overt social and military power tactics. His third suggestion is that the power establishment retained some oppressive, elitist views. Finally, Button observes that political activity by pressure groups remains, although many groups have adjusted to a new political environment.

We have already considered class and partisan alignment and dealignment but have not yet explained what we mean by pressure groups. Definitions generally include most of the following: that they are highly organized and hierarchical groups, defending their members self-interest, exerting pressure within the political system, but not seeking elective office for themselves, or presenting a programme covering a wide range of policies. This means that trade unions are usually described as pressure groups within a wider trade union movement, which is often described as an 'old' social movement. Yet trade unions have undergone a period of dramatic change since the early 1970s and are now very different to the pressure groups within the early labour movement of 100 years ago.

Since the 1970s, British governments have imposed many restrictions on union activities. Unions have tended to be unsuccessful in confrontations with employers and, when unions challenged government decisions, courts usually passed judgements in favour of the government. Divisions of opinion between unionists have become more apparent with the obligation to conduct rigorously monitored ballots before industrial action. The Labour government (1997–) has not reversed this legislation and has adopted an 'arm's length' approach to the unions. In the period between 1997 and 2005 the number of jobs in the British economy has grown considerably but manufacturing jobs – the traditional 'core' of trade union activism – have declined by about one million.

The decline of heavy industry and manual work means that a larger proportion of union members are now white-collar, non-manual workers. Overall membership declined quite dramatically during the early 1980s and has not shown a significant increase since then. As a result several unions have tried to consolidate their strengths by amalgamating to form a few 'super' unions.

The types of issue espoused by unions have also changed, largely because of their changing membership and constraints on industrial action. While still primarily concerned with economic issues, they have shifted from the traditional emphasis on social class inequalities and now involve themselves more in equal opportunities and welfare in general, including the protection of their members from discrimination on the basis of gender, ethnicity, disability or age, bullying in the workplace and fears about health and safety. They have been very active in promoting links with other workers within the European Union and campaigning for a stronger application of the EU Social Chapter.

'New' political issues

It is important not to accept too easily what may be a rather simple image of changes that are still taking place. Nevertheless, it is possible to identify a growing concern (in 'new' politics and 'new' social movements) that has less to do with social class and more to do with wider examples of inequalities (e.g. women's liberation; racial issues; children's rights; gay liberation; elderly, poor and disabled people; animal liberation; anti-roads protests; anti-hunt saboteurs; 'eco-warriors'), wider moral issues, rights and oppression.

Theoretical distinctions between old and new social movements tend to be raised by European writers (rather than those in the USA) because Marxist ideas, class-based analysis and class-based conflicts have been more influential in Europe, where their relative decline has been particularly noticeable. However, new social movements cannot be seen as simply a European phenomenon, because they are often perceived as emerging from the protest movements of the 1960s, and these had a great impact on many non-European countries (e.g. the black civil rights movement in the USA). These new movements articulate a sense of moral outrage against the uncontrolled tendencies of established political systems, emphasizing the importance of self-management and personal autonomy and values that are universalistic rather than class-based (e.g. environmental risks are faced by everyone).

Although new social movements usually include pressure groups (e.g. Greenpeace, Friends of the Earth and others within the 'green' movement) and may even be associated with a political party (e.g. the Green Party), they often consist of loose, fluid networks with decentralized, open, democratic structures. Indeed corporatism, elitism and political partisanship are often seen as potentially deradicalizing influences. Yet their activities are often well planned and they may be expert in using the media to mobilize public opinion (e.g. Greenpeace).

Karl-Werner Brand looked at cyclical aspects of new social movements:

> The mobilisation cycles of NSMs and their precursors find an exceptionally fertile ground in times of spreading cultural criticism. Such times heighten public sensitivity to the problems of industrialisation, urbanisation, commercialisation, and bureaucratisation. They temporarily upset the hegemony of the materialist conception of progress, thus giving way to a broad spectrum of anti-modern reactions and reform movements.
>
> (Brand cited by Dalton *et al.* 1990: 39)

These concerns have led to new interests in the study of civil liberties and citizenship (McKie and Bindman 1994). In keeping with some aspects of 'new' politics are new academic debates about communitarianism (in the USA, e.g. Etzioni 1993), which emphasize a balance between the rights of individuals and their responsibilities to the community. Although criticized for its occasionally paternalistic stance, communitarianism aims to remove severe impediments to community relationships; for example, providing education for parenthood, helping parents to help themselves, and devolving considerable government power to a local level.

Another important difference between 'old' and 'new' politics and social movements is in the change from a politics that focuses on material issues to a politics that seeks cultural change. For example, the women's liberation movement aims to change not only material and social inequalities between women and men but particularly the attitudes that lie behind them. This involves enlightening men and women and empowering women in their social and personal lives. Similarly, the gay liberation movement seeks to change social inequalities and the attitudes that support them. For some movements this involves provid-

Figure 5.6 Two Greenpeace activists abseil down Nelson's Column in Trafalgar Square, London, after unfurling a huge banner shortly before the Canadian prime minister, Jean Chretien, was due to arrive to reopen the newly refurbished Canada House (courtesy of PA News)

ing a strong cultural backing to support their supporters; for example, in the gay liberation movement, this involves the movement's own newspapers and magazines, pop music, night-clubs and other local and national groupings. Here can be seen an emphasis on both political change and improvements in the quality of life. It can also be seen that there is likely to be an overlap as some individuals support a number of movements, for example ecofeminism, gay feminists, Greenpeace's involvement in environmental and peace movements.

Pressure movements

It is difficult to label some movements as either 'old' or 'new' social movements; a third form of political grouping may be seen as including some of the features of each style of movement. Tonge (1994) identified five characteristics of a pressure movement:

1 It is concerned with political aims.

2 Its aims are limited to single-issue campaigns.

3 It may possess a class base, but not a class force.

4 It is likely to adopt a highly centralized form.

5 It is likely to by-pass political parties as agents of change.

He concluded that, although he could define the anti-poll tax movement of 1989–90 as a pressure movement, it would be difficult to find others. Yet many groups cannot easily be identified; for example, the 'Countryside Alliance', and anti-motorway and anti-road-by-pass groups.

> The countryside march this week was puzzling. What were they all doing there together? There were wealthy landowners and the peasants they still keep in penury; fox hunters and the farmers who put up barbed wire to keep them off their land; the people who've left the city for a peaceful life in idyllic rustic surroundings alongside those who are tearing down hedgerows and putting up hideous prefabricated barns. They didn't seem to have much in common except a general, rancorous discontent with the rest of us. It's as if all the people whose names begin with the letter 'R' had got together to complain that nobody else understood them.
>
> (Simon Hoggart, 'Nothing in common apart from a loathing of commoners', the *Guardian* 7.3.98)

Stop and think

➤ Consider the trade union movement, women's liberation movement and black civil rights movement in the USA. How would you label each of them: for example, a pressure group, 'old' social movement, 'new' social movement, pressure movement, or something else?

➤ Why did you choose that particular label?

Extreme forms of political action

Within any political organization – for example, a political party or a pressure group – there are likely to be several flanks, representing differences of opinion about policies and/or action. For example, 'dark greens' are particularly determined in their efforts to maintain an environmentally friendly lifestyle, and some have been accused of caring more about the environment than about people. Extremism is obviously a relative concept, and this may reflect on the larger group. When extremists create a radical flank it can either discredit the image of the whole movement or indirectly support the moderates' case by suggesting that political decision makers have little to fear from moderate elements. Malcolm X provided a figurehead for the extremist Nation of Islam but explained how he felt that his group of radicals could help the whole black civil rights movement in the USA.

> I want Dr King to know that I didn't come to Selma to make his job difficult. I really did come thinking that I could make it easier. If white people realise what the alternative is, perhaps they'll be more willing to hear Dr King.
>
> (Malcolm X 1965, quoted in Haines 1988: 1)

Martin Luther King was not easily impressed and predicted that,

> The more there are riots, the more repression will take place, and the more we face the danger of a right-wing take-over, and eventually a fascist society.
>
> (Martin Luther King, quoted in Haines 1988: 1)

Indeed, there were deeply ideological differences between these two figureheads of the black civil rights movement and such differences remain. Whereas most civil rights activists were campaigning for greater integration in the USA, the Nation of Islam has pursued a policy of black separatism, anti-white racism and anti-semitism. In 1995 it played an important role in organizing the Million Man March of over 400,000 black men to Washington in protest against the negative stereotyping of black men. As women were excluded from the march the organizers were criticized for their apparently sexist attitudes, despite the marchers' public pledge to respect their wives and lead better family lives.

It is easy to see how this form of fundamentalism can emerge as a reaction to de-traditionalization (see pp. 166–7, Giddens on democratization) and to the type of moral idealism associated with new politics. Some radicals may even feel that their peaceful methods have been unsuccessful and that the only alternative is to use violence. In his deprivation theory, Gurr (1970: 24) proposed that 'the potential for collective violence varies strongly with the intensity and scope of relative deprivation among members of a collectivity.'

There is also the possibility that radical flanks can attract individuals who join because they are more interested in violence that in the movement's aims. Terrorism aims to inspire terror by using violence, or the threat of violence, intimidation and a rejection of compromise. This means that some political systems answer that description and the old problem of distinguishing between freedom fighters and terrorists remains. It is likely that relationships between political systems, social movements and political violence will vary considerably.

Stop and think

➤ Consider the extent to which each of the following political groups is likely to spawn violence:
(a) pressure groups; (b) 'old' social movements;
(c) 'new' social movements; (d) pressure movements.

➤ Would you describe the African National Congress (before the end of apartheid) as: (a) a terrorist organization; (b) a group of freedom fighters;
(c) some sort of social movement?

➤ How would you label South African governments during the time of apartheid?

So what do we mean by politics?

It is understandable if you are now feeling even more confused about the nature of politics and the meanings of various terms. We have seen narrow and wide definitions of politics, how the personal can become political, how democracy could be democratized and how we are influenced by 'action at a distance'. Indeed, citizenship and rights could be narrowly defined when people were less aware of globalization. Even the style of politics may have changed from 'old' to 'new' politics, from emancipatory or materialist politics to life politics or post-materialism. The start of the chapter was concerned with citizens' rights, but more has emerged on citizens' obligations and lifestyles. You should now be able to study such issues further with a more critical approach than the brevity of this chapter could allow.

Summary

➤ A narrow definition of politics emphasizes formal political structures, including international bodies such as the UN and EU and British institutions such as the monarchy, Parliament and the civil service. A wider definition would encompass political theories and processes, including voting and other forms of political participation.

➤ Basic classifications of political parties and governments divide them into right-wing or left-wing. However, this categorization is far from straightforward: totalitarian states can be either extremely right-wing or left-wing, and fascist movements and leaders have appealed to those who would see themselves as basically left-wing. The new Labour government elected in 1997 has moved away from the traditional right-wing/left-wing division with its promotion of the concept of a 'third way'. Political, or ideological, positions are best understood in multi-dimensional terms.

➤ Political participation suggests an involvement in political decision making. In modern mass societies, studies of political participation have focused on patterns of voting. Models of voting behaviour include the party identification model, which emphasizes the influence of background on voting, the rational choice model highlighting the voter's self-interest, and more complex models of relationships between social background, policy preferences and choice of political party.

➤ Political decision makers are usually more middle-class, highly educated and wealthy than the general population, and much more likely to be male and white.

➤ Despite talk of class dealignment, class continues to be an important determinant of voting behaviour. Gender has become less important, while religion and ethnicity – especially in the Muslim community – has become more significant. Age has always played a part, but it is difficult to establish whether there is generational voting or cohort voting. As important as the distribution of the vote among parties is the varying propensity of groups to vote.

Summary (continued)

➤ Changes in the nature of political parties and the movement away from strong political loyalty and commitment to one political position have been seen as evidence of a 'new' style of politics. The old style of politics was characterized by class loyalty to one party, trade union support and political pressure groups; the new style is associated with a decline in the relationship between social class and party loyalty and with a growing interest in civil liberties and citizenship.

Links

The section on international political institutions, pp. 172–175, can be read in conjunction with pp. 45–451 of Chapter 11, Global Issues in Sociology.

The social background of MPs, pp. 183–185, can be related to the discussion of the privileged in Chapter 6, pp. 235–236.

 ## Further reading

The best place to start are some good textbooks on British Politics:

Ian Budge *et al.* (2004) *The New British Politics*, 3rd edn, Harlow: Pearson Longman.

Bill Jones *et al.* (2004) *Politics UK*, 5th edn, Harlow: Pearson Longman.

Some other useful books on British politics include:
Anthony Birch (2002) *The British System of Government*, 10th edn, Routledge.

Bill Coxall *et al.* (2003) *Contemporary British Politics*, Palgrave Macmillan.

Patrick Dunleavy *et al.* (2003) *Developments in British Politics 7*, Palgrave Macmillan.

HMSO, *Social Trends* (for 'social indicators').

John Kingdom (1999) *Government and Politics in Britain*, Polity.

Looking further:
John McCormick (2002) *Understanding the European Union*, 2nd edn, Palgrave.

Neill Nugent (2003) *The Government and Politics of the European Union*, 2nd edn, Palgrave.

Theodore Lowi and Benjamin Ginsberg (2002) 2nd edn, *American Government: Freedom and Power*, 'brief' 2nd edn, Norton.

Gillian Youngs (1999) *International Relations in a Global Age: a Conceptual Challenge*, Polity.

Try to read a 'serious' daily (once referred to as 'broadsheets', but many are now 'compacts', as they like to call themselves) and a Sunday newspaper: *The Times, Financial Times, Daily Telegraph, Guardian, Independent, Sunday Times, Observer.* There are also important weekly magazines: *The Economist, New Statesman, Spectator.*

 ## Web sites

There are a number of important web sites:
The UK Parliament: **www.parliament.uk**
British Government: **www.number-10.gov.uk**
Scottish Parliament: **www.scottish.parliament.uk**
General page of links: **www.keele.ac.uk/depts/por/ukbase.htm**

Most of these newspapers and magazines above have free online versions, for example:

➤ The *Guardian* and the *Observer*: **www.guardian.co.uk**
➤ *The Times* and *Sunday Times*: **www.timesonline.co.uk**
➤ *The Economist*: **www.economist.com**

There are a number of British and international news sites:

➤ British Broadcasting Corporation (BBC): **www.bbc.co.uk**
➤ Cable News Network (CNN) (American international news station): **www.cnn.com**
➤ Deutsche Welle (German-based European news in English): **www.dw-world.de**
➤ Aljazeera (Arabic news station – English language site): **http://english.aljazeera.net/HomePage**

Activities

Activity 1

A case study

Present a case study of one pressure group (e.g. Greenpeace), social movement (e.g. the Green movement), pressure movement (noting problems of defining the anti-poll tax campaign and anti-road protesters as such), or terrorist organization (e.g. the IRA).

Your central question will be: what has been the role of . . . [name of movement or group] . . . in a changing political environment?

You can consider how this particular movement/group has influenced, and been influenced by, the continually changing political scene. How has it responded to its circumstances? This provides an opportunity to consider features of the movement/group, while drawing together appropriate aspects of the whole chapter (and additional reading) to provide the necessary depth. The features could include how it fits (or does not fit) definitions of (and theories about) movements and other groups; its origins, aims, organization and tactics. Be selective in your references to the rest of the chapter (or book); thinking carefully about the relevance of various theories to the central question.

Your emphasis should be on discussion, rather than description, and you should avoid 'padding' with irrelevant detail.

Activity 2

Inglehart's theories about changing political values and levels of interest

Evidence from the 21 countries surveyed in both 1981 and 1990 indicates that, though they may vote less regularly, most publics are *not* becoming apathetic; quite the contrary, they are becoming increasingly interested in politics. As Figure 5.7 shows, political interest rates rose in 16 countries and fell in only four. The findings are unequivocal, and they contradict the conventional wisdom about mass apathy. Another good indicator of political interest is whether or not people discuss politics with others. Here, too, the predicted rise in conventional participation is taking place. The proportion of the population that discusses politics rose in 17 countries and fell in only three (with one country showing no change).

From 1981 to 1990 the percentage reporting that they had signed a petition rose in 16 countries and fell in only four. When we examine trends over a still longer time period, the results are even more dramatic. Four of the countries that were included in both waves of the World Values survey were also surveyed for the 1974 Political Action study (see Barnes *et al*. 1979: 548–9). In all four cases (the United States, Britain, West Germany and the Netherlands), we find even larger increases from 1974 to 1990 than we do from 1981 to 1990.

How do we explain declining rates of voter turnout and falling political party membership, in light of these findings? The confusion over whether participation is rising or falling arises from the fact that we are dealing with two distinct processes: elite-directed participation is eroding, but more autonomous and active forms of participation are rising.

The decline in voter turnout reflects a long-term intergenerational decline in party loyalty. Although the younger, better-educated birth cohorts show higher rates of political interest, political discussion and so forth than their elders, they have *lower* levels of party loyalty. Surveys from a number of Western European countries reveal that the post-war birth cohorts have considerably lower rates of party loyalty than the elder cohorts. This finding parallels a pattern of intergenerational decline in party identification that has been found among the American electorate during the past two decades.

Although their higher levels of education and politicization predispose them to identify with *some* political party, the younger relatively post-materialist cohorts have less incentive to identify with any specific political party

Activities (continued)

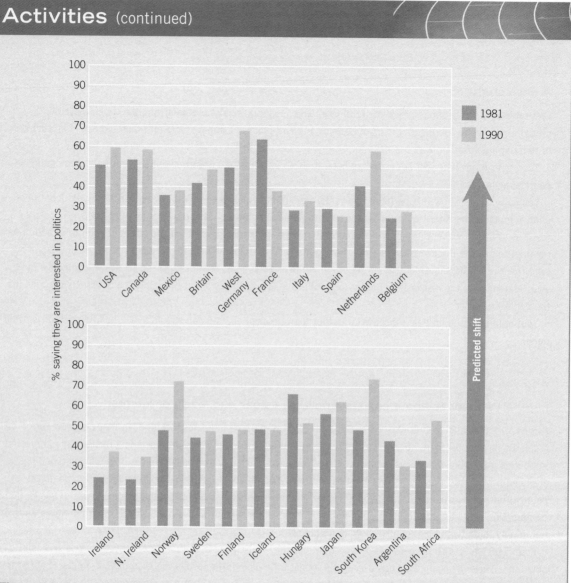

Figure 5.7 Percentages saying that they are interested in politics, in 1981 versus 1990, in 21 countries

Source: Inglehart 1997b, Table 10.8, p. 308. Data from 1981 and 1990 World Values surveys

among the available choices. The established political parties were grounded in an era dominated by social class conflict and economic issues and tend to remain polarized along these lines. For the older cohorts, religion and social class still provide powerful cues in establishing one's political party loyalties, but the younger cohorts' loyalties are less strongly influenced by social class and religion.

Even more important, however, is the fact that the younger birth cohorts are relatively post-materialist. This makes them less amenable to accepting the authority of hierarchical, oligarchical organizations like the old-line political parties.

Source: Ronald Inglehart 1997b, *Modernization and Postmodernization: Cultural, Economic and Political Change in 43 Societies*

Activities (continued)

Questions

1. What does Inglehart mean by (a) 'elite-directed participation' (see p. 178, about elitism); and (b) 'oligarchical organizations' (see p. 178, about oligarchies)?

2. Do you agree with Inglehart's theories that (a) there has been a 'long-term intergenerational decline in party loyalty'; and (b) 'younger birth cohorts are relatively post-materialist'?

3. How have political parties reacted to post-materialist ideas?

4. Can your own political attitudes be explained by Inglehart's theories and/or by any of the theories described in this chapter?

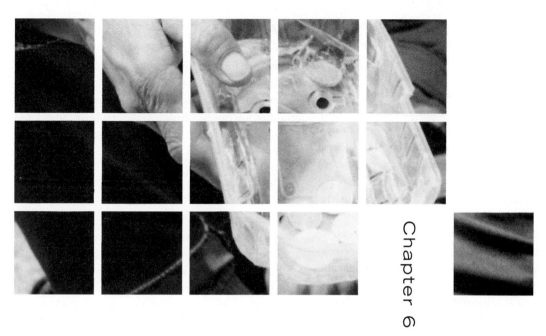

Chapter 6

Social stratification and class

I conceive that there are two kinds of inequality among the human species: one, which I call *natural or physical*, because it is established by nature, and consists in a difference of age, health, bodily strength and the qualities of the mind and the soul; and another, which may be called *moral or political inequality*, because it depends on a kind of convention and is established, or at least authorised, by the consent of men. This latter consists of the different privileges, which some men enjoy to the prejudice of others; such as that of being more rich, more honoured, more powerful, or even in a position of exact obedience.

(J.-J. Rousseau, quoted in Bottomore 1965: 15)

In a class society everyone lives as a member of a particular class, and every kind of thinking, without exception, is stamped with the brand of a class.   (Mao Zedong 1966: 2)

Key issues

➤ What are the major forms of stratification?

➤ What explanations have social scientists offered for the advantages and disadvantages that follow from membership of particular social classes?

➤ Is class analysis still useful in understanding social structure and social opportunities?

Introduction

Stop and think

➤ What kinds of inequalities can you identify which are natural or physical?

➤ Which ones would you regard as moral or political?

➤ Do you feel that you are a member of a particular social class?

➤ If so, which class and what influence does it exert on your life?

➤ If not, do you feel that you are a member of any other sort of social grouping that affects your everyday life?

While more and more people own more and more consumer goods than ever before, we do not have to look very far to find evidence of gross inequalities. Some people can afford to live in large houses with two or more expensive cars to drive around in, while others live in overcrowded and run-down accommodation or sleep rough and will never own a car.

The examination of inequalities has been a major (if not the major) area of sociological inquiry; issues of inequality are central to many social theories and are the key to understanding the different social opportunities available to different social groups and individuals. Sociologists suggest that the origins of inequality can be found in the cultures and social structures of societies themselves. This is not to deny that there are innate and natural differences between people and that such differences contribute to inequality; however, the sociological approach emphasizes how cultures and social structures can create and maintain individual inequalities.

In this chapter we focus on how inequality in societies leads to systems of social stratification, particularly stratification by social class. Chapters 7 and 8 look at stratification by gender and race.

A closer look

Inequality and stratification

Although not synonymous these terms are often used interchangeably. *Inequality* refers to differences between people in terms of their abilities and rewards. We notice these differences from an early age. Why am I stronger than my brother? Why is my sister smarter than me? We become aware of their social implications as we grow up. Why do some people get better jobs? Why are some jobs paid more highly than others?

Inequality leads to *social stratification* when people are ranked hierarchically according to their possession of attributes such as income, wealth, power, age, gender and status. This sort of ranking leads to groups of people being classified into layers or strata – like geological rock formations – hence the term 'stratification'. Stratification can be thought of as referring to structured inequalities that persist over time.

Inequality and stratification profoundly affect the quality of people's lives and can make the difference between, say, working in a well-paid job or being unemployed, eating well or going hungry, owning your own home or living on the street, living to an old age or dying young.

Systems of stratification

While our focus is on stratification in contemporary society, the origins of social inequality can be traced back to ancient times. Historically, four systems of social stratification can be identified: slavery, caste, estates and social class.

Slavery

The oldest and most extreme form of stratification involved the enslavement or ownership of others as a result of conquest, trade, kidnapping, hereditary status or the repayment of a debt. The early civilizations of Babylon, Egypt and Persia relied heavily on slave labour, as did the Greek and Roman empires. Between the fifteenth and nineteenth centuries the industrial and financial might of modern European powers was directly related to the trade in African slaves. This slave labour was crucial to the economic development of the New World and the establishment of black populations in the Americas and the Caribbean.

Although in earlier civilizations slavery was sometimes only temporary, with individual slaves occasionally enjoying high status and the opportunity to earn their freedom, usually it was a permanent state whereby an individual was the property of someone else for whom he or she worked with no prospect of reward, freedom or legal protection. Despite being abolished in the British Empire in 1833, slavery has by no means disappeared. In 1984 the United Nations investigated claims that the West African former colony of Mauritania still allowed 100,000 people to be kept in slavery. Anti-Slavery International has continued to monitor the use of forced labour as well as child prostitution on a global scale.

Caste

The caste system is mainly associated with Indian society and the Hindu religion. It involves a complex and strictly defined division of labour in which occupations are assigned to one of four closed status groups (*varna*). Rank order is not necessarily related to power or money but rather to traditional values which place the Brahmin priests at the top and those responsible for 'unclean' tasks, known as 'untouchables', as outcasts below the four main castes. There is no possibility of social mobility, as these positions are determined by birth. Indeed, a person's

Case study

27 million slaves in the world today

Since 1839 Anti-Slavery International has campaigned for an end to slavery around the globe. A fundamental abuse of human rights and the most extreme form of exploitation, slavery still exists on every continent with rich and poor countries involved in the trade. Since 2001, Anti-Slavery International has worked closely with Free the Slaves, its sister organization in the United States.

According to these organizations millions of men, women and children are bought and sold, bartered and exchanged and even given away as gifts. Although the shackles and chains we associate with the African slave trade are gone, slavery, bondage and serfdom still exist in the twenty-first century and its victims end up as domestic slaves, forced labourers and prostitutes. In West Africa children are kidnapped and sold for as little as $20 to be sold on for $350 or more to traders from richer neighbouring countries. The modern slave trade in women (known as odalisques), which exists between the poorer parts of the Indian subcontinent and the richer states of the Middle East, sees women changing hands for between $3,000 and $10,000. At the beginning of the twenty-first century, Dr Charles Jacobs who is President of the American Anti-Slavery Group claimed that there were over 27 million slaves worldwide and quoted a report from the CIA which estimated that 50,000 slaves were being smuggled into the US every year.

According to Anti-Slavery International's *Annual Review 2004*, the most common forms of slavery today are:

➤ **Bonded labour** This affects millions of people. The person is forced by poverty, or tricked, into taking a small loan vital for survival that can lead to a family being enslaved for generations.

➤ **Forced labour** Where a person is forced to work under the threat or use of violence or other punishment.

➤ **Forced marriage** Where girls and women, married without choice, are forced into a life of servitude often dominated by violence.

➤ **Worst forms of child labour** This affects an estimated 179 million children around the world in work that is harmful to their health and welfare.

➤ **Human trafficking** The fastest growing form of slavery today. A person – woman, child or man – is taken from one area to another in order to be forced into slavery.

➤ **Slavery by descent** In which people are either born into a slave class of are from a 'group' that society views as suited to being used as slave labour.

See the following websites for more information about slavery, human trafficking and child labour:
www.antislavery.org
www.iabolish.com
www.anti-slaverysociety.addr.com
www.unicef.org

Questions

1. *Using the web links mentioned above, examine one form of contemporary slavery in depth.*
2. *How would you account for the persistence of slavery?*

---

position is believed to be based on what was achieved in a previous incarnation. As a result of these beliefs, it is held that the structure of society is divinely ordained and individuals are obliged to accept it and to carry out their duties within it 'without ambition to change' (*dharma*).

These beliefs are further reinforced by taboos governing social interaction, pollution and marriage. Despite being officially abolished in 1947, this system still survives, especially in rural areas, as do the religious beliefs that have underpinned it for the past 3,000 years. The term 'caste' has also been used to describe societies based on racial segrega-

tion such as South Africa under apartheid and the southern states of the USA prior to the civil rights movement.

Estates

In the feudal system of medieval Europe a ranking of status groups known as estates became the dominant system. The three major estates were the aristocracy (headed by the divine monarch), the priesthood and the commoners (peasants, servants, artisans, etc.). This system was closely related to property and political power with land ownership as the key. In a relationship of rights and obligations known as *noblesse oblige* the commoners were allowed use of land in return for providing service and rents to their landlord, who in turn promised protection and support. Just as the tenant was a vassal (dependant) of the lord, so the lord was in debt to the monarch. This interlocking system, of rights and obligations was seen as divinely ordained. However, the estate system was not as strictly tied to religious belief as the caste system, and some historians have argued that feudalism allowed for a degree of social mobility, especially in the towns.

Social class

In the previous systems of stratification the social position of an individual was fixed by law, custom or inherited status. These positions were reinforced by a set of norms which clearly governed the relationship between members of the different groups; group membership was often ascribed at birth. Such systems are characterized by very little social mobility and are sometimes referred to as 'closed' societies because the life prospects of individuals are predetermined. Under the process of industrialization the traditional aspects of these stratification systems

Figure 6.1 Noblesse oblige

Cartoon by Ian Hering

gave way to a more open system which was characterized by competition and a higher degree of social mobility. Customary divisions and traditional distinctions were replaced by 'class' distinctions based on property and authority. Class position is therefore largely determined by an individual's place within the economic system and is to some extent achieved. Ideally such a society should become a *meritocracy* (a hierarchy based on achievement and ability) in which class origins are irrelevant to where an individual is 'placed' in the economic system. However, despite this conception of society as a hierarchy of positions based solely on merit, most sociologists still regard modern industrial societies as being stratified on the basis of social class. Indeed, the idea that contemporary societies can be and are divided into classes is one which is not only popular with sociologists but also shared by members of society at large. A large part of this chapter will be taken up with a fuller discussion of the meaning of class and of its continuing importance in modern society, while the chapters on Education, Politics and Health also make extensive use of the connection between social class, social processes and the quality of life.

Explanations of stratification

Inequalities between people and the stratification of entire societies have always required some form of explanation. Such explanations often tend towards either justification or condemnation and as such can be regarded as ideologies rather than theories. From ancient times these explanations have emphasized divine, natural or social intervention, while more recently (post-Enlightenment) the moral assumption that we are all born equal (in an increasingly divided world) has only increased the speculative interest in this debate.

Divine explanations

Peter Berger has claimed that religion has a special authority when it acts as an ideology of justification, 'because it relates the precarious reality constructions of empirical societies with ultimate reality' (quoted in Daly 1991: 132). This notion of 'ultimate reality' can be applied to various forms of inequality. The Indian caste system is supported by the Hindu belief in reincarnation and the identification of social rank as a sign of spiritual purity.

The twin concepts of *karma* and *dharma* are central to this moral justification of a closed social system:

> Karma teaches a Hindu that he or she is born into a particular caste or sub-caste because he or she deserves to be there as a consequence of actions in a previous life. Dharma, which means 'existing according to that which is moral' teaches that living one's present life according to the rules (dharma) will result in rebirth into a higher caste and thus ultimate progression through the caste system. Both existing inequalities of caste, therefore, as well as any possibility of change in the future, are related to universal religious truths and are thus beyond the reaches of systematic sociological examination.
> (Crompton 1993: 2)

Similar justifications were provided for the estates system by the Catholic Church, which sanctified the feudal hierarchy with the argument that it reflected the celestial order of things and blessed the king with a divine right to rule.

> One of the greatest achievements of the Middle Ages was the development of this idea of a universal human society as an integral part of a divinely ordered universe in time and in eternity, in nature and supernature, in practical politics and in the world of spiritual essences.
> (Southern 1988: 22)

This universal human society laid great stress on duty and order and allowed for little social mobility. 'Everyman had his station in society, and few men were allowed to sink very much lower or to rise very much higher than the station into which they were born' (Southern 1988: 43). To seek for personal improvement through the pursuit of wealth was condemned as a sin (of avarice), while poverty was cherished as a humble virtue. Such ideas may have originated in the Middle Ages, but they persisted into the Industrial Revolution and the age of the rise of capitalism.

In 'primitive' societies religious explanations were used to come to terms with phenomena which were beyond understanding, but gradually these beliefs and explanations became justifications and legitimations for keeping society as it was. Thus, for example, in the sixteenth and seventeenth centuries, the idea of a 'great chain of being' existed in which the social hierarchy of Gods, kings and bishops, lords, freemen and serfs was argued to be natural and God given. Similarly, in the eighteenth and nineteenth centuries many people thought it was largely senseless to try to do anything about poverty since it was God who had created the rich and the poor, and it was therefore immoral and ungodly to try to change things.

(Thompson 1986: 36)

Religious explanations have been used to justify both racial and sexual inequality. The relationship between religion and race has always been troublesome. In those societies that depended on African slaves for their economic power, theological debates raged over the 'humanity' of black Africans. The Dutch Reformed Church in South Africa persistently sanctioned apartheid from the pulpit. In its 'Statement on Race Relations, no. 1' (November 1960) the Dutch Reformed Church stated that it 'could not associate itself unreservedly with the general cry for equality and unity in the world today'. Its statement after the Sharpeville riots of the same year made clear its approval of separate development (apartheid):

> The Nederduitse Gereformeerde Kerk has made it clear by its policy and by synod statements that it can approve of independent, distinctive development, provided that it is carried out in a just and honourable way, without impairing or offending 'human dignity'.
>
> (UNESCO 1972: 178)

The universal subordination of women throughout history has also been explained and approved of by almost all religions. Whether it is through creation myth, spiritual teachings or ritualized practice, the subjugation of women by men has often been given the status of holy law. O'Faolain and Martinez (1979) have shown that holy teachings and practices have provided powerful ideological support for the oppression of women. In many representations of The Great Chain of Being, Man is always closer to God while Woman separates Man from the Beasts. In the 1579 version reproduced in Figure 6.2, women are absent altogether.

Naturalistic explanations

From ancient times to the present day the explanations of differences between individuals and groups in terms of natural differences have been popular. It appeals to 'common sense' to suppose that the differences and similarities which appear at an early age between members of the same family are caused by nature. Whether a child is regarded as 'a chip off the old block' or 'the black sheep of the family', the cause can be easily accommodated within a model that explains physical, psychological and

Figure 6.2 The Great Chain of Being. From Didacus Valades, *Rhetorica Christiana* (1579). In such representations of a divine order, all forms of natural and social species are ordained their place in the hierarchy

Source: Reproduced from Fletcher (1999)

intellectual characteristics in terms of genetic inheritance. It is a short step to assume that all inequalities within society are part of the same natural condition; 'boys will be boys' is used to explain why brothers are treated differently from their sisters; the idea that the aristocracy have 'blue blood' in their veins is taken to mean that they were 'born to rule'. There are important differences between different types of natural explanation; biological and psychological explanations, for instance, are not interchangeable.

As with divine explanations, appeals to the laws of nature can operate as very powerful conservative ideologies. While Aristotle was insistent that the domination of both slaves and women by freemen was a condition ordained 'by nature', so Plato argued that the clear differences between the three basic classes of human stock in an ideal society should be maintained by a form of state-regulated eugenics.

World in focus

Beyond God the Father

Mary Daly (1991) has argued that world religions (and Christianity in particular) are part of a conspiracy to retain the status of women as a 'sexual caste' through their own consent via the process of 'sex role socialization', which hides the truth of their caste status. Daly suggests that 'the entire conceptual systems of theology and ethics . . . have been the products of males and tend to serve the interests of sexist society' (Daly 1991: 4).

The biblical and popular image of God as a great patriarch in heaven, rewarding and punishing according to his mysterious and seemingly arbitrary will, has dominated the imagination of millions over thousands of years. The symbol of the Father God, spawned in the human imagination and sustained as plausible by patriarchy, has in turn rendered service to this type of society by making its mechanisms for the oppression of women appear right and fitting. If God in 'his' heaven is a father ruling 'his' people, then it is in the 'nature' of things and according to divine plan and the order of the universe that society be male-dominated.

Within this context a mystification of roles takes place: the husband dominating his wife represents God 'himself'. The images and values of a given society have been projected into the realm of dogmas and 'Articles of Faith', and these in turn justify the social structures which have given rise to them and which sustain their plausibility . . . however, change can occur in society, and ideologies can die, though they die hard.

As the women's movement begins to have its effect upon the fabric of society, transforming it from patriarchy into something that never existed before – into a diarchal situation that is radically new – it can become the greatest single challenge to the major religions of the world, Western and Eastern. Beliefs and values that have held sway for thousands of years will be questioned as never before.

(Adapted from Daly 1991: 14)

Questions

1. In what ways is traditional religion patriarchal?

2. Can you think of any religious beliefs or practices which illustrate this?

3. What does the controversy over women priests in the Church of England tell us about the extent to which the women's movement has successfully challenged patriarchal religious beliefs?

4. How would you feel about being married by a woman priest?

The importance of selective breeding for the maintenance of a stable class structure (especially in the face of a population explosion among poor people) was stressed in the work of Francis Galton and his admirer Cyril Burt. Both believed that individual talent (and its absence) was essentially inherited and that the unequal rewards found in society were no more than a reflection of this natural distribution of ability throughout the population. If social classes existed, that was merely a reflection of groupings in nature. The Eugenics Movement was also concerned with the issue of racial purity and campaigned for the sterilization and incarceration of disabled and mentally ill people as well as the introduction of strong immigration controls. In the nineteenth and early twentieth centuries the threat to the Anglo-Saxon stock (in Britain) was identified as Celtic and Jewish. Later this fear was extended to African and Asian people. Early on in Britain's imperial history scientists were ready to explain the differential treatment of other racial groups in terms of natural differences between the races. This led to the development of what Peter Fryer (1984) has called 'pseudo-scientific racism', which is clearly linked to attempts to demonstrate that differences in intelligence, aggression and personality have a racial origin. During the twentieth century the work of some psychologists has been used to suggest that the social failure of some racial groups is the result of inferior IQ.

In 1916 Lewis Terman introduced the Stanford–Binet Test by highlighting its capacity to distinguish between the

Case study

Plato's Republic – the world's first dating agency?

In Plato's ideal world the social structure depended upon the reproduction of the three key classes (Guardians, Auxiliaries and Labourers) for which he used the metaphor of precious and base metals (Gold, Silver and Bronze). In order for these 'natural classes' to be reproduced without mishap, Plato argued for the abolition of marriage and the family and sexual selection to be organized by the state through the regular celebration of 'mating festivals' at which the classes would be kept apart in order to maintain their genetic purity;

For guardians, sexual intercourse will only take place during certain fixed times of year, designated as festivals. Males and females will be made husband and wife at these festivals for roughly the duration of sexual intercourse. The pairings will be determined by lot. Some of these people, those who are most admirable and thus whom we most wish to reproduce, might have up to four or five spouses in a single one of these festivals. All the children produced by these mating festivals will be taken from their parents and reared together, so that no one knows which children descend from which adults. At no other time in the year is sex permitted. If guardians have sex at an undesignated time and a child results, the understanding is that this child must be killed.

(From: www.sparknotes.com)

A closer look

Eugenics and the Eugenics Movement

Eugenics refers to the improvement of the human race through genetic policies that would discourage certain people and social groups who were felt to be 'inferior' from breeding and encourage others, who were thought to be more intelligent or superior in some way, to breed.

By the late nineteenth century, scientific interest in the new fields of genetics and evolution led to a Eugenics Movement, which had a powerful influence on many areas of social investigation and policy, particularly in the USA and Europe.

abilities of different racial groups in the USA and expose the 'feeble-mindedness' of some groups in particular:

Their dullness seems to be racial, or at least inherent in the family stocks from which they come. The fact that one meets this type with extraordinary frequency among Indians, Mexicans and negroes suggests quite forcibly that the whole question of racial difference in mental traits will have to be taken up anew . . . Children of this group should be segregated into special classes . . . They cannot master abstractions, but they can often be made efficient workers . . . There is no possibility at present of convincing society that they should not be allowed to reproduce . . . they constitute a grave problem because of their unusually prolific breeding.   (quoted by Kamin 1977: 374–7)

This debate grabbed the headlines again in the early 1970s when psychologists such as A.R. Jensen (1973) began to repeat the claim that black Americans were intellectually inferior to whites. In the early 1990s Charles Murray and Richard Herrnstein initiated a return to the arguments with their claim that black people in the USA scored on average 15 points below whites in IQ tests. In their book *The Bell Curve: Intelligence and the Class Structure* (Herrnstein and Murray 1994), they argue that a three-part class structure has emerged based on inherited intelligence. Society is dominated by a 'cognitive elite' (IQ 125+) and serviced by a middle class of average IQ, beneath whom a largely black underclass with IQs of 75 or less survive and multiply (*The Observer* 23.10.94).

The historical subordination of women and the domination by men of all positions of economic and political power have been given similar treatment by biologists and psychologists who sought to show that gender differences can be traced back to the natural differences between men and women. (According to this view, women achieve very little outside their caring role

A closer look

Social class and race: the underclass

Characterized by poor IQ and educational failure, the 'underclass' becomes a breeding ground for 'welfare queens' and criminals. Although Herrnstein and Murray (1994) assert that they are more concerned with social class than race, the racial implications of their work are clear, especially in a society where terms like 'underclass' and 'crime' are codes for white Americans, meaning 'black'. As Haymes (1996) has argued, this research is an attempt to pathologize and criminalize black Americans as one step towards a 'final solution' of social problems which scapegoats black urban youth in particular.

'By using intelligence as a 'neutral' medium, Herrnstein and Murray are able to claim surreptitiously that Blacks are biologically predisposed to violent criminal behavior, linking criminality with race. Making this connection allows the authors of *The Bell Curve* to use crime to talk covertly about the black body as being menacing. In other words, Herrnstein and Murray link their explanation of crime with Western racial discourse.' (Haymes 1996: 244)

In *The Race Gallery*, Marek Kohn (1995) has shown that this racial discourse about the biological elements of social class is not restricted to American society. Since the collapse of the Soviet Union and its satellite states, there has been a rebirth of nationalism which draws on Romantic notions of *Volkgeist* and an emerging 'race science system', both reminiscent of the earlier pronouncements of European Fascism. In countries such as Hungary, Romania and Slovakia this ideology is largely directed at Romany Gypsies. Once again pseudoscience is being used to identify an ethnic group as a genetically inferior class, to blame them for society's ills and to make them the focus of social intervention. In 1992 Istvan Csurca, leader of the Hungarian Road movement, conflated the concepts of class and race to express this idea of a biologically created underclass in extreme and fatalistic terms.

'We can no longer ignore the fact that the deterioration (of the Hungarian nation) has genetic causes as well. It has to be acknowledged that underprivileged, even cumulatively underprivileged, strata and groups have been living among us for far too long. Society now has to support the strong fit-for-life families who are prepared for work and achievement.' (Quoted in Kohn 1996: 187)

within the family because they are physically weaker, emotionally unstable and intellectually inferior.)

Nineteenth-century phrenologists argued that in terms of head shape the areas responsible for love, approbation and secretiveness were larger in the female, but less well developed than those for aggression, self-sufficiency, firmness and ingenuity. Later attempts to locate the source of the differences targeted the brain, hormonal balance and genetically transmitted differences in intellect and personality.

By 1914 the German psychologist Hugo Munsterberg concluded that the female mind is 'capricious, over-suggestible, often inclined to exaggeration, is disinclined to abstract thought, unfit for mathematical reasoning, impulsive [and] over-emotional' (Fairbrother 1983). As Hugh Fairbrother has pointed out, such conclusions have a strong whiff of male prejudice about them and very little to do with scientific rigour:

> What we need to do is remind ourselves constantly that our behaviour is not only, or even mostly, at the whim of our physique and physiology. As social beings we share responsibility for each other's behaviour. We create the sexist society which in turn spawns sexist science. . . . The crude stereotypes of 'male' and 'female' that the scientists set out to validate have changed and continue to change.
>
> (Fairbrother 1983: 8–9)

In the modern age the advances in technology have meant that the 'harmless' speculations on genetic engineering of Aristotle and Plato have become distinct and disturbing possibilities, not only in the prophetic pages of Aldous Huxley's *Brave New World* (1932) but also in the real world of genetic engineering and social policy. Hitler's *lebensborn* policy of eugenic breeding to create a 'super race' was the flip side of the 'final solution' coin.

> All the good blood in the world, all the Germanic blood that is not on the German side, may one day be our ruin. Hence every male of the best Germanic blood whom we bring to Germany and turn into a Teutonic-minded man means one more combatant on our side and one less on the other. I really intend to take German blood from wherever it is to be found in the world, to rob and steal it wherever I can.
>
> (Heinrich Himmler, speech to officers of the Deutschland Division, 8 November 1938, quoted in Henry and Hiltel 1977: 143)

The Swedish nation was shocked to learn in 1997 that their Social Democratic governments had been practising a

Case study

Is 'Eve' the world's first clone?

The birth of the world's first cloned human was condemned by British scientists today as another example of the 'sordid depths' to which maverick physicians will sink. The claim by Clonaid announcing Boxing Day's arrival of a baby girl called Eve, born by Caesarean section, will prompt 'revulsion and disgust' throughout the world and will see 2003 go down in history of mankind as the Year of the Clone, Dr Patrick Dixon claimed.

Dr Dixon, a leading expert on the ethics of human cloning, described today's news as 'totally inevitable', with separate US and Chinese teams also claiming that they have created large numbers of human-cloned embryos for medical research (see below). He warned that it would all mark a watershed when the world would suddenly realize that science is spinning out of control.

'We don't know yet . . . whether the claim about Eve is fact or fraud but one thing is clear. There's a global race by maverick scientists to produce clones, motivated by fame, money and warped and twisted beliefs,' he said. 'Today's announcement is totally inevitable and we can expect a number of other births of clones to be announced over the next few weeks.'

He said that physicians across the world were propelled by 'private passions and weird emotions' with the determination to deliver a cloned baby to any man or woman who wished to 'duplicate themselves or recover the dead'. The cloning industry, and today's announcement, was worth tens of millions of pounds, he said.

Dr Dixon added:

'The baby born has been born into a living nightmare with a high risk of malformations, ill-health, early death and unimaginable severe emotional pressures. We should be very concerned for Eve's welfare.

Can you imagine what it will be like for a 12-year-old daughter to look at her mother and realise she is seeing her own sister? For Eve to look at her own grandparents around the Christmas table and to see her parents? Can you imagine what kind of freak show she will be regarded as for her entire lifetime?

What will it do to her sense of personal identity, knowing that she's only a copy of someone else who is much older?'

To read more about this debate follow the links at web page http://www.globalchange.com/eveclone.htm

Question

1. *What might be the implications for personal identity formation of knowing that one was a clone?*

---

programme of enforced sterilization for 40 years between 1935 and 1975. The campaign targeted ethnic groups, criminals, the mentally retarded and alcoholics and over the period approximately 63,000 men and women were either paid to take part or offered the operation as a means of achieving a quick release from prison, qualifying for state benefits or retaining custody over their existing children.

In California scientists have engineered 'super kids' using sperm banks and artificial insemination, and the prospect of cloning identical families is well within the scope of current genetic technology. 'Problem populations' may be dealt with through birth control and immigration legislation. Rather than being old-fashioned philosophies or creations of science fiction these ideas are now more powerful and potentially dangerous than they have ever been.

Social explanations

Within sociology various explanations have been offered for the persistence of social inequalities. Much emphasis is placed on the role of personal experience, culture and deprivation in explaining why some individuals succeed and others fail, while the openness of the opportunity structure is also a crucial part of the debate. For the moment, however, we concentrate on the purposes and consequences of inequality for society from three perspectives: the functionalist model, the libertarian model and the egalitarian model.

The functionalist model

Derived primarily from Durkheim's analysis of the division of labour, the functionalist model argues that social inequality is an essential part of modern society so long as recruitment is based on merit and rewards are fairly distributed. If this can be achieved social cohesion (rather than resentment) will result because it is seen (by the majority) as providing just reward for those who perform jobs of high social value. To some extent this view echoes the belief that market forces can be relied on to produce a 'spontaneous order' (see 'libertarian model' below), but it clearly possesses a moral dimension with references to social consensus, fairness and merit. For this reason, Durkheim, who is popularly typecast as a conservative thinker, argued against the inheritance of property on the basis that it gave unfair advantage to the offspring of wealthy families.

Developing Durkheim's concern with the moral aspects of inequality, Talcott Parsons maintained that the 'spontaneous order' is not simply a product of market forces but also the result of social consensus ('normative order') over the most important skills (such skills might be bravery, hunting or intelligence) and the extent to which they should be differentially rewarded. Davis and Moore argued that stratification is both inevitable and functional in any society which requires its most important tasks to be carried out efficiently:

> Social inequality is an unconsciously evolved device by which societies insure that the most important positions are conscientiously filled by the most qualified persons.   (Davis and Moore 1967: 48)

By compensating those who train to become qualified for the most important positions, this system ensures that the most able individuals are allocated to the key roles in society and motivated to work hard while they are employed in them. As a result social efficiency is maintained while the high value placed on certain skills is reinforced. At the centre of this model is the assumption that competition for the key places is open to all and that roles are allocated according to individual merit. This is clearly summarized in Turner's model of 'contest mobility'.

> Applied to mobility the contest norm means that victory by a person of moderate intelligence accomplished through the use of common sense, craft, enterprise, daring and successful risk taking is more appreciated than victory of the most intelligent or the best educated. . . . The contest is judged to be fair only if all the players compete on an equal footing. Victory must be won solely by one's own efforts.
> (Turner 1961: 183)

Saunders (1987) has argued for a return to this model, maintaining that as long as people are guaranteed political and legal equality, the best system must be one in which everyone has an equal opportunity to be unequal. In his discussion of the relationship between meritocracy, inequality and fairness, Saunders draws on evidence from a survey of public attitudes which suggested 90 per cent support for the ideal that 'people's incomes should depend on hard work and ability' and concludes that social inequality is not only an effective means of running the economy but also a force for social stability:

> This strong support for meritocracy . . . reflects the fact that most of us understand that inequality is not necessarily 'unfair' – it depends on whether it is justifiable with reference to individual talent and individual effort. If we are convinced that, by and large, those who have the ability and who make an effort can usually find success, and that those who do not will not generally prosper, then the basis is laid for a society which should be able to function reasonably harmoniously. Meritocracy does have a problem in dealing with the social consequences of failure, but this need not be catastrophic as regards social cohesion provided the competition is known to have been fair. Ninety per cent agreement is not a bad basis on which to build and sustain a moral social order.
> (Saunders 1996: 90)

In his discussion of meritocracy, Saunders points out that the functionalist approach has been criticized from the political right (libertarian) and left (egalitarian).

The libertarian model

The libertarian model, which is closely associated with individualistic and naturalistic explanations, emphasizes the importance of an open and free market for talents and abilities so that those with the most marketable skills are rewarded for their ability and motivated to work hard and compete with others for the highest rewards. Neo-liberal economists (sometimes known as 'the New Right') have argued that unequal reward encourages self-interest and competition, which in turn sponsor personal initiative and technological innovation. Capitalism is seen as a dynamic system which gets the best out of individuals by rewarding talent and hard work and penalizing feckless and idle people. As a result we all benefit from the inspiration of creative individuals and harnessing the power of their ideas and effort. Whether we approve of them or not we inhabit a world which has been greatly influenced by individuals such as Henry Ford, Richard Branson and Rupert Murdoch. Without an unequal reward structure we would never have heard of any of them or enjoyed the benefits of mass-produced motor cars, the Virgin Megastore and satellite TV. According to writers like Friedrich Hayek (1976) Milton Friedman (1962) and Robert Nozick (1974), any attempt to tamper with the 'spontaneous order' generated by the capitalist reward structure serves only to reduce the 'social energy' produced by inequality.

On the surface there seems to be a strong similarity between the idea that the market should be left to determine who gets what and the functionalist conviction that merit should be rewarded. However, the logic of the marketplace has no time for notions of fairness or just reward, particularly where these may impede the freedom of people to do what they will with their talents or their money. For Nozick, people may reap whatever rewards come their way so long as they are entitled to them as earnings or as gifts. Whether people deserve their luck or not does not enter into the argument; millionaire lottery winners, professional footballers on £80,000 per week or windfall profiteers cashing in on the vagaries of the stock market should not be denied their entitlement simply because it is not fair. As Hayek points out, this is an argument about freedom, not fairness; in general the market will reward highly those people who have rare skills and talents, but there is no guarantee that this will happen and sometimes the highest rewards go to those whom we feel least deserve them; as with the lottery winner our response should be 'good luck to 'em' because, as the advert says, one day 'It could be you'. In a free society people should be left to make the most of their talents and reap whatever rewards they can get so long as they do not exploit others or break the law:

> However able a man may be in a particular field, the value of his services is necessarily low in a free society unless he also possesses the capacity of making his ability known to those who can derive the greatest benefit from it. Though it may offend our sense of justice to find that of two men who by equal effort have acquired the same specialized skill and knowledge, one may be a success and the other a failure, we must recognize that in a free society it is the use of particular opportunities that determines usefulness ... In a free society we are remunerated not for our skill but for using it rightly.
>
> (Hayek quoted in Saunders 1998: 190)

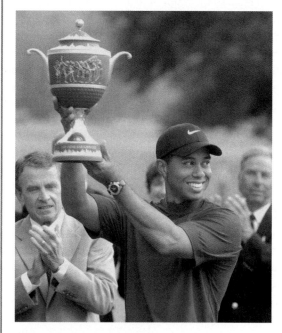

A closer look

Tiger Woods

Tiger Woods ranked number 2 in the Forbes Celebrity 100 for 2004 and is the highest paid sports personality in the world earning $80 million in that year alone. According to Forbes.

His winless streak in golf's majors is at seven and counting, but Tiger still managed to win his fifth straight PGA Tour Player of the Year award in 2003. Despite his recent stumbles on the fairways, it's still good to be Tiger. He's the world's number one ranked player, earns $70 million a year in endorsements and is about to marry Swedish former nanny/model Elin Nordegren.

www.forbes.com/maserati/celebrities2004/

Figure 6.3 Tiger Woods

The egalitarian model

While the libertarians and the functionalists accept that there are natural differences in talent among the general population but disagree over the extent to which rewards should be unequally distributed and the role of fair play in the allocation of these rewards, the egalitarian argument rejects the principle of unequal reward and the notion of natural differences on which it is founded. The so-called natural differences between people are created by the social priviledges and disadvantages inherent in an unequal society, and reinforced by differential educational opportunities in particular. Consequently the wide differences in reward in society are not a fair reflection of natural differences in ability or effort but a manipulation by those in positions of power to reward themselves at the expense of others. Instead of encouraging fairness, social cohesion and harmony, this model suggests that inequality of reward promotes a dysfunctional world in which the middle and upper classes revel in their superiority and the poor resent their failure. These views are clearly close to those expressed by thinkers on the political left, who believe that all people should be treated equally, but they are also to be found among 'progressive' sociologists, who have condemned the functionalist model as an ideological justification for the *status quo*.

Melvin Tumin's (1967) attack on the 'principles of stratification' outlined by Davis and Moore (1967) is well documented elsewhere; essentially his argument challenges the assumption that some positions are inherently more important than others, and that stratification provides an efficient mechanism for attracting the most talented individuals in society to these positions. Instead of promoting functional efficiency and fairness, such systems can be socially divisive and dysfunctional, promoting resentment, demotivation and conflict, while the skills and talents that are encouraged by unequal rewards have little to do with intelligence or social worth:

> Wealth and power tend to accrue to those who are ruthless, cunning, avaricious, self-seeking, lacking in sympathy and compassion, subservient to authority [and] willing to abandon principle for material gain.
> (Chomsky 1972, quoted in Anderson 1974: 82)

As a result, systems of stratification encourage self-perpetuating elites, who pass on their privileges through inherited wealth, private education and inter-marriage. As Bottomore (1965) pointed out, social stratification operates to resist the dynamics of openness and social change:

> Indeed, it would be a more accurate description of the social class system to say that it operates, largely through the inheritance of property, to ensure that each individual maintains a certain social position, determined by his birth and irrespective of his particular abilities.
> (Bottomore 1965: 16)

The arguments of Tumin (1967), Bottomore (1965) and Chomsky (1972) clearly indicate a lack of agreement with the fundamental idea of modern, stratified societies as meritocracies. Instead they would see Turner's model of 'sponsored mobility' in which status is ascribed rather than achieved as being more appropriate:

> Sponsored mobility . . . rejects the pattern of the contest and substitutes a controlled selection process. In this process the elite or their agents who are best qualified to judge merit, call those individuals who have the appropriate qualities to elite status. Individuals do not win or seize elite status, but mobility is rather a process of sponsored induction into the elite following selection.
> (Turner 1961: 183–4)

Even when the egalitarians concede that there are natural differences in ability and aptitude, they see no reason to accept that this is a fair basis for rewarding people differently. In response to Saunders' argument in favour of a meritocracy, Marshall and Swift put forward the view that ending up with the right genes is no more fair than winning the National Lottery and should not be rewarded as such:

> It [is] particularly apt to ask whether an inherited characteristic – genetically determined intelligence – is an appropriate basis for reward at all. A crucial issue here would seem to be the distinction between those attributes for which the individual can claim responsibility and those which are his or hers merely by chance. If someone possesses particular talents or skills merely as a result of the natural lottery then it is not clear how justice is served by rewarding such possession.
> (Marshall and Swift 1993: 206)

Stop and think

➤ Using the three social perspectives (functionalist, libertarian and egalitarian) assess the following cases from each one:

a) Ingvar Kamprad, the head of Ikea overtook Bill Gates as the 'richest man in the world' when the drop in the value of the dollar against the Swedish krona boosted his wealth to $53bn.

b) The world's biggest lottery winner ($315m).

c) A 16-year-old playworker earning £4.10 per hour.

d) A disabled 18-year-old receiving incapacity benefits of £56 per week.

Theoretical concepts of class

The discourse of class has become one of the key concepts through which we can begin to understand [the modern world]. Class, therefore, is a major organising concept in the exploration of contemporary stratification systems.   (Crompton 1993: 4)

Slowly but surely the old establishment is being replaced by a new, larger, more meritocratic middle class . . . A middle class that will include millions of people who traditionally see themselves as working class, but whose ambitions are far broader than those of their parents and grandparents . . . I believe we will have an expanded middle class, with ladders of opportunity for those of all backgrounds. No more ceilings that prevent people from achieving the success they merit.
                    (Tony Blair, quoted in the *Guardian* 15.1.99)

These two quotes highlight quite contradictory stances on the importance of class in contemporary societies. In the first, class is seen as an essential aspect of such societies whereas Tony Blair's comment suggests that class is becoming less important, with an individual's position increasingly based on that person's own ability. As we mentioned when looking at systems of stratification (pp. 208–9), sociologists would tend to support Crompton's comment and emphasize the continuing importance of social class in modern societies. The 'discourse of class' continues to have a wide and general usage. In thousands of different ways we generate and interpret clues about ourselves and others which indicate class position. How we dress, speak and eat are all indicators of social class. The concept of social class is part of our culture; embedded in this culture are judgements about how we earn our money and what we purchase with it, how we educate our children and where we spend our leisure time.

Marx and social class

Marx died with his aim of providing a precise definition of social class an unfinished project. Nevertheless, the concept remains at the centre of his work. Unlike Durkheim, who rarely used the term, or Weber, who gave it specific and limited meaning, Marx saw class not only as a descriptive device but also as a way of understanding how society and history interact, the maintenance of social order and the dynamics of social change. Sometimes he talks of 'Society . . . splitting up into *two* great hostile camps'; on other occasions he says that 'wage labourers, capitalists and landlords, form the *three* great classes of modern society.' In more empirical mood Marx allows for six different groups (in Germany) and seven (in Britain), where the working class can be subdivided into productive (factory workers) and non-productive (servants). In his mention of 'intermediate' classes Marx seems to anticipate some of the arguments developed later in Wright's discussion of 'contradictory class positions' (see

Case study

The Duke of Westminster's housing estate

In 1937 the Duke of Westminster made a present of the Page Street housing estate to the Westminster Council on the condition that it should be used exclusively as 'dwellings for the working class . . . and for no other purpose'. Almost fifty years later the 1985 Housing Act gave sitting tenants the 'right to buy' council rented property. Westminster Council attempted to implement this policy, but ended up in the High Court when they insisted that the phrase 'working class' no longer had any meaning. The current Duke of Westminster successfully defended his ancestor's wishes when Mr Justice Harman ruled that parliament 'does not determine the meaning of those words in ordinary English speech'. He concluded that the term was 'as valid today as when it was made'.
                    (The *Guardian* 27.11.90)

Questions

1. What do you think the Duke of Westminster meant by 'working class'?

2. What does the term 'working class' mean to you?

3. What evidence is there that the public still think in terms of social class?

p. 221). To understand the different ways in which Marx used the term we can distinguish between *objective* and *subjective* class position.

In Marx's work, then, social class is not simply a category to describe the measurement of social inequality, it

A closer look

Objective class position

For Marx, a person's class can exist independently of their awareness of it and affect them in ways they are not conscious of. In this sense class operates as a social force which influences opportunities, governs relationships (between groups) and transforms conflict into change.

As Lee and Newby (1983) have pointed out, Marx used this notion of objective class position both theoretically and empirically. First, it was used to explain the inevitable antagonism that would develop between the bourgeoisie and the proletariat as a result of their diametrically opposed interests and the gradual proletarianization of society, work and politics. The eventual outcome of this class conflict would be a revolutionary transformation of society and the victory of socialism.

Second, objective class position was used in a more static and descriptive way to provide a snapshot of the various social classes actually in existence at any particular time without making much comment on the relational aspects of these groupings. This explains why Marx can describe the existence of several classes alongside his more theoretical attempts to explain the importance of the two dominant ones.

Subjective class position

Although Marxism is often accused of being structuralist and deterministic in its emphasis upon the objective nature of social class, Marx himself clearly realized that antagonistic interests did not automatically guarantee social conflict and revolutionary change. People had to be conscious of their interests and committed to achieving them; only when this *class consciousness* developed could a class be transformed from a 'class *in* itself' to a 'class *for* itself'. This development of a class consciousness involved people in an ideological struggle in which 'false consciousness' is replaced by class awareness and a revolutionary consciousness. In the *Manifests of the Communist Party*, Marx makes it clear that workers will achieve nothing until they share a common consciousness.

is a dynamic force used to explain social change. As the processes of deskilling and proletarianization shape a homogeneous class of workers sharing similar experiences of work and lifestyle, Marx expected that they would also come to a common understanding of their political interests. The radicalization of working-class politics was seen to go hand in hand with proletarianization and, it was argued, would lead to the revolutionary transformation of society through class-based action.

In the more deterministic strands of Marxist thought, especially at the turn of the century, this revolutionary outcome is assumed to be an automatic result of the forces of history (historical materialism), while in later versions, following Lukács, the role of class consciousness and ideology are given a more significant part to play in class conflict and revolutionary struggle. The essential question here concerns the extent to which working-class people have a conscious role to play in making their own history or whether they are simply moulded in a deterministic manner by events. This debate within Marxism hints at later sociological interest in the concepts of 'structure' and 'agency', which are given particular attention in Giddens's (1973) work on 'structuration'. For the sociological discourse on the significance of class structure in modern society which concludes this chapter, the objective and subjective elements in Marx's writings are crucial because they set the agenda for the subsequent debate; Marx's ideas on proletarianization, class consciousness and radicalization are challenged by sociologists who feel that the processes of fragmentation, social mobility and embourgeoisment explain the inadequacies of the Marxist concept of class and the failure of communism.

Weber and social class

Like Marx, Weber did not finish his analysis of the concept of class, but he did give a more complete picture of what it meant to him by distinguishing the 'multidimensional' aspects of stratification. According to this view, society cannot be stratified by economic factors alone; status and party coincide and overlap with class as alternative bases for stratification. John Hughes (1984) has argued that rather than reducing inequality to economic factors, Weber regarded *power* as the primary relationship between unequal groups in society with class representing only one form:

> Power, according to Weber, is the ability of an individual or group to get what they want even against the

opposition of others . . . Power can be divided into three spheres of activity: the economic, the social and the political. Within each of these, individuals can be grouped according to the amount of power they are able to command. (Hughes 1984: 7)

These three spheres of activity are more commonly referred to as class, status and party, and we need to examine each one to understand the extent to which Weber differed from Marx on the issues of class and stratification.

Class

It is not surprising that Weber did not share Marx's beliefs about social class. Weber had a commitment to the possibility of value-free sociology and cautiously welcomed the growth of capitalism and bureaucracy as the inevitable progress of rationality. He was also a Christian with some faith in the possibility of social reform. However, his writings on social class show that he was in close agreement with Marx on the importance of economic classes and the shape that these classes took at the end of the nineteenth century. Weber defined class in clear economic terms and accepted that it often provided the basis for shared social position, life chances and political action. He defined 'class situation' as:

> The typical chance for a supply of goods, external living conditions, and personal life experiences, in so far as this chance is determined by the amount and kinds of power, or lack of such, to dispose of goods or skills for the sake of income in a given economic order.
> (Weber, quoted in Edgell 1993: 12)

Like Marx, he accepted that 'class situation is by far the predominant factor' in determining social position with ownership (or lack) of property being the 'basic categories of all class situations'. As a result Weber acknowledges the existence of positively and negatively privileged classes, separated by a growing middle class. His description of the prevailing class structure resembles that put forward by Marx:

> [Weber] identified as 'social classes' (a) the working class as a whole; (b) the petty bourgeoisie; (c) technicians, specialists and lower-level management, and (d) 'the classes privileged through property and education' – that is, those at the top of the hierarchy of occupation and ownership. In short, at the descriptive level, Weber's account of the 'class structure' of capitalist society is not too different from that of Marx.
> (Crompton 1993: 30)

In four other respects, however, Weber's views on social class formation and class action are very different from those espoused by Marx: first, class situation is not simply determined by property relationships, but by the shared life chances that people enjoy (or are denied) as a result of the value of their skills and possessions in the marketplace. This means that the possession of particular skills or qualifications may be just as important as the possession of property in determining class situation. It also implies that a person's class position will change with fluctuations in the market.

Second, class position is associated with potential for consumption (income) rather than the relationship to the mode of production.

> For Marx, class relationships are grounded in exploitation and domination within *production* relations, whereas for Weber, class situations reflect differing 'life chances' in the *market*. (Crompton 1993: 30)

This emphasis on consumption and lifestyle is central to Weber's idea of status.

Third, despite his apparent agreement with Marx over the four essential classes of capitalist society, Weber's definition allows for 'multiple classes' because he recognized 'important differences in the market situation of all groups, especially with respect to the various skills and services offered by different occupations' (Hughes 1984: 7). This means that on top of the differences between his four main classes he also emphasizes possible differences *within* these classes. Instead of society becoming polarized into two simple homogeneous classes, Weber's view was that the number of different classes would multiply with the expansion of society. Thus, Weber's conception of the social stratification structure in general, and the class structure in particular, is extremely complex and pluralistic.

Fourth, Weber rejected Marx's *dynamic* view of social class. He did not see class conflict as inevitable, nor did he accept it as the engine of historical change. Weber believed that people are essentially individuals and their class situation is only one of many possible sources of consciousness and political activity. Classes were seen as (merely) representing possible and frequent bases for communal action.

While Marx saw something inevitable in the connection between class position, class consciousness and political revolution, Weber was quite cynical about the political potential of the working classes and very pessimistic about the direction of world history. Working-class people could just as easily be motivated by patriotism and religious fervour as they were by class interest. He believed that rationally organized capitalism was more likely to dominate the future than revolutionary socialism.

Status

For many writers, Weber's greatest contribution to the stratification debate is his view that social differences can be as important as economic ones in the identification of social position even if the two seem very closely related:

> 'Classes' are stratified according to their relations to the production and acquisition of goods; whereas 'status groups' are stratified according to the principles of their consumption of goods as represented by special 'styles of life'!   (Weber, quoted in Hughes 1984: 8)

Although you may feel that 'lifestyle' is determined by class position, Weber says this is not necessarily the case:

> Money and an entrepreneurial position are not in themselves status qualifications, although they may lead to them; and the lack of property is not in itself a status disqualification, although this may be a reason for it.   (Weber, quoted in Ritzer 1992: 128)

Status position is derived from the prestige or 'social honour' which the community attaches to a particular individual or role as well as the expected 'lifestyle' that attaches to it. A community will judge someone's social status according to cultural standards like education, occupation, speech and dress, as well as the more obvious trappings of a privileged lifestyle.

Weber's concept of 'status group' has allowed modern sociologists to recognize that factors like age, gender and race are related to 'life chances' in much the same way as class differences are and, for the individuals concerned, may be even more important.

Party

Just as the social order is given autonomy from economic forces, so Weber argues that the political sphere cannot be reduced to economic interests either. In this third arena of Weber's stratification system, people exercise control over others and inequalities of power become another way in which differentiation manifests itself. Sometimes people will organize themselves into political parties which represent their economic interests (e.g. the parliamentary Labour Party), but this is not the only basis for political organization. When political power results from such organization it can be used for the benefit of party members at the expense of other groups in society. In the former Soviet Union, for example, party membership was closely related to social status and economic privileges.

Corruption scandals in Western democracies emphasize this point: political power may be used as a device to increase economic privilege and social differentiation. In developing societies, too, political power may be a source of economic privilege. On the other hand, political policy may be directed towards social reform and the eradication of economic inequality. In both cases, political power is not simply the reflection of economic relations but appears to have a life of its own which sometimes runs in the opposite direction.

Stop and think

Class, status and power – what's the difference?

➤ Awarding a mark for each occupant (with 1 as the lowest and 8 the highest) rate the following for 'class', 'status' and 'power'.

Name	Class	Status	Power
Bill Gates $140m per week			
Melanie Brock – Nurse of the Year 2004			
George Bush – multi-millionaire and President of USA			
Playworker on £4.10 per hour			
Duke of Westminster – worth £5bn			
John Palmer (jailed fraudster) worth £300m			
Mother Teresa of Calcutta – chose a life of poverty to help the poor			
The Beckhams – worth £65m			

Modern concepts of class

The debate over the concept of class has continued. The main contemporary contributors derive their inspiration from both Marx and Weber, with some clearly representing a neo-Marxist position and others proclaiming a neo-Weberian stance. In the middle there are those who attempt to use Weber's insights to 'round out' Marx.

Nicos Poulantzas

In the face of changes in modern society, the apparent failure of communism and the emergence of humanistic Marxism, structuralist writers like Louis Althusser (1969) and Poulantzas (1979) argued for a return to 'scientific Marxism'. This was largely an attack on individualism and subjectivism within Marxism and sociology, but it was also an attempt to re-emphasize the importance of class position as determined by the mode of production. For Poulantzas, classes are defined not by shared life chances or market situation but by their *role* in the production of *surplus value*. Consequently, those groups who appear to be 'working class' because of similarities in pay and working conditions with other workers cannot be included unless they are directly involved in the production of surplus value. On the political and ideological levels these classes may support one another and pursue the same interests, but they may not be classified together at the economic level. Instead, Poulantzas distinguished between productive and unproductive labour, with only those directly involved in production being allowed the classification 'proletariat'.

Erik Olin Wright

Wright is another neo-Marxist whose ideas developed not only in response to the work of Poulantzas (1979) but also as an attempt to provide an operational concept of class for use in empirical study. He followed the example set by fellow American Marxist Harry Braverman (1974) when he developed a more flexible 'class map' than Poulantzas' (1979) rigid 'production model'. In Wright's view the structure of class relations in modern capitalism is defined not primarily by economic production but also by power relations, i.e. control of the workplace and work processes. By including this factor of control in his analysis, Wright allows a much more complex model to develop, which is based on Marxist notions of exploitation and control but also allows for the ambiguous nature of class relationships that develop between different groups in a complex society.

> According to Wright, the two major classes have unambiguous locations with respect to all three dimensions [of control]. The capitalist controls investment, organises labour power and decides upon the nature of the productive process. The proletariat, on the other hand, is excluded from all forms of control. Other classes, however, have contradictory locations, the new middle class most of all.   (Hughes 1984: 13)

The concept of 'contradictory class locations' was used to accommodate managers, small employers and self-employed workers into his 'class maps'. In his later works Wright attempts to recognize that over and above the exploitative power of the owners, the middle classes also found themselves in positions where they could exploit others (Edgell 1993: 17–27).

In his recent contribution, Wright (1997) moves much closer to a Weberian notion of class, which he acknowledges 'does not dramatically differ from the class typology used by Goldthorpe' (p. 37). Goldthorpe's occupational scale is outlined on page 225.

Frank Parkin

Probably the best-known exponent of the neo-Weberian perspective, Parkin (1972) has made clear his opposition to Marxist concepts of class. Embracing Weber's idea of status he has argued that ownership of property is only one means of social differentiation and identified occupational status as the most significant criterion for distinguishing between groups in society.

> The backbone of the class structure, and indeed the entire reward system of modern western society, is the occupational order. Other sources of economic and symbolic advantage do coexist alongside the occupational order, but for the vast majority of the population these tend, at best, to be secondary.
>
> (Parkin 1972: 18)

In Parkin's model the major distinction appears to be that made between manual and non-manual jobs, with higher professionals at the top of the hierarchy of occupations and unskilled workers at the bottom. Instead of society being driven by class conflict, struggles between status groups are more important. In the battle over resources, those who monopolize economic and cultural assets strive to maintain their privileged position through a process Parkin calls 'social closure'. While the lower-status groups attempt to improve their situation through strategies of 'usurpation', the elite-status groups will resist attempts at equality and social mobility by employing a variety of techniques of social 'exclusion' which effectively deny access to the less desirable social groups. As a result, class boundaries are not created by some objective relationship to the means of production or market situation but out of the strategies and techniques adopted by competing status groups. As Simon Raven boasted in a recent Radio 4 interview: 'A good club, a good regiment, a good college or a good school; you can only make one by keeping people out.'

Stop and think

➤ Exactly what strategies do you think status groups adopt on a day-to-day basis to maintain their own prestige and exclude others? See p. 241 'The establishment' and p. 243 case study 'The overclass'.

Table 6.1 Runciman's 7 class model

Class	Size in 1990
Upper class	<1%
Upper middle class	<10%
Middle middle class	15%
Lower middle class	20%
Skilled working class	20%
Unskilled working class	30%
Underclass	5%

Source: Runciman 1990: 389

W.G. Runciman

Following Weber, Runciman (1990) has taken the three major stratifying elements in society to be 'ownership' (of property), 'control' (of power/authority) and 'marketability' (of skills), but instead of associating each source of privilege with a particular class he has argued that these criteria for differentiation cut across simple class boundaries, producing a much more fragmented model of the class structure in which the differences within broad classifications are celebrated rather than disguised. The result is a seven-class model in which a small 'upper class' shares a dominant position with regard to all three criteria. At the other end, a significant 'underclass' is identified, members of which possess no property, exercise no control over events and have few marketable skills. The two extremes are separated by two broad classes ('middle' and 'working'), internally differentiated by variations in access to property, authority and skill.

Anthony Giddens

Giddens (1973) puts forward a model of the class system which is very close to Weber's. In this model the power that people enjoy in the bargaining process derives essentially from their 'market capacities' (i.e. the value attached to their possessions and skills). He suggests that modern societies tend towards a three-class model in which class position is determined by market capacity:

Class	*Market capacity*
Upper class	Capital ownership
Middle class	Educational credentials
Working class	Labour power

Giddens is aware of cultural variations on this model and acknowledges the internal fragmentation that can occur within each group (e.g. the distinction between professional, technical, managerial and clerical workers within the middle class), but he still prefers to simplify the class system into its three major components, based on 'the possession of property, qualifications and physical labour power' (Edgell 1993: 53).

In his ideas on 'class structuration', Giddens is concerned with the ways in which individuals contribute towards a class-based social reality through their actions and beliefs. He is aware that people derive status from their position within a hierarchical division of labour in which some occupations are generally esteemed and others looked down upon. Within these occupations and through the performance of work roles some have more control than others and this emphasises notions of superiority and inferiority, which we also associate with ideas of social class. Finally, the way in which we spend our money can be seen as an expression of class differences in taste and lifestyle. Furthermore we can reinforce the importance of social class division by passing on property, skills and privileges to our children.

Over the following 20 years Giddens has changed his emphasis and aligned himself with a less class-based approach to politics and social democracy sometimes referred to as the 'third way' (for a useful discussion of these ideas and how they have influenced political thinking in Europe and the USA see http://www.sociologyonline.co.uk/politics/Giddens_3way.shtml). His new ideas involve a more individualistic approach in which class differences count for little; some individuals may experience more barriers to success than others, and some have more opportunities, but this is no longer determined by a thing called 'class' and is not experienced as such. In the constant and rapid changes brought about by technological change and globalization, life is far more unpredictable and social destinations far less related to their origins (Best 2005: 44–5).

Operationalizing the concept of class

Apart from the theoretical problems posed by the concept of class in sociology, there is also much disagreement over its categorization for the purposes of empirical study. This is an important issue, because if sociologists cannot agree on the best way of operationalizing social class (i.e. turning the concept into a measurable variable), they will use different methods for classification and measurement and end up with data which are not comparable. If this is the case, apparent changes in social life like voting behaviour or social mobility patterns may be nothing more than distortions created by changes in our definition and measurement of social class.

Official definitions of 'social class'

The earliest attempts to classify economically active groups in society did not involve class analysis at all. The first UK census in 1801 simply adopted general and vague categories of general employment:

➤ agriculture;

➤ manufacture, trade and handicraft;

➤ others.

Such a scheme may have been useful for assessing proportional shifts in the working population, but it made no attempt to classify people according to their position within the economic and social hierarchy. The revised census of 1851 simply increased the range of categories of employment and only added to the confusion. It was not until 1911 that the classifications were revised again 'to represent as far as possible different social grades'. The five grades that were introduced formed the basis of what we now know as the Registrar-General's scale and is 'the nearest thing we have to an official definition of "social class"' (Nichols 1979: 158).

Up until 1981, the occupational scale was based on social status but after this date was revised to reflect the level of skill demanded by an occupation (Roberts 2001: 24). By the time of its demise in 1998 this scale had been expanded to six main grades which managed to encompass most occupations and still appeared to reflect the traditional ideas of social status and skill associated with different jobs.

A closer look

Registrar-General's scale (pre-1998)

1   Higher level professionals, managers and administrators.

2   Lower level professionals, managers and administrators.

3a   Lower level white collar workers.

3b   Skilled manual workers.

4   Semi-skilled manual workers.

5   Unskilled manual workers.

The General Household Survey is a seven-point scale which identifies people by socio-economic groups and is used for some official investigations, while the advertising industry uses a six-point guide to social position which emphasizes consumer potential:

A Upper middle class.

B Middle class.

C Lower middle class.

D Skilled working class.

E Semi-skilled working class.

F Low level of subsistence.

In sociology the occupational scale has become adopted as the most convenient means of converting the problematic concept of social class into a variable which we can easily use. In Goldthorpe's work this neo-Weberian approach is clear to see. He identified 'market situation' and 'work situation' as the important determinants of class consciousness and used an occupational scale for his important empirical studies of class consciousness (Goldthorpe *et al.* 1968; 1969) and social mobility (Goldthorpe *et al.* 1980). His revised version shows how 'social classes' reflect gradations in the workplace and the labour market (Goldthorpe *et al.* 1980).

In the 1990s social scientists in the UK were invited to revise the official scale, and the eventual compromise, based upon the Registrar-General's scale and that proposed by Goldthorpe, was designed by Rose and O'Reilly (1997) and officially adopted by the Office for National Statistics in the following year. The basis for classification of occupations is to place together those that share:

i) similar 'market situations', i.e. rewards; and

ii) similar 'work situations', i.e. levels of control, responsibility and autonomy in the workplace.

A closer look

Goldthorpe's class scheme (revised version)

1 *Classes I and II* All professionals, administrators and managers (including large proprietors), higher-grade technicians and supervisors of non-manual workers.

2 *Class III* Routine non-manual employees in administration and commerce, sales personnel, other rank-and-file service workers.

3 *Class IVab* Small proprietors, self-employed artisans and other 'own-account' workers with and without employees (other than in primary production).

4 *Class IVc* Farmers and smallholders and other self-employed workers in primary production.

5 *Classes V and VI* Lower-grade technicians; supervisors of manual workers and skilled manual workers.

6 *Class VIIa* Semi-skilled and unskilled manual workers (other than in primary production).

7 *Class VIIb* Agricultural and other workers in primary production.

The eight class scale is now the official class scheme for the UK.

A closer look

The Office for National Statistics socio-economic classification analytic classes

1 Higher managerial and professional occupations:

   1.1 Large employers and higher managerial occupations.

   1.2 Higher professional occupations.

2 Lower managerial and professional occupations.

3 Intermediate occupations (e.g. clerks, secretaries, computer operators).

4 Small employers and own account workers.

5 Lower supervisory and technical occupations.

6 Semi-routine occupations (e.g. cooks, bus drivers, hairdressers, shop assistants).

7 Routine occupations (e.g. waitresses, cleaners, couriers).

8 Never worked and long-term unemployed.

Source:
http://www.statistics.gov.uk/methods_quality/ns_sec/

David Rose is currently on secondment to the Institute for Social and Economic Research developing a new socio-economic classification for the EU. Harmonization of class scales across Europe would make comparative research more valid.

Advantages of using occupational scales

The occupational scale incorporates the idea of social status and recognizes the growing importance of the 'middle classes' against the decline of the ruling and working classes.

In modern societies occupation has become 'the primary status-fixing device'. In modern mass societies characterized by large impersonal bureaucracies and a complex division of labour, occupational position becomes a shorthand method for recognizing others. It is often the first question that we ask someone we are meeting for the first time.

In order to measure the possible influence of social class on life chances it is necessary to have some generally agreed means of categorizing people. Much valuable research has been conducted using occupational scales and the data produced have been used to inform debate and influence policy making.

Criticisms of occupational scales

Occupational scales confuse 'class' and 'status'. In this merging of two distinct terms, the emphasis shifts away from 'property relations' and 'the process of production' in favour of 'prestige' as the main measure of social position.

Occupational scale is a *descriptive* device which is good at providing static snapshots of the occupational hierarchy, but it does not *explain* the relations between classes. This criticism comes from Marxist writers, who believe that class division, class conflict and the dynamics of class struggle are obscured by scales which simply rank the working population by prestige.

Although they appear to offer a neat solution to the difficulty of operationalizing the concept of class, occupational scales are extremely problematic for four reasons.

First, people may be classed together by occupational group despite large differences in reward and prestige *within* each occupation, for example junior hospital doctors and consultants in private practice.

Second, different occupations may be placed in the same social grade despite differences *between* those occupational groups, for example Goldthorpe has been criticized for including managers, high-grade technicians and professional workers in Class 1 along with 'large proprietors' (Edgell 1993: 32).

Third, accounts based on occupational scale target the working population and, by definition, overlook those who have retired or do not have a job; for example how should we class students, housewives and those engaged in voluntary work? It is also difficult, in such schemes, to classify the 'idle rich', who may live by an invested income but not have a recognized occupation. Nichols (1979: 165) has referred to the absurdity of 'a sort of bald class structure' which has a 'working class' and a 'middle class' but 'nothing on top'.

Fourth, feminists have attacked scales such as Goldthorpe's for classifying women according to the occupation of the male head of household and producing 'gender blind' accounts of social structure and social change so that women are seen as 'peripheral to the class system'. Writers like Oakley and Oakley (1981), Stanworth (1984) and Crompton (1989) have argued for a more 'gendered' approach to the class structure by replacing the 'head of household' classification with one which recognizes the increasing contribution of women in the workplace (see p. 226).

Stop and think

➤ What kinds of assumption do you make about people based on their occupation?

➤ What assumptions would you make about individuals in these occupations: (a) professional footballer; (b) doctor; (c) sociology lecturer; (d) secretary? (Consider political views, leisure activities, tastes.)

The class structure in modern society

Whether it is still useful to talk of a class structure is a matter of continuing sociological debate; this debate is informed by the theoretical positions outlined in the previous section and by empirical research based on the attempts to operationalize the concept of class.

The demise of class

In the latter half of the twentieth century, the traditional notions about the significance of social class have been questioned. Such questioning has been inspired not only by Weberian-influenced criticisms of Marxism – by writers such as Parkin (1972), Dahrendorf (1959) and Pahl and Wallace (1988) – but also by those such as Saunders (1987; 1996) who reject Weber's conception of class along with Marx's on the basis that 'they continue to employ essentially nineteenth century ideas to analyze late twentieth century conditions' (Saunders 1987: 319). According to this general viewpoint it is claimed that changes in the structure of society, the nature of work and the formulation of consciousness have reduced the value of class analysis so that, according to Pahl, 'class as a concept is ceasing to do any useful work for sociology' (quoted in Crompton 1993: 99). In their book, *The Death of Class*, Pakulski and Waters (1996) have even suggested that in today's world 'the class paradigm is intellectually and morally bankrupt'.

In general this position is based on the following factors:

1 changes in the quality of life;

2 social reform and the idea of 'citizenship';

3 changes in the organization and nature of work;

4 social mobility and the fragmentation of class structure;

5 the end of ideology and the embourgeoisment thesis.

Changes in the quality of life

According to Marx, the 'pauperization' of the working class was an essential condition for the survival of capitalism and its eventual downfall. However, since the 1950s the living standards of many working people have improved due to wage rises and the increasing cheapness of basic goods and mass-produced consumer items. For skilled workers who have retained their jobs and especially for those 'work-rich' households which have more than one income, material lifestyle has clearly improved. The relative affluence of these groups has promoted an optimistic notion of workers becoming incorporated into a diamond-shaped 'middle mass' society. Pahl (1989) argues that patterns of consumption have replaced productive activity as the means of fixing social identity and position:

If the symbol of the nineteenth century city was the factory chimney, the equivalent symbol at the end of the twentieth century in Europe and North America is the shopping mall. (Pahl 1989: 718–19)

The fact that many working people can now afford the 'luxuries' previously associated with well-off people as well as buying their own houses and shares in public utilities is taken as further evidence of the existence of the 'affluent worker' and the limitations of the 'pauperization' thesis. In this 'property-owning democracy' the assets are no longer concentrated in the hands of a capitalist elite but shared to such an extent that people who come from working-class backgrounds and occupations 'have a direct or indirect financial stake in capitalist enterprises, and most companies are owned directly or indirectly by millions of workers' (Saunders and Harris 1994: 1).

In the USA, George Bush has talked up the idea of Americans becoming members of an 'Ownership Society'. In a speech (16.12.2004) he made clear his belief that economic investment has social benefits:

I love the idea of people being able to own something . . . People from all walks of life, all income levels are willing to take risks to start their own company . . . And I like the idea of people being able to say, I'm in charge of my own health care . . . I particularly like the idea of a Social Security system that recognizes the importance and value of ownership.

Quoted by Joshua Holland (2005)

Social reform and the idea of 'citizenship'

In 1963 T.H. Marshall published the text of his now famous lectures on citizenship and social democracy. He argued that the social and political reforms of the nineteenth and twentieth centuries, the establishment of a welfare state and the belief in 'Keynesian' economic policies meant that a liberal democratic state had emerged which reflected and guaranteed the interests and rights of all people in society. No matter what class people belonged to they enjoyed the same rights of citizenship. Within liberal democracies, people had civil and political rights that guaranteed their freedoms before the law as well as the opportunity to participate in the political process, but what was special for the citizens of such democracies was their right to a decent standard of living established through the welfare state. The battle for 'social citizenship' was seen as an essential part of the war against capitalism; its aim was to assist 'the modern drive towards social

equality' and reduce class antagonism. According to Marshall, social citizenship would establish

a general enrichment of the concrete substance of civilized life, a general reduction of risk and insecurity, an equalisation between the more and less fortunate at all levels – between the healthy and the sick, the employed and the unemployed, the old and the active, the bachelor and the father of a large family. Equalisation is not so much between classes as between individuals within a population which is now treated for this purpose as though it were one class. Equality of status is more important than equality of income.

(Marshall 1963, quoted in Jordon 1984: 110)

As well as providing a 'universal right to a real income', Marshall's social citizenship had at its centre the right to a decent education, which in turn would widen opportunities and increase rates of social mobility. Under such circumstances it was envisaged that the sharp divisions of capitalism would be reduced and the resulting class antagonisms removed. This idea of citizenship is crucial to the 'third way' developed by Anthony Giddens (1998) in response to the demands of the 'late modern' age and the policies pursued by social democratic parties across Europe, the Americas, Australia and post-communist Russia. Through the extension of 'dialogic democracy' to all parts of society it becomes possible for all people to feel that they have a part to play in creating a 'state without enemies'. The policies of 'social inclusion' pursued by New Labour in Britain since 1997 are a good example: by targeting families, schools and sport it is felt that people from the most deprived communities can feel that they are equal citizens in a democratic world (see p. 223).

Changes in the organization and nature of work

In the traditional model of the class structure, people were clearly stratified according to their position within the system of production. The decisions about planning, investment and development would be made by those who owned and therefore controlled the means of production (factories, mines, railways, for example). This class of manufacturing entrepreneurs employed large groups of workers whose labour power was essential for the production of mass-produced goods. Entire communities emerged which were solely dependent on traditional industries and skills. Within these communities work was often regarded as central to a person's status, and the identities of male workers were inextricably bound up with the work they did.

At the end of the twentieth century many traditional industries have declined to the point of extinction. In Britain the steel industry, coal-mining, shipbuilding and deep sea fishing have all but disappeared. The service industries which have replaced them (in areas such as banking, leisure and retail) require different types of skills and different attitudes towards work. People are now told not to follow 'a trade' but to pick up as many 'transferable skills' as they can in order to take advantage of the new pick 'n' mix job opportunities thrown up by an ever-changing economic environment. No one can expect a job for life and everyone needs to be able to adapt. There are many consequences of these changes for the modern class structure, but two in particular stand out.

First, the emergence of a new middle class, which has, at the top end, taken over some of the administrative functions of the entrepreneurial class of owners and at other levels has expanded through the development of the professions and the rapid increase of the non-manual sector. This has given rise to the idea that apart from a very few rich people at the top and an increasingly marginalized underclass at the bottom, society is now characterized by a large and contented middle class. Despite there being little sociological evidence for this 'middle-class classless' society the idea has been extremely popular with social commentators and politicians (Edgell 1993: 119); it is certainly true that the majority of working people are now to be found in what may be loosely termed middle-class occupations.

Second, within this growth of non-manual, service sector jobs another pattern has emerged – the replacement of men by women. Whereas women in the first half of the twentieth century were largely excluded from the economic structure by their roles as wives and mothers and the 'ideology of domestication' that accompanied these roles, the penetration of women into the labour market and their increased importance as family breadwinners has been remarkable. The Labour Force Survey published in September 1993 found that most new jobs being created are part-time and filled by women (in the latter part of 1992, 80 per cent of the new jobs on offer in Britain were part-time and 80 per cent of these jobs were filled by women).

This 'feminization' of service work has several implications for the debate about the class structure. Women workers have been at the forefront of the occupational shift from manufacturing to service industries, so that as men in traditional industries are made redundant they are replaced in the occupational structure by women in a range of 'non-manual' occupations. Despite the evidence that many of these women are being recruited into low-paid and part-time routine jobs, the non-manual nature of the work creates the impression that the class structure is becoming more middle class. Although many women may go to work simply to make ends meet, where their income combines with other household incomes, sociologists such as Pahl and Wallace (1988) have argued that 'work-rich', dual-income families, who enjoy relatively high living standards, emerge. Again the impression of a new middle-class family being created by changing patterns of work and income has established itself; this reinforces the impression that modern society is increasingly dominated by middle-class households able to afford a middle-class lifestyle.

Social mobility and the fragmentation of class structure

The growth of a new middle class and the increasing opportunities for social mobility for people from both middle-class and working-class origins has led to the idea that the homogeneous and polarized classes of the traditional model have become so fragmented by differences in skill, pay and consciousness that it no longer makes sense to talk of a class structure. According to writers like Dahrendorf (1959), the traditional upper class has undergone a process of decomposition largely as a result of increasing share ownership and a *managerial revolution* which has effectively seen ownership and control of the means of production slip from their grasp (see also Burnham 1945; Galbraith 1967).

At the same time the working class has become fractured by differences in employment opportunities and pay. Not only are there divisions between skilled, semi-skilled and unskilled workers but also an underclass of 'work-poor' families has emerged characterized by unemployment and poverty (Smith 1992). This idea of fragmentation clearly undermines the Marxist notions of class formation and class consciousness and has been used to support the argument for the growth of a new middle class. However, it has been argued that even the middle mass of society is becoming increasingly fragmented by differences in skill and pay and that this has created a hierarchy of differentially rewarded status groups who see the social structure in very different ways (Roberts *et al.* 1977).

In his polemic against the 'British obsession' with class, Lord Bauer (1997: 1) argues that 'it remains part of contemporary political folklore that a restrictive and divisive class system is the bane of this country [which acts as] a major barrier to economic progress . . . and also a significant source of justified social discontent.' In rejecting what he sees as a stereotypical view of modern Britain Bauer contends that 'In Britain, class distinctions do exist, but they are not, and rarely have been, significant barriers to social or economic mobility.'

This view is supported by Saunders (1996), who claims that the research into social mobility by Glass in the 1950s and Goldthorpe *et al.* in the 1970s and 1980s distorts and exaggerates the influence of class background on social destination. From his own research, Saunders concludes that society is 'unequal but fair' and also argues that the meritocratic ideal that 'people's income should depend on hard work and ability' shares widespread support among the British public. In his own analysis of social mobility rates, Saunders (1997; 2002) uses data collected from the National Childhood Development Study, which has been monitoring the achievements of a cohort comprised of all the children born in the same week in Britain in 1958. As these children would have been assessed for ability and aptitude at regular intervals, Saunders analyzes this personal data and comes to the conclusion that, if we use IQ and motivation scores in childhood as our predictors of mobility (rather than social class), we find that the social destination of individuals have more to do with their ability than their social advantages or shortcomings. Upward and downward mobility reflect individual differences rather than social ones. These views are supported by psychologist Daniel Nettle (2003) who also analyzed the data from NCDS research.

The German sociologist Ulrich Beck (1992) has taken these ideas even further in arguing that the predictable patterns of class-related privilege and achievement have been replaced in the modern world by a lack of certainty about the future which confronts all young people. In the 'risk society' of late modernity the young generation leaving school and college face a world no longer characterized by the class-based certainties of an orderly industrial society revolving around work, family and local community. Instead they perceive social achievement as a matter of individual risk taking and social position as an outcome of these decisions. In the absence of any real community or class consciousness, people are left to deal with a rapidly changing world alone. In this sense Beck argues not that class is unimportant but that it is no longer perceived as relevant as an explanation or as a basis for action. In similar vein, Furlong and Cartmel conclude that:

In the 1990s the traditional links between the family, school and work seem to have weakened and young people embark on journeys into adulthood which involve a wide variety of routes, many of which appear to have uncertain outcomes. Because there are many more pathways to choose from, young people may develop the impression that their own routes are unique and that the risks they face are to be overcome by them as individuals rather than as members of a collectivity.

(1997: 29)

The end of ideology and the embourgeoisment thesis

Despite predictions of a proletarian revolution made by Marx, the failure of the working class to develop a 'class consciousness' which has translated into 'class action' has led many sociologists to challenge the basic assumption that class position, consciousness and political action are automatically linked (Rose 1988). Instead of becoming committed to a radical value system, most working people have rejected rebellion in favour of a more individualistic set of attitudes towards social change. In attempting to explain why workers do not necessarily adopt radical attitudes, Gordon Marshall and colleagues (1988) have distinguished between theories of working-class ambivalence and theories of working-class instrumentalism.

Theories of working-class ambivalence

The political passivity of workers is explained in relation to the fragmentation and middle mass arguments mentioned above. On the one hand it is suggested that a fragmented working class becomes heterogenous and divided and as such cannot achieve its role as a revolutionary class. On the other hand, it is argued that sections of the working class become incorporated into the dominant value system and subordinate to it. This view was clearly expressed in the *embourgeoisment* thesis put forward to explain the decline in working-class support for the Labour Party in the 1960s. According to this thesis the increasing affluence of working-class family life undermined the attraction of radical or social democratic policies for change. Being able to afford the trappings of a middle-class lifestyle had encouraged working-class people to become more conservative. This thesis was partially revived in the 1980s to explain the dramatic success of consecutive Conservative governments in appealing to the 'collective acquisitiveness' of some sections of the working class.

Theories of working-class instrumentalism

In their famous study of affluent workers in Luton, Goldthorpe and colleagues (1968) set out to test the embourgeoisment thesis and effectively demonstrated its limitations as a general economic explanation for the political behaviour of a whole class. Essentially they noted that despite economic improvements, the workers in their study had not become 'middle class', nor had they become conservative. They did conclude, however, that a 'new working class' had been created in the post-war environment of full employment, citizenship and consumerism; their goals were increasingly 'privatized' (home-centred) and their political strategies were still collective but clearly instrumental. In other words, affluent workers were prepared to support their trade unions and vote Labour as long as this guaranteed their affluent lifestyle. It has been the defection of this group of skilled manual workers to the Conservatives since 1979 after promises of tax cuts, 'right-to-buy' schemes for council tenants and the privatization of public utilities which kept the Labour Party out of power for 18 years.

In their attack on the Marxist model of class and class consciousness, Pahl and Wallace (1988) refute the deterministic approach as 'simple-minded' and romantic. They argue that the decomposition of the working class along with the dealignment of politics caused by Thatcherism has shown that there are other determinants of political outlook. Drawing on the research of sociologists and political scientists at the University of Essex (Marshall *et al.* 1988) as well as their own study of family life and class in the Isle of Sheppey, Pahl and Wallace argue that the class alignment of working people has been 'fractured' by changes in occupational structure and lifestyle. Four factors in particular provide alternative sources of social identity:

1   An increasing number of people are 'non-working' class and depend increasingly on state benefits for their income. It is their experience of unemployment that crucially affects their consciousness.

2   The increasing numbers of women in the workplace means that traditional (male head of household) notions of work, identity and class consciousness have to be re-examined.

3   Differential access to private and public services means that differing patterns of consumption appear which may be seen as a more important source of consciousness than occupation. Home ownership, private education, private health care and the ownership of shares may all become points of departure from a traditional class alignment.

4   In the world of work itself further divisions have occurred which are related to the form that work takes rather than the nature of the job. A self-employed maintenance worker may have very different views from one who works for somebody else. Whether that person was employed in the private sector or the public domain may also affect political attitudes.

As a result, it is argued that the 'cultural privatization' of home-centred working-class lifestyle can result in the demise of class identification and class politics. This view is developed further by Pahl and Wallace, who suggest that social identity and consciousness is too complex to be reduced to social class. The social world is experienced through the everyday life of families and it is people's own experiences of their domestic life cycle which forms their consciousness of the real world: 'Social images, we suggest, may be constructed less in terms of class and more in terms of family and personal biography' (Pahl and Wallace 1988: 136). These findings anticipated Beck's ideas on the decline of class consciousness in the 'risk society' discussed earlier (p. 229).

The Isle of Sheppey study found little evidence of any radical consciousness ('rebels in red'), nor did it discover the widespread deference often associated with privatized workers ('angels in marble'), but the collective identity it did come across took rather surprising forms. First, steel plant workers on the island had combined against pickets from other plants to defend their jobs rather than join in a broader struggle. (The defection of the Nottinghamshire miners during the national strike in 1983–84 is perhaps a better-known example of a similar phenomenon.) Second, trade union membership and organization were purely instrumental and were not linked in any traditional way to the Labour Party. Indeed, trade unionists were as likely to be actively involved in the Conservative Party – although the popularity of the Conservative Club seemed to rest on the price of beer as much as anything else! Third, the general collective identity had deep historical roots which went beyond class and touched on the themes of nationalism and patriotism. The victory celebration at the end of the Falklands War in 1982 was seen as an example of 'relatively spontaneous collective action'.

Alongside this rather conservative form of collective identity Pahl and Wallace (1988) also claim to have discovered 'a strong element of working class individualism', a resentment of 'less respectable' families and a deep-rooted commitment to the values of domesticity. It was within this broader social consciousness that the politics of 'dynamic conservatism' made its mark at the end of the 1970s with the rise of 'Thatcherism':

> She presented herself to the working class as the champion of the taxpayer against the Treasury, the worker against the trade union, the council tenant against the landlord and the citizen against the state.
>
> (Jenkins 1987: 53)

This populist ideology seemed to strike a chord with many working-class people who felt that the Labour Party had let them down and that ownership of property was an important means of 'getting on'. The stereotype was tracked down to its home in Essex where 'Basildon Man' had turned against his working-class roots to vote for the Conservatives throughout their period in office (1979–97). In their two-part study of this phenomenon, Hayes and Hudson (2001) explain how Basildon represents a post-war social experiment: attracting its new residents from the working class heartlands of the East End of London, Basildon was from the outset 'an overwhelmingly working-class town' characterized by 'a strong sense of individualism and self improvement' (2001: 11). At the end of the 1970s Mrs Thatcher swept to power on the promise of extended home ownership but it was felt by some political pundits that 'Thatcherism had wrought some deeper, more permanent change in the attitudes and outlooks of working class people' (2001: 38). Between 1981 and 1996 home ownership in Basildon increased from 53 per cent to 71 per cent and in their first study in 1992 Hayes and Hudson did find some evidence of a more family-centred approach to life which may have been related to a more instrumental attitude to politics and a revolt against Labour;

> In 1992 Basildon's skilled workers associated the Labour Party with poverty and welfare, hopelessness and failure. They saw it as the party for losers. Basildonians said they wanted to help themselves rather than wait around for someone else to sort out their lives. Many saw that Labour was a barrier to taking control of their lives and making something of themselves. For a period, through thick and thin, the pronouncements of the Tories had tapped into their aspirations.
>
> (Hayes and Hudson 2001: 19)

During the final ten years of the Conservative government, Bev Skeggs (1997) conducted an ethnographic study of 83 working-class women from a town in the northwest of England. Her interviews revealed a high level of insecurity as the women raised concerns about their identities and aspirations. Although they were aware that they did not possess the 'airs and graces' to be considered middle class, they also sought to distance themselves from the 'dirty and dangerous' stereotype of working-class life and its negative associations with loose morality, irresponsibility and poor educational standards. Seeing themselves as 'respectable' they tried to 'disidentify' with the traditional image and aspired to more positive self-images through marriage and vocational (as opposed to academic) education.

> Class is experienced by women as exclusion. Whereas working-class men can use class as a positive source of identity, a way of including themselves in positively valorised social category . . . this does not apply for working-class women . . . Overall (this) is a study of how social and cultural positioning generates denial, disidentification and dissimulation rather than adjustment. It is a study of doubt, insecurity and unease: the emotional politics of class.   (Skeggs 1997: 74–5)

Although one of the respondents (June) uses the term to try and make sense of her new and 'respectable' position she ends up rejecting 'class' as a useful concept:

> No, I don't think I'm working class at all now. Not after we bought the house and that . . . I expect I'm now middle class . . . but it's like when we go to Dave's business dos, but I don't really feel like some of them, you know the real bosses' wives with all their talk and that. I sometimes feel really frightened to speak in case I show him up. I expect they're really middle class so I'm not really like them, but I'm not like the rest of our family without two pennies to rub together. You know, I just don't think class is a very useful term. I think I'm probably classless. You know I'm not really one nor the other. I don't really fit.   (1997: 77)

In the 1990s Terry Clark and Seymour Martin Lipset analysed the significance of social class as an international phenomenon by comparing changing trends in the United States, Western Europe and the emerging nations of the old Eastern bloc. In their view the decline of hierarchy in the three major areas of social organization (referred to as 'situses of stratification') had seen a decline in the importance of social class; the democratization and differentiation of the workplace, government and family life had led to the decline of class as a determinant of lifestyle and opportunities which rendered the idea of class 'an increasingly outmoded concept . . . appropriate to earlier historical periods'.

They concluded that societies are now characterized by 'fragmentation of stratification' which can be summarized as:

> the weakening of class stratification, especially as shown in distinct class-differentiated life styles; the decline of economic determinism, and the increased importance of social and cultural factors; politics less organised by class and more by other loyalties; social mobility less family-determined, more ability and educational-determined.
>
> (Clark and Lipset 1996: 48)

Utilizing many of the arguments outlined above, Pakulski and Waters (1996) also claim that class has lost its significance with people rejecting class as a basis for social grouping preferring alternative sources of social identity such as ethnicity, gender and age. In a very Weberian analysis they argue that in contemporary 'first world' societies a series of technological and social changes have ushered in a 'post-industrial' age in which the old class-based communities and identities have disappeared. As the traditional industries of mining, steel production and ship building have declined the service sector has expanded. In consequence the traditional skills of labour power have been replaced with those of a 'knowledge economy' and people feel less distinguished by the division of labour. On top of this the wider distribution of wealth and income and the increase in property ownership has created a society no longer organized around class but 'status conventionalism' in which social esteem and identity are derived from patterns of consumption. Inequalities in income clearly still exist but the attention has shifted away from how people earn their money to an assessment of how they spend it. As Abbot puts it:

> For Pakulski and Waters, contemporary societies are stratified, but this stratification is achieved through cultural consumption, not class positioning in the division of labour. It seems that they are claiming that the differences between, say, a skilled worker from Luton, who drives a Ford Escort, lives in a semi-detached house worth between about £80,000 and £100,000 and who goes on package holidays to Spain, and an Oxbridge-educated lawyer living in Hampstead, who drives a Mercedes, has a house worth £200,000 and who holidays in private rented villas in Tuscany, are purely issues of status: it is not that they are members of different classes. It is all a matter of style, taste and status (prestige), not of location in the division of labour.
>
> (Abbot 2001: 7)

(These arguments are rejected by Houtt *et al.* (1996), whose position is summarized on p. 256.)

Stop and think

> ➤ Summarize the problems that may arise in trying to 'measure' the following indicators of the importance of social class: (a) changes in quality of life; (b) the importance of social reform; (c) changes in the nature of work; (d) the extent of social mobility; (e) the extent of working-class instrumentalism.

The persistence of class

Many sociologists, particularly those adopting a Marxist perspective, would reject the conclusion that class analysis is no longer useful, although few would argue that the class structure has been unaffected by social and economic change. From this point of view the major divisions in society are ones of class. These divisions still affect life chances and have a major effect on the way that people see themselves and the structure of society.

> The view that class is dead derives from a very narrow and misleading understanding of class. Properly understood, class points to fundamental social divisions that cross-cut Britain and all other modern societies. Taken along with the closely interlinked themes of gender, race and ethnicity and age, class defines the nature of social stratification, which remains the sociological key to understanding the structure of society.
>
> (Scott 1994: 19)

Despite the differences already mentioned sociologists who have been influenced by Marx and Weber still talk of three major classes and emphasize the underlying conflict in the relationship between these classes. In examining the extent to which social class is still important we look at some of the evidence and arguments that suggest that the upper, middle and working classes continue to be important and distinct groups in modern society.

In his review of social class in modern Britain, Ken Roberts (2001) argues that class still matters and that the evidence is 'overwhelming' particularly with regard to the key indicators of opportunity: wealth, health and education. His comments on the five key arguments for the 'demise of class' are worth summarizing;

1 **Changes in the quality of life** Roberts accepts that society has become more affluent and that wealth and income have been redistributed since the war. However, he points out that, despite increases in property ownership among working-class households, this often refers to assets for personal use such as houses and cars as opposed to investments from which an income can be derived, such as shares. Against the view that we have all become mini-capitalists, he points out that only about half the population 'has any significant share in the country's wealth' with less than 20 per cent owning shares. Added to which concentrations of wealth and disparities in income still exist. 'The fact that many workers have some assets, and many capitalists also work, does not necessarily prove that there is no longer a glaring class division between them' (2001: 179).

2 **Social reform and the idea of citizenship** Democracy and the development of the welfare state may provide the opportunity for everyone to be involved in the political process and to ensure that health, education and social security are properly funded, but that does not mean that rights or benefits are enjoyed in equal measure. As Titmuss pointed out in the early days of the welfare state, equal citizenship rights do not guarantee a more equitable distribution of opportunities or rewards (see Alcock *et al.* 2001). In education, for example, it is still the case that middle-class families tend to get a better share of resources, particularly when it comes to higher education. It is also the case that important services such as medical care, housing and education exist outside of state provision for those that can afford them and as such reinforce class differences rather than reduce them.

As Anne Phillips points out no democratic political system can be separated from the socio-economic system in which it is rooted and the privileging of certain interests which flow from it:

> The . . . conditions of corporate capitalism constrain the exercise of popular control, making the supposed freedom and equality of citizens a desperately unbalanced affair . . . The point here is not just that the wealthy find it easier to disseminate their views, to finance newspapers, launch pressure groups, lunch prime ministers. More troubling (because it is more systematic) is the fact that all governments depend upon the process of capital accumulation as the source of incomes, growth, and jobs, and must therefore ensure that the economic policies they pursue do not undermine the prosperity of the private sector. This structural privileging of corporate power means that the democratic playing field is never level.   (Phillips 1999: 17–18)

3 **Changes in the nature and organization of work** Pakulski and Waters' arguments that there has been a shift from manufacturing industry to a 'knowledge economy' based upon educational qualifications rather than industrial skills are given short shrift by Roberts who dismisses such ideas as 'plain bunk' (2001: 17) because they ignore the relationship between class position and educational achievement in the first instance and the tendency of such differentials to reinforce the class divisions in society in the long term. As Bourdieu has pointed out, educational qualifications are an important source of cultural capital and as such operate as a clear means by which social divisions are maintained. In Fiona Devine's (2004) ethnographic account of the strategies employed by middle-class families in Boston and Manchester to ensure the educational advancement of their own children it is clear that the perennial dinner party angst around schooling is treated as a serious aspect of the contest between individual families and social classes for places in the most prestigious schools. In her limited set of interviews with the parents of children from middle-class homes (24 doctors and 24 teachers) she shows the significance attached to education for social advancement and the lengths to which middle-class parents will go to ensure that their kids get the educational advantages they require. In other words we slip behind the rhetoric of 'meritocracy' to appreciate the social reality of self-recruitment and self-advancement from a middle-class point of view. As such, it succeeds in revealing 'the micro foundations of . . . macro reproduction' (Reed 2004).

4 **Social mobility and the fragmentation of the class structure** Despite the arguments of Saunders and others that we live in a meritocratic society in which the inequality of rewards reflect inequalities in ability and motivation, there are many sociologists who argue that achievement is still based upon social factors and that the changes in the class structure have been much exaggerated. (See Roberts 2001: Chapter 8 for a useful review.)

In the statistical analysis of Glass (1954) and the Nuffield study of Goldthorpe *et al.* (1972) it was suggested that social mobility rates in absolute terms (the overall movement between occupational groups) and in relative ones (the chances of groups from different backgrounds to move up or down when compared with one another) were not great. There has been some movement, especially into the expanding intermediate sector and between adjacent groups, but there was also evidence of high levels of self-recruitment at the top and bottom with very little evidence of a genuine 'rags to riches' meritocracy in operation. The social destiny of young men was seen to be clearly linked to the occupational status of their fathers. Goldthorpe (1996), Breen and Goldthorpe (1999) and Savage and Egerton (1997) dismiss Saunders' conclusion that intelligence and motivation account for patterns of mobility and self-recruitment, arguing instead that 'success' and 'failure' in the job market are still related to cultural and economic advantages rather than individual ones.

In fact, after seven years of Labour government the Prime Minister's own strategy unit admitted that the chances of people from lower-class backgrounds improving their chances in the job market had got worse rather than better. As Andrew Rawnsley reported:

No one seems to have a comprehensive explanation for why birth, not worth, has again become such a key determinant of life chances, not just in Britain, but across the advanced industrialized countries, not excluding so-called classless America.

One reason, I suggest, is that those already enjoying membership of the middle class have got more adept, energetic and aggressive about ensuring they bequeath that privilege to their offspring. Another reason is that, while the number of higher status and earning occupations is increasing, the pool of available jobs is not growing fast enough to let in many incomers from the bottom of the heap. A further factor is the number of people trapped in economic inactivity, like the many on incapacity benefit who say they would actually like to work, or stuck in insecure jobs which offer no skills development and little possibility of escape from low incomes.

There are compelling reasons to be concerned about the seizing up of social mobility. It ingrains poverty in crime-ridden sink communities. It hurts the economy when we fail to harness the potential talents of everyone with a contribution to make.

And if there aren't the opportunities for people to advance through effort, then they become impoverished, not just financially, but in aspiration. Government has to have a better answer to poverty of ambition in deprived areas than dangling the remote hope of winning the jackpot at a super casino.   (Rawnsley 2004)

In line with Roberts we may think that people have better opportunities today than they did in the past but the sociological evidence tells a different story:

As far as we can tell, the rate of social fluidity, meaning the social mobility that is not structurally inevitable on account of class differentials in birth rates and changes in the proportions of positions at different levels, is roughly the same at the beginning of the twenty-first century as it was at the beginning of the twentieth. Modern social classes have never been closed groups . . . But most people have ended up, and continue to end up, in either the same class, or in a class close to where they were born. In any case, social mobility transfers people between classes without necessarily weakening the roots of class division.
          (Roberts 2001)

Describing this as 'one of the most startling discoveries in the whole of sociology' Roberts argues that over time and between modern societies it is 'the absence of major variations' which is most apparent.

Despite the different explanations on offer (individual ability versus social advantage) there seems to be general agreement that the chances of social and economic advancement are restricted and the patterns predictable:

It is equally startling that this finding, one of sociology's firmer conclusions, has been ignored by virtually all social-policy makers, and by many sociologists who continue to act as if they expect modest interventions in education or labour markets to bring about a significant redistribution of life-chances between the social classes.
          (Roberts 2001: 224)

5 **The end of ideology and the embourgeoisment thesis** The idea that working-class people were becoming more affluent led to the idea that they would adopt more middle-class lifestyles and eventually a middle-class outlook on life including more conservative political attitudes. Roberts dismisses such simplistic thinking by pointing out that it is flawed on three grounds:

i) Income and assets may have improved in absolute terms but this is true for all groups so that in relative terms the inequalities in income between the classes still persist.

ii) Consumption patterns may change but so do people's perceptions of the status attached to goods and property. As items which were once regarded as exclusive become common they lose their associations with a middle-class lifestyle. Cars, holidays abroad, home ownership and TV sets were all symbols of high status which most people have come to expect as part of a normal standard of living. At the end of the day 'a washing machine is a washing machine is a washing machine'.

iii) Workers who have incomes comparable to those of middle-class professionals still earn their money in a different way, have a different experience of life and continue to see themselves as working class. In cultural terms it is unlikely that by becoming affluent, workers automatically disassociate themselves from their roots and see themselves as middle class.

These ideas are explored in more depth in the next section (pp. 248–58) where we look at the work of Goldthorpe and Lockwood, Fiona Devine, Hayes and Hudson, Simon Charlesworth and Bev Skeggs.

In conclusion, Roberts argues that despite the changes that have occurred class still remains a key factor in shaping lifestyles, opportunities and attitudes and that people still tend to use class as a means of understanding who they are. With regard to the related argument that people now have a range of alternative and competing claims on their identity (see Payne 2000), Roberts acknowledges the higher profile of gender, race, nationality and age as a basis for group membership but points out that these status differences are still striated by class.

In the remainder of this section of the book we look more closely at the composition of the three major classes themselves.

The upper class

Traditionally the upper class is associated with ownership of property and in particular the ownership of land. The landed aristocracy began to be replaced in the nineteenth century by those whose economic power derived from manufacturing industry, retail and banking, although a certain amount of overlap occurred between these interests. More recently it has been argued that a 'managerial revolution' has stripped this class of its power to control events and that a new managerial elite of administrators has taken over.

Occupational scales tend to obscure the existence of the 'super rich'. Research is thin on the ground with rich people tending to keep details of their wealth secret, so it is easy to be persuaded by the idea that this group has all but disappeared. However, there is clear evidence that as a class it has adapted in order to survive and even become more powerful through a diversification of interests.

A closer look

Every year *The Sunday Times* publishes the 'Rich List' (see Table 6.2), which documents the changing patterns of wealth in Britain and identifies the richest individuals and families who make up the 'super rich'. According to the 2004 figures, Roman Abramovitch was the richest man in Britain with a fortune of £7.5bn just lagging behind the Albrecht family who were the richest family in Europe on £22.3bn but their combined wealth could not match that of the Wal-Mart founding Robson family who were estimated to be worth £54bn. Since 2004 it has been reported that IKEA boss, Ingvar Kamprad, has leapfrogged to the top of the pile. However, the collective wealth of the 1,000 or so richest individuals in the 'Rich List' is in excess of £202 billion and there are still concentrations of considerable wealth in Britain, so that it takes a personal fortune of at least £400m to gain admittance to the Top 100 club.

To access the Rich List go to The Times Online at http://www.timesonline.co.uk

Table 6.2 The 11 richest in the world

				2004 wealth	2003 wealth
1	Robson Walton[1]	America	Retail (Wal-Mart)	£54.2bn	£54.6bn
2	Bill Gates	America	Software (Microsoft)	£25.3bn	£26.9bn
3	Warren Buffett	America	Investments	£23.3bn	£20.2bn
4	Karl and Theo Albrecht[1]	Germany	Supermarkets	£22.3bn	£16.9bn
5	Cox Forrest Jr and John Mars[1]	America	Confectionery	£16.9bn	£19.8bn
6	King Fahd[1]	Saudi Arabia	Oil	£13.5bn	£13.2bn
7	Barbara Cox, Anthony and Anne Cox Chambers	America	Media	£12.1bn	£13.6bn
8	Prince Alwaleed	Saudi Arabia	Investments	£11.6bn	£11.7bn
9	Paul Allen	America	Software (Microsoft)	£11.4bn	£13.3bn
10=	Sheikh of Abu Dhabi	Abu Dhabi	Oil, investments	£10.8bn	£10.5bn
10=	Johanna Quandt[1]	Germany	Cars (BMW)	£10.8bn	£8.6bn

[1] denotes family wealth
Source: Times Online 18.4.2004

Table 6.3 This year's top 10 in the UK

1	Roman Abramovich	£7,500m
2	The Duke of Westminster	£5,500m
3	Hans Rausing and family	£4,950m
4	Philip Green	£3,610m
5	Lakshmi Mittal	£3,500m
6	Sir Richard Branson	£2,600m
7	Kirsten and Jorn Rausing	£2,575m
8	Bernie and Slavica Ecclestone	£2,323m
9	Charlene and Michel de Carvalho	£2,260m
10	David and Simon Reuben	£2,200m

Source: Times Online 18.4.2004

The 2004 Rich List is made up of . . .

1,022 men; 78 women; 751 of the richest 1,000 entries are self-made millionaires; 249 inherited their wealth. There are . . .

190 in land and property
120 in industry, metal bashing, engineering, steel making
104 in banking, insurance, stockbroking, finance
85 in retailing (not food)
74 in media, television and films, publishing, novels
69 in food retailing, food production, drinks
62 in computers, software, telecoms, mobile phones
62 in construction, housebuilding
59 in hotels, leisure, health and fitness, sport
44 in music
37 in car sales, wholesaling, distribution
31 in business services, recruitment, office support
29 in transport
26 in pharmaceuticals, healthcare
8 in internet services

There are 39 new entries worth £100m or more and 109 worth less than £100m.

The oldest person in the list is Sir Julian Hodge, 99, who with his family has a fortune of £48m, and the youngest is Nina Hagen, 22, who is worth £225m.

In view of the continued concentration of wealth, writers including Miliband (1969), Scott (1991) and Westergaard (1995) in Britain and Barron and Sweezy (1968) and Zeitlin (1989) in the USA have argued that the managerial revolution is more imagined than real. The idea that the managerial elite are a group of essentially neutral technocrats operating in the public interest is roundly rejected. The modifications of the class structure in recent times have not altered its essential nature:

> Property, profit and market – the key institutions of a capitalist society – retain their central place in social arrangements, and remain the prime determinants of inequality.   (Westergaard and Resler 1976: 17)

At the apex of these key institutions remains a dominant class of between 5 and 10 per cent of the population who derive their position from property ownership and the control that they exercise over resources and other people's lives:

> The core assumptions of our society (property, profit and market) are firmly in line with the interests of one small group. That group comprises top business people and large property owners. It also includes those who

Case study

Dwarfs and giants

There is another way of looking at the overall income distribution . . . It involves thinking of a parade of the whole population passing before our eyes in a period of one hour. Each person's height is determined by their income such that the person with the mean income has the mean height (say 5'9"). Someone with income half the average would have a height half the average, and a person with income twice the average would be twice as tall as the average. Now suppose they pass before us in order of income (and therefore height) with the poorest (shortest) first until the last second of the sixtieth minute when the richest (tallest) person passes . . .

The first few seconds will actually see a few upside-down people with negative incomes and therefore negative heights. These will be the self-employed who are making losses from their businesses. And then for the first couple of minutes tiny dwarfs of under a foot or so will be passing. The heights of those passing will initially rise quite quickly, reaching 2'4" after six minutes. But then there will be a long parade of dwarfs whose height will increase very slowly, only reaching just

over 2'10" (or half average height) by the end of the twelfth minute. Most of those passing at this point will be on social security benefits of some sort.

In the next 18 minutes, taking us up to the half hour, the height of those passing continues to rise gradually, reaching about 4'9" when the half hour is reached. Half-way through and we are still looking down on people nearly a foot shorter than the average. The average height is eventually reached in the thirty-seventh minute, with the height still growing fairly gradually. At this stage, we are seeing mainly working people.

At about the three-quarters-of-an-hour mark, something happens to the parade. The heights of the people passing by start rising much more quickly. It took half an hour for everyone under 4'10" to pass. It then takes another 18 minutes for the height of the parade to reach 7'8". This is the height of people passing with just 12 minutes to go before the hour is up. But over just the next six minutes, the height rises to nearly 10', and in the last few minutes, the heights start rising very quickly indeed. By the time we get into the last minute, 15'6" giants are passing by. But it is not until the very last few seconds that the

real giants are striding past. A merchant banker or chief executive of a large company with a gross income of £1 million per year (say) and net earnings, therefore, of about £12,000 per week would be towering up in the sky at a mighty 265' or 88 yards tall, over one-and-a-half times as high as Nelson's Column.

Even above the highest-paid executives and employees will be a few entrepreneurs and aristocrats. The very richest in the country are not salaried employees. They either own their own companies (like Richard Branson) or large parts of the country (the Queen, for example). Unfortunately, none of our data contain information on this particular group of the population. When Pen first wrote of the parade, he estimated that John Paul Getty was the richest man in Britain and attributed to him a height of at least ten miles.

(Adapted from Pen (1971)
by Goodman *et al.* (1997)
Inequality in the UK)

Questions

1. *Transfer the above figures onto a graph that represents height (in yards and feet) against time (60 minutes).*

2. *What does this tell us about income inequality in the UK?*

---

derive substantial privilege from their association with this central cluster: the highly prosperous and well established professions, the senior ranks of officials in public service . . . Capital with its associates is still the effective ruling interest. It is not just one elite among several.   (Westergaard and Resler 1976: 252)

This homogeneous view of a capitalist class has been modified more recently by models which suggest a variety of interests constituting a powerful group at the top whose ownership of property confers power. Giddens (1986: 159) has identified three categories of rich people in Britain:

1 *Jet set rich*   This includes writers, sports professionals and rock stars who amass large fortunes very quickly as a result of well-marketed publicity. This group represents a very small section of the wealthy and would not normally be regarded as part of the capitalist class. An example is Paul McCartney.

2 *Landowners*   People whose fortunes have been largely inherited, their estates having been passed down over generations. The concentration of land ownership means that a small group of landed families are still prominent. Because of the responsibilities and costs involved in maintaining such estates, as well as the legal restrictions covering such property, members of this group are not as wealthy as they may appear and do not control the kind of liquid assets which make other rich people very powerful. The Duke of Westminster is an aristocrat who inherited both land and title.

3 *Entrepreneurial rich*   A group who derive their position from the ownership of stocks and shares. The concentration of ownership of these resources puts the control of manufacture, banking, insurance and the retail trades in the hands of a very few people. Although they may not be as wealthy on paper as some aristocrats, these people control assets that give them substantial power. Richard Branson and Roman Abramovitch are examples.

John Scott (1991; 1997) has researched the exclusive 'business class' at the centre of the major enterprises which dominate British economic activity. In his view, the landed aristocracy and the highly paid are not necessarily members of the business class simply because of their affluence. The important consideration for Scott is the involvement of wealthy and influential individuals who hold key positions ('economic locations') at the centre of capitalist activity.

> Capitalist economic locations are positions within a structure of ownership and control over property, and there are two bases for location within the capitalist class: direct participation in control through personal property holdings and administrative participation, as directors and executives, in the impersonal patterns of control through which business enterprises are ruled.
> (Scott 1991: 8)

Behind the rise of joint-stock companies and institutional share ownership there still exists a core of capitalists who represent a business class. Scott suggests that this group may be classified in the following manner:

1 *Entrepreneurial capitalists*   Through their personal property holdings they enjoy direct control over corporate policy in one organization where they have a major or complete stake. The Moores family's domination of the Littlewoods empire is a good example.

2 *Rentier capitalists*   They have less day-to-day involvement with company policy, and their personal investment is spread over a range of different companies. Return on investment rather than control is the major consideration – they 'speculate to accumulate'. They have multiple shareholdings and make their money out of share dealing. By their nature, such individuals tend to work behind the scenes and so are not very well known.

3 *Executive capitalists*   They have official full-time positions (e.g. chairman) within organizations but do not necessarily hold a large or controlling stake in the business. The senior executives of large concerns such as ICI, British Airways and British Telecom would fit this category.

4 *Finance capitalists*   They enjoy multiple non-executive directorships across a range of separate companies. These people are not simply passive shareholders but might represent the interests of big financial institutions on the boards of large companies and as a result may be regarded as a sort of 'inner circle' of the British business class.

Although Scott has indicated a more differentiated model of the upper class than that offered by Westergaard and Resler (1976), for instance, he is clear that they still represent a privileged group in society:

> Occupants of all these capitalist locations are able to secure advantaged opportunities and life chances for themselves and for their families and they are able to live a life of privilege.   (Scott 1991: 10)

According to Scott, this group survives *as a class*, despite the transformation of capitalism from personal to impersonal forms of ownership, because of a series of 'networks' which bind these people together socially, politically and economically to the exclusion of others. Scott shows that through intermarriage and kinship, private schooling and an exclusive lifestyle the establishment continues to assert itself as a sort of 'private welfare state' (Crompton 1993: 193). Similarities of social background, club membership and political affiliation (to the

Case study

Inequalities of wealth and income

There are two common measures of economic fortune and they are often confused.

Wealth refers to assets such as land, shares, houses, cars, jewellery, etc., and under some circumstances they can be more useful than having money in the bank. It is also important what type of assets we own as houses and cars are for personal use while stocks and shares are an investment. A car will almost certainly decline in value over time while houses and shares will usually go up.

Inequalities in wealth have generally decreased over time. In Britain an official report (Babb et al. 2004) claimed that 'over the twentieth century as a whole, the distribution of wealth became more equal. In 1911, it is estimated that the wealthiest 1 per cent of the population held around 70 per cent of the UK's wealth. By 1936–38, this proportion had fallen to 56 per cent, and it fell again after world war two to reach 42 per cent in 1960' (quoted in Carvel 2004). By 1991 this trend had fallen to its lowest ebb (17 per cent) before it began to reverse itself.

According to figures released since then, the top 1 per cent (the wealthiest 600,000 individuals in Britain) owned assets worth £355bn in 1996 but this had doubled to £797bn by 2002 and their share of the nation's wealth had increased from 20 per cent to 23 per cent. At the other end, the share of the poorest 50 per cent shrank from a high of 10 per cent in 1986 to 5 per cent in 2001.

In a review of recent research by the American economist Paul Krugman, Chris Hamnett claims that 'wealth inequality has returned to the level of the golden age of American capitalism from the 1870s to 1929'. By comparison the wealth gap in the US is even greater than that found in Britain or the rest of Europe:

The US is even more unequal than Britain in both income and wealth. In the US, the top 1 per cent of wealth owners owned one-third of total wealth in 1983 but this had risen to 38 per cent by 1998, and the top 5 per cent owned 59 per cent. By comparison, the bottom 60 per cent owned less than 5 per cent of total wealth.

What is remarkable about the US is that the group which has increased its share is just the top 1 per cent of wealth owners. The other 99 per cent have seen their share fall. This is very different from Britain, where the top 50 per cent have all gained, and it supports Professor Krugman's claim that America is moving back towards the gilded age of capitalism.

(Hamnett 2004)

Income refers to the non-marketable wealth which a person earns through wages, salaries, dividends, pensions or benefits. Most forms of income are taxed either at source (direct taxation) or through taxes such as VAT on our purchases (indirect taxation). It is important to distinguish between the disposable income someone earns after tax and gross or pre-tax earnings. It is also important to understand that direct taxation tends to hit those on higher incomes while indirect taxation has more impact on poorer households. In general the gap in incomes in the UK is less well-marked than the wealth gap but is still very unequal.

Since the start of the new millennium, the issue of 'Fat Cat' pay has never been far from the headlines with shareholders and trade union officials quick to criticize the relentless rise in pay for those at the top. In 2002, Income Data Services reported that the average pay increase for the leading executives of those companies listed on the FTSE 100 had been 9.7 per cent for the year. This meant annual earnings of £1.6m on average for top executives and £600,000 for the directors of these top companies. The biggest winners that year were

Table 6.4 Distribution of wealth					
United Kingdon	1976 %	1986 %	1991 %	1996 %	2001 %
Most wealthy 1%	21	18	17	20	23
Most wealthy 25%	71	73	71	74	75
Most wealthy 50%	92	90	92	93	95

Source: Inland Revenue

Case study (continued)

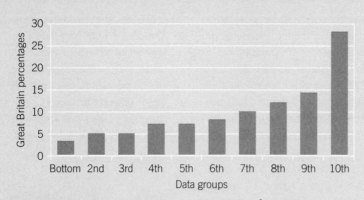

Figure 6.4 Shares of total disposable income[1], 2002/03

[1] Equivalized household disposable income before housing costs has been used to rank individuals. See Appendix, Part 4: Equivalization scales.

Source: Babb *et al.* 2004: 43

Luc Vandevelde, who got a cash bonus of £1.36m for stopping the rot at Marks and Spencers, and David Crossland, who achieved a 70 per cent pay rise from MyTravel despite a huge loss on the value of its shares. Despite calls for government regulation, the trend continued and in the following year Lord Simpson of Dunkeld and John Mayo walked away from the collapse of Marconi with a combined compensation package worth £3.7m, while American businessman William Aldinger managed to negotiate a 'Golden Hello' at HSBC worth £37m (Tran 2003). The Office for National Statistics issued a report in 2004 which showed that 'the pay of the richest 10 per cent of earners rose 4.3 per cent in the year to April to £825 a week – nearly double the average of £422 a week while the pay of the poorest 10 per cent rose only 4.1 per cent to £230 a week'

(Seager 2004). The rate of increase appears to be shrinking but 4.3 per cent of £825 is worth a lot more than 4.1 per cent of £230.

An international comparison

Using the Gini coefficient it is possible to compare inequalities across societies. The closer a society is to 0, the more equal it is in terms of income distribution. As we can see the UK and the USA appear to have the highest levels of income inequality. In countries such as the UK it is increasing, while in Italy it slows down over the 1990s; in the USA it remains high but unchanged.

Questions

1. *How might income differences become translated into social inequalities?*

2. *What factors might explain the differences in income inequality between societies?*

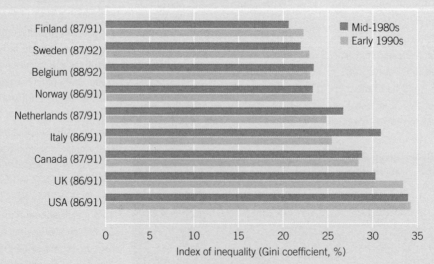

Figure 6.5 Income inequality in mid-1980s and early 1990s

Source: cited in Hills 1997, reported by permission of the Joseph Rowntree Foundation

Conservative Party) mean that these people see themselves as a class and act as one. As Crompton concludes:

> The upper class in capitalist societies *does* manifest all the signs of being both conscious of its material interests and capable of protecting them.
>
> (Crompton 1993: 198)

A closer look

The establishment

The establishment is not simply a group of people; it is a group of people allied around certain social institutions. These institutions are the Conservative Party, the Church of England, the public schools and ancient universities, the legal profession and the Guards regiments . . . In its informal aspect the establishment is the 'old boy network', the system of social contacts which stem from family and education. Such contacts 'are maintained largely in an informal manner by membership of the London clubs, by the social round of dinners and parties as well as, more formally, in business meetings and at official events'. The contacts which constitute this informal network of social relationships are important in the determination of the life-chances of those who go through the public school and Oxbridge system. Their contacts 'both facilitate their careers and enable them to have more influence in the posts where they eventually land'.

(John Scott 1992, quoted in Giddens 1992: 88)

The middle class

The term 'middle class' is one of the most misused in the sociological dictionary. It is used in everyday language to denote a variety of social, economic and cultural phenomena. It can be used to signify a wealthy lifestyle, a managerial occupation or cultural snobbery. In sociology its meaning is not much clearer; it has been used as a catch-all category for anyone found in the intermediate strata of industrial society or to describe and identify a particular set of social values.

In the eighteenth and nineteenth centuries the term tended to refer to those people who made a living from the trade and manufacture of goods and inhabited the middle ground between the landed aristocracy and the poor. As their economic power increased so did their political aspirations. In some countries (e.g. France) they led successful revolutions against the aristocracy,

establishing republican governments and exerting their own economic and political domination. In Britain, integration and reform led to the gradual merger with the aristocracy to form what is loosely referred to as the 'upper class'. In both situations the class that had been in the middle was now at the top, which made the continued use of the term even more confusing. According to Marx, the industrial bourgeoisie had become the new ruling class in opposition to the other major industrial class (the proletariat). In between he also recognized a class of small traders, self-employed artisans and landlords, whom he referred to as the petit bourgeoisie. However, as economic competition and the growth of monopolies forced them out of business, Marx expected that this group would eventually sink into the proletariat as society divided more clearly into 'two hostile camps'. As we have noted (p. 220) Weber disagreed fundamentally with Marx here and predicted an increase in the growth of the middle class as an intermediate status group. In the twentieth century the number of people in 'non-manual' occupations has undoubtedly grown at the expense of traditional manual occupations. The percentage of the working population in manual occupations is now lower than 50 per cent in many industrialized countries, with the non-manual sector representing anything between 50 and 60 per cent. This shift has been accompanied by a growth in female employment in the service sector and increasing levels of education and social mobility:

> With the general rise in living standards, the spread of higher education and the transformation of Britain from an industrial to a service economy the middle classes, however defined, have made up an increasingly large proportion of the population.
>
> (Williams 1986: 112)

Over time, then, the term 'middle class' has ceased to be used to define a class (of manufacturers and traders) and been applied instead to a status group who are distinguished by the non-manual nature of their work and whose attitudes and values differ from those of the traditional industrial working class. In 1948 Herbert Morrison generalized the middle class as 'that varied section of the community that works with its brain rather than its hands'. They were also seen to be better paid and to have earned a salary (paid into a bank account) rather than a weekly wage (placed in their hand). Along with this they were more likely to have a mortgage and to pay income tax. Some of these distinctions between manual and non-manual workers may have diminished in significance but the middle class is still defined in economic and social terms.

Sociologists and advertisers refer to the middle class as those who inhabit grades A, B and C on an A–E scale, where the distinction is still drawn between skilled manual (C2) and skilled non-manual (C1) occupations.

As this non-manual status group is so broad it is unhelpful to talk about all non-manual employees as if they belong to one homogeneous and conscious middle class, sharing similar economic, social and political interests. As a result, most writers seem to accept that the differences within this group are as important as the similarities that may exist:

> It is, indeed, much more accurate to talk about the *middle classes* rather than about one single middle class. There is an enormous difference in income, status and lifestyle between the stockbroker at the upper end of the upper middles and the shorthand typist hovering uncomfortably between the ranks of the lower middle classes and the skilled manual workers.
>
> (Williams 1986: 112)

Since the 1950s a distinction has been made between the 'old' middle class, whose position derived from property, and the 'new' middle classes, which include a range of 'white-collar' occupations. There is some dispute about the future of the old middle class, but it is clear that some small-scale entrepreneurs have survived. Optimists believe that this class may reassert itself as a result of government support for small businesses and enterprise initiatives. However, the high failure rate of such initiatives and the collapse of small businesses as a consequence of the recession and a jittery banking sector may lead us to question the long-term revival of a petit bourgeois class. Early research by Savage et al. (1992) suggested that the class position of the self-employed might be an unstable transition from redundancy to unemployment with over half lasting less than 10 years in their trade. However, recent figures show that after a poor time of it in the 1970s the numbers of self-employed in the labour market rocketed by 45 per cent to over 10 per cent of the workforce by the 1990s. In their review of the 1980s, Fielding (1995) concluded that after 10 years, approximately 62 per cent remained in self-employment. In comparing this with his own assessment of the period 1971–81, Savage concludes that the *petit bourgeoisie* are becoming a more secure, distinct and visible group in British society (1995: 3).

The 'new' middle classes, on the other hand, have been dramatically successful in expanding their size and influence. There is little dispute that the service sector has grown, and that professionals, managers and administrators have become a significant part of the occupational

structure. This growth has created a demand for new groups of specialists whose function is to service the emotional and cultural needs of the new middle classes. Media pundits, psychotherapists, fashion designers and health gurus are part of this 'new petite bourgeoisie', which has blossomed in response to an ever-growing appetite for difference in the postmodern age of mass consumption (Crompton 1993: 179–80).

Where this may end up is unclear but Roberts feels that despite its cosmopolitan appearance, patterns of inward mobility from lower-class groups may begin to slow down as the middle class consolidates itself and sorts out some notion of group identity:

> We have seen that the new middle class has expanded strongly since the mid-twentieth century. During this growth, it has become more diverse in ethnic and gender composition, and is equally mixed in terms of its members' social class origins. During the twenty-first century the middle class is likely to remain just as mixed, if not more mixed, in terms of gender and ethnicity, but it will definitely become increasingly self-recruiting. It is only at this stage that that any characteristic forms of consciouness and politics are likely to solidify. Perhaps the most important point to grasp about the new middle class is that it is still in formation. (Roberts 2001: 168)

The service class

This section of the 'new' middle classes is that which is closest to the capitalist or upper class by virtue of the control and servicing functions that it carries out on behalf of the upper class and because of clear differences in income, education and lifestyle which mark it out from other non-manual groups, but similar to the dominant group in society. As a result, this group clearly has 'a stake in the *status quo*' although there is continuing debate about whether it is so privileged that it has become part of the dominant class.

An attempt to make sense of the factors that confuse our analysis of the middle classes at this level can be found in the work of Mike Savage et al. (1992). According to their view it is possible to understand the lifestyle and structuring of the upper middle and service classes in terms of the different assets that they possess. These are property, cultural and organizational assets, which are the key to their success and the life chances they and their families enjoy. These assets also correspond to the formation of different groups within the middle class and may explain the differences in cultural outlook at this level.

Property assets

Property is the most important form of asset. It is easy to store and quick to utilize; it represents the most obvious way in which members of this class can establish themselves and get things done. Although property assets are most obviously connected with the formation of the entrepreneurial classes, they can also be important in establishing and maintaining the class position of members of the service class – some of whom enjoy six-figure annual incomes and lucrative share options. In their study *Inequality in the UK*, Goodman *et al.* (1997) conclude that inequalities in income distribution have widened since the 1970s, with the top 10 per cent of the population earning as much as the bottom 50 per cent. This trend was confirmed by the research of the economist John Hills who studied the growing inequalities in income between 1996 and 2003 in Britain. According to the *Observer's* Heather Stewart,

> About 40 per cent of the total increase in income between 1979 and 2003 went into the pockets of the top 10 per cent of Britain's earners. Between them they

now take home more than the whole of the poorest half of society.   (*Observer* 7.11.04)

The overnight fortunes made in the City after the Big Bang in 1986 also provided the basis for the formation of a young and upwardly mobile sub-class. The 'yuppie' phenomenon may have been short-lived but it demonstrates the enduring power of property assets to affect class formation. Because, in Savage's model, this group is almost indistinguishable from what we have already called the upper class, it is safe to assume that they exist within (or on the fringes of) the network which Scott identified as the establishment. Private education, intermarriage, membership of exclusive clubs and the Conservative Party are all badges of 'social exclusion'. Savage, however, identified a postmodernist trend among the yuppies of the 1980s whereby cultural taste is less determined by traditional patterns of consumption and is more hedonistic and eclectic in nature. The old divisions between high cultural forms and mass culture disappear in the free market of commodity choice as new patterns of consumption and taste emerge (see Chapter 2, pp. 93–7 on postmodernism).

Case study

The overclass

The following extract is taken from a feature on an exclusive housing estate in Buckinghamshire, made up of five houses and known as 'The Gate'. The people who live there have used their wealth to ensure that they are 'socially excluded'.

> Meg is interrupted, mid sentence, by an electronic chirruping. 'Oh damn, that's The Gate,' she explains, jumping up. The Gate, along with the winking red eyes in the corner of each room, are symbols of Meg's status: one of the socially excluded . . .
>
> One of the five houses behind The Gate – which is spoken of in reverential terms by residents – can be yours for a million-plus. On the drive of one house are a

Mercedes sports car, a Range Rover and a Rolls. One resident has homes on the West Coast of America, Spain and Bermuda.

'Opulence is the norm here,' says Meg. 'The concentration of wealth is really something.'

The people who live here, then, are not socially excluded through lack of money. On the contrary their wealth allows them to cut themselves off from society's mainstream. All the luxury-house building companies report an increased demand for scaled communities for the gated garrisons of the 'overclass' – a term included in an Oxford University Press dictionary published last month.

Meg's road is private. The children go to private schools.

There is a private, 10-acre wood and more cars than people. The infra-red motion sensors in their homes are linked directly to the local police station . . .

The families behind The Gate are the lead characters of the Thatcherite dream, people who worked their way, up – self-made, hard-working, risk-taking, entrepreneurial. When Tony Blair says the UK needs more millionaires, these are the people he is talking about. Conchi and husband Peter own a satellite TV firm. Gordon and Pat, a semi-retired Irish couple, built a computer company. Meg's husband, Eddie runs a medical products firm . . .

Celebration of their success means detachment from the less

Case study (continued)

successful. Status plays a part. 'People say "Wow, you've got a gate" when they visit,' says Meg. Security, too – though the scale of the protection seems ill-matched to the threat posed by the communities beyond The Gate. The enclave is in the heart of the most prosperous part of the country . . .

According to Professor Tony Giddens, director of the London School of Economics: 'If you allow a situation to develop in which some people cut themselves off, then you pose a threat to the very fabric of society.

'In effect there are two forms of social exclusion – voluntary and involuntary.' in the UK, some gated communities have opted for moats and portcullises to deter the outsider, a powerful echo of a time when society was fractured into baronies, and communities lived in fortresses, safe from marauders.

Giddens says that while the government cannot ban such gated estates, it can work to bring down some of the non-physical barriers.

'We need to foster institutions that enhance the sense of collective identity – which is why I am not in favour of a minimalist welfare state. And we need to do more to lower the hurdles between state and private schools for instance . . .'

'We are in danger of creating a structural breach in society,' says Giddens.

The inhabitants of Gateland deny the charge . . .

Meg says the self-made nature of the inhabitants is a safeguard against rebellion. 'People who have got here because of hard work and risk-taking are less likely to lose sight of the needs of others – of where they came from.'

But Giddens worries that over time, the separation of this group may grow. 'It is one thing to work your way up from humble roots to these places, quite another to grow up in them.'

Currently, the overclass is defined simply by money and a desire to be cut off. If the group begins to have shared political objectives, then a class in the real sense of the term could develop.

(From: R. Thomas 'Rich – And Excluded', *Observer* 20.9.98)

Question

1. *What sort of problems or difficulties might such exclusive developments cause for*
   (a) those who live in them;
   (b) the rest of society?

Cultural assets

Along with property, and sometimes instead of it, the 'cultural capital' achieved through exclusive and high levels of education can become the key to membership of the professional wing of the service class. This professional middle class clearly takes advantage of the education system to secure the cultural advantages that can lead to social success. These assets may not be as fluid or as effective as property, but a 'good education' is an investment in the future which can withstand inflation and the vagaries of the marketplace.

In the longitudinal '7 Up' study conducted by Michael Apted for British TV, a socially diverse group of seven-year-olds from 1963 are revisited every seven years to see if there is any truth in the maxim 'Give me a child until he is seven and I will give you the man.' By 1998 most of them are still willing to be interviewed for the '42 Up' episode. One of them, Andrew (who attended Charterhouse – one of the 'top' Public Schools in England – and

Cambridge University where he studied law) regards education as the most important investment his parents could have made for his future. Echoing the findings of Fiona Devine's study (page 233) he says:

> Education is very important . . . you can never be sure of leaving your children any worldly goods but at least you can be sure that once you've given them a good education that's something that no one can take away.

However, as opportunities for access into Higher Education increase, academic qualifications may count for less as employers become more interested in personal qualities such as character, appearance and manners. In a study by Nuffield College Oxford, it is suggested that education as the great hope for a more meritocratic society may be misplaced as individuals are employed for their ability to get on with clients and customers; the skills required are nonetheless social and tend to favour those with a middle-class background where such qualities are the norm. As one of the authors of the Oxford Study, John Goldthorpe puts it:

> If you are selling high-value things like real estate, you will be interacting with middle-class people and you will do better if you are familiar with their style, manners, etc. . . . It's not much use having some graceless anorak, however impressive his or her degree. The attributes that these people have from their family background have some real commercial use. It's not nepotism. Employers know what they want.
>
> (Cited in *The Economist* 2004)

As a result, cultural assets have enabled a powerful professional middle class to emerge 'alongside but subordinate to [the] propertied class' (Scott 1994: 2). As this group is high on cultural capital but low on economic assets, it is not surprising that in terms of consciousness and lifestyle they can be seen as different from the propertied middle class. This is especially true of those professionals who work in the public sector, who may have different tastes as well as unexpected political allegiances. Their lifestyle has been described as healthy, intellectual and culturally radical; Wynne (1990) called this group 'sporters' because of their ascetic and athletic lifestyle. In political terms they are also less likely to support the Conservative Party. Whereas top professionals have been described as a 'conservative force' this does not apply to all members of the professional middle class. Research has shown that while top professionals in the private sector who are employed within an entrepreneurial model tend to be Conservative, those who work in public service areas like health and education may support and become actively involved in the Labour Party (Callinicos and Harman 1987: 40–5; Crompton 1993: 204–5).

Organizational assets

The least valuable form of asset are those skills that relate only to the organization being served. Although administrative skills have made managers, as a class, indispensable to large organizations (see p. 228), they provide only a short-term and inflexible basis for membership of the service class. Managers may become redundant as a result of restructuring or new technologies and discover that their skills are no longer required anywhere else. This makes organizational assets alone a very unstable guarantee of middle-class position and lifestyle, especially in Britain, where the managerial middle class has historically been recruited separately from those with cultural assets. This may explain why the children of managers are likely to be well educated and are encouraged to 'trade' their organizational assets for cultural ones. As a result, the children of managers are more likely to become professionals than to follow their parents into management (Savage *et al.* 1992: 148).

The lower middle class

The other element of the 'new' middle classes is a lower or intermediate class which is comprised of lower-paid non-manual workers engaged in routine white-collar work. While some writers seem happy to lump this group together with other members of a general middle class characterized by their ownership of educational and technical qualifications (Giddens 1973; see p. 288), there is widespread disagreement among sociologists about the class position of routine non-manual workers. Some would argue that the pay, status and working conditions of these workers make them a distinct 'intermediate' class occupying the social territory between the service class and the working class; others, however, would prefer to see them as part of a broader working class which makes no distinction between mental and physical labour. In essence this debate concerns the process of *proletarianization*, which Marx predicted as the fate of industrial capitalism. Colin Ward provides a clerical worker's view of office routine:

> One occupational hazard facing a clerk is always the sense of futility he [*sic*] struggles against, and is more often just overwhelmed by. Unlike even the humblest worker on a production line, he doesn't produce

---

A closer look

We argue that, once a person's place in the relations of production is taken as the key to his or her class position, then three groups of white-collar workers must be distinguished: 1. a small minority who are salaried members of the capitalist class, participating in the decisions on which the process of capital accumulation depends; 2. a much larger group, the 'new middle class', of highly-paid white-collar workers, most of whom occupy managerial and supervisory positions intermediate between labour and capital; 3. the majority, routine white-collar workers having as little control over their work as manual workers, and often less well-paid. The crucial conclusion we draw from this analysis is that the growth of this third group represents the expansion, not the decline, of the working class.

(Callinicos and Harman 1987: 9)

anything. He battles with phantoms, abstracts; runs a paper chase that goes on year after year and seems utterly pointless. How can there be anything else other than boredom in it for him? (Ward 1972: 22)

Westergaard and Resler (1976) maintain that the apparent growth of this 'middle class' is really no more than an expansion of opportunities for low-paid drudgery with little prospect of promotion. This is especially true for women who have 'moved from domestic service jobs and skilled manual work into semi-skilled jobs in offices and factories' (1976: 294). Crompton and Jones (1984) have emphasized the continuation of deskilling in the workplace and the proletarianization of the social and economic position of white-collar workers. Crucial to this process is the 'feminization' of clerical work and the

Case study

Middle-class professionals are Britain's hidden poor

The plight of Britain's hidden poor – middle-class professionals who have slipped down the social scale – is highlighted in a report published today.

It shows that 3.8 million people, 14 per cent of the country's professional classes, are living on incomes below the poverty line.

For a single person this could mean an income as low as £114 a week.

The report paints a grim picture of the lives of a group that can include teachers, nurses, managers, social workers, solicitors and musicians, as well as others who have social standing but few or no formal qualifications.

The report, published by the Elizabeth Finn Trust, which gives financial support to almost 2,000 people a year, including those struggling on low incomes in retirement, was based on a poll of 10,000 adults plus 450 of its clients.

It talks of a 'vicious circle of decline' prompted by factors including money troubles, lack

of work, family breakdown, poor health and inadequate pensions.

A major problem for some of the group identified by the charity is their lack of formal educational qualifications 'in an increasingly meritocratic society' where 'who you know' is no longer a guarantee of financial or social status.

Only 6 per cent have a university degree, compared with a national average of almost 12 per cent, and a third have no university qualifications at all.

'Among the professional classes, one-quarter leave school without five good GCSEs,' says the report. 'Whereas once this group may have got into the workforce through their connections, this will be increasingly difficult in a world where qualifications are paramount.'

The value of pensions is also a cause of anxiety. 'With the ageing population, we will see an increase in the numbers of retired professionals who are in an ever more precarious position as a result of the increasing uncertainty of personal and company pensions,' continues the report.

'With increasing longevity, their pensions are squeezed at

the other end too, since it means that annuities are paying out increasingly smaller amounts, as the money has to stretch further.'

The report concludes that members of the group are less likely to be in work: 40 per cent of them compared, with 56 per cent of the total adult population and 70 per cent of their professional peers. They are also more likely to be on benefits.

On the whole they tend to be in worse health and are more likely to suffer with problems involving drink or drugs, anxiety, depression, blood pressure, heart problems and strokes . . .

'Overall it seems likely that the professional classes will polarise more in the future, with the educated and the better networked leaving others less fortunate than themselves behind in the workplace and social and leisure life.'

(David Ward, the *Guardian* 26.7.04)

Question

1. *Using the ideas covered in this section on the 'new' middle class (pp. 242–247), which group are most likely to find themselves amongst the 'hidden poor'?*

restricted opportunities for women in these organizations relative to men (see p. 228).

The proletarianization thesis has been attacked by sociologists influenced by the Weberian perspective. In their view those in white-collar occupations form a distinct 'intermediate class' who can be clearly distinguished from the service class above them and a manual working class below (Goldthorpe *et al.* 1980). In his early *Blackcoated Worker* study, David Lockwood (1958) argued that despite a deterioration in relative pay and status, clerical workers enjoyed better job security, pension provision and promotion prospects when compared with manual workers. In his revised edition, Lockwood concluded that changes in the workplace may have benefited white-collar employees:

> Regardless of the extent to which clerical work may be said to have been proletarianised, there are no grounds for thinking that the majority of clerical workers have experienced proletarianisation. The promotion opportunities of male clerks and the fairly rapid turnover of female clerks more or less guarantee that this is not the case. Secondly, the view that clerical work itself has undergone widespread 'degradation', as a result of rationalisation and mechanisation, is not one that has found much support. Indeed, the most detailed recent surveys and case-studies of the effects of the new technology lead to just the opposite conclusion: namely, that reskilling, even job enrichment appear to be the most general consequences.
>
> (Lockwood 1989: 250)

Support for this view has been provided by the research of Stewart *et al.* (1980), whose study of male white-collar workers showed that for over 50 per cent of their sample, clerical work was a route to promotion and social mobility. By the age of 30 less than 20 per cent were still in clerical work, which led them to conclude that in the experience of most clerical workers proletarianization did not characterize their work. This view has been endorsed by Marshall *et al.* (1988), whose research shows very little evidence of deskilling and proletarianzation among clerical workers but indicates a fragmentation within the lower middle class between this group and personal service workers (e.g. shop assistants), for whom the process of proletarianization is more significant.

There are clearly problems in using a term like 'middle class' to accommodate all those people who neither own property nor work with their hands. Although the term is used widely in everyday language, its use within class analysis is fraught with difficulties which stem from the fragmentary and contradictory nature of the group who make it up. Abercrombie *et al.* provide a clear summary of these difficulties:

> We conclude that the category of occupations conventionally identified as middle class contains a small number of identifiable, potentially cohesive fractions whose members share many conditions. The service class, still expanding, holds an advantageous position in most respects. Despite its internal differences it stands apart from other fractions, comprises perhaps 30 per cent of the occupied population, and shows no sign of relinquishing its privileges. Its lower ranges overlap with the routine white-collar group beneath, which has neither the control over work nor the rewards of higher managers and professionals. Lower managements, parts of the lower professions and technicians nevertheless still have better market and work conditions than clerks or shop assistants. The conditions of routine white-collar workers are also varied, but while the best-rewarded of them have advantages over manual work, the differences are reducing. The petite bourgeoisie is set apart, distinctive in its economic, social and cultural orientations, but despite its recent growth it has limited power and its privileges are precarious. Some independent small proprietors, particularly those selling cultural and professional services, prosper greatly, but others in traditional avenues like shopkeeping and the building trades are unlikely to be much better off financially than skilled manual workers.   (Abercrombie *et al.* 2000: 182)

The working class

We have already noted that the idea of an homogeneous manual working class with its roots in traditional forms of manual work, community culture and political allegiance has come under attack as a result of technological and economic change. These criticisms also brought into question the relationship between class position, class consciousness and class action. As a result, the revolutionary role of the working class has been rejected in favour of models which stressed working-class ambivalence and instrumentalism. However, the idea that the decline in the number of people working in some areas of industrial production means saying 'farewell to the working class' (Gorz 1982) has been challenged by many sociologists and Marxist writers, who have argued that the working class has simply been transformed by changes in the structure of the labour market. The nature of work, reward and lifestyle of these workers still distinguishes them from others, while the political consequences of these changes may have been exaggerated. While acknowledging the disagreement over the nature of the working class in modern society, we attempt to categorize the broad groups who may be said to constitute the working class: a traditional working class; an expanded working class; and an underclass.

The traditional working class

This group is made up of people (usually men) who work in the traditional areas of industrial production. In the past these industries have included textiles, steel production and coal-mining; more recently light engineering and the car industry have formed part of this changing area of the economy. Classical sociological studies of family life, work and the community have painted a homogeneous and possibly romantic stereotype of a working-class culture dominated by the male pursuits of sport, drink and trade union politics, but characterized also by a strong matriarchal family and sense of community (Dennis *et al.* 1956; Tunstall 1962; Young and Willmott 1957).

It has been argued that by the early part of the nineteenth century in Britain a strong working class with its own distinctive culture had emerged. Working-class people were conscious of their membership of this culture and their separate interests as a class (E.P. Thompson 1968). According to Callinicos and Harman (1987) these interests developed into a fully fledged class consciousness based on collective values and action as a result of 'three waves of industrial struggle' between 1850 and the 1930s. This old manual working class established the basis for collective action through a variety of organizations such as family, community, trade unions and the Labour Party.

Since the 1950s the homogeneity and strength of purpose of the traditional working class has been under attack from the processes of 'embourgeoisment' and 'privatization'. Goldthorpe *et al.*'s (1968; 1969) classic study of 'affluent' workers in Luton repudiated the idea that the working class had adopted middle-class norms and values as a result of a more affluent lifestyle (see p. 230). However, their conclusion that a 'new working class' had emerged who were more interested in a privatized lifestyle and an instrumental attitude to work (and politics) has also been criticized. At the time John Westergaard (1970) disputed the idea that increasing materialism made workers less interested in class action (in fact he suggested the reverse). In the early 1990s Fiona

Devine returned to Luton in order to test the 'new workers' hypothesis in the aftermath of a protracted recession and a decade of Conservative government. Her conclusions suggest that Goldthorpe *et al.* had 'exaggerated the extent of change in working-class lifestyles . . . [and] incorrectly gave primacy to changing working-class norms and values' (Devine 1994: 7). Workers moved to Luton in search of jobs and affordable housing (not to become socially mobile) and, once there, retained ties of kinship and friendship with communities as far afield as Northern Ireland, Scotland and the southeast of England. These workers identified with the concerns and aspirations of other workers (especially the threats of redundancy and unemployment) and felt that trade unions and the Labour Party were a 'collective means of securing working class interests'. What had appeared as a 'new' working class in the 1960s had all but vanished in 20 years.

A similar conclusion was drawn by Hayes and Hudson (2001) in their comparative study of Basildon. We have already noted that 'Basildon Man' had been heralded as the new face of working-class politics and that there was some evidence in the 1992 study that workers were becoming more privatized and family centred and less likely to trust the Labour Party (p. 231). However, this shift towards the conservatism of the Thatcher government was short-lived and 'skin deep'. In their 1997 follow-up study Hayes and Hudson discovered 'no rooted ideological shift in the outlook of Basildonians' and suggest that voting for the Conservatives was 'more to do with a rejection of Labour than a positive embrace of Thatcherism' (2001: 38). Despite the claims that Basildon workers had become more individualistic and middle class, Hayes and Hudson conclude that this was exaggerated by the media and that the idea they represented a new wave of embourgeoisment a myth (see Table 6.5). In any event the 1997 election saw a Labour Government returned to power and a victory for their candidate in Basildon with one of the biggest majorities in its electoral history.

Although Basildon workers did not see work as central to their identities or aspirations and class was not a basis for political action (trade union membership for example was in decline), they did see social class as an important part of their heritage and recognized class-based discrimination as a feature of modern life which affected their life chances.

Bev Skeggs (2003) also discovered contradictory trends in her analysis of class attitudes amongst white working-class women. Despite the fact that the women in her study tried to distance themselves from those aspects of working-class life, culture and self which they did not regard as

Table 6.5 The truth about Basildon Man

Media image	Reality 1992	Reality 1997
Tasteless: shell suits for men, short skirts and large 'hoop' earrings for women	Some truth in this choice of clothes but it is based on relatively low earnings	Ordinary or smart dress
Loads of money	64% less than £15,000 pa	60% earning less than £15,000. Relatively poor
Conservative	Yes. That is, they voted Conservative, but 24% rejected all Conservative policies	No. They voted New Labour and 39% rejected all Conservative policies. They are increasingly disengaged from politics.
Classless	75% describe themselves as working class	73% describe themselves as working class

(Hayes and Hudson 2001: 14)

'respectable', they were also aware that they lived in a society in which life chances relate to class structure and that their cultural responses enabled social class differences to be reproduced. In much the same way as Willis (1977) has argued that working-class lads contribute to their own reproduction as working-class adults, so these women were aware of the inequalities of social life, their cultural responses to this situation and the impact this had upon their own chances of progress:

> Class was completely central to the lives of the women. It was not only structural, in the sense that the division of labour organized what economic opportunities were available for them, or institutional, in that the education system was designed on this basis and operated through a multitude of operations of capital transformations and trading. By using Bourdieu's metaphors of capital and space the study mapped how a group of white working-class women were born into structures of inequality which provided differential amounts of capital which circumscribed their movements through social space. These movements were not imposed but put into effect by the women who utilized the forms of capital to which they had access in an attempt to put a floor on their circumstances. They did not have access to . . . those forms of capital which are convertible in an institutional system, such as the cultural capital of the middle classes, which can be converted and traded-up through education and employment into symbolic capital and economic reward. They made the most of what they had but it rarely offered good trading potential . . . Lack of alternatives was one of the central features of being working-class; they rarely had the potential to re-valorise their classed subjectivities.   (Skeggs 2003: 161)

Rather than examining aspiring working-class men from Basildon or women from Greater Manchester for evidence of change, Simon Charlesworth (2000) returned to the roots of industrial Britain to see what had become of those people left behind by the technological revolution. He returned to Rotherham (grimly referred to as 'Deadman's Town') where industrial decline and unemployment are the order of the day and an impoverished culture the legacy. Adopting a phenomenological approach he is keen to get 'to the heart of working-class people's experience' and understand their responses to the situation they find themselves in from *their* point of view. Rather than disappearing he finds working-class experience and an awareness of it only too prevalent:

> For the working class, themselves, for whom the economically marginal and socially excluded are family members and neighbours, they have had to deal in the most palpable way with the decline of their own economic role and social position. Since the early 1980s, the gradual decline of the culture of the working class has been one of the most powerful, telling developments in British society. The bleakness of English society, what lies around us in the faces of the urban poor everywhere, emerges from this context, and yet there have been few accounts of the transition and consequences from amongst those who are unable to buy their way out of the conditions and into the protected elite spaces of the English middle and upper classes.   (Charlesworth 2000: 2)

Despite attempts by middle-class intellectuals (some of whom are sociologists) to render the term meaningless, social class retains a powerful role in the understanding of social life for those the other side of the divide:

If one engages with working people one finds a profound sense of the centrality of a common experience of their living conditions and of the society in which they live. This experience is obvious in every constitutive moment in which the society is made and remade and in which the conditions of exclusion and marginality, of hardship and humiliation, are achieved through all the totality of affinities and repulsions that modulate the contours of English social structure.

(2000: 154)

These people rely upon their narrowly defined and un-demanding culture as a means of survival but are limited by it in turn; a cultural response which deals with frustration and boredom through instant gratification of the physical pleasures available is not one which is likely to enervate or engage. As one neatly puts it, these pleasures are pretty basic and easily summarized as 'some nice snap t' 'ave a good trough at; plenty'r beer, a shag, some decent kip an' a good shit, the'r in't much mo'ore t' life' (2000: 279).

In Charlesworth's view the economic decay of the area has infected the culture. Marginalized and redundant, people no longer seem proud of their heritage or positive about the future. He expresses his disquiet in terms which are grim and pessimistic:

They may be biologically alive but they do not have access to the resources, symbolic as well as economic, to have a life. They are the zombies that British culture has created by condemning them to a living death of a stigmatized, abject, being.   (2000: 281)

Although the number of people employed as manual workers in the traditional industries has clearly fallen, this does not eradicate their significance as a class. Manual workers still play an important role within the economy and continue to account for a large proportion of the workforce. Depending on how we define manual workers, this group still constitutes around 50 per cent. In some parts of the world the proportion is even lower (approximately 40 per cent in the USA) but in areas of recent industrialization the manual working class will continue to constitute the majority class.

The pay and life chances of manual workers have remained a significant part of working-class experience. Despite the fact that some white-collar workers take home less pay than some manual workers, it is still clear that *on average* the comparison favours those in non-manual occupations.

The *New Earnings Survey* showed that manual workers depended far more than other groups on over-time payments for their total earnings and that they worked longer hours. It is also still the case that manual workers enjoy fewer privileges at work (time off, sick pay, holidays) and have lower levels of job security. They have fewer opportunities for promotion and they are less likely to belong to pension schemes. As a consequence, manual workers are also less likely to enjoy the life chances available to other groups in society. In the areas of health, housing, education, social mobility and leisure, major differences still occur which reveal the significance of being 'working class'. As Ivan Reid's (1989 and 1998) work demonstrates, individual life chances are still tied to class background with very little likelihood of improvement for those at the lower end:

It is difficult to see that political activity and social change in the 1980s has done much other than to sustain, or even increase, existing class differences. Indeed the large body of unemployed, especially the long-term, may be seen as a new class whose deprivations are many and severe. There is, in short, no evidence to suggest that class differences are anything but alive and well at present and that they will feature prominently . . . into the 1990's and beyond.

(Reid 1989: 397)

An expanded working class

As noted earlier the 'proletarianization' debate raised the issue of the class position of the lower middle classes. It has been argued that as the nature of work has changed to increase the demand for routine clerical and service workers, the conventional distinction between manual and non-manual work has been rendered useless. Instead the view of neo-Marxist writers like Callinicos and Harman (1987) is that the routine nature of this work and its relatively low levels of pay and status make this form of employment virtually indistinguishable from manual labour.

In the 'hierarchically structured' world of white-collar work they estimate that a prestigious group of administrators and managers has emerged who represent between 10 and 15 per cent of the workforce and operate as part of the 'service class' (they use the term 'new middle class'). Below the minority are an 'intermediate grade' of administrative and clerical staff (approximately 15 per cent of the workforce) who aspire to membership of the 'new middle class' but in reality exist just above those on 'routine manual grades' and as a result must be regarded as simply another group of 'exploited workers'. Alongside this group has emerged a strata of lower professionals

Case study

Pay differentials

In the year to April 2003 average gross weekly earnings of full-time employees rose by 2.4 per cent to £475 per week (see Figure 6.6). The gap between top and bottom is clear to see but the traditional division between manual and non-manual occupations is still evident.

At the top end are managers and senior officials while the lowest paid include workers from the 'personal services' sector such as health care assistants and hairdressers.

These figures are taken from the *New Earnings Survey* – a sample survey of the earnings of employees in Britain carried out in April each year by the Department of Education and Employment and covering all industries and occupations.

Questions

1. Using Figure 6.6, identify the data that supports the view that a division between manual and non-manual incomes persists.
2. Identify any evidence which challenges this view.

Occupational group[b]	Average gross annual pay (£)[a]	Average gross weekly pay (£)	Percentage increase April 2002– April 2003	Average hourly pay excluding overtime (£)	Average total weekly hours	Average weekly overtime hours
Managers and senior officials	42,164	747.5	2.1	19.28	39.0	0.4
Professional occupations	33,741	650.7	2.1	18.02	36.3	0.5
Associate professional and technical occupations	27,627	527.9	2.1	13.63	38.5	1.0
Administrative and secretarial occupations	17,560	338.4	4.2	8.98	37.5	0.6
Skilled trades occupations	21,060	412.4	3.7	9.43	42.6	3.3
Personal service occupations	14,146	282.9	3.2	7.18	39.2	1.6
Sales and customer service occupations	14,912	288.9	–1.7	7.41	38.8	0.9
Process, plant and machine operatives	19,113	373.8	4.4	8.15	44.8	4.7
Elementary occupations	15,824	306.0	3.9	7.01	42.6	3.4
All occupations	**25,170**	**475.8**	**2.4**	**12.03**	**39.6**	**1.6**

Figure 6.6 Levels of pay by occupational group;[c] Great Britain; April 2003

a Annual earnings estimates relate to employees who have been in the same job for at least 12 months, regardless of whether or not their pay was affected by absence.

b Occupations are coded according to the Standard Occuptaional Classification 2000.

c Employees on adult rates whose pay for the survey period was unaffected by absence.

http://www.statistics.gov.uk

such as classroom teachers and lower-paid nurses, who also exert little control over their work and have only their labour power to rely upon. In conclusion they argue that 'the restructuring of industry has produced a restructuring of the working class, not the growth of a new class alongside and comparable in size to the working class' (Callinicos and Harman 1987: 86). If the surviving blue-collar workers and the lower grades of white-collar and routine non-manual workers are combined together they represent an 'expanded working class' which accounts for 70 per cent of the working population.

The underclass

In the debate over the persistence of the working class, the idea of a growing underclass has emerged which relates to a variety of sociological and political issues. In this discussion we shall have to overlook many of these important issues and focus on the relevance of the underclass to class analysis. In particular we are concerned with the way in which the underclass is defined and with its relationship to the wider class structure.

The idea of an underclass is not new. Marx used the term *lumpenproletariat* in the nineteenth century to refer in disparaging terms to a 'surplus population' living in the most destitute conditions. The writings of Mayhew (1949) and Booth (1889) also painted lurid and frightening portraits of life among the 'dangerous classes' in Victorian London (Chesney 1991). In the twentieth century the term 'underclass' was coined in order to make sense of the experiences of those living in the black ghettos of the USA or the townships of South Africa. This racial dimension has always made its application to British society problematic, but since the 1960s the term has been widely used to refer not only to inner-city deprivation among ethnic minority groups (Rex and Tomlinson 1979) but also to those suffering from the urban decay found on many of the (predominantly white) postwar housing estates on the fringes of major cities.

Writers like Giddens (1973) have used the term broadly to describe those people in modern capitalist society who survive in a twilight world between unemployment and the secondary labour market. But Runciman (1990) and Field (1989) prefer to highlight welfare benefits as the key to defining the underclass. As Field puts it:

> I accept that Britain does now have a group of poor people who are so distinguished from others on low income that it is appropriate to use the term 'underclass' to describe their position in the social hierarchy.   (Field 1989, quoted in Murray 1990: 37)

He goes on to suggest that the underclass includes three main groups: 'the very frail, elderly pensioner; the single parent with no chance of escaping welfare under the

Case study

Poverty: UK and Europe

The definition of poverty is problematic but most commentators accept that in an affluent society it makes little sense to use 'absolute' definitions which may be applied to parts of the world where people have to go without food and shelter. Consequently, relative definitions are used which compare living standards against the average income. Depending on our judgement of where the line should be drawn we end up with different figures for those thought to be living in poverty. In Figure 6.7 below from *Social Trends* we can see what the level of poverty might be using 60 per cent, 50 per cent and 40 per cent of the median income as our poverty line.

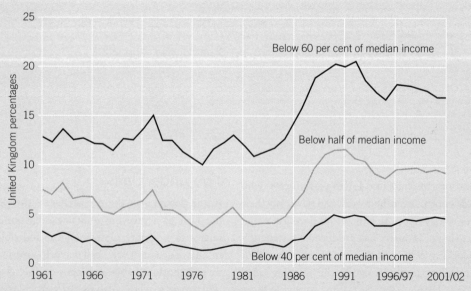

Figure 6.7 Percentage of people whose income is below various fractions of median income[1,2]

1 Equivalized household disposable income before housing costs. See Appendix, Part 5: Households Below Average Income, and Equivalizations scales.
2 Data from 1993/94 onwards are for financial years; data for 1994/95 onwards exclude Northern Ireland.
Source: Institute for Fiscal Studies in *Social Trends 34*, 2004: 85

Case study (continued)

By using this technique it is also possible to compare poverty levels in Britain with those in other European countries. We can see from (Figure 6.8) that Portugal appears to have the highest proportion of its households living below the EU median (set at 60 per cent) while Luxembourg has the lowest.

While this translates as 49 per cent of the Portuguese households falling below the EU median, in Luxembourg only 1 per cent did. In Britain, Sweden, Finland and France approximately 15 per cent of households fell below the 'EU poverty line'.

For a useful discussion of poverty thresholds and other issues related to poverty see **www.poverty.org** which is maintained by the New Policy Institute and supported by the Joseph Rowntree Foundation.

Question

1. *How would you account for the European differences in poverty levels suggested in the chart below?*

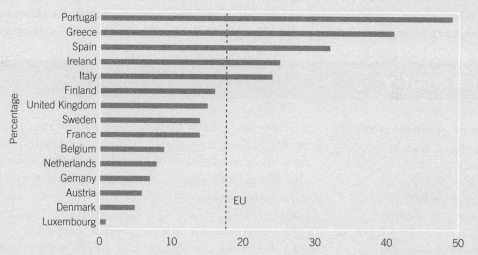

Figure 6.8 Percentage of people with incomes[1] below 60 per cent of the EU median: EU comparison, 2000

1 Equivalized disposable income in each country.

Source: European Community Household Panel, Eurostat in *Social Trends 34*, 2004: 85

existing rules . . . and the long-term unemployed' (Field, quoted in Murray 1990: 39).

Smith makes a case for defining the underclass in *structural* terms which are specifically related to legitimate opportunities for regular work:

> The underclass are those who fall outside [the] class schema, because they belong to family units having no stable relationship at all with the 'mode of production' – with legitimate gainful employment.

> (Smith 1992: 4)

According to this view structural changes which are a direct result of economic recession have led to long-term unemployment becoming a way of life for many people.

Changes in benefit rules and cuts in welfare expenditure have increased the likelihood that this way of life will be characterized by poverty, while the gap between 'work-rich' and 'work-poor' households increases. Studies have indicated that a growing number of people in Britain are living on or below the poverty line. The Joseph Rowntree Foundation report *Income and Wealth* (1995) concluded that inequalities of income and opportunity were widening: the 'top' 10 per cent were becoming better off and the 'bottom' 10 per cent worse off. These findings are supported by the Department of Social Security report *Households Below Average Income* (1994), which showed that the poorest tenth of the population suffered a 17 per cent fall in real income between 1979 and 1992 while the richest tenth enjoyed an increase of 62 per cent. It also highlighted an increase in the number of people living in poverty. Overall, 13.9 million children and adults (25 per cent of the population) were living below the official poverty line of half the average income after allowing for housing costs in 1992, compared with 5 million (9 per cent of the population) in 1979.

In contrast to this structural perspective a more controversial point of view has developed which stresses the *cultural* aspects of the underclass. This view can be seen as making a distinction between the 'respectable' and the 'rough' (or 'undeserving') working class. These ideas emerged in Oscar Lewis's (1960) work on the 'culture of poverty' in the 1950s and were apparent in Sir Keith Joseph's policy initiatives in the 1970s, which targeted the 'cycle of deprivation' (see Walker 1990: 51). In the 1980s the work of Charles Murray became part of a New Right perspective on poverty which identified the emergence of an anti-social ghetto culture:

During the last half of the 1960s and throughout the 1970s something strange and frightening was happening among the poor people in the United States. Poor communities that had consisted mostly of hardworking folks began deteriorating, sometimes falling apart altogether. Drugs, crime, illegitimacy, homelessness, drop out from the job market, drop out from school, casual violence – all the measures that were available to the social scientists showed large increases focused in poor communities. As the 1980s began, the growing population of 'the other kind of poor people' could no longer be ignored, and a label for them came into use. In the US we began to call them the underclass.   (Murray 1990: 2–3)

Case study

Third of children in the North-West live in poverty

Almost one in three children in the north-west of England is living in poverty, according to figures released yesterday.

The latest statistics from the End Child Poverty coalition show that 450,000 of 1.5 million children in the region are living below the breadline.

Research for the coalition, which brings together more than 75 organisations such as Barnardo's, the Children's Society and the Royal College of Nurses, found that in 215 wards at least 30 per cent of children were living on benefits.

Of these poorest wards, 75 were in Greater Manchester, 66 in Merseyside, 46 in Lancashire, 15 in Cumbria and 13 in Cheshire. Among the worst-affected areas were Blackfriars in Salford, where

60.8 per cent of children live on benefits, Hulme in Manchester, where the figure is 68.5 per cent, Princess in Knowsley (69 per cent) and Granby in Liverpool (71.9 per cent).

The coalition says that overall, 3.6 million children (28 per cent of the UK child population) are living in poverty. The proportion of children living below the breadline rose from one in 10 in 1979 to one in three in 1998 . . .

The effect of poverty reduces life expectancy. A boy living in Manchester can expect to live seven years less than a boy in Barnet. A girl from Manchester can expect to live six years less than a girl in Kensington and Chelsea.

Jonathan Stearn, the director of End Child Poverty, said: 'The fact that 450,000 children in the north-west are living in poverty – the highest number in any part of England outside London – is a blight on the region.

'Such high levels of poverty shame a prosperous country like ours. We are talking about children who often don't have warm winter coats, weatherproof shoes, and don't have three square meals a day.'

Figures from the charity in Yorkshire and North Lincolnshire showed that the worst-affected areas were the Manor Estate in Sheffield, where 53 per cent of families live on benefits, and Hull's Myton ward, where the figure was 54 per cent. A third of the 1.1 million children in the region are living in poverty.

(Helen Carter, the *Guardian* 12.3.05)

Questions

1. How would you explain such levels of child poverty in the north-west of England?

2. Why should poverty have any impact on life expectancy?

When asked to apply his ideas to Britain, Murray found no difficulty in discovering a similar group defined by their 'deplorable behaviour' rather than their structural position. This sub-culture not only marks them off from the respectable working class but also serves to transmit underclass membership from one generation to the next:

> I am not talking here about an unemployment problem that can be solved by more jobs, nor about a poverty problem that can be solved by higher benefits. Britain has a growing population of work-aged, healthy people who live in a different world from other Britons, who are raising their children to live in it, and whose values are now contaminating the life of entire communities.
>
> (Murray, quoted in *The Sunday Times* 26.11.89)

A slightly more sympathetic view, which still adopts a culturalist perspective, is that of Ralph Dahrendorf (1992), who argues that, partly through choice but also due to changes in long-term unemployment and family structure, there is now a distinct category of people who are redundant to the needs of modern capitalism and are in danger of falling out of the social and political system altogether. As such they challenge the idea of 'citizenship' discussed earlier (p. 227) and indeed represent a threat to social order.

In different ways these writers have used the term 'underclass' to denote a group in society which exists below or beyond the traditional class structure. The term itself indicates that they should be seen as a distinct class; however, few sociologists would agree that people who are poor, marginalized and out of work should be treated as a separate class with its own identity, interests and lifestyle. Although Dahrendorf popularized the term in Britain, he is adamant that 'there is no technical or proper sociological sense in which this particular category can ever be called a class' (1992: 55). Marxists such as Stuart Hall (1977) and Weberians such as Ray Pahl (1984) would agree that, despite being largely excluded from the opportunity structure of society, it is misleading to represent the underclass as a permanent and stable class, conscious of its own interests. Rather it has tended to be seen as constituting a fraction of the working class, despite the fact that it may have a distinct social character in terms of ethnicity, gender, age and cultural attitude.

Although it has excited a good deal of theoretical interest, the underclass has not been subjected to much empirical scrutiny. However, Anthony Heath (1992) used information from the 1987 British Election Survey and the 1989 British Social Attitudes Survey to study the attitudes of members of the underclass, investigating orientation to work and political attitudes of two samples (the long-term and the short-term) of the underclass. He concluded that it was difficult to identify the underclass as a distinct community with negative attitudes towards family values, work and other mainstream institutions.

'Class is dead; long live class'

In this chapter we have examined the concept of social stratification and, in particular, the relevance of social class. Discounted by many writers as an outdated notion more suited to the 'two nations' of nineteenth-century Britain, it retains for many sociologists a significance in the twenty-first century that has hardly been diminished by social, economic or political change. As Scott puts it, 'class remains the sociological key to understanding the structure of society' (1994: 19).

For Scase (1992), the relevance of class for ordinary people may be somewhat vague, but for sociologists 'it remains a concept that is vital for understanding the structure of present-day capitalist society'. As a Marxist, he argues that it is not possible to contemplate society without reference to the role played by social classes in the formation and maintenance of capitalism:

> The analysis of class is inherent to the study of capitalist society. Western industrial societies are capitalist and, hence, their economic development is determined by the interplay of class forces of one kind or another. The fact that the prime objective of capitalist corporations is to make profits means that they are characterised by relations of exploitation and control and, hence, consist of class relations . . . It is for this reason that social class will continue to remain central to sociological analysis. (Scase 1992: 81)

To some extent this view is matched by Edgell (1993), who emphasizes the importance of social class as the major source of structural social inequality. The significance of social class as the basis of social identity and political action may have been diluted over time but this is largely due to the power of capital and the relative weakness of the 'propertyless classes'. Instead of raising the question of the extent of class consciousness in contemporary society we should be questioning the assumption that society has become a classless meritocracy:

> The main obstacle to the establishment of a multi-class or non-egalitarian classless democratic society is the persistence of class inequalities . . . Hence, what needs to be explained is not the presumed demise of class, but the tenacity of class-based patterns of inequality and politics, and much else besides. In the meantime, class rules and classlessness remain a dream rather than a reality.   (Edgell 1993: 122)

Houtt *et al.* reject the arguments of Clark and Lipset (see p. 232) that the concept of class has been rendered obsolete by the fragmentation of stratification in the workplace, government and family life. They argue that Clark and Lipset have confused social class with social status, which diverts our attention away from the enduring inequalities of wealth and power with vague

references to the decline of hierarchy. By returning to the three 'situses' of economics, politics and family life outlined by Clark and Lipset, Houtt *et al.* argue that social class is still related to social opportunities and lifestyle in all three areas of social organization.

While they acknowledge the changing and complex nature of social class in modern societies, they insist that it still maintains a key role in understanding social relations:

> The persistence of class-based inequalities in capitalist societies suggest that in the foreseeable future the concept of class will – and should – play an important role in sociological research . . . As citizens and sociologists we would very much like to live in a world in which class inequalities have disappeared. But . . . class society is not yet dying, and truly classless societies have not yet been born.   (Houtt *et al.* 1996: 58–9)

World in focus

'All comrades are equal but some are more equal than others': Inequality in the People's Republic of China

55 years after the foundation of a classless society in China, observers have commented upon the increasing gap between the rural poor and a new elite of wealthy entrepreneurs in its major cities. In this report, by Paul Mason, a top class restaurant is used as a metaphor for what is happening across the country as a whole:

> The local nickname for the Jincaicheng Restaurant is 'The Aircraft Carrier'. With 220 tables, 700 staff and 27,000 square metres of floor space, it is the biggest restaurant in Tianjin.
> It's designed to cater for a wide range of customers – from

working-class families on a big night out, to China's new elite.
> It is the perfect place to observe the new class structure of China and we spent time behind the scenes with three people whose lives revolve around the business.

The trainee waitress Yang Ming

It was the household chores Yang Ming didn't like. On her grandmother's farm she used to

Figure 6.9 Yang Ming

draw water from the well, collect the firewood and watch the cows. Now she has swapped farm clothes for a waitress's uniform – and the eight rooms of the family farm for a bunk bed in Tianjin, China's third biggest city. She lives in a dorm with 29 other young women and earns 300 Yuan a month: that is just £20.
> She has no intention of going back. She told me: 'Living in the village restricts what you see and learn. Some girls stay in the village all their life until they get married. I don't want that kind of life.'
> She's travelled 2,000km from Hainan Province, an island in China's deep south. In Tianjin everything is different: the temperature is sub-zero, the food is heavy, the customers brash:
> 'It was a bit hard to adapt to the discipline. At first we had to ask permission to leave the

World in focus (continued)

restaurant. And time off was limited. The management were worried about our safety – especially because we're women and we're not used to the city. But as time's gone by we've settled down: now we have one day off a week.'

Yang Ming's journey from the farm to the city is one that 140m Chinese peasants have made already. Migrants are now a major force within the Chinese workforce – they make up 600 out of the 700 workers at Jincaicheng Restaurant where Yang Ming lives and works.

By the time China's market reforms are complete, 300m more will have hit the road. As long as they keep coming, at the rate of 10m a year, those on the bottom rung of the employment ladder will, like Yang Ming, have to work for next to nothing.

For Mu Xing Ha, head chef in one of the restaurant's three main kitchens, life is getting sweeter all the time. He's 35 and he's been a chef since he left school. The market reforms have globalized the tastes of the clientele and the sources of the fish: forget the fish market – he does his wholesale buying now at the airport.

'Before customers came to the restaurant just to eat. Just to fill in their stomachs with food. They didn't want vegetables or seafood much. Nowadays, customers are choosing a variety of food to meet their tastes. They're ordering meat, seafood, vegetables and salad, etc. They're

demanding top quality ingredients for every dish, and they're trying different kinds of cuisine.'

When he started, in the 1980s, the most a chef could earn was 600 Yuan a month. Now he earns 6,000 – 20 times the wages of a waitress, and he's only half-way up the management hierarchy.

It's a wage gap that illustrates one of the most pressing problems for China's rulers – while GDP per person is rising, the country is now one of the most unequal on earth.

The chief executive Ma Ya Cui

Ma Ya Cui's income, as Chief Executive, is undisclosed. From the look of her loft-style apartment in the city's new waterfront development zone, it is safe to assume it's a lot higher than the chef's.

Mrs Ma is not a classic entrepreneur: she's been appointed manager of the restaurant by TEDA, the state-owned investment group that set up the restaurant last year, on premises left vacant by a failed, state-backed department store.

Figure 6.10 Ma Ya Cui

Before the restaurant she helped run TEDA's hotel, and its football team.

'I've been involved in state-run businesses for the past 20 years,' she says. 'My philosophy's to be loyal to the Party, because I am a senior manager. I also have to be loyal to the company. In other words, my mottoes are loyalty and obedience.'

Whatever else this is, it's not free market capitalism.

The wealth gap is growing fast in China. According to the World Bank, it's among the most unequal societies on earth. Social unrest is rising too – though it rarely makes the official media outlets . . .

China's rising wealth effect is being generated not just by market reforms but by massive state intervention and cheap money. It's created a kind of social escalator – it moves faster at the top than at the bottom, but once you're on it, for now, the only way is up.

The problem is, two-thirds of China's population haven't even got a foot on the bottom step. And no one wants to contemplate what might happen if it should ever stop.

(Paul Mason, BBC's *Newsnight* 7.3.2005)

Questions

1. How does the Jinchairy Restaurant serve as a metaphor for what is happening in China?

2. Why should market reform and wealth creation lead to social unrest?

The relevance of class analysis, particularly in areas such as health, housing and education, remains clear. However, as indicated in our discussion of Weber, social class is not the only means by which social inequality is transmitted. Since the early 1970s sociologists have become more aware of the relative importance of gender and race as the bases of structured inequality and discrimination. These two areas are examined in Chapters 7 and 8.

Summary

➤ Historically most societies develop some form of stratification system.

➤ Most sociologists regard modern industrial societies as being stratified on the basis of social class.

➤ Sociologists have provided various theoretical 'class maps' and class categories based on Marxist, Weberian and functionalist models.

➤ The significance of social class in the latter half of the twentieth century is a matter of continuing sociological debate.

➤ On the one hand, it has been argued that changes in the structure of society have reduced the importance of class as a tool for sociological analysis.

➤ On the other hand, while acknowledging that the class structure has been affected by social and economic changes, there is evidence that social class continues to affect lifestyle, opportunities, consciousness and behaviour; the upper, middle and working classes continue to be important divisions in modern society.

Links

This chapter has strong links to Chapter 2 on sociological theories, particularly the section on Marx and social class, pp. 55–57.

Social class is a factor that strongly influences life chances and opportunities and features in the chapters on work (4), health (10), education (14) and crime (16).

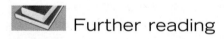 Further reading

Crompton, R. (1993) *Class and Stratification*, Cambridge: Polity Press.
A detailed examination of the complexities of class and status, especially recommended for pursuing this area of study beyond foundation undergraduate level.

Goodman A., Johnson, P. and Webb, S. (1997) *Inequality in the UK*, Oxford: Oxford University Press.
A recent empirical study of inequlity in the UK.

Lee, D. and Turner, B.S. (1996) *Conflicts about Class: Debating Inequality in Late Industrialism*, London: Longman.
An important assessment of the relevance of class in late twentieth century Britain.

Payne, G. (2000) *Social Divisions*, New York: St Martin's Press.
A useful introduction to the debates surrounding social divisions including class, gender, ethnicity, age, disability and so on.

Reid, I. (1998) *Class in Britain*, Cambridge: Polity Press.
An excellent review of the correlations between class position and life chances that covers areas such as wealth, pay, health, education and housing.

Roberts, K. (2001) *Class in Modern Britain*, London: Macmillan.
A useful review of the debates around class structure and mobility in contemporary Britain.

Scott, J. (1991) *Who Rules Britain?* Cambridge: Polity Press.

Scott, J. (1994) *Poverty and Wealth: Citizenship, Deprivation and Privilege*, London: Longman.

Scott, J. (1997) *Corporate Business and Capitalist Classes*, Oxford: Oxford University Press.
One of the few sociologists to undertake a comprehensive analysis of the rich and powerful, these are summaries of the patterns of wealth and poverty distribution in the UK and abroad.

Smith, D. (1992) *Understanding the Underclass*, London: Policy Studies Institute.
A collection of readings from the key contributors to the underclass debate, such as Dahrendorf, Murray and Field.

Regular sources of updated empirical material are in the journal *Labour Research*, publications of the Child Poverty Action Group and *Social Trends*.

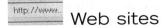 ## Web sites

www.statistics.gov.uk
Provides much data on class-related trends in the UK.

www.inequality.org
A US-based site which highlights the concentration of wealth, income and power in the USA.

www.trinity.edu/~mkearl/index
A fascinating sociological trawl through cyberspace – clicking on 'social inequality' provides many sources of information and weblinks (largely American).

Activities

Activity 1

Value, status and (in)dispensability

Occupational scales

Attempts to reconcile the differences over class and status in evaluation of an individual's position in society have generally involved classifying people according to their job based on the assumption that some jobs are more prestigious/important than others. Rate the following jobs in order of importance from 1 (most important) to 6 (least important): coal-miner; electrician; refuse collector; director of advertising agency; nurse; high court judge.

Are you a worker?

What is a worker? That's the question . . . provoked by our criticism of the Greenham Common protesters as predominantly middle class.

Ann Roderick, for example, naturally enough feels insulted when she is put – as a school teacher – in the same category as 'vicars' wives'.

The issues raised here are very important. A majority of the workforce in Britain, along with other advanced industrial countries, does white-collar work. Does that mean, as ruling class propagandists (and even some socialists) claim, that the working class is disappearing?

Class

The answer depends, obviously, on what you mean by class. Academic sociologists attach a great deal of importance to status – to how the job is seen by those doing it, and by others. Historically, there has certainly been a difference of status between manual and white-collar jobs. This is reflected in the fact that even today most white-collar workers work shorter hours and enjoy better pension rights than their manual counterparts.

Activities (continued)

Does this mean that they belong to different classes? Not according to Marx. For him, a person's class position is determined by his or her relation to the means of production. And this relationship is crucial because control over the means of production gives you the power to exploit the labour of others.

Equally, lack of such control makes you liable to be exploited. So, anyone who is compelled by their economic position to sell their labour-power is, according to Marx, a worker. A worker is someone who has the choice between working and starving because they do not control the means of production.

Control

From this standpoint a shorthand typist or word-processor operator is as much a worker as a miner or engineer. Both . . . must sell their labour-power to live.

So what has happened in the past 40 years is that the structure of the working class has changed. There are fewer manual workers in industries such as mining and manufacturing, but more typists and other clerical workers.

The size of the working class has increased overall, not shrunk . . . Most white-collar workers are not middle-class.

But this isn't the end of the story. All white-collar workers aren't middle class, but some of them are. Those that form what is sometimes called the 'new middle class'.   (Alex Callinicos, *Socialist Worker* undated)

Questions

1. What criteria did you use in 'rating' the six occupations? Which of these criteria were objective and which subjective?

2. Does the order coincide with classifications based on the conventional division between manual and non-manual occupations?

3. The article by Alex Callinicos looks at problems with the division between manual/working-class and non-manual/middle-class occupations. What difficulties do you think there are with this method of categorizing occupations?

Activity 2(a)

The underclass

The underclass spawns illegitimate children without a care for tomorrow and feeds on a crime rate which rivals the United States in property offences. Its able-bodied youths see no point in working and feel no compulsion either. They reject society while feeding off it: they are becoming a lost generation giving the cycle of deprivation a new spin . . . No amount of income redistribution or social engineering can solve their problem. Their sub-life styles are beyond welfare benefit rises and job creation schemes. They exist as active social outcasts, wedded to an anti-social system.   (Charles Murray, *The Sunday Times* 26.11.89)

Questions

1. What evidence can you find to support Murray's view?

2. What 'solutions' do you feel Murray would offer to deal with the problem of an underclass? What criticisms can be made of this approach?

3. There have been various publicity stunts by Conservative politicians who have claimed that they and their families have managed to live quite adequately for a week on income support. Find out how much you would get on income support and work out how you would spend your weekly payments. What kind of changes would you have to make to your current lifestyle? What are the strengths and weaknesses of approaching a social problem in this way?

Activities (continued)

Activity 2(b)

Investigating the rich

Using *The Sunday Times* Rich List (which can be found at The Times online **http://www.timesonline.co.uk**) find out the answers to the following questions;

1. *Who is the richest man/woman?*

2. *Who is top of the pops?*

3. *How many aristocrats are there?*

4. *Identify oldest/youngest.*

5. *Which forms of wealth creation tend to dominate the list?*

6. *How has the creation of wealth changed over time? – you will need to track down previous Rich List & Forbes (see below) information to do this.*

7. *Identify an individual from the Rich List – find out as much as you can about them, how they made their money and what they do with it.*

See also the Forbes listing for the richest people in the world at **http://www.forbes.com/billionaires/**

How rich are you? Go to the Care International Website **http://www.globalrichlist.com/index.php** and find out.

Gender

Kate: We are told that there are only two genders in the world, and I'm saying that just doesn't make sense. There is nothing else in nature that is two and only two, everything else has all these limitless possibilities but for some reason we figure there are only two genders and I'm saying there are more . . .

Interviewer: Are you really saying any more than that old classical idea that there is a bit of male and a bit of female in all of us?

Kate: I would say what I'm saying incorporates that idea, that yes we have a man and woman in us but I'm saying that there is so much more than that, I'm saying that outside the realm of men and women there are other identities and why limit ourselves? Why not be able to explore more identities? What is a man? What is a woman? Why do we have to be one or the other? Those are questions that aren't asked in this culture . . . Whenever you have something of two, a binary, there's going to be an imbalance and in this culture and in most cultures in this world women have come up short, men have oppressed women.

(From an interview with Kate Borstein, Woman's Hour, BBC Radio 4, September 1994)

Key issues

➤ What is the difference between sex and gender?

➤ What are the major theoretical approaches to gender differences and inequalities?

➤ How are femininities and masculinities constructed in different areas of social life?

➤ What are the major gender divisions in the contemporary world and how do they reinforce the subordinate position of women in society?

➤ How does gender interact with other social factors such as 'race' and ethnicity; sexuality; social class and disability?

Introduction

The interviewee above, Kate Borstein, is the author of *Gender Outlaw: On Men, Women and the Rest of Us* (1994); she describes herself as a transgender person and male to female transsexual and, in the interview, she clearly states that our concepts of gender are fixed on a binary proposition, in fact, a binary opposition – that of masculinity and femininity being separate and opposite experiences and identities. To avoid being treated as a 'man' or 'woman' is clearly a struggle. Gender is a key factor which shapes social behaviour and social institutions. Yet gender differences are something that we often take so much for granted, that seem so 'normal' that they often remain invisible to us.

A closer look

Sex and gender

In the 1970s sociologists began to make a distinction between sex and gender.

Sex is taken to mean some sort of anatomical differences between men and women and has been defined as

> The biological aspects of a person involving characteristics which differentiate females and males by chromosomal, anatomical, reproductive, hormonal and other physiological characteristics.   (Lindsey 1990)

Gender has been defined not as a fixed biological category but a socially created construct, which

> involves the social or cultural and psychological aspects linked to males and females through particular social contexts. What a given society defines as masculine or feminine is a component of gender.   (Lindsey 1990)

This distinction between sex and gender implies two concepts that can be separated unambiguously; it also implies that while gender is shaped by social factors, biological sex is not and is based on an assumption that there are two distinct biological sexes. Some sociologists and natural scientists question these rigid distinctions.

Sex = Gender?

. . . gender is usually described as socially constructed, and sex as biological. The categorizing of all human beings as 'male' or 'female' is left unquestioned. However, this does not always fit with local realities. For example, cultures of eunuchs in India, travestis in Brazil, ladyboys in Thailand or transgender in the USA all suggest that there is more to sex than just male and female. Perhaps ideas of sex are socially constructed too?

'You don't need genitals for politics. You need brains.' Shabna Nehru, the first eunuch politician to run for parliament in India (*New Internationalist*, issue 328, October 2000)

Figure 7.1 Eddie Izzard challenging gender 'norms'
© Getty/Dave Bennett

Stop and think

➤ Think about walking down the main street of any Western city or town. What gender distinctions are there between shops and between departments in shops? What gender distinctions are there among the staff in shops? Are most shoppers women or men? Are most car drivers women or men? Are most van and delivery drivers women or men?

➤ What other gender distinctions between women and men might you see on the street?

Connell (1987) describes the street as a 'gender regime', which he defines as 'The state of play in gender relations in a given institution is its gender regime' (1987: 120).

The gender regime consists of the social relations based on distinctions between women and men. The street is a place where meanings about gender are communicated and rules and patterns concerning gender are reinforced. Yet what goes on in the street cannot be understood in isolation; social settings and institutions are interconnected. Connell points out that all social settings including formal organizations and more informal ones have gender regimes:

Compact formal organizations like schools perhaps have particularly clear gender regimes, but others have them too. Diffuse institutions like markets, large and sprawling ones like the state, and informal milieux like street corner peer-group life also are structured in terms of gender and can be characterized by their gender regimes.   (Connell 1987: 120)

He stresses that it is impossible to identify a select group of social institutions that are concerned with gender, because 'gender relations are present in all types of institutions' (Connell 1987: 120). So wherever we look we cannot escape gender relations. It would be impossible in one chapter to explore the wide range of gender regimes that make up the social world we inhabit. Here we can focus on only some of these gender regimes, to illustrate some key issues and approaches in the developing field of the sociology of gender.

Traditionally sociology neglected gender as a factor that shapes our social experiences. Feminism, in its struggle to understand women's oppression, has placed gender on the broader sociological agenda. Increasingly it is recognized that gender is a crucial factor in shaping individual experience and identity, as well as social institutions, and must be taken into account by sociologists for a full understanding of all social processes. Maynard (1990) argued that the study of gender was reshaping sociology, and by the 50th anniversary of the British Sociological Association in 2001 her view was shared by several past presidents of the Association who when asked about the highlights and lowpoints in British society over the previous 50 years cited feminism as a highlight (*Network 2001*, 80). In addition as Whitehead and Barrett state:

we would go so far as to suggest that feminism was the single most powerful political discourse of the twentieth century ... one of the direct consequences of feminist thinking and action has been to expose and highlight the power, position and practices of men ... feminism puts men and masculinities in a critical spotlight ...   Whitehead and Barrett (2001: 3)

The sociological study of gender shows that gender shapes the experiences of women and men differently in many areas of social life and remains a source of inequality in society.

Explaining gender differences

Although feminism may now be accepted as a main strength of sociological work it has not always been the case, nor have feminist insights been accepted uncritically. Sociology has attempted to explain gender differences in a number of ways and here we will look at: biological explanations and their critiques; and socialization explorations and their limitations for explaining both female and male experience. We will also consider how the very discourses employed by society assist in the shaping of gender identity and 'norms'.

A closer look

Difference and inequality

Two key themes recur in sociology theory and research on gender: difference and inequality.

➤ **Difference** concerns how distinctions are made between women and men. Various theoretical approaches have been proposed to explain these differences. Sociologists have been concerned with examining how different social relationships, institutions and processes distinguish between women and men and create meanings about femininity and masculinity.

➤ **Inequality** concerns how gender distinctions are linked to inequalities, hierarchy and power relations. Sociologists have examined whether social distinctions between women and men create or reinforce inequalities between them, and the unequal distribution of resources and/or access to opportunity.

Feminist sociologists have developed and established the sociological study of gender. They have argued that distinctions between women and men have placed women at a disadvantage and have been central to the subordination of women. Gender differences are part of a social structure which ascribes more power and status to the male gender. There is a now a whole range of sociological research and theory, including that of pro-feminist male sociologists, which highlights that, although gender relations are dynamic and changing, gender inequalities persist in various areas of social life, including the labour market and the household. More recently this work has moved forwards to examine how other identities, such as ethnicity, sexuality, etc., interplay with gender to create inequalities even within a single gender.

Born to be a man/woman

Sociologists have concerned themselves with the biological category of sex because sex differences have often been proposed as explanations for the differences in social roles performed by women and men. Essentialist, or biological, arguments attribute the different social roles performed by women and men to underlying biological structures, particularly reproductive differences or hormonal difference. The 'natural' differences between women and men are seen to contribute to an organization of social relations in which women nurture and men go out to work. Biologically, deterministic explanations of sexual difference have a long history in scientific and pre-scientific thinking, though the form of the biological arguments has changed over the years as scientific techniques and knowledge develops. Essentialism and biological determinism

are umbrella terms for a range of approaches which emphasize biological factors. In the 1950s the functionalist sociologist Parsons argued that there are natural differences between women and men which mean they are suited for particular roles in society (Parsons and Bales 1955). This sex-role theory, particularly dominant in the years from the Second World War until the re-emergence of feminism in the 1970s (feminist movements had existed in Western and other societies, e.g. in India, from the 1880s to the 1930s), asserted that women have an instinct to nurture which suits them for an 'expressive' role in the nuclear family; whereas male biology, which leads men to be more aggressive and competitive, means that men are suited to an 'instrumental' role in the family, providing economic support and links with the outside world. As such, biological differences were seen to constitute a practical and 'natural' basis for the sexual

Case study

They just can't help it

What kind of brain do you have? There really are big differences between the male and female brain, says Simon Baron-Cohen. And they could help explain conditions such as autism. Do you have a male or female brain?

Are there essential differences between the male and female brain? My theory is that the female brain is predominantly hard-wired for empathy, and that the male brain is predominantly hard-wired for understanding and building systems. I call it the empathising–systemising (E–S) theory.

Empathising is the drive to identify another person's emotions and thoughts, and to respond to these with an appropriate emotion. The empathiser intuitively figures out how people are feeling, and how

to treat people with care and sensitivity. Systemising is the drive to analyse and explore a system, to extract underlying rules that govern the behaviour of a system; and the drive to construct systems . . .

According to this theory, a person (whether male or female) has a particular 'brain type'. There are three common brain types: for some individuals, empathising is stronger than systemising. This is called the female brain, or a brain of type E. For other individuals, systemising is stronger than empathising. This is called the male brain, or a brain of type S. Yet other individuals are equally strong in their systemising and empathising. This is called the 'balanced brain', or a brain of type B. There are now tests you can take to see which type (E, S or B) you are. Not which

type you'd like to be, but which you actually are. A key feature of this theory is that your sex cannot tell you which type of brain you have. Not all men have the male brain, and not all women have the female brain. The central claim of this new theory is only that, on average, more males than females have a brain of type S, and more females than males have a brain of type E . . .

The evidence for a female advantage in empathising comes from many different directions. For example, studies show that when children play together with a little movie player that has only one eye-piece, boys tend to get more of their fair share of looking down the eye piece. They just shoulder the girls out of the way. Less empathy, more self-centred. Or if you leave out a bunch of those big plastic cars that kids can ride on, what you

Case study (continued)

see is that more little boys play the 'ramming' game. They deliberately drive the vehicle into another child. The little girls ride around more carefully, avoiding the other children more often. This suggests the girls are being more sensitive to others.

Baby girls, as young as 12 months old, respond more empathically to the distress of other people, showing greater concern through more sad looks, sympathetic vocalisations and comforting. This echoes what you find in adulthood . . .

When asked to judge when someone might have said something potentially hurtful, girls score higher from at least seven years old. Women are also more sensitive to facial expressions. They are better at decoding non-verbal communication, picking up subtle nuances from tone of voice or facial expression, or judging a person's character.

There is also a sex difference in aggression. Males tend to show far more 'direct' aggression such as pushing, hitting and punching. Females tend to show more 'indirect' (or 'relational', covert) aggression . . .

How early are such sex differences in empathy evident? Certainly, by 12 months, girls make more eye contact than boys. But a new study carried out in my lab at Cambridge University shows that, at birth, girls look longer at a face, and boys look longer at a suspended mechanical mobile. Furthermore, the Cambridge team found that how much eye contact children make is in part determined by a biological factor: prenatal testosterone. This has been demonstrated by measuring this hormone in amniotic fluid.

. . . We, of course, know that, with time, culture and socialisation do play a role in determining a male brain (stronger interest in systems) or female brain (stronger interest in empathy). But these studies strongly suggest that biology also partly determines this.

The theory is saying that, on average, males and females differ in what they are drawn to and what they find easy, but that both sexes have their strengths and their weaknesses. Neither sex is superior overall . . .

Simon Baron-Cohen, the *Guardian* 17.4.2003. Simon Baron-Cohen is the director of the Autism Research Centre, Cambridge University.

Question

1. *What do you think of this argument? What evidence could you produce to support or refute it?*

---

division of labour. Biological theories also often present heterosexuality as the 'normal' and 'natural' expression of human sexuality, and identify women and men as having different sexual needs and desires.

Biological explanations are now marginalized within sociology, but they still abound in our culture and new biological theories are often proposed. For example, Moir and Jessel (1989) in their book *Brain Sex* bring together, what they argue, is evidence to support pre-natal hormone theory.

Moir and Jessel argue that at around six weeks, when the male fetus begins to produce hormones different from those of the female, key differences are laid down. As the brain is developing in the male fetus, male hormones, chiefly testosterone, are released; these shape the body and brain in a particular way which in turn determines thought processes and emotions. At adolescence, during puberty, another rise in male hormones exaggerates and confirms these differences. They argue that these changes in the brain have a real effect on personality and capabilities. To simplify, these hormonal differences mean that in effect the wiring of the brain is different in women and men. In women language and social skills are controlled by both sides of the brain whereas in men these are controlled by the left side. This has profound effects on personality and abilities. Men are more single-minded, they are able to ignore anything but factual information thus enabling them to focus and make decisions more quickly than women. These differences impact on the contemporary social structure and this theory can be used to explain a range of contemporary gender differences. For example, women are not in top jobs because they do not have the same drive to be on top; men are more aggressive and competitive:

the pursuit of power is overwhelmingly and universally a male trait . . . to rise in the hierarchy, men are much more prepared than women to make sacrifices of their own time, pleasure, relaxation, health, safety and emotions. (Moir and Jessel 1989)

Yet Moir and Jessel are keen to stress that they are not presenting a theory of female inferiority; women should be seen as different but not inferior and they emphasize that women's verbal and people skills should be increasingly valued in the labour market. More recently, psychological studies have entered the ether of the public media as the example from the *Guardian* shows (see p. 266).

For many years sociobiologists have provided a whole range of theories for gender differences, connected to Darwin's theory of evolution. Desmond Morris (1977), a popular sociobiologist, connects much of social behaviour to evolutionary drives and proposes a model of human development that is linked to his belief in 'man the hunter'. In this model, in pre-history women remained at the base camp with the children while the men went off to hunt as a result of men's higher levels of testosterone, which lead to greater aggressiveness and physical strength. As a result of evolutionary selection males with more aggressive qualities have left more copies of themselves and females with more maternal genes have been selected.

A key criticism of these essentialist approaches is that they are biologically deterministic and neglect social influences on behaviour (Bem 1993; Oakley 1972). They also neglect how biological features themselves interact with the environment in which it is situated: sociobiology 'massively underestimates the contribution of cultures and histories to that interaction' (Bem 1993).

Biological approaches also assume rigid distinctions between women and men and rely on the assumption that the categories 'women' and 'men' are universal groups sharing a universal biology and personality. (See 'A closer look' below for a different view, one that shows gender roles as malleable.) Hence these theories do not account for diversity. They do not account for biological women who display masculine behaviour and take on masculine roles and biological men who display feminine traits, except to define them as biological deviants. There

A closer look

An alternative view of evolutionary selection

In a similar vein to Morris, Leibowitz (1986) offers a different perspective to explain the sexual division of labour, not based on 'man the hunter' but on 'woman the mother'. Her argument is that the development of projectile weapons by primitive societies increased the availability and amount of animal produce, resulting in an increased demand for hearth skills such as preparing hides, cooking meat and making cooking utensils. As these skills were new and complex children needed to be trained to develop proficiency, and children where tutored in the skills they would use as adults. Given that females would spend more time at the hearth than males in adulthood, due to the physical restrictions both of pregnancy and child rearing, instruction in these new skills was directed at female children rather than at boys. As such, Leibowitz contends that females became more skilled in these areas and boys were taught other skills to compensate, generally those requiring physical strength rather than dexterity.

Although both Leibowitz and Morris reach the same conclusion – male manual strength and female nurturing being the successor genes – their explanations are different as they begin from different assumptions. Morris begins with the assumption that male strength and aggression were the valued attributes, whereas Leibowitz has male hunting skills arising from a greater valuing of the hearth skills of females. Both are based on biological roles, both have biology shaping social roles and both indicate the value-laden approach inherent in each writer.

A closer look

Mead's New Guinea study

Mead's (1935) famous study in New Guinea of three different groups of tribal peoples – the Arapesh, Mundugumor and Tchambuli – provides an example of variation. Among the Arapesh both female and male were gentle, passive and sharing. There was not a rigid definition between the responsibilities and personalities of women and men, and there was a more egalitarian community. Among the Mundugumor there was more defined sexual division: men were aggressive, hostile and dominant and women were responsible for child care and subordinates. Among the Tchambuli peoples Mead found what could be interpreted as a reversal of conventional Western gender behaviour: men had a greater responsibility for domestic labour and care of the young and adorned themselves, whereas the women had a greater involvement in leadership and food hunting and were more aggressive.

is a great deal of autobiographical evidence from individuals who feel that their gender identity does not correspond to their biological sex or who feel restricted by a culture that allows gender identity to be expressed only in terms of the female–male dualism. Further, sociologists point to the variation across cultures of what it means to be a woman or man. There is a great deal of anthropological and sociological research evidence which shows cultural variation in gender roles.

Within many contemporary societies women are effectively performing conventional male roles in, for example, the military; similarly, men can be found involved in child care and non-traditional masculine work. Some socio-

logists have argued that we have become blinkered by gender distinctions. In our culture we make a rigid distinction between female and male and then judge everyone in relation to this dichotomy and attempt to place them within one of two categories. We impose social meanings onto our human biology. In the 1970s Oakley (1972; 1974b) argued that it was misleading to think in terms of two distinct sexes and more useful to think in terms of the female and the male being placed at the ends of a continuum with overlap. Many sociologists now challenge the notion of two distinct sexes and propose that the male–female dichotomy itself is a social construct. Look now at the Case study below.

Case study

Refusing to be a man

John Stolenberg (1990) parodies the social distinctions between men and women that are made in our culture and the importance that is assigned to biological differences.

I'd like to take you, in an imaginary way, to look at a different world, somewhere else in the universe, a place inhabited by a life form that very much resembles us. But these creatures grow up with a peculiar knowledge. They know that they have been born in an infinite variety. They know, for instance, that in their genetic material they are born with hundreds of different chromosome formations at the point in each cell that we would say determines their 'sex'. These creatures don't just come in XX or XY; they also come in XXY and XYY plus a long list of 'mosaic' variations in which some cells in a creature's body have one combination and other cells have another . . . The creatures in this world enjoy

their individuality; they delight in the fact that they are not born divisible into distinct categories . . .

These creatures are not oblivious to reproduction; but nor do they spend their lives constructing a self-definition around their variable reproductive capacities. They don't have to, because what is truly unique about these creatures is that they are capable of having a sense of personal identity without struggling to fit into a group identity based on how they were born. These creatures are quite happy actually. They don't worry about sorting other creatures into categories, so they don't have to worry about whether they are measuring up to some category they themselves are supposed to belong to . . . perhaps you have guessed the point of this science fiction: anatomically, each creature in the imaginary world I have been describing could be an identical twin of every human being on earth. These creatures in fact, are us – in every way

except socially and politically. The way they are born is the way we are born. And we are not born belonging to one or other of the two sexes. We are born into a physiological continuum on which there is no discrete and definite point that you can call 'male' and no discrete and definite point that you can call 'female' . . .

What does all this mean? It means, first of all, a logical dilemma: Either human 'male' and human 'female' actually exist in nature as fixed and discrete entities and you can credibly base an entire social and political system on those absolute natural categories or else the variety of human sexedness is infinite.

(Stolenberg 1990: 33–6)

Question

1. *Do you believe that male and female are fixed, separate identities in relation to (a) sex; (b) gender? If not, what are the implications for our daily social interactions?*

Sociologists have engaged in the 'nature–nurture' debate on whether differences in personality, behaviour and social roles between men and women are the product of biological or sociocultural factors. Are women and men naturally different or are they made so by the society they live in? This debate has been of particular importance for feminist writers, who have argued that certain interpretations of women's biology have been used not simply to mark out their difference from men but to justify their subordinate and secondary status and to exclude women from certain areas of society. Gender inequality refers to this inequitable allocation of social status, opportunity and resources (economic, political and social) on the basis of gender.

There has also been a concern that the male sex has been taken as the norm and women have been defined as deviant, lacking, second rate or, as Simone de Beauvoir (1974) argued, 'other'. In the 1980s and 1990s, some sociologists have been concerned that on the basis of gender men have also experienced restriction, for example being defined primarily as breadwinners has meant they have been deprived of involvement with child-rearing and nurturing activities.

Stolenberg (1990) suggests that humans have imposed one of many interpretations on a set of biological characteristics and that difference rather than sameness has been emphasized. Birke (1992) explores the idea of sex differences, arguing that there are differences between women and men, but these are massively exaggerated. She also stresses that scientific work on differences usually takes an average but within the population as a whole there are individuals who deviate from these averages, for example female bodybuilders, who have a much greater muscle mass than many men.

Birke (1992) has pointed out that it is difficult to make a firm separation between fixed biological sex and culturally shaped gender, and encourages us to think how the biological and social interact. She identifies two key problems with the concept of biological causes of difference: it treats biology as a fixed concept and excludes other factors. Biological factors are themselves socially constructed. Physical characteristics can be shaped by the social. For example people's physical strength can be shaped by dietary and exercise programmes. With the example of pre-natal hormone theory (1992) testosterone leads to aggression, but the process is two-way because aggressive behaviour leads to the production of testosterone. Birke (1992) argues that gender identity is a continual process of construction and reconstruction. Rather than biological factors and cultural factors being treated separately they should be viewed as 'interacting' factors. What is important is how humans culturally interpret biology and how the biological is shaped by the social.

Many sociologists have doubted the reliability of 'objective' scientific results which claim to connect behaviour to biology or nature. Bem (1993) notes how science has historically provided unreliable evidence of differences between men and women, specifically evidence of women's inferiority. Feminist writers among others have pointed out that scientific knowledge itself is not value-free but can be shaped by cultural, political and ideological values (see Letherby 2003, Chapter 1 for discussion of this point).

The theory of *vitalism*, popular in the late nineteenth century, is an example of this type of now discredited scientific work. This theory proposed that humans have a vital electrical force and the amount of energy within us is constant. Nineteenth-century scientists argued that women's reproductive function drew vital energy from the brain, limiting intellectual capacity. This was used by writers such as Edward Clark (1873) in *Sex in Education* to argue that higher education was not suitable for women: education would divert energy from the development of women's reproductive organs, which would be damaging to women's health.

The argument that science can be a vehicle for ideological beliefs and can be utilized to justify various forms of inequality has formed an important part of feminist criticisms of many biological theories. Even if there are biological differences between women and men this does not explain why the male gender has higher status; to understand this we have to look to social and political factors.

Social construction of gender

The predominant view in sociology has been that many of the differences between women and men are the product of social and cultural processes, not biology. Yet, the earliest works on social learning were firmly based in biological notions of gender appropriate learning. Sex-role theory developed out of structural functionalism (see Chapter 2) and, as with other roles within structural functionalism, it was argued that sex-roles were both associated with a certain status within society while simultaneously providing a text, a script, for that role. Such texts, providing instruction on appropriate behaviour and attitudes, need to be learnt, and this is achieved through the process of socialization. As such, sociologists have focused on gender as a learned set of behaviours and have explored the social processes through which we all learn to be either feminine or masculine. A whole range of social processes have been identified as sites where gendered categories of femininity and masculinity are constructed. Sociologists have explored the diverse meanings attached to femininity and masculinity, so much so that there has been a shift towards talking about femininities and masculinities (we shall examine this shift in more detail on pp. 275–7).

Learning gender

According to social learning theory we learn what is considered gender-appropriate behaviour via socialization, which begins at birth. Girls and boys experience gender socialization in different ways, learning appropriate behaviours, personalities and gender roles and developing their own gender identities (own feelings and consciousness).

Sociological and psychological research has paid attention to various components and stages of gender development. In the 1970s and early 1980s particularly there was a mass of research which examined the differential learning processes of boys and girls. This included studies of such things as post-natal care, books and magazines, clothing and toys. Many researchers have reported that there are different practices or expectations in relation to girls and boys which encouraged or reinforced 'feminine' behaviour in girls and 'masculine' behaviour in boys.

Stop and think

➤ Social learning theory assumes that in our culture there are certain roles, behaviours and characteristics that are stereotyped as either 'feminine' or 'masculine'. Examine the list of characteristics below and decide for each one whether they are considered desirable for a woman or man in British society generally.

Affectionate	Tender	Sensitive to	Warm
Flatterable	Gentle	others'	Yielding
Analytical	Leadership	needs	Individualistic
Cheerful	abilities	Strong	Does not
Self-reliant	Makes	personality	use harsh
Forceful	decisions	Ambitious	language
Soft-spoken	easily	Childlike	Dominant
Independent	Sympathetic	Athletic	Loves children

➤ Was it easy to allocate characteristics to categories?

➤ If you were asked to allocate them in line with your own opinions of women's and men's personalities and capabilities rather than what is considered more desirable and appropriate in British society generally, would there be differences in how you allocated them?

➤ Did you feel that some could not be allocated to a discrete category?

➤ Tick those traits that you would use to describe yourself. Have you ticked mainly 'masculine', mainly 'feminine' or a mix of both traits?

These characteristics are taken from the Bem Sex Role Inventory (BSRI). Bem (1993) stresses that the traits that were included on her inventory were not selected on the basis of how females and males describe themselves but 'on the basis of what was culturally defined as gender appropriate in the United States in the early 1970s'. She determined this by asking a sample of US citizens whom she saw as her 'cultural informants' to identify for each of the traits whether they were seen as more desirable for a woman or a man 'in American society generally'. Bem went on to develop the BSRI using these traits; the inventory involves individuals assessing their own personalities. From the results of her work Bem has argued that humans are androgynous, expressing a range of 'feminine' and 'masculine' traits. She also argued that those people who were androgynous were more psychologically healthy than people who expressed more rigid feminine or male traits. Bem favours a social approach to understanding gender differences; her work suggested that women and men express a range of 'feminine' and 'masculine' traits yet also acknowledged that there are sociocultural factors which encourage feminine behaviour for women and masculine behaviour for men; this rigid socialization is restrictive, making it difficult for individuals to express whatever aspects of their personalities they feel, be these deemed 'feminine' or 'masculine' in our cultures.

Girls and boys come out to play

Socialization influences surround us everywhere: from messages we receive from our families, in school, from peers and from the media. The exploration of how girls learn to be women was a very important early focus for feminist theorists, who showed how feminine gender roles and dominant ideologies of femininity have been restrictive for women, channelling them into social roles to which lower social status is attached. There has also been a concern that the male sex has been taken as the norm and women have been defined as deviant, lacking, second rate or, as Simone de Beauvoir (1974) argued, 'other'.

While gender studies began with a concentration on girls and women to balance their absence from, or when present, often inaccurate, social scientific views, it is not the case that only women 'have' a gender. Masculinity has been studied since the 1950s, though it was only in the 1980s that the pro-feminist New Men's Movement turned the focus onto a critical study of masculinities. A commonality in the critique of both femininity and masculinity is the way that sociologists have examined how socialization has been employed to present and preserve hegemonic views of both. See below.

A closer look

Hegemony

A term originally devised by Gramsci (see Chapter 2) to explain and describe how one social group – in Gramsci's case, an elite social class – through the usage of political power and ideology can achieve dominance over other groups. The important aspect for sociology is the usage of ideology to obtain assent rather than the use of force. In discussing hegemonic femininity and masculinity sociologists mean the ideology of the 'ideal' forms. Interestingly, hegemonic influences are more frequently used to describe the forces around masculinity than femininity – though ideal types exist in most cultures.

Dominant notions of femininity have emphasized passivity, dependence, emotion and nurturing characteristics, which have often disempowered women. Many feminists have pointed out that these characteristics are not inherently negative but have been denigrated and unvalued. Socialization into roles that stress romance, marriage and motherhood have been seen as particularly restrictive and as providing an effective way of obtaining female subordination, by consent. Hence it has been crucial for feminists to explore how femininity is constructed and to challenge these processes. Sharpe (1994a [1976]) in *Just Like a Girl* mapped out the process of gender socialization for girls. She found that children's activities performed in the home which distinguished between girls and boys, and parental expectations, rehearse girls and boys for future roles. Girls were encouraged to be girlfriends, wives and mothers with primary responsibility for domestic labour. Although they expected to engage in paid work this was seen as temporary or secondary and the jobs they aspired to were conventional low-paid female jobs; girls were being encouraged to have limited aspirations and hence restricted choices. Sharpe went back to speak to young girls and boys in 1991 and repeated the research she had carried out originally in 1972. She found that in terms of teenage girls' views and expectations:

> **While their range of job expectations showed surprisingly little change, there were striking differences in attitudes to education, marriage and family life. Change was also evident in girls' personal opinions. They now placed a greater stress on equality with men, and on their own needs. I was greatly impressed by their comparative assertiveness and confidence, and their strong belief in women's ability to stand on their own two feet and not have to depend on, nor be dominated by, men.** (Sharpe 1994b: 15)

While men may have been the key subjects of sociological research, they had not been approached as gendered beings (Morgan 1981) until more recently. As well as feminist writers examining the social construction of masculinity, increasingly masculinity is receiving more attention from male sociologists. Some men listened to feminism and have responded with new ways of understanding men's behaviour. Masculinity is taken to be socially constructed: being a man is considered something that men become rather than an innate property of the male sex. It has been argued that the hegemony around masculinity operates not to teach what masculinity can be but rather what it is not (Donald 1992) although Morgan (1994a) still found the dominance of

Case study

There's a good girl

Marianne Grabrucker (1988) recounted her experience of attempting to bring up her daughter free from gender stereotyping. In writing a diary she became aware of the subtle ways in which she treated her daughter in a specific way simply because she was a girl and also the other social forces that conspired to teach her child gender consciousness. Despite her own efforts not to relate to her daughter in a sex-typed way she found that there were many influences outside her control in the social environment that communicated messages about gender difference. The child responded to advertisements and gender hierarchies she saw in her everyday environment; for example she saw mainly men on motor bikes and hence associated these with men. Children's literature which challenges gender sterotypes has been produced: Babette Cole's (1988) book *Princess Smartypants* is the story of a princess who scares off all her suitors and sets them unachievable tasks so she can spend her life on her own doing her own thing. However, cultural images that provide alternative messages tend to be the exception in children's books, games, films and television programmes.

Question

1. What influences exist today that spread messages regarding appropriate gender 'norms'?

the male breadwinner role to exist as late as the 1990s. Nonetheless, modern studies of masculinity examine the different experiences of masculinity in and across society (see Whitehead and Barrett 2001).

Feminists had pointed out that traditional masculinity often disempowered women and led to their subordination. Masculinity was therefore approached as problematic and certain aspects of male behaviour particularly so – men's violence and aggression, their sexual activity and their domination of women. Hearn (1987) identifies men as the gender of oppression and points out that they oppress other men as well as women. The study of men and masculinity has attempted to explore the processes that lead to this domination and to recognize the emotional costs to men of their dominance as well as to women (Seidler 1989).

It has been recognized that although feminism has challenged men's domination no fundamental changes in gender relations can take place without changes in men. Seidler (1989) has considered the consequences for men of what he identifies as the dominant Western form of masculinity, which is taken to be natural to men. He argued that far from being natural this is a relatively recent historical development. In this model of masculinity, the male mind has come to be seen as separate and superior to the body, masculinity is identified with reason, objectivity and superior mental power. Masculine identity is tied closely to the 'public' realms of work and political life. The consequences of this identity for many men is that they are restricted in developing a more personal sense of self and this makes it hard for men to recognize their own or other people's needs. Dominant masculinity stresses aggression, assertion, competition and reason rather than emotion. Within this model of masculinity, for men to acknowledge their emotional needs is seen as weakness. Men are then locked into a competitive struggle to prove their masculinity. This has implications for male sexuality. Seidler argues that as part of this competitive struggle men approach sex as something closely connected to individual achievement and something which signifies their position in the pecking order of masculinity. Male sexuality is part of the development of a masculine identity in which sexuality is seen in terms of power and conquest. Sex becomes a way of proving manhood.

Phillips (1993), in *The Trouble with Boys*, described what she saw as the cruel transition to manhood that boys undergo. She argues that in our society we are still raising boys to find and express themselves by standing alone, appearing strong, being independent and proving themselves through competition. In contrast girls are encouraged to develop relationships and gain affiliative skills. It is at the level of emotional relating where the most profound effects of gender can be seen; girls spend hours practising emotional skills, whereas boys' energies are directed towards mastering physical skills.

Stop and think

➤ Compare this to the male and female brains theory which states that these are already inherent traits merely reinforced through usage.

Although boys obviously have feelings they are rarely taught to identify and understand them. The feelings they do practise are feelings of competition and aggression. These may serve boys well in the world of competition but fail them in other settings and, as Donald (1992) warns, when winning becomes too important, it has societal as well as individual costs. As such, it is argued that boys and men find it hard to recognize vulnerability: signs of tenderness and need make them uneasy; they deal with this by competing and appearing not to need. From this viewpoint men are seen as emotionally crippled.

The beauty myth

A recurring theme in the work on the representation of women in the media is that women's physical bodies are represented in a particularly limited way. In films and magazines women's bodies are likely to be 'glamorous', 'beautiful', 'sexy' and 'thin'. Some theorists argue that the media play a key role not only in constructing notions of feminine ideals of beauty to which women are encouraged to aspire but also in feminine socialization.

The beauty industry has been identified as a set of practices and ideas which restrict women's lives. Feminist work on fashion, beauty and adornment has tended to interpret women's concerns with these practices as a product of ideologies of femininity designed to control women's lives, undermine women's autonomy and the development of unities between women by establishing competition between women (Chapkis 1986; Wolf 1991; Ussher 1997). The feminine ideal is impossible to achieve because the images and icons of the beauty industry are themselves fabricated and also because the ideal is constantly being redefined with a waif-like thin body in one year and a buxom look the next. Beauty and fashion culture have been seen as closely intertwined with capitalist relations:

> Feminists in the second wave originally explained the fashion culture in terms of patriarchy in league with capitalism. Femininity in this analysis is false consciousness.   (Gaines 1990: 4)

The 'fashion, beauty, diet' industry is identified as big business within capitalism and also serves to reinforce differences between women and men and undermine, control and restrict women. Feminists such as Naomi Wolf (1991) feel that the beauty myth has taken over other ideologies in undermining women's confidence. The beauty myth involves ideal standards of feminine beauty and body shape to which all women must aspire. For Chapkis (1986), this ideal is white, youthful and able-bodied. Hill-Collins (1990) points out that not only are eternally defined standards of beauty 'white', which can create anxieties for black women, who cannot live up to the white-skinned, blue-eyed, straight-haired ideal, but also this white ideal exists only in opposition to the black 'other'. This illustrates how women's experiences vary depending on their racial identity, and how gender ideologies interact with a wide range of factors including race. It also illustrates the reality that women are a diverse group with differential access to social power and prestige.

> Judging white women by their physical appearance and attractiveness to men objectifies them. But their white skin and straight hair privilege them in a system in which part of the basic definition of whiteness is superior to blackness.   (Hill-Collins 1990: 79)

Wolf (1991) argues that the beauty myth is the most insidious ideology yet undermining girls and women individually and collectively. At work and at leisure women can never fully be themselves and focus their energies, as they must always be concerned about how they present themselves, anxious about whether they match up to the 'beauty myth'. For Wolf, the 'beauty myth' plays a key role in controlling and undermining women. The pressures to aspire to the 'beauty myth' reduce women's confidence and sap their energies. Young girls may no longer prioritize getting married but they want to look like and perhaps become supermodels. So the diet industry and cosmetic surgery thrive on exploiting women's anxieties and insecurities. As Davis (2003) notes cosmetic surgery is gendered practice as surgeons are almost exclusively male and patients largely female. She argues that men will never seek surgery to the same extent as women (except for hair transplants) because men's bodies are constituted as bodies that 'do' rather than are 'done to'.

Hill Collins (1990) stresses the importance of self-definition and the creation of a new aesthetic for beauty based on individual uniqueness. Yet Ussher (1997) suggests that women can be critical of the 'beauty myth' and still get pleasure from 'doing femininity'. She cites Susan Douglas who writes

Figure 7.2 Qian, a student from Beijing who has had cosmetic surgery on her eyelids and cheeks, was crowned the winner of China's first pageant for such 'man-made' beauties
© Getty/AFP/Frederic J. Brown

I don't read a *Vogue* or *Glamour* . . . I enter them. I escape into them, into a world where I have nothing more stressful to do than smooth on some skin cream, polish my toenails and lie on a beach.

(Douglas 1995: 251)

As Ussher herself adds

[I]n a post feminist world, where women are supposed to reject traditional models of femininity and be independent and strong this is transgression (and therefore pleasurable) indeed.   (Usher 1997: 68)

Men in crisis?

As men have been placed under the microscope some people have talked about a crisis in masculinity, as conventional masculinity is challenged. Feminism not only demanded changes for women but also identified a need for men to change. To what extent men have changed is much debated. In the early 1990s the media began to talk about the 'new man'. This construct is typified by a man

who plays an active role in parenting and domestic labour, takes his partner's sexual needs into consideration and is generally in touch with his emotions (Collier 1992).

Sharpe (1994b), while arguing that the expectations and views of girls in the 1990s have changed distinctively since the 1970s, believes that boys have not moved as far: 'Unfortunately boys growing up today have less egalitarian expectations. Although they are being made aware of the issue of gender equality inside and outside the schools, boys are unlikely to make it a priority in their own lives' (Sharpe 1994b: 15). Yet, MacInnes (2001, originally 1998) believes that some social changes have occurred in Western societies since the Second World War; in particular he argues that the male breadwinner ideology is in serious decline:

In countries where women form a substantial part of the labour force, male breadwinner ideology has all but collapsed in terms of popular support for its core idea . . . A clear relationship stands out between the level of women's labour market involvement and men's loss of faith in breadwinner ideology . . . This is not evidence of the arrival of sexual equality in material or ideological terms, but it is evidence of dramatic change.

(MacInnes 2001: 321)

Stop and think

➤ Think about the books you used when learning to read. Were there gender messages within them?

➤ Think about the messages you received about your gender from family and friends. Were these gendered? If so how? Who did you receive such messages from? If they were not gendered why do you think this was so?

➤ When you were young what did you think you might do when you grew up? Do you think your choices were influenced by hegemonic views of masculine and feminine careers?

Femininities and masculinities: discourses of gender

Much of the sociological work on femininity and masculinity has adopted a socialization perspective, in which the main concern has been how people learned gender stereotypes and internalized them. Although many sociologists accept that gender is learned and that socialization plays a key role, an increasing number have pointed to the problems with taking a straightforward learning approach. Social learning theory acknowledges that gender roles and

A closer look

Gender as historical product

Bob Connell argues that masculinity is a recent historical production, only a few hundred years old and one routed within European notions.

'All societies have cultural accounts of gender, but not all have the concept 'masculinity'. In its modern usage the term assumes that one's behaviour results from the type of person one is. That is to say, an unmasculine person would behave differently: being peaceable rather than violent, conciliatory rather than dominating, hardly able to kick a football, uninterested in sexual conquest, and so forth.

This conception presupposes a belief in individual difference and personal agency. In that sense it is built on the conception of individuality that developed in early-modern Europe with the growth of colonial empires and capitalist economic relations.

But the concept is also inherently relational. 'Masculinity' does not exist except in contrast with 'femininity'. A culture which does not treat women and men as bearers of polarized character types, at least in principle, does not have a concept of masculinity in the sense of modern European/American culture.'

(Connell 2001: 30–31, originally 1995)

identities are not fixed and may change over history and across cultures. Walby (1990) argues that this approach still operates with a static and unitary conception of gender differences: femininity is one set of characteristics that girls and women learn and masculinity another set that boys and men learn. She argues that this takes insufficient account of the different forms that femininity and masculinity can take and hence it does not account for diversity among women and men. This approach implies that each person is equally conforming to gender ideology and does not explore how masculinity and femininity vary according to a whole range of social factors such as class, age, race and ethnicity. It treats people as relatively passive in their acquisition of gender identity. The emphasis on the passive learning of dominant ideology does not adequately recognize that people may resist, reject or subvert dominant meanings about gender.

This has led to an exploration of the varied content of femininities and masculinities and a shift in emphasis from examining simple sex stereotyping to exploring the *processes* by which a range of femininities and masculinities

are constructed. This shift is the product of a recognition that there are different messages about female and male behaviour, communicated for example via the media and education, and not simply one ideology. Sociologists examine how social structures act as vehicles for transmitting these different ideologies or discourses of gender (Walby 1990). This does not mean that all ideologies have the same power and influence; indeed some theorists acknowledge that some ideologies are more dominant and powerful than others. We can find advertisements that are not quite so gender-stereotyped and do not simply portray women as wives, mothers or sex objects. These advertisements can be understood as providing alternative messages about femininity. Yet we can still find many conventional notions of femininity communicated in advertising, women talking about their experience with washing powder products and endless examples of 'beautiful' women sexualized to sell a whole range of products. Approaches to the construction of gender which try to identify the varied messages/ideologies about gender Walby refers to as *discourse theory*.

Post-structuralist approaches to gender argue that the polarity of gender is hegemonic in its dualism but the difference with socialization lies in the way in which post-structuralism emphasizes the way in which language, discourses, constructs this dualism. Davies (2002, originally 1989) describes the ways in which children are restricted to situating themselves within one gender or the other through the influence and usage of linguistic forms. However, she also argues that this is not a wholly passive activity but rather one in which children are agents in their own construction of what it is to be female or male, feminine or masculine.

A closer look

John MacInnes (2001, originally 1998) has questioned the way in which social scientists have focused upon describing the socialization processes through which gender identity, in this case masculinity, is created. This has led to attempts to use these analyses to adjust and adapt socialization to produce androgynous gender identities. MacInnes sees the main question as being . . . 'what has made people including sociologists, psychoanalysts and popular journalists imagine that individuals possess gender? How have they come to see the connection between sex, self and society in this way?'

(MacInnes 2001: 326)

Femininity has been identified in the past very much as a set of characteristics and behaviours that women learn and which then constrain women's lives. Yet some researchers have explored how femininity and feminine identification can be part of social identification from which women can gain positive identity and meaning. Similarly, although masculinity was originally approached as a fixed set of characteristics which disempowers women and restricts men, it has been acknowledged that men may feel uncomfortable with some constructs of masculinity and that there are many alternative masculinities. Questions have been raised about the extent to which all men conform to the traditional model of masculinity and whether all men are uncaring and insensitive to the needs of others.

Morgan (1992) emphasizes that there are a range of 'masculinities'. For example, he points out that middle-class masculinity places emphasis on success at work whereas working-class masculinity, although incorporating the role of breadwinner, places great emphasis on physical strength and prowess. Likewise, Brod and Kaufman (1994: 4) remind us that we 'cannot study masculinity in the singular, as if the stuff of man were a homogenous and unchanging thing'.

Stop and think

> What characteristics do Prince William, Denzil Washington and Julian Clary share?

> In what ways are they different?

> Do you think it is accurate to describe them as sharing similar 'masculine' traits?

Post-structuralist and postmodern thinking have had a key role in shifting debates within sociology about gender away from simple social learning theory. Social learning theory identified a clearcut binary division between a category 'male', perpetuated and internalized via a process of learning masculine traits, and a category 'female', perpetuated via a process of learning feminine traits. Post-structuralist theorists argued this did not allow for differences among women, men, resistances or choice. Post-structuralism emphasizes that meanings about gender and gender identity are fluid, historically and socially constituted. Butler (1990), an influential post-structuralist feminist, favours:

> those historical and anthropological positions that
> understand gender as a relation among socially con-
> stituted subjects in specifiable contexts.

Gender is not fixed but variable and changes at different times and in different social contexts. She described gender as 'performative': we all act out a gender performance, some of us may act out a more traditional one, others might not. Those that run counter to the traditional or hegemonic are subversive performances/identities which can lead to what she calls 'gender trouble' as they confound and challenge the norm and present alternative identities.

Some post-structuralist theorists have argued that some cultural developments, such as the development of information technology, are not simply reinforcing rigid meanings about gender but present an opportunity to challenge these, giving individuals the opportunity to explore gender identities (Harraway 1991). The Internet has been identified as a cultural site where traditional gender identities can be confounded and transcended as users take on new gender identities in cyberspace. Hence a biological 'female' who identifies as heterosexual may adopt a male bisexual cyber identity (Di Marco and Di Marco 2003).

In line with post-structuralist thinking on the self, for Butler (1990) gender identity is not fixed or rigid but free-floating and does not represent some essence of the self but a performance. Butler has been associated with queer theory, which although often growing out of debates about gender and sexuality has at its centre the view that identity can be reconstructed. The word 'queer' is seen here to represent whatever is seen to be at odds with those identities and ideologies which claim validity, normality or dominance.

Sex, sexuality and relationships

Sex is everywhere you look: on television, in magazines and on advertising billboards selling everything from cars to ice cream. This cultural obsession with sex has been reflected in a considerable and diverse sociology of sexuality; we can only touch on some key debates here. Feminists and lesbian and gay theorists have argued that sex is a political phenomenon tied up with power relations. Many feminists have been keen to analyse sexual relations and intimate relationships and their implications for women and women's oppression.

Surveying sex

Considering the public interest, there is limited large-scale social research on sexual activity. Until the publication of *Sexual Behaviour in Britain* (Wellings *et al.* 1994) anyone who wanted information about human sexual behaviour based on large-scale research had to look to the work of Kinsey *et al.* (1948; 1953) or Masters and Johnson (1966; 1970). The 1994 study was more extensive and more characteristic of the general population than the Kinsey study. The sample of 18,876 people interviewed was representative of the British population in terms of social class, education, ethnic background, age and region. The survey produced a vast amount of descriptive information about reported sexual behaviour. It also raised a whole range of methodological issues concerning the study of sexual behaviour. For example, the survey found that six in every hundred men said they had had some homosexual experience in their lives. Some gay activists have stressed that these numbers may be an underestimation because respondents questioned about 'partners' may have counted only long-term relationships. They also said that the home interviews used by the researchers would have led to an underestimation, as 'Closeted Gays are unlikely to admit their homosexuality to a total stranger who turns up on their door and asks them personal questions about the intimate details of their private life' (Peter Tatchell, quoted in I. Katz, 'Rights Group scorn one in 90 gay survey', the *Guardian* 22.1.1994).

Despite media which often seem saturated with sexual imagery, sex as a serious topic of conversation is still taboo in many contexts. This is exacerbated by powerful discourses which construct only certain expressions of sexual desire and behaviour as normal and acceptable. Hence some gay, lesbian and bisexual individuals may not feel able to come out in a homophobic society. This creates difficulties for social researchers as many people may not want to talk about their sexual experiences or may not feel able to talk openly or honestly about them.

Stop and think

➤ Why do you think there has been limited research on sexual behaviour? If you were asked to research patterns of sexual behaviour among the British public what methods would you use?

Normal sex?

Sexuality is often defined as a natural instinct or drive which is part of the biological make-up of each individual and demands fulfilment through sexual activity.

This view of sexuality as a natural biological entity is referred to as *essentialism*. Much essential thinking links sex as a natural instinct to reproductive activity. Weeks (1986) points out that in this approach there is a clear link between biological sex/gender and sexuality:

> Modern culture has assumed an intimate connection between the fact of being biologically male or female (that is having appropriate sex organs and reproductive potentialities) and the correct form of erotic behaviour (usually genital intercourse between men and women). (Weeks 1986: 13)

This view leads to a distinction between the sexual needs and desires of men and women; men are defined as having a stronger sex drive than women and a natural tendency to promiscuity. According to this discourse human sexuality is rooted in biology and a normal sex drive is a heterosexual drive intended for procreation. Any deviation is considered to be pathological. Thus lesbian, gay and bisexual women and men have been defined as deviant, unnatural, perverse and not real women or men.

> We learn very early on from many sources that 'natural' sex is what takes place with members of the 'opposite' sex. 'Sex' between people of the same 'sex' is therefore, by definition, 'unnatural'. (Weeks 1986: 13)

Heterosexuality is the norm in this model for both women and men, and sex is properly expressed in stable, monogamous, ideally marital relationships.

Weeks has been a key critic of essentialism. He rejects any approach that does not consider the social and historical forces that shape sexuality and which does not acknowledge the diversity of sexual identity and desire. He rejects the idea that there is a true essence of sex, an 'uninformed pattern' which is 'ordained by nature itself' (Weeks 1986: 15). He argues that it is simplistic to reduce a complex pattern of sexual relations and identities to biological factors.

Butler (1990; 1993) challenges the assumed causal links between sex, gender and sexual desire. She argues that who individuals desire is seen to lead on from being masculine or feminine, and desire is usually constructed as being towards the other gender. She challenges heterosexuality as the only valid form of sexual desire: it is merely one configuration of desire but one that has come to seem natural. Once these links are challenged then not only is gender fluid but so is sexual desire. She is one theorist who challenges all forms of sexual norm: 'It's not just the norm of heterosexuality that is tenuous. It's all sexual norms.' (Judith Butler, quoted in Osborne and Segal 1994.)

Constructing sex and sexuality

There are a whole body of theorists who agree that our sexual desires may seem to be natural yet our sexual responses and identities are actually socially constructed (see Weeks 2000). We learn not only patterns of behaviour but also meanings attached to such behaviour. Our sexual feelings, activities, the ways in which we think about sexuality and our sexual identities are all the product of social and historical forces. Sexuality is shaped by the culture in which we live; religious teachings, laws, psychological theory, medical definitions, social policies and the media all inform us of its meaning. Our sexuality is also influenced by whether we are disabled or able bodied and by our age. This does not mean that biology has no influence: limits are imposed by the body and we experience different things depending on whether we have a vagina or a penis.

Yet the body and its anatomical structure and physiology does not directly determine what we do or the meaning this may have. The body gains certain meanings only in particular social contexts. Different parts of the body can be defined in different ways. For example, in the 1960s a new cultural context emerged with liberal attitudes that supported sexual liberation for women: the 'G-spot' was discovered, books were published and classes held to help women explore their bodies and find the G-spot; the physical anatomy of women was the same as before but it had a different social significance. This particular part of the body was given sexual meaning and this constructs desire.

Foucault and discourse theory

Foucault (1981) has been very influential on the social constructionalist position. He argued that there was no one truth about sex and that various discourses – law, religion and in particular medicine and psychiatry – have produced a particular view of the body and its pleasures, a set of bodily sensations, pleasures, feelings and actions which we call sexual desire. It is these discourses which shape our sexual values and beliefs and meanings attached to the body. Sex is not some biological entity governed by natural laws but an idea specific to certain cultures and historical periods. Sex and how we make sense of it is created through definition and in particular the creation of categories such as heterosexual and homosexual, lesbian and so on.

Weeks (1986, 2000), like Foucault, stresses that sexual identities are historically shaped. He has been concerned with the ways in which sexuality generally and homosexuality in particular has been shaped in a complex and ever-changing history over the past 100 years. He cites his influences as feminists, lesbian and gay activists and Foucault. His hypothesis is that the sexual categories that we take for granted, that map the horizons of the possible and which seem so 'natural' and secure and inevitable, are actually historical and social labels. He has stressed that it is important to study the history of sexuality in order to understand the range of possible identities, based on class, ethnicity, gender and sexual preference. He argues it is reductionalist to reduce the complexities of reality to an essentialist biological truth. Sexual identity is not achieved just by an act of individual will or discovered in the recesses of the soul.

Several feminists of different persuasions have questioned those feminist analyses of sexuality, which they feel have portrayed women as simply disempowered sexual victims (Segal 1994; Roiphe 1994). Some have argued that women can be empowered agents of heterosexual desire and have claimed that it is misleading to distinguish between male sexuality as simply and always exploitative and female sexuality as inevitably passive. Indeed such a distinction has been identified as reinforcing traditional discourses of women's sexual being as asexual. To deny female heterosexual pleasure comes full circle and presents women as somehow more pure and virtuous sexually than men by nature. To stress sexuality as a form of social control has meant a neglect of its pleasures (Vance 1992). Segal (1994) stresses that women in heterosexual relationships may have ambiguous relationships with men and with their sexual identity. Yet to acknowledge this should not lead to a denial of pleasure for all women. There has been limited examination of female desire and pleasure. Feminism should present a space for women to explore their sexuality rather than feel policed and restricted. These different positions on female heterosexuality have led to various disagreements between feminists.

Some theorists have revisited certain forms of erotic expression, for example the consumption of pornogra... and sado-masochistic practices, which had prev... been dismissed by many feminists as male-defi... of sexual expression. Competing analyses b... identifying these as potential areas of ... pleasure and spaces for women to e... (Assiter and Avendon 1993). (Se... debates about female sexuality...

Both heterosexuality a... social constructions. So...

there is no essential homosexual experience, that gay history is complex and the experience of being homosexual varies. Indeed the use of the term 'homosexual' to describe a certain type of person is a relatively recent phenomenon (Foucault 1977; Weeks 1990, 1991b, 2000); in many historical periods a woman who had sex with another woman would not think of herself or be regarded as lesbian.

A closer look

As Jeffrey Weeks (2000: 239) notes, despite the New Right Political concern (in both the UK and America) with social authoritarianism on moral issues which led to real setbacks for a more humane and tolerant order, the 1990s [and 2000s] have seen 'a recognition of the importance of the freedom of individuals to choose their own ways of being' influenced not least by the lesbian and gay politics of the past 35 years. Yet, despite shifts in attitudes towards gay men, lesbians and bisexuals, 'sexual citizenship' is still not equally experienced by all (Bell and Binnie 2000). As Davina Cooper notes:

'Heterosexual demonstrations are so naturalized they remain unapparent – wearing wedding/engagement rings, talking about marriage/honeymoons/dating, kissing/holding hands in public places. However, analogous signifiers of sexuality by lesbians and gay men, lacking a naturalized status, remain highly visible, and are constructed as flaunting.'

(Cooper 1998: 133)

Stop and think

➤ In your own family (of origin or partnership), who does the majority of the housework and childcare and who maintains relationships with family and friends and buys and writes cards for birthdays and religious festivals?

➤ What does this tell you about women's and men's roles within the family?

A closer look

'Doing gender'

'Sociologists have suggested that gender should be seen not as a set of static attributes and behaviour, but in terms of a process – 'doing gender' – where an individual's gender is continually being re-established, sustained, or modified . . . 'Doing gender' will involve displaying the emotional skills, capacities and propensities to do emotion work in a manner appropriate to the chosen gender ideology' (Duncombe and Marsden 1998: 218).

In her study of marriage Hochschild (1990: 44–66) argues that women are forced to live the family myth because of the continued gender imbalance of power in marital relationships and writes that whether women's emotion work is seen as 'a matter of denial . . . [or as] intuitive genius', it 'is often all that stands between . . . a wave of broken marriages'.

Love and marriage

In his book *The Transformation of Intimacy* (1992a) Giddens suggests that equalization in men's and women's

mplications
en women
es empirical
that men
artnerships;
e concern-
child care
Drawing on
(1998: 211)
long-term
themselves
image that

279

However, recent studies suggest that there might be individual variations among men and women and how they do emotion work (e.g. Duncombe and Marsden 1998) and despite continuing inequalities in both the private and the public spheres it is now more acceptable for women and even expected (at least in the West) that they maintain a public identity independent of home and family.

Sexual desire and gender

The work of Foucault, although recognized as very important by feminists, has been criticized for not paying enough attention to the way gender influences sexual

World in focus

'Cyber-chattels' and 'Maid to order'

Opportunities for independence for women have implications for intimate relationships and for relationships between women and men. Differences between women are relevant here with income, ethnicity and country of origin all being relevant to one's life chances and opportunities as the following examples indicate.

Cyber-chattels: buying brides and babies on the net

Those seeking a bride are offered a 'choice of women' who, according to Scholes (1999), can be 'broken down' into four categories – Asia, Latin, multi-ethnic and Soviet-based. Yet, by 2002, other regions of the world such as Africa had been added to the list. Prospective buyers are warned of the extra financial outlay attached to women of certain nationalities: 'Whereas a Thai is unprepared for cold German winters – one has to buy her clothes – a Pole brings her own boots and fur coat. And she is as good in bed and as industrious in the kitchen' (Scholes 1999: 168).

The popular discourse surrounding men who buy brides is that they are pathetic and inadequate, unable to attract a woman by the more accepted routes of Western courtship. However, Jedlicka's study of American men seeking mail-order brides found that 94 per cent of the men were white and 50 per cent were college educated. Most were economically and professionally successful, with 64 per cent earning more than $20,000 a year and 42 per cent in professional or managerial positions (Jedlicka 1988, cited in Glodava and Onizuka

1994). So, stereotypically at least, it appears that these men were likely to be 'eligible' to women in their own communities and country . . . [Thus] it is possible to argue that the issue is not whether the men themselves are appropriate husband material but . . . that they themselves have rejected contemporary Western marriage and partnerships.

Popular discourses surrounding women who offer themselves as brides are frequently judgmental and disapproving, often positioning the women as victims of their husbands and agencies. However, rather than viewing all women on mail-order Internet sites as victimized and exploited, it is possible to argue that, for some, seeking such a match may be an act of agency. Admittedly it may be interpreted as an act of limited agency, for truly free women would not need to seek such a marriage, but it may be the only kind of agency available to women who are entrapped in social and economic structures which limit their life opportunities. Evidence from the USA supports the conclusion that women are seeking improved life chances by offering themselves on 'bride' sites, for they 'for the most part come from places in which jobs and educational opportunities for women are scarce and wages low' (US Government Report on the Mail-Order Bride Industry, at www.wtw.org/mob/mobappa.htm) (pp. 70–71) (adapted from Letherby and Marchbank 2003: 70–71).

Maid to order

'We scrub your floors the old-fashioned way', boasts the brochure from Merry Maids, the largest of the residential cleaning

services that have sprung up in the last two decades, 'on our hands and knees.'

In a society where 40 per cent of the wealth is owned by 1 per cent of households, while the bottom 20 per cent reports negative assets, the degradation of others is readily purchased. Kneepads entered American political discourse as a tool of the sexually subservient, but employees of Merry Maids, the Maids International, and other new corporate-run cleaning services spend hours every day on these kinky devices, wiping up the drippings of the affluent.

Housework . . . was supposed to be the great equalizer of women. Whatever women did – jobs, school, child care – we also did housework, and if there were some women who hired others to do it for them, they seemed too privileged and rare to include in the theoretical calculus. All women were workers, and home was their workplace . . .

One thing you can say with certainty about the population of household workers is that they are disproportionately women of color . . . Of the 'private household cleaners and servants' it managed to locate in 1998, the Bureau of Labor Statistics reports that 36.8 per cent were Hispanic, 15.8 per cent black, and 2.7 per cent 'other'. Certainly the association between household cleaning and minority status is well established in the psyches of the white employing class . . . [an experience retold be Audre Lorde] 'I wheel my two-year-old daughter in a shopping cart through a supermarket . . . and a little white girl riding past in her mother's cart calls out excitedly, "Oh look Mommy, a baby maid"' (adapted from Ehrenreich 2002: 85–92).

desire and identity. Many researchers have argued that men and women have different attitudes to sex and relationships. Shere Hite (1981; 1993) has examined men and women's sexual behaviour and attitudes to sex. She claimed that although men were diverse in their feelings, attitudes and sexual experience, they were more likely than women to claim that their sense of self-identification was gained through sex.

Male sexuality: power and anxiety

Brittan (1989) proposes that in masculine ideology real men are heterosexual, sexually active, initiators of sexual relations and have a powerful sex drive. Many theorists have argued that men's sexual identity is in some way shaped by masculine ideology. Sexuality has been defined

Case study

Dominant masculinity and rape

Since the mid-1970s feminists have drawn attention to the high levels of violence that women experience at the hands of men. Kelly (1988) found that most women have experienced some form of sexual violence; she identified a continuum of violence, from verbal harassment to rape and murder, which she argues acts to instil fear and control women.

To explain rape feminists have turned their attention to the broader context of unequal gender relations, the social construction of masculinity and a culture which condones violence against women. Some theorists have directly linked the construction of dominant masculinity and male sexuality to violence against women, including rape (Radford *et al.* 1995). The view that, for men, sexual expression is linked to conquest and maintaining power and control has been utilized to understand the violence women experience from men. A recurring theme in the analysis of male sexuality is that as part of their socialization men learn to separate sex from emotion, that they must be dominant in sexual relations and that they learn to see women as sexual objects to please men.

Rape is understood as an act which exerts power over and controls and disempowers the victim. Rape acts to keep women in their place. A key point Brownmiller (1976) made was that rape is not purely a sexual act, where the rapist derives sexual pleasure, but an act of power designed to control and humiliate. In this type of approach rape is not a biological drive or a purely sexually motivated act it is an act of aggression and hostility and it flourishes where cultures encourage it (Scully 1990; Russell 1990).

Feminists have also pointed out that in many cultures women are sexually objectified and this objectification has been crucial in the legitimization of the sexual abuse of women by men. The ability to distance oneself from the person involved in the sexual encounter, to objectify the other person, to ignore the needs of the other and meet one's own desires are key features of an abusive relationship. John Stolenberg identifies objectification as part of the process that leads to violence:

The depersonalization that begins in sexual objectification is what makes violence possible for once made a person a thing, you can do anything to it you want.

(Stolenberg 1990: 59)

Tim Newburn and Elizabeth Stanko (1994a) argue that men not only victimize women but they also victimize each other; thus it is necessary to consider the experience of men as victims of sexual violence (including rape) as well as oppressors.

This focus on violence emphasizes male sexuality as a source of power. However, some researchers point out that male sexual identity is diverse and to reduce male sexual activity purely to an expression of power and control is simplistic and universalizes male experience. Sex can have a range of meanings for men, including anxiety (Seidler 1991).

Questions

1. *Violence against women is often considered to be 'women's own fault'. Why do you think this is the case?*

2. *What sort of so-called inappropriate behaviour by women is cited in these cases?*

as important to male gender identity because within this ideology genital sex has been a way of confirming masculinity. For Metcalf and Humphries (1985) this identity involves performance and conquest as sex becomes another area in which men feel that they have to prove themselves. Seidler (1989) suggests that if a man has not had sex with a woman there is a great deal of pressure on him to pretend that he has had sex to prove his masculinity; sex and masculinity are inextricably linked. Seidler (1991) has stressed that the way men approach sex is often shaped by a dominant notion of masculinity:

men should deny their emotions and feeling within relationships. As sexual relations are often intimate, men fear losing control of their feelings and feel uneasy, and this may make them withdraw after sexual contact as a strategy to prevent emotions and feelings coming to the fore. Some theorists have stressed that for men sex is related to maintaining control, power and conquest. The key to being a true man in masculine ideology is being in control and exerting power; this applies in sexual relations.

Kelly (1988) and Daly and Wilson's (1988) examination of homicide reveals the use of men's violence to

Case study

Teenage pregnancy and parenthood

Although teenage pregnancy is not a recent phenomenon in the UK it is an issue that is receiving more attention than ever before. Young mothers are not only stereotyped as a burden on the state (see e.g. Phoenix 1991) but despite evidence to the contrary (see Phoenix 1991; Ussher 2000) teenage mothers are stereotyped as bad mothers and their children severely disadvantaged. As Kent (2000) adds in both cases it is the so-called loose morals of these women which is in question and in each case moral discourses are harnessed to define the 'competent'/'incompetent' and/or 'fit'/'unfit' mother. Arguably though it is not the age of the woman that is the primary issue but the fact that younger pregnant girls/woman are more likely to give birth outside marriage. Hollway (1994) suggests that the *Male Sex Drive* discourse and the *Have/Hold* discourse each affect the dominant views of young unmarried mothers. The *Male Sex Drive* discourse implies

that men have biological urges and women's sexual needs are subservient to this male sex drive. Moore and Rosenthal drawing on Hollway suggest that:

> According to this discourse, women who openly exhibit an interest in sex are considered to be inferior and amenable to exploitation, as loose women who deserve all they get.
> (Moore and Rosenthal 1993: 87)

The *Have/Hold* discourse on the other hand implies that sex is only considered appropriate within a committed heterosexual relationship sanctioned by marriage. The young pregnant woman/mother has a problematic social identity. Her bump/baby is itself a stigma and sets her aside as other – as 'inappropriate' – according to dominant sexual and political discourses. Even earlier than this young women may be sanctioned for their arguably 'sensible' choices. As Luker argues:

> contraception forces a woman to define herself as a person who is sexually active. Planning

specifically suggests not only that a woman has been sexually active once, but that she intends to be so again. A woman who plans is actively anticipating intercourse; in the terminology of the women interviewed, she is 'looking to have sex' . . .

If she is frankly expecting sex, as evidenced by her continued use of contraception, she need not be courted on the same terms as a woman whose sexual availability is more ambiguous. For many women, the loss of this bargaining position outweighs all the benefits of contraception.

> (Luker 1975, cited by Petchesky 1985: 218)

Thus, young women's experience of pregnancy and motherhood takes place in a 'damned if you do and damned if you don't' context (for further discussion see Wilson *et al.* 2002).

Question

1. How many negative st
   of young mother
   of? Are you
   in th

control their female partners across industrial and non-industrial societies. While they argue that the killing of women is relatively rare, the widespread use of violence is not. While men's violence to women is usually characterized as 'losing control' or flying into a 'blind rage', all the evidence suggests that both battered women and the men who batter tell the same story, that men's behaviour is used as a means of control. On the other hand although men do experience violent attacks by women this constitutes the smallest proportion of men's assaults and men are much more likely to be victims of physical and sexual violence from other men (Newburn and Stanko 1994a).

Female sexuality: pleasure and pain

A key feminist demand has been the right for women to have freedom of sexual expression and choice; implicit in this is an assumption that female sexual expression has been more tightly controlled than men's and that women have had less power in sexual relations. Although research in the 1990s suggests that young women are taking more control in heterosexual relationships and making greater demands, it seems that women and men are still caught up in power relations.

Many have argued that there is an enduring sexual double standard whereby men are judged positively if they engage in sexual encounters, whereas women are judged negatively. Sue Lees (1986; 1993) in her interviews with young adolescent girls found evidence of this double standard in the 1980s and 1990s. Young girls who got a reputation for 'sleeping' with men would be labelled 'slags', whereas girls who got a reputation for not engaging in sexual relations were labelled 'tight', 'drags' or 'lessies'. Lees argues that this verbal abuse not only demonstrates the ⸱ double standard but also serves as one wa⸱ ⸱ female sexuality. Karin A. Martin⸱ ⸱y adolescents have sex su⸱ ⸱nd that the teenage ⸱ ⸱ sexual intercourse ⸱ y had sex before ⸱ ⸱friends.

⸱ ⸱ ⸱ower relations
⸱ ⸱s and these
⸱ ⸱ exploited
⸱ ⸱ d a great
⸱ ⸱ntrol in
⸱ ⸱aginal
⸱ ⸱asm.

Some theorists stress that the way sexual relations have been institutionalized through heterosexuality has served to control and oppress not only lesbian, gay and bisexual men and women but all women (Rich 1980; Jeffreys 1990). For some individuals, heterosexuality and the social relations that accompany it (such as marriage) have been crucial to the persistence of male dominance. Other theorists have explored the complexities of women's experiences of both the pleasures and dangers of sex. They have rejected theories which define all women as sexually passive and men as sexual aggressors.

Representing gender: media and popular culture

In contemporary Western society media is all around us and is influential in many ways. Douglas Kellner (1995) argues:

> We are immersed from cradle to grave in a media and consumer society . . . The media are forms of pedagogy that teach us how to be men and women; how to dress, look and consume; how to react to members of different social groups; how to be popular and successful and avoid failure; and how to conform to the dominant system of norms, values, practices and institutions.
>
> (Kellner 1995: 5)

Sociologists have examined how gender differences are represented in the media and how the media have shaped meanings about gender and gender identity. Winship (1986) argues that women's and men's lives are culturally defined in markedly different ways; what we read or watch and how it is presented to us reflect and are part of that difference. Media representation is political because different groups have more power to produce representations and definitions which may serve the interests of those particular groups. Feminists have argued that women have had less control over cultural representation.

Some sociologists have approached the media as a site where stereotypes about gender, dominant gender ideology and gender inequalities are reinforced. Women are represented in a restrictive and stereotypical range of ways, as sex objects or in a peripheral or supporting way. The representation of women is determined by the 'male gaze': that is, women are represented in ways that suit men's interest and pleasures. Feminists are concerned that the cultural representations of women as weaker and less capable than men not only create barriers for women in many spheres of society but also justify and contribute to inequality. There have been demands for a wider range of representations of women of varying age, race and class, and for women to have a greater role in the production of media of all forms.

Since the 1980s the construction of masculinity in the media has received attention. Although men may have a greater presence in the media, some theorists have been critical of the narrow definition of masculinity in popular cultural forms and have considered how representations of women shape men's views and treatment of women. As well as being produced through social practices and relations, masculinity 'is produced through cultural and ideological struggles over meaning' (Jackson 1990: 223). Some theorists have pointed out that while it is crucial to examine the restrictive ideologies of gender constructed by the media, it is important to recognize that men and women are not simply brainwashed by the media but may resist, criticize and subvert the information and messages conveyed.

There has also been a shift towards acknowledging that people will read and make sense of media texts in varying ways. Various writers have argued that the media are not simply vehicles for patriarchal ideologies: there is space in the media for the 'female gaze', for women to express their viewpoints and experiences and hence resist restrictive stereotypes and present alternative images (e.g. Gamman and Marshment 1988; Ussher 1997). Popular culture does not simply serve capitalism and patriarchy, 'peddling false consciousness to the duped masses' (Gamman and Marshment 1988: 1) and the media can be seen as a site of struggle where many meanings are contested and where dominant ideologies can be disturbed. It can provide a site for alternative meanings; representations can be produced that are challenging and subversive.

Stop and think

> Can you think of television programmes or particular characters which provide identification for women and challenge sexism and gender stereotypes?

Magazines

Walk into any newsagent and you will be confronted by a massive array of magazines clearly targeted at specific audiences in terms of gender and age. There is a vast range of titles for women including both weekly and monthly magazines and the proliferation of titles has led to fierce competition between magazines. There are also several men's general interest magazines in addition to the more special interest magazines focusing on cars or sport, for example. In recent years we have seen the rise of the 'celebrity' magazine focusing on the lives and activities of well-known people and by contrast an increasing focus on the 'true-life story' in magazines where the focus is on the lives of ordinary people.

Stop and think

> List magazines aimed at the following social groups: (a) young girls/young boys; (b) teenage girls/teenage boys; (c) young women/young men; (d) mid-life women/mid-life men.

> What is it about the magazine that identifies it as being aimed at a particular group?

Reading gender: women's magazines

Women's magazines are often read for leisure purposes; feminist writers have argued that they should not be trivialized but approached as a cultural form which informs us about the social world and as such is part of relations of gender, femininity and inequality. Women's magazines and the role they play in constructing femininity have been interpreted in a range of ways.

McRobbie (1982) argued that girls' and women's magazines define and shape women's lives and expectations at every stage of their lives from childhood. Her research into girls' youth culture led her to examine the magazines that young girls consumed, specifically *Jackie*. Beauty, fashion, boys and pop stars formed the main staples of *Jackie*. Indeed this almost exclusive focus on personal romance problems, fashion and pop led McRobbie to claim that these magazines communicated the message that all else was of secondary importance to girls. The stories contained in *Jackie* focused on romance and emotions, with such themes as a girl must fight to keep her man, you cannot trust another woman and, despite this, being a girl and romance itself are fun. McRobbie describes an ideology of adolescent femininity, the most pervasive element of which was the focus on finding and going out with a boyfriend. She refers to this ideology as 'romantic individualism' and sees it as a powerful influence on young girls; the message in *Jackie* is that, although they may seek advice from their friends, girls are on their own in the search for boys and once they find a boy they can move away from the world of girls. She claimed boys are not exposed to this type of pressure in the same way and felt that 'This whole ideological discourse, as it takes shape through the pages of *Jackie*, is immensely powerful' (McRobbie 1982: 282). *Jackie* is no longer produced but has been replaced by several other magazines aimed specifically at teenage girls. Arguably the messages remain the same but the focus on sex is more explicit.

Some analysts have pointed to the similarity of images, representations and ideologies of femininity contained in women's magazines. Ferguson (1985) argues that magazines perpetuate the 'cult of femininity'; indeed she describes them as the high priestesses of this cult, which defines what it is to be a good and real woman. The magazines lay out the rituals, rites, sacrifices and obligations which women must maintain. Rituals attached to beautification, child rearing, housework and cooking are all part of this cult. Ferguson examined women's magazines from the 1940s to the 1980s and claimed that although the rituals change slightly, the cult of femininity remains fundamentally unchanged. Until the late 1970s the dominant themes were 'getting and keeping your man', 'the happy family', 'self-help',

'be more beautiful' and the 'working wife is a bad wife'. Ideal femininity was represented in the self-reliant, resourceful, domesticated wife and mother who kept herself looking good for her man. In the late 1970s and 1980s many of these themes endured but there was one new theme for the emerging 'new woman': this was 'the working wife is a good wife' economic activity was now compatible with femininity. There is, she accepts, some differentiation, yet overall the messages about femininity still fit within the same parameters. On the surface the range of messages and the roles and expectations have widened beyond the earlier emphasis on romance and marriage but to be complete and satisfied a woman is still expected to get a man and be a successful wife and mother. The magazines contain two conflicting messages: show the world you are someone yet at the same time ensure you are a good wife and mother. These conflicting messages are the product of socio-economic changes, such as women's increasing role in the labour market and changing attitudes to sex and marriage. Women's magazines do not just reinforce and teach women traditional and emergent beliefs about the place of women in society; the covert message of the cult is that there is

Case study

Mothers: the bad and the good

As Kath Woodward (2003) notes media reports often focus on mothers as good or bad, with examples of bad mothers including those who abandon their children, leaving them at home while they go on holiday, or who selfishly put the interest of their own careers before the care of their children. Woodward adds that fathers are rarely subjected to the same kind of scrutiny or classification as 'bad' parents in similar cases. In 2002 one mother in the UK was sent to prison for failing to ensure that her daughters attended school, although there was no mention

of a father. In addition women's magazines, alongside other Western media, frequently feature 'celebrity' mothers. As Woodward notes:

A variety of supermodels such as Kate Moss, pop singers such as Victoria Beckham (Posh Spice) and Jordan, actors, the merely famous, and several women whose pregnancies and births (predominantly by Caesarean section) are of interest because they are rich and occupy public media space are included . . . Magazines often run mother and daughter fashion features at Christmas time . . . The upmarket fashion magazines also feature famous women

such as Jerry Hall who clearly demonstrate that it is possible to retain the body of a supermodel after having four (glamorous, attractive) children . . . What is new is that the women are not otherwise very different from their non-pregnant or non-maternal selves in what they wear and in looking sexually attractive. Successful motherhood is encoded as 'well-off and sexually attractive' . . .

(Woodward 2003: 23–30)

Question

1. *What stereotypically defines a 'good mother' and a 'good father'? Can you account for the differences?*

a feminine way of being that all women share and that women are fundamentally different from men (Ferguson 1985). Kath Woodward's (2003) focus is on motherhood in the media and she argues that a new figure of motherhood emerged in the 1990s and that this 'independent' mother was an amalgam of previous figures of caring and working mothers. In addition 'independent' motherhood adds sexuality to motherhood.

Consumption dominates women's magazines, which are packed with advertisements for and articles on beauty goods, food ingredients and so on. The emphasis on consumption can be understood on two different levels. Winship (1986) proposes that in the 1950s women's magazines educated women about their role as consumers, a work which reflected not only their femininity but also their class status and the kinds of individuals they were. Women's magazines still provide this advice and take this role seriously, but at same time they are concerned with making money and with creating a culture of individuality. Advertisements tap into dreams and fantasies, and magazines make these obtainable via the purchase of a product; pleasure is increasingly something we buy. Winship suggests that magazines provide a whole range of pleasures to women: the quality and look of the magazine, identification with heroines, exciting creativity, peeping in on the lives of the rich or the troubles of everyday people.

Several theorists have acknowledged women's pleasures in consuming certain forms of popular culture and indulging in feminine behaviour. Women's magazines can act as both vehicles for dominant ideology and bearers of pleasures (Ballaster *et al.* 1991; Ussher 1997). Many women's magazines are popular because they do contain contradictory messages and these resonate with the contradictions of women's lives. A magazine may contain a radical article on sexual harassment at work but this will be set against articles which reinforce ideologies of domesticity and romance. Ballaster *et al.* stress that women's magazines must be understood as a cultural form in which definitions and understandings of gender difference have been negotiated or contested rather than taken for granted and imposed; in them femininity is something which is not simply fixed but something which is struggled over and contested.

Dutch sociologist Joke Hermes (1995) felt that many studies of women's magazines had not really let women speak for themselves; indeed some had denigrated women readers, presenting them as a brainwashed group in need of feminist enlightenment. She focused on the views of readers, exploring the meaning of the magazines in the

context of readers' daily lives. She identifies herself as influenced by postmodernism and sees readers themselves producing meaning rather than just absorbing it passively from the texts: each individual brings with them different views and a range of identities. Hermes carried out ethnographic research and interviewed 80 Dutch and British women about their experiences of reading a range of women's magazines; she analyzed the different ways women interpreted and talked about magazines, identifying recurrent themes or repertoires. The magazines enable women to explore their wide range of 'selves'. The magazines are used to 'learn about other people's emotions and problems, in other cases readers are more interested about their own feelings, anxieties and wishes' (Hermes 1995: 41) so women empathize with others and recognize themselves in stories and articles. Both repertoires 'help women to gain a sense of identity and confidence, of being in control or feeling at peace with life, that lasts while they are reading but dissipates quickly when the magazine is put aside' (Hermes 1995: 48). Although there are many different reasons why women read magazines, it is important not to overestimate their cultural significance. Unlike some feminists, Hermes argues they are not central to shaping gender identity. The most important aspect of the magazine for readers was that it blended in with other obligations, duties and activities.

Stop and think

➤ Compare a woman's weekly magazine, a woman's monthly magazine, a magazine aimed at teenage girls and a 'celebrity' magazine. How many versions of womanhood can you identify? Can you identify any contradictions between these versions of womanhood?

Reading gender: men's magazines and other media

Sociologists have commented on the role of the media in constructing masculinity. Easthope (1986) stresses that 'the masculine myth' saturates media and popular culture: 'there is a natural and universal masculine identity based on strength, competitiveness, aggression and violence.' He argues that men internalize these features and a key source of the conscious and unconscious process of learning masculinity is in popular culture. Within films, advertising, comics and popular music lyrics, men are presented as masterful, in control of both nature and women, physically strong and heterosexual. The action heroes of the late twentieth century and early twenty-first century seem to live out this myth. Although Easthope acknowledges that men do not swallow the image whole-sale, he suggests it is difficult for them to escape some influence on their gender identity:

> Clearly men do not passively live out the masculine myth imposed by the stories and images of the domin-ant culture. But neither can they live completely out-side the myth since it pervades the culture. Its coercive power is everywhere – not just on screens, hoardings and paper but inside our own heads.
>
> (Easthope 1986: 167)

In the UK *The Beano* comic has been popular with boys and to a lesser extent girls for many years. Easthope considers how two contrasting characters who generally appear in the same story, Dennis the Menace and Walter, communicate messages about desirable male behaviour. Walter is presented as very weak, soft, pathetic and 'girly', whereas Dennis is physically strong, tough and daring:

> Dennis and his mates keep getting into trouble; Walter and his softies play nursery rhyme games . . . The pairing of Walter and Dennis gives the dominant codes for masculine and feminine across a wider range of boys' behaviour.   (Easthope 1986: 31)

Gender analyses of men's magazines, apart from porno-graphy, are less developed than women's magazines; indeed it is only since the late 1980s that a modern group of general interest, glossy 'men's magazines', has emerged. Titles such as *GQ* and *For Him* contain articles on health, sport, fashion and personal care, women, sex and employment. Collier (1992) points out that the depiction of masculinity in these magazines has received little attention. He scrutinized them to see if their presenta-tion of men and masculinity depicted the 'new man', the caring, child-centred, sensitive man, so talked about in the media; he found there were different and contradictory messages about masculinity:

> the masculism of the new men's magazines involves two simultaneous and contradictory developments. On the one hand the rewriting of an old and familiar and traditional masculinity; and alongside this not-ably with regard to work, sexuality and fatherhood the development of a masculinity which in some respects rejects out and out sexism and seeks instead progres-sive, non-oppressive relations with women, children and other men.   (Collier 1992: 35)

A closer look

Unmasking masculinity

David Jackson (1990) considered the comics he read as a boy in terms of their role in constructing his masculine identity. In the late 1940s he avidly read *Rover*, *Hotspur* and *Wizard* and felt that they played a 'small but significant part in the ideological construction of my masculinity' (Jackson 1990: 223). Reading comics was his key leisure interest after playing football; indeed many of the stories focused on sporting successes or adventure. Characters such as the Cannonball Kid presented a win-at-all-costs rounded superhero. The comics contained lots of actions but few words; events took place in the public arena rather than in a more personal sphere. These comics appealed to young boys' fantasies about achieving 'a fully formed masculinity through physical strength and competitive performance' (Jackson 1990: 127). At the time he was reading these comics he was insecure about his masculine identity, disappointed at the frailty of his body and experienced bullying from other boys. Part of his strategy to deal with this was through the fantasy of the stories in his comics. What grew out of this was the striving to appear more manly that shaped his notion of what it was to be a man:

> Boys' comics prepared the way for a 'natural' acceptance of a striving, individualist energy and a single determination to win at all costs.
>
> (Jackson 1990: 240)

He found that paid work, material success and economic power remain fundamental to the 'dominant form of masculinity on offer by the magazines'. He compared the ethos of the magazine to that of the corporate busi-ness world. Issues of sexuality were up-front, explicit and humorous; in the same way that women's magazines construct conflicting notions about female sexuality, men's magazines express a 'deep ambiguity about male sexuality'. Men are presented as both sexually and emotionally vulnerable yet sexually powerful, in control and dominant. Many images of women in the magazines draw on the soft porn genre and present women as sex objects. The magazines celebrate a heterosexual mas-culinity. He found similar confusion and contradiction regarding fatherhood: the 'ideology of new fatherhood' present in some magazines addressed issues of shared parenting and represented men as active fathers. Yet at the same time masculinity is presented in terms of material and economic success, which he suggests relies on and endorses the privilege, hierarchy and material benefits which accrue to men. For Collier, there is a tension in the new men's magazines' depiction of masculinity. They have been informed to a certain extent by feminism and the anti-sexist men's movement but in the end

> the failure to address the need for structural change and their own reliance on higher earning advertisement revenue which produces a consumerist-defined masculinity results in a little more than updated version of the old man.   (Collier 1992: 38)

As with 'independent' motherhood it seems that ideal manhood is now linked with fatherhood (Freeman 2003).

Yet, some new men's magazines are not even attempting to redefine masculinity. *Loaded*, launched in 1994, is aimed at and presents the image of the 'new lad' and has one of the largest circulations for a men's magazine. It contains features on partying, including lots of beer drinking, sport (particularly football), features and interviews with famous 'beautiful women' and male heroes.

A closer look

Why every man should have one

The media has become flooded with representations of high profile men publicly exhibiting affection for their young children and explicitly promoting their self-image as 'good', involved fathers . . .

'Why every man should have one' (*Sunday Times* 28 May 2000), pictures the footballers David Beckham and Dennis Wise holding their babies like trophies alongside a strikingly intimate photograph of the British prime minister, Tony Blair, lying beside his newborn son. Such open displays of paternal affection are now commonplace, with newspapers and magazines presenting a myriad of visual and textual images of pop stars, actors, sportsmen and politicians proudly parading their offspring and making enthusiastic pronouncements on the virtues of fatherhood.

(Freeman 2003: 44)

Women are presented as sex objects and there are many soft porn images of women's bodies. Real men get 'loaded', 'shag' women and watch football. This magazine stakes out the bounds of a particular type of masculinity

World in focus

Advertising

In a perfect world, advertisements would be created by members of a particular society and consumed by the members of the same society. However . . . globalization has altered the process. Often the advertisements in foreign countries are created in American and Western styles. In addition, the creative people concerned often have received their training in American and British universities or interned in Western ad agencies, so the forms of representation, particularly of women, often take on globalized or transnational patterns.

Some of the main criticisms of women's image in advertising in developing countries are similar to those of the developed world:

1 Women are depicted as less intelligent and competent than men.

2 Women are shown as being servants to men.

3 Women are shown as objects of sexual pleasure.

(Consumer Association of Penang 1990: 80)

As one Korean author put it:

For thirty years, media have been taken to task for reproducing and reinforcing stereotyped images of women. Yet unfair representations of women in media prevail worldwide. Sex stereotyping has been so deeply ingrained, even glorified, that the women themselves have become desensitized to their own inferior portrayal. The prospects appear even gloomier as the globalization of media progresses

(Kyung-Ja-Lee 2000: 86; Frith and Mueller 2003: 234–5)

through features and advertisements. As Jackson Katz (1995) argues:

> Advertising, in a commodity-driven consumer culture, is an omnipresent and rich source of gender ideology. Contemporary ads are filled with images of 'dangerous' – looking men. Men's magazines and mainstream newsweeklies are rife with ads featuring violent male icons, such as uniformed football players, big-fisted boxers and leather-clad bikers. Sports magazines aimed at men, and televised sporting events, carry millions of dollars worth of military ads. In the post decade, there have been hundreds of ads for products designed to help men develop muscular physiques, such as weight training machines and nutritional supplements.
>
> (Katz 1995: 135)

In addition stereotypical images of women are also used to sell products to men just as they are to women.

Health

When speaking of gender differences in relation to health and illness the oft-quoted phrase 'women get sick and men die', still has some truth in it but it over-simplifies the complex relationship between gender and health (Annandale 1998; Miers 2000). Male life expectancy is less than that of women in all but a few Asian countries. In Western countries, however, the male mortality disadvantage has slipped and is relatively small at the beginning of the twenty-first century (Doyal 1995; Miers 2000). It is also important to reflect critically on the reasons for the differences that do exist. Women live longer, and their use of health services increases with age; and higher consultation rates over a lifetime would therefore be expected especially when visits related to menstruation, pregnancy, childbirth, post-natal care and menopause are taken into account. Furthermore, as Miers (2000) notes that women appear to find it easier to discuss their own health and may find it more socially acceptable to do so and Watson (2000) suggests that psychosocial factors, such as how men and women evaluate symptoms, are also important.

Stop and think

> ➤ List the words used to describe (a) a healthy person and (b) a sick person. Which of these words are used more generally to refer to women and to men?

Men and health

The main causes of lower life expectancy for men lie in higher deaths for coronary heart disease, lung cancer and chronic obstructive airways disease, accidents, homicides, suicides and AIDS (Miers 2000). Men are more likely to die of occupationally related illnesses, men engage in more physical risk taking than women, and accidents and homicides have always been a feature of masculine rather than feminine behaviours. In addition, cigarette smoking has, hitherto, been a major cause of male death (although in the 1990s male and female smoking rates in the UK began to even out), men drink more than women, and men are more likely to die of alcohol-related deaths (including those in motor vehicle accidents). However, men's higher level of exercise participation may counteract some of the health disadvantages apparently resulting from men's less healthy lifestyles (Miers 2000).

Arguably, the prevailing explanations for such differences, in both medical and lay discourse are that men's poor health results from their trying to live up to a macho image and lifestyle which is itself dangerous to health. From this perspective much ill-health among men is a consequence of lifestyle. However, as Watson (2000) notes, the challenge to change male behaviour and resist stereotypical masculinity is problematic because it presumes that masculinity is a unitary construct and that all men benefit equally from being male in a patriarchal society.

Women and health

Just as men's dangerous lives are thought to be detrimental to their health, women's mental and physical weaknesses are thought to be of major significance to their ill-health. Statistics suggest that about twice as many women than men suffer from a mental disorder. However, yet again, in reality things are more complex as there are distinctive gender patterns associated with different mental phenomena. For example, anorexia nervosa is a predominantly female condition and women report rates for anxiety, phobias and depression twice as often as men. However, substance use disorders are more common among men than women and diagnoses of schizophrenia, paranoia or mania do not show a gender preference (Doyal 1995; Busfield 1996). The labelling of an illness or a condition as 'women's business' has serious medical, social and emotional consequences for women as van Balen and Inhorn's (2002) comment on infertility (a condition that is often viewed to have its routes in psychological 'disorders' and therefore to be women's rather than men's business) demonstrates:

> women worldwide appear to bear the major burden of infertility, in terms of blame for the reproductive failing; personal anxiety, frustration, grief, and fear; marital duress, dissolution, and abandonment; social stigma and community ostracism; and, in some cases, life-threatening medical interventions.
>
> (van Balen and Inhorn 2002: 7–8)

Despite enduring stereotypical views of women as weak and helpless, work, both paid and unpaid, as noted elsewhere in this chapter, is a significant aspect of women's lives. Yet most research concerned with the relationship between work and ill-health has focused on male-dominated occupations. It is widely believed that female jobs are neither physically hazardous nor stressful but recent research into nursing and clerical work demonstrates otherwise (Doyal 1995). This sexist bias in occupational health research is further extended by traditional assumptions of women's weaknesses, reflected in the fact that, although a significant amount of research has been conducted to determine whether or not menstruation interferes with women's capacity to work, there has been much less interest in how women's work affects their experiences of menstruation (Doyal 1995).

Although we know that being a 'good' wife and mother can make women sick the hazards of domestic work are even more hidden. Evidence suggests that women prioritize the needs of other family members allocating them more resources and caring for them to the detriment of their own health, often because this is expected of them (e.g. Doyal 1995; Abbott and Wallace 1997).

Overall then although differences between male and female patterns of health and illness do have some basis in biology these patterns are more complicated that biology alone can explain (Doyal 1995). Sociologists accept the significance of biology; in addition they look for social explanations of health and illness. Thus, it is important not to rely on sexist stereotypes of 'male' and 'female' illnesses and problems.

Stop and think

➤ The front covers of the magazines *Men's Health* and *Women's Health* depict young, stereotypically attractive and physically fit people. What does this and the advertised features tell us about what health means to men and to women?

World in focus

Infertility

Although infertility is a global rather than merely a Western concern it is often portrayed as a 'yuppie complaint of little concern to the rest of the world' (van Balen and Inhorn 2002). In reality van Balen and Inhorn suggest that 'infertility' is:

> a global phenomenon with some proportion of every human population – estimated at 10 per cent on average – affected by the inability to conceive at some point during their reproductive lives.
>
> (van Balen and Inhorn 2002: 7)

Similarly, Doyal (1995) (drawing on WHO data) suggests that between 8 and 12 per cent of couples are affected worldwide and adds that in many parts of the 'third' world the incidence is much higher, reaching 50 per cent of the female population in some countries in sub-Saharan Africa. The experience of 'infertility' in Western and non-Western cultures is different too. As van Balen and Inhorn (2002) note, Western-generated high-tech 'infertility' treatments (and indeed other medical interventions to help achieve reproductive control) are unavailable to the vast majority of people in developing countries. In many societies ancient medical beliefs and traditions (which often date back thousands of years) are commonplace. Furthermore, these practices are often embraced by individuals in the West instead of or alongside scientific medicine:

> more than ten per cent report having used alternative medicine – including New Age healers, magical stones and crystals, religious amulets, and pilgrimages to places of worship – to overcome their childlessness (van Balen and Inhorn 2002: 10).
>
> (Letherby 2003b: 175)

Figure 7.3 An example of a men's health magazine

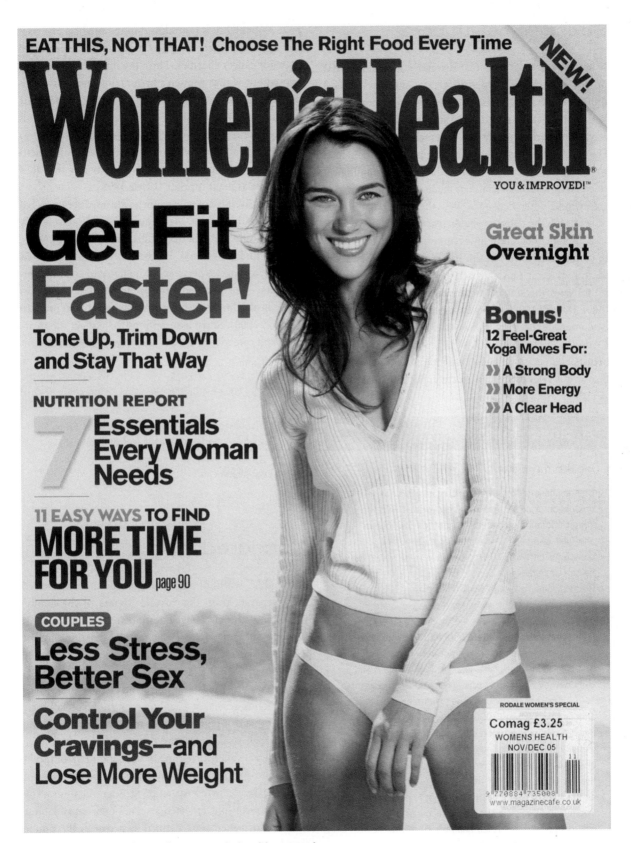

Figure 7.4 An example of a women's health magazine

Sexism in health care

It has long been argued that diseases and illnesses that proportionately affect men in greater numbers receive more resources than those that affect women more often. Writers now argue that it is not just that 'men's diseases' are taken more seriously but that male patients are too. Doyal (1998) argues that the continuing failure to include women in sufficient numbers either in epidemiological research or in clinical trials has made it difficult to investigate gender differences or to assess the overall significance of gender in the delivery of effective care.

Although men sometimes appear to find it difficult to communicate with health professionals, women seem to find it even harder, both because of their socialization and the stereotypical views that others have of them (Doyal 1998). One example of sexist treatment is women's experience of breast cancer. Wilkinson and Kitzinger (1994) argue that the cultural emphasis on breasts as objects of male sexual interest and male sexual pleasure is relevant within treatment. They suggest that

'page 3' mentality is reproduced in the medical and psychological literature, as well as in the material produced by major cancer charities. Thus, the implicit assumption throughout is that women's breasts are there for men's sexual pleasure, with the woman who has a mastectomy described as mutilated or disfigured. However, it is important not to assume that women are completely passive in health-care encounters as women (and men) resist and challenge treatment and behaviour that they experience as inappropriate (Coyle 1999).

Obviously, it is not only women who are disempowered by the health service. Male members of economically and ethnically marginalized or disadvantaged groups are likely to find it hard too. Furthermore, because of their reluctance to access services, white heterosexual middle-aged men – the 'so called' privileged group – are visible in public health literature but relatively invisible in practice (Watson 2000). Sexist assumptions then affect the treatment and care available both for women and for men.

A closer look

Health manuals

One response to sexism in health care has been the production of books that have been written with the aim of informing individuals about their own bodies and their own health. A number of them hit the bookstores in the 1970s (perhaps the most well-known being *Our Bodies Our Selves*, first published by the Boston Women's Health Book Collective in 1973) These were written by women and were grounded in women's experiences. However, as Hockey (1997) notes, these early texts were relevant mostly for white middle-class audiences. It was not until the 1980s that books aimed at black, lesbian, working-class and older women began to appear. There are less books even today specifically concerned with men's health although, as Watson (2000) notes, during the 1990s men's health was an increasing concern within the media with reports on increasing stress and incidences of cancer and declining fertility and reluctance to visit the doctor. In turn all of this has led to further debate on the state of men's health and what to do about it. One recent attempt in the UK to encourage men to pay more attention to their health has been the production of a men's health manual modelled on the car manuals produced by Haynes.

Stop and think

➤ Do fictional television programmes such as *ER* and *Casualty* confirm or challenge stereotypical beliefs of gendered health behaviour and experience and sexist health care?

Gendered labour

The 'public' world of paid work has often been referred to as separate from the 'private' sphere of the family, yet feminist theorists have questioned this notion of two separate spheres, arguing that gender relations in the labour market are related to gender relations in the family and household. For example, Garmarnikov *et al.* (1983) claim that domestic labour performed to a greater extent by women is crucial in enabling men to devote all their energies to a competitive labour market.

Although challenging the notion of separate public and private spheres, feminists have pointed out that the public–private dichotomy has had a very powerful ideological role in constructing gender relations. The public–private split reflected a sexual division of labour within which men were defined as active in the public world and paid work, and women were defined primarily as domestic labourers located in the private sphere of the home. Feminist theorists and male sociologists in the field of men's studies have argued that this division has had a central role in defining femininities and masculinities. For feminists it has meant that women have been excluded from, and placed at a disadvantage in, paid employment; for some theorists of masculinity it has meant a restrictive definition of masculinity. Historically, Western masculinity is defined by men's breadwinning role and men's relationship to the public sector. Morgan (1991) argues that employment provides a key site for understanding men; it has been a key source of masculine status and prestige.

Unpaid labour

Before we turn our attention to paid employment it is important to examine unpaid labour. Gender relations in the household interact with and shape paid employment. Throughout the world both women and men perform unpaid labour; a large proportion of this is domestic labour. Feminists have stressed that this labour is real work and can be taxing in ways that paid work is not. Oakley (1974b) carried out in-depth interviews with 40 London housewives. She found that women spent an average of 77 hours per week on housework. She applied the criteria used by industrial sociologists such as Goldthorpe and Lockwood (Goldthorpe *et al.* 1968; 1969) to the work performed by housewives and found high levels of dissatisfaction, monotony, loneliness and feelings of low status. Numerous studies have shown that despite some shift towards equality, women still perform an unequal share of domestic labour in the home and child care. Despite the claim by sociologists Young and Willmott (1975) that, as a result of more women going out to work, the division of labour between women and men in domestic spheres was changing with the family taking on a symmetrical form, much research reveals persistent inequality. Fawcett and Pichaud (1984) detailed the cost of child care to individuals in terms of time and found that the time cost was overwhelmingly borne by mothers. The Family Policy Studies Centre report *Inside the Family* (Henwood *et al.* 1987) found that women were still primarily responsible for domestic and caring tasks: although 50 per cent of couples claimed to share child care, women were mainly or solely responsible for almost three-quarters of all housework. Jowell and Witherspoon (1985) similarly found that women performed more domestic labour but they also found what other researchers have noted – a gendering of tasks.

Weelock (1990) examined in what ways the divisions of domestic work between wives and husbands changed when men became unemployed. The 30 working-class couples with children she interviewed in Sunderland, Wearside (UK) were representative of social and economic trends in the area, where opportunities for manual workers had declined but low-paid women's work remained relatively buoyant. She examined the relationship between economic restructuring and the internal dynamics of the household. She hypothesized that under such family circumstances, gender roles would change as men out of work would have more time to undertake domestic work while women, being in the labour market, would have less. She found substantial change with men taking on a considerable proportion of domestic labour in 20 per cent of households, some change in 47 per cent of the cases, no change in 13 per cent and regressive change in 10 per cent. She concluded that on the whole unemployment leads to a positive change in the distribution of domestic work as men demonstrated a degree of flexibility and responded pragmatically to the overall changing family/work situation. She noted that there remained a gendering of domestic jobs: some tasks were gender-segregated and others gender-neutral. Washing up, tidying up, using the vacuum cleaner and making beds tended to be gender-neutral; cooking the main meal and thorough cleaning were almost exclusively female, and washing clothes and ironing were done predominantly by women. Tasks with a managerial element like shopping and handling the household budget were done predominantly by women. Predominantly male tasks included gardening, mowing the lawn, household repairs and taking the rubbish out. Wajcman (1983) in a study of women who worked full time also found this: husbands perform certain domestic duties, but they are different from those that women do in that they are neither routine nor continuous but involve a few tasks, at intervals and often outdoors; female tasks are regarded as less skilled. Where gender difference between partners is not an issue, such divisions of labour are diminished: in her examination of lesbian households, Gillian Dunne (1998) found that most lesbian relationships were based on both partners working in the public sphere. As such, the responsibilities for home tasks were much more flexible than in traditional heterosexual households being based on principles of egalitarianism, especially when there were dependent children in the household.

Household and family responsibilities also involve broader caring obligations, particularly in relation to sick, elderly and disabled relatives. Women are the major

Case study

Food for thought

Despite the flamboyant male chefs who feature in many television cookery programmes, the *British Social Attitudes Survey* (Jowell *et al.* 1992) found that in 70 per cent of households women mainly made the evening meal, in 9 per cent of households men mainly did it, and in 20 per cent of households it was a shared task. Interestingly, 54 per cent thought that the task should be shared equally. Mennell (1992) suggests that men can cook but have more choice as to whether they do or not, and may do an occasional special meal, whereas many women have no option, having greater responsibility for the day-to-day family cooking. Cooking in our culture remains part of the ideology of wifeliness or motherhood. Women are expected to cook food which their partners or children like and hence adapt their food choices to suite these tastes. Research throughout the world has found that when food is scarce, women will often reduce their own portions first. In underdeveloped countries in which food is limited, women are more likely to suffer malnutrition (Wells 1993).

There is limited research on the gendering of food choice available at present; however, one contemporary issue that has received some comment is the consumption and non-consumption of meat (Timperley 1994). Among the three million vegetarians in the UK, there are more women than men (5.8 per cent of women as opposed to 3.2 per cent of men),

and young women constitute the largest growing proportion of vegetarians (16 per cent of teenage girls). Some theorists have linked this to inequality, masculinity and male dominance.

Meat to live

Even in the nursery, we are fed the image of the king in his counting house who consumes four and twenty blackbirds, while his queen dines daintily on bread and honey. So money, meat and masculinity are indelibly juxtaposed on impressionable minds. According to Carol J. Adams in *The Sexual Politics of Meat* it is an insidious method of perpetuating patriarchy: 'People with power have always eaten meat' . . . Meat is a symbol of male dominance. The implication is that by eating animal muscle, human beings increase their own muscle mass . . . During the Second World War, when meat supplies for civilians were strictly rationed, the per capita consumption of meat within the armed forces was approximately double that of the civilian population. An army marches on its stomach and its military puissance depends on that stomach being fed meat. Fifty years on the link between carnivorism and clout is just as strong. The Meat and Livestock Commission's multi-million pound 'Meat to Live' advertising campaign features athletic bronzed beefcakes exuding vigour and vitality from hoardings and the pages of lifestyle magazines. The unsubtle message is that if a guy wants pecs and sex, he'd better stick to steak.

Much of this is rooted in the tradition of man as hunter. And it follows that if man is hunter, woman must be gatherer. In other words, he brings home the bacon but she picks the mushrooms that accompany it . . . Women are as a rule more directly concerned with the purchase and preparation of food and with the health and well-being of their families. They have traditionally reserved the pick of the first class protein for their menfolk, which often meant going without themselves . . . Even the very metaphor of food reflects this masculine/feminine divide. Weighty topics are described as 'meaty' and are 'beefed up'; bravery is red-blooded behaviour. In contrast vegetables are dull, unexciting and intellectually improving. Quite apart from the positive/negative implications, there is an active/passive subtext: men as aggressors and initiators, women as passive recipients.

(Timperley 1994: 24)

Questions

1. In the extract on meat, which of the author's points do you agree with and which do you disagree with?

2. The preparation of food involves labour; does gender influence the preparation of food?

3. How is what we eat shaped by gender relations?

4. In the households that you have experienced, who has done the food preparation? How do you explain the arrangements in those households?

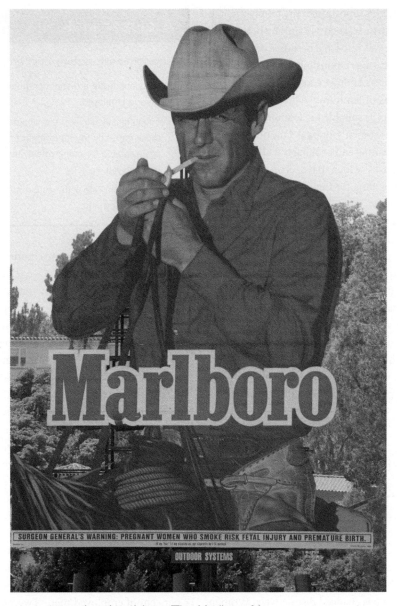

Figure 7.5 Gender stereotypes in advertising – The Marlboro Man
© Getty/John Chapple

providers of unpaid health care in the home (Graham 1984a); about 75 per cent of adults caring for elderly relatives are women. Finch and Groves (1983) argue that caring is central to women's lives. It is the medium through which they gain admittance into both the private world of the home and the public world of the labour market. It is through caring in an informal capacity (as mothers, wives, daughters, neighbours and friends) and through formal caring (as nurses, secretaries, cleaners, teachers and social workers) that women often occupy their place in society.

Other inequalities in the household have been identified in the areas of economics, decision-making and leisure. Pahl (1989) argued that the family is not simply a unit of consumption in which resources are shared equally; power relations exist which determine how those resources are allocated. Pahl found among the couples in her study that the most common model of decision-making involved women making day-to-day domestic decisions but men making the infrequent but important household decisions. Pahl points out that women may have control over household budgets but this by no means ensures them a position of power. Men's greater economic power was reflected in the greater share of family resources they received. Green *et al.* (1990) found in their research on women's leisure that men were still able to claim as a right a high proportion of the family income for their personal leisure use, such as drinking in the pub, while women's leisure was restricted because they still had greater domestic and caring responsibilities and tended to have access to less money. Another constraint on women's leisure were ideologies of femininity which defined only certain leisure pursuits as suitable for women.

On a global scale women's unpaid labour not only includes child care, cleaning and cooking but also involves a whole range of tasks which have economic value, such as gathering cow dung for fuel in Ladakh, India, or trading goods in Lagos. The UN *Fifth Annual Human Development Report* (quoted in the *Guardian* 8.8.1995) on women's economic status in more than 80 countries found that two-thirds of women's work and a quarter of men's work are unpaid and constitute 70 per cent of the world's annual global output of $23,000 billion. This research revealed that women work on average 13 per cent more than men, yet there are marked differences between countries. In Italy, women work 28 per cent more compared with 2 per cent less in Denmark; in rural Kenya women work 35 per cent more and in Nepal 5 per cent more. Women's labour in all its forms seems to be undervalued.

Paid labour

The sexual division of labour has changed dramatically since the Second World War; references to male bread-winners and housewives are misleading and conceal a diverse and complex range of social relations (Allen and Walkowitz 1987; Pascall 1995; Walby 1990). Pascall (1995) argues that since the mid-1970s women's position in the UK labour market has changed distinctively. Women have increasingly entered paid employment and by 2001 formed 44 per cent of the workforce, an increase of 1.5 per cent in the past decade (Twomey 2002). In the United Kingdom, 69 per cent of women and 79 per cent of men of working age are in paid employment, constituting a decrease in the difference between women's and men's employment rates from 14 per cent to 10 per cent in the decade from 1991 (*Labour Force Survey* 2001). This is not only through shifts towards gender equality but also because of economic restructuring: manufacturing jobs have declined whereas employment in the service industries has increased. Men have traditionally dominated many sectors of manufacturing, whereas women have been concentrated in the service industries, hence many of the new jobs created have been taken by women.

A closer look

Economically active and employed

Statisticians make a distinction between economically active and employed:

➤ Economically active = the whole labour market, those currently in employment and those of working age available for employment, though currently unemployed.

➤ Employment rate = the actual number of persons in paid employment.

These changes have led some commentators to argue that a 'genderquake' is taking place, that women are gaining equality at last and even that an emerging shift in power from men to women is taking place. Yet feminist researchers have argued that despite significant changes in the patterns of female and male employment women are still disadvantaged in paid employment compared with their male counterparts. These persistent inequalities are linked to the different types of work that women and men perform: men and women are largely segregated into different occupations. In the UK, women remain concentrated in a small range of roles: administrative and secretarial (24 per cent of all employed women); personal services (14 per cent) and sales and customer services (12 per cent) account for half of all women's employment, yet the same sectors only provide 12 per cent of men's occupations. In addition, women also work 'differently' from men and, despite restructuring, men's employment remains mostly in full-time posts while a sizeable minority of women work part time: 43 per cent of employed women compared to 8 per cent of employed men (Twomey 2002).

What women work part time?

In the UK there is a strong relationship between women working part time and motherhood, in particular the mothering of young children.

Age of youngest child	% of working mothers working part time 2001
0–4	67%
reducing to	
16–18	45%
Overall employment rate for women with dependent children	65.4%
Overall employment rate for women with no dependent children	72.2%

(Source: Twomey 2002)

The segregated labour market

Horizontal segregation describes the tendency for women and men to be concentrated in different occupations (Hakim 1979). In the UK in the 1980s, Martin and Roberts (1984) found that 63 per cent of women were in jobs done only by women and 81 per cent of men were in jobs performed solely by men. As shown by Twomey (2002) women remain concentrated in a narrower range of occupations and sectors of the economy than men, and tend to be the majority of part time workers.

Stop and think

> ➤ List six occupations you would describe as female-dominated and six as male-dominated. Why do you think these jobs are 'gendered'?

Beware: A note on statistical recording

Beware here the limitations of statistical records. Historically 'estimating the labour participation rates of women is fraught with difficulties given the discrepancies in census data available' (Marchbank 2000: 41) as often the part-time work of married women was not fully documented (Roberts 1988). It is impossible to quantify, but it is the case that even today not all family businesses record all members as working and for some women, and younger adults of both genders, working in the family business can be yet one more strand of unpaid work (Afshar 1989; Delphy 1984).

However, gender is not the only division in the labour market: paid employment is an area that demonstrates the interaction of gender with a whole range of other factors. Black feminists have pointed out that black women have had a different relationship with the labour market than white women; this differential positioning is the product of historical, economic and ideological factors. Whereas white women have found themselves excluded from paid labour and defined as domestic workers, Afro-Caribbean women, since slavery, have been seen as the 'mules of the world', capable of heavy work. Different ideologies of femininity have shaped the experiences of black and white women. Afro-Caribbean women have always worked, which is still reflected in their higher rates of economic activity. Phizacklea (1994) argues that labour markets across Europe are both gendered and racialized, even in traditionally female employment sectors such as home work. In fact, both men and women from ethnic minorities are less likely than white men and women to be in employment; in the UK this is especially so for Pakistani and Bangladeshi women. Comparing Pakistani and Bangladeshi women's rates of employment with those of white women showed that, in 2003, 72 per cent of white women worked while only 22 per cent of Pakistani and Bangladeshi women are similarly recorded (Hibbert and Meager 2003). However, when employed, men and women from ethnic minorities in the UK are no less likely that whites to work in managerial or professional activities (Hibbett 2002).

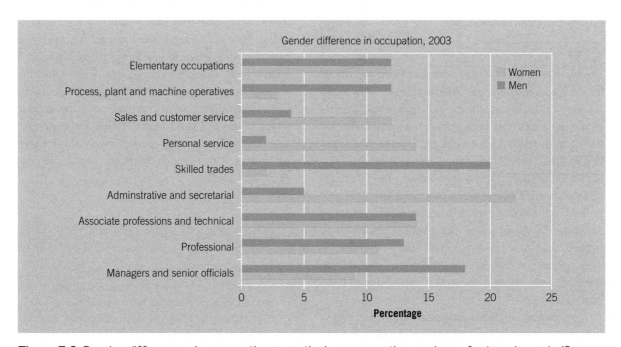

Figure 7.6 Gender differences in occupations: continuing segregation or signs of a 'genderquake'?

A closer look

Migrant workers

The exploitation of domestic migrant workers, which attracted some media attention in the 1990s, illustrates how gender, race and nationality interact. Migrant domestic workers, predominantly women from the Third World, come to Britain with families who act as their employers. They find themselves in a highly vulnerable position as the conditions under which they reside in the UK, laid out in current immigration law, class them as visitors and not residents. Tied exclusively to the employer with whom they came to the country, they have no independent right to work, which often traps them in exploitative working conditions.

Britain's Secret Slaves, a report commissioned by Anti-Slavery International (1993) and Kalayaan, which campaigns for the rights of domestic workers, found that they worked long hours for low pay and often experienced a range of abuses. In their study 89 per cent of workers were subject to psychological abuse and 33 per cent suffered physical abuse. If workers leave the family or the family discontinues their employment, they are classified as illegal immigrants and face deportation. With no right to work legally, illegal low-paid work is the only option. The experiences of these workers highlight the claim by bell hooks (1989) that to understand women's oppression we have to acknowledge the differences between women in order to explore the complex interaction of gender, class, race and the international relations of subordination and domination.

Vertical segregation describes how the division of labour between occupations is paralleled with that within them (Hakim 1979). When women and men work together in the same sector or organization, men are higher up the job hierarchy in better-paid, high-status conditions. Even in the twenty-first century we still find this vertical segregation: although women have broken into many male-dominated areas of employment they are still under-represented and virtually absent from high-status positions. The 'glass ceiling' describes the phenomenon whereby women are progressing into high-status professions but are not making it to the top jobs even though they are as talented and able as the men who hold those positions.

A whole range of disadvantages face women in organizations. Recruitment and promotion practices tend to operate against women. Even though, in many countries, it now violates equal opportunities legislation, some employers have continued to ask female interviewees if they plan to have children or marry or make decisions based on the assumption that they will and that this will affect their job performance. An Institute of Management Survey, *The Key to the Men's Club*, Coe (1992) also found that women in management make more sacrifices than men and that many women managers have opted out of having children; the image of the woman boss was still a stereotypical one of a harridan in tweeds or a vamp power-dresser in suit and stilettos. In the UK, at the end of the 1990s, one-fifth of men said they would find it difficult to work for a woman and gave reasons ranging from women simply do not make good managers to women crack under pressure.

Even where such outright prejudice is absent, there remain institutional barriers. The structure of work remains very 'masculinized', that is, it is based upon notions of male breadwinners who are free to work full time and who have no other commitments. However, there have been changes to working patterns to a degree: in the UK in 2003, 27 per cent of women and 18 per cent of men worked in jobs which allowed for some flexibility (e.g. flexitime, job sharing, term time only contracts, etc.), a total of around 6 million UK adults (*Labour Force Survey* 2003). Nonetheless, even when a greater degree of flexibility is legally provided, such as Nordic schemes regarding leave of absence for child care, patriarchal notions of gender are hard to challenge. In a study of Denmark, Finland, Iceland, Norway and Sweden, Kaul (1991) found that fathers utilize their rights to parental leave to a very limited extent: for many the reason they choose not to is a fear of jeopardizing their career, of being thought of as not serious enough about their job. In other societies, where no such provision exists, parents often have to find child care to cover them for long hours and work-based crèches are quite rare. While men too are parents the majority of those whose work pattern is determined by parenthood are women (Marchbank 2000).

Stop and think

> ➤ Is there any evidence to support the idea that if more women are in senior positions they (a) act as role models; (b) actively help other women in their careers; (c) bring new skills and approaches to their work?

Parent status, child care and pay

Across the world men have a greater rate of economic activity than women (see Figure 7.7). In the UK in recent years there has been a growth in part-time work, a growth that has been greater for men than women. There is a distinct pattern to men's part-time work, the largest proportion of part-time working men are either under 25 or over 50, due to most of them being either students or approaching retirement (Hibbert and Meager 2003). Unlike men, British women who work part-time come from across all age groups. There is a distinct connection between women's part-time work and their parenting status: those with young children are more prevalent in the part-time labour market, and this trend decreases with the increasing age of the youngest child. Of working mothers of children under five, 67 per cent work part-time but this falls to 45 per cent for those whose youngest child is over 16 (Twomey 2002). Given that only 32 per cent of childless women work part-time it is clear that motherhood is a major factor in part-time economic activity; conversely fatherhood does not seem to be a factor in men's reasons for working part time. White women are also more likely to work part time than ethnic minority women, showing that although ethnic minority women have lower employment rates overall, they are more likely, when in employment, to work full time (Hibbett 2002).

Gender is not the only factor affecting employment patterns of parents: the nature of a society also has influence as does its employment culture and rates of female employment generally. A study of the European Union in the 1990s showed that in 1995, across the EU, one-fifth of all working mothers held a part-time job, yet variations existed: in both the UK and the Netherlands the proportion was nearer two-thirds and in other countries such as Portugal, Spain, Italy and Greece the percentage of employed mothers who held part-time posts was 15 per cent or less (European Childcare Network 1996). Yet employment cultures do not provide all the answers as it has been shown that the link between the rate of employment of childless women compared to the rate of the employment of mothers in any one European Union state is weak, that is, mothers' chances of employment are not always necessarily better in those countries that have high rates of women's employment and are not always poor in those with low rates of women's employment (Marchbank 2000: 82). A factor that does affect the employment of mothers is the availability of affordable child care and a greater range of benefits for working parents.

In fact, it has been shown that across Europe there is a strong link between the availability of public child care and the number of women who are mothers of under-fives and economically active (Marchbank 2000: 80).

Pay

In a capitalist society the pay that people receive is a measure of the value of their labour. Compared with their male counterparts, women workers get less for their labour than male workers across the world (see Figure 7.7). Focusing on the UK, the gender pay gap is overall 40 per cent, that is women earned 60 per cent of men's wages in 2002 (see Figure 7.7). This is partly due to the greater tendency of women than men to work part time. However, a gap remains even when men and women work full time: in 2001 the average gross hourly earnings of women were less than 82 per cent of those of men, an improvement upon 1991 when women earned less than 78 per cent of men's pay (Twomey 2002). This gender pay gap remains because the areas in which women workers are concentrated are paid less than those areas in which the majority of men workers are found.

These differences in pay persist despite the existence of legislation in many countries. In Britain, the Equal Pay Act was passed in 1970 and came into force in 1975. In its original form, it had little impact as there was evidence that employers deliberately introduced segregation by gender in jobs where there had been none before to avoid giving female workers equal pay. In 1984 the Act was amended to refer to jobs of equal value; it was hoped that comparisons could be made across jobs and many women performing jobs in which traditionally few men have been employed would come within the scope of the Act. While some individual cases have been won, problems with the legislation remain. Many women are unaware of the existence of legislation or reluctant to make claims because of the fear of victimization by colleagues and employees. More fundamentally, differential pay is related to the structure of the labour market and the Equal Pay Act has had little impact on this structure.

Explanations for gender segregation in the labour market

A range of explanations have been put forward to explain gender segregation in the labour market and specifically why women generally undertake jobs which are relatively

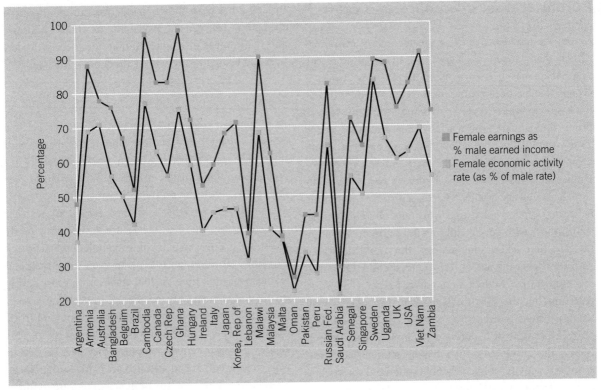

Figure 7.7 Gender differences in earnings and economic activity rates, selected countries 2002

low paid and which are perceived as having low levels of skill:

➤ economic theories;
➤ Marxist and feminist approaches;
➤ capitalism and patriarchy: the dastardly duo;
➤ sexuality on the job.

Economic theories

Sinclair identifies 'orthodox economic theories' as being influential because of the important role they play in 'determining the ideology and policies according to which the economy is run' (Sinclair 1991: 3). These theories focus on the supply and demand for female labour within the economy to understand women's position in the labour market. One example is human capital theory.

Women have less human capital than men; they get paid less because they have less skill and labour market experience as a consequence of freely chosen decisions to allocate more of their time to other domestic responsibilities. Women's work as carers of children prevents their acquisition of qualifications and labour market experience. Human capital theory attempts to explain occupational segregation as well as low pay: women choose those occupations for which their lesser skills will give the best reward

and in which they will be least penalized for their intermittent work patterns. This theory assumes that women believe that they will spend fewer years in the labour market than men. The occupations in which women are concentrated require fewer skills and have fewer penalties for interrupted work patterns which women choose to pursue. This is the type of approach to the labour market taken by the Institute of Economic Affairs, whose report *Equal Opportunities: A Feminist Fallacy* (IEA 1992) proposed that the Equal Pay Act and anti-discrimination legislation weaken the freedom of contract between employer and employee and undermine equality before the law.

This theoretical approach fails to account for women who have equal experience and training (equal human capital) but are not appointed to certain positions or fail to get promotions when placed against lesser or equally qualified men; that is, they ignore the evidence of sexual discrimination in the labour market. It also assumes that skill is an objective category, that there is consensus about what is skilled work and that all skills are recognized as such. Human capital theory completely neglects the structural factors within the labour market and outside that place women at a disadvantage in the labour market. It is to these structural factors and social relations that other theorists have turned.

World in focus

Gender discrimination not a lack of human capital

Julia Chambers discusses how different approaches have attempted to explain the changing labour relations in rural India.

One of the central ironies of changing labour relations in rural India has been the fact that though several field studies indicate that, on the whole, male rural labourers are able to transfer to NAE (non-agricultural employment) and also to demand higher agricultural wages from their employers, the same is not true of female rural labourers. Various studies have highlighted the very striking differences between trends in female and male employment especially following liberalisation (1991). While a large amount of both female and male labour was pushed out from rural NAE and back into agriculture after 1991, this was far more the case for female labour than it was for male labour. Some authors conclude that this sharp gender differentiation indicates poor rural women's lack of education, in relation to men. [Kapadia] . . . argues, however, that while this is clearly a major factor, there are more fundamental socio-cultural factors that lie behind both (a) rural women's comparative lack of education and (b) rural women's lack of employment opportunities in NAE, in contexts where rural men are equally lacking in education. In other words, gender-based discrimination is a very large part of the story.

Chambers quoting Kapadia, K. (2000), World Bank, Policy Research Report on Gender and Development, *Engendering Development*, Development Research Group

---

Phillips and Taylor (1980) argue that skill definitions are saturated by sex bias. The work of women is often deemed inferior simply because it is women who do it. They argue that we need to rethink the meaning of skill itself and that it is the sex of those who perform the work rather than its content which leads to its identification as skilled or unskilled. Skill is not an objective category, rather it is 'an ideological category imposed on certain types of work by virtue of the sex and power of the workers who perform it' (Phillips and Taylor 1980: 80). In other words it is a social construct.

Several feminists have noted that women's work does not get labelled as skilled because such jobs generally involve quite short periods of training, or use skills that, it is assumed, women learn informally within the home (e.g. cooking). Feminists have stressed that much of the work that women perform is an extension of the nurturing and caring work that they are culturally expected to perform in the home. Further, just as women are more likely to do the emotion work at home in intimate and familial relationships female-dominated occupations often include elements of emotion labour (Hochschild 1983). These sorts of skills are seen as natural feminine skills, rather than developed through experience. However, even work that entails long periods of training, such as hairdressing, still does not get labelled as skilled. Phillips and Taylor (1980) made the point that what has been labelled skilled is the outcome of a continuous battle between male craft workers and capital over the control of production.

Marxist and feminist approaches

Economic analyses such as that of Marx examine the ways in which men sell their labour and employers benefit from the surplus value of that labour. Despite a virtual absence of women from Marx's analysis many feminist Marxists have attempted to adapt Marxian theory to include the position of women. Various Marxist theorists acknowledge that women's labour is exploited and some suggest that this can be understood by considering how the labour market is itself split into two key sectors which provide very different experiences and opportunities. Barron and Norris (1976) identified two segments in the labour market:

➤ *Primary sector*: skilled secure work, good pay and working conditions, promotion prospects.

➤ *Secondary sector*: unskilled, poor working conditions, insecure pay, few prospects.

Employers segment the labour market as part of a divide-and-rule strategy to control the workforce. They utilize pre-existing social divisions based for example on gender or ethnicity. Women are concentrated predominantly in the secondary sector, easily fitting into this sector because they will work for less money as they are not so committed to paid work because of their domestic roles. Women frequently leave work of their own accord and are less likely to join trade unions, making them easier to dispense with; the social distinction between the sexes means women are demarcated from men and this becomes a useful way of dividing the labour force (Barron and Norris 1976).

This approach pays little attention to the role of men in excluding women from work and the role of trade unions in maintaining the segmented labour market. Dex (1985) argues that it is inaccurate as some women are employed in the so-called 'male' primary sector and also there are distinctions between women workers themselves. Some models have been developed which are more complex and propose a high degree of segregation rather than a twofold division, with many different labour markets arising as employers seek to divide and rule the labour force. However, feminists have been unhappy with this type of approach as it fails to take into account the fundamental effect that gender has on the labour market.

Marxist feminists also explain the experience of women in the labour market as the outcome of the capitalist economic system yet they identify the exploitation of women's labour as central to the functioning of capitalism and hence to the subordination of women. In much Marxist feminism the sexual division of labour in the family and family ideology have been seen as crucial in placing women at a disadvantage when they enter the labour market. There are a range of explanations proposed by Marxist feminism.

Marx had noted that capital accumulation required a *reserve of labour* to prevent workers from being able to bargain up their wages and conditions in times of increased demand for labour. Beechey (1978) applied this theory to women, arguing that they constitute a flexible reserve of labour which can be brought into the labour market when boom conditions increase the need for labour and let go to return to the home in times of recession. This type of approach has been applied to Western women's employment during the two world wars, when, due to the shortage of male labour, women were required and encouraged to enter the labour market, particularly in munitions factories, and to engage in trades which had

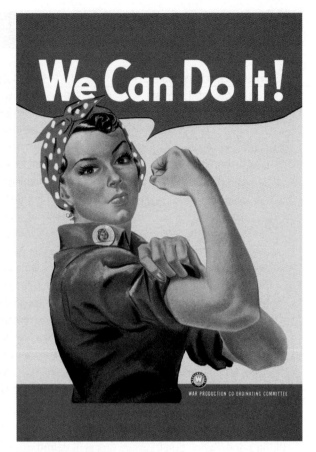

Figure 7.8 'Rosie the Riveter'
© Getty/Time & Life Pictures

been a male preserve. Images such as 'Rosie the Riveter' (in this case from the US) were part of the wartime strategy to encourage women to enter the labour market. Women were 'let go' at the end of the war to make way for the returning men (in some cases forced out by law), and governments were able to utilize ideologies about domesticity and motherhood, women's suitability as wives and mothers and the need for mothers to rear their children and also about men's right to work.

Marxist feminists generally have been criticized for focusing simply on the needs of capitalism and for paying insufficient attention to patriarchal relations and how these impact on the labour market. Hence the role of male workers and trade unions in constructing a gendered labour market has been ignored.

Cythia Cockburn raises this issue:

We can see that men and their unions do share responsibility with employers . . . Though they have sometimes paid lip-service to the idea of equal pay for females (as indeed most do today), they have never made it part of their industrial strategy.

(Cockburn 1983: 200)

World in focus

Women's employment in Russia

After decades of paying lip service to the principle of sexual equality, Russia has reverted to unashamed male chauvinism. Now the small but growing band of Russian feminists is having to stand up for their rights as Western women did 20 years ago. Thirty-nine million Russian women, about half the female population, have jobs, but so dire are the economic prospects in the newly democratic Russia that the position of women in the workplace is being challenged. Sex discrimination comes close to being official policy. Last month the labour minister, Gennady Melikyan, asked, 'Why should we employ women when men are unemployed? It's better that men work and women take care of children and do housework, I don't want women to be offended, but I don't think women should work while men are doing nothing.'

Small wonder that women account for 70 per cent of the 600,000 people so far registered as out of work, and that employers can get away with placing job ads that specifically discourage women applicants. Yelena Yershova, chairwoman of the independent Gaia Women's Centre, is furious with Mr Melikyan. 'If any minister in the West had spoken as he did, it would have been political death for him,' she said. 'But we will fight, because 10 million women in Russia are bringing up children on their own and have absolutely no choice but to work.' . . .

One of the public organisations which has the right to see and comment on draft legislation [is the Gaia Centre]. Ms Yershova, 59, founded it in 1990 when she retired from her job as an academic at the Institute of USA and Canada . . .

'I was impressed at how much American women have managed to achieve for themselves compared to women in the Soviet Union, where the laws on paper at least, were good. Now that is changing. Even the right we had we are losing.' Ms Yershova is particularly concerned about a draft law, which . . . would make the family, rather than the individual, the most important unit of Russian society. 'This may sound innocent,' she said 'but all totalitarian societies focus on the family, at the expense of the individual.'

Ms Yershova said she believes that Russia, with its increasingly influential Orthodox Church, could be heading down the conservative path taken by Catholic Poland. When it comes to sexism, Russian women are their own worst enemies, she admitted. Throughout the Soviet era they bore a heavy double burden, doing most of the house work while going out to work as well. Now in these times of acute economic crisis, they are under heavy pressure simply to survive. So it is tempting for them to surrender to men's suggestions that they stay at home.

Gone are the women railway workers and tractor drivers of Soviet propaganda, she says. Beauty contests, clubs teaching etiquette to wives of wealthy business men, prostitution, pornography are features of post-communist Russia.

(Helen Womack, 'Why employ women when there are men out of work? It's better that women do housework', the *Independent* 21.3.93)

Questions

1. How could you apply the reserve army of labour theory to these changes in Russia?

2. Why do you think some women have achieved greater success in the USA?

Capitalism and patriarchy: the dastardly duo

Some feminists have tried to understand women's position in the labour market as a product of both the economic relations of capitalism and patriarchal gender relations; this reflects a broad change of direction in socialist feminism. Hartmann (1981) argued that segregation by sex and women's low pay can be explained only by exploring the way patriarchy and capitalism work together to form a system which she referred to as *patriarchal capitalism*. The basis of male power in this social system is men's control over female labour, in both the family and the labour market. Segregation by sex in the labour market has secured male dominance and men's demand for a family wage ensures that men have higher wages and economic power in the household. She argues that men have organized via trade unions to exclude women from certain areas of work. Capitalist employers have benefited from this arrangement chiefly by obtaining women's labour cheaply in many areas of the labour market.

Walby (1986) has also taken a dual-systems approach but she stressed that patriarchy and capitalism are two separate systems which interact together in a variety of ways, and not always harmoniously as Hartmann proposed. Walby suggested that these two systems have conflicting interests over women's labour. Men dominate in the labour market but this is in tension with capitalist relations as employers are keen to exploit all forms of labour and particularly women's. Women's access to paid work on an equal basis to men would give women greater power and hence undermine patriarchy and male privilege. Walby identifies a pattern of struggles and compromises between employers and male workers and examines a range of historical and contemporary events to illustrate her theory. For example, she considered the Factory Acts passed in the late nineteenth century. Women were entering factory employment in large numbers and capitalists were happy to use their labour. Yet this threatened the patriarchal family. In excluding women, male workers and trade unions did not simply have the health and safety of women workers at heart but the dominance of male workers. Eventually a compromise was reached: women were excluded from certain sectors of the labour market, for example from mining in the UK. Although groups of women opposed this exclusion their voice was not heeded.

Cockburn (1985) has considered how trade unions have organized to exclude women from certain areas of the labour market. Her study of the printing trade found that historically the print trade unions have organized to resist women's entry into the trade and also how male workers via trade union struggle have shaped work processes themselves in a way that constructs that job as masculine. The workers felt that the presence of a woman doing a job devalued that job and she argued that the entrance of women into male jobs, for the male workers, disturbed the world as it should be, demarcated by gender.

Sexuality on the job

Adkins (1995) has argued that explanations of the differential experiences of women and men in the labour market fail to acknowledge the centrality of sexuality in the labour market. Her work, based on research in the tourism industry, has led her to explore how relations of sexuality are central in constructing women and men as different types of workers. She argues that feminists have concentrated on how women's labour is controlled through women's exclusion from jobs and wages or via segregation within jobs. All gender divisions in the labour market are seen to stem from this control: capitalism structures jobs into a hierarchy and then patriarchal control of women's labour restricts women's access to these jobs. Adkins argues that the hierarchy itself 'is intrinsically structured by patriarchal relations' and that the labour market is more gendered than dual-systems approaches suggest.

The labour market is not only a site of inequality but also a site where meanings about gender and sexuality are constructed. Adkins noted that jobs in hotels were gender-segregated, with positions such as receptionists and housekeepers being performed by women and porters and kitchen hands by men. Yet she also points out that the job specifications for posts at the hotel provided by personnel not only demonstrated this segregation but laid out certain qualities which were expected for 'female' and 'male' posts. Occupations in which women were concentrated required similar specifications; one specification that was not requested for male posts was 'attractiveness'.

Stop and think

➤ What are the key differences in qualities required for 'female' and 'male' jobs? Why are these different?

Adkins argues that the control of women's labour in tourism involves sexuality and the compulsion for women to be what she refers to as 'sexual workers'. Women and men may do the same job, but they are different kinds of workers, as women's work involves 'sexual servicing':

> Men and women were constituted as different kinds of workers within these workplaces even when they were located in the same job. To be workers women had to be 'attractive workers' and carry out forms of sexualized work, whereas men did not have to do this. Thus . . . women not only took orders, served food and drinks and cleared tables, they (and only they) also provided sexual servicing for men, both customers and co-workers. Women were thus not only 'economically productive' but also sexually productive workers. The fact that it was only women who were required to carry out sexual servicing as a condition of their employment shows that men and women participated in the two workplaces with substantially different relations of production.
>
> (Adkins 1995: 147)

Adkins describes the gender relations at 'Funland' to illustrate her notion of sexual servicing work. The majority of female staff were employed as catering staff or retail assistants, as waitresses, checkout workers or bar staff. Male workers were employed to run the rides as operatives; this role was defined as a male job because of its associations with strength and technology, although all rides were mechanized and repairs were carried out by a specialized repair team. The only women operatives were on the children's rides; these were young women who had been perceived as more 'butch'. Catering staff were predominantly female and were expected to present themselves in a particular way; there was an explicit feminine look with 'feminine' make-up which the female workers were expected to adopt. Some male catering staff had been sacked for reasons of hygiene but none had lost his job for simply not appearing the right way, as had happened to female staff. Adkins argues that this is part of the service women workers provide. Female bar staff found themselves allocated a uniform which they had to wear, including a short skirt, and the bar manager told the women they had to wear their blouses off their shoulders. Hence they were

Case study

Masculinity and the military

David Morgan (1994b) points out that meanings about femininity and masculinity in the labour market are not uniform. Focusing on masculinity he argues that there are a range of meanings within organizations and in different occupations. The military is an example where masculinity is most directly 'constructed, reproduced and deployed'. The warrior/soldier is a key symbol of masculinity and is associated with

aggression, courage, a capacity for violence, and, sometimes, a willingness for sacrifice. The uniform absorbs individualities into a generalized

and timeless masculinity while also connoting a control of emotion and a subordination to a larger rationality.

(Morgan 1994b: 166)

The organization is designed to produce a particular notion of masculinity; training entails the actual disciplining of the body, control, subject to danger and physical deprivation, and military culture contains entrenched sexism, racism and homophobia. Yet Morgan points out that even in this organization there is a complex range of masculinities. The military is a hierarchical organization: at different levels group solidarities develop, perhaps around race and class, and there may be resistance to official

models of masculinity and conflicts between masculinities. The increasing entrance of women into the military upsets the association of only the masculine with armies and the soldier. He stresses that battle and war themselves also provide 'the opportunity for the display of other characteristics more conventionally associated with the feminine than the masculine'. There is a whole body of literature which demonstrates care for others, fear and grief experienced by soldiers involved in war.

Question

1. *Consider how modern armies might deal with the increasing numbers of women in combat roles. What might this mean for masculinity?*

required to present themselves in a sexualized manner in a way that male bar staff did not have to. Adkins provides just one study of an organization which exposes how gender and sexuality are constructed in the labour market and shape the choices and opportunities of workers.

Increasingly, theorists are treating the labour market as a site where meanings about femininity, masculinity and sexuality are constructed. Some researchers have turned their attention to the ways in which female and male behaviour is constructed. Several researchers have considered how aspects of women's work require certain 'feminine' qualities, including the sexual attractivness of women workers. Broadbridge (1991) examined female sales assistants' perceptions of their work, experience of pay and working conditions and prevalent assumptions about skill and expected behaviour in a number of department stores in central London. She argues that the customers expect good-quality personal service, which may include product knowledge, submissiveness, friendliness and an attractive appearance. Shop assistants are expected to possess these characteristics, to dress in a business-like manner and to wear their make-up in a par-

ticular way, with more stringent expectations for women selling cosmetics. Broadbridge argues that these characteristics are fundamental in the construction of the female shop assistant as an essential ingredient of the consumer package. She argues that a sexual element also characterizes the relationship between shop assistants and customers. Sexual harassment of female assistants by male customers was frequently reported but the women believed that they had to grin and bear it. Expectations and responses to assistants vary according to gender, with customers tending to behave more respectfully to male assistants.

Stop and think

➤ Consider the different kinds of work in a restaurant, a shop, an office, where you are studying. What jobs are performed mainly by women and mainly by men? If they are performing a similar or the same job do they perform them in different ways? What are the expectations for female and male workers in these areas of work?

Summary

➤ The sociology of gender has been developed by feminist writers concerned with how gender differentiation has meant the subordination of one sex, women, who have been assigned certain gender characteristics and roles. Gender is socially constructed. Both men and women are gendered beings.

➤ Sexuality is also socially constructed, which has implications for the relationships between women and men and for the oppression of women and some men.

➤ The media have constructed meanings about femininity and masculinity and can shape people's gender identities. Some theorists identify magazines as a vehicle for promoting conventional and oppressive meanings about gender, others point to a more complex range of messages about femininity and masculinity. People read magazines in different ways and construct different meanings.

➤ Health is a gendered phenomenon. Health behaviour and experience is influenced by biology and by the social construction of masculinity and femininity. There is evidence of sexism in health care.

➤ Some progress towards equality for women, in the household and in the labour market, has been achieved but inequality persists. Gender ideologies still structure labour market choices and opportunities for women and men. The labour market is a site where meanings about femininity and masculinity are constructed and reinforced.

➤ Gender is a crucial social factor in producing adequate explanations of social behaviour and the organization of social institutions. Gender relations have been researched in all areas of social experience. This is reflected in the fact that many chapters in this book consider gender; and perhaps one day there will not be a separate chapter such as this one in sociology textbooks – if gender distinctions and divisions are eroded and gender studies becomes fully integrated into sociology.

Links

This chapter has strong links to Chapter 2 – the discussion of Marxist/feminist approaches, pages 303–306, and with the section on Marxist feminism on pages 75–77, while the section on Foucault and discourse theory, pages 279–280, links with p. 93 in Chapter 2.

Issues of gender and the mass media, pages 284–290, are also considered in Chapter 17, pages 699–702.

 Further reading

Anthias, F. and Yuval-Davis, N. (1993) *Racialized Boundaries: Race, Nation, Gender, Colour, Class and the Anti-Racist Struggle*, London: Routledge.
This book considers how race interacts with gender among other factors to shape social experience. It summarizes black feminist criticisms of much feminist theory and explores the relationship between gender, race, class and nation.

Brod, H. and Kaufman, M. (eds) (1994) *Theorizing Masculinity*, London: Sage.
This collection of papers, written by some key writers on masculinity, spans a range of diverse topics which include a variety of approaches to theorizing masculinity.

Cosslett, T., Easton, A. and Summfield, P. (1996) *Women, Power and Resistance: An Introduction to Women's Studies*, Buckingham: Open University Press.
A clear introduction to contemporary research and directions in women's studies.

Jackson, S. and Scott, S. (eds) (1996) *Feminism and Sexuality: A Reader*, Edinburgh: Edinburgh University Press.
A collection of readings from a range of feminist writers concerning key debates about sexuality that have preoccupied contemporary feminists. Each reading is placed in the broader context of relevant feminist debates on sexuality.

Kimmel, M.S. and Messner, M.A. (2004) *Men's Lives*, 6th edn, Boston and New York: Pearson.
A collection of articles focusing on men's lives (particularly in the US) in both public and private spheres. Topics include boyhood, family life, sexuality, health, the media.

Richardson, D. and Robinson, V. (1997) *Introducing Women's Studies: Feminist Theory and Practice*, 2nd edn, London: Macmillan.
A comprehensive introductory text with chapters on a wide range of areas of women's experience, including feminist theory, education, history, motherhood, health, work, family, representation and popular culture, sexuality and violence. Each chapter outlines and summarizes key research, debates and theories.

Sharpe, S. (1994) *Just Like a Girl*, 2nd edn, Harmondsworth: Penguin.
An updated version of Sharpe's 1976 study of how girls learn to be women, this text provides an insight into the social construction of femininity and the changing experience of growing up female in Britain.

Walby, S. (1990) *Theorizing Patriarchy*, Oxford: Blackwell.
As well as developing her own feminist analysis of gender relations and women's subordination, Walby reviews a range of approaches to gender relations and divisions in paid employment, household production, the state, culture, violence and sexuality.

Weeks, J. (2000) *Making Sexual History*, Cambridge: Polity.
A detailed consideration of the rethinking of sexuality by historians and sociologists.

Williams, C.L. and Stein, A. (2002) *Sexuality and Gender: A Blackwell Reader in Sociology*, Oxford: Blackwell.

 Web sites

www.library.wisc.edu/libraries/WomensStudies
This site provides an extensive list of resources relevant to issues concerning gender and women's studies; it also includes brief notes on those resources. It also provides links to relevant magazines, newspapers and women's organizations.

www.sosig.ac.uk
An entry portal to many issues and topics.

Activities

Activity 1

Women's and men's magazines

Select three or more magazines – at least one that is seen as a woman's magazine and one as a man's (and you might include one magazine you have read and one you have never looked at).

Questions

1. What does the title communicate? What about the cover?

2. Look at the checklist below – what topics does the magazine feature?

Beauty/make-up/personal grooming	People (a) ordinary (b) celebrities
Fashion	Paid work/careers
Fitness	Parenting
DIY and home décor	Sport
Cookery/food	Offers/competitions
Politics and social issues	Fiction
Feminism and women's rights	Holidays/travel
Personal relationships	Consumer items
Sex	Sewing/craft work
Others (please list)	

3. What written style does the magazine adopt – chatty, racy, investigative or serious?

4. To what type of reader do you think the magazine is addressed? (Consider age, socio-economic status, etc.)

5. What would you say are the key interests and concerns of the people who read the selected magazines?

6. What messages about femininity and masculinity are communicated in this magazine? Is there one particular ideology that you can identify or are there varying discourses about femininity and masculinity?

7. Carry out an interview with a woman and a man who read one of the magazines. Why do they read it? Do they agree with all the features? Are they critical of any aspects of the magazine?

Activity 2

Personalizing gender

Write your own autobiography focusing on gender relations and how they have affected your life.

Among other areas and aspects of your life you might consider (a) relations with and between family members; (b) the importance of gender relations at significant stages of or events in your life – births, weddings, going to new schools, joining clubs, starting work and so on.

Question

1. How did gender influence your schooling, the jobs you have done or are hoping to do, your leisure pursuits – what you do and what you would like to do?

Chapter 8

Race

The irony of 'race theories' is that they arise almost invariably from a desire to mould others'
actions rather than to explain facts.

(Barzun 1937: 284)

Key issues

➤ What are the main sociological theories of
race and racism?

➤ How have notions of ethnicity and
nationalism helped to reproduce and maintain
racial divisions and inequalities?

➤ How do the employment, housing and
educational experiences of ethnic minorities
differ from those of the white population in
Britain? What explanations are there for such
differences?

➤ How does policing of black communities
differ from policing of white communities?

Introduction

Imagine a world in which people are classified and graded
according to eye colour. Those with brown eyes enjoy
proportionately better housing, employment conditions,
education and social status. Those with blue eyes are
frequently, though not exclusively, marginalized in political life, absent from high-status occupations, and are
portrayed in the media as problems that the brown-eyed
population has to, at best, tolerate. Blue-eyed people
protest about the treatment they receive from the brown-
eyed population but are disillusioned by the bias they see
in the institutions and political laws of the land; even
their protests are defined by politicians and newspapers
in negative terms. The situation seems hopeless, though
there are moves within the blue-eyed communities to
resist and challenge this discrimination.

Such a situation seems absurd and fantastical; no
society, surely, would organize itself according to something as trivial and unimportant as eye colour. Yet if we
replace the word 'eye' with 'skin' and the adjectives blue/
brown with black/white, the descriptions in the passage
start to take on meaning and relevance. Even when physical difference would appear to have little relevance in
defining the way that people are classified – for example,
with the Jewish population and with the citizens of the
former Yugoslavia – racial and ethnic prejudices shape
how we see, and consequently treat, other people.

It is a mark of the highly contested nature of the word
'race' that its status in social theory still remains the
subject of controversy. (Brah 1994: 806)

The treatment of people according to perceived differences of class, sex, religion or age forms the basis of much sociological analysis and debate and the concept of 'race' has long been recognized as an important factor in social interaction but one which is extremely difficult to define. Yet whatever the problems of defining such terms as 'race', 'racism' and 'ethnicity' (which we shall address later) there can be no doubt that the issues connected with these ideas have a real and profound effect on people's lives on a daily basis. They experience racist violence and discrimination, they have to endure racist taunts and to cope with a society in which they are often portrayed as 'other', as inferior, different, threatening, 'not British'. There is also a more positive side to 'race', a sense of identity and pride which for example might be reflected for people of African descent in the emergence of black studies. But it can be difficult to appreciate when people belonging to ethnic minorities often struggle to get a good education, a job or even adequate housing.

Modern Britain: identities of tradition and translation

Much of the discrimination which members of ethnic minorities experience stems from the prejudice that they are not properly 'British', but as Cohen (1994) illustrates in his book *Frontiers of Identity: The British and the Others* the construction of the British identity has been a long and complex one:

> Multiple axes of identification have meant that Irish, Scots, Welsh and English people, those from the white, black or brown Commonwealth, Americans, English-speakers and even 'aliens' have had their lives intersect one with another in overlapping and complex circles of identity-construction and rejection. The shape and edges of the British identity are thus historically changing, often vague, and to a degree, malleable.
>
> (Cohen 1994: 35)

This issue of national identity is not specific to Britain but can be found across the US, Australia, parts of Europe and the emerging Rainbow Nation of South Africa. In all these societies the issue of national identity gets confused with those of race and culture. In the early days of post-colonial immigration into Britain, for example, the response of the 'host' society was very much based upon racial difference as the basis for social exclusion. Racial minorities were defined and treated as something 'other than British' and in response identified themselves with these perceptions, as Black, Asian, Chinese, West Indian and so on. To put it crudely, if you were not white it was difficult to lay claim to a British identity even if you were entitled to a British passport and spoke English. Consequently many black people argued that if they were to be treated as different by the dominant culture there was no point in trying to be anything other than 'black' and began to celebrate this as a source of personal and group identification which also provided some sort of stability in a world offering few choices (African-Americans, Australian Aboriginals and French Algerians would share such sentiments). Such identities have been described as 'traditional' because they attempt 'to restore their former purity and recover the unities and certainties which are felt as being lost' (Hall *et al.* 1992: 309).

Over time, however, a series of changes have undermined the certainty of traditional identities; new generations are born and raised within the 'host' culture, individuals and groups become socially and geographically mobile, biological and cultural mixing occurs, globalization erodes the barriers between peoples and cultures, new patterns of migration emerge and cities become increasingly cosmopolitan and pluralistic.

Consequently the fixed and homogenous ethnic and national identities of the past are being replaced with a range of choices made available within a transitional and hybrid culture. This has been described by Robins as a shift from 'Tradition' to 'Translation' and is summarized by Stuart Hall:

> This (possibility of Translation) describes those identity formations which cut across and intersect natural frontiers, and which are composed of people who have been *dispersed* forever from their homelands. Such people retain strong links with their places of origin and their traditions, but they are without the illusion of a return to the past. They are obliged to come to terms with the new cultures they inhabit, without simply assimilating to them and losing their identities completely. They bear upon them the traces of the particular cultures, traditions, languages and histories by which they were shaped. The difference is that they are not and will never be *unified* in the old sense, because they are irrevocably the product of *several interlocking histories and cultures*, belong at one and the same time to several 'homes' (and to

no one particular 'home'). People belonging to such *cultures of hybridity* have had to renounce the dream or ambition of rediscovering any kind of 'lost' cultural purity, or ethnic absolutism. They are irrevocably *translated* . . . They are the products of the new *diasporas* created by the post-colonial migrations. They must learn to inhabit at least two identities, to speak two cultural languages, to translate and negotiate between them. Cultures of hybridity are one of the distinctly novel types of identity produced in the era of late-modernity, and there are more and more examples of them to be discovered.   (Hall *et al.* 1992: 310)

In her book *Mixed Feelings*, Yasmin Alibhai-Brown explores the consequences of such hybrid options by examining the experiences of British children of 'mixed parentage'. As the title suggests the response is varied: some interviewees positively loved the way they looked, others remained confused and a few wished they had never been born. In her chapter on identity, children of 'mixed parentage' refer to themselves variously as 'British', 'White', 'Black', 'Mixed-Race', 'Third Race', 'Brown Peach' and 'Beige'. One woman had even invented the special term 'inbetweeny' to celebrate her unique status. Brown concludes:

It is foolish to generalise about mixed race families or to impose strong but false categories on them. Debates about identity and family rights go back to the sixteenth century. What is new however is that we now have a critical mass of young Britons who see themselves as mixed–race and who wish to challenge many of the assumptions that have been made about them for four centuries. They do not wish to be labelled by others. They do not wish to be subsumed by others. Most of all they do not wish to be patronised by those who always seem to know their needs should be. This is why the identity and terminology has become increasingly important when the issue of mixed race is raised.

(Alibhai-Brown 2001: 124)

With regard to the issue of national identity, it is interesting to note that in the first survey of such attitudes by the Office for National Statistics, the majority of black and Asian people living in Britain now see themselves as 'British':

Four out of every five people from the black Caribbean community living in Britain described their national identity as British, English, Scottish, Welsh or Irish. Three-quarters of the Indian, Pakistani

A closer look

Colin Wong – Chinese, European, English or Scouser?

'My parents arrived in England in the early 1960s . . . from Hong Kong with three daughters, one son and their aspirations for a different life. They settled in rented accommodation in Liverpool, with friends and other family members living nearby, working long poorly paid hours in various jobs in local Chinese restaurants and shops.

'Growing up in a large family was bliss; even with all the usual sibling dramas it was tremendous fun. Being bilingual was the norm; we spoke Cantonese with our parents and English with others.

[At primary school] 'I do not recall enduring any of the name-calling that my working family continued to experience in the shop. Ethnic differences were never really highlighted to me at primary school, so I grew up just being me. Labels only started being attached once I reached secondary school.

'It was really only at that time that I began to consider my cultural and ethnic identity. As if overnight, the duality of my life became evident: I attended Anglican schools, yet my home life reflected Buddhism; I celebrated Easter and Christmas, yet my family also celebrated festivals such as Chinese New Year; I believed in God, yet I continued to make offerings to other deities; I spoke English but also Cantonese . . .

'During my teenage years it was difficult to decide on my true identity . . . I felt English, but adversaries would remind me of my differences to them . . . I felt Chinese, yet I had never been beyond the UK.

'However, on my first visit to Hong Kong for a vacation I felt instantly comfortable with the people, the place, the language and the culture. Within hours, I submerged myself as a 'local' although the real locals spotted my Scouse-accented Cantonese immediately! Strange, but whenever I visit Hong Kong, I never feel like a tourist.

'So – who am I?

When I complete Ethnic Monitoring Forms, I tick the Chinese box. When I clear Customs at the airport, I walk through the European channel. When I look in the mirror, I do not see a Chinese face or an English face . . . I just see plain Me.'

(Colin Wong is Associate Director of the Undergraduate ITT Programme in the Education Deanery at Liverpool Hope University)

and Bangladeshi communities identified themselves in the same way. Among people of mixed ethnic origins the figure was 87 per cent and 81 per cent in the 'other black' category, those originating from outside Africa or the Caribbean. They included many born in Britain and describing their ethnicity as black British in recent official surveys.

[The] ONS data [also revealed] only 27 per cent of people in Scotland described themselves as British, with the rest preferring to identify themselves as Scottish. In Wales 35 per cent said they were British and 62 per cent Welsh.

The ethnicity report showed the group least likely to identify themselves as British were those recording themselves as 'other white', including Europeans and Americans. Less than 40 per cent of this group said they were British, English, Scottish, Welsh or Irish.

Less than half the black African group and 'other Asians' originating from outside the Indian subcontinent or China gave that answer. The figure for the Chinese community was 56 per cent.

The ONS said: 'People from the white British group were more likely to describe their national identity as English, rather than British. However, the opposite was true of the non-white groups, who were far more likely to identify themselves as British.

'For example, two-thirds (67 per cent) of Bangladeshis said they were British, while only 6 per cent said they were English, Scottish, Welsh or Irish.'

(John Carvel, the *Guardian*, 8.1.2004)

Black Britons – hidden from history?

One of the most widely believed myths which has contributed to a climate of prejudice and discrimination is that the black presence in Britain dates no further back than the 1950s and postwar immigration from the Caribbean. In fact there have been black people in England for hundreds of years and in the eighteenth century there were as many as 20,000 who came as seamen or as the children, slaves and servants of returning planters and colonial administrators. Far from all being dependent on their white masters, a significant proportion were successful and independent, enjoying their own social scene in London of balls, parties and concerts (Gerzina 1995). During the eighteenth and nineteenth centuries black communities grew up in many of Britain's western seaports, especially those connected with the slave trade such as Bristol, Cardiff and Liverpool. Many black people fought (and died) for Britain in both world wars, as did Asians and Jews.

Case study

The wonderful adventures of Mary Seacole

Mary Jane Seacole (née Grant) was born in Kingston, Jamaica, in 1805 of a Scottish father and a Jamaican mother. During her Jamaican upbringing she acquired the knowledge of traditional Creole medicine which had evolved from the herbal medicine that slaves had brought with them from Africa. In the boarding house which her mother ran Mary developed her medical skills, which were much in demand from European naval and military personnel stationed in Jamaica. In 1840 she embarked by herself on travels which took her first to Central America, where her medical reputation was further enhanced by her success in dealing with cholera and yellow fever epidemics. In 1854 she volunteered to assist the British army fighting in the Crimea. Despite official rebuttals she set up on her own initiative a 'British Hotel', where she both nursed the sick and provided food for healthy soldiers. She won many admirers for her courage in going into the field of battle to attend the wounded. All her efforts were entirely self-financed and in the end the war bankrupted her. She was rescued from debt by a high-profile campaign in her support in London. In 1857 her account of her travels in Central America and the Crimea, published under the title *The Wonderful Adventures of Mary Seacole in Many Lands*, became a bestseller. She died in 1881 in West London.

Question

1. *Why do you think Mary Seacole is not as well known today as Florence Nightingale?*

It is important to see Britain's current race relations problems in a historical context, because as Fryer (1991) points out in his book on *Black People in the British Empire*:

> There is no more significant pointer to the character of British society than the exclusion of black people from our history books . . . Without knowing something about black history we can neither understand the world of today nor see the way forward to the world of tomorrow . . . By disguising or glorifying the true history of colonialism, and by writing black people out of British history, the official historians have marginalised and thus further oppressed those whose history they have distorted or concealed. Their distortions and omissions have had the clear purpose of maintaining the existing power structure.
>
> (Fryer 1991: 11–13)

Though writing about black people in this instance, Fryer's argument could just as easily be applied to Jews, Asians, Irish and many others who have all contributed to the multiracial and multicultural nature of Britain but have been equally marginalized and discriminated against. As Miles (1993) has reminded us, racism against black people has long coexisted with racism against Irish and Jewish people.

Contemporary British racism is often explained as the legacy of a colonial history which could justify itself only by the assertion of the biological inferiority of black people but, as Miles points out, the economic and social circumstances of Jews in the nineteenth and twentieth centuries cannot be understood in terms of colonialism or the reification of skin colour (Miles 1990). Whereas the black American writer W.E.B. Du Bois had predicted that the 'colour line' would be the defining problem of the twentieth century, Modood (2005) has suggested that the characteristic division of the twenty-first century is likely to be about religion and in particular the conflict between the cultures of the West and Islam. In recent years, the phenomenon of Islamophobia (see World in focus below) has become recognized as one of the clearest expressions of racial intolerance in a different and growing form.

World in focus

Islamophobia

The infamous attacks on the Twin Towers in New York on 11 September 2001 and the London Underground network in July 2005 brought Muslim terrorism and suicide bombers into the world consciousness and has led to an increase in anti-Muslim feeling and actions across the Western world. Indeed those events are seen as a key date and turning point in recent history and are routinely referred to as 9/11 or 7/7 – with phrases such as 'Post 9/11' used and understood around the world. Islamophobia has become a widely used term and a major form of racial intolerance. The three extracts below illustrate the recent growth of this phenomenon. They are from different sources of information – an academic text, a news review and a campaigning website. Read them and consider the questions below.

Intolerant Britain

In the post 9/11 climate . . . Islamophobia in Britain, according to a report published by the Commission on British Muslims and Islamophobia (CBMI) (a think-tank set up by the Runneymede Trust) in May 2004, is becoming increasingly institutionalized . . . Police stop and search practices were singled out as a key indication of institutionalized Islamophobia in the post 9/11 climate because more than 35,000 Muslims were stopped and searched in 2003, with fewer than 50 charged. Three years ago, only around 2000 Muslims were stopped and searched (Doward and Hinsliff 2004). Several sources cite a 300 per cent increase in police stop and search techniques against 'Asians' in Britain between July 2003 and July 2004 . . . The chair of the CBMI, Richard Stone, suggested that in this climate of institutionalized Islamophobia, 'if we don't take positive action to embrace the young Muslim men in this country, we are going to have an urgent problem . . . we are going to have real anger and riots with young Muslims pitched

▶

World in focus (continued)

against the police (Doward and Hinsliff 2004 . . .

According to Alexander (2003), the emergent spectres of religious 'fundamentalism' and the threat of terrorism now mean that Muslim young men are becoming increasingly inseparable from the image of violence, which is evidenced in the explosion of the riots in 2001 . . .

The post 9/11 climate is both a culture of fear and a culture of indignation in which established and asylum-seeker migrant communities are viewed with suspicion. In this context, the benevolence of the UK's immigration and asylum policies and championing of multiculturalism (especially in the British tabloids) is being thrown back in the taxpayers' faces. This is clearly fertile ground for Far Right political manipulation . . .

The former Conservative Prime Minister Baroness Thatcher commented in an interview to *The Times* published on 4 October 2001 that she 'had not heard enough condemnation from Muslim priests' of the September 11 attacks. Baroness Thatcher was keen to present the attacks on the USA as an exclusive Muslim problem: 'the people who brought down those towers were Muslims and Muslims must stand up and say that it is not the way of Islam . . . they must say it is disgraceful'.

(McGhee 2005: 99–101)

UK 'Islamophobia' rise after 11 September

Muslims in one of the UK's most ethnically diverse cities have suffered an increase in racist abuse and attacks since 11 September, according to research. An academic survey of racist incidents in Leicester supports fears that the UK is witnessing a rise in Islamophobia – fear or intolerance of Muslims because of their religion. Earlier in the year, a European Union anti-racism research agency warned there was anecdotal evidence of a rise in Islamophobia. The research by the University of Leicester is the first detailed study into the actual effects of 11 September on a Muslim community.

Research findings

Racist and religious attacks in Leicester rose dramatically after 11 September, the university's research found, before dropping back during 2002. Attacks included abuse hurled at children on their way to school or women shopping, to one reported incident where a baby was tipped out of a pram. One man reported that he had eggs thrown at him outside a supermarket and then had to run as a car was driven at him . . .

Dr Lorraine Sheridan who conducted the research for the university, said that she had been shocked by what she had found . . .'The people behind the attacks think that Muslims are outside and they are different.

What is of most concern is that this is happening in Leicester, a leading multi-ethnic city which is supposed to be a model for the rest of the UK.'

. . . Leicester University surveyed the experiences of all the major religious faiths as part of the research which also included Stoke on Trent. The survey involved detailed questionnaires of experiences since 11 September 2001. Approximately 500 people responded, the overwhelming number being Muslims. The study examined levels of both racial and religious discrimination and incidences of 'implicit' racism – where people may deny being racist but treat other ethnic minorities differently.

(BBC News Online 29.8.2002)

Raising awareness

The presence of Muslims in Britain has been one that dates back over a century. Today Islam is the fastest growing religion in the history of the world. Britain's UK 2001 census confirms that, with more than 1.6 million UK Muslims (2.7 per cent of the population), Islam is now this country's second largest faith after Christianity.

British Muslims are a diverse and a vibrant community and they form an essential part of Britain's multi-ethnic, multi-cultural society. Despite their contributions, however, British Muslims suffer significantly from various forms of alienation,

World in focus (continued)

discrimination, harassment and violence rooted in misinformed and stereotyped representations of Islam and its adherents – the irrational phenomenon we have come to know as **Islamophobia**.

Islamophobia has now become a recognized form of racism . . .

In the wake of September 11, in the UK alone, within a space of two weeks, there were more than 600 cases of Islamophobic

harassment, violence and criminal damage . . .

The Forum Against Islamophobia and Racism (FAIR) was founded in 2001 as an an independent charitable organization – our aim is to work towards establishing a Safe, Just and Tolerant Britain in which Islamophobia and racism have no place.

(http://www.fairuk.org)

Questions

1. *Why do you think Muslims might be an 'easy' target for racial intolerance and violence?*

2. *How would you rate the reliability of the three extracts? (Consider the extent to which the comments are based on fact and/or research evidence.)*

Theories of race

Pseudo-scientific theories of race

The attempt to classify *Homo sapiens* into distinct biological types corresponding to racial groupings can be traced back at least as far as the nineteenth century and is in part a legacy of the Enlightenment – an intellectual movement of the eighteenth century which sought to apply rational and 'scientific' methods to all areas of human experience. The French anatomist George Cuvier and his associate Charles Hamilton Smith sought to link physical differences to distinct temperaments, and the Comte de Gobineau in the 1850s attempted not only to describe the differences between groups of people but also to explain them by dividing all of humankind into three distinct groups – 'white', 'black' and 'yellow'. He believed that these three groups had specific racially determined, cultural characteristics so that whites had superior intellects, blacks were mystical and the 'yellow races' were cunning and sly.

Michael Banton (1987) identified three main types of theory which classify human beings in terms of different biological or racial groups:

1 *Race as lineage* The idea of race as lineage originated from Christianity and the belief that all human beings are descended from Adam and Eve. After the expulsion from Paradise and various other disasters such as the Flood, humans were scattered across the

WATCH OUT–THE MASTER RACE ARE IN TOWN

globe, which resulted in distinctive lineages or races. These races developed physical characteristics which corresponded to their geographical environments. As Banton says, the message was 'each people was adapted to its own environment and therefore should stay where they were'.

2 *Race as type*   The theory of race as type was based on the belief that racial differences had occurred from earliest times and were either the result of a natural catastrophe or an act of God. These ideas were developed especially in North America, resulting in Nott and Gliddon's *Types of Mankind* (published in Philadelphia in 1854) which asserted not only that there were also different types of human being, which behaved differently from one another but also that these groups were naturally antagonistic to one another.

3 *Race as subspecies*   This theory, combining elements of the other two, originated with the work of Charles Darwin and the publication of *On the Origin of Species* in 1859, in which he explained the differences between humans with the theory of evolution. According to this theory humankind is a species which through a process of natural selection has developed from a common origin into a number of distinct subspecies or races which are constantly evolving to adapt most effectively to their environment – the survival of the fittest. 'Social Darwinism' also encompassed the idea that certain subspecies or races were less developed and therefore inferior to others according to a classification system elaborated by Herbert Spencer, an English sociologist of the nineteenth century (Andreski 1971).

The limitations of race as biology

Such biological theories of race seek to link *genotype* – the underlying genetic differences between groups of people – with *phenotype* – physical characteristics such as skin or hair colour which are a result of the interaction between genotypes and the environment. Rapid advances in genetic science, however, make this increasingly problematic. According to Steve Jones (1991), a leading geneticist who has reappraised biological theories of race in the light of these advances, there is no genetic justification for distinguishing different races even though there are genetic differences between groups of human beings. We know that human beings are the product of as many as 50,000 genes (sometimes described as the building blocks of the human organism) but changes in fewer than ten genes determine skin colour and there is far greater genetic diversity (about 85 per cent of those variations which occur) between individuals from the same country than there is between countries within the same continent (about 10–15 per cent):

> The overall genetic differences between 'races' – Africans and Europeans, say – is no greater than that between different countries within Europe or within Africa. Individuals – not nations and not races – are the main repository of human variation.   (Jones 1991)

Case study

Biology as destiny

Contemporary sociobiology is in many ways a modern reworking of some of the ideas of social Darwinism. The work of writers such as Desmond Morris (1968; 1977), Konrad Lorenz (1965; 1973) and Richard Dawkins (1976; 1977) can be seen as representing a resurgence of theories which attempt to explain the world through reference to genetic variations which shape personality traits and social behaviour. Sociobiology sees a propensity to hostility and violence between humans who look 'different' from one another (as formerly in South Africa for example) as rooted in genetic structures which act as fixed determinants of behaviour. Richard Dawkins, a prominent sociobiologist, argues that:

> Conceivably, racial prejudice could be interpreted as an irrational generalisation of a kin-selected tendency to identify with individuals physically resembling oneself and to be nasty to individuals different in appearance.
> (Dawkins 1976: 108)

Question

1. Sociobiology could be seen as providing a 'scientific' or 'rational' explanation for the existence of racist beliefs, and, most importantly, for hostile and racist behaviour. What do you think are the dangers involved in explaining racist violence in this way?

Jones goes on to say that there can be no scientific basis for genetic or biological theories of race and that 'much of the history of the genetics of race – a field promoted by some eminent scientists – turns out to have been prejudice dressed up as science.' This leads us inevitably to wonder why such ideas were so widespread and so popular for so long and it is difficult to escape the conclusion that not only did they bring with them a comforting sense of innate superiority but also they legitimized the process of colonial expansion of the nineteenth and early twentieth centuries, a process which often had disastrous consequences for the people being colonized.

The social construction of race

As mentioned earlier there is considerable debate about the definition of the concept and indeed the use of the word 'race'. While most sociologists would reject the scientific validity of the concept of 'race' there is a recognition that the widespread belief in the idea of 'race' and its influence on the way people interact justifies its use as a social category:

> Social categories depend for their existence on the subjective definition given to them by social actors. Race is no exception. So long as it exists in the minds of men [*sic*] there will be race relations problems to study. (Rex 1970: 192)

There have been a number of attempts to explain the continuing use of the concept of 'race' in a social context which draw on social psychological theories of group behaviour and personal stereotypes and prejudices. Of the more explicitly sociological theories it is worth examining the theory of race relations and Marxist and neo-Marxist theories of race and racism.

Race relations

The race relations perspective attempts to explain the different treatment accorded to ethnic minorities in their relations with the rest of society. Analysis focuses on situations in which members of minorities are defined by their distinctive identities and social treatment (Rex 1970: 160) and this is generally at least in part defined by their status as immigrants. Thus society is seen at certain points in time as racially stratified and 'disfavouring' certain races in the allocation of housing, employment

opportunities and education provision. As Miles (1989) points out, the problem with the race relations approach is that it leads to a situation in which the minority group is inevitably classified as 'racially disadvantaged' with social action directed towards helping the 'victim(s)' overcome the conditions associated with their racial status. The race relations model has frequently been applied in the field of social policy and in government legislation and has been adopted by the media when reporting incidents such as inner city riots involving black youths. However, though it ostensibly recognizes the social factors which contribute to race conflict and discrimination, it can also be interpreted in such a way that it leads to a 'blame the victim' attitude:

> Difficulty in race relations arises from the speed of the arrival of immigrants and their concentration in certain areas. This has led to social changes being imposed on the people already living in those areas, who perhaps find it hard to accept them.
> (Reginald Maudling 1971, quoted in Miles and Phizacklea 1984: 73)

Neo-Marxist accounts of race and racial discrimination

While Marxism has, for theorists such as Cedric Robinson (1983) and Paul Gilroy (1987; 1993a), been equated with Eurocentric, economistic accounts of black experiences, the accounts examined in this section do represent genuine attempts to explain patterns of inequality in society through reference to social and economic factors. In short, Marxist theories of racial discrimination move away from a concern with physical differences and innate personality traits towards an investigation of the relations between racist beliefs and the capitalist social system.

In addressing Marxist theories of race and racism, we can see how many accounts in this tradition see both racist practices and beliefs as the product of the capitalist class system while having the function of reinforcing capitalist class relations (see e.g. Cox 1970; Wallerstein 1983). Such accounts take the concept of class as their starting-point with racial oppression defined as a tool of the 'capitalist' classes. In dividing the black worker from the white, through racist beliefs and discriminatory practices, the working class is conceptualized as effectively split in two and a black 'underclass' created.

Writers such as Cox (1970) and Wolpe (1980) address (through reference to the systems of slavery and apartheid, respectively) what they see as an intrinsically economic motive for the creation and application of racist beliefs. In the case of the former, the supply and exploitation of black labour is understood as stemming not simply from racist attitudes but from a combination of demographic and economic forces (Mintz 1974). That beliefs about the intrinsic inferiority of blackness were mobilized to explain and legitimize the exploitation of African slaves is not denied, but the priority of economic motives and practices retains a primary role.

How, then, might Marxist accounts of race explain the continued disadvantages faced by the black population in Britain today? While race and racism are perceived to be important factors in explaining the specific type of discrimination encountered by black and Asian people in the labour market, it is the nature of the capitalist accumulation process that is of primary importance. For Marxists, capitalism exploits the worker regardless of race or gender: it is only when supply of labour exceeds demand that exclusionary practices which draw on racism may occur (Miles 1989: 128; Fevre 1984).

Contemporary Marxist theories of race and racism are useful in addressing the relationship between racist beliefs, practice and the broader social structure. Where the contributions of Marxism are not so clear is in relation to the apparently autonomous and independent nature of racist beliefs. In defining racism as shaped by economic forces, the potential of racist practices themselves to shape economics is not considered in any depth. Furthermore, the continued expression of racist beliefs by employers and workers which are to the detriment of the capitalist system through encouraging rioting and conflict is difficult to explain (Sivanandan 1990).

Neo-Marxism and the new racism

A number of sociologists based in the Centre for Contemporary Cultural Studies in Birmingham developed a neo-Marxist approach to race and racism (see for example their study The Empire Strikes Back 1982). They argued that racism pre-dated colonialism and was shaped by a variety of historical and political factors as well as economics. They believed it was important to take into account the part played by ethnic minorities in resisting and challenging racism and that the nature of racism was not fixed but dynamic and con-

stantly changing. They also identified a new form of racism which was not centred on the biological superiority and inferiority of different 'races' but saw the different cultures of Afro-Caribbean and Asian immigrants as a threat to the 'British' way of life. According to this view, being truly 'British' was a question not simply of citizenship but of embracing 'British' culture and values.

Paul Gilroy, who was one of this group, developed these ideas further in There Ain't No Black in the Union Jack (1987). Gilroy sought to examine 'race' and ethnicity in conjunction through his theory of race formation, a process by which groups continually redefine themselves and organize themselves around ideas of race.

Theories of racism

Although there is much discussion in sociology textbooks of the difficulties involved in defining racism, there is no shortage of definitions available including the psychological theories of the Frankfurt School and Marxist theories of institutionalized racism. The concept of *racism* refers to beliefs and social practices which draw directly or indirectly on the belief that there are racial groups which have distinct physical or cultural characteristics which are usually but not exclusively defined in negative terms.

Michael Banton (1997) defines it in the following historical terms:

1   The doctrine that race determines culture (1933).

2   The use of racial beliefs and attitudes to subordinate and control a category of people defined in racial terms (1967).

3   A historical complex, generated within capitalism, facilitating the exploitation of categories of people defined in racial terms (1970).

4   Anything connected with racial discrimination (1980).   (Banton 1997)

One distinction which it is helpful to make is that between racial prejudice – the holding of racist views and beliefs – and racial discrimination – the unfavourable treatment of a person or persons because of their real or imagined membership of a particular 'race'. Different theoretical perspectives have attempted to explain racial discrimination in, for example, the areas of housing, education and employment by focusing on specific aspects of racism such as beliefs and values or social practices, and in the following sections we shall look at these areas of discrimination in greater detail. In considering the most extreme form of discrimination – racist violence – however, it is not possible to make this distinction between beliefs and action:

> A vast majority of racist incidents are perpetrated by people not affiliated to any racist organisation, and without clear, elaborated (political/ideological) racist frameworks of thought. These incidents are racist, however, because the victim(s) are attacked because of the colour of their skin, or because of their alleged nationality, religion or colour.   (Witte 1996: 11)

Stop and think

➤ What role does racism play in understanding racial discrimination in employment in Marxist accounts?

➤ How would Marxism explain the different employment positions of black and white workers? Which is the most important factor, class or 'race'?

➤ Why do writers such as Robert Miles place inverted commas around 'race' and not class?

Racism and the state: institutional accounts of 'race' discrimination

Political or state-centred accounts of racism derive in part from the Marxist theorization of race, yet choose to focus in more detail on the covert incorporation of racist beliefs and attitudes into social and political policy. The existence and perpetuation of racial difference in the social structure is explained through reference to the effects of state policies which result in the exclusion of subordinate groups in society.

Described and defined in the writings of theorists such as Blauner (1972), Sivanandan (1982) and Hall *et al.* (1978), the notion of institutionalized racism reflects an attempt to move away from the individual as the focus of attention in understanding how racism works. To quote from Blauner:

> The processes that maintain domination – control of whites over non-whites – are built into the major social institutions thus there is little need for prejudice as a motivating force. Because this is true, the distinction between racism as an objective phenomenon, located in the actual existence of domination and hierarchy,

and racism's subjective concomitants of prejudice and other motivations and feelings is a basic one.
>
> (Blauner 1972: 10)

Drawing on a combination of racist sentiments, notions of Britishness and the nation-state, xenophobia and political strategy, British political policy since the postwar migration experience is defined by writers in this tradition as inherently racist in nature. Rejecting a common-sense race relations perspective, Miles and Phizacklea (1984), for example, examine the ways in which racism in the sphere of political policy defines black people as a 'problem' in need of legislation. Through building such beliefs into policy directives and party political debate, while claiming that they represent the sentiments of the people, racism is covertly reproduced at the level of the state and the individual.

To take one example, Hall *et al.* (1978) considered how social problems such as crime and violence have become racialized through state and media discourses. In creating a moral panic around the myth of the 'black mugger' in the 1970s, they argued that themes of immigration and personal safety became fused into one. Miles and Phizacklea, too, examine the strategic location of the threat to the (white) British citizen in discourses of race and culture, and address the role of the media in the institutionalization of racist explanations for manufactured social problems. Indeed, media representations of the muggings – which in fact constituted only 0.9 per cent of total recorded serious crimes in London in 1981 – can be seen as contributing to a social definition of a perceived problem in racial terms. Witness the *Daily Mail* on the crime problem in Handsworth:

> All the sentenced youths are either coloured or immigrants and live in one of Birmingham's major problem areas. Police and social workers have been battling for years to solve community problems in Handsworth, where juvenile crime steadily worsens and there are continuous complaints about the relationship between the police and the predominantly coloured public.   (*Daily Mail* 21.3.1973)

Texts and discourses of the state – specifically government inquiries – are described by Gilroy (1987) as in part reflecting the strength of the state institution to both define and solve what, exactly, constitutes the race problem. In this way, Gilroy sees the state as playing a crucial role in the reproduction of racial discrimination. In the Scarman Report on the relationship between crime, the police and the community, which was published in response to the inner city disturbances in Brixton in April 1981, the link between racial categorization and policy formation is striking:

> Many agencies are equally responsible for the communal good and find themselves locked in conflict with black adolescents. I am sure that the solutions lie in the sharing of perceptions not only with these agencies but, more vitally, with those who have managed to gain the trust of the black teenager.
>
> (Scarman 1982)

In relating patterns of racial discrimination to an understanding of the role of the state, and state institutions, such accounts ascribe the state system a central role in the following social practices:

➤ the defining and racialization of social problems;

➤ the development of social and political policy which reproduces racism through its location of black people as the 'problem' and which inhibits the promotion of a genuinely anti-racist political agenda;

➤ the reproduction of an institutional and structural framework which is strategically geared towards the privileging of a white, colonial experience (in, for example, the racist teaching of black culture in schools).

Before looking at the position of black people in Britain, we will introduce the concepts of ethnicity and nationalism and consider some of the recent theoretical debates around them.

Ethnicity

Ethnicity is used in ethnic relations literature to refer to a sense of cultural awareness and identity within groups that share a common history or heritage. In contrast to biological theories of race, the process of cultural identification or, more frequently, *non*-identification, has a determining role in explaining the different social experiences of black and white people. Issues of common identity and cultural difference are mobilized to account for the fear and hostility of the host population towards the ethnic other; in constructing boundaries between the self and the other, ethnicity is the key cultural variable.

> Ethnicity refers generally to the perception of group difference and so to social boundaries between sections of the population. In this sense ethnic difference is the recognition of a contrast between 'us' and 'them'.
>
> (Wellman 1977: ix)

Different experiences of black and white people in areas, for example, of housing and employment are thus explained for writers in the ethnic relations framework through reference to exclusionary practices which derive from both self-identification, and other (mis)recognition, of cultural differences.

While the ethnic relations focus represents a significant shift away from the implied biological associations of the race relations approach in addressing the relation of cultural characteristics – of dress, customs, religion, food – to practices of social exclusion, there remain serious theoretical problems with this approach (see Miles 1982: 71). As with racial labelling, the notion of ethnicity and ethnic groups conveys a sense of closure, of a homogeneity that is unchanging and impenetrable; questions of class and gender differences *within* ethnic groupings are not considered in any detail. Moreover, there are grounds for concluding that the notion of ethnicity is little more than the outcome of a race plus culture formula: in short, the sociobiological claim that culture is itself ultimately determined by phenotypical or physical features.

New cultural theories of 'ethnicity' and difference

The second tradition associated with the notion of ethnicity is to be found in the work of contemporary writers such as Stuart Hall (1992) and Homi K. Bhabha (1990). Such approaches are less concerned with explaining the *structural* inequalities experienced by the black population than with the reproduction and maintenance of the race notion in society. Indeed, it can be suggested that it is only through understanding the processes of labelling, identity and resistance that the motives behind continued discriminatory practices can be understood and ultimately challenged.

We shall briefly examine the approach of Stuart Hall (1992) as representative of a shift towards the analysis of what he terms 'new ethnicities'. As with writers in the early 'ethnicity school' (e.g. Wellman 1977), Hall's definition of ethnicity locates culture and history as core elements in the formation of identity:

> The term ethnicity acknowledges the place of history, language and culture in the construction of subjectivity and identity, as well as the fact that all discourse is placed, positioned, situated, and all knowledge is contextual.
>
> (Hall 1992: 257)

And yet the 'new cultural analysts' differ from those writing in the shadows of the race relations perspective through a focus *not* on ethnic boundaries and exclusion, but on the possibilities for the mobilization of cultural ethnicity as a liberating force. We are *all* ethnically located – black and white – and in recognizing the diversity of all cultural experiences, can work towards breaking down the negative connotations of blackness, otherness and race in society.

More recent work in this tradition (Cohen 1994; Sampson 1993) has addressed further the concepts of the self and the other. Cohen has suggested that otherness need not refer exclusively to 'blackness' but must take on board other types of 'ethnically specific identities' and other types of prejudice (for example, anti-Irish prejudice, anti-semitism). The implications of expanding our understanding of who 'makes up' the ethnic other are, for Cohen, potentially problematic when considering the concept of *racism*. For in aggregating a limitless number of ethnicities as subject to the process of racism, there is a danger of:

Stretching the elastic band of 'racism' around a fatter and fatter bundle of related (yet importantly distinct) phenomena so thinly that the band is in grave danger of snapping and flying off out of sight.

(Cohen 1994: 194)

One proposed solution to this problem is found in the work of David Goldberg (1993). Through adopting the term 'racism*s*', as opposed to the singular 'racism', the complexity and diversity of 'otherness' can be retained while at the same time recognizing that 'exclusionary practices' face all who are defined as other.

One of the strengths of work which addresses the *complexities* of ethnicity and race is that the complexities of racism, exclusion and discrimination are also addressed. Just as the 'other' is not to be seen as a homogeneous and unified group, so too should racism (or racism*s*) be understood as meaning different things to different people, at different points in time. As argued by Cohen, however, we must be careful, in recognizing the differences between those who are defined *as* 'different', that the defining characteristic of 'otherness' is not ignored.

Case study

Ethnicity – the new racism?

In 1935 two British academics, Julian Huxley and Alfred Haddon challenged the increasingly popular racist ideologies of the day in a book entitled *We Europeans*. They argued that the discredited biological concept of 'race' should be replaced with the socially defined notion of 'ethnic group' in the hope that this would undermine ideologies of racial supremacy. In the long run however, the idea of racial difference has survived and is often confused with the concept of ethnicity; as Hazel Croall has pointed out 'Social relationships become racialised when racial differences are assumed to be

significant' (1998: 161) and if cultural badges of difference are mistaken for biological ones we may simply end up with what Martin Barker (1981) has labelled the 'new racism'. In the discussion below, the persecution of groups on the basis of ethnicity is examined through the work of Marek Kohn and Michael Ignatieff.

By the 1930s, the idea of 'race' as a meaningful biological concept had been established through the work of eugenicists in the US and Europe who, in the name of 'racial science', argued that the innate characteristics of individuals were related to their racial origins. By studying the physiological differences of these groups and identifying their intellectual,

psychological and physical traits it would be possible to identify the strengths and weaknesses of each racial group. These physiological differences usually bring to mind differences in skin colour, body size and shape but in many parts of the world it is not physical differences but cultural ones which are seen as significant. In regions such as Central and Eastern Europe where the black/white dichotomy is not in evidence, it is ethnic group membership which is more important as a mark of difference although racial terminology is still often used and many ethnic groups are talked of as if they are racial ones (the search for the 'Hungarian gene' continued well into the twentieth century).

Case study (continued)

In his work on 'racial science', Marek Kohn (1996) demonstrates the universal power of racial discourse whatever we choose to call it. In Europe, for example, attitude surveys have revealed that the Roma (gypsies) are 'the most unpopular ethnic groups in each country polled'. Using evidence from Slovakia, the Czech Republic, Hungary, Romania and Bulgaria, Kohn concludes that 'hostility to the Roma might therefore be considered one of the principle characteristics of racism in East and Central Europe' (1996: 183). Since the middle ages the attitudes and actions of a land-based peasantry towards the nomadic Romani has always been hostile, in the nineteenth century Cesar Lombroso argued that gypsies were innately criminal because they were 'so low morally and so incapable of cultural and intellectual development' and even under Soviet rule the common perception was that 'gypsies were untidy, anarchic and archaic, requiring modernization in the same way that horses required replacement by tractors' (1996: 192). With the re-emergence of post-Soviet nationalism it is not surprising to discover that gypsies continue to be identified as outsiders:

> In the vision that prevails in Central and Eastern Europe . . . nationhood depends on the bond between land and people, hitherto based on the peasant way of life. This implies that the Roma are not an authentic people. (1996: 194)

In 1993 a pogrom in the Romanian village of Hadareni demonstrated how powerful such beliefs can be; following a fight villagers with the help of the police revenged themselves on the local Romani by kicking to death two gypsies being held in custody, burning 13 houses and killing another man. Following the incident a local resident said:

> We're proud of what we did . . . We did not commit murder. How could you call killing Gypsies murder? Gypsies are not really people, you see. They are always killing each other. They are criminals, sub-human, vermin. And they are certainly not wanted here. (1996: 184)

In *Blood and Belonging*, a work almost exclusively concerned with ethnic division, Michael Ignatieff (1994) examined the impact of nationalism and national identity on societies characterized by ethnic division. His research took him to the former Yugoslavia, the Ukraine, Germany, Quebec, Kurdistan and Northern Ireland. In all cases it was not obvious 'racial' characteristics which inspired conflict and persecution but cultural differences and the closer the physical resemblance between groups the more violent the response to ethnic division:

> Nationalism is most violent where the group you are defining yourself against most closely resembles you. A rational explanation of conflict would predict the reverse to be the case. To outsiders at least, Ulstermen look and sound like Irishmen, just as Serbs look and sound like Croats – yet the very similarity is what pushes them to define themselves as polar opposites. Since Cain and Abel, we have known that hatred between brothers is more ferocious than hatred between strangers.
>
> (Ignatieff 1994)

As Ignatieff says with regard to the civil war and ethnic cleansing in the former Yugoslavia, 'A Croat, thus, is someone who is not a Serb. A Serb is someone who is not a Croat. Without hatred of the other, there would be no clearly defined national self to worship and adore.'

> (Cited in Marsh *et al.* 1998: 259, 262)

Questions

1. In your own words describe the difference between the concepts of 'race' and 'ethnic group'.

2. What evidence is provided in the work of Kohn and Ignatieff to support Barker's idea of a 'new racism' based upon ethnic group membership?

3. Why do you think the Romani are a target for persecution in Central and Eastern Europe?

4. How would you explain Ignatieff's observation that nationalist violence is at its most extreme where the groups in conflict are similar in appearance?

Postmodernism, ethnicity and difference

A further tradition associated with new cultural theories of ethnicity and difference is that of postmodernism. Postmodern approaches to explaining ethnicity are distinctive in their concern to avoid categorizing and defining what, or whom, make up different ethnicities. They are concerned to move away from notions of ethnic *groups* in favour of a more flexible and less restrictive focus on the *individual* as defining, for her or himself, what is meant by 'race' or 'ethnicity'. So fluid and shifting is the process of ethnic identity, say postmodernists, that attention should be directed to people's own definitions of ethnicity, in contrast to attempts by sociologists to fit people into predefined ethnic groups. Writers such as Jonathan Rutherford (1990) address how the differences and diversities *between and within* experiences of ethnicity should be seen not as restrictive to an understanding of human relations but as creating insights which are potentially liberating, rather than limiting. In celebrating difference, then, postmodernists see ethnicity as highly individualistic, historically changeable and ultimately allusive. Attention should be directed, say writers in this tradition, to the pleasures of diversity and the freedoms that a greater understanding of oneself as one ethnicity among many may bring.

Postmodern theories of ethnic identity represent a positive break with theorizations of black people as victims requiring care and understanding by the 'white community'. Moreover, the focus on the *cultural* nature of new ethnicities would appear to finally break away from the limiting associations of race and physical chracteristics.

Their approaches, however, have been criticized by writers such as Callinicos (1993) as profoundly idealist and insensitive to the continued oppression suffered by those defined as different from the white majority. Celebration of cultural diversity and difference are of little comfort for those excluded from the labour market on the grounds of such perceived difference.

Case study

Forget black, forget white. EA is what's hot

It stands for 'ethnically ambiguous', a term embracing a whole new generation, from US mega-stars to Brixton clubbers, who have grown up colour-blind.

In the Plan B bar in Brixton, the DJ plays black R&B music in a part of town once seen as 'Black' but the crowd is mixed. They regard themselves as Generation Ethnically Ambiguous. While many blacks and Asians are casting aside the old ethnic labels as crude and outmoded, many white youngsters are embracing so-called 'black' lifestyle and culture in fashion, grooming, music, sport and language. As Nurj Khan, a nurse from Camberwell, explains. 'Trying to define people by the old race labels just doesn't work any more. Look around you. Can you pigeonhole these people? To me, that doesn't undermine the fact that culture and heritage are an integral part of life, but there is more to it than just colour.'

In the movies and the worlds of fashion and pop music, this fusion of culture and appearance has been well marketed in response to changes in America and the UK . . . Almost one million young Britons identified themselves as members of more than one race or of 'no race' in the most recent census, the first in which respondents could choose their ethnic origin. 'Mixed Race' is now the third largest ethnic minority group in Britain and is set to become the biggest over the next decade.

As blacks and Asians move away from colour-based labels, observers say that white youngsters are moving towards traditional black lifestyles, creating the new 'blended' youth.

'Black urban culture has become the mainstream culture,' says journalist and social commentator Paul McKenzie. 'It represents the triumph of the immigrant black community.'

As with all social trends, the first people to pick up on the rise of Generation EA have been media and entertainment groups. This can clearly be seen in the casting of mixed race movie stars and the 'racially-indeterminate, melting pot aesthetic' characterizing the cat walks of the fashion world. It is also beginning to have an impact on pop music; after years of

Case study (continued)

churning out lily-white, blond-haired, blue-eyed boy and girl bands, the music industry is remixing looks as fast as it remixes singles.

Multiracial bands such as the Sugababes are replacing the likes of Boyzone and Westlife. Even mega-stars are deliberately tweaking their looks, playing with audiences' perceptions of their origin. Among male stars, Eminem and Justin Timberlake, who are white, claim that their music is as 'black' as songs by such US rappers as P. Diddy or 50 Cent.

Ambiguity sells, marketing experts say, not only because it – helpfully – covers all bases but because it suits the times. 'There is a current fascination with the racial hybrid,' says Sean Pillot de Chenecey, a London-based trend analyst and researcher who has worked for Levi's and Coca-Cola. 'For the marketing industry, the focus is on trying to reflect the blending of cultures. It's about art imitating life.'

The transition from segregated cultures to multiracialism is now so marked that some believe the time has come to dismiss race altogether as a useful social indicator. US academic Evelyn Hammond, a professor of the history of science and Afro-American studies at Harvard, recently told the *New York Times* that race was an 'invented concept' used 'to categorize perceived biological, social and cultural differences between human groups'.

In Britain, Michael Eboda, editor of the black newspaper *New Nation*, says, 'The barriers between black and white are really coming down.'

While, at the Commission for Racial Equality, Trevor Phillips agrees: 'The CRE is not just here to go about shouting "racism, racism, racism". I want to bring the word integration back into fashion because I think it is what is going on already. Public bodies need to catch up with real life and work out how to take things even further forward.'

Back on the streets of Brixton, what do those in Plan B bar make of these claims? Is Generation EA a reality? In the multiracial, pluralist culture in which we now live, does race still matter, or has the new climate of crossover, fusion and cultural diversification relegated colour to the margins?

Nick Leader, a 25-year-old research consultant who has travelled from Hampstead, north London, to party with his friends, says: 'People don't make a distinction now because the distinction is dissolving – culturally and even at times physically.

'We are the new mix. We are the remix generation.'

(Adapted from John Arlidge, *Observer* 4.1.2004)

Question

1. *Using contemporary Britain as an example, what evidence is there to support or refute Leader's notion of a 'remix generation'?*

One final area that needs to be addressed within new cultural theories of ethnicity and difference are recent attempts that address questions of difference and exclusion through an examination of the white racialization process. In seeking to 'unpack' the many varied ways in which the 'self' is constructed, writers across a wide range of disciplines (for example, feminism, education and postcolonial studies) have explored how whiteness, defined as a 'privileged ethnic standpoint' (Fine *et al.* 1997), is continually established in social relationships, identities and political policy, and across social institutions such as schools and the health service.

Researchers who address questions of 'whiteness' stress the importance of questioning the 'normality' of whiteness and white culture as 'natural'. As Ruth Frankenburg puts it:

to speak of whiteness . . . refers to a set of locations that are historically, socially, politically and culturally produced and, moreover, are intrinsically linked to unfolding relations of domination. Naming whiteness displaces it from the unmarked, unnamed status that is itself an effect of dominance. Among the effects on white people both of race privilege and of the dominance of whiteness are their seeming normativity, their structured invisibility. (Frankenburg 1993)

While writers such as Roman (1993) and Lipsitz (1995) acknowledge that whiteness, like 'blackness', is a social and cultural construction, it is suggested that issues of colour and racial identity have to be addressed in order to understand how race privilege is conferred. It is only then that steps can be taken towards the formation of a 'positive non-racist White racial identity ego status' (Fine *et al.* 1997: 199).

Writings on whiteness are useful because they focus attention on the construction of white privilege – an area that had previously been neglected within the field of race and ethnicity – and how white people have historically 'possessed' the social, cultural and political institutions of society. Where there may be a danger in this approach is if the voice of 'whiteness' becomes self-indulgent, with 'white studies' establishing itself as an academic discipline at the expense of the formation of serious anti-racist strategies.

Immigration to Britain since 1945: a study in race relations

The history of immigration to Britain since 1945 and the legislation which has been introduced both to control it and to cope with its perceived effects on British society

provide a fascinating opportunity to examine ideas of structural racism and to look at the ways in which a climate is produced in which the racialization of social problems occurs. Though we do not have the space here to go into this history in the detail it deserves (and this has been done very adequately elsewhere: see Further reading on p. 352) one thing is apparent from a very quick glance at the legislation listed: there is considerably more legislation which curbs immigration than that designed specifically to improve race relations or reduce discrimination.

Stop and think

> Why do you think this is? What do you think might be the main problems involved in drawing up legislation which promotes good race relations?

On examining this legislation in chronological order it becomes clear that irrespective of which party was in power, British policy towards immigration since 1962 has

Case study

Legislating race

Some key Acts concerning immigration and race relations since the Second World War:

British Nationality Act 1948

Made a distinction between British subjects who were (a) citizens of the United Kingdom and (b) colonies and Commonwealth citizens, but both groups retained the right to enter, settle and work in Britain. Citizens of the Republic of Ireland retained the right to unrestricted entry and settlement.

Commonwealth Immigrants Act 1962

Withdrew right of entry of all Commonwealth immigrants unless

they (a) were born in the UK, (b) held UK passports issued by the government or (c) were included on the passport of someone exempted from immigration control under (a) or (b) (Macdonald 1983: 10–12). Effectively it distinguished between British citizens in general and those from the Caribbean and Asia. A voucher system was instituted for those who did not qualify, classifying people according to whether they already had a job or particular skills which the UK needed.

Race Relations Act 1965

Banned discrimination on grounds of 'race, colour or ethnic or national origin' in places of 'public resort' such as hotels, restaurants and public transport. It also made it illegal to incite racial hatred

through speech or written word. The Act was criticized for failing to cover discrimination in the crucial areas of housing and employment and for being 'toothless': between 1965 and 1969 only fifteen cases went to court and of those five involved members of the Black Power movement (Witte 1996). The Race Relations Board set up in February 1966 established local centres for reporting discrimination but most of the complaints received proved to be outside its jurisdiction.

Commonwealth Immigrants Act 1968

All citizens of the UK or colonies with a British passport became subject to immigration controls unless they had one parent or

▶

Case study (continued)

grandparent born, naturalized or resident in Britain.

Race Relations Act 1968

Extended the provisions of the Race Relations Act 1965 to cover employment, housing, commercial and other services but still did not cover the police (who dealt with complaints internally) and though the Race Relations Board was given the power to institute legal proceedings it had to provide substantive evidence that discrimination had taken place.

Immigration Act 1971

All aliens or Commonwealth citizens who did not qualify under the terms of the Commonwealth Immigrants Act 1968 could now enter Britain only with a work permit, which usually had to be renewed after twelve months. Unlike the voucher system, these permits did not grant permanent residency or the right of dependants to settle. Immigrants had the right to apply for citizenship after four years but the Home Secretary also had the right to deport anyone who might be seen as a threat to the public good. In effect it put Commonwealth citizens on a par with any other aliens who wanted to come into the UK.

Race Relations Act 1976

Made indirect discrimination illegal. This meant that if for example employers advertised

a job stating that all applicants had to be born in the UK they could be charged with indirectly discriminating against members of ethnic minorities unless they could provide a reasonable justification for so advertising.

The Commission for Racial Equality was established to promote racial harmony. It was given greater powers than its predecessors and has had some success initiating new legislation and exposing discrimination in a wide range of institutions as well as raising awareness of racial issues.

British Nationality Act 1981

Established three categories of UK and colonies citizens: (a) British citizens; (b) citizens of British dependent territories; (c) British overseas citizens. By stating that British citizenship could pass to children born overseas only if their parents were born in the UK it effectively discriminated against first-generation settlers from Asia and the Caribbean. The Act also stated that people married to British citizens had to be resident in the UK for three years before they could apply for citizenship.

Immigration Act 1988

Took away the right of dependants of men who had settled in the UK before 1973 to join them unless there was proof that they would not be dependent on state benefits.

Asylum and Immigration Act 1993

Designed to streamline procedures and to eliminate so-called 'economic refugees'. In late 1995 Home Secretary Michael Howard promoted a Bill designed to streamline procedures further by introducing a 'white list' of countries presumed to be safe so that any appeal for asylum from a country on the list would automatically be rejected.

Race Relations (Amendment) Act 2000

Strengthened (rather than replaced) the Race Relations Act 1976. It met recommendation 11 of the Stephen Lawrence Inquiry Report (that the full force of the race relations legislation should apply to the police – see p. 348). It also outlawed direct and indirect discrimination and victimization in all public authority areas that were not covered by the 1976 Act.

Asylum and Immigration Act 2004

This reforms the UK asylum-seeker system. It includes provisions which unify the immigration and asylum appeals system, deal with undocumented arrivals and those people who fail to comply with steps to co-operate with documentation, create a system of integration loans for refugees and tackle sham marriages.

progressively diminished the right of entry and settlement in the UK of Commonwealth citizens and has consistently discriminated against black and Asian people. Despite the passing of a number of Race Relations Acts designed to improve community relations the underlying assumption which this legislation is based on (and the often openly stated belief of policy makers and politicians) was, and still is, that these community relations had become a problem only because too many black immigrants had been 'let in' and were threatening the British way of life. It is impossible to know to what extent popular, common-sense perceptions of black immigration as a threat influenced policy and to what extent the legislation which was passed confirmed these fears. Certainly politicians and the press did little to assuage people's concern that the black immigrants coming in brought an alien culture with them which would undermine British traditions and values and that they would prove a drain on the newly created welfare state.

In the immediate aftermath of the Second World War the acute shortage of labour meant that for a short time companies such as London Transport actively recruited in the West Indies and labour immigrants of all kinds were welcomed. In fact, though much publicity was given to the arrival of 417 Jamaicans aboard HMS *Empire Windrush* in May 1948, the most important source of migrant labour in this period was Europe and, in particular, Ireland: 'between 1945 and 1951 between 70,000 and 100,000 Irish people entered Britain' (Solomos 1989).

As soon as the number of black and Asian Commonwealth immigrants began to increase in the 1950s, however, public attitudes began to change. As Solomos observes: 'throughout the 1950s the debate about immigration in parliament and the media began to focus on the need to control black immigration' (Solomos 1989).

The Notting Hill riots of 1958 are often seen as marking an important point in the racialization of social, economic and law and order issues; although there is

Case study

For their own sakes: stop them now!

The media played a significant role in establishing a link between social and economic deprivation and threats to law and order on the one hand, and the presence of the black migrant communities on the other. Often this causal connection was established implicitly in newspaper articles as in the Sunday newspaper *The People* on 25 May 1958, where an article was headed 'For their own sakes stop them now!' The article continued 'With the greatest possible urgency *The People* now asks the government to put a bar against the free admission of coloured immigrants in Britain. We are not yielding to colour prejudices. But the wave of immigrants rolling over our shores has now

risen to threatening proportions' (quoted in Witte 1996).

'I think it means that people are really rather afraid that this country might be swamped by people of different cultures. The British character has done so much for democracy, for law, done so much throughout the world that if there is any fear that it might be swamped, then people are going to be rather hostile to those coming in.'

(Margaret Thatcher 30.1.1978, quoted in Solomos 1989: 129; Fryer 1991: 397)

Kilroy unveils immigration policy

Ex-chatshow host Robert Kilroy-Silk has attacked UK policy on immigration saying Britain's open door approach is hitting low wage 'indigenous' workers.

The Veritas leader said the only people to benefit from immigrants from places like Poland were employers, landlords, members of the 'metropolitan elite'.

The MEP said his party would only admit foreigners who were required because they had specific skills to offer.

And he argued asylum cost £2bn a year for 14,000 successful applicants.

(BBC News Online 14.2.2005)

Question

1. The extracts show that between 1958, 1978 and 2005 little has changed in terms of some people's perception of the threats posed by black immigration. Do you think people still hold these views today? To what extent do you think Britain is a multiracial, multicultural society?

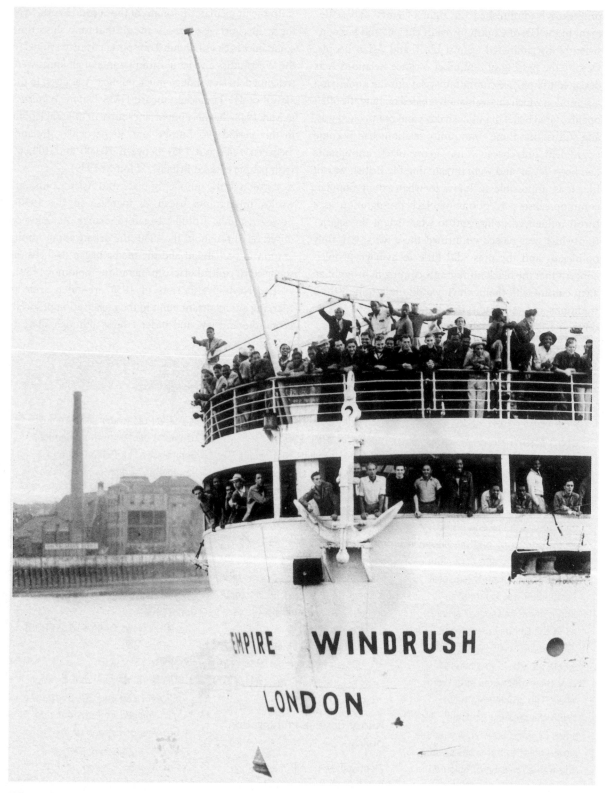

Figure 8.1 417 Jamaicans arrive on *Empire Windrush*, 1948
(Courtesy of Hulton Getty)

evidence to suggest that this process was already under-way, the riots certainly brought race and immigration issues to the top of the public and political agenda and were used by those calling for stronger immigration controls to justify their arguments. These arguments were developed even further by Enoch Powell in his infamous 'Rivers of Blood' speech, which he delivered in Birmingham in April 1968. In it he claimed, 'As I look ahead I am filled with foreboding. Like the Roman, I seem to see the River Tiber foaming with much blood' and he went on to warn that immigration was causing 'a total transformation to which there is no parallel in a thousand years of British history'. This transformation meant that white Britons 'found their wives unable to obtain hospital beds in child-birth, their children unable to obtain school places, their homes and neighbourhoods changed beyond recognition, their plans and prospects for the future defeated.' The speech cost Powell his place in the Shadow Cabinet, but a poll carried out in May 1968 showed that 74 per cent of those polled agreed with him.

Views like these have played an important part in shaping the experience of black and Asian people in Britain and in the next section we look at the consequences of this process of racialization.

Racial inequality in Britain

Table 8.1 reproduces the ethnic origin question in the United Kingdom's 2001 population census. The same categories are now being utilized for the purposes of

Table 8.1 The population of Great Britain

Ethnic group	Thousands	%
Indian	1,502	1.8
Pakistani	747	1.3
Bangladeshi	283	0.5
Black Caribbean	566	1.0
Black African	485	0.8
Chinese	243	0.4
Mixed	674	1.2
Other ethnic minorities	578	1.0
White	52,481	91.9
Ethnic minority*	4,623	8.1
All population	57,104	100

*Ethnic minority = all non-white groups
Source: 2001 Census

ethnic monitoring. For instance, when people are arrested by the police in Britain their ethnic origin is now recorded. Those under arrest must ascertain with which category they identify themselves. This may well create problems for those who identify themselves in ways the classification does not allow. Many persons within the South Asian parental generation would prefer to be classified by religion. Conversely, it is likely that their children (before long) may object to being classified by their parents' country of origin (possibly preferring to be identified as Muslims, Hindus or Sikhs). Others may desire the category 'black British' or one that represents an intermediate identify between black and white.

The PSI surveys

The Policy Studies Institute (and its predecessor, called the Political and Economic Planning (PEP) group) has produced national surveys of ethnic minorities in Britain since the 1960s. The first survey was published in 1966 and since this date it has become a sophisticated source of information on the subject.

When the first survey was commissioned very little was known about a population of migrant origin, who at the time numbered less than 1 million. In 1991 the census counted three million members of ethnic minority groups and they and the topic of 'race' are a major area of study in British social research. The PSI surveys remain the only large-scale national studies designed exclusively with the aim of increasing our knowledge about the circumstances of ethnic minorities and how they compare with those of the white population. They concentrate on discrimination and disadvantage in employment, education, housing, physical and mental health, lifestyle and cultural identity. They complement the data provided by other sources such as the census and the Labour Force Survey.

When the first survey was produced in 1966 the main focus of concern was discrimination. The first Race Relations Act, which mirrored American civil rights legislation, had been passed; while it prohibited segregated access to public services such as restaurants, discrimination in areas such as employment and housing remained not only in the legal context but also in overt ways through notices stating 'no coloureds'. The first survey, besides interviewing people about their perception and personal experience of discrimination, devised objective tests of the extent of discrimination (Daniel 1968). For example, white and ethnic minority actors, impersonating job applic-ants, applied to the same real job vacancies to discover the extent to which the white but not the minority actor were offered jobs. The tests conclusively established that racial discrimination was widespread, and the survey was one of the influences which led to the second Race Relations Act of 1967, outlawing direct discrimination in employment, housing and other fields. Since then discrimination testing has been extended and repeated a number of times, and has consistently shown the persistence of discrimination, even though it was illegal (e.g. Brown and Gay 1985: Simpson and Stevenson 1994).

It was clear from the first survey that the inequalities between whites and the minorities were not just produced by face-to-face discrimination but were the outcome of structural disadvantages. Minority groups had different qualifications and skill levels, for instance. Indirect discrimination also reduced black and Asian people's chances of success: for example, some employers gave preference in recruitment to relatives of existing employees, thus perpetuating an all-white workforce. The focus of racial equality in the 1970s therefore shifted to comparing outcomes, regardless of whether they were produced by discrimination or not, to see if the disadvantages faced by the minorities were lessening or persisting. The survey of 1974 found considerable inequality between whites and ethnic minorities in employment and housing conditions (Smith 1977). It was, in turn, one of the influences behind the third Race Relations Act (1976), which broadened the concept of discrimination to include indirect discrimination which refers to the unintended effect of policies and practices, such as those of employers when filling job vacancies.

The third national survey, undertaken in 1982, had a larger sample and widened the comparative socio-economic basis of analysis. While in many respects minority groups were in a much worse position than the white population, there was evidence of upward movement in job levels (Brown 1984). Although the focus of race relations research in the early 1980s was still on a dualistic perspective, distinguishing between the minorities as a group and the white majority, the third survey also provided evidence that some minorities were reporting different experiences from others.

The fourth national survey of ethnic minorities was undertaken in 1994 by the Policy Studies Institute and Social and Community Planning Research and published in 1997 under the title 'Ethnic Minorities in Britain: Diversity and Disadvantage' (Modood *et al.* 1997). This involved a nationally representative sample of 5,196 people of Caribbean and Asian origin who were interviewed in detail, together with a comparative sample of 2,867 white people. Each survey has broadened the scope of investigation of its predecessor. In general, it found that while there had been progress towards developing multicultural equality, there is a growing diversity between differing ethnic minority groups in terms of their experiences and position in contemporary British society. Essentially, it showed that some ethnic minority groups, for instance Pakistanis and Bangladeshis, continue to face severe disadvantages while others, such as African Asians and Chinese, have reached a position of broad parity with the white population.

In the rest of this chapter we examine racial differences in the areas of employment, and housing and then conclude by discussing in some detail an area of continuing contention: the policing of black communities.

Employment

Racism and racial discrimination account for most of the discrepancies in the employment statistics of black people. Generally, the over representation of blacks on the unemployment register and in low paid jobs still prevails, and now there is consistent research data to verify this in the private as well as public sectors . . . there will no doubt be a steady growth in black business, but this is not going to resolve the economic crisis faced by the black community.

(Bhat *et al.* l988, cited in Skellington 1992: 132)

Periphery to metropolis: migrant labour and inequality

According to Cashmore and Troyna (1990) the system of domination, which characterized the historical experience of empire, produced a well-regulated supply of labour

Table 8.2 Employment rates, percentage of people aged 16 and over		
Ethnic group	Women %	Men %
White	55.1	67.7
Black Caribbean	55.0	55.7
Indian	49.6	64.6
Chinese	44.6	52.9
Black African	42.8	51.0
Pakistani	21.0	52.3
Bangledeshi	16.6	48.6

Source: 2001 Census

from the periphery (colonies) to the centre of the system – the metropolis. In the early period of the empire, labour transference from the periphery to the centre was achieved by force – through slavery. However, in more recent times migrants have moved voluntarily to the centre:

> On, and for some time after arrival, the migrants tend to be disadvantaged relative to the metropolitan population and are compelled to accept only the undesirable jobs. Thus, migrants are almost disproportionately represented in the lower grade employments.
>
> (Cashmore and Troyna 1990: 74)

Migrants tended to be utilized in the public service sector. Wage levels here trailed behind those in the private sector. Migrants were also channelled into industrial jobs characterized by low pay, long hours and 'unpleasant' working conditions (C. Brown 1992: 47). Such conditions correspond to the conditions described in the 'secondary' labour market.

The dual labour market theory

This model, advocated by writers such as Piore (1973), suggests that the labour market is divided into primary and secondary sectors. The primary market, characterized by high pay, security, good prospects and good working conditions, attracts the 'stable' worker. Conversely, the secondary market, characterized by low pay, insecurity and poor working conditions, attracts 'unstable employees – women, ethnic minorities and other marginal and relatively docile groups' (Blackburn and Mann 1981: 77). In this scenario the 'stigmatized' minority groups find themselves caught up within a vicious circle. They can obtain jobs only in the secondary labour market and their over-representation within this market merely serves to reinforce their inferior social status (Richardson and Lambert 1995: 78).

Colin Brown (1992) suggests that for both employers and the indigenous workforce the invitation to immigrant workers was not an open one; rather it was a 'last resort'. This point was made clear by employers in the interviews during the first of the Political and Economic Planning Studies:

> The initial decision to employ them was almost invariably taken reluctantly, apprehensively and after a perhaps prolonged struggle with shortages of staff and unsuccessful attempts to recruit enough white employees. Inevitably the sectors in which circumstances had forced employers to accept coloured employees, through the shortage of white personnel,

had been those of acute manpower shortage or those in which the type or location of the jobs were especially unattractive to white people.

> (Daniel 1968, quoted in C. Brown 1992: 47)

Immigrants: the new reserve army of labour

According to Marxist writers Castles and Kosack (1973), immigrants form the new industrial reserve army of labour in the metropolitan centres. Capitalism creates a situation of underdevelopment in former colonies which in turn produces large reserve pools of cheap labour to be drawn on as required when metropolitan centres experience labour shortages. This, as we have seen, happened in the postwar period in Britain. The employment of immigrant workers has important socio-political functions for capitalism. Migrants do not simply enter a class society; they have an impact on it. For Castles and Kosack (1972) a division is created between immigrant and indigenous workers along 'national' and 'racial' lines. Working-class cohesion is divided because

> **Many indigenous workers do not perceive that they share a common class position and class interest with immigrant workers. The basic fact of having the same relationship to the means of production is obscured by the local workers' marginal advantage with regards to material conditions and status.**
>
> (Castles and Kosack 1972)

This marginal advantage enjoyed by indigenous white labour creates, for large sections of the working class, 'the consciousness of a labour aristocracy, which objectively participates in the exploitation of another group of workers' (Castles and Kosack 1972).

In Castles and Kosack's analysis, indigenous workers do not regard immigrant workers as comrades but as an alien presence which poses an economic and social threat. The fear is that they will take jobs from white workers and will be used by employers to force down wages and break strikes. Castles and Kosack point out that such racialism not only prevents working-class unity but also aids capitalism in its programme of 'divide and rule'.

Discrimination and employment in contemporary Britain

By the year 2000, over half the black population had been born and educated in Britain. Consequently the position of black people in the labour market in contemporary Britain cannot be explained in terms of low aspirations of immigrants. Evidence suggests that inequalities in the labour market are largely caused by racial discrimination.

Patterns of discrimination in employment

> If you can't be looked at and be seen as white, then you're going to be disadvantaged in employment. It's as simple and easy as that.   (Oppenheim 1993: 116)

Elizabeth Burney (1988) stated that black workers in Britain were no better off than they were before the second Race Relations Act became law in 1968. Her report concluded that in the absence of positive action members of ethnic minority groups would consistently fail to be part of mainstream economic life (Burney 1988, cited in Skellington 1992: 133). Colin Brown (1992) claims that no evidence was produced during the 1980s to suggest a drop in the extent of discrimination in the labour market. Research carried out by Brown and Gay in 1985 in London, Birmingham and Manchester found that at least one-third of private employers discriminated against both Afro-Caribbean and Asian applicants (C. Brown 1992: 60).

The 1988 BBC TV series *Black and White* used secret cameras to record 'real' attitudes of 'ordinary' people living in a 'typical' British city (Bristol). Two reporters, one black (Geoff Small) and one white (Tim Marshall), spent two months monitoring discrimination in employment, housing and accommodation and leisure. The series highlighted the often invisible nature of direct, deliberate discrimination:

> The landlady of the Ashley Arms, for example, who was not just nice, but seemed to go out of her way to explain exactly how and when the bar jobs had gone, turned out to be giving me an elaborate brush-off; but I would never have suspected, had it not been for our concealed camera, and the follow-up visit of Tim, who was promptly told that the job was still open.
>
> (Geoff Small, *The Listener* 14.4.88)

Studies suggest that young blacks and Asians have been excluded from those government training schemes that are most likely to lead to permanent employment (C. Brown 1992: 61). For example, the Youth Employment and Training Unit (YETRU) claimed in 1989 that

---

Case study

My life as a secret policeman

Mark Daly spent months working as a policeman in Manchester. His fellow officers were unaware that their colleague was, in fact, an undercover journalist who was trying to discover if racism lurked among their ranks.

> I am a BBC undercover journalist and 18 months ago I began the application procedure to join Greater Manchester Police.
>
> In 1999 the Macpherson Report branded London's Metropolitan Police institutionally racist. The report, which followed the Met's failure to successfully prosecute a gang of white youths for the murder of Stephen

Lawrence, found ethnic minorities in Britain felt under-protected as victims and over-policed as suspects.

The year before, the then chief constable of Greater Manchester Police took the bold step of admitting that his own force was institutionally racist.

We wanted to see what steps were being taken to eradicate

this. But more importantly, we needed to see if they were working. The only way we could find out what was really happening was to become a police officer – asking questions openly as a journalist would not have uncovered the truth.

Working undercover using the latest hi-tech covert filming equipment meant I could expose any of my fellow officers who held racist views or behaved in a racist manner.

And on 27 January this year, I had my first day of training as PC 2210 Daly. After five months of intensive training I was, for eight weeks, a fully operational PC working the beat.

Case study (continued)

I believe that at no time did my position as a journalist undermine or affect the way I carried out my duties with the public as a police officer . . .

In my time within the police, I encountered dozens of probation officers and senior officers, most of whom do their job with the highest of professional and ethical standards. I make no attempt to tar all officers with the same brush.

But the covertly filmed evidence against some of these men – and the allegations are not confined to GMP officers – is compelling. What I found was a police service trying very hard – and failing – to put its house in order.

The majority of the officers I met will undoubtedly turn out to be good, non-prejudiced ones intent on doing the job properly. But the next generation of officers from one of Britain's top police colleges contains a significant minority of people who are holding the progress of the police service back.

Racist abuse like 'Paki' and 'Nigger' were commonplace for these PCs. The idea that white and Asian members of the public should be treated differently because of their colour was not only acceptable for some, but preferable. I had become a friend to these men. They trusted me with their views. And they believed I was one of them . . .

(Mark Daly, BBC News Online 21.10.2003)

10 officers resigning and 12 more facing displicinary action.

Chief Constable Michael Todd and Deputy Chief Constable Alan Green of Greater Manchester Police met journalist Mark Daly and producer Simon Ford last week.

The documentary revealed racism at a police training college in Cheshire.

Mr Ford said: 'We had a very consistent meeting with the police.

'It's rare for a programme to have the amount of impact that *The Secret Policeman* has had, but if we can be of use in helping the police deal with racism then that's part of the job of the BBC in building public value.'

(BBC News Online 7.3.2005)

Extremity

It was at the Police National Training Centre in Warrington, where trainees from 10 forces in the North West and Wales spend 15 weeks, that much of my material was garnered.

The extremity of some of the racism I encountered from these recruits beggared belief.

Police and BBC in racism meeting

Senior police chiefs and the BBC have met to discuss progress made on issues raised by a television documentary about racism in the force.

The 2003 screening of The Secret Policeman led to

Question

1. Mark Daly's covert investigation identified racism amongst police recruits (trainees and not serving police officers). To what extent do you think it is fair to suggest that this is evidence of 'institutionalised racism' in the police service?

---

racial discrimination was widespread on Youth Training Schemes (YTS) – most notably among 'prestigious' employers that had outlets in large cities where black communities are concentrated (Skellington 1992: 137–8).

The Gifford Report (1989) examined 'race relations' in Liverpool. Among its area of focus were inequality and the struggle for jobs in the city. Examples of incidents often encountered by job centre staff highlighted the discriminatory practices of would-be employers. They included:

The employer who said the vacancy was filled once he saw the applicant was Black.

The employer who said the vacancy was filled once he heard the applicant speaking on the telephone with a non-English accent.

The employer based in the South Liverpool area who will not use the Toxteth job centre (South Liverpool) for filling vacancies.

(Gifford 1989: 136)

Stop and think

➤ Why is discrimination in the workplace difficult to detect?

➤ Why might it be detrimental to people to claim that they were discriminated against at work?

➤ Why might people not realize they had been discriminated against in the workplace?

Black women and the labour market

In general Black women are to be found in the lower echelons of all the institutions where they are employed, where the pay is lowest and the hours are longest and most anti-social. In accordance with gender divisions, Black women tend to be employed in particular sectors of the Welfare State: catering and cleaning, nursing and hospital ancillary work.

(Mama 1992: 83)

Studies of postwar migration have often presumed that female migration to Britain was a 'passive following of menfolk' (Peach 1972). Conversely, Doyal *et al.* (1981) contend that while that this was partially true, a substantial number of Caribbean and African women migrated independently. Migrant female labour, following the patterns of migrant male labour, tended to occupy low-paid jobs vacated by the socially mobile indigenous workforce.

Doyal *et al.* (1981) contend that immigrants constituted a source of cheap labour in the NHS. In contemporary Britain, black nurses are disproportionately represented in unpopular specialist areas such as mental health and genetics (Radical Statistics Health Group 1987). Mama points out that public expenditure cuts in the NHS since the early 1980s have disproportionately affected black workers across the board. Additionally, 'persistent discrimination ensures racist recruitment patterns in those areas being expanded and developed' (Mama 1992: 84).

Mama contends that black women's role as workers (most notably in the African and Caribbean communities) is particularly important because they are more likely to have unemployed partners and more dependants than white women (Mama 1992: 85).

Discrimination and the professions

Thus far attention has been focused on inequality in the less prestigious areas of the labour market. However,

it would be misleading to assume that all black labour is located in low-status occupations. Research in the late 1980s and early 1990s has focused on discrimination in the professional sphere of the labour market. Areas of direct and indirect discrimination included accountancy (CRE 1987a), graduate employment (CRE 1987b) and journalism (Alibhai 1990).

Labour Force Survey (LFS) statistics for the years 1987, 1988 and 1989 show that 41 per cent of employed men of Indian origin were located in professional and managerial positions compared with 35 per cent for the white population.

A 1991 survey of 15,000 young (under 35) black people found that 30 per cent of respondents were qualified to degree level and a quarter held professional or vocational qualifications. Despite this, two-thirds of the men and one-third of the women surveyed claimed they had experienced discrimination in work and in promotion (Skellington 1992: 142).

Unemployment

Unemployment rates have been consistently higher for black people and other ethnic minority groups than for white people. During the period 1989–91 the male unemployment figure for black people and other ethnic minority groups stood at 13 per cent – almost double the rate for white people (7 per cent). The pattern in unemployment rates for women was similar: 12 per cent compared with 7 per cent (House of Commons, *Hansard* 21.5.1992).

High rates of unemployment particularly affected people from Bangladesh and Pakistan. In 1989–91, the figures stood at 21 per cent for men and 24 per cent for women (House of Commons, *Hansard* 21.5.1992). In 1989–91, 22 per cent of young men (aged 16–24) from

Table 8.3 Unemployment rates, percentage of people aged 16–74

Ethnic group	Women %	Men %
White	3.8	5.6
Chinese	5.4	5.5
Indian	6.2	6.1
Black Caribbean	7.8	14.9
Black African	12.2	14.2
Pakistani	14.5	13.6
Bangladeshi	16.5	15.9

Source: 2001 Census

Case study (continued)

Racism, discrimination and the criminal justice system

The Bar

In 1990, Kate Muir examined the situation relating to black lawyers at the Bar. Although a Bill had become law in November 1990 outlawing race discrimination at the Bar, it was unlikely to make any difference to black lawyers 'in the world of old boys' committees and Oxbridge degrees which constitute the legal establishment'.

Muir focused on 'sets' (groups of barristers sharing 'chambers'). Describing the situation as 'legal apartheid', she argues that black sets are treated as inferior, inefficient, 'poor relations' by the white sets. Ethnic minority sets tend to be less busy than their white counterparts and tend to specialize in less lucrative and prestigious areas such as family and criminal law and commercial law.

Muir pointed out that in 1988, 182 chambers had no black members. In 1989, out of a total of 269 chambers which responded to a Bar Council survey, 16 contained 53 per cent of all non-white barristers. Muir maintained that a non-statistical way of describing the situation was 'ghetto'.

(Adapted from Kate Muir, 'Legal apartheid', *Correspondent Magazine* 11.11.1990)

The judiciary

➤ 15.8 per cent of court judges are female.

➤ 3.4 per cent of court judges are from minority ethnic groups.

➤ 59 per cent of law graduates are female.

➤ Only 7 per cent of High Court judges are female.

➤ In 1998–99, 20.1 per cent of all appointments to courts were women.

➤ By 2002–03, that figure had risen to 22.4 per cent.

➤ In 1998–99, 3.1 per cent of all appointments to courts were black or Asian.

➤ By 2002–03, that figure had risen to 6.4 per cent.

➤ In Canada, a quarter of judges in federal courts are women.

So, for many members of ethnic minorities, the face of British justice looks very white. In many parts of the criminal justice system, black and Asian people are significantly under represented. And the higher up the promotion ladder you go, the fewer people you encounter from ethnic communities.

In the police, very few blacks and Asian officers have risen to the rank of superintendent. And while the legal profession is becoming more diverse, top judges and QCs are still overwhelmingly white.

Question

1. *What measures might be taken to increase the numbers of people from ethnic minorities in the judiciary?*

---

black and other ethnic minorities were unemployed, compared with 12 per cent of young white men. The figures for young women were 19 per cent and 9 per cent respectively (House of Commons, *Hansard* 21.5.1992).

In 1989–91, the unemployment rate for ethnic minorities with high qualifications stood at 6 per cent compared with 3 per cent for white people with the same qualifications. The unemployment rate for ethnic minorities with 'other' qualifications stood at 13 per cent compared with 6 per cent for white people with similar qualifications ('Ethnic origins and the labour market', *Employment Gazette*, Department of Employment, February 1993). (This section is cited in Oppenheim 1993.)

The 1994 PSI survey found that unemployment rates for men (the percentage of economically active persons without work) varied between groups. Among men under retirement age, approximately 15 per cent of whites were unemployed. The proportions of Chinese, African Asians and Indians were within the same range (9, 14 and 19 per cent respectively). In contrast, Caribbean men had an unemployment rate double that of whites, 31 per cent, and Bangladeshi and Pakistani rates were even higher at 42 and 38 per cent respectively.

Female unemployment rates were generally lower than men's. The same ethnic pattern occurs as for men but the differences are smaller. The Chinese had the

A closer look

Multi-cultural Britain – room for improvement?

As Director of the Centre for the Study of Ethnicity and Citizenship at Bristol University, Professor Tariq Modood has researched patterns of inclusion and discrimination in education, employment, etc., and discovered a complex set of arrangements in which some ethnic groups do well in education (notably Indian and Chinese) while others (Bangladeshi women and Afro-Caribbean men) do not. These differential trends are reflected in patterns of employment. In a report on employment prospects in 2000, he concluded:

Overall, there are both positive and negative elements within the British experience . . . Sophisticated quantitative analyses, careful differentiation between groups, linkages between ethnicity, religion, class and gender, new analyses of racism, including 'new' racism, cultural racism and Islamophobia, suggest that while there may be no singular 'black–white' divide, 'race' and ethnicity continue to shape economic as well as wider socio-cultural divisions in Britain. Research shows that by most measures, racial disadvantage is declining and the circumstances of the minority groups are diverging. Some groups are poorly placed in educational and occupational hierarchies, others have overtaken the white population in the acquisition of qualifications, in business ownership and in entry to some prestigious professions, though perhaps all minorities are underrepresented as managers in large establishments. This overall picture reveals employment patterns for some sections of ethnic minority groups which are far better than that painted by surveys in previous decades, which had shown a general confinement of ethnic minorities to low skilled, low paid work.

   Whilst the causes of this development are many, it is not unreasonable to suppose that one part of the explanation is the role of equal opportunities policies in breaking down barriers of discrimination and disadvantage . . . The British experience has been that legal and administrative measures, voluntary policies, and the pressure on organisations from the collective actions of workers have all been necessary to bring about progress in the processes of integration of immigrants and ethnic minorities into employment.

(Wrench and Modood 2000: can be found on http://www.ilo.org)

lowest rate (6 per cent) followed by whites (9 per cent), African Asians and Indians (12 per cent) and Caribbeans (18 per cent). Pakistani and Bangladeshi women had a similar rate of unemployment to their male peers (39 and 40 per cent respectively) (Modood *et al.* 1997: 89).

Racial disadvantage continues to be a fact, even if it does not apply to all ethnic minority groups. This disadvantage is attributable partly to discrimination in employment. Controlled tests, whereby white and ethnic minority persons respond to advertised vacancies for which they are equally suitable, have been conducted since the 1960s and tend to reproduce the result that at least one-third of private employers discriminated against Caribbean applicants, Asian applicants or both (Daniel 1968; Smith 1977; Brown and Gay 1985; Simpson and Stevenson 1994). Discrimination is found not just in face-to-face encounters, or in telephone calls, but also in tests using written applications where it is clear from the applicant's name or biographical details that they are or are not white (Noon 1993; Esmail and Everington 1993). The Commission for Racial Equality continues every year to publish findings of direct or indirect discrimination in the practices of specific employers, and sometimes whole professions or industries, such as accountancy (CRE 1987a) or hotels (CRE 1991). The number of complaints of racial discrimination made by individuals to the CRE and to industrial tribunals has risen over the years (CRE annual reports). One in five of the minority ethnic respondents in the PSI Survey 1994 said they had been refused a job on racial grounds, nearly half of whom had had this experience at least once in the previous five years (Modood *et al.* 1997: 149).

Housing

Black people in Britain generally live in worse housing than white people, largely as a result of direct and indirect discrimination. Whether they are home owners, private tenants or council tenants, Black families are more likely to live in accommodation which is older, more crowded and situated in areas regarded as less desirable.

(Gordon and Newham 1986: 20)

Skellington (1992) points out that the general improvement in housing conditions in Britain since the 1950s has benefited ethnic minority groups along with the rest of the population. However, major disparities in housing outcomes still exist. From the late 1980s and into the 1990s a series of reports from the Commission for Racial Equality

(CRE) has highlighted covert and overt discrimination in housing policies and practices, including institutional racism, which has created and perpetuated ethnic minority disadvantages in housing (Skellington 1992: 93).

At the risk of over-generalization, we can distinguish two basic types of housing in Britain: private housing, including home ownership or private renting, and public or local authority housing, conventionally termed council housing. We look briefly at these two housing sectors and consider factors that might lead to racial inequalities within them.

Prejudice and discrimination in the private sector

Discrimination occurs in the private sector of housing through the actions and attitudes of what Skellington (1992: 109) terms 'key individuals'. These individuals include vendors, landlords and landladies, estate agents and building society officials. Their subjective racism may attempt to exclude black people from specific neighbourhoods.

In their research in Liverpool and Birmingham, Karn *et al.* (1983) identified stereotypical views among mortgage lenders that West Indians and Asians will want to purchase property only in specific areas where their communities are located. Moreover, the white population will not want to buy or even remain living in such areas (cited in Ginsburg 1992: 119).

In Bedford, Sarre *et al.* (1989) identified a process whereby the institutionalized stereotyping of mortgage applicants by building society officials produced a 'status hierarchy'. Prospective Italian and Asian buyers were viewed positively whereas Afro-Caribbeans were defined in negative terms as 'unreliable and disorganised [and] having irresponsible attitudes to finance . . . they are judged to have failed to display the thrift and resourcefulness so highly valued by the building society movement' (Ginsburg 1992: 119).

Subjective racism may also be linked to institutional practices. Ginsburg (1992) points out that building society officials, solicitors, surveyors and estate agents operate within frameworks which often lend themselves to institutional racist practices. Moreover, institutional racism in the owner-occupier sector can be defined as the product of a combination of common-sense, subjective racism and structural forces:

> The exclusion of certain areas, property or people with low or insecure incomes has a common sense financial and administrative legitimation, to the extent that a building society manager can claim that lending on such properties or to such people is too risky . . . black people on average have lower incomes than white people, a feature of structural racism.
>
> (Ginsburg 1992: 119)

Skellington (1992) contends that while signs stating 'No Blacks' or 'No Irish' may have disappeared in the wake of race relations legislation, evidence suggests that racial bias persists in the private rented sector. The CRE (1990) report *Sorry, It's Gone* showed that one in five accommodation agencies in 13 locations discriminated against ethnic minority group applicants. Moreover, one in 20 private landlords and landladies also discriminated against these groups.

Research in Bristol for the TV series *Black and White* illustrated the often invisible nature of subjective racism:

> As the filming progressed it struck me more and more that there was no real way of knowing how to interpret people's behaviour. As we went after flats . . . some of the people who were nicest to my face, who went out of their way to be helpful, were the ones who were discriminating.
>
> (Geoff Small, *The Listener* 14.4.1988)

Stop and think

> ➤ What influence could (a) estate agents and (b) building society officials have on patterns of housing for white and black people?

> ➤ Why might they try to exclude black people from specific neighbourhoods?

Prejudice and discrimination in local authority housing

Administrative processes in local authority housing departments – as with building societies and estate agents – have resulted in the unfavourable treatment of black people. These processes cannot be explained solely in terms of subjective racism among individual staff within such institutions. Rather they are legitimized by a combination of negative stereotyping of black people and a failure to recognize their specific housing needs. Ginsburg (1992) suggests that racial inequalities in housing that are linked to the practices of local housing authorities can be defined in terms of institutional racism. He argues that institutional racism in the area of council housing manifests itself in three major forms. First, there is the desire to match specific tenants to specific properties. A report on the allocation of housing in Tower Hamlets, east London, highlighted a process of 'ghettoization' that was most notable among the Bengali community: 'The view that all social security and black tenants should be put together on certain estates was expressed to the researcher on several occasions by different [council] officers' (Philips 1986: 34).

In a similar vein, a Commission for Racial Equality study in Liverpool in the late 1970s revealed that black people were allocated to the least desirable estates in the city. The study also highlighted the number of instances where black applicants were subject to overt racism by council officers. A West Indian male stated: 'After seeing a vacant flat I went to the district office where I was told the flat was not "for your kind of people"' (CRE 1984: 80–1).

A follow-up study in the mid-1980s provided further evidence of direct discrimination with black applicants nominated to housing association property being treated less favourably than white applicants in terms of the property they received (CRE 1989, cited in Ginsburg 1992: 112). This study found that white people were twice as likely to be offered new properties than black people, were four times more likely to be offered purpose-built properties, and four times as likely to get an offer of a council house with a garden. Liverpool Council was subsequently taken to the High Court by the CRE in 1993 for failing to comply with CRE directives to end discrimination in housing allocation in the city.

Second, housing officers anticipate that there will be racial harassment directed against black tenants by established white tenants on certain estates:

> Certain estates have been regarded as unsuitable for black tenants mainly it seems because of white tenants' objections to cooking smells . . . Some council employees may have been prepared to let white tenants dictate the pattern of housing allocation.
>
> (Philips 1986: 34)

Ginsburg suggests a 'head to head' merger of subjective and institutional racism. Discrimination against those who are perceived as a threat to the 'smooth running' of estates creates 'institutionalised acceptance of racial harassment or the threat of it' (Ginsburg 1992: 114).

Third, there are the value judgements of council officers who identify a 'deserving' and 'undeserving' status. A study in Nottingham in the mid-1970s revealed that on average black families were larger in size than white families and therefore required larger properties. The council did not have many larger properties available and those it did have were in varying states of disrepair. As a consequence, black people waited longer for housing or rehousing from overcrowded accommodation. Furthermore, they tended to be offered the 'poorer' properties by housing officials (Simpson 1981: 257).

Ginsburg points out that this particular manifestation of institutional racism which ignores the particular

Case study

Gentrification: perpetuating inequality

The process of 'gentrification' has been cited as perpetuating inequality in housing in contemporary Britain. 'Gentrification' refers to the middle classes moving into areas of towns and cities that have become run down. Private landlords are encouraged to sell their large rundown properties to property developers for high prices. The properties are then renovated and sold or rented out to better off, middle-class tenants from outside the area.

The run-down areas that become gentrified tend to be in inner-city areas and to have high concentrations of ethnic minority groups. Invariably these ethnic minority populations are forced to move to accommodation outside the gentrified area, which has now been priced beyond their means. On average, Black people have lower incomes than white people and therefore are effectively excluded from enjoying the benefits of living in gentrified areas. Jacobs (1988) comments that in Britain, as in the USA, the process of gentrification 'has had the effect of reinforcing the relative deprivation of ethnic minorities'.

(Jacobs 1988: 111)

Question

1. *To what extent has gentrification produced new forms of 'ghettoisation' in contemporary Britain?*

housing needs of black families is common to many housing authorities. Moreover, large families have traditionally been viewed as 'less deserving'. The notions of deserving, less deserving or undeserving have adversely affected not only black people but also Irish people, single mothers and unemployed people (Ginsburg 1992: 112–14).

Government housing policies and inequality

Ginsburg has commented that government housing policies have played a structurally racist role in producing inequality in housing in Britain. Since the mid-1970s both Labour and Conservative policies have focused on home ownership and withdrawal of support from council housing and council tenants. Government support for home ownership has included housing improvement grants, capital gains tax exemption and mortgage tax relief – all of which have differentially benefited higher income groups, among whom black people are poorly represented (Ginsburg 1992: 120).

The promotion of council house sales since the Housing Act 1980 has further amplified inequality. Over 1.25 million local authority dwellings have been sold since that Act was passed; those homes that have been sold tend to have been on 'better' estates with, for instance, their own gardens, again effectively excluding black applicants:

> These estates are populated mostly by white working class households who benefited from the racialised allocation policies of the previous decades. Thus local institutional racism of the past combined with contemporary central government policy produce a powerful inegalitarian effect.   (Ginsburg 1992: 121)

A closer look

Table 8.4 Ethnic group:[1] by tenure, 2001–04[2]: England

	Owned outright %	Owned with mortgage %	Rented from social sector %	Rented privately[3] %	All tenures (= 100%) (millions) %
White					
British	30	42	19	9	18.0
Irish	25	35	27	13	0.3
Other White	26	31	17	26	0.8
Mixed	11	39	32	18	0.2
Asian					
Indian	27	53	8	12	0.3
Pakistani	24	48	13	16	0.2
Bangladeshi	9	26	55	10	0.1
Black					
Black Caribbean	13	37	42	8	0.2
Black African	2	21	47	29	0.2
Chinese	14	39	12	34	0.1
Other ethnic groups	17	29	31	23	0.2
All households	29	42	19	10	20.4

1 Ethnic group of household reference person.
2 Combined data for 2001/02, 2002/03 and 2003/04.
3 Includes tenants in rent-free accommodation and squatters.

(Survey of English Housing, Office of the Deputy Prime Minister in *Social Trends* 35, 2005)

Questions

1. *Summarize the patterns of housing for the main different ethnic groups.*

2. *What are the main differences between the Black, Asian and White groups?*

3. *What are the differences within those ethnic groups?*

4. *What explanations can you suggest for those differences?*

Furthermore, cuts in public expenditure on the maintenance and construction of council housing represents another facet of structural racism which directly affects black people and thus perpetuates inequality. According to the Chancellor's Autumn Statement in 1988, public expenditure on housing was cut by 79 per cent between 1979 and 1988: 'The restraint in spending on council housing allied with council house sales has solidified and extended the racial inequalities already existing.'

Centre, twilight and periphery: housing classes

In Chicago in the 1920s, Robert Park, Ernest Burgess and Roderick McKenzie (1923) identified clear, demarcated sections of the city that were occupied by specific groups. These sections were found to form roughly concentric zones spreading out from the city centre. Park and his colleagues categorized these zones. The central area was essentially a business zone. This was surrounded by a zone of transition – an area characterized by run-down, dilapidated property and a general air of social disadvantage, with poverty and crime prevalent. Beyond this zone they identified three others, one occupied by the working classes and the other two by the 'privileged' classes. In this model the more powerful and affluent sections of society obtained the more desirable property at the periphery of the city.

Park and Burgess's model was adapted by Rex and Moore (1967) for a study in the 1960s based on the Sparkbrook area of Birmingham. Rex and Moore identified specific types of resident that corresponded to specific spatial zones of the city. The upper middle class, for instance, lived in large houses in peripheral areas away from industrial locations. By contrast, ethnic minority groups tended to be concentrated near the centre of the city, in twilight zones. These twilight zones were similar to the zones of transition identified in Chicago: they were run down, crime-ridden and generally undesirable places to live. People living in such areas had limited access to the more desirable forms of accommodation in the outer spatial zones. In these cases, it is the city itself that generates inequalities which are separate from and additional to inequalities that occur in other areas such as work and education.

Moving away from the traditional Marxian approaches, which identify two main classes in terms of their relationship to the means of production, Rex and Moore adopt a more flexible, Weberian approach which identifies a variety of classes according to their 'market situations' – and one such market is housing. Thus they introduce the notion of 'housing classes' (Richardson and Lambert 1985: 73).

In this scenario an individual might occupy a powerful position in the labour market but this does not necessarily reflect power and influence in the housing market. Therefore:

> A Pakistani worker might be relatively well qualified and have a position of seniority that pays well; but he [*sic*] may still be crushingly disadvantaged in his access to desirable housing. The opposite case may hold for a white labourer who has reasonable quality accommodation. (Cashmore and Troyna 1990: 108)

Housing, racial harassment and inequality

> Racial attacks, racial harassment and the threat of them at home are thus very significant in perpetuating racism and racial inequalities in housing in contemporary Britain. (Ginsburg 1992: 124)

> An Asian woman who reported a series of attacks to the police was stopped in a lift on a Merton estate by a man with a knife who threatened to kill her if she went to the police again. (Gordon and Newham 1986: 22)

> A three-year-old boy suffered a broken leg after he was run over by a youth on a bicycle. The incident took place on a council estate in Wandsworth, South London. The boy's mother has suffered racial abuse for three years. She has had blood smeared on her front door, stones thrown and pellets fired at her. This was one of 24 cases reported to the Wandsworth and Merton Racial Harassment Unit over a two-week period.
> (Gordon and Newham 1986: 22)

Skellington (1992) argues that up until the mid-1980s the response of most councils to allegations of racial harassment or direct attacks on white estates was to treat them as private matters between neighbours. Ginsburg (1992) points out that the major policy issues for local housing authority departments in such cases are the removal (transfer) of victims and the removal (eviction) of perpetrators. The former is the easier option, while the latter response is only rarely adopted: 'Victim transfer is disastrous as a long-term solution, yet it is being widely implemented' (Ginsburg 1992: 125).

Skellington suggests that in such cases black tenants are usually transferred back to overcrowded estates which contain large populations of minority ethnic group tenants. Action by housing departments against the perpetrators of racial harassment on housing estates is rare. Problems relating to legal interpretations and definitions of racial harassment have resulted in few councils taking such action.

In 1984 Newham became the first local authority to evict a white family for the persistent and violent harassment of its Asian neighbours. However, by the end of 1987 only six cases had been brought against white tenants and only three of these had succeeded in forcing the eviction of the perpetrators of racial violence and harassment.

Stop and think

➤ Why might local councils not wish to take action against tenants accused of racial violence/harassment?

➤ Do you think racial harassment should lead to eviction? Explain your answer.

The policing of black communities

A history of oppressive relations 1919–59

The defining of black people in Britain as a 'problem' is not a new phenomenon. In the period between the First and Second World Wars the expanding black communities of maritime cities such as Liverpool and Cardiff were seen as 'an unwanted presence by the various levels of government, including the police' (Cashmore and McLoughlin 1991: 22).

Racial disturbances, traceable as early as 1919 in Cardiff, Newport, Glasgow, Tyneside and east London, resulted in calls for the repatriation of black seamen.

Case study

Homelessness

The risk of becoming homeless is higher for people living on low incomes, for people from ethnic minorities and for single parents.

(Oppenheim 1993: 53)

The growth of homelessness in Britain in the 1980s and 1990s has particularly affected black people – both families and young single people – as the following findings demonstrate.

In 1988 research in London found that minority ethnic group households were up to four times as likely to become homeless as white households.

(NACAB 1988, cited in Skellington 1992: 99)

A CRE study spanning the period 1984–85 in Tower Hamlets suggested that a process of overt institutional racism affected homeless Bangladeshis. In particular, it found that there

were 'significant differences' in the period spent in temporary accommodation by Bangladeshis in comparison to white people. Evidence also suggested that Bangladeshis were offered inferior temporary accommodation often miles away from the area.

(CRE, cited in Ginsburg 1992: 122–3)

Young people, and most notably young single people, are particularly susceptible to homelessness. A survey of 24 London boroughs in 1989 highlighted the problem. In Brent and Southwark, for example, a disproportionate number of the single homeless were young and black. There was also evidence to suggest that an increasing number of the single homeless were young Asian women.

(SHIL and LHU 1989, cited in Skellington 1992: 99)

A more recent study by Centrepoint, Soho in London

(1992) that focused on young people who stayed at their night shelter during the period 1981–91 found that 36 per cent were from black and ethnic minority backgrounds.

(Oppenheim 1993: 88)

The effect of homelessness on educational attainment was highlighted by an HMI survey in 1990. It found that 'homeless children tended not to be enrolled at school, were frequently absent, performed relatively poorly in class, and suffered from low self-esteem and expectations.'

(cited in Skellington 1992: 99–100)

Question

1. What steps might be taken at government level to respond effectively to homelessness amongst people from black and ethnic minority communities in Britain?

Studies carried out in the late 1920s suggested a relationship between black men, crime, prostitution and disease. During this period the police not only actively involved themselves as 'key local spokesmen' in favour of repatriation (Rich 1986) but also actively engaged in the harassment of black people through the enforcement of the 1925 Special Restriction Order on 'alien seamen' (Ramdin 1987). Cashmore and McLoughlin (1991: 23) conclude that the labelling of black people as a source of social problems during this period laid the foundations for the subsequent relationship between the police and the black communities in Britain.

The arrival in postwar Britain of non-white immigrants in large numbers from 'New Commonwealth' countries served to heighten the perception that black people were a problem. John Solomos (1989) suggests that the police played a key role in the construction of this image. He points to a 'manifest racial prejudice within the police force dating back to the early stages of migration' (Solomos 1989: 101).

Police handling of the Notting Hill riots in 1958 was strongly criticized by some commentators of the period for its heavy-handed, abusive and openly prejudicial treatment of black people. The long-term implications of such policing was summed up by Herbert Hill in 1959:

> Repeatedly one is given a sense that these people feel completely deserted and that, if effective and reasonable forms of protest and redress are not provided, irrational forms of protest and explosions of anger are inevitable.
>
> (Herbert Hill, *New Statesman* 9.5.1959)

In the period that followed these 1958 riots the policing of black communities was described by Hunte (1965) as 'malicious and exceptionally hostile' in his report *Nigger Hunting in England?* so called after a spate of anti-black operations which the Brixton police themselves called 'Nigger hunting' (Witte 1996). Some writers have pointed out that this facet of law and order represented the 'hard' side of a policing designed to implement a ruling class's assimilation and integrationist ideology, which was, in turn, based on a 'colonialist-paternalist' mentality (Cashmore and McLoughlin 1991: 24). In this scenario those sections of the black communities which refused to respond to the 'hard sell' of assimilation were defined in terms of an ongoing threat to social order. Consequently new strategies were devised to counter this threat.

Mugging: the 'problem' redefined in the 1960s and 1970s

Popular media images of black youths in inner-city areas had, by the end of the 1960s, established a link between black youth and crime. The link was redefined in the early 1970s as public concern was focused on the spectre of the 'predatory' black mugger. Hall *et al.* (1978) explain that the mugging panic heralded a call for the re-establishment of law and order. This emphasis on law and order was not directed at black youth alone but at the wider sources of political, social and economic unrest which 'threatened' the fabric of the postwar consensus. Such sources of conflict included politicized youth protest, women's movements, industrial unrest and an acceleration of violent protest in Northern Ireland. For Hall, the crisis of the black mugger is directly linked to a broader crisis – a crisis within capitalism itself. From this period 'Black youth became a metaphor for every fear and anxiety that existed in British society' (Cashmore and McLoughlin 1991: 27).

A confrontational approach in the 1970s and 1980s

From the early 1970s onwards violent confrontations between black youths and the police became regular occurrences in inner-city areas (Solomos 1989: 101). Paul Gilroy explains that the subsequent fear and anxiety generated by the mugging crisis enabled the police to justify a move towards a more authoritarian and aggressive approach to inner-city policing. The eventual outcome of such policing was seen by Cashmore and McLoughlin as 'the civil disturbances of the 1980s' (1991: 27).

Stop and think

- ➤ Why do you think black seamen, in particular, were considered a problem in the early 1900s?
- ➤ Why do you think that black youths, in particular, were signified as a threat in the 1970s and 1980s?

Urban violence in the 1980s

The 'riots' of the 1980s have exerted considerable influence on debates surrounding the politics of 'race' in contemporary Britain. They have played a key role in discussions which focus on reforms and policy changes designed to stop the reoccurrence of such events. We consider four broad explanations:

> the role of the police;
> urban deprivation;
> political exclusion and marginalization;
> a 'cry for loot'.

The role of the police

It is difficult to assess the extent to which the events of the 1980s were a consequence of the relationships between the police and local black communities. Cashmore and McLoughlin (1991) suggest that the 'authoritarian' and 'racist' features of inner-city policing were ultimately responsible for producing the violent protests that characterized the 'civil disturbances' of the 1980s.

The Scarman Report (1982), which not only focused on the Brixton disorders of April 1981 but also considered the disorders that occurred elsewhere in the summer of that year, drew attention to the strained relationship between the police and local black youths: 'Tension between the police and Black youth was, and remains, a fact of life in Brixton' (Scarman 1982: 3:23). Furthermore, Scarman maintained that the disorders of 10 April 1981, which preceded the more serious rioting of the 11th, were 'a spontaneous act of defiant aggression by young men who felt themselves hunted by a hostile police force' (Scarman 1982: 3:25).

Similarly, some accounts of the riots of 1985 drew attention to the potentially explosive relationship between the police and black youths. In their examination of the causes of rioting in Toxteth, Liverpool, in 1985 Solomos and Rackett highlighted the tense relationship between the police and black youth: 'As in Brixton and Handsworth, police relations with youths, and especially young black people were a significant factor in the explosive mixture' (Solomos and Rackett 1991: 48).

However, although the Scarman Inquiry made reference to the 'tense' relationship between police and black youths, it did point out that this was one face of a complex set of variables which created 'a predisposition towards violent protest' (Scarman 1982: 2:38).

Urban deprivation

Unemployment and urban deprivation featured prominently as issues during the 1980 and 1981 disturbances in Bristol, London, Liverpool and Manchester and in the 1985 disturbances in Birmingham and north London. Media representations created images of 'urban decay',

'tinderbox cities' and 'ghetto streets'. In a parliamentary debate on the 'civil disturbances' of July 1981, Roy Hattersley, the shadow home secretary, rejected the idea that the police were instrumental in 'sparking' the riots:

> I do not believe that the principal cause of last week's riots was the conduct of the police. It was the conditions of deprivation and despair in the decaying areas of our old cities – areas in which the Brixton and Toxteth riots took place.
>
> (Hattersley 1981, cited in Solomos 1989: 111)

Political exclusion and marginalization

The Scarman Report highlighted the feelings of powerlessness and political marginality endured by the black community in general and black youths in particular:

> In addition they do not feel politically secure. Their sense of rejection is not eased by the low level of Black representation in our elective political institutions . . . Rightly or wrongly, young Black people do not feel politically secure, any more than they feel economically or socially secure.   (Scarman 1982: 2:36)

Analysis of urban unrest in the USA also emphasized political marginality as a factor which influenced involvement in violent protest (e.g. Skolnick 1969; Fogelson 1971).

However, it has been pointed out that this line of argument was kept off the public agenda by those in power because it defined the disorders and disturbances in terms of political responses to political exclusion rather than as irrational acts of criminal elements (Solomos and Rackett 1991: 53).

> The attempt to depict the riots as irrational was very important. It denied legimitimacy to the rioters, their actions and their views. It made them events without a cause.
>
> (Kettle and Hodges 1982, quoted in Solomos 1989: 114)

A 'cry for loot'

The ideology which denied a legitimacy to arguments highlighting the political marginality of black communities also denied a legitimacy to analyses suggesting that poverty, unemployment and deprivation were factors in precipitating the riots.

Enoch Powell rejected outright notions that social and economic deprivation were the key factors and major causes. Without actually using the term, he argued that 'race' was the main causal factor (Solomos 1989: 105). Right-wing discourse articulated by commentators such as Geoffrey Partington (1986) claimed that anti-racist education policies produced a 'new racism' which fostered 'hatred of British institutions, values and beliefs' (P. Gordon 1988: 99). In an article in the *Journal of the Police Federation*, Partington (1982) claimed that the roots of the riots could be traced to classrooms which adopted anti-racist teaching: 'Long before violence erupted on the streets there was uproar in the playground, corridors and classrooms. Provocation of teachers preceded and

paved the way for harassment of police' (quoted in P. Gordon 1988: 99).

Geoffrey Dear, at that time chief constable of the West Midlands force, defined the 1985 riots in that area in criminal terms as a 'cry for loot' rather than uprising against harsh inner-city policing or unbearable social conditions (Solomos and Rackett 1991: 59).

Other right-wing arguments emphasized the supposed 'pathological nature' of the West Indian family, again defining the 'riots' as something which went beyond the government and the police.

Case study

Black people and the criminal justice system

The criminal justice agencies – the police, the courts, prosecution, probation and the prison service – all have a major Public Sector Agreement target to be achieved by 2008. This is focused on reassuring the public, reducing the fear of crime and anti-social behaviour and building confidence in the criminal justice system without 'compromising fairness' According to the *Black Manifesto* in 2005 this reflects the ministerial priority which had seminal place in the Macpherson Inquiry in 1999. However, the manifesto argues that such good intention is in discord with the reality of disproportional black criminalization across the criminal justice system.

➤ In 2004, 24.6 per cent of the prison population were from black communities.

➤ The average population of African and Caribbean prisoners has risen by 113 per cent since 1994.

➤ In 2004 black Africans or Caribbeans were six times more likely to be arrested than white people.

➤ Asian people are only slightly more likely to be arrested than white people.

➤ Criminalization of black communities is further illustrated by the discussion on ID cards. The *Black Manifesto* contends that ID cards will further lead to the marginalization and demonization of black communities.

➤ Stop and search figures according to 2005 statistics showed that in 2002/3, black people were 6.4 times more likely and Asian people almost twice as likely to be stopped and searched by the police than white people.

➤ Black communities, particularly the UK's Muslim population, have suffered from disproportionate numbers of arrests and detentions.

➤ Anti-terrorist legislation such as the ATCSA (Anti-Terrorism, Crime and Security Act 2001)

sanctioned the indefinate imprisonment at Belmarsh Prison of foreign terror suspects without trial. This coupled with The Prevention of Terrorism Bill 2005 arguably have increased Islamophobia in the UK.

➤ The *Observer* Sunday 27 March 2005 reported that black or minority ethnic communities were three to four times more likely to be subject of racial attack and reported 12 racist murders in the last four years.

➤ Racist incidents recorded by the police have risen steadily from just over 10,000 in 1996/7 to about 50,000 incidents in 2001/2.

➤ In 2003/4 the number of racist incidents recorded by the police rose to 52,694 (+9.7 per cent) (British Crime Survey Data 2004).

(Black Manifesto 2005)

Question

1. *How can the criminal justice system serve ethnic minority communities more effectively?*

Black police officers: recruitment and retention

A survey conducted by *Today* newspaper in the autumn of 1990 showed that out of the 51 police forces in Britain only 1,308 officers (0.9 per cent) were drawn from ethnic minority groups. In 1998 ethnic minorities within the police service were still only represented by less than 2 per cent, and there were no black or Asian chief constables.

In the wake of the 1999 publication of the report of the Macpherson Inquiry into the investigation of the murder of black teenager Stephen Lawrence, Jack Straw, then Home Secretary, set recruitment targets for the police based on the size of the local minority ethnic population. The minimum target was set at 1 per cent.

A year later in February 2000 the *Guardian* reported that more than a third of police forces in England and Wales had failed to hire a single extra black or Asian officer in the year since the Inquiry report had demanded a rapid increase in recruitment. In fact the *Guardian* further reported that the number of ethnic minority officers had actually fallen in nine of the 43 forces in England and Wales. Only the Metropolitan Police had managed to recruit significant numbers of black and Asian officers – 184 – more than twice the number taken on by all the other forces.

In 2003 new Home Office figures showed that although the total number of ethnic minority officers rose by 410 (13 per cent) during 2002, in nine out of the 45 forces in England and Wales their numbers remained the same or had fallen in the last year. The figures showed the Cumbria, North Yorkshire and North Wales forces remained nearly all white, with fewer than 10 officers from an ethnic minority out of more than 1,000 in each force.

Such initiatives were the latest in a long line of attempts to improve minority ethnic representation in the police service that stretched back to the mid-1970s.

Holdaway in his 1996 research on recruitment goes some way in explaining cultural and structural factors that deter potential black and Asian recruits from considering a career in the police service:

> The attractiveness of a police career to a black or Asian person is not immediate. Highly publicised individual cases where a black person has received poor treatment at the hands of the police; question marks about the handling of riots; concern about how one will be treated by future police colleagues; and other related issues will be weighed in the balance when a police career is considered.   (Holdaway 1996: 142–3)

Further research in 1997 on retention rates within the police service of black and Asian recruits showed minority ethnic officers having to cope with continued racist remarks and banter and harassment. There was a potentially vicious cycle of exclusion which Holdaway argued was difficult to break. The problems were particularly acute where the occupational culture was centred on activities from which some officers were excluded. For example, some Muslim officers felt unable to participate in activities centred on the consumption of alcohol while their lack of participation was viewed by some officers as an unwillingness to commit to the team. Mason (2000) reminds us that such examples highlight how easy it is for exclusionary processes to operate even in the absence of deliberate discrimination.

Urban violence: the picture since the 1980s

Solomos (1989) argued that in the years since 1981, rather than addressing the causes of unrest, the government has become preoccupied with the building of defences. Consequently the police have been provided with increased resources, training and equipment with which to 'deal with' urban unrest and riots when they occur. And with right-wing political and ideological beliefs becoming firmly entrenched throughout the 1980s and into the 1990s and beyond the prospects of social disadvantage and institutional racism being addressed at national level have been further reduced (Solomos and Rackett 1991).

In the absence of 'radical' and imaginative reforms Solomos and Rackett pointed to the likelihood that 'during the 1990s there would be further outbreaks of violent unrest' (1991: 63).

This prediction seems to have been well founded, as the rioting in Bradford in 1995 illustrated. In June 1995, following on from an incident in which the police removed an Asian woman and her child in the Manningham district of Bradford, there were two nights of violent disturbances between Asian youths and West Yorkshire police. The causes of the disturbances are complex. Manningham is one of Britain's most disadvantaged areas. Unemployment in 1995 among Asian males was over 50 per cent. Were they related therefore, to widespread unemployment, intense poverty and consequent alienation or to the defence of an Islamic community? Were they the result of a widening gap between Asian youth and elders? The increased use of drugs and pornographic activity among Asian people had led the

police to adopt what was viewed in the area by some as 'heavy-handed methods' in order to combat the problem. Therefore, were the disturbances a response to insensitive policing techniques?

In 1993, the then Metropolitan Police Commissioner, Sir Paul Condon, urged police to be 'intolerant of racially motivated attacks, intolerant of those who indulge in racial abuse and intolerant of those who use hatred and violence as the tools of their political expression' (*Independent* 1.3.1993). These words and sentiments have been put to the test in a number of high-profile cases since then.

A closer look

Race relations and the police – a chronology

1964 First non-white applicant interviewed by the Metropolitan Police

1966 Three candidates from 'visible minority' appointed as police officers

1968 Metropolitan Police establishes its community relations branch

1973 Race and community relations training is introduced into initial probationer training

1974 Approximately 80 non-white officers serving nationally

1985 PC Keith Blakelock killed by rioters at Broadwater Farm, North London

1989 Racial Attacks Group produces first guidelines on dealing with racial attacks

1994 Ethnic monitoring of stop-and-search policy introduced

1994 Black Police Association set up

1995 Ethnic monitoring of service delivery by the police and criminal justice agencies introduced

1995 Stephen Lawrence stabbed to death at bus-stop in Eltham, south London

1997 Police Complaints Authority report into Lawrence case highlights weaknesses in investigation management skills, communication and first-aid training

1997 HM Inspector of Constabulary report into community and race relations highlights deeper problems of racism in the ranks

1997 Home secretary announces judicial review of investigation into Stephen Lawrence's death

1997 Police Promotions Examination Board sacks 13 black actors used in role-playing tests because white officers are unable to deal with them objectively. The Home Office reverses the decision

1998 ACPO's (Association of Chief Police Officers) race and community relations committee publishes guidelines on more comprehensive race relations strategy

1998 Race and Violent Crime Unit at Metropolitan Police set up in July in response to controversy over Lawrence murder investigation. It will now reinvestigate the death of black musician Michael Menson

1999 Inquiry into death of Asian student Ricky Reel will hear evidence from Police Complaints Authority on police objectivity

1999 Publication of the report of the Macpherson inquiry into the investigation of the murder of black teenager, Stephen Lawrence. The report determined that institutional racism and police prejudice served to undermine the murder investigation

1999 The Scottish Executive, the devolved government for Scotland, issued an action plan to guard against institutional racism based on the recommendations of the Macpherson Report

2000 12-year-old Daminola Taylor was murdered in Peckham, south-east London

2001 Riots in Bradford, Burnley and Oldham

2003 *The Secret Policeman* BBC television documentary places the media spotlight once again on institutional racism within the police service

In 1995 black teenager Stephen Lawrence was murdered in London by a gang of white youths. The judicial inquiry into the Metropolitan Police investigation of the case headed by Sir William McPherson reported in February 1999 against a backdrop of allegations of incompetence, bias and racism. The inquiry made recommendations for reforms in all areas of policing, including recruitment policy, the investigation of racially motivated crimes and the external relationship between the police and black and Asian people.

The claim by Stephen's father, Neville Lawrence, that there are serious questions/doubts in the ability of the police to investigate racially motivated crimes was supported by Home Office figures released in the latter part of 1998. These figures showed that a large majority of black and Asian people in the United Kingdom believed that the police were failing them.

Following on from this in the summer of 2001 there were further riots in the UK in Bradford, Burnley and Oldham. They were described as a manifestation of a 'summer of discontent' by some media commentators. In May 2001 disturbances in Bradford between white and Asian youths saw 80 police officers injured. There were further violent confrontations between white and Asian groups and the police in Oldham and Burnley.

In July 2001 violence broke out in the city centre of Bradford after crowds from an Anti-Nazi League rally discovered that National Front sympathizers were gathering in a nearby pub. There were violent confrontations between white and Asian groups which resulted in two stabbings, 120 injured police officers, 36 arrests (13 whites and 23 Asians) and millions of pounds worth of damage.

Six days after the July riots in Bradford, Lord Ousley published the results of a six-month investigation – commissioned before the riots – into race relations in Bradford, entitled 'Community Pride not Prejudice'. The report painted in its own words a picture of a 'city of fear'. It suggested the city's schools had done little to promote understanding between ethnic groups. The report also highlighted a complex mix of segregation, policy failings and the heavy-handed policing of inner-city communities.

In December 2001 a government-commissioned report 'The inquiry by the Community Cohesion Review Team' highlighted the 'shockingly' divided communities stoked by far-right extremists which led to the summer riots in Bradford, Oldham and Burnley.

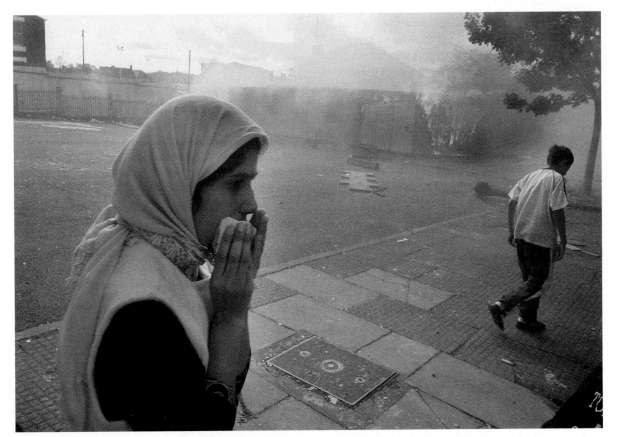

Figure 8.2 An image from the Burnley riots
© Getty/AFP/Odd Anderson

Furthermore, as the study below indicates, there remains deep suspicion between ethnic groups concerning the underlying agenda of official responses to incidents of ethnic conflict and longer-term attempts to palliate ethnic and racial misunderstandings, contention and tension. Clearly – even in a country such as the UK, which prides itself on an integrated multicultural and multi-ethnic community – racial and ethnic tensions and mistrust continue to exist both on and below the surface.

A closer look

The South Asian Crime Unit: policing by ethnicity?

What lies behind the recent creation by the Metropolitan Police of a South Asian Crime Unit?

The [South Asian Crime Unit has been created as] a response to an apparent rise in crimes ranging from kidnapping and gun-use, to drug-running and passport scams with transnational links in human trafficking. Modelled on Operation Trident, a specialist unit focusing on gun crime in black communities, it is hoped that the South Asian Crime Unit will achieve a similar level of success . . .

The Head of the new unit, Assistant Commissioner Tarique Ghaffur, tells us that rising crime in . . . South Asian communities, will result in a network of ghettoes . . . [which] will become breeding grounds for . . . organised crime. [His statistics show] a 300 per cent increase in the number of murders involving South Asians in the last decade and a 41 per cent rise in drug crimes in the last five years. Almost 20 per cent of kidnappings in London last year involved South Asians . . .

Yes, if we take a step back for a moment, it is important to ask what this unit will actually do. For, whilst the above statistics may be deplorable, so is the fact that stops under anti-terrorism legislation rose by roughly 1,450 per cent between 1999 and 2003, a huge number of which were carried out on South Asians. Well over 90 per cent of these led to no further action. Or the fact that particular South Asian groups are four times more likely to be victims of a racist attack than whites. Or the fact that, in 2003, South Asians were two and a half times more likely to be stopped and searched under the Police and Criminal Evidence Act 1984 than whites.

Furthermore, it is important to understand the rapidly changing context of South Asian communities in Britain, within which the South Asian Specialist Unit has emerged. There has been a growing moral panic over 'lawless' Asian youths . . . There has been a perceived breakdown in what are commonly perceived as 'Asian traits' – strong family-ties that bind, a readiness to work hard at all hours and a strong sense of duty and obedience before the law.

In particular, a number of events in 2001 ensured that the already shifting stereotypical assumptions of 'Asian traits' were undeniably altered. The summer was beset by riots in northern towns and cities which tore asunder these comfortable beliefs. Here was a generation of Asian youths not prepared to stand by and watch racists march through their neighbourhoods, not prepared to be told that they did not 'belong here'. And if this did not put a different picture of 'being Asian' on the map, the events of 11 September that year certainly did. England was suddenly confronted with 'Asian anger' at home and Muslim terrorism abroad . . . a context in which the mistrust of . . . those perceived to be Muslim, flourished under the guise of 'anti-terrorism' and the rhetoric of 'law and order'.

With South Asians cast as Britain's new suspect community, we might expect that a policing unit focusing on this particular group would be at pains to ensure that the full protection and support of the law was available to it; that the unit would do its utmost to render itself democratically accountable to the very group it was trying to protect; and, at the very least, challenge the damning stereotypes that frame South Asians as the 'enemy within' in their own county. But, instead, we see a highly politicized imposition of punitive policing practices that focus on the number-one agenda of the day: illegal immigration.

Detective Sergeant Lawrence Gibbons, of the National Crime Squad, explained that gangs are obtaining British passports and profiling these to match the age and height of would-be 'illegal immigrants'. And this appears to be one of the key reasons for the creation of the South Asian Unit. Not, then, racist attacks against South Asians, but offences that South Asians themselves are said to be committing, provides the rationale for this Unit.

(Jon Burnett, Campaign Against Racism
& Fascism (CARF) 7.7.2004:
http://www.carf.demon.co.uk/feat58.html)

Questions

1. *What is the main purpose of the South Asian Crime Unit?*

2. *What does the writer think the Unit should be doing?*

3. *South Asians are referred to as 'Britain's new suspect community'; which communities have come under suspicion in the past?*

4. *Do you think that the £5m spent on the Unit is money well spent?*

Summary

➤ Many theories have attempted to explain 'race', racism and patterns of racial discrimination. Biological theories developed in the nineteenth century stressed physical differences in human characteristics displayed in different groups of people. This theoretical position underwent a revival in the 1960s and 1970s under the guise of 'socio-biological' theories that emphasized the importance of genetic variation in shaping both individual personalities and social behaviour.

➤ There are a number of sociological theories. The 'race relations' approach focuses on the types of relations experienced by minority groups. Society is seen as racially divided in a way that works in favour of certain ethnic groups and against others. Marxist theories highlight the relationship between racist beliefs and practices and the capitalist economic system. Racial oppression is seen as a tool of capitalism – a mechanism for splitting the working class thereby lessening its potential as a force for change. Political or state-centred theories examine how social and political policy excludes subordinate groups in society – through, for example, categorizing black people as particularly prone to commit certain types of violent crime.

➤ Other theorizations of race have stressed the importance of cultural identity in explaining the different experiences of black and white people, with the term 'ethnicity' used to refer to the cultural identity of particular minority groups. Culture and history are seen as the key elements in the formation of different cultural identities.

➤ Other migrant groups to Britain, including Jews, have experienced racial discrimination and prejudice. The racism directed against Jews and other migrant groups can be related to the rise of ethnic nationalism in the twentieth century.

➤ There is plenty of evidence of continued racial inequality in Britain. With regard to employment, large numbers of black people have worked in the British labour market since the 1950s, when migrants from the old colonies of the British Empire were recruited for low-paid and low-status work. These ethnic minority groups have been seen as part of a secondary labour market or a reserve army of labour, with less security and fewer prospects than the indigenous white population. Today, although the majority of the black population in Britain have been born and educated in Britain, marked inequalities remain. Racial discrimination in the labour market is indicated by research and reports from a variety of bodies including the CRE and the Gifford Report. Discrimination occurs in both manual and professional occupations.

➤ Although there has been a general improvement in housing conditions since the 1950s, there is still clear evidence of inequalities in housing between different ethnic groups and particularly between black and white people. In the private housing sector black people tend to be directed away from the 'better' areas and towards less prestigious and 'poorer' areas. Local authority housing policy tends to operate in favour of the family structure most common among the white population, i.e. small, one-generation families. These policies and strategies combine to ensure that black people live in poorer-quality housing in the less prestigious areas of Britain's towns and cities.

➤ The type of education received and qualifications gained are strongly influenced by social and ethnic background. Attainment levels of Afro-Caribbean children are well below those of the general population. Ethnic minority groups have been seen as suffering from the same disadvantages as the working classes.

➤ Black children are additionally disadvantaged by the Eurocentric nature of the curriculum, which helps to promote a poor self-image among black children.

➤ There have been a number of 'racial disturbances' in British cities in the last thirty years; these are part of a tradition stretching back through the twentieth century. Explanations for urban violence have highlighted the poor relationship between black communities and the police, the deprivation faced by black people living in run-down inner-city areas and the political marginalization of black people.

Links

The Case study on racism in the police service, pages 334–335, and that on policing black communities, pages 343–347, link to the broader discussion of police culture in Chapter 16, pages 632–634.

The discussion of black women and the labour market can be read in conjunction with the discussion of women and employment in Chapter 7.

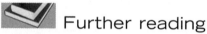 ## Further reading

Bowling, B. and Phillips, C. (2002) *Racism, Crime and Justice*, Harlow: Longman.
A detailed analysis of racism and the criminal justice process from crime and victimization to policing and punishment.

Braham, P. (ed.) (1992) *Racism and Anti-Racism: Inequalities, Opportunities and Policies*, London: Sage.
A detailed critical text which examines the nature and the extent of racial discrimination in contemporary Britain.

Cashmore, E. and Troyna, B. (1990) *Introduction to Race Relations*, London: Falmer.
A clear introductory text to the field of race relations that looks at key areas such as immigration laws, work, housing, education, rioting, fascism and the media.

Centre for Contemporary Cultural Studies (1982) *The Empire Strikes Back: Race and Racism in 70s Britain*, London: Hutchinson.
A radical account of racist practices and beliefs in Britain of the 1970s, written from a 'black' perspective.

Cohen, R. (1994) *Frontiers of Identity: The British and the Others*, London: Longman.
An accessible and fascinating examination of the way the identity of the British people is constantly redefined through various ethnic and national identities both within and outside the UK.

Fryer, P. (1984) *Staying Power: The History of Black People in Britain*, London: Pluto.
Provides a detailed history of black people in Britain.

Holdaway, S. (1996) *The Racialisation of British Policing*, Basingstoke: Palgrave Macmillan.

Holdaway, S. and Barron, A.-M. (1997) *Resigners? The Experience of Black and Asian Police Officers*, Basingstoke: Palgrave Macmillan.

Mason, D. (2000) *Race Ethnicity in Modern Britain*, Oxford: Oxford University Press.

Miles, R. (1989) *Racism*, London: Routledge.
Miles, R. (1993) *Racism after 'Race Relations'*, London: Routledge.
Racism provides a concise yet comprehensive historical account of the concept of 'racism'. Miles (1993) focuses on the multiple definitions of the concept of racism and contests the view that racism is experienced only by black people.

Modood, T. *et al.* (1997) *Ethnic Minorities in Britain: Diversity and Disadvantage*, London: Policy Studies Institute.
This is the fourth report from the Policy Studies Institute into the experiences of ethnic minorities in Britain. It provides a wealth of detailed information on the position of ethnic minorities in Britain in the 1990s; in particular it highlights the growing differences between the main ethnic minority groups.

Rex, J. and Mason, D. (eds) (1986) *Theories of Race and Ethnic Relations*, Cambridge: Cambridge University Press.
A good introduction to the 'race relations' tradition of analysis.

Skellington, R. (1992) *'Race' in Britain Today*, London: Sage.
This study focuses on various areas of contemporary debate and provides an insight into 'race' and discrimination in Britain today.

Witte, R. (1996) *Racial Violence and the State: A Comparative Analysis of Britain, France and the Netherlands*, London: Longman.
The first comparative study of racist violence in three major European countries covering the history, theory, policy and practice of state responses to racist violence.

 ## Web sites

www.ipl.org/ref/RR/static/soc
This is from the Internet Public Library and covers racism from all over the world.

www.blink.org.uk
Outlines the political, social and economic policy demands for Britain's black communities, from both a domestic and international perspective.

Activities

Activity 1

'Race', housing and the 'twilight zone'

Read the following extracts from Rex and Moore's (1967) study of Sparkbrook, Birmingham, in the 1960s (*Race, Community and Conflict*) and consider how their findings relate to areas you live in, have lived in or are familiar with. The questions at the end of the extracts ask you to apply Rex and Moore's model.

Race relations in the city

The most important contribution of Park and his colleagues, from our point of view, was their differentiation of the various residential zones of the city. It does not seem to us to matter very much whether these are to be regarded as forming concentric zones or as being arranged in sectors. [Their work] indicates the existence within the city of several important sub-communities . . . that of the lodging-house zone, that of the zone of working men's homes, that of the middle-class areas, and that of the commuters' suburbs . . .

We envisage a further stage of development characterised above all by the emergence of suburbia. This occurs when the lower middle classes . . . forsake the centre of the city for a way of life in which, with the aid of credit facilities, they may more closely approximate to the life of the upper middle classes. Their deserted homes then pass to a motley population consisting on the one hand of the city's social rejects and on the other of newcomers who lack the defensive communal institutions of the working class, but who defend themselves and seek security within some sort of colony structure . . .

In studying a zone of the city . . . we must find out who lives there, what primary community ties they have, what their housing situation, economic position and status aspirations are, what associations they form, and how these associations interact and how far the various groups are incorporated into urban society as citizens . . .

In many areas of his life, however, the immigrant finds himself not simply enjoying his social rights as a citizen, but having to satisfy his needs in the market. This is particularly true with regard to finding a job and a home . . .

Competition for the scarce resource of housing leads to the formation of groups very often on an ethnic basis and one group will attempt to restrict the opportunities of another by using whatever sanctions it can.

(Rex and Moore 1967: 8–16)

The zone of transition

We believe that in large measure what is happening in Birmingham is something which might happen in any West European or North American city . . .

Before we can begin to understand what the problems of the zone of transition or the twilight zone are, it will be necessary . . . to distinguish the different types of access to housing which are possible in a modern city.

We distinguish the following types of housing situation:

(1) that of outright owner of a whole house;

(2) that of the owner of a mortgaged whole house;

(3) that of the council tenant   a) in a house with a long life;

                         b) in a house awaiting demolition;

(4) that of the tenant of a whole house owned by a private landlord;

(5) that of the owner of a house . . . who is compelled to let rooms in order to meet his repayment obligations;

(6) that of the tenant of rooms in a lodging-house.

Activities (continued)

It is likely that these types of housing situation will have a definite territorial distribution in the city depending on the age and size of the buildings in different zones . . . The six housing situations . . . take the order 1–6 in a scale of desirability according to the status values of British society . . .

Situations (1), (2) and (3a) do not merely enjoy high prestige. They enjoy legitimation in terms of the value standards of the society as a whole. Situations (1) and (2) are legitimated in terms of the ideal of 'a property-owning democracy'; situation (3a) in terms of the values of 'the welfare state'. Situation (3b) is regarded as an unfortunate transitional necessity in terms of welfare state values. Situation (4) is of declining importance because of the gradual disappearance of the private landlord. Situations (5) and (6) are seen as highly undesirable in terms of welfare state standards, and especially in terms of public health standards. The number of those who can make the transition to situation (3a) is limited by the resources available and the standards which operate . . .

Local councils are likely to reflect the interests of the long-established residents who form the majority of their electorate. Thus a basic distinction is drawn between local people and immigrants, and between those with normal family situations and isolates and deviants. These will live in the lodging-house . . .

It will be the case, however, that for most people in the zone of transition, there is a sub community of some kind in which they feel culturally and socially at home . . .

In a strict sense this does not produce a ghetto. A ghetto would appear to imply a segregated ethnic community, and as we have seen the zone of transition includes ethnic communities, transitional people awaiting rehousing and isolates and deviants of all sorts . . .

Clearly this situation (in the zone of transition) is not a stable one. One possibility is that . . . the punitive policies of the host community and their elected representative might be checked by the active resistance of immigrants themselves. This later stage of development in the twilight zone may already have been reached in some American cities.

(Rex and Moore 1967: 272–80)

Questions

1. *Consider the town or city you live in – or the nearest to where you live. Use an Ordnance Survey or street map and divide it into 'housing zones'.*

2. *How easy was this to do? What problems did you face?*

3. *Describe the populations of each of your zones.*

4. *Where do different minority groups live?*

5. *What explanations can you offer for the spread of population?*

6. *How might the work of Rex and Moore help you to interpret the housing pattern – and particularly the position of minority groups – in your town? Can you recognize and locate the six types of housing situation distinguished by Rex and Moore?*

7. *How might the notion of a zone of transition or twilight zone help an understanding of the urban disturbances of the 1980s and 1990s (see pp. 347–9)?*

Activity 2

Is Britain a racist society?

Read the review of the opinion poll on race commissioned by BBC News Online below and consider the questions at the end.

Activities (continued)

Britain 'a racist society' – poll

More than half of Britons believe they live in a racist society, a major survey on race relations has suggested.

The opinion poll commissioned by BBC News Online also found that 44 per cent of those asked believe immigration has damaged Britain over the last 50 years.

But the ICM study goes on to suggest that most whites, blacks and Asians agree society is more racially tolerant than a decade ago.

The survey, part of a major BBC News Online series on race relations in the UK, also indicates widespread support for plans to introduce citizenship classes and English lessons for people applying to live in the UK.

It reveals that racism in the workplace is a major problem – with almost one in three blacks and Asians saying they believe racism has cost them the chance of a job.

But it also suggests widespread acceptance of mixed-race relationships. Half of all those asked say they would marry or have a relationship with someone from another race.

Tolerant

And when asked how they would feel if their child married someone from another race, most said the most important thing would be that they had found a loving partner.

The opinion poll, weighted to include the views of whites, blacks and Asians in the UK, is one of the largest surveys on race conducted in recent years.

More than half of each group said they feel that Britain is now more tolerant racially than it was 10 years ago.

But of all those questioned, 51 per cent said they felt Britain is a racist society. That view was shared by 52 per cent of whites and 53 per cent of blacks.

Among Asian respondents, 41 per cent said they believe Britain is racist compared with 45 per cent who rejected the suggestion.

Meanwhile, 47 per cent of whites said they felt immigration had harmed society in the last 50 years, compared with 28 per cent who felt it had benefited Britain . . . Gurbux Singh, chairman of the Commission for Racial Equality (CRE), said the poll showed a 'mixed response' from the public on race.

Victims

He said: 'Many of us agree that Britain is a modern multi-racial society, and welcome that. Yet, at the same time we think racism is on the increase.

'Ethnic minority respondents were more likely to feel they were the victims of racial discrimination than whites, showing very clearly the differences in their experiences of living in Britain to the majority of the population.'

But he said there were also positive findings from the survey, such as the 53 per cent who said they had friends from different racial backgrounds.

He said the most worrying findings were the suggestion from some that immigrants do not make a positive contribution to Britain.

'This is a worrying finding and simply belies the facts,' he said. 'Britain has been collecting different cultures, skills and people for centuries. From Marks and Spencer to the Mini motorcar, some of the most famous symbols of British success have come from people who were refugees and immigrants.'

(BBC News Online 20.5.2002)

Activities (continued)

Questions

1. What contradictions can you find in the results of the BBC poll?

2. How might they be explained?

3. What do you consider to be positive findings with regard to race relations in Britain?

4. What do you consider to be negative findings with regard to race relations in Britain?

5. Have you witnessed on experienced racism? If so, has it shaped your view of whether Britain is a racist society?

Activity 3

Researching race and ethnicity on the web

Using a range of sources on the web (Institute for Employment Studies, the Labour Force Survey, International Labour Organization, National Statistics Online, Department for Education and Skills, Sosig (http://sosig.esrc.bris.ac.uk/) etc.) see what data you can find to support Modood's view that educational and occupational opportunities have improved and find out what trends emerge in other countries.

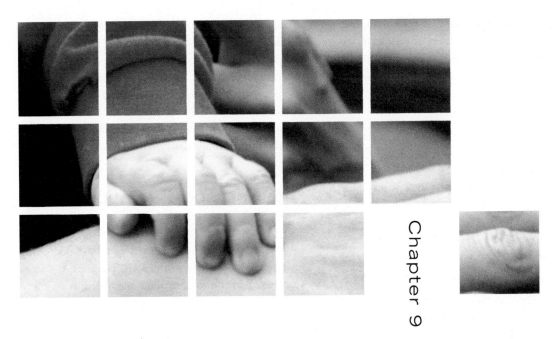

Chapter 9

Age

... the development of modern industrial capitalist societies brought increased awareness of age as a basis of social distinctions and greater segregation of age-groups. Whilst most societies have elements of age stratification, capitalism has promoted a distinct form of age inequality which rests upon the socially dependent status of the young and the old.

(Bradley 1996: 176)

Key issues

➤ How do we define and understand age? How does our understanding of age vary over historical time and in different cultures?

➤ How does age shape our identity? What sociological significance do we attach to the body and biological age?

➤ How do we separate different stages in the life course? For example, when does childhood stop and youth begin? How do we identify childhood, youth, adulthood and older age – what criteria are we using?

➤ What are the inequalities between different age groups? For example, why do adults tend to have more power than children and how do they maintain that power?

➤ What is the social construction of age-related behaviour? In what ways does our age provide us with opportunities or constraints? What does our age enable us to do, what might it stop us from doing, and why?

Introduction

Imagine a group of 18-year-olds spending an afternoon playing bowls followed by a few hands of bridge at the local bridge club, while a group of 75-year-olds go abseiling before an evening of clubbing at the local night club. Why does this sound strange? It does seem 'inappropriate' for people of those ages to engage in such activities but, we should ask ourselves, why is this the case? We consider these scenarios to be unlikely or somewhat perplexing because of the deeply held notions of age and acceptable age-related behaviour in a society like ours.

Clearly, we live in a world which is structured and ordered by age. Sometimes our age may inhibit us from doing certain things and, at other times, we are able to behave in particular ways because of how old we are. Thus, age can be both enabling and constraining. Our age may influence where we shop, what we buy and even how we pay for goods. For example, older people may prefer to pay by cheque, younger people may be more used to using switch or visa cards and children may use cash as they are less likely to have access to bank accounts. Our age may affect the types of books we read, the music we listen to, the television programmes we watch, the leisure activities we engage in. Thus our everyday lives are shaped to a certain extent by the way our age is understood and expressed in the society we live in.

Stop and think

➤ In what ways does age shape your identity?

➤ How do you feel if someone tells you that they think you look younger or older than you actually are, and if so, why might that be?

➤ Have you ever tried to appear older or younger than you actually are; if so, in what kinds of situations?

For a long time age has divided societies by distinguishing one group of people from another but, apart from some notable exceptions (e.g. Eisenstadt 1956; Mannheim 1952), age has only recently become a topic for sociologists (Bradley 1996). In the past it has been assumed that ageing is a biological process that 'naturally' affects everyone. Now it is recognized that age is also socially determined and that our experiences of age can depend on the society we live in. Different cultures attach a range of meanings and values to different age groups, and this affects the ways we behave as well as how we treat others. Thus, age can be seen as a social variable which is similar to other variables like gender, ethnicity and class. Age can differentiate how we are treated in society and how our lives are structured.

However, it is worth bearing in mind that age is only one of several social divisions which shape our lives. For example, our life experiences will vary according to whether we are rich or poor; male or female; black or white; young or old. These social divisions overlap and cut across each other, so we need to consider how one variable impacts on another particularly in relation to power and status. It is not enough to investigate what it is like to be old in society without recognizing, for example, that the life of an older woman from a working class background can be very different from that of an older middle-class man.

Thus, we live in an age-orientated world and this chapter begins by highlighting three main reasons why age is an important social category which should be considered alongside other social divisions such as class, ethnicity, disability and gender. Like these social divisions, age can act as a basis for social relationships, social stratification and discrimination. The chapter continues

by exploring three different ways of understanding age: chronological, biological and social age. The life course perspective is then considered before looking at the different ways that age can be used to organize societies. Subsequently, the chapter focuses on a detailed discussion of two stages in the life course: childhood and older age in order to illustrate the ways in which age is both socially and culturally constructed.

Age and social relationships

Societies are structured and organized by age in a variety of ways, for example age is used as a basis for group membership for certain institutions. These are known as aged-based institutions as their membership is linked to particular age groups. For example, older people may experience some of their old age living in a residential care home. Children are confined to many age-based institutions, the main one being school where pupils are segregated into year groups based on age rather than intellectual ability or interests. Furthermore, there is little mixing between different age groups at school (Ariès 1962) and, even during breaks, children tend to play with those in the same year.

Other age-based institutions for children include playgroups, nurseries and youth clubs. Some are also gendered, so boys may go to Cubs then Scouts when they are older, whereas girls may go to Brownies then Guides. Children's involvement in age-based institutions can create a peer group identity for children of similar ages. Consequently children are separated from much of the adult social world by spending a large part of their lives in age-related contexts with other children. In such ways children develop an understanding of 'appropriate' age relationships and build up knowledge of the ways in which the world is structured through age. They learn about power and authority by seeing the different status that is given to adults and children. For example, at school children soon discover that they should only speak to adults in certain ways. They may be told: 'you don't talk to a teacher like that', but in the playground they can behave more informally with their friends (Devine 2003). Thus children learn to treat different age groups in distinct ways.

Therefore, involvement in age-based institutions can create a sense of identity with those of a certain age group (or cohort). Karl Mannheim (1952) defined a 'generation' as a particular age group which lives through the same historical and social events. He argued that people of a similar age share a common historical experience and may develop a sense of social solidarity or common consciousness. Thus history and social change can impact differently upon our age-based experiences according to the generation we are born into.

Furthermore, our generational experiences can be reinforced by consumer goods such as music and clothes which are targeted to certain generations. Some fashions are perceived to be exclusive to specific age categories and tend to transmit age-related messages (Featherstone and Hepworth 1989). Attitudes can also mark generations as different from one another. Certain attitudes can be perceived as 'old fashioned' and out-dated, particularly when you hear older people talking about things that happened 'in their day'. An example of this is the changing perceptions towards disciplining children. Depending on their age, it is quite likely that, for your grandparents' generation, the beating of children may have been perceived as justified if the children involved had been disobedient. While for your parents' generation beating was perhaps considered too extreme but smacking was regarded as acceptable behaviour. In contrast, a younger generation are more likely to question the suitability of any type of physical punishment. Nowadays many people are opposed to the smacking of children which is reflected in the banning of corporal punishment in schools in 1986 in the UK and the banning of smacking in twelve European countries over the past thirty years (although debates are still ongoing in the UK regarding this issue). Thus, as Vincent argues, 'Generation is a cultural phenomenon; a set of symbols, values and practices which not only endure but unfold as a cohort ages' (2003: 115–116).

A closer look

Ageism

Johnson and Bytheway define ageism as 'the offensive exercise of power through reference to age' (1993: 205), and they suggest it includes:

➤ **Institutionalized ageism**: such as legislative discrimination excluding people over 70 from jury service. Age discrimination is also institutionalized in the labour market:

> It is common both for young job applicants to find themselves passed over for older, supposedly more mature applicants and vice versa, for older people looking for work to find younger, supposedly more lively, people preferred.   (Vincent 2000: 148).

➤ **Internalized ageism**: this occurs during social interactions, such as saying someone is 'childish' or calling someone an 'old bag' or an 'old fogey'. It involves systematic and negative stereotyping on the basis of a person's age. The underlying assumption is that people's experiences are determined only by their chronological age rather than taking into account their social competencies or the environment in which they live.

➤ **Benevolent patronage**: for example 'keeping an eye on the old folk' or being overprotective towards children. We tend to assume that all older people and all young children are vulnerable because of their age and thereby need adults to protect and care for them.

Age and social stratification

Age stratification involves the unequal distribution of social resources, including wealth, power and status, which are accorded to people on the basis of their age. Victor suggests that: 'Every society divides individuals into age groups or strata and this stratification reflects and creates age-related differences in capacities, roles, rights and privileges' (1994: 39). Key age groupings are childhood, youth, young adulthood, mid-life and old age (Bradley 1996). This chapter focuses mainly on examples from the two ends of the life course since childhood and old age tend to illustrate the ways in which, at least in British society, we attach less value and status to some age groups compared to others.

Age and discrimination

People can be discriminated against, or negatively stereotyped, because of their age and this is known as 'ageism'. As Vincent points out: 'Ageism, like racism or sexism, refers to both prejudice and discrimination; the first being an attitude, the second a behaviour' (2000: 148). Older people tend to suffer from ageism more than other age groups, as the process of ageing is often perceived with fear. We only have to look at the slogans on birthday cards to see the stigma attached to growing older. However, people of all ages can experience negative treatment because of their age: 'ageism places limits, constraints and expectations at *every* stage from birth onwards' (Johnson and Bytheway 1993: 204).

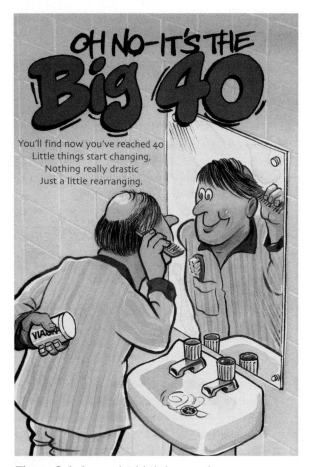

You'll find now you've reached 40
Little things start changing,
Nothing really drastic
Just a little rearranging.

Figure 9.1 An ageist birthday card

Consequently, we need to remember that ageism is not just directed at older people:

> Thus *all* older people are seen as less suitable for employment on the grounds that they are physically slow, lacking in dynamism, and not very adaptable to change; *all* younger people are suspected of being unreliable, reckless, undisciplined and prone to drug-taking and promiscuity. (Bradley 1996: 147)

Bradley (1996) concludes that age is a social division which can create inequality and difference because, on the basis of age, people have differential access to social resources, such as wealth, power and status. One of the main roles of sociologists is to understand social differences and try to explain social inequalities. This in turn can help policy makers try to minimize the negative treatment of those on the margins of society. In relation to age, children and older people are those most likely to be socially excluded. Britain is an ageist society and we tend to marginalize certain age groups, especially the very young and the very old. This will be discussed in further detail later in the chapter.

A closer look

Defining the majority and minority worlds

In this chapter we prefer to use the recent terms: majority world and minority world to refer to the developing world and the developed world respectively. These terms invite us to reflect on the unequal relations between the two world areas. The minority world consists of a smaller proportion of the world's population and land mass despite using the majority of the world's resources. Furthermore, by using the terms we are reminded that what happens in our society, in a minority world context, is not necessarily the way most of the world's population live their lives and that, with greater access to resources, we tend to experience more privileged lifestyles. Case studies from different parts of the majority world are used throughout the chapter to remind us that, like other social divisions, age is a cultural construction.

Majority world (in terms of population and land mass): Africa, Asia, Latin America

Minority world: UK, Europe, Australia, New Zealand, Japan, US and Canada

Ways of understanding age

There are three main ways of understanding age: chronologically, biologically and socially.

Chronological age

This is an important concept in the minority world. We are all very aware of how old we are in relation to others. We have birthdays to mark the number of years we have been alive. Our numerical age often determines our access to certain privileges or activities, some of which are linked to laws. For example, eligibility to drink alcohol in pubs or to vote depend on our chronological age. Our age means we are part of a certain 'cohort', which is defined as a set of people who are born at the same time (Vincent 2003). Policy makers need to know how many people are in each age cohort in order to predict levels of services which will be required. For example, they need to know what percentage of the population will be over 65 in ten years' time in order to estimate the provision of services such as hospitals and sheltered housing.

> ➤ What factors account for the rising proportion of older people in society?

> ➤ What social and political implications follow from these changes?

Nowadays people are living longer because of improved living conditions and health education, better nutrition and advances in medicine. Furthermore, in the minority world, both mortality and fertility rates have dropped (Wilson 2000), leading to what is known as an ageing population. This is when the average age of a population has risen and there is an increase in the proportion of older people compared with the rest of the society (Vincent 2003). In Britain, the numbers of older people have increased substantially over recent years:

> For the first time, people 60 and over form a larger part of the population than children under 16 – 21 per cent compared to 20 per cent. There has also been a big increase in the number of people aged 85 and over – now over 1.1 million, or 1.9 per cent of the population.　　　　　　　(National Statistics 2003)

Ginn and Arber comment that this

> has led to fears about rising costs of pensions and of health and welfare services used by older people, together with projections of a rising dependency ratio which has fueled the portrayal of older people as a burden on taxpayers.　　　(Ginn and Arber 1993: 6)

However, as they also point out, such attitudes are based on ageism and overlook the diversity of older people and their varied contributions to unpaid domestic and caring labour.

Biological age

Chronological age is linked to biological age which is based on physical development and the increasing maturity of the body. Biological age is the development over time of how our bodies should function, appear and perform. In terms of physical appearance, biological age is important. In the minority world, there is a strong notion of the youthful body as being central to looking good and people try to resist the signs of ageing (Vincent 2003). Medical science cashes in on this by providing cosmetic surgery, such as face lifts, liposuction and chemical peels, in order to try to make people look younger.

One of the reasons why people attempt to reverse the ageing process is because of society's response to biological age. Thus, it is not just about how you look but also about how people respond to the way you look. In British society there is a tendency to assume that notions of success and attractiveness are integrated and often linked to youthfulness. Hence, in a job interview, the young attractive candidate may have an advantage over the older, less attractive candidate even before saying a word. There is a stereotypical assumption that if you look young and attractive, you can be thought to be potentially more successful than if you look old and unattractive. Hockey and James indicate that this is not only experienced by women as even 'Men from their late teens onwards are increasingly aware of the role of a fit, well-groomed body in bolstering the adult individual's social power and status' (1993: 82).

Psychologists are particularly interested in biological age and they explore ideas about the biological and psychological development of individuals. At certain ages people are expected to be capable of developing specific skills, for example children are supposed to learn to walk and talk at particular developmental stages that are related to chronological and biological age. In contrast, sociologists are more interested in the significance attached to biological age and the ways in which the body is perceived:

> The body is lived, experienced, but is done so in ways which are profoundly influenced by social processes and shaped by particular social contexts. We do not simply have bodies that we do things with and to, but we *are* bodies, our sense of who we are is inseparable from our own body.　　　(Howson 2004: 12)

Thus sociologists are keen to explore the ways in which we experience and manage our own and other people's bodies (Shilling 1993). Shilling points out that bodily control is important for ensuring social acceptance, and children are socialized into the regulation of the disciplined body from an early age. It is also recognized that body image impacts upon how we feel about ourselves as well as how we experience our social relationships. Nettleton and Watson remind us that our bodily experiences change over time: 'The extent to which we are conscious of our bodies and how we feel about them will vary throughout our lives and within different social contexts' (1998: 2).

Social age

As well as considering different interpretations of the body and biological age, sociologists have a particular interest in social age. Social age refers to the social understandings and significance that are attached to chronological age. Ginn and Arber define it as 'the social attitudes and behaviour seen as appropriate for a particular chronological age, which itself is cross-cut by gender' (1993: 5). Social age concerns how you feel in relation to your life experiences and age group rather than fixed ideas based on numerical or biological age. For example, at 70 years of age, a person may be chrono-logically old, and biologically their physical develop-ment may reflect that age as they may have grey hair and wrinkles. However, socially they may feel 'young' and no different to when they were 40. They may still engage in the same activities and they might still be fit and healthy. Nevertheless, many people in society may expect their behaviour to reflect their biological age. For example, older people are supposed to 'grow old gracefully' and to avoid looking like 'mutton dressed up as lamb.' Social expectations place pressure on people to look, as well as act, their age.

Many ideas about ageing are social and can there-fore change. For instance, life expectancy in Britain has increased to 76 years for men and 81 years for women and this has affected our attitudes to chronological age. At the turn of the last century, in 1901, life expectancy was 45 years for men and 49 years for women (National Statistics 2003). Thus, when people did not live as long, 50 would have been considered very old, but nowadays, a century later, people are not perceived as very old until they are over 75.

Figure 9.2 A child soldier: an image which may challenge our assumptions about age
© Reuters/CORBIS

Stop and think

> ➤ Think of things that you did as a child or young person that you were not allowed to do. What activities or behaviour were seen as unacceptable for the age you were at the time?

> ➤ Consider who decided that you should not engage in such activities and why?

Ideas about age-appropriate behaviour are socially con-structed rather than based solely on biology. For exam-ple, what children can or cannot do tends to reflect their social age rather than their biological age. An eight-year-old can smoke: it is biologically possible but socially it is considered to be inappropriate for a person of that age. Usually it is adults, parents, policy makers or lawyers who decide what children are allowed to do at different ages largely because we perceive children to be immature, vulnerable and in need of protection. Thus the age at which people can drink alcohol, have sex, smoke or drive is often not based on their physical or mental abilities but on what society deems to be appropriate. These age-based norms are maintained by ideologies which are resistant to rapid change (Ginn and Arber 1993) but can change gradually over time. For example, in 1969 the age of majority was lowered from 21 to 18 years (Pilcher 1995: 72) and nowadays you can legally do most things by the time you are 18. Hence your biggest birthday celebration is likely to be your eighteenth whereas for your parents it was probably their twenty-first. This illustrates that ideas about age and the meanings we attach to different ages can change over time.

Similarly, ideas about age can change according to place: different societies have distinct age norms about what is perceived to be appropriate behaviour. In the United States the legal age for drinking alcohol is 21 but in Britain it is 18. The age of majority also varies in different countries, for example 18 in Austria, 20 in Switzerland and 21 in Malaysia. Therefore, we can conclude that age is a social construction: our understanding of age changes over time and space. The length of time that we live is a biological fact but the value we place on different age groups is a social construct. Our social experiences of age are affected by the social context in which we live. The way that age is socially constructed can change through history and in different societies and these issues will be explored in more detail in the sections on childhood and older age.

The life course perspective

Like age, the life course is a social construct and we attach meanings to different age groups, perceiving some as more important than others. The life course perspective is not the same as the life cycle model which is based on what is perceived to be the 'normal' path of human development. The life cycle sets out what is to be regarded as normal behaviour at different ages. For example, it is not normal to have a baby at 60 or before adulthood. If someone steps outside of this pattern, they are labelled as deviant (Becker 1963, see crime chapter). Thus the life cycle model is based on biological and chronological age; and is used mainly by psychologists and medical scientists. In contrast, the life course, used by sociologists, takes into account the socially constructed nature of human development and is based on social ageing. It does not suggest that biological and chronological development do not occur, but that we need to understand the social context in which they take place. Elder suggests that: 'The life course refers to pathways through the age-differentiated life span, to social patterns in the timing, duration, spacing and order of events' (1978: 21).

Hence, the life course is a socially defined timetable of events from birth to death which 'emphasises the interlinkage between phases of the life course, rather than seeing each phase in isolation' (Arber and Evandrou 1993: 9). Thus the process and experience of becoming old incorporates a notion of past and future. First of all you are born, then you are socialized from being a child to being an adult. The peak of the life course is adulthood (which is also the physical peak and the time

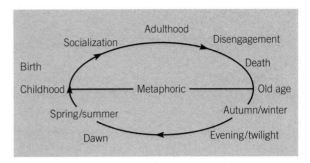

Figure 9.3 Schematic representation of the life course
(*Source*: Hockey and James 1993: 29)

for reproduction), and then you decline into old age and death. Hockey and James (1993) give a metaphorical comparison of this to indicate the values which we place on particular stages of the life course. Childhood is seen as something new and growing. It is metaphorically portrayed as spring or summer, to represent the growth and the dawn of a new life. In contrast, old age is seen as slowing down, metaphorically represented by autumn and winter. Coming to the end of life is compared to evening or twilight.

As we can see in Figure 9.3, in minority world contexts adulthood is perceived as the central and dominant stage of the life course, representing independence and power (see Case study on p. 364). Adulthood is what children are striving for and what older people are trying to hang on to. On either side of adulthood, on the margins, children and older people are more dependent and subordinate to the dominant social category of adults (Hockey and James 1993). Children are growing up and gaining independence. Their move towards adulthood is celebrated and perceived as positive. In the minority world, a frequent question which adults ask children is: 'What do you want to be when you grow up?' and this reflects that we focus on adulthood as the important stage of life, indicating that children's social status is marginal. In contrast, while children are growing up, older people are growing down and losing independence: their move out of adulthood is seen as unwelcome and negative (Pilcher 1995). Most people do not look forward to getting older and often try to disguise the ageing process, for example by using anti-wrinkle cream or hair dyes to conceal grey hair.

Thus, children try to look older and are pleased if someone thinks they are older than they actually are, whereas older people try to look younger and are pleased if someone thinks they are younger than they actually are. For example, you know you are getting old when

Case study

Adulthood

We have seen that adulthood is a sought-after status: the peak of the human life course. Yet paradoxically, it is rarely addressed by sociologists as a stage in the life course worthy of study in its own right. Whilst there are sociologies of childhood, of youth and of old age, there is no 'sociology of adulthood' (Pilcher *et al.* 2003). On the one hand, this is because adulthood is taken for granted, and many aspects of sociology indirectly address issues concerning adults without explicitly exploring the life course stage of adulthood. On the other hand, sociologists have an interest in studying marginalized social groups, so are more likely to focus on subordinate social categories when directly exploring the life course. However, it is worth bearing in mind that adulthood is a relatively vague and imprecise social category since it covers a wide range of chronological ages but, like other stages in the life course, it cannot purely be defined in terms of numerical age.

Adulthood has traditionally been associated with productive work roles, parenthood and citizenship rights. Consequently adulthood tends to be linked to notions of responsibility, independence and autonomy. In contemporary Britain, as in many parts of the minority world, adults hold a dominant position in the social world, including 'positions of importance in families and households, in the labour force, in political institutions, and so on' (Pilcher 1995: 87). However, we must remember that not all adults are equally powerful and an individual's experience of adulthood is shaped by class, gender, ethnicity, sexuality, disability and age. As Pilcher reminds us:

> Able-bodied, white, middle-class males in full-time employment are probably the most fully adult members of British society. Their advantageous structural position enables them to exercise their citizenship rights, their independence and autonomy, to a greater extent than can women, elderly or disabled people, children, the working class, or members of ethnic minority groups . . . Clearly, some grown-ups are more grown-up than others.
> (Pilcher 1995: 87–99)

The latter part of adulthood is often referred to as 'middle age', the period before old age, and has become recognized as a distinct phase of adults' lives. It is identified when signs of ageing begin to appear such as grey hair and the 'middle-aged spread', and for women it tends to coincide with the menopause. It is often linked to a change in parenthood such as when children leave home. In popular discourse this period can be referred to as the 'mid-life crisis': a time when people reflect on their family and work status while struggling to postpone the ageing process for as long as possible (Featherstone and Hepworth 1989). Thus although adulthood is constructed as the dominant powerful stage of the life course, it is important to bear in mind that, like other life course stages, it is not a constant status and it can be experienced in a variety of ways.

Question

1. As a child can you remember ever being eager to reach adulthood, the peak of the life course? If so, what features of adulthood were you keen to embrace and why?

---

you are pleased someone tells you that you look young. So, why is this? It is because we place value on the dominant social status of adulthood as a stage in the life course that symbolizes independence, autonomy and power (Hockey and James 1993). Thus, as Pilcher argues, 'The centrality of adulthood has less to do with its position mid-way through the span of human life than with its apparent *desirability*,' (1995: 81). Children like to rush towards adulthood and older people like to linger and hold on to it. The old and young are distant from the centre of social power. This can also be represented in a table (see Table 9.1) to show the centrality of adulthood compared with the marginality of childhood and old age in our society.

Table 9.1 Images of ageing in contemporary Britain

Childhood	Adulthood	Old age
Dependent	Independent	Decreasing independence
Lacking autonomy	Autonomous	Losing autonomy
Subordinate	Dominant	Becoming subordinate
Lacking power	Powerful	Losing power
Asexual	Sexual	Increasingly asexual
Vulnerable	Not vulnerable	Increasing vulnerability
Socialization process		*Infantilizing process*
Increasing personhood	Full personhood	Decreasing personhood

Source: Adapted from Hockey and James 1993

Table 9.1 indicates how age is perceived in our society and the ways in which we socially construct age by placing more value on some age groups than others. The life course perspective indicates that there is an age-based inequality in our society, where children and older people are marginalized in relation to adults. Sociologists are interested in exploring the unequal power relations between adults at the centre of society and children and older people on the margins of society. One of the key roles of the sociologist is to consider power and the way it is played out between different social groups in processes of domination and subordination.

We have seen that, in the minority world, childhood and old age are stigmatized and subordinated in relation to the dominance of adulthood. However, it is worth bearing in mind that people are rarely totally independent or dependent, but they may be independent in relation to some aspects of their lives and not to others. Thus, 'dependence and independence should not be seen as dichotomies, but as part of a spectrum which involves interdependence and reciprocity' (Arber and Evandrou 1993: 19). In addition, we should also remember that children and older people (and adults for that matter) are not all the same; they are not homogenous groups. They are often stereotyped as social groups, and this can mask the wide diversity of social experiences. As already mentioned, their lives will vary according to other important aspects of social differentiation, such as class, gender, disability or ethnicity.

One of the difficulties of studying the 'life cycle' is setting age limits to define the different social groups. Where do childhood, youth, adulthood and old age divide, and how distinct are they as different phases of people's lives? There are many competing definitions for all stages in the life course and the boundaries between them are

often blurred (see Case study on p. 366). For example, Abdalla (1988) describes children as less than 12 years old, and young people as between 12 and 18 years old; Bonnet (1993) defines children as less than 15 years of age; and the United Nations Convention on the Rights of the Child states that 18 years of age is the upper limit to childhood. Such wide age ranges to define the boundaries of being a 'child' or a 'young person' reflect that neat age-based categories are not easily set. Thus understandings of childhood and youth are linked to the social, economic and cultural context rather than to chronological or biological age. This emphasises why the concept of 'life course' is more appropriate than 'life cycle' as it recognizes that there are overlaps between different stages in the life course and there are no precise chronological markers of when one stage begins and another ends. Therefore, as Pilcher points out: 'it is important to remember that the life course is best understood as an interconnected and cumulative process' (1995: 82). In contrast to the life cycle, the life course takes into account both cross-cultural and historical variations.

Stop and think

➤ In Britain at what age can you (a) vote; (b) watch a PG category film unaccompanied; (c) be convicted of a criminal offence; (d) open a bank account; (e) leave school; (f) marry without parental consent; (g) buy a firearm; (h) become an MP; (i) qualify for a pension; (j) qualify for cheaper fares on public transport?

➤ How do these ages vary in different countries and at different points in history?

Case study

Youth transitions: from childhood to adulthood

Childhood and youth research widely recognizes that it is inadequate to consider the transition from childhood to youth to adulthood in terms of a linear progression from dependence to independence (Furlong and Cartmel 1997; Wyn and Dwyer 1999). Youth is an age group which is in transition from childhood to adulthood, and consequently young people's status is often ambiguous. In the minority world, due to changes in family structures, education and the labour market (see section below), youth transitions have become longer, interrupted and more complex. This has led to more options for young people as they may shift between work and education but it has also created much uncertainty and increased financial dependency on their parents (Furlong and Cartmel 1997). In the minority world young people are now more likely to undergo a series of transitions, moving in and out of independence and dependence in different contexts and in relation to different people (EGRIS 2001), yet still the ultimate goal is to achieve independence (Gillies 2000). Similarly, in a majority world context, the notion of 'youth transition' from dependent child to independent adult is problematic since young people negotiate and renegotiate their interdependence with their parents and siblings throughout the life course. Thus the notion of interdependence is a useful way of understanding how young people move in and out of relative autonomy and dependence (Punch 2002a).

Recently the use of the concept of 'transition' has also been questioned in minority world contexts and Gillies (2000) argues that there are three main drawbacks of using the term. First, it does not allow for greater recognition of the blurred boundaries between dependence and independence. Second, it tends to imply an individualistic transition while placing less emphasis on family interrelationships and, third, youth becomes conceptualized merely as a transitional period of change and instability rather than being a special category in its own right. However, despite these drawbacks, it is recognized that the concept of 'transition' can still provide a useful framework for exploring the ways in which young people are constrained and their decision-making processes in relation to their chosen school-to-work pathways (Gillies 2000). Apart from the school-to-work trajectories, youth transitions also include leaving home, starting a sexual relationship, having children and acquiring citizenship rights (EGRIS 2001). It is widely recognized that these transitions are interlinked and that it is important to take a holistic perspective in order to understand the interconnections between them (Wyn and Dwyer 1999). Therefore, this brief case study has shown that, like childhood, 'youth' is 'a *relational* concept, which refers to the social processes whereby age is socially constructed, institutionalized and controlled in historically and culturally specific ways' (Wyn and White 1997: 10–11).

Structural changes since 1970s leading to extended youth transitions

Labour market changes:

➢ decline in levels of employment (especially traditional heavy industries and the manufacturing sector)
➢ increase in levels of unemployment (young people are often perceived to lack skills and experience)
➢ a reduction in wages
➢ an increase in part-time and casual work
➢ decrease in entitlement to social security benefits
➢ increase in youth training schemes

Education:

➢ increasing numbers of young people remaining in full-time education

Family structures:

➢ increase of average age at first marriage
➢ increase of average age at first birth.

(Adapted from Pilcher 1995: 73–78)

Question

1. *In what economic and social contexts do you experience more dependence on family or friends? Do you think that people can ever live their lives totally independent of others?*

The social construction of the life course

We need to bear in mind that the life course, like age, is socially constructed. The process of ageing and the ways in which we perceive the very young or the very old are shaped by the attitudes of the society we live in. Our attitudes and understanding of different age categories are shaped by several interrelated factors: the social, political and historical context, ideologies, language and the media. Hockey and James comment that:

> the precise ways in which childhood is conceived, understood and ascribed with meaning in everyday social practice alters in relation to the economic and political demands of particular societies at particular historical moments.   (Hockey and James 2003: 15)

Similarly, the meanings we attach to adulthood and older age are also shaped by the politics and policies of a particular society located in time and place. Thus the specific social context in which people live will influence the ways in which different stages in the life course are understood at different points in historical time.

In turn, this leads to the development of ideologies which suggest what childhood or older age should be like for that society. For example, in Britain, partly because children do not engage in full-time work, it is commonly thought that childhood is meant to be the 'happiest days of your life', full of innocence and fun. However, it is not always like that in reality. Children can be miserable, they may hate having to go to school, and some have to care for older or sick parents. Not all of children's lives are based on dependence, innocence and carefree playtime. Similarly, in the UK, retirement tends to be thought of as a time to relax and for leisure activities. Yet some older people find not working a frustrating and boring experience, leaving them with feelings of uselessness. Thus our stereotypical views of childhood and older age are based on particular ideologies of society, and do not necessarily reflect realities.

Our images of age are also shaped by language and popular discourse. For example, older people are often told 'you're too old to act like that, act your age' whereas children are asked to 'stop acting like a baby and grow up'. People refer to certain behaviour as 'childish', and we tend to use an ageist vocabulary which reflects our

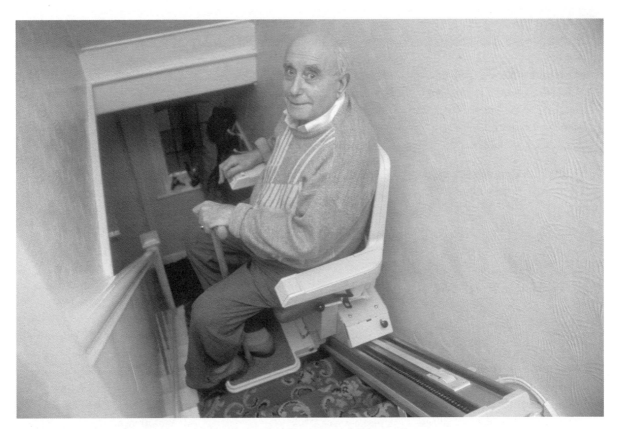

Figure 9.4 New technology can help to give elderly people independence
© Ulrike Preuss/Photofusion

ideas about age. Thus, the way language is used in every-day social interactions shapes our perceptions of age and this is also illustrated in media representations. The next time you watch television or read a magazine, look closely at how children and older people are portrayed, especially in adverts. Children tend to be depicted playing, happy and carefree, in contrast to older people who are presented as helpless and frail. Yet these particular images of children and older people reflect ideologies and stereotypes. The meanings we attach to different age groups are often part of adult discourses and representations which are expressed through language and imagery (Gittens 1998: 43). Thus, such discourses are often a reflection of adult power in society.

The important point to remember is that concepts of ageing are social constructions rather than simple descriptions of biological processes (Hockey and James 1993). The way we understand age and the life course is shaped by the social context, at a specific time in history. Thus, 'the life course is structured around cultural expectations of appropriate behaviour for people of particular ages' (Vincent 2003: 11).

Age as a cultural construction

Cross-cultural and historical comparisons remind us that what happens in our contemporary society is not the only way of doing things. Different cultures use age in distinct ways to organize their society. For example, the notion of time passing varies in different cultures. In Britain and in other parts of the minority world, numerical age and the measurement of time is important. The calculation of time passing structures our society and our access to certain activities such as work and school. Yet chronological age has not always been as significant as it is today and does not have the same relevance in other cultures. During industrialization the notion of structured time became more important when people were working in factories, having to clock on and work a certain length of time (see Chapter 4). Whereas, prior to that, families worked together on the land and time did not need to be so structured. In many pre-industrial societies, time is often marked by events rather than by counting numbers. The passage of time might be remembered by natural

World in focus

The following two cross-cultural examples indicate that different cultures can use age in distinct ways to organize their society.

Horizontal age relationships: Nyakyusa age villages

The Nyakyusa are cattle owners and cultivators living in the Great Rift Valley near Lake Nyasa in south central Africa. In this African society age dictates where people live and the power they have in society. Their villages are based on age rather than on kinship ties:

> The age-village starts when a number of herd-boys, about ten or eleven years old, build together at the edge of their fathers' village.

They have been practising building huts for some time, as small boys in other cultures do also, but when they reach the age of ten or eleven they actually go to live in their huts, sleeping and spending their spare time in them, though still going to their mothers' huts for meals. A boy should not and does not eat alone, but a group of friends eat together, visiting the mother of each member of their gang in turn. This system is regarded not only as being congenial to small boys (as with us) but also as moral. For the Nyakyusa eating with age-mates is a corner stone or morality, and a boy who comes home alone often to eat is severely scolded . . .

A boys' village starts quite small, with, perhaps, not more than ten or a dozen members, but it grows as young boys from the fathers' village, or from other men's villages in the neighbourhood, become old enough to join it. When the original members are fifteen or sixteen years old the village is usually closed to any further ten-year-olds, who must then start a new village on their own. Conditions vary with the density of the population in the neighbourhood and other factors, but generally the age-span within a village is not more than about five years, and a village numbers between 20 and 50 members.

World in focus (continued)

The boys who thus establish a village continue to live together through life.

(Wilson 1967: 219–20)

Vertical age relationships: Japanese society

In Japan, the ranking of individuals is more important for determining status and power:

For the Japanese the established ranking order (based on duration of service within the same group and on age, rather than on individual ability) is overwhelmingly important in fixing the social order and measuring individual social values . . . In this kind of society ranking becomes far more important than any differences in the nature of the work, or of status group. Even among those with the same training, qualifications or status, differences based on rank are always perceptible, and because

the individuals concerned are deeply aware of the existence of such distinctions, these tend to overshadow and obscure even differences of occupation, status or class . . .

In Japan once rank is established on the basis of seniority, it is applied to all circumstances, and to a great extent controls social life and individual activity. Seniority and merit are the principal criteria for the establishment of a social order; every society employs these criteria, although the weight given to each may differ according to social circumstances. In the west merit is given considerable importance, while in Japan the balance goes the other way. In other words, in Japan, in contrast to other societies, the provisions for recognition of merit are weak, and institutionalization of the social order has been effected largely by means of seniority;

this is the more obvious criterion, assuming an equal ability in individuals entering the same kind of service.

(Nakane 1973: 27–30)

In Japan, the rank of an employee depends on their qualifications and date of entry into the company. Thus, in the workplace, seniority is based on how long someone has been in the company rather than their chronological age. All those who join a large company at the same time form a club and socialize with each other. In contrast, in Britain, you are more likely to socialize with people your own age rather than those who started work at the same time as you.

Questions

1. *In what ways does age structure your life?*

2. *To what extent does British society enable or constrain you from doing certain things on the basis of your age?*

---

events such as the eclipse, a flood or a harvest or by social markers such as puberty or the first birth of a child.

Stop and think

➤ In British society can you think of any rituals which mark the entry into different stages of the life course? Compare them with rituals in other societies.

In some societies the actual age of the individual can be less important than their stage in the life course. Many traditional societies have 'rites of passage' to mark the movement from one status in the life course to another,

such as the onset of puberty. Ritual ceremonies are often used to mark this transition. In modern societies such transitions have become social events rather than formal rites of passage, although there are some exceptions such as christening and marriage ceremonies. Since these rituals change through history and in different cultures, this reflects the point that age is both a social construction and a cultural construction. In order to reinforce this key point, the remainder of the chapter focuses on two detailed examples of childhood and old age. Each example begins by indicating the ways in which childhood or old age are socially constructed and change over time, followed by a discussion of how they are also culturally constructed and change over place.

Social construction of childhood

Ariès was the first academic to criticize the idea of childhood as a fixed universal state, and his main argument was that childhood changes over time. He was well known for saying that: 'in medieval society the idea of childhood did not exist' (Ariès 1962: 115). He claimed that in the Middle Ages children were like miniature adults with the same style of dress, engaging in the same work and activities as adults. Ariès argued that, in the minority world, childhood gradually emerged from the fifteenth century onwards, only becoming established as different from adulthood in the nineteenth century once children were banned from working and compulsory schooling was introduced. He was not implying that parents did not love their children, but that child-rearing techniques were different. The differentiation between childhood and adulthood was based on the emergence of special clothing and literature for children, and the increase of schooling and new forms of work. Thus, over time, adult perceptions of childhood change and this in turn influences how children are treated and understood in society.

Ariès's ideas have been criticized because he was a social historian whose methods were somewhat controversial as he relied heavily on the images of children in paintings. His critics (e.g. Pollock 1983) argue that paintings may not depict how things are but how others think they should be or they may represent ideologies rather than realities. Nevertheless, some of his ideas were interesting and he was one of the first academics to show that the concept of childhood is a social construction: it is not universal and it changes over time.

Case study

Main influences of changing attitudes to childhood in Britain

Changes in family life   In medieval times family life was open, not private as it is today. Family and community life were mixed and children were integrated into the adult social world. Over time the family became a more self-contained private unit, moving from the public into the private sphere. Thus, children became less integrated into public life and adult contexts.

Changes in work   Before industrialization children carried out both paid and unpaid labour. Rural families tended to work the land together as a unit, including children. There was minimal separation between home and work (Pilcher 1995: 83). During industrialization, work and domestic life became separated, which meant that some children stopped working, but others began to work in the public sphere where they tended to be more vulnerable than when working for their families at home. Subsequently, after industrialization, laws were introduced with the aim of banning children from working by the end of the nineteenth century. Hence, the nineteenth century saw the growing dependency of children by denying them a source of income and by the beginning of the twentieth century children were no longer seen as workers (Hockey and James 1993). Consequently, industrialization led to a change in social relations and the emergence of children's dependency. Childhood became seen as a time when children did not work. It is important to remember that this was because of changing social relations, not because of children's physical abilities. It was not connected to their biological or chronological age but rather their social age. Thus, as a result of changing social attitudes, children no longer engaged in work and became seen as not fully participating in society.

Changes in education   In medieval times education was seen as open to all ages, not just children. The medieval school was more like a technical college with apprenticeships for all ages. The school system as we know it developed later, initially with a key role in moral instruction (Heywood 2001). In the seventeenth century there was a focus on the idea that the young were degenerate and in need of control. Gradually schools responded to this social problem by teaching religious values to pupils.

Case study (continued)

Hoyles (1979) notes that, although educational changes were important, children were affected differently according to their social class. Middle-class boys were the first young people to be constructed as 'children' and use education. This is because their parents had sufficient money to fund them and saw education as a way of providing opportunities for their children's future. The aristocracy did not use education as much because they had alternatives: other traditional jobs were available to them via their aristocratic networks, such as jobs in the army. In contrast, poor children continued to work and were the last to use education. During industrialization poor children worked in mills, factories and agriculture and there was a lot more resistance to viewing working-class children as a separate group from adults. It took some time to remove them completely from the workforce because they were perceived to be too useful. Thus this example indicates that social class can impact upon children's experience of childhood.

Ariès (1962) argues that with industrialization, the middle class developed new childhood ideologies. One such ideology was to perceive children as sweet and cute, romanticized as a source of amusement. A later ideology perceived them with concern because of their morally weak nature. These ideas came from religious notions about children being born without sin but being vulnerable to corruption. The outcome of this was that children were seen to be in need of guidance and control. Two notions were developed: that children need discipline and that children should be separated and protected from the adult world.

The school system developed as an appropriate separate place for children: an arena where they could be apart from adults, but also where they could be disciplined and guided. This often resulted in very harsh punishments, sometimes to the point of being cruel. Compulsory education was introduced in 1880 (Heywood 2001), and this contributed to the marginalization of children from

the workplace, because it meant that children had to go to school instead of work. Education not only segregated children from world of adults, but it also led to the economic dependency of children.

Changes in consumer products
As children became separated from the adult world, new markets for children were created. Children became a new group of consumers due to the commercial expansion of markets, such as book and toy industries, that were developed in the eighteenth century. Subsequently, a range of specialist services, and products for children were created, including different clothes, toys, books, films and games (Hockey and James 1993). Specialized markets for children reinforced the idea of childhood as a special period in the life course. Children became a separate and distinct consumer group.

Question

1. *In what ways do you think that new technologies, such as email, the Internet and mobile phones, have changed the nature of contemporary childhoods?*

In 1973, Hardman made a plea for children to be studied in their own right and not merely as passive objects of society (Hardman 2001). The 1970s witnessed the gradual rise of interest in the social studies of childhood, which developed through the 1980s, mainly in the disciplines of sociology and anthropology. Previous work on childhood had been concentrated mostly in the fields of developmental psychology and education, guided by models of child development and socialization. Thus, until recently, childhood studies focused on children's future worth rather than on their present worth as beings in their own right. Children were perceived only in terms of what they would or could become, and were regarded as by-products of other units such as the family or parents (Saporiti 1994: 193). Traditionally, childhood had been conceptualized as an incompetent, passive and dependent stage in the life course (Hockey and James 2003). The linear developmental model was taken for granted, based on growing competencies increasing with age. Recently, developmental theories of childhood have received widespread criticism: 'this approach both denies the agency of children and ignores the socially constructed character of childhood' (James *et al.* 1998: 173).

A closer look

The sociology of childhood

James and Prout (1990) offered a new paradigm for the sociology of childhood, highlighting six key features for understanding children and childhoods:

1 Childhood is understood as a social construction. It is not defined in biological terms of chronological age but varies across different cultures and societies. It is not universal but is subject to social and cultural interpretation.

2 Childhood is a variable of social analysis, in the same way as gender, class and ethnicity are considered essential components of social analysis.

3 Children's cultures and social relationships are worthy of study in their own right.

4 Children are not passive subjects but active agents in the construction of their own lives.

5 Ethnography is a useful and appropriate methodology to study childhood, allowing children to have a more direct voice.

6 The emergent paradigm involves a process of the reconstruction of childhood in society.

(James and Prout 1990: 8–9)

The 'new' sociology of childhood was consolidated in the 1990s focusing on the social construction of children's everyday lives in the present rather than on their future worth as adults. Previous developmental models of childhood did not take children's views into account and the focus was on the child 'becoming' an adult. In contrast, the sociology of childhood takes children's views seriously and considers children as social actors. Children are perceived as competent active beings who, within certain constraints, are capable of shaping their own lives. Thus the focus is on 'the experiences of being a child' (James *et al.* 1998: 208); the child as 'being' rather than 'becoming' (Qvortrup 1994). Such a framework facilitates sensitivity towards understanding children's issues from their own perspectives rather than imposing adult concerns and interpretations onto their lives.

It must also be recognized that the social construction of childhood needs to be understood at three different levels: the structural, the discursive and the situated (Jackson and Scott 2000). At the structural level, childhood is shaped by the institutions of the family, education and the state. The socio-economic context and the structural constraints of adult–child relations affect the opportunities and restrictions which children face in their lives (Lavalette and Cunningham 2002). At the level of discourse, representations and images of childhood shape common-sense understandings of childhood (Jenks 1996) which vary in different cultures. However, at an everyday, individual level, children are not passive actors in the face of either discourse or structure. Children act to shape and reshape structures and discourses particularly in their relations with others. They are social actors in the social construction of childhood, which is situated in everyday relations, as well as within structures and discourse. Yet it must also be recognized that:

> children's participation in constructing their own everyday world takes place within the constraints set by their subordinate location in relation to adults.
>
> (Jackson and Scott 2000: 154).

A closer look

Rights of the child

Article 12: State parties shall assure to the child who is capable of forming his or her own views the right to express those views freely in all matters affecting the child, the views of the child being given due weight in accordance with the age and maturity of the child.

(UN Convention on the Rights of the Child 1989)

Perceiving children as social actors means that their own views should be sought when constructing knowledge about their daily lives (Mayall 2002). There is now wide recognition that children should be listened to and their perspectives should be taken seriously. The 1979 United Nations Year of the Child provided much impetus to child research (Boyden and Ennew 1997: 9). Such interest has continued to increase as a result of the 1989 United Nations Convention on the Rights of the Child, which has been almost universally ratified except in Somalia and the United States. The Convention has 54 Articles covering the following broad areas of rights: survival, protection, development and participation. As well as defining the social, economic, cultural, civil and political rights of children, the Convention outlines the duties and responsibilities of governments and other adults to children and their families. Article 12 focuses on the importance of children being able to express their views freely and having them taken into account in matters which concern them. Children's perspectives should be listened to not only because they have a right to be heard and are capable of expressing themselves, but also because 'only by hearing from children themselves is it possible to learn about their particular childhood experiences' (Boyden *et al.* 1998: 170).

Stop and think

➤ In what ways and to what extent are children's interests represented in these social institutions: (a) the family; (b) different forms of media; (c) religion; (d) politics; (e) education; (f) the law?

➤ In discussing this you may find it useful to compare and contrast possible responses from adults and children and compare these institutions across time and cultures.

Characteristics of modern childhood in Britain

We have seen that changes in family life, education, work and consumer markets have led to what we understand as modern childhood today. In Britain, as in most societies of the minority world, childhood is perceived as a distinctive and special stage in an individual's life. Children are regarded as 'other': a distinct social group, set apart as a special category with specific needs, different from adulthood (Pilcher 1995). Children tend to be separated from much of the adult world such as spending much of their everyday lives in aged-based institutions with their peers. Thus what began as separation from the adult world then led on to marginalization, resulting in a construction of childhood as a stage of dependence and subordination to adults. Children experience social, political and economic dependency. Furthermore, their lives are largely controlled by adults (Mayall 2002). They are subject to parental control in the family and to teachers' control in schools. Thus much of their lives is spent under adult surveillance.

There are two polarized views of children in modern society. On the one hand, they are perceived as vulnerable and innocent, in need of protection from the harsh adult world. On the other hand, they are seen to be vulnerable and corruptible, in need of control. In Britain, as in many other parts of the minority world, childhood is considered as a time dedicated to play and to school, but not to work: a period free from adult responsibilities. As mentioned earlier, this social construction of childhood leads to the view that children are meant to be happy and lack responsibility. Yet this is the idealized image of

A closer look

Research with children

In the past most childhood research tended to gather second-hand information about children's lives from parents, teachers or other adult carers. Nowadays it is widely accepted that children's own perspectives should also be sought on issues that concern them. However, most societies do not have a culture of listening to children, so how can their views best be heard?

The challenge is to strike a balance between not patronising children and recognising their competencies, whilst maintaining their enjoyment of being involved with the research and facilitating their ability to communicate their view of the world. A combination of techniques can enable the data-generation process to be fun and interesting for the participants as well as effective in generating useful and relevant data . . . Some children prefer to draw, others to write or talk. As preferences and competencies vary from child to child in the same way as they do from adult to adult, it is impossible to find the ideal methods for research with children.

Using a range of methods, both traditional and innovative, can help strike a balance and address some of the ethical and methodological issues of research with children. Like other child researchers I found that using a variety of techniques was valuable: to prevent boredom and sustain interest; to prevent biases arising from over-reliance on one method; to triangulate and cross-check data; to evaluate the usefulness of different methods and to strike a balance between traditional and innovative methods . . .

It should also be acknowledged that it is misleading to talk about 'child' and 'adult' research methods, since the suitability of particular methods depends as much on the research context as on the research subjects' stage in the life course. The choice of methods not only depends on the age, competence, experience, preference and social status of the research subjects but also on the cultural environment and the physical setting, as well as the research questions and the competencies of the researcher . . . Perceiving children as competent social actors does not necessarily mean that research should be conducted in the same way as with adults. This is because many of the reasons underlying potential differences stem from children's marginalised position in adult society or from our own adult perceptions of children rather than being a reflection of children's competencies.

(Punch 2002b: 337–8)

childhood in the minority world which is often presented as universal, and it is important to realize that it is an ideology and not necessarily a reality (Boyden 1990).

However, some argue that children are oppressed, that their lives are too controlled, that they are not valued and are too dependent on adults (Hood-Williams 1990). Furthermore, the dependence of children on adults is widely recognized but the idea that adults are, or can be, dependent on children is frequently ignored or under-estimated. In the minority world, since most children go to school and do not work full-time, they tend to be economically dependent on their parents. However, Leonard (1990) observes that parents in the UK can be emotionally dependent on their children for 'love, loyalty, obedience and moral support' (1990: 67). She suggests that children give meaning to adults' lives and are central to adults' definition of self. Children also create many jobs for adults in terms of child-care and schooling. Oldman (1994) argues that adults in the UK may be dependent on children for their employment.

Therefore, adult–child relations are complex, and should not merely be seen in terms of independence versus dependence. Elements of exchange in reciprocal relations between adults and children should be con-sidered (Morrow 1994). Adults' and children's lives are interrelated at many different levels; adults are often not fully independent beings (Hockey and James 1993). It is too simplistic to use the notion of dependency, whether of children on adults, or adults on children, to explain the complexity of adult–child relationships. Adult–child relations should be explained in terms of interdependence that is negotiated and renegotiated over time and space, and needs to be understood in relation to the particular social and cultural context (Punch 2001a).

Many of the characteristics of modern childhood in Britain are found in other minority world societies, but not in all cultures. This definition of childhood is relatively recent, thus illustrating that childhood is a social con-struction and the way it is understood varies over time. Furthermore, as we shall see in the following section, it is a cultural construction; the way childhood is understood also varies over space.

Cultural construction of childhood

The notion of a universal childhood only exists in so far as it is a generational category present in all societies. That is, childhood is a structural form and a social status in both minority and majority world contexts. However, as Qvortrup argues, we need to bear in mind that: 'There is . . . not one, but many childhoods' (1994: 5). The multi-plicity of different childhoods requires them to be placed within their particular historical, geographical and cultural context. For example, Blanchet (1996) shows how children in Bangladesh are indulged and protected when very young. However, they are treated somewhat severely between the ages of about 10 to 20 in order to prepare them for the harshness of adult life. Similarly, Stafford comments that children in a fishing village of Angang in Taiwan are often subject to teasing and harsh treatment by adults in order to teach them to be 'clever, resilient or tough' (1995: 179). In the majority world, where many children work, parents may be economically dependent on their children. For example, Boyden (1990) notes that in some countries children can be the main or sole income-earners in the household. Children are often the only source of social and economic support for their parents in old age. Thus relations between children and adults in the majority world tend to be more interdependent than the genera-tional relationships of families in the minority world.

In the majority world many children work and can be proud about being active contributors to the mainten-ance of their households. Children tend to be perceived as competent workers and they are encouraged to take on adult responsibilities from an early age. Much of their work teaches them useful skills for their future and is perceived to be a central part of their childhood. How-ever, in popular and media discourses majority world children who work from an early age, 'burdened with adult-like duties and responsibilities' (Kefyalew 1996: 209), tend to be conceptualized as miniature adults (Boyden et al. 1998). This is because the notion of the globalization of childhood based on minority world ideals continues to persist, where childhood is perceived as a time for play and school but as incompatible with work (Boyden 1990). Childhood is considered as a special time when we need to be protected, often resulting in exclusion from the world of adults, especially from adult responsibilities of work. The popular conceptualization of children who do not live up to such idealism is that they have 'abnormal' childhoods (Edwards 1996). While not denying that some child work can be extremely exploitative, recent academic studies have shown that work is central to many majority world childhoods and that it is not necessarily detri-mental, often having both positive and negative effects (Boyden et al. 1998; Woodhead 1999).

Thus, in a global context, it is more common for chil-dren to work and go to school than to have a childhood dedicated to play and school. Rather than perceiving majority world children as having 'abnormal' childhoods, it should be remembered that children in the minority world tend to experience more privileged, protected childhoods compared with most of the world's children. It is also worth remembering that although most children in the majority world work, this does not mean that they have no time for play; many combine the activities of play with both school and work (Woodhead 1999). For example, rural Bolivian children tend not to have access to manufactured toys because of limited financial resources and the relative isolation of countryside locations but, to compensate, children use their own resourcefulness to make their own toys (Punch 2001a). They use the natural environment and materials that are available to them, such as stones, water, mud and maize (see Figures 9.5 and 9.6). They integrate their play activities with work and school, for example by playing on the way to and from school or while taking animals out to pasture (see below).

Nevertheless, this is not to say that all children who work in the majority world have happy childhoods. There are also many street children, child prostitutes and child soldiers who live in particularly difficult circumstances. The important point to bear in mind is that we should not see childhood in poor countries, and children who work, only in a negative light. We should be aware that simplistic stereotypes of childhood hide the complex realities of children's lives. Thus, although the social construction of childhood in Britain means that we perceive work as something negative and potentially harmful for children, we have to remember that these are merely our ideas of what childhood should be like. After all, we should not forget that in our society we force children to go to school and do not let them work full-time. Who is to say what a 'normal' childhood should consist of?

Thus there is not one universal childhood, but a diversity of childhoods that exist both between and within different cultures. Simplistic distinctions between majority world and minority world childhoods are problematic because children's lives vary according to a range of factors such as culture, class, gender, age, ethnicity, disability, religion and birth order. For example, in Hecht's (1998) research with street children in Brazil, he differentiates between the protected, nurtured childhoods of the rich and the independent, nurturing childhoods of the poor. As a social category childhood exists in all societies but attitudes towards it can be different, so the ways of being a child and the ways it is understood by adults vary. It is important to consider the particular circumstances in which children live their childhoods. The historical, cultural, economic, social and geographical context shapes how different childhoods are understood and experienced. Therefore, childhood is both a social and a cultural construction as it varies over time and space.

World in focus

Childhood in rural Bolivia

It is useful to consider examples of childhood in different parts of the world to highlight that the minority world construction of childhood is not universal. Research in rural southern Bolivia illustrates that the concept of childhood varies cross-culturally:

Most of the children in Churquiales face the same broad constraints of relative poverty and geographical isolation. The opportunities for waged employment are limited, and schooling is available only for the first six years of primary education. The community is relatively isolated, having limited access to the mass media, as there is no electricity and no television, and communication networks are not extensive. The main form of transport is foot and there are no cars. There are no push-chairs for young children, so they are tied by a shawl and carried on their mother's back. As soon as they can walk they are encouraged to get used to walking long distances and from as young as three years old they can be expected to walk several miles if necessary. Children cover a lot of ground every day as they walk between their home and school, go to the hillsides in search of animals or firewood, fetch water from the river and carry out regular errands for their parents to other households or to the shops in the community square . . .

In order to provide for the family's subsistence requirements, the households in Churquiales

World in focus (continued)

have high labour requirements in three main areas of work: agriculture, animal-related work and domestic work. In the countryside many jobs have to be done every day, such as caring for the animals, food preparation, and water and firewood collection. The household division of labour is divided according to sex, age, birth order and household composition (Punch 2001b). Children are expected to contribute to the maintenance of their household from an early age. Once children are about five years old parental expectations of their household work roles increase, and children are required to take on work responsibilities at home. As they acquire skills and competence their active participation in the maintenance of the household rapidly increases.

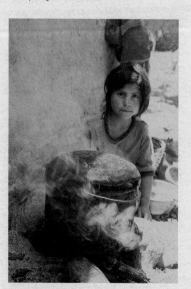

Figure 9.5 A young Bolivian girl cooking
© Samantha Punch

Bolivian children in rural areas carry out many jobs without question or hesitation, often readily accepting a task and taking pride in their contribution to the household. In addition, some household tasks, such as daily water and firewood collection, are such a regular part of their daily routine that they accept responsibility without having to be told to do them. Water collection is a child-specific task, usually carried out by young children as it is a relatively 'easy' job which children as young as three or four years old can start doing. They may begin by only carrying very small quantities of water (in small jugs at first), but by the time they are six or seven years old they can usually manage two 5-litre containers in one trip. Since children are assigned this job from a very early age and it has to be carried out at least once or twice everyday, children know there is no point of trying to avoid doing something which is very clearly their responsibility. I observed that children frequently accepted responsibility for such tasks and initiated action to fulfil them rather than merely responding to adults' demands. Their sense of satisfaction for self-initiated task-completion often appeared to be greater than when they were asked to do something.

So, children in rural Bolivia are not only expected to work and are given many responsibilities but they are also aware of the importance of their contribution and often fulfil their duties with pride. Parents encourage them to learn new skills by giving them opportunities to acquire competencies and be responsible. Parents do not expect to have to remind children constantly of their tasks and may threaten them with harsh physical punishment if their obligations are not completed. Children are encouraged to be independent: to get on with their jobs, to combine work and school, and to travel large distances within the community unaccompanied. In addition, children are also expected to maintain interdependent family relations by contributing to the survival of the household. Furthermore, parents teach their children to try to be relatively tough, for instance not to cry if they fall over and hurt themselves, not to sit on adults' laps or be carried on mothers' backs once they are over about three years old, and to be able to look after themselves and younger siblings when parents are away from the household.

(Punch 2001a: 25–28)

Questions

1. What were the opportunities and constraints which shaped your experience of childhood?

2. Consider the responsibilities you had as a child. Did you perceive them as a frustrating burden or did they enhance your sense of pride and achievement?

Social construction of old age

Stop and think

➤ Think of terms we use in everyday language to describe older people. What kind of images do they conjure up?

➤ In what ways are such images positive or negative about the ageing process, and are they gendered (i.e. are different images used to refer to older men compared with older women)?

For many people, growing old can be a time of social withdrawal and loss – loss of job, income, health, independence, role, status, partners, friends and relatives. Old age can be experienced as a time of loneliness and social isolation. It is commonly believed that older people are 'burdens', being dependent on medical and social services. Yet old age can also be associated with having greater life experience and being 'wise', such as when grandchildren look up to the worldly wisdom of their grandparents. However, many of the negative generalizations of older people mask the diversity of their varied experiences. As Victor argues:

> Although the realities of ageing do not fit the commonly held stereotypes, the myths about ageing continue to find common currency and expression in everyday life. (Victor 1994: 78)

This is reflected in the popular terms used to describe older people, such as 'being past it', 'little old ladies' and 'old biddies'.

Most images of older age indicate that in minority world societies older people tend to be marginalized through negative stereotypes which reflect 'the experience of bodily decay or mental deterioration' (Hockey and James 1993: 79). As previously mentioned, young bodies tend to be considered more beautiful in British society, so physical ageing is often perceived in prerogative terms. In particular, images of ageing tend to marginalize older women more than older men (Biggs 1993). This is partly because physical appearance is seen as more important in society for women than for men (Arber and Ginn 1993) so, when women lose their physical attractiveness, they are more stigmatized than men. Victor (1994) explains why there is a double standard of ageing:

Growing older is less problematic for a man because masculinity is associated with qualities such as competence, autonomy and self-control. These valued attributes withstand the ageing process much better than the qualities for which females are desired: beauty, physical attractiveness and childbearing ... Later life is a time when men become grey-haired, distinguished, wise and experienced whilst women are typified as worn-out, menopausal, neurotic and unproductive.

(Victor 1994: 82)

It is important to recognize that in relation to gender and ageing women suffer from both sexism and ageism (see Case study). For example, they are more likely to be living in poverty as their pensions tend to be less than those of men. Women are also more likely to live longer than men, since life expectancy for women is higher than for men which means they are more likely to end up living alone in later life or to end up in residential care (Biggs 1993).

Stop and think

➤ Do you think that future cohorts of older women will have higher expectations regarding their position in society than previous generations? If so, why?

➤ In what ways do you think older women in future generations might be able to resist the patriarchal ideal of femininity?

Retirement

The experience of retirement has become one of the defining features of old age in the minority world. In the UK, the age of retirement (65 for men and 60 for women) is an arbitrary age which 'bears no relationship to the nature of the individual's personality, vitality, biological condition and mental acuity' (Holmes and Holmes 1995: 53). There is no particular decline in physical or mental abilities at this chronological age, and many older people can still be both mentally and physically capable at 60 or 65. However, the notion of the pensioner, the retired older person who receives a pension, tends to be how many older people become defined, hiding their individual identity. Yet we need to be aware that older people are not a homogenous group (Arber and Evandrou 1993; Phillipson 1998). For a moment, compare yourself to someone 25 years older than you and imagine how you

Case study

The double standard of ageing

Arber and Ginn (1991) argue that growing older has a different significance for women compared with men:

Itzin (1990) sees the double standard of ageing as arising from the sets of conventional expectations as to age-appropriate attitudes and roles for each sex which apply in patriarchal society. These are conceptualized by Itzin as a male and a female 'chronology', socially defined and sanctioned so that transgression of the prescribed roles or of their timing is penalized by disapproval and lost opportunities. Male chronology hinges on employment, but a woman's age status is defined in terms of events in the reproductive cycle. She is therefore 'valued according to sexual attractiveness, availability and usefulness to men' (Itzin 1990: 118). The social devaluation of older women occurs regardless of occupation or background, or of the fact that after childrearing they have potentially twenty-five years of productive working life ahead.

Because women's value is sexualised, positively in the first half of life, negatively in the second, it depends on a youthful appearance. Sontag (1972) observes that while men are 'allowed' to age naturally without social penalties, the ageing female body arouses revulsion. The discrepancy between the societal ideal of physical attractiveness in women and their actual appearance widens with age, whereas the signs of ageing in men are not considered so important. This double standard is most evident and acute in the conventions surrounding sexual desirability, as shown in the taboo on asking a woman her age, and in the contrasting attitudes towards marriages where the husband is much older and those (few) where he is much younger. The former practice is socially approved, or at least forgiven, as is the desertion by husbands of their middle-aged wives for younger women. But an older woman who marries a young man is censured as predatory and selfish. Unlike the older man who is admired for this capture of a young bride, the older woman is condemned because she has broken the convention that men remain dominant. Since age seniority generally implies authority, women remain minors in their conjugal relationships (Sontag 1972) . . .

The double standard of ageing is not merely a matter of aesthetics: it is 'the cutting edge of a whole set of oppressive structures (often masked as gallantries) that keep women in their place' (Sontag 1972: 38). Itzin concurs; men's preference for wives younger than themselves at *all* ages shows that the devaluation of women as they age has less to do with appearance than with the sexual division of labour and of power (Itzin 1990).

(Arber and Ginn 1991: 41–3)

Question

1. *Think of some examples of well-known women, such as actresses or politicians, and consider the extent to which they suffer from the double standard of ageing in comparison with men in similar situations.*

would feel if you were constantly referred to as being part of their social group. It seems a bit ridiculous to consider that people who are 25 years apart share many similarities, but it is what we tend to do to older people. Society often sees them all as just part of one big group of pensioners. Yet the group of retired people over 65 can represent a number of different generations. Trying to suggest that the life of a 65-year-old is similar to that of a 90-year-old, merely because they are both in the age of retirement, is not appropriate.

A closer look

Appropriate terminology

The term 'older people' is a more suitable expression than the more static and homogenized terms of 'pensioner', 'the elderly' or 'old people' since it implies variety and suggests a range of different ages (Wilson 2000).

Retirement has become the norm in Britain and is experienced in a variety of ways. Research has shown that, if people are dissatisfied with retirement, it is usually related to their loss of income and reduced social contacts rather than missing the job itself (Victor 1994). Satisfaction with retirement is linked to increased opportunities for leisure activities and greater freedom. However, the experience of retirement is affected by social class (Biggs 1993; Vincent 2000). A middle-class person will be more likely to have a good pension, health insurance, own home and car as well as savings to spend on new activities. In contrast, a working-class person will be more likely to have sparse savings, receive an inadequate state pension, and be unable to afford a good lifestyle. Thus they will be more likely to experience retirement as a time of poverty. The problem of poverty in old age can be acute and older people feature prominently in the poorer sections of all societies (Vincent 2003). For example, according to the Office for National Statistics, a total of 3,000 women and 2,000 men aged 75 and over in Britain have neither central heating nor sole use of a bathroom (not including residents of communal establishments). Financial hardship may also be intensified by ill health and isolation (Bradley 1996). A growing proportion of older people live alone: 14.4 per cent of all households in the UK, of which two-thirds of these (68.2 per cent or 2,129,000 older people) have no access to a car (National Statistics 2003).

Consequently, the experience of retirement, like that of ageing, is extremely diverse and cross-cut by factors such as age, gender, class, marital status, disability and ethnicity (Victor 1994). For example, class can also affect the likelihood of an older person suffering from poor health or becoming dependent. However, the persistence of inappropriate negative stereotypes of older people masks the diversity of their experiences and can result in both discrimination and prejudice against them (Victor 1994). Phillipson argues that in order to understand the complexity of life in old age we should explore the ways 'in which people "resist" rather than succumb to the pressures associated with growing old' (1998: 139). We should also take account of older people's contributions to society by recognizing that some continue to work or learn (such as by embarking on Open University courses), and many still provide material and emotional support within their families and communities through voluntary and unpaid services. Thus, as Victor (1994) suggests, it is more appropriate to consider notions of interdependence between generations and throughout the life course, rather than a more linear conception of independence and dependence at different life stages. We should not perceive old age to be 'naturally' problematic by focusing only on 'the "burdens" of pensions, caregiving and intergenerational equity' (Wilson 2000: 160). We need to move beyond stereotypical assumptions by also considering the benefits of old age and older people's positive experiences and contributions to society:

> Older people should be seen as repositories of cultural wisdom and expertise, craft skills and local knowledge – things that are valuable to all. However, it is important to avoid romantic stereotypes of old age, since elders can also be repositories of prejudice and ancient animosities as well as the positive side of tradition.
>
> (Vincent 2003: 168)

A closer look

Table 9.2 Different perspectives of retirement

1950s:	Concern that withdrawal from work may lead to social and mental health problems
1970s and 1980s:	Promoted as a means of coping with mass unemployment
1990s and 2000s:	Fragmented and flexible pathways into retirement: redundancy or disability pathways, forced or voluntary early retirement, informal care or unemployment pathways and state retirement

The contested nature of sociology

Table 9.2, based on Phillipson's (1998) work, indicates that over time different sociological arguments emerge in relation to specific issues. Initially there was concern that retirement would impact negatively on people's lives. This view then shifted to perceiving retirement as a positive way of coping with mass unemployment. More recently it has been recognized that there are multiple routes into retirement and that it may be experienced in both negative and positive ways. These different perspectives reflect the complexity and shifting nature of sociological understanding which is often debated and may change over time.

Stop and think

> ➤ Give examples of older people who continue to play leading roles in areas such as the arts, politics and law in contemporary society.

> ➤ In what ways do they challenge negative stereotypes about older people?

A closer look

Sociological perspectives of ageing

Some writers approach the study of ageing from different theoretical perspectives. Each 'theory' or way of understanding the ageing process is given a different name, such as:

Disengagement theory Cumming and Henry argue that 'Disengagement is an inevitable process in which many of the relationships between a person and other members of society are severed and those remaining are altered in quality' (1961: 211). As the ageing process develops, older people are believed to become increasingly self-preoccupied while society prepares for their final 'disengagement' of death in order to minimize the social disruption it may cause (Phillipson 1998).

The political economy of old age This theory strives to understand the relationship between the ageing process and the economy. Townsend (1981) refers to the concept of 'structured dependency' which perceives older people to be excluded from work as well as having a restricted access to a range of social resources resulting in their dependent status and increased likelihood of living in poverty. The loss of a productive role in the economy and increased welfare dependence can result in old age being perceived as a social problem (Howson 2004: 149).

'Ordinary theorizing' Gubrium and Wallace (1990) suggest that researchers should listen carefully to the questions that older people raise when they are being interviewed. They argue that, in research, older people should not merely be perceived as passive respondents; it should be recognized that 'they develop facts and theories of their own, and the relevance of these deserves wider recognition' (Phillipson 1998: 26).

Cultural construction of old age

We have seen that in Britain and other societies of the minority world ageing is devalued and not esteemed (Hockey and James 1993). We need to bear in mind that the disadvantages of old age are not universal or fixed:

> A decline in strength and a changing physical appearance may be inevitable in old age, but the degree and meaning of change are very variable. The actual impact of physiological changes depends on whether the environment is hostile to disabilities or supportive . . . The cross-cultural approach to the study of ageing shows that most of the attributes of old age are culturally determined. For example, it is not 'natural' for older men or women to live in poverty, or to take care of grandchildren, or to spend time in religious contemplation, but it is easy to believe it is if we are locked into one culture only. (Wilson 2000: 3)

Retirement pensions are by no means universal and globally many people continue working until they are no longer physically capable. There are widespread beliefs that in the majority world old age is revered and once older people are unable to work, they are cared for by their families. Some cultures have more positive attitudes towards the ageing process but this does not necessarily mean that all older people in those societies will be treated with respect and importance. Featherstone and Hepworth (1989) note that high status tends to be accorded to those who had power, wealth or status when they were younger.

In some traditional cultures, there can be a tendency to offer older people higher respect and status. For example, some societies worship their ancestors and it tends to be older men who carry out important ritual ceremonies. Elders can be perceived to achieve almost godlike status, for example in Ghana older people are a symbol of deity and so, if you offend them, you are thought to offend the gods. The traditional Hindu perception of ageing illustrates the benefits of older age in that culture: 'being old means being more saintly, gaining greater respect and possibly achieving a better position in the next life' (Wilson 2000: 23). Wilson (2000) also points out that in Islamic and Asian countries there can be very strong religious or philosophical beliefs that older parents should be greatly respected. These cultural beliefs, along with a lack of available pensions, often leads to families rather than the state providing support for older people. For example, in Japan there is a strong sense of duty towards older people, and children (usually sons and daughters-in-law) are generally expected to provide economic and social care for older parents. However, because of falling birth rates and greater longevity, Japan has the largest ageing population in the world and is increasingly concerned whether families will be able to continue to provide support for older people.

Thus, older people can be treated well and may have more power and status in the majority world. However, we need to be careful not to romanticize old age in such cultures, as not all older people in traditional or religious communities will be treated well:

Even among very small-scale societal types such as hunters and gatherers (or tribal horticultural peoples), a wide variation exists in how older people are evaluated and dealt with. Some such societies regard their older citizens as revered personages to be carried on one's back as communities move over the landscape, while others see them as excess baggage to be left to the elements when they can no longer keep up.

(Sokolovsky 1990: 2–3)

In addition, widespread poverty can make it difficult for some people to care for the older generation. As Wilson reminds us, 'not everyone has a family and, further, not

World in focus

Older age in Inuit culture

Holmes and Holmes (1995) describe how processes of modernization have impacted upon the role of older people in Inuit culture. Inuits live in a harsh cold environment, mainly surviving on the subsistence activities of hunting sea mammals and fishing. Traditionally, older people have held positions of high status and respect within their communities. Younger family members frequently consulted them about improving their hunting skills, choosing marriage partners and settling family disputes (Holmes and Holmes 1995: 149). Older people played an important role in educating children, particularly in economic skills, and were believed to have special knowledge and spiritual power. The Inuit culture developed food-sharing practices in order to ensure that the older people would be cared for. For example, some foods were prohibited to be eaten by hunters and were reserved for those who could not hunt for themselves

(Holmes and Holmes 1995: 153). However, because of contact with Europeans, the traditional Inuit system has begun to experience some effects of modernization. Some of the recent changes are positive, such as access to basic services of running water and electricity, but generally the impact on the role of older people has been negative. For example, the subsistence food-sharing practices are beginning to be replaced by more commercial hunting. Older people are losing some decision-making power and respect as elected councils with younger people are being formed. Education has become more formal, and children now attend school rather than relying on informal education from their grandparents. This has even led to a language barrier between older people who speak Inuit and children who learn English at school:

The result is very little intergenerational communication or learning. However, much of the knowledge the old people

traditionally have imparted is now largely irrelevant anyway, and both grandparents and grandchildren know it.

The elderly have also lost other traditional functions. Store-bought goods have eliminated the need for old people to make such things as weapons or clothing, and maintaining new mechanical and electrical gadgets requires skills they have never acquired. The elderly at one time performed magical services and taught young people magic songs, formulas, and techniques, but the coming of Christianity has done much to destroy belief in or use of such phenomena. In the larger communities, curing activities and midwife duties have been taken over by trained medical personnel.

(Holmes and Holmes 1995: 157)

Question

1. In what ways has the modernization process impacted upon the lives of older people in the UK?

all families are dutiful, let alone harmonious' (2000: 26). Hence, even when old age is perceived positively, not all older people will occupy a privileged position. Furthermore, we need to take into account that increasingly the values associated with old age in majority world countries are diminishing in their importance:

> Wisdom, spirituality and magic powers were seen as attributes of long experience or nearness to death. Now the spread of materialism, industrialization, urbanization and Westernization have led to the breakdown of religious authority and family solidarity and the devaluation of the wisdom of the old.
>
> (Wilson 2000: 10–11)

Recent social changes, such as the spread of mass education and the introduction of new technologies, tend to impact negatively on the social status of older people as their traditional knowledge is no longer valued to the same extent. With the growth of industrialization, more people move from rural areas to cities in search of new jobs and it can mean that older people are left behind in rural communities. Thus traditional patterns of caring may also be affected as extended family networks are broken. However, again we need to recognize that not all aspects of modernization and globalization have negative outcomes. Some older people in the majority world may benefit from improved standards of living and an enhanced economic status if welfare systems are also introduced. Consequently, we should explore the diversity of older age in different cultures rather than accept the taken-for-granted ideologies. In particular, we should consider the ways in which age intersects with gender, class, disability, ethnicity and geographical location (especially whether urban or rural location), thereby producing a range of experiences for what it means to be old. Old age is a social construct which differs according to the meanings attached to the ageing process in a specific social and cultural context.

Old age and childhood in Britain

We have considered childhood and older age as being both social and cultural constructs. In this section we shall explore some of the broad similarities and differences of the treatment of children and older people in contemporary Britain. They are both marginal social groups whose lives vary according to class, gender, disability, ethnicity, etc. Nevertheless, there are some general ways

Table 9.3 Comparing and contrasting old age and childhood in Britain

Similarities	Differences
Lack power	Temporality
Dependency	Length of time
Asexuality	Financial dependence
Voiceless	Negative stereotypes
Resistance	
Economic dependence	
Social exclusion	

in which we can compare and contrast these two stages in the life course. These are summarized in the Table 9.3 and then discussed in further detail.

Similarities of marginalized social groups

Both children and older people lack power, autonomy and independence in relation to the more dominant social category of adults (Hockey and James 1993). Children and older people are often perceived as being dependent on adults, in need of care, vulnerable and asexual. They tend to be seen as reliant on others, sometimes described as burdens. Furthermore, they are often treated as if they are unable to speak for themselves. Their voices are silenced as adults take over and may speak on their behalf. For example, during a visit to a health clinic the parent is likely to discuss their child's illness with the doctor rather than allowing the child to speak directly for themselves. Similarly, at a residential care home, the adult son or daughter often speaks to the care staff on behalf of their older parent who is resident.

Despite lacking power in relation to adults, children and older people both have strategies of resistance to compensate for their relative powerlessness. They do not passively accept adult power and control over their lives. Such coping strategies may include feigning illness to avoid doing something they would rather not do, or refusing food. For example, Waksler's (1996) research in the UK indicates that children may lie, fake illness, have temper tantrums or act extra cute in order to cope with and control certain aspects of their lives. Reynolds' (1991) study of children in the Zambezi valley, Zimbabwe, refers to children's strategies of negotiating relationships in order to secure help for their future. She also highlights children's rebellion in defying adults' wishes, with reference to gambling, smoking and refusing to do certain tasks.

Alternatively, both children and older people may distance themselves from the role of cared for: children look after younger children, and older people might care for those who are older than themselves. Hockey and James (1993) suggest that some older people use their actions and speech as a way of distancing themselves from their own frailty. For example, they resist referring to themselves as 'old' and, in some residential care homes, older women visit and help to care for other residents who are frailer than themselves. This then increases their sense of power as other people become dependent on them. Both age groups also have the power to shock. For example, older people might take delight in causing trouble in care homes, and young children may like the attention they get if they swear or say something rude at the family dinner table in front of relatives. These are forms of resistance which they use to counteract their lack of power in relation to more powerful adult social actors.

Both children and older people also experience economic dependence as their access to work is restricted. They are either excluded from work or, if not, their choice of work is limited to low-paid, low-status work which is often irregular or temporary, such as paper rounds or baby sitting for children and gardening or domestic cleaning for older people. This is because there is compulsory retirement for older people and compulsory schooling for children. Work shapes people's social identity and self-esteem which means that exclusion from work can lead to social marginalization as well as economic dependency. Their limited incomes mean that they are less able to participate as active consumers in society. Furthermore, work provides access to social life and friendships, so both children and older people do not experience these additional opportunities for socializing. They tend to be confined to an age-based social life: children with their peers at school and older people in bridge clubs or bingo halls.

Differences of marginalized social groups

Perhaps the main difference between these two social groups is the temporality of childhood. Compared with old age, childhood is a transitory state as children grow out of dependency (Hockey and James 1993). In contrast, once older people move away from adulthood, their dependency is permanent and they remain on the margins of society. The length of time for these two stages in the life course may differ. At most, childhood tends to be perceived as finishing at 18 years of age but old age could last for more than 40 years. Thus old age can represent more than double the time span allotted to childhood. It is also worth bearing in mind that, as adults, we have all had experience of being part of the marginalized group of children, but as yet we do not have any personal experiences of being older and this can affect how we understand the two groups.

The economic dependence of the two social groups is also different. Children are usually financially dependent on their parents whereas older people are more likely to be dependent on their own savings or pensions. The final difference between childhood and old age as stages in the life course is that there appear to be more negative stereotypes about older people compared with children. Thus, although in Britain both groups are devalued in relation to adulthood, old age suffers greater denigration than childhood.

Figure 9.6 A South American child 'being mum'
© Samantha Punch

Summary

- Age is used in all societies to differentiate individuals in both positive and negative ways. For example, as Wilson points out: 'Experiences of ageing can be disabling (we, who are old, cannot do this because we are old) or enabling (we, who are old, have experience and know better)' (2000: 7).

- The social significance attached to biological age is of interest to sociologists. Generally, in the UK and in much of the minority world, the ageing process is perceived negatively as something to be feared and avoided for as long as possible. However, although we define the later stage in the life course in negative terms this does not mean that old age is universally perceived as having low status. We need to analyze critically different case studies, rather than merely accepting the values of our own culture.

- Childhood and old age in the minority world tend to involve a loss of autonomy and these examples indicate that age is a social and cultural construction.

- Age is cross-cut by other forms of social differentiation such as class, gender, ethnicity and disability.

- Age differentiation not only varies between different cultures but also within societies and throughout history. Therefore the construction of age changes over time and place.

Links

The section on childhood and children's rights can be related to the discussion on child abuse in Chapter 13, pages 537–539.

The discussion of work and industrialization on pages 368–370 are developed in Chapter 4, particularly pages 144–152.

 Further reading

Hockey, J. and James, A. (2003) *Social Identities across the Life Course*, Basingstoke: Palgrave Macmillan.
This account shows how the ageing process throughout the life course shapes our sense of identity. It includes discussions of childhood, youth, middle age and older age.

Holmes, E.R. and Holmes, L.D. (1995) *Other Cultures, Elder Years*, London: Sage.
This book offers a comparative perspective on ageing by providing a range of cultural examples including Inuit, Samoa, the United States and American ethnic groups.

Maybin, J. and Woodhead, M. (eds) (2003) *Childhoods in Context*, Chichester: John Wiley & Sons.
A well-written, accessible and comprehensive book which explores childhood and family life, historical perspectives, youth transitions and the different arenas of school and work in both minority world and majority world contexts.

Pilcher, J. (1995) *Age and Generation in Modern Britain*, Oxford: Oxford University Press.
This books provides an excellent overview of the key aspects of childhood, youth, adulthood and older age in British society.

Vincent, J. (2003) *Old Age*, London: Routledge.
An excellent and up-to-date discussion of key concerns in relation to old age: poverty, globalization, intergenerational conflict, consumerism, health and identity.

 Web sites

Age Concern
http://www.ace.org.uk/
This organization aims to improve the quality of life for older people in the UK. The web site includes research, recent news and campaigns.

Centre for Policy on Ageing
http://www.cpa.org.uk/
This organization is concerned with the analysis of public policy as it affects older people, and the web site offers relevant publications, research findings and an information service.

Save The Children
http://www.savethechildren.org.uk/
This organization aims to enhance children's rights and to improve the quality of life for children worldwide. The web

site is an extensive source of publications, research, policies and recent news relating to children's health, education, poverty and exploitation.

UN Programme on Ageing
http://www.un.org/esa/socdev/ageing/
This web site has useful information regarding the ageing of the world's population. It also provides a database on relevant policies and programmes.

Activities

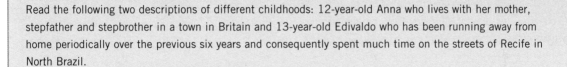

Read the following two descriptions of different childhoods: 12-year-old Anna who lives with her mother, stepfather and stepbrother in a town in Britain and 13-year-old Edivaldo who has been running away from home periodically over the previous six years and consequently spent much time on the streets of Recife in North Brazil.

Activity 1

A middle-class urban 'nurtured' British childhood

Interviewer: And what do you think it's like being a stepdad?

Anna: I think it must be quite good, because he treats me like his child and, like, I go to his family's house.

. . . And he gives me my pocket money and buys me Christmas presents, and just, like, normally treats me like my own Dad does. He disciplines me. And if I'm scared or something. He helps me with my homework if I don't understand something. [Section here on how she plays out with her mates.]

Interviewer: So you have a lot of independence?

Anna: Yes. My Mum doesn't mind where I go provided I tell her where I'm going. So if my friends I'm hanging round with say, Let's go down to [x], I either phone my Mum or I go home and ask my Mum if I can go and have some money to go with. And if she says, No, that means no – I'm not going; then I stay in and watch TV or just go out to play in my area, but if she says, Yes, I do, I get what I need and go to [x].

Interviewer: Do you get money regularly so you can go by bus and –

Anna: Yes.

Interviewer: Is that irrespective of what you might have to do?

Anna: I do housework, I clean dishes, do the Hoovering. But sometimes I get money for it, it depends on, if I've been really good the whole week. But occasionally if I need money my Mum will give it me if she's got it. But if she's got like £1 in her purse she'll say, OK take it. But I'll say, No, it's OK I'll stay in . . .

Interviewer: So do you get on with your Mum – cos you said you did with your, both your fathers?

Anna: Yes, she's my best friend.

Interviewer: What sorts of things do you do with her?

Activities (continued)

Anna: I go out with her, to visit friends. I went with her to see the *Titanic*. And when my stepdad's out, we watch videos, we move the couch in front of the TV and we get loads of snacks and we watch TV, stuff like that, we watch movies together. [Section about gender issues at school.] I like school, I love coming to school. I don't want to leave school ever!

Interviewer: Are there some things you specially like about school?

Anna: I like being with my friends. I like most of my lessons, but there's no particular. I like dance and PE [more about subjects at school, and afterschool clubs, and a homework club].

Interviewer: So school's an important part of your life?

Anna: Yes. Most people just go home after school. They think I'm mad because I stay on. But sometimes I walk home with my friends, and then I get all my homework done and then I go out. And, like, every night I get my bag ready, so when I get up I can just [set off to school with it].

Interviewer: Yes, so is it up to you how you arrange your time after school?

Anna: Yes, so long as I let my Mum know. (Mayall 2002: 95–96)

Questions

1. What constraints and opportunities does Anna face in her everyday life?

2. In what ways does Anna indicate that she is a competent social actor, able to negotiate her autonomy and relationships on a daily basis?

Activity 2

A poor urban 'nurturing' Brazilian childhood

I only ran away from home because of my stepfather. He beat me with a wire cable, left me all cut up, then he threw water and a kilo of salt on me. When I would run away I'd go all over the place. I spent two days with a truck driver, then he said, 'Go away now,' so I left. I stayed in the city and met a lot of kids and that's how I started learning about street life.

I think I have way too much experience now. The street doesn't have anything to offer you except experience. In the street we learn how to live because at home we get spoon-fed everything. It's not like that in the street. In the street we have to work to have something. That's what the street teaches you.

Tobias: In the street, do you roam with a gang?

Edivaldo: If you hang out with a gang, it's worse than being alone, because, look, in a gang it's the strongest one who wins. If I'm weak and, say, I steal a watch, the biggest guy in the gang is going to say, 'Hey, that watch is mine, I'm going to sell it.' That's why I prefer to roam alone. I only went around with a gand once, because when I'm with a group, the group wants to fight to see who's strongest. If you get caught in the middle of something you're in trouble. The one time I was with a group I got stabbed.

I've run away from home twenty-nine times. I've always come to Recife when I run away from home. I'd get a ride with the trucks. Sometimes I'd hide under the spare tire. You know how trucks have that extra tire in case one pops? I'd hide back there and come to Recife all hungry.

The first time, I was seven years old. That's when I started learning about street life. My mother came to Recife and spoke with the police. She sent the police out after me, and she even offered a reward for the person who found me.

Activities (continued)

The second time I went to the Shopping Center in Boa Viagem. I asked a guy for money. He said he didn't have any and walked away. But then he came back and bought me food and asked if I wanted to work in his house. I said yes and I went to live there. I stayed for two days and then my mother found me. She got a whole bunch of kids together and gave them money so they would tell her where I was. I liked it there. I would have stayed. I went back twice [to see the man] but he already had another boy living there and when I went the third time he had left for São Paulo.

I went back to Caruaru and stayed for two months. Then I ran away again, but my mother didn't come to look for me. I stayed in the street in the center of the city for three days. Later I went home because I hadn't really learned what street life is about.

The fourth time was when I learned how to sniff glue. I got together with a bunch of kids and started sniffing, and I got used to it. So I just started running away from home to sniff glue. It's a vice, you know. It's not that I like it, you get to be a prisoner of glue.

Tobias: What do you mean?

Edivaldo: It's a temptation that hits you: 'Come on, sniff glue, sniff.' And you end up sniffing.

Tobias: And what happens when you sniff glue?

Edivaldo: You get high and start seeing things that aren't in front of you. That's what hooks you.

Tobias: What happens if you sniff every day and then all of a sudden you stop? How do you feel?

Edivaldo: You get a fever, a headache, you feel like dying.

Tobias: Does sniffing glue make you hungry?

Edivaldo: Yes, but only when you stop sniffing. Sometimes you sniff to kill the hunger, because when you're hungry and you sniff, the hunger goes away. But if you stop sniffing, the hunger gets you again.

Tobias: I've noticed that some kids sniff glue after eating. Why do they do that?

Edivaldo: It's so that you don't mess up your lungs, because if you eat and then sniff on a full stomach, it's not so bad for you. But if you sniff on an empty stomach, the air from the glue fills up your belly.

(Hecht 1998: 28–29)

Questions

1. *What constraints and opportunities does Edivaldo face in his everyday life?*

2. *In what ways does Edivaldo demonstrate that he has developed coping strategies for managing his precarious life on the streets?*

3. *What are the similarities and differences of the two childhoods presented here?*

4. *Compare and contrast the two accounts in relation to the following themes: responsibility, autonomy, education, family life and adult–child relations.*

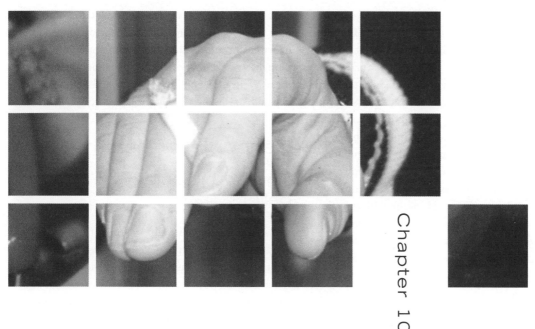

Chapter 10

Health and illness

Twenty years ago, the mention of health and illness would probably have invoked thoughts of hospitals, doctors, nurses, drugs and a first aid box. Today, however, it would probably conjure up a much broader range of images which could well include healthy foods, vitamin pills, aromatherapy, alternative medicines, exercise bikes, health clubs, aerobics, walking boots, running shoes, therapy, sensible drinking, health checks and more. Health, it seems, has become a ubiquitous motif in our culture. Health and illness receive considerable attention from the mass media: television, radio, magazines and videos all devote considerable space and time to health-related issues. Information and knowledge about health and illness are thus no longer just the property of health 'experts'. Everyone has at least some experience and knowledge.

(Nettleton 1995: 1)

Key issues

➤ How do different concepts of health impact on behaviour?

➤ How is health care organized?

➤ What are the major determinants of health?

➤ How are health and illness socially produced?

Introduction

Over the last 50 years, there have been impressive advances in medicine, and much progress in the provision of health care. Antibiotics and vaccination programmes have diminished the threat of infectious disease and improv-

ing technology has enabled surgeons to transplant hearts, lungs and kidneys. More recently, these advances have been seen as more problematic: increasing welfare spending has led to political debate about the future of publicly funded health care systems; the development of antibiotic-resistant diseases and the appearance of new diseases such as AIDS have generated a questioning of the role of medicine, and ethical debate surrounds new technologies such as genetic testing and *in vitro* fertilization.

Stop and think

➤ How has your experience of illness and health care differed from that of your parents, or grandparents? You may want to think about childhood disease, experiences of hospital, information about health and the use of alternative therapies.

If we go back 150 years, there have been even more dramatic changes in the health of the populations of Western countries. In 1841, life expectancy at birth in the UK was 40 years for men and 42 years for women. In 1991, it had risen to 72 years for men and 77 for women. This increase has been largely due to the decline in infectious diseases such as tuberculosis, cholera and typhus, which were prevalent in the nineteenth century but have almost disappeared in Western countries today. Although medical technologies have developed to prevent and control these diseases, including immunization and antibiotic drugs, the rapid decline in infectious disease rates is largely a result of improved social and environmental conditions and better nutrition: most treatments and preventive measures were developed in the second half of the twentieth century, by which time the death rates from infectious diseases had already declined (McKeown 1979).

However, these improvements in the health of the population have been unevenly distributed. Our chance of living a long and healthy life is influenced by a range of factors, from our own behaviour (such as smoking, or engaging in dangerous sports) and individual genetic make-up to the environment we live in and our access to health services. Figure 10.1 illustrates these.

Stop and think

➤ How do these factors impact on your own health? Which factors have the most influence?

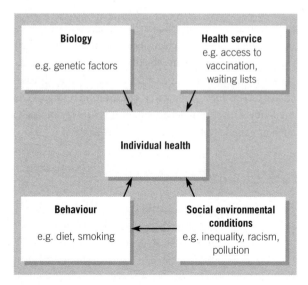

Figure 10.1 Factors influencing health

This chapter examines the social production of ill health: how social, cultural and economic factors impact on the distribution of ill health across populations. First, though, it is necessary to explore in more detail what we mean by 'health', and how our beliefs about the causes of ill health are influenced by social and cultural context.

Concepts of health
The anthropology of health beliefs

Not all societies separate 'illness' from other kinds of misfortune that might happen. Gilbert Lewis, in his account of health beliefs of the Gnau people from New Guinea, found that the word for ill, *wola*, also meant evil, harmful, bad or dangerous (Lewis 1986). People with long-term illnesses or disabilities were described as *biwola*, which also meant aged or old. There was no specific word that could translate as 'illness', because the concept of ill health was not a separate one for the Gnau. They had no specialized healers, and any adult could carry out the treatments that were available. Sickness was seen as a result of evil spirits, and getting better relied on defeating these spirits. The Azande (see Case study) also saw misfortunes such as illness as a result of outside forces – in their case witchcraft. Systems of thought which tend to do this are called *externalizing systems*. Other cultural beliefs about health and illness see the primary causes of illness as internal to the body. These are called *internalizing systems*. Traditional Chinese beliefs are one example, where health is seen as an equilibrium between 'hot' and 'cold' (Wheeler and Tan 1983), and maintaining health and treating disease involve re-establishing a balance.

When serious disease occurs, sufferers often ask 'why has this happened to me, and why now?' Although Western medicine has sophisticated explanations of how diseases are caused, and how to treat them, it cannot answer this question. Some traditional non-Western cosmologies do account for the particular occurrence of illness, and thus account for illness as a personal and social misfortune, rather than just a physical problem.

Stop and think

➤ Listen carefully to conversations about illness between your friends and family. How do explanations and beliefs differ from those of the Azande?

Case study

Azande beliefs about misfortune

Evans-Pritchard was an anthropologist who lived with the Azande in Sudan in the 1920s and described their belief system. The Azande saw misfortune arising from two sources: either the breaking of taboos or witchcraft. All misfortune, whether lack of success in hunting, or illness, or death, could potentially be explained as the result of witchcraft. Indeed, all adult deaths were attributable

to witchcraft, and there was no concept of a 'natural' death. Sickness was often seen as the result of witches, who could slowly consume a victim's body over time. Injuries were also caused by witches: 'A boy knocked his foot against a small stump of wood in the centre of a bush path . . . and the cut . . . began to fester. He declared that witchcraft had made him knock his foot against the stump' (Evans-Pritchard 1976: 19–20). Witchcraft did not explain the general causation of misfortune (this boy explained

the dirty cut as a cause of infection) but it did explain the particular, or why the stump of wood happened to be there just where the boy was walking, and why this cut festered when many others heal without problem. Witchcraft thus explained what for Evans-Pritchard were mere coincidences of time and place.

Question

1. *What equivalents to witchcraft do modern societies use to explain misfortunes?*

Lay definitions of health

The beliefs shared by non-professionals are called *lay beliefs*. They are just as complex in Western societies as they are in cultures such as those of the Azande, and may not correspond closely to the beliefs of medical professionals. When Mildred Blaxter (1990) carried out a survey to find out how behaviour and social circumstances affected the health of people in Britain, she started by noting an initial problem, which was trying to define what 'health' was. She distinguished three different ways in which people talked about health.

First, there were *negative* definitions, in which health is seen as merely the absence of disease. Some people describe themselves as healthy because they have no symptoms of illness. However, there were also other ways in which people commonly identify health. Second were what could be called *functional* definitions. Here, health is seen in terms of abilities, such as being able to work or go to school. In this sense, people described themselves as healthy if they were able to carry out their normal activities. Third were *positive* definitions of health, which tried to identify health as more than merely the absence of disease but as a positive state of being fit, or strong, or feeling 'full of life'. The World Health Organization defines health using a positive definition:

a state of complete physical, mental and social well-being, and not merely the absence of disease or infirmity.
(WHO 1978)

The types of definition Blaxter identified are typical of the responses found in other research. The ways in which we think about health are complex and are influenced by our culture, our experiences and circumstances. Claudine Herzlich (1973) looked at how middle-class people in France talked about health and found that although *illness* was seen as external (either germs or environmental hazards came from outside the individual to make them ill), *health* was seen as something internal, coming from within the person. Again, she found different kinds of concepts of health, with 'positive' definitions emphasizing equilibrium, or the body and mind being in harmony.

Ideas of health as a positive state are as important, then, as the notion of the absence of disease. However, a positive state of good health is difficult to measure, and most information about the health of populations and individuals is actually about 'disease'. In the UK, the Office for National Statistics publishes annual reports of the numbers of people who die each year of different diseases, and hospital records provide data about how many people are treated. There is less information about how 'well' or healthy people feel.

Biomedical concepts

To some extent, this is because medicine has traditionally been less concerned with 'health' and more with disease. What is disease? For most medical professionals, a disease is some kind of abnormality in the structure or function of the body. Disease is often conceptualized in biomedicine as deviation from a norm: for instance in the amount of a hormone that is circulating, or the normal peak flow capacity of the lungs.

Having a 'disease' does not necessarily mean that a person feels ill. For instance, essential hypertension (or high blood pressure not caused by any particular disorder) is, when found on examination, diagnosed as 'disease'. Many patients would not be aware that they were 'ill', as they would feel no symptoms, and the high blood pressure would only be noticed when measured. High blood pressure is a risk factor for coronary heart disease but, given that people's blood pressures are distributed along a continuum, and indeed the measured blood pressure of any individual patient will vary over time, there is no clear cut-off point when high blood pressure unambiguously presents a threat to health. The definition of a 'normal' blood pressure is somewhat arbitrary. In fact, there are differences even between European countries in terms of treatment for blood pressure. In Germany, for instance, low blood pressure is taken seriously as a 'disease' and widely treated, because it is seen as responsible for such problems as chronic fatigue. In Britain, few doctors would treat low blood pressure as a 'disease'.

Similarly, patients can suffer from an illness without having a recognizable 'disease'. A large proportion of people who visit their general practitioner appear with symptoms which disrupt their lives (such as chronic tiredness, headaches or nausea) but which cannot be diagnosed as 'caused' by an illness. Conflict over whether particular symptoms are caused by diseases or not can become overt, such as the public debates about whether repetitive strain injury (RSI) or chronic fatigue syndrome (sometimes called myalgic encephalomyelitis, or ME) are 'real' diseases. Sufferers have had to campaign to get such diseases recognized by the medical profession and the wider public:

> The misunderstandings and prejudice which surround [ME] have engendered a climate of disbelief which adds immeasurably to the distress and misery experienced by the sufferer. We in the ME Association believe that the burden of illness should not be borne by the sick

and disabled . . . [and are] campaigning to have ME recognised for the devastating organic illness which it is, so that sufferers are afforded the same facilities and support as those affected by other disabling illnesses.

> (ME Association Home Page)

The difficulties of finding adequate support for an illness which is not widely recognized as a 'disease' are described by this young woman with ME:

> It was in 1988, at the age of eleven, I first became ill . . . I developed the familiar symptoms . . . chronic fatigue, violent headaches, visual disorders, severe joint pain, swollen glands, depression, etc. I was sent to numerous specialists for various tests: eyes, blood, urine, allergies, X-rays and even a brain scan. I saw a paediatrician who suggested the problem stemmed at school, which of course it didn't. I was then treated for irritable bowel syndrome, migraine and depression . . . it wasn't until 1992 . . . that the diagnosis was confirmed as ME.

> ('Rachael's story' on the BRAME web site)

So even within Western medicine there is no easy equation of either dysfunction or abnormality with ill health. There are social, cultural and political factors which influence how some differences are categorized as diseases. There is an International Classification of Diseases, which is used to code different causes of death so that rates can be compared internationally and across time, but the content of this has changed historically. Sudden infant death syndrome, for instance, was only formally recognized in Britain from 1971, and became a category of the International Classification of Diseases in 1977. Before then, deaths of infants from no known cause were classified as accidents, or suffocation, or from unknown cause. Another example is homosexuality, which was once classified as a 'disease', until a meeting of the American Psychiatric Association voted in 1973 that it should no longer be seen as an illness (Morgan *et al.* 1983).

The International Classification of Diseases is also more detailed in its classifications of causes of death in developed countries than less developed countries. For instance, there are a large number of categories for describing various kinds of fall (such as from a cliff, from a wheelchair, from a bed, from a commode) but very few categories for describing the kinds of accidents more likely to happen in less developed countries (Bowker and Star 1999).

Biomedicine as a belief system

As we have seen, the ways in which we, as lay people, think and talk about health are culturally produced. What we are less likely to have considered is that this is also the case for health professionals. We are used to accepting that the medical professional's view of health, illness and disease is the 'real' one. Further consideration, however, soon reveals that things are not quite as simple as this. For example, in the UK we have seen a recent increase in the availability and use of a variety of 'complementary' or 'alternative' therapies (this will be discussed further in the section on 'folk remedies' on pp. 403–5). The very existence of other systems demonstrates that biomedicine is only one of many ways of understanding and treating health, illness and disease. The words 'complementary' and 'alternative', however, illustrate the dominant position that allopathic or biomedicine currently occupies. How has this position become so taken for granted? It certainly has not always been this way.

Shifting paradigms

Modern medicine is a product of the scientific age. In the medieval world-view the cosmos was thought to be a series of concentric layers (like an onion). In the centre was the Earth, next water, third, air and, fourth, fire. Beyond this were the Moon and then other celestial bodies. The elements were thought to move 'naturally' towards their allotted realm and thus needed no further explanation. This was a teleological, or purposive, worldview. The natural world, therefore, was not subject to control by people but only to the laws of nature.

With the advent of the 'Age of Exploration' during the seventeenth century these ideas began to change. The newly emerging world view needed a new mode of explanation, one which established not the *purpose* of things but their *cause*. This way of thinking made it possible to seek to control the natural world by establishing its patterns and regularities. This *predictability* led, in turn, to the production of more general laws, such as those of Galileo and Newton.

This change is what Kuhn (1962) termed a 'paradigm shift'. The new form of reasoning was based on the assumption that things work (or happen) because there are underlying processes which can be discovered. 'Natural law' based on sensory observation was no longer felt to be a sufficient explanation in itself. Instead 'nature' was conceptualized as akin to an enormous and complex mechanism, such as a clock, subject only to physical laws which were external to the interests or wishes of people. This form of explanation is known as the 'machine metaphor'. This kind of world-view allowed for the development of modern medicine based on the principles of the new scientific rationality. Medicine began to be seen as a science instead of an art.

> ## Stop and think
>
> ➤ Ideas about 'natural law' have not entirely died out. Think of some examples of when 'it's human nature' or 'it's unnatural' are offered as explanations in themselves. Why are such explanations popular?

Modern medicine and mind–body dualism

As has become apparent from our look at health beliefs in other cultures, beliefs about the workings of the body are informed by the conceptual framework of the society in which they occur. This is just as true for our own social world, although easier to notice in other cultures. In the seventeenth century, the philosopher René Descartes extended the new principle of 'mechanical philosophy'. He suggested that there was no necessary correlation between the physical world and our sensory experience of them, thus allowing for the philosophical separation of the physical and the spiritual worlds. Further, he applied this to the human body, describing the body as a machine, a machine that performs all the physiological functions of man (*sic*) (Osheron and Singham 1981). While this explanatory model has been criticized and developed, it is still enormously influential. We see our 'selves' as separate from our bodies and our bodies as a piece of technical equipment to be maintained, serviced and finely tuned for maximum performance. Equally, illness occurs when some part of our bodies 'breaks down' and treatment is sought in terms of repair to the part. In the conceptual framework of modern medicine the body is a machine and the doctor a mechanic.

This is a vastly over-simplified picture. However, the point to be made is that what we take for granted as 'the truth', for instance that our bodies are made up of a number of internal organs which 'operate' as part of a system of circulating blood, is only one of many possible explanations of how human bodies 'function' and a comparatively recent one at that. Thus biomedicine can

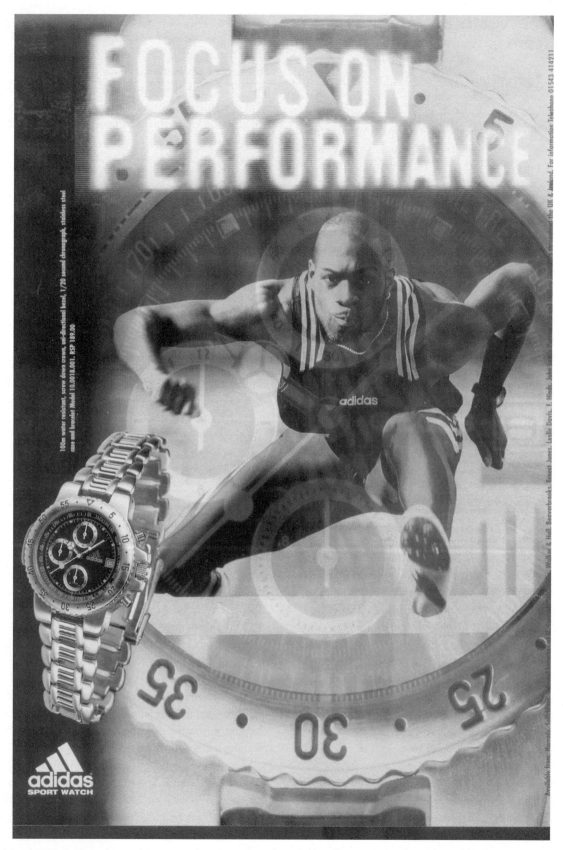

Figure 10.2 Adidas advert depicting the human body as machine

be understood as a belief system, albeit one that has achieved almost global dominance.

Illness as deviance

The sick role

> When someone [from the Gnau] is sick in the critical sense . . . his behaviour is conspicuously changed. It is not only altered by the physical effects of disease but also by the conventions for behaviour. He shuns company and conversation; he lies apart, miserable in the dirt or inside a dark hut, the door shut; he rejects certain kinds of normal food, tobacco and areca nut; he eats alone; he begrimes himself with dirt and ashes. Further degrees of this behaviour are seen in severe illness; more extreme restrictions of food are applied, men . . . lie stark naked.   (Lewis 1986: 121)

People in modern urban societies may not cover themselves with ashes when ill, but they do act in certain ways that are seen as appropriate for ill people. Illness is not a biological state, but a social role. In the 1950s, the American sociologist Talcott Parsons (1951) outlined the norms that govern illness behaviour, and professional responses to it, in modern society. Although he was writing 50 years ago, and his account has been criticized, many of the elements of what he called the 'sick role' are still relevant today.

His analysis started with two assumptions. First, he saw the patient–doctor relationship as a social system, governed by norms about appropriate behaviour. Second, illness, claimed Parsons, is basically a kind of deviance, and is therefore potentially disruptive to the social order, as all deviance is. Parson's sociology was in the *functionalist* tradition: he saw society as a functioning whole and was concerned with how the social order was maintained, and how various institutions in society – in this case health-care institutions – function to contribute to this maintenance. From this perspective health is highly prioritized in modern democracies: indeed it is a 'functional prerequisite of the social system'. If people are to achieve their potential, and be equally able to compete in a meritocracy, they need to be healthy. Health is a basic requirement of being able to fulfil our normal social roles as parents, workers or students. Illness is potentially disruptive because it provides an opportunity to leave the labour market: to withdraw instead of competing.

The medical system, that is, the social institutions which provide medical care, functions to cope with this disruption and the 'sick role', a socially sanctioned way of being ill, functions to constrain these potentially dysfunctional properties of illness. Parsons described the patient's side of the sick role as being structured by two rights and two obligations. The two rights were:

1 Sick people are allowed to give up their normal activities (going to work, school).
2 They cannot be blamed for their incapacity.

The 'right' of exemption from normal activity is clearly relative to the severity of the illness and often requires legitimation from a medical practitioner, such as getting a sick note from the GP for more than a few days absence from work. Illness, for Parsons, was a morally neutral state and the sick role absolved the sufferer from any blame for their condition. People who are seen as legitimately sick cannot be expected to get better by an act of will. In this respect, says Parsons, the sick role is quite different from other deviant roles, as the person in it is not held responsible. Given that there are these 'rights' attached to the sick role, then there is a need for balances to make sure it is not abused. There are also two obligations on sick people:

1 To get well as quickly as possible.
2 To seek competent care and co-operate with medical help.

The sick person has to see the state of being ill as undesirable and one to be left behind as soon as possible. Legitimate claims to the sick role can only be made if the person sees health as their objective. The sick person does not have the proper knowledge and skills to cure themselves, so they are obliged to seek proper professional help, such as from a doctor. The normal sanctions which would apply to people who do not fulfil their social obligations do not apply. Even the minimal self-care obligations such as brushing your hair or getting dressed in the morning do not have to be done when legitimately ill.

Stop and think

> ➤ Think of examples of behaviour which would normally incur sanctions (either legal or social) unless the perpetrator were seen as legitimately 'sick'.

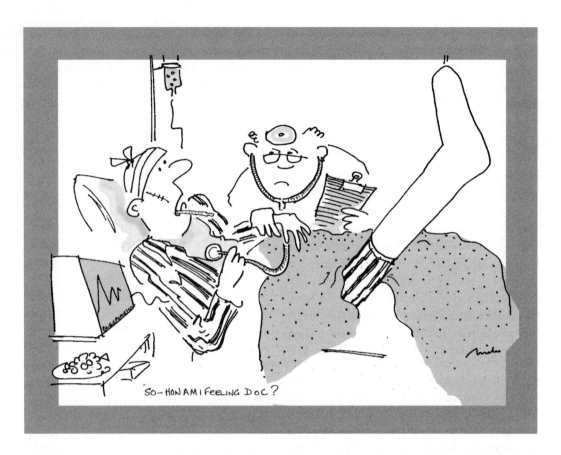

SO - HOW AM I FEELING DOC ?

A closer look

Should treatment be equally available to all?

More hospitals are likely to adopt a formal policy of limiting vital heart surgery to non-smokers because of financial pressures and increased waiting lists, a leading specialist on medical ethics said yesterday.

Commenting on reports that heart surgeons in Manchester and Leicester were turning away smokers who refuse to give up, Dr Richard Nicholson said 'This is not surprising. In the long term it is the kind of decision that will be made much more frequently as the pressure on society not to waste health-care resources increases.'

Dr Nicholson, editor of the *Bulletin of Medical Ethics*, said such policies were similar to those adopted in the early days of liver transplants, when alcoholics were excluded. 'It is an interesting ethical question for much wider debate,' he said. 'In one respect it is a crude and utilitarian approach to a problem [of limited resources], but if you believe that everyone has a right to health care and the treatment they need then such policies pose a real dilemma.'

According to newspaper reports, surgeons at Groby Road Hospital, Leicester, and Wythenshawe Hospital, Manchester, have turned away smokers who refuse to give up and are giving priority to non-smokers on the waiting list (*Independent* 24.5.93).

You must not allow your views about a patient's lifestyle, culture, beliefs, race, colour, sex, sexuality, age, social status or perceived economic worth to prejudice the treatment you give or arrange . . . You must not refuse or delay treatment because you believe the patient's actions have contributed to their condition, or because you may be putting yourself at risk.

(The General Medical Council, Duties of a Doctor 1998)

Question

1. *Should patients be treated equally irrespective of whether their actions contributed to their disease? Give reasons for your answer.*

There are some limitations to Parsons' account of the sick role. One is that it only really applies to short-term illnesses, such as infections. For those with more long-term health problems, such as arthritis or diabetes, the obligation to 'get well' is not appropriate, as there may be no 'cure'. Parsons has also been criticized for portraying the sick role as part of a functioning system and not accounting for the potential conflict around legitimation. Doctors do not only sanction claims to the sick role in a social sense, they may also have a legal role in terms of sanctioning access to benefits for those with long-term sickness or disability.

With a shift in focus to behaviour as a determinant of health, there is a moral sense in which we are increasingly held to blame for some of our illnesses. This was dramatically illustrated by newspaper coverage of AIDS in the early 1980s, when some were seen to be 'deserving' because of their behaviour. It continues in debate around such issues as whether smokers should be entitled to free treatment for conditions they are seen as responsible for.

Despite the many limitations, the idea of a 'sick role' still has great usefulness. It draws our attention to the way in which behaviour is socially patterned. Perhaps more significantly, it also has force as a normative ideal: we still expect not to be held morally accountable for our illnesses (and are often outraged by doctors who do make moral comments) and we often feel reassured by illness which has been legitimized by a professional.

Stigma

If illness is deviance, it is clear that some illnesses are more deviant than others, and those suffering become 'stigmatized' as somehow different from the norm. The classic study of stigma was by Erving Goffman (1963), who used a wide range of case studies and autobiographical sources to define stigma as 'an attribute that is deeply discrediting' and included in this category attributes of race, sexuality and criminality as well as ones of illness or disability. A stigma, argued Goffman, 'spoils' social identity because it causes a gap between 'virtual' social identity, which is the one we assume that others have, and actual social identity. We assume that 'nothing unusual is

Case study

'Normal rubbish': patients in casualty

Roger Jeffrey (1995) found that staff working in casualty departments described their patients as either 'good' patients or as 'rubbish'. Good patients were those who allowed staff to practise specialist skills (such as trauma surgery) or who presented unusual and interesting symptoms. The 'rubbish' were a more diverse category including tramps, alcoholics, attempted suicides, those with minor injuries which could have been self-treated, or those who could have gone to their GP. Jeffrey utilized Parsons' concept of the sick role to identify what the 'rubbish' had in

common. All, he said, broke at least one of the sick role rules and were not, as the casualty staff saw it, legitimately 'sick'. Suicide attempts and alcoholics, for instance, were seen as responsible for their own illnesses, and were often not co-operative with medical help. Those with trivial injuries had often been at work for several days before attending, so demonstrating that they were not abdicating their normal responsibilities. Some patients in the 'rubbish' category were frequent attenders, especially the tramps, and were seen as not trying to get well, but instead seeking to stay in the sick role. Although all patients were treated professionally, Jeffrey notes that those described as 'normal rubbish'

were more likely to have to wait longer, and were treated less sympathetically by staff. Patients, he says, may be well aware of these attitudes, and may attempt to present themselves as legitimately sick, for instance by stressing the accidental nature of an injury, or by stressing their need to get it fixed so as to get back to work.

Questions

1. In what other situations might there be this kind of negotiation over the legitimacy of the sick role?

2. How do you react to Jeffrey's description of staff attitudes? Do you think patients still expect professionals to treat them as 'morally neutral'?

happening' until something disrupts that expectation. Goffman described two kinds of stigma:

1 *Discrediting* stigmas are the obvious ones, such as facial disfigurement, or the use of a wheelchair. The problem for the person stigmatized is managing interaction between themselves and the 'normal' person, as it is potentially disrupted because of awkwardness. Stigmata break our expectations of social intercourse, and the stigmatized person feels uncertain about how they will be treated.

2 *Discreditable* stigmas. Here the problem is managing the information, as this kind of stigma is not obvious in social interaction but is potentially disruptive if discovered. Examples might be a criminal record or history as a mental patient. Scambler and Hopkins (1986) found that fear of the consequences of disclosing their diagnoses created considerable information-management work for people with epilepsy and their families. One in two of those they interviewed had not told their spouse their diagnosis at the time of marriage, and only one in 20 had disclosed their diagnosis to employers.

When there is an encounter between someone who is stigmatized and one who is not (the 'normals', as Goffman calls them), there is the potential for seriously disrupted social intercourse. At one level, this is just the normal day-to-day embarrassment we may feel when our expectations have not been met, and most of us at one time or another have been on both sides of that encounter, either having to cope with information that we feel might discredit us in the eyes of another, or feeling embarrassed when we encounter someone 'different' in an unexpected way. However, some of those with disabilities or certain chronic conditions are potentially defined by that condition and it becomes a 'master' status. Goffman argued that it then has the potential to impact on all interactions, and on self-image, becoming internalized as what he called a 'spoiled' social identity. A stigma then becomes a dominating social role, so that, whatever else anyone does (their professional role, or family responsibilities), they are principally defined by their stigmatized role – as an epileptic, or as a wheelchair user.

Clearly stigma is socially situated. Attributes that are discrediting in one situation are not in others. Homosexuality, being a drug user or being a single mother are all attributes which in some cultures or subcultures might be discreditable but in others are the norm, or not potentially stigmatizing.

Stigma: socially excluded groups

Goffman was primarily interested in how attributes such as disability impact on the minutiae of social interaction. At the cultural level, there are also questions about why certain attributes come to be stigmatizing in the first place. Why, for instance, is a death from AIDS thought of as so stigmatizing that it is still often recorded as leukaemia? The answer lies to some extent in the association of AIDS and HIV, particularly in the early days of its identification, with socially excluded groups. Thus HIV was (and is) found to be most prevalent among gay men, intravenous drug users, sex workers in developed countries and people living in the sub-Saharan countries of Africa. All these groups of people are seen as socially marginal and, as such, pose a threat to the established 'normalcy' of white, middle-class, heterosexual Europeans and Americans. At its most extreme this discourse represented AIDS as divine retribution for 'going too far' against a so-called 'natural order'. That this is so is illustrated by the well-known photograph of Princess Diana embracing a gay man with AIDS. If this were a morally neutral act there would have been no value in the photograph. As it was, it served to illustrate her charity, compassion and liberalism.

Of course, not all those with HIV are regarded as socially deviant and these 'innocent victims', for example haemophiliacs, are contrasted with those who are held responsible for their own infection. This is perhaps why it has become so important to know *how* the infection was acquired, so that moral blame can be apportioned. There have been many analyses of the cultural discourse around AIDS and HIV, particularly surrounding the early media coverage. As Tamsin Wilton (1992) notes, even liberal commentators lapse into contrasting 'the public' (i.e. 'normal people') with 'AIDS sufferers'.

Another trait in the non-sociological literature is to describe people with AIDS and HIV as 'victims' or 'sufferers' and this, as with the literature from the disability rights movement, has been criticized as disempowering and infantilizing. People with AIDS as with (other) people with disabilities have expressed the wish to be known as just that, *people* who just happen to be disabled.

Stigma has been a useful concept for sociologists to use to understand the relationship between social reactions and individual attributes. However, it has been argued that this focus on social interaction has meant that the more immediate practical problems of living with disability or chronic illness have been underestimated. More recently, there has been growing interest in how people cope with

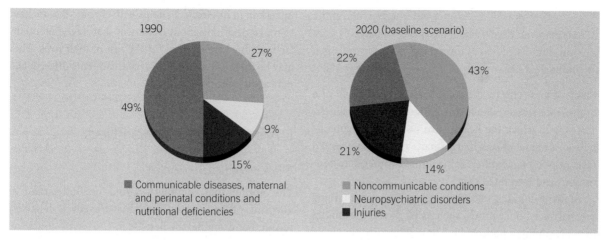

Figure 10.3 Global chronic disease burden – 1990–2020 (by disease group in developing countries)
Source: http://www.who.int/dietphysicalactivity/media/en/gsdoc_principles_charts.pdf

long-term medical conditions, and the limitations of the health and welfare services in providing for their needs.

Living with chronic illness

Until the late 1930s, in industrialised countries, as in Third World countries today, the prevailing and often terrible afflictions were due to bacteria and parasites – the so-called acute disease . . . [Today] what people are sick from mostly are the chronic diseases. They include the cancers, arthritis, and a great host of others that are currently incurable.   (Strauss *et al.* 1997: 2)

In their book on how work in medical hospitals is organized, Anslem Strauss and his co-workers note that one key problem is that medical work is still structured as if most medical problems were acute illness rather than the chronic conditions which are now far more prevalent. The term 'chronic disease' covers a diverse range of conditions, such as diabetes, asthma, arthritis, depression and cancer. Although the symptoms of chronic conditions and the impact these have on everyday life are varied, chronic diseases do share certain features:

➤ they present long-term health problems;

➤ they often present multiple health problems;

➤ there is usually no 'cure', only treatment for symptoms;

➤ there may be great uncertainty about how the illness will progress and when;

➤ they potentially cause major disruption to the lives of sufferers and their families.

Table 10.1 Percentage of people reporting a long-standing illness in Britain, 2001

Socio-economic group	Male (%)	Female (%)
Managerial and professional	27	26
Intermediate	31	32
Routine and manual	37	36
Never worked and long-term unemployed	32	33

Source: Walker, A.; O'Brien, M.; Traynor, J. *et al.* (2002) *Living in Britain: Results from the 2001 General Household Survey*, London: TSO

Chronic disease is also rapidly becoming the major health challenge for developing countries. As Figures 10.3 shows, the World Health Organization have predicted that by 2020, chronic disease will have overtaken communicable disease as a contributor to ill health in developing countries.

In high-income countries, most of the population will experience some chronic illness at some point in their lives, and many of us will end up living with chronic illness. As Table 10.1 shows, in the UK one in four of professional groups and one in three of unskilled manual labourers report some long-standing disease.

Psychological effects of chronic illness

Kathy Charmaz interviewed people in the United States with quite severely restricting illnesses. They described lack of self-worth as one of its fundamental effects. She describes the suffering as one of loss of self, crumbling away of . . . former self images without the simultaneous development of equally valued new ones – the cumulated loss of former self-images results in a diminished self-concept.   (Charmaz 1983)

Many of these effects, she argued, are a direct result of a health-care system which concentrates on acute illness. The way in which the health-care system uses acute illness as a model means that patients receive fragmented care, responding to different symptoms, rather than continuous and integrated care.

In many cultures, self-worth comes from maintaining normal social obligations, such as work responsibilities or maintaining a household. Those with chronic illness view themselves as dependent, as they become increasingly reliant on family and friends, feeling themselves to be a burden and potentially wearing out support. Medical treatment itself may be isolating, especially interventions such as renal dialysis, which are not only time-consuming but also focus the patient's attention on themselves as an ill person.

Charmaz describes a feedback between the different sources of suffering. For instance, the chronically ill person may not go out because they feel stigmatized, and thus restrict their opportunities for constructing a valued self. They may no longer work, or may severely restrict other activities, such as social engagements, so that they can continue working. Maintaining support networks of friends takes energy – energy that those with chronic illness may not have. So even if the person with a chronic illness has no obvious stigmatizing attributes, they will still suffer from decreased participation in the world. At the very time when they need more human contact, both for support and to bolster a flagging self-image, they become less capable of maintaining relationships.

Stop and think

➤ In what ways does the organization of modern society reinforce these effects of chronic illness?

In Parsons' account of the sick role, the patient was conceptualized as largely passive, apart from seeking help, and ignorant, in that they had to turn to 'experts' for help. For those with chronic illness, this is not an adequate model of encounters with health professionals. Most become 'experts' in their disease, how the symptoms affect them, and which therapies help. Many chronic diseases have no cure, and medical treatment is symptomatic and perhaps

uncertain in its effects. Patients with chronic disease have to make decisions about treatment that have potentially far-reaching implications for the rest of their lives. They may be therefore more critical of treatments offered, and may appear less compliant.

Living with disabilities

The medical model

The notion that 'disability' could be understood as anything other than an individual tragedy is relatively recent. For example, the first Open University course on 'dis-ability' was run in 1975 and was located in the 'cure or care', health and welfare disciplines (Finkelstein 1980). This departed from the notion of individual tragedy and instead located disability within a social and environmental context, distinguishing between functional limitation (handicap), bodily (or mental) imperfection (impairment) and the social restrictions which occur as a consequence (disability).

A closer look

Definitions of disability

WHO definitions of impairment, disability and handicap

impairment loss or abnormality of psychological, physiological or anatomical structure or function.

disability any restriction or lack of ability to perform an activity in a manner within the range considered normal for a human being.

handicap disadvantage for a given individual, arising out of impairment and disability, that limits or prevents the fulfilment of a role that is normal (depending on age, sex and social and cultural factors) for that individual (WHO 1980).

The Disabled People's International (DPI) definitions

Impairment functional limitation within the individual caused by physical, mental or sensory impairment.

Disability loss or limitation of opportunities to take part in the normal life of the community on an equal level with others due to physical and social barriers (DPI 1982).

So an impairment is some kind of bodily problem, such as short sight, the congenital absence of a limb, scars from burns, or high blood pressure, whereas the term 'disability' refers to functional ability. Not all impairments cause disabilities. High blood pressure, for instance, or burn scars, may not restrict normal activity. The term 'handicap' in the WHO model refers to social roles so, again, not all disabilities cause handicap. Being short-sighted does not necessarily interfere with the ability to carry out most normal roles. This is where not only cultural values (about 'normal' social roles for men and women in particular societies) but also environmental factors have to be considered. Having even the slightest impairment can, for instance, make it very difficult to use public transport in many cities. Conversely, there are impairments which do not cause disabilities but do cause handicaps, such as dis-figuring scars which have no impact on ability but which may seriously interfere with social roles because they are stigmatizing.

Relationships between the three concepts are clearly affected by social, cultural and environmental factors (such as wheelchair-accessible buildings, whether manual labour is the only work available). This nevertheless remains rooted in a medical model of disability which seeks to either cure or to care, that is to 'normalize'. The underlying assumption remains that to be disabled is to be abnormal, and that to be abnormal is undesirable.

The social model

Many people with disabilities take issue with the WHO model and its assumptions that there is a 'biological' basis to disability. Rather than seeing it as biology that 'disables' people, they argue that:

> it is society which disables physically impaired people. Disability is something imposed on top of our impairments by the way we are unnecessarily isolated and excluded from full participation in society.
>
> (Oliver 1996: 33)

Disability activists and academics have focused on the social causes of oppression, at a number of levels. An early essay by Paul Hunt (1996) identified the ways in which people with disabilities challenge the norms and cultural assumptions of society, by their very differences. Such cultural assumptions include the equation of 'worth' with economic usefulness, and that normality should be a goal. Others have seen the roots of disability in the particular organization of Western capitalism, with the exclusion of many people with disabilities from the workforce. These more materialist accounts stress the social ways in which those with impairments are excluded: from workplaces that are inaccessible to those with wheelchairs, from education that relies on good eyesight to benefit, and from built environments that assume a standardized body shape. Disability can also be seen as a social construct in the sense that it is the arbitrary medical definitions of impairment and welfare classifications which 'create' statistics such as 'there are approximately six million disabled people in Britain' (Shakespeare 1998). Everyone is 'impaired', and there are degrees of difference: it is just that some differences are socially labelled as 'disabilities', and these differences have social consequences. Impairment, in this more social model, is thus not inevitably disabling: it is no more than a description of a particular physical body. What disables are the restrictions that particular kinds of social organization place on particular people.

A further challenge from the disabled people's movement has been the criticism of the notion of 'independence' as a normative goal. In modern societies we are, of course, interdependent: we cannot manage to feed and clothe ourselves without relying on a vast network of other people and organizations. Similarly, we are all dependent on many aids for mobility and communication. Few of us could function without telephones, transport, ladders, tools and so on, and many of us cannot function at all well without glasses, or medication, or other aids. Why then, are some mobility aids stigmatizing? One of the aims of the disability movement has been to try to counteract the stigmatizing imagery used routinely, certainly by charity advertising, but also in health promotion, in which pictures of 'accident victims' in wheelchairs have been used to promote safe driving. These have been criticized by wheelchair users as confirming stereotypes that this is in itself a terrible thing to happen.

The social model of disability rejects the assumption that to be disabled is a personal misfortune. Mike Oliver (1996) suggests that the medical model could be called the 'personal tragedy' theory of disability, whereas the social model could be called the 'social oppression theory'. This is not, he argues, merely a matter of language: the assumptions built into the medical and social models translate into policy, with a medical model suggesting interventions that aim to prevent or cure disabilities, or compensate people for the 'tragedy' they have experienced. A social model would imply social policies which focus on redressing oppression.

Recent developments

Within the disabilities studies literature there have been recent critiques of the social model (see Shakespeare 1998). While they acknowledge the importance of having refocused away from the medical model of care or cure (often at any cost) and towards disability as a social construction, they feel that the 'lived experience' of impairment has been ignored. They suggest that social and environmental manipulation cannot alone remove all the limitations imposed by impairment, for example the experience of pain. As Crow (1996) notes 'impairment means the experience of our bodies can be unpleasant or difficult' (Crow 1996: 209, quoted in Chappell 1998: 216). However, many of the social model theorists are wary of this approach in case it leads back to the old individualistic models.

Chappell (1998) argues that both these approaches (that is, the social model and the recent critiques of it) fail to take into account the experience of people with learning difficulties. 'Disability' has come to mean the opposite of 'able-bodied' and thus those with learning difficulties have been implicitly excluded. She is not, however, arguing that this is inevitable: rather that both the social model and its recent critique can be developed to include people with 'normal' bodies but 'impaired' minds.

Stop and think

> How often are disabled people portrayed in the mass media? (You may want to consider soap operas, documentaries, newspaper and magazine articles.) To what extent do these portrayals fit the medical or social models? Why do you think certain disabilities are more stigmatizing than others?

The debates about what disability is, and how it should be defined, make it very difficult to estimate the number of people with disabilities. In most countries, the only figures easily available are of those claiming some kind of benefit. As these rates reflect the changing rules of the benefit system, they are not particularly useful for looking at trends over time.

Health care

Which institutions exist to manage health care in modern society? The health-care system is characterized by a complex division of labour, with increasingly specialized professionals offering care. However, most health work does not happen in the formal health-care sector but in the home, where we maintain our own health. This section examines how health care is organized at a general level, and the next goes on to look specifically at the professional sector.

Sectors of health care

Arthur Kleinman (1978) proposed a model of health-care systems in which three separate but overlapping sectors could be identified (see Figure 10.4). Traditionally, the folk sector has attracted the most attention from anthropologists looking at non-Western societies, where this sector is large. It consists of those healers who are specialized, but not professionals. With the rising number of 'alternative' practitioners in Western countries, there has been more interest in this sector.

The informal sector, in which most health care happened is the largest sector. The popular sector is non-specialized and consists of all the routine health maintenance and treatment done by lay people for themselves and their families.

The professional sector includes those who are professional healers. In Western society, these are those trained in the biomedical tradition. In other societies, it can include professionalized traditions such as Ayurvedic practice in India, or traditional Chinese medicine.

In modern Britain, the overlap between the professional and folk sectors is getting larger, as more general practitioners (GPs) begin to refer to practitioners such as herbalists and homeopaths in the folk sector, or even begin to employ them within their own surgeries.

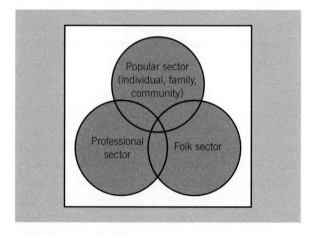

Figure 10.4 Kleinman's model of health-care sectors

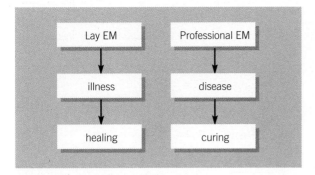

Figure 10.5 Explanatory models

Kleinman argued that in each sector there would be different *explanatory models* (EMs) of illness (see Figure 10.5). An EM refers to how illness is understood (what causes it, how symptoms relate to causes, what effects it has) and how it is managed or treated. Sometimes there are clear conflicts between explanatory systems, when the professional doctor, for instance, has a very different understanding of what causes disease than the patient. A distinction often made in medical sociology is between illness and disease: illness is what the patient suffers from, and disease is what the doctor treats. In Kleinman's account they relate to different activities, where curing is about eliminating the disease, but healing is a rather more social process involving making the patient 'better' in a more holistic sense.

Folk sector

The 'folk sector' usually refers to those health-care practices which appear to derive from 'traditional' or 'non-Western' beliefs about the origins and causes of health and illness: that is, their epistemology differs from that of 'modern scientific medicine'. Thus they encompass 'old wives tales' at one end of the spectrum (a collection of *ad hoc* remedies and recommendations which have been 'passed down' historically by word of mouth) and acupuncture at the other (a highly systematized body of knowledge which requires specialist training). In effect, biomedicine, having claimed a privileged epistemological status and having received almost universal acceptance of this position of dominance, has rendered all other systems of health care as (necessarily) marginal.

This does not mean, however, that their significance has dwindled. Rather, there has been an increase in the popularity and acceptance of many 'alternative' therapies and an attendant debate within medicine (and sociology) as to the impact of this. Sharma (1996) reviews some of the research on the use of complementary therapies and suggests that people tend to consult for chronic conditions and where biomedicine has failed to offer much improvement. The majority of patients choose a practitioner on the basis of lay referrals from friends, and many use a variety of different therapies, including biomedicine.

Studies on complementary medicine use suggest that a growing number of people in Britain turn to specialized healers outside the biomedical 'professional' sphere. In the last two decades we have seen a rapid growth in the use of alternative or complementary therapies. These might include osteopathy, homeopathy, acupuncture, hypnosis and herbalism. These are all techniques which, although classified as part of the 'folk' sector in the UK, might, in other contexts, constitute the 'formal' health-care system.

It could be argued that this growth is a consequence of the growing disenchantment with medicine. There has been considerable debate over the potential impact of this on medicine: will it undermine its dominant position or even lead to its ultimate demise? In fact, it seems that neither is likely. Many facets of this debate can be spotted in the different ways in which these 'alternatives' are described. Perhaps the most common term has been 'alternative medicine', which signifies that this is clearly different from the usual medical practice but still 'medical' in some sense. Similarly, 'complementary medicine' suggests that it is to be used in *conjunction* with rather than *instead* of biomedicine. Later came the descriptor 'therapies'. This (more accurately) reflects the different epistemological basis while retaining the notion of a therapeutic intervention.

Historically in Europe almost all 'health care' took place in the folk sector: that is, outside of a single, unified body of formal professional knowledge. Physicians and priests (who were, by law, always men, as university training was restricted to males) provided spiritual comfort and guidance, but symptomatic relief could be found from a variety of sources. These can be loosely divided into the three sectors of physicians, surgeons and apothecaries.

Margaret Pelling (see Stacey 1988) has described in detail the plurality of healers to be found in seventeenth-century Britain. Indeed many healers were women. Some were midwives, but others were 'wise women' who were often practised in the art of herbalism (see Figure 10.8). Using the remarkably well-preserved and comprehensive records for Norwich (then the second largest city in England) Pelling was able to demonstrate that there was a great deal of publicly available 'health care' which drew on many different 'knowledge bases'.

Figure 10.6 A Chinese herbalist shop
© Bob Krist/CORBIS

Healers in Norwich between 1550 and 1640 included:	
22	Doctors of medicine, or practitioners of physic
46	Members of the Norwich Barber Surgeon's Company
34	Other surgeons and barber surgeons
13	Women practitioners, including midwives
5	Itinerants
1	Astrologer
3	Bone setters

Figure 10.7 Margaret Pelling's healers of Norwich
Source: Stacey 1988: 41

Among the itinerants would probably have been fore-runners of the modern dentist, the tooth-drawers who travelled the country offering their services. They were a source of entertainment and spectacle in the villages they visited. They were practitioners of all kinds of surgery and their craft included phlebotomy. The theory that underpinned their practice was derived from the system of 'humours' (see below).

The classificatory system identified by Helman (see Case study, p. 405) is not by any means unique to his sample. Rather, it is situated in the once prevalent 'humoral theory', where the world was conceived in terms of:

➤ four basic elements: fire, earth, air and water;

➤ four basic qualities: heat, cold, dry and dampness;

➤ four humours: blood, phlegm, yellow bile and black bile;

➤ four personality types: sanguine, phlegmatic, choleric and melancholic.

In this system the key to health was to maintain the optimum balance of the four humours in relation to the other aspects of the world. Illness was the effect of too much or too little humoral activity.

Recourse to elements of this theory are still to be found in colloquial English and also in many other 'folk' models. Snow (1974) found this model operating in her interviews with poor black American women living in the 'Deep South'. This, she believes, can be 'traced back

Case study

Folk systems in contemporary society

There are many traces of these 'folk systems' apparent in contemporary Britain. One well-known study by Cecil Helman, a practising GP in one of the London suburbs, documents the coherence and prevalence of a particular construct, 'feed a cold, starve a fever', among his patients (Helman 1985). From his research he constructed a 'folk' model which divided illness into four categories: whether it made you feel 'hot' or 'cold' and whether the symptoms you experienced were 'wet' or 'dry'. 'Colds and chills', in this classification, are qualitatively different from 'fevers and infections': they have different causes and thus require different kinds of treatment.

Colds and chills were seen as being a consequence of skin (particularly heads and feet) being exposed to cold or wet weather or to sudden changes in temperature. This construct will be familiar to many readers, particularly those brought up in the UK by white English-speaking parents. Treatment takes the form of warming foods and drinks and tonics to 'build up' the body, not just physically, but also in terms of its 'resistance' to disease.

Fevers, by contrast, were felt to be the consequence of exposure to 'germs' (which are, by definition, bad). This is a normal hazard of life as there are always felt to be 'bugs going round'. People with them, however, (for example, flu) do have a responsibility for keeping themselves apart and to 'not spread their germs about'.

Treatment for these 'hot' conditions involves expelling the 'bug' from the body through, for example, plenty of fluids (flushing it out) or expectorants (coughing it up) or through fasting (starving it out).

The importance of this piece of research is not only that it demonstrates that these 'folk beliefs' are still very much in evidence as at least one level of explanation of an individual's misfortune but also that it shows that GPs also refer to lay health beliefs in explaining illness. Indeed the epistemological boundaries are frequently blurred.

Questions

1. Can you think of an example from your own experience when two 'explanatory systems' are mixed?

2. What phrases do people use to express the dangers of being exposed to cold or wet weather?

---

from humoral pathology via Spanish folklore and then via Mexican and Puerto-Rican folklore, into American cultural ideas' (Snow 1974).

Similarly, Thorogood (1990), in her research with Afro-Caribbean women in London, found a whole range of traditional remedies in recent if not current use (see Figure 10.8). These could be divided into categories including those suitable for correcting humoral imbalances in 'hot' and 'cold' and West African conceptions of 'blockages' as well as those deriving from the French, Spanish and English cultures of the old colonial powers and those of contemporary Britain.

The informal sector

Despite the attention given to the formal health-care sector, most health care happens in the 'informal sector': that is, it is not part of professional practice. Indeed, the majority

of symptoms people experience are either ignored or receive non-medical attention (see Table 10.2). This may take the form of self-medication with orthodox medications or with 'folk' or alternative remedies.

Stop and think

➤ What examples of health care carried out by 'lay people' can you think of?

A great deal of 'informal care' is provided by women, and this relates to the gendered division of labour. As much feminist scholarship has demonstrated, 'caring' is considered 'women's work' and as such is considered of less worth. It is no accident that the same word, *nursing*, means both breast-feeding and caring for the sick. It is assumed that mothers have responsibility

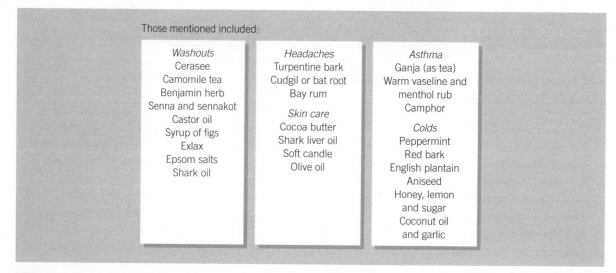

Those mentioned included:

Washouts
Cerasee
Camomile tea
Benjamin herb
Senna and sennakot
Castor oil
Syrup of figs
Exlax
Epsom salts
Shark oil

Headaches
Turpentine bark
Cudgil or bat root
Bay rum

Skin care
Cocoa butter
Shark liver oil
Soft candle
Olive oil

Asthma
Ganja (as tea)
Warm vaseline and
menthol rub
Camphor

Colds
Peppermint
Red bark
English plantain
Aniseed
Honey, lemon
and sugar
Coconut oil
and garlic

Figure 10.8 Caribbean home remedies

for the health of their family (including their husband or male partner) and this is reflected in advertising campaigns as well as in social policy (for example, the payment of benefits).

Indeed, for the most part women *do* take responsibility for the health and care of others, as to be kind and caring is seen as part of the essential business of being a woman (see Chapter 7). This gendered division of responsibility is mirrored in the formal health-care sector, where caring work, or nursing, is predominantly carried out by women.

One of the difficulties about acknowledging caring as work is that the tasks and duties which constitute 'caring' are also those which are usually also done out of 'love'. This makes it extremely difficult to put a monetary value on them but it also implies a reciprocal relationship of duties and obligations on the part of the 'cared for' which is deemed a 'natural part of family life'. It may be that one reason that patients often feel they want to express more personal gratitude to their nurses by giving them flowers or chocolates is in order to acknowledge this more intimate aspect of caring and to discharge some of their obligations.

Lay referral

In a later section we move on to the third sector: the formal or professional sector. First, though, it is worth considering how ill people make the decision to seek professional help. The answer to this is not as obvious as it seems. Kasl and Cobb (1966) reviewed some of the literature on how people make the decision and found that the severity of their symptoms played only a minor part. Indeed, many studies have found that there is an 'illness iceberg' (see Table 10.2), where only a small, and not necessarily the most severe, proportion of symptoms reach the doctor.

It could be argued that most of these symptoms are trivial and not worthy of a doctor's attention. However, there is little difference in terms of severity between those symptoms which do reach a doctor's surgery and those which do not. Many of the unreferred symptoms in the community are those of serious disease (Epsom 1978) and would benefit from treatment. The issue of how people do decide which symptoms need some kind of medical attention is clearly not just a matter of symptoms

Table 10.2 **The illness iceberg**	
	Number of people
No symptoms	49
Symptoms, but took no action	188
Symptoms, took non-medical action	562
Saw general practitioner	168
Hospital out-patient	28
Hospital in-patient	5
Total	1,000

Source: Wadsworth *et al*. 1971

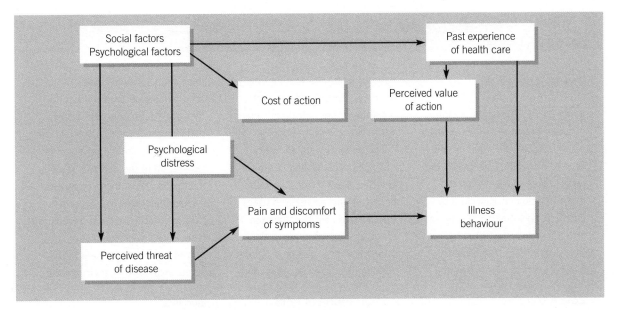

Figure 10.9 Kasl and Cobb's (1996) model of illness behaviour

or severity; there are many other factors which impact on the decision to seek help.

Kasl and Cobb (1996) modelled all the other factors which influence the decision, including social and psychological factors, past experience of the health-care system, and the perceived costs and benefits of health-seeking behaviour. A simplified version of their model is shown in Figure 10.9.

In this model, the actual pain and discomfort of the symptoms are only one influence on the eventual illness behaviour, and they are themselves influenced by social factors. The part in the middle of this diagram, with the cost and benefit of the action, often gets somewhat simplified into what is known as the *health beliefs model*. In this framework any health-related behaviour, such as going to the doctor, getting a cervical smear, eating a low-fat diet or taking exercise, can be seen as a result of an individual balancing the perceived costs and benefits of that action, in terms of the risk posed by the threat to health. The costs might be financial, even in a publicly funded service (such as the cost of taking a morning off work to go to the doctor, or perhaps to pay for child care), but it might also include social costs. Finding time to go to an exercise class may be more costly for a working single parent than for a young man with no dependants. There might also be psychological costs. Fear of dentists may be a cost to take into account against the perceived benefit of regular dental checks, or an unwillingness to face the possibility of cancer may be a cost to balance against the reassurance of a mammogram.

Social factors

As Kasl and Cobb's (1966) model suggests, the relationship between 'beliefs' and illness behaviour is considerably more subtle than a simple version of the health beliefs model implies. How do people make assessments of the costs and benefits? How do we decide when the potential benefits outweigh the costs? These assessments are likely to be at least in part culturally determined in that they are bound up with our learned ideas about the meaning of illness. At the top of Kasl and Cobb's model are the cultural and social factors that they hypothesize would influence the 'perceived threat of the disease' as well as the 'perceived value of any action'.

Psychological factors

Different individuals have different thresholds of self-referral. Psychologists have identified one set of attitudes which explains some of this behaviour: the *locus of control* (Rotter 1966). The locus of control refers to how far people see themselves, rather than other agents, as in control of what happens to them. Those who consider that their health is largely an outcome of their own actions are described as having a high *internal locus of control*. Those who are more fatalistic, seeing health or illness as largely a matter of luck, or the actions of others, have a high *external locus of control*. Theoretically, those with a high internal locus of control are more likely to use preventive services such as screening and more likely to engage in health-related activity such as taking

Case study

Irving Zola

Irving Zola (1973) examined the question of how ill people become patients, given that there seems little to distinguish symptoms that do get taken to the doctor and those that do not. How do they decide to seek treatment? He was also interested in cultural factors that might affect that decision-making process. He interviewed patients who were waiting in an American hospital out-patient department for their first appointment with the doctor. These patients were all either Irish Catholics, Italian Catholics or Anglo-Saxon Protestants, the largest ethnic groups who used that hospital. He hypothesized first that most people experience symptoms for a long time before seeking help: they accommodate them, and only when this accommodation breaks down do they seek help. Zola asked these patients about their symptoms, the presence of pain and experiences leading up to the decision to visit the doctor. From these interviews he identified five what he called 'triggers' to the decision to seek care. These were not physiological, in that they did not relate to the actual symptoms or their severity.

Zola's triggers to the decision to seek medical help

Trigger	Example
The occurrence of an interpersonal crisis	The breakdown of a relationship, or a bereavement
The perceived interference with social or personal relations	An adolescent who sees acne as a barrier to a full social life
Sanctioning	A parent or partner persuades the patient to visit the doctor
The perceived interference with vocational or physical activity	Eyesight deteriorates to the point a typist can no longer do the job
The temporalizing of symptomology	'If it's still hurting at the end of the week, I'll visit the doctor'

Questions

1. *What groups of people are most likely to seek help at an early stage?*

2. *What groups might be more reluctant to seek help? Why?*

exercise and not smoking. These psychological orientations are also influenced by social and cultural factors. In modern societies, such as Britain, self-determination has a high cultural value, whereas fatalistic views are more marginalized.

The professional sector

The professional sector of the health system is very significant in modern society. The National Health Service, for example, is one of the largest employers in Britain, with over 900,000 people directly employed. Health-care costs consume a high and increasing proportion of the welfare budget, accounting for over £33 billion in 1995–96 (DoH 1997). The professional sector is prestigious (medical doctors enjoy high social standing) and the vast majority of the population have some contact with health professionals at some point in their lives.

The emergence of the hospital

In the Middle Ages hospitals were religious institutions which cared for pilgrims and others in need of rest, as well as the sick. The hospital as we would recognize it today, as a centre for medical treatment and training, emerged in the early nineteenth century. In Britain, the first hospitals were in provincial towns, and were established by the newly emerging wealthy middle classes, who wanted 'good causes' to invest in and to display both their wealth and their philanthropy. These hospitals were originally used only by the poor, while the wealthy would still have a doctor to visit them in the home. Gradually, though, they became central to the organization of modern medicine. This shift from the home to the hospital as the major site of care had many implications, not only for how health care was delivered but also how professionals were trained and even the content of medical knowledge itself. Michel Foucault and Nick Jewson have both written about the role of the hospital, and have somewhat different arguments about its significance.

Foucault's account of the role of the hospital

Michel Foucault (1976), in *The Birth of the Clinic*, looks at the emergence of the hospital in Paris in the late eighteenth century and argues that the shift in locus of medical care, from the patient's home to the hospital, enabled a new kind of medical knowledge to be produced. One precondition for this new knowledge was an understanding of 'anatomy' and the gradual breaking down of taboos against the dissection of corpses. This brought with it a radical change in the way in which disease and death were conceptualized. In the sixteenth and seventeenth centuries, disease was perceived as an external agent that invaded the body. The new understanding was

of disease and death as part of life: disease was part of the organs and functions of the body itself.

Foucault called this the 'clinical gaze'. This phrase implied a particular way of seeing bodies and the diseases they carried which penetrated them, examining them for the underlying pathology. For Foucault, the clinical gaze was a facet of a new kind of power, which relied on surveillance and inspection. As hospitals became teaching institutions, rather than merely hospices for the poor or infirm, doctors had access to large numbers of patients to examine, compare and, if they died, dissect. For Foucault, the hospital is just one example of the kinds of institution which developed in modern secular societies (the school and the prison were others) which were sites at which the state could control the population. The new kind of power they represented was not based on the absolute sovereignty of the king, as in previous regimes, but on a more pervasive and controlling power which acted on individual subjects. Foucault called this *disciplinary power*.

The model for disciplinary power was Jeremy Bentham's panopticon, a plan for an ideal prison. In the panopticon the cells are arranged in a ring around a central tower, from which a guard could see any inmate. Windows from the tower to the cells were shuttered, so the prisoner would never know when they were being watched but instead

Figure 10.10 Florence Nightingale at Scutari
(Artist: W. Simpson courtesy of Mary Evans Picture Library)

would have to assume that surveillance was continuous. The classic Nightingale hospital ward has elements of this, in that patients are arranged so that they are visible from a central nursing station, and their bodies subjected to the various examinations and inspections of the new medical knowledge.

Foucault's analysis is at the level of discourse: what it is possible to say and know, and how it is said, and indeed how and what we see when we look. He starts his book *The Birth of the Clinic* with a quote from Pomme, a medical writer from the middle of the nineteenth century, who describes how he cured a hysteric by making her take 'baths for ten or twelve hours a day, for ten whole months'. At the end of this treatment, Pomme saw:

> membranous tissues like pieces of damp parchment ... peel away with some slight discomfort, and these were passed daily with the urine; the right ureter also peeled away and came out whole in the same way ... The oesophagus, the arterial trachea, and the tongue also peeled in due course. (Foucault 1976: 1)

No modern doctor would use this treatment, or indeed even recognize the disease of hysteria. More importantly, though, Foucault argues that the modern doctor would *see* the body, and its constituent parts, in an entirely different way. The new medical 'gaze' is not just an act of looking, it also involves the techniques of physical examination and, more significantly, it makes the invisible signs of pathology visible, providing a way of seeing the anatomy of the body in a new way. Thus the anatomy which is mapped in books such as *Gray's Anatomy* is not, for Foucault, an unchanging reality, always there but only recently discovered, but rather a product of a specific discourse. David Armstrong (1983) described how the anatomical atlas directs the student to 'read' the body:

> The fact that the body became legible does not imply that some invariate biological reality was finally revealed to medical enquiry. The body was only legible in that there existed in the new clinical techniques a language by which it could be read. The anatomical atlas directs attention to certain structure, certain similarities, certain systems, and not others and in so doing forms a set of rules for reading the body and for making it intelligible. In this sense the reality of the body is only established by the observing eye that reads it. The atlas enables the anatomy student, when faced with the undifferentiated mass of the body, to see certain things and ignore others. In effect, what the student sees is not the atlas as a representation of the body but the body as a representation of the atlas. (Armstrong 1983: 2)

Jewson's account of the role of the hospital

Nick Jewson takes a more Marxist approach to the changes caused by the new hospitals. He focuses on the *modes of production* of medical knowledge, by which he means the social factors inherent in the relationship between the client and the provider of that knowledge (Jewson 1976). Jewson discusses 'cosmologies' of medical knowledge, by which he means something similar to Foucault's discourse. A cosmology is a conceptual structure which frames the kinds of things that are known, what questions may be asked and the kinds of answers that are offered. For Jewson, however, these cosmologies are not merely cultural artefacts but are produced within certain economic relationships. Medical knowledge is thus intricately tied to the kinds of economic relationships which give rise to it.

Before the end of the eighteenth century, argues Jewson, the major mode of production was what he calls 'bedside medicine'. Bedside medicine was not characterized by any one unifying theory, but by schools of thought: there were many conflicting accounts of disease and healing. However, what these different medical theories had in common was their focus on symptoms as experienced by the patient: the manifestations of illness rather than its underlying causes. It was a holistic approach, taking all the factors of a patient's experience into account to find the original cause of the illness. Medicine was essentially person-oriented. The practitioners were fragmented, and their livelihood depended on the goodwill of their patrons: the patients. The status of the clinician was dependent not on their clinical skills, defined by an autonomous profession, but on the status of their patrons.

With the rise of the hospital, says Jewson, this mode of production was replaced by one of hospital medicine, which rested on a new relationship between the sick patient and the practitioner. First, social roles were now prescribed rather than being negotiated between individual patrons and practitioners. They were prescribed so that the practitioners had the respect and deference that had been won by organizing as a coherent profession. A new object of medical cosmology emerged here: the disease, rather than the sick patient. Hospital medicine did not view the ill person holistically but in terms of the specific causes of their diseases and what organs of the body were affected. The key to diagnosis was now physical examination and investigations, rather than the verbal reports of the patient.

By the beginning of the nineteenth century, then, medical education had been institutionalized at the hospitals, replacing the theoretical education of Oxford and Cambridge and the apprenticeships that had preceded them. In Britain, this development was consolidated by the 1858 Medical Act, which established the General Medical Council to regulate the medical profession on behalf of the state, and to oversee medical education. It was this Act that perhaps finally established medicine as a profession, as the council was to keep a register of qualified medical practitioners. It made it illegal for anyone but a registered medical practitioner to call themselves such and joined all recognized healers onto one register, while excluding practitioners such as herbalists.

The demise of the hospital?

By the end of the twentieth century, the centrality of hospitals has come under increasing threat. There has been an increased focus on primary and community care in both national and international policy, partly as a result of the rising costs of the hospital sector. The average length of hospital stays has reduced, with a decrease in the number of in-patient beds and an increase in the number of procedures that can now be done as 'day cases'. In 1960, the average length of stay in NHS hospitals was 36 days: by 2000, it had fallen to five days (Yuen 2001). The declining number of beds and length of stay in modern hospitals presents a problem for medical education, traditionally centred on the 'ward round' and bedside instruction (Atkinson 1981), and medical students are increasingly taught in the community as well as in the hospital.

> ### Stop and think
>
> ➤ What examples can you think of where care or treatment has moved from the hospital setting?
>
> ➤ What do you think are the advantages and disadvantages of these changes?

By the 1980s in Europe and the United States there were calls for action to provide better care in the community for people with long-terms needs. Perhaps one of the biggest problems with the implementation of community care as a policy is the rather nebulous concept of 'community'. 'Community' embodies the notion of shared goals and values, of everyone working together. It has been used in policy terms to evoke the opposite

of the term 'institution', which has come to symbolize remote, impersonal detachment. 'Care' too has complex meanings and usage. Alone it symbolizes humanitarian values – to care for someone is seen as a way of expressing love and tenderness – but to be 'in care' is not redolent with such warm overtones. It is instead more equivalent to 'institution' in that it conjures up state-organized services which, almost by definition, do not care for or about people. These issues are well summarized in this passage from Means and Smith (1994):

> But where does the positive power of the term 'community care' come from? Baron and Haldane argue that it flows from the fact that 'community' is what Raymond Williams (1976) calls a keyword in the development of culture and society. From the ninth century BC through to the present time, Williams is able to trace the use of the term 'community' to lament the recent passing of a series of mythical Golden Ages. Each generation perceives the past as organic and whole compared to the present. As Baron and Haldane point out, the term 'community' thus enables 'the continuous construction of an idyllic past of plenty and social harmony which acts as an immanent critique of contemporary social relations'. Thus the call by politicians and policy makers to replace present systems of provision with community care feeds into this myth by implying that it is possible to recreate what many believe were the harmonious, caring and integrated communities of the past. (Means and Smith 1994: 5)

There have been a number of criticisms of these community care policies (Dalley 1996). The first is that they have, in the past at least, been seen as a relatively cheap option in comparison with the costs of institutional care. Second, not all 'dependencies' are equally amenable to community care and community care is often practitioner/ policy maker defined, not client-led. Finally, they are based on the notion that privacy and independence are desired and achievable only within a 'family', that is, that caring is essentially a private business. This latter criticism clearly has implications for those who are deemed to have responsibility for the care of 'dependent people', that is, the 'carers', of whom most are women (Graham 1986).

There has been a great deal of discussion about the effect of these policies on women, who bear the majority of the responsibility for domestic labour and the assumptions embedded in the policy about women's role in social, political and economic life. It has also assumed not only the desirability but also the prevalence of heterosexual nuclear families.

However, despite the rhetoric and indeed policies which herald a new world of care in and by the community it is unlikely that we shall witness the demise of the hospital. Indeed, hospitals are likely to continue as important sites of training and care for some time to come. In a later section we consider the role of medicine in society in more detail, but first we turn to the idea of medical dominance and the debate about the nature of 'professions'.

The division of labour in the professional sector

Medical dominance

So how did 'medicine' emerge as a coherent profession from this mixture of systems? It was unlikely that it was as a result of having any superior healing powers than, say, lay healers. Rather, there were a number of social factors – for example, the rise of scientific medicine as a dominant discourse – and with it the rise of the hospital as an organization together with the growing role of the state during the seventeenth and eighteenth centuries, which in combination have brought about the dominance of the profession of medicine.

Medicine is not the only profession: there are non-medical professions such as lawyers and accountants, and sociologists have attempted to identify the features and core characteristics which distinguish them from other occupations. These are generally agreed to be:

➤ a specialized body of knowledge;

➤ a monopoly of practice;

➤ autonomy to define the boundaries and the nature of their work;

➤ a code of ethics which regulates relationships both between professionals and between professionals and their clients.

Case study

Healers in Britain in the past

Until relatively recently, there was a plurality of healers in Britain. Among these were three main formalized sectors. *Physicians* were university trained and their role was to examine, diagnose and prescribe. They were not allowed to make up or dispense drugs. Physicians were very few in number as there were only two universities in Britain (Oxford and Cambridge), only men were allowed to study and only wealthy families could afford to send their sons there. This small group formed the College of Physicians in 1518. Their knowledge was based on the Galenic theory of humours and legitimized through reference to learned authors, rather than experimentation and empiricism. Indeed, anatomical

dissection in Britain was (in theory, at least) exclusively the monopoly of the Company of Surgeons, who were allowed to dissect the bodies of hanged felons, until the Anatomy Act of 1832 allowed dissection of bodies from workhouses and made possible the widespread teaching of anatomy by dissection (Richardson 1989).

Medicines and other remedies were provided by *apothecaries*, tradesmen who organized into a separate guild, the Society of Apothecaries, in 1617. This gave them a monopoly over the manufacture, sale and application of drugs and separated them from grocers, who had previously also traded in drugs. Although officially not allowed to diagnose, it seems likely that apothecaries took on the role of physician for the lower classes.

The third main branch of healer, which was to form the basis of the modern system of medicine, was the organization of *barber surgeons*, craftsmen who learned by apprenticeship rather than university study. They were the first group to organize and by 1800 had become the Royal College of Surgeons. In London, Henry VIII first licensed the physicians and the barber surgeons, while in the country bishops had this authority. Although this appears as a fairly formal tripartite system, it seems likely that in practice this was not so rigid.

Questions

1. *Suggest ways in which modern-day chemists and doctors act in a similar way to these early examples of healers.*

2. *What are the main differences?*

For example, doctors derive authority from their practice of specialized skills, their theoretical knowledge, their state-legitimated monopoly over practice and their ideology of 'service' to individual patients. However, these are neither necessary nor sufficient conditions for all claims to professional status. Doctors and vets, for example, have codes of ethics which oblige members of the profession to take an oath which binds them to putting the patients' interests first, while dentists do not. Nurses have a register but are considered a 'semi-profession', separate, but not equal to, medicine.

Stop and think

➤ Why do you think dentists did not have to take an oath?

➤ Why are nurses considered a semi-profession?

Occupational strategies and the professionalization of nursing

It is commonly held that nursing, since becoming a profession (the first register was set up in 1919) has progressed to become a higher-status, centrally recognized health-care profession. Yet the crucial distinction between nursing and medicine remains: that of curing versus caring. Nursing's professional bodies are caught in a double bind: in order to be of high status the profession must lay claim to clinical and curative skills, but in order to remain as 'nursing' the practice must be centred on caring for, not curing, patients.

This dilemma has been addressed in part by the conscious formation of a body of theoretical knowledge, the nursing process (Macfarlane 1977), which is particular to nursing and distinct from medicine. To some extent, this has also been the rationale behind more recent developments in nurse education, for example the replacement of old apprentice-style ward-based training of 'pupil' nurses with degree education in many countries.

Women in nursing

There are, however, clear gender dimensions to this division. In Britain, the Victorian constructions of upper-class femininity ensured that women were considered unsuitable candidates for higher education in general and the GMC, in excluding women from registering, merely enshrined in its regulations what, with a few notable exceptions, had been usual practice anyway.

Nursing, as opposed to healing, was a less contentious sphere as it was seen as an extension of women's domestic role. As a consequence no special skills were deemed necessary for it and during the eighteenth and nineteenth centuries it became the domain of working-class women who were not caring for a family of their own. Their reputation as drunken and untrustworthy meant that nursing was not seen as a job for respectable women (e.g. the nurse employed to 'guard' Mrs Rochester in Charlotte Bronte's *Jane Eyre*).

Nursing as a paid occupation for middle-class women arose during the nineteenth century not only (if largely) as a result of the professionalization of medicine and its barring of women but also because of a demographic change which resulted in 'an excess of spinsters'. 'Respectable' women who could not be married were able instead to find financial security in an occupational sphere deemed acceptable, for example, as a governess or nurse.

These were the factors behind Florence Nightingale's campaigning for the recognition of 'the nurse' as a suitable job for a (middle-class) woman. The story has it that she deliberately did not suggest that nurses were equivalent to doctors as a way of ensuring support for her plans from the professional medical men. Nightingale proposed that to be a good nurse was to be a good woman. Thus by the end of the nineteenth century medicine and nursing had divided into two separate professions, each profoundly gendered (see Table 10.3). This gender division persists today, with women constituting the majority of the nursing workforce (see Table 10.4) across the world.

Men in nursing

As nursing is equated with caring, and caring with femininity, any man in this role is by definition acting outside the discourse of masculinity. The exception to this is in psychiatric nursing, where nurses are deemed to need physical strength to manage potentially difficult patients. In these cases nurses are presumed to be male.

Table 10.3 Staff directly employed by the NHS, 1998

	Male (%)	Female (%)
Nursing, midwifery and health visiting	12	88
Medical and dental	67	33
Administration and estates	25	75
Management and support	42	57

Source: DoH (1999)

Table 10.4 Number of male and female registered nurses in selected countries

| Country | Number (per cent) of registered nurses in the workforce who are: | | | |
	Male	%	Female	%
Canada	11,467	(5)	220,045	(95)
Denmark	1,865	(3.5)	50,327	(96.5)
Germany	10,000	(2)	450,000	(98)
Iceland	25	(1)	2,300	(99)
UK	50,000	(10)	450,000	(90)

Source: International Council of Nurses (http://www.icn.ch/)

Indeed, in mainstream nursing very few men remain at practitioner level. Men in nursing are far more likely than their female equivalents to achieve management posts. Salvage, writing in 1985, documents that 'there is only about one male to every 19 female nursing auxiliaries and assistants (1980 figures, England only) . . . In senior jobs . . . nearly half the top management and education posts [are] occupied by men' (Salvage 1985: 35).

Thus, despite the entry of increased numbers of men to the profession in recent years (the GNC only documented this between 1955 and 1971, during which time the percentage of men rose from approximately 5 per cent to 10 per cent of the nursing workforce in the UK), the male nurse remains an anomaly.

The nurse/doctor binary pair are perceived as forming a complementary whole, mirroring the ideal-type heterosexual couple:

Medicine and nursing came to be seen as complementary activities in the sense that if nursing was feminine, medicine was masculine: the nurse was the ideal woman, the doctor the ideal man. His intelligent, active, pragmatic qualities were appropriate for the aggressive treatment of disease but not compatible with caring.

(Salvage 1987: 66)

Stop and think

➤ How are nurses and doctors represented in children's and in classic literature; in films; and in TV programmes, both fictional and documentary?

➤ Do these representations support traditional notions of women and men? Do you think that these representations are changing to any extent?

'Race' and the division of labour in health care

Just as there is a clear gender hierarchy in health-care professions, so, in the UK, there are clear divisions along lines of ethnicity. Again, the unequal access of minority ethnic doctors to higher-status medical specialties is well documented (Smith 1980), although there is no comparable literature on dentistry. However, this divide also exists within nursing: women from black and minority ethnic backgrounds are more likely to be found in the auxiliary grades. During the mass recruitment of Caribbean and Irish nurses to the NHS in the 1960s, many black nurses were encouraged to sign up for state enrolled nurse (SEN) training rather than SRN (state registered nurse) without it being made explicit that this was a 'second-rate' qualification (Bryan et al. 1985). The World in focus box on p. 415 illustrates how global forces contribute to this ethnic division of labour internationally. It remains to be seen what the impact will be of nursing having become a degree course. Alongside this has been the increase in the numbers of white, middle-class women entering medicine who might, in earlier times, have been obvious candidates for nursing. Thus there is a gender and a race hierarchy within and between every stratum of health care.

The organization of society, in terms of its structure, clearly has an impact on the organization of medicine. However, the impact of medicine and health care on the organization of society and the experience of daily life has been the subject of further sociological enquiry. The next section considers the role of medicine in society.

The role of medicine in society

As we have seen, the discipline and profession of medicine has become increasingly important in the way society is organized. This has led many theorists to speculate on the role of medicine. Is medicine an unequivocally good thing? Or does medicine have dysfunctional effects on individuals and society? Are there simply unforeseen consequences of the rapid expansion of medicine in society?

Early critics such as Elliot Freidson and Irving Zola writing in the late 1960s and early 1970s pointed to the way the discipline of medicine had come to dominate expanding tranches of social life: areas which law or religion previously had regulated. This is termed *medicalization* and refers to the way in which 'social problems' are turned into 'medical problems', for example drunkenness, becomes alcoholism. Ivan Illich, a radical Catholic priest

World in focus

Globalization and health professionals

Globalization is discussed in detail in Chapter 11. This is the process by which the world is becoming one interconnected marketplace for ideas, goods, technologies and, increasingly, people. The health care workforce is one labour market that is becoming increasingly international. There are some benefits to this, with professionals travelling to increase their skills and experiences, and sometimes earning relatively high salaries which contribute to their home economies. It has been estimated that the million Filipinos who work abroad (many of them as nurses) contribute £3.75 billion to their country's economy each year (Batty 2003). For the richest countries, recruiting staff from overseas has become a necessary response to shortages of home-trained professionals. There are a number of reasons for this. In countries such as Saudi Arabia and other Gulf states, low rates of participation of women in the workforce and relatively recent expansion of the health care services mean there are very few nationals working as nurses: about 85 per cent of nurses in Saudi Arabia are foreign. In countries such as the US and the UK, high rates of staff turnover and low morale within the public sector contribute to difficulties in recruiting national clinical and nursing staff. In the UK, for example, about a quarter of the doctors employed by the National Health Service were trained abroad, and about 13,000 overseas nurses were registered in 2002. Hospitals in the UK, especially in the South-East, are increasingly reliant on recruitment from overseas to maintain services: one London trust surveyed by the Royal College of Nursing in 2003 reported that it recruited staff from 68 different countries (see Figure 10.11).

The global movement of people is not, though, a politically neutral one: inevitably, it has contributed to increasing international inequalities in health. The advantages for populations in rich countries can be devastating for the health care systems in poorer countries. There is a chain by which the best-funded health care systems 'poach' nurses trained overseas. Nurses trained in the UK and Ireland, for instance, leave the relatively under-funded National Health Service to work in the United States. The UK recruits nurses

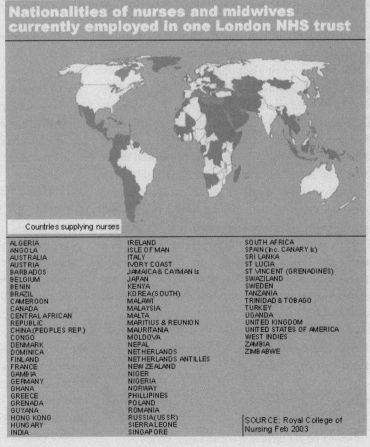

Figure 10.11 Nationalities of nurses and midwives currently employed in one London NHS Trust

Source: Royal College of Nursing February 2003, from the *Guardian* web site

World in focus (continued)

from South Africa, which in turn recruits from more impoverished African countries. Those countries with the least well-funded health care systems, which can least afford to loose their trained professionals, then have nowhere to turn to staff their own systems. For instance:

➤ Nelson Mandela had to appeal to Britain to stop 'poaching nurses' after over 6,000 left South Africa to work in the UK between 1997 and 2002.

➤ Zambia has lost 550 of the 600 doctors it has trained since independence in 1964 (Fouch 2004), and 60 per cent of newly qualified doctors left Ghana to work abroad between 1985 and 1994.

➤ Even in the Philippines, which has traditionally trained a surplus of nurses, so many have left that many operating theatres there are now staffed by trainee nurses (Batty 2003).

In recent years, the British government has attempted to

introduce ethical recruitment policies, by banning the active recruitment of nursing and medical staff from countries that are short of trained professionals. However, it is difficult to legislate for private hospitals and care homes, and estimates suggest that since 2001, when the ban was introduced, some 5,000 nurses from South Africa and other African countries have registered in Britain, often via 'backdoor' routes of working initially for private hospitals (Carvel 2004).

---

who worked in South America and became a critic of many modern institutions, took this view even further. He argued that medicine not only dominated too many aspects of social and moral life but that, far from providing the cure for all our ills, it was actually making us sick. He pointed to all the 'side-effects' of medication and to post-operative complications, for example, as well as to the major unforeseen consequences of medical intervention, such as the case of thalidomide. This proliferation of medically induced illness he called 'iatrogenesis'. He also felt that the promise of medical 'wonder cures' had falsely raised public expectations and that the prestige and status associated with medicine and doctors had created a debilitating dependency on 'experts', undermining the autonomy and ability of lay people. For Illich medicine had 'gone too far' and was about to reach its nemesis (Illich 1975).

Contemporary fears over MRSA, the antibiotic-resistant bacterium found in some modern hospitals, would seem to bear out many of Illich's predictions.

Stop and think

➤ How far do you agree with Illich's views? Do you think that the benefits of medicine are now outweighed by the cost? What other examples can you think of?

There have been many critiques of this thesis. Navarro (1983), writing from a Marxist perspective, criticizes Illich for taking an individualistic and utopian view. For Navarro, most ill health is a consequence of the capitalist mode of production. Others have pointed to the benefits of medical intervention and feel it is unrealistic to condemn all medicine.

Medicine and social control/deviance

Other social theorists have concentrated on the role 'medicine' plays in the regulation of society in general. One area in which this critique has been prevalent is that of mental health. Thomas Szasz (1961), writing in the 1960s, was one of many in the 'anti-psychiatry' movement who pointed to the way 'madness' was a label applied by society to those who did not 'fit', and that this varied according to historical period and culture. For example, in the early twentieth century 'unmarried mothers' were deemed 'mad', or at least 'mentally unstable'. The anti-psychiatry movement (which included both patients and former practitioners) argued that psychiatry was not being used to 'cure' people who were sick but to control those who were considered deviant.

This thesis has been extended by many social scientists (particularly criminologists), who point to the way drugs are used to 'correct' many aspects of 'deviant behaviour' from the use of ECT in mental hospitals (e.g. see the film *One Flew over the Cuckoo's Nest*) to the administering of ritalin to 'hyperactive' children, or to the prescription of valium to 'depressed housewives'. They argue that the very 'disease categories' themselves are created by this process of 'medicalization'. For example, boys now labelled as having 'attention deficit disorder' may once have simply been thought of as naughty.

In a society where to be sick is more acceptable than to be bad, this process may come as a relief, for wilful deviance is a crime and implies punishment whereas unintended deviance is 'illness' and implies treatment. As we have seen in the earlier discussion of Parsons' 'sick role', the role of 'sick person' confers certain obligations, such as a willingness to be treated.

Health, medicine and social regulation

Foucault, in *Madness and Civilisation* (1965), also studied the way 'madness' was socially constructed and took the notion of 'medicalization' even further. He showed how 'punishment' had given way to 'treatment' and how that implied the need for constant surveillance and monitoring. This is seen as the basis for new forms of power which extend throughout the whole of society. He described what he calls the 'clinical gaze' (see p. 409) as having moved beyond the hospital and the clinic into many and diverse sites such as our schools, workplaces and homes. In this view, we are all 'medical subjects', making decisions about many aspects of our daily lives in relation to whether or not something is healthy.

Stop and think

> ➤ Are there areas of social life you feel should not be subject to medical scrutiny? Why? Are your grounds moral, political or social? Can you think of any examples from your own lives?

Health services in Britain

Across the world, formal health care systems are funded in a number of different ways. In the United States, there is some public provision through the Medicaid and Medicare programmes, funded from general taxation revenue, but for most of the working age population, health care is paid for privately through a combination of insurance and out-of-pocket payments. In Western Europe, most health care systems are funded through either social insurance schemes or taxation revenues. In the UK, the National Health Service is an example of a publicly funded system paid for largely through taxation revenue. This section takes the development of the National Health System as an example of how formal health care systems have emerged in modern societies.

The development of the NHS

The development of medicine during the nineteenth century led, as we have seen, to a proliferation of registered medical practitioners: doctors, dentists, midwives and nurses, as well as opticians and pharmacists. Thus most formal health care in Europe was now located within the biomedical model. Nevertheless, the provision of health care was piecemeal and either private or voluntary. For example, in Britain the well-off would employ a doctor to visit them at home, even for operations, while the poor would rely on the services of a 'voluntary hospital'. Voluntary hospitals were staffed by doctors who practised privately but gave up some sessions each week to instruct medical students and to gain experience of 'interesting' cases. Voluntary hospitals depended on charitable donations and benefactors to keep running. As medical science developed, the voluntary hospitals became increasingly selective in the type of patient they would take.

The 'destitute sick', that is, the chronic sick or those with infections, were dependent on the workhouses set up under the Poor Law Act, where they were initially housed in infirmary wards and subsequently in purpose-built infirmaries. These were the first examples of the public provision of hospitals. As the twentieth century progressed, these purpose-built hospitals increasingly employed their own salaried medical staff and ceased to be regarded as a Poor Law service.

Recruitment for the Boer War at the end of the nineteenth century had highlighted the poor health and physical fitness of potential soldiers. This contributed to the formation of various health and social policies aimed at improving the health of the population, for example the 1906 Education (Provision of Meals) Act, which led to the provision of school meals, and the 1907 Education (Administrative Provision) Act, which led to the setting up of the school medical service. By 1911 the prime minister, Lloyd George, had introduced the National Insurance Act. This enabled all working people earning less than a certain amount (£160 p.a.) to sign up with a local general practitioner for free health care, although this did not include hospital care. This facility did not, however, extend to the spouse (usually wife) or the children of the worker, or to those who were not in paid work such as elderly or unemployed people.

By the 1940s about half the population were insured under this Act, and this signified a major development in the involvement of the state in the provision of health services. Thus by the outbreak of the Second World War there was a proliferation of health services and of legislation which laid the foundation for a welfare state in Britain. This was accelerated by the collective experience of shared risks and resources during the war itself.

It was recognized that comprehensive social and economic planning was required and that the state needed to take the major responsibility for the provision of health and welfare services. The result was the Beveridge Report of 1942. In this the 'five giants' to be tackled on the way to post-war reconstruction were identified as disease, ignorance, squalor, idleness and want, each to be tackled by the new welfare legislation. The 1946 National Health Service Act was to address the problem of disease, while other Acts, such as Education in 1944, National Insurance in 1946, Housing in 1946 and National Assistance in 1948 (which finally laid the Poor Law to rest) were to address the other areas.

The NHS from 1948

Aneurin Bevan, the Labour health minister who published the National Health Service Bill in 1946, was renowned as a great orator, a 'fiery Welshman' and a political radical. His vision was of a service where the very best of health advice and treatment would be available to all, regardless of their ability to pay: that is, to 'universalize the best' rather than guarantee the minimum (as was the case with the contemporary social security legislation). This utopian vision, however, soon foundered. The 'pool of ill health' which it was envisaged would place an initial burden on the NHS never seemed to reduce. In 1951, in order to supplement the funds raised by taxation, the Labour government introduced the first charges – for dentures and spectacles – and Bevan, along with Harold Wilson and John Freeman, resigned from Attlee's government in protest. In 1952 charges for dental treatment and prescriptions were introduced for those not exempt.

Indeed, as time went on and there were more developments in medical science, more illnesses became available for treatment. In addition to this the population was beginning to live longer, thus creating an expanding and unforeseen demand on the resources of the NHS.

Private provision

In Britain, most health care is provided through the NHS, and the private sector has been small. However, there are a number of areas in which the private provision of health care has been important, and there was increased political pressure during the Conservative administration in the early 1990s to reconsider the role of the state in the provision of health care. Hospital support services, such as laundry, catering and domestic services, have been put out to tender since 1983, and many private companies now provide these services within NHS hospitals. The Conservative reforms of the NHS, which were enacted in the 1991 NHS and Community Care Act, left the NHS as the major provider of health care but did introduce a 'market' model to the system, with a split between providers (the hospital and community trusts) and purchasers (the health authorities) in an effort to introduce private sector mechanisms to encourage efficiency. In theory, providers would compete to provide services in a locality (with other NHS and also private providers), so increasing quality and reducing costs. In reality, the health sector does not work like a market in other goods, and there were many problems with this model. However, some commentators have seen its introduction as evidence of a greater commercialization in the NHS.

Commercialization could be seen to be happening in terms of the charges that can be made for certain services. Although charges have never provided a large proportion of NHS revenue, they have tended to be raised by recent governments. Dentistry raises 25 per cent of costs through direct charges to patients. The rationale for direct charges is partly that charges deter trivial attendances, in that they introduce an element of self-rationing into publicly provided health care. The other way of looking at this, though, is that they may have a deterrent effect, and that people in need of services may not get them.

One trend of interest is the increasing range of 'alternative' or 'complementary' practitioners who in theory provide front-line services. It is estimated that one in seven of the British population visits alternative practitioners

Table 10.5 UK spending on NHS, private and other health care			
	NHS £m	Private £m	Other[1] £m
1980	11,257	355	615
1985	17,154	738	1,190
1990	28,426	1,623	1,919
1995	41,853	2,808	3,919
2000	57,037	4,927	5,265

1 Includes spending on over-the-counter pharmaceuticals and spectacles
Source: Yuen, P. (2001) *OHE Compendium of Health Statistics*, 17th edition, 2005–06, Radcliffe Publishing

(Saks 1994). Given that very few of these practitioners, or those of other complementary professions, work for the NHS, most consultations and treatments have to be paid for on a fee-for-service basis.

There are also an increasing number of people who use private facilities for acute care, such as operations which have long waiting lists on the NHS. Most of this is paid for through insurance schemes. Between 1982 and 1987, the number of people who held a policy for private medical insurance doubled, and it has grown, but more slowly, in the period since then. In 1996, 6 per cent of the population of Britain held a policy (*Social Trends* 1998). The majority of these are company schemes, so managers, employers and professionals are more likely to be covered than those in manual occupations.

Stop and think

➤ Suggest what the advantages and disadvantages are of private medicine for (a) the state; and (b) the patient.

Social structure and health

Global inequalities shape our chance of having a long and healthy life. The Would Health Organisation contrasted the case of Japan, the country with the longest life expectancy, with Sierra Leone, where male life expectancy is only 32 years:

> While a baby girl born in Japan today can expect to live for about 85 years, a girl born at the same moment in Sierra Leone has a life expectancy of 36 years.

The Japanese child will receive vaccinations, adequate nutrition and good schooling ... Growing older, she may eventually develop chronic diseases, but excellent treatment and rehabilitation services will be available; she can expect to receive, on average, medications worth about $550 per year and much more if needed.

Meanwhile, the girl in Sierra Leone has a low chance of receiving immunizations and a high probability of being underweight throughout childhood. She will probably marry in adolescence and give birth to six or more children ... One or more of her babies will die in infancy, and she herself will be at high risk of death in childbirth. If she falls ill, she can expect, on average, medicines worth about $3 per year. If she survives middle age she, too, will develop chronic diseases but, without access to adequate treatment, she will die prematurely.   (WHO 2003)

For the poorest countries in the world, health status will only improve with higher standards of living. For countries with a higher standard of living, it seems that the health status of the population is less influenced by absolute wealth of the country and more by how that wealth is distributed within the population. Inequalities in health within the populations of developed countries are perhaps more difficult to explain than those between countries, as most of the population have access to vaccinations, adequate nutrition and schooling. There are also global inequalities in vulnerability to pollution risk, with many thousands of people (12,000–15,000) dying and injured as a result of the Bhopal gas tragedy at the Union Carbide pesticide plant in India in 1984, widely regarded as one of the worst commercial industrial disasters in history. Sociologists, and those from other disciplines, disagree about how to explain inequalities in health. Debates around potential explanations centre on how to interpret the evidence, and on the theoretical perspectives brought to bear on that evidence. These are important dedates, as how we explain inequalities in health clearly shapes the kinds of health policies advocated. If, for instance, we see different health outcomes as the result of behavioural differences, we might advocate health education to change behaviour, whereas if we adopt a more materialist perspective and explain health inequalities as an outcome of economic structures, we might focus more on advocating redistributive fiscal policy. The next section focuses on inequalities in health in the UK, as one example of a developed country with persisting gaps between the health status of the richest and poorest members of society to explore these different explanations.

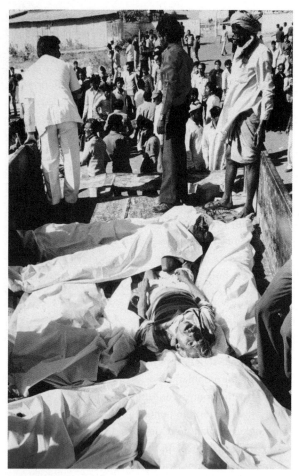

Figure 10.12 Victims of the Bhopal gas tragedy in India 1984

The social production of health

It has long been recognized that health is influenced by living and working conditions. Over 150 years ago, Frederick Engels arrived in Manchester and was appalled at the conditions in which the working classes lived. He found it unsurprising that more than 57 per cent of working-class children died before their fifth birthday, whereas only 20 per cent of those from the higher classes did.

> The manner in which the great multitude of the poor is treated by society today is revolting. They are drawn into large cities where they breathe a poorer atmosphere than in the country; they are relegated to districts which, by reason of the method of construction, are worse ventilated than any others; they are deprived of all means of cleanliness, of water itself,

since pipes are laid only when they are paid for, and the rivers so polluted they are useless for such purposes . . . [they] are worked every day to the point of complete exhaustion of their physical and mental energies . . . How is it possible, under such conditions, for the lower classes to be healthy and long lived?

(Engels 1995)

People in British cities today, on the whole, enjoy clean water, good sewage disposal, clean air and access to health services. However, there are still large gaps between the health of those from the middle and the working classes. Table 10.6 shows mortality rates for men and women in England and Wales, showing the continuing gap between those in the highest and lowest social classes.

In the 1970s, the British government was concerned that, despite the National Health Service, there still appeared to be such inequalities in health. They commissioned a report, known as the Black Report after Sir Douglas Black, the chairman of the Commission which produced it.

The Black Report

The Black Report (Townsend *et al.* 1988) suggested that in overall terms social inequalities in health did not only still exist but there was also some evidence they were getting wider. Men and women born into Social Classes IV and V had twice the risk of dying before retirement age than those born into Social Class I. The differences were apparent at every stage of the life cycle, and for most major causes of death. There were also persistent social class differences in reports of chronic illness, the use of the health services and in health-related behaviour. The Black Report considered four potential explanations for these differences.

1   *The artefact explanation*   This explanation suggests that both 'health' and 'class' are artificial variables, and the relationship between them may be of little causal significance. One contributing factor is the reduction in the size of the unskilled and semi-skilled manual social classes as a result of rising levels of white-collar employment. If we are comparing differences over time, so this argument goes, we are not comparing like with like. Jones and Cameron (1984), for instance, argued that as the Registrar-General's classification was originally designed to measure social class differences in ill health, it is not surprising that it does so. They suggest that sometimes occupations have been allocated to

Table 10.6 All cause death rate: by social class and sex

England and Wales	Rate per 100,000 people		
	1986–92	1993–96	1997–99
Males			
Professional, managerial and technical	460	379	347
Skilled non-manual	480	437	417
Skilled manual	617	538	512
Skilled, semi-skilled and unskilled manual	776	648	606
Non-manual	466	396	371
Manual	674	577	546
Females			
Professional, managerial and technical	274	262	237
Skilled non-manual	310	262	253
Skilled manual	350	324	327
Skilled, semi-skilled and unskilled maunal	422	378	335
Non-manual	289	257	246
Manual	379	344	330

Source: Longitudinal Study, Office for National Statistics

social classes not on the basis of any theory of social classification but on the basis of their mortality rates. There have certainly been significant changes to the classification of occupations. Clerks, for example, were classified in Class I in 1911 but III by the 1931 census, as a rise in education had meant that clerical work was no longer an elite occupation. Postmen and telephone operators were reclassified Class III to IV in 1961, while aircraft pilots moved in the opposite direction from III to II.

However, even if we accept that the Registrar-General's system is flawed, there are some compelling reasons to accept that there is a 'real' relationship between social class and health outcomes. One piece of evidence to support this comes from what was known as the Whitehall Study (Marmot *et al.* 1978), which studied 17,000 civil servants and their mortality rates from heart disease over seven years. When different grades of worker were compared, those in the lowest grade had a 3.6 times greater risk of dying from heart disease than those in the highest grade. This difference was not explained by differences in health behaviour, such as smoking rates or diet. As civil service employment grade is not subject to the problems of measurement as the Registrar-General's scale, this does suggest that there is something about being in a lower social class which causes a higher mortality.

The other explanations considered by the Black Report did accept that there was a causal relationship between social class and health.

2 *Natural and social selection explanation* This explanation theorizes that the healthier you are, the more likely you are to experience upward social mobility, so the higher social classes have a disproportionate number of hardy, robust individuals who will experience lower mortality rates. Conversely, the weaker members of society will drift down the occupational hierarchy to make up the lower social classes. For some diseases, such as schizophrenia and bronchitis, there can be associated downward social mobility. However, most researchers question whether social selection explains much of the observed social class differences in health. It cannot account for the social class differences in health found in childhood, when there is not much social mobility but very great differences in mortality. For unintentional injuries (which are the leading cause of death for children over one year), for instance, there is a fivefold greater risk of dying for those born in Social Class V families compared with those in Social Class I (see Table 10.7).

The last two explanations offered by the Black Report both assume that health status is the dependent variable: that there is something to do

Table 10.7 Death rate per 100,000 children, aged 0–15 in England and Wales, 1989–92	
Social class	Death rate
I	16.5
II	15.8
IIIN	19.1
IIIM	34.3
IV	37.8
V	82.9

Source: Roberts *et al.* 1998. *Injury Prevention* 4, pp. 10–16, reproduced with permission of the BMJ Publishing Group

Table 10.8 Prevalence of cigarette smoking by sex and socio-economic group, Great Britain		
Socio-economic group	Male (% smokers)	Female (% smokers)
Managerial and professional	21	18
Intermediate	29	26
Routine and manual	35	31

Source: Walker *et al.* 2002

with being in a lower social class that causes a greater mortality rate. Figure 10.13 shows the continuing gap in life expectancy at birth between professional and manual occupations.

3 *Cultural or behavioural explanations* At its crudest, this explanation says that there is something about the culture of lower social classes that is unhealthy. Evidence comes from information we have about such things as smoking behaviour (see Table 10.8) and the kinds of diet people eat.

4 *Materialist explanation* A *materialist* explanation is one that prioritizes economic factors. There are several kinds of materialist explanation. One holds that material conditions (such as poverty or

homelessness) are still a direct cause of increased mortality in modern society, despite the general rising standard of living. Although it may not be convincing to argue that the poorest workers do not have enough resources to fulfil their basic needs, which Engels suggested was true in the nineteenth century, there is an argument that they may be relatively disadvantaged in terms of avoiding the risk factors for disease.

Stop and think

➤ Can you suggest how material factors could influence health in terms of (a) accident rates in childhood; and (b) diet?

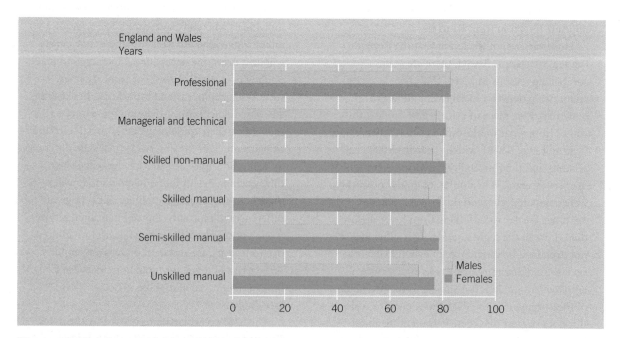

Figure 10.13 Life expectancy at birth: by social class and sex, 1997–99
Source: Longitudinal Study, Office for National Statistics

Case study

Roseto: a town in the USA with low mortality

Researchers noted that Roseto, a town in Pennsylvania, had low death rates compared with neighbouring towns. Rates of death from heart disease, for instance, were 40 per cent lower, although there were no differences in the rates of smoking, exercise or diet. However, the town did have one noticeable difference: a closer, more cohesive community that was descended from Italian immigrants

who came to the USA in the 1880s. There were high levels of social support, and social norms which countered ostentatious displays of wealth. This meant that there were not wide disparities in access to resources, as the community provided mutual support. During the 1960s, young people began to leave the town and the community ties loosened. Egalitarian norms broke down, as increased affluence led some members of the community to buy expensive cars and houses.

The health advantage of living in Roseto disappeared in the same period, and death rates became comparable with those in neighbouring towns.

(Wilkinson 1996; Bruhn and Wolf 1979)

Questions

1. How might the lower death rate from heart disease in Roseto be explained?

2. Why did this change after the 1960s?

There are overlaps between the cultural and materialist explanations, and they differ perhaps most in emphasis, with the cultural explanation seeing behaviour as the important variable, which is, at least in principle, chosen by an individual, whereas the materialists see behaviour as a result of social forces over which the individual has no control. Hilary Graham's work on women and smoking (Graham 1987), for instance, looks at the ways in which behaviour might be influenced by material factors. Smoking might help women in poverty to cope because it is a relaxation, a uniquely adult experience for mothers whose main interaction is with small children and it may be a legitimate way of having a break.

Social capital and health

Other materialist explanations look not at the direct effect of material factors on the individual but at the pattern of inequality in society and its impact. Recently, there has been an interest in looking at whether it is inequality itself that causes ill health, rather than absolute levels of incomes, or access to resources. Wilkinson (1996) has argued that international data suggest that in countries where there is the greatest inequality in wealth, there are the lowest life expectancies. In Britain, during the periods after the world wars, both periods of greater equality in income, there was a growth in life expectancy. Obviously this data does not prove cause, but it does suggest that

we might look not at *absolute* material disadvantage but *relative* disadvantage to explain health inequalities.

That social structure has a profound influence on health has long been recognized. Durkheim's study of suicide (Durkheim 1963) argued that suicide rates increased as social integration decreased, and Wilkinson's work follows in this tradition. He uses the concept of 'social capital' to explore why there is a relationship between inequality and health outcomes, suggesting that the mechanism may be a psycho-social one, in which experience of inequality, and the stress and anxiety it engenders, have effects on the health status of individuals (Wilkinson 1996: 214–15).

Ethnicity and inequality

Another social structural influence on health outcomes in many societies is ethnicity. There are a number of ways of explaining the relationships between ethnicity and health outcome in societies such as Britain.

The role of ideological considerations has been largely ignored in health and health service research on Black populations. There are two main trends in research and writings on Black people's health. One is a vehemently 'culturalist' approach, where realities are constructed and explained in terms of 'cultural differences' – differences usually equated with deviance and

Case study

The rickets campaign

One example of health-promotion policy which illustrates the 'pathologization' of ethnic minority culture was the DHSS rickets campaign in the 1970s. This identified rickets as an 'Asian' problem and, despite the lack of any one factor which explained the re-emergence of rickets in poor families in Glasgow in the 1960s, focused on trying to change behaviour. British Asians were encouraged to eat foods which had been fortified with vitamin D, such as margarine and breakfast cereals, and to expose themselves and their children to more sunlight. It was decided not to fortify chapati flour with vitamin D, although fortification had been the main way in which rickets had been eliminated in the 1950s. The campaign did not address material constraints, although poverty had been seen as the key cause of rickets in the wider population 20 years earlier. Maggie Pearson argues that these kinds of campaign reinforce a victim-blaming approach to health problems, and present black and ethnic minority culture as alien and pathological.

(Pearson 1986)

Question

1. Can you think of other health campaigns that 'blame the victim'?

---

pathology . . . The second approach is of supposedly benign epidemiology, the notion of an unconcerned, value-free observer making objective pronouncements on the basis of carefully collected evidence which uses rigorous scientific methodology. This is a prized tradition in clinical medicine and the scientific researcher who dismisses such 'irrelevancies' as 'race' and class is much applauded for upholding the traditions of good science.   (Ahmad 1993: 2)

Waqar Ahmad notes how the social structure disadvantages black and ethnic minority people's health because it limits their access to the prerequisites of good health: access to jobs, decent education and good quality housing (Ahmad 1993: 1). In the above quote, he points to the ideological assumptions of much research on ethnicity and health: that it assumes either that 'other' cultures are pathological, or that 'race' is not important, or that racism is not a 'health' issue.

Material factors cannot explain all the differences in health outcome between different ethnic communities in Britain. Table 10.9 shows infant mortality rates for children born to mothers from some ethnic communities, illustrating that although babies born to mothers from Pakistan do have a high mortality rate, those born to mothers from Bangladesh (who share similar profiles of occupation and housing) are protected. Why should this be? Gantley and her colleagues (Gantley *et al.* 1993) suggest that one protective factor could be child-care practices in Bangladeshi households, where babies are rarely left alone and sleep next to parents. This, they suggest, may lead to a lower rate of sudden infant death syndrome, the most common cause of death for children under one.

Table 10.9 Infant mortality rates	
Country	Infant mortality rate (deaths per 1000 live births)
Angola	191.2
Nigeria	98.8
Pakistan	72.4
India	56.3
Brazil	29.6
Russia	15.4
USA	6.5
UK	5.2
Japan	3.3
Sweden	2.8

Source: The World Factbook 2005 (www.cia.gov)

Ethnicity and the experience of health services

Racism impacts on how users of health-care services experience care, and on the quality of service they receive. Isobelle Bowler (1993) found that midwives stereotyped patients of south Asian descent, and saw them as 'different' and lacking in 'normal' maternal instinct. Lack of awareness of different cultural traditions and communication difficulties increased the problems faced by south Asian mothers, and Bowler suggests that this influenced the care they received in terms of pain relief during labour and offers of contraceptive advice.

Brent Community Health Council concluded in 1981 that 'racism penetrates every aspect of the NHS, from its recruitment policies to its assumptions of the superiority of white diets, family systems, traditions of healing and approaches to child rearing; from mythologies about black "pain thresholds" to eligibility for NHS treatment.' Chris Smaje has suggested that there are three ways in which racism directly impacts on service delivery:

1 *Direct racism* where a health worker treats a person less favourably simply by virtue of the latter's ethnicity.

2 *Indirect or institutional racism* where although ostensibly services are provided equally to all people, the form in which they are provided inevitably favours particular groups at the expense of others.

3 *Ethnocentrism* where inappropriate assumptions are made about the needs of people from minority ethnic groups on the basis of majority experience (Smaje 1995: 110).

Smaje argues that, although there are many instances of direct racism within health-care delivery, the problems of ethnocentrism are more complex and do result in less satisfactory services for people from ethnic minority communities.

Stop and think

➤ What areas of service provision may be particularly susceptible to ethnocentrism? Give reasons for your answers.

Gender

How does gender impact on health experiences? There are a few 'health experiences' that women have which relate to their specific genes or biology, for example those related to childbirth and menstruation. Similarly, there are some conditions specific to men, for example testicular cancer and muscular dystrophy. The main differences in health experience, however, are related to the social construction of gender: that is, the ideas we, as a society, have about what is expected of men and women.

The puzzling aspect of health and gender is that, although women report more illness than men, they live longer. In Britain, life expectancy has been greater for women than for men since the seventeenth century (Nathanson 1984), although it is only in the twentieth century that the gaps between life expectancy for men and women became large and are seen as in need of explanation. Increasing differences in male and female mortality in the developed countries have been attributed to reduced rates of death in women from childbearing, and greater mortality in men from cardiovascular disease and cancers. Higher levels of cigarette smoking among men during the early part of the century account for some of their relative disadvantage. However, the general question of why women appear to be advantaged in terms of mortality has not yet been adequately answered. Contributing factors are likely to include:

➤ *Biology* Is there a hormonal difference which protects women? Some researchers have suggested that the extra X chromosome carried by women confers some protection, in part making them more resistant to disease in childhood (see Nathanson 1984).

➤ *Behaviour* Are men more likely to take risks, such as smoking cigarettes, or taking part in dangerous sport, or violent activities?

➤ *Social and environmental causes* Ingrid Waldron (1985) suggests that men are more likely to engage in hazardous occupations and to be socialized into behaving in ways that involve more 'risk-taking'.

➤ *The use of health services* Women tend to consult doctors more often, and may be more likely to use preventive health services. However, for most major causes of mortality, there appear to be few differences in the use of curative medicine (Waldron 1985).

The statistics for *morbidity* (illness episodes), however, suggest that women have more illness than men, or at least report more illness (see Table 10.10). On yet another level, it may be that, as we have seen, women are expected to take responsibility for family health and might therefore have higher rates of GP consultation. If we also take into consideration the socially produced gender roles, we know that it is more acceptable for women to show weakness and to seek help, and seeking medical help for illness is no exception.

Finally, we might suggest that some aspects of women's lives and experience are more likely than men's to be *medicalized*. This has been well documented in

Age group	Male	Female
0–4	16	11
5–15	13	12
16–44	22	29
45–64	44	50
65–74	47	55
75+	64	67

Table 10.10 Reported acute sickness: average number of reported days of restricted activity per year, by sex and age group

Source: ONS (1998)

Stop and think

➤ To what extent do you think that gender differences in health experience are a consequence of nature or nurture?

relation to childbirth and reproduction (see e.g. Oakley 1980) and also in the arena of mental health (Showalter 1987). For example, women who present with mental health problems are more likely than men to be given prescriptions for anti-depressants or tranquillizers. Men, however, are more likely to have alcohol-related accidents and it is likely that drinking alcohol is a more socially acceptable response to stress for men than it is for women.

It is difficult to say how gender impacts on health simply because it is very difficult to establish for certain causal relationships between single variables. How much of a person's experience is determined by their gender, ethnicity, class, disability, sexuality, age or other social attribute is perhaps the wrong question. Our experience of health and illness is a complex interaction of these and probably many other factors. Indeed, as we have sought to show in other sections of this chapter, 'health' and 'illness' are themselves contested concepts.

Summary

➤ 'Health' and 'illness' are contested concepts, with a range of meanings. There are cultural differences in how societies classify health and illness, and what the causes of illness are thought to be.

➤ Western biomedicine has been very successful as a system of knowledge about health and illness. Rooted in ideas of scientific rationality, and the identification of specific causes of 'disease', biomedicine arose in the eighteenth century and has achieved a legitimacy not afforded to other belief systems.

➤ Despite the dominance of biomedicine, there are areas of conflict. Lay and professional accounts of illness experience may differ, and there are potential conflicts over what is labelled a 'disease'. The rising interest in complementary therapies demonstrates the persistence of alternative conceptions of health.

➤ Sociological approaches to health and illness include the study of illness as a kind of deviance and a focus on stigma. More recently there has been a growing interest in 'illness narratives' or how people account for the experience of ill health, and in the study of medicine as a facet of the disciplinary society.

➤ Most health care happens in the informal sector, within people's homes, and is disproportionately carried out by women. The vast majority of symptoms are dealt with by self-care. The decision to refer some to health professionals is influenced by a range of social, economic and psychological factors.

➤ The rise of the hospital has been central to the development of modern medicine and the success of the medical profession. At the beginning of the twenty-first century there are some indications that the status of the hospital may be in decline, with more emphasis on community care and preventive medicine.

Summary (continued)

➤ Despite the existence in Britain of a National Health Service, there are still vast social divisions of health outcomes. Social class divisions in mortality and morbidity are probably the result of material factors. Experiences of the health service are likely to be influenced by gender and ethnicity, as racist and sexist ideologies influence the provision of care and how it is delivered.

Links

The discussion of stigma, pages 397–8, is based on Goffman's work, which is examined more fully in Chapter 2.

The division of labour in health, pages 412–14, relates to the role of women in employment generally considered in Chapter 7.

Inequalities in health care, pages 420–1, link with the coverage of social stratification and class in Chapter 6.

Further reading

Bury M. and Gabe, J. (eds) (2004) *The Sociology of Health and Illness: A Reader*. London: Routledge.
This collection has classic and more recent readings on health beliefs, inequalities, professional and patient interactions, chronic illness and disability and the politics of health care.

Green, J. and Thorogood, N. (1998) *Analysing Health Policy: A Sociological Approach*, Harlow: Longman.
Taking key issues in British health policy as examples, this book illustrates how sociological approaches can illuminate where policies come from, how they get implemented and how well they work. It includes a chapter on researching health policy and case studies from research.

McKeown, T. (1979) *The Role of Medicine: Dream, Mirage or Nemesis?* Oxford: Basil Blackwell.
A fascinating analysis of how mortality from infectious disease has fallen in Western countries, with an assessment of the relative roles of modern medicine and environmental factors

in the production of health. This text also provides a good introduction to some key concepts in medicine and public health.

Nettleton, S. (1995) *The Sociology of Health and Illness*, Cambridge: Polity Press.
A readable text introducing the key areas of the sociology of health and illness, which includes accessible accounts of contemporary theoretical approaches as well as some of the more traditional ones.

Stacey, M. (1991) *The Sociology of Health and Healing*, London: Routledge.
Margaret Stacey traces the emergence of biomedicine historically and in the context of healing traditions in other societies. She examines the division of labour in health care, including the informal sector, and the role of medicine in terms of capitalist development. Informed throughout by a feminist approach, the book ends with a consideration of human reproduction in the twenty-first century.

Turner, B. (1987) *Medical Power and Social Knowledge*, London: Sage.
Bryan Turner links developments in medical sociology with wider theoretical approaches in the social sciences in this analysis of medicine and its role in modern society, including Talcott Parsons and Foucault.

 ## Web sites

www.nhs.uk
is the official web site for the British National Health Service. It provides historical and background information on the NHS and a search facility to research related sites.

www.who.int/en/
is the World Health Organization web site and gives information on health topics, research and publications from round the world and provides links to hundreds of related and relevant sites.

Activities

Activity 1

Health, illness and the media

Look at a range of media, including TV, women's and men's magazine, and newspapers.

List the extent to which health and illness issues are covered. Summarize the way these issues are covered. Are there any key themes in these media representations? How do different media approach these issues?

Take one character from a gel 'soap' with which you are familiar. Draw up a 'health profile' for that character using the ideas and concepts you have come across in this chapter. For example, how might their health be affected by factors such as race, gender and class? What might be the relative impact of biological, material, social and cultural factors?

After considering the soap character, you could try out the same exercise on yourself, a friend or someone in your family.

Activity 2

Health promotion campaigns

Collect some examples of recent health promotion campaigns and then consider the following questions:

- Are they taking a structural or an individual approach to behaviour change?
- What kinds of people are represented and how are they represented?
- What, if any, groups of people are being specifically targeted?
- How effective do you think each of the campaigns you have looked at might be in changing people's behaviour?

The discussion of medicalization has shown areas of private and public life that have become objects of medical scrutiny. What do you think of the argument that health promotion is a form of social and/or moral regulation? Do you think making 'healthy choices' should be a matter for individual conscience or for government intervention?

As a follow up to your consideration of health campaigns, draw up a list of things people do which they know to be 'bad' for them. What reasons can you suggest for people knowingly indulging in 'unhealthy behaviour'?

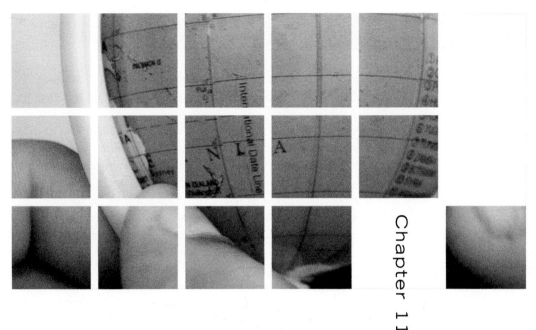

Chapter 11

Global issues in sociology

There are only two families in the world, as a grandmother of mine used to say: the haves and the have nots.
(Cervantes, *Don Quixote*, quoted in Simpson 1994)

Key issues

➤ What are the strengths and weaknesses of sociological theories of development?

➤ What explanations do sociological theories offer for the continuing economic disadvantages experienced in many societies?

➤ What is the extent of global inequality?

Introduction

Today we appear to accept as fact that we live in a globalized world. As indicated above, just thirty years ago international travel was for the most part limited to either the middle or upper classes, or to members of the working class whose work took them overseas, most usually while serving with the British armed forces or as merchant seamen. For members of the working class,

travel was very much limited. Today this has radically changed. World travel is a practice increasingly facilitated by cheap airfares and a growing number of so called 'budget airlines'. As Kevin Meethan (2001) points out international tourism has grown at a phenomenonal rate in the past two decades, leading to a global revolution in tourism. This is perhaps best illustrated in the Figure 11.1 below which shows the number of visits overseas taken by UK residents and the number of visitors from overseas to Britain in the period 1980 to 2004.

While this data does not concern itself specifically with tourism, and as a consequence neither confirms nor refutes Meethan's claims, it does demonstrate quite a phenomenal growth in the rate at which the British travel in the late twentieth and early twenty-first centuries. However, there is, as Meethan indicates, significant evidence to demonstrate that this travel (and tourism) is far more regionally localized and far less widely globalized. As indicated above, the growth of low-cost airlines in the UK such as EasyJet and Ryanair, or 'Jet Blue' in the USA, have all facilitated population mobility and travel. Increasingly, low-cost airlines cater for short-haul

Case study

Life as local – growing up in the 1960s

In the 1960s and 70s when I was growing up life appeared to have a familiarity to it. It was known, it was predictable and it was above all local. For most of my family the idea of foreign travel, of even meeting people from the far side of the planet was largely unheard of. When someone from another country did enter our lives, this was strange, unusual and different. Such strangers were viewed as exotic people. Moreover, where I lived it was unusual to see black people, and I have to say such individuals were met with a significant degree of suspicion and even hostility. Members of my family did 'go to sea' and had travelled with the British merchant navy to far-flung parts; this was something of a working-class tradition for the men of my community. Going to sea was part of the way of life for some and one of the few opportunities for foreign travel. Many came back with exotic stories of far-off places. My older sister had ventured on one of the early package holiday tours to Spain, bringing all the family back Sangria and sombreros. For the most part we lived in a localized world in which what we did, what we produced and what we consumed appeared to have existed locally. At a consumer level British brands dominated the things we bought from the clothes we wore to the cars we drove. Marks and Spencer was the height of fashion

and reigned supreme and the Co-op shop was the place we bought most of our food; car ownership was rare, but growing, and even here it was dominated by British makes such as Rover, Austin, Humber, Rolls Royce, Ford and Vauxhall (the latter two of these being arms of General Motors and Ford US, and Rolls Royce is now part of the German-owned BMW Group). Politicians even encouraged this with slogans like 'I'm backing Britain'. The TV we watched was largely dominated by British-made comedies, dramas and children's programmes. Yet even these programmes offered tantalizing glimpses of the wider-world out there, epitomized by the children's TV programme 'Blue Peter' with its annual adventure to Africa, India, Honk Kong or Canada.

However, this was also a time of profound change; the certainties that we had grown up with were rapidly fading. The British merchant fleet was shrinking, replaced by ships flying flags of convenience. The merchants navy was less and less an option for men of my generation to follow. This was also matched by the slow demise of the local shipyards, workplace to numerous relatives, as ever more foreign-registered and -crewed ships were built in Japan or Korea. More and more the products we consumed on a daily basis took on an international feel; new brands were marketed as being more sophisticated and improved than those we

had previously bought. Alongside this came the availability of new consumer goods such as washing machines, dishwashers and fridge-freezers, mostly made overseas. In turn we became more adventurous in our tastes for food and drink; our national diet appeared to be changing, becoming much more international. The expansion of the supermarket sector brought an abundance of exotic fruits, vegetables ready-prepared meals. In the 1980s and 90s we saw the rise of the Delia Smith generation and ever more complex meals made at home from recipes in cook books and foods from our supermarkets In comparison with British made cars we'd previously driven, the new foreign cars proved both cheaper and often far more reliable. Our TV and cinemas increasingly showed programmes and films from the USA. Without realizing it my life and the lives of my family and community were becoming globalized. The first signs of seismic shifts had occurred and they resonate increasingly today. But it is the effect of these shifts and their consequences that will form the focus of this chapter.

Questions

1. *In what ways might globalization be said to be driven by consumption?*

2. *What products have you recently purchased that might illustrate this?*

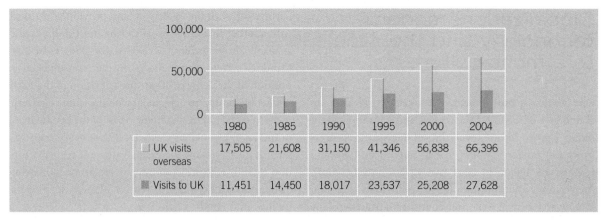

	1980	1985	1990	1995	2000	2004
☐ UK visits overseas	17,505	21,608	31,150	41,346	56,838	66,396
▓ Visits to UK	11,451	14,450	18,017	23,537	25,208	27,628

Figure 11.1 Visits from and visits to the UK (1000s)
(*Source*: UK Office for National Statistics February 2005)

destinations such as 'bachelor parties' in Barcelona, or 'hen parties' in Amsterdam. In the USA in the period 1990–99 overseas travel increased by more than 67 per cent with an annual increase in travel of 5.9 per cent (US Bureau of Transportation 2004). However, up until quite recently the growth in travel and tourism was largely dominated by the middle and upper income sectors of the British and US population. Increasingly it has become more affordable and thus open to the masses. As such there is a tension here between the environmental impact of the growth in highly polluting air travel and the freedom of increasingly affluent individuals. (It is well recognized by environmentalists that short-haul air travel is the most polluting form of travel as the fuel required for take off and landing is far greater than that required to keep an aircraft in the air, as such long-haul travel is, less environmentally damaging.) Matched by the growth in low-cost air travel has been the dramatic increase in the number of passports the British government issues. In Britain there are more than 47.5 million passport holders; nearly 82 per cent of the British population have a passport (British Passport Office, February 2005). In the USA there are no official statistics on the number of passport holders, but reliable evidence indicates that there 18–20 per cent of the US population hold passports. Clearly governments issuing passports gain from the revenue that this generates, along with the multiple service industries that support such travel, from the taxi to the airport to the travel insurance industry.

From the evidence presented here in terms of travel, the British are increasingly a globalized people. We appear willing, certainly in comparison with citizens of the USA, to travel far and wide. Equally, in terms of material consumption, the localism evident in my youth, with the exception of some niche brands, such as Bovril and Oxo cubes (both of which are near impossible to obtain on the west coast of the USA), has now vanished, subsumed under international ownership such as Nestlé or Kraft, one a Swiss company, the other a US food group. In 2004 the NGO 'Action Aid International' reported that the top 30 global food retailers, including Tesco in Britain and Wal-Mart in the USA, account for well over a third of world grocery sales. We increasingly eat and drink the foods and beverages that our European or even North American neighbours consume. We have become far less parochial and far more cosmopolitan in our tastes for food and drink, no doubt partly inspired by our increasing number of foreign adventures. We drive similar, if not identical cars, albeit on the other side of the road. Moreover, our consumption patterns are increasingly influenced and shaped by the growth of global media and advertising; I can now sit in my hotel room in such far away places as San Francisco, USA, or Sharm El Sheik, Egypt, and watch my favourite Premier League side lose yet again. Our world, that is to say the affluent Western world (more of the other world later), is the world of Levi's, a world of Gap, a world of Coca-Cola, McDonald's, H&M, a world of Oil of Olay.

Stop and think

➤ Look at the consumer goods in your house. How many different countries of origin/manufacture can you locate?

➤ Compare the goods and clothes you buy and use to those that your parents and grandparents bought and used when they were your age in terms of where they were made.

Globalization, modern technology and the race to a mono-culture

Our world is also a media saturated world with an abundance of satellite TV channels and a multiplicity of radio. The worldwide ownership of television sets grew from 190 million in 1965 to 850 million in 1994 and reached 1.3 billion in 2004 (www.NationMaster.com). As Macionis and Plummer (1998) point out, television is now watched in over 160 countries, attracting daily audiences in excess of 2.5 billion people, with major areas of recent growth being in Central and South America, Africa and Asia. In the 1960s there were three terrestrial TV channels, BBC1, ITV and BBC2. Indeed BBC2 was a new and radical innovation when it launched on 21 April 1964. Today, through satellite or cable, the average British home has access to well over 200+ TV and radio channels, a number which is growing weekly, rather than yearly. Much of the content of these channels is international (read American) in nature: from the Disney channel for small children to what appears to be the non-stop 'Friends' channel or MTV for my teenage son to the History channel for more serious people like me. To facilitate this growing global audience for television there is in constant geostationary orbit a belt of satellites – mostly controlled and developed by the USA, Japan and Germany – which facilitate telephone, radio and television contact with every part of the Earth. These satellites monitor weather patterns, provide instantaneous communications between countries and assist trade and capital flows. Satellite communication allows other economic and cultural dimensions to be added to the process of globalization. Since the early 1990s, many satellites have been launched, in particular as China and European nations enter the space race, with the explicit intention of widening the market for capitalist goods and services. Featherstone (1991b) points out that this may result in the increased repression or submersion of national culture in favour of a highly commercialized materialist and capitalist culture. Such developments inevitably further the reach of capitalist values and its attendant consumer-based culture. In the late 1980s the Hong Kong movie mogul Sir Run Run Shaw launched a communications satellite on the back of a Chinese space rocket. This satellite, named 'Star', has a 'footprint' that extends over China, South-East Asia and as far as India, broadcasting to an audience and market in a total of 38 countries. In 1992 Rupert Murdoch's News Corporation entered into partnership with the owners of Star, providing Murdoch with another forum for broadcasting most of his readily available programming developed for BSkyB. In 2004 Murdoch's News International further consolidated its position in the delivery of satellite television to the Asian market by signing an agreement with the Chinese government to deliver agreed content. Most of the people living in Indian cities such as Calcutta, if they have access to a satellite dish, as many increasingly do, now regularly tune into Star; it is quite common to see arrays of satellite dishes pointed skywards to receive Western soap operas dubbed into Hindi.

Much of the complex technology and computer chips which support these satellites is produced in the developed world, although in the late 1990s and the early part of the twenty-first century production of these chips has moved eastwards to India and China. However, an imbalance still exists and the current technological lead held by the West has led some to believe that new forms of colonialism are developing. Electronic colonialism and consumer colonialism have no national boundaries, are not controlled by national governments and answer only to the owner of the satellite and the producer of the broadcast images. The satellite owners and broadcasting companies have been quick to utilize the opportunities offered by globalization, but so too have manufacturers and advertisers. Global advertising growth has been phenomenal in the past two decades. As the United Nation's 1997 *Human Development Report* pointed out:

> In 1986 there were only three developing countries among the 20 biggest spenders in advertising. A decade later there were nine, and in spending relative to income Colombia ranks first with $1.4 billion, 2.6 per cent of its GDP.   (United Nations 1997)

In 2004 the global spend on advertising had grown to $370 billion, with the USA alone accounting for $169 billion spent on advertising (www.Brandweek.com) To give some idea of how much this is, in 2003 the GDP of Afghanistan was $20 billion, of Iraq $37 billion and of Sweden, a Western developed country, $238 billion. Advertising, then, is very big business.

The US soft drinks company Coca-Cola was the first to break into truly global advertising of its products. Jingles such as 'I'd Like to buy the World a Coke' (first broadcast in 1971) demonstrate how both product and culture are being packaged for a global audience. Advertising companies who promote Coca-Cola world-wide have done so through a process of 'globalization', adapting their global campaigns so that they do not affront the local sensibilities of particular local societies. TV adverts in the Philippines or Korea less frequently show smiling American kids on skateboards drinking Coke and more often Asian children in 'culturally specific settings' enjoying a Coke. In fact these ads are mostly written and produced in the USA using suitable-looking bilingual actors. Coca-Cola is now the most widely known (and used) consumer product in the world. Its advertising message is simple, its product immediately recognizable and its taste the same in every part of the world. Where Coca-Cola led others have followed. Products such as Kodak film, Levi jeans and McDonald's hamburgers have all become household names and household products across the globe.

Should we see such developments in a totally negative way, as unavoidable results of progress? Such pessimism ignores the essential diversity of human cultural practices that fight against such homogenizing influences. As Giddens (1990) acknowledges, while the process of globalization may indeed be driven by the accumulation needs of capitalism, its effects on people may be unintended and result in reactions not necessarily beneficial to capitalism. We must not expect the expansion of multi- and transnational corporations operating within the cultural field, such as Sony, EMI or Disney, simply to produce an unchallenged degree of global cultural uniformity. As Street (1997) points out, many transnational corporations are responsible for selling national or local culture back to their own localities, quite simply because this is what people demand. Thus such transnational corporations must be in tune with their markets and must not push a cultural uniformity which will be rejected at the national or local level. Indeed, as he further suggests, during much of the postwar period, international regulatory organizations such as the EU and UNESCO have acted to control cultural flows and, for the most part, restrain the power of multinational and transnational corporations. In France, Street believes the Ministry of Culture is a key player in political and cultural life, its central aim appearing to be to resist what it sees as the insidious forces of cultural globalization. As the 2004 HDR stated in relation to such attempts to resist the foreign cultural onslaught:

Under the cultural exception (*l'exception culturelle*) introduced during the Uruguay Round of trade negotiations and resolutely defended by the French government of the mid 1990s, the state promotes and pays for the production of Gallic culture, a successful example of public support for the culture industries.

The government subsidizes the production of televised versions of French fiction, a popular staple of public television. France imposes a 40 per cent minimum quota of French language radio transmissions. These measures have created opportunities for artists who might otherwise not have been able to crack the domestic market and have made France the largest film producers in Europe, effectively countering the competition from Hollywood.   (United Nations 2004: 99)

As we can see from this example, multinational corporations and certainly those belonging to Hollywood USA are prone to political control. For Featherstone (1991b), the development of a global culture may offer the prospect of unity through diversity in which the increased level of cultural contacts can draw people together in realization of their common aspirations.

There are other aspects of this process of global communication and the way the mass media can enact cultural change: it may also work in the opposite direction. If you scan the various satellite channels of any home today you will find a growing number of channels aimed at specific 'niche' markets, including the various ethnic minorities present in Britain. Many of these channels provide programming which originates in the former home country of these communities, allowing them to keep in touch and be informed and educated about what is going on there. For Lull (2000) this represents a process of 'transculturation' in which migrants often carry with them an identification with, and the active practising of, cultural norms and ways of life from the places they left behind. This perhaps best demonstrates that globalization isn't always a one-way street from the West to the rest of the world, but can allow for the creation of diversity and maintenance of distinct cultural identities separated from a real geographical location.

One of the most fundamental elements to change us from our very localized world to members of a global community has been that of the revolution in information technology. The dramatic growth of the World Wide Web in the last decade has profoundly altered many aspects of our lives and will perhaps be one of the defining factors of the future. The World Wide Web has the very real potential to empower, but is itself open to manipulation and control. In China, for instance, certain web sites, such as those relating to the 'Falun Gong', a movement which gained popularity and challenges the government on its human rights record, have been blocked. In Saudi Arabia many Western web sites, in particular those containing pornographic, or even semi-pornographic imagery, together with anti-Islamic web sites are blocked. We must also remember that there is an economic cost to access the web, the cost of the hardware and the telephone link which is still beyond the vast majority of the world's population.

The picture painted here appears to be one of certainty that my life and the lives of many in the affluent West and even the developing world have been changed through the process of globalization and that change has been an improvement: the abundance of choice and the growth of consumerism and communication. However, this is to accept a one-dimensional view of such change, seeing globalization as a positive. This approach would not be out of step with the ideas of leading politicians of our day.

In a major economic policy speech in San Fransciso on 26 February 1999 former President of the USA Bill Clinton said that:

Since 1945, global trade has grown 15-fold, raising living standards on every continent. Freedom is expanding: for the first time in history, more than half the world's people elect their own leaders. Access to information by ordinary people the world over is literally exploding.

Because of these developments, and the dramatic increase in our own prosperity and confidence in this, the longest peacetime economic expansion in our history, the United States has the opportunity and, I would argue, the solemn responsibility to shape a more peaceful, prosperous, democratic world in the twenty-first century.

We must embrace the inexorable logic of globalization – that everything from the strength of our economy to the safety of our cities, to the health of our

A closer look

One world or many?

The **First World** refers to affluent industrialized and developed societies. The USA, Britain, France, the Netherlands, Germany and others, such as Japan from the mid-1960s onwards, are examples of First World countries.

The term **Second World** was first applied to the communist or socialist societies of Eastern Europe, and later included Cuba and countries of communist Asia. Second World societies might be industrialized, as demonstrated by the former Soviet Union, former East Germany and Hungary. However, these nations had failed to reach the rates of social and economic development reflected in high levels of consumption and general affluence within the First World.

The term **Third World** has considerable symbolic meaning. It was first used by French sociologists and demographers and meant, quite simply, the third level of the world – 'le tiers monde'. In using such a term the classical sociological ideas of writers such as Spencer, Durkheim and even Marx, with their implication that there exists a natural gradient from poor to rich, undeveloped to developed, appears to be accepted. As an English-language concept Third World was first popularized within British sociology by Peter Worsley (1964). Worsley rejected the seemingly negative connotations associated with the concept 'Third World' adopted by the French in favour of a much more sympathetic emphasis, although even the idea of support and sympathy for the Third World could be construed as patronizing or insulting. For many French and British sociologists the world could indeed be divided

into three. In the strict academic sense employed by sociologists and economists, the concept 'Third World' means those societies that have yet to undergo industrial development, or those in the process of developing but still with some distance to go before they could be considered industrialized. Any nation outside the economic orbit or control of either the USA or, until the early 1990s, the former Soviet Union was seen to be a Third World nation, ranging from societies such as Brazil, which had large industrial sectors and pockets of affluence, to those nations that were utterly destitute with little if any economic growth.

Prior to the collapse of communism a new term was added – the **Fourth World**. This even more pejorative description makes a distinction between those Third World societies which have the potential to develop, such as many oil-rich societies, and those societies that appear destined to remain non-industrial and poverty-stricken: societies such as Bangladesh, Afghanistan and Ethiopia were all once regarded as Fourth World societies, simply because of their dire poverty.

Since the late 1980s with the collapse of communism the term 'Third World' is still used but it remains to be seen for how long. These societies can be regarded as 'super-poor'. As a concept 'super-poor' can be said to unite not just countries sharing common conditions, but disparate groups in several societies. Thus many women in Third World societies can be said to be 'super-poor'. Their lives are marked by economic inequality and second-class status in already deprived societies. In reality they suffer a dual burden of social stigma and social exculsion, simply because of their gender.

MAKEPOVERTYHISTORY

MAKEPOVERTYHISTORY is a campaign alliance consisting of organisations (especially charities), religious and political leaders, celebrities and members of the public aiming to put pressure on the political and economic leaders of the world to end conditions that they see as perpetuating poverty, particularly in Africa. Of particular importance to the campaign was to target the G8 – a meeting of leaders of the 8 wealthiest governments in

the world – summit in Gleneagles Scotland in July 2005. The campaign specifically called for an end to what is regarded as an unjust global trading system and a cancellation of third world debt. A large number of events and campaign initiatives coalesced around the summit, including the LIVE8 concert and a mass rally of 225,000 people in Edinburgh.

Go to the web address for MAKEPOVERTYHISTORY at: http://www.makepovertyhistory.org/ and answer the following quesions:

1. *How many children die every day as a result of extreme poverty?*

2. *What do MakePovertyHistory argue is the solution?*

3. *Why did they target the G8 summit?*

4. *The* Pressureworks *web site is 'about using the tools of popular culture . . . to wake up the world' Do you think that the LIVE8 concerts achieved this?*

people, depends on events not only within our borders, but half a world away. Globalization is irreversible.

Just two years later the new US President George Bush speaking during a National Radio address to the American people during a G8 Economic Summit on 21 July 2001 said that:

What some call globalization is in fact the triumph of human liberty stretching across national borders. And it holds the promise of delivering billions of the world's citizens from disease, hunger and want.

In Britain politicians such as Chancellor Gordon Brown, whilst less effusive of globalization, see it as both inevitable and necessary for British economic growth and prosperity.

Some critics say the issue is whether we should have globalization or not. In fact, the issue is whether we manage globalization well or badly, fairly or unfairly. And we have a choice. Globalization can be for the people or against the people. Just as in any national economy economic integration can bring stability or instability, prosperity or stagnation, the inclusion of people or their exclusion, so too in the global economy.

Managed badly, globalization would leave whole economies and millions of people in the developing world marginalized. Managed wisely, globalization can

and will lift millions out of poverty, and become the high road to a just and inclusive global economy.

(extract of speech by Gordon Brown Chancellor of the Exchequer to the Federal Reserve Bank, New York, in November 2001)

Stop and think

➤ Many of the terms and concepts (such as 'third world') used to describe poor and less affluent countries have pejorative overtones. How might such language condition our perceptions of non-Western societies?

➤ Think of the ways in which such societies are described by the media. Is the language used judgemental or neutral?

Globalization: something old, something new?

Is globalization something radically new and positively advantageous? Or has it always been with us? For globalization to occur there must be some concept of a planet united by links of trade, transport and communication. It is assumed that the real origins of globalization come with the various voyages of discovery that started toward the very end of the fifteenth century, and that, most importantly, these voyages were the products of adventurous European societies eager for conquest and commerce with the East. In essence this Eurocentric view tells us that globalization was a condition created and determined by the West towards the rest of the world. However, this can be challenged in any number of ways. In a recent book, *1421: The Year China Discovered the World*, Gavin Menzies, a former submariner in the Royal Navy, details the way in which in 1421 a vast Chinese fleet consisting of more than a hundred ocean-going 'Junks' and thousands of sailors were sent out by the Emperor Zhu Di 'as envoys to the barbarians'. Piecing together the evidence from a wide range of sources in China and as far afield as the Vatican Library, the University of Wisconsin Library, the National Archives of Portugal and archaeological evidence from the West Coast of the USA, Menzies puts forward compelling evidence that the Chinese had in the first three decades of the fifteenth century discovered Australia, charted the coastline of Antarctica, sailed up the Sacramento river in what is today California and established settlements on the eastern side of America around the area we know as New England. Why should this matter? We assume that discovery of the 'New World' came with Christopher Columbus in 1492, that Australia was discovered by Capitan Cook in 1770 for the British crown. Yet as Menzies notes:

> Columbus, da Gama, Magellan and Cook were to later make the same 'discoveries' (as the Chinese) but they all knew that they were following in the footsteps of others, for they were carrying copies of the Chinese maps with them when they set off on their own journeys into the 'unknown'. (Menzies 2002: 12)

The point here is not who discovered America or Australia first (or even if you can 'discover' something which is already inhabited), but how we see the process of global expansion as being a uniquely European phenomenon. It carries with it our prejudices and superiority towards other societies and as such fails to understand both the historical and contemporary dynamics of the process itself. In commanding his navy to 'seek out and humble the barbarian' Zhu Di was simply following a logic that dictated an expansion in communication and trade. Indeed, the so called European voyages discovery outlined above also followed the same imperative of communication and trade. The very nature of humanity might be seen in the desire to communicate, dominate or trade which has existed since the dawn of the earliest civilizations

in Mesopotamia, Greece, Egypt and Rome. Each of these ancient empires existed in their own globalized world, with networks of domination, trade communication and commerce between geographically separated societies. To be sure many of these civilizations existed as military empires, but it does not deny their scope or their achievements. Since the earliest days of human civilization there have been networks of trade and commerce that have spanned the world, in effect a form of globalization that has existed for millennia. The travels of Marco Polo in the thirteenth century were predicated on the basis of finding viable trade routes to Cathay and the spice-producing areas of the East, his travels determined by consumer demand in early renaissance Europe.

Yet many scholars of globalization see it as a uniquely modern phenomenon, a product of either the expansion of the British empire in the late eighteenth and nineteenth centuries, as defined by Niall Ferguson (2004), or the post-war era, the period in which the USA's development as a superpower occurred at the same time as globalization started to take off.

Sociological theories of development

Modernization theory

Walt Whitman Rostow (1960), a US economist and historian, is the leading exponent of modernization theory, a theory of development which he described as a non-communist manifesto. The key to modernization theory is the idea that all modern capitalist societies, such as the USA, have a system of cultural values that makes them advanced. The cultural values of capitalism are held to be those of openness, democracy, innovation, individualism and achievement. The cultural values of primitive and agrarian societies are held to be those of control, anti-individualism, anti-democracy and anti-achievement. Needless to say the long boom following the end of the Second World War allowed the growth in global economic dominance of the USA; everything from baked beans to disco was shaped by the USA.

Rostow believed that while some communist countries had engaged in the process of development, even modernization, their cultural values in essence prevented them reaching the final fifth stage; ultimately they would have to develop the cultural values of capitalism or slip back to an earlier and less-developed stage. Moreover, Rostow believed that it was possible for Third World societies to

A closer look

Rostow's five stages of development

1 The traditional society

The most basic form of all societies, this does little more than economically survive, shrouded in mysticism, pre-scientific, with rigid social hierarchies and a weak division of labour.

2 The preconditions for take-off

In this form of society the division of labour increases as population increases, freeing up social organization, in turn allowing for the growth in knowledge, innovation and specialization. Very important to this stage are revolutionary developments taking place in agriculture that allow the growing urban population to be fed without the usual cycle of famine.

3 The take-off

In this society manufacturing industry has started to emerge and a complex division of labour exists, dependent upon an increasingly complex system of economic organization and distribution.

4 The drive to maturity

For Rostow, this is a crucial period in which the forces for modernization are allowed to develop, or else society would slip back into a state of economic decline and rigidity. In this period a society defines the economic direction it will take.

5 The age of high mass consumption

At this point in the economic evolution of a society, affluence has become widespread. The division of labour is now at a highly refined level in which the full potential of the population is utilized, providing both high economic rewards and levels of satisfaction for workers. Equally, it is a society, in which the emphasis is now placed upon consumption of goods and services, including social welfare.

(Adapted from Rostow 1960)

goods and services produced in the developed world. As the developed world moved to service-based industry, a new world economic division of labour would emerge, with industrializing and developing societies providing many of the simple manufactured goods it required.

For Rostow and other modernization theorists it was important that developing societies overcome the obstacles to modernization that exist within their own society. They must rid themselves of outdated structures, institutions and practices; they must accept the value systems employed in successful Western capitalist societies. Modernization theorists such as McClelland (1961) have suggested that the process of change would come not only through diffusion of capitalist values to these societies but also through trade, cultural exchange and commerce. Modernization theory argues that the more rational and clearly better practices and forms of organization employed in the West will gradually filter through into these societies.

Clearly modernization theory has within it a highly *ethnocentric* vision of the world: capitalism is seen as 'good' and socialism 'bad'. Such a view should not surprise us, for the ideological climate of the USA in the 1950s was one of fundamental opposition to all things communist; this was the decade of the 'McCarthy witch-hunts'. US society was effectively engaged in a struggle with the Soviet Union and communist bloc for economic, political and military world domination.

Linked to this theoretical perspective is that of Convergence Theory. This idea of convergence rests firmly upon the Weberian notion of 'rationalization'. This whole approach sees little to differentiate capitalist and communist (or rather 'state capitalist societies' such as West and East Germany). However, where modernization theory can be seen as an anti-communist polemic by Rostow, convergence theory is more neutral. It was developed by sociologists such as Daniel Bell (1988) with his thesis on the 'End of Ideology' and Clark Kerr (Kerr *et al.* 1962) who in his book *Industrialism and Industrial Man* claimed that: 'The same technology calls for the same occupational structure around the world, in steel, textiles and transport' (1962: 84). This theoretical perspective appears to be far more neutral in its approach to the whole process of change than is modernization theory. Societal differentiation, specialization and integration follow in its wake; secularization, rationalism and individualization all become hallmarks of industrial society, be they capitalist or communist. Thus for both modernization theorists and convergence theorists an inescapable logic demanded a linear path to modernity and progress.

develop and become capitalist in much the same way as the USA. As the Third World societies became capitalist and advanced, the USA, Britain, France, Germany and other developed nations would derive benefits from this process of modernization. The expansion in industry in the Third World would produce new markets for the

As with much sociological theorizing, modernization theory was a specific product of its place and time. It appeared to represent the ideological triumph of the advance of Western economies, in particular the growing economic power of the USA. In the 1960s this domination both in the wider economic world and at the level of sociological analysis began to be challenged. The challenge appeared to emerge on two levels: economically and ideologically. At the economic level US dominance started to be challenged by new international competitors. The rise of Japan in the postwar period (itself dependent on massive US aid in an effort to create a stable Western-style democracy) produced a society in which economic enterprise flourished. In Europe, West Germany (with similar US aid) had become a significant economic force by the 1960s. These alternative centres of economic growth provided a measure of counterbalance to the American economic hegemony. However, at an ideological level, some developing societies rejected capitalist materialism in favour of a state socialist option as the mechanism for development: countries such as Cuba, Vietnam and some African countries provided illustrations of the rejection of American dominance.

Underdevelopment theory

In many ways these approaches to the concept of globalization have elements of the theories first developed by André Gunder Frank. Frank, writing from a distinctly left-wing ideological position, sought to challenge the central orthodoxy of modernization theory (Frank 1967). For Frank, Rostow's theory of modernization (as noted above) simply provided academic smog behind which a process of domination and exploitation, as rigid and destructive as that which occurred in the nineteenth century under imperial and colonial expansion, was justified. Moreover, the idea that by adopting the necessary cultural values Third World societies may themselves become modern was anathema to Frank.

While he accepted that the rich West could be regarded as developed, and that most other societies must be seen as underdeveloped, these conditions did not exist in isolation from each other, but rather were fundamentally joined. The developed, and modern, condition of a small number of Western societies was in effect dependent upon the deliberate underdevelopment of the majority of other societies. Quite simply, for there to be rich nations, poor nations had to be kept poor. For Frank this was a contemporary process as well as being a historical fact.

Modern capitalist societies could have become so only through their exploitation of other societies in the past. Frank stated that historically capitalism created a chain of exploitation that reached from the centre, or what he terms the 'metropolis', the capitalist West, to the edge, or 'periphery'. The peasant farmer of the Third World and the capitalist manufacturer of the West existed under one mode of production: the capitalist mode.

According to Frank, capitalism has polarized the world into what he terms the central metropolis and the peripheral satellites. Satellite societies channel what they produce to the centre, but even within these satellites there are centres which are fed into by the outlying satellites' areas. Thus there is a gigantic chain of capitalist exploitation linking individuals at both the centre and the periphery: impoverished peasant producer and affluent Western consumer. At each stage those above will exercise economic power and control over those below. As power increases closer to the centre, the centre is able to use the surplus it extracts from the periphery for its own ends.

In Frank's model there is a process of the 'development of underdevelopment' which is deeply rooted in the sands of history.

Stop and think

> Take an everyday food item such as tea, coffee or sugar and trace the steps from the original agricultural production to the processing and manufacture of this item, to its distribution and sale, and ultimately to your table. Where was the item originally grown/produced?

> Who produced it?

> What was its cost in its raw form?

> Where was it exported from?

> Which companies were involved in its processing and packaging?

> What is the cost of the item to you the consumer?

> Does this help us to understand what Frank had in mind?

> By tracing the steps from the periphery to the centre can you see any underlying weaknesses in Frank's model?

For Frank the obstacles to development by societies on the periphery are numerous, both external and internal. Externally, the centre will not allow the development of the periphery, because this will in turn reduce the level of

A closer look

Frank's underdevelopment theory

Capitalist world metropolis

The cities of London or New York are examples of the very heart of the capitalist world system to which the maximum surplus or profit is drawn, supporting fabulous wealth and affluence for those at the very centre.

These are cities in the Third World from which products (often raw materials such as coffee, tea or copper) are exported. São Paulo in Brazil, Lagos in Nigeria and Chittagong in Bangladesh are examples, with pockets of vast wealth and affluence existing alongside deprivation and misery for the masses.

Regional centres

Here goods, mostly in the form of raw materials, are brought and traded. It is often in these centres that the multinational companies purchase goods and natural resources used in manufacturing.

Large landowners/merchants

These act as middlemen between the producer and the regional centres. Often large landowners will rent out their land to peasant producers at high prices, inducing crippling debt for the peasants that can be paid off only through even harder work, and sale of the items to the landowner/merchant.

Small peasants/tenants

Those who either own or rent the land on which they work producing goods that are sold to the merchants, but managing to retain only a very small fraction of the real values of what they produce.

Landless labourers

In some cases local landowners or even multinational corporations such as the North American giant United Fruit will employ workers to work their land. In this way the relationship of the worker is simply one of wage slave with no control whatsoever over what is produced.

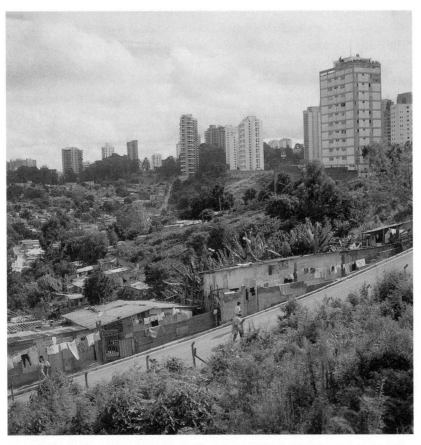

Figure 11.2 São Paulo, Brazil, where wealth and affluence exist alongside deprivation
(Photograph © David Lomax, courtesy of Robert Harding Picture Library Ltd)

exploitation and surplus that is extracted by the centre. So, for example, if mass consumer goods such as cars are produced at the periphery this will add unwelcome competition to the same industries at the centre. It is only when the capitalist industrial centre switches its production to other goods and services that it will allow production of the old goods to take place at the periphery.

In Brazil and Mexico, for example, Frank accepts that car manufacturing has been allowed to develop. However, these facilities mostly produce models that are outdated, for example VW Beetles in Mexico. The Beetle is a very popular car in Mexico, frequently used as a taxi cab, and VW has also found a small niche market in the USA by exporting to enthusiasts. The same may be true, Frank argues, for commodities such as coffee, tea and sugar. If coffee was processed and packaged in the countries in which it was grown much of the profit from the 'value-adding processes' of such processing and packaging would be lost to the company selling the coffee to the supermarkets of the capitalist world metropolis.

Processed goods are often re-exported back to the country where they originated in their raw form. Most of the instant coffee drunk in Brazil, for example, is provided by one of two large multinational companies, Nestlé, based in Switzerland, which produces Nescafé, and United Foods, the US manufacturer of Maxwell House coffee. As shown above, the Action Aid Report indicates that a number of companies dominate world food production and act in ways harmful to producers in the developing world. At the periphery it is often the agents or employees of these large multinationals (the export managers, shipping agents and government officials) who form the base of the consumer market for Western goods, often living lifestyles very similar to those of their counterparts at the centre. The West employs structures and systematic policies that prevent development taking place in the periphery. The refusal to export technology such as machine tools, computers and processing equipment is an example of this. Such external formal barriers are not the only tools employed by the West; others include protective tariff barriers to prevent goods produced at the periphery undercutting those produced at the centre.

Many Western companies will actively create at the periphery structures which have a vested interest in maintaining the chain of exploitation. Internally, groups exist which depend upon their link with the centre – local landowners, politicians and the military, for example. According to Frank they will often form an alliance with the centre to prevent opposition developing. Indeed, the unflattering term 'banana republic', meant to signify a

backward and corrupt society, was originally coined to explain the control exercised by US fruit companies, such as United Fruit, over Latin American countries. Countries like El Salvador and Nicaragua were under the control of local oligarchies or families, who were paid employees of such US companies. So the term 'banana republic' is more an index of exploitation and control than a description of a corrupt and primitive country.

As an alternative explanation to both modernization theory and more recent ideas of globalization, underdevelopment theory believes that the only real way forward to economic growth and prosperity for the majority would involve breaking the chains that link the periphery to the centre. In the past some attempts have been made to do this; thus the nationalization of the Suez Canal in 1956 by the radical Arab nationalist leader Gamal Abdel Nasser, president of Egypt, led to an invasion by the combined forces of Britain, Israel and France. For Frank, such independent action by small countries should be avoided in favour of a more co-operative and unified approach between exploited nations. This could be done through the formation of *cartels* such as the Organization of Petroleum Exporting Countries (OPEC). Indeed, OPEC is an example of how societies previously exploited by the West can gradually gain a position in which they are able to use their natural resources against the developed world. In 1973 OPEC trebled the price of oil overnight, forcing countries like the USA, Britain and Japan into economic recession. The effects of the oil crisis are still with us in the 1990s, symbolized by the growth of nuclear power, the exploration and development of North Sea oil reserves and moves towards ever-increasing levels of fuel efficiency in cars, in an attempt to move away from externally produced forms of energy to a position of near self-reliance.

During the 1970s OPEC was very successful both economically and politically: countries such as Saudi Arabia, Iran and even Nigeria provided an example of how change might be accomplished. However, it can be argued that OPEC was a victim of its own success: in forcing the West to acknowledge its dependence on oil, many Western capitalist societies sought to reduce such dependence, which in turn lowered world demand for oil and weakened OPEC. Thus the strategy of cartel development does not appear to offer the success of economic independence envisaged by Frank. Additionally, while the West became less reliant upon oil as its major source of energy, efficiency measures and substitution (i.e. the development of North Sea oil and nuclear power in Britain), many Third World countries felt the full effect of the oil price rise.

In this way, the action of OPEC in 1973 and 1980 hit the poorest nations harder than the richest.

Another and perhaps far more direct strategy for development was through social revolution and a move towards independent development via *socialism*. Socialism, Frank assumed, would rid peripheral societies of the massive internal inequalities that existed. Cuba in the late 1950s and early 1960s was an example of the Frankian message in practice – social revolution leading to a new and more equal social structure. Cuba's revolutionary leader Fidel Castro pledged to Cuban citizens that Cuba would no longer be a puppet of US imperialism and multi-national corporation control. The revolution in Cuba enjoyed widespread popular support and, even today, in the face of continued US hostility, a significant degree of support for the Castro regime remains. Yet in reality the revolution in Cuba depended to a large degree on the economic and military support provided by the Soviet Union. With the increasing economic strains faced by the Soviet Union in the mid-1980s, leading to its eventual collapse in 1990, the level of economic support and subsidies to peripheral socialist states vanished. Since the 1960s the USA has maintained an economic blockade against Cuba that has prevented Cuba exploiting its own natural resources and full economic potential. Living standards in Cuba have continually dropped; discontent and counter-revolutions have been prevented only by an exodus of people to the USA. At first this exodus was gradual and orderly but during the summer of 1994 economic conditions in Cuba deteriorated so badly that an estimated 1,200 people per day were leaving. Many of these individuals took to the high seas on rafts made of little more than inner tubes and wood. The US Coast Guard estimated that of the 1,200 leaving per day, only 800 were picked up or made it to the USA: the human cost of the economic blockade has been very high.

Despite the communists winning a long and bitter war of national independence, first against the French, then against the USA, Vietnam has suffered a similar economic blockade to that imposed on Cuba. For the most part, the USA says that it will lift its blockade only if the communist government in Vietnam accept policies of economic liberalization and moves towards 'democratization'. In Vietnam at least, economic collapse has been avoided only by policies of economic liberalization and the development of capitalist markets.

A development in Vietnam, which is being followed in African countries such as Malawi and Zambia, is that of eco-tourism. In the early 1990s under the communist government's policy of economic liberalization, large tracts of land were given over to the formation of national parks. Much of the money to finance such schemes came from the United Nations or the World Bank. However, this has forced the indigenous population to move out for Western-style tourist hotels to move in.

Stop and think

> What do you understand by the term eco-tourism?
> What might be the dangers of implementing such a policy?

World system theory

Writing a few years after Frank, Immanuel Wallerstein (1979) sought to enhance the idea implicit within Frank's work that a world system existed which was based upon the Marxian idea of the 'capitalist mode of production'. Central to Wallerstein's model was the concept of the 'social system'. The history of the world, he argued, could in effect be seen not as the development of distinct nation-states that are exploited by other nation-states, as in Frank's model, but rather as the evolution of quite distinct social systems. Essentially these social systems resemble Marx's modes of production, although in Wallerstein's model there are three modes of production, rather than Marx's five.

Wallerstein argued that it may be possible for some peripheral societies to move to the semi-periphery, while other semi-peripheral societies are forced to the periphery by changes in the world economic conditions and, importantly, by decisions made at the capitalist core. This world system came into existence at about the same time as the colonization of the New World and the European agricultural revolution. Over the following centuries this system became ever more refined and complex. As with Frank, for Wallerstein control of this system lies at the core, with those nations that are economically and politically able to control the periphery. These nations are basically the technologically advanced West, including nations such as Japan, and they are able to use the powers they have to maintain their position of dominance and control over the periphery. In turn the periphery is economically reliant upon the centre. Under the world economic system the same basic economic principles, those of capitalism, apply everywhere; however, at the same time a significant degree of political heterogeneity is allowed among those nation-states encompassed within it. Under this system the political structure and freedom enjoyed within any society is limited by the economic control exercised by the global economic system. In this model clearly there appears to be a return to the Marxist orthodoxy of 'economic determinism' in which non-material factors play no part: the economy is the motor of social change.

It may be possible to apply some of Wallerstein's ideas to Britain. It is often said by commentators on the political left that Britain is ultimately under the control of the world monetary system, most effectively through organizations such as the International Monetary Fund (IMF), and even through economic speculators, who can influence, if not dictate, social and economic policy for Britain. Thus the economic power of, say US or Japanese bankers can force the pace of social and political change in any society, including Britain. An example of a British government being forced to adopt economic policies not of its own choosing came on 16 September 1992 when currency speculators, and in particular one man, George Soros, 'broke the pound' (*Guardian* 4.12.1992) and forced a withdrawal of the British currency from the European Monetary System. This compelled the Conservative government to adopt economic and political policies which it had previously rejected. The period between 24 August 1992, when share values fell by £10 billion, and December 1992 illustrates the volatility of financial capitalism and global financial markets.

Wallerstein's model may help to explain the significant level of exploitation that takes place in many Third World countries by reference to their place in the wider international division of labour. It possibly allows us to understand the way political structure and internal mechanisms of control may vary from nation to nation but are ultimately subordinated to the global capitalist economies. In many ways, Wallerstein's model is a highly pessimistic analysis of the global economic system, arguing that control is removed from democratically elected governments and placed in the hands of the impersonal forces of capitalism. Such a position (as we shall see) is not without its critics.

Articulation of modes of production

One of the key elements stressed by both Frank and Wallerstein was that the world was now encompassed by the capitalist system. For Frank, even the poor peasant

farmer living in Chile, growing coffee beans for sale to the developed world, was part of a system of capitalist exploitation. In effect, he argued, there was now only one mode of production, capitalism, a system that was rigid and unbending in applying the same economic logic throughout the globe. Wallerstein's world system theory introduced a degree of flexibility that went beyond Frank's original ideas: different political systems were allowed to operate, but one overarching and all-powerful economic system remained in control – capitalism. In Wallerstein's model, political and social policies may be adopted in one country as long as they do not impinge on the operation of the world capitalist system itself.

Writers such as Ernesto Laclau (1977), following on from the pioneering work of French anthropologists such as Rey (1976), felt this argument was both inaccurate and misleading. Laclau challenged the idea of a distinct capitalist core and periphery. He believed that while capitalism may exist in the centre, at the periphery different modes of production existed. For Laclau the simple test of whether capitalism existed at the periphery was to ask what relations of production existed there. For Laclau it was impossible to regard the relationship of the peasant farmer, who decides what to produce and when to produce it, to the landowner as equivalent to the relationship that existed between a worker on a production line and the owner of that factory at the developed capitalist core. In each of these modes of production there are specific social and economic relations of production. Although these may result in both the production line worker and peasant being at the bottom of the economic ladder, to say they are both on the same ladder is, for Laclau, totally misleading. The relationship to the ownership of the means of production, be it the land or the factory, is quite different in each case. In essence Laclau challenges Frank's argument (and to a considerable degree Wallerstein's) in suggesting that the relations of production that exist at the periphery are not, and need not be, capitalist for the process of exploitation to take place. Laclau argued that capitalism would use different modes of production for its own ends; it did not need to expand its own direct economic control and its form of economic relationship directly to the periphery in the way that Frank assumed it must. Moreover, the way that capitalism used different modes of production at the periphery was very sophisticated and far more complex than allowed for in either the Frankian model or in Wallerstein's world system model.

A good example of how the process of articulation works is provided by an examination of *labour migration*

A closer look

Laclau's notion of the process of 'articulation'

This is a concept first developed by Laclau in his critique of dependency theory. In dependency theory Frank and Wallerstein both made the assumption that only one global mode of production existed – capitalism. For Laclau, it was possible to have several modes of production operating at the same time across the globe. A mode of production, in classical Marxist terms, is an integrated system that links together complex economic, productive and social forces. In capitalism the mode of production involves specific economic, social and productive relationships between worker and owner of the means of production which signifies that they are in opposition to each other. Under feudalism these relationships will vary. Thus it is possible for non-capitalist modes of production to exist apart from, but be used and articulated by, capitalism without becoming capitalist. In this way it is in the interests of capitalism to preserve the feudal mode of production if this serves capitalism or at least does not act in opposition to it. Thus Laclau's focus on Latin America allowed him to describe the mode of production that existed there as semi-feudal. Capitalism simply accentuates and consolidates such exploitation for its own ends.

Laclau accepts that there is a real division between the capitalist centre and the underdeveloped periphery, and that peripheral countries perform vital services and roles that allow the affluence of the developed world to be sustained and even expanded. In essence a key function performed by the periphery is the provision of an indirect wage for the developed world. In the developed world workers are not only paid a wage by their employer but also receive certain indirect amounts of income in the form of welfare services such as education, hospitals and social security payments, the so-called indirect wage. This indirect wage is paid by the state to the workers and their dependants. For the most part these indirect wages fulfil a number of functions, ensuring that workers are educated to a high enough level to enable them to take their place in the process of production and that the workforce is fit and healthy. It can also function to buy off potential discontent by higher living standards. Thus the social security net that exists in many Western capitalist societies, and which provides the indirect wage, to a certain degree prevents the immiseration of the workforce and the potential for working-class discontent and revolution. (The term *immiseration* was coined by Marx and is the process by which the poor become poorer.)

(LM), where workers are drawn into the centre, that is the heart of capitalism, to perform the menial unskilled and low-paid jobs that the capitalist system is built upon, and which, at least during times of economic boom, Western workers are reluctant to take. They are paid a wage by their employer, but this is often very low by Western standards. While they perform a vital function in the labour process of capitalist economies they are not provided with any substantive form of indirect wage. Examples of the type of employment that such migrant workers perform is work in the service sector – catering, cleaning, household domestic work, transportation and textiles. However, the capitalist economic cycle necessarily includes both booms and slumps; as demand fluctuates within capitalism the migrant workers are the first to be laid off (and often sent home, away from the centre) during periods of economic recession. As they have no citizenship rights, and may often be deprived of even basic civil rights in their host country, it is relatively easy to dispense with their services at short notice and with very little fuss. Forced to return to their own country, they are paid no social welfare benefits or wages by the capitalist centre and must either depend upon their savings or eke out an income through the existing economic structure (e.g. subsistence farmers hawking goods in large cities). When the capitalist centre or core returns to a phase of economic boom, these displaced workers are drawn back into the capitalist economy. In this way the real costs of the worker are not met by capitalist employer or the society at the centre, but rather from the pre-capitalist, or articulated, mode of production.

In Laclau's (1977) model of articulated modes of production, capitalist economies are given a level of flexibility which allows them to sustain high living standards at the cost of continuing poverty and deprivation in the Third World. Any attempt at development by Third World nations is prevented by the economic control of the capitalist centre, when developed societies operate policies of import substitution, or play one society off against another, restricting economic development. The only way that non-capitalist societies might develop would be by a radical change in the world system that actively encouraged far greater equality between nations. This would require sacrifices on the part of the rich societies that they appear to be unwilling to make.

While the articulation of modes of production model is a useful analytical tool that seems to explain a number of different situations, it does have its own inherent difficulties. It fails to recognize significant differences between peripheral countries. There is a tendency in Laclau's work

Case study

Guest workers

The guest-worker system used in many European countries, particularly Germany and Switzerland, illustrates articulation in operation. A more widespread and disagreeable form of LM is found in South Africa and many southern states of the USA. Under the now abolished 'pass laws' of the previous apartheid regime in South Africa, it was illegal for most black workers to live in 'white areas'. Yet some white employers required their domestic servants to be available 24 hours a day, if required. Even those black workers excluded from the pass laws and legally resident in white homes were often provided with only very basic accommodation, living away from their families, whom they would only see on their days off. In post-apartheid South Africa illegal migration from surrounding countries, such as 'super-poor' Mozambique, has helped to fuel the nationalist reaction on the part of black South Africans. Such migrations of large numbers of workers serve to depress already low wages, further aiding black unemployment and anger, which the current post-apartheid ANC-led government is finding difficult to control.

In the USA many 'illegal aliens' from Mexico and Central America are employed in fruit harvesting or as domestic servants, low-paid workers undertaking very menial jobs. Their illegal status excludes them from any of the civil, political or social rights enjoyed by citizens. In 1995 in California the position of such labour migrants was made even more insecure by the passing of Proposition 187. This was a California law removing the right to welfare, education and medical treatment to the children of illegal immigrants. This change to the law has been viewed by many other southern US states as one possible way of reducing their welfare expenditure. As with the European guest-worker system, it is increasingly easy to dispense with such workers when required if they have few if any civil, political or welfare rights.

Questions

1. *What are the pressures that brought about the 'guest worker system'?*

2. *What sort of pressures might lead to its decline?*

to see the world as divided between the capitalist mode of production and the articulated non-capitalist mode of production. The former comprise a small number of Western societies, while the latter are the majority of the world's nations. In reality, its critics argue, there is as wide a level of variation between peripheral societies as between core and peripheral societies. At the periphery there are societies quite different from each other in terms of economic, political and social structures.

There is evidence that non-capitalist or pre-capitalist societies can take their own path to capitalist development, for example Japan during the post-war period. With the help of US capital, Japan transformed itself from a semi-feudal and rigidly controlled society into a modern and vibrant capitalist economy. Indeed, so strong is the Japanese economy and industry that both North America and Europe have called for some form of restrictions on Japanese exports lest their own industries collapse under the weight of competition. Japan's example is in turn being followed by many of the so-called 'tiger economies' or NICs (newly industrialized countries) of South-East Asia. The fact that some societies are able to transform themselves into modern, advanced capitalist economies suggests that the rigid division of the globe into capitalist and non-capitalist modes of production is both misleading and inaccurate.

Modernization theory, convergence theory, Frank's development of underdevelopment model, world systems theory and the idea of 'articulated modes of production', as developed by Laclau, were attempts at understanding what we now increasingly regard as globalization. As such they are historically located in a period in which two dominant economic, ideological and political systems went head to head: capitalism and communism.

As noted above some writers such as Ferguson sees the process of globalization as developing in its modern form in the nineteenth century. For some writers the most important period of globalization is historically much closer to home and signalled by the collapse of the Berlin Wall in 1989 and the worldwide collapse of communism. This appeared to herald the final victory of capitalism over the only alternative economic system in place since the end of the Second World War. This is the point at which the process of globalization becomes, for these writers at least, embedded as the dominant world economic, political and social trend It led the Harvard historian Fukuyama (1989) to publish an article entitled 'The End of History?' In this article, which was widely discussed in the corridors of power in Washington, Bonn, London and Tokyo, Fukuyama proposed that the economic and ideological struggle between communism and capitalism had now been won by capitalism. Free trade and the growth in political democracy fashioned in the mould of America all appeared to indicate the inescapable facts; only one economic system existed, capitalism, and Western-style (read US-style) democracy was the only way in which freedom, happiness and economic prosperity could be achieved for the majority of the world's population. Indeed, this view is clearly epitomized in the words of the politicians quoted above. However, there is a dualism to the idea of globalization, an alternative perspective in which the flip side of economic expansion, Western style democratic institutions, a Hollywood style culture and western consumption patterns all see their antithesis.

Globalization as a contested concept

As a concept the term 'globalization' has been in popular use since the early 1960s, partly due to the technological revolution that occurred as a result of the space race between the USA and the former USSR. From the military competition between these two superpowers a revolution in communications technology occurred with the launch of satellites to carry sound and video across the globe. These satellite communication, changes in telecommunications, computing and information technologies at this time led to the emergence of what Marshall McLuhan (1962) termed the 'global village', giving the concept of globalization its first real academic currency.

However, sociologically, the idea of globalization has a much older history than the sixties space race. The origins of the term *globalization* can be found within classical Marxist sociology. Marx referred to capitalism as a global process, while Lenin in his study of imperialism saw the globalization of capitalism as dependent upon the expansion of imperialism by societies such as Britain and Germany. But what does the term 'globalization' mean?

Is globalization a process, a condition or an outcome? Due to its widespread use, it is important that sociology defines and understand what globalization stands for. Held and McGew (2003) argue that:

> Globalization, simply put, denotes the expanding scale, growing magnitude, speeding up and deepening impact of transcontinental flows and patterns of social interaction. It refers to a shift or transformation in the scale of human organization that links distant communities and expands the reach and power relations across the world's regions and continents.
>
> (Held and McGew 2003:)

In similar vein, Cohen and Kennedy (2000) adopt the definition developed by Albrow (1990) that 'globalization refers to all those processes by which the peoples of the world are incorporated into a single, global society'. However, they recognize that globalization is an ongoing project, bringing ever increasing levels of change. These changes are long in the making and impact on different locations, countries and individuals in a highly uneven manner. Such changes have nevertheless increased in scope and intensity and, for Cohen and Kennedy, have occurred at an accelerating rate in the last decades of the twentieth century. Moreover, these transformations need to be understood as mutually reinforcing and as occurring more or less simultaneously.

The views articulated by Cohen and Kennedy indicate a need in sociology for some sort of sociology of 'one world', something Giddens (1990) also appears to be arguing for in his suggestion that globalization reflects 'a growing interdependency of world society'. The changes implied by this view of globalization are quite profound, suggesting the creation of a world society in which the image of nation-state and national identity may give way to worldwide social interaction (we will return to this idea further on). There are however those who challenge the concept of globalization itself. Hirst and Thompson (1999) are critical of the breadth and depth of globalization in the late twentieth or early twenty-first centuries, seeing this process less as one of globalization and more of Westernization. In this context Hirst and Thompson are arguing from a similar left-wing position as Frank cited above. However, unlike Frank, for Hirst and Thompson globalization is in essence an ideological smokescreen behind which Western liberal governments can preach mutually beneficial free-trade while exercising even greater degrees of economic control and dominance via their hold over investment capital. This critique of globalization may be seen itself as an extension of the previous Marxist analysis of monopoly capitalism. Moreover, for writers such as Weiss (1998) globalization existed at a far greater level and with far fewer impediments in the nineteenth century than it faces in the twentieth and twenty-first centuries. Indeed for Weiss globalization may even be in retreat. In all of these models there is less economic openness and freedom between trading blocs than is alleged by the term globalization: the power of the multinational corporation, protected as it is by both national governments and supranational authorities such as the European Union, is more powerful in dictating the rules of the game (free trade) than at any other time in the past.

This view of globalization accords well with the writings of Rosenau (1990) who sees it as more than a process of merely the shifting of power between nation-states but rather involving a radical change to the very idea of the nation-state itself. Rosenau argues that the intense pace of change exhibited by the forces of globalization makes the idea that nation-states can exercise power independently very uncertain. He believes that as capitalism becomes truly global the very idea of the nation-state, with its fixed boundaries and fixed structure, must be challenged. For Rosenau the main imperative of globalization has been the process of technological development brought about by capitalism.

Stop and think

Look around your home or college and list any consumer electronic items.

➤ Do the product names sound high-tech or Asian?

➤ Where were these goods made?

➤ How much do they cost?

➤ Find out if the cost has dropped or risen since it was purchased.

What distinguishes capitalism from other economic and social systems is its flexibility, versatility and, for Rosenau at least, its central use of technological innovation in pushing cultural, ideological and economic barriers back. Clearly then for some writers, such as Fukuyama, the process of the 'globalization' of the world economy is synonymous with the triumph of capitalism and it is assumed that Western societies play a leading, if not key, role in this process. What marks this process of globalization off from the expansion of 'capitalism' in the past is the way in which the previous division between the 'developed' (north) and the 'underdeveloped' (south)

is no longer applicable. For Sklair (1991), globalization acts at three levels – economic, political and cultural–ideological. Transnational corporations (TNCs) such as Shell Oil and the North American telephone company AT&T operate at not only a global economic level but also global political. Their desire to accumulate profits through the development of new oil fields or markets for telecommunications have had significant impacts on nations with oil within their territory, or without developed systems of communication. Companies such as Shell and AT&T are virtually able to dictate the terms under which they will exploit such oil reserves or install telecommunications systems and for the most part they are able to extract agreements that reinforce their position of global importance. The question of relations between TNCs and Third World governments was graphically illustrated by the controversy surrounding Shell's activities in Ogoniland in south-east Nigeria following the execution of Ken Saro-Wiwa and eight other environmental activists in November 1995.

In the modern global world, knowledge, finance, manufacturing and even crime know no national boundaries. Just as capital or manufacturing can flow easily from one country to another, so too can global tides such as drugs and the associated criminality flow from one part of the world to the next. Moreover, to fight such tides of worldwide criminality, global policing is now emerging. In July 1994 the United States Federal Bureau of Investigation (FBI) opened an office in Moscow with the aim of exchanging information with its Russian counterpart, and to gather intelligence information which might be useful to other organizations such as Interpol, but perhaps more importantly to attempt to stay one step ahead of organized crime operating at transnational and even global level.

With the internationalization of capitalist production, social relations have become international rather than simply national. As an example of this the British computer company ICL has subcontracted its software design to a company in Pune, India. Here qualified software designers are paid the equivalent of about £3,000 per year, ten times less than an equivalent worker in Britain would earn. UK customers of ICL software are put through to the Pune engineers when they make telephone enquiries in Britain.

As noted above, one of the most important implications of the process of globalization is the potential weakening of national autonomy and the further strengthening of supranational bodies such as the EU, OECD, IMF, G8 and WTO. Paul Kennedy (1993) argues that all governments are losing their control over the nation-state, a process aided by the ever growing concentration of economic power in the hands of TNCs, political control in the hands of supranational organizations such as the EU, WTO or G8 and cultural independence through the impact of technology in the form of satellite communications and media. Susan Strange (1996) offers further support to this analysis by indicating that actions are taking place in which control shifts from weak states to powerful states, from independent states to markets and from labour markets to financial markets and the control exercised by multinational capital. However, evidence to support the shift in power to such supranational organizations is far from conclusive. Writers such as D. Gordon (1988) argue that decisions made at the level of the nation-state still maintain an impact at the level of operation of international capital. This can perhaps be illustrated by the strategy of the British government during the 1980s and 1990s to attract inward investment into the UK in the face of attempts by other European Union countries to do the same. The British government utilized a number of devices, including tax concessions, financial inducements and infrastructure projects, to attract several Japanese car companies such as Honda (Swindon), Nissan (Sunderland), Toyota (North Wales) and BMW

World in focus

Workers without boundaries: outsourcing and the new flow of jobs from the developed world

Of central concern in recent years in Britain has been the process of outsourcing, that is to say the movement of production, and quite recently service sector provision to developing parts of the world. In the past central to the process of globalization was the movement of industrial production, most usually environmentally polluting, with low wages and labour intensive to the Third World. The process of globalization in this context allowed an international division of labour to take place in which high paid, knowledge intensive and highly skilled jobs remained in the developed West, while other jobs moved to the developing world where labour costs are low, trade unions were powerless or non-existent, environmental regulation was either minimal or absent and the overall cost of production was a small fraction of the profit that

could be made from the production of the goods manufactured. This process was led by large multinational corporations such as Ford, IBM General Motors, Union Carbide. Indeed the very real human cost of this shifting of production to the developing world was evident with the environmental disaster which occurred in Bhopal, India, in 1984. A toxic gas leak from the Union Carbide chemical plant covered the city in a deadly fog resulting in the death of over 20,000 people. The environmental impact of this leak remains today with ongoing law suits against the company by the government of India and those in Bhopal who remain affected.

While many of the Western world's more polluting jobs have been exported to the developing world, there appeared to be an assumption made in the developed world that many traditional white collar jobs would be exempt from this process, protected by the barriers of language, distance and corporate necessity. However, in recent years the process of

outsourcing in the service sector has become a major aspect of globalization.

Much of the service sector outsourcing that takes place involves the relocation of service support to English-speaking parts of the developing world, most notably to the Indian sub-continent. This process has accelerated as service-based providers, such as insurance companies, banks, telemarketing and enquiry-based services, have been relocated from North America and Britain to India. Known as 'Business Process Outsourcing' call centres in India have become a new white-collar factory floor, employing nearly a half-a-million people, contributing well over $3.5bn to the Indian economy in 2003 and growing at the rate of 60 per cent per year.

Companies as diverse as British Gas, General Electric (one of the largest US multinational corporations), HSBC, UK National Rail Enquiries, AXA Insurance and Barclaycard all operate in India. The reasons are not hard to find.

World in focus (continued)

New technological developments such as the Internet, cheap telecommunications and above all an abundance of low-paid highly qualified English-speaking graduates makes the movement of call centres from the USA and Britain a logical step for large companies wishing to cut costs. The cost of employing an English-speaking graduate working an eight-hour shift is a little over £140 per month. In Britain a call centre worker earning the basic minimum wage (many earn in excess of this) would be £4.85 per hour giving an average monthly wage of £754. Often the British worker would be far less well educated and qualified than their Indian contemporary. The protection afforded British (and even American) workers by health and safety legislation, employment protection laws and representation by trade unions is largely absent in Indian call centres. Workers are often paid not by the length of shift, but rather the number of successful calls they deal with during their shift. Meal breaks and toilet time are all rigorously controlled.

The majority of the employees are women who work long and arduous shift patterns. As New Delhi, India (where many of the call centres are based), is $5^{1}/_{2}$ hours ahead of London, $10^{1}/_{2}$ hours ahead of New York and $13^{1}/_{2}$ hours ahead of San Francisco many of the women will be starting their day late and finishing in the middle of the night or the early hours of the morning, clearly playing havoc with their family lives, not to say their own biological clock and psychological health.

Workers at these call centres are made 'culturally aware' of customers they are dealing with by having clocks showing the 'local time', together with appropriate national or regional weather forecasts. More often than not they will have been through training sessions which employ showing soap operas to communicate the complexities of localized British and American culture. While such jobs might be seen as low paid by British standards they are quite often paid much more than an ordinary Indian worker might expect to receive.

For the most part while there has been a considerable level of opposition to the process of outsourcing in recent years this has been ameliorated by the idea that just like the old 'sunset industries' that relocated to the developing world, many of the jobs that have recently been outsourced in the service sector are low paid and low skilled, and of low value to the UK economy. Politicians such as Gordon Brown, Chancellor of the Exchequer, believe that they will be replaced by high skilled, higher paid and more valuable forms of employment for the economy. However, such has been the success of outsourcing at this lower level that many high-tech companies are also moving elements of their service provision off-shore. Quite recently Reuters, the financial news organization which has been part of the British media establishment since 1851, moved part of its business operation to Bangalore, India. The unit which has moved to India covers financial journalism and data-reporting, a highly profitable part of Reuters provision. Reuters made the move after recognizing that they could provide the same information business services to many medium- and large-scale British and American clients at 60 per cent less than it cost providing the same service from London.

producing the Mini (Midlands). The current precarious demand for cars in world markets means that without such inducements these multinational companies would find themselves in very difficult circumstances. TNCs have just as much to gain by adopting flexibility and compromise towards national governments as there is in bullying them. Gordon argues that a mutuality exists in which the power and role of the nation-state should not be underestimated. However, as Held and McGrew (2003) point out, there is a complex process taking place in which control is neither fully lost, nor maintained. What we have, they argue, is a reconfiguration of the relationship between the nation-state and its external environment, be it financial, militarily or political. Alliances are sought and some control is ceded in the dance of maintaining some degree of sovereignty and the exercise of power within national boundaries. Clearly, the closer to the centre of financial, political and military power, the greater degree of self control and autonomy the nation-state can retain. Thus it is far easier for Britain to exercise some degree of control and autonomy through its key membership of organizations such as the G8, the World Bank, the IMF and OECD than it is for countries such as Turkey or Romania. However, even the USA, the only remaining 'superpower', must enter into a complex process of negotiation, diplomacy and compromise to ensure its needs are met. This is clearly illustrated in the ways which the USA sought the help of the EU in resolving tensions with Iran over its potential development of nuclear weapons during early 2005. Similarly the USA has sought wide international support in the so called 'war on terror' following the attack on the World Trade Towers on 11 September 2001. More often than not the stage for the complex dance between the nation-states of the twenty-first century takes place within the global organizations that are an increasing feature of everyday life in the twenty-first century.

An equally radical, but differently put critique of globalization comes from the opposing political perspective. It is best articulated by the Peruvian economist Hernando de Soto (2000), who while not in complete agreement with writers such as Hirst, Thompson and Weiss, comes very close to their analysis. Hernando de Soto argues as they do that in reality globalization has failed due to the inherent protectionism of the developed world to deliver improvements in living standards, economic opportunity or advancement for the vast majority of the world's population. Indeed, like Gordon, he believes a degree of autonomy still exists at the national level (at least at the level of the nation-state in the developed north). In effect de Soto, like Marx, takes a materialist approach to the nature of human society. However, unlike Marx, Hirst, Thompson and Weiss, de Soto believes that material self-interest and the need to accumulate and protect wealth are the driving forces of economic change and improvement. It is at this point that he departs from more overtly left-wing writers.

As an example of why Hernando de Soto believes the process of globalization has 'failed' he takes the plight of the peasantry of many parts of the developing world. For de Soto all peasants are by nature capitalists and therefore interested in economic self-improvement, creating and sustaining wealth and it follows in the principles of free trade.

The cities of the third world and the former communist countries are teaming with entrepreneurs. You cannot walk through a Middle Eastern market, hike up to a Latin American village, climb into a taxicab in Moscow without someone trying to make a deal with you. The inhabitants of these countries possess talent, enthusiasm, and an astonishing ability to wring a profit out of practically nothing. They can grasp and use modern technology. Otherwise American businesses would not be struggling to control the unauthorized use of patents abroad, nor would the US government be striving so desperately to keep modern weapons technology out of the hands of third world countries. Markets are an ancient and universal tradition: Christ drove the merchants out of the temple two thousand years ago, and the Mexicans were taking their products to market long before Columbus reached America.

(Hernando de Soto 2000: 4)

For de Soto free trade has been at the heart of human existence since the development of settled communities. Societies have evolved on the basis of trade within their immediate boundaries: as trade expands, so do these boundaries, leading to a process of global trade and globalization. In the post-war period the expansion of world trade has allowed the developed world to become rich and prosperous. This has been achieved by export-oriented economies. In recent years this has led to the current rules of the game (trade agreements between the developing and developed world through agencies such as NAFTA and WTO) effectively locking the peasants out of the game by providing unfair barriers to access and protectionism for those already part of the process (large Western companies or agribusiness). Thus the USA and Europe are able to import only those goods and services that they need and which do not compete against their own goods and services, while they export at vast subsidy goods and services to the developing world at unfair levels. A good example of this are the subsidies given to European, Japanese and American farmers. Under the Common Agricultural Policy (CAP) in Europe each cow is subsidized to the tune of £446. In the USA the Federal government provides an even larger level of subsidy to its farmers at a cost of £587 per cow. Yet in Japan the level of national government subsidy to farmers is so large that every cow in Japan costs Japanese taxpayers £1,419. (These figures are based upon 2004 prices and $/£ exchange rate). Given these levels of subsidy it would be impossible for peasant farmers in Africa, Asia or South America to supply beef to the US, European or Japanese markets. A similar situation applies to many other basic commodities or foodstuffs ranging from wheat to cotton. Equally, the dice is further stacked against Third World farmers by

A closer look

Global organizations

IMF (International Monetary Fund)

This is made up of 184 member countries and has its headquarters in Washington DC. The chairman of the IMF is usually nominated by a process in which the leading lending countries to the fund, such as the USA, Britain, France, Japan and Germany, take the lead. As such it is often regarded as the rich countries' central bank. This world financial organization was set up by the USA after the Second World War to provide economic support for industrial expansion primarily in the West, but from the 1960s onwards provided loans to countries in the developing world such as Brazil and Mexico. Usually loans provided by the IMF come with strings attached. There are strict rules on overdrafts and loans, but these are far harsher than high street banks would impose; for example, they demand economic, political and social change in societies receiving loans.

World Bank

Effectively an arm of the IMF, the World Bank grants loans to Third World countries. As with the IMF and developed societies, rules on lending are strict. However, during the 1960s a generally flexible expansion in credit took place as the world economy expanded. Many Third World and developing nations borrowed heavily at what were then favourable rates of interest. Following the oil price rises after 1973, interest rates climbed and the cost of servicing such loans became immense. More loans were taken out to pay back the interest on earlier loans. In the late 1970s and early 1980s some Third World countries threatened to default on their loans unless interest rates were reduced. As a result an international banking crisis ensued from which we are only now recovering.

G8

This group of leading industrial economies comprises the USA, Japan, Germany, France, the UK, Italy, Canada and Russia. The G10 group also includes Belgium, the Netherlands and Sweden. During the 1990s, Russia attempted to gain access to this 'club'

in the hope of influencing global economic policies. It was refused entry due to what were termed 'structural deficiencies in the Russian economy', most probably the lack of truly developed capitalist markets and 'liberal democratic freedoms'. It would appear that Russia has now made sufficient progress in developing its capital markets, property and legal systems to join what became G8 in June 2002. In January 2005 Britain took the chair of the G8 a point at which the British Chancellor Gordon Brown said he would push for an agenda of change in terms of Third World debt through a new 'Marshall Plan' (see below).

OECD (Organization for Economic Co-operation and Development)

Formed by a larger group than G7, the OECD includes countries such as Iceland, Finland, Denmark, Sweden, Switzerland and New Zealand. OECD reports on individual member economies are taken seriously, not only within the organization but also by the country itself.

GATT (General Agreement on Tariffs and Trade)

Under the Bretton Wood Agreement of 1948, post-war Western governments decided that the only way to prevent a future war was by free trade between nations. This would allow a general rise in living standards for all Western societies, thus preventing the rise of fascism as in the 1930s. Since the 1980s leading capitalist countries such as the USA have tried to further liberalize world trade and open up markets in the developing nations. GATT no longer exists, but has been replaced by the WTO (see below).

Uruguay Round

The most recent agreement within the GATT nations will allow an expansion in the level of world trade by the removal of import barriers between nations. For some developing nations there is a real fear that their emerging industries will be swamped by competition from the developed nations, in particular in the fields of new technology.

A closer look (continued)

WTO (World Trade Organization)

The WTO was set up in January 1995 and currently (February 2005) has 184 members made up a wide range of developed, developing and under-developed countries. This organization will take over responsibility for policing world trade from GATT; like so many international or regional bodies it is based in Washington, DC. Its formal role is to monitor world trade and employ sanctions against those member nations which impede free trade. The WTO provides the assurance to its members that the agreed rules governing world trade will be followed by all member states, thus it provides assurance and confidence in world trade. So, for example, if a Western country sees its products being copied and sold by a developing society that is a member of the WTO it can ask the government in question to take action or, failing such action, the WTO can impose sanctions on that country until compliance is met.

NAFTA (North American Free Trade Agreement)

This is an agreement signed by the USA, Canada and Mexico to open up their countries to each other's goods and services. During 1993, while NAFTA was being negotiated, the US trade union movement launched a political campaign to derail it, arguing that NAFTA would lead to the export of US manufacturing jobs as companies relocated in Mexico to take advantage of low wage rates.

EU

The EU was originally formed in 1957 out of an agreement by Germany, Belgium, France, the Netherlands and Luxemburg to regulate trade between them. The United Kingdom attempted to join the then Common Market in the mid-1960s, but was originally vetoed by the French, eventually joining in 1973. Membership now stands at 25 countries, the most recent countries to join are Cyprus, the Czech Republic, Estonia, Hungry, Latvia, Malta, Poland, Slovenia and Slovakia, in May 2004. The population of the European Union now stands at 500 million. The EU has an organization becoming increasingly important in co-ordinating and regulating trade policy environmental policy, social welfare, health and safety issues and consumer policies within the EU.

NGOs

Non-Governmental Organizations are charitable and voluntary organizations, sometimes known as 'private voluntary organizations' or 'voluntary relief organizations'. These organizations are central players in helping the people of the developing world. Historically they have their origins in the philanthropic organizations of the nineteenth and twentieth centuries. Good examples of NGOs include OXFAM: founded in 1942 to help the people of war-time Greece, the Oxford Committee for Famine Relief currently operates in 70 countries worldwide and spends well over £120 million annually in development relief, education and reconstruction in the developing world. A large proportion of money spent by OXFAM is generated through charitable giving and through the network of 700 OXFAM shops found on many UK high streets. Greenpeace, with its focus on environmental issues, and Amnesty International, with its emphasis on human rights, reflect the diversity of NGOs. Médecins Sans Frontières (MSF) is a French-based emergency medical aid organization operating in well over 80 countries worldwide and is essential in providing medical and humanitarian assistance during times of disaster or emergency. NGOs have in recent years grown in both their scale and importance. The financial help and support they bring is matched by the level of support they enjoy in the developed world. Quite often NGOs act as both political pressure groups on national governments and international organizations, such as the IMF and WTO, as well as acting as catalysts for change in their own right. The importance of the NGO community was clearly demonstrated following the 2004 Boxing Day Tsunami when a large number of NGOs from across the developed world mobilized their resources to help those affected by the disaster. The NGOs had a significant impact in mobilizing Western public opinion and forcing many governments to act quicker than they might have otherwise done so.

their lack of control over what they produce. The Action Aid International Report cited above, indicates that in Peru one TNC controls 80 per cent of the milk produced by farmers and that five TNC's control 90 per cent of the world grain trade. This is graphically illustrated in the following quotes taken from the Action Aid International Report:

'I feel cheated by the operations of Twifo Oil Palm Plantation because I do not understand the deductions they make. When you doubt the figure they will not explain it to you . . . There is no effort to correct mistakes quickly, if at all. We just accept what the officials give us.' Kwando Osae, a palm oil small holder who supplies a Unilever plantation in Twifo Ntafreaso Ghana.

'They're not bothered about receiving milk from those who sell little, they want those who produce a lot more to reduce their number of suppliers and make gains in volume.' Baldur Friederich a dairy farmer from Rio Grande do Sul, Brazil, describing his experiences of selling to Parmalat.

(Action Aid International 2004)

It is not surprising, therefore, that de Soto argues that there is a real need to free the farmers of the Third World from control by the first, to allow them real access to Western markets through trade liberalization. This argument is given currency by Western politicians, such as Gordon Brown, quoted above, who during a visit to Africa in January 2005 advocated the liberalization of trade between the developed and developing worlds, such as Africa. For Gordon Brown, as with Hernando de Soto, the idea of self-improvement using capitalism and the market is alive and well in Africa. What is lacking

is simply the access to Western markets by unfair trade practices. Liberalizing trade would have benefits both to those in the Third World (i.e. allowing them to prosper through the production and sale of goods, mostly foodstuffs) while at the same time creating markets for Western goods. For Gordon Brown it is essential that this process of liberalization be allowed to take place: affluence in Africa quite simply equates, in a globalized world, to affluence in Britain.

Hernando de Soto also argues there is a further negative side to this process in that unless we find ways of allowing the participation of those at the bottom they may well seek alternatives to playing in a global free market and begin to subscribe to alternative ideologies. Such ideologies are available as alternatives to capitalism and often involve preaching the abandonment of capitalism and materialism by those who feel least loyalty to it. As a consequence of this de Soto believes that the resurgence of militant Islam, Communism and extreme forms of nationalism all demonstrate a real frustration with the unfair practices of the West and offer real possibilities which already impact on the West in terms of the growth in Islamic terrorism and the production of illegal consumer goods such as drugs.

In similar vein Stiglitz (2002) a Nobel Prize winner for economics, former economic adviser to President Bill Clinton and Vice-President of the World Bank believes that while the general public of many developed Western societies such as Britain, the USA and Europe want a global economic system that is fair and balanced, providing real opportunity to the poor of the developing world, the power of multinational capitalist groups, such as software giants or drug companies, shape national and international trade policies and agreements.

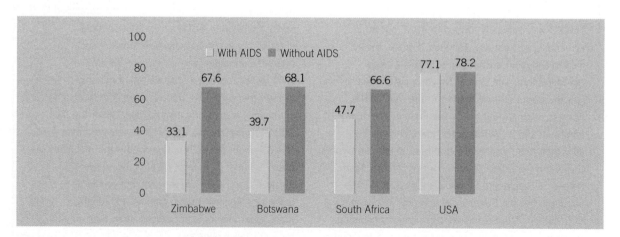

Figure 11.3 Life expectancy at birth with and without AIDs
Source: United Nations Human Development Report 2004

In the West an individual suffering HIV/AIDS will often receive treatment through socialized medicine in Britain on the NHS. As such these socialized medical systems pay large amounts for major drugs such as £110 for Zidovidune, £80 for Lamivudine and £72 for Stravudine (per treatment). However, generic versions of these drugs are available at £13, £7.70 and £2.70 respectively (2004 prices and $/£ exchange rates). Western drug companies refuse to supply or license these drugs to developing countries such as South Africa, the Philippines or Thailand for fear that supplies will 'leak back' into the West and undermine the gigantic profits they make. As such WTO-brokered trade agreements with the developing world often preclude medicines. Similar arguments can be applied to software giants such as Microsoft, who during 2004 licensed a number of 'cut-down' versions of the famous computer operating system Windows XP and the Office suite software. This was done in an effort to combat the seemingly epidemic nature of software piracy in countries such as Russia, Romania, Poland and China. These cut-down versions are, however, not available in the Western world, where consumers have to pay full price for most Microsoft products, thus contributing to the fortunes of the world's second richest man, Bill Gates. As both Stiglitz and de Soto point out, it is through actions such as these

Stop and think

Of the money spent on HIV/AIDS research and treatments, 90 per cent is spent in the 'developed' world where only 8 per cent of the sufferers live.

➤ Why do you think this is?

➤ What do such statistics tell us about global inequalities?

Case study

HIV/AIDS

It is a fact that HIV/AIDS is a worldwide problem, but this problem affects the developing world to a far greater extent than the West.

As a global problem there are few that are more immediate and apparent than the growing numbers and spread of HIV/AIDS infection. For the most part HIV/AIDS is a disease of the blood and bodily fluids, transmitted by these fluids from individual to individual and requiring either unprotected sex or contaminated blood supplies. In a little over twenty years HIV/AIDS has gone from 452 cases reported in 1982 to 5.8 million in 1998, with just under 40 million cases recorded in 2004 (the UK population is just under 60 million, so this gives an idea of the scale of the problem). The United Nations calculated that there were a little

over 39.4 million people living with HIV/AIDS in 2004 and that around 4.9 million new infections occur each year. More worrying still are the large numbers of children with the infection, calculated at 2.2 million. The UN estimated that in the 2002 over 3.5 million people died from the effects of HIV/AIDS. While there is at present no known cure for HIV/AIDS there are drugs (see above) which can both delay and suppress its long-term effects and allow sufferers to live relatively long and normal lives. In the USA an individual infected with HIV/AIDS can expect to live a normal life well into their late 60s or early 70s. In the developing world, few reach the age of 45 once infected. Moreover, less than one in ten of those infected in the developing world have access to these drugs, while nearly all sufferers in the

developed world have access.

While HIV/AIDS is a global problem and nearly every country has some recorded cases of the infection, its effects disproportionately hit the developing world hardest. Despite the fact that the disease was first identified in San Francisco in 1978, the vast majority suffering the effects of HIV/AIDS live in sub-Saharan Africa, with 28.5 million recorded cases, South and South-East Asia with 5.6 million recorded cases, Latin America with 1.5 million cases and Eastern Europe and Central Asia with 1 million recorded cases. The UN recognizes that in some countries, such as South Africa, Mozambique, Botswana, Zambia, Thailand and the Philippines, HIV/AIDS infection has now reached epidemic proportions. HIV/AIDS is now becoming a real issue in China,

➤

Case study (continued)

the country with just over one-fifth of the world's population. In 2002 the UN estimated that 1.1 million people were infected with the virus in China, showing a 67 per cent increase in the number of infections over the past two years. In India, the country with the second largest population, the UN estimates that nearly 4 million people are infected.

Globalization is part of the problem for the spread of HIV/AIDS and in particular flows of migrant workers (mostly men) between different countries. In sub-Saharan Africa HIV/AIDS is at pandemic levels carried by migrant male workers. Often these male workers living away from their wives and families for months or even years have unprotected sex, only to infect their wives when they return home. Indeed HIV/AIDS rates are now climbing faster among

women in many parts of the developing world.

It is not just the effect of the illness on individuals in the Third World, but the economic and social impact of the disease. As many of the men in such regions often have to travel to seek work, women are left on the land to raise crops and produce food. Increased rates of illness among women are leading to a reduction in the amount of food grown as the labour force reduces. Social and community breakdown results, as children left orphaned after their parents die from the disease rely on their grandparents or other relatives to care for them or on the overstretched resources of the states. In China, where the disease is a late arrival, but with similar migratory flows of male workers from the land to the cities, a similar situation to sub-Saharan Africa is emerging.

Figure 11.4 An HIV/AIDS victim

Question

1. *In what ways is education the key factor in the fight against HIV/AIDS?*

---

that the balance of forces weighs towards the developed West and against the under-developed South.

While much of the academic analysis focuses on the negative aspects of globalization, such as the over-arching power of MNCs and their ability to bring about economic shifts and economic decline in one place being matched by economic expansion and growth in another, Giddens's (1990) view contains within it an optimism hitherto lacking within academic analysis. As noted above, for Giddens, the process of globalization has the potential to empower and unite citizens as well as to divide them. So while the process of globalization of industry or the mass media might allow vast wealth or influence to accumulate in the hands of a small minority of 'global' entrepreneurs, the potential for human understanding of problems common to everyone, such as increasing population growth, pollution and threats to the environment, are the more positive side of globalization.

Topographies of globalization

Today one of the most apparent aspects of globalization is the process of urbanization or the rise of the city, and in particular the so-called 'Global City'. Rates of urbanization have increased dramatically in the last century, but in particular in the last three decades of the twentieth century. Cities such as Mexico City, Cairo, Shanghai and New Delhi have all expanded at unprecedented rates. Indeed, cities such as Cairo and New Delhi have populations larger than some European countries. Moreover, as the impact of globalization takes effect and development accelerates in many previously Third World countries, their cities increasingly adopt Western forms. Physically, there appears little to differentiate the cityscape of places as geographically separated as New York, Kuala Lumpur, Berlin, Shanghai, Tokyo or London. While each may have their 'signature' landmark features, all seem to be driven toward a similarity of style and organization that reflects an increasingly mirror like outlook. As with the other aspects of globalization this is not accidental, but must be seen as a conscious product of human actions, political and economic decisions. The city is seen by some writers (including Simmel and Tonnies and, more recently, Zukin 1991) to represent modernism in its purest form. Cities are sites where unplanned social interaction takes place and as a result where social change occurs. As Braham and Janes (2002) point out, cities are spaces in which the bonds of traditional community and social control fail to operate, or operate at a weaker level.

Clearly for many of the architects, city planners and political leaders of these global cities, there is a competition to be the biggest and the best, to have the tallest buildings, the fastest metro or the best cultural facilities. Cities thus represent national pride, prestige and power; they are as much symbolic spaces as they are physical spaces. In the run up to the 2008 Olympic Games Beijing is being transformed from a typically Asian city, one with a distinct Chinese identity in its architecture, with lots of small houses closely packed together, and with unique and defined quarters and communities, to a 'World City', one that can take its place alongside New York, Chicago,

London, Paris or Berlin. The bulldozers and urban planners are at the time of writing at work and the traditional Chinese heritage that has lasted for more than 2000 years is being replaced. Moreover, many of the architects of the cityscape that is being created here are American or European. This new urban landscape, with its shopping malls, high-rise apartment style housing and ever larger office blocks and commercial and corporate headquarters is little different from the other world cities.

Figure 11.5(a) The New York skyline

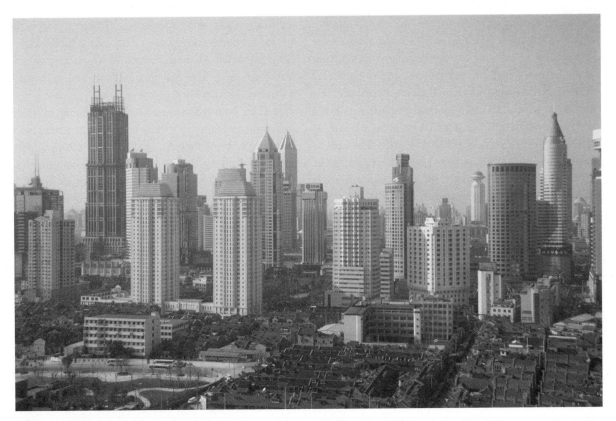

Figure 11.5(b) The Shanghai skyline
© Liu Liqun/CORBIS

For sociologists, unlike geographers or other social scientists, the city was and is much more than a collection of buildings, of transport infrastructure or of a means of communication. Cities can be seen as the living breathing nature of society, reflecting the complex social interactions that make up society. Perhaps the major distinguishing feature of modern life is that above all it is urban.

As noted above, the city, in the writings of early social theorists such as Tönnies, Simmel, Durkheim, Weber and Engels, became at one and the same time the exemplar of progress yet also the place where some people lived in filth and squalor. It was the site where the traditional and subjective bonds of kinship, family and locality gave way to formalized social relations bound up with the onward march of rationalization and capitalism. In many respects the global cities of the twenty-first century mirror many of the complex social problems and issues that the Victorian cities of the industrial revolution held, the very cities which themselves gave such an impetus to the birth of sociology.

For Robert Park (Park *et al.* 1923), writing in the 1920s and pioneer of the Chicago School of Urban Sociology, the city, compared with the rural setting, required new forms of thinking of social organization and social relations. City was a metaphor for the changing nature of social life; moreover this social life existed in a myriad number of forms. The city is a melting pot of society. Whereas for Simmel and Tönnies the city was the site of the isolation of the human spirit, for Park the city, and in particular the neighbourhood to which an individual belonged, was the site at which the individual identity was supported and nurtured, the physical distinctness of neighbours, as identified in Park's vision of 1920s Chicago. The various neighbourhoods of Chicago were a reflection or statement of human difference. However, this is not to assume that Park believed in the harmonious nature of urban existence: far from it. For Park the city was riven with tension, disorder and above all conflict, and it becomes the locus for struggles over power, political, economic and social. Moreover, as the city expands the very complexity of these power struggles increase as well.

However, as with Tönnies and Weber, but above all leaning heavily toward the analysis of Simmel, Park believed that a process of impersonal control, mediated through political and legal force, provides order against the potential chaos that can emerge. The growth of the city and urbanism transformed the landscape of Western Europe and North America. It helped to unleash both the material and mental productive forces of capitalist society. To be sure, the urban slum conditions endured by most of the poor, as described by writers such as Engels, Mayhew or Zola, were quite dire: high rates of infant mortality, disease and criminality, massive poverty and social deprivation. But alongside came a new dynamic relying on the complex interaction of individuals and the transforming and quite dramatic productive changes they brought with them.

As noted above, the global city of the twenty-first century can be said to represent a third phase of urbanism and one which sociology is only starting to come to terms with. This third phase of urbanization is perhaps reflected in a number of ways, not least of which is the popular cultural image of the global city epitomized in the film *Blade Runner*, the Los Angeles of the future in which a very myriad of languages, combinations of English, Japanese, Cantonese and Spanish reflecting overlapping cultures styles of life coexisting in a dark dystopian images of all-pervasive media, and overcrowding and gigantic buildings that dominate landscape and lives. The alternative and very real image is of the coexistence of gleaming glass-clad skyscrapers alongside shanty towns, something increasingly seen in the developing world from New Delhi, to Durban, to Shanghai. These cities are chaotic and disordered, a juxtaposition of the regularity and clinical order of early twentieth century modernist architects such as Le Corbusier. However, for many in the developing world the reality of the global city is far from this modernist, or even postmodernist vision. Urbanization is a global phenomenon and cities such as Cairo, Mexico City, São Paulo and Lagos all have exploding populations, most of them living in abject poverty, struggling on a daily basis to make ends meet. In many respects they are similar to their counterparts in industrializing Europe of the late nineteenth and early twentieth centuries. They are drawn to the cities in search of work as the land on which they labour is made unproductive in the face of imports of basic agricultural products from the West.

The United Nations predicts that within the next 25 years some 300 million Africans will migrate from the land to the cities. The consequences of this for public health and the general well-being of these people is quite marked. Cities in the developing world are places where infectious disease such as TB, cholera and above all HIV/AIDS are spread. As in the development of urbanism in the West during the nineteenth century, the loosening of the social bonds and moral sanctions of the rural community faced in the new urban landscape brings with it many opportunities to the individual, but also many potential dangers.

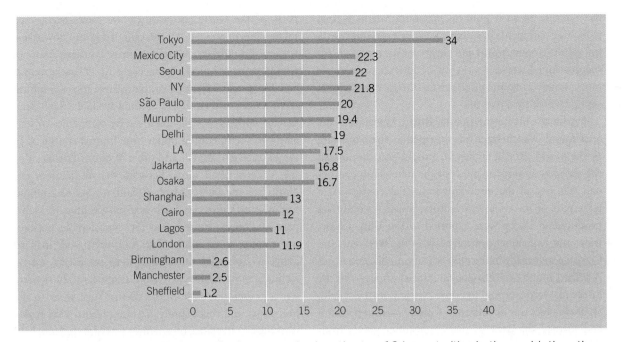

Figure 11.6 World cities: Tokyo to Osaka are ranked as the top 10 largest cities in the world; the other cities shown are for comparison

(*Source*: www.citypopulation.de)

For Manuel Castells (1989) the new global city exists outside the boundaries of the nation-state; in many ways these new global cities are more akin to the city states of Renaissance Europe: Venice, Florence or Paris. These cities are, for Castells, tied in to 'networks' or 'space flows' in which the consequences of decisions made on the other side of the globe all have their influence felt in the global city many thousands of miles away, but in turn these global cities are part of the network itself and can tie in to the flows of information and in turn shape them.

In this way the 'computer component' manufacturers of Beijing and the software writers of Seattle will have their lives dictated to by the bankers of London, New York or Los Angeles. This perhaps helps explain why many politicians in the West are less concerned about the flow of industrial jobs to the developing world, while the control of based industries remains firmly located in the affluent West. Indeed, as Castells' work implies, information is the most important aspect of production, rather than labour. In essence we now live in a knowledge or information economy. This perhaps also indicates that in the future the struggle for resources will be as much a struggle for access and control of information networks as to physical goods, products and raw materials. For the moment, however, the developed world appears content to allow a new worldwide division of labour to take place with developing countries taking on those aspects of industrial production which are no longer viable in the high-tech high-wage economies of the West. Control of information flows and the technologies which support this are, as Castells indicates, central to the power of capital.

If the new modern and advancing global cities of Shanghai, New Delhi and Kuala Lumpur and Tiapia reflect the impact of globalization at built environmental level perhaps the most fundamental shift from east to west that has taken place in recent decades is the whole-scale shift in manufacturing of consumer goods that has occurred, as the logic of a new world division of labour as indicated above. The wave of urban change that is spreading through cities in the developing world is itself being fueled and shaped by global changes taking place at the same time.

The new workshop of the world

As noted above many Western politicians see globalization as a necessity, one in which free trade and the movement of traditional industry (sometimes called sunset industries) relocate to parts of the globe where labour is cheap. Indeed, the rhetoric of such political pronouncements is that globalized competition is beneficial to everyone: work for the developing world and cheap consumer goods for the developed world. As such it is difficult to extricate our national economic interest from the global networks we find ourselves a part of.

During the nineteenth century Britain (specifically the area round Manchester) was regarded as the workshop of the world. British industrial production dominated the world economy for much of the nineteenth century and was one of the dominant industrial centres for a large part of the twentieth century. Steam locomotives produced in Derby were exported to the USA, China, India and Argentina; some are still in use 80+ years on. Cotton goods made in the mills of Bolton, Blackburn and Bradford found markets globally. British shoes from the Midlands were exported to the empire and further afield. Sheffield steel was an industry with a world reputation and formed the basis of many consumer goods from ships to kettles to cars. British-built ships supported the dominance of both the British merchant navy and the Royal Navy well into the early twentieth century. But Britain was not alone in the twentieth century with its emphasis on industrial manufacture. The economies of France, Germany and, especially, the USA all relied heavily on the manufacture and sale of industrial and consumer goods. In the mid- to late twentieth century the USA became the new workshop of the world. In the twenty-first century all that has changed again with the processes of globalization having found a different new 'workshop of the world', this time in China, located on the Pearl River Delta of Guangdong Province, south-east China. The consequence of this for British industry has been enormous as the examples in the World in focus box on p. 459 indicate.

The international body that regulates world trade is the WTO (see above). This governs the rules by which world trade runs. In 2002 140 countries belonged to the WTO; in 2004 this had grown to 184. Some countries including Russia and Saudi Arabia have yet to qualify for inclusion. China was allowed to join in 2002 and as a result now has far better trading rules with the West, so making its exports easier and flows of capital into China simpler.

A key aspect of globalization is the way it has opened up opportunities to Western companies and increasing numbers of Western workers. While outsourcing has shifted many traditional industries to China, India and the Far East, there has also been a migration, at least on a temporary basis, of workers from the West to these parts of the world. Increasingly we have, in the last thirty years or so seen the creation of a group of workers without boundaries. Moreover, these workers, many of whom have technical, engineering or IT backgrounds are able to move from geographical area to geographical area as work and contracts become available. Such peripatetic workers may be employed by companies or self-employed or operating under time-limited contracts. In the oil industry British and other Western European or US workers often move between the oil-fields of the North Sea, the Gulf of Mexico, Saudi Arabia, Kazakhstan or the South China Sea. Such workers will often be highly paid and away from home for considerable periods, for months if not years. They will often work in hard dangerous occupations such as deep sea divers, oil rig technicians or engineers. In the summer of 2004 there was a graphic example of the cost of such work to the individual and their family. Liverpool-born Ken Bigley working as a freelance oil engineer was captured and held by an Iraqi terrorist group. The group demanded the withdrawal of British forces occupying the southern part of the country. After several weeks of detention, played out through the international media and by means of the World Wide Web, Ken Bigley was executed. In a very real way this highlights the dangers such workers may put themselves into by following their work and that in a globalized world terror groups are adept at using new technologies and the World Wide Web as a tool against the affluent developed world. In many was reflecting, in part at least, some of the arguments put forward by Hernando de Soto.

In May 2004 the European Union expanded to 25 members with the inclusion of Poland, Cyprus, the Czech Republic, Estonia, Hungry, Latvia, Malta, Slovenia and Slovakia. As noted above, this brought the population of the EU to over 500 million. One of the consequences of this growth has been increased flows of workers from eastern to western Europe. In Poland, Hungry and the Czech Republic a ready pool of educated workers, many in middle-class occupations such as doctors, nurses and medical technicians, became available for the health services of Germany, France and Britain. As a consequence of this process of enlargement Britain has been able to ease the shortage of key workers in the NHS by importing Polish, Hungarian and Czech doctors, nurses, medical technicians and dentists. While such flows of workers provide immediate economic or social benefits, easing the pressure on the NHS, they have adverse effects in their own countries, where the health case systems suffer shortages of such expertise.

World in focus

China as the new 'workshop of the world'

In 2003 the company which produced the famous 'Dr Martens' footwear decided to relocate production out of the UK. The company moved its production to China with the closure of its Nottingham factory and the shedding of 1,000 jobs. The reasoning behind this is quite simple: cost. In China workers are paid just over £70 per month to produce the Chinese version of Dr Marten's boots, this is one-tenth of that paid to the workers they replaced in Nottingham. Moreover, the manufacturer selected to produce this footwear on behalf of the Dr Martens Company also produces footware for Adidas, Nike, Timberland and Reebok. Adidas, a German company, Reebok, a British company, and Nike and Timberland, both American companies, have outsourced production to the Taiwanese conglomerate Pou Chan.

This process of outsourcing from the West to China and other far eastern countries is nothing new, but is accelerating. In the USA the supermarket giant Wal-Mart is the world's biggest single customer of manufactured goods from China. Moreover, it is China's eighth largest trading partner on a worldwide scale, dwarfing trade between China and Sweden, the Netherlands or Belgium. Wal-Mart employs 1.3 million workers in the USA. Wal-Mart has revenues of $256 bn, and accounts for just over 2 per cent of US gross domestic product. Wal-Mart is also expanding its operations into China, with a programme of store openings started in the major city of Shanghai. It hopes to bring the American shopping experience to the newly wealthy citizens of China.

In Britain the B&Q chain of DIY stores sources $1 bn worth of products from China each year. Many of the power tools, garden furniture and electrical goods sold by B&Q are now produced in China, rather than in Britain, Europe or the USA. Many of the famous name products such as Black and Decker (a US company) are in effect produced in China, in and around Guangdong Province. B&Q, like Wal-Mart, has also expanded its operations into China by opening stores across the country. As in Britain, the newly affluent Chinese workers have an appetite for consumption and especially, like many of their Western counterparts, for DIY.

But go further along the British high street, into most German department stores or any US shopping mall and you will find a similar story. As Gordon Brown acknowledged during a visit to China in February 2005, nearly 70 per cent of the world's microwaves and 90 per cent of the world's kettles are produced by manufacturers in the Guangdong Province of China. It is no surprise that China's economy has been growing at over 8 per cent per year during the late 1990s and the first four years of the twenty-first century. But this manufacturing boom has also been aided by one key export from the developed world: capital. Britain invests more in China than any other European country. Only Japan and the USA invest more in China than Britain. British investments in Chinese manufacturing are immense with $18 bn invested in 2003, up from $13 bn in 2002. Increasingly the pension funds many people rely on in Britain are being invested in China. As such the retirement prosperity of workers who once produced British manufactured goods are now dependent upon the production of those same goods in the factories of China, which are then exported back to the West! One other potential negative here is that every dollar that British capitalists invest in China is a dollar less invested in Britain. This is a key issue for the British trade union movement in the early twenty-first century. But as noted above British and many other Western politicians and governments see globalization as positive, calling for increased liberalization, rather than regulation.

Resistance to globalization

Globalization as a process, as we have seen above is one which leads or should lead to the gradual erosion of barriers across the globe. It implies a freedom of movement of money, products, information and even people. As we have seen above, one aspect of this process for many British workers is to make them geographically mobile, in search of opportunities on the other side of the planet. But such an idea of globalization implies unrestricted freedom of travel for everyone. Whilst this may be the case for international businessmen, entrepreneurs and even technically qualified workers from the West, travel of people from the other direction is not always possible.

For example, Jeremy Rifkin (2001) is highly critical of the process of globalization arguing that it simply magnifies the already existing gap between rich and poor countries and has in turn created such imbalances that many in the developing world can only resolve their own economic needs through migration to the wealthier countries. We have seen the consequences of this illustrated in the past two decades. In the 1980s the plight of the Vietnamese boat people demonstrated how these people experiencing poverty and oppression in their homeland took to the open South China Sea, sometimes in very small and unseaworthy craft in a desperate attempt to find security and prosperity in the developed world. This scenario was repeated in the early to mid-1980s when a similar situation was played out in the waters off the coast of Florida with the exodus of economic and political refugees from Cuba to the USA. Similarly in the late 1990s refugees from Afghanistan where picked up in over-crowded cargo boats in the Indian Ocean, off the coast of Australia, a country where they had sought to make a new life. In southern Europe there has been a steady flow of refugees and economic migrants across the Mediterranean from countries such as Albania and even Russia, Afghanistan and Pakistan. These so called 'boat people' have one thing in common: the desire to risk life and limb on the high seas in search of a better life in the developed and affluent west. In all these cases their fate was to be detained in internment camps. Some have been lucky and have been allowed to stay in Italy, Hong Kong and Australia and other countries; many, however, have not. In the USA economic migrants regularly attempt to cross the Rio Grande River, the border between several US southern states and Mexico. Such illegal migrants are often captured and swiftly processed only to be returned to Mexico. Moreover, these illegal migrants try again and again; such is their desire for a better life in the USA.

In February 2004, 23 illegal Chinese workers were drowned while cockle picking in Morecambe Bay, trapped by the high tides and treacherous quick sands of the bay. These Chinese workers had illegally entered Britain and were under the control of so-called 'Snake-head Gangs' criminal organizations based in China that smuggle people across international borders and supply illegal cheap labour to the West. Such gangs, be they Chinese gangs, Romanian or Russian Mafia, supplying the sex trade of the West, or the illegal people smugglers of Mexico, all make vast amounts of money by trading on the desperate dreams of those wishing for a new life in the affluent West. As we have seen above, quite often that dream turns sour.

However as Rifkin argues, such is the scale of these attempts that many Western media outlets and even some right-wing politicians see such population movements as a flood of humanity that will overwhelm the West. Headline-grabbing stories paint dire pictures of countries overrun by outsiders. As Rifkin points out such an exodus has also had other equally negative effects, such as the cultural backlash that often occurs in the host country when it sees the influx of immigrants with 'different' forms of culture. Refugees, economic migrants and others seeking a better, more secure and less repressive life in the West have often met with hostility, racism and abuse, fed by the headlines of the press and claims of some right-wing politicians. Increasingly in the West, as Rifkin points out, the barriers are going up. It is becoming harder and harder for the flows of population that once marked the period of world economic expansion at the start of the twentieth century. Countries such as the USA no longer ask;

> Give me your tired, your poor, your huddled masses yearning to breathe free, the wretched refuse of your teeming shore. Send these, the homeless, tempest-tossed to me. I lift my lamp beside the golden door.
>
> (inscription at the base of the statue of Liberty in New York)

Instead such migrants are met with tight immigration and boarder controls, often leading to their swift return. In February 2005 the British government announced a policy of tightening immigration controls into Britain. The British government would in the future utilize a points system similar to that adopted by the Australian government in the 1980s. Each prospective migrant to the UK would be assessed against a sliding scale of employment. Those who hold skills or professional qualifications which are in short supply in Britain would be given easy access. Those migrants with low or no skills would not be allowed into the country. In reality the right to entry is equivalent to at least a couple of 'A' levels. Moreover such migrants, once they passed the labour market test, would be required to demonstrate that they have sufficient command of the English language and of British history and culture. If they pass all these tests they would be allowed to stay for a period of five years, after which their case for permanent residence would be reviewed.

Often, the case is that there is such open and real hostility towards those who do make it from the developing world to the affluent West that they are not able to integrate into their host communities. As a result they seek solace and support within distinct migrant communities. In cities such as Berlin, London, New York and Paris there are well-defined 'exiled communities' living lives little different from those they left behind.

Some may even reject many of the cultural aspects of life in the West with its emphasis on materialism and consumerism, retreating into their traditional cultures. In France in 2004 a law was passed banning the wearing of religious symbols in public places, including schools and many public buildings. This law was brought in in an attempt to reinforce the traditional boundaries between the state and religion in France, reflecting the secular nature of French society. The result, however, was to make illegal the wearing of traditional religious dress, such as the Islamic headscarf, in French schools. As a result protests from the Islamic community in France met with widespread hostility in the French media and protests

by Islamic groups were broken up by the often violent action of the French police. The *Human Development Report* 2004 states:

> Those fearing that immigrants threaten national values make three arguments: that immigrants do not 'assimilate' but reject the core values of the country; that immigrant and local cultures clash, inevitably leading to social conflict and fragmentation; and that immigrant cultures are inferior and if allowed a foothold would undermine democracy and retard progress, a drain on economic and social development. Their solution is to manage diversity by reducing flows and acculturating immigrant communities.
>
> (United Nations 2004: 100)

Islamaphobia and other forms of racism and intolerance evident from the above example is a reality in many European countries. Minority groups are regularly attacked and suffer abuse and racism. However, this is to passively accept that migrants to the West are locked in a simple and well-defined 'alien cultural identity'. Both the UN report cited above and Giddens (1991) point out that identity is never fixed and simple, but rather mediated by the changing social conditions within which individuals find themselves. Individuals, whether immigrants or native-born citizens, often have overlapping and multiple identities. However, reactions against such immigrant communities, as noted by the UN HDR, in this sense reflect at best ignorance, or at worst a denial, that incomers into a society cannot hold both pre-existing and newly overlapping cultural identities. As Held (1999) points out, our national and cultural identities are complex and fluid. In this context it is quite easy to be a Muslim and patriotically French at the same time, or a British Hindu and a supporter of the Indian cricket team when it plays England in a test match at Old Trafford.

At a more political level resistance to globalization is predicated on the basis of a desire to protect what are seen as vital national interests: the economy, language or cultural symbols. Ironically this can have the effect of uniting those who exist at traditionally polar ends of the political spectrum. In the USA left-wing radical Ralph Nader, environmentalist, consumer champion and Presidential third candidate in 2000 and 2004, is highly critical of the process of globalization and has adopted a similar logic to right-wing business entrepreneur and billionaire Ross Perot. Both favour a much more openly protectionist policy on the part of the US government to protect US jobs and industry. In Europe a similar situation also exists with rejection of the move towards

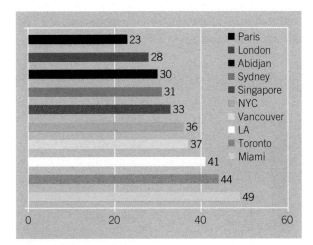

Figure 11.7 Top 10 cities by share of foreign born (%) population
Source: United Nations 2004: 99

greater European integration and the adoption of a single European, globally traded currency. In Britain members of the Labour party, such as Dennis Skinner and Frank Field, advocate a rejection of such economic integration which is little different from the policy espoused by the radical political grouping UKIP, the United Kingdom Independence Party. In France the National Front, headed by far-right politician Jean-Marie Le Pen, identifies itself with a rejection of cultural globalization and anti-Americanism which in part, at least, mirrors the hostility of the French government to such a process. Anti-globalization protests have taken place thoughout the world, most notably in Seattle in 2000. Such protests are widely supported and mobilization often takes place by means of the very tools of globalization itself: telecommunications and the World Wide Web. Within the developed world globally we are seeing new forms of civil protest and civil unrest. There are wide coalitions of groups from human rights organizations, to environmental groups to anti-capitalist movements allying themselves against globalization.

Rates of development

Many Western politicians believe that the solution to global poverty can only come through the process of globalization. Yet despite the fact that the UN has shown that global poverty appears to have reduced in recent years (most of this reduction due to the economic explosions in China and India) the gap between rich and poor countries has grown wider since the 1960s. In this sense, and as Stiglitz, Hernando de Soto and others have argued, globalization has been a failure.

Simpson (1994) argues that gross domestic product (GDP) can be used as a measure of the wealth and degree of development of a society. In effect the GNP of a society is the total value of the goods and services produced within that society. Thus tables which give the GDP per person of various societies give a very good idea of the overall wealth of one society in comparison with another. However, as Simpson cautions, such figures do not indicate how that wealth is spread within a society; a society can be very rich, but with massive differences between the people at the top and the bottom.

As shown on p. 463 (Figure 11.9), the annual reports of the United Nations in the form of *HDRs* provide a comprehensive guide to global human development. These reports rank countries on a Human Development Index (HDI), in effect measuring criteria such as life expectancy, adult literacy and real gross domestic product (GDP) per person to give an overall picture of the world today. Countries are grouped according to their scores in one of three bands: High, Medium or Low Human Development.

Figure 11.9 shows how little has changed in recent years. It is true that India has moved from being a low human development nation, to a medium development nation, but the affluence and wealth enjoyed by the developed countries, such as Britain, remains fairly locked in the West. It is far better to be living in the developed West, in terms of overall human development, than it is to be living in the developing world.

As with overall human development (Figure 11.9 combines all factors that go toward human development: health, access to income, clean water, housing, sanitation and education, etc.) Figure 11.10 shows that glaring gaps remain between life expectancy levels in the developed world and the developing world.

In the West or developed world universal primary and secondary education, with its emphasis on universal literacy, is taken as a norm, as part of our rights. In the

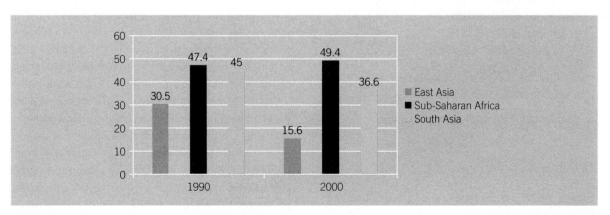

Figure 11.8 Percentage of people living on $1 or less per day

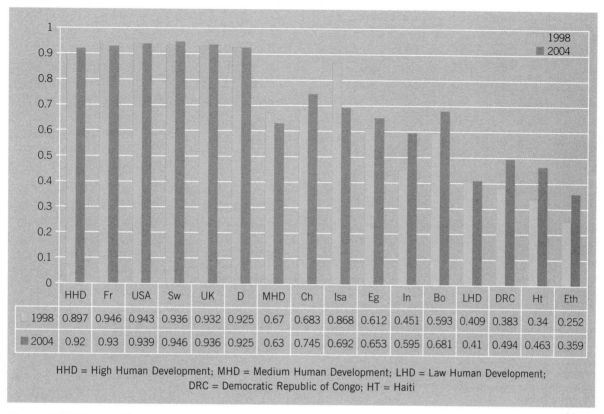

	HHD	Fr	USA	Sw	UK	D	MHD	Ch	Isa	Eg	In	Bo	LHD	DRC	Ht	Eth
1998	0.897	0.946	0.943	0.936	0.932	0.925	0.67	0.683	0.868	0.612	0.451	0.593	0.409	0.383	0.34	0.252
2004	0.92	0.93	0.939	0.946	0.936	0.925	0.63	0.745	0.692	0.653	0.595	0.681	0.41	0.494	0.463	0.359

HHD = High Human Development; MHD = Medium Human Development; LHD = Law Human Development;
DRC = Democratic Republic of Congo; HT = Haiti

Figure 11.9 Human Development Index (HDI)

Source: 2004 Human Development Index, United Nations Development Programme (UNDP) New York, USA

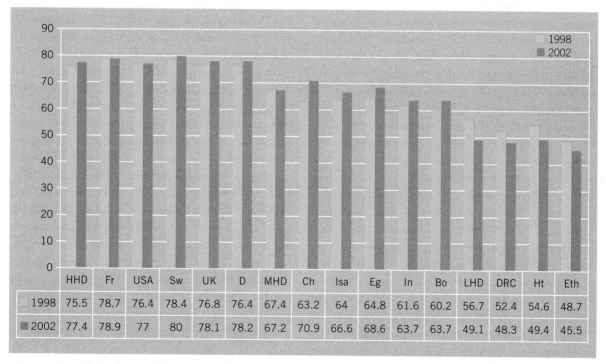

	HHD	Fr	USA	Sw	UK	D	MHD	Ch	Isa	Eg	In	Bo	LHD	DRC	Ht	Eth
1998	75.5	78.7	76.4	78.4	76.8	76.4	67.4	63.2	64	64.8	61.6	60.2	56.7	52.4	54.6	48.7
2002	77.4	78.9	77	80	78.1	78.2	67.2	70.9	66.6	68.6	63.7	63.7	49.1	48.3	49.4	45.5

Figure 11.10 Life expectancy at birth (years)

Source: 2004 Human Development Index, Oxford University Press, New York (for United Nations)

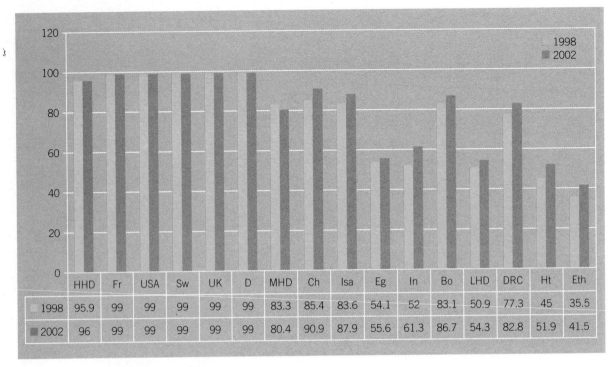

	HHD	Fr	USA	Sw	UK	D	MHD	Ch	Isa	Eg	In	Bo	LHD	DRC	Ht	Eth
1998	95.9	99	99	99	99	99	83.3	85.4	83.6	54.1	52	83.1	50.9	77.3	45	35.5
2002	96	99	99	99	99	99	80.4	90.9	87.9	55.6	61.3	86.7	54.3	82.8	51.9	41.5

Figure 11.11 Adult literacy rate (%)

Source: 2004 Human Development Index, Oxford University Press, New York (for United Nations)

developing world, as Figure 11.11 shows, such levels cannot always be attained, but many countries do try.

As with the earlier graphs, Figure 11.12 showing real GDP per capita exemplifies the reasons behind why human development in the developing world lags so far behind that of the developed West: it comes down quite simply to affluence and wealth. The West has maintained its affluence and high standard of living, while the rest of the world follows in its wake and tries to emulate it.

As the 2004 report points out, an explosion in consumption has taken place in the past two decades, but what is clear is that while some societies, such as India and China, have, through a process of dramatic industrial expansion, started to pull themselves out of poverty, the vast majority of countries in the developing world have been unable to perform the same trick. The 2004 Report notes that India, Bangladesh, Cambodia, Jordan and others have all had a reduction in the number of people living in poverty. It remains a sad fact that the poorest of the world's population have failed to secure a slice of the increase in wealth that has occurred. The same report indicates that countries such as Pakistan, Morocco and Zimbabwe have all shown a net increase in the numbers living in poverty. While the benefits of globalization have been extended beyond the previous narrow confines of the developed world, this extension has not gone much

further. In terms of wealth the HHDI countries account for just over 16 per cent of the world's population, but own 80 per cent of the world GDP. MHDI countries, which now comprise 44 per cent of the world's population, own just 17 per cent of world GDP and LHDI countries with 40 per cent of the world's population have only 3 per cent of the world GDP.

So while the affluent world has maintained or improved its situation, measured against a variety of indicators from the *Human Development Reports*, many, in particular those belonging to the Low Human Development countries, have fallen behind or failed to keep pace with global improvements. Moreover, even in those countries which have seen a general improvement in their HDI performance, the benefits of such improvement have not been uniform or spread across these societies. In India, the new wealth and affluence that comes with the outsourcing of Western service industries such as call centres, has not spread far beyond a largely educated English-speaking middle-class sector of Indian society, a sector which accounts for little over 10 per cent of the population of India. In China, the explosion of manufacturing still hides a massive problem of unemployment and underemployment with the ever increasing migration of the rural poor into the large cities and towns, placing ever more strains on Chinese central and local government.

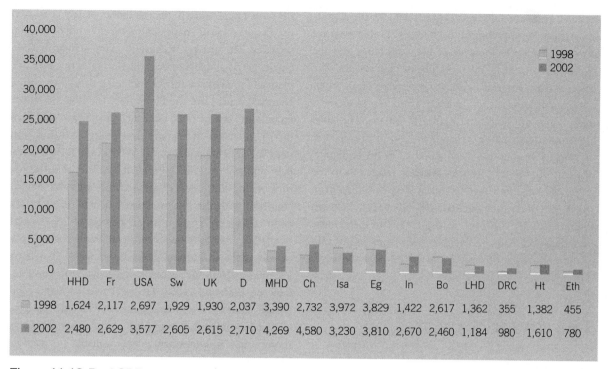

Figure 11.12 Real GDP per capita ($)

Source: 2004 Human Development Index, Oxford University Press, New York (for United Nations)

With well over 1.2 billion people in 2000, according to the 2004 *HDR*, just over 47 per cent of the Chinese population live on less than $2 per day, while in India, with a population of just under 1 billion, 80 per cent of the population live on the same amount or less.

The world population currently stands at a little over 6.3 billion, having grown from just over 2 billion in the 1930s. With well over 4.4 billion people living in the developing world, just over 2.6 billion of them still lack basic sanitation, more than 1 billion do not have a decent roof over their heads and nearly 1 billion children have an inadequate daily diet, leaving them hungry and lacking essential nutrition. The world remains one of rich and poor. The richest 20 per cent of the world's population consume 45 per cent of all meat and fish, 58 per cent of all energy, and 84 per cent of all paper, and own 87 per cent of all road vehicles. The same 20 per cent of the world's population produce over 50 per cent of the carbon dioxide emissions into the atmosphere, not simply polluting the space above their heads but globally increasing the so-called greenhouse effect. The USA, which accounts for a little fewer than 5 per cent of the world's population, produces 25 per cent of the world's pollution. Of the annual 2.7 million deaths from air pollution, over 2.1 million occur in developing countries.

By looking at the real level of GDP for a society, as indicated above from the 2004 *HDR*, we can start to understand the ability of that society to feed itself. The poorer a society, the less its ability to pay for the importation of food. The richer a society, the more it can spend on food. Countries such as Ethiopia, Afghanistan and Colombia use their precious agricultural land in the production of agri-exports, attempting to earn foreign currency which will allow them to survive. As noted above, the process of globalization has led to the opening up of domestic markets to foreign competition in many developing countries. Thus in many sub-Saharan African countries, such as Kenya, Uganda and Tanzania, farmers find it very difficult to compete with cheap and often subsidised foods from the USA and Europe. As noted above agricultural subsidies provided to many Western food producers have a dual effect, securing the domestic market, while allowing for the overproduction of foodstuffs, which are often dumped in the Third World at below world market prices. In these countries the majority of their populations live on meagre diets while people in the developed world are fed a wide variety of foodstuffs.

Average calorie intake per individual varies considerably between rich developed societies and poor developing nations. Food and calorie intake are related to life expectancy: the lower the amount that a society is able to spend on food, the lower the average life expectancy and the higher the rate of infant mortality in that society. The basics that any individual needs to survive are clean water, adequate diet and shelter. In many Third World societies these basics are becoming harder to obtain. The 2004 *HDR* indicates that the number of under-nourished people in the HHDI countries is so small as to be negligible, while in the MHDI countries a steady reduction in the numbers of malnourished has taken place dropping from 19 per cent of the total population to 14 per cent between 1990 and 2001. However, in the LHDI the percentage of under- and malnourished has risen from 30 per cent of the population of these countries in 1990 to 31 per cent in 2001.

Third World debt

During the 1960s and early 1970s many Third World countries borrowed massive amounts from the IMF, World Bank and commercial Western banks with the hope of boosting their own economic activity and thus forcing development to occur. However, the expected expansion in world trade never occurred. Indeed, in 1973 the dramatic rise in oil prices led to a world debt crisis which affected both the developed and developing worlds. The tight fiscal policies adopted by many Western nations had two effects on Third World nations: first, an increase in their own debt level forced them to abandon or significantly reduce their aid levels to the Third World; and, second, they were much less willing to accept imported goods from Third World countries.

In the early 1980s many Western banks started to believe that these Third World countries would have difficulty paying off their loans. The cost of loans had risen dramatically in the years following 1973, with interest payments becoming an increasing burden. In many cases countries had to take on new loans to help them pay off their earlier loans. The repayments on new loans can account for 10–15 per cent of export earnings. These problems were illustrated when Mexico defaulted on its international debt in 1982, leading to the Third World debt crisis. Latin American countries were among those that faced the largest debts – Mexico $103 billion, Brazil $117 billion and Argentina $59 billion. The cost to individuals in these countries was disastrous. Individual incomes fell by 1.5 per cent per year during the 1980s, while in the West individual incomes were growing at

the same rate. Linked to the international debt crisis were the fiscal crises of many Third World and developing societies. The attempt to sustain living standards while paying external debts forced inflation rates to climb dramatically in many countries, including Brazil, Argentina, Nigeria, Algeria and the Philippines (in 1990 Brazil had an inflation rate of 1,000 per cent). In 2002 a World Bank report indicated that many developing countries were net exporters of capital to the West in the form of large debt repayments. The 2004 *HDR* indicates that the cost of servicing these debts has risen for large numbers of countries with the biggest impact being felt by MHDI countries seeing a rise from an average of 2.9 per cent of GDP in 1990 to 5.5 per cent of GDP in 2002. The cost of such debt in human terms is immense. In Ghana, an African economic success story, growth rates doubled between 1985 and 1995 – far faster than in many other African countries. However, to service its external debt, Ghana has to spend one-third of its export earnings, money that is consequently not available for schools, health or food.

Aid

In 2002 the USA provided nearly $1.3 billion in foreign aid; in cash terms it is the largest aid donor to developing countries. Although this is an increase from the $1 billion it gave in 1992, it still represents less than 0.13 per cent of its gross national income, and the real amount it provides has fallen from the 0.21 per cent of its GNI that it gave in 1992. Simpson (1994) points out that since the early 1970s most major donor nations have substantially reduced their aid budgets in real terms.

A number of NGOs have been at the centre of attempting to ease the burden of debt faced by the developing world. Jubilee 2000, an increasingly important and independent NGO and political pressure group, with a wide-ranging membership across British society, has been at the forefront of pressurizing the British government into action on Third World debt. They have called for programmes of debt reduction and an increase in aid alongside viable political, economic and social support for Third World and developing countries. They reject the aid and trade link that has been a hallmark of Western government policies to the developing world. Among the key supporters of Jubilee 2000 has been the singer and Third World political activist Bob Geldof, inspiration behind the 1984 Band Aid concerts. In April 2004 Geldof said that:

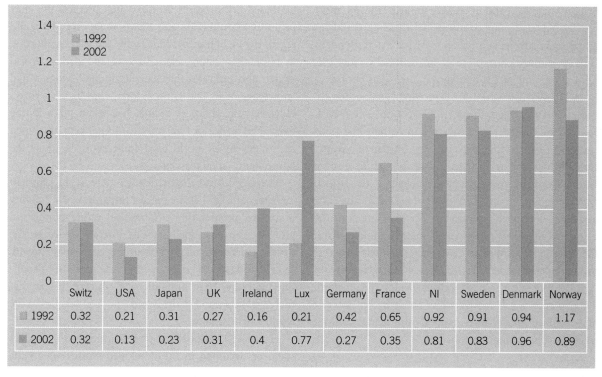

	Switz	USA	Japan	UK	Ireland	Lux	Germany	France	NI	Sweden	Denmark	Norway
1992	0.32	0.21	0.31	0.27	0.16	0.21	0.42	0.65	0.92	0.91	0.94	1.17
2002	0.32	0.13	0.23	0.31	0.4	0.77	0.27	0.35	0.81	0.83	0.96	0.89

Figure 11.13 Aid to the developing world by developed countries as a percentage of GNI 2004
Source: Based on data from *HDR* 2004

Today we are imposing so many impossible conditions, in the form of benign interference, which in truth actually prevent them developing. Perhaps it's not conscious but this is the manner in which all wealthy countries have always behaved. That's what was so unusual about the United States Marshal Plan which after the Second World War rescued Britain and Europe. Yet the truth is that, without taking away from America's legendary generosity, the Marshall Plan was devised to further America's self-interest and security. The US at that time needed a viable trading partner for their uniquely booming post-war economy.

(Bob Geldof, speech entitled 'Why Africa', St Paul's Cathedral 21.4.2004)

Yet the support and increased aid called for by Geldof and Jubilee 2000 have not really materialized. It is true that in the late 1990s change started to take place, but previous trends have dominated. Only a small number of countries (including Britain during the late 1990s and early twenty-first century have increased their aid budget in real terms. Other countries, notably the USA, Germany and France, have all reduced their aid budgets in real terms.

Yet we should not be complacent. In Britain, as in most developed countries, aid is linked to trade. Donations of aid give the impression that the rich nations are indeed helping their less fortunate friends. In reality aid is often a double-edged sword. In the 1990s Britain gave substantial amounts of aid to the MHDI country Indonesia, a large part of which was based on trade, in which the aid was used to purchase British-made goods. In this case a substantial amount of the aid given was used to purchase Hawk Jet training aircraft for the Indonesian airforce. Despite these aircraft being unarmed and designated for 'peaceful purposes' they were quickly modified by the Indonesian government for military use against separatist rebels in Ache Province of the Indonesian archipelago, the province that suffered most when the tsunami hit on 26 December 2004, with many tens of thousands dying. Similarly, the British government through the European Union has given large amounts of aid to the Palestinian Authority, which resulted in orders for British made Land Rovers for the Palestinian police.

The international community has been active in helping the developing world recover from its burden of debt. In 1996, in a joint initiative of the International Monetary Fund and the World Bank, a new fund was set up, the Heavily Indebted Poor Countries initiative (HIPC). This initiative was endorsed by the member countries of the IMF and World Bank, the USA and

Britain included, and it aimed to help the 38 most heavily indebted poor countries. Of these 38 countries 32 of them are in sub-Saharan Africa. At the end of 2004 24 countries are still receiving debt help under this fund to the tune of $54 billion over a ten-year period.

In January 2005 the UK Chancellor Gordon Brown, speaking at a forum of the developed countries in Davos, Switzerland, called for further action to help the poor countries of the world escape from the burden of poverty. He called for a new 'Marshall Plan' for the developing world. Gordon Brown acting on behalf of the British government in its capacity as chair of the G8 during 2005 asked the developed countries to write off much of the Third World debt, thus freeing many countries from the burden of debt that has hampered their progress in the post-war period (see MakePovertyHistory on p. 435). We must ask, as indeed Geldof did in April 2004, is such a call motivated as much by self-interest and the need for a market in goods and services, as out of genuine humanitarian concern?

The demographic time-bomb

Perhaps one of the biggest challenges facing a globalized world is that of population growth and decline. Whilst the Western world's population remains static or declines, rates of population growth in the developing world have been maintained or increased. This is perhaps best illustrated by the fact that in Western countries, such as Italy, pensioners will outnumber employees by 2030. In the same period, India, which has already reached a population of 1 billion, will add a further 335 million, equivalent to the total employable population of the United States and the European Union combined.

Why are there such glaring disparities between the affluent West and the developing world? In the West birth rates have declined as economic prosperity has increased. Conversely in the developing world in an effort to maximize their income many families increased the number of children they had out of economic necessity. In 1950 the annual growth in world population was 28 million per year; by 1960 it was 72 million. By the year 2000, annual population growth reached 94 million: the number of babies born each year is equal to the population of Germany, or one-a-half times the population of United Kingdom. UN statistics show that in 1991 there were 5.3 billion people in the world; in 2004 there were 6.4 billion; by 2050 there will be 8.9 billion people. The

US-based organization World Watch predicts this may be an underestimation and that population levels could reach 10–14 billion by 2050, with the biggest increase in population taking place in Asia and Africa. World Watch also indicates that globally in 1960 women had an average of six babies each; today that figure is three. However, the sharpest decline has taken place in the developed world. In 1960 only 10–15 per cent of women in the developed world used contraceptives, today the figure stands at 60 per cent.

The UN World Population Conference in Cairo in 1994 recognized that the biggest threat to world stability is not the proliferation of arms but rather population growth. The developed nations offered advice to the developing nations on ways of curbing population growth. As with aid, such advice appears to be more out of self-interest rather than humanitarian concern, a fear that there will be a flood of the world's poorest peoples to the world's richest nations.

Figure 11.14 shows that population growth rates are static or declining in the developed world, but in the developing world they are increasing by close to 2 per cent per year – a doubling of the population every 35 years. While the rate of population growth is now slowing, demonstrated in the above table by declining rates for most countries in the period 2040, rates of growth will continue to remain higher in the developing and impoverished world.

It is clear that in those societies with expanding populations some form of action is needed to reduce population growth. The developed world commands the majority of the world's income, but in many Latin American countries, poor, half-starved children roam the streets, often searching rubbish bins for scraps of food, stealing to survive. In February 2005 the United Nations put forward a proposal that all humans born on planet earth should have their births registered. Registration would serve the purpose of allowing more accurate population statistics to be made, planning for schools, health and food to be put into place, and above all to accord invaluable citizenship rights to many of those who simply officially do not exist. The growth of population in many Third World countries has led to children being seen as a burden, rather than as valued members of their society. Without the acknowledgement of their existence such children are prone to exploitation such as in child labour, the sex industries or as child slaves. Such has been the large number of these children and their 'perceived threat to public order' that in some right-wing Latin American countries death

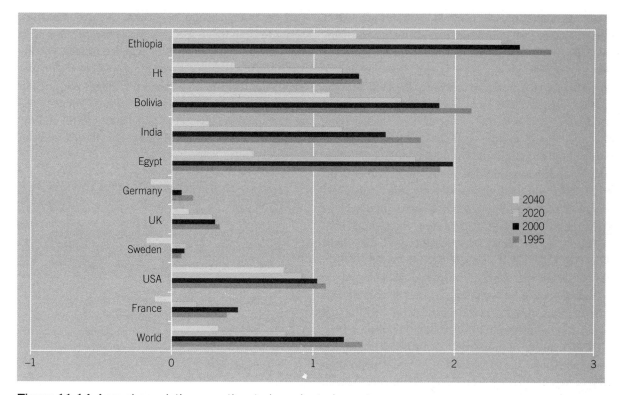

Figure 11.14 Annual population growth rate by selected country

Source: Based on data supplied in *World Population Prospects: The 2002 Revision United Nations (data for 2020 and 2040 are based upon current United Nation projections)*

squads routinely shoot these children and dump their bodies in rivers and sewers, believing that they have done society a favour by ridding it of vermin. In India it is estimated that, despite child labour laws, 55 million children are forced to live as little more than slaves. Often these children work twelve hours per day, seven days a week, producing carpets, pottery, leather goods and other items for Western markets.

Part of the solution to the demographic time-bomb is the greater empowerment of women with regard to their reproductive life. However, in many societies, both developed and less developed, cultural barriers, in particular lack of education, prevent women having access to and making decisions over contraceptives and abortion. At the 1994 Cairo conference the Vatican and Islamic delegates joined forces in condemning any weakening of traditional family structures and encouragement of what they perceived as permissive behaviour. However, Catholic doctrine no longer appears to be a significant deterrent to birth control. As we have seen above, Italy, for example, has one of the lowest birth rates in the world.

However, the demographic outlook is not all bleak. As was demonstrated at Cairo, some countries have had remarkable success in introducing programmes to reduce population increase, even traditional Catholic countries

in Latin America. In Mexico population growth rates have fallen from 1.64 in 1995 to 1.45 in 2004 and are projected to fall to 0.03 in 2050. Similarly in Argentina rates have fallen from 1.27 in 1995 to 1.17 in 2004 and are projected to reduce to 0.28 in 2050, and in Brazil rates have fallen from 1.36 in 1995 to 1.24 in 2004 and to 0.08 in 2050. Falls in population growth rates are dependent upon a number of factors, not least of which is the availability of contraceptives and sexual health education. This has in turn led to increasingly innovative ways of delivering contraceptives and the family planning message to the population of many countries.

India's most populous state has hit upon a new way of spreading the message about family planning and cut its booming population – the postman. Postal workers more used to delivering letters and parcels will now pop condoms and even the pill through the doors of residents in Uttar Pradesh's Argra and Ferozabad districts . . . Postal workers will gain an extra £1.50 per month for their efforts plus a £1.50 performance bonus. (the *Guardian* 19.10.2000)

In the early nineteenth century Thomas Malthus argued that any attempt to increase the living standards of the poorest section of the population above subsistence level was bound to fail because it would lead to an increase in the general or total population that would be unsustainable. Since 1950, the growth in world trade, the impact of the so-called 'green revolution' in agriculture and the use of technology has prevented the type of global catastrophe predicted by Malthus from occurring. However, there is disagreement as to the effects of these demographic changes. Some bodies such as the UN Food and Agriculture Organization (FAO) believe that high yields and the further application of technology to agriculture will ensure that growth in population is matched by growth in food levels. Other organizations such as Greenpeace and World Watch believe the technological quick fix can no longer be applied. Indeed, they argue that the further use of science and technology in the form of the genetic engineering of crops and the increased use of inorganic fertilizers will lead to a real deterioration in the 'carrying capacity' of the planet. More recently in a similar Malthusian vein the Optimum Population Trust (OPT), made up of prominent scientists and academics, has called for a drastic reduction in world population levels, arguing that the world can only in effect sustain

half the current world population. Natural resources, access to clean water, space and sustainable environment can only be maintained if the population falls. For the UK, the OPT is calling for a reduction from the present population level of 58.9 million in 2004 to 30 million at the start of the twenty-second century. For the OPT at least, only the reversal of population growth and the dramatic curtailment of the process of globalization can save the planet.

Stop and think

➤ What do you think the implications of population growth are for (a) natural resources; (b) climatic and environmental effects; (c) food supplies; and (d) levels of poverty?

➤ As the wealthy nations retain and increase their share of global wealth, for individuals in Third World societies more members in the family may mean the difference between survival or death. Why do you think this is so?

Summary

➤ Early sociological theories of development aimed to explain the 'development' of societies; the sociology of development has reflected this notion of the superiority of the advanced, capitalist world, for example, the hierarchy of 'worlds' from 'First World' to 'Fourth World'.

➤ Modernization theory illustrated this ethnocentric thinking and was criticized by Marxist-influenced writers such as Frank (underdevelopment theory), who 'blamed' the rich capitalist nations of the West for exploiting the rest. Other theories that have emerged as critiques of these positions (such as world system and articulation theories) have themselves emphasized the crucial role of the capitalist mode of production.

➤ Globalization is a concept illustrating the growing interdependence of world economies and therefore societies. The decline of communism following the fall of the Berlin Wall has been interpreted by writers such as Fukuyama as evidence that capitalism is the only economic system able to offer Third World countries a path to a developed status: liberal democracy and capitalism have passed the test of time. Globalization is reflected in the increasing domination of the world economy by transnational capitalist companies. This process has weakened the autonomy of nation-states.

➤ In spite of growing world interdependence, global inequality (specifically the gap between rich and poor nations) shows little sign of diminishing. This inequality is reflected in (among other things) the food eaten and the life expectancy rates in different countries. Expansion of the world economy and world trade has led many of the economically weaker nations to borrow from the richer ones. The cost of repaying these loans has had disastrous consequences for such nations.

Summary (continued)

➤ For the past five or more centuries there has been an implicit assumption that progress (most often material progress) is both desirable and sustainable. The West, more by good fortune in being the first to develop manufacturing technology, has been able to maintain a steady increase in living standards, material prosperity and economic growth. However, since the 1960s there has been a gradual shift in sociology away from grand theories, or meta-narratives, be they pro- or anti-capitalist. Our new understanding of the process of globalization presents us on the one hand with a stark realization of the potential for planetary catastrophe while on the other hand allows some room for optimism. In attempting to understand the effects of Western materialism and consumerism on the cultural practices and lifestyles of the Third World, sociology can also offer a critique of such practices and lifestyles in the capitalist world.

Links

The section on 'the new workshop of the world', pages 457–9, links to examples of work in different cultures provided in Chapter 4.

The discussion of HIV/AIDS, pages 453–454, links to the comments in Chapter 10, page 398.

 ## Further reading

Cohen, R. and Kennedy, O. (2000) *Global Sociology*, London: Macmillan.
This provides an up-to-date clear introduction to globalization.

Hulme, D. (1990) *Sociology and Development: Theories and Practice*, London: Harvester Wheatsheaf.
This is particularly good on the complexities of agricultural production in the developing world.

Lemert, C. (ed.) (1993) *Social Theory: The Multicultural and Classic Readings*, Oxford: Westview.

Worsley, P. (ed.) (1991) *The New Modern Sociology Readings*, Harmondsworth: Penguin.
Both these books include a range of useful readings which will provide you with an introduction to and flavour of the work of writers discussed in this chapter – both 'classical' and more recent development theorists.

Schlosser E. (2002) *Fast Food Nation*, London: Penguin.
An interesting, provocative and amusing examination of the history of fast food and its impact on popular culture as well as its global reach.

Simpson, E.S. (1994) *The Developing World: An Introduction*, 2nd edn, London: Longman.
As well as providing a great deal of up-to-date data on rates of development, fertility, mortality, etc., Simpson introduces the basic issues of development in the Third World and examines how particular nations are attempting to secure sustainable economic development.

Wheen, F. (2004) *How Mumbo Jumbo Conquered the World*, London: Harper Perennial.
This is a wide ranging attack on everything from Thatcherism to Postmodernism and Globalization. While being a very funny read and written in an easygoing style, Wheen conveys some very serious arguments.

 ## Web sites

www.makepovertyhistory.org
Is the web site of a campaigning group, whose work is introduced on p. 435 above.

www.worldbank.org
Is the web site of the World Bank Group, whose mission is to fight poverty and improve living standards in the developing world.

www.worldwatch.org
Is the web site of World Watch Institute which researches into environmental, social and economic trends and produce a wide range of up-to-date publications.

Activities

Activity 1

Third World images

The image of the Third World supported by modernization theory is one in which war, poverty, famine, disaster and drought are either natural disasters or self-inflicted wounds which visit these societies on occasion. These disasters or social upheavals are often explained in terms of the general inefficiency or even corruption common to such societies or because of their lack of rational values or scientific or professional processes of management.

Such views are not uncommon and often condition the way that we see and relate to the Third World. The Band Aid concert to raise money for the starving people of Ethiopia in 1984 or the Oxfam appeals in the 1990s for help in Somalia or Rwanda appear to deny the West and developed world any part in creating such situations. Charitable appeals ask us to respond in humanitarian ways, but while they are generally hugely successful in terms of raising money they do little to prevent those problems recurring. Our attention to such disasters is often brought about by media coverage, including media appeals by the rich and famous on behalf of charities. Such appeals are intended to prick our consciences and then ease them by credit card payments over the phone.

Search through a selection of recent newspapers for stories, features or adverts which relate to Third World countries.

Questions

1. What images are portrayed of the particular societies? Do you feel these images are accurate?

2. Are any explanations offered for the situations or conditions being described?

3. What sort of response is being invited from the reader?

4. What do you think are the advantages and disadvantages for Third World countries of accepting charitable aid from the West?

Activity 2

Understanding dependency

This activity is intended to help develop an understanding of the concepts surrounding sociological theories of development. A useful way of helping to identify or empathize with the predicament of dependent nations is to consider the options that are open to individuals when they are financially dependent on others and the effects which the choice of particular options might cause. Does it make things better or worse? Do the long-term effects outweigh the immediate benefits?

Imagine that you are at the end of the first year of your course and now have a large overdraft at the bank. Next year you know that such an overdraft will entail bank charges.

Questions

1. What strategies might you adopt to resolve this problem? What effects would such strategies have? List these strategies and effects in the two left-hand columns one the chart.

2. Are there equivalent strategies open to national governments. What effects would such strategies have for these governments? List the strategies and effects suggested for governments in the two right-hand columns on the chart.

Activities (continued)

Individual		National	
Strategy	**Effects**	**Strategy**	**Effects**
Example: Sell your possessions	Low price for goods. May have to replace later at inflated prices. Poorer lifestyle	Example: Sell off national assets	National assets controlled by outside interests

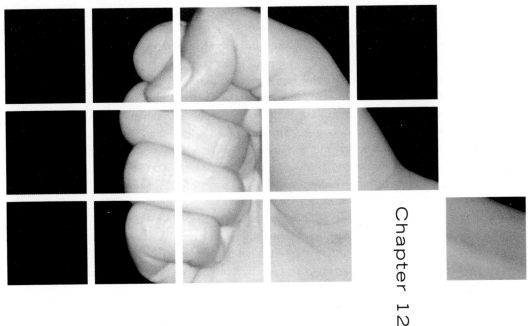

Chapter 12

Nationalism

If people behaved in the way nations do they would all be put in straitjackets

(Tennessee Williams)

Key issues

➤ How do we define nations and nationalism?

➤ How do notions of language, culture, ethnicity and history relate to the idea of a nation?

➤ How have sociologists theorized about nations and nationalism?

➤ What is citizenship and how does it relate to nationalism?

➤ How are people socialized into national identities?

➤ What is the role of gender in shaping national identities?

Introduction

There are a number of terms in this book that seem straightforward enough until one comes to think about them. Nation is one that seems especially difficult as it is at once rather more abstract and rather more common place than a number of other terms at issue. The same is true of related terms national identity, nationality and nationalism. If we leave aside the internal distinctions that need to be drawn between these terms and pursue at a general level the problem of definition with nation, such a contrast exists in respect to gender. Gender has an everyday reality in a way that nation does not. Gendered roles in the home, for instance, shape the domestic division of labour. It can therefore affect what a woman does and what a man does not do, and vice versa, from the time they wake in the morning to the time they go to bed at night. Of course, an awareness of different household tasks does not mean that they are recognized and analyzed in terms of sociological understandings of gender. However, there may well be some sense of injustice and inequality, particularly but not exclusively on the part of the woman, and certainly at the very least awareness that there is a gender contrast. Such an everyday awareness of gender is not generally true of nations and nationalism, the subject of this chapter.

Being a member of a nation does not have an immediate relevance the moment one gets out of bed in the morning. As an individual goes about their everyday concerns – school, college, work, etc. – belonging to a nation, being a national, probably seems of rather distant importance. There are important exceptions to this. For example, being a Palestinian in most Israeli-occupied parts of Palestine, Gaza and the West Bank, means a daily reality of Israeli Army patrols, checkpoints, evictions and shootings. But such actions take place in the relatively rare context of two nationalisms that claim the same territorial area rather than the more common quarrel over the exact position of borders. On a rather different level, an awareness of nationality may come into focus and occupy our thoughts before an international sporting event such as the football World Cup. For the most part, however, being a national does not occupy our thoughts and influence our actions in a way that other identities do.

At the same time 'nation' is everywhere both in relation to state institutions, government-controlled industries and the obligations and rights of the individual. In many countries, France and the USA for instance, national flags routinely fly outside public buildings, inside school rooms, in public spaces and from the roofs of private houses. The term 'national' is coupled with others to indicate what exists only within the geographical remit of the country, something that applies to all across the land and a collection that is equally 'ours': the national electricity grid, national holidays and the National Gallery. In order to work, to claim most benefits and to be educated in a given country, we must be a 'national citizen' of that state. More dramatically, every time we travel we are aware that we must prove our nationality by producing a passport upon entry to another country. It is wise to prevent this discussion going any further, however, as it obvious that there are important distinctions between national citizenship and national identity. The former may be largely a matter of convenience – a practical necessity for travel, etc. – the latter the stuff of pride. The general point is that although nations and nationalism may not in ordinary circumstances weigh upon our minds and influence our activities like other subjects covered in this book, its assumptions are crucial to the organization of social, political and, to a lesser extent, economic life. Moreover, everybody has some notion of what a nation is.

Stop and think

➤ What nation do you feel you belong to?

➤ How does it affect (a) your daily behaviour and (b) your view of life?

A closer look

Nationalism: good or bad

Some may find this question rather strange. Are we really concerned with questions that are political and moral in sociology? Is it not the case that the outlook of the individual will determine this? His or her feelings about their own nation will figure large. However, it is important to try and establish some way in which the positive and negative aspects of nationalism might be assessed. There are, moreover, grounds for doing this as nationalism is not a constant in human history. We are entitled to ask 'what has been its impact'. No serious scholar of the subject would claim that nations have always been around, certainly not in the sense that we now know and understand them. If, for the sake of argument, we accept that nationalism as a popular ideology has been around for approximately the last two hundred years, we might go about answering this question by drawing up a balance sheet of the deeds that have been done in the name of nation. In doing so we would probably place under a minus column acts of hate: wars, invasions and ethnic cleansing. In the plus column we would list some of the creations that have been inspired by love of country: pieces of music, works of literature, poetry, architecture and sporting success. On a more mundane level we might cite the attachment an individual has to the countryside of his or her nation, a sense of pride in the achievements of a nation's historical figures and the enjoyment of its particular dishes and drinks. More simply still, this would extend to a certain sense of well-being people have in the company of their countrymen, a feeling that, for all the faults of their nation, this – both people and place – is where they are at home, where they belong. Viewed in this way nations and nationalism are key to the psychological stability of the individual. A nation is, in the words of a poet, 'The place that has to take you in when you have to go there.' We have only to consider the predicament of the asylum seeker, who no longer has a nation and has to seek sanctuary elsewhere, to understand the importance of having a home nation. Considered in this way nationalism is simply part of the human condition, something whose absence would drastically impoverish what it is to be alive: well-being through togetherness.

Such balance sheets between the good and the bad of nationalism are perhaps inevitable but rather simplistic.

A closer look (continued)

First, it is wrong to attribute everything that takes place under the banner of nation, whether good or bad, as motivated purely by nationalism in a narrow sense. The word 'nationalism' is often applied indiscriminately to complex realities. Consider the example of sporting success. We know that love of country does motivate athletes, but can this motivation be neatly separated from the egos and bank balances of many international sportsmen and women? As with individuals, so with wider historical events. For instance, it is legitimate to refer to twentieth century independence struggles of African and Asian countries against European empires as nationalist. But any serious analysis of them would have to take proper account of the role of other ideologies of the independence movements, especially socialism, and the political and economic motives of local elites. Similarly, it is problematic to explain away something like a war by applying the word nationalism. During the early 1990s it was common to hear journalists say that the bloody break-up of Yugoslavia was caused by ethnic nationalism, as if that was really all the analysis that was needed. Indeed nationalism clearly was central to the emergence of antagonistic separatist movements within the federation that had existed since 1945. Nobody could seriously argue otherwise. However, that is not the whole story of the war: far from it. It is quite impossible to separate strictly nationalist political motivation – principally the pursuit of an ethnically homogenous independent state – from the self-agrandizement and enrichment that occurred at both local and regional levels. Power hungry politicians, in some instances former Communists, quickly draped themselves in rival national flags in order to bolster their personal standings as 'socialist' Yugoslavia collapsed. On the ground, both paramilitaries and civilians could share the material rewards of ethnic cleansing if they were victorious: the neighbour's car, television and life savings. The only price to pay was to turn a blind eye to the actual killings and subsequently keep quiet. And then there were those who simply liked a fight, the dirtier the better, who revelled in the chauvinistic machismo and the semi-pornographic gun culture of war. So the break-up of Yugoslavia was about nationalism, but also opportunist politicians, gangsters, unemployed football hooligans and, only a little more charitably, human weakness. So nationalism should not be considered a sort of analytical magic talisman that explains everything.

Second, such a division between the good and the bad begins to break down after a little reflection. Take war as an example, a probable first inclusion on the minus side of things. Aside from a few psychopaths, who would seriously claim that death and destruction are in themselves good things? But if war might be generally considered a bad thing, it is necessary to quickly point out that the fighting of wars is part of the historical glory of nations. Invariably wars – whether victories or defeats – are depicted by a nation's historians and remembered in popular consciousness as struggles that are forced upon them: defensive campaigns that had to be fought because the nation was imperilled. But having been so provoked, having been forced to take up arms in self-defence, the positives of nation come to the fore: the self-sacrifice, the valour, the sheer toughness and determination of a people united in opposition to a common enemy. This shades into gendered notions of military manliness and romance.

The actions and emotions associated with the positive are frequently given a separate name: they are termed patriotic rather than nationalistic. The contrasting connotations of these terms are indeed powerful. Take the closing scene form one of the best known films of the twentieth century, *Casablanca*. As the French police sergeant walks from the airfield with Sam (Humphrey Bogart), who has just shot a Nazi officer thereby enabling his former lover (Ingrid Bergman) to escape German-occupied Morocco, he says, 'You know, Sam, I think you have the makings of a patriot.' If he had said 'nationalist' rather than 'patriot' the connotation would have been wholly different; indeed in the context it would have illogically implied the very thing the Second World War was being fought against by the Allies: fascism. As the use of the term nationalism conjures up hate and violence so its pointed use is deceitful. For instance, Fox News uses the term nationalism – as well as Islamic fundamentalism – to describe the attacks on American soldiers and the Iraqi police force in occupied Iraq. The word is not applied when referring to the motivations of the Bush Administration. The assumption is that they have nationalism, we have patriotism. However, all that the use of 'patriotism' does is to replace the plus heading. It only superficially makes clear the distinction between the good and bad in any list we might try and draw up. It does not deal with the problems identified above of how discreet a category nationalism really is and how the good and the bad merge. For that reason it only serves to confuse matters and is not therefore a useful distinction.

There is another way of thinking about the good and the bad in nationalism: identify certain nationalisms that fall into one camp or the other. This is more or less what one scholar, Liah Greenfeld (1992) tried to do in a much discussed if highly controversial book, *Nationalism: Five Roads to Modernity*. According to Greenfeld certain

▶

A closer look (continued)

nationalisms, especially the English (and by extension British) and American cases, are, for various historical reasons, inherently democratic. Others, notably German and Russian nationalisms, are inherently undemocratic. Of the German nationalism, Greenfeld states in a line that quickly became notorious, 'The moment German national identity was born Germany was ready for the holocaust' (Greenfeld 1992: 176). Most critics thought this line an incredibly simplistic understanding of the complexities of the historical process.

Other 'good' nationalisms are expounded by those who would seem to have a certain national case to make in their writing. The Scottish sociologist David McCrone does not make clear his attachment to Scotland in his principal book on his country, *The Sociology of Scotland*. However, the final chapter consists of an energetic account of how the civic and multicultural nature of contemporary Scottish nationalism is a model of a new globalized world of nations – a world of nations without nation-states as he puts it. McCrone does not even mention things like racism and xenophobia in Scotland. We really rather get the impression that Scottish nationalism is just a 'good nationalism'. Now it is clearly possible to try to identify a positive trend in a particular nationalism and make the case that it is increasingly politically relevant. It is quite another thing to overlook other less attractive features of a given nationalism. We might say that all countries have different tendencies within them and all have different varieties. Therefore it would be wrong to try to categorize

a nationalism wholesale. Many would have some sympathy with the ambivalent feelings of the playwright Denis Potter. These are his thoughts about England shortly before his death in 1995:

> Sometimes I get out of bed and I don't know whether I'm right-wing or left-wing, to be honest, because I feel the pull of both. I feel the pull of tradition, and I love my land, I love England, and when I'm abroad, I genuinely feel homesick. I've always loved my country, but not drums and trumpets and billowing Union jacks and busby soldiers and the monarchy and pomp and circumstance, but something about our people that I come from and therefore respond to. And I expect other people to do it of their own backgrounds and nations and cultures, too.

Ultimately, there is really no way round the issue of nationalism good and bad. All one can to do is to acknowledge that it is both of those things. It is inherently contradictory or, more accurately put, Janus-faced – a head with two faces, one benign, one grotesque. It is a source of motivation that provides human togetherness and creativity and at the same time furthers division and ultimately destruction. It creates spectacle and enjoyment and motivates hatred and war. It is simultaneously incredibly flexible and transportable across time and space, an ideology that can shape the basic assumptions of movements and parties that are political enemies. These points will become clearer as we consider the given components of a nation.

This chapter is concerned with trying to define what a nation is, with looking at how sociologists and others have tried to understand the rise of modern nations and in looking at how people learn to be national and acquire a sense of national identity. It covers the relationship between nationalism and citizenship and discusses crucial questions like nation and gender/sexuality. First, however, it is necessary to deal briefly with an issue that is raised by the very use of the term: nationalism.

What is a nation?

When trying to understand nations and nationalism it is necessary to try and distinguish between myth and reality. This can be difficult because on the one hand nationalism is taken for granted, a common sense reality without being an everyday concern. On the other hand,

because national identity is a matter of pride for many people, to suggest that nations are somewhat or largely mythical can cause offence. Nations, the people who constitute them, tend to take their existence for granted and are unhappy about this suggestion. Myths, however, should not be taken as the opposite of reality as not all of them are strictly untrue. The point about a myth is that it that it is thought to be self-evidently true. The credence given to them derives from their perpetuation as a popular narrative; a myth is something that people believe because others, such as family, peers, the wider society, say so without question. Looking critically at the myths that surround nations is not an attempt to suggest that they are mere fictions that gullible people adhere to because they are somehow comforting. Looking critically, however, it is essential for a proper sociological approach to the subject. Certainly when coming to what a nation is we have look beyond the claims of nationalists. We have to ask whether what is taken for granted now has always been the case, and to distinguish between what is seemingly natural and what has occurred as a result of social and political engineering and transformation. And we have to question if what is thought to be typical applies to anything like the majority of the nation in question. The nation involves, I suggest, all of the things below. But we must look at each of them with caution.

Territory

A novel feature of contemporary nations is that they are strictly demarcated territories, patches of land controlled by a state in the name of nation. This contrasts with the existence of nomadic tribes and more loosely defined kingdoms and empires for long periods of human history. Certainly kingdoms and empires were about lands, frequently viewed as the personal property of the king and his noblemen, and separated by natural geography like rivers and seas. However, the policed borders of the nation of the twentieth and twenty-first centuries with their arrays of fences, checkpoints and guards are historically recent. The key requirement of the international traveller today is a passport. One-hundred-and-fifty years ago passports did not exist. A traveller could come and go pretty much at will. Now practically every inhabitable square kilometre of the world is parcelled up among the 220 states that control it. They put in place an ever increasing variety of measures to try and regulate human movement between nations.

The principal claim to controlling a territory is historic habitation: we were here first, put bluntly. Nationalism is about the historical justification of geographical residence. This applies as much to historic nations as it does to settler nations and those that were created relatively recently. Therefore the justification of the Japanese, the Australians and the Kenyans is that they belong in that area of the world's surface: it is theirs because they have been there generation upon generation. It makes very little difference to this justification whether the period of time is known to be one hundred or one thousand years. Nor, in the case of settler nations, does it make very much difference to a sense of pride and belonging, what the circumstances of arrival were. Do black Jamaicans and many white Australians feel at least as much attachment to their countries, although their ancestors were forcibly taken there as slaves or convicts, as, say, New Zealanders? There are other ways in which nations and nationality are understood and granted. The notion of national citizenship is about geographical residence, but not formally about historical habitation. Rather, it is about belonging and the conferment of privileges and obligations through national allegiance – being a national and being seen as one by putting something into a country if you like. But as with most things in this subject there is no dichotomy here: national citizenship through residence frequently operates in tandem with notions of nationality attained through historic habitation.

Clearly a national land is not simply a practical space to exist. As indicated above, an attachment to nation often includes the love of a distinctive area of natural beauty. Anyone who has lived abroad for a period of time may well have experienced nostalgia for the landscape they left behind and see it as the defining feature of their nationality. But landscape is not usually just a pure environment. In nationalist discourse territory and people combine. In notions of national character we consider below how the features of national natural environment, together with its climate, create notions of dominant personality types. How relevant such notions are in an age when increasingly people live in town and cities is, of course, open to question.

It would be both pointless and wrong to try to disprove all national narratives of original habitation. However, various important qualifications should be made. First, we should be wary of political claims designed to further national political advantage. As Nigel Harris comments in relation to Malaysia they often rely upon a certain historical myopia:

> When the Malay leaders of Malaysia assert that the Malays are 'bumpiputras', sons of the soil, and therefore should be accorded privileges as against the Chinese and Indian Malaysians, only the unkind would point out that the Malays were also immigrants from an earlier period, and that no one has paid any attention to the claims of the real indigenous peoples, the Dayak and other tribes of the forestland.   (Harris 1992: 9)

Second, as indicated, the claim to original habitation overlooks the cumulative and profound impact of migration in human history. Third, the land of a people is not something that has just happened like evolution, peoples have not just grown up with borders always strapped around them. The positioning of borders has been the result of wars, conquests, empires and diplomacy. The borders of most European countries have remained the same since 1945. But before that they were subject to various historical revisions as a result of war. African, Latin American and most, if not all, Asian states were the product of

European empires. In many instances the borders established by colonialists were quite arbitrary, grouping and dividing tribal groups. So we should be sceptical of any suggestion that national territories are just natural.

Language

In the Tower of Babel nations developed through God's introduction of different languages to sew confusion. Clearly nations are 'about' languages. Germany is the nation where German is spoken as distinct from France where French is spoken, unlike Spain where Spanish is spoken and so on. A national language obviously allows mutual comprehension amongst its inhabitants. Although this does not in itself guarantee a sense of togetherness, of community, it is all but impossible if people cannot communicate with each other. But a national language is not just a practical matter of communication. It is also a literary language in which fiction, poetry lyrics, are composed. A love of language is usually, though obviously not always, a love of one's own language. For some, most famously the great German romantic nationalist Godfried von Herder, a national language captures the history and spirit of a people (Herder 1969). For him a language is not just a mutual means of expression so much as an embodiment of the experience and essential character of a nation. He thought that the spectacle of the German middle classes of the late eighteenth century desperately trying to educate their children in French because of its supposed superior qualities was not only pathetic but a national betrayal. We do not have to follow Herder in this exclusivist conception of language to recognize that in order to grasp the full nuances and references of a language, especially as it pertains to humour, an individual has to grow up speaking it.

However, while nations are clearly about national languages, if we look critically at the issue we can see that the matter is not so straightforward. For the most part this is true that nations have a single national language, but this is not always the case. If there is no single national language it at least places a question mark over the assumption that all members of the nation can automatically communicate with one another. In some cases, like Canada, where there are officially two languages, French and English, this is a recognition of the division within the nation. However, Switzerland has three state languages, French, German and Italian, and it is one of the most stable European countries. The only threat to its unity in recent years was over the divisive issue of women's right to vote in local canton

elections, not over some language concern – whether or not one of the languages, and by extension its speaking constituency, is being discriminated against in some way. Simultaneously, a number of nations speak the same language. English is the official language of, among other countries, Britain, Australia, India and the USA. Spanish is the national language of the whole of Latin America with one or two exceptions, notably Brazil that shares Portuguese with its former European colonial master.

A common language does necessarily blunt national distinctiveness and pride. Do the Irish feel any less Irish for instance because they speak English? Indeed, where neighbouring nations speak the same language this can appear to increase animosity in some instances, rather than lead to a feeling of togetherness. In the case of the Balkan countries, Serbia and Croatia, that were until 1991 part of the federal Yugoslav state with several other regions of that area of southern Europe, their languages are all but identical. Since 1991 Croatian linguists have gone to great lengths to try to extend the minor differences between the languages, but that does not alter the fact that if a Serb and Croat were to meet they would have no difficulty in communicating with each other. A common language did not stop Serbs and Croats (and Bosnians), sometimes neighbours, killing large numbers of their 'enemy' nationality during the break-up of Yugoslavia, 1992–95. One of the ironies of that bitter civil war is that Serb and Croat war crime suspects held at a jail in Holland near the International Tribunal for War Crimes in the Former Yugoslavia at the Hague, freely communicate with each other while they await trial in what they refer to as 'our language' (Drakulic 2004: 173–83).

But as a common language exists across borders some nations, specifically nation-states, will sometimes go to great lengths to ensure that a single language is spoken throughout its territory. A major part of the whole process of nation-building in the nineteenth century and twentieth century Europe was to ensure that a single language became intelligible across the whole nation. The key means of doing this was the provision of universal primary education that taught the nation's young a grammatically uniform language. Prior to the advent of universal state education much of the labouring population had grown up illiterate and speaking either a regional dialect or a minority language that made communication with other sections of the population problematic or impossible. We sometimes hear today people in London say that they cannot understand people from Liverpool or Newcastle. However, if placed together in a room it is almost inconceivable that they could not have a conversation, even if the participants had especially strong regional accents. If they had sat together as late as 1870 it is likely they would have had genuine difficulty making themselves understood given the influence of regional dialects. Other agencies played a part in the spread of national languages, the military and state broadcasting institutions, but above all education was vital in creating single national languages where in practical terms they had not really existed. Other cases were more dramatic than the English. When Italy was unified in 1861 only two per cent of its population spoke Italian.

We should note that the spread of national languages over the last two hundred years has not just been about 'teaching the lower order to speak properly'. In some countries during certain periods the upper classes have largely spoke a language distinct from the mass of the population. Russian aristocracy in the eighteenth century prided themselves on their distinction from the common peasant mass of the country by generally conversing in French, the then European *lingua franca*. It was only in the nineteenth century that emerging middle-class nationalists insisted that the nation as a whole should speak a single language.

As education systems have been central to 'ironing out' regional dialects they have, in some instances, also actively suppressed minority languages. In French schools for instance, into the 1950s children could be punished for speaking in one of a number of regional rural languages like Breton that they learnt as their first language at home. Trying to root out non-official languages extended in some instances in the twentieth century to making it an imprisonable offence to speak it. In Turkey until recently speaking Kurdish in public was deemed a crime. This was part of the attempt by the Turkish government to officially deny even the suggestion that there was a substantial Kurdish minority population within Turkey that claimed an independent state. More recently, partly in an attempt to liberalize Turkey in order to apply to join the European Union, Kurdish is now tolerated and even officially recognized as a minority language.

This indicates that nation-states are not just concerned with imposing a national language in the interests of the greater nation. In some instances they may extend the rights of particular languages in order to try to preserve the wider nation, or at the very least, the survival of its wider territorial existence. For example, the provision of Welsh as the first language in Wales through the Welsh Language Act of 1993 has had the effect of reducing Welsh demands for independence from the United Kingdom. Britain may not be particularly united over anything

very much any more, but it is unlikely that the Union of England, Ireland, Scotland and Wales will completely disintegrate in the near future. In the general election of 2005, the Scottish National Party failed to make substantial gains and Plaid Cymru in Wales slightly declined. However, if the Welsh were denied the right to speak Welsh in schools and other public places, and children were expelled for voicing it in the classroom, it is likely that demand for outright independence would rise. So granting language rights to minority nationalities within a wider nation-state can actually be a way of securing its future. The point is that in both instances it is the nation-state that is crucial to the use of a language.

Stop and think

In the USA English is becoming a second language in some areas. In Los Angeles, for example, there are more people who speak Spanish as a first language than English. The city has recently elected its first Hispanic mayor.

➤ Can you think of any other examples where the national language is being displaced by another?

➤ Does it, as some claim in the USA and elsewhere, serve to undermine the stability and coherence of the nation through eroding a basic feature of nations – the ability to communicate with each other?

➤ Or is it just inevitable in a globalized world that urban populations will increasingly speak a diversity of languages while being able to communicate in English?

➤ Would you describe your own language as regional? If so, from what region?

➤ What words and phrases do you and your family use that are specific to your local language?

Culture

Language is a key aspect of the wider phenomenon of culture. Indeed, most people recognize that nations share certain common cultural pastimes that serve to distinguish them one from another. Such pastimes are traditional in that they have been practised historically and handed down through the generations. Again we should note that traditions of course exist; as indicated above in looking at nations critically we are not seeking to suggest that they are mere fictions. It is the case that there are traditional musical forms, song, food, forms of dress and sporting pastimes that are distinct by nationality. There are serious

Figure 12.1 Different national cultures on the UK high street
Source: Nicola Chilvers, photographer

problems however, in any assumption that traditions are always or even usually historical, typical or unique.

It is not difficult to think of cultural pastimes in contemporary Britain that are anything but historical but which are certainly popular. For instance, it is now almost a cliché to say that chicken tikka masala is the typical dish that the nation eats, as popular perhaps as fish and chips. Now the type of curry usually eaten in Britain may be much anglicized or 'repatriated' as one sociologist puts it (Appadurai 1990: 305), that is, adapted to the British palate, compared with that found in the Indian subcontinent. But leaving this aside, the key point is that it was hardly known a hundred years ago. 'Going for a curry and a few lagers' (originally a German beer) maybe typically British but it is the product of only recent history, specifically of post-imperial immigration to Britain after 1945 – something that took place to the consternation of some British nationalists. The case of curry is only one illustration of how national traditions can be of very recent origin. Another national food, pizza, thought of as typically Italian in fact only acquired such a reputation with efforts to introduce a common cuisine among the people of the region that became Italians in the nineteenth century. To extend the famous saying of D'Azelglio, 'Now we have created Italy we must make the Italians' – by baking pizza together.

It is perhaps in the nature of cultural pastimes that they can become widespread very quickly. If people

enjoy the activity in question they seldom pause to consider whether or not it has been practised for ten years, or a hundred or a thousand years or, indeed, what the motivations were of those responsible for introducing it in the first place.

Sociologically we have to ask, to return more specifically to national traditions, how and to what extent do such traditions establish social cohesion within a group. We have to look at how they legitimize institutions, status or authority and whose particular purposes they serve (Hobsbawm and Ranger 1983: 9).

A contrary, but equally important, question is how widespread a cultural practice really is within a given nation. The images that fill the popular mind of a typical form of cultural practice are often something of a stereotype. When asked for 'the typical' traditions of a given group people often refer to some apparently authentic mental image, usually one with rural connotations. For example, when asked for what is typically Spanish or Irish they might refer to flamenco and the ceilidh. If pressed on what is typically English they might have to cite morris dancing. Now obviously such dances do exist and young people continue to learn them, but invariably they are dances that originated in village communities and rural lifestyles. Young people are obviously now more likely to dance to the electronic rhythms that fill the clubs and discos of modern cities the world over.

Case study

Halloween

Take a non-national 'tradition' – the current razzmatazz surrounding Halloween seems to have escalated in recent years with the spread of the scary costumes, trick or treat and

now cards. Halloween itself is an ancient pagan festival but ten years ago far less fuss was made of the 31 October. Not that this matters much to the children who love dressing up and getting sweets. They are the products of cultural exposure to America and

the huge commercial activities seized upon by firms eager for a new market.

Question

1. *Can you think of any other national traditions that have emerged fairly recently?*

Finally, there is the issue of how distinct a cultural tradition really is. How many important things are there that are really unique to particular nations? Some pastimes only find expression through the very fact that they are global. In contemporary England football, specifically the World Cup and European Championships, is one of the few things that seemingly unites the nation, if only for a week or two – though there are undoubtedly issues about whether or not, in particular, Asians can fully participate in the rituals like displaying the cross of St George that now accompany tournaments. However, the ability of England to take the field and play foreign opponents is obviously due to the fact that it is played elsewhere. In fact, with a handful of important exceptions, football is the most popular game in most of the world. Football is a global game that gives rise to international competition – that sometimes spills over into nationalist violence and even war. Other aspects of global culture are clearly not bound up with the rivalry of nations. Few aspects of consumption – what we wear, eat, listen to – are entirely free of any national connotation. Contemporary dance music might be an example. Indeed, many corporate brands, like McDonald's and Nike, are synonymous with America, their country of origin. But this does not stop young people the world over wearing the same sports shoes and clothes and eating in the same fast-food restaurants. (The sociological approach towards culture is discussed in Chapter 1, pp. 20–3.)

Racial origin

The idea of race has been much discredited. In terms of biology, specifically genetics, it has very little going for it as it places a high level of importance upon a very small degree of human diversity. So in a sense there would seem little point in proceeding with discussion: if race has no reality then the idea of racial nations has no reality.

However, this avoids the fact that people believe in race and assign much importance to belief. Moreover, whatever the inner reality revealed by genetic testing, it is not the case that peoples are identical in appearance. So in a discussion of nationalism we must consider it. I use the term 'race' below in preference to 'ethnicity' so as not to confuse matters with the generally positive cultural rather than biological connotations of the term. However, in much of the academic discussion of nationalism the term 'ethnic nationalism' is used rather than 'racial nationalism'. The term 'ethnic cleansing' – the term given for driving out another nationality from a territory – has, unfortunately, become commonplace in recent years. 'Ethnic' is used in preference to 'racial' because an ethnic nationalism tends to place a primary emphasis upon a fundamental group similarity through common descent, rather than innate physiological differences.

Within Europe this approach to defining membership of a nation was, until recently, officially that of Germany and most Central and Eastern European countries. Put bluntly the approach was either you are German or you are not. Being German was defined by parental lineage and culture, but the two were the same: culture, in the final analysis, was in the blood. As a result, it was impossible until fairly recently for somebody whose parents were a nationality other than German to acquire German citizenship other than by marrying a German. So the second generation of Turkish immigrants who came to Germany in the late 1950s were unable to become fully German and thereby acquire the full range of benefits of that nationality: residency rights, some social security benefits, etc.

This principle of national inclusion and exclusion – who is allowed in and who is not – has been an area of massive importance for many countries. For instance, after 1991, when Croatia declared independence from Yugoslavia, it declared that all those within the region and beyond were Croat if they could prove their ethnic authenticity. Therefore, if an individual was born and lived in Bosnia Herzegovina or Serbia but had a parent who was born within the territory deemed to be Croatian, and was Catholic, they might apply for Croatian nationality. However, if somebody was actually born in Croatia but was classed as Serbian, not only was their right to claim Croatian nationality much reduced, they risked losing their job. This happened to a substantial number of Serbs in the Croatian region of the Balkans despite the fact that, in some cases, their families had lived in that area of the Balkans for hundreds of years.

But it is not only countries like Croatia that have applied the 'German principle' of nationality in recent history. Britain changed its post-war policy of allowing all former colonial citizens – inhabitants of the British Empire – to apply for British citizenship in 1971, to only those who could prove their British nationality by virtue of the British birth of their parents or grandparents. This was intended to allow full citizenship and therefore crucially the right to enter the UK and settle to whites of British ancestry in, in particular, Australia, Canada and New Zealand, but to keep out the rest (Spencer 1997).

Few, if any, countries maintain a strictly racial definition of nationalism, but it remains central to understandings of nationalism in many countries in the world, notably Japan and China. And the notion that nations are racial-based entities is not just an official classification; it is one that chimes with the most rudimentary understandings of nations: you are of that national group with that label because you come from there and you look that way. Such an outlook has a certain intuitive logic. If it had no basis in reality it is difficult to see how nations could in any sense be thought to exist. Moreover, we must go further in insisting that it is the case that nations – even modern 'cosmopolitan nations' like Britain and France – do have a definable racial basis as measurable by their predominant ethnic composition. If we were to measure the *average* genetic make-up of the British it would be distinct from, say, the Chinese.

This rather obvious point is different to the contention, both official and popular, that nations are definable by any kind of pure blood line that is akin to an extended family. In fact, there can be no defence of a common pedigree. Nations are composites, the heterogeneous products of waves of immigration. This is obviously true in relation to nations that were established in the nineteenth century such as Brazil and Peru. It is the case that a definable white European ruling class dominates economically and usually politically, but this does not mean that the nation as a whole could be thought homogeneous. In fact, the suggestion would be thought absurd. Part of the self-image of the USA is as an immigrant nation so the idea of it being an ethnic nation is a misnomer. However, despite massive racial inequality in the USA it is clear that the hold of the economic and political elite, the so called WASPs (white Anglo-Saxon Protestants) is being undermined by the diversity of, in particular, its major cities. Despite the fact that the current US President, George W. Bush, was born in Connecticut and is more a member of the WASP establishment than the Texan one, the current American government is notable for its multiracial make-up. But there are good reasons to be sceptical of any claim to an ancient and stable population core even with older European nations. In the case of the English, if one leaves aside Scottish, Welsh and Irish (the single biggest source of immigration to the UK) influences upon 'English stock', one can identify historically, among others, German, Scandinavian and French eras of migration and settlement. Within modernity, approximately the last two hundred years, immigrants have settled here from most parts of Europe. Over the last sixty years new Commonwealth citizens have come in substantial numbers from, in particular, the Caribbean and the Indian subcontinent. More recently, asylum seekers and others have come from a variety of countries inside and outside of Europe.

Now this in itself certainly does not mean that England can be considered a giant melting pot in which everybody can and does consider themselves to be English regardless of their background. Some immigrant groups have maintained a high degree of ethnic exclusivity. Nevertheless, it is the case that one in five of children at primary schools in British cities is reckoned to be of mixed ethnicity – and, moreover, one or both of these parts may in themselves be composites. The current fashion for delving into one's family history frequently throws up the fact that a relative of three, four or five generations back came to England from somewhere else. Nationality defined as ethnic purity simply does not make much sense. It is probably a better idea to view nations as hybrids.

This does not mean that national groups have no genuine claim to a territory on the grounds of original habitation – 'we were the first here so this is our land' as it might be put – but it can make its application problematic, especially where there is dispute over the matter. For instance, the Zionist claim that contemporary Israelis make up the historic population of that region of the Mediterranean coast, conveniently overlooks the genetic heterogeneity of the Jewish people and of course the very existence of the Palestinians.

History

Nations are historical entities. This applies to the relatively mundane aspects of everyday life discussed above such as language and culture. They are passed on from generation to generation without much of a second thought. But history more properly, and as discussed here, applies also to the grander aspects of a nation's past: wars, occupations, famines, migrations. A nation is that group that knows something of key shared moments it has experienced. Without any kind of a sense of history it is difficult to see how nations exist in a meaningful sense as there can be no sense of collective history. Without history nations would be mere aggregates of people whose only possible perceived connection is that they happen to share the same geographical space.

History in this sense is not strictly academic history as taught in schools and universities. It is as much a history of the pub and the football stadium. 'Two world wars and one world cup', 'No surrender to the IRA scum' and 'Rule Britannia' are chanted by some English football fans to remind themselves and others of the nation's twentieth century triumphs over Germany, British rule in Ireland and its wider imperial past, but it is unlikely that most of those who give voice in the stadium have any great knowledge of the historical detail of these things. That is not the point. Their importance is that they are part of the general assertion – together with the national anthem – to continue in the same vein, of 'England, England, England!'.

A slightly different example of national remembering is that of the Second World War. Memories of 1939–45 have faded over the last few years with the passing of many of those who lived through and fought in the war, including, as it has only recently been fully acknowledged, servicemen and women from British colonies in the Caribbean and Asia. However, through a combination of sources – official and unofficial, consisting of family oral history, Remembrance Sunday marches to memorials and church services, the wearing of poppies, war films, documentaries, TV sitcoms, magazines, the armed forces themselves, museums – the memory of that period has been kept alive, 'lest we forget their sacrifice'. The same is true for other nations, sometimes with other wars, all over the world. At the symbolic heart of many nations is the tomb of the unknown soldier – an anonymous representative of those who laid down their lives for their nation when called upon to do so.

But while nations remember episodes in their past that they can take pride in with genuine justification, it is necessary to point out that, as the Frenchman Ernest Renan famously put it, they are 'getting history wrong' and 'forgetting history' (Renan 1990). It is not that everything in national histories from the nationalist perspective is factually incorrect, but there is a tendency towards distortion given nationalist priorities. Sometimes this may involve revision of the historical record. One example is the way in which Franjo Tudjman, the first president of Croatia, 1991–99, started his political career by writing a history of the Croatian fascist regime of the Ustache in 1941–45 that considerably scaled down the official Yugoslav estimate of how many Serbs had been killed. More interesting, though, because the mechanisms are more subtle, is the way in which mental images of a period are built up. The Second World War is a good example. The image that developed during the post-war era was very much one of togetherness on the domestic front in a united British effort against the Nazi enemy who seemed to be on the brink of invasion. Undoubtedly this did exist: people did sing songs in tube stations during the blitz, share food together and more readily strike up conversations with strangers. Young men did willingly join the armed forces. Children from the industrial towns were well looked after by country people. Home guard units were formed that would have fought to the last man. However, this picture is exaggerated. It leaves out the fact that the government did not initially want civilians to use underground stations as air raid shelters and ignores the evidence that considerable looting took place after German bombing raids; nor does it include the knowledge that there were significant numbers of deserters from the army during the war. The popular story of the war did not, until recently, acknowledge that many children experienced extreme cruelty and sexual abuse in the countryside or that most units of the home guard were incompetent (Tiratsoo et al. 1995).

A complete history of the period of the Second World War would take these type of things into account, as indeed histories now do. One can see, however, how the dominant national view of the past has difficulties incorporating less rose-tinted images.

National character

A lot of the above discussion is related to the idea of national character – the idea that nations have rooted in their history and culture distinct patterns of consumption, personality and self-expression. Possibly belief in national character is less marked than it once was, but it is common enough to hear somebody refer to an individual, an action or a product (a film perhaps) of another nationality or even their own as, for example, 'Typically English' or 'Typically Scottish'. Problems might arise if the speaker is asked to define what they mean, but that would spoil the vague reality of the stereotype. For instance, if somebody said a certain individual was 'typically Italian' or 'a real American' we would probably have some idea what they meant. Until recently football commentators would account for a style of play as a reflection of nationality: the cynical foul of the Italian, the mechanical organization of the German defence, the English determination, the suspect temperament of the Nigerians, the Brazilian flair, and so on. And of course it is the case that there are differences between nations. Who would wish to deny that there are differences in behaviour and choice of pastime between, say, the Americans and Japanese despite roughly similar levels of income and technology? Furthermore, many would claim that the world would be a rather predictable and boring place if peoples were uniform in character. So once again our concern should not be with denying completely the existence of this aspect of a nation. Rather we should look critically at national character.

Within academic sociology one rarely finds mention of national character now. This has not always been the case. In the post-war period there was a boom in cross-national surveys designed to try and discern average differences between peoples. The American sociologist Inkeles (1997) has spent much of his life trying to discern what he calls the 'modal personalities' of nations through questionnaires on things like parenting and attitudes towards authority. This empirical approach is influenced both by social psychology and social anthropology. There is another tradition in the social sciences that is more concerned with relating character to the wider conditions of the nation in question. This approach has its roots in the eighteenth century Enlightenment where thinkers like Voltaire believed that climate was key in a people's temperament, or, for the Scottish philosopher David Hume, national character was to be explained by the morals – the culture – of a society. During the nineteenth century both emphases, climatic and sociological, are found in the great study of American society by de Tocqueville (1995). Thinkers like Max Weber thought national character important, emphasizing the importance of how one class group could popularize its accents and manners across the class structure (Weber 1958). More recently in post-war European sociology, Norbert Elias (1996) tried to understand the German personality type of Hitler's Third Reich.

This involved, among other things, an examination of the general historical forces that he thought had shaped the German people and, in particular, the kind of sadistic attitudes encouraged among young gentlemen in the late nineteenth and early twentieth centuries.

So, national character is not just a 'lazy generalization', it is also an idea with an academic history. Why is it then that we need to be sceptical about its application? The first reason was indicated above in the discussion on culture. It is that a conception of national character is necessarily an overgeneralization. The attempt to define a typical Italian or German or Australian is fraught with all kinds of problems. A stereotype in the form of a given set of overriding personality traits can be problematic for even a single individual. Often we will hear somebody described as 'tough' or 'sympathetic' when we know that such a description only captures one aspect of their character. When applied to a whole population the problems are obviously far greater. Then there is the issue of regional characteristics – whatever generalization that might be made about nationality should be qualified by the particular characteristics of people from a certain geographical area. Related to this is class and gender. National character glosses over cultural differences between classes. Is it really the case that it is possible to blend the English upper classes and working classes into a single categorization? With gender, even taking into account that sometimes we hear references to 'typical Frenchmen' as opposed to 'typical Frenchwomen', there are problems in a formulation that rarely takes into account differences between the men and women. Finally, and again to return to the coverage of culture, the claim that there are distinct national characters fails to take into account the possibility that globalization is not only giving rise to similar patterns of culture worldwide – fast food, music, etc. – but also a similar personality type. One perhaps orientated above all else to acquiring consumer goods.

Stop and think

➤ Why might governments try to influence the way the history of their nation is told?

➤ Can you think of any examples of how this has occurred?

➤ How would you describe a typical (a) British, (b) Irish, (c) American person?

➤ Are your descriptions based on evidence?

A closer look

So what is a nation?

How can we define a nation? We have to be critical in doing this and sift through the reality of what nations claim about themselves. A definition has to take into account both myth and reality: what people believe to be the case and what we know to be the case looking objectively at the matter. Among the many definitions, the following from the Czech historian, Miroslav Hroch, has sufficient flexibility to enable us to do this. Like all definitions that of Hroch does reflect certain influences, in his case a central European/German approach to nations and nationalism. For Hroch a nation is three key things. First, it is a group of people who can communicate linguistically and culturally. Second, it is a group of people who have a sense of shared history within a given territorial area that informs their present togetherness and collective future or destiny. Put succinctly, to use the definition favoured by Hobsbawm (1990: 9) and Gellner (1983: 1), the political unit should correspond to the cultural one. Third, it is a group of people who have a sense of horizontal unity – that is a unity that exists despite differences in wealth, status and power. Nationalism is the assertion of the primary importance of the nation – the nation outweighs other considerations. It may pertain to economics, culture, sport and international relations. In all instances, whether big or small, macro or micro, such an assertion involves politics. It involves a recognition of the historical past as historical destiny, and taking them sufficiently seriously to put forward claims for cultural organization, diplomatic interests and so on. This limited but important definition will become clearer as we consider how key thinkers have approached an understanding of nations and nationalism.

Sociology and the study of nationalism

Nationalism, until fairly recently, has not been of major concern to academic sociology for two main reasons. First, because traditionally the arena for study has been 'society', and more specifically its various components: the family, the education system, religion and so on. This has been challenged to some extent in recent years by the emphasis on global sociology – the acknowledgement that societies are not self-contained entities but are influenced in all kinds of ways by global forces that wash over them. But in general when students have studied sociology at school, college and university the concern has been state and society. Students in Britain have studied British state and society, French students French state and society and so on. This has meant that the whole issue of national identification and belonging has largely been overlooked. In so far as sociology has had a comparative dimension it has been of the differing internal development of contrasting states and societies.

Second, nations and nationalism have not been much considered because academic sociology, throughout its hundred-year history, has been much influenced by its so-called founding fathers: Marx, Weber and Durkheim. None of these thinkers had a great deal to say about the subject. Obviously all of them acknowledged that there were such things as nations and nationalism. Durkheim and, on occasions, Marx voiced occasional pride in their respective French and German national backgrounds. For Weber being German was the single most important political and personal issue throughout his life. It is possible to go further and say that a concern with Germans and Germany lay behind his famous work, *The Protestant Ethic and the Spirit of Capitalism* (Barbalet 2001: 164). Contrary to what people sometimes say, the book is not primarily about the respective influences of Catholicism and Protestantism on the work ethic. Essentially, it is concerned with different national varieties of Protestantism: why English Calvinism was more conducive to capitalist take-off than German Lutherism. But that does not mean that he came up with anything approaching a full account of nationalism. He only made a few remarks on the subject here and there.

In so far as these thinkers did talk about nations and nationalism they tended to do so either as an extension of their general sociology or in expressly political terms. Marx thought that nationalism would become less relevant as a single capitalist market reduced the particularities of the world. He talks in *The Communist Manifesto* of how national peculiarities, together with particular religious differences, would be swept away by the onrush of capitalist uniformity. While he thought this a general process, he particularly welcomed the death of small, 'non-historic' nations. By contrast, he speculated elsewhere about the importance of workers in imperial nations such as Britain realizing that they would never be free unless they recognized that they were complicit in the domination and exploitation of other nations, especially the Irish. Durkheim welcomed nationalism when he thought that it was serving to cement the solidarity of society, such as at the outbreak of the First World War in 1914 (Lukes 1973: 547–61). Weber, the most ardent nationalist of the three founding fathers, nevertheless rejected the dominant nineteenth-century idea that national belonging was based upon a common ethnic descent. Although some of his writings suggest otherwise, he thought that nations were above all social and political things: they exist because people believe in them, not because they are natural (Weber 1958: 171–3). A key sociologist whose writings on nationalism are worthy of consideration in themselves, rather than in relation to wider issues of their work, is George Simmel. Simmel's writings on conflict (1955: 100) provide interesting and original insights into the way in which nations, and groups more generally, actively seek some of degree of conflict up to and including war in order to retain and further internal cohesion. However, his writings on this subject are not particularly well known. The major interest in his work in recent years has centred on his understanding of the city in modernity.

So there is not much in classical sociology to have given rise to an interest in nationalism. Those academic writers who did directly consider it in the nineteenth and twentieth centuries were generally philosophers and historians, though that does not mean that their thoughts are irrelevant to sociology. Some of the theorists who we shall shortly consider are not professional sociologists but historians and political scientists; the study of nationalism is inevitably multi-disciplinary. However, it does explain why sociology has not been greatly concerned with nationalism. Given this it is sensible to begin this section with more recent considerations of nationalism, about which there has been considerable debate over the last few years.

The perennialist and modernist approaches to nations and nationalism

It is difficult to outline this position with any precision because it is not one that finds favour with academic considerations of nationalism, although some writers do appear to have given it voice. For example, the one-time French Marxist Regis Debray puts it thus: 'We must consider the national phenomenon within general laws regulating the survival of the human species . . . against death. Against entropy' (1977: 28). In other words nations are intrinsic to humanity; they are part of human nature and therefore outside of history. Actually, even the most

ardent nationalists do tend to periodize their nation. They set a date, usually a fairly definite one, as to when their nation came into being, its birthday. That established, the task for the nationalist historian is to chart the rise of the nation, noting its trials and tribulations, its great leaders, a particular golden age, internal strife, wars, possibly invasions and migrations. The assumption is that at all times the nation is there as a given: something that is central to the lives of all those who live within it. The nation might lie dormant for a period of time but awakes – or will awake at some time in the future – to begin in earnest the next chapter in its proud history.

As this story of the nation inevitably takes place after an initial point of departure, Debray is wrong even in relation to those who are the most likely to agree with him. But, leaving that aside, the assertion that nations are natural phenomena is a key aspect of the perennialist approach: they just *are*. Nations are characterized by a common genealogy, a common culture, a national character that runs along beneath the surface of history. We looked at these assumptions critically above so there is no need to repeat the criticisms of this approach here.

This approach to nations and nationalism is rejected by writers who take what is generally known as the modernist approach. It can be considered the direct opposite of the perennialist approach. Rather than seeing nations as ancient entities modernists point to their far more recent existence. They are in general sceptical, in some cases contemptuous, of the claims of nationalists about language, culture and so on. This is because they suggest that what is taken to be the stuff of nation is generally of more recent origin. Modernists point to the transformations of modernity to explain nationalism. Without the various ruptures associated with it – capitalism and industrialization, political upheaval, modern empire, the rise of the middle classes – there would have been no nations as we currently recognize them. Beyond this general but profound claim the approaches of modernist writers differ. Below we will look briefly some of the main positions.

Modernist position 1: Gellner

Ernest Gellner's approach to nationalism takes a wide historical sweep, the big picture, through an anthropological methodology. In his principal study of the subject, *Nations and Nationalism* (1983), he looked at the general rise of nations by observing crucial changes in everyday life. He did not think that key historical events, such as wars and revolutions, are of central importance to the rise of nations and nationalism, but he tried to identify more gradual but profound developments in human societies. His contention is that prior to the coming of industrialization – a very general term that Gellner used to refer to commercialization, urbanization and the advent of bureaucracy, not just factories and production – nationalism, the idea that there are discreet nations that combine government and culture within a territorial area, was not an idea that made much sense. Therefore, nations did not really exist in any meaningful sense: it was nationalism that created such entities. Nationalism only has a function or a definite purpose in the context where there is a need for a common culture to correspond to a definite territorial area where everybody is, at least formally, on the same footing. A common culture provides a single level playing field for interaction and competition based *formally* upon merit. By interaction Gellner is thinking of a medium of communication, a language. By competition he is primarily concerned with the labour market, with competition for jobs. The nation becomes the only viable arena in which interaction and competition can take place.

Prior to industrialization in Europe in the nineteenth century there existed in Europe and elsewhere a peasant culture that was at once undifferentiated and local (Gellner 1991). It was undifferentiated because it had key things in common across time and space. Thus a traveller passing across medieval Europe at, say, the start of the fifteenth century would probably not have observed a great deal of difference between the numerous various village communities he witnessed. Such changes that there were in language, dress, custom or typical foods would have been explicable by climate and terrain, not nation. If he were able somehow to repeat the journey a hundred years later not a great deal would have changed. The rulers of such societies – landlords, kings and emperors – had little or no interest in the culture of the grey faced and generally poor inhabitants of the peasant villages. Peasant culture – language, pastimes, etc. – were largely irrelevant to them. Feudal rulers may have had some limited concern over religious practice, but that was the extent of their awareness of peasant life. Their interest in the peasantry did not much extend beyond tax collection. Meanwhile, the peasant's limited outlook did not really extend beyond the boundaries of the local community. What possible interest could such an individual have in establishing common bonds with people outside of the immediate village community that he or she neither knew nor cared about?

All of this changed with modernity and the associated developments, including the anonymity of the city, the impersonality of modern state bureaucracy and the meritocracy of the modern career in which people are thrown together from a variety of geographical and social backgrounds. In such circumstances a common national culture becomes vital to allow societies to work or, to use a term Gellner was comfortable with, to *function*. This is true in practical terms – above all with communication, language – but also at a psychological level. Responding to the criticism that his approach to nationalism cannot explain the passions of national identity, Gellner countered that they arise when there is a lack of congruence (a fit) between state and culture (1997: 84). Therefore, if an individual is placed in the situation where their culture is out of political alignment with the state in which they live – as in an empire, an occupied country or a federal arrangement – they may resort to violence in order to try and achieve a resolution, that is a state that is at one with their culture. That is not primarily a matter of feeling that their culture is not being officially recognized in itself, but the reality of being discriminated against in all those things that the dominant culture allows: citizenship, jobs, etc. So nationalism as a movement of political opposition to a state focuses on achieving a specific state of affairs, a nation-state where culture does not hinder and discriminate against a people.

We should note that Gellner's explanation of national identity works best with national opposition movements – movements against empire, federation, etc. – rather than with established nations. But the strength of nationalist passions was not in his view a product of the depth of their history. For instance, in a now famous debate with Anthony Smith in 1995, he pointed out that the fact that the Baltic state of Estonia did not really exist at all as a nation at the beginning of the nineteenth century does not mean that the identities its inhabitants subsequently acquired as Estonians were any less real than those of older nations. Simultaneously he was quite dismissive of the idea that nations are natural or inevitable. He was fond of pointing out that among the many that now exist there are many instances of ancient peoples, of nations, that are gone and all but forgotten (1983: 45–7). The fact that some 'made it' into existence historically while others did not was not due to them being intrinsically more worthy of success. Those that we are familiar with today are not any more or less real than those that have disappeared. Rather, it so happens that the historical process literally and without sentiment swept some nations off the map. Their peoples were dispersed and absorbed by others.

Gellner thought that as nationalism was specific to industrialization over the last two hundred years, there was nothing inevitable about it being around forever. On the contrary, he thought that a slow, curve towards industrial convergence was discernible that would dim the glare of nationalism. The early and middle of period of industrialization was responsible for the intensity of nationalism, above all war. Now, if only among the advanced economies of the world, a general level of affluence is serving to sap the cultural energy of nationalism as peoples adopt similar lifestyles, use common technologies and so on.

Stop and think

➤ Give examples of nations that existed in the past but do not now.

➤ Find out why they have ceased to exist – at least in the same form as they were previously.

Modernist position 2: Benedict Anderson and *Imagined Communities*

Benedict Anderson's account of nationalism, as contained in his famous book *Imagined Communities* first published in 1983, is probably the most influential account of nationalism in the social sciences. This is probably due in part to the fact that the very term, 'imagined community', was taken up and freely used by people influenced by postmodernism who did not want to deal directly with the political realities of nationalism, but wanted to emphasize that they were vaguely critical of it. To call a nation an imagined community indicates that at some level nations are seen as socially constructed. So as the writing on nationalism proliferated in the 1990s one would often read in academic journals 'I understand nations as imagined communities'. Now there is always a danger when a term is used very loosely, as something that purportedly explains everything actually explains nothing. This does not mean that Anderson's actual writings on nationalism are in any way the worse for this; only that we should be careful about the excessive use of the term 'imagined community'.

It is worth noting first that Anderson is in some ways rather impressed by nationalism. In a sense it is impossible not to be, given the scale of its achievements, both positive and negative. The immediate prompting for the writing of *Imagined Communities* was his realization that even states in Asia, specifically Vietnam and China, which claimed to be socialist descended into war in the late 1970s. But it is possible to detect a positive note in Anderson's writings about nationalism in his discussion of its differences with racism. He sees the dreams of historical greatness of the nationalist as very different from the narrow, ahistorical hatred of race and racism. In a famous quote he elucidates the difference:

> The fact of the matter is that nationalism thinks in terms of historical destinies, while racism dreams of eternal contamination, transmitted from the origins of time through an endless sequence of loathsome copulations outside history.   (Anderson 1983).

In short, according to Anderson, racism is about a group's supposed particular biology whereas nationalism is about a particular historical rise to greatness. There are good reasons to be skeptical about this claim. Among other things that Anderson overlooks is the fact that many nationalisms have explicitly relied upon an idea of racial national greatness, and most nationalisms rest to some extent of an idea of ethnic exclusion.

While Anderson is impressed by this aspect of nationalism he also sees it as in some senses respects doctrine that is closer to a religion than a political ideology. He thinks nationalism occupies the same psychological space as religion. Nationalism can be about hatred but Anderson suggests it is equally about love, sacrifice and courage. How many things, he asks, are there that people are prepared to devote their lives to besides their nation (1983: 17–18)? The symbols of nation have a collective aspect. Anderson does not mention Durkheim, but the way in which he describes the commemoration of nation is similar to how the great French sociologist analysed religion. Anderson suggests that when wreathes are laid and heads are bowed at the tomb of the unknown soldier people remember the collective dead of nation. As nations owe their present existence to what came before, the living 'reality' of the nation is confirmed. This is similar to how Durkheim thought that the fundamental role of religion is to strengthen their society. When people gather together to pray and so on they are primarily bringing to mind, specifically to the collective conscious, a belief in their own togetherness under God.

There are other similarities between Durkheim's conception of religion and the very notion of an 'imagined community'. Anderson uses the term to get at the way in which people can conceive of an essential togetherness with others beyond their immediate locality and therefore experience. Prior to nationalism the community was that of the village or town, their kinsmen were those of whom they had personal knowledge. People may have had some vague allegiance to a distant king and a wider religion, but the idea that people living beyond their locality could have been 'the same as them' would have been thought ridiculous. In fact, it would not have been considered in the first place. In the face of all of this, nationalism insists that people separated by time and space, differentiated by occupation, status and power nevertheless have a common overriding nationness. They, indeed we, are literally one people. Thus individual A and B may have little in common: they live five hundred (or five thousand) miles apart, have different jobs and lives. Yet from the point of view of the nationalist they are both just as much French or Russian or American or Japanese or whatever nationality it might be. Of course, in reality the right of nation is rarely so inclusive. The most dramatic illustration of this is that when the founding fathers of the American constitution declared 'We, the people . . .' they did not mean that portion of the population who were black. More generally, claims to national membership have frequently been qualified by class, ethnicity and region. Some are more national than others, others are not really national at all. However, this is not the point Anderson is concerned with. His contention is that nationalism involves a massive shift in outlook, an imaginary leap.

As most modernists, and indeed writers associated with other positions, Anderson sees the development of capitalism as the crucial backdrop to the rise of nationalism. Within this general backdrop he identifies three things in particular.

1 The key role of 'print capitalism', the invention and subsequent mass circulation of printed books, newspapers and periodicals, to the rise of nations. It is through the printed word that the imaginings of the nationalist might spread. Of particular importance to nation building in nineteenth-century Europe was the role prepared by an emerging class of people who owed their livelihood to writing in their national language, a language distinct from the official language of state. Anderson has in mind people like grammarians and lexicographers who standardized languages and compiled dictionaries in an effort to make them stand as viable alternatives to German, French or Russian. A little later such people formed national academies of language that served to act as the official protector of the given language.

In some instances the national language in question was basically a peasant vernacular that was spoken by peoples of different ethnic backgrounds over an indeterminate geographical area, which was not of much importance to those who subsequently extolled its newfound historical virtues. Also important to the development of national languages were other purveyors of language like government officials and school teachers. Finally, literary writers, poets, philosophers and historians were crucial to providing an intellectual justification for nation.

2 Anderson identifies empire as the context for the emergence of nations. The first wave of nationalist revolt was that of Creole cliques in Spanish Latin America during the first half of the nineteenth century. These were indigenous national groups that sought independence from the Spanish king because their career path and status were blocked – their road to Madrid as the centre of the imperial nation – because they were not considered fully Spanish as they were not born in Spain or they were of mixed Spanish and Indian blood. Their motivation to break away from the Spanish empire was to create a state, a nation-state, where formally achievement was based upon merit. Later in Europe, the Russian and Austro-Hungarian empires acted as the nursery for nationalities with, as mentioned, intellectuals playing a formative role. More recently, principally in the twenty-year period after the Second World War, European empires across Africa, the Middle East and Asia acted as the crucible for another wave of national liberation, sometimes violent, sometimes peaceful, as countries such as India, Jamaica, Indonesia and Algeria gained independence. *Imagined Communities* was written before the most recent wave of independence was achieved, that of the peoples of the Soviet bloc under Russian domination. But the analysis of the central role of empire to nation would obviously permit this. Indeed, it could easily be extended to the present day given the contemporary relevance of American empire and imperialism.

3 A third key ingredient to the rise of nations and nationalism in Anderson's view is 'official nationalism'. Anderson takes this term from Seton-Watson, the historian who much influenced Anderson in the writing of *Imagined Communities.* This refers to the attempt by established ruling classes to use nationalism to bolster their legitimacy

and popularity. The period that Anderson sees as particularly important to this is the latter part of the nineteenth century and the early twentieth century when, in particular, the monarchies of Europe embraced the populist potential and reach of nationalism. The way in which the British and Russian royal families did so through acquiring the symbols of imperial greatness and, in the British case, actually changing their name in 1916, are especially good examples. The process might not have been wholly cynical but was certainly convenient to Europe's old order faced with the strains of modernity and the rise of mass labour movements pledged in principle to international solidarity. Again such analysis is not controversial or new. Moreover, the attempt by monarchs and governments to use nationalism to shore up their support is of ongoing relevance. However, it does place Anderson some way from Ernest Gellner, who was dismissive of the idea that elites and ruling classes could really exercise very much influence over what the lower orders think.

Over the last twenty years Anderson has written widely on other issues in the study of nationalism, especially through various case studies of Indonesia and the Philippines. Although he has not made any explicit departures from the analysis set out in *Imagined Communities*, other emphases have been added to those set out above. Of particular interest is his identification of the importance of long-distance nationalism because of its contemporary importance. Anderson thinks that exile and displacement act as key forces in nationalist sentiment. He sees this as an historical aspect of nationalism that has become more important in our now global world. In the past immigrants were usually absorbed, at least to some extent, as a citizen by the nation they settled in. However, nation-states today struggle to do so, leaving the immigrant free to maintain an often romanticized attachment to the country of their real or more imagined or distant origin through the Internet, web site, text, telephone call and international flight. Simultaneously, the political importance of long-distance nationalism has become more apparent and pronounced. Among many possible examples on offer, Anderson mentions the role of the Croatian diaspora in Canada, America and Australia to Croatian independence in 1993, and the role of political exiles from Poland and the Baltic states in the USA to their new, non-communist governments, after the revolutions of 1989.

Modernist position 3: Eric Hobsbawm

Eric Hobsbawm's stance towards nationalism is the most critical of the various modernist accounts. While Gellner conceded to being moved to tears by the folk music of his native Czech Republic and Anderson grants nationalism a certain historical grandeur, Hobsbawm has little time for its historical claims and political pro-grammes. Of course, he recognizes that nationalism played a fundamental historical role in building nation-states during the nineteenth and first part of the twentieth centuries. But apart from a few favourable remarks about multiracial nation building in South Africa since the end of apartheid, Hobsbawm is dismissive of the idea that it is a valid political doctrine in the new millennium. That is because he thinks that its time has gone, it has played out its historic role and has now only limited relevance in our globalized world. This is not the only reason why Hobsbawm is contemptuous of nationalism. As a historian he thinks that it is based on false premises, that much of the history of the nation as written by nationalists is bad history. In fact, he claims to the dismay of some, it is impossible to be a nationalist and write good history as nationalism involves an almost unconscious commit-ment to shape a view of the past that corresponds to a favourable political and cultural outlook. Put simply, the nationalist writes history to serve the present rather than do justice to the past. Finally, we should note Hobsbawm's continuing commitment to Marxism as important to his view of nationalism.

Of all the modernist writers on nationalism, Hobsbawm is the most attentive to the issue of whether or not nations as we now know them are pre-dated by the earlier historical forms, by ideologies like religion or by ethnicity. In the light of a careful consideration of intimations of nationalism through proto-nationalism' (i.e. hints and suggestions of the development of national consciousness before nationalism fully emerged on the scene), he is quite convinced that it is impossible to make a definite connection between nations before the age of nationalism and nations after that crucial turning point. In fact he boldly declares that they are not stating that it is, 'Nations do not make states and nationalisms but the other way around' (1990: 10). More widely, he sees the creation of modern nations as part of the wider process of what he calls the long revolution of the nineteenth century, the period from 1789 to 1914. This was a giant movement in human affairs that was powered by the dual revolutions at the end of the eighteenth century – the revolution in political organization and thinking and the industrial revolution (see Chapter 1).

Similarly, Hobsbawm is dismissive of the idea that there is a direct connection between ethnicity and nationalism. This argument that we will examine in more detail below claims that although nationalism in the form of a popular belief in the primacy of the nation is of recent origin, there are definite links to older tribe-like formations called ethnicities. Ethnicities share with nations, in the estimation of those who think there is a link between ethnicity and nationalism, several common features, above all a collective memory. Hobsbawm thinks that the idea that modern nations are the outgrowth of ethnicities is simply wrong. For one thing the nineteenth century exponents of nations – the political leaders and intellectuals – conceived of nations as something quite different from the various local allegiances that people had. In the first instance this is undoubtedly true. The liberation period of nationalism in the nineteenth century that gave rise to the birth of nations like Italy was about overcoming what its leaders saw as the numerous petty local divisions of that region of southern Europe. However, as Hobsbawm himself recognizes, this liberation phase of nationalism was based on the belief that only certain nations qualified for self-determination. Towards the end of the century the threshold principle – size, economic potential, history – was replaced by the political demand from all-comers for national independence. Many of these smaller nations – the Basques in Spain, for example – constituted an ethnic approach to nation. But even this does not prove a connection. Hobsbawm's contention, as we saw above, is that nationalists generally make up their history to serve their current purposes. Therefore, the fact that aggregates of people subsequently come to believe that they are part of a group with roots that can be traced back through history does not mean that this was the case. Thus during the war in Yugoslavia in the early 1990s, when it became fashionable and frankly easy for those who knew little or nothing about the region to refer to the 'ancient hatreds' of the various warring parties – principally the Serbs, the Croats, the Bosnian Muslims and the Kosovan Albanians – Hobsbawm was adamant that there was nothing constant in the history of the peoples that predisposed them to conflict. Rather an explanation for the Yugoslav civil war had to be sought in, among other things, the use of history as propaganda by the political leaders of Serbia and Croatia in particular.

So Hobsbawm is quite convinced of the modernity of nationalism; or rather that nationalism is a product of modernity. Beyond this his analysis follows a fairly standard historical path. As indicated, he sees nationalism's take off in the late eighteenth century when the French Revolution fired the notion that peoples rather than monarchies were the basis of nations. Understandably this subversive doctrine, with its obvious implication for parliamentary democracy, was viewed with some alarm by Europe's autocratic leaders who only became confident in embracing nationalism somewhat later in the nineteenth century when they felt that its once revolutionary adherents – principally among the middle classes – had become sufficiently conservative to make it a useful means of bolstering their popularity with, in particular, the emerging industrial working classes. Hobsbawm, like Anderson, refers to this as official nationalism. This period is characterized in his estimation by the 'invention of tradition': the attempt to ground and normalize practices through the insistence that they are historical. The term the 'invention of tradition' – like that of 'imagined communities' – has undoubtedly been loosely and much overused; it is, in fact, the title of a famous book edited by Eric Hobsbawm and Terence Ranger. It consists of a number of studies that analyze how, from the end of the eighteenth century, attempts were made in a variety of countries and contexts to justify the existence and importance of artifacts, institutions and social practices by creating the impression that they were of long historical convention. In fact, they were far more recent, in some cases having been cooked up by their proponents virtually overnight. In Hobsbawm's view the invention of tradition came to the fore as nationalism fully entered the consciousness of, in particular, the European peoples in the period before the outbreak of the First World War in 1914. In Britain, for example, the monarchy was invented, or rather reinvented, as a popular institution in the context of the growth of the British Empire. Some years later, in 1907, the Boy Scouts movement began life under the leadership of General Baden-Powell. This rather distinctive youth organization proposed a series of activities for boys – camping and so on – all of which were supposedly of great national tradition. They were not, but this did not particularly matter to the thousands of boys in Britain who enjoyed doing them and probably had some vague notion that this was the very stuff of being British.

In the subsequent period, the twentieth century from 1914, Hobsbawm sees nationalism as a fundamental factor in what he refers to as the age of extremes. He doesn't resort to the crudity of simply blaming nationalism for the colossal mass murders of the twentieth century, but he thinks that its move away from liberalism towards the political right and the politics of race was fundamental to the rise of fascism and the Second World War. Less critically he identifies nationalism in the Third World as key to the break-up of European empires after the Second World War. Probably because of continuing political allegiances to state communism he was critical of the view that nationalism was responsible for the break-up of the Soviet Union and its extended empire, preferring to blame the failure of Communist Party leadership in general and the last president of the USSR, Mikhail Gorbachev, in particular (Hobsbawm 1992). As indicated above, he now sees nationalism as an historically spent force. He obviously recognizes people still have great allegiance to nations, that nationalism can mobilize people to war in places like Yugoslavia and, more positively, can unite and build nations as in South Africa since apartheid. However, he thinks that the historic role of nationalism in building and securing nation-states and in carving them out from empires is now finished.

A state is a central organization that is responsible for the affairs – political, economic, social, legal and cultural – of a given geographical territory. He argues that nationalism typically takes the form of a political movement that develops as a reaction against imperial power, a liberation movement that seeks to unite various peoples in wider nation-state formation and a political attempt to bolster the popularity of an existing state. Beyond this identification of nationalism, specifically nationalist politics, as revolving around the state, Breuilly contends that it is impossible to identify a monocausal understanding of nationalism. Instead detailed comparative histories are required to illuminate how nations arose.

The ethno-symbolist approach of Anthony D. Smith

For the sake of clarity it is tempting to present this approach to nationalism as the direct opposite of the modernist approach as set out through its various proponents, above. In fact this is not the case as Anthony D. Smith is not a crude perennialist or nationalist. He does not think that nations have essentially been around for ever; his case is considerably more sophisticated and based on an enormous knowledge of the subject matter. Nevertheless, there are profound differences between Smith and the modernist position. Smith's academic career has consisted largely of the attempt through numerous books and articles to clearly define the shortcomings of the modernist approach and, by way of contrast, outline his own distinctive approach. He thinks, contrary to the claims of modernist writers, that we should pay proper

attention to the *longue duree* – the long duration, or, we might say, maturation – of nations.

Smith has framed much of his writings as reactions against the modernist position because of its influence in the academic study of nationalism. Indeed, as a one-time postgraduate student of Ernest Gellner, Smith was initially concerned to demonstrate the importance of modernity in the construction of nations (1971). However, over the last twenty-five years for various reasons he has increasingly tried to emphasize the crucial role of history before modernity in the construction of nations. There are several reasons why he thinks that modernists are altogether too dismissive of the longevity of nations. For Smith the enormous and deep-rooted power of nationalist ideas require recognition of the ties of nation that precede and run through modernity. When the nationalist leader refers to a people's glorious past and the key importance of its culture – often in the face of an assumed external threat – it may well be that there is some myth in their claims. Smith's contention is that there is generally a historically deposited perception – not just superficial sentiment but a more profound perception based upon collective memories, loyalties and identities – that predisposes a people towards the appeal. As he puts it speaking of the nationalist,

> Their interpretations must be consonant not only with the ideological demands of nationalism, but also with the scientific evidence, popular resonance and patterning of particular ethno histories . . . between an active national present and an often ancient ethnic heritage, between the defining ethnic past and its modern nationalist authenticators and appropriators. In this continually renewed two-way relationship between ethnic past and nationalist present lies the secret of the nation's explosive energy and the awful power it exerts over its members.

More specifically, in relation to the creation of Pakistan in 1947, Smith makes the point that,

> Pakistan, both as a name and as a national state, was quite clearly 'invented', the name by a student in Cambridge, the national state by Jinnah's party. But the idea of a Pakistani state would have had no collective force or meaning, unless the mass of Muslims in Northern India had already acquired a vivid sense of common ethnicity based on their shared religion, one which differentiated them from other Indians. In some form, given the strength and geographical concentration of Muslim sentiments in the subcontinent, it was probable that something like Pakistan would have formed in an age of political nationalism and communal self-assertion.   (Smith 1998: 130)

So, for reasons we will shortly consider, there must be something there, some raw material for nationalists to work on. Nation-building, crucially its invention of tradition aspect, will by implication have limited impact unless some sort of deep-seated chord is struck with a people.

It is important to note that Smith's assessment of the role of ethnicity to nations and nationalism was something that occurred in his work prior to the 'return to the national question' as one Marxist put it in the late 1980s. Actually, this phrase is highly misleading: there never was a 'return to the national question', it had always been there. Nevertheless, it was certainly the case that the power of nationalism – with all its positives and negatives – was no more evident in the revolutions throughout Russian-dominated 'communist' Eastern Europe and the break-up of the Soviet Union itself and Yugoslavia. Now without entering the complex history of this period, Smith would have had at least some justification in claiming that history had validated his approach. No doubt he felt that this would have been rather crude and opportunistic; a feature of his writing is that it is very much based in the academic study of nationalism without easy references to passing contemporary events. Nevertheless, we can perhaps see the role of the events unfolding across Europe in his 1991 book *National Identity*, in the claim that there is a dominant ethnic basis to the stability of a state and that nationalism is not waning in power. As noted, Eric Hobsbawm claimed at approximately the same time that the global capitalism was slowly undermining the political basis of nationalism with the result that the end is now in sight. Smith countered that, on the contrary, there is no sign that it is beginning to weaken in power and importance. Smith's approach, based upon an underlying sociological understanding of its role in memory and identity, has increasingly appeared over the last fifteen years to have been more accurate.

So how does Anthony Smith understand the rise of nations and nationalism? As noted, Smith is not a perennialist. In common with modernist writers he emphasizes the role of political revolution, capitalism, the development of the military and the advent of modern bureaucratic states in the rise of modern nations in the nineteenth century. This process took place at different periods of time in different areas. In doing so two contrasting types of nation formation are evident: territorial and ethnic. Territorial formation generally occurred in western Europe and involved an orientation to nation achieved by a ruling dynasty, a royal family, to draw in a wider population to a conception of nationhood based

upon law, citizenship and national culture within a given geographical area. This is distinct from ethnic nationalism that was more concerned with genealogy – the 'family history' of nation – and folk custom. As usual in Smith's writing, there is a concern not to exaggerate this contrast but to qualify it. Thus he recognizes that an ethnic orientation to nation can become the vehicle for the pursuit of a territorial nationalism and that the given aristocratic core of a territorial nationalism has an ethnic dimension. In fact, it acts as an *ethnie*.

Taking this point, that ethnicity always has a role in the formation of nations even where this is less pronounced because of the territorial orientation, we should emphasize in a little more detail what Smith is concerned with in using this term. Ethnicity supplies this link between nations in the modern sense and older human group formations which provides a historic continuity and accounts for important contemporary features. A non-hostile although ultimately quite severe critic of Smith, Ernest Gellner, once described this link as akin to an 'ethnic navel' or belly button (Gellner 1996: 357). In other words nations have surviving evidence on their bodies that in social and cultural terms they came from somewhere. Ethnicity provides a relationship of past to present, from the pre-modern eras where, as Smith concedes, nationalism did not exist, to a world dominated by the assumptions of nationalism. Crucial to this is the symbolic dimension. Smith identifies a number of group practices that come to define a group and have a lasting influence. He is concerned with such things as myths, rites, duties, customs, laws and ideas concerning destiny. These give rise to collective norms of thought and behaviour that come to define a group to itself and others.

Put by themselves references to the existence of pre-modern collective memories and so on can seem rather impressive. But simultaneously a theoretical argument – and Smith's approach is one designed very much to develop an overarching theory of nations and nationalism – always runs the risk of becoming vague and abstract in its quest to construct a wider framework that captures the empirical reality. Similarly, Smith's general contention that a middle way must be sought between modernism and perennialism appears as a balanced, sophisticated and therefore reasonable position to take. Yes, he argues, of course the forces of modernity were crucial to the rise of nations and nationalism, such things have not been around ever. And yes, obviously tradition, so crucial to the historical justification of nations, has been invented. Given the evidence no one could seriously deny it. The point Smith wants to make is that tradition only resonates where it strikes a chord with existing historical beliefs and popular social practices. It is somewhat easier to make this sort of claim than demonstrate it in any verifiable way. However, in such books as *The Ethnic Origins of Nations* (1986) and *National Identity* (1992), Smith has attempted to demonstrate how in the pre-modern world ethnic groups, *ethnies*, developed symbolic dimensions of themselves that have definite equivalents amongst modern nations.

Citizenship

There are a number of issues to consider under this heading. Some that might be covered here have only a tenuous relationship with nationalism so for the sake of clarity we will only deal with those that have a fairly obvious connection. For instance, we will not discuss how organizations such as voluntary bodies and charities are dealt with in school citizenship classes in Britain. Nor will we deal with the kind of things that an informed and responsible citizen should know. These are aspects of the wider definition of citizenship. Citizenship as discussed here concerns the rights and responsibilities of people because they are thought to belong to the national community.

Narrow definitions of rights and responsibilities principally emphasize the legal aspects in a form of contract: the right to liberty and freedom of association, for instance, in return for the obligation to keep the law. However, both in its original formulation and classical formulations citizenship has a wider sphere of meaning. For the ancient Greeks it implied freedom from chaos. Chaos was understood both as internal and external disorder, the latter being through the threat from barbarian hordes. Therefore, even in this initial notion of citizenship, there was an explicit message that citizenship was not a universal condition, but applied to a particular group, the Athenians. In its classical eighteenth-century articulation through its most famous exponent, Jean Jacques Rousseau, there was a similar stress upon freedom, in this case freedom from tyranny as exercised by absolutist governments. This was to be achieved through liberty within a government, something Rousseau thought relied upon an active body of citizens. So concern and involvement in society – in return for rights but not simply in expectation of a given return – have always been the hallmarks of good citizenship.

It is not, therefore, overstretching the point to say that there is a direct line between citizenship's theoretical foundations in political philosophy and what it is associated with today: an interest and sense of responsibility with the well-being of others and the environment in which one lives. The arena of concern is typically the local community as conceived as the locale – the town, the city or the immediate residential area – in which a citizen lives. However, although there is an obvious connection between the immediate identity of the individual citizen and local community, this is reinforced by and extends to a wider sense of community, a community that is coextensive with the state, a state that bounds a nation or, in some instances, several nations.

So the state is the medium through which citizenship meets the issue of nationality and nationalism. It does so in three interrelated ways.

1 The state – the government, the law, the police, the judiciary, the civil service, the army, educational and health services – acts as the mechanism that provides the individual with rights and seeks to ensure they understand and carry out its rules. Rights in themselves vary from the negative conception of citizenship that is principally concerned with guaranteeing the liberty of the individual from possible interference from external bodies, especially the state itself, to a more positive conception that posits that the citizen is entitled to a range of welfare services. The point for our purposes is that the state is not an abstract body but one specific to the particular nation. In theory the state is organized in the contemporary world so that its jurisdiction or rule extends over a definite geographical area that comprises the nation, usually, although not always, a single nation.

2 The nation is obviously not just a zone of convenience, an arbitrary construct to draw a line around a human group that makes it definable and thereby possible to organize for the provision of rights and responsibilities. The nation is conceived as a cultural thing, something that people have an identity with, a feeling of belonging. So the idea of citizenship is premised – to some extent regardless of the actual model of citizenship and nationality, the nature of which we will shortly consider – on the idea of citizenship for 'our' people. Citizens of a given state will usually consider that they should enjoy certain rights because they observe certain duties and obligations. Duty and obligation are conceived in formal terms like obeying the law, but also through displaying a basic loyalty to the nation

in which the citizen belongs. So it is not *just* a case of obeying the law to be a citizen: the expectation of the nation – the nation as collective of people – is that those people within it, its citizens, will give something back through identity and involvement. Of course, for the mass of people, giving something back in the sense of identity is not an issue that would occur to them or would even make much sense if put in these terms. The average Spaniard, for example, may or may not contribute a great deal to his or her community, but they have at some level a sense of identity and Spanish citizenship. The issue of citizenship is in some senses of particular concern to those who reside in a state but who do not automatically enjoy its benefits.

Stop and think

➤ Suggest the rights that a government owes to its citizens.

➤ What duties and obligations are owed in return from citizens to the nation?

➤ Give examples of how you, as a citizen, (a) benefit from the government/state, and (b) have duties and obligations to perform.

3 The obligation to fulfil, at least publicly, a sense of national identity or cultural belonging is strongest in nations that have had historically a strong sense of citizenship based, in theory, on the idea that the nation is comprised of those that reside within its geographical borders. France and the USA, both constitutional republics created through revolutions, have a nationality principle that formally maintains that at least in principle all those within its territory are considered citizens. This is usually referred to as civic national citizenship or *ius soli*. However, even formally with respect to French and US nationality law, citizenship is also based upon a differing principle: *ius sanguinis*, the ethnic nationality of an individual's parents. Thus if a child is born to French or US parents who live outside their countries, the child will be entitled to French or US nationality. The nationality laws of most countries in fact involve a combination of the two principles: nationality by a juridical pact to confer citizenship based upon geographical residence and nationality by right of birth. This is the basis of the famous, though now less frequently used, distinction between civic and ethnic nationalism. The former holds out the possibility of naturalization: an immigrant acquiring citizenship through living in a country for a period of time and, possibly, fulfilling certain requirements. The latter insists that only those who are born into the nation can be considered citizens: you are either a national or you are not. The typical given contrast has been between the once ethnic nationalism of Germany and the civic nationalism of France.

Now the fact that this distinction between *ius soli* and *ius sanguinis*, between civic and ethnic nationalism is less well used than it was is not to say that it is without any foundation, though there are complications that make it far from precise. Until 1992, it was only possible to acquire German nationality through marriage to a German national. As a result, Turkish immigrants who had in some cases moved to Germany in the early 1960s were unable to obtain German nationality. More importantly, their children were also unable to do so despite the fact that they had been born in Germany. By contrast, in France hundreds of thousands of immigrants from all over Europe and former French colonies migrated to France in the post-war period and acquired, either automatically or after a period of residence, nationality and citizenship. More important to this contrast is the fact that arguably the world's most powerful nation is in both image and reality a country of immigrants. It is often remarked that the USA resembles not so much a giant melting pot so much as a patchwork of ethnic communities, retaining and indeed periodically 'rediscovering' the identity of their immigrant pasts. What is actually much more remarkable is how the national identity of wave after wave of immigrants of numerous countries has been assimilated into an all-embracing American one. So we should be attentive to the civic and ethnic aspects of nationality as clearly it is of importance.

However, we should be careful about blanket descriptions for two reasons. First, even in respect to nation-states where the principle of civic citizenship, like the USA and France, is most strongly entrenched to the extent that it is an aspect of national identity, it has enjoyed something of a chequered history. In the USA citizenship was denied to black people until the 1960s in large parts of the country. Despite the formal abolition of slavery in 1865 following the American Civil War, a formal and informal system of apartheid existed – segregation in schools, restaurants, public transport and often exclusion from voting in elections – in southern states in particular, following a vicious backlash against integration and indeed against the very notion that black people were members of the same nation as white people. With respect to immigration, not only was it restricted to relatively small numbers for the half century after 1924, but there was for a time in the 1920s a quota system that specified the number of immigrants to be allowed from different countries according to a racial estimate of IQ. Would-be immigrants from the supposedly intelligent races of northern Europe were looked upon more favourably than the supposedly less intelligent ones of southern European countries.

France today is hardly a country of integration through an inclusive citizenship. On the contrary, ethnic division within its major cities is as obvious and profound as anywhere in Europe, including Germany which, as we discussed earlier, had an overtly ethnic approach to nationality for much of the twentieth century. With Germany it is quite wrong to try to draw a straight line between the well-known horror of Germany's past and its ethnic definition of German nationality and citizenship. We cannot so easily view German history as an unfolding consequence of racial nationalism. It is not the case that Germany has consistently throughout

Case study

Citizenship in Revolutionary France

In the French case, the principle of civic inclusion through residence rather than birth actually had some relevance prior to the Revolution of 1789. While the Revolution was undoubtedly a crucial step in establishing the notion that a sovereign nation is composed of a people through its citizens as residents, its new administration quickly insisted that the French were actually those who were native speakers the language. This had the intended effect of excluding both immigrant newcomers and minority language speakers who predominately lived in rural regions outside the central Parisian region the country. The fact that France's most famous leader after the revolution, Napoleon, was himself a Corsican and therefore not a native speaker of French is only a historical irony. The title of a famous book about the French in the second part of the nineteenth century, *Peasants into Frenchmen* (Weber 1976), indicates that an

attempt was only made to extend Frenchness, with respect to both culture and citizenship, some time after the French Revolution. Thereafter, various other attempts to impose a more directly ethnic interpretation of French nationality and citizenship have been made as part of an ongoing tension over quite what it is to be French.

The issue surfaced over Jewish inclusion in the nation during the famous Dreyfus affair of the 1890s. The trial exposed those within the French establishment who considered Dreyfus guilty almost because he was Jewish. More recently the leader of the French National Front, Jean-Marie Le Pen, declared at the beginning of the football World Cup in 1998 that as the French team was largely composed of immigrants and the sons of immigrants, they could not feel fully what it is to be French and therefore play as well as 'real' Frenchmen. The French National Front asserts that French nationality is based upon race rather than residence. When the side lifted the World Cup four weeks later to

national rejoicing, Le Pen was forced to concede that he was wrong; a footballer did not have to be ethnically French through birth in order to give everything and win football matches for France.

The tradition within French nationalism which insists that citizenship is based upon residency is clearly a more inclusive one than an ethnic assertion of nationality. However, it is in principle and practice an approach to nationality that has difficulty accommodating other cultures and traditions. In other words it is opposed to multiculturalism. The view of all the mainstream political parties is that immigrant groups must not display the symbols of identity that serve to differentiate them from others in public institutions. This issue recently came to the fore in France in relation to the wearing of the hijab, a headscarf (and also Jewish orthodox scull caps, orthodox Christian crucifixes and Sikh turbans) by Muslim girls in French schools. France has more Muslims than any other European country. The principal argument in favour of

Case study (continued)

Figure 12.2 The French football team winners of the World Cup 1998

the ban was that as France is a secular state, school children should not be allowed to wear something in the classroom that marks them out as part of a separate group. To be French they must conform to the dress requirements of French schools. A majority backed the banning of the hijab in the referendum that decided the issue.

Now this move should not be simplistically understood as simply a reflection of racism. Many people opposed to the wearing of the hijab in French schools sincerely believe that ethnic division in French society will only be deepened by the overt display of religious affiliation. However, it is also undoubtedly true that the opposition to the

hijab reflects widespread hostility to Islam as a non-French religion of immigrants.

Question

1. *To what extent should minority traditions, like wearing headscarves, be tolerated in schools, workplaces and elsewhere?*

history formally excluded immigrants and minorities from nationality and citizenship. Obviously anti-Semitism existed in Germany prior to the rise of Hitler and the Nazis. Some Germans would have denied that the Jews could properly be Germans at all. This was a necessary factor to the subsequent holocaust – Jews (and Gypsies and others) were deemed not only racially unworthy of German nationality but of life itself. However, a paradoxical feature of the holocaust was that it took place in

a European country where large numbers of Jews were well integrated and generally successful. Moreover, for the most part they considered themselves good Germans as well as being Jewish. Some of those who perished in the gas chambers in the early 1940s had willingly fought in the German Army during the First World War.

Few if any nations have either an exclusively ethnic or an exclusively civic approach to nationality and citizenship. Neither *ius sanguinis* or *ius soli* should be considered in isolation from the historical context. The policy of the state towards immigration and the general attitude towards foreigners and ethnic minorities cannot be neatly read as a simple reflection of formal ethnic or civic approach to nationality and citizenship. Moreover, within every nation there will be competing understandings of nationality. At the fascist extreme in the United Kingdom there are those who continue to claim that the basis of nationality is whiteness. For them birthplace is irrelevant. Such an understanding of nationality is summarized well by the rhetorical question, 'If a dog is born in a stable does that make it a horse?' Others would distance themselves from such a self-evidently racist approach to nationality, but simultaneously question the extent to which ethnic minorities can fully be considered culturally English or Welsh or Scottish. Others hold out the promise of an integrated multicultural society based upon a citizenship that can foster mutual respect. But even this seemingly most tolerant of approaches to nationality has implicitly some assumption of exclusion. It has to do so if it is allied to a nation-state. The fact of the matter is that all versions of citizenship from the most liberal to the most narrow and overtly racial exclude some people while including others.

National identity and socialization

In the previous section we have indicated how people acquire nationalist ideas, or, it might be better put, a national identity. This is an important if strangely overlooked subject in the literature on nationalism. There has been, for instance, much debate in recent years over theories of nationalism. Aspects of this discussion have dealt with this question but few thinkers have directly addressed it. However, it is important to understand the way in which we acquire a national identity through socialization. The very concept of socialization has been somewhat discredited of late because it is thought too static and restrictive a way of understanding the ideas and actions of individuals. While this criticism is overstated it is true that certain qualifications have to be made about the process of socialization in relation to national identity. First, while there is no doubt that most people consider themselves to be members of a particular nationality, it is also true that the answers tend to vary when they are asked to define the attributes of their nationality. If five people were stopped on the street and all stated that they were proud to be English, they would still, in

all likelihood, produce rather different answers about why they felt such pride, the key characteristics of their nationality and so on. Such confusion would be replicated to varying degrees for all nationalities. So socialization does not produce uniformity.

Second, national identity – like any identity – is not a permanent presence of uniform importance. For example, the weight a single individual gives to being a parent, a Liberal-Democrat voter, a second-generation Indian, a Sikh, a British citizen, a small businessman, a resident of Stockport, a supporter of Manchester City will vary upon the particular context and conjuncture. A particular identity is given focus at particular personal and wider historical points in time. Moreover, a given national identity can be reconfigured and reinterpreted by both individual and group. The meanings attached to being British, for instance, may change markedly over a single individual's lifetime as he or she is forced to rethink what any given identity actually means. This may not take the place of a profound event. The quote above from Denis Potter (see p. 478) – 'I feel the pull of tradition, and I love my land, I love England, and when I'm abroad, I genuinely feel homesick' – is probably not the sort of remark he would have made as a young man. However, we should not exaggerate how much time people devote to reformulating their identity.

Third, much of the content of national identity is not explicit. It is taken for granted by the individual, seen as really rather obvious, too obvious in fact to require articulation, it just 'is'. In a particularly interesting book on nationalism, *Banal Nationalism*, Michael Billig (1995) considers the way in which we almost unconsciously assume a fellow feeling with our compatriots and undertake national traditions. Billig's contention is that nationalism is not just there when there is a big political issue. News events – wars, revolutions and so on that have a directly national dimension – tend to be viewed as phenomena that are rather separate from our everyday lives. But it is just because the assumptions of nationalism are so commonplace that we take them for granted and fail to question them. Nationalism exists at a more subtle and thereby more powerful level than we assume. For instance, we do not have to consider the reasons and significance of supporting a fellow national in an international athletics competition, even if we have little knowledge or interest in the particular event and had never even heard of the competitor before. If we were to ask a TV viewer to explain why they wanted the athlete to win, a likely uncomprehending look would convey the answer: 'Isn't it obvious why I want her to win?' Similarly with national traditions.

Thus when Americans gather together for Thanksgiving, explicit thoughts of doing so as Americans would perhaps seem rather misplaced. Certainly it would make little sense if this was put to them in a direct manner: of course Thanksgiving is an American tradition; it is so obvious it almost goes without saying.

Stop and think

➤ When did you first begin to feel your national identity?

➤ What incidents in your life have strengthened, or weakened, your identification with a that national identity?

The above examples illustrate the wider debate around the subject of identity, something that has rather preoccupied academics in recent years. The issue for discussion here is of the agencies through which ideas of national identity are formed. The list below is not exhaustive and overlaps considerably.

1 *The family*   Here we would need to distinguish between, on the one hand, traditions that are national in an everyday sense but nonetheless have a cumulative and profound influence upon a sense of national identity, while not being directly reducible to 'nationalism' alone. On the other, there are more direct messages of national identity that children receive from their parents and other family members. The former would include aspects of dress, cuisine and rituals of holiday rituals. Such cultural distinctions exist despite the pervasiveness of a global consumer capitalism supplied by Disney, McDonald's, Nike and so on. The prevalence of direct messages varies enormously between different societies. There is reason to think that they are strong in nations that are or have been recently in conflict with another or those that are (or at least consider themselves to be) oppressed. For instance, a recent documentary on Palestine, *Death in Gaza*, featured a four-year-old Palestinian girl who, at the prompting of her mother, said that she hated Israel and wants to kill Jews. Apparently a number of members of her family had been killed by the Israeli Army operating in occupied Palestinian territories. It would not be difficult to find similar sentiments about Arabs among Israelis who had lost relatives to suicide bombings. In Northern Ireland there is evidence

that children as young as four have a definite notion that they are members of one or other of the rival national communities (Connolly, *et al.* 2002). But even in nations that are not locked in conflict with others, the family still acts as a forum through which history is often conveyed. How many children have, for instance, picked up on the national likes and dislikes of their fathers while watching international football matches?

2 *Religion*   The second agency, religion, is in itself directly and usually primarily conveyed through the family. While it is difficult to generalize about the importance of religion to national identity, we can say that at a general level organized religions are rarely free of a national emphasis. It would of course be remarkable if that were not the case as they operate in national contexts. But in many instances religions are as, or more, important for the nationalist political role they play as purely as spiritual authorities. This is true of world religions, such as Catholicism and Islam, as it is true of religions, such as the Russian and Serbian Orthodox Churches, which take their very name from a nation. Catholicism has been integral, indeed synonymous, with Irish, Polish and Croat nationalisms. In contemporary Iraq and across much of the Middle East, political opposition to the USA, Israel and the official authoritarian regimes invariably takes a national form that is expressed through an Islamic medium. Even Osama Bin Laden, the leader of Al Qaeda, the international Islamic terrorist network, allegedly pledged to establish a world caliphate (Islamic state), began his rise to prominence through publishing texts that voiced first and foremost his opposition as a Saudi national to US presence in 'our', Saudi, national land.

Quite how nationalism will be conveyed by the religious leader – the priest, bishop, minister, imam and so on – will vary somewhat. In some cases, especially Christian churches, the religious icon and national symbols may be placed together. The relevant religious leaders may include an overtly national political message in the address given to their followers. In some formal aspects of a particular service the importance of God and nation may be stated. For example, in a Serbian Orthodox baptism it is stated that it is the parents' duty as both Serbs and Christians to bring their children up to be like them. In many countries, organized religion directly

Figure 12.3 The juxtaposition of nationalism and religion: Poles mourn the death of Pope John Paul II

influences schooling. In situations of national conflict the message may be particularly stark. For instance, until recently in many if not all schools in Northern Ireland the religious figures in the school, the priest or the minister, would tell children that the Christianity of those on the other side, religious and national, Catholics or Protestants, was suspect. Quite possibly such messages will extend the claim that they are sinners and therefore will not enter heaven. It is impossible to know how important such indoctrination is compared with other forms of information, but it certainly played a part in the enmity that exists between the communities.

A place of religious importance may also be a site of national importance. The religious pilgrim is at the same time a national one. The popularity of Medjugorje in Yugoslavia as a Catholic shrine, following claimed sightings of the Virgin Mary by Catholic schoolchildren there in 1981, coincided with the rise of Croat nationalism in the subsequent period. Many of those who made their way there in

that period and thereafter no doubt did so because of the political importance the site took on. The burial site of General Franco, Spain's military ruler for much of the twentieth century, *Los Valle de los Caidos* outside Madrid, has become a place of pilgrimage for the small but significant number of Spaniards who mourn the passing of the austere Catholicism of his era, and hark back to the strictures of the authoritarian Spanish national identity he personified.

3 *The school* The school is itself a mechanism by which national ideas are inculcated into the young. It is a particularly important one because in most societies children are legally required to attend school. The extent to which the books and other learning materials of the classroom are nationalist in a direct sense will vary. At one time in Britain, most schools would have a map of the world on the wall, with the British colonies clearly indicated. The history of Britain's wars with both France and Germany (and French wars with Germany), as written in most history books, would unequivocally portray Germany as the aggressor. Today messages of national greatness are less overt. Indeed, some people think that school history, in particular, should be considerably more patriotic. Newspapers like the *Daily Mail* in Britain insist that the great benefits that Britain brought the world through empire should be stressed. But even if national messages are now less explicit than in the past they are still there in a modified form. And, perhaps inevitably, the history British school children mainly study is of 'us' – 'we' study *our* British history. In some societies, school education has a more explicit and direct nationalist agenda. In the Israeli-occupied territories of Palestine, for instance, Palestinian school books are explicitly negative in their coverage of Israelis in particular and Jews in general (Bedein 2004).

4 *Youth organizations* Voluntary youth organizations should be mentioned as playing an important part in the formation of national identity. In Britain, in particular, the Boy Scouts and Girl Guides have played a historical role in nurturing a sense of national identity (see p. 493). Other organizations in Britain and elsewhere have relied upon more overtly militarist forms of nationalist propaganda or have been extensions of the state armed forces. In authoritarian regimes, of both the political left

and right, youth organizations have either been placed under state control or set up by the government to bolster its own support. In Nazi Germany the Boy Scouts became the Hitler Youth in the 1930s. Although it should not for a moment be considered comparable to the Hitler Youth it is interesting to note that governments continue to try to foster national inclusion and citizenship through youth organizations. Americorps, set up by Bill Clinton in the 1990s, and continued by George W. Bush, is a recent example of this.

5 *The media* We should mention the importance of the media to constructions of national identity. As the media chapter in this book makes clear, we should be wary of simplistic assumptions that peoples' consciousness and outlook is directly shaped by the messages they receive from the media. One would need to discriminate between the various sources that are available to an individual. That said there can be little question that it does have a considerable influence. For instance, one might wish to question to what extent newspapers in this country like the *Sun* and the *Daily Mail* are motivated by national interests as opposed to the sectional interests of class, political ideology and/or the commercial interests of their owners, but there can be no doubt that, for instance, their relentless opposition to European enlargement influences a significant section of public opinion. The editors of such newspapers would no doubt say that they merely articulate the views of their readership that the EU is a superstate run from Brussels by the French and Germans that seeks to subdue ancient British freedoms. But, regardless of the extent to which they lead or reflect public opinion, certainly play an important part in a clearly national aspect of politics in Britain. As concerns the broadcast media, national broadcasting companies have played a fundamental role historically in establishing and maintaining a sense of togetherness, of an imagined community in the sense used by Benedict Anderson. In some cases it has been fundamental to accentuating national antagonism. In the former Yugoslavia, for instance, it was crucial to producing the ethnic hatred that preceded and accompanied the civil wars of the early 1990s (Thompson 1999).

It has, of course, become fashionable to claim that the monopolistic control of state and traditional private media has become anachronistic in the age of the Internet and satellite technology. The hold of such organizations over a given group of people, some critics argue, through a traditional ideology like nationalism has been weakened as an aspect of the general undermining of the nation-state in the global age. Without wishing to deny the novel importance of the Internet as a global media form, it is important to recognize that most people continue to receive most of their information from established sources like newspapers and national broadcast news. Simultaneously, the fact that the World Wide Web is inherently global does not of course mean that the content reflects that. All that it means is that the content, of say, anti-European tabloid newspapers are available to an English-speaking audience across the world, for those who should wish to read it and have the means to do so. So, too, with the widely right-wing web sites and radio shows of political and religious groups in the USA.

6 *Sport* Finally, we should mention sport as a fundamental way in which national identity is conveyed. Indeed, in some cases it may well be the most important of ways that provide people with a sense of national identity. As the national team takes the field in an important game everybody within the nation is afforded the sense that they are united in their hope that they will win. Basic to this process it is the usually unquestioned assumption that the national team in question represents us and has the privilege as well as the pleasure to play for 'us'. It is all but obligatory, too, for members of whatever sporting side it might be to declare that they consider it an honour to represent their country. The captain may add that he or she is especially proud. The success or failure of the individual or team reflects upon us. On occasions when it is thought that the national side has not tried to win sufficiently hard the reaction of the general public can be damning. Similarly, the general off-field behaviour and conduct of a team and its supporters is thought to represent the nation. A footballer may be praised or condemned as a role model for children.

The official ethos of international sport, especially the Olympic Games, is that regardless of how intense the competition may be, it ultimately serves to foster good relations between the people of different nations. The reality of much sporting

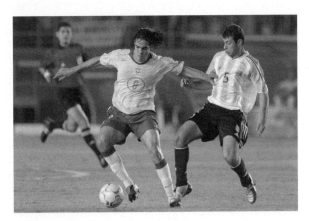

Figure 12.4 A South American football match

competition is rather different. In fact, the enmity and occasional violence of some certain sporting rivalries have been fundamental to hostile national identities. This is particularly apparent between national neighbours where sporting fixtures take on great importance. In southern Latin America, for instance, central to popular nation-building in the twentieth century were football matches, perhaps better put as 'football clashes', between the neighbouring countries of Uruguay, Argentina and Brazil (Mason 1995). The games sometimes had serious diplomatic reverberations. None as dramatic, however, as the 1968 'Football War' between El Salvador and Nicaragua when fighting broke out between the armies of the two states following a match.

As sport can further national identities through antagonism, so it can reveal fault lines within the nation by bringing to the fore the ethnic and exclusive aspects of a nationalism. The usually short-lived fervour surrounding the English national football team in international tournaments is, unfortunately, something most British Asians have at least some difficulty in relating to.

Gender and nationalism

As in most areas of social life, there has always been a 'gender dimension' to nationalism. However, until the intervention of feminist-influenced writers in the early 1990s, it was almost totally absent from academic discussion. Scholars were probably aware of the way in which some nations have feminine symbols and indeed were

often referred to as 'her', but there is little in the older literature on this sort of issue. When writers remarked upon metaphors of rape in relation to cultural imposition of a hostile culture, as with nineteenth-century German nationalists with French cultural influences (Kedourie 1960), the wider question was not mentioned. However, over recent years there has not only been a growth in the number of general discussions and case studies of this subject, but a slow recognition that the consideration of gender is crucial to understanding nationalism. Much the same could be said about sexuality. However, it is rather more difficult to identify with any great clarity precisely what the relationship is. Here we indicate some of the general interconnections. In all cases, the link to gender is explicit in some nationalisms at certain points in time, although it is usually implicit in all cases.

The first way in which women are formally positioned in nationalism is as child bearers, specifically as biological reproducers of nation. This is not an obvious means of simply continuing the species, but a political onus falls upon women to take up a primary and defining role as mothers to produce babies. This usually involves confirmation that a woman's place is the home. This message is particularly acute in authoritarian nationalisms that have few qualms about involving themselves in family matters, and thereby dissolving the distinction between the public and the private. An extreme example of this would be the demand that women returned to the home in order to produce babies in Nazi Germany for the good of the *volk*. This injunction was backed by a series of welfare benefits to encourage reproduction. Such a call to have children for the nation is also discernible within pro-natalist nationalisms where there is a perceived or actual decline in the birth rate (see Pryke 1998). There are numerous examples of this. In Communist China after the revolution of 1949, women were encouraged by Chairman Mao to have as many children as possible to outbreed the imperialist enemies of China in the West. More recently, given the massive growth in the Chinese population, the legal requirement is that family size is to be limited to one child per couple in urban areas. In some instances, though not the Chinese one, the state has insisted that for the greater good of the nation higher rates of fertility are essential among certain class sections of the population. The eugenics movement in Great Britain in the late nineteenth and early twentieth centuries was preoccupied by the implications for nation and empire of the rise in birth rates for what it considered the racially least fit sections of the population, the urban poor. It proposed various unsuccessful measures for boosting the birth rate of the educated middle class including a national dating agency for brainy people.

Closely related to the responsibility of women in some nationalisms for boosting population growth is the role of mother to the future's countrymen and wife to the man of the nation. The maintenance of tradition is afforded to the woman as she socializes the nation's young in the culture and history of the nation. Simultaneously, it is her given role to provide for the man through running the family home. Home is not simply a practical arrangement but takes on a wider symbolic importance with many nationalisms – the nation as home, returning to the national home. In times of war when the nation is under threat women have been expected to guard the home front (while sometimes simultaneously taking up jobs that men might otherwise do). 'Keep the home fires burning' was one of the maxims of the Second World War, the imagery of the phrase being that as the men of nation took up the call to arms and fought the German aggressor, so their women would be keeping up the domestic front and waiting faithfully back home. The moral disapproval of women who transgress the boundaries of acceptable behaviour, especially during times of war, can be severe. In extreme cases, such as for women accused of having sex with the enemy, this has involved their routine public humiliation. French girls accused of sleeping with German soldiers during the French occupation of France in the Second World War were shaved after liberation and paraded naked around towns and cities.

The result of the symbolic role of women in nationalist discourse is ambiguous. On the one hand, nationalism has served to justify the division of labour between men and women. On the other, it has contributed to the status and sometimes dominance that women have had within the confines of the home, even in particularly patriarchal nations.

The issue of sexuality is impossible to disentangle from gender. We have already noted the image in nationalist discourse of women as at once fertile and faithful. The emphasis this implicitly places upon heterosexual sex within marriage as the only acceptable form of sex has been furthered by some nationalisms that assert that other forms of sexuality like homosexuality and even masturbation are inimical to the interests of the nation. The prohibition of homosexuality has been especially strong within religiously oriented nationalisms. It was considered simply un-Irish in the closed Catholic autarchy of Eamonn De Valera's Ireland during the mid-twentieth century. In other cases, homosexuality has been identified by Third World nationalist leaders as a vice of the decadent West, something opposed to the development priorities they affirmed. Masturbation has been similarly branded as a national ill. Famously the founder of the Boy Scouts movement, Baden-Powell, thought it indicative of urban impurity among boys, a physical and moral form of degradation that was threatening the implosion of nation and empire.

As indicated, it has often been the case that nationalisms have identified certain sexual practices with other nations, those quite different from their own. This extends to a sense of threat of enemy sexuality usually hinging around a stereotype. A range of stereotypes circulate of the particular national sexualities – peoples as especially erotic or by contrast particularly cold – and not all of them are in any real sense related to a national opposition. However, it is noticeable that some of the most vivid contrasts are related. Although the juxtaposition is probably not as strong as it once was, a recurring theme of British, specifically English, stereotypes of the French is that they are dangerously oversexed. Terms for certain sexual practices that were not quite English were given to them such as French kissing and Frenching. By contrast, the French have historically tended to depict the English as seriously repressed and thus inclined to perversions like masochism that express their inhibitions. Such stereotypes are due to historical cultural development, climatically derived notions of national characters and also intermittent wars over the last thousand years. Notions of deviant sexuality among both French men and women were especially marked in English depictions of their Gallic foes after the French revolution when invasion from the continent was feared (Gibson 1995).

Further to the way in which war produces stereotypes, is the way in which gender and sexuality are configured in notions of nations as either soft or hard, feminine or masculine. During the First World War, for instance, France depicted herself in propaganda as violated through the barbarism of the German armies, an integral part of this being the rapes its soldiers committed. The numerous cartoons that circulated drew a contrast between the masculine aggression of the Prussian soldier and the innocent feminine vulnerability of Marianne, in itself a revealing French symbol of purity and toleration (Harris 1993).

Summary

➤ Until recently sociology has not generally considered nationalism due to its concentration on a given society and the fact that its founding fathers had little to say about the subject.

➤ Nations and nationalism are crucial both for the identity of individuals and groups and, through the nation-state, the organization of society.

➤ Nations have definite objective features like languages and cultures. However, we should be careful to distinguish myth from reality in examining them. Many of the claims of nationalists about the antiquity of a people, its original habitation, the timelessness of a language, its glorious history, its unique character are much exaggerated, and often simply wrong. National movements and states from the nineteenth century onwards were crucial to disseminating national myths.

➤ It is useful to consider a nation as a group that shares a feeling of horizontal and historical togetherness by dint of common culture located in a single geographic area.

➤ The principal debate in the study of nationalism in recent years has been over the modernity of nations. Perennialists argue that the nations are ancient, even timeless, entities. Modernists, by contrast, argue that nations are the product of modernity. According to the particular writer, this involves emphasizing the importance of the industrial revolution, the role of the intelligentsia in inventing tradition and the role of the nation-state in the making of the nation. By contrast, an ethnic origins approach argues that although nations are modern entities, an ethnic antiquity exists through organization and memory.

➤ Nations and nationalism have an important relationship with citizenship through the relative importance they place upon the attainment of nationality through birth or residency.

➤ National identity is not something we are born with, but learnt through socialization. The family, school, religion, youth movements and sport are all important vehicles for conveying an everyday sense of nationality.

➤ Nations make important assumptions about gender and sexuality. Their claims inform women about the duty to reproduce within the magic circle of nation, while 'being national' is an important component of masculinity.

Links

The section on language and culture, pages 480–483, links back to the discussion in Chapter 1, pages 20–29.

The issues surrounding racial origin raised on pages 483–484, are also looked at in Chapter 8.

 ## Further reading

Anderson, P. (1991) *Imagined Communities: Reflections on the Origins and Spread of Nationalism*, 2nd edn, London: Verso. A brilliant and colourful exposition of the rise and power of nationalism.

Gellner, E. (1983) *Nations and Nationalism*, Oxford: Blackwell. A good first book to read on nationalism and a highly influential modernist account by one of the most eminent scholars of the subject.

Hobsbawm, E. (1994) *Nations and Nationalism Since 1780: Programme, Myth and Reality*, Cambridge: Cambridge University Press. Because of the weight of historical detail this is a difficult book, but it actually combines strong general findings with a wealth of fascinating facts.

Ozkirimli, U. (2000) *Theories of Nationalism: A Critical Introduction*, Basingstoke: Palgrave Macmillan.
A strong overview of the debates within the academic study of nationalism.

Smith, A.D. (1991) *National Identity*, London: Penguin.
Anthony Smith has written numerous books on nationalism that state and restate, with great erudition, essentially the same 'ethnic origins' approach. This is a concise example.

Spencer, P. and Woollman, H. (2002) *Nationalism: A Critical Introduction*, London: Sage.
An excellent book, challenging and at the same time comprehensive.

Web sites

http://www.nationalismproject.org/
Contains some definitions of nation, overviews of the principal approaches to the subject and extensive reading lists.

http://www.suc.org/index.html
It is predictable and therefore a little unfair to use a Serbian web site as an example of nationalism, but that of the Chicago-based Serbian Unity Congress is a particular instance of the use of history for nationalist purposes. Some mirror images can be found in the web site of the Croatian American Association **http://www.caausa.org/links.htm**

Activities

Activity 1

Flags and national pride

The article below concerns Turkey, specifically the Turkish flag. There have, however, been similar reactions in recent history over the burning of flags of other countries. During the Vietnam War, American peace campaigners sometimes burnt the Stars and Stripes to display their disgust over US military actions. But this was too much even for many opponents of the war, let alone the mass of the American public. In 1971, Marcy Taylor, a 25-year-old from San Francisco, dashed into an anti-war demonstration and smothered a burning flag with her bare hands. She became a national heroine and celebrity. Read the article and consider the questions below it.

ANKARA – A botched bid Sunday by a few teenagers to burn a Turkish flag during a Kurdish celebration has led to a patriotic backlash with unprecedented public displays of the national symbol. 'We will not tolerate any insult against our flag,' an angry shopkeeper in the residential Cankaya district here said Thursday. 'Trying to burn it is out of the question – everyone should know this.' A huge Turkish flag – a white star and crescent on a red background – was taped to the window of his grocery store. 'This is unheard of: Turks trying to burn their own flag,' said an incredulous Abdulkadir Delibas, 25. Turks take great pride in their national emblem, which for them is a symbol of the 1919–22 war of independence and its leader, Mustafa Kemal Ataturk, the founder of the modern Turkish republic.

Private homes and businesses are often bedecked with flags on national holidays, but the spontaneous reaction to Sunday's incident has surpassed even the most patriotic Independence Day displays. Balconies, verandahs, windows, taxis, city buses, banks and businesses here and in other major cities – even the vast, labyrinthine covered bazaar in Istanbul – are festooned with the star and crescent emblem.

The incident that sparked it all occurred Sunday in Mersin, a port city on the southern Turkish coast that is home to large numbers of Kurdish refugees from the southeast who fled the war there between the army and the rebel separatist Kurdistan Workers Party (PKK) between 1984 and 1999. During celebrations in Mersin of Newroz, the traditional Kurdish New Year, a group of teenagers manhandled and tried to burn a Turkish flag in front of TV news cameras. Newroz, which marks the summer equinox and the arrival of spring, is celebrated across Turkey and particularly in the Kurdish-populated southeast, has often provided an excuse for pro-PKK demonstrations.

Activities (continued)

This year too, tens of thousands of people participated, many chanting slogans and demonstrating in favour of the PKK and its leader, Abdullah Ocalan, now serving a life term for treason. But contrary to previous practice – reflecting the kinder, gentler Turkey trying to break out of its authoritarian cocoon as it aspires to join the European Union – police this year did not intervene. But by Thursday, they had arrested half a dozen people in connection with the outrage, the youngest aged only 12 and the others in their teens.

First to react to the TV footage that shocked the nation was the powerful army, which waged a 15-year-war against the PKK that claimed 36,500 lives.

In a strongly worded statement, the general staff described the event as an act of 'treason' by 'so-called citizens'. The media and the entire political establishment – including the pro-Kurdish DEHAP party – denounced the outrage as a surge of patriotism gripped the country. Thousands of flags were distributed freely and TV channels placed the symbol on a corner of their screens. The flag is protected by a strict law that provides fines and jail time for all offenders – whoever places it where it can be sat or trod upon, or insults, burns, tears or throws it to the ground.

The fervour was such that newspapers began calling for moderation, fearing incidents between Kurds and Turks. Analysts were afraid such demonstrations could harm Turkey's EU bid, with accession talks due to begin on October 3. 'There is a general feeling of "enough is enough" among the population that defines its national identity as Turkish,' commented a columnist for the liberal daily Radikal. The incident, she wrote, reflects mounting anti-Kurdish 'racism' in the country, which should be openly discussed if a solution is to be found.

(Source: www.turkishpress.com 24.3.2005)

Questions

1. What do you think it is about this action, the burning of the national flag, that triggers such hostile reactions?

2. Flags are widely displayed in a number of different contexts. What were the issues at stake for the Turks who reacted with such indignation to the burning of their national flag?

3. How might you contrast the issues at stake with this incident to:

   a) the mass display across America of the Stars and Stripes after 9/11;
   b) the display of the national flag by Poles in Rome and in Poland itself after the death of the Polish pope;
   c) the display of the cross of St George from cars, taxis and houses before and during recent international football tournaments that the English team has taken part in?

4. The article refers to how this incident might 'harm Turkey's EU bid'. Do you think that the response of Turks is natural and, given this, acceptable? How might it hinder this bid?

Activity 2

National character

The passage below is taken from the first part of an essay entitled 'England Your England' by George Orwell. The full piece is called *The Lion and the Unicorn: Socialism and the English Genius* (Orwell 1968 [1941]). The gist of this passage is that 1) nationalism is an enormously powerful motivation that can cause people to try to kill one another; 2) this is more than international politics alone as there are real differences between people; 3) national character is a product of the fusion of the objects and practices of everyday life and the psyche of a people; 4) national character determines what sort of events happen in the country in question. Read it and consider the questions that follow.

Activities (continued)

As I write, highly civilized human beings are flying over my head, trying to kill me.

They do not feel any enmity towards me as an individual, nor I against them. They are 'only doing their duty', as the saying goes. Most of them, I have no doubt, are kind-hearted law-abiding men who would never dream of committing murder in private life. On the other hand, if one of them succeeded in blowing me to pieces with a well-placed bomb, he will never sleep any the worse for it. He is serving his country, which has the power to absolve him from evil.

One cannot see the modern world as it is unless one recognizes the overwhelming strength of nationalism, national loyalty. In certain circumstances it can break down, in certain circumstances it does not exist, but as a positive force there is nothing to set beside it. Christianity and international socialism are weak as straw in comparison with it. Hitler and Mussolini rose to power in their own countries very largely because they could grasp this fact and their opponents could not.

Also, one must admit that the divisions between nation and nation are founded on real differences in outlook. Till very recently it was thought proper to pretend that all human beings are very much alike, but in fact anyone able to use his eyes knows that the average of human behaviour differs enormously from country to country. Things that happen in one country could not happen in another. Hitler's June Purge, for instance, could not have happened in England. And, as western peoples go, the English are very highly differentiated. There is sort of backhanded admission of this in the dislike which nearly all foreigners feel for our national way of life. Few Europeans can endure living in England, and even Americans often feel more at home in Europe.

When you come back to England from any foreign country, you have immediately the sensation of breathing different air. Even in the first few minutes dozens of small things conspire to give you this feeling. The beer is bitterer, the coins are heavier, the grass is greener, the advertisements are more blatant. The crowds in the big towns, with their knobbly faces, their bad teeth and gentle manners, are different from a European crowd. Then the vastness of England swallows you up, and you lose for a while your feeling that the whole nation has a single identifiable character.

But talk to foreigners, read books or newspapers and you are brought back to the same thought. Yes, there is something distinctive and recognizable about English civilization. It is somehow bound up with solid breakfasts and gloomy Sundays, smoky towns and winding roads, green fields and red pillar boxes. And above all, it is *your* civilization, it is *you*. However much you hate it, you will never be happy away from it for any length of time. The suet puddings and the red pillar boxes have entered into your soul. Good or evil, it is yours, you belong to it, and this side of the grave you will never get away from the marks that it has given you.

(Orwell 1941)

Questions

1. *Is it possible to talk of definite national characters in the twenty-first century?*

2. *Is this concept of any relevance for sociology?*

3. *What sort of forces can be identified that have perhaps made it less relevant now than when Orwell was writing in the mid-twentieth century?*

4. *Assuming there is at least something to Orwell's contention that 'anyone able to use his eyes knows that the average of human behaviour differs enormously from country to country', what explanation might one give for this other than national character?*

5. *Leaving aside the possible criticisms of national character, how would you define it for the national group you consider yourself to be part of?*

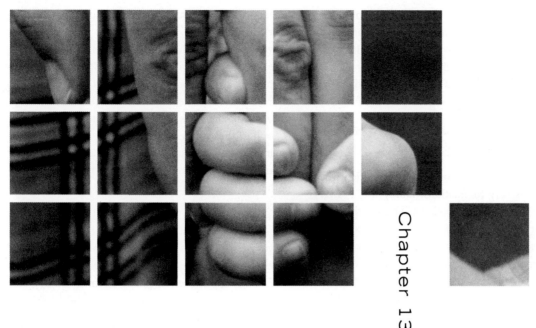

Chapter 13

Families and family living

My father was frightened of his mother; I was frightened of my father, and I am damned well going to see to it that my children are frightened of me.

(George V, quoted in Donaldson 1976: 10)

The stereotype of the family epitomised by the husband as the sole wage earner, wife as full time housekeeper and mother with dependent children living at home (that is, the family which is featured almost exclusively in the advertising world), in fact comprises only a minority of households at any given point in time.

(Henwood *et al.* 1987: 3–4)

Key issues

➤ What problems arise in trying to define concepts such as the family and marriage?

➤ What is the relationship between family patterns and wider social and physical environments?

➤ Does the rise in rates of divorce and cohabitation mean that the family and marriage are no longer valued?

➤ How are specific groups affected by social expectations within the family and society at large, for example single parents, homosexual couples and step-families?

➤ What are the major areas of debate within the sociology of the family?

Introduction

Families can be sites of conflict, tension and arguments, yet may also be sources of love, caring, support, affection, commitment and a sense of belonging as well as involving relations of responsibility, obligations and duties. Thus family living can be both positive and negative, and often provokes ambivalent feelings and emotions in all of us.

The family is regarded as one of the most basic and important institutions in society. In fact, what the family is, and should be, is regarded by some as such unquestionable common sense that it became central to the British prime minister's call for a return to traditional values in 1993, a theme that was intended to run through all areas of government policy in the years to follow:

It's time to get back to basics: to self-discipline and respect for the law, to consideration for others, to accepting responsibility for yourself and your family, and not shuffling it off on the state.

(John Major's address to the Conservative Party Conference, November 1993)

This strong emphasis on traditional family values has been reinforced by the Labour government:

We cannot say we want a strong and secure society when we ignore its very foundations: family life . . . Every area of this government's policy will be scrutinized to see how it affects family life. Every policy examined, every initiative tested, every avenue explored to see how we strengthen our families.

(Tony Blair's first major Conference speech, the *Guardian* 1.10.1997)

However, the fact that some felt a moral crusade to strengthen family values was needed at all reveals that contemporary British society is experiencing considerable social change in relation to attitudes, values and structures concerning family life. Recent changes in family living include increasing cohabitation and divorce, remarriage (serial monogamy), reconstituted or step-families, lone parents, joint custody, abortions and two-career households (Jagger and Wright 1999). As we shall see in this chapter, such changes in family structure can create demands for new government policies and the increased diversity of family forms often sparks intense public and academic debate. It is interesting to note, however, that unlike other European countries, we in Britain do not have a minister with special responsibilities for

'the family' or a coherent programme for 'family policy' (Morgan 1998).

Even the apparent bastion of traditional British values – the Royal Family – conforms to these general trends. Of the Queen's four children, one is divorced, two are divorced and remarried. These details became the subject of media debate when Prince Edward's engagement to Sophie Rhys-Jones was announced in 1999. Of her six grandchildren, four are being brought up by lone parents and two are in a reconstituted family with their mother and stepfather. As Cheal points out, their family lives have become closely scrutinized:

Inside information, or rumours, about the personal lives of royalty has helped to sell huge numbers of newspapers, magazines and books. Today, the details of family life are often public business on a grand scale.

(Cheal 2002: 16)

A glance at some contemporary media forms also reflects awareness of the transition. In most popular television soap operas, for example, how many families fit the nuclear model of once-married parents living happily with their two children under one roof? (It is however argued later in this chapter that a more comprehensive analysis of the media shows that an ideological model of the family is still portrayed as the desirable norm.)

Clearly, then, the family is an exciting area of sociological study, particularly when set in a comparative context over time and culture. Research has shown that all societies exhibit some form of family and marriage arrangements. At the same time, however, while it can be argued that the family is universal, the form that it takes is subject to enormous variation. Bernardes (1997)

Figure 13.1 The royal family
© Getty/Scott Barbour

Figure 13.2 The BBC's Royale Family

reflects this variation by referring to the range of 'family pathways': movements through and between differing patterns of household and family living. If we take a single multicultural society such as Britain, it is evident that there are many forms of family life and that the nature of the family has changed over the years. These forms of family are examined in this chapter.

Stop and think

➤ Complete this sentence. The family can be defined as . . .

➤ What difficulties arise in attempting to come up with a definition of the family?

Defining the family

It is inappropriate to talk about '*the* family' as if there is only one universal type; although it is more appropriate to talk about 'family life' and to explore the many variations of family life in contemporary society. Let us try to give a preliminary definition of what we mean by 'the family'. While we all operate with a common-sense understanding of what we mean by the family, once we try to define the family it soon becomes obvious that it is not so straightforward. Such an exercise highlights the enormous cultural variation in the forms of family life.

Most sociological textbooks give a definition of the family. Here are two examples:

> The family has been seen as a social institution that unites individuals into cooperative groups . . . Most families are built on kinship, a social bond, based on blood, marriage or adoption, that joins individuals into families. (Macionis and Plummer 2002: 436)

> A family is a group of persons directly linked by kin connections, the adult members of which assume responsibility for caring for children.
>
> (Giddens 2001: 173)

Behind such definitions lie some common assumptions of the family. Giddens' definition stresses the idea of parental responsibility. Traditionally this was broken down by gender, such that the father was seen as the main bread-winner while the mother was expected to take on the main role in child-rearing and running the home. Aspects of social policy have reinforced the idea of fathers taking responsibility for supporting the family (for example the Child Support Agency: see p. 526). Over time this cultural expectation has been challenged and many women take on a dual role.

There is no agreed definition of the family, and recent definitions tend to be broad in order to recognize the growing complexity of different family forms, including lesbian and gay families:

> A household is a residential group whose members usually share some basic tasks (like cooking). A family may or may not also be a household, but is usually distinguished by formal ties of 'blood' and marriage. However, 'family' also connotes ties of love and affection, commitment, and obligations whether these are formally recognised or not.   (Van Every 1999: 178)

Thus families are not just about who they are but what they do, such as caring, sharing resources, meeting respons-ibilities and fulfilling obligations (Silva and Smart 1999). Bernardes (1997) emphasizes that families are constructed, the result of everyday lived realities. Such a view is similar to the family practices discussed by Morgan (1996) who argues that families are a product of daily interactions, routines and transactions which may be both enabling and constraining. Thus our family relationships can be experienced as a mixture of love and hate, burden and duty, care and protection, approval and disapproval.

A cross-cultural perspective shows that definitions of childhood and adulthood are not universal, with conse-quences for assumptions about roles and responsibilities within the family (see Chapter 9, Age). Assumptions about parental responsibility and relationships between mem-bers of the family tend to vary across different societies and even within different cultural groups within society. Therefore, as Jagger and Wright remind us:

> The groupings that are called families are socially con-structed rather than naturally or biologically given. Families and family relations are, like the term itself, flexible, fluid and contingent. They encompass a whole variety of historically and culturally specific types of domestic arrangements and kinship systems.
>
> (Jagger and Wright 1999: 3)

The nature of marriage has changed in Britain in terms of the overall increase in divorce. We now talk about 'serial monogamy' referring to patterns of marriage, divorce and remarriage. There has also been a decline in the over-all number of marriages and a rise in the number of births taking place outside wedlock.

Stop and think

> ➤ Define (a) monogamy; (b) polygamy; (c) polyandry.
>
> ➤ Why do some societies practise polygamy?
>
> ➤ What do you think are the advantages and disadvantages of monogamy, polygamy and arranged marriages?

Birth rates outside marriage

There has been a dramatic rise in the number of births outside marriage. According to the Office for National Statistics (ONS 2004), in 1980 nearly 12 per cent of all births were outside marriage but by 2002 the figure had reached 41 per cent. However, as Denscombe (1998: 20) points out, four out of five such births are registered with both parents identified and, in most cases, with both living at the same address. As well as the increasing proportion of children born outside marriage, more women are deciding not to have children or to have them later in life and to have fewer. Recent figures show that only 11 per cent of women born in 1925 were still childless by age 35, but this increased to 25 per cent of women aged 35 who were born in 1965 (ONS 2004). This pattern is expected to continue and is linked to women's increased participation in the education and labour market as well as the wider choice and effectiveness of contraception.

Obviously such changes in child-bearing trends may be due to a variety of factors and are likely to have an impact in the future on the structures and patterns of family life. In China the impact of government policy restricting families to one child only is being felt. It is now being predicted that the concept of 'aunts' and 'uncles' (as blood relatives) will be meaningless to the next generation.

A common assumption about the family is that marri-age involves having children. Young married couples are often asked when they are planning to 'start a family'. In some societies and communities the expectation and pres-sure to procreate can be more explicit, with child-bearing regarded as a couple's duty and a part of their responsibility to the community or state. In France, child-bearing is encouraged through legislation, while in Singapore tax incentives have been used to encourage graduates to marry and start families. Many traditional religious and ethical codes regard child-bearing as a natural consequence of marriage and include prayers in wedding ceremonies that the couple will be blessed with offspring.

Many people see having children not so much as an obligation or even a choice but as a right. Archard (1993: 97) discusses how human rights charters have recognized the right of adults 'to found a family' as referring to both bearing and bringing up children. (Archard examines the limits and contingencies regarding this right, including concern for the well-being of the child and the consequences for society of any birth – 1993: 98.) Partly as a result of this view of child-bearing as a right, there continues to be extensive research and development in the field of biological and genetic engineering.

Cross-cultural comparisons of family legislation, religious customs and kinship patterns show the significance of social context for different types of family structures. In analyzing the different forms of family within society, sociologists make the distinction between the nuclear and extended type of family. The *nuclear family* is often referred to as 'immediate family' – parents and children living in the same household. The *extended family* goes beyond this to include wider kin such as aunts, uncles and grandparents. One feature of industrialization is the weakening of extended family ties as younger members of the family become socially mobile and move away from home for work and to set up their own nuclear family (see pp. 517–19).

Sociological research has shown that as societies change and evolve, so does the nature of the family. Expectations and assumptions about the family are constantly changing and it is impossible to study the family as a unit in isolation from wider developments in the

Case study

Foetal eggs: a fertile ground for debate

These extracts are taken from the letters page in *The Guardian* on 6 June 1994. They illustrate public concerns about the use of genetic engineering and parenthood.

Recent advances in reproductive technology have done much to enable some of those hitherto unable to have children to become parents. These developments have given hope to some, while causing many to consider the ethical and moral dilemmas created by our newfound ability to control aspects of our reproductive potential . . .

Clearly there is a need for a wide ranging and informed debate . . . However we must take care to ensure debate is not clouded by excessive anxieties about the possibility of abuse by a few at the expense of significant benefits for many others.

The debate on the ethics of genetic engineering is taking place with too narrow terms of reference. The reason why the concept of eugenics is unacceptable . . . is that it means making decisions for other people about their procreation – people without power to object . . .

Overpopulation, defined as too many poor people, means that we in the North, who have our fertility checked by sheer consumerism, applaud sterilisation programmes and condoms galore (megabusiness!) for states which are still in fact colonies and cannot afford to listen to their own indignant populations . . .

Genetic engineering is the latest focus for capital investment. Its application involves the need

for control by laws and the state . . . but not by the millions of women who are never consulted when patriarchy acts 'for their good', 'to give them choice' and divide them into wombs, foetuses, eggs, each with a claim to life which sets the woman's rights against the 'properties' in her own body . . .

We are back to eugenics: imposing a reductionist, patriarchal view of procreation and scientific 'progress' on an earth full of powerless people, when all that is needed to improve the human stock is food, shelter, freedom from want and war.

Questions

1. *What ethical and political viewpoints are being put forward here?*

2. *How are traditional views about parenthood being challenged?*

nature and structure of society. Politicians recognize this when they use the welfare of the family as an indicator of the general health of society and express concern over figures that seem to suggest that the family as we know it is in decline. Those who mourn the apparent demise of the family tend to work with two further assumptions about the family: first, that the family is a positive and desirable part of society and that it is good for its members; and second, that where there is evidence of the negative side of the family this is a relatively new phenomenon and the traditional family did not experience it. Both of these assumptions have been challenged by sociologists.

The ideology of the family

'Family ideology' in contemporary society is the idealized image of the family that tends to be the basis of our common-sense understanding of what the average family is or should be:

> An *ideology* provides collective definitions of what a 'normal' family is thought to be, what is a 'proper' marriage, and what it means to be a 'good mother' or a 'good father'. Family ideologies are held out as ideal ways of living. (Cheal 2002: 72)

Several institutions are responsible for shaping a particular ideology of the family including the state (in terms of the assumptions about the family conveyed in welfare or educational arrangements), political parties (in terms of political structures and policies), legal systems (in terms of the structures and assumptions behind family law) and the media (in terms of its portrayal of family life).

The influence of ideology can be illustrated by a closer examination of media projections of the family. Abercrombie and Warde (1994) refer to commonly accepted media stereotypes of the 'cereal packet family' as the 'typical' normative family: two fairly young parents and their two children (a girl and a boy). The family is seen as a harmonious refuge, a unit of consumption, a 'good thing'. The ideology of the family corresponds to a functionalist model in that it is regarded as a positive social influence, beneficial both for its members and for society as a whole.

Marxists have criticized the ideology of the family as being distorted and biased and raising false expectations:

> The ideology of the family would have us believe that there is one type of family, one correct way in which individuals should live and interact together . . . An

ideology that claims there is only one type of family can never be matched in reality, for it represents an ideal to which only some can approximate, and others not at all. (Gittins 1993: 167)

Stop and think

➤ Find examples of the 'typical' family in, for example, adverts, holiday brochures, Christmas ads, women's magazines, including exceptions that prove the rule.

➤ What are the typical roles of adults and children, women and men in these representations?

➤ In your view how close is this image to reality?

The power of the concept of the ideology of the family lies in the fact that it is taken for granted rather than being subjected to constant reappraisal. What makes it all the more important to consider the ideology of the family is the fact that it often does not represent the reality of how individuals interact together: 'It is this gap between ideology and reality which signifies the assumed "crisis" in the family' (Coppock 1997: 75). However:

> it manifests just enough similarity to people's life situations to make it seem tangible and real to most. Thus the never-married, the divorced, and the childless can at least identify part of the 'ideal family' with a past childhood or family distorted in memory, and feel that their own 'failure' has been an individual failing rather than an unrealistic ideal. (Gittins 1993: 165)

Changing family patterns
The role of the extended family

We tend to accept that the nuclear type of family is both a natural and a normal arrangement for society. It is the yardstick against which 'abnormal' or 'alternative' types of family (such as one-parent families) are measured. However, sociological research reveals that the patterns of family life are far from constant and are subject to changes in line with changes in wider society. While it is true that today most people live in a household of three or more people, there has been a rapid increase in the number of people living either alone or with one other

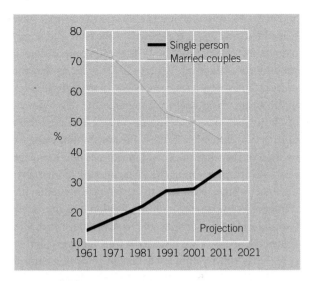

Figure 13.3a Trend to single person households (as a percentage of all households, GB)
Source: Denscombe 1998: 21

person. This trend is expected to continue. Between 1971 and 2001 the number of one-person households almost doubled from 17 per cent to 31 per cent (Office for National Statistics 2001) and is predicted to increase to 36 per cent in 2016 (as shown in Figure 13.3).

Morgan warns against interpreting this change as equating with the decline of the family:

> While households may often contain family relationships, such relationships nearly always cut across different households. The young person living in a single person household, for example, may continue to maintain relations with his or her parents, brothers or sisters, located in other households. The argument that there is no such thing as 'the family' refers to the fact that we are dealing with a relatively fluid set of relationships and the feelings and obligations that are sometimes associated with these relationships.
>
> (Morgan 1998: 9)

One of the best-known studies of changing family patterns in Britain was carried out by Young and Willmott (1957) on working-class communities in east London in the 1950s. Like other family and community studies in the 1950s (e.g. Firth 1956; Kerr 1958), this classic study highlighted the strength of kinship networks. Young and Willmott found that the traditional extended family kin network weakened as younger members of the family moved from Bethnal Green to housing estates like Greenleigh in outer London and set up their own nuclear form of family. ('Kinship networks' covered all the relatives whom a person knows to exist, in all the families to which they

are linked, such as through marriage as well as family of origin.) In Bethnal Green Young and Willmott found that traditionally most married couples had lived close to their parents-in-law and maintained virtually daily contact, particularly mothers and daughters, whose relationship tended to be strong and vital. In this way the extended family had functioned as a mutual reciprocal support service, an arrangement threatened by change:

> In a three-generation family the burden of caring for the young as well, though bound to fall primarily on the mothers, can be lightened by being shared with the grandmothers. The three generations complement each other. Once prise out two of them, and the wives are left without the help of grandmothers, the old without the comfort of children and grandchildren.
>
> (Young and Willmott 1962 [1957]: 197)

The effect of increasing levels of occupational and geographical mobility was to erode close-knit networks. It brought the transition from the characteristic extended family to the smaller nuclear pattern. This type of nuclear family was more self-contained with greater emphasis placed on conjugal relationships (the relationship between husband and wife).

The family and industrialization

Young and Willmott's study illustrated, as later research has borne out, that changes in the physical and social environment can have enormous impact on patterns of kinship. Their final passage in 1957 sent out warning signals to town planners designing new housing and aiming to create new communities:

> Even when the town planners have set themselves to create communities anew as well as houses, they have still put their faith in buildings, sometimes speaking as though all that was necessary for neighbourliness was a neighbourhood unit, for community spirit a community centre. If this were so, then there would be no harm in shifting people about the country. . . . But there is surely more to a community than that. The sense of loyalty to each other amongst the inhabitants of a place like Bethnal Green is not due to buildings. It is due far more to ties of kinship and friendship which connect the people of one household to the people of another. In such a district community spirit does not have to be fostered, it is already there. If the authorities

regard that spirit as a social asset worth preserving, they will not uproot more people, but build the new houses around the social groups to which they already belong.   (Young and Willmott 1962 [1957]: 198–9)

Many out-of-town overspill estates and high-rise housing blocks in the 1960s came under severe criticism for having destroyed family and community life by failing to acknowledge the significance of geography and environment for family networks.

Taking a longer-term historical perspective, historians such as Laslett (1972) and Anderson (1971) have carried out research which reinforces the effect of external environmental changes on family life. Their research suggests that before industrialization kinship was much less strong

and that the onset of industrialization may well have helped to bring about the growth of the extended family pattern. By comparing family size and composition in pre-industrial England, Laslett (1972) suggests that the nuclear family may have been a significant factor in helping to bring about and accommodate the development of industrial society. Anderson (1971) analyzed later nineteenth-century family life in Preston, finding evidence by then of the importance of kinship ties and exchange relationships in meeting the challenges of industrializing society. Thus in contrast to the popular myth that the changes accompanying industrialization are inevitably harmful to family networks, the research suggests that in Britain the opposite was historically true. Indeed, Willmott (1988) has since commented that the strong extended

Figure 13.3b The traditional extended family is still a feature of contemporary society
Source: Jose Luis Pelaez, Inc./Corbis

family bonds found in Bethnal Green did not exist a hundred years earlier but rather emerged as a result of changes in the economy and housing patterns.

Since the 1960s the traditional urban kinship pattern in Britain has continued to weaken:

> A number of changes have broken the old order: high levels of geographical mobility, redevelopment of the inner areas of Britain's cities and industrial towns, changes in the family and marriage, and the increase in the number of wives going out to work (reducing their contacts with their mothers).
>
> (Willmott 1988: 44)

Willmott points out, however, that while families may no longer live physically close to one another there is still close contact between them and relatives continue to be the main source of informal support and care. In follow-up research based on families in north London, Willmott (1988) found that families helped each other in areas such as child care, babysitting, lending money and supporting older relations and that class differences were not marked in this. High contact is facilitated by the car, the telephone and public transport systems.

Willmott concludes that although Western kinship systems are based on choice – such that individuals can choose whether or not or the degree to which they maintain contact with wider kin – what is significant in British society is the fact that the family continues to survive, indeed to flourish. In support of a functionalist approach, Willmott implies that this is because the family continues to fulfil an important role within contemporary society.

> The most striking feature of British kinship, now and in the past, and in both urban and rural environments, is its resilience ... kinship has continued, as it still continues, to supply the ties and support that people need. Throughout British history it has proved to be a national resource of great value. This has been possible because of its power to adapt to greater mobility and to the demands and opportunities of an increasingly urbanised world. (Willmott 1988: 46)

Marriage, divorce and cohabitation

Family breakdown and divorce are a significant part of contemporary family life and affect all levels of society. Despite the increasing rate of divorces and the greater

social acceptance of the vulnerability of relationships, the breakdown of marriages among rich and famous people regularly attracts sensational media attention. This suggests that there is still a certain amount of stigma associated with the break-up of a family, even where a split may be seen as being in the best interests of all concerned. Nevertheless, the increase in divorce has not detracted from the popularity of marriage, cohabitation and the attraction of family life, which seems to reinforce the view that the ideology of the family is as strong as ever. As Dimmock points out:

> Despite the current concern about the uncertain future for marriage and the family, statistics suggest the majority today still seek a union of two people – 80 per cent wanting children – ideally for many years.
>
> (Dimmock 2004: 193)

Here we shall examine trends in marriage, cohabitation and divorce and consider the sociological explanations behind them.

Divorce rates

In Britain there was a steady increase in the divorce rate since the Second World War until it peaked in 1993. In 1971 there were just under 80,000 divorces and this

---

A closer look

Divorce terminology

It is important to adopt a careful and critical approach to any statistics presented on divorce and the terms used.

Divorce rate number of divorces compared with the number of marriages in any one year.

Divorce petitions number of requests for divorce.

Divorce absolutes number of marriages fully terminated by law.

As Nicky Hart (1976) points out, the statistical rate of divorce in England and Wales is not a full measure of the incidence of marital breakdown since not all separated couples seek legal termination through the courts. Others may separate without recourse to the law or else maintain an 'empty-shell' marriage, continuing to live as husbands and wives but with no real quality of relationship left.

Figure 13.4 The Osbournes
© Neal Preston/CORBIS

Case study

Royal attitudes to marriage and divorce

Henry VIII broke away from the Roman Catholic Church in order to divorce his first wife, Catherine of Aragon, his older brother's widow; he married a further five times.

George IV had two wives at once; he separated from the second, Caroline of Brunswick, and went back to the first, Mrs Maria Fitzherbert, a Roman Catholic.

Victoria had nine children with Prince Albert, most of whom married into other European royal houses.

George V married Mary of Teck after her original fiancé, his older brother, died.

Edward VIII relinquished the throne after 325 days in order to marry divorcée Wallis Simpson, saying 'I now quit altogether public affairs and I lay down my burden'.

Princess Margaret was prevented from marrying a divorcé, Group Captain Peter Townsend, but later divorced Antony Armstrong-Jones.

Princess Anne married and divorced Mark Phillips, then married Tim Lawrence.

Prince Charles married Lady Diana Spencer, who was descended from the Stuarts via an extra-marital liaison of Charles II; they separated after revelations about his relationship with Camilla Parker Bowles. This led to debates about his future as king and head of the Church of England. The Royal Marriage Act 1772 limits the monarch's freedom to marry, divorce or remarry (for example the monarch may not marry a Roman Catholic).

Prince Andrew married, then separated from, Miss Sarah Ferguson.

Public opinion In a *Daily Mail* opinion poll (12 December 1993), 70 per cent polled said they would oppose Prince Charles being king if he HAD stayed married and kept Camilla as his official mistress. However, if he had divorced Princess Diana and married Camilla then 64 per cent would have opposed his succession. Since Princess Diana's death there was increased media interest in the prospect of Prince Charles remarrying. Prince Charles married Camilla Parker Bowles in 2005.

Prince Edward married Sophie Rhys-Jones in June 1999.

Question

1. *How closely do you think changing royal attitudes towards marriage and divorce reflect those of the general public?*

---

figure rose to 180,000 in 1993 (ONS 2004). While the divorce rate increased, the number of marriages fell from around 459,000 in 1971 to just over 286,000 in 2001. As a result of fewer marriages taking place, the number of divorces began to drop in the 1990s, falling by 13 per cent to 157,000 in 2001 (ONS 2004). Similar trends of declining marriage rates and the prevalence of divorce and cohabitation are evident throughout Europe.

Are some couples more prone to divorce than others? On the basis of present trends it is estimated that four in ten marriages will end in divorce (Gibson 1994: 30). Some marriages are statistically more likely to end in divorce, including teenage marriages, couples who start their child-bearing early, couples with four or more children, local authority tenants and couples with relatively low incomes.

Stop and think

➤ What do these statistics tell us about divorce and remarriage?

➤ What factors do you think might help to explain recent trends in marriage and divorce in Britain?

In explaining divorce rates, sociologists examine the wider social, economic and legal context of marriage and divorce. Such factors help to explain why the rates have risen as much as they have. A more complex analysis also challenges simplistic conclusions such as the view that marriage is entered into less seriously or is no longer highly regarded.

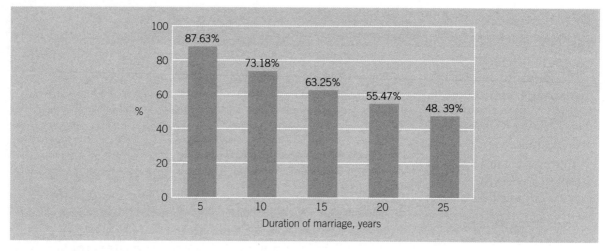

Figure 13.5 Divorce rate – the proportion of marriages surviving 5–25 years
Source: Denscombe 1997: 19

One factor that has contributed to the increase in divorce is that legal changes have made divorce easier. This suggests that the rise in divorce may not reflect the breakdown of marriage so much as the opportunity for broken marriages to be officially terminated. Following the Matrimonial Causes Act 1923, under which women were given equal access to divorce, the number of petitions rose from 2,848 per year to 4,784. The number of petitions rose dramatically after the Legal Aid Act 1949, which made divorce accessible to larger numbers of people by introducing financial aid for paying solicitors and court fees.

The Divorce Reform Act 1969 altered the concept of and grounds for divorce; there is no longer in law the idea of guilty parties but rather marriages can be terminated on the basis of irretrievable breakdown. Provision was also made in this Act for divorce after specified periods of time (two years with the agreement of both parties, five years where only one agrees). Fletcher (1988) points out that the aim of this legislation was not only to bring the law into closer touch with the social realities of marital breakdown but also to serve and support the family in society. According to the Law Commission the aim was

> to buttress rather than undermine the stability of marriage, and, when regrettably a marriage has broken down, to enable the empty legal shell to be destroyed with the maximum fairness and the minimum bitterness, distress and humiliation. (Fletcher 1988: 2)

The number of divorces also rose dramatically between 1984 and 1985 following the introduction of the Matrimonial and Family Proceedings Act 1984. Couples no longer have to be married for at least three years before they may petition for divorce, but may do so after their first anniversary. Thus while in 1981 1.5 per cent of British divorces occurred within the first two years of marriage, by 1991 this proportion had multiplied sixfold to nearly 10 per cent (ONS 1994: 38). By 1996 the proportion of marriages ending in divorce within ten years was 3 per cent for those married in 1951, but 23 per cent for those married in 1981. 'The stark message from *Population Trends* is that fewer than half of all marriages occurring in the late 1990s will survive for 25 years' (Denscombe 1997: 19).

Stop and think

> ➤ While changes in the law are significant, the rise in divorce cannot be attributed solely to this. Legal changes only make it possible to end a marriage which has already failed. What changes in social and religious attitudes can help to explain the increase in divorce rates?

Another factor which may help to explain the increase in divorce is the changing status and attitudes of women. Women are more independent economically and socially and the increase in the number of wives petitioning for divorce shows that they are more able and willing to take steps to end unsatisfactory relationships. Some analysts suggest that women now expect more from marriage and are less willing to accept relationships with men who are unwilling to participate in household tasks and responsibilities. Furthermore, in the past marriage was linked to material interests whereas now it is more concerned with romantic love. Thus the satisfaction of personal needs and desires can become more important than cultural traditions or religious codes of conduct. Nevertheless, although traditional conventions have decreased, they are still important:

> Despite the increased prevalence of cohabitation, weddings remain important to many people in many places because they provide the opportunity to publicly demonstrate a private commitment to a long-term relationship. (Cheal 2002: 55)

Increasing cohabitation

Just as divorce has increased, so has cohabitation. However, it is worth bearing in mind that 'Divorce rates might be high but we have no idea how stable cohabitation is' (Van Every 1999: 179). A survey into the history of marriage in more that 30 European nations since the Second World War (Lord 1992) (carried out by the charity One Plus One: Marriage and Partnership Research) found that half the couples marrying in England and Wales live together first. The report predicted that the rest of Europe may increasingly follow the Swedish and Danish model, where

> the vast majority of people live together before marriage, nearly half of those aged thirty are not expected to marry at all, one in two marriages end in divorce and half of all births occur outside marriage.
>
> (Lord 1992: 2)

While cohabitation tends to be less stable than marriage and most cohabitees eventually marry, there is evidence in Scandinavia that cohabitation is becoming more popular than marriage and that in Sweden cohabiting resembles marriage more closely, exhibiting 'greater permanency and childbearing' (Lord 1992: 2). The increased rate of cohabitation partly explains why the average age of marriage has risen to 29 for men and 27 for women (Kiernan 1992). By 1995 in Britain one in four of all women aged 18 to 49 who were single, widowed, divorced or separated were found to be cohabiting. The implication of this, as the report predicts, is more children in Europe will in future be brought up in single parent families, predominantly by their mothers.

> In countries with high rates of relationship dissolution, a substantial proportion of children will be brought up by mothers alone for much of their childhood. If this trend continues the only indissoluble relationship will be between mothers and their children. (Lord 1992: 2)

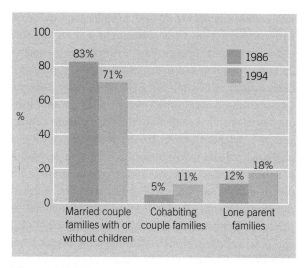

Figure 13.6 Types of family: with head aged under 60, GB (excludes all people living alone)
Source: Denscombe 1997: 18

This emerging trend along with rising divorce rates raises the question of the welfare of children and the effects on them of marital break-up and single parenthood. Dimmock states that in Britain today approximately 25 per cent of children under 16 years of age experience their parents' divorce (2004: 195). Studies on the effects of divorce have found that compared with children in unbroken families, children involved in divorce perform less well at school and have more behavioural problems. The damage done to children by marital conflict occurs long before divorce and lasts long after it. Kathleen Kiernan found this in analyzing the findings from the National Child Development study of 11,000 children born in 1958. She argues that young people are more likely to leave lone parent households and step-families at a younger age than those living in traditional nuclear families. She also suggests that they are more likely to have children earlier, have lower educational attainment and fewer employment prospects.

More recently there has been some research which explores children's perspectives of their parents' divorce. Moxnes' (2003) study showed that in Norway after the divorce, children found that a decline in household income, change of residence and having step-parents were difficult and stressful processes but that with sufficient time and support from their parents, they learned to cope. In contrast, children who felt they were not listened to or involved in any of the negotiations felt increasingly vulnerable and lonely. Similarly in Robinson *et al.*'s (2003) research in the UK children were discovered to be resilient and able to cope but they needed adequate information in order to help them to understand and adapt to the new situation. The children in their study said that they experienced their parents' divorce as a period of emotional turmoil and upset, but that they appreciated being actively involved in managing post-divorce changes. Co-parenting is increasingly perceived as an appropriate way of enabling children to maintain regular contact with both parents. However, the sharing of child care forces separated parents to continue to co-operate and work together, which can be emotionally problematic after divorce (Allan and Crow 2001). Furthermore, children can experience the moving between two households as tiring, time-consuming and requiring much emotional and practical effort to maintain competing demands on their use of time and space (Robinson *et al.* 2003; Smart *et al.* 2001).

Single parent families

Van Every (1999) reminds us that while sociologists have explored many aspects of modern nuclear families, we know comparatively little about other family structures although recent research has begun to address this gap (e.g. O'Donnell 1999; Ribbens *et al.* 2003; Silva and Smart 1999). One of the most dramatic changes in the nature of families in Britain since the 1960s has been the increase in the number of single parent families and associated social concern about the welfare of family members. This means that organizations such as the Office for National Statistics have to operate with a wide definition of the family: 'A family is a married, or cohabiting, couple with or without children, or a lone parent with children' (ONS 1994: 35). In Britain today there are around 1.5 million lone parents who are bringing up 2.3 million children which totals just over one-fifth of all households with dependent children that are headed by lone parents (Daniel and Ivatts 1998). The 2001 General Household Survey indicated that this number of lone parents bringing up children almost doubled from 12 per cent in 1981 to 23 per cent in 2001 (ONS 2001). Overall the 'traditional' family unit has declined, constituting only two in ten households by 1994. 'The most common type of household is not a married couple with dependent children; it is a married couple with no dependent children' (Denscombe 1998: 18).

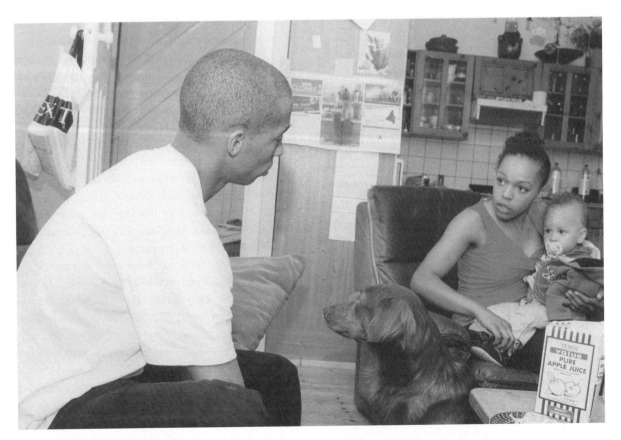

Figure 13.7 Teenage parents
© Ulrike Preuss/Photofusion

A number of factors help to account for the increase in single parent families, including the rise in divorce and births outside marriage. There has been a lessening of the stigma associated with births outside marriage, partly as a result of secularizing influences. Younger parenting is also a feature of single parenthood. According to the Office for National Statistics births outside marriage are more likely to take place at a younger age than those inside marriage. For example, in 2000 'women giving birth outside marriage were more than four years younger than their married counterparts' (ONS 2003b).

The increase in single parent families not only challenges the stereotype of the 'normal' family but also generates much discussion about the roles of parents and the moral welfare of children within different family arrangements. Some see the decline in marriage and the rise in the proportion of single parents as symptomatic of a diminishing sense of parental responsibility, particularly on the part of fathers given that most single parents are women. The concern centres especially on the well-being of children growing up in the absence of two parents and raises again the important issue of the primary function of the family in nurturing children. The implication is that where the influence of one or both parents is missing, children are in some sense deprived. The question is: is it better to be brought up by both parents in an unhappy environment or by one parent alone? It is in this context that the language of the rights of children and the corresponding responsibilities of parenthood are often stressed.

Case study

Effects of family breakdown

Man loses fight to prove child is his

The Court of Appeal yesterday refused to order blood tests to determine the father of a young child, saying it was better to let her live in ignorance than risk upsetting her family life.

The tests were being sought by a man attempting to prove the girl, born after his affair with a married women, is his child.

The woman, named only as Mrs F, said her husband was the father, although she accepted that, at the time of conception, she was also having a sexual relationship with the other man. She and her husband are bringing up the girl, the court was told.

In an appeal against an earlier High Court ruling, the applicant, known as Mr B, argued it was best for the child to know the identity of her natural father . . . He argued that in the future, the girl could unwittingly marry a blood relation. Further, he said that she could develop a disease for which treatment depended upon knowledge of her genetic make-up . . .

But Lord Justice Balcombe, sitting with Lord Justice Nolan and Lord Justice Kennedy, dismissed these arguments, pointing out that the girl had been brought up 'as a child of the family of Mr and Mrs F.' Lord Justice Balcombe said: 'Now, and for the first few years of her life . . . [the child's] physical and emotional welfare are inextricably bound up with the welfare of the family unit of which she forms a part: any harm to the welfare of that unit, as might be caused by an order for the taking of blood tests, would inevitably be damaging to [the child].'

Afterwards, the applicant . . . said: 'My argument . . . is to do with the truth. What the court is saying is that it is all right for this child to go on being told things about her origins which those telling her know are almost certainly untrue.' He had started the action because 'I feel I'm being deprived of my daughter and . . . my daughter is being deprived of me.'

The Children Act had appeared to ensure that a child would be brought up by 'two natural parents', but in practice 'it still seems to be so much in favour of the mother,' he said. In future, mothers would be able to say 'I don't want this man to be declared the father.'

(The *Independent* 6.2.1993)

Questions

1. What assumptions are illustrated in this article in relation to (a) the needs of children; (b) the needs of fathers?

2. What are your views on these assumptions?

Child Support Agency

Social policy in Britain reflects such assumptions about the family and has been graphically highlighted by the foundation of and ensuing debates about the Child Support Agency. This was set up in 1993 with the aim of ensuring that fathers contribute towards their children's upbringing as well as saving government expenditure on income support to lone parents. The launch was seen as 'a recognition that the traditional family structure is breaking down and mark[ed] a break with the permissive attitudes over parental obligations towards their children' (*The Times* 10.2.1995).

However, the establishment of the agency brought widespread and vigorous reaction. Within a matter of months it was accused of insensitivity and inefficiency in the way it conducted and followed up its calculations. Groups representing single mothers were unhappy about being forced to claim maintenance from absent fathers from whom they wished to break contact, while groups representing fathers claimed that the agency failed to take account of men's financial circumstances in assessing contributions. It soon became apparent that in order to achieve its targets the agency was focusing on those fathers who were already keeping up payments rather than pursuing the vast majority of absent fathers who never paid at all.

The effects of the foundation of the Child Support Agency were far-reaching. It was blamed for a number of male suicides and the break-up of several second marriages, all of which eventually led to demands for a review. To this end an active campaign of lobbying and demonstrations was supported by mushrooming pressure groups such as the Campaign Against the CSA, Families Need Fathers, Absent Parents Asking for Reasonable Treatment (APART) and the National Campaign for Fair Maintenance. Eventually modifications were introduced, including the phasing in of new payments over a longer period.

An interesting aspect of the public debate around the Child Support Agency was its focus on fathers' abdication of responsibility and the reaction this generated in relation to fathers' sense of rights and needs in relation to parenting.

Stepfamilies

Family policy and law shape the ways in which family life is understood. In Britain there has been a shift towards emphasizing the importance of biological parenthood in the context of increasing divorce, remarriage and reconstituted families. This raises questions in relation to the role and expectations of stepfamilies. Like other family forms, there are definitional difficulties as to what exactly constitutes a stepfamily. Since members can cut across several different households and boundaries may be blurred, there can be differing perspectives on who counts as family. For example, as Ribbens *et al.* (2003) point out, a new stepfamily may include a non-resident parent and their partner, step-grandparents and other kin. Furthermore, some people may not readily recognize themselves as being part of a stepfamily.

Allan and Crow (2001) argue that as distinct family histories are brought together, the sense of solidarity and unity can be more complex to develop compared with families based purely on blood ties. This can lead to divided loyalties and perceived interventions from 'outsiders'. Bernardes summarizes some of the key tensions which may have to be resolved in stepfamilies:

> There may be conflicts between children and their step-parent, especially revolving around the extent to which the child and step-parent 'accept' each other and how far the child 'accepts' the adult taking on the role of 'mother' or 'father'. There may be disputes between the new partners in which children manipulate loyalties; there may be disputes between different 'classes' of children. Beyond this, there may be dispute and confusion about the roles of grandparents and previous spouses.   (Bernardes 1997: 164–165)

Thus relations with stepfamilies can be difficult to manage, highlighted over issues such as time and attention, financial resources and contact with a non-resident parent. In addition, attempts to work out these issues may be exacerbated with intensified emotions of resentment and jealousy on behalf of the parent and/or child concerned. Step-parenting can be a difficult role to negotiate and may include heightened tensions in relation to the appropriate manner of child rearing, especially disciplinary issues. Research has shown that different strategies can be employed. Some step-parents try to replace the non-resident biological parent whereas others do not attempt to do so. However, not only is there limited research on this aspect of family living, but stepfamilies also lack normative role models and can be ill-prepared for the reparenting role (Bernardes 1997).

Thus stepfamilies can be based on contradictory expectations and tend to be contingent relationships dependent on the ways in which individuals manage their new roles. Members of stepfamilies are not automatically accepted on the basis of the legal context of remarriage, but have to 'earn their place' and negotiate good relationships achieved through social practices rather than ascribed by formal status (Ribbens *et al.* 2003). In their research on step-parenting in the UK, Ribbens *et al.* (2003) were somewhat surprised to find that rather than defining themselves as a different and new form of family, many stepfamilies sought to develop traditional family ties. Most rejected the term 'stepfamily' and placed continued importance on the 'family' consisting of responsibility, team effort, togetherness and commitment. It was felt that the investment of time and fairness towards all family members would encourage the creation of solidarity. Thus in their study, family 'may be seen as fixed by blood or marriage ties, or as something that develops over time' (Ribbens *et al.* 2003: 50). Their research also found consistent class differences: middle-class stepfamilies revealed that they perceived biological parental ties as being crucial whereas in working-class stepfamilies the social practices of the current household were more important than biology. Thus their study emphasized the continued importance of the family which is cross-cut by notions of class as well as gender and generation.

There are many different ways of being a stepfamily so we need to refer to stepfamilies rather than 'the stepfamily' (Ribbens *et al.* 2003). Certainly not all stepfamilies are problematic, and many of the tensions and difficulties which they face are not necessarily very different from those of intact families but they may become more intense and complex:

> It can be recognised that within stepfamilies the interests of the different members are less uniform; the sets of relationships which need to be managed are broader; and the sense of family cohesion is less secure than in natural families. Equally, some stepfamilies 'work' much better than others.   (Allan and Crow 2001: 161)

Homosexual families

Research into homosexual families illustrates the diversity of styles of relationship that can be described as constituting an alternative to the family and, as O'Donnell (1993: 191) points out, shows the danger of simplistic stereotyping of homosexual couples. Lesbian and gay families present a key challenge to traditional family life as they clearly depart from the norm of the heterosexual ideal (O'Donnell 1999). Furthermore, as Allan and Crow point out:

> Indeed many gay couples, whether male or female, actively strive for relationships which are marked by *difference* from dominant heterosexual patterns.
> (2001: 106).

First, lesbian and gay relationships are often constructed as 'families of choice' (Weiss, Donovan and Heaphy 1999) whereby a sense of belonging and long-term companionship are created. However, because such relationships are not bound by conventional understandings of marriage and a legal framework, they are more contingent upon continuing satisfaction, which tends to result in more reflexivity and negotiation around commitment and responsibility (Allan and Crow 2001).

Second, same-sex relationships are not constrained by the norms and assumptions associated with traditional gender roles. For example, Dunne (1999) argues that while lesbian couples still have to negotiate their relationships to avoid inequalities, they can work towards a more egalitarian social world where power is not rooted in conventional roles and expectations of gender. Similarly Weiss *et al.* (1999) discuss the ways in which same-sex relationships enable men and women to express their masculine and feminine identities in alternative ways. However, Silva and Smart suggest that the distinctiveness of same-sex relationships may 'increasingly be shared by newly emergent patterns in heterosexual relationships where commitment may be a matter of negotiation, rather than ascription' (Silva and Smart 1999: 8).

One of the important points to remember is that homosexual families, like heterosexual families, are diverse. Yet most non-heterosexuals continue to experience 'some form of informal discrimination, ranging from enforced self-censorship to physical attack' (Weiss *et al.* 1999: 97). Some same-sex couples seek the same rights of social recognition as heterosexuals couples (including pension rights, inheritance, marriage), while others fear that egal recognition may impinge on the flexible and egalitarian nature of their relationships resulting in unnecessary power struggles (Cheal 2002). Thus some gays and lesbians would like to be able to marry and others prefer to retain their status of difference.

The subject of homosexual families tends to become contentious when children are involved and questions are raised about their welfare. Some homosexual partners (particularly women, who are more likely to gain custody than men) may previously have been married or have children either from unmarried relationships or from artificial insemination. Reflecting the dominant ideology of the family, many people instinctively feel that children will suffer from being raised in the absence of either a father or mother. There is some evidence that gay and lesbian parenting is no more damaging than heterosexual parenting (Tasker and Golombok 1991) yet often this evidence tends to be disregarded in the legal process. As O'Donnell argues:

> Although some changes in the legal perspective can be identified, such as an increased willingness to recognise parenting existing outside marriage, the law still tends to emphasise traditional concepts in its construction of the family and thus adopts an exclusive approach to its construction of the family, denying recognition and validity to what are perceived to be 'abnormal' forms. The emphasis placed upon marriage as the source of family status excludes homosexuals (and transsexuals) who cannot validly marry and whose relationships with each other are devalued.
>
> (O'Donnell 1999: 94–95)

Thus while there has been an increasing, if somewhat reluctant, recognition of homosexual relationships as an alternative family form, public debates about non-heterosexual marriage, parenting, custody and adoption continue to be highly contested. This remains an area for ongoing research and feeds into the wider debate about the ideal family and the most desirable social arrangement for the socialization of children. It also relates to the question of whether it is preferable for children to grow up in the company of two parental figures as opposed to one, as in the case of single parent families.

This brief overview of changing kinship arrangements has indicated how very varied are the forms of modern family life and how changes in the wider economic, moral and social structures of society continue to shape family patterns. As Morgan (1994a) states:

> Older sociologies of the family, based around the model of the traditional nuclear family, are becoming less and less appropriate. This is not to say that, in the light of these trends, the family is 'dead'. Indeed most people will continue to spend part of their lives within a nuclear-family based household. Yet these other trends can no longer be taken as minor departures from the norm but as signifying the complex strands of family and domestic life in modern society.
>
> (Morgan 1994a: 113)

Theoretical perspectives on the family

Two contrasting approaches to the family are provided by the consensus and conflict approaches within sociology. Both schools of thought regard the family as a central institution within the structure of society, but they differ in so far as one focuses on the more positive aspects of the family and the other concentrates on its negative features.

Functionalist views of the family

A functionalist approach tends to assume that any institution that exists in society plays a positive part in maintaining the social equilibrium and harmony in society. Functionalists ask what functions are provided by the family and how these are beneficial both for individual members of the family and for wider society.

At the most basic level the family functions to provide new members for society through reproduction. It is seen as the initial stable environment in which to rear children, who learn through the process of socialization to become acceptable members of society. Parsons (1954; Parsons and Bales 1955) has described this as being one of the main functions of the family in modern society. Chapter 1 described the significance of the family in providing a developmental framework by illustrating the deprivation associated with the denial of such an environment. Parsons sees the family as also functional for adult members in that it stabilizes adult personalities. By this he means that wives and husbands give each other emotional support and work together in a mutually complementary relationship. Writing in the 1950s, Parsons reflected traditional assumptions about husbands being the breadwinner and wives chiefly taking on the domestic role (Parsons 1954; Parsons and Bales 1955).

Sociological research on the family examines the roles and relationships between wives and husbands within the family and how those roles have been affected by wider social changes such as industrialization, the increased involvement of women in the workforce ('feminization' of labour) and unemployment among male workers. Some functionalists, including Willmott and Young, argue that as families move from being extended to being more

Stop and think

➤ Give examples of the complementary domestic roles fulfilled by women and men within the family.

➤ How far in your experience is it true to say that as families change the relationship between wives and husbands has become egalitarian?

isolated, nuclear and privatized the relationship between wives and husbands adapts to become more egalitarian with both partners working and sharing household tasks. Young and Willmott (1975) call this the 'symmetrical family'.

Despite changes in the nature of society that accompany social processes such as industrialization and modernization, functionalists believe that the family is as important as ever today. They resist suggestions that it is in danger of decline or dying out and focus rather on the way in which it is able to adapt and accommodate itself to the requirements of contemporary society.

> Functionalism is a theoretical approach which stresses the positive benefits of families. Families are therefore often described as adaptive systems, which respond creatively to the stresses that are caused by unmet needs. Functionalist sociologists also argue that the reason why families exist is because of the functions which they fulfil . . . According to this point of view, families are thought to be still evolving today in order to help us cope with our changing economic and social environments.
>
> (Cheal 2002: 8–10)

Given its predominance within sociology up until the early 1960s the functionalist approach to the family has been very influential. Thus in the 1950s and early 1960s public sentiment was dominated by the assumption that 'society rested on the basic domestic group of the family' (Fletcher 1988: 3). Indeed, the sense that the family and marriage might be in a state of moral decline and decay was interpreted as a serious threat to the security and survival of society in general:

> The family [was regarded as] the very foundation of society, and since the family was now in dangerous disarray, so was the entire moral order of society.
>
> (Fletcher 1988: 3)

While functionalists today would recognize that the family has seceded many of its traditional roles, which have been taken over by agencies of the state such as schools, and health and welfare services, they would still maintain that it is a fundamental and desirable feature of society. This sentiment is echoed in public debates and calls for a return to 'traditional family values'. Changes in the 1990s in health and welfare systems in Britain which favour a minimal role for the state and stress a greater role for the community have shifted the responsibility for many of the traditional functions back on to the family. As Cheal's quotation illustrates, in view of continuing social change functionalists see the family adapting and modifying its structure to the needs of society. Thus while its form continues to change, its necessity does not.

Critical views of the family

In the late 1960s a range of alternative ideological positions on the family rose to prominence. Though each was distinctive they shared in common a radically different perspective on the family to that of the functionalists. Radical/critical sociologists challenged traditional functionalist assumptions about what they regarded as an over-idealized image of the family. They focused instead on the more constraining and oppressive features of family life. Their analysis may appear at first sight to be quite extreme in that it challenges many of the basic assumptions about the family that we tend to take for granted. In our society we tend to assume that the family is a good thing and it can be difficult for us to question when we take for granted that it is a positive aspect of our lives:

> Typically, family life is thought to be warm, intimate, stress reducing, and the place that people flee to for safety. Our desire to idealize family life is partly responsible for a tendency either not to see family and intimate violence or to condone it as being a necessary and important part of raising children, relating to spouses, and conducting other family transactions.
>
> (Gelles 1997: 1)

The scope of the conflict perspective in sociology is very broad, and a critical approach to the family encompasses a variety of approaches including Marxism, radical psychiatry and feminism. What all these approaches share in common is a focus on the more negative aspects of family life and the idea that the family may not be beneficial for all its members. This has led some to advocate the break-up of the family. While this may seem a rather extreme conclusion based on exceptional cases rather than the norm, these alternative approaches have helped to provide a balance to the rather over-optimistic, conservative and biologically deterministic approach that dominated functionalist sociology of the family up until the 1960s.

Marxist approaches

In keeping with the emphasis on dominant and subordinate groups in society and the location of conflict within the structural composition of society, Marxists regard the family as yet another institution promoting dominant societal values and perpetuating the exploitation

Case study

Changing functions of the family

Traditional functions of the family	How these functions were fulfilled	Are these functions still fulfilled today?
Procreation and regulation of sexuality	Reproduction of family members. Ensures continuity of society and constrains sexual desires within the context of marriage. Reinforces heterosexual norms.	Changing sexual attitudes and behaviour. Increase in cohabitation and pre-marital sex as well as alternative sexualities. More women deciding to limit family size or not to reproduce at all.
Affectional/emotional function	Marriage exists primarily for companionship as lifelong emotional tie. Parent–child relationship regarded as basis for other relationships in life. Family relationships seen as basis of emotional security and bonding in contrast to competitive contractual relationship in wider society.	Many relationships today are short term, e.g. rising divorce rate, more serial relationships. Nature of relationship between parents and children changing in context of emphasis on children's rights. Although relationships are changing, the need for affection/emotional security remains an important function.
Economic function	Family traditionally a unit of production in pre-industrial society – largely a self-sufficient unit sharing work tasks and the benefits of labour. Economic production has moved from home to factory/outside services. Family becomes unit of consumption; emphasis on family consumer items such as family car, TV, holidays, etc.	Growth of welfare state seen as taking over some of the economic function through provision of benefits, e.g. income support. However, recent dismantling of the welfare state means that the family is again becoming an important resource for economic survival, e.g. parents funding children through education; family members as carers.
Welfare/protective function	Linked with the economic function; family traditionally seen as source of protection and support for dependants, e.g. the young and the old. With the expansion of the welfare state and the decline of the extended family this appeared to be a declining function.	Even within the welfare state many benefits and services assume the primary role of the family as the basis of support. Such expectations have increased as funding has been reduced since the 1980s and the focus shifted on to 'community' care (i.e. the family and mostly women).
Socialization	Traditionally the family was seen as the key agent in passing on basic skills and knowledge. Psychologists emphasize the primary role of parent–child relationship as providing the basis for other relationships in society. Education and media systems reinforce and sustain this function, which continues throughout the individual's life.	Functionalists still stress this as the basic function of the family in contemporary society. Political and religious affiliation are still influenced by family socialization, though there is more emphasis on individual choice and flexibility.
Social status	Family ascribes several aspects of social status – age, sex, birth order, ethnicity, religion, class. However, in modern society emphasis is on achieved status rather than ascription. There is scope for individuals to be socially mobile and change from their family status of origin.	While the emphasis on individual growth and achieved status remains important, ascription, heredity and 'who you are' is still influential in many political, occupational and social circles (e.g. 'old boy network').
Recreation and leisure	Leisure pursuits within the family can influence children's development. The increase in leisure time brought recognition of the family as a unit of recreation and consumption, e.g. DIY, home videos and holidays.	Although the family leisure industry has grown, many recreational activities still take place outside the home and family, e.g. with the peer group.

of subordinate groups by upholding the norms and values of capitalist society.

> The policy of promoting the nuclear family as the source of social justice and social cohesion is flawed. It fails to recognise that this kind of family is in fact a site of disadvantage, subordination and oppression for its members, particularly women.
>
> (Bilton *et al.* 2002: 245)

In *The Manifesto of the Communist Party* (1848), Marx and Engels outline their views of the family as a reflection of bourgeois interest and control.

> On what foundation is the present family, the bourgeois family based? On capital, on private gain. In its completely developed form this family exists only among the bourgeoisie . . . The bourgeois claptrap about the family and education, about the hallowed correlation of parent and child, becomes all the more disgusting, the more, by the action of modern industry, all family ties among the proletarians are torn asunder, and their children transformed into simple articles of commerce and instruments of labour.
>
> (Marx and Engels 1848, quoted in Fletcher 1988: 54)

Stop and think

➤ Do you agree with Marx and Engels that family relationships are determined by class and economic situation?

In defending the family, Fletcher (1988) is keen to add that Marx and Engels were not advocating the abolition of the family *per se* but rather the improvement of the monogamous family:

> [Marx] was certainly not 'anti-family' in his personal life, and . . . this was no inconsistency with his own and Engels' view of the family in society in general. It was the bourgeois family – and all those traditional family-types in societies of the past which entailed the exploitation of women as property – to which they were opposed. (Fletcher 1988: 79)

In other works Engels took an evolutionary view of the family, arguing that the form of family life changed as the mode of production did. In early communism property was collectively owned and the private family as such did not exist. There were no rules restricting promiscuity. It was only when private property developed that the monogamous nuclear family emerged to protect men's inheritance

by ensuring their rightful heirs. Engels thus traces the subordination of women back to the emergence of private ownership, whereby women became economically dependent on men and thus subject to them within marriage.

Engels believed that the end of exploitation within the family would be guaranteed only in a truly communist society, where individuals would return to living arrangements that existed before private property developed. True equality between the sexes would come where tasks were communally shared.

The Marxist view of the family was further developed and applied to modern capitalist societies in the 1960s and 1970s by such writers as Louis Althusser, who sees the norms and values of family life as part of the ideological state apparatus being used to further reinforce the exploitative nature of capitalist society. In the interests of capitalism other institutions such as the media encourage ever greater consumption by the family, setting up ideals of the modern family as one equipped with the latest consumer goods – the washing machine, video, mobile phone, DVD. Marxists see these as false needs created to serve the interests of producers and keep the capitalist economy ticking over rather than being in the genuine interest of consumers.

Stop and think

➤ Examine examples of current advertisements in different forms of media (magazines, television, radio). What consumer goods are being promoted and how far do the adverts reflect or challenge stereotypes about the family?

➤ In what ways do the norms and values of the education system reinforce the ideology of the family?

Within a Marxist perspective, Gittins (1993) states that the ideology of the family is pervasive in modern industrial society:

> Organisations are said to be run 'like a family', the highest compliment a man can receive is that he is 'a good family man' (women are never accorded the compliment of being 'a good family woman', as by definition they are assumed to be just that). The notion of the family informs the education system, the business world, asylums, the media and the political system. (Gittins 1993: 155)

Yet she adds that this conceptualization of the family evolved historically only as part of the development of the industrial bourgeoisie during the late stages of capitalist development. Despite its appeal as a universal ideal achievable by all, Gittins argues that the ideology is a false one since it is rooted in a class-specific, patriarchal outlook:

> Family ideology has increasingly purported to be egalitarian, yet it remains based on notions of gender, age and authority that are by definition unequal. The ideal that families are egalitarian, like the ideal that class no longer divides society, has enjoyed considerable support, even if it seldom tallies with reality.
>
> (Gittins 1993: 159)

Gittins' analysis provides a good illustration of the Marxist notion of false ideology; the 'ideal' family is used to distort and disguise the real economic basis of exploitation:

> Family ideology implicitly presupposes a relatively secure economic base: the husband should be able to support the family by his income alone, the household income should provide adequate shelter, food, comfort, space, and consumer durables, the wife should be able to cease paid work when she has small children . . . everyone is supposed to aspire to a certain kind of family life, while the realities of economic inequality make it virtually impossible to achieve the ideal.   (Gittins 1993: 161)

The value of the Marxist approach is that it emphasizes both the powerful ideology of the family in society and the structural relationship between the economy and family life, a consideration that has not been ignored in the development of sociological (particularly feminist) approaches to the family. Morgan (1994a) describes how changes in the formal paid economy have impacted on the family (in terms of the repercussions of more women working and high male unemployment), while the definition and measurement of family life has started to recognize labour within the home.

> The increasing tendency to write of 'the household' rather than the 'family' reflects an increasing willingness to see family relationships as having economic, and not simply emotional significance. Put another way, economic life is not simply what takes place in the sphere of paid employment outside the home. It is also within the household that economic activity takes place, in the unpaid labour of housewives and mothers, of fathers and husbands and, indeed, of children. The use of the term 'emotional labour' in relation to caring work is indicative of this growing recognition of the work which often takes place unnoticed within the home.
>
> (Morgan 1994a: 122)

World in focus

The impact of globalization on family life in India

The post-industrialization period in the West led to dramatic changes in religious beliefs, family structures, family size, work ethic, morals, economics, education, literature, health, politics, human rights, medical and scientific research and several other areas of human concern . . .

It has been argued that globalization will lead to a process of Westernization and modernization and that all the developing countries will eventually come to imbibe the Western values of individualism, rationalism, humanism, empiricism and secularism, thus becoming ultimately indistinguishable from the Western countries . . .

That certain Western values, as a result of globalization, will impinge on the people of Asian cultures is inevitable. Insofar as economic affluence is concerned, this is already evident by the significant changes that are noticeable in India. Affluent Indians in the urban areas of India have begun to adopt Western ways of living, including living in high-rise blocks, condominiums (with swimming pools and tennis courts), furnishing their homes in modern Westernized styles, membership of exclusive Western-type clubs, Western culinary preferences, modes of dress, artistic and other esthetic preferences, driving imported luxury cars, increasing use of communication and information technologies, and last but not least, foreign travel . . .

However, as soon as one starts to dig deeper and observe the day-to-day lives of families at home, the picture changes: the observable similarities, so easily noticeable from the

World in focus (continued)

outside, seem merely cosmetic – not unlike a new, conspicuous patchwork on an ancient family heirloom. The house, although furnished in modern Western style, is still dominated by a temple or a shrine. The family members, one finds, usually eat their meals together, the home-cooked food often conforms to the families' indigenous regional culinary habits, family life still tends to operate in a hierarchical order. Although children 'enjoy' a certain degree of latitude in expressing their views and opinions, and although the children are not any less indulged than they were in the past, deference to the

views of the elders to a large extent is taken for granted and remains unquestioned. Collective activities, in which all family members are expected to participate – visiting relatives, entertaining relatives, performing prayers and *pujas*, participating in all the religious rituals (e.g. the mundan [tonsure] ceremony, the sacred thread ceremony, betrothals, marriages and festivities) – are still an integral part of family life.

One of the most important factors that distinguishes Indian families from Western (English or American) families is the fact that children (sons), upon reaching maturity,

are *not* expected to leave home and set up their own lives.

(Laungani 2004: 100–101)

Questions

1. *What kinds of collective activities did you participate in with your family when you were a child? To what extent do you still engage in family events?*

2. *What impact do you think recent social changes have had on contemporary family practices? For example, in what ways have modern technologies (e.g. microwaves, DVD players, mobile phones) and changing working patterns (e.g. more women participating in the labour market) shaped family life?*

Feminist approaches

Marxist themes of exploitation within the family and society are taken up by feminists, who highlight the continuing exploitation of women in capitalist societies, not least in terms of the way in which their contribution to the bulk of private domestic work remains unrecognized, unrewarded and undervalued labour. Sheeran (1993) points out the overlap between Marxist and feminist approaches:

> Marxist and radical feminists argue that the family is both an 'ideological construct' and a repressive, socially-produced reality, which helps to perpetuate capitalism and/or patriarchy. Such criticisms are overtly anti-family, and argue that women have been forced into taking responsibility for child care by that 'agent' of the state, the patriarchal family.
>
> (Sheeran 1993: 29)

More fundamentally, feminists challenge the idea that the sexual division of labour within (and indeed outside) the family is based on biological and genetic predispositions, so that women are 'naturally' more domesticated and men

are 'natural' providers. Feminists and many others would argue that this sexual division is culturally determined (and hence, in this case, exploitative), as are many of the assumptions about relationships between women and men which are institutionalized within marriage or less formally through cohabitation arrangements. Traditional prescriptions about gender-related behaviour within the family and marriage are often supported by religious beliefs and customs. For example, in some Muslim communities men are permitted more than one wife (the condition being that they treat them all equally) and have easier access to divorce.

Feminists argue that in Western societies, despite secularization and legislation giving women equal access to divorce and the ownership of property, the family and marriage are still arenas for the exploitation and subordination of women. In Britain many couples still opt for a ceremony in which the bride is 'given away' (symbolically from the property of one man to another) and choose to pledge vows in church based on the traditional assumption that the husband is the head of the family and that the woman's duty is to obey.

Stop and think

➤ Examine the rituals, prayers, blessings and hymns of different Christian marriage ceremonies. What assumptions about the roles of women and men within marriage are implied?

➤ Compare these with the procedures in a registry office marriage and in marriage ceremonies practised by different religions.

Oakley (1974a) has analyzed the traditional role of the housewife as a feature of women's exploitation within the family. Despite the socialization of women as homemakers, Oakley reported that as well as being unpaid labour, women found housework dull, monotonous and unfulfilling. It provided little job satisfaction and was accorded low status ('I'm "just a housewife"'). This sort of analysis led to calls for housework to be recognized as a form of labour by being paid.

Women increasingly opt for a career, resulting in their having a 'dual role'. This often generates a need for child-care support outside the home with associated financial implications. However, the increase in the number of women going out to work has not resulted in the sharing of domestic responsibility. Feminists have described the role that women have continued to play as the major provider of care within the family regardless of the diversity of forms that the family may take. Sheeran (1993) points to the centrality of this 'female-carer core unit' today, historically and across different cultures.

> In households with male and female partners, most males have a relatively small amount of interaction with the children, even when both partners work. Many female partners only work part-time so that they can look after the children. Making child care arrangements, and staying off work when children are sick is also largely the woman's responsibility. Men tend to 'help' rather than assume full responsibility, and then only with the more enjoyable aspects of child care.
>
> (Sheeran 1993: 30)

Research into the phenomenon of the 'new man' and into roles within the changing nature of the family has found that it is still women who are doing the housework and providing child care. Women's jobs still tend to be regarded as secondary within the family and women are more likely to give up their jobs to rear children.

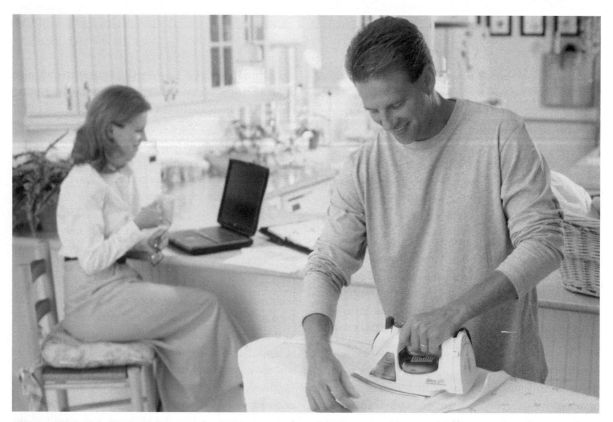

Figure 13.8 The 'new man'
© Michael A. Keller Studios, Ltd./CORBIS

This role of women as chief providers of care has become more significant in view of recent developments in the field of social policy which have re-emphasized the importance of the family as a source of care and support. There has been a reversal of the trend towards state support for sick and disabled people through the provision of institutional care and the welfare state and calls for the community to become the basis of support. 'Community' tends to mean in practice 'family', which generally means women:

> Janet Finch points out that the increasing use of terms such as 'caring' and 'care in the community' obscures the fact that caring involves work and, in many areas at least, the work of women.   (Morgan 1994a: 119)

A feminist perspective is particularly significant to the sociology of the family. It highlights the centrality of women within the core domestic unit, the changing attitudes to and roles of women in the spheres of marriage, divorce and cohabitation and the increasing significance of their role as carers within the community. Although the central female carer role is not inevitable (rather it is a cultural construct as opposed to being immutably biologically determined), its virtual universality is such that the sociology of the family cannot proceed without taking account of the roles and experiences of women.

Interpretative approaches

In keeping with an interpretative approach some radical psychiatrists have examined the micro-level relationships between children and adults within the family. The advantage of their contribution to the sociology of the family, particularly in the 1960s and 1970s, was their focus on the individual experiences and face-to-face relationships of members within the wider family group. Even functionalists such as Fletcher, though critical of their conclusions, acknowledge the value of this perspective:

> One fundamental significance of the Laing, Cooper, Esterson school . . . was that they had validly seen the importance of the sociological perspective for the understanding of individuals and their problems.
> (Fletcher 1988: 29)

These writers agree with critical approaches that challenge the positive assessment of socialization within the family (as argued by functionalists) and focus on pathological situations where the family prevents individuals from achieving personal freedom. Laing and Esterson

(1970) and Cooper (1972) argue that parents can over-protect the young and smother individuality. Love can be used as an emotional weapon to manipulate children or partners. The family sometimes creates barriers between itself and the outside world – a kind of 'us and them' mentality. Such authors condemn the institution of the family and the socialization process which trains children to accept indoctrination and subordination in later life.

The family as a social problem

The shifting focus provided by radical analysts of the family since the 1960s has shed light on what many have referred to as the 'dark side' of the family. Many cases of violent crime, and statistically most murders, take place within the home. Domestic violence and child abuse have both been underestimated and 'brushed under the carpet' in the past. Partly this is linked to a reluctance to accept that the family can be simultaneously a site of violence as well as love, and partly there is a notion that we should not intervene in the private world of the family. The discourse of family privacy can lead to family problems being perceived as personal troubles for individuals to sort out rather than as public issues which the state should address (see Wright Mills 1959).

Feminists have largely been responsible for raising public awareness of the potential for women's and children's oppression in the family. They exposed the possibilities for conflict, violence and inequality in the family, thereby challenging the myth of family ideology and the notion of the 'family as a safe haven'. They argued that the existence of unequal power structures within the family could lead to male physical and sexual violence against women and children (Fiorenza and Copeland 1994). For feminists, the legitimation of male dominance in the private sphere can result in the normalization of violence within the home. They strongly argue that issues such as domestic violence and child abuse are thus social problems which reflect structural inequalities of power within the family. However, as we shall see in the following sections, others argue that these are individual problems occurring only in certain pathological or 'dysfunctional' families (Jamrozik and Nocella 1998). This debate of the extent to which family problems are personal troubles or public issues is a key to understanding the different ways in which domestic violence and child abuse have been explained.

Domestic violence

Domestic violence began to be recognized as a serious social issue in the 1970s: while the phenomenon of battered women was not a new one, its recognition as a social problem requiring a political response was (Jamrozik and Nocella 1998). The term 'domestic violence' covers a variety of behaviours ranging from verbal and emotional abuse to physical attack, including sexual assault and rape. Dobash and Dobash (1992) argue that violence between adults in the home is systematically and disproportionately directed at women, and that such violence is the extension of the husbands' control over their wives:

> Within the family the use of physical force and violence has traditionally been a prerogative of men who were given the rights and responsibilities over all members of households, including women, children.
>
> (Dobash and Dobash 1992: 267)

Thus, this control is historically and socially constructed. In other words, violence against women in the home can be explained by looking at the history of the family and the status of women in society. So although battered husbands do exist, 'wife-beating' is comparatively more common.

Domestic violence is a widespread form of crime which is notoriously under-reported and thus underestimated in official statistics. Stanko cites one estimate that only one out of 270 incidents of wife abuse is ever reported to the authorities (1992: 187). Many victims are afraid or too ashamed to report it. Some victims may blame themselves, an attitude reinforced by suggestions that domestic violence is part and parcel of marital life and a private family matter that should not be interfered with by outsiders. 'To hear battered women recount these experiences is to hear stories of abuse which are often characterised as the "normal" interaction of intimate couples' (Stanko 1992: 186).

In the past cases of domestic violence (referred to as 'domestics') were not always taken seriously by the police who tended to consider wife-battering as a private family matter rather than a criminal offence (Foreman and Dallos 1993). Police rarely arrested batterers, and the court system rarely convicted them. There was even a certain amount of victim-blaming where the victims of domestic violence were perceived as weak individuals who allowed the abuse to take place or it was assumed that they must have provoked the violence or even perhaps deserved it (Gelles 1997).

Figure 13.9 Domestic violence
© Tom & Dee Ann McCarthy/CORBIS

Researchers have suggested that other key members of society – doctors, social workers, neighbours, parents and so on – have played a part in perpetuating the cycle of domestic violence by failing to confront it or by shifting responsibility back onto the victim.

Thus there was a traditional denial of the problem until the 1970s when the feminist movement played a key role in defining the issue of domestic violence as a social problem which required a collective solution. They perceived it as being based on the unequal power relationships between men and women in society as reflected in family structures (Fiorenza and Copeland 1994). Their initial response was to provide immediate help and shelter for battered women by providing refuges for them as a place of safety (Dobash and Dobash 1992). The first refuge was founded in 1972 in Chiswick. Their broader aim was to raise public awareness of male violence in the family which gradually began to filter through to policies of intervention and popular consciousness (Foreman and Dallos 1993).

In contrast, the government has preferred to define the problem of domestic violence as a psychological one rather than as a sociological one, using causal models to explain it as a result of individual character disorders rather than having structural causes (Jamrozik and Nocella 1998). The state preferred to define it as a problem caused by pathological individuals often as a result of drug or alcohol misuse. Thus, the state's response was to provide much larger 'service' centres which were run by a range of different professionals who also offered services for the batterers, such as drug and/or alcohol treatment and psychiatric counselling. Their aim was to work towards family reunification and they tended to individualize the problem.

As we can see, the way a particular group defines a problem and the particular explanation they give to it, in turn affects the kind of action they propose as a solution. Refuge shelters began with a commitment to radical social change but became transformed into professional services dealing with individual problems, which led to redefining the image of domestic violence. Thus, using the terminology of Wright Mills (1959), we could say that, before the 1970s, domestic violence had always been considered a private trouble. Subsequently the women's movement identified it as a social problem and for just over a decade it was a public issue. However, once the state became more involved, it was redefined as a personal trouble in order to avoid the creation of a large-scale moral panic about the potential for male violence in a male-dominated society.

In the decade following the emergence of wife-battery as a social problem, there was a large increase in the number of shelters for victims as well as a rise in public funds that were spent on the issue. Eventually there were some legal changes and an increase in police co-operation which has resulted in more protection for victims and the recognition of domestic violence as a crime. However:

> There is little real commitment to relieving some of the stresses, financial, occupational and/or housing, that families experience and which can contribute to violence. Likewise, encouragement and opportunities for women to escape from violent relationships are lacking. Instead, most women are still likely to feel the situation would have to be very dire before they would choose to escape.   (Foreman and Dallos 1993: 34)

Consequently, on the one hand, the feminist movement was successful: public awareness was raised and action was taken. On the other hand, it was only a partial victory because their initial aims of addressing the issue of male domination in society became lost as the state reinterpreted the problem as an individual, pathological one rather than as a structural, societal one (Jamrozik and Nocella 1998).

Child abuse

Today society has become more open and responsive to the phenomenon of child abuse. The acknowledgement of the more sinister side of family life has brought a shift of emphasis in favour of listening to children and taking account of their experiences within the family. In previous eras children were not regarded as vulnerable members of the community but treated as adults and only gradually did a sense of their needs and rights come to be identified as an issue of social concern (see Chapter 9). T. David (1993) records the historical foundations of legislation and organizations specifically focusing on children:

> When one considers the difficulties working class men – and then women – had in gaining the vote and in gaining rights as human beings and citizens, it is hardly surprising that children's rights have been neglected. In fact, child abuse was first brought to the headlines in 1874 under the auspices of an animal protection campaign in New York. A young girl named Mary Ellen, who lived with her adoptive parents, was regularly beaten and neglected by them. Her neighbours became concerned, though the adoptive parents saw no fault in their actions, as they 'owned' the child. The case was eventually brought to the attention of Henry Bergh, the founder of the Society for the Protection of Cruelty to Animals who brought a court action against the parents. Although there were more laws relating to the protection of animals than children at the time, the case was won on the basis of Mary's human rights, not – as is sometimes thought – because Mary Ellen was a member of an animal species. The lawyer who was hired by Henry Bergh subsequently precipitated the development of a new movement, the Society for the Prevention of Cruelty to Children, in December 1874.
>
> (T. David 1993: 10)

It was this that led to the foundation of the equivalent National Society for the Prevention of Cruelty to Children (NSPCC) in the UK.

In examining concepts of childhood and children's rights, Archard (1993) shows that the problem of detecting and dealing with child abuse rests on the link between the discovery and definition of abuse:

> In all the talk of child abuse as a new problem, two related mistakes are often made. The first is to think that child abuse itself, rather than its recognition and

description, is a modern phenomenon. The second is to believe that child abuse is more extensive than in the past, whereas what, in fact, has increased is the reporting of abuse. This in turn may be ascribed to the explicit acknowledgement by society that child abuse does exist and that an account of it can be rendered.

Significantly, what has been 'discovered' is a certain kind of abuse, and this has helped to determine the ways in which 'abuse' is defined, explained and dealt with. The standard case of abuse, at least in the 1960s and 1970s, was that of a child's physical maltreatment, most often leading to serious injury, by an adult within the child's family. What may probably not be considered abuse is, for instance, that a child is brought up within a significantly poorer household than its contemporaries.

Consequently, everything depends on how 'abuse' is defined and this depends on what the definition is required to do.   (Archard 1993: 147–8)

As the quotation from Archard implies, there are many different interpretations of child abuse, reflecting both the variety of perspectives on this subject and the range of behaviour which is regarded as constituting forms of abuse. The NSPCC and the National Children's Homes (NCH) recognize and keep statistics on four types of abuse: physical abuse, sexual abuse, emotional abuse and neglect.

Since the 1990s cases of child abuse along with child neglect have become familiar news stories covered in the media. The public recognition that child abuse takes place, the lifting of the 'taboo' against open discussion and the move in favour of listening to children all help to account for the dramatic increase in the rates of recorded child abuse, not only in Britain but also internationally. The extent of the problem in Britain is illustrated by official statistics, though these are likely to give only a partial picture:

Department of Health (DoH) statistics for the end of March 1990 indicate that around four children in every 1000 aged under 18 in the UK were on child protection Registers. Furthermore, according to the NSPCC (1989), the number of cases of child abuse registered by them doubled during the mid-1980s, from 1115 in 1985 to 2307 in 1987. Those who work in the field know that this may represent only the tip of the iceberg, ie those cases where concern had become so great and the evidence so certain that the children in question were registered.

(T. David 1993: 4)

It is likely that many cases remain unrecognized and unrecorded due partly to a misplaced sense of shame or embarrassment on the part of the abused or even due to threats made by the abuser in the event of the facts becoming public. However, it is difficult to estimate the number of child abuse cases for two main reasons: namely, it depends on the definition used and how the information is obtained (Saraga 1993). How do you go about counting something which is often not reported? There is no uniform agreement in defining child abuse. Difficulties with definitions and measurement have led to a wide range of different estimates of the size of the problem (see Gelles 1997). Comparing different research is also problematic because some studies count the number of deaths from abuse, others the number of physical injuries and others focus on sexual abuse.

Statistics imply that levels of abuse are higher in poor and working-class areas. However, David suggests that this may be due to higher detection rates as a result of close monitoring rather than real incidences (1993: 13). It is more significant to note that abuse occurs in all strata of society, and that increasingly, older children are being found to be abusing younger ones (T. David 1993: 5), a shocking recent example being the James Bulger case in 1993. Teachers and other professionals working closely with young people can potentially monitor children's behaviour for signs of distress.

Like domestic violence, there are alternative accounts of child abuse, and the different explanations lead to different suggestions of ways to solve it. One of the key questions is to what extent the actions of the perpetrator are seen as deliberate. In other words, are the perpetrators individually responsible for their actions or are the social structures of society to blame in any way? Theories seeking to explain child abuse can be categorized broadly as biological, medical, psychological, sociological and political (T. David 1993: 38–9). The medical explanation was developed in the 1960s by paediatricians who defined the battered baby syndrome (Parton 1985) and related it to the individual illness of the perpetrator. With this medical view, the problem was seen to be behavioural and the explanation was thought to be found in the personality and family background of the abuser. The paediatricians emphasized the individuality of the perpetrator, the 'diseased' person who could perhaps be cured by therapy (Saraga 1993). This disease model suited the paediatricians because they could offer a solution based on treatment and there would be a crucial role for doctors. Hence there was a certain amount of professional self-interest in defining the problem in this way (Parton 1985).

Psychologists also put forward an individualized explanation but their views were linked to the intergenerational transmission of violence, often known as 'the cycle of violence' (Gelles 1997). This is when it is thought that people who are victims of child abuse are disproportionately more likely to become abusing parents themselves. In contrast, sociologists would say that these are inadequate explanations of child abuse. They would argue that it is a social and political issue rather than one of individual or family pathology. For example, the social structural model suggests that physical child abuse is linked to stress caused by poverty and material deprivation (Corby 2000). This is not to say that poverty directly causes abuse, and we need to recognize that abuse also occurs in affluent families. However, as Saraga (1993) argues, people who live in poverty are more likely to experience economic and social stress which may lead to parents taking their frustrations out on their children.

Another sociological view is the social–cultural perspective which stresses the importance of unequal power relationships, highlighting the generally low and oppressed status of children in society. Children are subordinated and there is a routine use of power by adults over children. Children are relatively powerless and can be considered as the 'property' of parents (Saraga 1993). As a result violence against them can become normalized and accepted in society: 'violence is a socially sanctioned general form of maintaining order and that it is approved of as a form of child control' (Corby 2000: 147). Thus some commentators suggest that the protection and reinforcement of family values is problematic in that it reinforces the very institution which is the source of conflict. A potential solution would be to address the power structures of society and take seriously the issue of children's rights, such as by banning all physical punishment of children including the use of smacking. This perspective suggests that a broad change is needed in the way we treat and control children in society (Corby 2000).

As we have seen, there are a range of possible interpretations for explaining child abuse and we need to bear in mind that there are most likely diverse causes which are to blame. While certain factors, like the inequalities of social structure, are important they do not provide adequate explanations on their own as not all powerful adults abuse less powerful children. Thus, rather than focus on single-factor explanations, it is necessary to consider a combination of factors because problems like child abuse and adult domestic violence are complex issues.

Public concern over the phenomenon of child abuse has expressed both the sense of moral outrage and perhaps the community's awareness that it bears some sort of responsibility for allowing such behaviour to persist. David asks: 'If children feel that no-one close to them can be of help, that they need to resort to phoning someone they do not know on a helpline, what kind of a society do we live in?' (1993: 4). Some commentators have stressed that both preventive action and collaborative co-operation between those in the fields of health, social services and education (T. David 1993: 6) are important if family life and the most vulnerable members of the community are to be supported.

The interesting point to note is that if problems like child abuse and domestic violence are individualized then the abuser is blamed, rather than blaming 'normal' attitudes in society towards women and children. Individual responses to social problems lead to the maintenance of existing power relations. Furthermore, it is worth remembering that problems are more likely to be seen as individual where the group with the problem is more powerless and less able to contest the definition of their problem (Jamrozik and Nocella 1998). In contrast, if a problem is acknowledged as a public issue, then a collective response is required to address the power inequalities which may underlie the abuse. However, the extent to which a problem may be seen as individual or collective will vary not only across time and place but also according to who is defining or interpreting it.

The ever-changing family

Perhaps because people have higher expectations than ever of family life, the family in all its forms continues to play a vital part in society.

> Perhaps the biggest change in families and family ideology is that now more is expected from marriage, childrearing and sexuality than in the past. Moreover, as family ideology has become stronger over time, by definition the reality and the ideal become further and further apart ... Without family ideology it would be possible to reconsider and reconstruct the realities of relationships between men, women and children and to work towards more equal and more caring ways of living and working together.
>
> (Gittins 1993: 165–8)

This chapter has illustrated how difficult it is to provide a straightforward definition and analysis of the 'family' given its ongoing modification in the context of social change.

We cannot speak of 'the family' as if it were a static and unchanging thing. Rather, it is better to use the word as signifying the character of a complex series of processes over time. Thus, instead of talking of 'the family' we should speak of 'family processes', 'family living' or 'family life courses'. In this way we will come to recognise that family life is always subject to change and variation, that change is at the very heart of family living.   (Morgan 1994a: 124)

Morgan's statement shows that diversity is as important a feature of family life today as any other. Within this diversity it is important to take account of the experiences of family life through a range of perspectives. You may research further into the distinctions between and within households based on gender, age, ethnicity and class. A cross-cultural approach broadens the possibilities even more in an age when we are increasingly exposed through the media and technological advance to alternative value systems and lifestyles.

This chapter has stressed the more negative features of the family and the prevalence of extreme violent forms of behaviour such as child abuse and domestic violence. Such awareness counterbalances naive views of

> ### Stop and think
>
> ➤ Next time you are in a supermarket, look more closely at the people shopping. What does this tell you about family life today? Does it illustrate family diversity?
>
> ➤ Look at the products on sale and any special promotions. What assumptions, if any, do they make about family life?

the family which focus simply on its positive attributes. An alternative focus also challenges the pervasive ideology of the traditional nuclear family, 'a social construct which is often held up as both the norm and the ideal, perpetuated by many media, from television dramas and advertisements to children's reading schemes' (T. David 1993: 27). The realities of family life demand that we weigh up carefully arguments on both sides of the debate about whether the family is a good or bad thing and in fact demonstrate that the complex and various nature of family life in modern society precludes any simplistic conclusions.

Summary

➤ While all societies exhibit some form of family arrangement, norms and values vary widely across and within generations and cultures. Defining the meaning and expectations associated with concepts such as 'family' and 'marriage', is less straightforward than we often assume.

➤ Research into the transformation of family patterns within Britain clarifies the influence of changing social and physical environments. The processes of industrialization and urban development, for example, have been associated with the evolution from nuclear to extended families and later the relinquishing of close kinship ties.

➤ Despite these changes, theorists within the functionalist school maintain that the institution of the family remains a fundamental feature of society that is able to adapt and evolve in function according to societal needs. Conflict theorists tend to focus on more negative interpretations of the family as an arena of power relationships and social control stifling the individuality of members.

➤ Trends in marriage, divorce and cohabitation illustrate the continuing dynamism of family patterns. Despite evidence of rising divorce rates and the increasing popularity of cohabitation in Britain and beyond, the evidence suggests that this does not signify the declining popularity or expectations of marriage. The rise in lone parenthood has triggered further public debate and policy regarding the most beneficial family arrangements for the welfare of children and parents.

➤ Understanding the family as a social problem involves considering the extent to which problems such as domestic violence and child abuse are interpreted as private troubles or public issues.

Links

The section on feminist approaches is related to issues discussed in Chapter 7 on gender.

The section on child abuse can be related to the discussion of childhood and children's rights in Chapter 9, pages 370–376.

 ## Further reading

Allan, G. and Crow, G. (2001) *Families, Households and Society,* Basingstoke: Palgrave Macmillan.
Written in a very accessible style, this book explores key changes in relation to family living including demographic changes, leaving home, cohabitation and marriage, lone-parent families and divorce, stepfamilies and households in later life.

Bernardes, J. (1997) *Family Studies: An Introduction,* London: Routledge.
Bernardes updates the now traditional sociological material on the family and industrialization and consider post-industrial and postmodern forms of family.

Cheal, D. (2002) *Sociology of Family Life,* Basingstoke: Palgrave Macmillan.
An extremely clear and well-written text which brings to life key issues in the sociological study of family life, drawing on a range of cross-cultural examples.

Jagger, G. and Wright, C. (eds) (1999) *Changing Family Values,* London: Routledge.
Based on feminist perspectives, this book examines contemporary issues in relation to family values, including single mothers, masculinities, same-sex families and implications for social policy.

Silva, E. and Smart, C. (eds) (1999) *The New Family?,* London: Sage.
This explores new forms of family by focusing on family practices. It includes chapters on lesbian and gay households, parenting after divorce, gender and generation.

http://www. Web sites

Centre for Research on Family, Kinship and Childhood
http://www.leeds.ac.uk/family/
This web site has information on the centre's research activities and key findings relating to a wide range of projects.

Centre for Research on Families and Relationships
http://www.crfr.ac.uk/
This research centre has a main office at the University of Edinburgh, with partners at Glasgow Caledonian University, and the Universities of Aberdeen, Glasgow and Stirling. The web site provides many online reports and briefings of recent research projects.

Department for Education and Skills
http://www.dfes.gov.uk/childrenandfamilies/
This government web site offers information on a range of family issues including child protection, family policy and teenage pregnancy.

National Statistics
http://www.statistics.gov.uk/
This web site is an invaluable resource of a range of statistics indicating the changing nature of different family structures.

Activities

Activity 1

Social policy and the family

Sommerville (1982) claims that in those countries in which the government encourages a variety of social bonds by offering some support to families, sharing child-rearing and presumably also the care of the elderly, life in families is thriving in a way which is not happening in those societies where support is haphazard.

(T. David 1993: 35)

Social policy in Britain reflects certain assumptions about the family and members' roles and responsibilities. Collect information on current legislation and welfare benefits and analyze the assumptions that underpin them in the light of the discussions covered in this chapter. You may wish to discuss what amendments, if any, you would make were you in a position to influence policy.

Useful sources will include advice leaflets and benefit forms available from the local Department of Social Security and details of current legislation from the media.

Activity 2

Family breakdown

Breakdown of family can lead to life of crime, says Bottomley

The community and the family must first look to themselves when society breaks down, Virginia Bottomley, the only woman member of the Government to address the Tory conference, said yesterday.

Mrs Bottomley, the Health Minister, was winding up a debate on the family, during which Geoffrey Dickens MP received loud applause when he called for the castration of rapists and child abusers.

Mrs Bottomley said: 'Time and again, from so-called joyriders to horrific instances of child abuse, when the basic cohesiveness of the family unit breaks down, crime, degeneracy, violence and horror break to the surface of our society. When parents give up caring, children, sometimes literally, run riot. Too many young people drift easily into a life of crime'.

She said the family was the basic building block of society, and the Government would go on producing policies to support it. . . . Mr Dickens, MP for Littleborough and Saddleworth, called for the recruitment of more experienced people into social work – 'grannies who would stand no nonsense'. He also called for legislation to castrate child abusers and rapists on second conviction. (The *Guardian* 12.10.1991)

Public and political concern about the single family is associated in the minds of many with concern about the ultimate welfare of society. Those who interpret the single parent family as symptomatic of the breakdown of the family and communal values are more likely to see a link between changing family forms and the increase in society's crime rates, particularly in the area of juvenile delinquency. The views expressed by a Conservative minister at the party's annual conference reflect this sentiment.

Questions

1. *The statements quoted from Virginia Bottomley's speech indicate the view that there is a very clear and direct relationship between the changing nature of the family and rising crime rates. What evidence is there of this if you examine recent crimes which have been featured in the media?*

2. *What effect do you think recruiting 'grannies who would stand no nonsense' to the social services would have on those who used these services?*

Chapter 14

Education

We adults destroy most of the intellectual and creative capacity of children by the things we do to them or make them do. We destroy this capacity above all by making them afraid, afraid of not doing what other people want, of not pleasing, of making mistakes, of failing, or being wrong. Thus we make them afraid to gamble, afraid to experiment, afraid to try the difficult and the unknown. Even when we do not create children's fears, when they come to us with fears ready-made and built-in, we use these fears as handles to manipulate them and get them to do what we want. Instead of trying to whittle down their fears, we build them up, often to monstrous size. For we like children who are afraid of us, docile, deferential children, though not, of course, if they are so obviously afraid that they threaten our image of ourselves as kind, loveable people whom there is no reason to fear. We find ideal the kind of 'good' children who are just enough afraid of us to do everything we want, without making us feel that fear of us is what is making them do it.   (Holt 1990: 274)

Key issues

➤ What are the main sociological approaches to the study of education and what problems do they identify?

➤ How has the sociology of education helped to inform education policies?

➤ In what ways do social class, gender and ethnicity affect educational achievement?

Introduction

The opening words for this chapter come from John Holt, whose book *How Children Fail* is still read by educationalists over forty years after its original publication. These words serve as a reminder that, although education is ideally about personal growth and creativity, its effects can sometimes be destructive. Growth can involve emotional pain and can be challenged by criticisms, fears, withdrawal and rebellion. There are also competing theories about how that growth and creativity should be managed and the purpose of education in serving either the needs of the individual or the needs of the state. Yet, even if our personal experiences of education seem to be mainly negative, and if that negative impression is reinforced by what we read in the sociology of education, it is still possible to be interested in the problems unearthed and even more fascinated by debates about the possible solutions to those problems.

This balance between negative and positive aspects of education is used in the structure of this chapter. We shall start by looking at how sociologists have used various perspectives in their critical analyses of education. Here we get a largely negative impression of some of the problems associated with education, and often the sociology of education has stopped at this point. These theorists have felt that their role was to describe what existed and not to concern themselves with what 'could be'. However, contemporary studies of education are concerned just as much with prescription as description. Debates about how many of these problems could be tackled via educational policies are in many ways more constructive and positive, but they do tend to highlight even more difficulties than those initially identified.

To return to personal experiences, Holt suggested that the learning process could be anything but straightforward. It could even be perceived as involving 'one step forward and two steps back'! Our formal education does not simply teach us uncontroversial 'facts'; schooling also includes hidden messages or unofficial rules that must be understood if we are to succeed in education. Jackson (1968) called this unofficial learning the 'hidden curriculum' and Hargreaves (1978) described it as the 'paracurriculum'. Aspects of this unofficial learning and personal experiences of education can teach us that we are valuable, intelligent individuals, or that we are worthless and 'dim'. Sociologists sometimes talk about personal aspirations being 'warmed up' or 'cooled down'. This can be seen, for example, in the experiences of some black girls in British schools, whose aspirations could have been 'cooled down' by the force of their negative school environment.

> Children were presented with a world view in which blackness represented everything that was ugly, uncivilized and underdeveloped, and our teachers made little effort to present us or our white classmates with an alternative view. Having been raised on the same basic diet of colonial bigotry themselves, they simply helped to make such negative stereotypes and misconceptions about us more credible.
>
> According to them, we 'could not speak English' and needed 'special' classes where our 'broken' version of the language could be drilled out of us. We were quiet and volatile. Best of all, we were good at sports –

physical, non-thinking activities – an ability which was to be encouraged so that our increasing 'aggression' could be channelled into more productive areas.

(Bryan *et al.* 1987: 93)

Notice the suggestion that this could discourage *some* black girls! It is not simply a case of a certain cause having a predictable long-term or short-term effect, as we respond to our experiences in a variety of ways. Bryan and colleagues entitled their article 'Learning to Resist' because they found that many black girls were not prepared to accept this negative conditioning and instead used education as a source of personal liberation.

Stop and think

> ➤ Think of illustrations of your personal 'growth' or 'regression'. Do you perceive your own experience of schooling mainly as a process of 'warming up', 'cooling down', or neither? Was this process straightforward?
>
> ➤ Interview another student about his or her experiences.
>
> ➤ To what extent can we associate the roots of these positive and negative educational processes with individual action or with the social structure?

In considering whether someone is 'bright' or 'dim', we should be aware that there are many types of intelligence (for example, a quiz champion who cannot cook a meal, an autistic child who can make rapid mathematical calculations) and a wide variety of educational experiences and outcomes. Howard Gardner (1983; 1993) challenged the notion of a single type of intelligence by writing about multiple intelligences: those that are typically valued in schools (linguistic, logical-mathematical), those associated with the arts (musical, bodily-kinesthetic, spatial) and 'personal intelligences' (interpersonal, intrapersonal). There are also a variety of ways of assessing abilities.

The sociology of education shows us that individual 'failures' or 'successes' are socially as well as personally constructed, that knowledge is socially constructed and that the identification of intelligence is a social and subjective process.

> I regard as the prime postulate of all pedagogical speculation that education is an eminently social thing in its origins and in its functions, and that, therefore, pedagogy depends on sociology more closely than any other science. (Durkheim 1956: 114)

A closer look

Assessment

In sociology the use of concepts such as 'intelligence', 'knowledge' and 'ability' is regarded as problematic. Our 'common sense' may tell us that such things can be identified and measured (and we may see this as a prime function of our own education) but those professionals with a responsibility for their measurement are often acutely conscious of the practical problems involved. A brief consideration of how the purpose of assessment influences the methods that are used demonstrates how complex this topic is.

To start we could ask if the purpose of the assessment is summative or diagnostic. **Summative assessment** aims to describe an individual's current intelligence/knowledge/ability. This may lead to a grading, or some other type of summary or label (for example, a second-class honours degree). Yet, even a descriptive assessment of this kind can lead to a variety of results. Objectivity is very difficult to achieve, and examiners may disagree about what questions should be asked, what skills should be tested and how results should be interpreted. **Diagnostic assessment** is likely to include a summative assessment but will go further by providing an indication of what the next stage of the learning process should be (for example, by identifying special educational needs). Positive action can be taken, but again we can reasonably ask how objective the assessor's recommendations can be.

The degree of objectivity must also be considered in the selection of a standard, or standards, against which individuals are to be judged. When **criterion-referencing** is used there is some sort of list of criteria available to provide guidance concerning the standard that has been reached. An individual is assessed according to how the criteria have been satisfied, and the assessment can be made by a tutor or by the student (e.g. self-assessment using a tutorial on computer). When **norm-referencing** is used the performance of one individual is ranked in comparison with that of others. Usually the aim of this approach is to ration the number of 'passes' or qualifications (for example, in the use of an 11+ examination to allocate children to a limited number of grammar school places).

Questions

1. What type of assessment is most likely to be used for the following:

   (a) a driving test;
   (b) admission to university;
   (c) music grades;
   (d) qualifications at school leaving age;
   (e) assessment of students' knowledge of sociology?
   Give reasons for your answers.

2. Do you think the types of assessment are fair?

A closer look

Influences on different national education systems

1 *Different economic structures*, including systems of skills formation and numerous economic indicators such as unemployment, income distribution, and wage costs.

2 *Different geo-political and geo-cultural influences*, 'the broad cultural traditions in the major regions of Europe, stereotypically represented as universalism in France and southern Europe, cultural particularism in Germany and the German-speaking states, communitarian solidarity in Scandinavia and liberal individualism in the UK and Ireland' (Green, Wolf and Leney 1999, p. 26).

3 *Different labour market organization*.

4 *Different political and institutional traditions*, France and southern European states are seen as having state-centred policies and relatively centralized forms

of educational administration, German-speaking states having more decentralized or federal systems, an emphasis on regional control of education and well-defined roles for employers, the Scandinavian states being influenced by neo-corporatist and communitarian ideas, resulting in a shift towards local control of education, and England (and to a lesser extent other UK countries) being influenced by laissez-faire liberal traditions, weak social partnerships and a history of voluntarism and local autonomy in education.

(Adapted from Green, Wolf and Leney 1999: 25–6)

Questions

1. How do these four features apply to the four British 'nations' of England, Wales, Scotland and Northern Ireland?

2. How might these differences affect education in the four 'nations'?

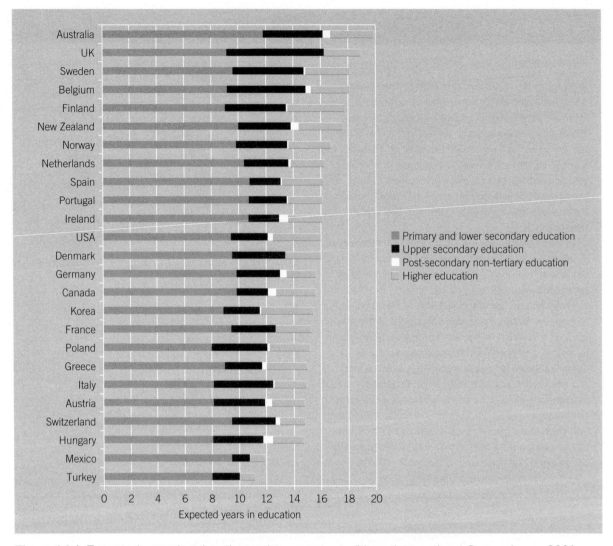

Figure 14.1 Expected years in education under current conditions, International Comparisons, 2001
Source: www.dfes.gov.uk

Figure 14.1 demonstrates how in OECD (Organization for Economic Co-operation and Development) countries even the total number of expected years in primary, secondary and higher education ranges widely between countries, from 11.5 years in Turkey to 20.0 years in Australia. Many other states do not provide any formal system of education, and arrangements for the provision of education within an individual state will vary according to constantly changing political, economic and social contexts.

Not only are educational systems and structures influenced by their social and political context but what we learn about our physical and social environment is selective and influenced by social norms.

How a society selects, classifies, distributes, transmits and evaluates the educational knowledge it considers to be public, reflects both the distribution of power and the principles of social control.

(Bernstein 1971: 47)

We have already seen Bryan *et al.*'s (1987) complaints about racial bias and negative conditioning and will later consider ways in which a biased curriculum can impact on individual experiences, but you may take some time at this point to consider other ways in which educational knowledge can be selective.

Sociologists commonly use a wide definition of education, to include informal education in the home and

A closer look

The problem of credential inflation

College degrees, once the possession of a tiny elite of professional and wealthy individuals, are now held by more than a fourth of the US population. But as education has expanded, the social distinctiveness of the bachelor's degree and its value in the marketplace have declined – in turn increasing the demand for still higher levels of education. In fact, most problems of contemporary universities are connected with 'credential inflation'.

In 1910, less than 10 per cent of the population obtained, at most, high school degrees. They were badges of substantial middle-class respectability, until mid-century, conferring access even to the managerial jobs. Now, a high school degree is little more than a ticket to a lottery in which one can buy a chance at a college degree – which itself is becoming a ticket to a yet higher lottery.

Such credential inflation is driven largely by the expansion of schooling – like a government's printing more paper money – rather than by economic demand for an increasingly educated labor force. Our educational system, as it widens access to each successive degree, has been able to flood the market for educated labor at virtually any level.

Many people believe that our high-tech era requires massive educational expansion. Yet the skills of cutting-edge industries are generally learned on the job or through experience rather than in high school or college. Compare the financial success of the youthful founders of Apple or Microsoft, some of them college dropouts, with the modest careers of graduates of computer schools.

Furthermore, a high-tech society does not mean that a high proportion of the labor force consists of experts. A more likely pattern – and the one we see emerging today – is a bifurcation of the labor force into an 'expert' sector – perhaps 20 per cent – and a much larger range of those with routine or even menial service jobs. (Collins 2002)

Questions

1. Have you any personal experience of credential inflation?

2. What problems in universities could be caused by credential inflation?

3. Do you agree with Collins's claim that qualifications have become tickets in a lottery?

4. What arguments can be made for and against the claim that 'our high-tech era requires massive educational expansion'?

---

elsewhere. As education is part of the process of socialization, and influenced by other agencies of socialization, studies that separate it from other parts of society are severely limited. In Chapter 13 we saw how important the family is to our whole experience of life, and the influence of the family on our educational experiences can hardly be overestimated. However, sociologists are likely to reject claims that intelligence is primarily innate and inherited biologically from our parents. Instead they will emphasize the ways that families influence educational achievement after birth and the social labelling of children according to their background.

Schooling in Britain

In this chapter we concentrate on formal education in schools, colleges and universities. While this is a large enough area in its own right, it is important to bear in mind that we learn a great deal outside formal education – from parents, friends, the television, and so on. We will look at the kinds of schools provided in Britain and the origins of that provision, then consider some of the problems sociologists have identified and debates about how those problems should be dealt with. As we do so you should consider the extent to which the issues we encounter in British education could also exist in other countries.

Origins of the current schooling 'system'

Such a diverse range of schools exists in Britain that the term 'school system' no longer seems as appropriate as it was in the 1950s (when most children were educated in a bipartite system of grammar and secondary modern schools) or 1960s (when comprehensive schools were more common). During the 1940s and 1950s the one point on which most politicians and educationalists were agreed was that social origins could have a profound, and often negative, effect on educational achievement. To tackle this problem some favoured the sort of competitive access to secondary education offered by the tripartite system (i.e. grammar, secondary modern and technical schools), and this was the system that was originally promoted by the Education Act 1944. This Act was introduced in wartime, by a coalition government and with wide-scale public support. For the first time it provided free secondary education for all and therefore created a 'ladder' of educational opportunity for working-class children. The three types of school planned for a tripartite system were originally presented as being of equal value but offering different types of education to suit different abilities. Planners aimed to provide 'parity of esteem' for all children but, partly because few technical schools were provided, the reality was that children were seen as 'passing' the 11+ examination and going to a grammar school or 'failing' and going to a secondary modern school.

Criticisms of what was largely a bipartite system gradually gained strength during the 1950s and 1960s. These were mainly concerned with two assumptions: first, that intelligence could be assessed accurately at the age of 11; and second, that abilities would be fixed for life. It was found that relatively few children from working-class backgrounds were 'passing' the 11+ to find a place on the 'ladder' of educational opportunity and that girls were often discriminated against in the allocation

of grammar school places. There were also regional disparities in the provision of grammar school places, making it more difficult to 'pass' the 11+ examination in some areas than in others. During the 1960s increasing numbers of secondary modern school pupils passed GCE O Level examinations. This meant that some 11+ 'failures' left school better qualified than some grammar school pupils.

During the 1960s the tone of sociological research seemed to become more radical and egalitarian as educationalists grew more persistent in their claims that changes in the school system were not enough to improve working-class opportunities. Among others, work by Douglas (1964), Halsey *et al.* (1961) and Jackson and Marsden (1963) emphasized the need to make schools more accessible to working-class parents and to involve parents more fully in their children's education. This coincided with a period of Labour government and political initiatives aimed at generating greater equality: for example, Circular 10/65 (Department of Education and Science 1965) instructed LEAs to replace a bipartite system with comprehensive schools and the Plowden Report (Central Advisory Council for Education: CACE 1967) recommended the introduction of educational priority areas (to provided compensatory education for children living in poor areas).

Case study

Extracts from the speech made by James Callaghan, Ruskin College, 1976

I am concerned on my journeys to find complaints from industry that new recruits from schools sometimes do not have the basic tools to do the job that is required.

I have been concerned to find that many of our best trained students who have completed the higher levels of education at university or polytechnic have no desire to enter industry . . .

There is no virtue in producing socially well-adjusted members of society who are unemployed because they do not have the skills. Nor at the other extreme must they be technically efficient robots. Both of the basic purposes of education require the same essential tools. These are basic literacy, basic numeracy, the understanding of how to live and work together, respect for others, respect for the individual. This means acquiring certain basic knowledge, and skills and reasoning ability. It means

developing lively inquiring minds and an appetite for further knowledge that will last a lifetime. It means mitigating as far as possible the disadvantages that may be suffered through poor home conditions or physical or mental handicap.

(quoted in *Education: Journal of Educational Administration Management and Policy* 22.10.1976: 333)

Question

1. Do you agree with James Callaghan's definition of the two basic purposes of education?

By the mid-1970s economic issues had become upper-most in political debates, as economic crisis followed economic crisis. This was reflected in a new emphasis on the role of education in serving the needs of the economy; this emphasis was labelled the 'Great Debate', and continued into the twenty-first century. The starting date is generally cited as a speech by the then Labour Prime Minister James Callaghan at Ruskin College, Oxford, in October 1976. To say that one speech was solely responsible for the Great Debate would be a gross simplification, but it was followed by a period of intense political activity around a theme of 'vocationalism' that accelerated throughout the 1980s and the 1990s. Some educationalists have noted in particular the way that politicians have criticized education for in some way 'failing' the nation – Ball (1991) called it a 'discourse of derision' – and we can see signs of this discourse emerging in Callaghan's speech.

Until the 1980s a rather fragile process existed by which education policy was generated via negotiations between three groups: local councils and their local education authorities (LEAs), central government, and teachers' representatives. This came to be known as the 'triangle of tension' (Briault 1976). Teachers also had considerable freedom to decide what should be taught in class; so much so that the curriculum was often described as a 'secret garden'. Local education authorities had the main responsibility, and some freedom, in deciding what kinds of schools should be provided in their areas. They had always been influenced by directives from central government but maintained some flexibility in their responses. For example, after a Labour government issued Circular 10/65 in 1965 some Conservative LEAs were so effective in stalling the move to comprehensive secondary education that their areas still have a largely bipartite system.

However, a major shift of influence took place as the previous 'triangle of tension' was replaced by the allocation of more power to central government, at the expense of LEAs and teachers. This shift was sustained by the 'discourse of derision' (Ball 1991) and its allocation of blame for educational 'failures' to LEAs and teachers. Conservative governments (1979–97) gradually reduced the amount of influence LEAs had on the type of schools provided in their areas (for example, by promoting grant-maintained schools and city technology colleges) and acquired a tighter control of LEA spending. To a certain extent the influence of Labour-controlled LEAs was incompatible with the policies of central government. For example, the policies of the Labour-run Inner

Figure 14.2 Catering for cultural diversity
© Getty/AFP/Alessandro Abbonizio

London Education Authority (ILEA) were seen as a major challenge by the Conservative government, which abolished it. During the mid-1980s teachers' unions took industrial action, in protest not only about their pay but also about conditions of work and changes in the education system. The government responded by withdrawing their negotiating rights. Efforts by LEAs, teachers' unions and other interest groups to promote stronger versions of equal opportunities were suppressed by government policies favouring a diverse range of opportunities within a varied school 'system'.

Since the election of a Labour government in 1997 the varied schools system has remained, although the School Standards and Framework Act 1998 initiated change more in keeping with the ideas of New Labour. Schools previously funded by LEAs, churches or central government (i.e. grant-maintained) were newly designated as, respectively, 'community', 'voluntary' and 'foundation' schools. Unlike past Labour governments, New Labour did not instruct LEAs to replace selective schools with comprehensive schools but, instead, laid down a procedure for parents to vote on future admission arrangements at local grammar schools and allowed some specialist schools to maintain selection for a minority of their intake. Places at non-maintained schools which were partly or wholly paid for by central government (assisted places) were gradually withdrawn, and more money was directed at the reduction of class sizes in primary schools.

It is interesting to note that an end to grammar schools is no longer seen as a central tenet of Labour policy and seems to have been replaced by a new version of the previous government's emphasis on parental choice. Whereas the last Conservative government emphasized parental rights and freedoms, New Labour emphasizes parental rights and obligations, with home–school contracts setting out mutual responsibilities and expectations. The aim is to help parents to improve their parenting skills and to link education policies to wider efforts to reduce social inequalities and 'social exclusion'. An emphasis on parental obligations can also be seen in the Labour government's introduction of means-tested fees

for higher education. New Labour broke away from the commitment previous governments had to free education for full-time students in higher education. In doing so it has met with large-scale public scepticism concerning its commitments to both increasing the number of graduates and reducing social inequalities.

Relationships between government, LEAs and teachers have also changed since 1997, as communications between them seem to have become more effective. Although central government still retains its extensive powers, it is prepared to negotiate, and doors closed by the previous government have been opened. Labour favours the devolution of some powers to regional assemblies and (the mainly Labour-controlled) LEAs, it has encouraged LEAs to apply for extra funding as education action zones and has introduced a General Teaching Council, which teachers hoped would provide them with more autonomy. However, teachers have complained that the 'discourse of derision', with its increasing emphasis on accountability, has left them facing new forms of control and associated feelings of guilt about their imperfect performance.

Case study

Performativity in education

Stephen Ball described 'performativity' as a

technology, a culture and mode of regulation, or even a system of 'terror' in Lyotard's words, that employs judgements, comparisons and displays as a means of control, attrition and change. The performances of – individual subjects or organisations – serve as measures of productivity or output, or displays of 'quality', or 'moments' of promotion or inspections. They stand for,

encapsulate or represent the worth, quality or value of an individual or organisation within a field of judgement.

(Ball 2004: 143)

A teacher quoted by Jeffrey and Woods said,

I don't have the job satisfaction now I once had working with young kids because I feel every time I do something intuitive I just feel guilty about it. 'Is this right; am I doing this the right way; does this cover what I'm supposed to be covering; should I be doing something else; should I be more structured; should I have

this in place; should I have done this?' You start to query everything you are doing – there's a kind of guilt in teaching at the moment. I don't know if that's particularly related to Ofsted but of course it's multiplied by the fact that Ofsted is coming in because you get in a panic that you won't be able to justify yourself when they finally arrive.

(Jeffrey and Woods 1998: 118)

Questions

1. *Discuss the effectiveness of performativity as a way of monitoring and improving teaching standards.*

Development of sociological explanations and theories

We now consider the main sociological approaches to the study of education and the problems they identify. Sociological perspectives (see Chapter 2) can help to make sense of educational provision and processes, but critical analyses of education have often limited themselves to describing problems, without concerning themselves with solutions. We shall follow this application of familiar sociological explanations and theories with a short analysis of themes that are more particular to the study of education policies.

As the aim here is to follow a basically developmental approach, we shall start, as early sociologists tended to start, with an emphasis on the social structure. Writers such as Durkheim were concerned with establishing the relatively new study of society and with arguing the merits of a sociological study of education at a time when education was largely seen as a matter for individuals only. This structural approach emphasizes the role of education in maintaining consensus and continuity in society, and is often primarily descriptive. However, other writers, such as Karl Marx, have emphasized the use of education as a means of perpetuating or shifting structural inequalities within society, focusing their attention on education as a source not only of continuity but also of conflict and change.

These structural concerns could be viewed as over-deterministic if they ignore the reactions of individuals to their educational experiences. We have already noted that some individuals can 'learn to resist' the negative influences within education. This emphasis on interaction will be considered in more detail when we look at interpretative approaches. The dynamic relationship between structural and interpretative approaches will be acknowledged when we look at recent movements towards a synthesis of these theoretical positions.

Case study

Durkheim: education and sociology

In sum, education, far from having as its unique or principal object the individual and his interests, is above all the means by which society perpetually recreates the conditions of its very existence. Can society survive only if there exists among its members a sufficient homogeneity? Education perpetuates and reinforces this homogeneity by fixing in advance, in the mind of the child, the essential similarities that collective life presupposes. But, on the other hand, without a certain diversity, would all co-operation be impossible? Education assures the persistence of this necessary diversity by becoming itself diversified and by specializing. It consists, then, in one or another of its aspects, of a systematic socialization of the young generation. In each of us, it may be said, there exist two beings which, while inseparable except by abstraction, remain distinct. One is made up of all the mental states which apply only to ourselves and to the events of our personal lives. This is what might be called the individual being. The other is the system of ideas, sentiments, and practices which express in us, not our personality, but the group or different groups of which we are a part; these are religious beliefs, moral beliefs and practices, national or occupational traditions, collective opinions of every kind. Their totality forms the social being. To constitute this being in each of us is the end of education.

(Adapted from Durkheim 1956: 114–16)

Questions

1. Can you find any examples of education policies that have as their 'principal object the individual and his [sic] interests'?

2. Why did Durkheim regard diversity (and the provision of diversity via education) as necessary in order to promote social cohesion? (See Chapter 2 for guidance.)

Structural explanations: consensus and continuity

Consensus perspectives emphasize the important role of education in socializing the individual to fit into, and perpetuate, the social system. Although society has been created by people, individuals are seen as being born into a society which already has an identity of its own, and education as serving the function of passing on the collective consciousness, or culture, of that pre-existing society. This approach is most commonly associated with functionalist perspectives and Emile Durkheim. In the extract on p. 551 we can see Durkheim urging his readers to accept what was a relatively unorthodox idea at the time, that education had a social, rather than just an individual, reality.

As a socialist Durkheim was concerned about social inequality, but as a positivist he also believed that the role of sociology was to describe society without aiming to change it. Functionalist approaches to education have therefore been portrayed by their critics as being rather conservative: analyzing the functions of education in maintaining an efficient and stable social order. They have also tended to adapt to the context of the time, more recent writers focusing on the study of classrooms and schools as social systems.

Parsons, for example, was primarily concerned with the problem of first:

> how the school class functions to internalize in its pupils both the commitments and capacities for successful performance of their future adult roles, and second of how it functions to allocate these human resources within the role structure of the adult society.
>
> (Parsons 1959: 297)

Parsons was aiming to integrate structural and interpretative approaches by emphasizing how the social structure influences the roles of individuals within the education system. His work is relevant in both sociology and psychology, and is an example of how unrealistic it is to make sharp distinctions between structural and interpretative approaches. Nevertheless, Parsons' work is more often cited in the sociology of education as a 'structural functionalist' approach simply because he does not emphasize the routine small-scale classroom interactions that provide a focus for interpretative approaches. He was interested in the 'patterned expectations' (rules and regulations) that have developed, governing how individuals should behave in order to maintain social order

A closer look

Four functional requirements of society

Adaptation

Education adapts itself and individuals to changes in the cultural, technological and physical environment. It helps to emancipate the child from dependence on the family.

Goal attainment

Education helps individuals to identify and realize their personal and collective needs. Differentiated achievements can contribute to an effective division of labour.

Integration

Education provides some coherence between the relative influences of, for example, family, legal system, church, employment and the wider economic system. It helps individuals to identify themselves within a wider social system.

Latency or pattern maintenance

Educational processes lead to the reproduction of common values and social norms. It teaches us not only how to conform but also how to think.

and continuity. More specifically, education is seen as serving the four functional requirements that all societies have in order to survive.

Here we can see a continuation of Durkheim's positivist approach, with its emphasis on description rather than criticism. Its implication that education contributes towards a meritocratic system (in which pupils' educational achievements are based only on ability and effort) has been severely challenged as research has repeatedly highlighted the profound effects of social inequalities on educational outcomes. Critics have also argued that education can contribute to both social cohesion and social conflict, and that education does not necessarily serve the needs of either the economy or the individual. There are, moreover, no clear and agreed sets of 'needs' that can be functionally fulfilled. In general, functionalist images of society have been seen as being so unrealistic that they should either be dismissed or be adapted to suit reality.

It would, however, be wrong to assume that functionalist approaches to education are no longer influential. Some aspects have indeed been adapted or developed more fully to incorporate criticisms. For example, theories about social dysfunction (Merton 1938) help to explain how education can not only fail to serve the needs of society but also actually work against the interests of society. It can also reasonably be claimed that it is just as important to observe the role of education in maintaining society as to observe the manifestation of conflict within education.

Structural explanations: conflict and change

Conflict perspectives emphasize inequalities of educational opportunities and the need for social change. These have varied from the revolutionary writings of Marx and Engels to more moderate appeals for reforms within the existing social system. Classical Marxists have emphasized the primary influence of the capitalist economic infrastructure and the secondary role of education in perpetuating the necessary supportive ideology. In the box we can see Marx and Engels' condemnation of education as a means by which the state maintains a capitalist system and its associated inequalities.

Marxist influences continue today but have (like functionalism) been developed and adapted to the changing historical context. They have probed more deeply into the processes by which inequality is perpetuated through education. For example, writing about *Schooling in Capitalist America*, Bowles and Gintis (1976) analyzed the correspondence between children's experiences in school and the inequalities they encounter as adults in the workplace. In this way the school is seen as introducing and reproducing the inequalities of social class that are perpetuated in a capitalist system, normalizing them in the process so that the working class are hardly aware of them (and therefore in a state of false consciousness).

Alienated labor is reflected in the student's lack of control over his or her education, the alienation of the student from the curriculum content, and the motivation of school work through a system of grades and other external rewards rather than the student's integration with either the process (learning) or the outcome (knowledge) of the educational 'production process'. Fragmentation in work is reflected in the institutionalized and often destructive competition among students through continual and ostensibly

---

A closer look

Marx and Engels: education and the state

The communists have not invented the intervention of society in education; they do but seek to alter the character of that intervention, and to rescue education from the influence of the ruling class.

The bourgeois claptrap about the family and education, about the hallowed co-relation of parent and child, becomes all the more disgusting, the more, by the action of modern industry, all family ties among the proletarians are torn asunder and their children transformed into simple articles of commerce and instruments of labour. (Marx and Engels 1976 vol. 6: 502)

Equal elementary education? What idea behind these words? Is it believed that in present-day society, (and it is only with this one has to deal) education can be equal for all classes? Or is it demanded that the upper classes also shall be compulsorily reduced to the modicum of education – the elementary school – that alone is compatible with the economic conditions not only of the wage workers but of the peasants as well? . . .

'Elementary education by the state' is altogether objectionable. Defining by a general law the expenditures on the elementary schools, the qualifications of the teaching staff, the branches of instruction, etc., as is done in the United States, supervising the fulfilment of these legal specifications by state supervisors, is a very different thing from appointing the state as the educator of the people! Government and church should rather be equally excluded from any influence on the school. (Marx 1891, *Critique of the Gotha Programme*, quoted in Feuer 1969: 170–1)

Questions

1. How could education transform children into 'simple articles of commerce and instruments of labour'? Could aspects of your education be interpreted in this way?

2. Compare these views with those of Durkheim. What are the similarities and differences?

---

meritocratic ranking and evaluation. By attuning young people to a set of social relationships similar to those of the workplace, schooling attempts to gear the development of personal needs to its requirements.

(Bowles and Gintis 1976: 131)

Stop and think

➤ What influences have you had on the content or style of your education (a) at the age of 8; (b) at the age of 12; (c) now?

➤ List any aspects of schooling that are essentially (a) cooperative; (b) competitive.

Yet even in what is often defined as a structural approach, Bowles and Gintis (1976) were looking not only at the social structure but also at the way that small groups and individuals related to each other in schools. This makes it difficult to see where a structural approach may end and an interpretative approach start, and divisions between these approaches become even more spurious when we consider the work of Paul Willis. Willis (1977) analyzed the attitudes of a group of working-class 'lads' during their last year at secondary modern school and their first year in the workplace and, in the process, greatly enhanced our understanding of how the 'correspondence principle' identified by Bowles and Gintis could work in practice. Willis's analysis is considered in more detail below (pp. 555–6).

Pierre Bourdieu provided another explanation of how analyis at a structural level could illuminate our thinking about social inequalities and their effects on our educational experiences. This involved the identification of various types of capital.

The focus of writers working within a Marxist tradition (and critical theorists in particular) has also shifted to an emphasis on hegemony and the role of the ideological superstructure in perpetuating social inequalities. For example, Althusser (1972) saw education as playing a vital role within the ideological state apparatus, perpetuating inequalities by conditioning the masses to accept the *status quo*. Similarly, feminists have examined the features of education that perpetuate and legitimize gender inequalities (see e.g. Arnot 1986; Byrne 1978; Deem 1978; Kelly 1981; Kenway and Willis 1990; Stanworth 1983).

One feature that many of these theoretical developments have in common is an emphasis on the use of education as part of a process of liberation. This can be seen in the earlier quote (p. 544) from Bryan *et al.* (1987), where we saw that black girls described their educational experiences as being primarily defined by their blackness in a negative way. The title of their article, 'Learning to Resist', suggests that children do not automatically accept this sort of labelling. They (and their teachers) may resist negative

A closer look

Cultural capital

'Capital can present itself in three fundamental guises: as economic capital, which is immediately and directly convertible into money and may be institutionalized in the form of property rights; as cultural capital, which is convertible, on certain conditions, into economic capital and may be institutionalized in the form of educational qualifications; and as social capital, made up of social obligations ('connections'), which is convertible, in certain conditions, into economic capital and may be institutionalized in the form of title of nobility.'

Bourdieu criticized economists and functionalists for emphasizing the value of education in terms of national productivity and society as a whole. In doing so they ignored the influence of cultural capital and were 'unaware that ability or talent is itself the product of an investment of time and cultural capital'.

'This typically functionalist definition of the functions of education ignores the contribution which the educational system makes to the reproduction of the social structure by sanctioning the hereditary transmission of cultural capital.'

Bourdieu observed that access to further and higher education in order to acquire more knowledge and qualifications was influenced by all three forms of of capital.

'Differences in the cultural capital possessed by the family imply differences first in the age at which the work of transmission and accumulation begins . . . and then in the capacity, thus defined, to satisfy the specifically cultural demands of a prolonged process of acquisition. Furthermore, and in correlation with this, the length of time for which a given individual can prolong this acquisition process depends on the length of time for which the family can provide him with the free time, i.e. time free from economic necessity, which is the precondition for the initial accumulation time which can be evaluated as a handicap to be made up.'

(Bourdieu 1997: 183–98)

Question

To what extent do you agree with what Bourdieu had to say about (a) whose interests are served by education; (b) connections between educational process, the labour market and national productivity?

influences and not only use education as a source of personal empowerment but also bring about minor or major changes in educational processes. In order to achieve any real depth in our understanding of education we must therefore look at how individuals relate to structural constraints and at their experiences of small-scale interaction.

Interpretative influences

From the late 1970s onwards the influence of Weber and other action theorists was becoming more noticeable in educational research. More sociologists started to present findings based on classroom observation and interview data, the best known of these in Britain being provided by Ball (1981), Hargreaves (1967), Lacey (1970) and Willis (1977). They were trying to understand the meanings that individuals and groups attached to their behaviour, and to interpret their findings at a theoretical level. However, it would be a simplification to depict these as just inter-

pretative studies when often they have been motivated by an interest in how structural inequalities are maintained by educational processes. This interest in showing how many 'interpretative' studies of classroom interaction incorporate 'structuralist' issues could be seen as a natural progression from the work of Weber (1964: 88–120) and part of a general move towards the triangulation of methodological and theoretical perspectives.

Paul Willis' (1977) research has already been mentioned as it relates quite closely to the 'correspondence principle' described by Bowles and Gintis (1976) (notice that his book was published a year after theirs). Willis acknowledged the use of both structuralist and interpretative approaches at the very beginning.

> The difficult thing to explain about how middle class kids get middle class jobs is why others let them. The difficult thing to explain about how working class kids get working class jobs is why they let themselves.
>
> (Willis 1977: 1)

Case study

Willis: *Learning to Labour*

It is essentially what appears to be their enthusiasm for, and complicity with, immediate authority which makes the school conformists – or 'ear 'oles' or 'lobes' – the second great target for 'the lads' [the first target is the teachers]. The term 'ear 'ole' itself connotes the passivity and absurdity of the school conformists for 'the lads'. It seems that they are always listening, never doing: never animated with their own internal life, but formless in rigid reception. The ear is one of the least expressive organs of the human body: it responds to the expressivity of others. It is pasty and easy to render obscene. That is how 'the lads' liked to picture those who conformed to the official idea of schooling.

Crucially, 'the lads' not only reject but feel superior to the 'ear 'oles'. The obvious medium for the enactment of this superiority is that which the 'ear 'oles' apparently yield – fun, independence and excitement: having a 'laff'.

[In a group discussion]

PW   . . . why not be like the 'ear 'oles', why not try and get CSEs?

–   They don't get any fun, do they?

Derek   Cos they'm prats like, one kid he's got on his report now, he's got five As and one B.

–   Who's that?

Derek   Birchall.

Spanksy   I mean, what will they remember of their school life? What will they have

to look back on? Sitting in the classroom, sweating their bollocks off, you know, while we've been . . . I mean look at the things we can look back on, fighting on the Pakis, fighting on the JAs [Jamaicans]. Some of the things we've done on teachers, it'll be a laff when we look back on it.

(Willis 1977: 14)

Questions

1. Most of 'the lads' got jobs when they left school in the early 1970s. Consider the implications of Willis's findings today.

2. Were there similar groups to 'the lads' in your school? Were any of these groups, or members of these groups, female?

However, you can see the essential features of interpretative sociology, as he uses 'the lads' own words and tries to communicate their own sense of reality (see Case study, p. 555).

Willis's interests reflect common sociological interests in pro- and anti-school sub-cultures, the self-fulfilling prophecy and the 'hidden curriculum'. Put simply, teachers' expectations about how well or how badly individuals will behave are likely to influence that behaviour. Pupils are likely to internalize their teachers' expectations and make them their own, eventually matching their behaviour to the predictions made. Expectations may be derived not only from teachers but also from families, friends and society in general; in this way, social inequalities can be perpetuated by low self-esteem.

Willis, however, adds depth to this sort of scenario by illustrating 'the lads' creative interaction with social constraints as well as the processes by which they reached a predictable structural location. This creative process has been more recently illustrated by Anoop Nayak (2003), who discovered that, over 25 years after Willis's research, 'local lads' in school sub-cultures still preserved a traditional white working-class masculinity and the grammar of manual labour. This was through a modern 'curriculum of the body', as exemplified through the rituals of football fandom, which provided an illusion of stability in insecure times. (Other well-known studies of the self-fulfilling prophecy include Holt (1969), Rosenthal and Jacobson (1968) and Spender and Sarah (1980).)

Willis's 'lads' may be seen as taking a rather predictable route but what about the black women interviewed for 'Learning to Resist'? Fuller (1980) also found that a group of black girls in comprehensive school created an anti-school sub-culture but still valued academic achievement as a form of resistance.

Unity and diversity in the study of education

Developments in sociological theories about education seem to have moved towards a synthesis of structural and interpretative perspectives. For example, critical theory has Marxist origins but emphasizes the ways that language reproduces or transforms culture. Like classical Marxist approaches it advocates changes in education to reduce social inequalities, but it also emphasizes individual rather than social class, empowerment in recognition of the increasingly diverse nature of society and the fragmentation of social classes.

Other approaches also mix theories and techniques. Feminists share a common concern about gender inequalities in society (i.e. a structural emphasis) but the diverse range of, sometimes competing, feminist theories often seem to share little else. Like feminism, postmodernist ideas challenge even basic assumptions about education.

> Postmodernism does more than wage war on totality, it also calls into question the use of reason in the service of power, the role of intellectuals who speak through authority invested in a science of trust and history, and forms of leadership that demand unification and consensus within centrally administered chains of command.
>
> (Giroux 1992, in Halsey et al. 1997: 118–19)

Indeed, if you look at what has been said in this chapter about competing social influences on shared knowledge and education systems you may also share a sense of confusion about our ability to theorize in any way. Yet Giroux argues that modernist, postmodernist and feminist theories offer valuable opportunities for rethinking learning processes and relationships between schooling and democracy.

> To invoke the importance of pedagogy is to raise questions not simply about how students learn but also how educators (in the broad sense of the term) construct the ideological and political positions from which they speak. At issue here is the discourse that both situates human beings within history and makes visible the limits of their ideologies and values. Such a position acknowledges the partiality of all discourses so that the relationship between knowledge and power will always be open to dialogue and critical self-engagement.
>
> (Giroux 1992, in Halsey et al. 1997: 128)

According to Giroux this partiality of discourse does not exclude an agenda for using education in a transformative and political way. Here he explains how, to him, sociological theories about education are inextricably linked to education policies.

> A radical pedagogy and transformative democratic politics must go hand in hand in constructing a vision in which liberalism's emphasis on individual feedom, postmodernism's concern with the particularistic, and feminism's concern with the politics of the everyday are coupled with democratic socialism's holistic concern with solidarity and public life.
>
> (Giroux 1992, in Halsey et al. 1997: 128)

Sociological approaches to education policy

We have seen how educational studies have become more 'political', encompassing not only their traditional interests in educational problems but also increasingly emphasizing debates about how those problems should be tackled. In order to clarify current political debates about educational issues we shall consider the two main themes of equality/inequality and uniformity/diversity. This is because policy makers' perspectives will vary from those favouring an extremely uniform education system (e.g. with the same sort of schooling provided for all) to those favouring an extremely diverse system. Similarly, policy makers will vary from those favouring extreme notions of equality (egalitarianism) to those favouring extreme notions of inequality (biological determinism). The theme of equal (or rather unequal) opportunities is already well established in educational studies and, although debates about uniformity/diversity are certainly not recent, they assumed greater prominence along with an increasingly diverse school system and their relevance to postmodernist ideas.

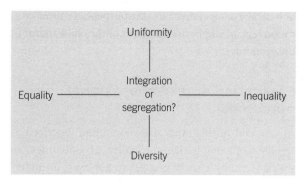

Figure 14.3 Educational policy making: a model of key themes and polarities

Equality or inequality?

There seems to be an almost universal assumption that 'equal opportunities' are a 'good thing' much in the same way that 'democracy' is regarded as a 'good thing'. Yet if we try to clarify these concepts it is likely that individual interpretations of these terms will differ. In educational studies there is a wide range of views as to what 'equal opportunities' means based on different assumptions about human nature (e.g. that we are basically competitive

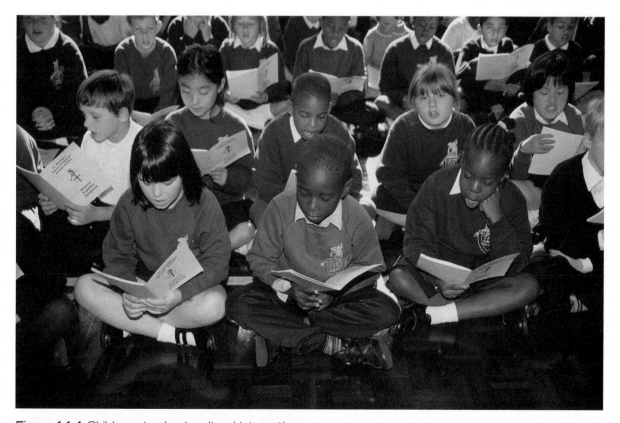

Figure 14.4 Children at school: cultural integration
© Christine Osborne/CORBIS

or basically co-operative) and the purpose of formal education (e.g. to emphasize the needs of the child and/or of the economy).

Egalitarian approaches: equal outcomes

At one end of this range are views often described as 'egalitarian', emphasizing equality of outcomes, in which identifiable social groups are not over- or under-represented among high or low achievers. This means that the proportion of a social group represented among university graduates (and also among those without qualifications) should correspond with the proportion of that group in the whole population; for example, if 50 per cent of the population is female, about 50 per cent of all graduates should be female. In the sections on social class, gender and race we shall see how far we are from such equal outcomes.

Egalitarian arguments have supported the need for compensatory education, such as the educational priority areas promoted by the British Plowden Report in 1967. In other words, some children are seen as needing extra resources and extra help in an effort to compensate for wider social inequalities.

According to egalitarian approaches, social inequalities cannot be tackled by education alone. A new educational power base and other changes in education (such as anti-racism, anti-sexism and anti-heterosexism) are promoted, but egalitarians present these as just part of the necessary shift towards a more equitable and caring society in general. The use of education for personal empowerment fits egalitarian images of enlightenment and emancipation.

> Education has also been seen as a means to social emancipation. It is through education that socialists and feminists, for instance, have come to know their everyday unhappinesses aren't the fault of personal inadequacies but are common experiences, shared by others, and produced by particular social arrangements.
> (Johnson 1983: 20)

Critical theorists and action researchers have encouraged individuals not only to acknowledge but also to challenge the forces that oppress them, and nowhere can this be seen more forcefully than in the writings of Paulo Freire. Freire worked among poor farmers in northern Brazil during the 1960s. In *The Pedagogy of the Oppressed* he said that they were trapped in a 'culture of silence' by being in an economic and social situation in which

critical awareness and responses were virtually impossible. What was needed was teaching as a partnership and dialogue through which people could 'achieve significance as people' (Freire 1972: 61).

> Conscientization is a permanent critical approach to reality in order to discover it and discover the myths that deceive us and help to maintain the oppressing dehumanizing structures.   (Freire 1976: 225)

In Britain, Freire's approach was adopted by Doreen Grant (1989) when she worked with parents and children in a Glasgow slum. Here she explains her emphasis on a dialogue between participants:

> In the context of under-achievement in school, the ultimate goal of such dialogue is an improvement in children's learning. But there are intermediate goals. Parents need to work through hidden fears and feelings which block successful involvement in their children's education. Positive feelings have to be strengthened in two areas: pride in their role as educators of their own children, and interest in widening their own knowledge base and personal scope. The parents are, therefore, the central participants with their own children, with each other and with professional educators.   (Grant 1989: 132)

At first glance this looks very similar to the British Labour government's emphasis on the need to improve parenting skills (including their skills as educators). Efforts to do this include the introduction of a National Institute for the Family to focus on family and parenting issues, encouraging local self-help groups, a freephone helpline for parents and an expanded role for health visitors in advising the parents of children up to 10 years old. A 'Sure Start' programme also brings together education, health and child development agencies to promote the welfare of pre-school children and their families.

> Sure Start will work with parents to help them promote the physical, intellectual and social development of their children. The programme will break down the barriers between the different approaches to the family and the child in the crucial early years, and will operate alongside our children and early years strategies.
> (David Blunkett, Education and Employment Secretary, quoted in the *Guardian* 24.7.1998)

This looks like a remarkably egalitarian approach but must be considered alongside claims that New Labour's emphasis on parenting skills and the family in general is focused on an interest in training individuals for responsible citizenship, rather than on tackling the social inequalities emphasized by Friere. In order to evaluate such claims it would be necessary to study Labour policies and draw on the communitarian ideas espoused by Etzioni and others (see Etzioni 1993; Demaine and Entwistee 1996).

Stop and think

➤ How could these debates about the role of parents be interpreted from different theoretical perspectives? (You might consider functionalist, Marxist and feminist perspectives.)

Equal access

A second interpretation of equal opportunities describes a co-operative system in which equal access to a high-quality education, with equal resources, is provided for all. The image is of a broad staircase to which all should have access; it is this sort of definition that supports the provision of comprehensive schools attended by children of all abilities and (in theory) all social backgrounds.

In the past this approach was seen as quite radical because of its emphasis on equal treatment for all, irrespective of social origins. Although still popular, in Britain it is limited in its application to social class inequalities by the existence of a diverse range of schools, and its success is more noticeable in policies relating to gender and racial issues. For example, British efforts to ensure that individuals are not discriminated against on the grounds of gender or race include the Sex Discrimination Act 1975 and Race Relations Act 1976. Proposals such as these, couched in terms of equal access, were able to gain more popular and political support than some of the more radical (egalitarian) action promoted by the Equal Opportunities Commission and Commission for Racial Equality. The 'discourse of derision' (described by Ball 1991) helped to generate a climate that was generally disparaging of anti-sexist and anti-racist ideas but could tolerate 'weaker' versions espousing equal access.

Legislation may therefore be more successful in generating less discriminatory practices than in changing public attitudes. It is more difficult to foster fundamental changes in public attitudes and the educational culture as a whole. In Britain there have been many other initiatives since the 1970s in which the aim of changing attitudes had to take a back seat to the achievement of equal access. For example, the Girls Into Science and Technology initiative aimed to encourage more girls to take science and technology courses, and had some success, but was less successful in challenging the high status often associated with 'male jobs' or the low status associated with 'female jobs' (Kelly 1981).

Competitive access

A third approach involves the idea of a competitive system in which only a few children can find a place on the narrow ladder to success. Superior educational provision is seen as being rationed according to ability, the less able being provided with the sort of education that will equip them for relatively undemanding working lives. This sort of approach has supported the provision of scholarships (or the 11+ examination for entry into British grammar schools) and rests on two assumptions – that intelligence can be identified at an early age and that basic aptitudes do not change considerably over the years.

We have already considered assessment by norm-referencing as a form of selection for places on this narrow ladder and the criticisms of the bipartite system that eventually led to the introduction of comprehensive schools. The next move is to consider the market-led form of competitive access associated with New Right political policies.

Parental choice

A long period of Conservative government in Britain (1979–97 when some other English-speaking countries also had New Right governments) brought a new emphasis on parental 'choice' and an uncritical approach to inequalities in education. From this perspective, more egalitarian approaches to equal opportunities are unrealistic and impractical. They are unrealistic because they do not accommodate our competitive natures, and they are impractical because they demand too much action from the state via the education system. Margaret Thatcher's criticisms of the 'nanny' state were supported by her conviction that the state, and therefore education, could and should do very little that interferes with individuals' private lives.

> The [Conservative] government views inequality as being helpful to incentives at both ends of the income distribution and does not regard gross inequalities in income and wealth as a problem.
>
> (Walker and Walker 1987)

Although similar to the third approach (competitive access) because of its emphasis on competition, this fourth approach no longer sees competition as being only between children but also between parents, who are expected to act in their children's best interests by sending them to the best possible schools. The ultimate aim is to provide a free-market education system in which only those high-quality schools that attract parents will survive. As schools and families become more self-sufficient, the pressures of education on the state should decrease and consumer-led education should lead to optimum consumer satisfaction:

> the 1944 Act was profoundly alien to Conservative philosophy. The idea that state officials should allocate children to different kinds of school, on the basis of the decisions of experts about what kind of occupation they are best fitted for, is part of the philosophy of socialism and the planned society. The Conservative tradition is surely one of individual families making decisions for themselves.   (Lynn 1970: 32)

Stop and think

> ➤ New Labour has also shifted from 'the philosophy of socialism and the planned society' towards an emphasis on parental choice. How did this shift take place?

Brown (1989: 42) called this perspective the 'ideology of parentocracy'. However, an emphasis on competitive access does not allow parents complete freedom of choice, or eliminate selectivity on the part of the school. Some popular schools had to adopt stringent criteria for the selection of pupils, and 'parental choice' raises uncertainties about who is really being selected in this sort of competitive system: is it parents or their children? Choice is also limited by practical and economic factors.

Inequality: biological determinism

Our earlier extract from Durkheim presented criticisms of the then orthodox view that educational achievement was entirely based on individual ability, and that this ability was determined at birth. However, Jensen (1969) and Eysenck (1971) claimed that educational attainment was heavily influenced by biology. Many (perhaps most) people regard themselves as naturally 'bright' or 'dim'! This sort of approach often appeals to our common-sense

assumptions and provides a simple explanation of, and justification for, social inequalities. However, sociology challenges common-sense assumptions and, although accepting that some aspects of educational ability may be biologically determined (for example, the abilities of autistic children), it is clear that sociologists would reject absolute notions of biological determinism.

Uniformity or diversity?

Although the theme of equal opportunities is well established in the sociology of education, debates about uniformity and diversity reflect a growing emphasis on policy issues. Many different types of school are currently provided in Britain, and the fragmentation of educational provision is in keeping with current postmodern theories about the fragmentation of society in general. In other words, it would be wrong to associate educational diversity only with government policies without also acknowledging other social trends. One of these trends is the common concern of politicians and academics from many perspectives that ever-increasing demands on the state leave it overburdened or overloaded. Efforts to reduce government responsibilities for education were in keeping with New Right policies favouring greater self-sufficiency and the 'rolling back of the state'. Yet, writing from a left-wing perspective, Habermas (1971a) observed the problems of an overburdened state and associated them with a legitimation crisis in capitalist societies. All of this might suggest that a shift towards the fragmentation of educational provision is inevitable but, again, it is not as simple as that.

In Britain during the 1980s and 1990s there were concurrent moves towards both diversification and uniformity in education. For example, the Education Reform Act 1988 included elements of diversity and uniformity: provisions for schools to apply for grant-maintained status and 'opt out' of local education authority (LEA) control; details concerning the reorganization of education within the Inner London Education Authority area after its abolition in 1990; limitations on the influence of LEAs on further and higher education; the introduction of a centrally determined national curriculum, and a requirement that all children in maintained schools should attend an act of collective worship.

The school curriculum was constrained by central directives and the educational power base shifted away from LEAs to central government control. In theory Conservative governments were commited to reducing state

Case study

A typology of admission policies

Model 1: Zoned comprehensive
In principle a mixed ability and mixed social intake, delayed specialization into vocational, academic or other tracks, a broad curriculum. There may be four ways of trying to achieve a mixed ability intake:

1   Children are obliged to attend their nearest secondary school and/or one linked to their feeder primary school. This works when local areas have a relatively mixed social composition.

2   Children are 'bussed' into zones in order to achieve a social balance. This has been an unpopular practice in some parts of the USA and has not been government policy in Britain (although there has been some bussing of students to integrated schools in Northern Ireland).

3   School catchment areas may be drawn up in ways that include a mixture of social and economic community types.

4   Parents may choose from a range of schools but their applications are judged by schools according to various selection criteria, in order to achieve a socio-economic balance.

Model 2: Open enrolment in comprehensive and partially comprehensive systems   This gives parents more freedom of choice and allows schools to compete with each other for students and, therefore, resources. However, an element of choice suggests diversification in the type of schools provided and this may contradict the principles of comprehensivization, which is based on the notion of equal entitlement to common learning experiences. In Britain diversifiacation has been encouraged without an emphasis on equality. Since 1997 the Labour government has allowed comprehensive schools to select up to 15 per cent of their pupils on the basis of ability and has retained grant maintained (now called 'foundation') schools and city technology colleges. This obviously promotes status differentiation between schools.

Model 3: Selection by ability
Children are selected according to an assessment of their abilities. This selection may be by examination, by teachers' recommendations or by a mixture of both. Germany has traditionally maintained a selective system for admission to its Gymnasien, Realschulen, Hauptschulen and Gesamtschulen. In Britain this is common in Northern Ireland, less common in England and Wales and quite rare in Scotland. Selection by ability does not allow for real parental choice, although some parents will make a great effort to ensure that their children go to a high status academic school.

(Adapted from Green, Wolf and Leney 1999)

Questions

1. *Consider arguments for and against the 'bussing' of students from one area to a school in another area.*

2. *Green, Wolf and Leney claim that, within the European Union, there has been growing pressure to move towards Model 2. Why might that be the case?*

3. *Do you favour one of the models? If so, why?*

---

involvement in education but in practice they increased central government control in many ways.

In theory the British Labour government elected in 1997 is committed to the decentralization of education in various ways, but in practice it has increased some forms of centralization. For example, a Labour government is inclined to share more powers with (mainly Labour-controlled) LEAs, and regional assemblies in Scotland, Northern Ireland and Wales may extend the distinctions between educational provision in the regions of the UK. However, the decision to introduce fees for students in higher education was taken by central government and had to be adjusted to suit four-year degrees in Scotland and three-year degrees elsewhere in the UK. The School Standards and Framework Act 1998 also included elements of diversity and uniformity: setting up a new framework of community, voluntary and foundation schools; supporting the phasing-out of assisted places by preventing LEAs from introducing similar, alternative schemes; setting up education action zones; establishing a code of practice defining the role of LEAs; providing central government with 'fresh start' powers to take over failing schools; empowering central government to take over failing LEAs; compulsory nutritional standards for school lunches; and limiting class sizes for infants to a maximum of 30.

The Labour government has maintained a national curriculum for state schoools despite its reservations when this was introduced by a Conservative government. Indeed, it now seems that opposition to the principle of a national curriculum comes mainly from Liberal Democrats, whose policies have traditionally maintained a strong emphasis on decentralization.

Stop and think

> What sort of assessment should be used in the national curriculum: descriptive or prescriptive, criterion-referencing or norm-referencing? (See p. 545.)

> Can a national curriculum be politically neutral?

Although some similarities between left-wing and right-wing policies have been identified, there are certain fundamental distinctions between their perspectives on education and you should at least start to consider how they relate to wider sociological theories and findings. Left-wing politicians (in both central and local government) are likely to emphasize stronger definitions of equality but are still faced with decisions about uniformity or diversity. An emphasis on egalitarianism and uniformity may lead to the state being overburdened by its responsibilities as it tries to reduce social inequalities, but an emphasis on egalitarianism and diversity may have inherent contradictions or, indeed, may just be a utopian dream.

Decisions about the segregation or integration of children within and between various schools also have to be made, and it is often difficult to identify the perspectives on which such decisions are based. For example, arguments about coeducational or single-sex education, schools for separate religious faiths, and the integration (in mainstream schools) or segregation of children with special educational needs are not clearly delineated along political lines. Pressure groups associated with any one of these issues could include members of all political hues and various sociological perspectives.

Stop and think

> Consider the arguments for and against (a) single-sex education (either within individual schools or via separate schools); (b) the granting of public finance to Muslim schools; (c) the integration of children with special educational needs within mainstream schools and the various ways in which this can be done.

Social groups and education

If you were asked to explain which social characteristics most influenced your educational experiences and achievements you would probably be rather baffled. Which was most significant: your gender, social class, ethnicity, religion, physical disability, geographical location? There is no simple answer; it is the same when sociologists study the relationships between social characteristics and education in general. The search for indicators of social class or ethnicity has to be combined with a sense of realism and an appreciation that individual experiences of social class or ethnicity may be very different. For these reasons, by the end of the twentieth century, sociological studies of education had become more concerned with the cumulative effects of social characteristics than with discrete social groupings. For example, the experiences of working-class black girls may be so different from the experiences of middle-class white girls that it would be unrealistic to suggest that 'gender' has had the greatest influence on their educational outcomes.

Why then are we providing an overview of findings concerned with the *separate* categories of social class, gender and ethnicity, especially when we have already considered them under other headings? This is partly in recognition of the sheer mass of data now available from studies in those three areas. Sociologists have also been able to provide valuable insights into the social labelling of individuals, continuous social trends (for example, the socio-economic origins of graduates) and dramatic shifts of direction (for example, gender differences in educational achievement). However, they are merely scraping the surface of the complex social influences on educational experiences.

Social class inequalities in Britain

We have already looked at conflict theorists' criticisms of the role of education in supporting social class inequalities and at functionalists' concern about the maintenance of a true meritocracy. Some interpretative/structural explanations of how inequalities have been legitimized and reproduced have also been considered. Different definitions of equal educational opportunities have also provided some understanding of how relative are ideas about inequality. It really is in the eye of the beholder!

More empirical data are therefore needed in order to evaluate the theories provided. In Britain, the 1950s and 1960s produced a series of official reports – e.g. Gurney-Dixon (CACE 1954); Crowther (CACE 1959); Newsom (CACE 1963); Robbins (1963); Plowden (CACE 1967) – which provided cumulative evidence of the relationship between father's occupation and educational outcomes. Concurrent support for official findings about social class inequalities was provided by sociologists (e.g. Bernstein 1971; Bourdieu and Passeron 1977; Bowles and Gintis 1976; Douglas 1964; Goldthorpe *et al.* 1980;

Halsey *et al.* 1961; 1980; Jackson and Marsden 1963; Rutter *et al.* 1979; Willis 1977) and by the end of the 1970s the evidence had become overwhelming. From the 1970s onwards we can see a long list of sociological findings in which the focus is more sharply placed on educational policy making, with an emphasis on social inequalities (e.g. Flude and Ahier 1974; Institute of Public Policy Research 1993; Karabel and Halsey 1977; Kogan 1975; Lodge and Blackstone 1982; McKenzie 1993; National Commission on Education 1993).

Yet, despite such activity and noticeable changes in class composition over the years, it is remarkable how consistent some findings still are. For example, the survey carried out for the Robbins Report (1963) found that 33 per cent of all respondents with fathers in the 'professional' group had a degree, compared with 1 per cent of respondents with fathers who were 'semi/unskilled manual' workers. Only 7 per cent with fathers in the 'professional' category had no qualification, compared with 65 per cent with fathers in the 'semi/unskilled manual' category (Robbins 1963: Table 2, p. 40). When these findings are compared with information for the year 2002 it seems that the imbalance remains (see Table 14.1 and Figure 14.6).

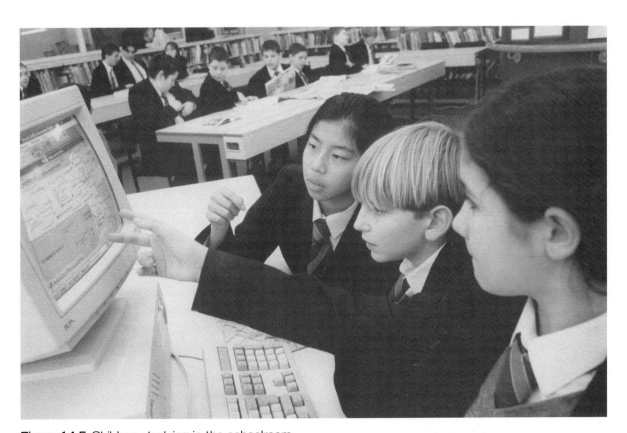

Figure 14.5 Children studying in the schoolroom
© Jacky Chapman/Photofusion

Table 14.1 GCSE attainment:[1] by parents' socio-economic classification,[2] 2002
England and Wales

	5 or more GCSE grades A*–C %	1–4 GCSE grades A*–C[3] %	5 or more GCSE grades D–G %	1–4 GCSE grades D–G %	None reported %	All %
Higher professional	77	13	6	..	3	100
Lower professional	64	21	11	2	2	100
Intermediate	52	25	17	2	4	100
Lower supervisory	35	30	27	4	4	100
Routine	32	32	25	5	6	100
Other	32	29	26	4	9	100

1 For pupils in year 11. Includes equivalent GNVQ qualifications achieved in year 11.
2 See Appendix, Part 1: National Statistics Socio-economic Classification.
3 Consists of those with 1–4 GCSE grades A*–C and any number of other grades.

Source: Social Trends 34, 2004, Table 3.9, p. 42

A closer look

Scott Lash has suggested that the production of information and communication goods has become 'the new axial principal of capital accumulation' (Beck *et al.* 1994: 129), replacing the production of heavy industry, and that the new middle class work as experts inside expert systems. As information and communication systems have become increasingly important in the workplace, those people with a low level of education and lacking in computer skills had started to be socially excluded.

Lash was impressed by theories about an underclass, arguing that at the turn of the century we had a 'two-thirds society', consisting of the expanded middle class, who worked in the information and communication sectors, the upgraded working class, who had adapted to the shift from manufacturing to information production, and those who had been downgraded from the classical (Marxist) proletariat to become the new underclass.

Question

1. *Do you agree with the claim that education and skills in information technology have replaced other aspects of production (e.g. work in heavy industry) as the key influence on social class?*

It has long been claimed that children from working-class families are less willing to 'defer gratification' and want to start earning a wage as soon as possible rather than stay longer in education (see Bourdieu's comments on social capital on p. 554). Yet the route to higher education has for a long time been effectively blocked for some by the lack of LEA grants for A-level students. Sociologists even observed a tendency to split young people into 'sheep and goats', with some being able to take the route to a high-status qualification, others resigning themselves to low-grade training for low-status jobs or long-term unemployment.

Some sociologists (e.g. Bourdieu) have suggested that the role of education is not simply to serve the economy by imparting knowledge but to provide a filtering or screening device by enabling employers to identify individuals with suitable personal characteristics (such as motivation, reliability and attitudes towards authority). Critics of this hypothesis argue that it tends to neglect the importance of formal qualifications; yet most educationalists are aware that, like money, qualifications tend to be devalued as more people have them (credential inflation) and employers regard personal characteristics (often called 'graduateness') as particularly important when selecting from many equally qualified job applicants.

Shortly after the election of the Labour government in 1997 a report called 'Learning Works' (the Kennedy Report, published by the Committee On Widening Participation in Further Education) addressed some of these problems and pointed to serious inequities between the funding of further and higher education. It argued that, although they generally came from more affluent backgrounds than other students, students in higher education received more of taxpayers' money and could also achieve a higher income after graduation. This point was later supported by the Report of the National Committee of Inquiry into Higher Education (Dearing 1998) and the

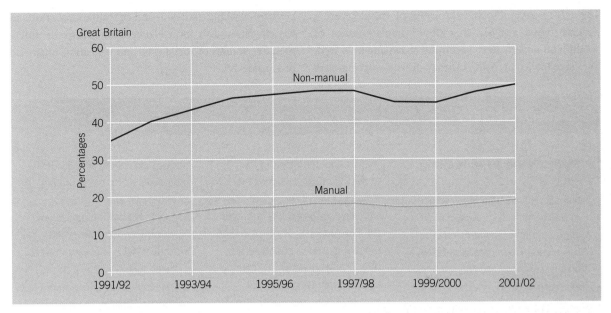

Figure 14.6 Participation rates in higher education: by social class[1], Great Britain
1 See Appendix, Part 3: Social class.
Source: Social Trends 34 2004, Figure 3.13, p. 45

government paper, 'The Learning Age: A Renaissance for a New Britain' (1998). The government therefore saw its effort to widen access to further education (including various initiatives for tackling literacy and numeracy problems) and lifelong learning in general as in keeping with its commitment to lessening social inequalities.

Education in Britain has never been widely based on egalitarian ideals. Under recent governments some schools have been able to thrive due to their popularity with parents and their position in published league tables. A growing dependence on fund-raising by parents for school resources also means that where a large proportion of pupils come from affluent backgrounds the school is more likely to prosper. Some schools in less affluent areas have become what are popularly known as 'sink' schools (i.e. unable to afford proper maintenance and with facilities that are barely adequate), with an intake of children whose parents cannot compete in a market system. Success in a market system has therefore relied more heavily on family background than did even the more moderate forms of competitive access.

This diversity of provision obviously meant a diversity of educational experiences. The proportion of children attending non-maintained schools increased from the 1970s to the 1990s (from 5 per cent in 1975/76 to 7 per cent in 1991/92: *Social Trends* 1994) but Conservative governments' support for private education was balanced by a lack of support for social provision at the other extreme. The 1980 Education Act introduced the Assisted Places Scheme, in order to support some children in private schools, but the same Act withdrew the statutory duty of LEAs to provide school dinners and milk. In contrast, we can see that since 1997 a Labour government has tried to reverse these trends: for example, the School Standards and Framework Act 1998 ended assisted places, set nutritional standards for school dinners, and introduced the fresh start programme and education action zones.

We have seen how unequal educational opportunities can be influenced by the dominant political ideology, but what about the reactions of working-class children to educational inequalities? Sociologists (e.g. Mac an Ghaill

1996: 171) have observed the irony of the decentring of class-based analysis at a time when extremes of wealth and poverty were becoming increasing polarized. We have looked at Willis's theory of why working-class boys got working-class jobs and at egalitarians' efforts to use education as a form of liberation. However, Interpretative studies of social class and education must also be considered.

Case study

Resistance to schooling

McFadden's analysis of resistance to school indicates how social class (and other social inequalities) can be studied in greater depth by linking structural and interpretative approaches.

The crucial point though – and one that brings questions of class and structure back into the debate – is that the rejection of the offers and advantages or schooling has differential class consequences. Aggleton (1987) found that middle-class students who resist schooling are advantaged in the labour market in general terms. The labour market defines class and advantage in the clearest sense (Weiss 1990). At a time of high youth unemployment, all of Aggleton's middle-class resisters were in employment six years after his study. They were involved either in service industries or in industries related to symbolic production and the arts. The available evidence suggests that resistance has differential racial, ethnic and gender consequences as well.

While middle-class resisters may still be advantaged, working-class students who comply may still be disadvantaged.

Willis's counter image to that of the voluntary walk onto the shopfloor. i.e. of 'Armies of kids' who have absorbed 'the rubric of self-development, satisfaction and interest in work', 'equipped with their "self-concepts" . . . fighting to enter the few meaningful jobs available, and masses of employers . . . struggling to press them into meaningless work' is as powerful and applicable an image now as it was then.

McFadden notes that Willis stressed the importance of language as one of the 'underworkings' supporting the continuity of social structures. Bernstein also regarded it as very important.

Essentially, Bernstein's work shows how power articulates through discursive practices and that schools, through their pedagogic practices – largely but not exclusively rooted in language – can limit the access of certain groups to the language of power and symbolic control.

Yet McFadden is not entirely pessimistic about educational constraints and feels that structuration theory (Giddens 1984) provides the conceptual tools needed to deconstruct such power relationships.

If, for example, gender/sexual and racial norms of behaviour are said to be reproduced through the actions of individuals, then there exists the possibility of anti-sexist and anti-racist actions, because no matter how narrow the options facing the individual there is always choice.

Taken together with Giddens' formulations about the nature of society and change, Bernstein's work enables us to see the way that students can be positioned within classroom discourse as either producers or passive receptors of knowledge. It also helps to illustrate how the pedagogic device can 'naturalize' state of affairs, silencing students' voices and allowing no access to the discourse relaying power. Without access to the means of knowledge production no means is available to change or challenge the 'symbolic boundaries regulating classroom practice' (Singh 1993: 40).

(McFadden 1996: 297–306)

Questions

1. Can you think of any examples of how in educational settings power (a) 'articulates through discursive practices', and (b) through 'pedagogic practices'? Think of your own educational experiences here.

2. How can students be 'producers' of knowledge, rather than 'passive receptors'? Again, relate to subjects you have studied and courses you have followed.

Gender differences in British education

There has been an increasing influence from feminist and anti-sexist approaches since the 1970s. Although many feminists will argue that not enough progress has been made, research into gender inequalities does seem to have had a greater influence on education policies than has research into social class inequalities. Apparently policy makers were prepared to accept stronger definitions of gender equality than of social class equality.

The Sex Discrimination Act 1975 can be clearly associated with an equal access approach to equal educational opportunities. It prohibited sex discrimination in admission to schools, in the appointment of teachers (with some exceptions for single-sex schools) and in careers advice. It also stipulated that neither boys nor girls should be refused access to 'any courses, facilities or other benefits provided solely on the grounds of their sex'. The national curriculum also emphasized equal access by tackling the problem of gendered subject choice – the tendency for girls to favour languages and boys to favour science subjects (except for biology, which has been more popular with girls).

Figure 14.7 The classroom jungle or catering for individualism?
© Getty/Catherine Ledner

A stronger, egalitarian approach to equal opportunities places more emphasis on equality of outcomes. Using this approach it is important not only to look at access but also to see whether males and females are equally represented at all levels of educational achievement. Even applying this sort of definition there are indications that, in education at least, gender inequalities are being transformed.

Tests of 7-year-olds have, since 1992, shown that girls achieve better grades than boys in English, maths, science and technology (*Social Trends* 1994: Chart 3.16). However, these findings did not come as a surprise to many educationalists. It had long been claimed that, in general, girls mature at an earlier age than boys and therefore achieve more during their early years at school. Boys have been expected to catch up at a later age. Girls often had to get better results than boys to 'pass' a norm-referenced 11+ examination. The problem with the 'catch-up' argument is that girls now achieve better results at the age of 16, and by 1995 had overtaken boys in A levels and Scottish Highers.

Since the mid-1970s more girls than boys have been achieving five or more GCSE passes in grades A to C (or SCE Standard Grades, or O-level grades A to C, or CSE grade 1). In 2004, 63.3 per cent of girls and 54.9 of boys in the UK achieved grades A* to C in their GCSEs and 23.7 per cent of girls and 21 per cent of boys achieved A grades in their A levels. This reflects a pattern that has lasted for over 10 years (see Figures 14.8 and 14.9).

These inequalities among school leavers have now made their way into further education (FE) and higher education (HE). Between 1970/71 and 2001/2 the number of students taking FE courses increased dramatically and female students accounted for most of that increase (see Table 14.2). By 1990/91 there were more females in both part-time and full-time courses.

The gender distribution of higher education students is also changing, although not quite so dramatically at the highest levels. Between 1970/71 and 1995/96 the number of students enrolling on HE courses more than trebled, with one in three young people entering HE in 1995/96 compared with one in twenty in the early 1960s. In 1970/71 there were twice as many male students as female students in HE, but by 2001/2 there were more females.

It is also interesting to note that the increased access of women to higher education is not just a British phenomenon. In the member states of the European Union the percentage of higher education students who were female increased overall from 46 per cent in 1985 to 50 per

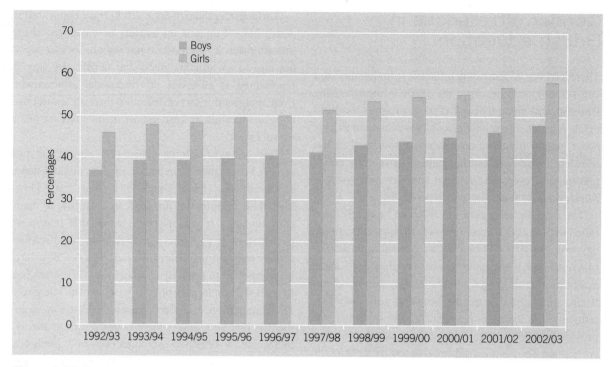

Figure 14.8 Percentage of pupils aged 15 achieving 5 or more GCSEs at grades A* to C, England, 1992/93 to 2002/03

Source: www.dfes.gov.uk, Chart A

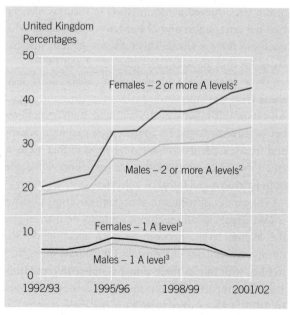

Figure 14.9 Achievement at GCSE A level[1] or equivalent, United Kingdom

1 2 As levels count as 1 A level pass. Data from 2000/01 are not on the same basis as earlier years, and data prior to 1995/96 refer to school pupils only.

2 Equivalent to 3 or more Highers.

3 Equivalent to 1 or 2 Highers. Includes those with 1.5 A levels.

Source: *Social Trends 34*: 2004, Figure 3.14, p. 45

cent in 1994, with rates varying in different countries (*Eurostat Yearbook 1996*: 99). At the same time female participation in higher education in the UK increased from 45 per cent to 50 per cent, in the USA it increased from 25 per cent to 55 per cent and in Canada it increased from 49 per cent to 51 per cent.

These developments seem rather surprising to sociologists, who have tended to assume that 'gender' inequalities really meant 'female' disadvantage. So what do we now mean by 'gender inequalities' in education and are boys now the disadvantaged ones? Developments must be set into a wider context by considering the educational achievements of all ages, and not just of the rising generation. In 2003, 13 per cent of men and 16 per cent of women of working age in Britain had no educational qualifications (see Table 14.3). It is taking a long time for the improved performance of female school leavers to make an impact on the dispersion of qualifications among the whole population.

The impact of these changes on gender inequalities in general will also be moderated by access to, and conditions in, the workplace; sociologists have found that there is no perfect link between educational achievement

Table 14.2 Students[1] in further and higher education: by type of course and sex

United Kingdom Thousands

	Males				Females			
	1970/71	1980/81	1990/91	2001/02	1970/71	1980/81	1990/91	2001/02
Further education[2]								
Full-time	116	154	219	569	95	196	261	559
Part-time	891	697	768	1,665	630	624	986	2,562
All further education	1,007	851	987	2,234	725	820	1,247	3,121
Higher education[2]								
Undergraduate								
Full-time	241	277	345	519	173	196	319	620
Part-time	127	176	193	263	19	71	148	412
Postgraduate								
Full-time	33	41	50	94	10	21	34	93
Part-time	15	32	50	133	3	13	36	153
All higher education[3]	416	526	638	1,009	205	301	537	1,279

1 Home and overseas students.
2 See Appendix, Part 3: Stages of education.
3 Figures for 2001/02 include a number of higher education students for which details are not available by level.

Source: Social Trends 34 2004, Table 3.11, p. 44

Table 14.3 Highest qualification held:[1] by sex and ethnic group, 2003[2]

Great Britain

	Degree or equivalent %	Higher education qualification[3] %	GCE A level or equivalent %	GCSE grades A*–C or equivalent %	Other qualification %	No qualification %	All %
Males							
White	18	8	31	18	12	13	100
Mixed	14	7	21	22	17	17	100
Asian or Asian British	20	6	17	11	24	20	100
Black or Black British	19	7	21	16	23	12	100
Chinese	29	4	19	9	28	10	100
Other ethnic group[4]	23	6	11	7	36	18	100
All	18	8	29	17	14	13	100
Females							
White	15	10	18	27	13	16	100
Mixed	21	9	17	21	15	17	100
Asian or Asian British	14	6	13	17	25	24	100
Black or Black British	13	12	16	21	24	13	100
Chinese	26	9	14	10	30	11	100
Other ethnic group[4]	14	9	11	10	34	22	100
All	15	10	18	26	14	16	100

1 Males aged 16 to 64, females aged 16 to 59.
2 At spring. These estimates are not seasonally adjusted and have not been adjusted to take account of the Census 2001 results. See Appendix, Part 4: LFS reweighting.
3 Below degree level.
4 Includes those who did not state their ethnic group.

Source: Social Trends 34 2004, Table 3.17, p. 47

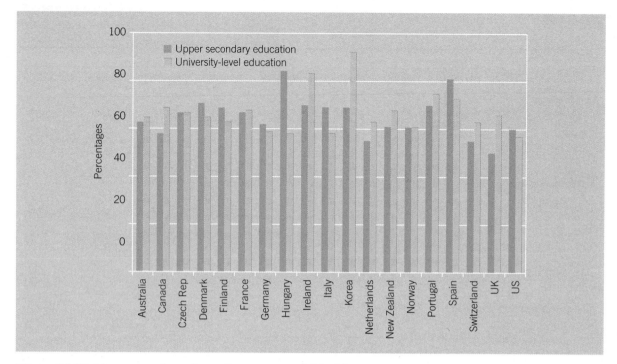

Figure 14.10 Mean annual earnings of women aged 30–44 as a percentage of earnings of men, by level of educational attainment, international comparisons (2001)
Source: www.dfes.gov.uk

and advancement in employment. This can be seen in the average annual earnings of women as a percentage of the earnings of men (see Figure 14.10). In most countries the gap in earnings narrows with increasing educational attainment, but in some it widens. The extent of the problem can be illustrated if we look at occupations in the field of education. Gender inequalities in the teaching hierarchy are long established, although there have been some improvements over time. For example in 1999 women made up over 70 per cent of the teaching force overall, and over 80 per cent of the teaching force in primary schools. Yet 58.5 per cent of primary head-teachers and 27.8 per cent of secondary headteachers were female. These figures (Hutchings, 2002) represent a gradual increase over time.

The impact of changes in educational achievement will also be influenced by the way that qualifications are dispersed between subject areas. The national curriculum has encouraged pupils to make non-gendered subject choices by obliging pupils to take English and another language (not popular among boys), maths and a science (not popular among girls) in their examinations at the age of 16. Some educationalists feel that changes in subject choice have still been rather slow; as, for example, biology is still a particularly popular science with girls and there are gender-based choices in technical subjects.

At A level (or Scottish Highers) students have more freedom to choose favoured subjects and gendered patterns still emerge.

The major problem associated with gendered subject choice is that some subjects are awarded higher status than others, and that the high-status subjects (maths, science and some technologies) are those favoured by boys. This means that, although females are achieving more qualifications, some of their qualifications are not awarded similar recognition to the fewer qualifications achieved by males. Those 'technologies' that are favoured by females, such as textiles and home economics, tend to be unfavourably compared with 'male' technologies, such as electronics and engineering. Educational achievements are given a social rather than an individual construction: the 'male' is regarded as the norm to which female achievements are compared. For example, keyboard skills assumed greater importance when they were associated with computers rather than secretarial work. Yet, as more women gained word-processing skills, that particular application of information technology also lost its relative status.

Although boys have tended to favour maths and science subjects and girls have favoured arts subjects, there have been some changes in subject choice at A level standard. Since 1970 an increasing number of

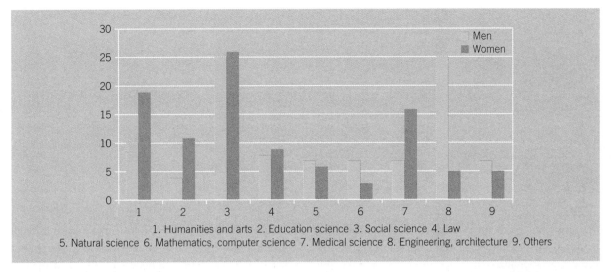

Figure 14.11 Fields of education chosen by students in tertiary education, by gender, 1997/8
Source: Eurostat Yearbook 2001

girls have chosen to take A levels in biology and maths (Statham *et al.* 1991: 151). However, these do not reflect the spread of subject areas or links with further and higher education which can be seen when we look at a summary of findings from countries in the European Union (Figure 14.11).

Gaby Weiner's (1985) summary of relevant gender-related strategies may provide a useful overall view of changes in the relationship between gender and education and how they relate to theories about equal opportunities. The 'equal opportunities/girl-friendly' approach is similar to what we have described as an equal-access approach to equal opportunities and reflects a fairly moderate interpretation of equal opportunities. This fits those government policies aiming to discourage gendered subject choice. By comparison, the 'anti-sexist/girl-centred' approach has a stronger egalitarian outlook and has secured less government support.

Despite the statistical data illustrating changes in achievement, structural approaches have to be supplemented by interpretative approaches to provide a comprehensive understanding of the nature of gender differentiation in education. For example, images of women and girls in textbooks and other educational resources have been monitored in order to challenge the normalization of stereotypes. Statham (1986) found that, when one mother tried to make all her own changes to a book her 5-year-old son was reading, she met an angry response.

In fact he was a bit upset when I went through a book which has a boy and girl in very traditional roles, and changed all the he's to she's and the she's to he's. When I first started doing that, he was inclined to say 'you don't like boys, you only like girls'. I had to explain that that wasn't true at all, it's just that there's not enough written about girls.

(Statham 1986: 46, 67, cited in Giddens 1989)

Nilsen (1975) analyzed 58 award-winning children's picture books and found that 21 of them included a picture of a woman in the home, while men were pictured at work or in various adventures, their image being associated with the public world of work and outside the home. She christened this domesticated representation of women the 'cult of the apron'. Yet, where is the 'cult of the apron' today? Although there is no room for complacency (and sexist images are still common in the wider media) continuous monitoring of resources by sociologists and educationalists has helped to promote more positive images of women in school textbooks.

Feminist studies have also raised awareness of sexism in classroom interaction and an understanding of how girls and women perceive themselves in education. For example, Stanworth (1983) and many others observed that boys tended to demand, and get, more of the teacher's attention in class and that girls tended to have unrealistic ideas about their own capabilities. Boys tended to over-estimate their own capabilities while girls tended to underestimate their capabilities.

Lees (1986) studied the attitudes of 15–16-year-old girls, from various social class and ethnic backgrounds, in three London schools. Her interpretative approach elicited

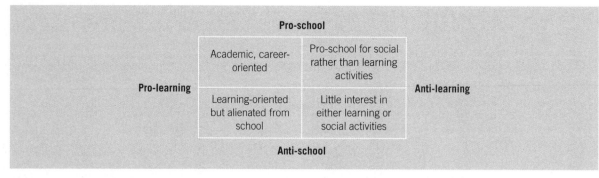

Figure 14.12 Girls' attitudes to schooling

the terms on which they described their sexuality and managed their social world and helped to explain how some girls rationalized their lack of achievement. Yet this now rather dated research still offers a possible model for the analysis of girls' achievements. She categorized the main attitudes of the girls she studied into four main groups (see Figure 14.12).

Stop and think

➤ What factors could influence pupils (female or male) to adopt each of the four types of attitude described in Figure 14.12?

➤ How useful would Lees' model (Figure 14.12) be for the study of boys' attitudes to schooling? See the findings by Willis (1977) and Nayak (2003) about the attitudes of anti-school sub-cultures of working-class boys (pp. 555–6).

The growing numbers of mature women students since the 1970s (see R. Edwards 1993: 6) has also meant that sociologists have become more absorbed in the educational experiences of women as well as girls. Using feminist methods this research has often been used as a source of empowerment for the subjects rather than straightforward academic analysis. For example, the Taking Liberties Collective (1989) published accounts of the educational experiences of over 50 women, recording how they had encountered 'oppression in men's education'. One of the themes emerging from this and other studies (e.g. Pascall and Cox 1993) is that mature women have perceived education as playing a dual role: their schools encouraging domesticity and low-status jobs, but further and higher education providing an escape route from traditional roles and into more rewarding jobs.

This emphasis on the empowerment of women through education has tended to dominate feminist research, but what of the gendered experiences of boys and men in education, and why are they falling behind in their educational achievements? Research into the construction of masculinity (e.g. Morgan 1992; Roper and Tosh 1991) has opened up new avenues for the sociology of education. In *Boys Don't Cry*, Askew and Ross (1988) studied the role of schools in the construction of masculinity, classroom dynamics, sexism in school structure and organization and women teachers' experiences. They argued that boys were victims of their own socialization, which involved learning to be aggressive and attaching little importance to academic discourse. Problems were identified in some boys' schools, where it was claimed that a traditional image of masculinity was reinforced by an authoritarian ethos. Askew and Ross also suggested strategies for working with boys and for in-service work with teachers, including the use of workshops, the adoption of anti-sexist initiatives and strategies for persuading boys to talk more openly and honestly. Arnot *et al.* (1997) also addressed these themes during a ten-year (1984–94) study of educational reforms and gender equality in schools.

> A number of new areas of concern relating to equality issues emerged during the project. One of the most common has pointed to an apparent loss of motivation among working class and black boys. It was claimed time and time again that as traditional areas of male employment have collapsed or altered, working class (and/or black) male students now tend not to see themselves as benefiting academically or vocationally from schooling. They appear to be less motivated than girls, therefore, and/or alienated from the classroom. Further, while working class boys seem increasingly to stay on into the sixth form, they tend to study for vocational qualifications such as GNVQ (rather than A levels). (Arnot *et al.* 1997: 143)

A closer look

Yes he can!

More research projects and strategies for tackling boys' achievement have emerged since the 1990s. For example, in July 2003 OfSTED published two reports on boys' achievement: 'Yes he can: Schools where boys write well' (HMI 505) and 'Boys' achievement in secondary schools' (HMI 1659). Another project was undertaken by researchers at Homerton College, Cambridge, who worked with over 60 schools in England for the 'Raising Boys' Achievement Project'. In August 2003 the Homerton researchers published their interim report in which they identified and evaluated strategies which were particularly helping to motivate boys. All of these reports acknowledged that improving boys' achievements is a complex matter, including a range of factors. The two Ofsted reports described the following characteristics exhibited by schools that had been successful in raising boys' attainment and writing skills.

➤ A positive learning culture that stimulates high standards, engages boys' interests, and insists on good behaviour. High expectations for all pupils with value placed on diversity of style and approach.

➤ Good teaching and learning – the Key Stage 3 National Strategy has been a catalyst for developments in these respects. Teachers are knowledgeable and enthusiastic about language with effective pastoral systems and extra-curricular activities.

➤ Good classroom management – i.e. behaviour was well managed, discipline was fair and praise was used frequently.

➤ Tracking and supporting boys' performance through good use of data and assessment which particularly values their work and always offers them clear advice on how to improve.

➤ Strategies focusing on literacy, which provides intensive support for reading, writing and literacy across the curriculum with careful selection of materials which appeal to boys. To improve writing, pupils are encouraged to write frequently and at length with a balance between support and independence.

(www.standards.dfee.gov.uk/genderandachievement/
understanding/faqs)

Some remaining problems and policies regarding gender and education centre around the theme of uniformity and diversity. For example, we have already briefly considered the question of whether or not education should be coeducational, but this debate is too large to be probed in depth.

Debates about uniformity and diversity have also encompassed concerns about how attitudes to sexuality are influenced by education. Clause 28 of the Local Government Act 1988 forbade local authorities from promoting the 'teaching in any maintained schools on the acceptability of homosexuality as a pretended family relationship'. Critics argued that this could encourage homophobia and the presentation of heterosexuality as a norm from which individuals must not deviate. Yet it was over 14 years before the clause was withdrawn. Not only does this also have implications for the social construction of knowledge but also interpretative sociologists have generated accounts of the experiences of homosexuals in academic environments. For example, Trenchard and Warren (1984) found individuals who had been expelled or referred to a psychiatrist when they 'came out'. Jones and Mahony (1989) provided an analysis of the historical background to this debate, including criticisms of the sociology of education for the way it had ignored the promotion of heterosexuality in the past. In 1998 findings were published from the first survey of homophobia in schools (commissioned by Stonewall and the Terrence Higgins Trust). Clause 28 seemed to have had some impact as, of about 1,000 schools taking part in the survey, only a quarter said that their teachers mentioned sexuality when talking about equal opportunities. More than 80 per cent of schools taking part reported that verbal bullying was common and more than 60 per cent of the respondents felt that schools were an appropriate place for providing information about homosexuality.

The study of gender and education is not only wide-ranging and confusing but also quite fascinating when we look at findings about the achievements of males and females. When the cumulative effects of social inequalities are considered we shall get a clearer impression of current debates within the sociology of education.

Ethnicity and education in Britain

'Ethnicity' and 'race' are confusing concepts. In general, too many studies of education and race could be justifiably accused of gross simplification because they

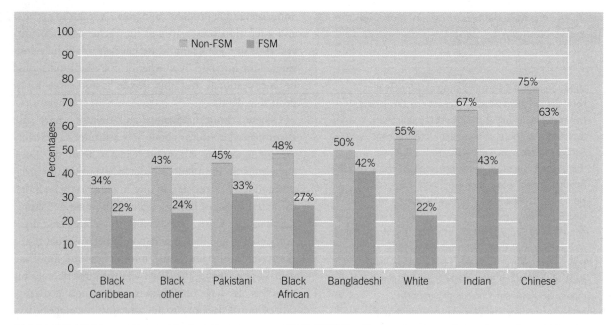

Figure 14.13 Proportion achieving five or more A*–C GCSEs, free school meals and non-free school meals, 2002
Source: National Pupil Database version 2, in Bhattacharyya, Ison and Blair, 2003, Figure 5, p. 12

have forced individuals into inappropriate, homogeneous categories and thus misrepresented the unique nature of our ethnic backgrounds. Despite the wide range of ethnic backgrounds in Britain, educational research has often categorized individuals into three main, and largely incomprehensible, groups – 'West Indian', 'Asian' and 'other'. It is easy to see why this happened. Sociologists study group behaviour and are, by the nature of their subject, obliged to assign individuals into groups. They are also concerned about inequality in education and make such distinctions in order to identify and measure inequality.

Sociologists have also labelled people as 'black' or 'white' in order to identify racism in education as being primarily based on skin colour, rather than cultural or ethnic identity. However, this raises the possibility that sociologists themselves could be accused of racism because of their tendency to use the categorization of 'black' to override any other personal characteristic and to label black children (and 'West Indian' children in particular) negatively as 'under-achievers'.

Research into ethnicity and education is therefore fraught with difficulties, first because of the problem of finding suitable ways of labelling groups; second, because there is a temptation to generalize from small samples; and third, because an emphasis on statistical data often means that qualitative differences in educational experiences are ignored. These reservations help

to explain why figures relating to various ethnic groups have been included in official, national statistics on education only since 1990–91.

We are left then with the central question: are educational outcomes most influenced by social class, gender, ethnicity or other factors?

In view of Britain's history of racial discrimination and prejudice we could reasonably ask whether ethnicity affects social class and, if so, whether research that intends to study 'ethnicity' is actually studying social class. For example, continuous research into school leavers for both the Rampton Report (1981) and Swann Report (1985) was carried out in five inner-city LEA areas where the educational attainment of every ethnic group in the study was lower than the national average. In their more recent research Bhattacharyya, Ison and Blair (2003) analyzed pupils by splitting them into eight ethnic categories and considering whether or not they were receiving free school meals (FSM, see Figure 14.13). They noted that

These differences may yet be attributable to socio-economic differences: the broad non-FSM category captures a wide range of socio-economic status and income which is not differentiated. Ethnic groups will vary in the extent of this range, with some ethnic groups containing many more people of higher incomes. However, socio-economic factors are not the sole explanation for lower attainment, as not all children from low-income families have low attainment at GCSE. For example, Chinese children eligible for free school meals, whilst a small group, are more likely to achieve five or more GCSEs than all other ethnic groups, except Indian non-FSM pupils.

(Bhattacharyya, Ison and Blair 2003: 11)

This obviously leads us to ask whether there were differences in the social class background of 'West Indian', 'Asian' and 'other' children, and some evidence of this was provided in 1986 by Eggleston *et al.* According to these findings 87 per cent of children from 'Afro-Caribbean' backgrounds had fathers who were manual workers, compared with 73 per cent of 'Asian' children and 69 per cent of 'white' children. This might suggest that some children were more disadvantaged by social class but, yet again, we encounter the problem of labelling children.

In 1985 the first national study (of England and Wales: Drew and Gray 1989) of the achievements of young black people found that the performance of 'Afro-Caribbeans' was better than in earlier studies, but still concluded that the results of this group had changed little between 1972 and 1985. However, the study went further by considering the relative influences of ethnicity, social class and gender. Drew and Gray (1989) found that social class explained more variation in examination performance than did ethnic group or gender, but the combined effects of social class, gender and ethnicity still left the larger part of the variation in performance unexplained. This suggested that other, unknown, factors were also significant.

More recently, Bhattacharyya, Ison and Blair (2003) considered, not only free school meals but also factors such as having English as a second language, special educational needs, children of refugees and asylum seekers, school exclusions, poverty, parental or pupil illness, racial abuse or harassment, lack of role models, unfamiliarity with the workings of the education system, 'teaching based on unfamiliar cultural norms, histories and points of reference' (2003: 22). They also considered the particular problems of traveller and gypsy/Roma pupils.

We have seen that girls have moved ahead of boys in their educational achievements and this raises questions about the comparative influences of gender and ethnicity. Driver (1980) studied five multiracial schools and found that 'West Indian' girls did better than 'West Indian' boys but that, among 'whites', boys did better than girls. It was also found that in these five schools 'West Indian' children performed better in their 16+ examinations than did 'whites'. This raised the possibility that individual school factors might have a significant influence on educational outcomes.

When we look at the working age population as a whole we can see that there are marked variations according to ethnic groupings and that (see Table 14.3) only in the 'Mixed' ethnic group were there more female than male graduates. There were the same or higher percentages of women as men with no qualifications, showing that the recent improvements in female attainment have not yet tipped the balance created by lower female attainment in the past.

The achievements of black women have been established long enough to feed through to statistics covering a wide age range. It is therefore reasonable to ask if there are more developments waiting to make a similar impact. For example, although Table 14.3 described the high proportion of working-age women in the Asian or Asian British group in 2003 without any qualifications, it is likely that the proportion will decline as younger generations have more impact over the years. Bhattacharyya, Ison and Blair (2003: 12) found in 2002 that more girls than boys achieved five or more A* to C grade GCSEs in *every* ethnic group.

This structural approach obviously raises various questions that can be investigated only by interpretative research. For example, Singh-Raud (1997) interviewed nine Asian girls aged 14–18 (three Muslims, three Sikhs and three Hindus) and reported on their diverse and conflicting views on education. He also (1998) surveyed 202 female Asian undergraduates (51 Sikhs, 52 Hindus and 99 Muslims) and found that they were increasingly asserting their rights to have a higher education. This was particularly evident among Muslim women. Parker-Jenkins *et al.* (1997) interviewed 100 Muslim women aged 16 to 25 in order to chart their career destinations and experiences. The title of their report, 'Trying Twice as Hard to Succeed', reflects some of their findings, but they also found that an apparently common religious identity contained diverse views and wide-ranging multicultural, multiracial and multilingual groupings. Some women said that religious leaders had told their parents not to let them attend university, while one woman reported that her parents had supported her studies because of the emphasis on education in the Qur'an. Again we can see the limitations of statistical data in helping us to develop a deeper understanding of educational experiences.

Sociologists have also taken an interest in the achievements of various ethnic groups at the top end of education, in further education and higher education. Research during the 1980s seemed to confirm the findings about

A closer look

Unsung success of Chinese pupils

Chinese pupils outperform their classmates in British schools because education and the spirit of competition are valued highly in the home, according to research. A two-year study of 80 British-Chinese boys and girls, 30 parents and 30 teachers found that studying hard was a way of life for youngsters and they were not ashamed to admit it. However, some teachers interpreted this as repression by pushy parents and believed Chinese pupils to be over-diligent and too quiet. While they perceived them as 'nice and polite' and 'hard-working' they also considered them 'withdrawn' and 'quiet'. Teachers were particularly negative about Chinese girls, deeming them too compliant.

The study, by Dr Becky Francis and Dr Louise Archer, of London Metropolitan University, found little attention was being given to Chinese pupils and their remarkable achievements. Chinese pupils outperform every other ethnic group in tests and exams, including the English at English. At GCSE 74.6 per cent achieved at least five A* to C grades in 2003, compared with a national average of 50.7 per cent. In Key Stage 2 tests, 83 per cent of Chinese children gained the benchmark level 4, compared with 78 per cent of Indian and 75 per cent of white pupils.

The study found that a key factor underpinning their success was the high value they placed on education. This was regarded as a defining aspect of British-Chinese identity and occurred irrespective of pupils' social class and gender. One pupil described it as 'school first, life after', while a parent said education was 'a way of life'. Chinese families also tended to compete against each other and this added greater impetus for academic success.

(Dorothy Lepkowska, 'Unsung success of Chinese pupils', *Times Educational Supplement* 27.8.2004).

Question

1. *Discuss the finding that some teachers were critical of their high achieving Chinese-British pupils.*

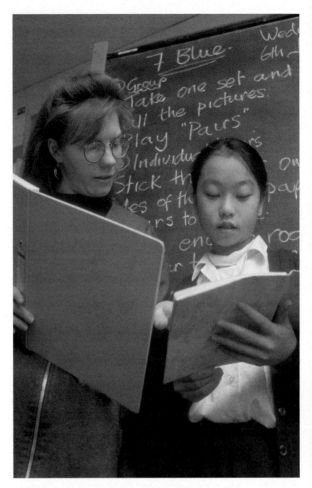

Figure 14.14 The value of education
© Jacky Chapman/Photofusion

education course than was general for the whole population. This finding has been supported by more recent research, which seems to strongly contradict earlier negative images of the achievements of 'West Indians' or 'Afro-Caribbeans' (see Table 14.3).

In 1994 the Policy Studies Institute published its findings about the different rates of entry of ethnic minorities into higher education in 1992. It considered the percentages of successful applicants from various groups and found radical differences in access to universities and polytechnics. When looking only at success in access to universities it was found that 'Chinese' and 'black African' applicants were over-represented compared with their presence in the population as a whole. 'Black Caribbeans' and 'Bangladeshis' were under-represented compared with their presence in the population as a whole. When looking only at success in access to polytechnics it was found that 'black Caribbeans' were over-represented compared with their presence in the population as a whole. However, the Policy Studies Institute (1994) indicated that

'West Indian' under-achievement in schools. Craft and Craft (1983) found that, irrespective of social class, 'West Indians' were under-represented in further and higher education. The Swann Report (1985) found that 1 per cent of 'West Indians', 4 per cent of 'Indians', 4 per cent of 'Asians' and 4 per cent of 'others' went to university. However, the report also found that a larger percentage of 'Asians' and 'West Indians' took some sort of further a simplistic cause/effect interpretation based on ethnic categorization is to be avoided, for example a larger proportion of 'black Caribbeans' applied for access to highly competitive courses (such as medicine and law) and to courses in a relatively small number of universities near to their homes. This meant that competition for places was not evenly spread. The socio-economic inequalities highlighted in the study fell disproportionately on certain ethnic minority groups.

Again we can see that analysis based only on statistical data is very limited. To achieve any sort of depth of understanding we must also apply an interpretative approach. For example, it is reasonable to ask whether language problems might inhibit the achievements of some children. Many children of 'Asian' origin appear to have thrived in education despite the fact that many of them have English as their second language; in comparison, earlier claims that 'West Indians' were underachieving seemed peculiar when so many of them had been raised with English as their first language.

Various writers have claimed that the language problems of 'Asian' children have been more easily recognized and treated more sympathetically than the language problems of 'West Indian' children. Children are expected not only to speak English in British schools but also to speak *standard* English or, even more specifically, what Bernstein (1971) called an 'elaborated code'. When children learn English as a second language they are taught the 'correct' grammatical constructions; when English is a child's native language, it may be spoken with a wide range of dialects and grammatical constructions. Labov (1969) maintained that non-standard English was different, rather than inferior, that it could have its own logical structure and could be very effective as a means of communicating complicated arguments. Edwards (1976; 1979) argued that Creole played an important role in the underperformance of West Indian children. Although the Creole spoken by many West Indian children (and children of West Indian parents) includes English vocabulary, it has different grammatical constructions and sound systems. These children are at a disadvantage not only because their Creole 'interferes' with their use of standard English but also because they have to endure the commonly held view that they are inarticulate: children who speak Creole are assumed to be speaking 'poor' English.

The influence of racist attitudes is difficult to gauge, but one of the women interviewed by Bryan *et al.* (1987) provides an indication of other factors that could affect the literacy of black children.

I had always liked reading, and could have really enjoyed literature at school. I suppose I liked the strange and different world I found in books, especially the ones about life as it was supposed to have been in Britain. This couldn't last though, because reading often became a nasty, personal experience. You would be getting deep into a story and suddenly it would hit you – a reference to Black people as savages or something. It was so offensive. And so wounding. Sometimes you would sit in class and wait, all tensed up, for the next derogatory remark to come tripping off the teacher's tongue. Oh yes, it was a 'black' day today, or some kid had 'blackened' the school's reputation. It was there clearly, in black and white, the school's ideology. The curriculum and the culture relies on those racist views.

(Bryan *et al.* 1987: 93)

Political perspectives on race and racism tend to encompass all of the approaches we have already encountered, ranging from egalitarianism to biological determination and including debates about uniformity, diversity, integration and segregation. Some right-wing perspectives take a 'colour-blind' approach, assuming that children from a wide range of backgrounds will be incorporated into the existing British 'culture', submerging their own cultural heritage in the process. A New Right emphasis accepts individual diversity but assumes that social cohesion can be maintained and promoted by the sound operation of market forces, without government intervention. However, the most extreme right-wing approach is obviously in favour of negative racial discrimination and enforced segregation of some sort.

Centre-ground and left-wing perspectives tend to involve more concern about racism and the negative effects of ethnic inequalities, but vary in their proposed solutions. A multicultural approach tends to assume that, if children can learn about cultures other than their own, a greater degree of tolerance will be cultivated, not only in the individual but also in society as a whole. This approach has been criticized for being naive in its understanding of the true nature of racism (caricatured as just being about 'saris and samosas'). It ignores the fact that many children who are born to indigenous 'British' families and in a British 'culture' (if that could be defined) suffer from covert or overt racism simply because they have black or brown skin. Anti-racists therefore argue that it is racism, rather than cultural diversity, that must be confronted. The role of education is to challenge racism in society as a whole by, for example, providing children with positive images of 'blackness' (Bryan *et al.* 1987).

However, a third (and there are probably more) approach tries to assimilate multicultural and anti-racist approaches. Interculturalism promotes a recognition and acceptance of the uniqueness of the individual and the superficiality of labelling anyone simply by skin colour, 'culture', social class, gender, disability, and so on.

It seems that, despite the problems involved in studying ethnicity and education, racism must be acknowledged as a fundamental problem and the role of education in the transmission or amelioration of racism must be considered. Studies of racism in schools are still beset with difficulties due to its often covert nature. There are, however, many 'victim reports' of the sort furnished by Bryan *et al.* (1987) and other studies into the nature of racist bullying and name-calling (e.g. Cohn 1988). Some of these were inspired, or commissioned by, Macdonald *et al.* (1990), who reported on the circumstances behind the racist murder of an Asian boy in a school playground.

If we try to simplify the findings of the Macdonald Report and allied research we are sure to fail, and this is a problem for the sociology of education in general. There seem to be no easy answers to our earlier question of whether educational outcomes are most influenced by social class, gender or ethnicity.

Stop and think

> It is easier to identify and categorize an individual according to sex than according to social class or ethnic group. How has this affected the introduction of education policies that (a) are egalitarian; (b) emphasize equal access; (c) promote inequality?

> Compare the policies of central government (on social class, gender and ethnicity) with local or independent initiatives that aim to reduce educational inequalities. How effective have local initiatives been and what challenges have they faced?

We can identify some themes and trends at a structural level, and can see some patterns emerging in small-scale interactions, but must still acknowledge education as a unique experience. Ethnicity, social class and gender must be recognized as sources of educational inequalities, but their effects and interrelationships must not be distorted by oversimplification. Even the improved educational performance of girls and women does not provide a regular pattern of educational achievement and more equal opportunities.

Other inequalities in Britain

Class, gender and ethnicity are probably the most highly researched influences on educational experiences but sociologists have now moved towards a greater appreciation of influences that have been relatively ignored in the past. The Warnock Report (1978) raised the profile of children with special educational needs, and the Utting Report (1997) raised the profile of children in the care of local authorities.

Before 1978, children with special educational needs were usually educated in 'special' schools and apart from the majority of children in 'mainstream' schools. A movement towards the greater integration of children with special needs into mainstream schools has brought with it a greater appreciation of the diversity of special needs. Some acknowledgement of this can be seen in changes in the discourse about special educational needs, with a shift from an emphasis on 'integration' to an emphasis on a stronger sense of 'inclusion'. This is in keeping with the wider political discourse about social inclusion and social exclusion. However, it is clear that structural changes are not enough and that education can play an important

A closer look

Educating children in care

The social exclusion and educational problems of children in the care of local authorities (whether fostered or living in children's homes) have only started to be appreciated fully (see Armstrong *et al.* 1995). Children in care may be fostered or be living in children's homes, but in both cases the state has effectively taken the role of parent. Although it is estimated that at any one time there are approximately 50,000 such children in the UK (and it often costs more to support a child in care than to send a child to Eton), it was easy to ignore them in a society promoting ideas of a parentocracy.

In 1997 Sir William Utting produced a disturbing study of children in local authority care which led to the setting up of a ministerial task force, and in 1998 the Downing Street Social Exclusion Unit (SEU) considered children in community care as part of its wider remit. It found that three-quarters of children in care left with no qualifications of any kind and were ten times more likely than other children to be excluded from school. Many experienced several moves between homes and half of care leavers were unemployed.

part in generating a more genuine form of social integration. Oliver (1990) tries to explain what is needed:

All disabled people experience disability as a social restriction whether these restrictions occur as a consequence of inaccessible built environments, questionable notions of intelligence and social competence, the inability of the general public to use sign language, the lack of reading material in Braille or hostile public attitudes to people with non-visible disabilities.   (Oliver 1990: xiv)

This chapter ends with an image of educational inequalities in the UK so extreme that we may wonder why so little has been achieved during the twentieth century. Yet we have also encountered disagreements about both the meaning of 'equal opportunities' and the extent to which the state should control the educational experiences of its citizens. Perhaps it seems that this chapter has provided more questions than answers but it should now be clear that, although 'education is an eminently social thing' (Durkheim 1956: 114), it is still possible for individuals to become producers, rather than passive receptors, of knowledge.

Summary

➤ The sociology of education shows us that individual 'failures' are socially as well as personally constructed, that knowledge is socially constructed and that the identification of intelligence is a social and subjective process. Even the use of concepts such as 'intelligence', 'knowledge' and 'ability' is regarded as problematic: for example, qualifications tend to be devalued as more people have them (credential inflation).

➤ The nature of schooling in Britain has shifted from its 'secret garden' before the 1970s towards an increasing emphasis on accountability to parents and central or regional government. A discourse of derision criticized education for 'failing' the nation and, during the past 30 years, there has been intense political activity around a theme of vocationalism. A varied school system has emerged from successive governments' emphasis on parental rights.

➤ Sociological explanations and theories have developed from an early emphasis on the social structure towards a synthesis of structural and interpretative perspectives. Functionalist approaches have emphasized the role of education in maintaining consensus and continuity. Approaches emerging from Marxist influences have emphasized conflict and change within education and inequalities of educational opportunities within a capitalist system. Critical theorists have emphasized the role of education in supporting an ideological superstructure and perpetuating inequalities. Interpretative influences have included descriptions of how working-class boys have creatively interacted with their social constraints to generate self-fulfilling prophesies. Postmodernist ideas challenge even basic assumptions about education.

➤ Sociologists have identified important themes within debates about education policy. These include questions about equality and inequality, uniformity and diversity. Perceptions of equality include egalitarianism (emphasizing equal outcomes), equal access (to equal resources), competitive access (rationing access to superior education), parental choice (the ideology of parentocracy) and biological determinism (with its emphasis on inequality). There are also debates about how much uniformity or diversity, segregation or integration, there should be in education.

➤ It has been found that social class explains more of the variation in educational achievement than does ethnic group or gender. Findings about the influence of social class have also been remarkably consistent over time. These inequalities can be influenced by the dominant political ideology. Recently some sociologists have claimed that the acquisition of skills in information technology have become a key influence on social class.

➤ Gender inequalities in education have been transformed since the 1980s as girls have tended to achieve more than boys in education. Improvements in girls' performance have resulted from some policies reflecting an equal access approach (equal opportunities/girl-friendly) and some reflecting a more egalitarian approach

▶

Summary (continued)

(anti-sexist/girl-centred). In view of such progress for women, sociologists are asking why gender inequalities remain in the workplace (including the teaching hierarchy). They are also focusing on the role of schools in the construction of masculinity and some have argued that boys are victims of their own socialization: learning to be aggressive and attaching little importance to education.

➤ Research into ethnicity and education has been fraught with difficulties. These include forcing individuals into inappropriate categories and questions whether research that intends to study ethnicity is actually studying social class. However, the role of education in the transmission or amelioration of racism must be considered. Political perspectives on ethnicity and education include the full range, from egalitarianism to biological determinism and include debates about uniformity, diversity, integration and segregation. Some ethnic groups are over- or underrepresented in access to higher education. However, statistical data is limited in helping us to develop a deeper understanding of educational experiences: for example, the success of children of Chinese origin.

➤ Sociologists are continually moving towards a greater appreciation of influences on education that have been relatively ignored in the past.

Links

The discussion of sociological explanations and theories in relation to the role of education in society, pages 551–554, links to the broader theoretical approaches of Durkheim, Marx and other social theorists discussed in Chapter 2.

Issues around inequalities of educational achievement in terms of social class, pages 563–566, gender, pages 564–573, and ethnicity, pages 577–578, can be related to the general discussion of class, gender and race in Chapters 6, 7 and 8 respectively.

 ## Further reading

This chapter has shown that educational processes are constantly changing, and you should now appreciate the need to make your reading as up-to-date as possible. You should search out the most recently published books available and remember that by the time of their publication they will already be out-of-date in some respects. For this reason it is a good idea to search for up-to-date information in web sites, educational journals and magazines.

The many educational journals and magazines provide a useful resource for updating and expanding your existing knowledge of this area. Weeklies in the UK include the *Times Educational Supplement*, and the *Times Higher Educational Supplement* (see Web sites section for online access). Academic journals provide your best source of recent research findings, and sometimes focus on one aspect of education. Many of these are listed at **www.tandf.co.uk./journals/online.asp**.

 ## Web sites

Web sites include the following:

The United Nations Educational, Scientific and Cultural Organization (UNESCO)
www.unesco.org.education

The Organization for Economic Co-operation and Development (OECD)
www.oecd.org/topic/education

The Statistical Office of the European Communities (Eurostat)
http://europa.eu.int/comm/eurostat

The UK Government's Department for Education and Skills
www.dfes.gov.uk

The Social Science Information Gateway
www.sosig.ac.uk/roads/subject-listing/World-cat/soceduc.html.
www.educationarena.com

The Times Educational Supplement
www.tes.co.uk

Activities

Activity 1

Reforming education in Japan

Japan is to abandon its experiment with child-centred education, education minister Nariaki Nakayama has announced. The country's ruling coalition said it will overhaul Japan's education laws this year in an attempt to reverse what it sees as the policy failures of the past 20 years. But analysts say the about-face is a sign of panic only three years after the government introduced a liberal curriculum. It had cut the school week from six days to five, introduced 'softer' subjects such as general studies into the curriculum, and reduced students' workloads by 30 per cent.

At the root of the change appears to be the latest batch of international educational comparison scores, which caused uproar in Japan . . . In the 2003 Programme for International Student Assessment (PISA) tests, Japan slipped from eighth to twelfth place in reading, and from first to fourth in maths, among countries belonging to the Organization for Economic Co-operation and Development. 'The question of whether the government's policy of "education free from pressure" has caused a decline in academic ability in this country appears to have been answered,' said an editorial from the right-leaning *Yomiuri* newspaper. However, Japan did come second in science and fourth in problem-solving. One aim of the liberal curriculum was to teach children to identify and solve problems by themselves rather than simply fill their heads with facts. Another was to reduce the pressure on students.

The minister admitted to reporters that to find the increased class time he may have to reintroduce Japan's six-day school week, which was phased out three years ago. He has also suggested that it is time to reintroduce common assessment tests, which were used in all schools in the 1950s and 1960s but were stopped because it was thought they encouraged too much competition. Even more controversially, the ruling party also wishes to insert some kind of patriotism studies into the curriculum or at least demand that teachers instill a sense of 'love of the country' in their pupils.

(Michael Fitzpatrick, 'Minister pulls plug on liberal policies', *Times Educational Supplement* 4.2.2005)

Questions

1. *Look again at A closer look on p. 545 (Influences on different national education systems) and identify possible influences on the education system in Japan.*

2. *Look again at A closer look on p. 547 (The problem of credential inflation) and consider whether it is possible to have an 'education free from pressure'.*

3. *Discuss the relative benefits and problems associated with these shifts in education policy in Japan. What are your conclusions?*

Activity 2

Secular schools or faith schools?

Faith schools

Educationalists in saris, headscarves, robes and pinstriped suits came together in Edinburgh this week for the 15th conference of Commonwealth education ministers. Ministers from the 52 member states of the Commonwealth meet every three years to discuss issues relevant to the developed and developing world. Access, inclusion and achievement were the themes of this year's conference, with delegates examining how to close the gap which separates rich and poor countries.

Activities (continued)

Amartya Sen, master of Trinity College, Cambridge, and 1998 Nobel laureate, accused faith schools of breeding illiberalism and intolerance, and of narrowing pupils' horizons. These schools, he said, had become popular only because of the lack of facilities in other, non-denominational state schools. He added that they encouraged pupils to define themselves by religion alone, leaving them with a one-dimensional view of society.

'The importance of non-sectarian and non-parochial curricula that expand, rather than reduce, the reach of reason can be hard to exaggerate,' he said. 'We have to make sure that we do not have smallness thrust upon the young.'

(Adi Bloom, 'Countries seek to close wealth gap', *Times Educational Supplement* 31.10.2003)

Secular education

Last week 17 Muslim girls were sent home from a school in Lille for wearing the Islamic headscarf or hijab. This follows last month's directive from the French education minister, François Bayrou, banning 'ostentatious' religious symbols in schools. (Crucifixes and Stars of David are seen as discreet.) At the beginning of the school year four students at a lycée in the Paris suburb of Goussainville were excluded for wearing the hijab. Lessons were suspended following demonstrations by Islamic and human rights groups.

The practice of wearing the headscarf does not come from the Koran and the head of the Paris mosque has said that he does not believe it is obligatory for Muslim women to cover their heads. But many Muslims of both sexes feel it is an assertion of their cultural and religious identity and that the French state has no right to interfere.

The wearing of the headscarf is seen as a challenge to the French tradition of secular education established in the nineteenth century. French opponents of the headscarf in schools believe that it is demeaning to girls and marks them out from other students purely on the basis of their sex and religion.

Britain had its own row over the wearing of the headscarf when two girls were sent home from a school in Altrincham, Cheshire, in 1990. But the issue has never reached the proportions that it has in France, because the British school system does allow the expression of religious beliefs.

(The *Guardian* 1.11.1994)

A fortnight ago Mr Ferry [French Education minister] launched a *Republican Guide* for teachers to help promote anti-racism, tolerance, integration and the Republic itself. Last month the controversial law banning religious signs in schools was adopted, but it has already been challenged by a young girl in a *collège* [lower secondary school] who turned up for class in a headscarf, to the fury of staff who then went on strike.

(Jamey Keaten and Barbara Cassassus, 'Web war on anti-Semites', *Times Educational Supplement* 2.4.2004)

Questions

1. *Why do Britain and France have such different traditions regarding the promotion of secular or faith schools?*

2. *Consider reasons why parents might choose to send their children to faith schools.*

3. *Do you agree with Amartya Sen's criticisms of faith schools?*

4. *Do you agree with the French government's decision to ban 'ostentatious' religious symbols in schools?*

5. *Are some expressions of a religious faith acceptable in schools and some not?*

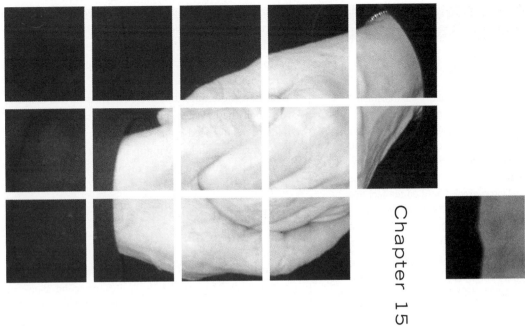

Chapter 15

Religion

Whatever any individual's religious beliefs may be, or even if there is some antagonism towards religion, it is difficult for anyone to deny that religions have had considerable impact on societies in all continents.

(Hinnells 1984: 11)

Key issues

➤ How should religion be defined and measured?

➤ What explanations have been given for the role of religion in society?

➤ How does religion affect our daily lives?

➤ What are the main debates about the decline and future of religion?

Introduction

We live in a world which has been and continues to be widely influenced, for good or ill, by religion. A glance at any week's newspapers and television news confirms that worldwide events are influenced directly or indirectly by religion. Religion is not just about churchgoing or Christianity, although early sociologists reflected their predominantly western Judaeo-Christian heritage in their writings. Religion affects virtually every area of social life, including dress, dietary habits, marriage customs, the types of schools and hospitals attended and the services provided therein, as well as attitudes to moral issues. It is therefore unsurprising that early sociologists were fascinated by religion and it was a central concern of early sociological research.

> Sociology has always had a strong interest in analysing the nature of those shared beliefs to which men [sic] attach some kind of priority of sacredness, and which provide the basic perspectives around which groups of individuals organise their life.

(Thompson and Tunstall 1971: 363)

Today there is as much interest as ever in exploring the centrality of religious beliefs in many communities and their pervasiveness across time and culture. The move into the third millennium, which was after all an event with roots in Christian history and tradition, has been the basis for much discussion about the past, present and future role for religion in society (see 'End of the world fever', below). Though the social context of beliefs has

A closer look

'End of the world' fever: A millennial event

What do you remember most about the transition to the third millennium? During the preparations for the millennium, much emphasis was placed on the Millennium Bug and ways of marking the event through monuments such as the Millennium Dome. It would be easy to forget that the event was actually historically a religious event, based on the fact that the Millennium marked the 2000th anniversary of Christianity. For this reason, millennial changeovers have also been marked by both religious celebrations and prophetic predictions about the end of the world.

In 998, the changeover was interpreted as heralding the coming of the Antichrist, and the outbreak of disasters including floods, famines, plagues and earthquakes. Although some of these predictions came true, the world survived and inspired efforts to consolidate Christian communities in Europe. The end of the second millennium was characterized by vigorous celebration plans as well as prophetic predictions in some quarters, particularly among those religious organizations with a millennial theme within their theology (that is, beliefs relating to the end of the world).

In 1997, 39 members of the Heaven's Gate cult committed suicide based on the belief that Comet Hale-Bopp was a prophetic omen; in 1993 in Waco, Texas, mass deaths also occurred among followers of David Koresh – the Branch Davidians – whose theology included millennial tones. While some predicted that the millennium would bring increased potential for religious fanaticism and religious terrorism, others including the mainstream Christian denominations focused on the changeover as a more positive opportunity for reflection, consolidation and spiritual renewal.

Millennial movements, however, are likely to persist. In 2003 the Pana Wave cult predicted that a close encounter with a 10th planet would set off earthquakes and tidal waves destroying most of humankind. Followers of its charismatic leader Yuko Chino drape themselves – and surrounding trees, bushes or crash barriers – in white fabric to protect themselves from electromagnetic waves allegedly directed at them by communist aggressors. The Pana Wave is one of increasing numbers of cults in Japan.

changed, the questions are similar: under what circumstances do religious beliefs arise, develop and decline? Do the social structures of different communities help us to understand the diversity of religious forms and experiences? The approaches of Marx, Durkheim and Weber to these questions are examined in this chapter. Although these writers predicted the gradual decline of religion in advanced industrial societies, religion appears to be surviving and reviving in many areas of the world in various forms and degrees of intensity.

The sociological approach to religion

Given the sociological aim to avoid bias and prejudice in the study of society, it is important to be aware of one's own attitudes towards religion and how these may impinge upon its study. For many people religion can be a sensitive, personal and emotive subject about which value-neutrality seems inappropriate.

The sociology of religion is not so much interested in weighing up the validity of particular doctrines but rather focuses on the social context and consequences of belief systems. Sociologists are interested in the ways in which beliefs are translated into social action.

> Sociological researchers set aside, for the purposes of the study, their personal opinions about religion and try to be as objective as possible in observing and interpreting the religious phenomena under study. From a sociological perspective, one religion is not superior to another. (McGuire 1992: 8)

Stop and think

> ➤ What assumptions or beliefs do you bring with you to the sociology of religion? Would you describe any of them as prejudices?

> ➤ How do your own beliefs differ from those of (a) your family; (b) your closest friends? Would you describe any of their beliefs as prejudices?

The ongoing sociological debate about whether it is possible and/or desirable to be value-free (see p. 108) applies to the sociological study of religion. A preconceived understanding of what is or is not 'religion' may be brought to bear in an assessment of the following sociological approaches to the definition and measurement of religion.

Defining and measuring religion

Sociologists acknowledge the inherent complexities in attempting to define and measure religion. Some researchers focus on adherence to particular beliefs or attending a place of worship in determining levels of religiosity. However, 'being religious' means different things to different people. This can become problematic for the social scientist attempting to quantify and compare religiosity within and across societies.

In a book examining forms of religious life, Durkheim (1976) argues that all religious beliefs share an important criterion, namely the clear distinction they make between two realms: the sacred and the profane. The sacred is not limited to gods and spirits but includes anything considered superior in dignity and power, protected and isolated through a sense of awe and thus treated with special respect. Durkheim elaborates on the sacred and profane in relation to religious beliefs and behaviour:

> The real characteristic of religious phenomena is that they always presuppose a bipartite division of the whole universe, known and knowable, into two classes which embrace all that exists, but which radically exclude each other. Sacred things are those which the interdictions protect and isolate; profane things, those to which these interdictions are applied and which must remain at a distance from the first. Religious beliefs are the representations which express the nature of sacred things and the relations which they sustain, either with each other or with profane things. Finally, rites are the rules of conduct which prescribe how a man [*sic*] should comport himself in the presence of these sacred objects.
> (Durkheim 1976: 40–1)

Durkheim proceeds to this definition:

> a religion is a unified system of beliefs and practices relative to sacred things, that is to say, things set apart and forbidden – beliefs and practices which unite into one moral community called a Church, all those who adhere to them. (Durkheim 1976: 47)

A key feature is Durkheim's identification of religion with society. He sees a parallel between dependence of the individual on the community and on the sacred, the gods being an expression of society itself.

> This reality, which mythologies have represented in so many different forms, but which is the universal and eternal objective cause of these sensations *sui generis*

out of which religious experience is made, is society. . . . If religion has given birth to all that is essential in society, it is because the idea of society is the soul of religion. Religious forces are therefore human forces, moral forces. (Durkheim 1976: 418–19)

Durkheim stresses that in seeing religion as something essentially social he does not regard it as a mere epiphenomenon, an unreal reflection of real material conditions (this is more the case with Marx's theory of religion and historical materialism). Rather, Durkheim sees religious sentiments, ideas and images as having an independent existence and life of their own. Once born of society, they develop laws of their own:

> They attract each other, repel each other, unite, divide themselves and multiply, though combinations are not commanded and necessitated by the condition of the underlying reality. (Durkheim 1976: 424)

It is for this reason that there is such a dynamic and varied pattern of religious life.

This emphasis on the real, autonomous existence of religion is a departure from Marx's definition of religion, which, though also seeing religion as socially grounded, attributes much more limited scope to it. For Marx, religion has no independent existence but is simply a fantasy (see pp. 599–601). By taking the individuals out of themselves religion forces them into self-alienation. Hence the task of explaining religion is the task of explaining social reality:

> Religion is only the illusory sun which revolves round man [*sic*] as long as he does not revolve round himself. . . . Thus the criticism of heaven turns into the criticism of the earth, the *criticism of religion* into the *criticism of right* and the *criticism of theology* into the *criticism of politics*.
> (Marx and Engels 1955: 42)

It is neither easy nor appropriate to consider Durkheim's and Marx's understanding of the essence of religion without examining the way in which they both locate their views in the social context and focus on the social role of religion. This aspect of their writings is discussed on pp. 590–601.

Stop and think

> ➤ How would a society without any religion at all differ from your own?

Figure 15.1 Buddist monks, Thailand
(Courtesy of Robert Harding Picture Library Ltd)

Weber (1963) provides an alternative definition of religion. He departs from an exclusive emphasis on the *social* grounding of religion and highlights the meaning of religion for *individuals*. Weber wrote far more about religion than Marx or Durkheim and his emphasis on meaning has inspired many theoretical contributions to our understanding of religion. In the sociology of religion his legacy is illustrated in the work of Berger (1967b) and Luckmann (1967), while researchers in the field of religious studies (e.g. Smart 1978) also refer to the phenomenological origins reflected in Weber's approach.

Weber stated that 'to define "religion", to say what it *is*, is not possible at the start . . . Definition can be attempted, if at all, only at the conclusion of the study' (Weber 1963: 1). For him the concern of the sociologist should not be the essence of religion; rather the task is to understand religion as part of meaningful human behaviour and explain its influence on other spheres of activity such as ethics, economics and politics. (Chapter 2 described how Weber's (1974) study of Protestantism is part of a wider analysis of capitalist ethical and economic behaviour.)

Weber's concentration on both the social context and the significance of meaning systems in the sociology of religion is illustrated in a broad range of works on the religions of China (Confucianism and Daoism), India (Hinduism and Buddhism) and ancient Judaism. Weber also studied Calvinism in *The Protestant Ethic*, which was more than simply a response to Marx's seemingly deterministic view of religion as being dependent on economic factors. Weber's study was part of a much broader analysis giving emphasis to the nature and significance of religious motivation; he concluded that religion can play a key part in helping to shape economic attitudes and behaviour.

Berger and Luckmann (1963) took up this interpretative approach linking the study of religion to the broader field of the sociology of knowledge. They saw religion as an attempt to make sense of reality through the development of a subjective world view. Luckmann (1967) reflects both Durkheimian and Weberian influences when he suggests that religion has an important function in helping individuals to make sense of the world around them. Berger (1967b) outlines his thesis of religion as the means by which a sacred external cosmos is constructed:

Religion has played a strategic part in the human enterprise of world-building. Religion implies the farthest reach of man's [sic] self-externalization . . . Put differently, religion is the audacious attempt to conceive of the entire universe as being humanly significant.   (Berger 1967b: 37)

Definitions of religion tend to be either substantive or functional. *Substantive* definitions try to uncover the essence of religion – what religion is. *Functional* approaches place more emphasis on the effect of religion

– what religion *does*. Such distinctions become significant when discussing whether religious ideas and practices are inevitable in society and in debates about secularization. For those operating with more inclusive definitions of religion – seeing, for example, apparently secular ideologies as functional equivalents of religion where they have the same effect – secularization is a limited possibility. Those examining the extent to which religion has declined, and areas where it competes with non-religious conceptions of the social order, are more likely to prefer exclusive definitions.

Linked in with these debates are discussions about measuring religiosity. Glock and Stark (1968: 253–61) differentiated five dimensions of religiosity which still apply today. These are indicators by which it might be possible to measure degrees of religiousness. Particular indicators may apply more to one individual, group or religion than others at any particular time. The five dimensions are belief, practice, experience, knowledge and consequences.

Types of religious organization

All religions involve a community of believers, but there may be variations in members' commitment, or in the way the community is organized. Like other organizations, religious institutions are constantly changing, in terms of both their internal structure and their relationship and status *vis-à-vis* the secular environment. At the same time there are clearly differences between the size, constitution and status of bodies such as the Anglican Church in relation to organizations like the Unification Church (sometimes referred to as 'the Moonies' after their leader Revd Sun Myung Moon).

Sociologists have devised a number of ways of classifying religious organizations. As well as being of academic interest, this has important legal and political implications. Barker (1989: 146) points out that many organizations actively seek either to attain or to avoid religious status in order to qualify for certain social advantages. In Britain, for example, religious bodies may qualify for tax exemption, so groups such as the Unification Church have actively claimed religious status. In the United States, however, where religious beliefs have traditionally not been taught in public (i.e. state) schools, some groups have sought to avoid the religious label so that their teachings can be communicated through the curriculum.

A closer look

Five dimensions of religiosity

The *belief* dimension refers to the core beliefs of a religion. *Practice* refers to acts of worship carried out either publicly through formal rituals (such as taking communion or attending prayers at a mosque) or privately (such as personal prayer or meditation). The *experience* dimension refers to the expectation that religiosity involves subjective feelings and perceptions, some personal sense of communication with the transcendental. This again varies within and between religions. Members of a Pentecostal Christian group, for example, may be encouraged to express personally the power of God through speaking in tongues, singing or crying aloud. By contrast, the kind of religious experience associated with those who have claimed to see apparitions of the Virgin Mary has often been discouraged by authoritative figures within the Catholic Church.

The *knowledge* dimension refers to the extent of understanding the basic tenets of a religion. This need not align with the belief dimension: one may study the teachings of a religion without believing them, or one may have faith without deep knowledge. The *consequences* dimension extends the idea of religious commitment beyond the first four criteria and focuses on their effects in everyday life. Muslims, for example, may be recognizable outside the mosque by the way they dress, their diet, the type of school they attend and their social and moral codes.

Questions

1. *Consider one religion. Give an example of each of Glock and Stark's five dimensions of religiosity.*

2. *How might each of these dimensions be measured?*

3. *What difficulties would arise in measuring these dimensions?*

There are four main categories of organization: *church*, *denomination*, sect and cult. Within the sociology of religion Weber (1963) made the original distinction between church and sect and inspired further research into the social characteristics of different types of religious organization (e.g. Troeltsch 1931).

The sociological terms such as 'sect' and 'church' may differ from the everyday usage and meanings of these terms, which may not be referring to the social characteristics defined below.

Church

In sociological terms a '*church*' is a well-established religious body. It maintains a bureaucratic structure (including a hierarchy of paid officials) and a formal distinction between religious officials and the laity. (In the Christian tradition this is illustrated by the authority of the priesthood in celebrating the sacraments and in Islam by the legal authority of the imams.) Through its links with the establishment, the church is generally integrated

Case study

Splitting the Church? The gay clergy controversy

The job of Archbishop of Canterbury has never been an easy one. Some, like Thomas a Becket, have been murdered. Others, most notably Thomas Cranmer, have met their end courtesy of the executioner.

Archbishops have been used as political pawns by monarchs, ridiculed as meddlesome priests by politicians and scoffed at as wishy-washy liberals by the media. Today, the 104th Archbishop, the most Reverend Rowan Williams, is facing his own crisis, this time within the Church itself.

The election of the first openly gay Anglican bishop, in the United States, came at the same time as another homosexual priest, Canon Jeffrey John, had his nomination as Bishop of Reading withdrawn at the request of the Archbishop.

With more traditionalist Anglicans, in Kenya, Nigeria and Australia, now setting themselves against liberals in the US and the

UK, Dr Williams has convened an emergency top-level meeting of bishops in October, to discuss the issue of gay clergy . . .

Dr Williams' major problem rests with his unique position. As Archbishop of Canterbury he is leader of the 77 million-strong worldwide Anglican Communion but, unlike the Pope, he has no power to force any of his 38 archbishops to submit to his will. The broad nature of the Church, which includes Anglo-Catholics, evangelicals and liberals, means that it is almost impossible for it to achieve unity on many controversial matters, including the ordination of women, human sexuality and relations with Rome.

The question today is: how can the Church accommodate both those like Archbishop Peter Akinola of Nigeria, who has called homosexual conduct 'lower than that of beasts' and the newly elected Bishop of New Hampshire, the openly gay Gene Robinson?

Dr Williams has met this matter head on. In July, delivering a

recent speech to the Church's parliament, the General Synod, he spoke frankly:

'There are several different "Churches of England" . . . they do not communicate with each other very effectively . . . they need to learn how to do this better if they are to fulfil their primary task of witnessing to God's transforming power,'

More recently, he has warned that the Church might have to break-up. 'Unity becomes finally unintelligible and unworthwhile when it itself ceases to be a theological category,' he wrote recently. 'Staying together is pointless unless it is staying together because of the Body of Christ.'

BBC News Online 3.10.2003

Questions

1. *List the arguments for and against the inclusion of gay bishops within the Anglican communion (consider theological, political and social arguments).*

2. *Which of these arguments do you consider most persuasive and why?*

into the wider economic and social structure of society: its beliefs and values are widely accepted by the population. It is part of the *status quo* and tends to be conservative, with an interest in maintaining traditions and its privileged position within the system. This emphasis on traditional values, however, can lead to some tensions as societal norms and morals evolve, as the example below, of the divisions within the Anglican Communion over the question of homosexual bishops, illustrates. Although all sections of the population may be represented in traditional church memberships, the higher-status groups in society tend to be overrepresented. The old saying that the Church of England is the 'Tory party at prayer' reflects this traditional association between the Church of England and the establishment.

Sect

Sociological research into *sects* and sectarianism has identified social characteristics contrasting with those of a church. Sects tend to be much smaller, more insular and more in conflict with, or even overtly rejecting, the values and behaviour of the church and wider society. A sect is usually a breakaway movement from a church, formed in protest to the established or orthodox traditions. Disputes may be centred on official doctrines, the interpretation of teachings, or questions around leadership and succession. Christian sects include Jehovah's Witnesses, Christadelphians and the Branch Davidians. Islamic sectarian movements include the Bahā'īs. In Judaism examples include the Hassidim, while in Buddhism there are followers of the Pure Land sect. Although these examples may be regarded as sectarian responses, they might not maintain all the features listed here; caution must be exercised in applying categorical labels.

Unlike churches, sects are more likely to require strict discipline and control of members and to perceive themselves as part of an exclusive community. They may withdraw from the surrounding society, thus reinforcing their marginality and sense of being set apart.

When attempting to define a typology of religious organizations such as sects, there may be a tendency to over-generalize and to ignore the enormous diversity between groups that fall into the category of sect. Wilson (1963) outlined a sevenfold typology of sects, which he

---

A closer look

Troeltsch's church-type and sect-type

A theologian and church historian, Troeltsch developed Weber's typology for the purposes of historical comparative analysis. Troeltsch (1931) was focusing specifically on church and sect types within Christianity, so it is harder to apply the typology to traditions such as Hinduism and Buddhism. His distinctions were also based on societies much more polarized and differentiated than those today:

Church-type	Sect-type
Large and universal; aims to embrace everybody	Small and particularist; fellowship with members but not outsiders
Individuals born into church; infant baptism	Members join voluntarily; conscious conversion
Grace through intervention of priest and sacraments	Grace through individual personal effort
World-accepting; stabilizes social order/established institutional set-ups	World-rejecting; avoids wider society
Top-down; develops from upper classes	Bottom-up; connects with those opposed to state and society
Asceticism seen as preparation for afterlife; means of acquiring virtue	Asceticism seen as means of direct union with God; expresses detachment from the world

Question

1. *Troeltsch's typology is located within a Christian theological and historical context. How helpful is this classification for understanding different types of religious organization today? (See also the traditional work of Neibuhr 1957, Yinger 1946 and Beckford 1975.)*

Case study

'NRMs': seeking to understand their appeal

Today there is as much interest as ever in the dangers of new religious movements, especially in view of groups such as Aum Shinrikyo, a sect which unleashed a fatal poison gas attack on the Tokyo subway in 1995. In 2003 the Japanese Government estimated that there could be more than 200,000 cults at large, many with profit as their main motivation.

Why are such movements popular in contemporary societies like Japan? Some point to factors such as the decline of spiritual certainty or economic decline eroding the confidence of a society that has measured its worth by work. Other explanations include the decline of parental authority and traditional moral values leading young people to seek alternative bases for security and spiritual fulfilment. The wish to understand and gain access to such groups and movements has always raised ethical and methodological questions for social scientists.

In 1990 one such movement in Britain, the Soka Gakkai, was studied by questionnaires and interviews. Wilson and Dobbelaere's study, *A Time to Chant* (1994), examined the social characteristics of British members of the movement, their beliefs and practices and the location of the movement in the wider social structure.

Soka Gakkai International was founded as a lay Buddhist organization in Japan in 1930. It was affiliated to Nicheren Shoshu, the largest sect in Japan, which followed the teachings of a thirteenth-century Buddhist monk. In 1991, however, while the research was being conducted, Soka Gakkai broke away from its parent body. Wilson and Dobbelaere were interested in the reasons for its impressive growth in Western secular society (at that time it had around 5,000 followers in Britain). In October 2000 the Secretariat of SGI-Europe stated that the membership in Britain was 6,200 with 39,980 across Europe. They concluded that part of the appeal of this religion was its practical, world-affirming and life-enhancing orientation rather than any sense of retreat from world affairs. The main form of religious practice is chanting, which is supposed to bring about tangible benefits, whether these be spiritual, material or communal.

Soka Gakkai in Britain is a largely urban movement of followers integrated into wider secular society, fulfilling their own careers and not segregated from wider family and friendship networks beyond the movement. Many members were in professional, cultural and caring occupations. They tended to have a high degree of educational attainment and to be slightly older on average than followers of some other new religious movements (members tended to be aged between 24 and 45).

Wilson and Dobbelaere concluded that the practical nature of this religion, with its endorsement of tangible rewards and a world-affirming lifestyle, helps to explain its success in contemporary Western society. In contrast to the moral economy of sinfulness, suffering and penitence associated with the work ethic and lifestyle of traditional religions such as Christianity, Soka Gakkai embraces the consumer society of spending, hedonism and individualism. While emphasizing personal responsibility, Soka Gakkai also encourages personal positive thinking and achievement in line with the enterprising culture of wider society.

As well as being of intrinsic interest as a social movement, the case of Soka Gakkai serves to warn us of simplistic over-generalizations about the nature and conduct of new religious movements. While it is sociologically useful to distinguish broadly different types of religious organization, it is important to avoid stereotyping as, for example, the media often tend to do when covering sensationalist news stories relating to cults.

(Adapted from Beckford 1985)

Questions

1. *Suggest reasons for the popularity of Soka Gakkai in the 1980s and 1990s.*
2. *How would you approach the study of new religious movements?*

hoped could also be applied to sects beyond the Western and Christian world. He classified sects in relation to *their response to the world*. The seven types of response were conversionist, revolutionary, introversionist, manipulationist, thaumaturgical, ('miracle-working') reformist and utopian. Wilson illustrates how important it is to analyse religious organizations in social context: when sects persist they always undergo processes of change and face challenges to their organizational features. Social realities to be faced may include changes in leaders and followers, the disappointment of eschatological hopes (e.g. Festinger *et al.* 1956: 152, 172) and declining commitment to original values, especially in protest movements.

Denomination

As sociologists of religion developed the original church–sect typology, they introduced the term *denomination* to refer to the advanced state of the sect once it loses its original fervour (Becker 1932) and becomes more world-accommodating (Neibuhr 1957). Denominations are a more established part of society without the conflictual characteristics of the sect. Sects are likely to be valid for one generation only; if they survive longer their organization adapts in order to maintain a routine existence within mainstream society. The relationship between the norms and values of the denomination and the majority religion of society tends to be one of coexistence and co-operation rather than conflict and challenge. However, denominational representatives may actively challenge the moral norms and values of mainstream society and urge their followers to re-examine their own beliefs and practices. Examples in Britain include historical pronouncements by the Roman Catholic Church about the teaching of sex education in schools and opposition by some Christian groups to Sunday trading. More recent examples include the Archbishop of Canterbury's criticisms of the Government's approach to war (2003) and of the treatment of prisoners in Iraq by coalition troops (2004).

Cult

While these examples are exceptions to the mostly peaceful coexistence of religious denominations in multicultural Britain, one type of religious organization generates consistent public hostility – the *cult*. While the term 'cult' is often interchanged in everyday conversation with terms such as 'sect' and 'new religious movement', within sociology there has been much discussion of the appropriateness of labels. The term 'cult' should be used cautiously because of its negative connotations. Cults contain some similarities with 'sects' in terms of size, leadership and lifespan, but the term embraces a large variety of groups outside the main religious traditions. Sociologists originated the category of 'new religious movement' (NRMs) (Barker 1989) to refer specifically to the spate of religious groups that grew very rapidly in North America and Western Europe in the post-war period of the twentieth century. However, it is a broad term used to cover a wide range of different religious groups, some more deserving of the negative reputation attributed to them than others. Some of the New Religious Movements studied by sociologists have included the International Society for Krishna Consciousness (ISKCON often known as 'Hare Krishna'), the Unification Church (also known as the 'Moonies'), Synanon, the People's Temple (founded by Jim Jones) and the Children of God.

> ### Stop and think
>
> ➤ Why did so many new religious movements gain popularity in the Western world in the 1960s and 1970s?
>
> ➤ Why do you think young people today may find alternative movements appealing and how would you approach their study?

The role of religion in society

Following on from their interest in the structure of society and the problem of social order, Marx and Durkheim tended to generalize about the universal role of religion in maintaining and reinforcing the *status quo*. However, there are important differences in their analyses and consequently in the way modern sociologists have developed their ideas. Today sociologists are less interested in looking for one all-embracing role that applies to all manifestations of religion in any time or place. Rather it is recognized that just as the form of religion varies, so does its role both within and across different social settings. Religion has a dual function both to bind and divide, to contribute both to social integration and to social conflict.

The integrative role of religion

Durkheim was one of the first sociologists to describe the function of religion in binding communities together. His main emphasis was on the level of the social structure and how religious beliefs and rituals bring people together, giving them a sense of unity and shared values. Durkheim's identification of religion with society focuses on its integrative effects. Religion's affirmation of collective ideals has been taken up by later analysts such as Bellah (1975) and Parsons (1971), who applied a functionalist approach to the study of religion in contemporary societies.

Today functionalist theorists assume that since most people in society follow religious beliefs and practices, and since societies on the whole function cohesively, religion must be playing a significant role in reflecting, sustaining and legitimizing the social order. As a key socializing agent religion transmits norms and values that help to hold society together. While the style and content of different religions may vary, what they share in common is a coherent system of beliefs and practices serving universal human needs and purposes.

Stop and think

> ➤ To what extent do you think such things as football and music have taken the place of religion in fulfilling people's needs for a coherent system of beliefs and practices?

Religious beliefs and ceremonies integrate individuals into social groups or communities in several ways by

- ➤ providing identity;
- ➤ expressing shared meanings and understanding;
- ➤ physically bringing worshippers together;
- ➤ prescribing moral norms;
- ➤ sanctioning changes of status;
- ➤ dealing with emotional stress or life crises.

First, religion helps by *providing identity*, a sense of who we are both in this world and in relation to the next. Wilson refers to how religion has 'answered the question "who am I?" for individuals and "who are we?" for groups' (Wilson 1982: 34).

Many people inherit affiliation to a religious group through their family, just as they inherit a sense of belonging to a kin group. Formal identification often takes place through a religious naming ceremony whereby an individual becomes formally accepted as a member of the community. In Christianity, for example, the first stage of membership is baptism or christening, when an individual traditionally adopts a Christian name (perhaps that of a saint). In Islam, although babies born of Muslims are automatically regarded as Muslims, membership of the *ummah* (the Muslim community) is signified by the name Muhammad (the name of the Prophet) or by the adoption of one of 99 names used to describe God, for example Rahim ('Kind') or Hafiz ('Protector').

As well as marking an individual's identity in this life, many belief systems include a strong sense of the past in terms of heritage and ancestry. This reinforces the uniqueness of both the individual and the group, which, through commemorative rituals, further enhances social solidarity. For Jews, the Hebrew Scriptures and regular festivals and ceremonies such as Passover and Hannukah, recalling events in Jewish history, reflect the belief that they are a chosen people whose special relationship with God marks them out from other communities.

Religious beliefs and practices can affect social behaviour in relation to customs associated with life after death. Both Marx and Weber were interested in how Christian beliefs about the afterlife affected the behaviour of people on Earth, albeit to produce either apathy or activity within the social and economic system. It is not only the various Christian concepts of heaven and hell which affect people's sense of destiny and social behaviour. Both Hinduism and Buddhism include the concept of reincarnation or rebirth, which helps to explain people's social situation and also functions to modify behaviour. Many Chinese communities believe that paying proper respect to their ancestors will secure their prosperity and welfare and bode well for the future. Beliefs about the continuity of life beyond physical death reinforce identity in the family group and can also strengthen social solidarity and social order.

Second, an interpretative approach to religion highlights the importance of religious symbols in *expressing shared meanings and understanding* among believers. Religious language, gestures, images and icons all have special significance to members partaking in rituals and ceremonies. This sense of mutual understanding and adoration unites worshippers and sets them apart from non-believers. Indeed it is the spiritual meaning and sacred significance bestowed by believers on to symbolic forms and actions which makes them 'religious'. Lighting a joss stick, kneeling in front of a statue or wearing particular

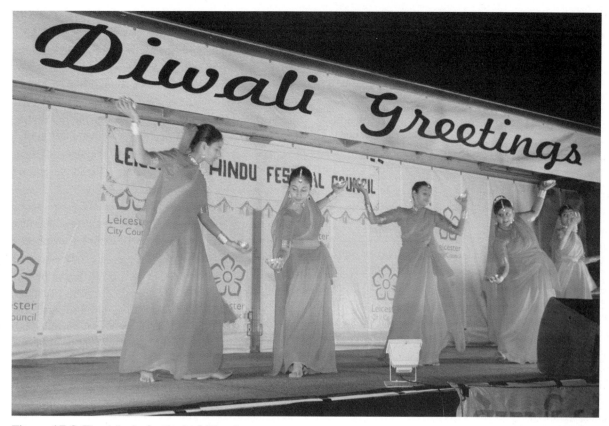

Figure 15.2 The Hindu festival of Diwali

clothes are actions that could have either secular or religious connotations depending on their context and the meaning attributed to them by participants.

Third, religious meanings and feelings cannot be directly observed. They can be 'seen' only in the physical actions of those translating beliefs into action. *Physically bringing worshippers together* in regular rituals and ceremonies binds members of a religious community together. Examples of annual occasions include Christmas, Diwali, Eid, Passover and Visakha.

The fourth way in which religion contributes to social cohesion is in *prescribing moral norms*; this refers to the role of religion in providing a sense of right and wrong. (This is explicitly recognized in the British education system, which emphasizes the teaching of religious education in schools as part of young people's moral education.) A belief in the afterlife is one factor influencing social behaviour. Some societies also develop legal codes incorporating systems of punishment for behaviour regarded as contravening God's law. In Islamic states the religious and civil law coincide and punishment is administered according to the strictures of the Qur'an. Most societies do not have a complete overlap between religious and secular law; the number of Islamic states where this is so is small. (Although the Organization of Islamic Conferences lists over 55 member countries as Islamic states, the majority of these would feature secular influences in areas such as the law.) However, even in largely secular societies such as Britain there are legacies of a religious heritage in the legal system, with many examples of laws and customs based on and still reflecting Christian interpretations of right and wrong. Furthermore, research shows that for many ethnic communities in Britain, religion plays an important part in influencing the way people live their lives (see Figure 15.3).

Stop and think

> Is it fair to conclude that in prescribing moral codes religion contributes to social cohesion? Or are there some instances in which this could lead to conflict? (You may wish to refer to the article on 'the gay clergy controversy and other contemporary world events (see p. 588) for this discussion.)

Fifth, religion often plays an important part in rites of passage, which alter sets of social expectations and responsibilities of individuals. Examples of such transitions include coming of age and marriage, which religious ceremonies mark by publicly *sanctioning changes of status* for the individual and reinforcing the norms and identity of the whole group. Rituals recognizing the change from childhood to adult status are ceremonies such as Confirmation within Christianity, Bar/Bat Mitzvah within Judaism and the Sacred Thread ceremony (*Upanayana*) within Hinduism.

Finally, given the functionalist emphasis on social order, this approach recognizes the important role that religion can play at times of social disorder, by *dealing with emotional stress or life crises*. Periods of social upheaval or uncertainty such as a death in the family, large-scale disaster or war may be anomic situations when individuals or communities question social norms and ask ultimate questions about the meaning of life and death. Religious beliefs may provide answers for those who believe that all events are part of God's will. Anthropologists (such as Malinowski 1926) argue that funerary and commemorative rituals function to restore social balance and gradually reintegrate bereaved individuals back into normal life.

In recent years, while there have been more 'secular' funerals featuring less traditional religious symbolism, there has also been a growth in symbolic ritualism in response to local or national tragedies. The laying of flowers at the scene of accidents, murders or disasters is an example of the continuing need to express loss and seek answers at a time of social distress, be it in traditional or quasi-religious terms. The response of the public after the Hillsborough football disaster in 1989

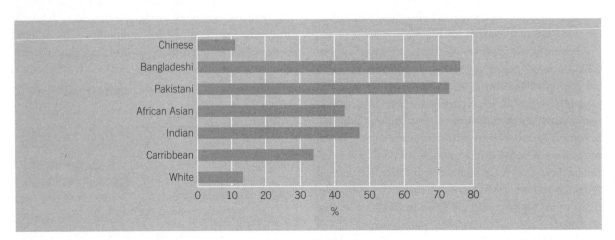

Figure 15.3 'Religion is very important to how I live my life.' Percentage agreeing with this statement
Source: Denscombe 1998: 48

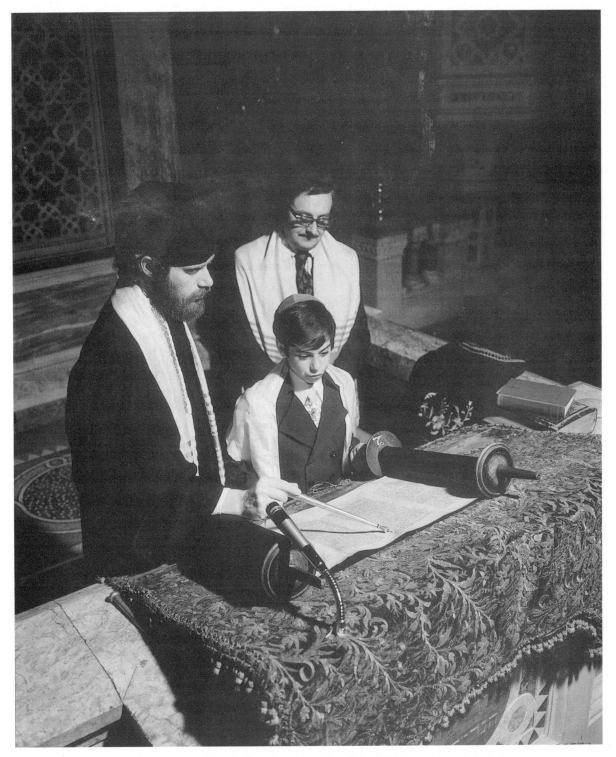

Figure 15.4 A Bar Mitzvah ceremony makes the transition from childhood to adult status
(Photograph © Chris Ridley, courtesy of Robert Harding Picture Library Ltd)

illustrated this most graphically as did the public mourning rituals following the 11 September attacks in 2001.

Religious beliefs, rituals and codes can uphold social solidarity and consensus, depending on the extent to which all members of society share the same values and belief systems. If this idea of consensus is questioned, however, religion may instead be interpreted as a negative force of social control with its beliefs, rituals and codes part of an

Case study

You'll never walk alone

Mass public grieving was most vividly illustrated in Liverpool after the Hillsborough disaster of 1989 when almost 100 Liverpool supporters were killed at an FA Cup Semi Final Match.

The most visible response in this first week was the visit of over a million people to Anfield, Liverpool's home ground. Large crowds had already gathered outside the ground when club officials opened the gates at noon on Sunday and began admitting people. By five o'clock the Kop end of the ground, where home supporters always stand, had become a shrine bedecked with flowers. The visitors continued to arrive from all over the country over the seven days of official mourning, queuing for hours in silent solemnity. The field of flowers gradually grew towards the centre of the pitch, whilst the concrete steps behind the goal were transformed into a carpet of scarves, pictures and personal messages. Scarves were also hung on the metal barriers, many of which became dedicated to the fans who had stood behind them week after week. School friends penned the names of their lost classmates on the walls outside the stadium. These messages expressed personal and communal grief as much, if not more than, any of the official ceremonies could have. For many people, visiting Anfield . . . brought their grief to the surface (Eyre 1989).

Questions

1. How far do you think traditional religious beliefs, rituals and codes function to integrate members in modern society?

2. To what extent do public mourning rituals after events such as the attacks on 11 September 2001 replace the role of traditional religion in fulfilling individual and social needs?

(In considering this extract and questions you might look back to the discussion of the public response to Princess Diana's death and funeral in Chapter 1 (pp. 21–22).)

imposed system of norms and values. Critics have suggested that a functionalist analysis is more appropriate to smaller-scale, less complex societies where the majority adheres more strongly to a unitary religious system. Where such consensus does not exist or is questioned, social expectation and pressure to participate in prevailing cultural norms might be regarded by individuals as an unwelcome imposition. Questioning particular beliefs or customs might even be interpreted as a rejection of all the wider community stands for. In modern or postmodern societies, characterized by a vast range of competing beliefs and practices, traditional functionalist analysis might seem less appropriate. However, functionalist theory has had a strong impact on the development of the sociology of religion. The main impetus for the development of this perspective was Durkheim.

Durkheim's study of religion

Durkheim's central concern in studying religion was the role it played in keeping societies ordered (see also pp. 47–48). He believed that just as cohesion was a basic requirement of all societies so was religion, operating as a kind of social cement binding individuals within the social system. Durkheim sought to discover the essence of religion by examining what he regarded as its most elementary form: the totem religion of Australian aborigines. Once he understood the essential characteristics of this religion he believed he could generalize about the religious character of any society.

Drawing on anthropological data of aboriginal society, Durkheim concluded that by regularly gathering together to worship the totem, the rituals reminded aborigines of their sense of unity, obligation and interdependence, all of which were imperative for the group's survival. The sacred significance attributed to the totem represented to Durkheim not so much the supernatural quality of the totem itself but rather the worship of the group's collectiveness. Through the tangible worship of the totem the more abstract quality of society was being essentially worshipped and reinforced.

While the aborigines did not think in terms of worshipping society, Durkheim believed that as a distanced observer he was able to make a more objective evaluation of the underlying significance of totem worship. As a positivist, Durkheim's sociological interest lies less in the subjective personal experiences of the individual or in the theological essence of religious belief; rather he is interested in the wider social context and general effect of collective religious behaviour. For him religion can be understood in terms of its sociological effect as the most basic 'collective representation' in society:

> The general conclusion . . . is that religion is something eminently social. Religious representations are collective representations which express collective realities; the rites are a manner of acting which take rise in the midst of the assembled group which are destined to excite, maintain or recreate mental states in these groups.   (Durkheim 1976: 10)

Following on from this understanding about the real nature of religion, Durkheim looked for examples of beliefs, values and rituals in modern society functioning in the same way as traditional religion.

> There can be no society which does not feel the need of upholding and reaffirming at regular intervals the collective sentiments and ideas which gave it its unity and individuality.   (Durkheim 1976: 427)

Durkheim regarded the national flag of a modern society as an equivalent of the totem in that it too represents the sum of a nation, a reality over and above all the individuals comprising a society and a symbol of national values given special or 'sacred' qualities. Durkheim reflected the rise of nationalism in his own country after the French Revolution, in which the ideals of liberty, equality and fraternity had been held up as national ideals. This reminds us that authors of sociological studies will to some extent be influenced by the cultural developments, norms and values around them. It also leads us to ask how applicable Durkheim's ideas are in contemporary societies.

The civil religion thesis

In 1967 the US sociologist Robert Bellah applied Durkheim's ideas to the United States and developed the sociological concept of 'civil religion'. The term had first been used by Rousseau in 1762 to refer to the religious dimension underlying the political order. Bellah extended it to the fundamental, universally accepted moral beliefs and values of a nation, in this case the United States. He argued that national values such as the ideals of freedom, justice, equality and democracy are given 'sacred' status in the Durkheimian sense in American civil life in the way that they are esteemed principles augmented within the national psyche and regarded with special respect. Just as the aborigines effectively worshipped their unity through regular rituals and ceremonies, so civic rituals in the United States function to bind together the nation through the celebration and commemoration of key national events.

Religious language and imagery have been applied to the sense of history and heritage of the American people with biblical analogies of a chosen migrant people settling in the promised land of their ancestors – the 'pilgrim fathers'. Bellah (1967) analyzed the content of presidential speeches and observed the frequent references to God in such statements as 'God bless America'. Contemporary examples of civil religion in symbols and action include the celebration of Independence and Thanksgiving Day, the Declaration of Independence, the Statue of Liberty and national shrines such as Mount Rushmore and presidential birthplaces.

Thus the nation's flag and other national symbols and ceremonies upholding American ideals serve to remind civilians of their loyalty to the nation, of their interdependence and reliance on basic standards and responsibilities within the community and of the fact that the nation stands as a collective ideal over and above the individual. Irrespective of ethnic, religious and other distinctions individuals are all part of the greater unity which is the US nation.

> Civil religion is the expression of the cohesion of the nation. It transcends denominational, ethnic and religious boundaries.   (McGuire 1992: 179)

In countries undergoing rapid social, economic and political change there is often increased potential for social dislocation and division at a time when traditional religious ties are being challenged by secular norms and ideals. Many countries in the East, and in Southeast Asia in particular, faced just such a situation as they underwent rapid capitalist development. In Malaysia, Singapore and Indonesia, for example, governments tried to mitigate what they see as potentially threatening effects of development by introducing ideologies and customs stressing national values and norms. In Malaysia the *Rukunegara* – a statement of national ideals – was formulated and regularly recited, while at the same time the celebration of independence day (National Day) and the construction of a national culture are examples of attempts to bind this multicultural nation over and above communal differences (Eyre 1995).

A closer look

Civil religion refers to 'any set of beliefs and rituals, related to the past, present and/or future of a people ("nation") which are understood in some transcendental fashion' (Hammond 1976). Civil religious ideologies, symbols and values are often reasserted in societies when security and social order seems threatened. Consider the following statement from Dynes writing about the period after the September 11 attacks.

'It has been a period when sainthood has been proffered to some political leaders instead of the usual threats of indictment or impeachment. It has elevated New York to a pantheon of sacred cities worthy of a pilgrimage, such as Jerusalem, Rome or Mecca. It has been a time when working class civil servants have replaced corporate executives as contemporary heroes . . . In recent years we have commemorated the anniversary of that event and, while the memorials have been diverse, one general theme has been evident. That the collective response was a collection of individual heroic acts, mirroring the traditional value on individualism in American society. Certain authority figures were seen as remarkable, holding a torn social order together. Those exceptional efforts hark back to the heroism celebrated in America's past.'

(Dynes 2003: 10)

Question

1. *How far do you think the various activities, political rhetoric, rituals and emblems seen after the attacks on September 11 have reflected the civil religion of the United States? In considering this question bear in mind that in order to qualify as examples of civil religion they should fulfil the following criteria:*

➤ The symbols and rituals operate at a national level uniting the nation.

➤ The symbols and rituals are set apart and treated with special respect; they are given 'sacred' significance.

➤ There are regular rituals and ceremonies which bring people together and function to remind people of their collectivity as a nation.

ence between Britain and the United States is that in Britain there is an established Church; in the coronation service the monarch becomes head of the Church and Defender of the Faith. In the United States no particular traditional religion is identified with the civil religion, but in Britain there has traditionally been a close association between the Church of England and expressions of nationalism; an illustration of this was the controversy caused by Prince Charles's statement (during a BBC television interview with Jonathan Dimbleby, 29 June 1994) that he would want to be Defender of *Faiths*, and more recently the controversy surrounding his divorce, revelations about his extra-marital relationship with Mrs Camilla Parker Bowles and discussions about whether he should be allowed to remarry. This 'church-sponsored' civil religion (Gehrig 1981) also embraces the royal family as part of the historical relationship between church and state.

Analysts of civil religion in Britain have identified ceremonial events such as the coronation, royal weddings, the Queen's speech on Christmas Day and other civic events involving a royal presence as examples of civil religion. Shils and Young (1956) studied the coronation of Queen Elizabeth II in 1953 and concluded that such an event not only expressed national values and sentiments but also united the British people in an act of national communion. They suggested that there was an underlying respect among the British people for the symbols of society and for the royal family as upholders of national values.

Stop and think

➤ How far do you think British society today is bound together by a church-sponsored civil religion reinforced by the royal family?

➤ What alternative national rituals and symbols, if any, do you think may function to uphold a sense of national values and bind British society together? Think particularly of examples which may fulfil this function when society may be experiencing a sense of threat?

Civil religion in Britain

How appropriate is the concept of civil religion for Britain? Are there regular rituals and symbols associated with national values which function to bind together the disparate elements of British society? One obvious differ-

Evaluating the concept of civil religion

While civil religion is a useful notion for measuring integration in contemporary societies, the vagueness of the concept makes it difficult to limit the various elements that could be included in a list of civil religious rituals.

Hughey (1993) sums up further difficulties involved in trying to accurately understand and measure civil religion:

> The Durkheimian analysis excludes from consideration the possibility that different groups may be differently committed even to orthodox values and that, therefore, the substantive grounds on which particular groups respond to these values may also be different. If a more empirically adequate understanding of the relationship between values and social order is to be attained, one must know not only that certain values and symbols have attained orthodox stature, or that they have been ceremonialised, but also which groups are most committed to those values, who controls the rituals, and what, if any, other institutionalised mechanisms for their support exist. One must also explore the substantive grounds on which particular groups respond to those values or participate in their ritual celebration. (Hughey 1993: 172)

This sort of evaluation forms part of a more general criticism of the functionalist approach to defining religion in terms of its effects. It has been suggested that the label of religion is too inclusive and should be restricted to those beliefs and rituals associated with a sense of the supernatural. A further criticism of the functionalist approach to religion is that it tends to overemphasize consensus and to underestimate it as a potential source of conflict. Within the sociology of religion a useful balance is provided by a Marxist analysis of religion.

The divisive role of religion

Marxist analyses of religion form part of a wider critique of social structures regarded as tools of control and manipulation used by dominant groups. It will come as no surprise to a student of sociology that Marx did not regard religion within capitalist society as redemptive in any way. Rather he believed it to be a powerful ideology used to express and reinforce class divisions within capitalist society. For Marx, salvation could be achieved only by individuals taking action within this world, not by continuing to depend on and give credibility to institutional structures or beliefs that try to explain and dismiss worldly experiences of oppression.

However, this interpretation of Marxism is by no means the full picture. In order to do justice to a conflict approach to religion it is necessary to look at how Marxist themes have been adopted by later scholars, including those focusing on the revolutionary potential of religion

as an agent of social change and not merely seeing it as an ideology supporting and reinforcing the *status quo*. Here it is helpful to remember that the twin themes of consensus and conflict are inevitable features of society and that something as complex as religion is likely to fulfil both integrative and divisive functions in contemporary contexts.

> The aspect of conflict is basically the obverse of social cohesion; a certain amount of conflict is part of the very structure that holds groups together. And because religion is an important way by which groups express their unity, it is also a significant factor in conflict.
> (McGuire 1992: 175)

Stop and think

> ➤ Is there a relationship between religion and social class? Do you think people from one class are more likely to be attracted to religion than those from another?

Marx's views on religion

Karl Marx not only shared with Durkheim a Jewish family background but also applied a top-down approach to the study of religion in so far as he felt it appropriate to consider religion's general contribution to the perpetuation of social order. However, whereas Durkheim's analysis seems to accept uncritically the role of religion in maintaining the *status quo*, Marx did not. Religion was seen as a distraction from the struggle towards the utopian new world of the communist order. Marx believed that a new society truly based on equality, fairness and freedom would have no use for the sort of exploitative ideas and belief systems encapsulated in religion. There would be no need of any such human ideologies to manipulate, pacify and control the masses.

It is important to be aware of the fact that most of Marx's writings were not directly related to religion. Unlike Weber and Durkheim he did not devote special attention to a study of religion or develop a coherent treatise on it. However, as Elster (1985: 504) points out, there are brief passages about religion scattered throughout his writing over 25 years in which he discusses his views on the nature, causes and consequences of religion. It is also important to appreciate that unlike Durkheim, and even more so Weber, Marx did not give credit to the many forms and varieties of religion across the world, tending rather to generalize from his own experience of religion in Western, capitalist societies based on a Judaeo-Christian heritage.

Marx's basic premise was that religion is a human phenomenon rather than a supernatural one. Religion arises in society out of human or social need, either as a spontaneous invention by the oppressed to make sense of their condition or as an ideology developed by the ruling class. Marx was influenced by the writings of Feuerbach (1957) and saw religion as a way that individuals could satisfy their needs in this world by imagining their fulfilment in a future world. Such an imaginary world is ruled over by a supernatural being in whom is realized humanity's supreme potentialities:

> The basis of irreligious criticism is: man [sic] makes religion, religion does not make man. Religion is indeed the self-consciousness and self-feeling of man who has not yet gained possession of himself or has already lost himself again. But man is not an abstract being lurking outside the world. Man is the world of men, state, society. This state, this society produces religion, an inverted consciousness of the world, because it is an inverted world . . . Religion is the realisation of the essence of man in the imagination because the essence of man has no true realisation. The battle against religion is thus indirectly the battle against that world whose spiritual aroma religion is.
>
> (Marx and Engels 1976 vol. 3: 175)

For Marx, religion cannot be divorced from the social context in which it is found, because the social context is the basis of both its origin and its form.

> If therefore we investigate the religion of a people, we are not really exploring a world beyond this world, but are examining symptoms that reveal the social diseases from which the people are suffering.
>
> (Acton 1967: 26)

Here again there are similarities with Durkheim in the sense that Marx seems to be explaining away religion by regarding it as purely of social origin. Many sociologists of religion today would challenge such an extreme and dismissive position.

Marx elaborates on the idea of religion as a reflection of and protest against distressing social conditions in what has become a well-known summary of his thought:

> Religious want is both the expression of and the protest against real want. Religion is the sigh of the oppressed creature, the heart of a heartless world, the soul of soulless circumstances. It is the opium of the people.   (Marx and Engels 1976 vol. 3: 175)

While the term 'protest' tends to conjure up images of engaged action and demonstration, in Marx's analysis the form of protest engendered by religion is more passive, a process of withdrawal from worldly involvement. He suggests that, just like a drug, religion can give the user temporary relief and even a temporary 'high', but in the long run the prognosis is not good.

Stop and think

> ➤ In what ways might the effects of religion be comparable to those of taking drugs? How appropriate do you think this analogy is in terms of the following:
>
> (a) gives an emotional and physical high; release from reality;
> (b) affects consciousness either through hallucination or distortion of reality;
> (c) leads to long-term effects of apathy, lethargy, inaction;
> (d) results in physical and psychological dependency.

Marx argues that religion not only has a narcotic effect on the masses but also functions for the dominant class in sustaining the *status quo*. Religion justifies for them their social and political status as well as maintaining their position by diverting the revolutionary potential of the oppressed.

> The social principles of Christianity justified the slavery of antiquity, glorified the serfdom of the Middle Ages and are capable, in case of need, of defending the oppression of the proletariat, even with somewhat doleful grimaces. The social principles of Christianity preach the necessity of a ruling and an oppressed class, and for the latter all they have to offer is the pious wish that the former may be charitable . . . The social principles of Christianity declare all the vile acts of the oppressors against the oppressed to be either a just punishment for original sin, and other sins, or trials which the Lord, in his infinite wisdom, ordains for the redeemed. The social principles of Christianity preach cowardice, self-contempt, abasement, submissiveness and humbleness, in short all the qualities of the rabble, and the proletariat, which will not permit itself to be treated as rabble, needs its courage, its self-confidence, its pride and its sense of independence even more than its bread. The social principles of Christianity are sneaking and hypocritical and the proletariat is revolutionary.   (Marx and Engels 1976 vol. 6: 231)

Marx was hopeful that the oppression of the masses would end. He predicted that capitalism would be overcome along with its unjust ideologies and false hopes. Once the social conditions of capitalism were overthrown there would be no need for false ideologies such as religion to compensate for social reality.

> To remove religion as the people's illusory happiness is to demand real happiness for the people. The demand for the abandonment of illusions about one's condition is the demand to give up a condition that needs illusion. The criticism of religion is thus in embryo the criticism of the vale of sorrows whose halo is religion.   (Marx and Engels 1976 vol. 3: 176)

His views of communism appear rather naive now that we have the advantage of historical insight into the limits of communism and the changes to the political and social landscape of eastern Europe over the last decade or so.

In 2003 pope John Paul II celebrated twenty-five years of his papacy. He had grown up and joined the priesthood in communist Poland before being elected head of the Catholic Church in 1978. Some believe he played a key role in the overthrow of communism in eastern Europe. However, he has been one among many religious leaders who have spoken out about what they regard as the evils of contemporary economic systems, both on the left and right. In 1993 Pope John Paul II gave an interview in which he criticized the extremes of both communism and capitalism. He also highlighted those strands of Catholic thought compatible with Marx's views:

> Communism has had its successes in this century as a reaction against a certain type of unbridled savage capitalism which we all know well. One need only take in hand the social encyclicals, and in particular the first, Rerum Novarum, in which Leo XIII describes the condition of the workers of that time. [This powerful encyclical, issued in 1891, asserted the rights of labour to just rewards and endorsed legislation, trade unions and co-operative organizations having this purpose.] Marx, too, described it in his own way. That's what social reality was like, without a doubt, and it was a consequence of the system, of the principles of ultra-liberal capitalism.'
>
> (Pope John Paul II, quoted in 'States of Savagery, Seeds of Good', the *Guardian* 2.11.1993)

Later in the interview he said:

> Of course, it was legitimate to fight against the unjust, totalitarian system which defined itself as socialist or communist. But it is also true what Leo XIII says, that

there are some 'seeds of truth' even in the socialist programme. It is obvious that these seeds should not be destroyed . . . The proponents of capitalism in its extreme forms tend to overlook the good things achieved by communism: the efforts to overcome unemployment, the concern for the poor.   (Ibid.)

Neo-Marxist approaches to religion

The statements from Pope John Paul II show that the relationship between religion and Marxism is a surprisingly complex one. Making simplistic generalizations about religions in historical or contemporary context, therefore, would be highly misleading. However, it would be equally misleading to leave a Marxist analysis here, since the classic interpretation of Marx's views on religion outlined so far has itself been subject to substantial reinterpretation. Neo-Marxists defend Marx's views on religion against misrepresentation and an overemphasis on religion's opiate effects. They suggest that Marx balanced this analysis by acknowledging a dynamic role for religion as a powerful agent of challenge and social change in society.

> The fact that religion is far from being in all cases a drug administered by the oppressors for the purpose of inducing resignation and inaction among the oppressed has long been clear to Marxists as well as to others . . . Thus repetition of a crude opium-of-the-people thesis has no scholarly justification, least of all if presented as the Marxist view of religion.
>
> (O'Toole 1984: 189)

Using Marxist themes, analysts focus on situations where religious and cultural ideologies are developed and applied as part of revolutionary struggle of the oppressed against injustice, using both violent and non-violent means. In South Africa, Latin America and Poland, for example, Christian activists have mobilized the poor and oppressed against the authorities. These activists combine Marxist and Christian strands in *liberation theology*, invoking the Christian Gospels to justify their resistance against poverty and exploitation in the name of human rights.

Since becoming Archbishop of Canterbury in 2002, Dr Rowan Williams and other Church representatives have frequently spoken in opposition to Government policy and cited the interests of the most vulnerable in society as legitimation for their beliefs and views (see the Case study on p. 603). From time to time such declarations lead to heated public debate about the role of the Church in society and criticisms of Church leaders 'meddling in politics'.

World in focus

Liberation theology

When I feed the poor they call me a saint; when I ask why they are poor they call me a communist.

(Dom Helder Camara, quoted on a CAFOD poster)

Liberation theology represents a radical engagement of Christianity with the world, with the intent to represent human freedom and God's gratuitous activity in the questions and issues of the day. As a radically new paradigm and departure from modern theology, liberation theology reflects and guides a Christianity that is identified with those who suffer, that represents a freedom of transformation, and that proclaims a God whose love frees us for justice and faith.

(Chopp 1986: 153)

In prefacing a documentary history of liberation theology (LT), Hennelly (1990: xv) states that its development sprang not from First World scholars in great universities but from small communities of the poorest and least literate men and women, first in Latin America and later in other parts of the Third World. Latin American theology first started to be identified as a

'theology of liberation' in the 1960s and has been inspired by the writings and actions of individuals such as Leonardo Boff (1987) and Gustavo Gutierrez (1973; 1990; 2001).

Liberation theology illustrates how a conflict approach to understanding and evaluating social reality can be compatible with a religious outlook and can actively bring about social change. Indeed 'the ideals and ideas of Liberation Theology specifically point[ed] to a transformative approach to religious action' (McGuire 1992: 241).

Dom Helder Camara (1909–99) was one of the most prominent figures associated with liberation theology, a fact which made him one of Brazil's most controversial clergymen. After the Second World War he became politically active in campaigning on behalf of Brazil's poor and oppressed and, through his activities and international travel, became a well-known international figure. Camara devoted much time to setting up charitable foundations and social projects and was a vigorous critic of the arms race. In 1964 he became Archbishop of Recife but this did not prevent him from clashing with the military

government which ruled Brazil in the 1960s and 1970s.

Many such dedicated priests, nuns and lay churchworkers were branded as left-wing agitators, were persecuted and even gave their lives fighting oppressive systems as part of their Christian vocation. They include Archbishop Oscar Romero, shot through the heart as he preached at Mass in San Salvador in 1980. Camara once had his home sprayed with machine gun fire.

On a visit to Brazil Pope John Paul praised the social concern of LT but criticized clerical involvement in politics. Speaking in 1989, Camara said: 'The world of the rich and the world of the poor; why do we not come again to the idea of the Creator and one family if we are brothers and sisters?'

After Camara's death in 1999, an official note of condolence from President Cardoza described him as a blessed man who dedicated his life to ecumenism, human rights and the fight for peace and solidarity. Camara's works and writings continue to have relevance in today's world.

The only legitimate war is the one that is declared against the underdevelopment and the misery. (Camara)

While it is important to recognize alternative strands in the Marxist analysis of religion, it is true to say that the 'opium-of-the-people' interpretation appears to be the strongest and most consistent element in Marx's writing. However, this has not prevented modern analysts from developing the emphasis throughout his work on the significance of differing interest groups and the power of ideologies in trying to understand and

interpret the role of religion in contemporary situations of social conflict.

Religion and social conflict

Media coverage of religion in contemporary world affairs usually highlights its role in social and political struggle. Religion is more 'newsworthy' when it is part of conflict

Case study

Religion and politics: the Church meddling?

February 2003 Dr Williams issues a joint statement with the leader of the Roman Catholic Church in England and Wales, Cardinal Cormac Murphy O'Connor, doubting the moral case for military action in Iraq during the second Gulf War. In 2004 all 114 Church of England bishops join in writing to Prime Minister Tony Blair to warn him of the damage to Britain's reputation caused by the abuse of Iraqi detainees.

February 2004 The Church of England General Synod condemns the exploitation of asylum seekers. It passes a motion condemning 'the exploitation of the poor and vulnerable by organized criminals engaged in people trafficking'. The Synod calls on the government to deliver an asylum system characterized by 'quality, speed and justice' and to ensure it did not present a 'negative image' of vulnerable people.

May 2004 In the lead up to local and European elections, various church leaders issue statements designed to influence voters. The Catholic Church for example, issues a 100-page booklet, *Cherishing Life*, stating voters should challenge candidates about their attitudes on a range of subjects of particular concern to the Church. These include anything that the Church regards as antithetical to life, such as abortion, euthanasia, IVF treatment and stem-cell research.

July 2004 The Church of England declares its support for a challenging proposal to tackle the threat of climate change. In a lecture entitled 'Changing The Myths We Live By', Dr Williams criticizes specifically 'the addiction to fossil fuel of the wealthy nations; this is what secures the steady continuance of carbon emissions, but it is also what drives anxieties about political hegemony'. He calls on the government to promote a new sense of public seriousness about environmental issues.

July 2004 The Church of England's General Synod votes to accept a report calling for prison to be used as a last resort. The Archbishop of Canterbury, Rowan William brands the government's penal policy 'scandalous'. He also accuses the three main political parties of 'point scoring' in the debate on criminal justice. Dr Williams condemns the government for overseeing a massive rise in the prison population and for locking up more vulnerable children and women.

Question

1. *Do you think it is right that religious leaders should be involved in political debates? Give reasons for your answer.*

than when it fulfils its expected role of integrating communities through rituals, worship and festivals. Even in situations where religion enhances community and belonging, it engenders a sense of insiders and outsiders, of 'us' and 'them'. In some social and political contexts these lines of division may be made explicit. The war in former Yugoslavia in the 1990s illustrated that even where religious communities have existed alongside each other relatively peacefully for many years, circumstances may combine to ignite a confrontation.

Such confrontation often continues for months or even years and can leave devastation as communities struggle with new configurations. In 1998 the World Disasters Report described the war in Sarajevo as having caused 'massive dislocation': 'Most of Sarajevo's substantial pre-war Serb minority has left and the population of the City, once famous for its multi-ethnic mix, is now predominantly Bosniak (Bosnian Muslim), a community with its own divisions. Even the language has changed, replacing Serbo-Croat with the trio of Bosnian, Croatian and Serbian' (World Disasters Report 1998: 82).

As this example illustrates, conflict within and between groups may be based not only on religion but also on economic, political, ethnic and cultural lines of social division. These factors overlap and it is difficult to isolate the extent to which any one is the main cause or influence. Indeed, different individuals involved in such conflicts may disagree about the significance of particular factors, whose significance may vary over time.

Stop and think

➤ Examples of twentieth-century conflicts involving religion in some way include the Holocaust, the 1950s Civil Rights movement in the United States, the Iran–Iraq war in the 1980s, the Gulf Wars 1990–91 and 2003, Arab–Israeli conflicts, the civil unrest in Indonesia (2004), Northern Ireland and former Yugoslavia and the 'War on Terrorism' (2001). To what extent were are these conflicts based on theological, religious, racial, political or other grounds?

➤ How far does religion overlap with other lines of social division and to what extent is it possible to distinguish between them?

In the above examples complex factors are involved and it is difficult to isolate the precise role and significance of religion. In other situations, however, religion appears to be the most central factor in a conflict based on specific theological, ethical or organizational questions. Where a religious belief system includes an exclusivist or particularist world view (that is the idea that its own religious outlook is the only legitimate one), it is likely that conflict with outsiders will arise. Examples of movements attempting to convert outsiders to particularist religions are the medieval Crusades and some missionary movements. In extreme cases refusal to convert ends in death (or martyrdom depending on your point of view).

Within any religious community disagreements may arise over questions of doctrine, ethics or leadership. Individuals who openly challenge officially defined doctrines may be labelled as heretics. They may be excommunicated from the official structures or break away from the main tradition to set up sectarian alternatives (see pp. 589–90). Schism occurs throughout the history of religion and might be seen as an inevitable consequence of institutions trying to reconcile competing demands of tradition and change. In the Church of England the debates and consequences relating to the ordination of women and homosexuality within the priesthood illustrate themes of religious and social conflict. Leaders of the main religious institutions expect to be challenged by grassroots members – within the priesthood or the laity – over issues of doctrine and ethics. In smaller religious groups, such as new religious movements, questions of succession may arise once the charismatic founders pass away. Resolving leadership challenges is crucial in determining the long-term survival of a movement.

In the wider arena of ethics, there are also many examples of religiously prescribed codes of behaviour being subject to negotiation, disagreement and difference. In contemporary societies standards of public morality are dynamic, constantly facing reassessment in response to the challenges provided by developments in the fields of science and technology. In the area of medical and sexual ethics, for example, there are ongoing debates about genetic engineering, euthanasia, contraception and abortion. Religious bodies often subscribe to particular ethical codes in relation to such dilemmas, though these may give rise to conflicting opinions and actions both within and between denominational boundaries. The media often give coverage to such controversies, particularly when religious authorities are being called on to inform public debates about ethical and moral standards.

Stop and think

➤ Think of examples of recent press coverage of public moral and ethical debates. How much space is given to religious perspectives? Are they presented in a predominantly positive or negative way?

This overview of religion and social division illustrates the various ways in which religion is associated with social conflict. It is important to develop beyond a classical Marxist interpretation in order to understand the rich complexity of religions in social context. The sociology of religion, having evolved beyond its founding theories, defies any simplistic deduction about the ideological function of beliefs. Both consensus *and* conflict are important features of religious life and any analysis that underplays the significance of either can be only partial.

Is religion dying out?

Many people today query whether religion can survive the onslaught of secularism. A hundred years or so ago, sociologists predicted the gradual decline and even disappearance of religion. While their ideas have received much support within the sociology of religion, it seems less appropriate today to talk of the demise of religion given its persistence as a political and cultural force in a rapidly changing world. We shall consider and evaluate the secularization thesis.

The term *secularization* carries many meanings, some of which imply a value-judgement. Originally 'secularization'

referred to the transfer of church property from ecclesiast-
ical to secular state control during the Reformation. In
Roman canon law it denotes the return of a person from a
religious order to the world. In some theological circles it
may refer to 'de-Christianization' and carry a negative sense
of loss, whereas critics who see religion as a false or harmful ideology (e.g. radical Marxists) may regard secularization as a positive process in the sense of enabling the
liberation of humanity's rational intellectual potential.

In sociological terms secularization is not intended to
carry any prescriptive judgements but rather refers to a
variety of processes associated with the gradual decline of
religion in society. It has been succinctly defined as 'the
process whereby religious thinking, practice and institutions lose their social significance' (Wilson 1969: 14).

Secularization is often identified with a more general
process which includes features such as industrialization,
modernization and rationalization. Thus while being
part of something greater, and involving many sociological features beyond the manifestation of religion *per se*,
the secularization process refers specifically to the transition from a society dominated by religious forms to one
marked by the increasing absence of religious influence
in social life (Berger 1967b: 113). Secularization has been
related to wider processes of 'modernization', though
current debates about 'postmodern' living have modified
theories of secularization.

Defining and measuring secularization in relation to
religion is hampered by similar problems to those that
beset attempts to define religion. While 'secular' tends
to be referred to as the opposite of 'religious', as with the
dichotomy sacred–profane, it is questionable whether
the distinction is so rigid: at what point does the secular
become the religious?

Stop and think

➤ How would you measure the extent of secularization
in your own community?

➤ What problems might there be with attempts at
measurement?

The myth of secularization?

Critics have questioned the value of the secularization
thesis for implying that we have moved from a religious
'golden age'. Glasner (1977) suggests that it is misleading

A closer look

'Cybergrace': the future of religiosity?

'Following Jesus's command to "go, therefore, and
make disciples of all nations" has never been easier.
No more exhausting crusades to faraway lands, no more
missions to the heart of darkness, no more trudging the
streets weighed own by a sandwich board: spreading the
word can now be done from the comfort of a computer
screen'. So states Milly Jenkins in reporting of the
growth of the Internet as a method of evangelization
and religious practice (*Independent* 28.4.1998).
As far back as 1987 Pope John Paul II recognized the
missionary potential of cyberspace, a forum which has
becoming increasing popular for those delivering and
receiving religious messages. Today every major religion
has a web presence. Many places of worship keep their
congregations informed via individual web sites. In 2004
a web-based community of worshippers – i-church –
was launched and recognized as a full Anglican church,
the first time for such a web-based congregation.

A whole range of traditional and newer religious
bodies are represented on this forum, which presents in
itself a fascinating arena for study. At the same time,
such trends remind us of the difficulty in accurately
measuring concepts such as secularization and
religiosity in more traditional ways, such as through
examining institutional membership and physical
attendance at places of worship.

to assume either that the historical past was one in
which people were more religious or that any decline that
has taken place has been uniformly spread throughout
society or the world. This brings us back to how we
define and measure religiosity in society. Statistics on
church attendance show that fewer people attend services
than in the past, but this does not mean that our ancestors
were more religious. In Victorian times, churchgoing was
strongly associated with respectability and people were
under considerable social pressure to attend church.
Campbell (1971) suggested that if public standards of
morality are referred to as the yardstick for measuring
religiosity, we should query designating the Victorian
period as a golden age of religiosity given its moral
attitudes to prostitution, for example.

Various phases in history such as the last years of the
Roman Empire and the Reformation can be identified as
'irreligious' to the extent that they were characterized by
much scepticism and heresy. Consequently, the implication within the secularization thesis of a past golden age

of religion has been seen by some as a myth. Glasner (1977) argued that the myth has been used out of context by those looking for an all-purpose explanation for the supposed ills of contemporary society. In challenging the idea that there has been a steady and irreversible fall in moral standards, these critics suggest that a linear conception of religious decline may be too generalistic and warn against oversimplification in any analysis of religion and social change.

Although there has been much debate about the difficulty of both defining and measuring secularization, as well as controversy about the extent of its impact, few would doubt that secularizing processes have been at work, not just in the West but increasingly as a global phenomenon. Since secularization can be seen as a multi-dimensional concept, the main aspects of this process will be examined.

The institutional decline of religion

As an institutional process, secularization includes the *decline in institutional membership and practice*; there has been decreasing participation in most forms of religious ceremony over the last 25 years or so, particularly within Christianity. The *UK Christian Handbook* (Brierley and Hiscock 1993) has shown that between 1975 and 1992 Church membership in the United Kingdom fell from an estimated 8 million (one in five of the adult population) to 6.7 million (one in seven). This figure had dropping to less than 6 million by the year 2000 (*UK Religious Trends* 2001), a factor partly reflecting demographic changes and the fact that the majority of churchgoers have been older. Denscombe (1998: 38) cites the following facts on membership and attendance from *UK Religious Trends 1997*:

➤ In the period since 1980, attendance at mass by Roman Catholics has fallen from 2.4 million to 1.7 million.

➤ Numbers on the electoral roll of the Church of England fell from nearly 2.2 million to less than 1.6 million during the period since 1980. Presbyterian membership, meanwhile, has fallen from 1.4 million to under 1 million and membership of the Methodist Church is down from 520,000 to around 366,000.

As regards church attendance the figures in Table 15.1 for Church of England attendances are from the CofE web site and show a continuing decline in the first years of the twenty-first century.

Given this general trend, more in-depth research has shown that the decline has been far from uniform; while some religious groups have declined rapidly, others have experienced periods of stabilization or even growth. Davie (1994) gives a good critical overview of religious constituencies.

Religious membership and attendance may not be accurate reflections of the religiosity of individuals: difficulties in using these criteria as accurate measures include the accuracy, reliability and interpretation of such data in terms of methods of collecting statistics and the relative importance within different belief systems of attendance at a place of worship. There are also problems in defining 'membership' of a religious organization. A one-off attendance at a meeting could be evidence of 'membership' for some religious groups, while irregular attendance indicates personal disaffiliation for other groups. The tenth British Social Attitudes survey in Britain for example, provided data on the proportion of people describing themselves as regular worshippers; only one in five would describe themselves as a regular Christian worshipper, while over one-third said they had no religion. The statistics suggest that compared

Table 15.1 Typical monthly church attendance 2001–03

All ages	2001	2002	Change 2001 to 2002	2003	Change 2002 to 2003
Average weekly attendance (AWA)	1,205,000	1,170,000	−3%	1,187,000	1%
Weekly lowest attendance	862,000	825,000	−4%	844,000	2%
Weekly highest attendance	1,708,000	1,682,000	−1%	1,704,000	1%
Average Sunday attendance (ASA)	1,041,000	1,005,000	−3%	1,017,000	1%
Sunday lowest attendance	774,000	733,000	−5%	755,000	3%
Sunday highest attendance	1,425,000	1,395,000	−2%	1,401,000	~
Usual Sunday attendance (USA)	938,000	919,000	−2%	901,000	−2%

Source: www.cofe.anglican.org

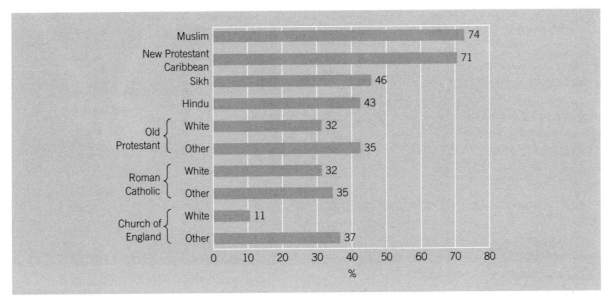

Figure 15.5 Religion and lifestyle: percentage of people who say that religion is very important to their way of life
Source: Denscombe 1998: 48

internationally, Britain is 'particularly low in terms of religious commitment' (Denscombe 1994: 23).

While the evidence suggests that there has been a decline overall in what is referred to as 'church-oriented' religiosity in Britain, this does not necessarily mean that people are no longer 'religious'. Indeed there remains a relatively high rate of belief in God among the general population, which Davie (1994) describes as 'believing without belonging'. Furthermore, when we look beyond the white population and the traditional Christian churches in Britain, there is evidence that religious belief and the influence of religion on lifestyle appears to be stronger (see Figure 15.5).

In institutional terms, secularization in Britain refers particularly to the decreasing *social and political influence of the Church of England*, including the Church's declining wealth and influence over areas of social and political life that in the past came under its jurisdiction and authority. With the development of the welfare state, the public sector increased its control over areas of social provision such as education, welfare and patronage of the arts, while the Church's involvement diminished. However, the Church's influence has not altogether disappeared. Indeed, since the 1980s the state's role in the public sector has been markedly reduced with the effect that the voluntary sector (including religious bodies) has increasingly re-emerged to try to fill the gaps in services that have accompanied the dismantling of the welfare state. Though the Church is unlikely to regain the wealth

and range of influence that it once had, the renewed need for its role as a provider of care within the voluntary sector is in part a response to the secularization process.

A closer look

Differentiation

The process whereby the Church has become disengaged from these different institutions of society and has become more specialized in relation to its main function of 'hatching, matching and dispatching' is known as 'differentiation'. Differentiation has been defined as 'the development of increasing complexity within organic systems or societies' (Giddens 1989: 738).

The decline of religious thinking

Referring back to Wilson's definition (p. 605), secularization reflects the decline of religious thinking in society. This has been related to the rise of scientific and rational modes of thought in advanced societies, which gradually replaced non-rational systems of belief such as religion. For some of the early sociologists this was seen as the logical conclusion to the Age of Enlightenment; religious

Table 15.2 Indicators of religious commitment, Britain compared with European average, 1990

Indicators of religious disposition	Britain	European average*	Indicators of orthodox belief	Britain	European average*
Often think about meaning and purposes of life	36	33	Believe in personal God	32	39
Often think about death	19	20	Believe in a spirit or life force	41	30
Need moments of prayer, etc.	53	60	Believe in:		
Define self as a religious person	54	63	God	71	72
			Sin	68	54
			Soul	64	61
Draw comfort/strength from religion	44	48	Heaven	53	42
			Life after death	44	44
God is important in my life	44	52	The devil	30	26
			Hell	25	23

Note: *Figures for equivalent countries provided by Dr D Barker, European Values Group
Source: Table adapted from Abrams et al. 1985: 60 and further adapted from Davie 1994: 78

ideas, symbols and values would gradually be replaced by instrumental values, rational procedures and technical methods (Wilson 1982). A clear parallel was drawn between the increasing secularization of society and processes of modernization; a modern advanced society would have no need for the irrationality of religion and reference to a supernatural God. Rather in time all would be subject to human influence and control. In such an advanced (and by implication superior) society, science would provide the explanations of the way the world functions, so enabling humanity to control all events within it.

Case study

Science, religion and health

This might be enough to give you a heart attack: there are now more than 250 'risk factors' for cardiac disease.

You know about the major risks – smoking, high blood pressure, a high-fat diet, physical inactivity and a family history . . .

Now there is another factor to worry about. The latest warning, in The Lancet last week, concerns colds and flu, which may increase the risk of heart attack for two weeks . . .

A further risk factor will come as no surprise to those who still believe, against all scientific evidence, that the heart is the seat of human emotion. While doctors have traditionally dismissed as Mills & Boon the old idea that we could die from a broken heart, research suggests otherwise.

In one study, 6,000 men and women with mildly to moderately high blood pressure were asked if they had ever been treated for depression. Those who had been were followed for five years and found to have twice the number of heart attacks.

The wise ones, it seems, turned to the Lord, because regular churchgoers have been shown to be at less risk. After interviewing several thousand patients, Dr Harold Koenig, director of the UK Duke Programme on Religion, Health and Ageing in North Caroline, is convinced that religion is a highly effective anti-depressant.

(From Illman 1998, 'You really can die of a broken heart . . . but psalms and sermons could save you', Observer 17.5.1998)

Question

1. As the extract shows, some scientists have found links between religion and health. To what extent do you think there can be links between physical, emotional and spiritual well-being?

To a limited extent this has happened: many natural and social events are explained by reference to scientific phenomena. Our ability to understand and control environmental, technical and medical developments has never been greater; most of the time we find no need to refer to supernatural explanations.

However, there is clearly a limit to the extent to which all phenomena are explicable in scientific and rational terms. The realities of death, war, world famine, earthquakes and environmental destruction bear witness both to the unpredictability of human behaviour and our inability to control all events. In terms of secularization both sociologists and theologians have pointedout that there are still fields of human action and inquiry which go beyond science in offering explanations for ultimate questions of human existence. There is continuing reference to religious and spiritual authorities for guidance in addressing moral dilemmas generated by a changing world. These factors help to explain the continuing need and survival of religious modes of thinking and expression.

In thinking about the future of religion, sociologists no longer assume that it might well die out but ask rather what form and role religion might take in the twenty-first century. Questions about the fundamental nature of religion and reasons for its existence were raised by the first sociologists, knowing that they were on the brink of unprecedented social and economic change. As we progress through the next millennium, the uncertainties surrounding global religious, political and economic transformation make the search for meaning, identity and destiny as relevant as ever.

Summary

➤ The sociology of religion focuses on the social context and consequences of belief systems. It attempts to define and measure religiosity but this can prove problematic across time and culture. Glock and Stark (1968) differentiated five dimensions of religiosity: belief, practice, experience, knowledge and consequence.

➤ Durkheim made a clear distinction between the sacred and profane and defined religion as 'a unified system of beliefs and practices relative to sacred things' which united its followers into a moral community or church. Once these beliefs had been created by society they acquired an autonomous existence of their own.

➤ Weber emphasized not only the nature and significance of religious motivation but also the influence of religion on other aspects of society including ethics, economics and politics.

➤ There are four main categories of religious organization: church, denomination, sect and cult.

➤ Religion can contribute both to social integration and to social conflict. Functionalist approaches have tended to emphasize religion's integrative effects and these ideas were developed further by Robert Bellah (1967) into the concept of civil religion. In contrast, the conflicts in the former Yugoslavia, Northern Ireland and the Middle East all illustrate instances where religion has played a divisive role.

➤ Marxist analyses of religion traditionally present it as a powerful ideology which expresses and reinforces class division and oppression, the 'opium of the people'. However, some neo-Marxists have recognized the revolutionary potential of religion as an agent of social change, as illustrated by the impact of liberation theology in parts of Africa, Latin America and Eastern Europe.

➤ Despite predictions of the decline and eventual disappearance of religion it still remains a powerful political and cultural force on a global scale and has resisted the forces of creeping secularization.

Links

The theorizing of Durkheim and Marx on the role of religion, pages 596–601, can be related to their broader theoretical writings examined in Chapter 2.

The integrative role of religion, pages 592–596, links to the discussion of cultural identity in Chapter 1.

 Further reading

Davie, G., Heelas, P. and Woodhead, L. (2003) *Predicting Religion: Christian, Secular and Alternative Futures,* Hampshire: Ashgate.

Religion in the contemporary West is undergoing rapid change. In this book twenty experts in the study of religion present their predictions about the future of religion in the twenty-first century.

Davie, G. (1994) *Religion in Britain since 1945: Believing without Belonging,* Oxford: Blackwell.

A significant contribution to the sociology of religion in Britain, tracing post-war patterns of religion. A key theme is 'believing without belonging' – the growing discrepancy between high indicators of religious belief in Britain and low statistics on membership and practice. This is a very readable book integrating both theoretical and empirical strands.

Halman, Loek and Riis, Ole (2003) *Religion in Secularising Society: The Europeans 'Religion' at the End of the 20th Century,* Amsterdam: Brill Academic Publishers.

The cross-national analyses of Europe's patterns of religious and moral orientations presented in this book are all based on the 1990 European Values study data. Use is also made of the 1995/97 World Values study. All the contributions show aspects of the religious and moral culture in contemporary secularizing societies.

Social Compass (Sage Publications).

This regular journal is the international review of the sociology of religion. It includes contributions from top analysts in the field and from all over the world. Recent editions have focused on the following themes: teaching and research in the social sciences of religion; religion, culture and identity; and state reconstruction of the religious field.

Web sites

BSA Sociology of Religion Study Group
www.socrel.org.uk
This study group within the British Sociological Association was founded in 1975 and has become one of the largest study groups within the association. It runs regular conferences and study days as well as an email discussion list. The group particularly encourages younger members and works to increase the profile of the sociology of religion within sociology.

Activities

Activity 1

New religious movements

To highlight one aspect of the variety of groups within the category of 'new religious movement', group the following organizations in relation to their theological roots: Western (i.e. Judaeo-Christian), Eastern (i.e. Hindu or Buddhist) or other (e.g. Satanic, New Age). You will need to do some library research in order to find out more about the beliefs of these groups and their activities. It is important to be critical about your sources and the perspectives they engender:

(a) Unification Church (Moonies); (b) Scientology; (c) International Society for Krishna Consciousness (ISKCON or Hare Krishna); (d) Soka Gakkai International; (e) Children of God (also known as The Family of God or the Family); (f) Bagwan Shree Rajneesh; (g) Branch Davidians (followers of David Koresh at Waco, Texas); (h) Church of Satan; (i) Findhorn Community; (j) Pan Wave.

Add to this list and discuss other similarities and differences between these groups in terms of their beliefs and practices.

The three classifications (Western, Eastern, other) are not the only ones which have been applied to religious organizations. Consider the application and methodological issues associated with the following ways of classifying religious forms: 'world religion'; 'established religion'; 'traditional religion'; 'messianic and millenarian movements'; 'official and unofficial religion'; 'popular/folk religion'.

Activity 2

Religious ceremonies

Observe a religious ceremony and give an account of the symbolic behaviour and its meaning for believers. You may choose one of the ceremonies referred to in this chapter or else a more regular religious gathering such as weekly worship or one relating to birth, marriage or death.

What norms are involved? (Describe observable forms of behaviour such as ritual, gestures, dress, speech and song.)

What values underpin these norms? (Investigate the symbolic meaning attached to forms of behaviour. Your research may involve asking participants or researching second-hand sources.)

How far do these ceremonies function to bind the community? Discuss whether such functions are more or less important in secular society.

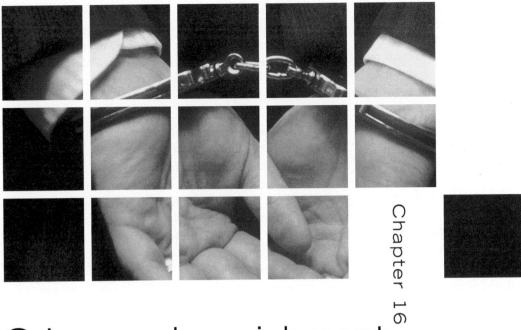

Chapter 16

Crime and punishment

The study of crime begins with the knowledge of oneself. (Miller 1945)

The standards of a nation's civilisation can be judged by opening the doors of its prisons.
(Dostoevsky 1860)

Key issues

➤ How has crime been defined and measured?

➤ How have sociologists tried to explain crime?

➤ To what extent is crime characteristic of particular social groups?

➤ What are the main aims of punishment?

➤ How have sociologists explained the role of punishment in society?

Introduction

Unconventional and criminal behaviour fascinates people. Many popular TV programmes, successful films and bestselling books are about crime and criminals, both 'real life' and fictional. Our interest is in criminal behaviour – what it involves and how it is done – and in what happens to the criminals – whether they 'get away with it' and what happens to them if they do not. However, while we like to watch and read about crime, and many of us break laws from time to time, relatively few of us will have been caught and prosecuted for our lawbreaking behaviour and even fewer will make crime a way of life and become professional murderers, smugglers or fraudsters.

This chapter looks at both crime and punishment, at the extent of crime, why some people and social groups are more likely to engage in criminal behaviour than others, how society controls crime and how it deals with those people who are caught. The role of the police in enforcing the law and the debates surrounding punishment of offenders are discussed. Punishment is examined as a key element of the sociology of crime; this is evident in the work of Durkheim, the major 'classical' theorist in this area. Durkheim highlighted the importance of crime for maintaining the collective conscience of society and emphasized how punishment exemplified this collective conscience at work. The first section of the chapter focuses on the sociology of crime and the second section centres on the sociology of punishment.

The sociology of crime
The relationship between crime and deviance

Before looking at sociological work on crime, we need to define and clarify our subject matter, particularly as crime is often examined as part of the broader field of the sociology of deviance and the terms 'crime' and 'deviance' are sometimes used interchangeably. Unconventional behaviour fascinates people; such behaviour might involve breaking the law or just fall outside the commonly held definition of what is normal and reasonable. This distinction helps us to distinguish crime from deviance.

Crime may be defined as an act that breaks the criminal law; it can be followed by criminal proceedings and formal punishment.

Deviance is a less precise concept than crime: deviance means any behaviour that differs from the normal. Thus deviant behaviour could be uncommonly good or brave behaviour as well as unacceptable behaviour, such as theft or vandalism. It could also be eccentric or bizarre behaviour, such as talking loudly to oneself or to no one in particular in public places. However, deviance generally refers to behaviour that is disapproved of and subject to some form of punishment, behaviour that is outside the rules of society and leads to a hostile and critical response from 'conventional society'. These rules might be legal rules – laws that have specific penalties established to punish those who break them – or social and moral rules – rules about how people should behave in public, for example.

In distinguishing between crime and deviance we have talked about breaking laws and not following conventional standards of behaviour or norms. *Norms* are the unwritten rules that influence people's behaviour. They are the ideal standards of behaviour that members of a social group share and form part of the culture of that society, such as the manner in which parents should treat their children and children their parents. Different groups within a society may have their own norms. While it is the norm in the UK to eat meat, being a vegetarian is not generally seen as unacceptable behaviour. Young people may hold quite different norms from older people and particular youth groups have norms that are distinct from other groups.

The definitions of crime and deviance as behaviour that is outside the laws or norms of society emphasize the importance of the reaction of others; such behaviour will usually produce some form of critical or hostile response from the wider society. However, laws and norms are not fixed; they vary from time to time and from place to place. Therefore behaviour which breaks them will also vary. So crime and deviance are *relative concepts*, which vary according to the particular social situation. Behaviour which is criminal in one country can be acceptable in another, for example drinking alcohol or having several spouses at the same time. Certain types of behaviour have been criminal at one period of time but not at others; homosexuality, for instance, has been decriminalized in many countries but still carries the death penalty in Iran.

Social reaction is of central importance in determining whether behaviour is categorized as criminal or deviant. No action is criminal or deviant in itself; it becomes so only if the society defines it as such, through the legal system or through the general acceptance of certain norms of behaviour. In modern societies killing is usually seen as the most serious of offences, but in the context of war killing can be seen as heroic and people may even be punished for not wanting to take part in killing, as happened to the conscientious objectors who were imprisoned in the First World War.

Crime is behaviour that deviates from conventional, accepted behaviour and can lead to formal punishment. Many other forms of behaviour contravene norms without actually breaking the law and becoming criminal. Transvestism is not a crime but may be considered deviant. While deviance is a broader concept that encompasses crime, criminal behaviour is not always seen as deviant. Making private phone calls on an office telephone is, strictly speaking, theft yet may be widely accepted as a 'perk' of the job.

The sociological study of crime

Crime encompasses such a vast range of activities that its sociological study is a massive and uncertain task. An unquantifiable, but clearly large, amount of crime is not generally known about. Burglars and fraudsters may not be caught; assaults, prostitution and illegal drug use occur on a far wider scale than is officially recorded. People who break the rules of society tend not to advertise themselves, which makes the study of this sort of behaviour more problematic than many other areas of sociological study. Some criminals do appear to enjoy publicity, but the majority of those who commit criminal actions attempt to conceal themselves.

The secretive nature of crime raises a number of problems for those wishing to study it. Initially, the researcher needs to find the subjects for study. How do we go about locating a group engaged in forgery, for example? Crime often occurs in conventional situations and the researcher has to be alert to this. In *Cheats at Work*, Gerald Mars (1982) studied the variety of crime in everyday work situations and found that fiddling and thieving were accepted practices in many occupations. One example that Mars cites involved 462 watch repairers being presented with an identical problem: a watch in perfect condition except for a small fault, a loose screw that could be easily tightened and that would be obvious to a scarcely trained repairer. Nearly half the sample

(226 repairers) responded to this 'problem' with diagnoses that lied, overcharged or suggested extensive and unnecessary repairs; many of the repairers suggested that the watches needed a clean and overhaul, in spite of their pristine condition. Mars called this the exploiting of expertise, when one person (the expert) has knowledge that others (the customers) do not have access to. Although not rare, employee theft is usually hidden, which raises problems for research.

Once a group or individual has been located it is necessary to convince them that they can safely discuss their criminal behaviour with the researcher. Their confidence has to be gained and it can take months to gain the trust of a professional criminal. Research into crime is thus likely to take comparatively longer and be more expensive than research into other areas of social behaviour. Other practical problems include the potential (physical) danger faced by researchers who investigate certain types of criminal behaviour and criminals – most obviously, violent criminals – and the fact that criminals are perhaps particularly likely to give false information – although this is not to suggest that lying is limited to criminals!

Case study

Crime and deviance: cultural and historical relativity

It is easily observable that different groups judge different things to be deviant. This should alert us to the possibility that the person making the judgement of deviance, the process by which the judgement is arrived at, and the situation in which it is made will all be intimately involved in the phenomenon of deviance . . .

Deviance is the product of a transaction that takes place between a social group and one who is viewed by that group as a rule breaker. Whether an act is deviant, then, depends on how people react to it . . . The degree to which other people will respond to a given act as deviant varies greatly. Several kinds of variation are worth noting. First of all, there is variation over time. A person believed to have committed a given 'deviant' act may at one time be responded to much more leniently than he would at some other time. The occurrence of 'drives' against various kinds of deviance illustrates this clearly.

(Becker 1963: 4–12)

Questions

1. Alcohol drinking and bigamy illustrate the relative nature of crime and deviance. List other types of behaviour that have been categorized as criminal or deviant in one society but not another.

2. Give examples of behaviour that has been criminal or deviant at different periods of time in the same society.

3. In looking at responses to crime and deviance Becker refers to 'drives' against certain types of behaviour. What types of crime or deviance have been subject to such drives in recent years in the UK?

As well as practical difficulties, researching into criminal behaviour causes ethical problems. The behaviour being studied is often widely condemned, which can cause moral dilemmas for the researcher over whether to reveal information that might help the authorities and could, perhaps, help to prevent others getting hurt. This problem is faced by other people who are entrusted with confidential information, such as doctors, lawyers and priests. Finally, it is not always easy for researchers to remain neutral and objective; they may feel sympathy or disgust depending on the particular topic being studied.

> ## Stop and think
>
> ➤ In view of the problems that the sociological study of crime faces, which methods of research might be most appropriate for investigating such behaviour? Why would they be appropriate?
>
> ➤ What particular problems would be faced by the different methods?

Why do most people conform?

Although many people break the law, few become regular offenders and most people are never found guilty of criminal offences. So why does the majority conform to the generally accepted standards of behaviour? This question can be answered by referring to two basic types of social control or restraint:

➤ *Informal mechanisms of control* centre around the socialization process: children learn that stealing, cheating and so on are wrong.

➤ *Formal mechanisms of control* involve legal and formally established sanctions, such as the law, the police and punishment system.

These control mechanisms do not exert a uniform influence on all individuals or groups. This can be illustrated by considering your own behaviour. Why do you follow the laws of society? If you follow laws because you agree with them and feel them to be right, this indicates the influence of informal control mechanisms. If you follow laws because of a fear of being caught and punished, the influence of formal control mechanisms is greater. Would you steal from shops if it could be guaranteed that you would not get caught? Answers of 'yes' to this question

would suggest that formal control mechanisms are the major determinant with regard to shoplifting, rather than a belief that the behaviour is wrong in itself.

Clearly it is not always easy to pinpoint exactly why we do or do not follow any particular action. Often the reasons reflect a mixture of informal and formal social controls, their relative importance varying with different circumstances. It might be very easy to steal from a family member or friend and not get caught, but most people would feel this to be wrong. Such feelings of disapproval would perhaps not exert such a strong influence over decisions as to whether to steal from less personal, larger victims. Stealing from a small corner shop may seem more personal than stealing from a supermarket which makes vast profits and expects a certain amount of theft or 'stock shrinkage'. However, it is more 'dangerous' to steal from a supermarket in that the chances of getting caught and prosecuted will be greater in the larger store.

Explaining crime

Explanations for why people break laws are of great public interest and over time a vast array of possible causes of crime have been suggested, such as inherited personality traits, poor housing, getting in with the 'wrong crowd' and inadequate parental control. More recently, there has been considerable controversy over the possibility raised by some scientists that individuals might have a genetic or inherited predisposition to certain types of behaviour and feelings that are more likely to result in criminal acts. But even these deterministic approaches do not deny the importance of environmental factors such as nutrition and deprivation.

Sociological theories of crime emphasize the importance of the social context: crime and criminals are viewed in relation to specific social conditions and opportunities. The review of theories in this section follows the conventional division of functionalist, interactionist and conflict-based approaches; these are broad schools of thought containing many variations and particular studies may not fall neatly into one perspective. Nonetheless, this division does enable sociological theories to be discussed in a chronological sequence. At the risk of oversimplification, functionalist approaches were taken issue with by interactionist and conflict theories in the 1960s and 1970s. More recent theoretical approaches have included elements of the interactionist and conflict perspectives in an attempt to avoid the limitations of one particular theoretical position.

Functionalist theories

Durkheim

The underlying characteristic of all functionalist-based theory is the importance of shared norms and values which form the basis of social order. Durkheim argued that deviance, and crime in particular, was a normal phenomenon in society, an 'integral part of all healthy societies'. Given that crime involves breaking laws, it might seem odd to argue that it is necessary for society. The emphasis of Durkheim's argument is that crime is inevitable and can be functional. His work is looked at in more detail in relation to the punishment of crime (pp. 644–6). The case study below illustrates how crime can not only encourage social change but also strengthen the generally held values and rules of a society.

Structural and sub-cultural adaptations

Durkheim's argument that crime is inevitable and functional does not explain the causes of crime or why certain people are more likely to engage in criminal activities than others. More recent functionalist theories, based on the notion of there being a general consensus of values and norms, have focused on and tried to explain the *causes* of criminal behaviour.

Robert Merton (1938) suggested that in situations where there is a strong emphasis on particular goals but the means for achieving these goals are not available for certain groups or individuals, *anomie* will result. This means that the rules that normally govern behaviour lose their influence and are liable to be ignored: the shared values and norms no longer determine behaviour.

Case study

Crime and the collective conscience

In the first place crime is normal because a society exempt from it is utterly impossible. Crime consists of an act that offends certain very strong collective sentiments . . . Imagine a society of saints, a perfect cloister of exemplary individuals. Crimes will there be unknown; but faults which appear venial (trivial) to the layman will create there the same scandal that the ordinary offense does in ordinary consciousness. If this society has the power to judge and punish, it will define these acts as criminal and treat them as such. For the same reason, the perfect and upright man judges his smallest failings with a severity that the majority reserve for acts more truly in the nature of an offense . . .

Crime is, then, necessary; it is bound up with the fundamental conditions of all social life, and by that very fact it is useful, because these conditions of which it is a part are themselves indispensable to the normal evolution of morality and law . . .

Crime itself plays a useful role in this evolution. Crime implies not only that the way remains open to necessary changes but that in certain cases it directly prepares these changes. According to Athenian law, Socrates was a criminal. However, his crime, namely, the independence of his thought, rendered a service not only to humanity but to his country . . .

Nor is the case of Socrates unique; it is reproduced periodically in history. It would never have been possible to establish the freedom of thought we now enjoy if the regulations prohibiting it had not been violated. At that time, however, the violation was a crime . . .

From this point of view the fundamental facts of criminality present themselves to us in an entirely new light. Contrary to current ideas, the criminal no longer seems a totally unsociable being, a sort of parasitic element. On the contrary, he plays a definite role in social life.

(Durkheim 1964: 67–72)

Questions

1. What are the positive and useful functions of crime suggested by Durkheim?

2. Suggest any other social functions that crime might perform.

3. Look at press and/or television reports of a recent criminal trial and suggest (a) the values reinforced by the crime; (b) the possible social changes that might follow from that case.

Merton explains criminal behaviour as resulting from a contradiction between the aspirations into which society has socialized people (the goals – in Western society material success is a generally held goal) and the ways that are provided for the realization of these aspirations (the means). In devising ways of adapting to this contradiction between what they want from society and the means they have available to get it, some people will turn to criminal behaviour, such as theft. This approach explains crime in terms of the structure and culture of society, rather than in terms of the individual; it laid the ground for explanations based on the notion of subculture and the argument that certain groups will be more liable than others to engage in criminal behaviour.

Albert Cohen's (1955) study *Delinquent Boys* is generally seen as the starting point for sub-cultural theories. Cohen takes issue with the view that delinquent behaviour is directly caused by the desire for material goals. Although some forms of crime and delinquency are centred on acquiring goods or money, a large amount of it is expressive (e.g. vandalism) rather than concerned with materialistic gain.

Cohen's explanation turns to the educational system. Schools, he argues, are middle-class institutions that embody middle-class values and goals. Individuals brought up in a working-class environment will be likely to desire the generally held goals but will have less opportunity to achieve them due to educational failure. Seeing the avenues to success blocked will lead to working-class boys suffering from what Cohen termed 'status frustration'. They will be likely to reject the school system and form a delinquent sub-culture. Delinquent sub-cultures, according to Walter Miller (1958), are based on a number of 'focal concerns' that reflect the values and traditions of 'lower-class' life; these focal concerns include 'toughness', 'excitement' and 'smartness'.

The sub-cultural approach stresses the collective response as crucial, rather than seeing criminal behaviour as an individual response to failure, as Merton argued. As Cohen puts it:

Delinquency, according to this view, is not an expression or contrivance of a particular kind of personality; it may be imposed upon any kind of personality if circumstances favour intimate association with delinquent models. The process of becoming a delinquent is the same as the process of becoming, let us say, a Boy Scout. The difference lies only in the cultural pattern with which the child associates.

(Cohen 1955: 13–14)

Another sub-cultural theory that stresses deprivation and develops from the work of Merton and Cohen is that of Cloward and Ohlin (1961). They argue that there is greater pressure to behave criminally on the working classes because they have less opportunity to 'succeed' by legitimate means. Working-class boys are liable to form and join delinquent sub-cultures, but there is more than one type of sub-culture. Cloward and Ohlin define these as:

- a criminal sub-culture, where delinquency is closely connected with adult crime;
- a conflict sub-culture, which develops where links with adult crime are not well established;
- a retreatist or escapist sub-culture.

Sub-cultural theories suggest that crime and delinquency can, ironically, represent conformity. In modern society there are a range of sub-groups with their own sub-cultures that include norms, values and attitudes that differ from and conflict with those of the rest of society. Conformity within such sub-groups will involve some form of deviance from and conflict with the wider society.

Stop and think

- Delinquent sub-cultures are typically described as male and working class. Can you think of examples of criminal, delinquent sub-cultures that do and do not fit this stereotypical picture, in terms of both class and gender?
- Cloward and Ohlin refer to criminal, conflict and retreatist sub-cultures. Give an example of each type.

Functionalist theories can be criticized for offering explanations of crime that are too generalized. Characteristics that are common to the working class as a whole are used to explain crime. Merton (1938) highlighted the importance of restricted opportunities to achieve material goals; however, restricted opportunities are very common and most people who suffer from them do not turn to crime. A similar point can be made with regard to Cohen's (1955) notion of status frustration and Cloward and Ohlin's (1961) explanation of delinquent sub-cultures.

Interactionist theories

Functionalist theories of crime tend to assume that there is a general consensus within society over what is right and wrong behaviour. The interactionist approach questions this assumption; it does not see criminals as essentially different from so-called 'normal' people. Many people commit criminal actions and it is therefore not easy to maintain a clear distinction between the criminal and non-criminal in terms of particular personal characteristics.

Labelling

Labelling theory is perhaps the key aspect of the interactionist perspective. The criminal is an individual who has been labelled so by society and interactionist theory centres on the relationship, or interaction, between criminals and those bodies or individuals who define them as such.

Howard Becker's (1963) study of deviance, *Outsiders*, contains one of the most quoted statements on the labelling perspective:

> Social groups create deviance by making rules whose infraction constitutes deviance and by applying those rules to particular people and labelling them as outsiders. From this point of view deviance is not a quality of the act a person commits, but rather a consequence of the application by others of rules and sanctions to an offender. The deviant is one to whom that label has been successfully applied; deviant behaviour is behaviour that people so label.
>
> (Becker 1963: 9)

Thus labelling is a process by which individuals or groups categorize certain types of behaviour and certain individuals. A deviant or outsider is a person who has been labelled as such, which raises the question of 'Who does the labelling?' The actions and motives of those doing the labelling are of as much, if not more, concern as those of the labelled. The focus on the process of labelling raises the issue of who has the power to define and impose their definitions of right and wrong on others. Giddens (1993) puts the interactionist position succinctly:

> The labels applied to create categories of deviance thus express the power structures of society. By and large, the rules in terms of which deviance is defined, and the contexts in which they are applied, are framed by the wealthy for the poor, by men for women, by older people for younger people and by ethnic majorities for minority groups.   (Giddens 1993: 128)

The emphasis on labelling is due, in part, to the interactionist interest in the political nature of crime and deviance. Laws are essentially political products that reflect the power some groups in society have, a power that enables them to impose their ideas about right and wrong,

normality and the like on the rest of society. Although the law applies to everyone, including the powerful, interactionists suggest that it is less frequently and vigorously applied to some people and groups: there is a selective enforcement of the law and a selective application of criminal labels.

The selective enforcement of the law was examined by Cicourel (1976) in his study of the way in which juvenile justice is administered in the USA. Cicourel found that particular groups are selected, processed and labelled as delinquent. White, middle-class youths are less likely to be identified by police and probation officers as being potential delinquents. The police are more liable to react towards those groups and individuals whom they see as being especially prone to engage in delinquent behaviour, often labelling such individuals before the actual committing of any act.

Labelling individuals will tend to mark them out. The knowledge that someone has been convicted for a violent crime, for instance, might well influence how you react to that person. Furthermore, individuals who have been labelled tend to view themselves in terms of the label and act accordingly. This produces an amplification or snowballing effect: the label becomes more firmly fixed and the person more attached to it. Interactionists argue that the social reaction, in terms of labelling, can actually increase or 'amplify' the criminal behaviour of the labelled individual.

A more general criticism of labelling theory is that it pays little attention to the original causes of crime and deviance. If crime and deviance is the result of labelling by others how does 'primary deviance' occur. In other words an initial deviant action could be seen as 'unlabelled deviance' (Tierney 1996). Tierney argues that although a rule or law might have been broken the individual has not yet been labelled so how can that action be deviant? In response it could be argued that deviant and criminal behaviour are actions which break established laws or rules and that the labelling of a particular individual need not occur for crime or deviance to exist. In other words it is quite possible for 'secret deviant' to exist.

The interactionist, labelling approach has also been criticized for focusing on the rules and laws themselves. Interactionists place great stress on social reaction; however, they do not really attempt to explain why certain actions are labelled as crimes and not others. There is little examination of who makes the rules. The relationship between power and crime is raised with regard to the selective nature of labelling, but is not really e...
Interactionism c...

Case study

High jinks and hooliganism: having a smashing time

It was a lovely evening. They broke up Mr Austen's grand piano, and stamped Lord Rending's cigars into his carpet, and smashed his china, and tore up Mr Partridge's sheets, and threw the Matisse into his water-jug; Mr Sanders had nothing to break except his windows.

Evelyn Waugh's account of the activities of the Bullingdon Club at Oxford University was written in the 1920s. The recent antics of James Sainsbury and other Oxford undergraduates suggest that little has changed since then. Sainsbury, heir to £124 million-worth of his family's grocery business, went out to dinner in June at Thatcher's restaurant, near Oxford, with fellow members of the Assassin's Club. They set fire to the table cloths, smashed crockery, threw food at the walls, vomited on the carpet and tore

curtains down. Sainsbury was fined £25 last week.

If James Sainsbury's hooliganism was in keeping with the traditions of his university, so was the gentle punishment which he received for his misdeeds. (When asked if he could afford the £25 fine and £25 prosecution costs, he replied: 'I expect I can manage it'.) Sean Paton, co-editor of the student newspaper *Isis*, thinks that too much fuss has been made about the Sainsbury case. 'James Sainsbury's a pretty harmless bloke,' he told me. 'He just does silly things when he's drunk. To his friends he's a pretty reasonable bloke.' Paton adds: 'I think it's all high jinks.'

Indeed, some upper-class and upper-middle-class parents actually approve of 'horseplay' (a word which is applied only to their class; when working-class youths behave in a similar manner they are called juvenile delinquents).

(Wheen 1982: 9)

Rules tend to be applied more to some persons than others. Studies of juvenile delinquency make the point clearly. Boys from middle-class areas do not get as far in the legal process when they are apprehended as do boys from slum areas. The middle-class boy is less likely, when picked up by the police, to be taken to the station; less likely when taken to the station to be booked; and it is extremely unlikely that he will be convicted and sentenced.

(Becker 1963: 12–13)

Questions

1. *Why might upper-class hooliganism be responded to in a different manner from working-class hooliganism, and by whom?*

2. *Becker and Cicourel highlight social class as a factor which influences whether or not a person is defined as criminal. What other social factors might influence such definitions? How might they do so?*

between people, on the 'drama' of the police station and courtroom, without investigating the importance of the social system itself. Interactionists look at criminals, the police and the legal system without examining the power underlying the system, without examining how power and decision making are distributed. These issues are central to the conflict explanations of crime.

Conflict theories

'Classical' Marxism

Marx did not write in detail or theorize about crime; working within a Marxist framework have from this perspec-

tive crime is seen largely as the product of capitalism, with criminal and anti-social behaviour indicative of the contradictions and problems inherent in the capitalist system. The basic motivations of capitalism, such as the emphasis on materialism and self-enrichment, encourage self-interested, anti-social and, by implication, criminal behaviour.

With regard to the control of crime, Marxists argue that the law expresses and reflects the interests of the ruling classes. Furthermore, there has been a great increase in the range of behaviour that has come under the control of the law. In their introduction to *Critical Criminology*, Taylor *et al.* (1975) point out that old laws have been reactivated and new laws created in order to control and contain an increasing range of behaviour seen as socially

Case study

The criminal law: recent legislation

The Criminal Justice and Public Order Act 1994

This Act brought massive changes to the criminal justice system. Essentially, it was an attempt by the then Home Secretary, Michael Howard, to deal with all the outstanding problems of criminal justice as he saw them. Not surprisingly, then, the provisions of the Act were wide-ranging. Among other things, the principle of a defendant's 'right to silence' was withdrawn and the power of the police to stop and search and to take intimate body samples was extended. Part Five of the Act dealt with public order offences. A series of clauses in the Act have effectively criminalized sections of the community which the government felt to be 'anti-social'. It became an offence to take part in a gathering of more than 20 people on a highway or any land without the owner's permission. Hunt saboteurs and squatters were criminalized, raves banned and New Age travellers had their sites taken away. This Act was a central plank of the Conservative government's policy on crime; indeed the Conservative Party's Campaign Guide in 1994 talked directly about a 'crackdown on squatters, "ravers", "New Age travellers" and hunt saboteurs'.

The Crime and Disorder Act 1998

One of the key elements of the current Labour government's thinking and policy towards crime and its reduction is an emphasis on 'community safety'. This is reflected in the Crime and Disorder Bill that it introduced in 1997 and that became law in 1998. This legislation required local authorities and other responsible agencies to formulate and implement strategies for reducing crime and disorder in their areas. It was the first opportunity for the (New) Labour government to implement its pre-election pledge to be 'tough on crime and tough on the causes of crime'. In particular it adopted a tough approach to youth offending. The proposal for curfews, for instance, will exercise greater control over the behaviour of young people, while the legal powers introduced to deal with behaviours not previously seen as criminal, termed 'ASBO' (anti-social behaviour order), widened the criminal net. Although there is no detailed definition of 'disorder' it would seem that it was being equated with anti-social behaviour and would be interpreted by local authorities to cover the things that people complain about, such as noise, litter and young people hanging about.

The Criminal Justice Act 2003

The Criminal Justice Bill was introduced by the government in November 2002 and became law in 2003. The focus of the Act is on the reform of sentencing arrangements and criminal procedures. The Home Office has described it as 'an integral part of the government's commitment to modernise the criminal justice system which at present is not bringing enough offenders to justice'. In attempting to do this, new types of sentences have been introduced to protect the public from dangerous offenders, including 30-year minimum sentences for some crimes. The length of prison sentences which magistrates can mete out rises from six to twelve months. Such new provisions are likely to lead to an increase in the already record prison population as magistrates adopt a tougher approach to sentencing.

Key points of the new Act include:

➤ changing the rules of evidence to allow the use of previous convictions where relevant and to allow reported (hearsay) evidence where there is a good reason why the original source cannot be present;

➤ making retrials of acquitted defendents possible in serious cases if there is new and compelling evidence;

➤ new longer sentences to ensure dangerous offenders remain in custody as long as they remain a threat to the community, new community sentences and new custodial sentences with periods of supervision in the community.

Questions

1. The pieces of legislation introduced above aim to tackle offending behaviour more effectively and to reduce crime. To what extent do you think they will be successful?

2. How might a Marxist perspective 'interpret' them?

problematic. The legal system is seen as reflecting economic interests; it is seen as an instrument that supports the powerful groups in society against behaviour that threatens or interferes with their interests.

An example of the way that the law reflects the interests of the powerful is the way in which the 'crime problem' tends to be equated with working-class crime, often of a fairly trivial nature, rather than the more significant, at least in financial terms, business and white-collar crime. Marxists argue that business crime is largely ignored by the legal system. There are some well-publicized exceptions, but these tend just to reinforce the impression that criminals are mainly from the working classes and that business criminals are not 'real' criminals – they are just doing 'what everyone else does'.

The way in which the legal system reflects economic interests is also illustrated by the relative power that different groups have to impose rules and their own definitions and interpretations of them on others.

> When, for example, is a particular behaviour – like drinking liquor or smoking pot – defined as deviant or illegal and when is it viewed as an 'alternative life-style' that individuals are free to accept or reject? Formal and informal social power play major roles in this definitional process. (Persell 1990: 159)

The Marxist argument that the legal system works in the interests of the powerful and against those of the working classes is returned to in our examination of theories of punishment (pp. 646–9).

New criminology and recent conflict approaches

Marxist explanations suggest that capitalism produces the conditions that generate criminal behaviour. Crime occurs because of economic deprivation and because of the contradictions that are apparent in capitalist societies. Working-class crime is a 'rebellion' against inequality and against a system that uses the legal process – including the law, the police, courts and prison – as weapons in a class war.

A number of writers who adopt a broadly conflict perspective have criticized the 'left idealism' of the basic Marxist approach and have developed a realistic approach to law and order. The left idealist position has been criticized for its apparent lack of interest in issues of policy. Lea and Young (1984), for instance, argue that, in contrast to the left idealist view, crime really is a problem for the working classes; and a problem that needs tackling with realistic policies and practices. This is not to deny the impact of crimes of the powerful, but to suggest that the working classes are most often the victims of crime – both crimes of the powerful and working-class or 'street' crime. In street crime there is an overlap between victims and offenders, with the working class forming the great majority of both groups. As Young (1992: 146) suggests, 'it is difficult to romanticize this type of crime as some kind of disguised attack on the privileged.' In her discussion of realist criminology, Croall (1998) emphasizes how in its attempt to understand crime, the left realist approach advocates the exploration of all the dimensions of crime – offenders, victims, the public and the state and its agencies, and the interrelationship between them. This provides a broader view of crime than other theories, in particular through recognizing the victim. The 'left realist' approach also highlights the widespread consensus there is about crime. Most people of all social classes are offended by rape, robbery, drug smuggling and so on; there is little evidence that the working classes see crime as a rebellion against the inequalities of capitalism.

Although rejecting any single cause of crime, the left realist approach does emphasize the role of relative deprivation. While there is no clear evidence that deprivation in itself produces crime, deprivation is a relative concept in that people have different expectations about what they deserve. As Croall (1998) puts it:

> They may compare their situation with others whom they would expect to equal – to a reference group. If these expectations are not met they may feel deprived – not absolutely but relatively. Unemployed youth may feel relatively deprived compared with employed youth and feel frustrated because they feel their unemployment is not their fault. Young members of ethnic minorities may experience deprivation in comparison to white youth . . . Members of some occupational groups feel deprived in comparison to others whose jobs they feel are of equal value. The executive may feel relatively deprived if denied the chance of promotion. (Croall 1998: 78)

While not all of these feelings of deprivation will lead to crime, they may do so in situations where legitimate ways of pursuing grievances are not available. This is perhaps particularly likely to be the case for groups or individuals who are socially or politically marginalized – such as the young unemployed or ethnic minorities.

Young and Mathews (1992) distinguish between what they term the realist and the radical positions. The classical Marxist approach is linked with radical notions

Case study

White-collar crime

The term white-collar crime is usually associated with scandals in the business world and sophisticated frauds. Croall (1992) adopts a broad definition of white-collar crime as 'the abuse of a legitimate occupational role which is regulated by law'. This includes occupational crimes committed by employees and corporate crime, where businesses or corporations exploit consumers and workers.

There are regular examples of notorious white-collar crimes such as the Guinness takeover in 1990, the collapse of the Bank of Credit and Commerce International in 1991 and the 'breaking' of the City of London's oldest merchant bank, Barings, in 1995. The Barings case involved Nick Leeson, one of the bank's general managers and the head of its futures operation in Singapore, allegedly entering into a series of fraudulent trades involving fictitious client accounts to try to cover up for substantial losses he had made on behalf of Barings. White-collar crime can also encompass 'accidents' like the sinking of the ferry *The Herald of Free Enterprise* in 1987. The ferry had sailed from Zeebrugge with its bow doors open – something that

should have been checked before the ship left port – and over 100 people were drowned when it sank. The ferry's owners, Townsend Thoreson, had a poor safety record. Although it could be argued that these kinds of crime are more serious and damaging to society than conventional crimes like burglary, white-collar crime tends not to be seen as part of a 'crime problem'. The public are more concerned about and afraid of being mugged or burgled than they are of being misled by bogus adverts or killed on a ferry. This is not to say that white-collar crime is ignored, but the media and public focus tends to be on the more spectacular frauds involving millions of pounds or on cases involving well-known personalities (Ken Dodd or Lester Piggot, for example).

Croall (1992) describes the considerable scope of fraud:

➤ *Tax evasion* commonly referred to as a perk. Often law-abiding taxpayers condone tax evasion by paying for services 'cash in hand'.

➤ *Trade description offences* the false description of goods, misleading bargain offers and other deceptive practices.

➤ *Weights and measures offences* including deceptive packaging and short measures.

➤ *Food and drugs offences* selling 'unfit' food.

Although unaware of it, most of us are probably multiple victims of white-collar crime. Many offences are commonplace and there is a thin line between normal trading and fraud and deception.

Questions

1. How does the relative power of different groups in society influence the way in which the following activities are viewed: (a) prostitution; (b) social security fraud; (c) providing false information to tax inspectors.

2. Why might business crimes and criminals be treated differently from other forms of crime?

3. Give an example of each type of fraud listed by Croall: (a) tax evasion; (b) trade description offences; (c) weights and measures offences; (d) food and drugs offences.

4. How often have you or your family been victims (or perpetrators) of these frauds?

that the criminal justice system does not work in the interests of the mass of working people and should therefore be abolished. A more accountable and efficient system of justice is not possible nor is it really desirable; the legal system is just another aspect of ruling-class domination that should be smashed.

This left radical view has been attacked by sociologists and criminologists writing from the left realist position.

Left realists point to the injustices that marginalize sections of the population and encourage crime. However, they realize that there are no magical solutions. Only socialist intervention will reduce the causes of crime fundamentally as these causes are rooted in social inequality; only a genuinely democratic police force will provide greater safety in the community. Young and Mathews (1992) point out that poor people pay dearly for inadequate protection; there is a need for an adequate criminal justice system that works in the interests of all social groups. Left realism is advocated as a social democratic approach to the analysis of crime and the development of effective policies to control it.

In this section on 'explaining crime' we have introduced a number of theories. All of them contain important insights and elements of 'truth', but it is unrealistic to expect to discover an ultimate explanation for such behaviour given the diverse range of activities encompassed by the term 'crime'. Why should an explanation for fraud by wealthy business people also provide an explanation for football hooliganism or burglary committed by drug addicts, for example?

The extent and pattern of crime

Official crime statistics in Britain are published by the Home Office and provide data on criminal offences recorded by the police. They play an important part in influencing government policies towards crime and its treatment. This section begins with a brief review of the trends in officially recorded criminal behaviour and then examines some of the problems associated with the use of crime statistics.

What do official crime statistics measure?

There are hundreds of possible offences ranging from murder to not paying one's TV licence. Recorded offences generally include only *notifiable offences*. These are the more serious offences; illegal parking, minor assaults, licence evasion and speeding, for example, are not notifiable. Notifiable offences are a measure of the number of crimes that are recorded by the police. It is not a measure of the real level of crime: many offences are not reported to the police, while others are not recorded if the police do not feel that there is enough evidence that a crime has been committed. Unrecorded crime is known as the 'dark figure of crime'. So official crime statistics provide only a partial picture of crime committed. Crime recording can start only when someone reports an offence to the police or when the police themselves discover an offence.

The official statistics indicate that there is an ever-increasing rate of crime. Recorded offences in England and Wales rose from around 3 million in 1981 to over 5.5 million in 2001/2 (*Social Trends* 2003).

Table 16.1 Recorded crime: by type of offence (thousands)

	England and Wales		Scotland		Northern Ireland	
	1981	2001/2	1981	2001/2	1981	2001/2
Theft and handling stolen goods,	1,603	2,267	201	171	25	42
of which: theft of vehicles	*333*	*328*	*33*	*23*	*5*	*12*
theft from vehicles	*380*	*655*	–	*40*	*7*	*7*
Burglary	718	879	96	45	20	17
Criminal damage	387	1,064	62	95	5	40
Violence against the person	100	650	8	20	3	26
Fraud and forgery	107	317	21	21	3	9
Robbery	20	121	4	4	3	2
Sexual offences,	19	41	2	5	–	1
of which rape	*1*	*10*	–	*1*	–	–
Drug trafficking	–	121	2	36	–	1
Other offences	9	65	12	25	3	1
All notifiable offences	2,963	5,525	408	422	62	139

Source: adapted from *Social Trends 28*, 1998 and *Social Trends 33*, 2003

The increase in recorded crime is not a recent trend. Radzinowicz and King (1977) found that the police in England and Wales recorded fewer than three crimes per thousand of the population in 1900; by 1974 they recorded four crimes per hundred of the population – a thirteen-fold increase in just over 70 years. Although the increases in crime appear startling, it is important to bear in mind that concerns over 'crime waves' are not new. The streets of London and other cities in the mid-nineteenth century were not havens of safety, ideally suited for a night-time stroll. Robbery and violence were commonplace, as the stories of Charles Dickens and other writers illustrate. Although official statistics demonstrate a rapid increase in crime, violent crime is not a modern problem.

As long ago as 1195 Richard of Devizes, in describing the London of his time, stated that

> No one lives in it without falling into some sort of crimes. Every quarter of it abounds in grave obscenities . . . If you do not want to dwell with evil-doers, do not live in London.

However, while crime is not new, the explosion in the data and information we now have about crime is. In contrasting the kinds of information available to criminologists today compared to fifty or so years ago, Maguire (2002) points out that virtually the only source of systematic information about crime in the 1940s and 1950s was the annually published Criminal Statistics. Since then the research capacity of the Home Office has expanded rapidly as have the number of criminological researchers in general. In addition, there are now massive electronic data sets, such as the British Crime Survey and the Offenders Index.

Just as crime is not a modern phenomenon, it is not particular to any one country. As Table 16.2 demonstrates Britain is by no means the most crime-prone nation in the world.

Problems with crime statistics

Although official crime statistics do not measure the real amount of crime, they are the basis for people's ideas about crime and criminals. The 'facts' about crime quoted in the media are assumed to provide an accurate picture of the extent of criminality. As Maguire (2002) puts it,

> despite the warnings of criminologists and government statisticians . . . these statistics are still treated by many politicians and journalists as an accurate

Table 16.2 Comparison of homicide in selected cities 1997–99

	Total homicides during 1997–99	Homicide rate*
London	539	2.36
Belfast	45	5.23
Edinburgh	29	2.15
Paris	139	2.21
Berlin	333	3.23
Dublin	76	2.37
Moscow	3,863	18.20
Sydney	200	1.70
Tokyo	420	1.17
Pretoria	1,512	27.47
New York city	2,074	9.38
Washington DC	802	50.82

*murders per 100,000 population of the city, average per year from 1997–1999

Source: International comparisons of criminal justice statistics, Home Office, 2001; adapted from Denscombe 2002

'barometer' of crime, and any sizeable rise in the figures they produce tends to receive widespread publicity and spark off arguments about police or government ineffectiveness or the need for sentencing changes.

(Maguire 2002: 334)

The official statistics are the end-result of a series of decisions by victims, the police and the courts about what action to take in particular situations; they are 'socially constructed'. The relationship between the real and recorded rates of crime is complex. Some indication of the gap between them can be seen by contrasting the official figures with those provided by the British Crime Surveys, which ask people, among other things, whether they have been victims of crime and if so what crimes. The British Crime Survey began reporting in 1982 and produced its ninth survey in 2001. It estimated a total of just over 19 million crimes in 1995, of which 41 per cent were reported to the police. While this might seem alarming the main reason people gave for not reporting offences to the police was that they considered them too trivial to waste police time. It is reasonable to assume that a much higher proportion of serious offences is known about by the police and included in the official statistics. The degree to which official statistics underestimate the actual level of crime depends, therefore, on the particular category of crime. Virtually all stolen cars are reported for the simple reason that this is the only way owners will get insurance compensation.

The social incidence of crime

Official statistics indicate that criminal behaviour is not randomly distributed throughout the whole population; some social groups commit more crime than others. In particular, crime is predominantly committed by young people. Over 70 per cent of offenders cautioned or convicted for indictable offences in 2001 were under the age of 25. The peak age of offending for males in England and Wales was 18 and for females 15 (see Table 16.3 below). Data on the social incidence of crime also indicate a relationship between crime and gender and crime and ethnicity: a relationship that is looked at in the following two sections.

Table 16.3 Offenders found guilty of, or cautioned for, indictable offences by sex, type of offence and age, 2001

England and Wales

	Rates per 10,000 population				
	10–15	16–24	25–34	35 and over	All aged 10 and over (thousands)
Males					
Theft and handling stolen goods	104	196	91	16	137.8
Drug offences	17	140	52	8	76.1
Violence against the person	31	70	26	7	47.0
Burglary	31	48	16	2	29.4
Criminal damage	14	18	6	1	12.5
Robbery	7	13	3	0	6.7
Sexual offences	3	4	2	2	5.0
Other indictable offences	11	95	50	11	65.0
All indictable offences	218	584	246	46	379.3
Females					
Theft and handling stolen goods	64	72	30	6	52.7
Drug offences	2	15	7	1	8.9
Violence against the person	10	10	4	1	7.8
Burglary	3	3	1	0	1.8
Criminal damage	2	2	1	0	1.6
Robbery	1	1	0	0	0.7
Sexual offences	0	0	0	0	0.1
Other indictable offences	3	19	12	2	13.8
All indictable offences	86	121	55	10	87.5

Source: Social Trends 33, 2003: 169

Crime and gender

There is a strong link between gender and both the rate of recorded crime and crime survey data. All the data indicate that crime is an activity carried out mainly by males. Over 80 per cent of those convicted of serious offences in England and Wales are males: in 2001 around 380,000 male offenders and 86,000 female offenders were convicted (*Social Trends* 2003). While women commit all types of offence, the proportion of male and female offenders varies according to the offence. Women only outnumber males in two offence groups: prostitution and failing to pay a TV licence. Although sexual offences, which include rape and indecent assault, are overwhelmingly committed by males, prostitution is generally defined as a female offence. The fact that women are more likely to be found guilty of not paying TV licences is partly due to women being more likely to answer the door to enforcers. Aside from these examples, men are more likely to commit every other category of offence (Croall 1998, citing Coleman and Moynihan 1996). The most common offences for both sexes are thefts. Shoplifting is often thought of as the 'typical' female crime but more males than females are convicted of it: '40 per cent of the convicted are female [but] many more women than men are shoppers, so that the proportion of women shoppers who shoplift is smaller' (Hart 1985: 299). Women commit fewer crimes of violence. In 2001 just 47,000 males were found guilty of, or cautioned for, crimes of 'violence against the person', compared with just under 8,000 women (*Social Trends* 2003). Out of a prison population of just over 73,000 in May 2003, just

under 4,500 (roughly 6 per cent) were female – and that figure has been growing in recent years, with there having been a 150 per cent increase in the number of females prisoners between 1991 and 2001, compared to a 40 per cent increase for men (Morgan 2002).

Women are also under-represented in the criminal justice system. As Table 16.4 shows, women made up less than a quarter of the number of police officers in England and Wales in March 2002.

In similar vein, the senior judges are still overwhelmingly male. Of the first 85 judges appointed since the Labour Party were elected to power in 1997 only seven were women.

Why do women commit less crime?

Heidensohn (1989) points out that in spite of the clear and persistent differences in rates of male and female criminality, it is only since the 1970s that sociological and criminological attention has turned to this issue.

Prior to this, explanations focused on the biological and/or psychological make-up of women. These studies, often written by men, argued that female biology determines their personality and makes them more passive and timid and therefore less likely to commit crime, which is an aggressive activity. The relatively few female criminals were seen as suffering from some sort of physical or mental pathology. In 1895 Lombroso and Ferrero argued that women were naturally less inclined to crime than men, and that those who did commit crimes were not 'really' feminine. Explanations emphasizing the physiological bases for females' criminality remained popular up to the 1960s (Cowie *et al.* 1968) and their influence can still be seen in the tendency to view women who commit crimes, and especially the more serious crimes, as 'abnormal' or pathological in a way that male criminals are not viewed.

Sociological explanations have argued that gender differences in crime cannot be 'reduced' to biological differences alone. As large numbers of women do commit crime it is difficult to maintain that females are innately less disposed to crime than males. In attempting to explain the gender gap in crime, sociologists have focused on the expectations and constraints that are placed on women by society and how the different role expectations for women and men lead to different patterns of socialization. This 'sex role theory' approach sees crime as more consistent with male roles – men, rather than women, learn the skills that are usually connected with certain types of criminal activity. Boys play with guns, learn how to fight and are more likely to be socialized for active and

Table 16.4 Police officer strength: by sex,[1] minority ethnic group, and rank[2]

England and Wales	Numbers		
	Males	Females	All minority ethnic groups
Chief Constable	47	6	1
Assistant Chief Constable	141	10	2
Superintendent	1,173	83	23
Chief Inspector	1,433	117	24
Inspector	5,717	479	99
Sergeant	16,621	1,953	369
Constable	79,351	20,137	2,844
All ranks	104,483	22,784	3,362

Source: Social Trends 33, 2003

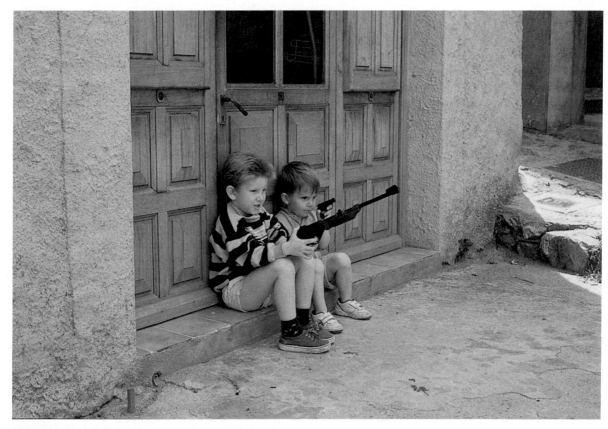

Figure 16.1 Boys playing with toy guns, Corsica: it has been argued that boys are more likely to be socialized for active and aggressive behaviour
(Courtesy of Robert Harding Picture Library Ltd)

aggressive behaviour. Burglary, for example, is an untypical female crime. It requires the criminal to be out alone on the streets at night, and to possess 'masculine skills' associated with being able to force an entry. However, 'women have got sufficient strength and skills to commit all sorts of offences which they hardly ever do commit. One does not need much strength to mug a small and frail old lady' (Hart 1985: 299).

A different approach to female criminality has been to focus on conformity and the pressures on women to conform. It has been argued that women, and girls in particular, are subjected to stronger social control than are men and boys. Girls are 'taught law-abiding behaviour and are expected to be non-violent, co-operative and docile' (Hart 1985: 300). Girls are expected to conform to a stricter morality by their parents and also by their peers (girls have to keep their 'reputations' in a way that does not apply to boys). Adolescent girls are likely to be allowed less freedom to go out and stay out than are their male peers. This will limit the opportunities they have to become involved in criminal and delinquent behaviour. As with the 'sex role theory', the argument that women

are subject to more restrictions and greater control is difficult to substantiate and is based on rather stereotypical notions about gender and appropriate behaviour for females and males.

Heidensohn (1989) summarizes the impact of feminist criminology on the study of women and crime. A major area of interest has been the criminal justice system and the alleged bias in favour of women – the 'chivalry' idea that male police officers and judges treat female offenders more sympathetically than they do male offenders. Heidensohn dismisses this idea and suggests that women offenders are more stigmatized than men. She argues that the much lower levels of women's recorded criminality compared to men's has significant consequences for those women who do offend (Heidensohn 2002). They are seen to have broken gender norms as well as social norms and the courts treat them as doubly deviant, as being both unfeminine and criminal by breaking laws. The social consequences of this can be women offenders losing their children, homes and partners. In examining reasons for the low rate of female crime, feminists have warned of the dangers of looking for all-embracing explanations.

Women's criminality, like men's, is mainly instrumental and related to economic goals; women can and do commit all crimes, including very serious, sometimes horrific, crimes such as terrorism and child murders.

An important feature of feminist work on gender and crime has been an emphasis on women's victimization. This is not to deny that men are victims but to highlight the different experiences of victimization according to gender. As Croall puts it:

> Men and women have different experiences of victimization. In respect of violent crime, for example, it has been seen from victim surveys that while men are more likely to be victimized in public spaces, women are more likely to be victimized at home.
>
> (Croall 1998: 138)

On the whole, domestic violence is perpetrated by men against women and children. Awareness of the problems of wife battering, child abuse and sexual assault has grown in the 1990s due in part to the work of feminist sociologists (see pp. 536–7). There has also been concern about the different ways that women and men are treated by the courts, for example men who kill a 'nagging' wife have been given derisory sentences in comparison with women sentenced to life imprisonment for killing long-term violent husbands.

In concluding her recent review of gender and crime, Heidensohn (2002) suggests that those studying this area perhaps need to ask different questions. Rather than trying to explain why women's commit rate is so low, the emphasis should be on why men's is so high. And research into the relationship between masculinity and crime is a fast-developing area. Feminists have argued that the aggressive and violent behaviour of men should be viewed as normal rather than unusual or abnormal in criminological theorizing. As Newburn and Stanko put it in their introduction to an edited collection of papers on masculinities and crime, 'The task is to use the developing understanding of masculine identities to make sense of male over-involvement and female under-involvement in criminal activities' (1994a: 4).

Crime and ethnicity

It is less easy to detail the link between ethnicity and crime than gender and crime because official statistics do not record the ethnic identity of offenders. However, the majority of studies in this area show that black people (of West Indian, Guyanese and African origin) are over-represented throughout the criminal justice process: they are more likely to be stopped and arrested by the police and to be sentenced to prison by the courts (Croall: 1998). Prison statistics do show a strong ethnic bias in that black males are much more likely to go to prison than white males; although 6 per cent of males over 21 are from ethnic minority groups, 17 per cent of male prisoners over 21 are from these groups. This over-representation in prison does not apply to all ethnic minority groups but is particularly the case for those of Afro-Caribbean origin (see Table 16.5). It is important to bear in mind that prison statistics cannot be used to demonstrate the rates of criminal behaviour as only a small proportion of offenders end up in prison.

With regard to policing and the criminal justice system, ethnic minorities are even less represented than women. In 2002 just over 3,000 of the 127,000 police in England and Wales were from ethnic minority backgrounds (just over 2.6 per cent); and while this represents a significant increase, only three out of 204 Chief and Assistant Chief Constables were of ethnic minority origin. We saw earlier (p. 627) how few women had made it to the senior ranks of the judiciary; ethnic minority representation is even lower, in 1999 ethnic minorities accounted for less than one per cent of judges with none at High Court level or

(see Table 16.5). We saw earlier (p. 627)

Stop and think

➤ Do you agree that girls are subject to stricter social control than boys by their families?

➤ Give examples from your own experiences.

➤ Does this continue into adulthood?

➤ Look at press or TV reports of recent criminal trials. What evidence can you find of the differential treatment of women and men? To what extent does it support the 'chivalry' idea?

Table 16.5 Prison population rates in England and Wales by ethnic origin (rate per 10,000 population)

	Males	Females	All
White	19.4	0.5	9.6
West Indian, Guyanese, African	144.0	9.9	76.7
Indian, Pakistani, Bangladeshi	24.3	0.4	12.4
Other/not disclosed	72.1	5.4	38.3
All ethnic origins	22.0	0.7	11.0

Source: Social Trends 24 1994: 162

above. Similarly, of the 1074 Queen's Counsels (senior barristers) in 2002 only 14 were from ethnic minority backgrounds, even though 9 per cent of the 130,000 barristers from whom QCs are drawn are from ethnic minority groups (Home Office 2002, Lord Chancellor's Department, Race and the Criminal Justice System).

In the USA, 36 states have executed people since the death penalty was reinstated in 1977. Black people are much more likely to be executed than whites. Although only 12 per cent of the US population is black, 42 per cent of the nation's condemned prisoners are black (Amnesty International 1998); and 290 of the 845 people executed since 1977 have been black (roughly 35 per cent).

Explanations for the relationship between crime and ethnicity

Historical background Bowling and Phillips (2002) argue that a historical perspective is necessary to understand current links between ethnicity and crime. Supposedly 'scientific' ideas about 'race' developed in the seventeenth century Enlightenment through the work of philosophers such as Kant and Hume. This period was seen as the 'age of reason', with civilization and progress associated

solely with white people and, specifically, northern Europe. Those people of other ethnic and cultural origins were seen as less rational, less moral and inferior. These notions of white supremacy encouraged the practice of slavery, and, although slavery ended in the early nineteenth century, the ideas of racial superiority and inferiority were embedded in British imperialism and colonial policies. It was a short step from these ideas to link 'race' with crime and Lombroso's work became representative of a new 'scientific criminology'. In his study *The Criminal Man* (1876) he argued that 'many of the characteristics found . . . in the coloured races are also to be found in habitual delinquents'.

Sociological explanations First, some of the difference in crime rates between whites and blacks may be due to *demographic factors*: there is a greater proportion of young people among ethnic minority populations, and black people are more likely to live in poor inner-city areas. However, research which has isolated age and socio-economic variables has indicated that such factors cannot be used to explain the higher rate of crime among West Indians (Stevens and Willis 1979, cited in Moore 1988).

Second, there may be some *racial prejudice within the police*, but this could not completely explain differences

Case study

Crime and different ethnic minority groups

The sociological study of crime and ethnicity should acknowledge that different ethnic minority groups have varying propensities to offend and differing relationships with the criminal justice systems. Most discussion of the crime and race issue has concentrated on Afro-Caribbeans and ignored other ethnic minority groups. Moore (1988) summarizes explanations for the low levels of criminality in Asian groups:

1 *Greater economic success* Asians, particularly Indians, have been relatively successful in business and commerce and are more likely to be in employment. Therefore, they suffer less from the marginality experienced by other young blacks.

2 *Stronger family and community* Asian families exert strict control over family members, which can limit the opportunities for criminal activities. In contrast, West Indian youths are more likely to leave their homes earlier and be free from the influence of close family ties.

3 *Different cultures* Asian cultures are clearly distinct from mainstream British culture and Asians are perhaps less likely to feel resentful about the difficulties they face in becoming part of this mainstream culture. Lea and Young (1984) argued that young West Indians feel more bitter when they are not accepted by the wider culture and are consequently more likely to turn to crime.

Question

1. To what extent do you feel that these explanations for lower levels of Asian crime hold good today?

in police arrest rates. The fact that the vast majority of serious crimes are reported by the victims rather than initiated by the police will limit the police's influence on reported crime rates.

Third, *race and political struggle* are rooted in Britain's colonial history. Britain controlled its colonial populations through force, slavery and 'education'. When immigrants from the former colonies were recruited to work in Britain in the 1950s, the conditions of the colonies were reproduced in the British inner cities. Black crime is seen as a continuation of the struggle against colonialism; the activities of young blacks are a form of rebellion. Crime is, then, a form of politics, a form of organized resistance (Moore 1988). However, there is little evidence that black people commit crime as a form of political struggle. Black youths appear to be as conformist to the values of the wider society as other young people. As Moore (1988) puts it, 'One must be suspicious when "experts" can read meaning into behviour that the actual participants are totally unaware of.'

Fourth, black people have been *marginalized* due to their lack of opportunities to achieve financial success; this encourages some of them to turn to crime. Cashmore (1984) argued that young blacks faced a situation where their aspirations (for consumer goods) were not matched by the reality of their economic situation (high unemployment rates). The outcome is that they are drawn into criminality. Again, this explanation lumps all young blacks together and does not take account of the variety of responses; only a small proportion of those who cannot achieve financial success turn to crime.

Having looked at possible explanations for crime and the extent and distribution of recorded crime we shall now focus on the control of crime; we shall look briefly at the role of the police before examining in greater detail the punishment of crime.

Controlling crime: law enforcement and the role of the police

In looking at why most people conform, we discussed two basic types of social control – informal and formal social control (see p. 616). The police are part of the formal control mechanisms of modern society. They are not the only agency of formal control; customs and excise, private security firms, store detectives and regulatory bodies such as factory inspectorates are all able to exert formal control over others. However, the police have a decisive role as the 'last resort' in the process of social

control. The police tend to be seen, and to see themselves, as the 'thin, blue line' protecting the majority of respectable citizens. The division between informal and formal social control is not absolute; although the police are the most visible agent of formal social control, much of their work is carried out in an informal manner. There is a considerable degree of flexibility and discretion in police work. As well as being perhaps the most visible agency of social control, the police are also the most expensive element of the criminal justice system. Around two-thirds of the £14 billion public expenditure on the criminal justice system in England and Wales is on the police compared with around a sixth on prisons.

The police and the public

The police are a segregated group in society. Public opinion varies from suspicion to hostility, and a major police problem appears to be relations with the public. The Policy Studies Institute (PSI) report *The Police and People in London* (1983) indicated that roughly half of the London population had serious doubts about the standard of police conduct. Everyday interaction between the police and public tends to do little to improve relations. Traffic patrol, for instance, provides many people with their only direct contact with the police; the attitude that 'they should be catching criminals not bothering me' would seem to be widely held.

A closer look

The clearance rate

The clearance rate is the percentage of crimes solved out of those reported. It is an official means of measuring the success and efficiency of the police and of comparing different police forces. If a particular police force or division had a 50 per cent clearance rate it would be solving ('clearing up') 50 per cent of the crimes reported to it. Thus, the higher the clearance rate the more efficient that police force is seen to be.

Questions

1. *The clearance rate varies from offence to offence. What kinds of offences will have the highest clearance rates and what the lowest? Give reasons for your answers.*

2. *What problems are there with using clearance rates as a measure of police efficiency?*

In examining what he terms 'cop culture', Reiner (1992) found that many police officers report difficulties in mixing with members of the public in everyday life. This relative social isolation encourages strong inter-group solidarity and mutual dependence, which tends to further their segregation. Occupational groups often mix together and have some measure of self-identification, but the police have a particularly high degree of occupational solidarity. This segregation encourages the development of a special code and sub-culture within the police, which we examine in the case study on police culture below.

As well as conflict with the public, relations between the police and the legal system are not always easy. The British legal system depends on the rule of law and the supremacy of Parliament (which makes the laws), and the police are required to maintain order under the rule of law. There is, though, a basic tension between the concepts of order and legality. Criminal law presumes innocence until guilt is proved. The police, however, tend to presume guilt. When arresting someone, the police officer will believe the suspect to be guilty. Furthermore, the police are likely to feel that the legal process makes their task increasingly difficult. The presumption of innocence is the first in a series of restrictions: the police are interested in actual guilt, which they believe they can recognize, rather than legal guilt. Court decisions to dismiss charges are especially likely to annoy the police, who will have spent time and effort bringing the case to court. When in court police officers face something of a role reversal in that they are subject to cross-examination, whereas they are usually questioning suspects themselves.

Case study

Police culture

The first extract summarizes some of the main findings of the Policy Studies Institute (1983) report into the Metropolitan Police force: a detailed examination of the world of the police officer in London. The second is taken from Robert Reiner's discussion of 'cop culture' in his study *The Politics of the Police* (1992).

The police and people in London

In contrast to the image of police work as exciting and dangerous (an image which the police themselves tend to stress), for most police officers, patrolling was invariably boring and somewhat aimless. A considerable amount of police behaviour can best be understood as a search for some interest or excitement. Officers on patrol might spend whole shifts without doing any police work apart from providing simple information. Even car patrolling might involve hours of doing nothing while waiting for calls. Occasionally a patrol car will be rushing from one call to another, but such occasions are unusual. This boredom and aimlessness is not apparent in popular portrayals of police work in the media, where there is a natural concentration on the interesting bits.

The desire for action is illustrated by the comment of one officer, who recounted how much he enjoyed the Southall race riots of 1981:

> It was a great day out, fighting the Pakis. It ought to be an annual fixture. I thoroughly enjoyed myself.

While some of this talk might be exaggerated, many police officers do not appear to object to occasional violent confrontations. And the comment on Southall illustrates another aspect of police culture – racism.

Racism

Racialist language was used by the police in a casual, almost automatic way and was commonly used over the personal radio. The report's authors heard one inspector say over the radio, 'Look I've got a bunch of coons in sight'. The report found that black people (but not Asians) were much more likely to be stopped by the police than white people.

Masculinity

The report describes a 'cult of masculinity' in the police force which has a strong influence on police officers' attitudes to women and toward sexual offences. Most of the women police officers interviewed felt that there was a prejudice against them; they felt that the importance of physical strength in police work was greatly over-emphasized and that they were regularly excluded from more interesting kinds of police work.

Case study (continued)

Many of the women officers have had to accept these attitudes. One recounted how an inspector at training school had said to her, 'Why don't you admit it, you're only here to get a husband, aren't you?' She had 'let it run off her back'.

Solidarity

There is a strong sense of solidarity among police officers and particularly among the small groups who work together. Calls for urgent assistance from police officers are always met with a massive and immediate response – all available cars would dash to answer such calls. However, this solidarity encourages officers to cover up for colleagues. On being asked whether he would 'shop' a colleague who had seriously assaulted a prisoner, one sergeant responded:

> No, I never would. If one of the boys working for me got himself into trouble, I would get us all together and I would literally script him out of it. I would write all the parts out and if we followed them closely we couldn't be defeated. And believe me, I would do it.

When questioned a bit further on his attitude, he said that the disciplinary system was unfair and he wouldn't stand by and let someone lose their job.

(Smith and Gray 1983)

'Cop culture'

The core of the police outlook is this subtle and complex intermingling of the themes of mission, hedonistic love of action and pessimistic cynicism. Each feeds off and reinforces the other, even though they may appear superficially contradictory. They lead to pressure for 'results' which may strain against legalistic principles of due process . . .

Suspicion

Most policeman are well aware that their job has bred in them an attitude of constant suspiciousness which cannot be readily switched off . . . Suspiciousness is a product of the need to keep a look-out for signs of trouble, potential danger and clues to offences . . .

Isolation/solidarity

The them and us outlook which is a characteristic of police culture makes clear distinctions between types of 'them' . . . The crucial divisions for the police do not readily fit a sociologist's categories of class or status. The fundamental division is between rough and respectable elements, those who challenge or those who accept the middle-class values of decency which most police revere . . .

Police conservatism

The evidence we have of the political orientations of police officers suggests that they tend to be conservative, both politically and morally. Partly this is a function of the nature of the job. The routine 'clients' of the police are drawn from the bottom layers of the social order . . . Furthermore, the force has from the start been constructed as a hierarchical, tightly disciplined organisation. Thus the police officer with a conservative outlook is more likely to fit in.

(Reiner 1992: 114–22)

Questions

1. How might the sort of police culture described above influence (a) the way the police carry out their job; (b) their relations with the public?

2. Do you think police officers should be subject to stricter rules of behaviour than other people?

The organization of modern policing

Effective policing depends on receiving information: the vast majority of recorded crimes are reported to the police by the public. The investigative policing common on TV portrayals is not the norm. However, the extent to which the police and public work together varies according to the style of policing; since the 1970s there have been two distinct styles, which seem to pull in opposed directions.

Community or consensus policing

The community sees the police as doing a socially useful job and supports them. This style is characterized by foot patrols, juvenile liaison schemes, neighbourhood watch and a generally 'softer' approach from the police. Here the police are likely to receive useful information from the public.

Military or 'fire-brigade' policing

Essentially this style of policing is without consent and with some hostility from the community. It is reactive and involves the use of guns, CS spray, surveillance technology and so on. The flow of information to the police is likely to be minimal and an important part of police activity will be random stopping and questioning. The police tend to concentrate on those people they feel to be 'typical criminals'; they make maximum use of stereotypes.

In the last 50 or so years, and particularly since the 1960s, there has been a changed context of policing with a number of factors combining to distance the police from the public. These factors include the increased use of technology by the police, initially the use of mobile patrols and radios, reducing the need for so many police officers 'on the beat'. There were growing concerns over police corruption and scandals, as a result of the exposures of senior police officers in the 1970s, that indicated systematic and widespread malpractice. The heavy handed policing of demonstrations, including anti-war demonstrations in the 1960s and industrial disputes in the 1970s and 1980s alienated sections of the population, most dramatically evidenced in the miners' strike of 1984–85 which polarized the police from large sections of the working population in the areas threatened with pit closures. The inner-city riots in the early 1980s in Brixton (London), Toxteth (Liverpool), Moss Side (Manchester) and elsewhere reflected an increased deterioration in the relationship between the police and sections of the population, in particular the young black population. Finally, the style of policing in Northern Ireland has affected attitudes across the UK, the images of a routinely and heavily armed police force there has helped undermine traditional notions of the British police. Waddington (1993) highlights how such pressures have tended to push contemporary policing towards the military style. It is difficult to prevent the continuation of 'fire-brigade' policing due to the sub-cultural emphasis on action and excitement; while 'the police persist in rushing from one reported incident to the next and spend little time in the proactive business of fostering links with the community' (Waddington 1993: 18).

The sociology of punishment

In this section we look at the relationship between crime, punishment and society. The examination of punishment as a social phenomenon provides a broader approach than that of 'penology', which focuses on the workings of specific institutions of punishment. Although punishment occurs in various social contexts – in the family, at school and at work, for instance – our focus is on punishment in the legal system.

The legal punishment of offenders is a complex process that involves law making, conviction, sentencing and administering penalties. The sociological examination of punishment has, therefore, to be wide-ranging. Legal punishment can have various aims, although its major purpose is to reduce the rate of crime. Punishment is seen as a means to an end, of controlling crime. Given that crimes still occur, and in ever-greater numbers, it could be argued that punishment has 'failed', but it is probably unrealistic to expect punishment to control crime.

Until the mid-twentieth century the main aim of punishment was to punish wrongdoers and there was little attempt to reform those who had offended. Punishments tended to be quick, harsh and public, with little pity wasted on lawbreakers.

During the 1950s and 1960s in Britain, reform and rehabilitation became key elements in what Garland (1990) has termed the 'ideological framework' of punishment. They provided a sense of purpose and justification for punishment, reflected in the introduction of a number of a new methods of punishment. Parole and suspended prison sentences were established by the Criminal Justice Act 1967 and community service orders and day training centres by the 1972 Act. These measures greatly extended the role of the Probation Service, which played a major role in many of the new initiatives that aimed to reduce and avoid custodial punishments: probation officers were responsible for supervising offenders on probation, parole, suspended sentences and community service orders.

In the 1970s optimism gave way to a general scepticism. Rising crime rates and the high percentage of criminals who reoffended raised doubts about the efficiency of 'modern' punishment. The emphasis moved away from reform; in 1980 'short, sharp, shock' sentences were introduced in detention centres and senior politicians advocated a hard-line approach to punishment.

Such initiatives have had little effect on the size of the prison population or on rates of recidivism. After a slight dip in the late 1980s, the prison population in Britain has continued to rise pretty steadily, with over 71,000 people in Prison Service establishments in 2002 (*Social Trends 33*, 2003). The number of people given immediate custodial sentences in 1999 was over 105,000 compared

to just under 80,000 four years previously (Home Office data, Annual Abstract of Statistics, 2002). The reason that the number of people sent to prison each year is greater than the prison population reflects the fact that most prisoners are sentenced to short sentences of less than one year and so not all would be in prison when the annual figure is calculated. With regard to repeat offenders and the rate of recidivism, it would seem that a relatively small number of offenders are responsible for a large proportion of offences. Of the 97,800 males who entered prison in 1999 almost 68 per cent had had previous convictions for 'standard list offences' (which includes all indictable offences plus some of the more serious summary offences), with 46 per cent having had three or more previous convictions (Home Office data, Annual Abstract of Statistics, 2002).

These kinds of figures and the concerns they raise about the punishment of offenders have highlighted questions about the aims of punishment, which we look at in the following section.

Case study

The politics of punishment: hard versus soft approaches

In the political arena, the debate about punishment has tended to polarize around the 'hard' versus 'soft' positions. Former Home Secretary Michael Howard was a strong advocate of the 'hard' position:

> Prison works . . . it makes many who are tempted to commit crime think twice . . . This may mean that more people will go to prison. I do not flinch from that. We shall no longer judge the success of our system of justice by a fall in our prison population.
> (Michael Howard, Conservative Party Conference, October 1993)

As well as being out of line with his recent (Conservative)

predecessors as Home Secretary – Kenneth Clarke, Kenneth Baker, David Waddington, Douglas Hurd, Leon Brittan and William Whitelaw all favoured a reduction in prison sentences, for minor offenders at least – Howard's comments have been criticized by those centrally involved in the running of our prisons. Lord Chief Justice, Lord Woolf, has said that sending more people to prison is the easy answer to concerns over increasing crime and would increase the likelihood of prison disturbances and riots. The former director general of the prison service, Derek Lewis, criticized the Home Secretary's call for stricter, more austere prisons and stated that he would not abandon the rehabilitative role of prisons.

This hard-line approach tends to be popular with the general public

and with certain sections of the mass media. Perceived 'softness' on crime tends to be seen as a sign of political weakness. In the face of the evidence (and reporting) of horrific crimes it is easy to see how hard-line, 'hang them high' approaches to punishment gain considerable sympathy and support.

The hard-line approach to punishment was highlighted by former Prime Minister John Major's comment on the supposedly lenient treatment of juvenile offenders serving custodial sentences, that 'we should understand a little less and condemn more.'

This approach appears to have been continued by the Labour administration of 1997 with its oft-repeated promise to be 'tough on crime and tough on the causes of crime'. The Crime and Disorder

The aims of punishment

We shall discuss five aims of punishment:

➤ deterrence;
➤ retribution;
➤ rehabilitation;
➤ incapacitation;
➤ reparation.

Deterrence

The utilitarian approach to punishment focuses on its 'usefulness' for society (utilitarianism is a doctrine that the value of anything is determined solely by its utility). If punishments deter offenders from reoffending or discourage other people from offending in the first place then their utility is apparent. There are two basic ways in which deterrence can work, described by Cavadino and Dignan (1993) as individual deterrence and general deterrence. *Individual deterrence* is when offenders find their punishment so unpleasant that they never repeat the offence for fear of that punishment. *General deterrence* is when offenders are punished not only to deter them from reoffending but also to encourage others not to commit similar offences. As the focus of deterrence is on frightening people into not offending, it is associated with severe penalties, such as long prison sentences.

While the theory of individual deterrence – that people 'refrain from action because they dislike what they believe to be the possible consequences of those actions' (Walker 1991) – seems plausible, it does not work well in practice. Offenders who have been subjected to harsh punishments should, in theory, be less likely to reoffend than similar offenders who received a less severe punishment. In practice the reverse seems to occur. The introduction of much stricter regimes in detention centres in the early 1980s had no effect on the reconviction rates of young offenders. Cavadino and Dignan point to research that suggests that offenders who suffer *more* severe penalties are more likely to reoffend: 'harsher penalties . . . could help foster a tough, "macho" criminal self-image in the young men who predominate in the criminal statistics' (1993: 34). This is not to argue that no offender is ever deterred by a harsh punishment but that there are other effects of punishment which will have a greater influence on offenders.

Walker (1991) suggests that the notion of deterrence with regard to punishment is imprecise. Are individuals deterred if they refrain from committing an offence at one time but then commit the same offence later, or in another place? The sight of a police car might deter the burglar for that particular night or the burglar might move to another street. Whether this sort of 'displacement' could be classified as deterrence is, Walker argues, rather doubtful.

The potential punishment is not the only factor influencing the would-be offender. Walker suggests that 'on-the-spot deterrents' that pose practical difficulties, such as effective security, high walls, large dogs and the like, will have a greater deterrent effect. More remote consequences, such as the 'stigma' of being known as a shoplifter, may also be deterrents.

Deterrence involves the individual weighing up a range of possible consequences of committing an offence, but it would 'work' only if that individual was tempted to offend in the first place; a person who is not tempted cannot be deterred. Walker (1991) argues that the key factor in assessing the effectiveness of deterrent punishments is that the person believes in the deterring consequences; some people will be deterred by quite remote possibilities. Walker uses the example of many parents not immunizing their children against whooping cough because of a minimal risk of brain damage. The effectiveness of deterrence can vary as the individual's state of mind varies. Normally law-abiding people might become undeterrable when sufficiently angry, drunk or jealous, and commit offences from which they would usually be deterred.

The fear of being caught and stigmatized is enough to deter some people from committing any offence, and the degree of harshness of the punishment attached to an offence is irrelevant. Others see punishment as part of the risk: 'if you can't do the time, don't do the crime.' Punishments can have some deterrent effect. If life imprisonment was the standard sentence for shoplifting or exceeding the speed limit, the rate of such offences would probably be significantly reduced. Cavadino and Dignan (1993) refer to the deportation of the entire Danish police force by the German occupiers for several months during the Second World War, leading to a spectacular rise in rates of theft and robbery in Denmark. However, aside from such extreme examples *there is little evidence that the type or severity of punishment has much influence as a general deterrent*. This argument is supported by the example of a Birmingham youth receiving a 20-year detention sentence for a mugging offence in 1973. This exceptional punishment attracted plenty of media attention, yet research comparing rates of mugging before and after that sentence, in Birmingham, Liverpool and Manchester, found that it had had no effect on the rate of such offences.

The old saying 'might as well be hanged for a sheep as a lamb' suggests that too severe a punishment for a relatively minor offence might drive the offender into committing more serious offences. Although offenders always run the risk of being caught, the chances of getting away with an offence (the amount of unrecorded and unsolved crime indicate these chances are pretty good) will greatly weaken the deterrent effect of any punishment.

The probability of conviction – offenders' own estimate of whether they will 'get away with it' – is a key influence on whether a particular offence is committed. The actual punishment seems to have less influence as a general deterrent than the offenders' estimation of the likelihood of detection.

Capital punishment

Capital punishment is often seen as the ultimate form of deterrence. Those who advocate the reintroduction of capital punishment for murder have argued that the death penalty would have a deterrent effect and lead to a reduction in serious crime. The view that capital punishment must be a better deterrent than any other penalty presupposes that the potential murderer rationally calculates the advantages and disadvantages of murder and is therefore deterrable. However, an estimated three-quarters of murders are committed on impulse, perhaps in a fit of rage or during a fight. Furthermore, it is questionable whether the supposedly rational murderer – for instance, the terrorist or armed robber – is so easily deterrable. They will tend to think that they have a good chance of getting away with their crime, and, particularly in the case of politically motivated murderers, they will often have some form of organization to help them escape detection.

It is possible that capital punishment does act as a deterrent in some cases, but it is difficult to recognize when deterrence works. There is little evidence that long-term imprisonment deters would-be murderers any less than capital punishment. There are other arguments concerning capital punishment that have nothing to do with its deterrent potential, including the belief that murder is so wicked that the death penalty is the only proper response, which illustrates the retributionary aim of punishment (see pp. 640–64). These beliefs may account for the fact that in a MORI poll carried out in 1994, 72 per cent were

(see pp. 640–64)

> ## Stop and think
>
> ➤ Do exemplary sentences work?
>
> ➤ Which of the following crimes have you committed?
>
>> ➤ theft of stationery or similar from the workplace;
>> ➤ using TV without a licence;
>> ➤ possession of illegal drugs;
>> ➤ buying goods that may have been stolen;
>> ➤ theft of a car;
>> ➤ drinking in a pub while under age.
>
> ➤ What would deter you from committing such crimes?

World in focus

Capital punishment: China and the USA

During 2002 at least 1,526 prisoners were executed in 31 countries and at least 3,248 people were sentenced to death in 67 countries. Of the executions in 2002, 81 per cent took place in China, Iran and the USA.

China outstrips world on executions

China executed more people in the last three months than the rest of the world did in the past three years, the human rights group Amnesty International says . . . The London-based group said China has put people to death not just for violent crimes, but also for offences such as bribery, embezzlement and stealing gasoline.

Using figures tallied from publicly available reports, Amnesty International said since an anti-crime campaign, Strike Hard, was launched in April, China has carried out at least 1,781 executions. In contrast, Amnesty International counted 1,751 executions in the rest of the world over the past three years. But only a fraction of death sentences and executions in China are publicly reported and the actual number of people put to death is far higher . . .

Most executions in China take place after sentencing rallies in front of massive crowds in sports stadiums and public squares. Prisoners are also paraded through the streets past thousands of people on the way to execution by firing squad in nearby fields or courtyards.

(BBC News Online 6.7.2003)

Figure 16.2 Awaiting execution

World in focus (continued)

The death penalty in the USA

Seventy-one prisoners were executed in the USA in 2002, bringing to 820 the total number executed since the death penalty was resumed in 1977.

Over 3,700 prisoners were under sentence of death as of 1 January 2002.

Thirty-eight of the 50 US states provide for the death penalty in law.

(Amnesty International 2003 – www.amnesty.org/pages/deathpenalty)

Table 16.6 US execution statistics by state and year (as at 10/03/03)

State	No. of executions	Year	No. of executions
Texas	310	1976	0
Virginia	89	1977	1
Oklahoma	69	1978	0
Missouri	60	1979	2
Florida	57		
Georgia	33	1980	0
Alabama	28	1981	1
South Carolina	28	1982	2
Louisiana	27	1983	5
North Carolina	27	1984	21
Arkansas	25	1985	18
Arizona	22	1986	18
Delaware	13	1987	25
Illinois	12	1988	11
Indiana	11	1989	16
California	10		
Nevada	9	1990	23
Ohio	8	1991	14
Mississippi	6		
Utah	6		
Washington	4	1992	31
Maryland	3	1993	38
Nebraska	3	1994	31
Pennsylvania	3	1995	56
USA	3	1996	45
Kentucky	2	1997	74
Montana	2	1998	68
Oregon	2	1999	98
Colorado	1		
Idaho	1	2000	85
New Mexico	1	2001	66
Tennessee	1	2002	71
Wyoming	1	2003	57 (to date)
Total executions since 1976	877		

Source: www.people.smu.ed

Case study (continued)

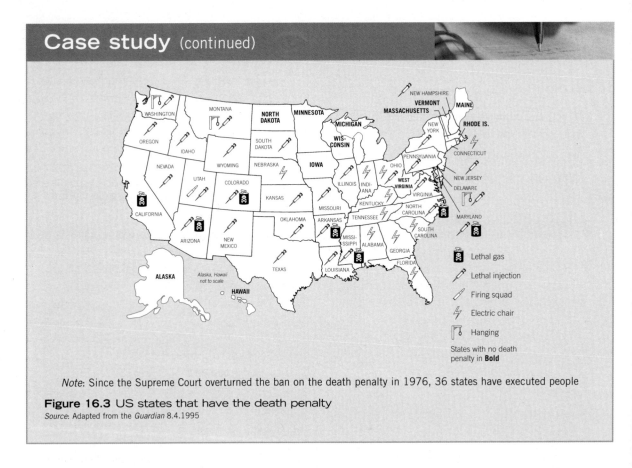

Note: Since the Supreme Court overturned the ban on the death penalty in 1976, 36 states have executed people

Figure 16.3 US states that have the death penalty
Source: Adapted from the *Guardian* 8.4.1995

in favour of reintroducing the death penalty, 24 per cent were opposed to it and 4 per cent unsure.

Retribution

Retribution is based on the revenge motive: 'an eye for an eye and a tooth for a tooth'. It originally meant the paying back of a debt and in the penal context refers to deserved punishment. It is often seen as the most important aim of punishment: certain offences deserve certain punishments and if criminals do not receive 'proper' punishment then law and order will break down. Linked with retribution is the belief that punishment should demonstrate society's condemnation of particular offenders; offences that excite the strongest condemnation merit the severest punishments. Although punishment cannot undo the harm done, it can make the victims of crime feel better and helps people to make sense of the senseless (in cases such as child abuse). Retribution emphasizes the denunciation aspect of punishment. The passing of a sentence acts to denounce the particular offence and can be seen as a public statement of disapproval; and the severity of the actual punishment demonstrates the extent of this disapproval.

The death penalty is a retributionary punishment that meets the desire for revenge. It can be argued that people who kill deserve to be killed themselves; crimes which are totally condemned by society are seen as requiring the severest possible punishment. However, retribution is not generally put forward as the most important argument for reintroducing capital punishment; rather the debate has focused on its deterrent effect (p. 637).

Stop and think

➤ Would a return to retributive punishment lead to televised executions?

➤ Suggest arguments for and against televised punishments.

Walker (1991) sees retribution as promising the certainty which the notion of deterrence and the utilitarian approach cannot provide. The retributive justification for punishment is clearly based on what a person has done. The idea of deserved punishment implies that the gravity of the offence should determine the severity of the penalty.

However, the extent to which harm was intended is a variable that affects the sort of punishment received: an accidental killing is not punished as if it were murder, even though the end result is the same. Furthermore, some offences might cause only a minimal degree of harm yet be seen to merit severe punishment: an attempted murder may do no actual harm but yet be punished almost as severely as a successful murder. As Walker puts it, 'incompetence does not mitigate'.

Some physical harms are clearly greater than others: injuries that lead to permanent disability are obviously distinguishable from minor cuts or bruises. The psychological harm caused by offenders is less easy to quantify. In the case of theft, the amount of money lost is not the sole factor: victims deprived of all their savings, whatever the total sum, will suffer far more than better-off victims who lose a similar amount. The feeling of violation following a burglary in one's home or a personal attack can be long-lasting, while shoplifting from large stores is liable to cause little personal suffering.

Stop and think

➤ Although incompetence may not be seen as a mitigating factor (something that might be taken into account to lessen the normal penalty), there are other factors which influence the punishment received. List as many factors as you can which you feel 'sentencers' should take account of when punishing offenders.

➤ Suggest reasons for and against these factors affecting a sentence.

Harm done is not the only factor that causes difficulty in applying the retributive idea to punishment. Assessment of the offender's character is often problematic. Walker refers to a case where the Court of Appeal reduced the prison sentence given for a serious insurance fraud because the offender, while on bail, had jumped into a canal to save a drowning boy. He suggests that 'spectacular behaviour seems to influence courts more than unobtrusive decency'. We have seen that it is difficult to quantify the suffering experienced by victims. A by-product of punishment is that people other than the offender will often unintentionally suffer from that punishment. If the offender has a family, imprisonment or fines will usually cause distress and hardship for innocent partners and/or children.

Rehabilitation

Rehabilitation is based on the belief that people can change: they are never beyond reform. Thus offenders can be taught how to be 'normal' law-abiding citizens; their punishment will make them less likely to reoffend. We shall use the terms rehabilitation and *reform* interchangeably, although strictly speaking reform refers to individuals being persuaded and given the space to change themselves, while *rehabilitation* involves a more planned and regulated treatment, for example a supervisor finds employment for offenders and monitors their progress. The focus is on how punishment can be used to 'correct' an offender's behaviour (indeed Walker uses the term 'correction' in preference to rehabilitation or reform).

Religious influence has usually emphasized the correction of the offender, but religiously motivated attempts at reform often caused as much hardship as the methods that they aimed to replace. Victorian reformers believed that prison should be a place where the offender might become a reformed person; they advocated long periods of solitary confinement during which time prisoners could examine their souls and consciences, spend hours in prayer and emerge purified; Bibles were made available in all cells.

With the growth in the study of crime, there have been strong arguments for more constructive and humane punishments, supported by groups campaigning against unjust and inhumane punishments, such as Amnesty International and the Howard League. However, revenge and deterrence justifications for punishment are still widely supported and public anxiety is easily aroused about the supposed softness of modern punishments. Whenever there are moves to release, or even discuss the release, of widely condemned prisoners there is immediately a massive media and public outcry. Before her death in November 2002, any consideration of parole for Myra Hindley, the Moors murderess, caused such widespread public and media anger that it was unlikely any government would have ever contemplated it.

In practice there has tended to be a balance between reform and retributivist themes; one or other theme becomes fashionable at particular times. Cavadino and Dignan (2002) suggest that there has been a revival of the rehabilitative approach in recent years, although the idea that methods of punishment could 'work' almost independently of the offenders having been replaced with an emphasis on how a specific punishment can be used to help offenders improve their behaviour. These newer approaches often centre around confronting offenders

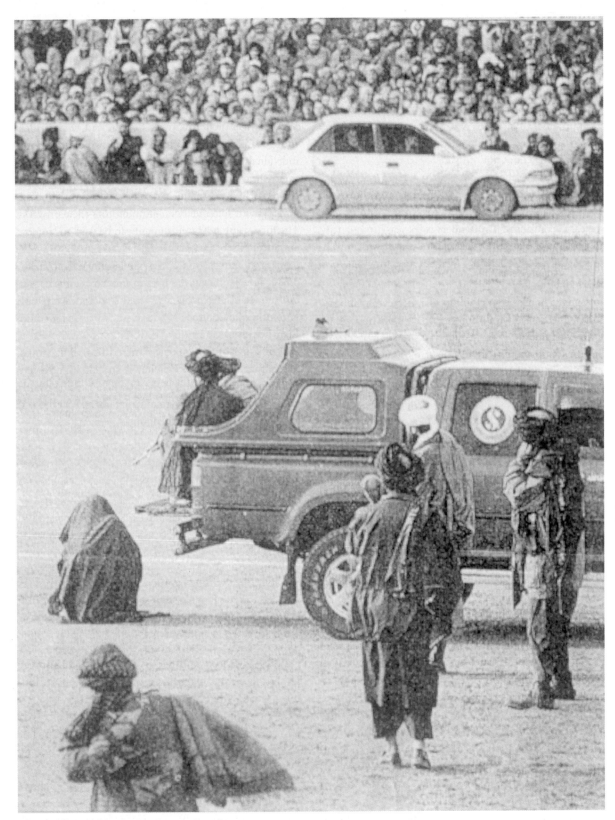

Figure 16.4 Eye for an eye in the Taleban's Kabul. Bahram Khan, 29, an accused murderer, kneels in the centre of Kabul's football stadium moments before being shot. At least 35,000 people turned out for the execution
Source: The Times 14.3.1998

with the consequences of their behaviour in the hope that they will choose to change both their behaviour and their attitudes towards offending. These ideas characterize the notion of restorative justice which is considered below.

The contradiction between reform-based and retribution-based punishments is a basic problem that faces any system of punishment. The lack of success of harsh punishments encourages reform measures, but these are felt by many people not to be a proper response to the harm caused by offenders.

In assessing the extent to which rehabilitation 'works', Walker (1991) points to the difficulty of ever being sure why a particular offender ceases to offend. It may be the stigma, the unpleasant memory of the punishment, the influence of family, friends or social workers. Even offenders who appear to be successfully corrected may still be involved in crime but have not been caught again. The difficulty in assessing reform-based punishments does not mean that 'nothing works'; some approaches may work with some offenders but not with others.

Uncertainty over the extent to which rehabilitation works led to the emergence of a justice model of punishment in the 1970s. Rehabilitative, treatment-based approaches included indeterminate sentences, based on the notion that when the treatment worked the punishment could end. However, the *justice model* argued that this gave too much discretion to 'experts' working in the criminal justice system and that punishment should be based on the seriousness of the offence; the rehabilitative approach was inherently unfair in that it treated similar offences in very different ways. Cavadino and Dignan (2002) highlight the abolition in 1982 of the indeterminate borstal sentence for young offenders (who were released any time between six months and two years according to how they had 'responded' to their punishment) and its replacement with a fixed-term sentence as evidence of the impact of the justice model on penal policy in Britain.

Incapacitation

Incapacitation means that offenders are prevented from reoffending, either temporarily or permanently, by the punishment they receive. In some societies this has taken the form of preventive detention, whereby people who are perceived as potential offenders or a political threat are imprisoned. This is clearly opposed to the basic notions of individual freedom. Milder forms of incapacitation

can result from a range of punishments. Banning people from driving should prevent them repeating motoring offences. Any form of detention or imprisonment ensures that the offender is unable to commit certain offences, at least for the duration of the sentence.

Reparation

Another aim of punishment is *reparation* or *compensation*. Reparation is based on the principle of *restorative justice* and the notion that crime affects communities and victims, who should therefore have a part to play in administering justice. This approach to punishment usually involves the offender being confronted with what they have done by being brought face-to-face with those they have harmed. Charles Pollard, chief constable of Thames Valley Police, sees this as a

> hugely powerful thing. There is nowhere for them to go. There is no defence lawyer giving lots of mitigation and trying to minimise the responsibility for what they have done . . . This is about coming face-to-face with the harm they have caused, and that has the impact of shaming the offender. But what's important is that it is in private and is what we call *reintegrative shaming* which means that once that person has really understood the impact they have had on others they are very ready to really think about how they are going to change their behaviour in the future. They are ready to think about how they are going to repair the damage to the people they have harmed whether by compensation, certainly by apologising, maybe doing some work for them. (Pollard 1998)

Pollard goes on to point out that the criminal justice system does not have a mechanism for people to apologize for their behaviour, and that an apology has to be the first and most important part of any form of reparation. In discussing the community conferencing scheme used in Thames Valley, he emphasizes how restorative justice gives victims 'a part to play in the system'.

If there is not an individual victim or identifiable victim for the offender to compensate, reparation could be made to society through some form of community service or by paying a fine into public funds. However, reparation is difficult to apply. Often the offender will not have the means to repay the victim; if a youngster commits an offence it is debatable whether the parents should be responsible for compensation. Nonetheless, in a high proportion of offences the offender and victim know one another; if they are brought together to arrive at a settlement it can be better and quicker for all parties, as well as cutting down on court workloads. Such an approach is generally seen as particularly suitable for minor offences such as car crime or damage to property. However, like other new methods, it tends to be seen by many as too soft a response to crime.

Sociological theories of punishment

Although punishment and justice has not been a major area of sociological inquiry, certain theoretical approaches provide the basis for the sociological study of punishment:

➤ punishment and social cohesion: Durkheim;
➤ punishment and class control: Marxism;
➤ punishment, power and regulation: Foucault.

Sociologists have examined punishment in social terms rather than as crime control. Garland (1990) points out that institutions of punishment such as prisons or community service orders are social artefacts reflecting cultural standards. Just as styles of building or music cannot be explained solely in terms of their obvious purposes of providing shelter or entertainment, so punishment has to be considered in historical, cultural and social contexts.

> ## Stop and think
>
> ➤ What social purposes other than the control of crime might punishment have?
> ➤ What specific penalties might achieve these purposes?

Punishment and social cohesion: Durkheim

In Durkheim's sociological analysis, punishment represented the 'collective conscience' of society at work and the examination of punishment would provide an insight into the moral and social life of the society. Durkheim believed that social order was based on a core of shared values and moralities (see pp. 43–4). Punishment provides a clear illustration of the moral nature of social order; it is not just about controlling crime. In Durkheim's

The Division of Labour in Society (1893), changes in the nature of punishment were seen as reflecting changes in the nature of social morality and social solidarity.

Durkheim emphasized the relationship between the punishment of crime and the maintenance of moral and social order. Crimes are moral outrages that violate a society's collective conscience; this violation produces a punitive reaction. As Durkheim puts it, 'crime brings together upright consciences and concentrates them'; crime provides an occasion for the collective expression of shared moral feelings (see p. 617).

The existence of social morality and social solidarity makes punishment necessary, in that it reaffirms moral and social bonds. Of course, punishment is not the only social institution that reinforces social morality and solidarity. Religion, education and family life all help to strengthen the collective conscience and to promote social cohesion; however, formal punishment enjoys a special place in Durkheim's work.

Durkheim acknowledged that the nature of punishment changes as society changes; he saw punishment as more important as a means of reinforcing moral and social order in less complex societies with a less developed division of labour. However, while methods change the functions of punishment remain constant. Although people are outraged by different activities over time, punishment as a social process has an unchanging character.

In contrasting simpler societies based on mechanical solidarity with modern societies based on organic solidarity, Durkheim suggested that the former are characterized by more severe and intense punishment. The intensity of the collective conscience in simple societies is reflected in the intensity of punishment. In modern, advanced societies, collective sentiments are less demanding; there is more scope for diversity and interdependence, so punishment for violations of the collective conscience is more lenient. The intensity of punishment reflects the nature of the collective conscience; as society develops the severity of punishment diminishes.

The link between punishment and morality is the key element of Durkheim's sociology of punishment. Punishment helps to prevent the collapse of moral authority and demonstrates the force of moral commands; its primary function is the reassertion of the moral order of society. Punishment is not an instrument of deterrence; the threat of unpleasant consequences just presents practical problems that stand in the way of the criminal's desires. Although in practical terms punishment has to be unpleasant, Durkheim saw this as incidental. The essence of punishment is the expression of moral condemnation.

Rituals of punishment

Durkheim believed that it was the rituals associated with punishment which specifically conveyed moral messages and helped to maintain social order. These rituals tend nowadays to centre around the courtroom drama. They include the wearing of wigs and gowns, the process of the trial, the passing of sentence (guilty or not) and the meting out of punishment. The focus on the courtroom is due in part to the decline in public, and therefore visible, punishments, such as public floggings or executions. Prisons and other institutions responsible for punishment tend to be closed to the public and the media. Of course there are rituals associated with imprisonment; in his famous study of total institutions, Goffman (1968) highlighted the rituals of initiation that serve to 'mortify the self', including the replacing of prisoners' names with numbers, the issuing of prison clothing, the shaving of heads and the restrictions on contact with the outside world. However, these rituals are undertaken to maintain the institution itself; they are done for an internal audience. As a consequence of this decline in public punishment, the focus of public and media interest tends to be on the trial of offenders and on 'who gets what' rather than on the detailed workings of the processes of punishment. Durkheim's emphasis on the rituals of punishment can be compared with his study of religion; it does not matter if a particular doctrine is true or not, the importance is the faith and the rituals which have social functions (see pp. 47–8).

Stop and think

> ➤ Which criminal trials have received detailed media coverage recently?

> ➤ How have the media reported these trials? How did it make you feel?

> ➤ To what extent might such trials strengthen the 'collective conscience'?

> ➤ Court cases and punishments can provoke a range of responses as well as social solidarity. What other responses might these trials have provoked?

Comment and criticism

Just as Durkheim's description of simple societies, characterized by mechanical solidarity, and advanced societies, characterized by organic solidarity, has been criticized as oversimplistic, so his history of punishment has been similarly criticized. Garland (1990) suggests that the historical transition from simple societies characterized by severe punishments to advanced ones characterized by lenient punishment is not really demonstrated by Durkheim; no account of any intermediate stages is given.

Garland also criticizes Durkheim's application of the notion of the collective conscience. A certain degree of order in society does not necessarily indicate a general commitment to shared moral norms; many people follow laws for practical reasons, to avoid punishments rather than because of moral commitment. This raises the question as to whether violations of the criminal law do really break genuinely held moral sentiments. Clearly there is some link between the law and popular sentiment; the laws protecting property and personal safety, for instance, are supportive of widely shared values. However, while there may be general agreement that rape and burglary are morally repugnant, there is considerable disagreement over the 'proper' punishment for such behaviour. And there is even less agreement over criminal offences which do not offend such strongly and widely held sentiments – crimes such as tax evasion or infringing copyright laws, perhaps. Punishments which deal with the most serious and shocking crimes – child murder for example – provoke the strongest feelings and the greatest moral outcry.

It seems clear that the punishment of crime produces emotional responses. Garland refers to the philosopher Nietzsche, who suggested that positive pleasure can be gained from punishment; it can gratify impulses of sadism and cruelty. The fascination with crime and criminals – witness, for example, the popularity of films, books, magazines and TV programmes on serial killers – can be seen as a gratification of repressed aggression as well as a reflection of horror and repugnance.

Stop and think

> ➤ Which crimes excite the greatest moral repugnance? Why do they?

> ➤ What forms of punishment express this moral condemnation and repugnance?

To what extent, then, is punishment functional for society? Certainly it performs some functions – restraining some types of behaviour and legitimizing some forms of authority. However, what is functional from one point of view may be dysfunctional from another. This is a criticism that is often made of functionalist work, which implies that there is a general agreement over what is functional or not and what should and should not be valued and appreciated. It could also be argued that punishment has dysfunctional as well as functional consequences. The fact that crime does produce emotional responses can encourage societies to direct their punishments towards the denunciation of particular criminal individuals rather than doing anything about wider social conditions that may give rise to crime. In addition, directing anger and punishment solely at the individual may also encourage the scapegoating and potential for harassment of specific groups of people.

The emphasis on general agreement ignores the obvious power differentials in the maintenance of order in society. Durkheim's work seems to ignore or at least underplay the fact that people are members of groups that can have opposed interests and to neglect the conflict between interest groups. Garland also questions whether Durkheim's theory is relevant to modern, advanced societies with a complex division of labour and where the moral order is not necessarily universal.

Durkheim's work has encouraged examination of the social processes of punishment; his work introduced the symbolic and emotional elements of punishment rather than just the narrow technical side. In arguing that punishment was necessary and functional for society, Durkheim realized that it had only a very limited ability to control criminal behaviour. It was this apparent contradiction – that punishment was politically and socially functional yet had little effect on actual criminal behaviour – that Garland argues is the crucial characteristic of punishment:

> This sense of being simultaneously necessary and also destined to a degree of futility is what I will term the *tragic* quality of punishment.   (Garland 1990: 80)

Punishment and class control: Marxism

Neither Marx nor Engels analysed the practices and institutions for the punishment of offenders; they wrote very little on crime and criminals and did not develop a theory of crime. Thus we have to look at the writing of later Marxist writers to provide us with a Marxist analysis of punishment.

The basic Marxist approach sees the economy as the key locus of power in society. The economic system determines all other areas of social life, including the legal system. Those groups who have economic power are able to ensure that social institutions work in a way that is consistent with their interests. Thus the institutions of the law and punishment come to reflect the interests of the dominant economic groups. Marxist analysis of punishment has tended to focus on the way in which elements of the superstructure support ruling-class power. The law works in the interests of some groups more than others: 'there's one law for the rich and one for the poor'.

Garland suggests that the Marxist analysis of punishment centres on the notion of class struggle and the ways in which the relationship between social classes shapes the form of punishment in a particular society. He highlights the work of Rusche and Kirchheimer as the best example of the Marxist interpretation of punishment. Rusche and Kirchheimer's major text, *Punishment and Social Structure* (1939), was not widely read when first published and it is only since its reissue in 1968 that their work has been taken up by Marxist criminologists and become more widely known.

Rusche and Kirchheimer provide a detailed history of punishment which emphasizes how the economy and, in particular, the labour market influence the methods of punishment in society. An illustration of their basic argument is provided by their account of the development of punishments such as galley slavery, transportation and hard labour. These 'new' punishments emerged in the sixteenth and seventeenth centuries alongside the early developments of a capitalist economic system. Labour power increasingly came to be seen as a vital resource and the harsh physical punishments, such as whipping, branding and execution, were replaced by punishments that involved productive, hard labour, and particularly work that 'free' people were unwilling to undertake. At this period there were vast amounts of land in the colonies that needed to be worked and the penalty of transportation was used to develop these areas. Transportation was initially offered as a commutation of capital punishment but by the early 1700s it was regularly used as a sentence for a range of minor offences. By the end of the eighteenth century the growing prosperity in the colonies led to the decline of this form of punishment; the free immigrants to Australia and elsewhere were not happy about criminal labour and convicts undercutting their wages, while the authorities felt that transportation was becoming little deterrent to criminals.

Case study

Rusche and Kirchheimer's theoretical approach to punishment

➤ Punishments have to be viewed as historically specific phenomena that appear in particular forms at different periods. This principle of historical specificity distinguishes Marxist accounts from Durkheim's view of punishment as something that performed essentially similar functions in all societies.

➤ The mode of production is the major determinant of specific penal methods in specific historical periods. Different systems of production will produce different methods of punishment.

➤ The particular forms of punishment are, therefore, social artefacts or constructions.

➤ Penal policy is one element within a wider strategy for controlling the poor. Punishment is seen almost exclusively as aimed at the control of the 'lower orders'. Rusche and Kirchheimer suggest that there were clear similarities between the way criminals were treated and the policies aimed at controlling the labouring masses. In the early industrial period the regime and organization of prison life was similar to the way workers were treated in factories and beggars and vagrants in workhouses.

➤ Punishment is a mechanism deeply implicated within the class struggle: 'the history of the penal system is the history

of the relations between the rich and the poor' (Rusche 1933).

➤ Although punishment is generally and conventionally seen as an institution which benefits 'society as a whole', for Marxists, in reality it supports the interests of one class against another. Punishment is (another) element and example of control that is hidden within ideological veils.

(Adapted from Garland 1990: 90–2)

Questions

1. *What do you think were the main similarities between prison and factory life in the early industrial period?*

2. *Think of examples of how 'different systems of production will produce different methods of punishment'.*

Comment and criticism

The priority given to economic explanations by Marxist writers such as Rusche and Kirchheimer has been criticized for understating the importance of political and ideological factors; religious and humanitarian influences on the development of punishment are accorded only secondary importance, for example. Furthermore, the emphasis given to class and class relationships tends to ignore popular attitudes to punishment. There is widespread support among the working classes for harsh punitive policies and little evidence that the working classes support criminals any more than other social groups, which Garland suggests casts doubt on a simple class conflict approach to punishment.

However, these comments do not refute Rusche and Kirchheimer's argument that economic relationships and the labour market can exert an important influence on penal policy and that the institutions of punishment can be seen as part of a wider strategy for managing the poor and working classes.

The essence of the Marxist approach is that the approach to and form of punishment is influenced by the strategies that the dominant, governing groups adopt towards the working classes. Punishment is not merely shaped by patterns of crime but by the perception of the working class, and the poor in particular, as a social problem. Rusche and Kirchheimer argue that the working classes have little commitment to the law or to the

Stop and think

Think of recent criminal cases that have received a lot of publicity.

➤ To what extent does class play a part in the way the public reacts to crime and criminals?

➤ How fair is it for Rusche and Kirchheimer to suggest that the working classes have little commitment to the law?

Case study

Rich law, poor law

The sociological study of white-collar crime lends support to the idea that the extent and severity with which the legal system is applied varies between different social groups. Dee Cook (1989) examined the different responses to tax and supplementary benefit fraud. She cited examples of judicial responses to defrauding the public purse by two different means – by defrauding the Inland Revenue by evading tax and defrauding the DHSS by falsely claiming supplementary benefit:

Two partners in a vegetable wholesalers business admitted falsifying accounts to the tune of £100,000. At their trial the judge said he considered they had been 'very wise' in admitting their guilt and they had paid back the tax due (with interest) to the Inland Revenue. They were sentenced to pay fines. A chartered accountant who defrauded taxes in excess of £8,000 was sentenced to pay a fine as the judge accepted, in mitigation, that his future income would be adversely affected by the trial.

An unemployed father of three failed to declare his wife's earnings to the Department of Health and Social Security (DHSS). He admitted the offence and started to pay back the £996 he owed them by weekly deductions from his supplementary benefit. He was prosecuted a year later and sentenced to pay fines totalling £210, also to be deducted from his benefit. Magistrates told him that 'this country is fed up to the teeth with people like you scrounging from fellow citizens'. A young woman defrauded the DHSS to the tune of £58: she served three months in custody as magistrates said she 'needed to be taught a lesson'.

(Cook 1989: 1)

In looking at why the law does not treat white-collar crime in the same way as conventional crime, Hazel Croall (1992) points out that white-collar crime is subject to different regulatory arrangements and these tend to be more lenient than those of the criminal justice system; regulatory bodies are less worried about securing convictions and more keen on settling disputes with a minimum of fuss and, often, publicity. This point is supported by Steven Box's (1983) comments on the deterrents for would-be corporate criminals.

For the most part corporate crimes are not/do not fall under the jurisdiction of the police, but under special regulatory bodies . . . In the UK, there are numerous inspectorates, commissions and government departments . . .

Although they all have powers either to initiate or recommend criminal prosecution, they are primarily designed to be regulatory bodies whose main weapon against corporate misbehaviour is administrative, i.e. (occasional) inspection coupled with (polite) correspondence. Corporate executives contemplating the possibility of being required to commit corporate crimes know that they face a regulatory agency which for the most part will be unable to detect what is going on, and in the minority of cases when it does, it will have no heart and few resources to pursue the matter into the criminal courts . . .

Criminal laws aimed at regulating corporate activities tend to refer to a specific rather than a general class of behaviour . . . they focus purely on the regulation broken and not on the consequences of that broken regulation. Thus the company responsible for the hoist accident at Littlebrook Dee power station were not prosecuted for the fact that five men died, but for the fact that the machinery was not properly maintained or inspected. For this they were fined £5000. In conventional crime . . . a person is charged with the consequences of his/her action; if someone dies as a consequence of being stabbed, the assailant is more likely to be charged with a homicide offence rather than 'carrying an offensive weapon'. The point of this fracture between the regulation broken and its consequences is that it facilitates corporate crime; executives need only concern themselves with the likelihood of being leniently punished for breaking regulations.

(Box 1983: 44–58)

Questions

1. What are the key differences between corporate and conventional crime?

2. To what extent do they provide a justification for the differential treatment of white-collar and business criminals?

dominant moral order in general and that it is therefore important for the criminal law and the punishments associated with it to make sure that crime does not pay. Punishments have to be severe and institutions of punishment such as prisons have to be unpleasant; indeed they have to be more unpleasant than the conditions that the worst off 'free' people are able to live in.

In contrast to Durkheim's view that punishment expresses the interests of society as a whole, the fairly simplistic review of the Marxist approach to punishment that we have presented here sees punishment as expressing ruling-class interests only. Although the criminal law and punishment does provide protection for the working classes as well as the ruling classes – protection against assault and burglary, for instance – it does not, according to Marxists, 'protect' against economic domination and oppression.

Punishment, power and regulation: Foucault

Foucault's (1975) *Discipline and Punish* has become one of the key texts in the sociology of punishment. Foucault sees punishment as a system of power and regulation which is imposed on the population: an analysis that overlaps with the Marxist approach and contrasts with Durkheim's argument that punishment is embedded within collective sentiments and therefore conveys moral messages. Foucault, however, focused on the specific workings of penal institutions – how they were structured and how they exercised control. This approach moves away from the examination of society as a coherent whole that can be analyzed by structural methods and to that extent Foucault's work could be described as phenomenological rather than Marxist (see pp. 91–3 on post-structuralism).

The historical issue that Foucault sets out to explain in *Discipline and Punish* is the disappearance of punishment as a public spectacle of violence and the emergence of the prison as the general form of modern punishment – hence the subtitle of the book 'The Birth of the Prison'. This change in the basic form of punishment took place between 1750 and 1820 when the target of punishment changed, with an emphasis on changing the soul of the offender rather than just the body, on transforming the offender not just avenging the crime. Foucault sees these developments as reflecting how power operates in modern society with open physical force and ceremonies associated with it replaced by more detailed regulation

of offenders; troublesome individuals are removed from society rather than destroyed; they are resocialized.

Foucault goes on to consider why imprisonment so quickly became the general method of legal punishment. He saw the development of the prison and imprisonment in relation to the growth of the human sciences. The prison practice of isolating and monitoring inmates ensured that they were studied as individuals with their own characteristics and peculiarities. To an extent, prison led to the discovery of the 'delinquent' – a person distinct from the non-delinquent – and, according to Foucault, to the rise of the science of criminology.

Foucault also argues that the creation of delinquency has been a useful strategy of political domination by dividing the working classes, enhancing fears of authority and guaranteeing the power of the police. Delinquency, which generally consists of relatively minor attacks on authority, is not a particular political danger and can, within limits, be tolerated by the authorities; furthermore, it produces a group of known habitual criminals who can be kept under surveillance.

Although Foucault did not develop a 'grand theory' in the manner of classic social theorists, such as Karl Marx, as mentioned above his work shares a Marxist appreciation of the importance for capitalism of labour power. In the context of punishment he considered how methods of punishment could be used to turn rebellious subjects into productive ones. For instance, in charting the emergence of prisons and prison regimes in the nineteenth century, he emphasized how they produced a new kind of individual 'subjected to habits, rules and orders'. This investigation of the development of prisons in the early nineteenth century was used by Foucault to help him explore the general themes of domination and how that is achieved and of how individuals are 'socially constructed'.

Foucault saw an extension of power and domination occurring through the methods of surveillance that were part of the design of the new prison buildings of this time. The panoptican designed by Bentham was a prison building constructed so as to allow for the constant observation and monitoring of 'progress' of all its inmates – essentially it was a circular building built around a central axis that allowed the guards to observe the inmates without themselves being observed. The aim of this design was to induce in the inmates the belief that they were under constant surveillance and although that classic sort of panoptican was never fully instituted, the ideas and basic approach behind it were integrated into the architecture of the new nineteenth century prison buildings. Foucault saw the prison as illustrating the basic principle of punitive and disciplinary power:

> The perfect disciplinary apparatus would make it possible for a single gaze to see everything constantly . . . the major effect of the panoptican: to induce in the inmate a state of conscious and permanent visibility that assumes the automatic functioning of power.
>
> (Foucault 1977: 173–201)

Stop and think

> ➤ In spite of the problems with prisons, Foucault suggests that prisons have important political effects at a wider, social level. What do you think these effects might be and how might they work?
>
> ➤ Foucault argued that observation could be used as a means of regulation and control. Give examples of how this might happen.

Punishment in modern society: the rationalization of punishment

Over the last two hundred or so years, makeshift forms of punishment have been replaced by centrally administered arrangements, with greater uniformity in punishment and the development of a penal infrastructure, due in part to the growth in population since the eighteenth century and the rising rate of crime. The range of professional groups working in the penal system – social workers, probation officers, psychiatrists, prison officers and governors – tend to see prisoners in terms of whether they are good or bad inmates on account of their institutional conduct, rather than as evil or wicked on account of the crimes they are being punished for. The punishments are administered by paid officials rather than the general public or, indeed, those personally affected by the offenders' actions.

This 'professionalization of justice' (Garland 1990) has altered the place and meaning of punishment in modern society. The institutions of punishment have become less accessible and more secretive as specialized professions have become involved. This trend toward rationalization runs counter to Durkheim's emphasis on the emotional nature of punishment – as reflecting an outrage to generally held moral sentiments. Indeed, this may help to explain why the public often feels frustrated by moves to release criminals 'early' – as evidenced by the campaign to ensure that the two 10-year-old boys who abducted and killed toddler James Bulger in 1993 remain in prison for many years and the opposition to periodic suggestions that, prior to her death in 2002, Moors murderer Myra Hindley (imprisoned in 1965) be considered for release on parole.

No method of punishment has ever managed to control crime or to achieve high rates of reform of offenders; it is unrealistic to hope that any methods will. Punishments fail because they can never be any more than a back-up to the mainstream processes of socialization. A sense of duty and morality, acceptable standards of behaviour and so on have to be learned and internalized, they cannot be imposed. 'Punishment is merely a coercive back up to those more reliable social mechanisms, a back up which is often unable to do anything more than manage those who slip through these networks of normal control and integration' (Garland 1990: 289).

Garland suggests that we should expect less from penal policy. Although sometimes necessary, punishment is beset by contradictions and irresolvable tensions:

> However well it is organized, and however humanely administered, punishment is inescapably marked by moral contradiction and unwanted irony – as when it seeks to uphold freedom by means of its deprivation or condemns private violence using a violence which is publicly authorized. (Garland 1990: 292)

Summary

➤ Crime is behaviour that breaks the criminal law and, if detected, may lead to criminal proceedings and formal punishment; it is distinct from the broader area of deviant behaviour.

➤ Those who commit crimes generally wish to keep their criminal behaviour secret. The methodological problems for the sociological study of crime include the difficulty of gaining access to such behaviour and of collecting reliable data from lawbreakers and the moral dilemmas that can face researchers who are confronted with behaviour which may, for instance, cause suffering to innocent victims.

➤ Crime has always fascinated people and explanations for it have been wide-ranging. Sociologists emphasize the specific social conditions and opportunities that are available to different groups. However, there is no one sociological position on crime.

➤ Crime has been seen as a response to the frustration felt by those who cannot achieve the 'success goals' of society (Robert Merton and Albert Cohen, for example); as a consequence of society, and particularly the agencies of social control within it, labelling certain forms of behaviour and groups of people as criminal (interpretativist approaches); and as a result of the power of the ruling, dominant groups to impose their standards of appropriate and inappropriate behaviour on other, less powerful groups (critical, Marxist theories).

➤ Criminal statistics indicate that crime has grown spectacularly in the twentieth century. However, these statistics have to be treated with caution: the extension of formal control mechanisms, such as more and better-equipped police and more laws, will clearly influence the amount of criminal behaviour that is known about. Criminal statistics also show that crime is a largely male preserve and that ethnic minorities, and especially black males, are more likely to be convicted and punished for criminal behaviour than other social groups.

➤ The police are the most visible formal agency of social control; the relationship between the police and public is of crucial importance in the control and subsequent punishment of criminal behaviour. A 'police culture' has helped to segregate the police from certain sections of the wider public, particularly young blacks.

➤ Legal punishment is the ultimate form of social control. There are different opinions over what should be the 'aims of punishment'. Deterrence, retribution and rehabilitation are three major aims that have been given more or less support and credibility by both governments and the public at different periods of time.

➤ There are various sociological explanations of the role of punishment in society. The Durkheimian approach sees punishment as helping to maintain social cohesion through strengthening the moral and social bonds of a society; the work of Foucault and the Marxist approaches have focused on punishment as a formal means for regulating the mass of the population and for supporting the power of the ruling classes.

Links

The section on 'explaining crime', pages 616–622, includes different theoretical approaches that are examined more generally in Chapter 2.

The discussion of policing, pages 631–634, touches on the issues of racism and policing considered in Chapter 8.

 ## Further reading

Becker, H.S. (1963) *Outsiders: Studies in the Sociology of Deviance*, New York: Free Press.

Cohen, A.K. (1955) *Delinquent Boys: The Culture of the Gang*, New York: Free Press.

Pearson, G. (1983) *Hooligan: A History of Respectable Fears*, London: Macmillan.

Young, J. and Mathews, R. (eds) (1992) *Rethinking Criminology: The Realist Debate*, London: Sage.

There is nothing like the 'real thing' and many of the original sources referred to in our examination of theories of crime are most accessible.

Cavadino, M. and Dignan, J. (2002) *The Penal System: An Introduction*, 3rd edn, London: Sage.

As well as looking at justifications and explanations for punishment, this book examines the specific elements of the penal system of England and Wales, including sentencing practices, imprisonment, non-custodial penalties and issues of bias within the criminal justice system.

Croall, H. (1998) *Crime and Society in Britain*, Harlow: Addison Wesley Longman.

Hester, S. and Eglin, P. (1992) *A Sociology of Crime*, London: Routledge.

Valier, C. (2002) *Theories of Crime and Punishment*, Harlow: Longman.

These three texts provide clear comprehensive introductions to the sociology of crime. Croall's text analyzes and describes various kinds of crime including violent and sexual crimes, organized and corporate crime and crimes of the state. Valier's study covers sociological theories of both crime and punishment.

Garland, D. (1990) *Punishment and Modern Society: A Study in Social Theory*, Oxford: Clarendon.

A comprehensive introduction to the sociology of punishment.

McLaughlin, E. and Muncie, J. (eds) (2001) *Controlling Crime*, 2nd edn, London: Sage.

Newburn, T. (2003) *Crime and Criminal Justice Policy*, 2nd edn, Harlow: Longman.

Two up-to-date overviews of the criminal justice system that include coverage of future policy issues such as the implications of privatization.

Maguire, M., Morgan, R. and Reiner, R. (eds) (2002) *The Oxford Handbook of Criminology*, 3rd edn, Oxford: Clarendon.

Comprehensive and up-to-date readings by key writers and researchers on criminology and the criminal justice system.

Marsh, I., Cochrane, J. and Melville, G. (2004) *Criminal Justice: An Introduction to Philosophies, Theories and Practice*, London: Routledge.

Part One provides an overview of the major philosophical aims and sociological theories of punishment and the developing perspective of victimology, while Part Two focuses on the main areas of the criminal justice system – including the police, the courts and judiciary and prisons.

Walker, N. (1991) *Why Punish*, Oxford: Oxford University Press.

This short, thought-provoking book looks at the justifications for and aims of punishment, grappling with the moral issues and dilemmas that they raise.

 ## Web sites

www.homeoffice.gov.uk

This is a major site that has substantial sections on crime and policing and justice and victims. It also includes a mass of statistics and research findings relevant to crime and its punishment.

www.crimetheory.com

As well as highlighting recent research on criminological theorizing, this site has an excellent archive of historical texts on the theory of crime – including Beccaria, Lombroso and Merton.

Activities

Activity 1

Explanations of crime

Rather than focusing on the individual characteristics of criminals, sociological theories of crime emphasize how the characteristics of the particular society play an important part in the explanations for crime. The following extract is from American sociologist Jack Levin (1993), who describes how the sociologist's 'eye' on crime differs from biological, psychological and common-sense explanations.

> Watching the evening news on television, I learn that a 35 year old man has murdered 23 people at a Luby's Cafeteria in Killeen, Texas. I read in the paper that a 'cannibal killer' in Milwaukee has strangled and dismembered 17 men. Then, I discover that the cities are burning again. The city of Los Angeles has gone up in flames following days and nights of rioting, looting and killing. Everyone is eager to understand why. So they consult the experts.
>
> Biologists and psychologists find their answers in the offenders themselves. Perhaps the mass murderer in Killeen had an undiagnosed tumour; maybe he had experienced severe blows to the head as a child. Perhaps the cannibal killer had been abused or neglected. He certainly had to be 'crazy', didn't he? And, the rioters must have been 'just plain rotten.'
>
> . . . [Sociologists] look at the structure and changes in American society that are possibly responsible for our growing problem of discontent and violence – . . . the breakdown in rules and regulations concerning moral behaviour, the high divorce rate and residential mobility . . . a high unemployment rate and a stagnant economy, and a collective belief that the ordinary American is powerless to control his or her destiny.
>
> Biological and psychological explanations are not necessarily incorrect. In fact, many serial killers may suffer from bad childhoods. Some rioters may have had brain disease. [But] someone looking only for psychological or neurological causes will focus on the perpetrator alone: Send him to prison, put her in the chair, give him surgery, treat her with anti-convulsant drugs, or see that he receives psychoanalysis or electro-shock therapy. From this viewpoint, only the perpetrator needs to change; the rest of us don't have to do anything.
>
> The sociological eye sees things differently. It does not deny the need to punish or rehabilitate violent offenders, but it also focuses our attention on ourselves and, so takes a much broader view. To reduce the level of violence, for example, we might consider changing laws, modifying the distribution of wealth, improving education, providing jobs that lead to upward mobility, reducing discriminatory practices, lowering the level of isolation in our major cities, improving our criminal justice system, or possibly even changing our values. As a society, as a community, as a group, we must make at least some changes, too.   (Levin 1993: xvi–xvii)

Questions

1. *The notion of the 'criminal type' is still widely held. What sort of characteristics form the common perception of the 'criminal type'?*

2. *Take an example of one particular criminal activity. What kinds of explanation for this would be offered by the different theoretical perspectives we have looked at?*

Activity 2

Crime and punishment

The second extract below, 'Prison inspections', is taken from the reviews of recent reports into particular prisons that are published in *The Howard Journal of Criminal Justice*. They suggest that some aspects of prison life have changed little since the nineteenth century, when Dostoevsky (the source of the first extract) was writing.

▶

Activities (continued)

First impressions

Those first few weeks, and indeed all the early part of imprisonment, made a deep impression on my imagination. The following years, on the other hand, are all mixed up together, and leave but a confused recollection. Whole periods, in fact, have been effaced from my memory. Generally speaking, however, I remember life as the same – always painful, monotonous and stifling. What I experienced during the first few days of my imprisonment seems to me as if it took place but yesterday. Nor is that unnatural. I remember so well in the first place my surprise that prison routine afforded no outstanding feature, nothing extraordinary, or, perhaps I should say, unexpected . . .

I experienced, moreover, one form of suffering which is perhaps the sharpest, the most painful that can be experienced in a house of detention cut off from law and liberty. I mean forced association. Association with one's fellow men is to some extent forced everywhere and always; but nowhere is it so horrible as in a prison, where there are men with whom no one would consent to live. I am certain that every convict, unconsciously perhaps, has suffered from this.

(Dostoevsky 1962: 21–3)

Prison inspections

The inspection at HMP Chelmsford disclosed 'a collective failure over a period of time of a number of senior members of the Prison Service to recognise and eliminate too many unacceptable practices and deficiencies in the running of the prison'. Among elements making Chelmsford 'dreadful' were 'the appalling and 19th century attitude to the treatment of young offenders' which the chief inspector felt may breach the UN convention on children's rights, and finance/staffing problems. Adult and young offenders were freely mixing in the same accommodation and 'it was not difficult to find young men of 17 clearly lost and often afraid within the prison'.

(*The Howard Journal of Criminal Justice* 1998: **37**, 1, 105)

The unannounced, follow-up inspection of HMYOI (Young Offenders Institution) Reading was critical, and the Chief Inspector (Ms Anne Owers) comments on the institution's failure to provide 'the environment that its young men needed'. There were dirty and cold cells, showers were in an appalling state and there was an ineffective incentives and earned privileges scheme. And, echoing a theme throughout the previous reports during this period, there was inadequate purposeful activity with little meaningful work that resulted in prisoners spending long periods in their cells. Crucially, Ms Owers also identifies 'an institutional and systematic lack of respect' between staff and prisoners.

(*Howard Journal of Criminal Justice* 2002: **41**, 5, 490)

Questions

1. What do you think may be the long-term effect on prisoners, prison warders and society as a whole of experiences and institutions such as these? How do you think they might affect you?

2. How might those who favour (a) retribution (b) rehabilitation respond to these extracts?

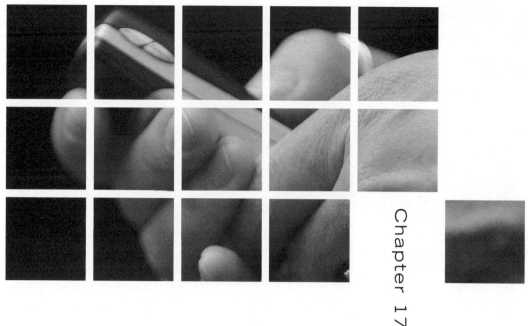

Chapter 17

The mass media

To understand day-to-day media use, it is necessary to take the whole ensemble of intersecting and overlapping media provision into consideration. Audiences piece together the contents of radio, television, newspapers and so on. As a rule, media texts and messages are not used completely or with full concentration. We read parts of sports reviews, skim through magazines and zap from channel to channel when we don't like what's on TV. Furthermore, media use, being an integrated part of the routines and rituals of everyday life, is constantly interrelated with other activities such as talking, eating and doing housework. In other words, media use is not a private, individual process, but a collective, social process.   (Bausinger 1984: 349)

Key issues

➤ How have the mass media developed and extended their influence in modern societies, particularly in Britain?

➤ What factors determine and constrain the content of the mass media?

➤ What are the major sociological explanations of the role of the mass media in society?

➤ How do the mass media influence social and cultural behaviour – in particular what is the relationship between the portrayal of violence in the media and violent behaviour?

Introduction

The importance of the media within society cannot be overestimated. We live in a media-saturated world where much of our social knowledge is gained through the channels of television, radio, cinema, video, books, newspapers, advertising, comics and home computers. The media have become an accepted part of our urban way of life: they give us news and entertainment, sell us lifestyles and reinforce social identities; we use them to educate ourselves and to communicate with one another. We spend much of our spare time and a lot of money on the media in one form or another, and much of it is taken for granted. 'The media are central in the provision of ideas and images which people use to interpret and understand a great deal of their everyday existence' (Golding 1974: 78). Twenty-five years later Briggs and Cobley extend this view to assert that 'as we move into the new millennium the media are increasingly a central part of our lives, our cultures and global economies' (1998: 4).

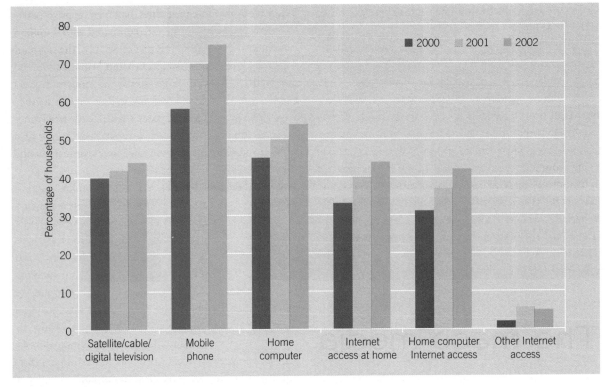

Figure 17.1 New technology in British households
Source: General Household Survey 2002

Stop and think

➤ Which of the following media do you use on a regular basis: daily newspapers; magazines; radio; television; video; home computer; the Internet?

➤ Which do you use most for news/information?

➤ Which do you use most for entertainment?

➤ Keep a diary for a week and record your use of the media. What patterns emerge? Are there any surprises? How much of your cultural world is 'situated' and how much is 'mediated'? (See O'Sullivan *et al.* on p. 660). How do you compare with your classmates?

It is clear from market research and social surveys that people in general depend heavily upon the media for information and entertainment. By looking at ownership of media hardware and the purchase of consumer items we can get some idea of the level of media saturation of modern society.

Once regarded as luxury goods and symbols of status, TV sets can be found in 99 per cent of households in Britain with over 80 per cent owning VCRs and CD players

and, since 2003, 31 per cent possessing a DVD player. Mobile phone ownership has increased fourfold in the period 1997–2003 to 70 per cent of households and there has been a similar rate of increase over the same period in the ownership of home computers (50 per cent) and Internet access (45 per cent). Figure 17.1 only takes us up to 2002 but shows the rapid growth in the areas of new technology.

Computer ownership and Internet access are linked to earnings with those in the top income group far more likely to own a home computer (see Figure 17.2). Sales of related consumer goods represent a billion-dollar market which has seen an increase in video tape consumption and CDs (and the demise of the vinyl disc). The computer games market also continues to expand with major competitors like Sega and Nintendo spending millions on developing new products. In contrast with this drive towards a more privatized leisure culture, the cinema increased in popularity during the 1980s, with 64 per cent of the population over seven years of age attending at least once a year. According to the British Council's web site (www.britfilm.com) there were 167.3 million visits to the cinema in Britain in 2003 – although this represented a 5 per cent fall from 2002's record total it remains an indication of a general revival of interest in the cinema.

Similar growth in the twenty-first century has been noted in the USA, Europe and Japan.

The level of interest in newspapers and magazines has remained high with 64 per cent of adults in Britain being regular readers of a daily newspaper and 71 per cent reading a Sunday paper. However, there has been an overall drop in readership over the past 50 years of an average two million readers per day and the 'red top' tabloids have taken the brunt with the *Daily Mirror* losing around 7 per cent and the *Sun* 5 per cent per year. In the Sunday market too the *Sunday Mirror, People* and *News of the World* are all losing readers. With audiences (especially younger ones) turning to alternative sources (TV, Internet, mobile phones) for their news, newspapers are also losing out to magazines which target the celebrity news once found in the tabloids:

> The gap between weekly magazines and newspapers has steadily closed, and they are competing to play increasingly similar roles. The impact is not an immediate or dramatic one – readers do not stop buying red tops. They just buy them a little less regularly.
>
> The competition in celebrity is obvious: 2.8m celebrity magazines are sold each week. For many women, celebrity news is the news, and weekly magazines deliver this news more reliably, and in a glossier way, than the tabloids can.   (Ewington 2004)

Women buy far more magazines than men (approximately 17 million per week in the UK, compared with 4 million bought by men). Within this market some of the standard weeklies (*Woman, Woman's Own* and *Women's Weekly*) are in decline, while those aimed at younger readers such as *Chat* and *Heat* are doing well. Women's lifestyle magazines have increased sales overall with newcomer *Glamour* topping the charts with sales of over half a million and older competitors such as *Vogue* just making the top ten with sales of 200,000.

The other staple diet in a gendered audience, once catered for by the tabloids through soft porn displays on page 3, can now be found in magazines which target 'football-loving, beer-swilling blokes'. Since the 1990s new magazines such as *Loaded* and *FHM* have emerged with a content which is 'openly juvenile and not ashamed of it' (*Observer* 13.11.1994). More recently this market has been assaulted by the arrival of men's weeklies *Nuts* and *Zoo*, which if any thing are attempting to outdo the competition by taking 'dumbing down' to a new low. With sales running at £7bn per year and advertisers spending over £2bn in this sector (in March 2003 newspaper advertising revenue fell below the £2bn mark for the first time in 70 years) it is clear that the magazine market remains vibrant while the newspapers struggle to come to terms with changing readership habits. (see Bell and Alden 2003: 19–23 and 33–35).

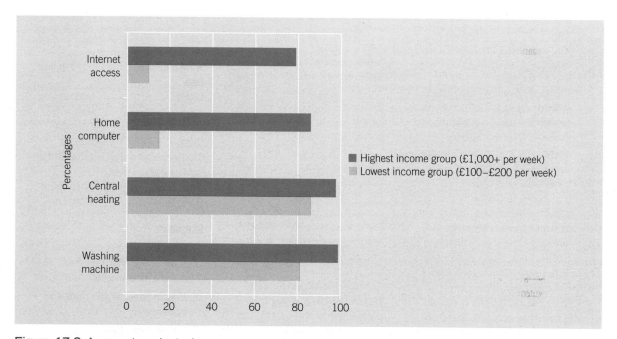

Figure 17.2 Access to selected consumer goods and services: by highest and lowest total weekly household disposable income group, Great Britain 2001–02
Source: Financial Times FT.com site, 14.04.2005

Case study

The loutish lad is dead: enter the caring lad in cashmere

The popular image of the young British male as a beer-swilling, loutish thrill-seeker has been declared dead by *Loaded*, the iconic 'lads' mag' that did so much to promote it.

Research commissioned by the title ahead of a relaunch this month shows that young men are aspirational, ambitious and, above all – sensible. The shift in values is reflected in their choice of role models, according to a survey of 6,000 18- to 24-year-olds carried out for *Loaded* by pollsters NOP.

The top five includes David Beckham, Jonny Wilkinson and Michael Owen; clean-living sportsmen who are more likely to be found on the training field than the dance floor. The only musician in the top five is the pop star Justin Timberlake.

The fifth name is Richard Branson, admired for creating a multi-billion-pound business empire without adopting the characteristics of a rapacious Gordon Gekko.

The contrast with the heroes of a decade ago is stark. When similar research was conducted in 1995, shortly after the magazine's launch, the list was dominated by hedonistic anti-heroes. Readers placed Paul Gascoigne, an alcoholic who later admitted beating his former wife, at number one, with his friend and occasional heavy drinking partner Chris Evans in second. They were followed by Oliver Reed and John Lydon, two infamous hell-raisers from previous generations, and the fey former Smiths frontman, Morrissey.

The survey suggests that young men today spend more time thinking about their careers. Nearly 85 per cent of respondents agreed with the statement 'I am ambitious' and 77 per cent agreed that 'planning the future is very important to me'. Having a good time is regarded as less important. When asked on what they would spend a free £1,000 windfall, 33 per cent said travelling but just 3 per cent said partying. Three per cent said they'd save the money, the same proportion as those who'd spend it on partying.

When a similar question was asked a decade ago, no one said they'd put it in the bank. Just 2 per cent said they'd spend it on their car and 33 per cent would spend it on clothes.

The new survey also found that men spend an average of £12 a month on grooming products including moisturiser and aftershave, compared with £6.90 10 years ago.

The survey suggests that young men are more materialistic. In 1995, just over half of the 18- to 25-year-olds said they wanted to be a millionaire by the time they were 30; in 2004, 79 per cent of 19- to 24-year-olds shared that aspiration.

The 'new lads' are likely to spend that cash on expensive designer clothes or luxury brands. Italian fashion labels Versace and Armani are cited as favourites. More than 6 out of every 10 respondents said it was important to keep up with the latest fashions.

According to *Loaded* editor Martin Daubney, young men admire successful figures, but are now unimpressed by bad behaviour. Famous figures who self-destruct are now regarded as 'losers' rather than 'characters' who should be applauded or emulated.

'Men will always love girls and beer, but now they also appreciate the need to moderate their hedonism to achieve their ambitions,' he said. 'In 1995 it was all about being talented and not giving a toss – these days more men appreciate why it's important to make the most of what you've got. Having fun is part of life, but not the only reason for it.'

James Brown, the former music journalist who founded *Loaded* in 1994, agreed that there appeared to be a change in the 'lad' image: 'I was at a 40th birthday party with my mates last week and a younger guy was wearing a cashmere jumper with a scarf in the pub.

That's the difference between then and now. My mates were stumbling around and drinking bottles of red wine. He was going home early.'

(James Robinson, the *Observer* 24.4.2005)

What they liked then . . .	. . . and now
Levi's	Versace
Ibiza	Goa
Oasis	Coldplay
Curry	Sushi
Vic Reeves and Bob Mortimer	Little Britain
Alcohol	Abstinence
Gary Oldman	Jude Law

Questions

1. What evidence is offered to support the view that 'lad culture' is changing?

2. How reliable do you think this evidence is?

3. Is there any evidence that Loaded has changed its direction?

Simply because people buy these products does not in itself tell us very much. Almost everyone owns a radio (or three) but how are they used and how many of us really listen? Social surveys reveal the hidden patterns in our viewing, listening and reading habits and they tend to confirm the fears of saturation suggested by the trends in media consumption. Not only do we rely upon the media as sources of up-to-the-minute information but also the media have come to dominate our leisure time.

Stop and think

> ➤ How would your life change without the media, if you did not have television, newspapers, advertising, radio and video? What would be the possible consequences for personal and social interaction? How often do you discuss films or TV programmes with your friends?

The point of such speculation is to emphasize the extent to which we depend on the media without really recognizing it. Consequently Masterman (1985) has argued that 'Media studies has become as important as reading' and identifies these reasons for its inclusion in the curriculum:

➤ high levels of media production, consumption and saturation within contemporary society;

➤ ideological importance of the media and their influence as consciousness industries;

➤ growth in the manufacture and management of information and its dissemination through the media;

➤ increasing penetration of the media into our central democratic processes;

➤ importance of visual communications and data handling in many areas;

➤ increasing cross-media ownerships which concentrate power and influence in fewer hands;

➤ increasing commercialization of the media environment, the privatization of information and the threat to public service obligations. (Adapted from Masterman 1985: 2.)

These issues are particularly relevant in a media-saturated world where the media have become so much part of our way of life that it is almost impossible to talk objectively about our relationship to them. As Postman has observed, the media are not only taken for granted but also mythologized into part of the natural order; the alphabet and the television set are no longer regarded as human inventions but, like trees and clouds, seen as elements of natural inheritance (Postman 1987: 167). Fiske and Hartley (1978) put their finger on it when they describe our problematic relationship to television:

> Everybody knows what it is like to watch TV . . . and it is television's familiarity, its centrality to our culture, that makes it so important, so fascinating and so difficult to analyse. It is rather like the language we speak: taken for granted but both complex and vital to an understanding of the way human beings have created their world.   (Fiske and Hartley 1978: 16)

This underlines the central place of the media within secondary socializing processes, to provide ideas and images which help to map out the contours of social reality, and to construct 'common-sense' meaning systems. For this reason it is probably not very surprising to discover that when *The Observer* put together its Power 300 to rank those people who 'more than any others, exert daily influence on the lives of people in Britain' they placed two media moguls, Rupert Murdoch and Bill Gates, alongside the prime minister in the top three (1.11.98).

Our main intention throughout this chapter is to provide a comprehensive grasp of the relationship between the individual, the media and society. Attempts by sociologists to emphasize the social role of the 'mass media' have led to some concern over the use of the term itself, which implies an undifferentiated and passive audience and encourages the simplistic belief that all media operate in more or less the same way with little recognition that individuals may use different media in different ways. We share these misgivings but retain the use of the term 'mass media' to denote the way in which most people rely on the media for much of what passes for cultural activity and information in the modern world.

The rest of this chapter focuses on the historical context of media development, the relationship between the media and society, the power of the media to influence attitudes and behaviour and the potential of audiences to interpret and respond to media texts.

The historical development of the mass media in Britain

Over time the mass media have come to play an increasingly important part in the everyday transmission of information and culture. These developments are largely due to technological inventions but are also influenced by social, economic and political factors. The invention of the printing press created the possibility of mass communication but it was only with the establishment of a free press and the right to a free education that an affordable daily newspaper became a reality. Similarly the worldwide potential of satellite or the Internet will remain unexplored for as long as the hardware can be affordable only by a minority or governments continue to practise official censorship. Nevertheless, there can be few people who have not been affected by the media; for many of us it is the main means by which we relate to one another. Knowledge based on direct experience and the oral transmission of culture are parts of a fading tradition in which face-to-face communication was crucial. What was once a culture founded in folk tales and contained within clear geographical boundaries has given way to an electronic revolution that respects neither time nor place. The world has been reduced to what Marshall McLuhan (1964) referred to as 'the global village', in which our culture becomes mediated rather than situated:

> Through [the] networks of direct interpersonal communication we participate in a *situated culture*. We may hear or relay news of recent events in the neighbourhood, likewise rumours, gossip, stories or jokes. We may attend and participate in local events, entertainments, family ceremonies or other rituals. These cultures of situation are primarily oral, by word of mouth relationships and . . . tend to be limited and defined in relation to a particular locale. In certain ways they embody elements of pre-industrial cultures, relatively small-scale forms of social interaction and groupings derived from the immediate, face-to-face environment and its daily experience. Since the mid-nineteenth century, however, we have increasingly learned to live not only in our situated culture, but also in a *culture of mediation*, whereby specialised social agencies – the press, film and cinema, radio and television broadcasting – developed to supply and cultivate larger-scale forms of communication; mediating news and other forms of culture into the situation. 'Our' immediate world co-exists with the mediated 'world out there'.
>
> (O'Sullivan *et al.* 1994: 12–13)

The rate and scale of these changes are also important aspects of the mediation of culture; as yesterday's technological miracle becomes today's obsolete gizmo, we begin to grasp how rapidly our lives become transformed by media technologies which we take for granted.

The 'mass media' cover a range of media formats and cultural forms from the days of the printing press to the more interactive technologies of today and include advertising, which as a cultural form permeates most forms of mass communication. We focus here on the most widely recognized technologies of the press and broadcasting but encourage you to explore the development of areas such as advertising, comics, music and the Internet.

The press

The early development of the British press occurred at a time of great social unrest and political struggle; the fight for the freedom of the press is often associated with the wider campaigns for individual liberty and workers' rights. In this struggle the newly emerging press was seen as a potential vehicle for political agitation and consequently became a target of government intervention. Using a combination of legal sanctions and covert operations the governments of the late eighteenth and early nineteenth centuries infiltrated, bribed and intimidated newspapers into political obedience. Tough laws of sedition and libel were available to deter political agitation, while the infamous stamp tax was used to ensure that newspapers were owned and read only by the well-off. This 'tax on knowledge' had the opposite effect to that intended and the government's attempts to control the established press simply sparked a proliferation of radical pamphlets and newspapers which were forced to operate as underground and clandestine organizations (*samizdat*). These papers were owned and written by political activists and they quickly became popular with the new industrial working class for whom they were intended.

In 1826, Cobbett's *Address to Journeymen and Labourers* sold over 200,000 copies, while his *Political Register* sold over 44,000 copies a week, compared with the 6,000–7,000 circulation of the London-based *Times* (Hall 1982). In 1831, the *Poor Man's Guardian*, carrying the slogan 'Published in defiance of the Law, to try the power of Might against Right', began a six-year run as the most notorious opponent of government tyranny, at times achieving sales of over 16,000 per issue. By 1836, Curran and Seaton (1991) have estimated, the 'unstamped press' was enjoying a readership of over two million in London alone, while stamped newspapers really struggled to compete: not surprising when we realize that one copy of *The Times* would have cost the average weekly wage of 7d (3p). The government appeared to accept defeat and eventually

Case study

The media in Britain 1945 and 1990

1945 There was no television. About ten million households had a radio set and most were run off the mains, not off a battery. The compulsory licence-fee was ten-shillings [50p]. You had a choice of two BBC stations. One was 'serious'; the other broadcast light music and entertainment. The nine o'clock evening news had an audience of half the population during the war, but this fell quickly in 1945. You could hear music at home on a wind-up gramophone with ten or twelve-inch 78 rpm bakelite records. Most people read one of nine London-edited 'national' morning newspapers. If it was the *Daily Mirror* or *Daily Sketch*, it was tabloid. Local evening papers were smaller, but more numerous. Even more people read a Sunday paper than a daily, often for the sport. The national dailies differed sharply in style between the low-circulation 'qualities' and the mass-circulation 'populars'. All nine were separately owned by press barons, such as Lords Beaverbrook, Kemsley and Rothermere. On the news-stands were several popular illustrated news and feature magazines: *Everybody's*, *Illustrated* and *Picture* Post. There were numerous general magazines and a growing market in women's weeklies and monthlies. You went to the cinema regularly.

Thirty million cinema tickets were sold each week. The short weekly 'newsreels', a mix of news and feature stories, gave a foretaste of TV news. Hollywood films predominated. In addition to the main feature, you saw a shorter, low budget 'B' movie.

1990 There was no escape from television. Three homes out of five had two sets and one person in six had three. ITV broadcast round the clock. Viewers had a choice of four channels and between them, BBC1, BBC2, ITV and CH4 provided some 450 hours of programmes a week. The licence fee was £71, all of which went to the BBC. ITV was paid for by advertisements, carefully regulated by the Independent Broadcasting Authority. We spent twenty-six hours a week watching TV: news, soaps, films, the House of Commons, endless studio discussion amongst politicians. Snooker was the most popular televised sport with only one team game [football] in the TV top-ten. We spent eight hours a week listening to the radio, but mainly whilst doing something else. The BBC had four national stations and thirty-two locals. There was a commercial station for most people and any number of overseas stations. Stations mostly broadcast music and 'chat'. BBC Radio 4 was news and talk; Radio 3 for classical music. You could listen almost anytime and anywhere,

especially with a Walkman headset. Music of high technical quality was available in the home through CDs, cassettes, LPs and pop-videos. Despite TV, most people still read a daily newspaper. Of eleven main dailies, six were tabloids with 80 per cent of the circulation. Your paper had 30–40 pages or more; a large proportion of features, pages of small ads and, increasingly, colour. The Sunday papers came in sections. Fewer people read an evening paper, primarily to see what was on TV. Half of us bought a local weekly paper, and three-quarters received 'free-weeklies'. The national dailies were bunched into eight ownership groups, headed by Murdoch, Maxwell and Rothermere. They had interests as international multimedia organisations; TV, radio, film, video, music and book publishing. Magazines were very popular, and station news-stands commonly displayed over 700 titles, including music and hi-fi, computing, body-building, sports and so on.

(Seymour-Ure 1992: 1–5)

Question

1. *There seems to be a world of a difference, yet these developments took place in only 45 years. Since 1990 you may have noticed media developments which should be added to an update of this snapshot; what would they be? Which have affected your own life most?*

abolished the stamp tax. This is often hailed as a great achievement in the struggle for democracy and referred to by some as a 'golden age' of British journalism which ushered in a transition from official to popular control (Koss 1973).

This 'liberalization' of the press is challenged by Curran and Seaton (1991), who argue that it is a political myth which disguises the real purpose of the reform: to destroy the popularity of the radical press, to enhance the power (and profitability) of the 'respectable' press, and to ensure that the newly freed newspapers were owned and controlled by 'men of good moral character, of respectability and of capital' (1991: 29). According to this perspective the commercial press did not come into being as a celebration of freedom but as a deliberate attempt at repression and ideological control:

> The period around the middle of the nineteenth century . . . did not inaugurate a new era of press freedom and liberty: it introduced a new system of press censorship more effective than anything that had gone before. Market forces succeeded where legal repression had failed in conscripting the press to the social order.   (Curran and Seaton 1991: 9)

By the end of the nineteenth century a newly educated working class provided a mass market which was satisfied by a range of commercial newspapers. The start-up costs were high but so were the returns on investment. Advertising revenue enabled the cover prices to fall dramatically and placed the commercial press in a strong position to see off radical competitors who refused to dilute their political seriousness and as a result were unappealing to readers and advertisers alike. By 1933 the left-wing *Daily Herald* was trading at a loss despite having the largest circulation in the Western world, indicating the crucial importance of advertising for newspapers irrespective of their popularity; it closed in 1964 with 8 per cent of market share. New types of newspaper emerged which were aimed at the literate working and lower middle classes but geared towards entertainment, consensus and patriotism. The *Daily Mail*, *Daily Express*, *Daily Mirror* and the *News of the World* all emerged as mass circulation newspapers for the lower-class reader, with *The Times* and the *Daily Telegraph* providing serious news for the middle and upper classes.

Behind these ventures were successful businessmen whose power was quickly recognized. As the ownership of the press became concentrated in the hands of four or five press barons and their dynasties, politicians became concerned about the influence of unaccountable proprietors who enjoyed 'power without responsibility'. By 1937, the four major players were Lords Beaverbrook, Rothermere, Camrose and Kemsley, who between them owned 50 per cent of national and local dailies and 30 per cent of the Sunday papers, including most of the popular titles. Although often referred to as 'the fourth estate of the realm' because of its independence from party politics and government influence, the British press was now controlled by men with very serious political ambitions. Beaverbrook and Rothermere, for example, used their newspapers to launch the United Empire Party as a challenge to the Conservatives in 1930; for Rothermere, this had turned into outright support of fascism by the end of the decade (Jenkins 1986: 24–5).

After the Second World War a Royal Commission was set up to investigate 'the growth of the monopolistic tendencies in the control of the press'. Despite its conclusion that concentration of ownership did not represent a threat to freedom of expression as long as the public got what it wanted, the issues of monopoly ownership, editorial freedom and political bias have continued to dominate discussion of the relationship between society and 'its' press and been the subject in Britain of two further Royal Commissions.

In the post-war period the great proprietors gradually disappeared from the scene and their 'crumbling palaces' fell into the hands of others amid intense competition and takeover. The personal fiefdoms of Beaverbrook and Rothermere became corporations run as businesses on behalf of shareholders who were primarily concerned with market share and advertising revenue. Control was seen to pass from powerful and interfering owners into the professional hands of editors and journalists committed to satisfying their customers and running an efficient business (Koss 1973). On the other hand, Curran and Seaton (1991) argue that some of the old barons clung on to their power well into the 1960s, by which time a new generation of 'interventionist proprietors' had emerged including one or two members of the old dynasties. While Vere Harmsworth (the third Viscount Rothermere) continued to run Associated Newspapers as a French tax exile, the new breed included Rupert Murdoch (News International), Robert Maxwell (Mirror Group) and Lord Stevens (who replaced Lord Matthews at United Newspapers). Lord Thompson (*The Times*), Tiny Rowlands (*The Observer*) and Conrad Black (who purchased the *Daily Telegraph* from Lord Hartwell in 1985) made up the other key players in this shake-up.

Curran and Seaton complain that this is not so much a period of 'market democracy' as one of concentration of ownership and corporate takeover resulting in the 'integration [of the press] into the core sectors of financial and industrial capital':

> The ownership of newspapers thus became one strategy by which large business organisations sought to influence the environment in which they operated. This strategy was pursued mainly on the basis of an arm's length relationship between newspapers and conglomerate newspaper companies during the 1960s. But in the more recent period, newspapers campaigned more actively for the general interests of big business, under closer proprietorial supervision. This development signified an important, long-term shift: commercial newspapers became increasingly the instruments of large business conglomerates with political interests rather than an extension of the party system.   (Curran and Seaton 1991: 101)

In the mid-1980s the press world was turned on its head by technological innovations which revolutionized the production process and the relationship of journalists to their work and one another. Computerization made traditional typesetters redundant and dragged the messy business of industrial newspaper production out of Fleet Street and into the shiny new world of Wapping. In theory this reduced production costs and opened up the press to new competition. For the first time in decades new titles were launched which appeared to challenge the monopolistic domination of the established press: *Today*, the *London Daily News*, the *Independent*, *Independent on Sunday*, *Sunday Correspondent*, *News on Sunday* and the *Sunday Sport* hit the streets in a flurry of marketing hype and hard-nosed competition, but the costs of breaking into the world of press monopoly were too great and by the mid-1990s only the soft porn *Sunday Sport* and its daily equivalent have survived intact; the *Sunday Correspondent* and *News on Sunday* collapsed within months, while *Today* was forced to close because it was losing so much money and *The Independent* was finally forced to accept a takeover bid from the Mirror Group.

What is interesting in all of this is the way in which a genuinely radical press has become depoliticized, commercialized and integrated into the economic and political core of society; a medium which began its life as a force for political agitation and social change has become part of the entertainment industry. As Hugh Cudlipp (one time boss of the *Daily Mirror*) commented in 1988, the 1970s ushered in 'the dawn of the dark age of tabloid journalism' in which 'proprietors and editors

... decided that playing a continuing role in public enlightenment was no longer any business of the popular press' (Pilger 1997: 18).

Economic gains secured by adoption of new technologies for production and printing and the move out to London's Docklands and regional sites have not stopped newspaper proprietors from seeking new ways to promote their newspapers. The nominal distinction between quality and tabloid format is slowly being squeezed by ever more ingenious attempts to attract new readers by introducing gimmicks, such as fantasy sport, bingo prizes and portfolios, sponsorship of downmarket TV game shows linked to game cards and, during the 1990s, the race to beat the competition through lower prices: for example, the price of *The Times* went down to 20p – less than half the price of *The Guardian* at the time.

Advertising revenue, boosted by circulation sales, makes newspapers viable so long as they can keep loyal readerships. The popular press is financed by its readers; two-thirds of its income derives from sales, only one-third from advertising. In the quality press – *The Times*, the *Guardian* and *Daily Telegraph* – this ratio is reversed. Although 60 per cent of adults read a daily paper, the increasing number of different newspapers and print media forces papers into a desperate battle to retain their market share. Roy Greenslade reported in 1998 that overall sales of all newspapers were in decline with a 300,000 drop in copies of 'dailies' and 700,000 for Sunday sales over a six-month period. In particular, 'the Sunday red-top market is disappearing in front of our eyes' (the *Guardian* 15.6.98). This decline in tabloid readership has been confirmed by circulation figures and a National Readership Survey which noted that sales were falling for all tabloids apart from the *Daily Mail*. This was partly to do with changes in Sunday leisure (shopping, TV sports coverage, relaxed licensing laws) and alternative sources of information (Internet, mobiles, magazines) (see *Mediaweek* 2000).

Ironically the 'market democracy' model seems to have led to a decline in journalistic standards and a growing concern over issues such as libel, chequebook journalism and the invasion of privacy. In 1989, the government set up a committee of inquiry, chaired by David Calcutt, after public complaints of sleazy tabloid journalism. The committee recommended the creation of a Press Complaints Commission to replace the voluntary codes of practice within the defunct Press Council. After several further reviews, and the 'odious' press treatment of the former heritage secretary David Mellor and the Princess of Wales, the final *Review of Press Regulation* came out in January 1993. Its main recommendations were that a statutory tribunal be set up to ensure conduct-code approval by the chief editors of all UK newspapers, to stop publication of offending material, impose fines and award costs and, finally, to create new criminal offences of unauthorized trespass and phone-taps, infringement of privacy and interception of telecommunications (National Heritage Select Committee 1993). The reaction from the editors themselves, however, was highly indignant. Peter Preston, then editor of the *Guardian,* said 'What is now being proposed is an all-purpose Government tribunal enforcing Government guidelines which will sit in judgment on the press year after year, coloured by the views of the Government of the day. That seems to me to be the complete antithesis of press freedom' (leader comment, the *Guardian,* 11.1.1993). Since the establishment of the Press Complaints Commission, Sir David Calcutt (and the majority of MPs surveyed in 1995) have called for statutory controls over the media (see p. 668). Despite these misgivings over the effectiveness of self-regulation, the PCC deals with over 3,000 complaints annually and it seems to have silenced attempts to introduce tighter controls; in March 2005 a Press Standards Bill failed to get support from government or opposition MPs.

Stop and think

> ➤ Despite the best efforts of government tribunals and individual campaigners, and frequent expressions of public outrage, the tabloid press in particular continues to publish sleazy and scurrilous stories. To what extent do you think a society gets the press it deserves?

Broadcasting

Since the 1920s technological developments in the electronic and broadcast media have transformed the communications environment and overshadowed the debates about the importance of the press. Although we should not overestimate the power of these new forms of mass communication by falling into the trap of 'technological determinism' (R. Williams 1974), it is clear that the instant and immediate nature of telecommunications and broadcasting have played a major role in the modernization of societies; they are essential elements in the creation of mass society and the globalization of culture and for many people represent the most significant link with social reality. In particular the ability of these forms to communicate in sound and images enhances their apparent power over the written word to convey 'how things really are'. This impression is so vital to the broadcasting media that no effort is spared to maintain it. In a *Late Show* review of the CNN coverage of the Gulf War it was revealed that 'live' transmissions from reporters in Baghdad were in fact based on information gained via telephone links to New York and London, where foreign correspondents and government officials had much more idea of what was going on (BBC2, 20 June 1995).

Television and radio broadcasting provision in the UK has undergone some important changes in the postwar period, and particularly so since the arrival of new technologies such as satellite broadcasting, cable and VCR. In many ways, TV and radio have become essential elements of everyday life so that it is difficult to imagine a time without them, but if we turn to the history of these media in Britain it is interesting to note how broadcasting, which began almost by accident, developed within a particular set of cultural, economic and political circumstances. Unlike newspapers, whose early evolution appeared in opposition to the state, broadcasting has always been subject to state regulation and control, primarily through the allocation of scarce channel frequencies. The incorporation of the early BBC under its Royal Charter gave it a degree of licensed independence, but the main paradox lies in the fact that the BBC remains economically dependent on, yet constitutionally separate from, the state. The constitution requires that it provides an impartial national service offering a mixed blend of programming 'news, sport, educational, religious and children's programmes' without the need for any advertising support for its production or transmission budgets. It is this commitment to high-quality public broadcasting for all which has led to conflict between the BBC and various governments, particularly when the prevailing attitudes are shaped by the enterprise culture and policies of deregulation. This tension between private enterprise and public service runs through the history of British broadcasting, but predictions that the BBC and Channel 4 were to be 'privatized' in the 1990s have not materialized. According to Negrine (1998) this resistance to deregulation and private competition 'reflects different socio-political traditions, economic forces (and) geographic features' to be found in Europe:

Unlike the US experience where radio broadcasting developed within a competitive framework with private commercially funded companies running the broadcasting services, European countries mostly favoured some form of state control over broadcasting as a way of avoiding the chaos in the airwaves which was characteristic of an unregulated system and also a way of ensuring that the 'public interest' was not overlooked.   (Negrine 1998: 225)

In March 2005, the UK government confirmed that the BBC would continue to be funded from a licence fee. This will be reviewed in 2016 when the BBC's Charter comes up for reconsideration.

Radio

Radio is often overlooked when we talk about the media, yet before the advent of television it was one of the main sources of news and entertainment in the home. Originally, the BBC was the sole provider of national programming on a public service model in the UK. This changed with the arrival of independent radio (IR) and is currently undergoing new changes with the advent of national commercial stations, the growth of community-based stations and changes in technology. According to Bell and Alden (2003) around 500,000 digital radios had been sold by the end of 2003 which has prompted the growth of digital radio stations both nationally and locally. The number of people now tuning into radio via TV has also grown (by 24 per cent in 2003) as the number of channels available increases.

The history and development of UK radio is under-researched at present, although Scannell and Cardiff (1991), Lewis and Booth (1989) and Crisell (1994; 1997) offer particular insights into how the arrival of radio created new, even unique, forms of national identity and domestic practices acting through the BBC. Golding (1974) and Curran and Seaton (1991; 1998) also offer accounts of the development of radio under the auspices of Lord Reith and the BBC. Beginning life as a 'wireless' version of the telephone, the radio very quickly emerged as a means of mass communication which needed regulation. In Britain this originally involved the British Broadcasting Company, the body set up by the manufacturers of radio sets and licensed by the Post Office to broadcast as a monopoly. The first director of the BBC was John Reith, a strict Calvinist who recognized the importance of the radio to act as 'trustee of the national

interest' and to defend middle-class standards of Christian morality. In 1924, Reith wrote in *Broadcast over Britain*:

> As we conceive it, our responsibility is to carry into the greatest possible number of homes everything that is the best in every department of human knowledge, endeavour and achievement, and to avoid the things which are, or may be, hurtful. It is occasionally indicated to us that we are apparently setting out to give the public what they think they need – not what they want. But few know what they want, and very few what they need. In any case, it is better to overestimate the mentality of the public, than to underestimate it.
>   (Reith 1924: 27)

By 1926 this private company had become a public monopoly (it became the British Broadcasting Corporation) which harnessed the 'initiative of business enterprise' to the 'concept of public service'. This particularly British notion of 'public service broadcasting' has until recently remained at the core of what the BBC stands for and, according to Asa Briggs (1961: 235–9), was based on four key principles:

- ➤ Programming was for public good not profit.
- ➤ National coverage for an undifferentiated community of the British people.
- ➤ Unified control through the 'brute force of monopoly'.
- ➤ Maintenance of high moral standards.

This model of public service radio broadcasting was how the BBC operated up to and including 1945, at a time when it was crucial to maintain national cohesion. The Home and World Services carried news programmes, while a specially created Forces Programme (comedy shows, big-band music and quizzes) became very popular with the UK listener. Following the war, the Light Programme, Home Service and 'highbrow' Third Programme emerged in recognition of the social class differences which still existed within the 'national' culture. According to Curran and Seaton (1991: 187) these three new radio stations coincided with the tripartite classification of schools to be found in the reformed education system. With some allowance for regional variations, however, the mission of the BBC remained 'to educate, to inform, and to entertain' within a national context:

> Because radio was directed at the home, it was the duty of broadcasters to thread their material into the fabric of family life without warping it; to diffuse ideas, information, music and entertainment without

being brashly intrusive . . . for whilst British broadcasters wished to preserve the individuality of their listeners, they recognised that radio had a unique potential for uniting the public to the private sphere of life, and it was for this reason that the programmes of national identity formed the backbone of British broadcasting.   (Scannell and Cardiff 1991: 14)

The 1960s brought a breath of sea-spray to the airwaves with the arrival of pirate radio, which was advertising-led and offered a mix of pop music and chat that was immediately popular with young listeners, unlike the middle-class production values of 'Aunty's' middle-of-the-road Light Programme. After pirate broadcasting was outlawed, it was decided to break the existing BBC radio system apart, and in its place to offer programmes geared to particular age and 'taste' groups, through Radios 1 (pop music), 2 (light entertainment), 3 (classical music) and 4 (news/current affairs/drama).

It is very likely that future competition for radio listeners will diversify into increasingly distinct age and taste groups, with the BBC's national AM and FM services (Radios 1, 2, 3, 4 and 5 Live) being squeezed not only by locally based BBC and IR stations but also by the new national commercial services, such as Atlantic 252, Classic FM, Virgin 1215 and Talk Radio UK. In the battle for the 'pop' audience the BBC saw its Radio 1 figures plummet from 17 million in 1992 to below 10 million in 2003. Although challenged by new commercial pop stations, Radio 1 has lost ground to its stablemate, Radio 2 which now grabs over 13 million viewers. In general terms the BBC still attracts the most listeners at national level while the commercial stations tend to be more popular with local audiences. Since 1984, when there were only 48 local commercial stations, the independent sector mushroomed to boast 248 by the year 2000 outnumbering the BBC by six to one. In total audience share, the commercial stations overtook the BBC in 1995 and increased their advertising revenue throughout the 1990s more than threefold to an annual total estimated at £500m in 2002. According to Crisell such success in the marketplace has done little to increase consumer choice or to challenge the BBC's claim to quality public broadcasting:

> Commercial radio has enriched output in one or two areas, notably pop and rock music, but not in many others such as documentary, features, drama, comedy and light entertainment, where the BBC's near-monopoly has been left largely unchallenged.
>
> (Crisell 1998: 115)

It is certainly a distant cry from the days of Lord Reith, when 'the great and the good . . . trooped into studios to educate and inform on every subject from unemployment to the Origin of the Species' (Scannell and Cardiff 1991, quoted in Curran and Seaton 1991: 138).

Stop and think

How good is radio?

Listen for at least an hour to each of the following:

- Radio 1
- Radio 4
- Radio 5 Live
- Talk Sport
- Your BBC local radio station
- Your Independent local radio station

➤ To what extent does each fulfill Lord Reith's original mission for public service broadcasting: 'to educate, inform and entertain' (see p. 665)?

Radio and everyday life

Radio is, essentially, a user-friendly medium. By its portable and accessible nature, it is so well integrated into everyday routines that it has become a backing soundtrack for many domestic chores or driving the car. For this reason it is often related to 'secondary' or 'tertiary' forms of media consumption, which do not require the concentrated activity of 'primary' use. Radio is also relevant to people's daily routines according to different times of day, particularly when there is less demand from other forms of media engagement like newspapers and television. It is not surprising to learn that 90 per cent of the British public listen to the radio on a regular basis and that it is a more popular source of information and entertainment than television during the daytime.

Radio is also seen as an essentially democratic medium, opening up scarce opportunities for listener feedback and public involvement through live radio 'phone-ins'. Different age, class and taste groups can be targeted much more effectively for advertising purposes, and the range of UK radio output, in this respect, is very wide, covering channels dedicated to news, current affairs, drama, features, sport and all types of music. This is more noticeable in the USA, where local radio stations are the norm and often focus exclusively on particular genres of popular music.

This 'narrowcasting' of 'format radio' is 'the life blood of commercialism' and in Crisell's view 'all but unstoppable'. Although it may provide some local flavour and diversity in popular music tastes 'it is hard to see how formats have increased or even matched the overall range of output which was once provided by the BBC networks' (Crisell 1998: 120).

Crisell goes on to argue that despite the apparent diversity offered by 'format radio' stations the output is a 'reassuringly uniform' blend of 'cosmopolitan culture' guaranteed by the syndication of pre-packaged programmes which are centrally produced by an industry where 'ownership (has become) concentrated among a few large groups' (p. 121). This leaves Radio 4 as the only surviving station for 'mixed programming' which treats radio as a 'primary' medium with a 'listening' audience to be 'spoken' to. As an outpost of genuine 'public service broadcasting' subsidized by a licence fee, Radio 4 continues to provide a range of programmes including news, current affairs, drama and comedy in a way which celebrates the dynamic and imaginative qualities of the spoken word. As such Radio 4 manages 'to reclaim for its audiences, situated as they are at the end of several centuries of predominantly "literate" culture, something of the archaic value and pleasure of listening to "talk or speech"' (Crisell 1998: 123).

Television

Most people spend some of their daily leisure time watching TV, which is, by far, the most popular form of home-based leisure with the average person watching approximately 27 hours of TV every week. Robert Kubey of Rutgers University has estimated that the average American spends 9 years in front of the TV in a lifetime and figures from Japan and Europe show similar patterns. In a MORI poll conducted for *Radio Times* in the UK, 54 per cent said that they would be lonely without the television although 67 per cent were prepared to admit that there was nothing worth watching. Having said that, viewing figures have had their ups and downs since the 1990s and both the BBC and ITV have had to face falling audience rates since the turn of the century although this may be partly accounted for by those turning to Sky, cable and digital stations. Whatever the precise picture might be, it is still the case that 'Television remains the number one leisure activity in the UK' (Bell and Alden 2003: 87). This is probably true across Europe and the USA although new technologies may have some

impact over the next couple of decades (see pp. 672–6). All social groups spend roughly a quarter of their viewing time on information and news, and 40 per cent view light entertainment and light drama, though there is a difference according to social class and gender.

Television viewing always involves mixed audiences, but there does seem to be a higher percentage of women viewers and an increasing scale of TV watching in the C2 and DE class groups. This is partly a result of an increased use of cable and satellite TV (see pp. 669–70). High-rating soap operas, quiz shows and news programmes tend to be watched by a complete cross-section without any skew towards a particular age group, sex or class. According to Barnett (1989), patterns of television viewing do not depend exclusively on the content or quality of the programme. There are many independent and unpredictable variables as well as the more obvious social and cultural ones.

Development of television broadcasting

Currently, British viewers have the choice of five terrestrial channels (BBC1, BBC2, ITV, Channel 4 and Channel 5) and 16 regional commercial TV companies, with S4C providing a Welsh-language service. Funding follows from the annual BBC licence fee, while independent TV and radio operate from spot-advertising revenue and programme sponsorship deals. The BBC sees itself as a particularly 'national' service, with regional and cultural variations, while ITV/IR developed from strong regional production bases, but sharing programmes with other companies across the independent network. Recent developments, such as Channel 4 and TV Asia, exist to cater for minority and multicultural interests. There has been a growth in both satellite and cable TV services which offer subscription-only programmes, such as sport, movies, cartoons, 'lifestyle' and MTV (music television); these are commercial enterprises competing with the terrestrial networks for a limited pot of advertising revenue.

Television started life in 1936 as the poor relation of radio at the BBC with a privileged audience of 20,000 Londoners. After the war the experiment resumed but TV licence sales had barely reached two million by 1953. The exciting potential of television was being explored and exploited by commercial broadcasters in the USA, but in Britain it remained under the control of an old-fashioned organization which had grown out of radio and tended to treat television as a 'wireless' with pictures.

By the end of the 1950s, however, television had become part of the 'mass media' and had supplanted radio as the more popular broadcasting medium. At a time when the disposable income of the 'affluent' working class had increased to the extent that they represented a large consumer market it was dangerous to ignore their tastes, which were becoming heavily influenced by the popular culture of North America (see Tunstall 1977: 100–1).

Independent Television in Britain grew out of the desire in the 1950s to challenge the monopoly of the BBC and to make money out of the advertising potential of television. This was a time of relative economic expansion and, under pressure from the commercial TV lobby, the Conservative government approved legislation for the creation of advertising-funded commercial television under an Independent Television Authority (ITA). Branded at the time by Lord Thompson as 'a licence to print money', the ethos of commercial television, and the later developments incorporated in the Broadcasting Act 1990, had been established.

The new commercial TV companies were allocated eight-year regional franchises and operated a system of 'pooling' programmes for transmission. The existing ITA was soon replaced by the Independent Broadcasting Authority (IBA), which licensed the regional companies and oversaw the transmission facilities. This federal system of local companies having strong regional identities helped to further encourage competition and diversity. However, the IBA held control of advertising. The US system of direct sponsorship was rejected and, in its place, spot advertising at set intervals was permitted to enable programme continuity and flow. Independent TV in this form prospered but grave concerns over the quality of programming resulted in a poor end-of-term report in 1962 from the Pilkington Committee, which complained that the ITV companies had failed to deliver good-quality public broadcasting. As a result, the BBC was awarded the third channel and BBC2 expanded into new areas of programme production, particularly with the arrival of colour TV in 1967.

In the 1980s the Conservative government began to explore the opportunities for deregulation and private enterprise in broadcasting which challenged the duopoly of the BBC/ITV networks. As a result of the Broadcasting Act 1981, Channel 4 was created from within the existing TV network. Like BBC2 it was to provide for minority tastes but was initially subsidized from the advertising profits of the ITV companies in an attempt to provide public service broadcasting via commercial channels.

Under the IBA the new channel was required 'to ensure that the programmes contain a suitable proportion of matter calculated to appeal to tastes and interests not generally catered for by Service 1 (ITV); to ensure that a suitable proportion of the programmes are of an educational nature; to encourage innovation and experiment in the form and content of programmes, and generally to give Service 2 a distinctive character of its own' (Blanchard and Morley 1982: 22). By mixing popular programmes with the 'risky and challenging', Channel 4 has become a successful alternative to the ITV companies with a 10 per cent share of viewers and taking over £300 million in advertising revenue in its first year as an independent operator (Peak 1994: 101).

The Peacock Committee considered alternative forms of funding the BBC but direct sponsorship via advertising was ruled out. However, the BBC was heavily criticized for waste and 'red tape', and the Peacock Report (1986) recommended that the Corporation should be opened up to commercial ideas and practices, 'enlarging the freedom of choice of the consumer and the opportunities to programme makers to offer alternative wares to the public.' Under the guidance of Michael Checkland, John Birt and Greg Dyke, the 1990s were a time of change and reorganization at the BBC, where the 'thrusting modernizers' battled it out with the 'fossilized fogeys' to give the BBC a more commercial feel and thus avoid privatization and the wholesale introduction of advertising in replacement of a licence fee. Writers such as Hargreaves have argued for a complete break with the past and an end to the licence fee (Williams 1994: 9) while the independent broadcasters regard it as unfair for a major competitor to get government sponsorship especially when the commercial terrestrial channels are expected to contribute to the idea of providing a public service (Sky is not bound by the same rules). In a poll conducted in March 2004 by ICM, public opinion was evenly split with 31 per cent supporting the retention of the licence fee, 31 per cent preferring the BBC to be funded through advertising (like ITV) and 36 per cent opting for subscription (like Sky); however, this does indicate that two-thirds would prefer an end to the existing arrangements. In defence of public service broadcasting it is argued that standards will fall and minority tastes will be axed should the licence fee be dropped in favour of an unregulated commercial system. This viewpoint is clearly expressed by the Campaign for Press and Broadcasting Freedom and is summed up by Tom O'Malley in their campaign to preserve public service broadcasting in general and the BBC in particular:

The BBC is a major part of our daily lives. It entertains and informs us across radio, the Internet and TV. It is a testimony to the success of the public funding of broadcasting. It is central to the development of the political and cultural life of the country. We need to build on this success to create a better, more democratic, more creative BBC in the twenty-first Century.

(O'Malley 2005: 3)

In 1990 the Broadcasting Act revolutionized the industry and in particular the dominance of the old ITV companies. Under the Act, broadcasting came under the remit of a new heritage ministry, committed to the idea of 'typically British' public service broadcasting. Furthermore, the Act obliged both the BBC and the ITV companies to contract out up to 25 per cent of their programmes to independent producers, which has meant a growth in the subcontracting sector, for example Hat Trick, Action Time, Zenith, Witzend and so on. The BBC came through relatively unscathed from the Act's implementation and its function was recognized as a necessary part of national public service programming policies. The Act's main effect was on the ITV companies, which were now to be licensed and regulated by the Independent Television Commission (ITC), whose members are appointed by the Heritage Secretary. The commercial broadcasters were required to bid for the right to operate as regional broadcasters, and franchises went to those who tabled the highest bids so long as they satisfied quality requirements. Several ITV companies failed to secure their existing franchises, while Channel 4 became an independent corporation in its own right, selling its own advertising in place of subsidy from within the ITV operating budget.

As Curran and Seaton (1997) point out, fears that the 1990s would introduce rampant commercialism and deregulation of national broadcasting were unfounded; the BBC and Channel 4 were protected from privatization, the Channel 3 companies were reminded of their public service obligations and in the auction of Channel 3 franchises, the ITC excluded 14 bids and rejected three of the highest bidders on grounds of quality (Curran and Seaton 1997: 330). Since the Communications Act of 2003, rules on TV ownership have been relaxed and in 2004 the final two independent companies gave up all pretence of representing regional broadcasting by merging into one large corporation – ITV. Rather than strengthening terrestrial public broadcasting it has been argued that this is simply setting up ITV for a foreign (probably US) take over.

Stop and think

> ➤ What assumptions about society lie behind the concept of public service broadcasting? How important is it in a period of rapid commercialization?

Cable and satellite broadcasting

As more and more homes link up to cable and BSkyB, the market dominance of the old BBC/ITV duopoly is being challenged. Major 'listed' sporting events like Premier League football, Benson and Hedges cricket and rugby league have been bought up to ensure that live coverage is exclusive to those able to receive BSkyB (Whannel and Williams 1993). In the long run the choices offered by 'pay to view' broadcasting and video on demand may take us to a future where all our telecommunications needs arrive through a modem connection to the family PC subsidized by spot advertising and sponsorship deals. In this kind of customer-led marketplace the future of public service broadcasting is open to doubt. As Granville Williams has pointed out:

We now have two different delivery systems into the home. We can watch BBC, ITV and Channel Four Television free at the point of use, or with the new delivery systems, such as cable, pay-per-view and television-on-demand, payment is made as we view. There is an important issue of public policy in the future relationship between the two systems, and at the heart of it is the continued provision of broadcasting free at the point of use.

(G. Williams 1994: 51)

Contrary to popular belief, cable broadcasting is not new to the UK. Many homes in the 1950s and 1960s were cabled up to receive radio and paid through subscription for the better-quality reception. The cable systems which are being installed across Britain in the mid-1990s were first established in Swindon and Milton Keynes. The go-ahead for cable and satellite services began with two Information Technology Advisory Panel (ITAP) reports in 1982, which led to the creation of the Cable Authority. It was decided that the future for television services would be better served by the market and, in particular, that government policy should be one of introducing and promoting competition so that the industry and the consumer could benefit.

At the same time the first steps towards satellite transmission were taken, where again the development in the UK was primarily market-driven, in contrast to other operations such as the Minitel service in France, which offers public access to a wide range of interactive communication services. The early initiative was taken by a consortium of television and publishing interests (the original British Satellite Broadcasting) but they were left at the starting-gate by Murdoch's gamble in creating Sky Television on European-owned transmission facilities. This venture required a great deal of heavy initial investment, partly subsidised by his profits from other publishing interests. The start-up costs of £2 million per week were largely off set by the £1 million in profits made by the *Sun* every week. However, the competition for subscribers left both BSB and Sky TV at a disadvantage, and they combined into the single BSkyB with Rupert Murdoch in control. It seems that Murdoch's gamble paid off, and his advertising profits will be used for other international forays into other areas, such as the Southeast Asian-based Star TV satellite as well as the development of digital TV with the French Canal Plus, which promises to open up the possibilities of interactive TV for the twenty-first century.

In domestic audience terms, Britain has virtually reached saturation point for broadcast programmes from domestic, cable and satellite companies. Viewers can enjoy a greater range of channels and broadcasting services which provide a wide range of 'thematic' programmes, such as box-office films, sport, lifestyle, cartoons, classic repeats, soaps and twenty-four-hour news as well as the traditional 'mixed' programming from the BBC and the ITC companies. According to Veljanovski (1991), this is a prime example of viewer sovereignty, which the new television marketplace is geared to provide:

> The viewer will no longer be restricted to a few general entertainment channels, but will be able to create his or her own viewing schedule at times which are convenient to them and not the broadcasters. In the absence of government restrictions on the spread of new technologies and programming, viewers will have greater choice, variety and access to more programmes. It follows that British broadcasting should move towards a market system which recognises that viewers and listeners are the best ultimate judges on their own interest, which they can best satisfy if they have the option of purchasing from the broadcasting services from as many alternative sources of supply as possible.
> (Veljanovski 1991: 14)

By 1995 the penetration of cable and satellite was lower than anticipated, with BSkyB dish sales running at around three million and cable links in approximately 700,000 homes. These are unevenly distributed, with a greater concentration in working-class homes. Curran and Seaton point out that in Britain cable and satellite TV accounted for only 8 per cent of total viewing by 1996 and that in the USA (whose model Britain has followed) more cable stations closed during the 1980s than opened; this situation is exacerbated in Britain, which leads the world in ownership of VCRs and where TV addicts seem to prefer the video as an alternative to (or an extension of) terrestrial television (Curran and Seaton 1997: 202). However, by 2004 Sky had 7m subscribers and cable 3.4m and, free from the duty to provide a public service, seems to be challenging ITV and BBC for a range of audiences.

The digital revolution: '57 channels and nothin' on' (Bruce Springsteen)

Since the mid-1990s there have been massive technological changes to the way the programmes are broadcast and experienced by viewers. In 1994 Granville Williams predicted that the developments in fibre optics and digitization will create a new interactive multimedia environment in which nothing will be the same again:

> Television, with its limited terrestrial and satellite TV channels, will be transformed into a two-way medium offering a superfluity of information and entertainment: movies-on-demand, video games, databases, educational programming, home shopping, telephone services, telebanking, teleconferencing, and even the complex simulations of 'virtual reality'.
> (G. Williams 1994: 12)

Since then the digital revolution in broadcasting has not only led to improved quality of reception but has dramatically increased the number of channels available and provided the opportunity to interact with TV in a variety of ways. The number of homes receiving digital transmission has steadily increased so that by 2004 over 50 per cent of households in the UK had digital TV. By the end of the decade the government intends to turn off analogue transmission altogether.

On the consequences of all this for society, opinion is divided between what Curran and Seaton (1990: ch. 14) call the 'neophiliacs' on one hand and the 'cultural pessimists' on the other. In the view of the neophiliacs we are moving towards a bright new post-industrial

I UNDERSTAND THE HANGOVER LACKS A LITTLE AUTHENTICITY!

Figure 17.3 Virtual escapism
Cartoon by Ian Hering

future (the Information Society) where the whole world is at our fingertips thanks to the Internet and the World Wide Web (WWW). Interactive communications will increase the opportunities for democratic participation and education, while authoritarian national governments struggle to control the flow of information. Customer choice becomes paramount as demand is stimulated and satisfied by a range of 'specialised narrowcast channels and services' (see O'Sullivan *et al.* 1994: 276–7). In reply, the cultural pessimists point to the inevitable decline of quality broadcasting and the damage done to cultural standards by the new forms of communication. Concentration of media ownership, the globalization of culture and the distortion of political power represent the unwelcome side of the new, media-saturated order. In the view of Graham Murdock (1990) we run the risk of creating a world where the principle of universal access to information is sacrificed in the interests of diversity of production and consumer choice. In a journalistic experiment, Stephen Pile subjected himself to the choice of 100 channels which subscription to Sky and ONdigital offer. After an enjoyable week during which he felt 'oddly unnourished' he concluded: 'ONdigital lets me select my own package

of channels, but does not carry many of the ones I want to see, whereas Sky carries them, but there is no package on offer that lets me select these without paying full price for a sea of dross' (*Daily Telegraph* 12.12.98).

The end-result may be a divisive fragmentation based on access to the skills required to travel the superhighway. As the poor and ill-educated are excluded from these skills they will become 'an unplugged, disenfranchised underclass' falling further behind 'a technological elite' (G. Williams 1994: 20). In their review of the impact of satellite TV on sport, Whannel and Williams (1993) come to a similar conclusion:

In summary, we are well on the road to a two-tier system of television sport. Terrestrial television will continue to feature a wide range of sports. But major events may be increasingly available only on satellite television, to those able to afford the dish, the channel rental and the pay-to-view fee. . . . Television sport from the 1950s to the 1980s could be seen as a form of social cohesion – developing a series of major national and international events and building an audience for them. These events – the FA Cup Final, Wimbledon, the Olympic Games and the World Cup – became major national shared rituals; events that large numbers of people watched simultaneously, and, symbolically, shared. The more recent developments are characterised by fragmentation. . . . As a result, audiences too, will fragment, and sport may no longer provide as many nationally shared rituals.　　(Whannel and Williams 1993: 4–5)

Stop and think

➤ To what extent has the prediction of Whannel and Williams come true?

➤ How many of these 'shared rituals' have been transferred to satellite coverage?

New media

Apart from the changes in media broadcasting, the technological developments mentioned above have had an impact on our lives in other ways. The invention of the DVD player spells the end of video while mp3 players make it possible to carry our entire music collection around on a 40 gigabite iPod. Linked to computer technology both have transformed the way in which we access, store and distribute information. In social terms, the two most important innovations have probably been the invention of the mobile phone and the emergence of broadband Internet provision. Both have contributed in different ways to the 'network society' predicted by the Spanish sociologist Castells (2000). In his work the revolution in information technology is as significant to our social experiences today as the industrial revolution was to those living in eighteenth-century Europe. The twin forces of digitalization and globalization have created a world in which we become increasingly estranged from fellow human beings and more dependent upon the virtual networks created through cybernetics.

The mobile phone has transformed not only the way we communicate with one another but also our social relationships and the ground rules for social interaction. Hans Geser has attempted a sociological analysis of the impact of the mobile phone on our lives and suggests that as they provide opportunities to escape the barriers to communication imposed by local and interpersonal settings and to increase our potential range of contacts,

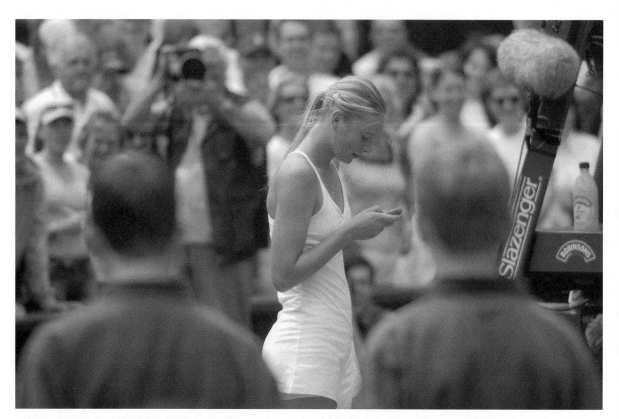

Figure 17.4 Maria Sharapova keeps Wimbledon waiting while she phones her mother

they may also alter the way we relate to one another in real time and space, what we referred to as *situated culture* at the start of the chapter.

This is particularly apparent in the impact that the 'unpredictable and uneasy intrusions of distant others' may have upon the interpersonal and intimate aspects of social life as well as the disruption caused to everyday interactions by the summons of a ringtone. Apart from turning the thing off, the recipient can respond in three ways:

1 *Flight*: the most drastic response is leaving the place of collocal (face-to-face) interaction for a corner or another room where the phone talk cannot be overheard.

2 *Suspension*: while remaining in the same physical location, the recipient suspends current activities or interactions for an undefined time.

3 *Persistence*: keeping current activities ongoing.

Whichever strategy for taking the call is made, the impact on the collocal interaction is inevitably disruptive for those on the receiving end:

> There can be something comical about the mobile user attempting the difficult task of managing a call whose purpose and emotional registers are at odds with those around them: the conversation with a lover on a train, or with an irate boss in a bar. Certain conversations can induce emotional and bodily responses, which may be quite incompatible with their perceptions of their physical location. Their participants often look as though they don't quite know what to do with themselves, how to reconfigure the tones of voice and postures which would normally accompany such conversations. The mobile requires its users to manage the intersection of the real present and the conversational present in a manner that is mindful of both. (Plant cited in Geser 2004)

As Goffman has pointed out rules governing our use of public space and for conducting private communication are taken for granted. The widespread use of mobile phones is beginning to rewrite these rule books. As Rob Stones has noted:

> It is difficult to sustain a mobile phone conversation in a public space without breaking either some of the rules of normal face-to-face interaction or the rules of civil person-to-person phone interactions.
>
> (Stones 2001)

Stop and think

➤ In which public spaces are mobile phones prohibited and why?

➤ What rules of 'face-to-face interaction' are disrupted by a mobile phone call?

➤ Do any disruptions annoy you more than others? Why?

➤ What calls are the most difficult to take in public spaces?

➤ Which of three strategies (flight, suspension, persistence) do you tend to use?

➤ Using the table below identify the consequences of adopting each strategy for ongoing face-to-face interaction and person-to-person phone interaction.

Strategy	Consequences for face-to-face interaction	Consequences for person-to-person phone interaction
Flight		
Suspension		
Persistence		

➤ Do you notice any difference in the strategies used by you and your friends?

➤ Are different strategies preferred by different social groups?

For a full discussion of these issues see Geser http://socio.ch/mobile/t_geser1.htm#5

The impact of the Internet is the other major development to have transformed our lives. Access to the Internet is not as widespread as mobile phone ownership but its social impact is far more wide-ranging. Recent developments – particularly through digital technologies and the introduction of broadband transmission – have enabled us to become amateur movie directors, our own disk jockey and private secretary. Apple have developed their own digital lifestyle suite of software (iLife) which delivers these possibilities through an ADSL connection to the Internet. David Fanning is the editor of *Macworld* magazine and his review of these developments is worth summarizing. After ten years of using the Internet he identified the following as the Top Ten uses by 2004:

1 *Shopping*   Amazon started it all as a bookshop but now their range of goods covers everything we would expect to find in a decent sized shopping mall. The high street has responded by developing their own web sites for online shopping. In 2004 online retail spending in the USA alone was approximately $144bn.

2 *Online gaming*   This allows players to master their skills and then compete with others in the virtual gaming community.

3 *Personal organization*   Software such as iCal allows the user to schedule appointments and organize an annual diary by event and date across the year. It can then be synchronized to a Palm computer or iPod to view (and edit) on the move.

4 *Watching TV*   Not only can we view TV broadcasts on our computer screens but it is also possible to use the Internet to program the recording of favourite programmes and replay them on computer. TV stations also offer the opportunity to watch again online important programmes we may have missed. The BBC also offers this facility for many of its radio broadcasts.

5 *Watching movies*   It is easy to order movies on DVD over the Internet for play on a home movie centre but it is also possible to download them directly and watch on your PC.

6 *Video conferencing*   Using iChatAV, it is possible to connect up with other PC and Mac users. Away from home or for business use it allows individuals to see each other while in conversation but does not cost the earth in telephone calls. It can also be used to stream video across the net making it possible to share film and TV with others.

7 *Surfing*   The Internet is a great place to idle away your time returning to web sites of particular interest which you have bookmarked (such as www.toffeeweb.com) or relying on others to do it for you; www.fark.com is one such which collects links to all things weird and wonderful in cyberspace.

8 *Amateur photography*   Digital cameras made it possible to import, edit and print your own photographs but now it is easy to share photos online and to use this technology to order prints from professional service providers such as Kodak.

9 *Audio entertainment*   Music and audio books can be downloaded, compressed and stored on hard disk. Using Napster, Limewire or iTunes it is possible to create a huge music library of mp3 files which can be downloaded onto mp3 players or burned onto CD/DVD. This is an area of most concern to the music industry particularly the prospect of illegal pirating of people's work. In view of online sales and the emergence of downloaded music it remains to be seen whether the high street retailing of music will survive.

10 *Pornography*   The top-shelf magazine will find it increasingly difficult to compete with the range of uncensored pornography available over the Internet. (Adapted from Fanning 2004.)

Case study

The Internet at its best . . . and worst

Cyberlibrary

As the Internet has expanded it becomes increasingly difficult to find what you want in the ocean of data sloshing around on the World Wide Web but in 2004 Steven Levy reported on the latest technological breakthrough at Google which promises to bring together the power of its search engine and the digitization of the printed page. At an average cost of $10 per volume it would be possible to integrate the world's greatest library collections into its indexes and provide free access to all who need it. The cost of digitizing the 15 million books held in these collections would be covered by pegging adverts to the search results and using the revenue to subsidize the project. As Levy says:

> Google's goal is to have *everything* at your fingertips, all the world's information digitized and instantly available to all who have a right to see it.
> (Levy 2004)

Yahoo are already reviewing a similar project for a video clip library.

Case study (continued)

Cyberporn

Although Fanning intended the last item on his list as a joke it is something that we should take seriously. It has been suggested that 'sex' is the most popular search term on the Internet and using 'porn' for a search in Google will get you almost 10 million hits. Not all of these are linked to porn sites as some of them will involve campaign groups against pornography but it is clear that the Internet provides an almost unlimited opportunity to access materials which may be seen as offensive and, in some cases, illegal. The images and video downloads offer incest, paedophilia and rape as part of a staple diet which would be banned if offered over the counter.

In 2001 several members of the Wonderland Club went to jail following an international police investigation of Internet child pornography across 12 countries. Almost a million images were traded online and men abused their own children for the entertainment of fellow members using video conferencing technology. Status within the club was achieved through the nature of abuse on offer. In a disturbing extension of the Right to Freedom of Expression which the Internet provides, sites such as Ogrish.com now serve up videos of murder, torture and the beheading of hostages alongside hardcore porn as part of everyday entertainment. In this sense the Internet may be seen to undermine general moral standards in ways which were previously unimaginable.

WAP technology

WAP is an attempt to bring the two developments of mobile phones and the Internet together and will enable customers to use their mobile phones to surf the Internet, access news items, interact with their computers and enjoy the audio and video services already available through the digitization of information. At present the handsets are cumbersome, the quality patchy and services expensive but by the time the next edition of this book is in print (if we are still reading books) it may be commonplace for the mobile phone to incorporate the functions of video camera, TV set, mp3 player and broadband-connected PC. Such visions of the future may be premature, however, as research suggests that 'mobile entertainment' is not what people want from their phones. As Mike Masnik reports:

> TV at home works because you turn it on and it works – and the user can sit back and relax while watching it. Radio in the car works, because you turn it on and it starts playing, and the user has no where else to go. On a mobile phone, there are other options, and if things cost too much and don't work as easily as consumer electronics, they'll find other things to do.
> More importantly, people still view their mobile phones as communication devices first. They buy them so they can talk to others or SMS others. Not because it lets them watch TV when they're away from home . . . In fact, study after study after study all seem to show that people want to use their phones to communicate . . .
> That isn't to say there isn't a market for mobile entertainment. In fact, it's likely to be a huge market – it's just that it has to be built on the foundation of communication and interaction, rather than broadcast. This is in the form of communicating with each other for entertainment purposes, interactive gaming, file sharing and other forms of entertainment that actually take into account that the user is mobile and connected – rather than stationary and isolated. Simply moving entertainment to a mobile device and calling it mobile entertainment is missing the point. If there's no reason for that entertainment to be mobile, there's no reason anyone's going to be willing to pay anything extra to get it.
> (www.thefeature.com 29/1/2005)

Questions

1. What are the likely advantages and disadvantages of the cyber library?

2. Do you think that cyber porn poses a threat to moral standards?

3. Would you welcome the forms of 'mobile entertainment' offered by WAP technology?

Case study

Broadband challenges TV viewing

The number of Europeans with broadband has exploded over the past 12 months, with the web eating into TV viewing habits, research suggests. Just over 54 million people are hooked up to the net via broadband, up from 34 million a year ago, according to market analysts Nielsen/NetRatings.

The total number of people online in Europe has broken the 100 million mark. The popularity of the net has meant that many are turning away from TV, say analysts Jupiter Research. They found that a quarter of web users said they spent less time watching TV in favour of the net.

The report by Nielsen/NetRatings found that the number of people with fast Internet access had risen by 60 per cent over the past year. The biggest jump was in Italy, where it rose by 120 per cent. Britain was close behind, with broadband users almost doubling in a year. The growth has been fuelled by lower prices and a wider choice of always-on, fast-net subscription plans.

'Twelve months ago high speed Internet users made up just over one-third of the audience in Europe; now they are more than 50 per cent and we expect this number to keep growing,' said Gabrielle Prior, Nielsen/NetRatings analyst. 'As the number of high-speed surfers grows, websites will need to adapt, update and enhance their content to retain their visitors and encourage new ones.'

The total number of Europeans online rose by 12 per cent to 100 million over the past year, the report showed, with the biggest rise in France, Italy, Britain and Germany. The ability to browse web pages at high speed, download files such as music or films and play online games is changing what people do in their spare time.

Broadband growth in 2004

Italy: 120%
UK: 93%
France: 70%
Switzerland: 42%
Spain: 33%
Germany: 33%

(Source: Nielsen/Netratings)

A study by analysts Jupiter Research suggested that broadband was challenging television viewing habits. In homes with broadband, 40 per cent said they were spending less time watching TV. The threat to TV was greatest in countries where broadband was on the up, in particular the UK, France and Spain, said the report. It said TV companies faced a major long-term threat over the next five years, with broadband predicted to grow from 19 per cent to 37 per cent of households by 2009.

'Year-on-year we are continuing to see a seismic shift in where, when and how Europe's population consume media for information and entertainment and this has big implications for TV, newspaper and radio,' said Jupiter Research analyst Olivier Beauvillian.

(BBC News Online 3.12.2004)

Questions

1. *Has access to broadband affected your use of the media?*

2. *What explanations can be given for the differences in broadband growth across Europe?*

The mass media and control

So far we have concentrated on the development of media technologies and institutions. In emphasizing the power and autonomy of media technologies there is a danger of falling into the trap of 'technological determinism'; as Williams (1974) and Winston (1998) have warned, this diminishes the importance of social, economic and political factors in the development and use of the media. By focusing on the idea that media institutions are driven by technological innovation we imply that society merely deals with the consequences of change instead of looking at the ways in which media technologies, society and culture shape one another:

New technologies are discovered by an essentially internal process which then sets the conditions for social change and progress. Progress, in particular, is the history of these inventions, which 'created the modern world'. The effects of the technologies, whether direct or indirect, foreseen or unforeseen, are as it were the rest of history. The steam engine, the automobile, television, the atomic bomb, have made modern man and the modern condition.

(R. Williams 1974: 13)

In the rest of this chapter we explore the wider relationship between the media, society, culture and power. The issues raised will include media freedom, censorship, social control, public responsibility and the ethics of media production; in particular, four areas will be emphasized. First, media and control – the extent to which media communicators and audiences are restricted by social, political, economic and organizational determinants of media production and consumption. Second, theories of media freedom and control – an examination of the different theoretical positions which analyze the relationship between the media, the audience and the structure of society. Third, media power – a brief review of the debates over the media's influence on culture and social behaviour, focusing on the relationship between media presentations of violence and violent behaviour. Fourth, the 'active audience' – we finish the chapter with a reminder that far from being an undifferentiated mass of brain-dead cultural dupes, the audience has the potential to discriminate, negotiate and resist media power: an important factor which is often overlooked in the way we talk about 'the mass media' and what it does *to* people.

As we noted when reviewing the history of the press, the issue of media freedom has been seen as crucial to the development of democratic societies. In opposition to 'authoritarian' and 'soviet' models of deliberate media control, McQuail (1994: 126–31) has noted the emergence of 'public service' and 'libertarian' models which emphasize the creative freedom of media personnel and the customer's right to choose. These ideas underpin the liberal and pluralist views of media production (see pp. 690–2) that are at the centre of the debate over the relationship between the media and democracy (Keane 1991). In its most idealized form this view exaggerates the investigative and creative freedom of individual journalists and broadcasters, who, according to Gans (1974), 'fight to express their personal values and tastes ... and to be free from control by the audience and media executives' (quoted in Lull 1995: 122). However,

as Gans recognizes, media personnel are also trained employees of large organizations as well as members of society. Whether producing hard-hitting news, dramatic fiction or alternative comedy there are institutional restraints placed upon what the media professional can and cannot do. As Brian Whitaker (1981) pointed out in his review of the production of 'the news', journalists and editors are not only gatekeepers of news events but also actively involved in the creation of news through the criteria by which they select 'newsworthy' stories:

> There is no limit to what might be reported. The number of observable events is infinite ... We often fail to realise what a very, very limited selection of events it is that appears on our table at breakfast time.

(Whitaker 1981: 23)

The criteria that govern this selection process involve individuals in making decisions, but they are decisions made in the performance of an organizational role which in turn has to be placed in the context of wider global and social factors which are economic, political and cultural in nature.

McQuail (1994) identifies a hierarchy of five levels of analysis for understanding the relationship of the individual communicator to the outside world (see Figure 17.5).

The range of factors or pressures that journalists have to deal with can be expressed in a different way which emphasizes the competing interest groups seeking to influence media decisions (see Figure 17.6).

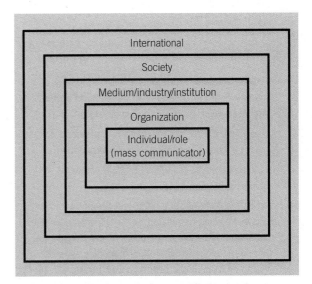

Figure 17.5 The relationship of the individual communicator to the outside world
Source: McQuail 1994: 189

677

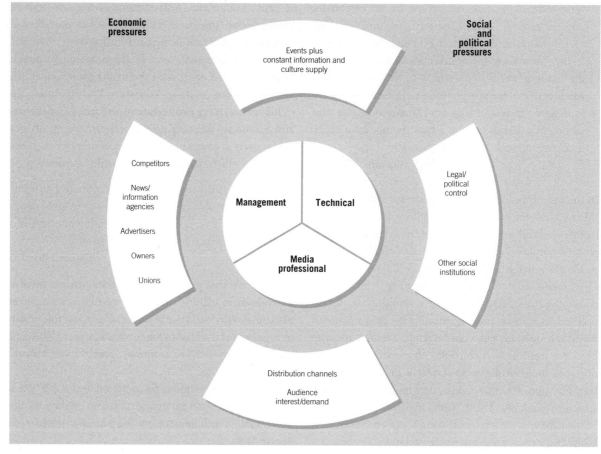

Figure 17.6 Pressures that journalists have to deal with
Source: McQuail 1994: 191

The various influences on media content can be referred to as 'determinants'. Some of these determinants operate internally and some are external to the media organization.

The external influences include economic, political and legal interventions, while the internal relate to the constraints inherent in the structure of media organizations.

Stop and think

> Provide examples of the ways in which the work of journalists or broadcasters can be analyzed at the five levels given by McQuail (Figure 17.5).

> How might the factors identified in the second model (Figure 17.5) influence news production?

> Find some recent examples of media personnel being constrained by these influences.

> When the *Daily Mirror* printed photographs of 'Iraqi prisoners' being humiliated by 'British troops' which turned out to be fakes, the editor, Piers Morgan, was forced to resign. Using McQuail's models, why do you think Morgan decided to go with the story in the first place and where do you think the pressures to resign came from?

External influences on media content

There are three main external influences:

> economic factors;

> political control;

> regulation.

Economic factors

In any market-led operation, audience demand is going to have a major impact on production. A privately run media enterprise has to produce profits for its shareholders. The only way to do this is to create a large

Figure 17.7 A fake photograph printed in the *Daily Mirror*

local press and, as cable and satellite broadcasting expand, in radio and television. Through the process of *vertical integration* companies have extended their operations into media distribution as well as production. BSkyB, for example, is involved not only in the production of television programmes but also in their transmission, while the Japanese electronics giant Sony has bought out software production companies, like Columbia, in order to have greater control over media consumption. This is part of a wider trend towards cross-media ownership on a global scale which is of great concern to media analysts distrustful of the concentration of a variety of media interests in the hands of a few powerful and extremely wealthy operators. In the USA a series of mergers and take-overs since 1993 have seen Paramount going to Viacom for $10 billion, Disney merge with CapCities/ABC for $19 billion and CBS taken over by Westinghouse for $5 billion. In 2001 the $165bn merger of AOL and Time Warner represented the biggest media merger in history. Two years later Newscorp aquired 19 per cent of Hughes Electronics for $6.6bn which gave them a broadcasting outlet in the USA for their global satellite operation. In Europe the empires of Murdoch and the Italian media magnate Berlusconi indicate the extent to which national and global conglomerates can dominate the media and entertainment industries. Following the collapse of communism in central and eastern Europe and the opening up of this market to Western investment concern has been expressed by the European Federation of Journalists that this will result in the development of an independent and nationally based media in this region. This globalization of the world media also applies to advertising, where a series of mergers and takeovers in 1998 have seen British agencies such as GGT and Abbott Mead Vickers taken over by the appropriately named US giant Omnicom. Other British agencies (the Media Business Group and Partners BDDH) ended up in US hands as a result of multimillion pound bids. 1998 ended with two of the world's biggest agencies (Dentzu and Leo Burnett) merging.

audience who are in turn attractive to advertisers by providing the kinds of product that people want to consume. In theory this is supposed to ensure competition and freedom of choice. Any media organization which tries to buck the market is asking for trouble: 'My concern is to give people what they want, not what improves them. Television does not make the times. It follows them' (Robert Giovalli, Head of Programme Planning at Finninvest, quoted in Keane 1991: 121).

The problem with the basic market model is that it exaggerates the power of the customer and ignores the influence of media owners and advertisers. Since the end of the nineteenth century the tendency in media ownership has been towards concentration rather than diversity, with large media conglomerates and powerful media moguls dominating the global village. Through the takeover of their rivals, large companies have expanded via a process of *horizontal integration* to establish their dominance in particular areas of the media – such as publication. By the same process in Britain, 90 per cent of the national press is in the hands of five major producers, with similar concentrations of ownership found in the

We can see that the new generation of media conglomerates encompass much more than the traditional mix of press and television and are now extending their ownership and influence into many related industries such as publishing, radio, film, video, recorded music, telecommunications, computers, advertising, marketing and public relations, cinemas, couriers, hauliers and even postal services ... We have a highly concentrated media in the hands of politically partisan owners who use their power to defend and advance

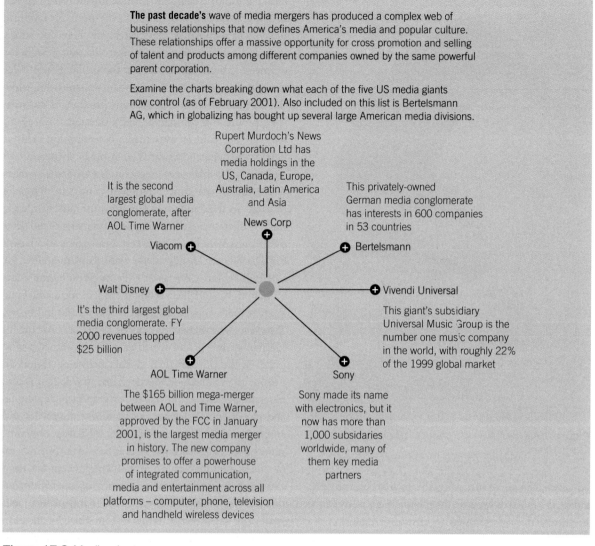

The past decade's wave of media mergers has produced a complex web of business relationships that now defines America's media and popular culture. These relationships offer a massive opportunity for cross promotion and selling of talent and products among different companies owned by the same powerful parent corporation.

Examine the charts breaking down what each of the five US media giants now control (as of February 2001). Also included on this list is Bertelsmann AG, which in globalizing has bought up several large American media divisions.

Rupert Murdoch's News Corporation Ltd has media holdings in the US, Canada, Europe, Australia, Latin America and Asia

News Corp

It is the second largest global media conglomerate, after AOL Time Warner

This privately-owned German media conglomerate has interests in 600 companies in 53 countries

Viacom

Bertelsmann

Walt Disney

Vivendi Universal

It's the third largest global media conglomerate. FY 2000 revenues topped $25 billion

This giant's subsidiary Universal Music Group is the number one music company in the world, with roughly 22% of the 1999 global market

AOL Time Warner

Sony

The $165 billion mega-merger between AOL and Time Warner, approved by the FCC in January 2001, is the largest media merger in history. The new company promises to offer a powerhouse of integrated communication, media and entertainment across all platforms – computer, phone, television and handheld wireless devices

Sony made its name with electronics, but it now has more than 1,000 subsidaries worldwide, many of them key media partners

Figure 17.8 Media giants
Source: www.wgbh.org

their commercial and political influence. Unrestricted ownership and control will lead to a narrowing of choice and the elimination of diversity in media at a local, regional and national level.   (G. Williams 1994: 52)

Go to http://www.pbs.org/wgbh/pages/frontline/shows/cool/giants/ and click on the links to see a breakdown of ownership for each conglomerate.

See also http://www.thinkandask.com/news/mediagiants.html

For a critical discussion of the concentration of media ownership see; www.globalissues.org/HumanRights/Media/Corporations/Owners.asp#MediaConglomerates MegaMergersConcentrationofOwnership

Gillian Doyle (2004) has analyzed the development of two key processes in the transformation of the media: *globalization* (the erosion of national boundaries to media markets) and *convergence* (the amalgamation of different media technologies through digitization):

The ongoing globalization of media markets and the convergence in technology between media and other industries has caused many media firms to adapt their business and corporate strategies accordingly. As traditional market boundaries and barriers have begun to fade away, the increase in competition among the media has been characterized by a steady increase in the number of perceived distributive outlets or 'windows' available to media firms.

As media markets have been freed up and have become more competitive and more international, the opportunities to exploit economics of scale and economies of scope have increased. Globalization and convergence have created additional possibilities and incentives to repackage media content for a global audience into as many different formats as possible (books, magazine serializations, television programme, video) and sell the product through as many distribution channels and to as many paying consumers as possible. Think about the range of products – books, films and toys – now available in the multimedia global Harry Potter industry, for example.   (Doyle 2004: 3)

Consequently, she argues that the bigger and more convergent organizations are best placed to exploit these opportunities and that this has led to a spate of mergers:

Highly concentrated firms which can spread production costs across wider product and geographic markets will, of course, benefit from natural economies of scale and scope in the media. Enlarged, diversified and vertically integrated groups seem well suited to exploit the technological and other market changes sweeping across the media and communications industries.

(Doyle 2004: 3)

Because of the impact these industries have upon our culture, our political views and our way of life, Doyle argues that this issue of media regulation and pluralism are crucial and not simply a matter of economic competition. Instead the general deregulation of media and the increasing opportunities for concentrations of ownership on a global scale pose a real threat to a genuinely inclusive and pluralistic media. Using the 2003 Communications Act in the UK as an example, she suggests that the battle may already have been lost:

Communications policy should encourage the economic strength of players in the media and communications sector. But economic or commercial factors are by no means the only, or indeed the most important, considerations tied up with public policy for the communications sector. If the UK government favours the ambitions of major commercial media players at the expense of pluralism, it is not clear how self-interested media corporations can be prevented from dominating ever-widening spheres of political decision making in the future.   (Doyle 2004: 4)

Although writers such as Veljanovski (1989; 1991) have sought to justify unrestricted cross-media ownership on the grounds that it stimulates competition by 'bailing out'

ailing newspapers, more critical commentators disagree. While ownership does not automatically imply control, there is much evidence from the history of media institutions and from the biographies of great media moguls such as Beaverbrook that owners have always sought to intervene in media production to further their own commercial and political interests or those of others whom they support (see e.g. Bower 1995; Coleridge 1994; Clarke and Riddell 1992; Jenkins 1986; Shawcross 1992; Tunstall and Palmer 1991).

In 1998 Rupert Murdoch's 'hands-on' style featured in a celebrated case of censorship when he objected to the criticisms of the Chinese government in Chris Patten's account of the handover of Hong Kong. The book, *East and West*, was due to be published by HarperCollins, which is owned by Murdoch's News Corporation, but it was clearly felt that the tone of the book could harm Murdoch's interests in the Far East satellite station, Star TV. The editor-in-chief of HarperCollins was suspended and *The Times* (also owned by News Corporation) failed to carry the story. This came as little surprise to 'Murdoch watchers', who could recall that BBC broadcasting was withdrawn from the Star TV satellite following its critical coverage of the 1989 Tiananmen Square massacre of pro-democracy demonstrators by government troops.

On the surface the power of media owners to intervene in media production is itself constrained by a countervailing economic force – the audience. Whatever their personal and political ambitions, owners are in business and have to respond to market pressure. Rupert Murdoch has shown himself to be a master in the art of giving the punters what they want. When he bought the ailing *Sun* newspaper from the Mirror Group for £800,000 in 1969 he targeted the youthful working-class audience ignored by the *Daily Mirror*: '[Murdoch and his editor] felt the *Mirror* had grown old with its wartime generation of readers. They identified the working class, postwar baby-boomers, now in their early 20s as their potential audience. These young people were anti-establishment, sexually experienced and watched a lot of television. Murdoch understood that TV was the new medium (rather than a rival medium) . . . and gave copious coverage to the TV programmes his target readers were watching' (Pilger 1997: 7).

The *Sun* quickly became the *Daily Mirror*'s biggest rival and overtook it in terms of sales in 1978. However, audiences can be volatile and in the late 1980s the *Sun* lost many readers following misjudged and false allegations about Elton John in 1987 and Liverpool fans during the Hillsborough tragedy of 1989. On Merseyside it has not recovered from the decline in sales. Fifteen years later the *Observer* reported:

Copies of the *Sun* were burnt in the city's streets and many newsagents refused to sell it. It has still not fully recovered: while the paper sells 3.3 million copies nationwide, it shifts only 12,000 in Liverpool. One rival publication calculated that, given an average cover price of 20p over 15 years, editor Kelvin MacKenzie's catastrophic misjudgment has cost owner Rupert Murdoch around £55 million in lost circulation.

(The *Observer* 11.7.2004)

Table 17.1 Per capita adverting expenditure per year in the five largest markets

	USA $	UK $	Germany $	Japan $	France $
1998	415.9	293.4	241.8	237.4	166.0
1989	291.6	191.1	175.4	234.9	129.7

(Cited in McRury 2002: 40)

Newspaper cover prices and 'pay per view' television rates are an important source of income, but it has often been said that the chief function of the privately owned media is to produce audiences for advertisers.

Advertising is a multibillion-dollar business, with independent broadcasters and newspaper companies caught up in an endless battle over ratings. McRury estimates that global expenditure on advertising is currently around $300bn per year with the USA accounting for about 40 per cent and Europe 30 per cent of global expenditure. If we look more closely at the breakdown we can see that there are contrasting patterns across the market place. During the final episode of *Seinfeld*, for example, NBC charged $2 million per 30 seconds of commercial broadcast and netted a record $40 million for one show (the *Guardian* 14.5.98). As Carlton TV's director of programmes told the *Daily Telegraph*, 'there is no place in prime time television for programmes which cannot achieve ratings

Case study

Newspaper owners and journalists

The extract below is taken from the letter of resignation that *Times* journalist Peter Kellner wrote in 1986 after *The Times* did not publish a column he wrote on Rupert Murdoch. It illustrates how newspaper owners can exert an influence on newspaper content – indirectly in this case through *Times* sub-editors not wishing to print any criticisms of the paper's owner.

Dear George
. . . On Sunday I told you of my intention to write my column for tomorrow's *Times* on Rupert Murdoch and the unions. You said that this might cause problems, but that there were no general rules covering this kind of piece and that the article would be judged on its merits . . .

You told me that there was no way the article could be revised to make it suitable for publication in the *Times* . . . Your message was clear: legitimate and robust criticism of the *Times'* proprietor is banned from its pages.

I understand your position, but have these comments to make on it:

First, your statement that there was no point even referring my article to Charles Wilson [the editor] demonstrates the oppressive environment in which Murdoch's journalists are now required to work.

Second, your comments about criticisms of proprietors in other papers are wrong. You seem to have forgotten Donald Trelford's public criticisms in *The Observer* of Atlantic Richfield at the time of the paper's sale to Lonrho . . .

Murdoch is not like any other media boss. He is different,

and worse, and has decisively broken the tradition that good journalists and their editors always strive to put the interests of their readers above those of their paymasters . . . Fine it is his paper. Now we all know where we stand, you can seek and may find columnists willing to write according to these rules. I regret that I cannot be one of them.

(Letter written by Peter Kellner, 11 February 1986, quoted in Seaton and Pimlott 1987: 252–4)

Questions

1. *In what ways and to what ends do owners and shareholders attempt to influence the content of 'their' newspapers or radio and television stations?*

2. *What kinds of constraints are there on this influence? How effective do you think they are?*

of six to eight million' (G. Williams 1994: 17). This places advertisers in a strong position to influence programming, production values and even the script: through 'product placement' some shows are thinly disguised commercials. Historical drama is not popular with TV programme makers because the opportunities for product placement or identification are limited. As Peggy Charren, president of Action for Children's TV, has pointed out: 'You can't make Marie Antoinette eat Domino's Pizza' (quoted in G. Williams 1994: 18). This is less of a problem in the UK, where product placement is strongly controlled by the Advertising Standards Authority.

In the USA, where television has always been a commercial enterprise, even news programmes have to be angled towards dramatic reconstruction of sensational incidents in order to boost audience ratings. K7, the Florida news channel, set a new trend for newscasting in the 1990s when it deliberately shifted towards news as entertainment.

A closer look

The most expensive advert of all time is thought to be a two-minute commercial for Chanel No. 5, directed by Baz Luhrman and starring Nicole Kidman. According to the rumours she is said to have been paid $12m and wore $42m worth of jewellery for the three-day shoot.

'Tabloid television' is the result, providing a diet of human interest and trivia with a heavy emphasis on violent crime. Special effects, background music and trained presenters work together to turn other people's tragedies into prime-time television; in the pursuit of ratings, sensation, excitement and drama replace the quest for serious news coverage (BBC2 *Late Show*, 25 May 1994).

In theory, the market-driven media model should guarantee customer choice and satisfy audience needs but

Case study

Children bombarded with junk food adverts

Children are being bombarded with advertising for junk food at the rate of 1,150 television commercials each day, researchers have found. The average child watches 20,000 adverts a year on children's television. Among food commercials, 95 per cent are for products high in fat, sugar and salt. The findings (in a TV documentary called *Fat Pushers*) come two days after the Government's chief medical officer said obesity in children had shot up by 25 per cent in eight years and now affects one in 10 six-year-olds.

The programme . . . blames Whitehall for failing to crack down on junk food advertising and for allowing it into schools. According to research for the programme, 48 per cent of schools now have

vending machines, largely selling sweets and crisps.

Last year, McDonald's spent £32.5 million on television advertisments, while Coca-Cola spent £13 million and Pringles £7 million. The programme suggests that it is money well spent.

While the Government maintains that children are wise consumers who are not manipulated by advertising, when the programme filmed a class of nine-year-olds watching adverts for foods such as Frosties and Dunkers, many of them clearly knew every word and gesture in the commercials.

Nick Barham, of the advertising agency Karmarama, said advertisers try not to talk about the food itself. 'These ads are no longer trying to sell the foods, which are of such poor nutritional value it's hard to say

anything good about them,' he added. 'Instead they're promoting a dream; a fun, exciting, seductive lifestyle.'

Although Tessa Jowell, the Culture Secretary, has decided that Britain will not follow other European countries and ban junk food advertising, the Labour MP Angela Eagle told the programme there was 'overwhelming' evidence that advertising was affecting what children eat. 'I would ban advertising of foodstuffs that are unhealthy to children,' she said.

(*Daily Telegraph* 1.5.2004)

Questions

1. What adverts/jingles can you still recall from childhood?

2. Do you think they influenced your diet?

3. What measures should the government take on junk food?

as Keane (1991) argues, the outcome ignores the needs and opinions of minority groups (1991: 84). In this relentless pursuit of advertising revenue the media become terrified of controversy and depth and learn to play safe:

> Advertising works in favour of advertisers and business and against citizens. It privileges corporate speech. Bent on maximising audiences and minimising costs, advertising ensures that material which is of interest to only a small number of citizens will at best be available on a limited scale. Advertising reduces the supply of 'minority interest' programmes, aesthetically and intellectually challenging themes and politically controversial material which fails to achieve top audiences and, hence, does not entice advertisers to open their cheque books.
>
> (Keane 1991: 83)

Stop and think

➤ Visit the Advertising Standards Authority web site on http://www.asa.org.uk/asa/ and discover what it does and how many complaints it handles per year. For a more in depth look at what they do take the College Guided Tour which covers many issues to do with advertising and its regulation.

Political control

In the twentieth century the potential of the media for political influence and control has been widely recognized. It is no accident that in times of political upheaval the fiercest battles are often for the control of the radio or television stations as warring factions seek to establish ideological as well as military supremacy (e.g. radio broadcasts whipping up racial hatred played an important role in Rwanda's slide into civil war and genocide in 1994 and in Serbia in 1998, where two newspapers were closed by the government because they refused to report Milosovic's 'climb down', in the face of NATO threats, as a 'victory'). The bombing in 1999 of the State TV Station in Belgrade, with the loss of 13 lives, was justified by NATO on the grounds that it was broadcasting propaganda.

In periods of political stability the media also play a major role in establishing and maintaining social order and political control. McQuail describes how the state in totalitarian regimes deliberately suppresses freedom of expression through official censorship while at the same time seeking to establish ideological hegemony through orchestrated propaganda campaigns. McQuail defines propaganda as 'the deliberate and systematic attempt to shape perceptions, manipulate cognitions, and direct behaviour to achieve a response that furthers the desired intent of the propagandist' (McQuail 2000: 425).

In the 1930s Hitler expressed his opinion on the importance of political propaganda in *Mein Kampf*, identifying two clear objectives in the battle for the hearts and minds of the masses: the silencing of critical intellectuals and the brainwashing of everyone else:

> All propaganda must be popular and its intellectual level must be adjusted to the most limited intelligence among those it is addressed to. Consequently, the greater the mass it is intended to reach, the lower its purely intellectual level will have to be . . . The art of propaganda lies in understanding the emotional ideas

World in focus

Television in Iran

Parliament in Iran, where clerics want to stop people watching television programmes they see as corrupting, yesterday passed the final parts of a bill which bans the private use of satellite television equipment.

The bill, which prohibits the import, distribution and use of satellite dishes, will become law when the guardian council, a parliamentary watchdog, ratifies it in a fortnight. That is considered all but certain.

The legislation empowers the Ministry of Islamic Guidance and Culture 'to safeguard cultural boundaries of the country and of its families against destructive and indecent satellite programmes'.

Iranians watching programmes with dish antennas have a month to dismantle the equipment or risk its confiscation and fines of 1 million to 3 million riyals (£360–1000).

(The *Guardian* 2.1.1995)

Questions

1. Why might satellite broadcasting pose such a threat to regimes such as these?

2. How might the content of satellite programmes be seen as corrupting to Iranian culture?

of the great masses and finding . . . the way to the attention and thence to the hearts of the broad masses . . . The receptivity of the great masses is very limited, their intelligence is small, but their power of forgetting is enormous. [Therefore] all effective propaganda must be limited to a very few points and must harp on these slogans until the last member of the public understands what you want him to understand by your slogan. ('War Propaganda', in Hitler 1969)

In the former Soviet Union the importance of the press for the purposes of agitation, propaganda (*agitprop*) and organization date from the victory of Lenin in 1917 and the subsequent domination of Soviet society by the Communist Party.

> The press is the strongest instrument with which, day by day, hour by hour, the party speaks to the masses in their own essential language. There is no other means so flexible for establishing spiritual links between the party and the working class.
>
> (Stalin, quoted in Whitaker 1981: 45)

However, such intentions do not always have the desired effect; audiences can react against deliberate attempts at ideological manipulation. Lull (1995) points out that many Chinese people ridicule and resist government propaganda:

> They detest the Communist Party's simple minded self-promotion, its blatantly biased news reports, the laughable TV 'model worker' programmes, the many exaggerated advertising claims about domestic products, and the unavailability of advertised foreign goods. (Lull 1995: 62)

A closer look

Film in Tibet

In Tibet the Dalai Lama is seen to be such a subversive figure by the Chinese government that possessing an image of him is treated as a political crime. A recent documentary, *What Remains of Us*, was shown at the Cannes Film Festival under strict security to protect Tibetans who had been filmed watching an illegal recording of their spiritual leader. The movie makers risked imprisonment themselves by smuggling a video of the Dalai Lama into the country and filming the responses of local people to his first appearance since fleeing the country in 1959. See *Students for a Free Tibet* web site: http://studentsfora.tempwebpage.com

In liberal democracies the freedom of the media is a much-valued principle but in practice there are still many restrictions imposed by the state. Politically sensitive and morally offensive material is often suppressed; the state also uses the media to transmit information (and misinformation) which serves its interests. This is particularly true in times of political crisis or war. During the First World War, for example, press coverage was tightly controlled and manipulated by the British government (Lovelace 1978). In the 1980s, similar criticisms were made of the news coverage of the Falklands War (Glasgow University Media Group 1985; Morrison and Tumber 1988), while Curtis (1984) is one of many writers to highlight the involvement of British governments in a 'propaganda war' over Northern Ireland.

According to Keane (1991), as the power of the media has grown so the need to curb and control their influence has increased. Since the First World War he notes the growth of 'the democratic leviathan', a range of unaccountable political institutions at all levels of government which combine to further state power at the expense of the citizenry. A key element in this process has been the control of the media, and Keane highlights the four types of political censorship of the media.

First, the British government can exert direct political censorship on the media. It can vet any sensitive material before it is released; the 'thirty-year rule' on Cabinet papers is an example of the automatic 'prior restraint' on information. It can also take legal action against journalists, radio stations and TV companies to prevent the dissemination of material already available or in production. This may include banning, shredding, burning or confiscating material. An example of this direct legal action was the 'Spycatcher' case in 1986, where the British government tried unsuccessfully to stop the publication of a book detailing the memoirs of Peter Wright (1987), a former member of the Secret Services.

Second, state officials have involved themselves in surveillance, infiltration and information management which has 'resulted in a well organised form of permanent political censorship at the heart of state power' (Keane 1991: 99). In 1995 newscaster Jon Snow revealed that in his first days as a journalist, MI6 (the UK Intelligence Service) had tried to recruit him as an agent because of his contacts with the radical student movement (Snow 2004: 90–92).

Third, governments may be 'economical with the truth' or deliberately orchestrate a campaign of disinformation. Tactics can include stage-managed briefings, denial of access to official sources and the leaking of misinformation. Those seeking to expose such activities can expect to find their careers destroyed. When in 1985 Clive Ponting, a civil servant, leaked a memo to the Labour MP Tam Dalyell which implied that a Conservative government minister had misled the House of Commons over the sinking of the *General Belgrano* during the Falklands War of 1982 he ended up in court but was found not guilty after a celebrated legal battle. Sarah Tisdall, also a civil servant, had been less fortunate the previous year when she leaked to *The Guardian* government plans for managing public opinion over the siting of US cruise missiles in Britain and received a six-month prison sentence. *The Guardian* was forced to reveal its source by threat of legal action.

Fourth, governments seek to use the media to influence public opinion: 'All governments seek to manage the news; to trumpet the good, to suppress the bad and to polish up the image of the Prime Minister' (Cockerell *et al.* 1984: 9). Through 'lobby system' briefings, public information campaigns and the manipulation of links with media organizations, governments and politicians use the media to market political policies and careers. Media organizations can scarcely afford to offend such powerful clients, with the result that TV and radio interviews often seem to reflect the demands of the interviewee rather than the interests of the public. Margaret Thatcher, for example, seemed unwilling to be interviewed by Brian Redhead on Radio 4 but positively enjoyed appearing on the *Jimmy Young Show* on Radio 2. Shortly after coming to power she singled out the editors of the *Sun* and the *Sunday Express* for knighthoods, while Victor Mathews, owner of the *Daily Express*, received a peerage (Shawcross 1992: 212). More recently Michael Moore has complained that by repeating the accusation that a link existed between Sadaam Hussein and Osama Bin Laden so often, the Bush administration managed to get the American public to believe that the two were allies. By the time war had begun a poll conducted by Knight-Ridder showed that 50 per cent actually believed that one or more of the hijackers on 9/11 were Iraqis. (Moore 2003: 56).

As a result of these trends in what might euphemistically be called 'information management', Keane (1991) suggests that Western democracies have become immune from public evaluation and criticism. Government officials have less interest in consulting the public and little belief in their right to know what is going on. The media have had to become part of a strategy of public deceit, or else face the consequences of legally sanctioned intimidation. The Official Secrets Act was extended in 1989 to gag government officials for life and to render it a criminal offence for a journalist to make a 'damaging disclosure'.

Simultaneously, Clause 28 has ensured that the public promotion of homosexuality by government employees is now an offence. An example of this official censorship was the dubbing of Sinn Fein members' voices between 1988 and 1994 in an attempt 'to starve [them] of the oxygen of publicity' (Gilbert 1992). However, Sinn Fein's leader, Gerry Adams, later commented that the actors assigned to speak his words were rather better at it than Adams himself!

Stop and think

Media democracy

The Media Democracy movement involves a variety of groups who campaign for a more representative media. Many of these organizations can be found on the Internet where interactive media technology is being used to challenge the power of the conventional media institutions. One of the pressure groups to check out is: http://www.mediademocracyday.org. A more general political web site which also covers the media is: http://www.opendemocracy.net

➤ Look them up and see if you can find evidence to support Keane's argument.

➤ Do you think such campaigns can bring about change?

Regulation

Most state control of the media is exerted through the law and voluntary codes of conduct entered into by media organizations and journalists and broadcasters. While the USA guarantees freedom of expression in its First Amendment and the European Convention on Human Rights does so in Article 10, British governments are not bound by such rights.

As Robertson and Nicol (1992: 3) observe in a 650-page book devoted to legal restrictions on the media, 'Free speech is what is left of speech after the law has had its say.' We shall touch briefly on these legal constraints and identify the more important regulatory bodies and codes of practice.

Regulatory bodies and codes of conduct

Through statutory laws and voluntary agreement, regulatory bodies have been set up to establish guidelines on 'public taste' and to maintain decent standards of

Case study

Legal restrictions on the media

Official Secrets Act

Under the Official Secrets Act 1911 the leaking of official information by civil servants was forbidden and the use of unauthorized material by journalists became a criminal offence. The police were given special powers of arrest, seizure and interrogation in cases where leaks occurred. After the 'Spycatcher' case it was replaced in 1989 with even tighter legislation, which meant that civil servants were bound by 'a lifelong duty of confidentiality' (Burnet 1992: 54) and journalists could be prosecuted for disclosing information 'damaging the security forces or the interest of the United Kingdom' (Robertson and Nicol 1992: 424). That revelations were 'in the public interest' was no longer an admissible defence. Following newspaper revelations in 1998 by a retired member of the Secret Services that MI5 had planned to assassinate Colonel Qaddafi of Libya, the British government tried unsuccessfully to extradite the agent from France to stand trial in Britain under the Official Secrets Act.

Blasphemy

In 1950 the crime of blasphemy was defined as 'any contentious, reviling, scurrilous or ludicrous matter relating to God, Jesus Christ or the Bible, or the formularies of the Church of England'. Since 1922 there has been one prosecution as a result of a private action brought by Mary Whitehouse against *Gay News* in 1977. *Gay News* lost the case, was ordered to pay costs and fined and the editor was given a nine-month jail sentence.

Obscenity

The Obscene Publication Act 1857, which empowered magistrates to confiscate and destroy immoral books, was amended in 1959 to make a distinction between erotic literature of genuine artistic merit and pornography. A number of show trials ensued, the most famous of which concerned *Lady Chatterley's Lover* by D.H. Lawrence in 1961, the *School Kids' Oz* (1971) and *Inside Linda Lovelace* (1976). Since then the law has largely been used against works glorifying violence and drug abuse, and hard-core pornography, though in 1991 it was invoked against the misogynist lyrics of rap artists

N.W.A. Films and videos came within the provisions of the Act in 1977 and 1979, respectively, and television and radio were covered by the Broadcasting Act 1990.

Contempt of court

In Britain there are strict rules governing the media coverage of court cases that are *sub judice* (under consideration). Though cases such as the trial of O.J. Simpson 1995 in the USA illustrate how difficult it is to reach a judgment that is fair and seen to be fair when there are not strict controls on the media, these controls can sometimes be used to avoid unwelcome publicity.

Civil law

Civil law covers private litigation relating to breaches of confidence, copyright and libel. At a secret hearing judges are requested to grant an injunction which, once granted, prevents anyone repeating the material covered by it. Where injunctions are not sought or granted and a libel action is successfully prosecuted, the aggrieved party can make a lot of money: Elton John £1 million, Jeffrey Archer £500,000 for example.

---

journalism. Pornography, violence, bias and invasions of privacy tend to be the main concerns of such bodies. However, the codes of conduct they try to enforce are seen by Harris (1992) as a minor part of the regulatory framework as journalists and broadcasters are more concerned with the constraints imposed by proprietors, advertisers, public demand and the law.

In Britain there has been some attempt by the press to safguard standards and deal with complaints from the public. Following post-war concerns over the effects of media ownership on free expression, it was suggested that a Press Council be formed which would ensure 'the highest professional standards' in journalism. After threats of government intervention, newspaper proprietors agreed to

Figure 17.9 The Press Council fails to curb tabloid trash
Cartoon by Mike Keating

support the Press Council, which was set up as a voluntary body in 1953. Over the next 35 years the Press Council struggled to impose its principles on a press which did not take it seriously. By 1989 agitation and threats of statutory control by MPs of all parties led to the Calcutt Report (1990), which threatened the press with a tribunal possessing legal powers of censorship unless the profession made some attempt to regulate itself. Under threat of government regulation the newspaper prorietors rushed to set up their own Press Complaints Commission (PCC). With a clear code of conduct covering six controversial subjects (accuracy and fairness, privacy, chequebook journalism, race reporting, financial journalism and disclosure of sources), the PCC deals with complaints from the public and publishes a quarterly bulletin of its judgements. However, the PCC has no power to restrain publication or even to insist on prominent public apologies. Robertson and Nicol (1992) are pessimistic about its ability to enforce decent standards of journalism or guarantee the privacy of individuals; they argue that it may be no more than a public relations exercise to avoid government intervention. This view was shared by Sir David Calcutt, who has dismissed the PCC as lacking teeth, independence and

public confidence. He has concluded that, incapable of self-regulation, the press requires some form of statutory complaints tribunal with the power to censor in advance material which may be in breach of a new code of practice (Curran and Seaton 1997: 368). By comparison, the Advertising Standards Authority (which provided the model for the PCC) has more teeth as a self-regulating body to ensure that adverts are 'legal, decent, honest and truthful' because it has the power to hurt advertisers in the pocket by forcing the withdrawal of offensive adverts (Robertson and Nicol 1992: 542–5 and 559–61).

With regard to broadcasting, the power of the spoken word and the moving image has always been considered more deserving of public control than written text. The broadcast media have a captive audience and the normal rules which cover the distribution of magazines and newspapers cannot be applied to radio and television programmes, which are beamed into our homes. The power of broadcasters has always been closely tied to government control through the granting of licences and the insistence on clear codes of conduct, particularly in relation to accuracy, impartiality and public taste. In Britain there are three major forms of control.

First, the Broadcasting Complaints Commission was set up under the Broadcasting Act 1981 and has the narrow function of investigating complaints of unfair and unjust treatment and the invasion of privacy. Unlike the PCC it has the power to enforce judgements.

Second, the Broadcasting Standards Council (BSC), established in 1988, has a much wider role which includes the monitoring of sex and violence on television and providing codes of conduct for the portrayal of sensitive and controversial material. Under the Broadcasting Act 1990 these codes were given statutory status. According to Robertson and Nicol this gives the BSC real power to influence programme content and is a far more serious constraint on the freedom of broadcasters:

> It is another external pressure on broadcasters to bring their professional judgements (about what the public interest requires to be seen) into line with official judgements about what the public does not need to be shown.   (Robertson and Nicol 1992: 606)

In 2003 the Communications Act in the UK relaxed the regulations on cross media ownership but increased the power to regulate standards of content. Ofcom (the body now overseeing broadcasting) has the power to enforce the public service obligations of broadcasters as well the power to fine them as much as £250,000 for 'breaches of taste and decency'.

>   (Bell and Alden 2003: 10)

Third, the licensing and censoring of films and videos (but not video games) has a long history of quasi-statutory regulation. The British Board of Film Classification, set up in 1912, has become a means of prior classification of films (U, PG, 15, 18, 18R); see http://www.bbfc.co.uk/ for definitions and is the chief censor of films shown in cinemas and broadcast on television. Since 1984, the power of classification was extended to video cassettes in the wake of concern over 'video nasties'. The Video Recording Act 1984 requires that all video material, including current affairs, sex education and television drama, receives certification before being sold in cassette format. Films which have already received an 18 or 18R certificate for cinema release do not automatically get approval for transfer to video; the *Evil Dead*, for instance, can be seen on the large screen but cannot be sold legally on cassette. Despite these attempts at prior censorship, it is still possible to bring court action against certified films for obscenity (e.g. *Last Tango in Paris*) or for local authorities to ban any film from cinemas within their jurisdiction (e.g. *The Life of Brian*).

Internal influences on media content

There are a number of factors that occur within media organizations and influence media production, including the social construction of 'media reality' by journalists and broadcasters working within media organizations. The 'reality' journalists produce has to be accounted for in terms of the practices of those who have the power to determine the experiences of others; these practices have to be placed within the context of media personnel working within bureaucratic organizations.

The organizational structure of the media means that media workers are constrained in two main ways. First, by the hierarchical and paternalistic nature of media organizations. As with any bureaucracy, the lines of authority are clearly marked and the interaction between journalist and editor and between editor and owner are of crucial importance. Second, the journalist relies on sources and contacts within other organizations. The story of journalism 'is the story of the interaction of reporters and officials' (Schudson 1991: 148).

Journalists are members of a profession governed by its own internal regulations (the National Union of Journalists' Code of Conduct). These regulations can be used as a defence against the more unscrupulous editors employed by newspapers. In his study of the BBC, Burns (1977) noted that for many journalists a commitment to professional standards can be a source of conflict with management. John Tusa's criticism in 1995 of John Birt's running of the BBC is a good case in point; Tusa as a foreign correspondent represented the old values of public service broadcasting, while Birt was much more market-driven.

The social backgrounds of media personnel are also important, because their social and educational backgrounds may simply reinforce the taken-for-granted assumptions underlying organizational definitions of 'newsworthiness' and 'professionalism'. According to US critics such as Lichter *et al.* (1986), the liberally educated 'media elite' in the USA are biased towards 'liberalism' (a dirty word in US politics during the early 1990s) and the Democratic Party. However, the white, male, middle-class profile of most media professionals has led others to provide a different interpretation:

> Journalists, who are better seen as bureaucrats than buccaneers, begin their work with a stock of plausible, well-defined and largely unconscious assumptions. Part of their job is to translate untidy reality into neat stories with beginnings, middles and denouements. The values

which inform the selection of news items usually serve to reinforce conventional opinions and established authority. (Curran and Seaton 1991: 265)

By definition, the experiences and perspectives of those groups who are not part of 'the club' are likely to be undervalued and under-represented. The formal training of journalists through degree programmes may serve only to reinforce this bias by recruiting into the profession those with formal academic qualifications.

Stop and think

> ➤ Try to find out whether journalists and broadcasters come from similar social and educational backgrounds. What sort of evidence could you use to do this?
>
> ➤ You could also try to find out the extent to which proprietors, editors and journalists represent a cross-section of society.
>
> ➤ Find out from your local or college career service what the entry requirements are for a future in journalism.

Perspectives on the mass media

In order to understand the relationship between media personnel, media organizations and social structure it is necessary to examine some of the major theoretical perspectives on the role of the media. The media have to be examined within the context of social interaction and social rules. These rules are formed within the structures of power in society and within this set-up the electronic media have a crucial role to play:

The special authority of electronic media, asserting and reinforcing endless streams of ideologically charged information is, without question, an impressive social force . . . Media help shape and maintain rules and the ideological predispositions underlying them because their unique and powerful technical capabilities and appealing content are the most effective means of information diffusion ever invented . . . By articulating ideological syntheses that promote certain perspectives and exclude others . . . the mass media help constitute and regulate social reality by structuring some of their audiences' most common and important experiences

. . . Mass media help break down distance between the macro social and the micro social. They bring public themes into private environments where they enter into and are influenced by local conditions, orientations, authorities and practices. (Lull 1995: 60–1)

Recognition of this 'special authority' of the media is not a simple acceptance of its social control function; it is the starting-point in an exploration of a range of perspectives which ask us to think about the relationship between the media and society in a variety of ways. These perspectives do not fit neatly under the conventional headings for organizing our ideas on social theory (as, for instance, in Chapter 2); we may wish to compare media perspectives in terms of their emphasis on materialist or culturalist factors. Whether these theories are expressed in optimistic or pessimistic terms is also important. McQuail (1994) has shown how difficult it is to talk about media theories as if they exist in a simple and agreed relationship with one another. The comparison of the *dominant paradigm* with *alternative paradigms*, which is the way in which we categorize different media perspectives below, is therefore only one way of presenting media theories. It may be helpful in providing 'the general structure of thinking about the mass media and society' (McQuail 1994: 93) but it can provide only a limited map of the area.

The dominant paradigm

Early theories tended to exaggerate the power of the media to influence behaviour and were strongly associated with fears of 'mass society': in particular, fears that developments such as mass education, mass communication and political democracy would cause the collapse of the old order and elite rule, leading to a fragmented society in which individuals suffer isolation and anomie, and the mob rule. The mass media were seen as part of this 'problem': 'Rather than being viewed as vehicles for enlightenment, popular education and the press are regarded as reducing intelligence to the level of the lowest common denominator' (Bennett 1982: 34). However, precisely because the new mass media dealt in the artefacts of mass culture they could also be seen as a popular means by which the masses could be integrated into the social consensus of the new order:

The links between popular mass media and social integration were readily open to conceptualisation in terms both negative and individualistic (more loneliness, crime and immorality), but it was also possible

Case study

The functions of the mass media

From the early work of Lasswell (1948), Wright (1960) and Mendelsohn (1966) a number of writers have identified the essential functions of the mass media. McQuail (1994) provides a summary of these media functions:

Information

- providing information about events and conditions in society and the world;
- indicating relations of power;
- facilitating innovation, adaptation and progress.

Correlation

- explaining, interpreting and commenting on the meaning of events and information;
- providing support for established authority and norms;
- consensus building;
- setting orders of priority and signalling relative status.

Continuity

- expressing the dominant culture and recognizing subcultures and new cultural developments;
- forging and maintaining common values.

Entertainment

- providing amusement, diversion and means of relaxation;
- reducing social tension.

Mobilization

- campaigning for societal objectives in the sphere of politics, war, economic development, work and sometimes religion.

(Adapted from McQuail 1994: 79)

Question

1. *Give an example of how the television and the national press might fulfil each of the functions listed by McQuail.*

---

to envisage a positive contribution from modern communications to cohesion and community. Mass media were a potential force for a new kind of cohesion, able to connect scattered individuals in a shared national, city and local experience. (McQuail 1994: 34)

The dominant paradigm which emerged tended to emphasize a positive view of modern society as liberal, democratic and orderly within which the media play an important role. These ideas found their early expression through the perspectives of functionalism and pluralism.

Functionalism

By responding to human needs, social institutions develop which are said to be functional for society as a whole. The mass media can be looked at in this way, with an emphasis on the ways in which they satisfy a range of social needs more effectively than alternative social institutions (e.g. church, family, school). The media according to this model are clearly involved in socialization, integration and the maintenance of social consensus.

[We are talking of] the ability of the media to bind together disparate and fragmented audiences into a classless community of individuals who feel others to

be their equals, with whom they can share news of events, television characters and fictional narratives.

(Keane 1991: 120)

Pluralism

Usually associated with theories of power and political participation (see pp. 175–8), the concept of pluralism has been adapted to explain the role played by the media in modern democracies. The pluralist model developed in direct opposition to the negativism of the mass society approach.

In the 1960s and 1970s the fears endemic to the mass society model were attacked by US writers such as Bramson (1961), Dahl (1961), Gans (1974) and Shils (1959), who argued that such distrust of the masses was elitist and undemocratic. Rather than fearing the totalitarian potential of mass society, these writers celebrated its power to liberate 'the cognitive, appreciative and moral capacities of individuals' and the various 'taste cultures' which make up a heterogeneous popular culture (Billington *et al.* 1991: 17). According to this view the media play a key role in the democratic process by providing access to information, stimulating open debate and giving all groups the opportunity to share their beliefs and tastes with

Case study

The liberal model of the mass media

O'Donnell (1981) suggests that this model has five key elements:

1 The freedom to set up media ventures ensures that a range of opinions and interests are represented.

2 Editorial freedom and professional standards of journalism underpin an effective media.

3 Public access to press and broadcasting allows individuals to express their opinions and criticisms – through, for example, letters to the editor, right to reply or phone-ins.

4 A commitment to balance, which ensures that all groups in society have access to the media and are fairly represented – through programming which reflects minority tastes and interests (Channel 4 was established in part to achieve this).

5 Market power enables the audiences to determine in the long run which media prosper and who goes out of business.

(Adapted from O'Donnell 1981: 546)

others. In exercising political and cultural choices in a democratic society the freedom of the media is crucial.

Whether this represents a normative theory (how things should be) or an actual model of how the media operate is debatable and relates to another key issue: how best to deliver a genuinely pluralist media. On the one hand is the belief that the media (and especially broadcasting) are so important to a free and rational society that they must be controlled for the public good. Hence regulations are imposed on ownership, offensive content and political balance. Public service broadcasting derives from this 'top-down' approach, with the BBC an obvious example. On the other hand, such 'nannying' of the public by the state is seen as a threat to liberty. According to the liberal market model, the only means of providing a diverse public with genuine freedom of choice is through a deregulated marketplace. This view was clearly expressed by Rupert Murdoch in his lecture on 'Freedom in Broadcasting' in 1989, which has been summarized by Keane (1991):

> Murdoch insists that market competition is the key condition of press and broadcasting freedom, understood as freedom from state interference, as the right of individuals to communicate their opinions without external restrictions. Market led media ensure competition. Competition lets individual consumers decide what they want to try. It keeps prices low and quality high, forces suppliers to take risks and to innovate continually, lest they lose business to rivals offering better, improved products. A privately controlled press and a multi-channel broadcasting system in the hands of a diversity of owners is a bulwark of freedom. (Keane 1991: 53)

This confidence in the ability of the market to provide real choice and a genuinely pluralistic media is supported by writers such as Whale (1980) and Veljanovski (1989), but it is rejected by Keane and others, who argue that the marketplace fails to provide genuine competition or free access to all media operations when it is dominated by a handful of global monopolies. Keane also rejects the idea that consumer choice and satisfaction are secured by a liberal market; some consumers are excluded by the purchase costs of media technology, others by their membership of minority groups who are not attractive to advertisers. The market becomes led by the demands of advertisers and the caprice of private owners and corporate decision makers. Choice exists within the confines of commercial viability and this often amounts to broadcasting more of the same in order to satisfy the 'mass audience' which the advertisers demand. In the long run this will lead to the 'Americanization' of the media and an increase in what Keane (1991: 64) terms 'garbage television' and 'satellite slush'.

Although critical of both the public service and liberal market models, Keane retains a belief in the potential of the modern media to provide:

> A radically new public service model which would facilitate a genuine commonwealth of forms of life, tastes and opinions. Communications media . . . should aim to empower a plurality of citizens who are governed neither by undemocratic states nor by undemocratic market forces. The media should be for the public use and enjoyment of all citizens and not for the private gain or profit of political rulers or businesses.

(Keane 1991: xi–xii)

Case study

Golden age: myth or reality?

In the 2005 Huw Wheldon lecture, sponsored by the Royal Television Society, Dawn Airey (managing director of Sky Networks) challenged the idea that TV standards had declined as a result of increasing choice and argued instead that new technologies have liberated the audience from the patronage of the BBC (see earlier discussion of Public Service Broadcasting and the emergence of digital and satellite TV on pp. 664–72).

> The opportunities for connecting with the audience in ways hitherto unimagined will produce programmes of genius that will exploit the medium's capabilities in ways we haven't even dreamed of. At some point we might be able to choose the ending of a popular drama instantaneously with the click of the red button. Or follow the path of an individual character rather than a linear storyline – much as computer games

already do. The one thing that is certain is that in this new era the best television will be saved from oblivion.

Today's personal video recorder has a memory of 160 gigabytes. That means it's capable of recording maybe 80 hours of programming. But the home entertainment systems of the future will be capable of storing thousands of hours of content, including perhaps every movie ever made, all available on demand at the press of a button in high definition quality.

No longer bound by the tyranny of the schedule, with programmes allowed their brief shining moment before being lost in the archives, a breadth of imagination and a depth of information will be available as never before. Television will at last be able to emulate one of the great achievements of civilization (and one that is all too often overlooked): the library. Everything will be available for all to see . . . If there is a

Golden Age of TV, then I believe that we're only just on the cusp . . . Rather than it being a 'social menace of the first magnitude' as Lord Reith suggested, television has become a powerful means of breaking down mass conformity in order to liberate individual choice . . . Viewers are no longer simply passive observers. Television has broken free from paternalistic rationing by an elite which once decreed what it ought and ought not to do. And, as it does so, the only path for those who work in the industry is to trust the viewers and the infinite choices that they are now capable of making.

There is no alternative because technology has finally set them free.
(For a full transcript of this lecture go to: http://www.rts.org.uk)

Questions

1. In what sense do the new technologies set TV viewers free?

2. What criticisms could be made of this argument?

Alternative paradigms

It is difficult to talk about an alternative paradigm as if it comprises a consistent set of ideas and perspectives that constitute a particular school of thought. The challenge to the dominant paradigm includes the work of Marxists, feminists and some strands of post modernism and cultural theory. There are, then, enough critics who reject the consensus underlying functionalism and the democratic assumptions behind pluralism to talk of an alternative, oppositional paradigm, which McQuail has summarized:

Most broadly, an 'alternative paradigm' rests on a different view of society, one which does not accept the prevailing liberal-capitalist order as just or inevitable or the best one can hope for in the fallen state of human kind. Nor does it accept the rational-calculative, utilitarian model of social life as at all adequate or desirable. There is an alternative, idealist and sometimes utopianist ideology, but nowhere a worked out model of an ideal social system. Nevertheless, there is sufficient common basis for rejecting the hidden ideology of pluralism and conservative functionalism.   (McQuail 1994: 46)

This approach grew out of the concern expressed by radical academics and critical theorists over the emergence of mass society and the rise of popular culture which echo those put forward by conservative thinkers. The first attempts to make sense of the media in modern society from a critical perspective were made by the Frankfurt School (and particularly Horkheimer, Adorno and Marcuse: see pp. 82–5), who argued that the media were a conservative force acting to replace working-class aspirations with a false and one-dimensional consciousness dominated by commercialism, individualism and false needs.

This pessimistic view was endorsed in the USA by C. Wright Mills (1956), who argued that the media were a powerful instrument for manipulation and control which operated in the interest of the 'power elite'. In Europe similar concerns were expressed through the writings of Althusser (1971), Barthes (1972) and the rediscovered works of Gramsci (1971). As a result, Marxists began to develop an interest in the cultural and ideological aspects of social life with an emphasis on the significance of the media and the emergence of popular culture. Although Marxist writers disagree with each other over the importance of ideology and the relationship of the media to the structures of power and ownership, the following seven elements of an alternative paradigm of the media can be highlighted:

> the political economy of the media;
> the media as ideological state apparatus;
> the media and hegemony;

> Glasgow University Media Group;
> the threat of technology;
> globalization;
> feminism.

The political economy of the media

This approach derives from the classical 'base–superstructure' model in Marxist thought, which focuses on the relationship between the economic base or infrastructure and the ideological superstructure. It emphasizes the power of the economy (through, for instance, owners, advertisers and media markets) to determine media content. This power has been enhanced by the moves toward deregulation and the concentration of ownership on a global scale. Such a view is concerned with the power of owners and advertisers to influence public agendas and media content and is sometimes known as the 'manipulative model' (Trowler 1988: 33–7). However, the critical political-economy approach also examines the economic forces which may constrain the extent to which influential individuals can meddle in the media.

Government and business elites do have privileged access to the news; large advertisers do operate as a latter-day licensing authority . . . and media proprietors can determine the editorial line and cultural stance of the papers and broadcast stations they own. [However, they] operate within structures which constrain as well as facilitate.   (Golding and Murdock 1991: 9)

Case study

The political economy model

A number of writers can be placed within the political economy model, including Bagdikian (1988), Collins, Garnham and Locksley (1988) and Miliband (1969). For Golding and Murdock (1991) this approach concentrates on three 'core tasks':

1 *The production of meaning and the exercise of power* This emphasizes the increasing control exerted over cultural production by large corporations and the failure of governments to regulate such developments.

2 *Political economy and textual analysis* The selection and promotion of particular cultural forms and discourses are determined by economic rather than cultural factors. The 'Americanization' of British TV, for example, is partly due to the need to fill increasing broadcasting space with cheap and cheerful imports (Tunstall 1977).

3 *Consumption: sovereignty or struggle?* This represents an attack on the assumptions behind the liberal market and pluralist approaches which celebrate the free choice of the audience and its ability to impose its own interpretation on cultural texts. As a result, the material and cultural barriers to free and equal access are explored.

The link between economic power and editorial control which this model takes for granted was well summarized by the famous American critic Noam Chomsky in the Massey Lectures delivered in 1988:

> Media concentration is high, and increasing. Furthermore, those who occupy managerial positions in the media . . . belong to the same privileged elites, and might be expected to share the perceptions, aspirations, and attitudes of their associates, reflecting their own class interests as well. Journalists entering the system are unlikely to make their way unless they conform to these ideological pressures generally by internalizing the values . . . those who fail to conform will be weeded out. (see Chomsky 1989)

The media as ideological state apparatus

In the writings of structuralists like Althusser (1969; 1971) and Poulantzas (1973) the state is seen as operating in an almost mechanical manner to reproduce the social relations of a class society. The involvement of individuals in this operation is irrelevant as it is the overall function of the apparatus of the state which is important and not the motivations, interests or activities of its agents. In this process social control is established through physical coercion (repressive state apparatus) or the power to persuade (ideological state apparatus). Along with the school and the church, the media are clearly regarded as having a key role in establishing ideological domination and false consciousness among those classes whose interests are not served by capitalism. In his attack on humanist Marxism and the Frankfurt School, Althusser established a model which saw all aspects of 'civil society' (family, church, media, for example) as extensions of state power, so that human consciousness and subjectivity are constituted by external forces created by the structures of society. Althusser (1969; 1971) admits that ideas have some 'relative autonomy' but he insists that in the last instance ideology is determined by the economic structure of society and the agencies of the state. It is against this rigid and mechanistic model that Gramsci's (1971) more flexible concept of hegemony has been adopted by European Marxists.

The media and hegemony

Although the concept of hegemony relates to the general discussion within Marxism about the ways in which dominant ideologies encourage a 'false consciousness' among the lower classes in society, it has also been applied to the role of the media in the transmission of popular culture, consumerism and national identity.

In his original use of the term hegemony, Gramsci (1971) refers to the 'dual perspective' whereby as well as using 'levels of force' those in power will also seek to establish 'moral and philosophical leadership' over the mass of the population by winning their active consent.

> The convictions of people are . . . not something manipulated by capitalists or put into the minds of the masses by them, but rather they flow from the exigencies of everyday life under capitalism. The workers, and others, hold the values and political ideas that they do as a consequence both of trying to survive and of attempting to enjoy themselves, within capitalism. These activities require money . . . mediated by ideological means, for people have to come to desire the goods for sale. Such desires . . . are not natural, not inborn . . . These desires to consume various products have to be constructed by ideological apparatus, especially in the mass media. (Bocock 1986: 32–3)

As Lull (1995) has pointed out, such a media-transmitted ideology establishes itself through two processes of mediation – technological and social. *Technological mediation* refers to the power of the media to influence human consciousness on behalf of consumer society. Advertising is a classic example of this:

> Selection of corporate spokespersons, visual logos, audio jingles, catchy slogans, the style and pace of commercials, special technical effects, editing conventions, product packaging, and the welding of print and electronic media campaigns . . . all combine to generate the desired result, selling capitalism's big and bright products and the political-economic-cultural infrastructure that goes along with them. (Lull 1995: 16)

According to this view, media personnel are not coerced or manipulated into deliberately misrepresenting social reality; they have become socialized into accepting the values and techniques of their profession and to a large degree believe in what they are doing and that they are giving the customers what they want.

Social mediation emphasizes the humanism of Gramsci's work by stressing the active involvement of people in the hegemonic process. If we are duped by the system we are partly responsible by virtue of our participation in the language and image systems which have been created by the media. In our everyday interaction with one another we give credibility to and reinforce 'media-transmitted ideology' by referring to its content and using its codes and incorporating its messages into our social discourse.

The admission that ordinary people have a part to play in creating and reaffirming their culture raises the possibility that the audience may also reinterpret, resist or reject the preferred messages of those responsible for media production and thus undermine the ideological control of those in power. This 'relative autonomy' in cultural production underpins the work of the Centre for Contemporary Cultural Studies (based at the University of Birmingham: see, for example, Hall and Jefferson 1976). Although they accept the Marxist idea that the media reproduce the relations of class society through the reinforcement of a consensus-based 'common sense', they reject the economic determinism of traditional Marxist models. The meanings of cultural texts are not

Case study

The people's music?

Despite the fact that popular music is produced and marketed by corporations for commercial reasons, it is also possible to regard some elements of popular music as a genuine attempt to wrest creative control and production away from the industry professionals and to produce ideas and music which challenge cultural and political conventions. As MacDonald (2003) argues we may run the risk of romanticizing the rebellious nature of pop music but some of it certainly set out to change public perceptions and attitudes – especially of the young:

> The first such outburst was the original rock'n'roll outbreak of the mid-fifties. This rebellious spirit reignited in the mid-sixties in the work of Bob Dylan and The Rolling Stones, intensified in the late sixties under the influence of LSD and New Left politics, and turned popular music into a counter-cultural phenomenon expressing itself in gigantic outdoor festivals in the years thereafter. A similar spirit drove the radical politico-theology of reggae Rastafarianism and the anarchistic Punk spasm of the seventies. Hiphop has carried a

rebellious torch since the early eighties, while the 'orbital' dance scene of the late eighties in the UK sparked a comparable enthusiasm . . . such eras come and go, being attached to wider social signifiers and deeper cultural upheavals than can be accounted for in purely creative terms. The creativity of rock music rides on a social background and takes much of its cut and colour from what's going on in the wider world. The individual cult figures involved are products of their time . . . popular music is a product of society first, a rebel festivity second (and always in passing).
(MacDonald 2003: vii–viii)

As an illustration of this point it is worth repeating what MacDonald has to say about the Beatles in the latter half of the 1960s. Today their work is part of the nostalgia industry, a trip to Liverpool is not complete without a visit to the Beatles Museum and Paul McCartney has been knighted for his services to the music industry but forty years ago . . .

Quality of consciousness was the key motif of the counter-culture's revolt against consumer materialism in the sixties, running, for instance, through the Beatles' work from *Revolver*

onwards and reaching a zenith with 'A Day in The Life'. The nub of the countercultural critique was that 'plastic people' of 'straight' society were spiritually dead. New Leftists spoke of 'consciousness-raising' while hippies offered a programme of 'enlightenment' through oriental mysticism supplemented by mind-expanding drugs. In today's pleasure-seeking world, introspection holds no appeal and the sixties focus on innerness is ignored or derided as a cover for nineties-style chemical hedonism. The truth was otherwise in 1965–69.
(MacDonald 2003: 220–21)

See also George McKay's (1996) *Senseless Acts of Beauty: Cultures of Resistance Since the 1960s* for an historical account of the counter-culture and its political manifestation in various movements such as free festivals, anti-road campaigns, 'new age' travellers, etc. For a critique see http://www.geocities.com/ aufheben2/auf_5_mckay.html

Questions

1. Do you think pop music has lost its rebellious nature?

2. Which artists in the contemporary pop music scene can be considered rebels?

pre-given but open to interpretation and negotiation and therefore never ideologically fixed.

This cultural flexibility allows writers such as Hall and Jefferson (1976) and Hebdige (1979) to argue that subcultural groups can express their resistance to dominant ideological forms through their cultural practices (for instance, music, fashion, language):

> Style in sub-culture . . . challenges the principle of unity and cohesion [and] contradicts the myth of consensus . . . It is this alienation . . . which gives the teds, the mods, the punks a truly subterranean style.
>
> (Hebdige 1979: 118–19)

In Branston and Stafford (1996: 151–4), Bob Marley's career is used as a case study to demonstrate how ideologies of domination can be opposed by reggae as 'rebel music'. However, they also show how in order to become successful Marley had to sign up to Island Records and replace the original 'Wailers' to develop the mainstream sound and star image required by the music business:

> Marley and the new Wailers presented a 'sweeter' and more rock-oriented sound to go with a seemingly less aggressive stance. Where 'roots reggae' set out to exclude whites and to attract an aware audience interested in discovering an African culture and African rhythms, Island was effectively marketing Marley as 'Bob Dylan or Marvin Gaye or both'.
>
> (Branston and Stafford 1996: 153)

It is also possible within the more liberal Marxist model to recognize the relative freedom of journalists and broadcasters to challenge the ideological consensus. In *Channels of Resistance* (Dowmunt 1994), a variety of media analysts reveal the ways that television producers around the world have managed to preserve their local identities against the threat of cultural imperialism and global homogenization. Although the contributors are not necessarily Marxist, their conclusions clearly reflect the dialectical notions of domination and resistance found in the concept of hegemony:

> The fact [of television dominance] does not stop us from imagining, developing and analysing alternatives . . . groups all over the world, in institutional and technological situations not of their own making, have begun to resist this domination in diverse and creative ways . . . Although the economic and political pressures on the global television system are strong, they are not totally determining. We can dare to imagine, and start to create, something different. (Dowmunt 1994: 15)

Glasgow University Media Group

Although it does not represent a particular element of Marxist theory of the media, the Glasgow University Media Group has provided much empirical evidence to support the view that the media tend to favour conservative representations of reality. In analyzing news coverage of industrial disputes, politics and warfare, it has focused on the ways in which political bias affects the structuring of the news, its content and the language used to report it:

> The essential thrust of our critique is not against media workers as such . . . Rather, it relates to the picture of society that the media construct with such remarkable consistency. We attribute this artificial and one-dimensional picture to the nature of organisations whose basic assumption is that our industrial, economic and social system operates to the benefit of everyone involved . . . unfortunately [this] involves the mass of the 'public' being misrepresented.
>
> (Glasgow University Media Group 1982: 144–5)

The Glasgow University Media Group have also become increasingly well known for developing new research methods relating production, content and reception. In a recent example of their work, Greg Philo examined the 'quantitative imbalance' in the flow of news between the Third World and the First and the negative representations of Africa in particular. By interviewing audience groups it was confirmed that the coverage had a predictable character and that it was perceived as such:

> Our own study showed that when the developing world is featured on British news, a high proportion of the coverage is related to war, conflict, terrorism and disasters. This is especially so for the main television channels, with over a third of coverage on BBC and Independent Television News (ITN) devoted to such issues . . . Some people were completely 'turned off' from the developing world (about 25 per cent of the sample), but the reason was in part the constant negative diet of images they were given. As one interviewee put it: 'Well every time you turn on the TV or pick up a paper, there's another [war] starting or there is more poverty or destruction. It's all too much.'
>
> (Taken from *An unseen world: how the media portrays the poor*. See http://www.unesco.org/ courier/2001_11/uk/medias.htm)

In his critique of the GMG, Shaun Best attacks the group for its positivist methodology (Content Analysis) and its theoretical approach (Marxist):

The Glasgow media group do not pose interesting questions because they have their answers in advance. Greg Philo has no concept of ideology. Ideology is merely news and views that he disagrees with. The whole argument of the Group is wrapped up in a romantic package about what life was like before the new right. One of the reasons why many people have embraced postmodern ideas is because of the total and complete intellectual collapse of Marxism as the basis of an explanatory framework for anything.

(From http://shaunbest.tripod.com/id8.html)

The threat of technology

While Marxist writers tend to blame those who control the mass media for cultural decline and political manipulation, other writers have argued that it is the technology itself which threatens cultural and intellectual life. In the 1960s Marshall McLuhan first warned that the new media technologies were transforming our relationships by promoting lazy and irrational attitudes. Whereas a culture based on reading books demands a level of rational concentration, the television has ushered in a 'couch potato' culture for the masses which makes very little demand on the individual other than turning on the TV set (McLuhan 1964; McLuhan and Fiore 1967).

In the 1980s, Postman (1987) returned to the debate with a blistering attack on television and the threat it poses to Western culture. He argues not that we are being deliberately misled or brainwashed by those in power but that we are conniving in our own cultural and political downfall through our demand for continuous entertainment:

> Our politics, religion, news, athletics, education and commerce have been transformed into congenial adjuncts of show business, largely without protest or even much popular notice . . . The result is that we are a people on the verge of amusing ourselves to death.
>
> (Postman 1987: 4)

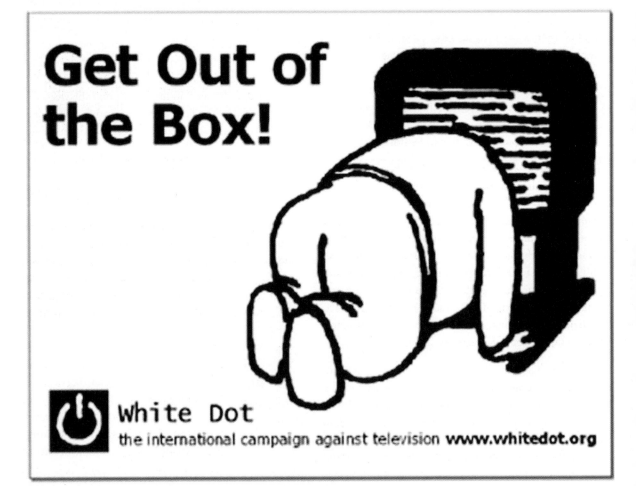

Figure 17.10 Turn off TV!
http://www.whitedot.org

Television clearly plays a central role in providing this endless stream of amusement but for Postman the real threat is not in the arena of entertainment (which is after all what television was invented for) but in the belief that television can operate as a serious medium for the transmission of culture and political debate:

> When a population becomes distracted by trivia, when cultural life is redefined as a perpetual round of entertainment . . . when, in short, a people become an audience and their public business a vaudeville act, then a nation finds itself at risk; culture-death is a clear possibility. (Postman 1987: 161)

Postman's argument is compelling but there are many who reject his 'doom and gloom' scenario, particularly those who feel that television can be a useful educational aid (including Masterman 1985; Cragg 1992; Fiske 1987; Fleming 1993). Lisa Jardine (1998), for example, has argued that instead of 'dumbing down' our culture, television dramatization of soap operas as well as classic texts can be used to inspire and enhance learning.

In his book, *Everything Bad is Good for You*, Stephen Johnson (2005) pokes fun at those who automatically assume that popular culture is inferior to literary culture and that TV must be bad for you. Instead he argues that the plots of TV dramas can be just as demanding as those found in literature and that video games are as intellectually stimulating as playing chess or reading books. In this satirical extract from his web site he turns the tables on those who condemn TV by proposing a world in which interactive technology came first and books have suddenly been discovered:

> Imagine an alternate world identical to ours save one techno-historical change: videogames were invented and popularized before books. In this parallel universe, kids have been playing games for centuries – and then these page-bound texts come along and suddenly they're all the rage. What would the teachers, and the parents, and the cultural authorities have to say about this frenzy of reading? I suspect it would sound something like this:
>
> Reading books chronically under-stimulates the senses. Unlike the longstanding tradition of game-playing – which engages the child in a vivid, three-dimensional world filled with moving images and musical soundscapes, navigated and controlled with complex muscular movements – books are simply a barren string of words on the page. Only a small portion of the brain devoted to processing written language is activated during reading, while games engage the full range of the sensory and motor cortices.
>
> Books are also tragically isolating. While games have for many years engaged the young in complex social relationships with their peers, building and exploring worlds together, books force the child to sequester him or herself in a quiet space, shut off from interaction with other children. These new 'libraries' that have arisen in recent years to facilitate reading activities are a frightening sight: dozens of young children, normally so vivacious and socially interactive, sitting alone in cubicles, reading silently, oblivious to their peers.
>
> Many children enjoy reading books, of course, and no doubt some of the flights of fancy conveyed by reading have their escapist merits. But for a sizable percentage of the population, books are downright discriminatory. The reading craze of recent years cruelly taunts the 10 million Americans who suffer from dyslexia – a condition that didn't even exist as a condition until printed text came along to stigmatize its sufferers.
>
> But perhaps the most dangerous property of these books is the fact that they follow a fixed linear path. You can't control their narratives in any fashion – you simply sit back and have the story dictated to you. For those of us raised on interactive narratives, this property may seem astonishing. Why would anyone want to embark on an adventure utterly choreographed by another person? But today's generation embarks on such adventures millions of times a day. This risks instilling a general passivity in our children, making them feel as though they're powerless to change their circumstances.
>
> Reading is not an active, participatory process; it's a submissive one. The book readers of the younger generation are learning to 'follow the plot' instead of learning to lead. (Johnson 2005)

Feminism

If the Marxist tradition tends to focus on the ways in which the media reproduce relationships and ways of thinking that are of benefit to capitalism, feminists concentrate on the ideological work carried out by the media on behalf of men. However, while the importance of gender has long been recognized in the field of cultural studies the feminist perspective has not always been treated as significant by media theorists. Van Zoonen (1991)

World in focus

The globalization of culture

In 1977, the author of this chapter arrived in Marrakech. The marketplace bustled with the activities of jugglers, musicians and storytellers but, in the shade of a streetside cafe, Berber tribesmen in traditional dress sipped mint tea and sucked on hookahs as they sat transfixed by the huge monochrome television set that dominated the small bar. As I drank my ice cold Coke, I realized that I recognized the characters on screen: it was an episode of the TV western series *High Chaparral* which had been dubbed in French (the colonial language) and sub-titled in Arabic (for the hard of hearing). The only thing missing was a Big Mac with fries!

Writers such as Baran and Sweezy (1966) had written about the economic and political domination of global markets and national governments by American multinational companies and this was also the year that Tunstall (1977) published his warnings about the Americanization of the world's media but the terms 'globalization' and 'cultural imperialism' were yet to be applied to the impact of Western media on local cultures and identities. Twenty-five years later the terrain has changed (there is now a McDonald's in Marrakech) but the issue remains the same; to what extent can local cultural traditions survive and resist the threat of cultural imperialism which accompanies the rise of the transnational corporation and the monopoly exercised over new media technologies by one or two global powers?

While the old multinationals that were located within nation-states, such as America or Japan, were subject to government regulation and owed some allegiance to their home base, the emerging transnational corporation has no parents and no obligations other than to itself (*see Chapter 00*). Using the latest information technologies it scours the globe in search of expanding markets and cheap labour.

The economic might of transnational production companies is paralleled in the media environment by the emergence of global giants in the shape of Sony, Disney, Time-Warner and Microsoft, and these corporations both convey the commercial ethos of the transnationals and impose their own cultural footprint (through news, information and entertainment) on countries which quite literally cannot afford to produce their own.

There are many who fear that this global influence is eroding local differences and cultural diversity and will lead to a form of cultural imperialism which threatens to engulf us all in a torrent of commercialism dedicated to spreading the gospel of Coca-Cola, McDonald's and Nike Sports Wear. Pessimistic writers such as Schiller

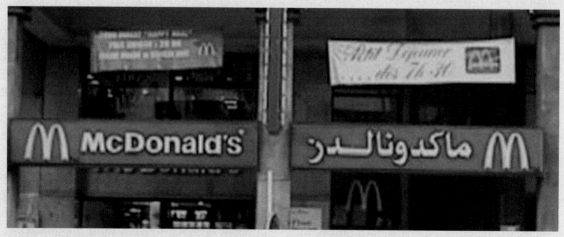

Figure 17.11 McDonaldization?
http://www.pitt.edu/~atsea/morocco.html

World in focus (continued)

(1989; 1993) argue that traditional cultures and national identities may be swept away by the rising tide of (largely) American values, aspirations and popular culture. The world has become a global village, and it is called America.

This grim view of a world in the grip of a homogeneous culture is not shared by many cultural commentators. James Lull (1993), for example, rejects the simplistic notion of 'cultural imperialism' as an irresistible force for uniformity as it entails the notion of passive audiences and acquiescent cultures. Following the ideas of Smith (1990) and Appadurai (1990) he argues that the idea of a 'global culture' is 'a practical impossibility' because the notion of culture refers to historical differences between peoples in terms of collective

beliefs, language and behaviour. As peoples around the world do not share a common past, language or experience it is a contradiction in terms to refer to a 'global culture'. It is further argued that cultures are dynamic processes, not fixed entities to be confirmed or replaced. In other words the post-industrial media conglomerates of 'the West' may dominate the transmission of modern culture but they do not control its reception or the way that it is used. In a process known as 'deterritorialization' cultures become separated from their geographical and social roots and transplanted into other cultural environments. The result is not global hegemony by a dominant Western culture but a transformation of all cultures (including the Western) by the

interplay between the local and the global. Big Macs in Marrakech is one side of this coin, Ladysmith Black Mombazo advertising baked beans on British television is the reverse. For a broader discussion of the interrelationship between the global and the local see Sreberny-Mohammadi (1991), Stevenson (1995) and Back (1997). Not surprisingly, for a computer mogul who has become the world's richest man, Bill Gates's book *The Road Ahead* (1995) is an unashamed tribute to the wonders of globalism.

Questions

1. *What examples of globalization have you come across at home or abroad?*

2. *Do you regard them as a threat to national or regional cutlures?*

---

argues that before the rise of the women's movement, the 'gendered' nature of culture was accepted as natural and consequently the use of gender as a mechanism for analysis was largely ignored by traditional and critical theorists alike. But consequent research such as Meehan's (1983) study of prime-time television revealed that in North American serials women characters were restricted to a limited number of stereotypical roles. However, Radway's (1984) work on romantic novels and Winship's (1986) study of women's magazines suggest a more supportive role in what is still a male-dominated culture. Similarly the work of Geraghty (1991), Hobson (1982) and Kilborn (1992) reveals that strong and positive role models for women exist in soap operas:

> Many of the British soaps . . . are marked by the presence of women – most of them no longer in the prime of youth – who have remained sturdily independent, in spite of sometimes quite strong social or family pressures to be otherwise. As such their judgement is respected and they often operate as confidantes or

advisors to the young, vulnerable or inexperienced. Bet Lynch and Rita Fairclough in Coronation Street are good examples of this particular type of strong woman. (Kilborn 1992: 47)

Although there is much agreement that the media play a crucial role in the gendering of culture there is little evidence of theoretical convergence among feminist writers (see pp. 70–9 on the different strands of feminist theorizing). We shall look briefly at how different feminist approaches have been applied to the media.

Liberal feminism

Women have been the victims of prejudice and stereotyping which are at the root of a gendered outlook for women as well as men. The limited role models and negative images that are offered by the media play an active part in reproducing dominant and traditional values and reinforcing the power of men and the absence of opportunities for women. The liberal solution is for women to compete with men for the powerful positions

Case study

A survey of women's magazines

In 1997 the Social Affairs Unit conducted a survey of women's magazines. Although one or two magazines, for example, Bella and Prima, were found to offer 'useful advice and pleasant entertainment' for the young mothers who form their readership, most magazines targeting the young 'Magazine Woman' of the 1990s were castigated. Magazines such as Marie Claire, Cosmopolitan and, in particular, Company were condemned for

ignoring traditional values, child-rearing and family life in an amoral diet of sex, fashion and sensationalism which trivialized the role of women and the issues which they face. They conclude: 'It is a depressing survey . . . the bulk of magazines . . . contain a dominant image of women as selfish, superficial and obsessed with sex'.

(The *Guardian* 24.11.97)

Questions

1. Applying the technique of content analysis (see p. 121) to one of the magazines

mentioned, examine the report's conclusion that 'Magazine Woman has escaped from the kitchen only to get as far as the bedroom'.

2. What criticisms would you make of the methodology used in the survey? (You will need a copy of the report by the Social Affairs Unit (1997) or the Media Guardian *review* (24.11.97).

3. How might the differing feminist approaches respond to the 'Magazine Woman' referred to in the study?

within the media and to educate journalists and broadcasters in the values of non-sexist media production. Janet Street-Porter's criticism (at the Edinburgh Television Festival, August 1995) of the media organization as a male, mediocre, middle-aged and middle-class 'broadcasting boys' club', reveals the extent to which individual women can feel powerless to change the system.

Radical feminism

According to this view the media are simply one more institution run by men for the convenience of men in a patriarchal society. As such the media demean women and overlook their concerns while actively encouraging female abuse through pornography and violence. The promotion of individual women within male structures which promote masculine culture is regarded as nothing other than a short-term gain for the individual career women concerned – sometimes dismissed as 'sleeping with the enemy'. Radical strategies on the other hand, entail women writers, producers and broadcasters co-operating to create their own alternative media. There have been some successful attempts to create independent publishers – The Women's Press, Virago and Pandora, for example – but Van Zoonen (1991) is pessimistic that this can be achieved without female broadcasters and publishers adopting masculine management styles in order to compete with men.

Socialist feminism

Adopting elements of the Marxist approach, socialist feminism uses class analysis to examine the economic position of women under patriarchal capitalism. The commercial pressures on the media are clearly recognized in this perspective as important constraints on the media reforms proposed by liberal feminists or the separate developments favoured by radical feminists. Power in the media is related to the economic structures of society and although in support of changes for women, the socialist feminists are also aware that the benefits of reform are most likely to improve the career opportunities of middle-class women.

Effects of the mass media

The debate over the power of the media to influence attitudes and behaviour goes back to the nineteenth century. It is a controversial area where strength of opinion often outweighs hard evidence; it has therefore become increasingly difficult to talk with any certainty about the power of the media to influence social behaviour. We cannot in this chapter do justice to the range of techniques used to research the effects of the media or to summarize the mountain of research findings amassed since the 1930s, but we can identify and discuss the major

Case study

The branding of the media

Advertisers may not be able to directly influence the choices consumers make but they can have some say over media content as well as ensuring that the line between plot and product become blurred. In her book, *No Logo*, Naomi Klein draws on recent history to make the point:

It is common knowledge that many advertisers rail at controversial content, pull their ads when they are criticized even slightly and perpetually angle for so-called value-addeds – plugs for their wares in shopping guides and fashion spreads. For example, S.C. Johnson & Co. stipulate that their ads in women's magazines 'should not be opposite extremely controversial features or material antithetical to the nature/copy of the advertised product' while De Beers diamonds demand that their ads be far from any 'any hard news or anti/love-romance themed editorial' . . . But the advertisers don't always get their way: controversial stories make it to print and air, even ones critical of major advertisers . . . [however] these same media show how deeply distorting the effects of branding can be on our public discourse – particularly since journalism, like every other part of our culture, is under constantly increasing pressure to merge with the brands . . .

The merger between media and catalog reached a new high with the launch of the teen TV drama *Dawson's Creek* in January of 1998. Not only did the characters all wear J. Crew clothes, not only did the windswept, nautical set make them look as if they had stepped off the pages of a J. Crew catalog, and not only did the characters spout dialogue like 'He looks like he stepped out of a J. Crew catalog,' but the cast was also featured on the cover of the January J. Crew catalog. Inside the new 'freestyle magalog', the young actors are pictured in rowboats and on docks – looking as if they just stepped off the set of a *Dawson's Creek* episode.

(Klein 2000: 39–42)

Question

1. What examples of 'branding' can you find in TV series and films?

---

areas of concern: the media's economic, political, and moral and social influences.

Areas of concern

Economic influence of the media

Apart from their potential for making money, the media are thought to possess the power to influence consumer choice. Billions of pounds are spent on advertising every year by companies seeking to improve their market share, and customers pay over the odds for the privilege. It is estimated that the average American child will have seen 350,000 commercials by the age of 18 (Brierly 1998: 46). *The Guardian* (18.9.1992) estimated that for every £1.50 spent in Britain on a top brand of coffee, 12 pence goes in profits and wages to the growers but 57 pence is accounted for by the advertising budget. In 1987, Gold Blend instant coffee launched its successful 'mini-soap' campaign, which saw sales rise by 15 per cent over the first year and by 40 per cent after five years (Cashmore 1994: 76). Despite its success the series was eventually dropped by Nestlé after 11 years and an increase in overall sales of 70 per cent in order to appeal to a more international market. By the same token, companies are terrified of bad publicity and will resort to the law to stifle public complaint. The organizers of the 'What's Wrong with McDonald's?' campaign (see http://www.mcspotlight.org) ended up in court for spreading anti-Mac propaganda. While it is clearly in the interests of advertising agencies to claim that publicity has a direct influence on consumer choice, there is very little evidence to support this. Brierly (1998) notes research showing that we can barely recall any of the adverts with which we are bombarded every day, while advertising pundit Winston Fletcher argues that for the amounts they spend advertising their brands, companies get very little in return. As someone who has worked in advertising for most of his life, he comes to the remarkable conclusion that 'at least 96 per cent of all advertising is wasted, but nobody knows which 96 per cent' (Fletcher 1992: 38).

Political influence of the media

Since the advent of public education and mass circulation newspapers, the role of the media in the coverage of politics has been regarded as important; however, it is with the introduction of broadcasting that the power of the media to influence opinion has been a key issue in political debate. Some of the earliest content analysis of newspapers was concerned with political bias and propaganda (Krippendorf 1980: 13–20). Original research into media effects concentrated upon the effectiveness of wartime propaganda (Hovland 1949) and the links between election campaigns and voting behaviour (Berelson *et al.* 1954; Katz and Lazarsfeld 1955; Lazarsfeld *et al.* 1944). Despite little evidence that the media can do much more than reinforce existing political attitudes, the media have been heavily involved in election campaigns since the 1950s; with strict controls imposed in some societies on the extent to which political parties may have access to broadcasting at election time.

The first politician to take advice on his election campaign from an advertising agency was Dwight D. Eisenhower, who paid for TV commercials to get his message across in the defeat of Adlai Stevenson in 1952. In 1960, the first real 'election by television' took place when John F. Kennedy and Richard Nixon debated the issues on both television and radio. It is widely held that despite a good performance Nixon came across poorly on television, largely due to his appearance, and that this cost him the election. This success was repeated in the 1964 election, when Lyndon Johnson was advised to use a negative advertising campaign against Barry Goldwater which highlighted the Republican's desire to use nuclear weapons in Indo-China. In what has become a classic example of the genre, the 'Daisy Girl' commercial shows a young girl plucking the petals from a flower as we hear the countdown to the launch of a nuclear warhead.

By the 1980s, negative campaigns and zappy commercials had replaced the more traditional approaches to electioneering. Political advertising and, to some extent, political discussion became reduced to the wisdom of what works on television. As Kern (1989) has argued, a political broadcast is deemed effective only if it is short, entertaining and capable of provoking a reaction.

These lessons have been learned in Britain, where, despite the restrictions on access to the broadcast media, the major parties engage 'spin doctors' to grab the soundbite and advertising agencies to manage the image (Jones 1995). Concern has also been expressed about the potential of television satire to influence political perceptions, with *Spitting Image* grabbing most of the attention; on the eve of the 1987 election the spoof *Election Special*, which included scenes of Thatcherites dressed as Nazis singing 'Tomorrow Belongs To Us', was delayed until after the polling stations had closed. After the election David Steel complained that the repeated trivialization of his SDP by *Spitting Image* had contributed towards undermining its credibility with the electorate. In general, however, the evidence suggests that for all the efforts by politicians to exploit or blame the potential of television, it is still the press which is more likely to influence voters. In his study of the 1987 general election in Britain, William Miller (1991) concludes that once party identification (partisanship) had been taken into account, the press had some influence in the swing back to the Conservatives, especially among tabloid readers:

> The influence of the tabloid press was particularly strong on those voters who denied being party 'supporters', even when they had a party preference. They made up half of the electorate. The Conservative lead increased by 50 per cent amongst politically uncommitted *Sun/Star* readers but not at all amongst politically uncommitted *Mirror* readers. Since *Sun/Star* readers as a whole were relatively uncommitted they were relatively easy to influence anyway but, in addition, the tabloids were particularly good at influencing their readers' voting preferences.
> (Miller 1991: 199)

Very few political analysts hold the view that the media can determine what we think or radically alter our political beliefs but argue instead that the media play a part in *reinforcing* existing opinions, *setting the agenda* for political discussion and *framing* the way in which the public perceives political events in general. The tabloid press cannot make die-hard Labour supporters vote against their own party, but by repeatedly placing the 1992 election in the context of Labour's tax plans they may have influenced the less committed voter to vote against a return to power for Neil Kinnock's party. The Labour Party complained that their defeat was a consequence of negative tabloid coverage, while the *Sun* announced the next day that 'It was the Sun wot won it'. However, by the election of 1997, many traditional supporters (broadsheet and tabloid) of the Conservative Party had turned against John Major's government and for the first time since the war the Labour Party enjoyed a slight advantage in terms of press support, which included a switch by Rupert Murdoch to Tony Blair's side. Since coming to power the Labour Party have continued to get

Table 17.2 Election 2005: What the papers said

Newspaper election endorsements

Newspaper	1997	2001	2005
The Sun	Labour	Labour	Labour
Daily Express	Conservative	Labour	Conservative
Daily Mal	Conservative	Conservative	Conservative
Daily Mirror	Labour	Labour	Labour
Daily Star	No party	Labour	Undecided
The Times	No party	Labour	Labour
Daily Telegraph	Conservative	Conservative	Conservative
Financial Times	Labour	Labour	Labour
The Guardian	Labour	Labour	Labour
The Independent	No party	Labour	Undecided

By Ben Hall. Tim Burt and Fiona Symon, *Financial Times* 14.4.2005

the backing of most of the press but in the 2005 election, support began shifting again (see Table 17.2).

In the US elections some concern was raised over the support for the Bush campaign in 2004 by the boss of Viacom, the parent company of CBS which is the major news channel in the USA. Sumner Redstone said that from a 'Viacom standpoint, the election of a Republican administration is a better deal because the Republican administration has stood for many things we believe in, deregulation and so on'. For the debate this caused see http://www.msnbc.msn.com/id/6173187/site/newsweek/. In Italy the prospect of having someone standing for election when he owns the major Independent TV broadcasting group is even greater cause for concern. Berlusconi owns Fininvest, a major shareholder in Mediaset which controls the three commercial terrestrial channels in opposition to the state-run RAI. This gives Berlusconi around 45 per cent of the audience share in a country which has a low level of newspaper readership and where the majority of people (87 per cent) depend more heavily on TV for their information about political issues than anywhere else in Europe. Fininvest also controls a leading national newspaper and a range of magazines. In 2002 the *Economist* reported:

Mr Berlusconi has yet to remove the ubiquitous conflicts between his private and public concerns. Because his companies are embroiled in almost every part of the economy, his failure to do so casts doubts on the motives behind so many of his projects, whatever their merits.

(From webpage http://www.ketupa.net/ berlusconi.htm)

In their analysis of 'globalization' Curran and Seaton (1997) touch on a different aspect of political influence; the impact of up-to-the-minute news coverage on the formulation of policy by governments. Particularly in the field of foreign policy they argue that national governments can be stampeded into hasty responses to world events simply to satisfy the media expectation that they 'do something'. The NATO bombing of Kosovo in 1999 by US and British war planes, as well as the invasion of Iraq, can be seen as examples of this.

Moral and social influences of the media

An area that has provoked particular concern has been the effects of media violence and pornography, especially upon children. Historically these fears about juvenile delinquency and the link between mass entertainment and moral degeneration predate the invention of the television set and the 'video nasty' by at least a century. Murdock and McCron (1979) remind us of this when they quote from a concerned observer in 1851, who warns of the corrupting and demoralizing influence of the theatre acting as a 'powerful agent for the depraving of the boyish classes of our towns and cities . . . which are so specially arranged for the attraction and ensnaring of the young' (quoted in Glover 1985: 372). In the 1950s the comic book became the focus of a moral panic in the USA over educational standards and deviant behaviour which ultimately led to the official censorship of horror and crime stories (M. Barker 1984). However, it is the issue of violence in the cinema, television and computer games which grabs the headlines in the 1990s.

Figure 17.12 Down with Kinnock

Source: News International

Figure 17.13 Up with Blair
Source: News International

Levels of screen violence are notoriously difficult to measure and comparisons have to be made with care (Gunter 1985). The SDP MP David Alton (now in the House of Lords) claimed in 1994 that by the age of 5 the average child will have witnessed 20,000 murders on television; Mary Whitehouse's National Viewers' and Listeners' Association (now renamed Mediawatch) monitored the output of the terrestrial channels in the first half of 1994 and concluded that 'broadcasters are promoting a relentless culture of cruelty and violence' (Denscombe 1994: 43). Studies by less partial bodies such as the Henley Centre (1993), the Broadcasting Standards Council (1994) and the Independent Television Commission (1993) all suggest that whatever the relative levels of violence on television, sex, violence and bad language remain an issue for many people, with 65 per cent feeling that there is still too much violence on television (Broadcasting Standards Council 1994).

In the run up to the 2005 General Election in the UK, the head of Mediawatch, John Beyer, wrote to each of the party leaders expressing his organization's concern over continued levels of violence and anti-social behaviour on TV. He complained that his researchers had monitored 177 films across the five terrestrial channels during 2004 and had 'identified 900 incidents involving firearms and 680 violent assaults'. Consequently he wanted to know what they intended to do to regulate such coverage:

Parliament legislates on a range of social and moral issues and these have yet to feature very much in the Election campaign. Many people care deeply about standards in entertainment and are concerned about the portrayal of violence, the use of obscene language and the display of nudity and sexual intimacy on television. We believe the quality of our culture matters and that television, in particular, is promoting violence and uncivilised behaviour which validates the social and criminal violence that disfigures our society. The latest statistics on the portrayal of violence on television again show that violence involving firearms is the most common followed by violent assaults – precisely those crimes that are on the increase.

Whether such concerns reflect a real threat or simply represent an imaginary moral panic is difficult to assess, but there is much hearsay evidence that violence on screen is a direct cause of copy-cat behaviour in society. In 1971, *A Clockwork Orange* was withdrawn from British cinemas by its director because of imitative violence by young gangs. In 1987, the Hungerford massacre was said to have been inspired by Michael Ryan's obsession with Rambo films. Three young men were convicted of a murder in Cardiff which followed repeated exposure to the film *Juice*, while the video of *Child's Play 3* was cited in the 1993 murders of James Bulger in Liverpool and Suzanne Capper in Manchester (see Newburn and Hagell 1995). Similar concerns were raised over the film *Natural Born Killers* and apparent 'copycat' killings in the USA and France, leading to much publicized court cases. The murder of London headteacher Philip Lawrence by a teenager has also led to the introduction of guidelines on screen violence being introduced in 1998 by a government convinced that screen violence and street crime are linked.

Case study

Copy cat killing?

Since 2000, other films have grabbed the headlines such as *The Matrix*, which has been related to several 'copycat killings' including the massacre of students at Columbine High School, and *Scream* which has been associated with many violent murders across Europe and North America;

in the States there have been at least 4 killings in which the film was cited as a trigger or where a *Scream* mask was worn by the killer. In England and in France there have been 3 reported cases and one in Belgium where a lorry driver put on a *Scream* costume before killing a 15-year-old girl with two kitchen knives.

(The *Observer* 9.7.2002)

Questions

1. What other films have been associated with 'copycat' violence?

2. How valid do you find the evidence that there is a causal link between film violence and real life imitation?

On a less serious level, the antics of cartoon characters such as Tom and Jerry, Ren and Stimpy, Beavis and Butthead and the Simpsons have all been linked to the incitement of violence, vandalism and anti-social behaviour; Mighty Morphin Power Rangers have also been accused of promoting imitative violence in the playground. Professor Provenzo at Miami University has found that of 47 Nintendo games monitored, only seven were not violent; much of the violence was directed at women with 'foreigners' most likely to be portrayed as villains (*Guardian* 4.11.1991). Since the early 1990s, computer pornography has been treated as a serious offence as children gain widespread access to acts of buggery, rape and bestiality via the Internet. Butterworth (1993) examined the impact of the new technologies on pornography and the emergence of what she calls 'virtual sex' in wider-ranging and more accessible formats. Catherine Itzin has claimed that such extreme pornography distorts the perceptions that boys have of women and can contribute to sexual violence:

> Many studies show that if teenage boys are repeatedly exposed to images where women are reduced to their genitals and presented as sexually voracious, passive and servile it desensitises them and increases callous attitudes towards women. Pornography is often a contributing factor in child sexual abuse, sexual harassment and forced sex. (quoted in Bouquet 1994: 2)

In March 1994, Elizabeth Newson, professor of developmental psychology at the University of Nottingham, claimed that the new levels of mindless violence occurring in society could be explained only by the 'easy availability to children of gross images of violence on video' (Newson 1994: 3). From her summary of research findings she suggested that video violence leads to identification and imitation among the young, but Newson's main concern was with the way in which vicious and cruel behaviour was portrayed as entertainment and amusement, encouraging desensitization. She quotes an American writer to emphasize the point:

> Not only do these films suggest that brute force is a prerequisite for manliness, that physical intimidation is irresistibly sexy, and that violence offers an effective solution to all human problems; today's movies also advance the additional appalling idea that the most appropriate response to the suffering of others is sadistic laughter. (Medved 1992, quoted in Newson 1994: 4)

It is true that many studies, especially those conducted under experimental conditions, support the view that violence on the screen leads to aggressive attitudes and violent behaviour, but whether this is the cause or the trigger of such behaviour is another matter. It should not surprise us that young offenders express an interest in films which sensationalize crime or that sex offenders show an interest in pornography, but this does not demonstrate any original cause, it merely suggests an attraction to the behaviour which has got them into trouble in the first place and accepts that the media play a part in the story. McQuail has summarized this link:

> The balance of evidence supports the view that media can lead to violent behaviour and probably have done so; these effects occur mainly as a result of 'triggering' of aggressive acts, imitation, identification with aggressive heroes and 'desensitisation', leading to a higher tolerance for real violence. (McQuail 1994: 334)

Critics of the violent effects model have argued that there is no clear evidence to prove a link between screen violence and social behaviour. After more than 1,000 studies, 'no satisfactory consensus has emerged', with different research techniques tending to produce contradictory results (Newburn and Hagell 1995: 8). The work of Hodge and Tripp (1986) and Gunter and McAleer (1990) has questioned the reliability of studies which show a causal link, while Cumberbatch has been a persistent critic of those who too readily accept the pessimistic warnings of media-induced violence (Cumberbatch and Howitt 1989). Cumberbatch has pointed out the relatively low levels of violence on British screens, especially in comparison with law-abiding societies like Japan, as well as refuting the evidence that short-term responses to media violence indicate long-term changes in behaviour. The horror stories so often quoted by the press and the largely discredited Newson Report mentioned above have been the subject of detailed examination (such as Buckingham 1996; Barker and Petley 1997), where much of the repeated 'evidence' for media-induced rape, murder and violence is denounced as popular myth inspired by tabloid journalists and high-profile moralists. In his recent summary of the continuing controversy surrounding 'media effects', Cumberbatch (1998) argues that much of the 'evidence' would not be out of place in 'an encyclopaedia of ignorance':

> The tip of the iceberg of knowledge about media effects is probably akin to a pebble on a mountain: the bit underneath is a colossal mass that geologically might turn out to be reasonably representative of the bit above, but might not bear any relationship to it whatsoever. (Cumberbatch 1998: 262)

Case study

Manhunt

Following the conviction of 17-year-old Warren Leblanc for the murder of 14-year-old Stefan Pakeerah in 2004, many high street stores, including Dixons, have removed the Rockstar game, Manhunt, from their shelves. Leblanc had savagely beaten his victim with a claw hammer and stabbed him several times after luring him into a local park. The defence had suggested that the motive was robbery but Stefan's mother argued that the violence had been linked to Leblanc's obsession with Manhunt, described by reviewer Dave Jenkins as 'perhaps the most violent, amoral video game ever made [in which] you're forced to sneak around a series of maze-like levels killing "hunters" and SWAT-team members as you go, using such unsavoury methods as suffocating them with plastic bags and cutting their throats with shards of glass.' Stefan's father described the game as 'a video instruction on how to murder somebody, it just shows how you kill people and what weapons you use'. Stefan's mother added: 'When one looks at what Warren did to Stephan and looks at the brutality and viciousness of the game one can see links.'

A statement from the game's publishers Rockstar North said: 'We extend our deepest sympathies to those affected by these tragic events . . . Rockstar Games is a leading publisher of interactive entertainment geared towards mature audiences and markets its games responsibly, targeting advertising and marketing only to adult consumers aged 18 and older . . . [We] submit every game for certification to the British Board of Film Certification and clearly mark the game with the BBFC-approved rating.'

A spokesperson for the British Board of Film Classification said the game had been given an 18 certificate. It was also the board's opinion that there were no issues of harm attached to the game and there was no evidence directly linking the playing of games with violent behaviour.

Professor Mark Griffiths of Nottingham Trent University, a psychology expert, said 'Research has shown those aged eight years or below do in the short-term re-enact or copy what they see on the screen. But there's been no longitudinal research following adolescents over a longer period, looking at how gaming violence might affect their behaviour.'
(Adapted from BBC News Online 29.7.2004)

Questions

1. *How convincing do you find that statement from Rockstar?*

2. *Does the research referred to by Professor Griffiths help us to draw any conclusions?*

After reviewing well-known anecdotal cases and the evidence of psychologists, psychiatrists and sociologists who favour the media violence hypothesis, Cumberbatch concludes that in the face of contradictory data, researchers have been extremely selective in their presentation of findings and overlook suggestions that the audience can handle the material to which it is subjected.

These conclusions are to some extent supported by the work of Gauntlett (1995), who suggests that the link between TV and juvenile crime has been exaggerated by a middle-class moral panic over social order which ignores the more obvious part played by unemployment and poverty. Noble (1975) has gone further by suggesting that some forms of television violence may have the cathartic effect of releasing feelings of aggression. This is a point of view also expressed by Yaffe and Nelson (1982) about the use of pornography in sex education and therapy sessions. However, they also point out that pornography can be used in different ways by different people and will have more than one set of consequences. They conclude that apart from the harmful effects of violent pornography on children, especially those who are already disturbed, 'pornography might be offensive, distasteful and a nuisance, but it did not appear to pose a threat to society' (Yaffe and Nelson 1982: xii). In his review of the research into the effects of pornography, Goode (1997: 225–30) dismisses the 'catharsis theory' as obsolete and false, but he is equally dismissive of the argument that pornography is by nature a form of violence against women. Following a trawl through a variety of statistical and experimental studies, Goode concludes that 'sexual explicators in pornography, by itself, is not a major determinant of male aggression against women.' However, the case of violent pornography is a different matter, and he agrees with Donnerstein *et al.* (1987) that 'exposure to violent pornography will increase aggression against women . . . it also plays a part in changing the way men think about women.' As Malamuth *et al.* have concluded:

> if a person has relatively aggressive sexual inclinations resulting from various personal and/or cultural factors, some pornography exposure may activate and reinforce associated coercive tendencies and behaviours . . . [although] high pornography use is not necessarily indicative of high risk for sexual aggression.
>
> (Malamuth *et al.* 2000: 79–81)

The contradictory evidence and the range of possible responses by different audiences to different stimuli make it difficult to draw firm conclusions. The debate over the effects of the media on children raises important issues about the nature of the society we want them to grow up in and the kind of people we want them to become but the evidence, quite simply, fails to resolve these questions; the remarks of Wilbur Schramm in 1961 are still true today:

> For *some* children under *some* conditions, some television is harmful. For *other* children under the same conditions, or for the same child under *other* conditions, it may be beneficial. For *most* children *under* most conditions, most television is neither particularly harmful nor particularly beneficial.
>
> (Schramm *et al.* 1961: 1)

Interpreting the evidence

Given the inconclusive nature of the evidence it is not surprising that several models have developed to explain the relationship between the media and its audience. While early models emphasized the power of the media, later work has concentrated on the ability of the audience to make its own sense of media texts through the processes of interpretation and negotiation. Similarly, there has been a shift away from short-term effects on the individual towards the long-term impact of media messages within different cultural contexts. The following represent some of the major theoretical positions which characterize the historical development of media effects research.

The hypodermic syringe model

Early ideas tended to be influenced by sociological positivism, behaviourist psychology and popular fears of mass society, all of which created the 'myth of media power'. Although, as McQuail has pointed out:

> this view was based not on any scientific investigation but on observation of the enormous popularity of the press and of the new media of film and radio that intruded into many aspects of everyday life as well as public affairs. (McQuail 2000: 417)

According to this view the media had the power to change attitudes and behaviour and the potential for pro-social as well as anti-social influence. The panic induced across America by Orson Welles' radio play *War of the Worlds* in 1938 is often quoted as a classic example of the power of the media to influence behaviour (Cantril 1940). Such deterministic ideas still inform modern debates about the use of the media, but as McQuail (1977) points out there are at least four methodological issues which prevent an acceptance of such a simplistic model:

1 The media are only one of many factors involved in the socialization process. When assessing the possible effects of the media we must also consider the influence of family, friends and schooling.

2 The media themselves consist of many forms which operate in different ways. When discussing 'the media' we have to specify which aspect we are referring to; broadcast media operate differently to the press, tabloid newspapers do not behave like broadsheets and so on.

3 A distinction must be made between effects ('any of the consequences of mass media operation, whether intended or not') and effectiveness ('the capacity to achieve given objectives'). The whole issue of the dichotomy between the intended message and the audience response to it is crucial to the later shift of interest away from the power of media texts towards the reader's interpretation.

4 We need to specify the level at which we are measuring media effects; the media may have influences on the individual, the group, the institution or culture in general. Before making general claims for the power of the media to affect behaviour it is important to be clear about the level at which they are operating.

The 'no effects' model

Empirical research soon revealed the shortcomings of the hypodermic syringe model, and it was recognized that the effectiveness of the media in getting its messages across depended on the personal influences affecting the perceptions of audience members. The direct consequence of this was the development of the 'two-step flow' model by Katz and Lazarsfeld (1955), which recognized that the way we interpret the media usually involves a process of negotiation with other members of the audience; instead of passively absorbing media output, we discuss with family, friends and even perfect strangers the programmes we have seen on TV or the stories we read in the press. In this model, opinion leaders emerge (in families, at work, in the pub) to help interpret the messages we are being sent; the simplicity of the stimulus/response relationship between media and audience was replaced by the complexity of human meaning and personal relationships.

A more extreme variant of audience power which diminished the significance of the media even further was the 'uses and gratification' model, which stresses the ways in which the media respond to the biological, psychological and social needs of the individual members of the audience (Blumler and Katz 1974). In an approach which has similarities to the dominant paradigm mentioned above (pp. 690–1) the media are seen as responsive to client needs. McQuail *et al.* (1972) looked at the way in which people use television in particular to satisfy a range of personal requirements; they concluded that at a general level, four types of gratification were provided for:

1 *diversion*: media as a form of escapism;
2 *personal relationships*: media as a means of providing companionship and the opportunity for social interaction;
3 *personal identity*: media as a device for confirming personal values and concept of self;
4 *surveillance*: media as a channel for information and ideas.

Stop and think

> ➤ Using the two-step flow model, who do you regard as the major opinion leaders who have affected your reading of media events at home? At college? At work? At play?

> ➤ Using the uses and gratifications model, provide examples of the four types of gratification identified by McQuail *et al.*

The emphasis of this approach has led to the criticism that it exaggerates the importance and independence of the audience (Elliott 1974), but it has also opened up the possibility of exploring the ways in which media texts may be interpreted (McQuail 1994) and the role of the individual consumer within an 'active audience' (Lull 1995).

Long-term effects

A rejection of both the hypodermic syringe model and the no effects alternative has encouraged the view that the media may influence us in many ways that are hard to measure and have long-term effects on our attitudes, creating new ideas or reinforcing existing ones rather than changing opinions we already have. When this is combined with the recognition that individuals belong to social groups, a new paradigm emerges which insists on placing media production and audience response within the context of a cultural effects approach which 'seeks to bring together both the way in which meanings are created by the media and the way in which these relate differently to the cultures of particular social groups' (Glover 1983: 380). Another way of interpreting the panic of Martian invasion which gripped Americans in 1938 is to go beyond the polarized debate (which blames the power of the media or the gullibility of individuals) and explore the interplay of various historical, situational and cultural factors which may lead us to understand the context within which, for some people, the panic took place. Such factors would include the relative newness of the radio as a medium for communication, the dramatic devices employed in the production of the play itself, the point at which individual listeners tuned in, the role of the 'opinion leader' within the family, the fascination with science fiction film and comics of the time, current speculation over the habitability of the planet Mars and the serious political situation in Europe as it drifted towards the Second World War.

A further aspect of the long-term view is the role played by the media in reinforcing negative attitudes through the stereotypical portrayal of particular groups by the media. In this the concept of representation is central because it recognizes the part played by the media in articulating and preserving the values and norms of wider society. Gill Swanson has defined representation as 'the way images and language actively construct meings according to sets of conventions shared by and familiar to makers and audiences.' However, the construction of these meanings takes place within a system of power which ensures that some representations enjoy greater legitimacy than others and are dominant; those without legitimate status become marginalized. Branston and Stafford (1996) discuss this power in their examination of the way in which stereotypes categorize and evaluate groups of people in such a way as to explain their social position in terms of the characteristics which form the basis of the stereotype. Briggs and Cobley (1998) argue that the way in which groups of people are represented not only affects the ways that they are seen by others but also influences the way they see themselves. Rather than adopting a Marxist perspective on ideology and 'false consciousness', they are more interested in 'the manner in which ideology underpins and endows with meaning the constituent components of our identities and what these entail.' What it means to be a woman, an Asian, gay, young, British or disabled all entail identities which are partially constructed through the discursive activities of the media.

Moral panics

One aspect of the 'media effects' debate is not so much concerned with its ability to influence behaviour in a direct manner but with the possibility that it can generate widespread feelings of anxiety and concern and exaggerate the risks that the public might face from particular threats or social groups (Goode and Ben-Yehuda 1994) Rather than acting as a cause of individual behaviour in the positivistic sense (see Hypodermic Syringe model above p. 711), this approach is more interested in the role of the media in creating a climate of fear in which we become sensitized to certain risks and not others. In general terms Gerbner (1995) has talked of the way in which the media obsession with violent crime promotes a 'mean world syndrome' which exaggerates the sense of insecurity, anxiety and mistrust that is characteristic of modern life. More specifically, however, the idea of 'moral panic' was originally developed to explain the demonization of young people as a social problem and the scapegoating of certain sub-cultural groups in particular.

First used by Jock Young to describe the impact upon public anxiety of the creation of 'drug squads' in the 1960s, the concept of *moral panic* was borrowed and extended by Stan Cohen (1972) in his classic study of mods and rockers and their treatment by the media and the police in the early 1960s. Like the Teddy boys before them, the mods and rockers were presented by the media not simply as symbols of youthful style but as an indicator of national decline. This approach reached fever pitch in

press coverage of the mod 'invasions' of various seaside resorts in 1964. These events were given front page prominence by national newspapers who referred to a 'day of terror' in which whole towns had been overrun by marauding mobs 'hell bent on destruction'.

Such spectacular reportage was generally exaggerated. For instance, in the case of the mod 'invasions' the initial violence and vandalism was minimal. Moreover, it is speculated that press coverage actually engendered and amplified subsequent disturbances. Stanley Cohen defined the moral panic which followed as a situation in which:

> A condition, episode, person or group of persons emerges to become defined as a threat to societal values and interests; its nature presented in a stylised and stereotypical fashion by the mass media, the moral barricades are manned by editors, bishops, politicians and other right thinking people; socially accredited experts pronounce their diagnoses and solutions; ways of coping are evolved [more often] resorted to, the condition then disappears, submerges or deteriorates and becomes more visible.   (Cohen 1972: 9)

In such situations distorted media coverage plays a key role in shaping events. Media attention fans the flames of an initially trivial incident and creates a self-perpetuating 'amplification spiral' which generates a phenomena of much greater significance and magnitude. In his work Cohen shows how media intervention gave form to these sub-cultural groups and represented them as threatening 'folk devils'.

In Pearson's (1983) work the idea is used to explore the fears generated by the emergence of urban gangs in the nineteenth century: Girroters, Peaky Blinders, Scuttlers and Hooligans were some of the gangs which gripped public attention at the time but Pearson concludes that:

> every era has its young gangs that catch the terrified imagination of the respectable. Every era also has its myth about a previous golden age of traditional values, a time when it was safer to walk the streets.
> (cited in Toynbee 1983)

Hall *et al.* (1979) applied the idea of moral panic to the criminalization of black youth in the 1970s while Bill Osgerby (1997) points out that Cohen's arguments could easily be applied to media treatment of the various forms of sub-cultural groups that have emerged since. From the skinheads of the late 1960s, the punks of the 1970s to the new age travellers and acid house ravers of the late 1980s and early 1990s. These youth sub-cultures have been subject to a process of stigmatization and stereotyping which have worked to popularize and lend substance to styles that were initially indistinct and ill-defined. Media intervention, therefore, gives youth sub-cultures not only national exposure but also a degree of uniformity and definition. As Osgerby points out:

> Without the intercession of media industries it is unlikely that sub-cultures such as Teddy Boys, Punks or Ravers would have cohered as recognisable cultural formations, instead remaining vaguely defined and locally confined stylistic innovations.
>
> (Osgerby 1997)

The active audience

Often overlooked in the debate about media effects is the ability of the audience to take control of the media and to respond to its messages in unpredictable ways. Because of its pluralist and individualistic overtones, this view has been unfashionable in sociological circles (see Elliot 1977; also in Marris and Thornham 1996: Reading 30). However, recent dissatisfaction with the amount of time and funds devoted to inconclusive research and the simplistic thinking about the media it encourages has led to a revisiting of the 'uses and gratifications' model and a more psychological approach to what we do with the

Case study

The hoodie – another moral panic?

In May 2005, the Bluewater shopping centre in Kent introduced a dress code for customers which bans youths wearing hoods and baseball caps from their private malls as such young men are seen as intimidating yobs who use the hood to conceal their identities during a day spent shoplifting.

Rachel Harrington, vice-chair of the British Youth Council, says Bluewater's decision demonstrates a growing demonization of young people. 'It's yet another example of a trend – tarring all young people with the same brush and overreacting to any behaviour by young people. You can understand a shopping centre's desire to please their customers, but it doesn't seem to me to be the best response. It's very easy to create the stereotype of the young thug as emblematic of society's problems, rather

than seek out the root of the problems.'

Angela McRobbie, professor of communications at Goldsmiths College, says it's the hoodie's promise of anonymity and mystery that both explains its appeal and provokes anxiety. 'The point of origin is obviously black American hip-hop culture, now thoroughly mainstream and a key part of the global economy of music through Eminem and others. Leisure- and sportswear adopted for everyday wear suggests a distance from the world of office [suit] or school [uniform]. Rap culture celebrates defiance, as it narrates the experience of social exclusion. Musically and stylistically, it projects menace and danger as well as anger and rage. [The hooded top] is one in a long line of garments chosen by young people, usually boys, and inscribed with meanings suggesting that they are "up to no good". In the past, such appropriation was usually restricted to membership of specific youth cultures – leather

jackets, bondage trousers – but nowadays it is the norm among young people to flag up their music and cultural preferences in this way, hence the adoption of the hoodie by boys across the boundaries of age, ethnicity and class.'

However, McRobbie concludes that attempts to ban such clothing will simply make it more desireable: 'Moral panics of this type have only ever made the item, and its cultural environment, all the more attractive to those who prefer to disidentify with establishment figures and assorted "moral guardians" and who enjoy the outlaw status of "folk devil".'

(Gareth McLean, the *Guardian* 13.5.2005)

Questions

1. Why would traders at Bluewater want to ban hoodies?

2. In what sense can this be seen as a 'moral panic'?

3. What is the cultural significance (attraction) of the hooded top to young people?

'You're just wearing that
so you can't come to the
shops with me'

Figure 17.14 Matt cartoon from the *Sunday Telegraph* 15.5.2005

media rather than what they do to us. Lull has argued that despite its mechanistic references to human needs, the uses and gratifications approach, through the research of McQuail *et al.* (1972) and Blumler *et al.* (1974), did show how 'various audiences . . . use media differently and for different reasons' (Lull 1995: 93). By accepting that psychological needs have a cultural dimension, Lull attempts to bring together the social and the psychological strands into a less deterministic approach to the study of communications which recognizes the critical abilities of 'the audience':

> In the end it is this tension between the ability of the mass media to influence thought and activity, and the strong tendency of individuals to use media and symbolic resources for their own purposes, that our theory of media, communication, and culture must accommodate.   (Lull 1995: 105)

This view underpins much of the thinking now to be found in cultural studies and is clearly reflected in the work of Fiske (1989), Ien Ang (1985; 1991) and Lewis (1990) on the relationship between popular culture and its audiences. Ang's book *Desperately Seeking the Audience* (1991) is a revolt against the perspectives and models which treat the audience as a homogeneous and passive bunch of 'couch potatoes' in danger of 'amusing themselves to death' or quite literally driving themselves mad. In her attack on this dominant thesis she argues that the 'viewers' perspective is almost always ignored' in preference to an 'institutional point of view' in which the actual audience is treated as 'an objectified category of others to be controlled' (Ang 1991: 4).

In order to provide an alternative 'microscopic stance', Ang argues that attention should focus on 'actual audiences' that inhabit the real world:

> The social world of actual audiences . . . [is] a provisional shorthand for the infinite, contradictory, dispersed and dynamic practices and experiences of television audiencehood enacted by people in their everyday lives – practices and experiences that are conventionally conceived as 'watching', 'using', 'receiving', 'consuming', 'decoding', and so on, although these terms too are already abstractions from the complexity and the dynamism of the social, cultural, psychological, political and historical activities that are involved in people's engagements with television. It is these heterogeneous practices and experiences of audiencehood that form the elements to be articulated in discourses of 'television audience'.
>   (Ang 1991: 13–14)

This approach requires an 'ethnographic thrust' which is genuinely concerned to produce an alternative body of knowledge 'that is constructed from the point of view of actual audiences' (p. 162). In an example of patriarchal remote control, Ang borrows the following account from Bausinger's (1984) study in which a woman talks of her husband's use of the TV: 'Early in the evening we watch very little TV. Only when my husband is in a real rage. He comes home, hardly says anything and switches on the TV.' According to Bausinger this is not a choice of programme but a well-understood family code for 'I would like to hear and see nothing'.

From this 'micro-situational' perspective the static viewing habits of 'the audience' revealed by empirical research are replaced by a more intimate approach which transforms our understanding of media use by celebrating 'the dynamic complexity of television audiencehood' and recognizing its diversity:

Television audiencehood is becoming an ever more multifaceted, fragmented and diversified repertoire of practices and experiences. In short, within the global structural frameworks of television provisions that the institutions are in the business to impose upon us, actual audiences are constantly negotiating to appropriate those provisions in ways amenable to their concrete social worlds and historical situations.

(Ang 1991: 170)

The active nature of the audience can be seen in many ways, whether it involves swearing back at *PopIdol* or *I'm a Celebrity: Get Me Out of Here* in the privacy of our own homes or the public demonstrations in Liverpool against the *Sun's* treatment of Hillsborough. In 1939, a dramatic, if extreme, example of audience power was demonstrated in Ecuador when an attempt to reproduce the *War of the Worlds* hoax backfired; the public took such exception to the joke that they burned the radio station to the ground, killing six members of staff!

Case study

Soap talk: using TV to negotiate identities

In *Television, Globalisation and Cultural Identities*, Chris Barker (1999) discusses the idea that ideologies are not simply imposed upon people by those in positions of power but created in an interactive environment which involves audiences in interpreting texts from popular culture and the 'television talk' which accompanies them. In Barker's view 'television talk' is an important part of establishing ethical and personal boundaries, particularly through the discussion of soap opera:

Soap talk is one of the ways in which [people] make intelligible and manageable the moral and ethical dilemmas that face them.
(Barker 1999: 132)

Following writers such as Barthes, Foucault and Gramsci, Barker argues that we make sense of the world around us and our relationship to it within the context of power and ideology but that audiences have the power to negotiate and resist the hegemonic attempts to control ideas through

the imposition of their 'preferred meanings' upon media texts. Such texts are 'polysemic' and as such can be read in different and oppositional ways. Although the media industry holds most of the cards when it comes to the *production* of media texts it is powerless to dictate their *consumption*. In this sense the power of the audience is important because they bring with them a range of common sense attitudes by which they interpret the messages they receive and play a major part in judging the relevance of these messages to their own lives. Television, for example, does not tell us how to act but

forms a resource for the construction of cultural identity just as audiences draw from their own sedimented cultural identities and cultural competencies to decode programmes in their own specific ways.   (1999: 112)

This means that our reading of texts is closely tied to the major identity elements of our 'self'. Studies of news programmes like *Nationwide*, US soaps such as

Dallas and the popular Australian soap opera *Neighbours* have suggested that our readings of such texts are influenced by cultural background and the identity components of class, gender, ethnicity and locality. In other words different people 'read' the same text in different ways depending upon the aspects of identity which are of most importance to them.

In Barker's study he uses *qualitative* research to examine

the role of television soap opera as a resource employed by British Asian and Afro-Caribbean teenagers [to show] how a specific group of persons deploy television as a resource for the construction of cultural identities [through] the formative nature of language as a resource in lending shape to ourselves and our world out of the contingent and disorderly flow of everyday talk and practice.   (1999: 119)

In other words, he records the conversations the sample have about soaps. This 'soap talk' provides the data by which he can examine the process of 'discursive production'

Case study (continued)

through which their 'multiple and gendered hybrid identities' are formed within British culture.

Through their discussion of soaps, certain themes, plots and characters emerge which contribute to the exploration of their own boundaries to personal identity because by expressing opinions on the behaviour of others they are really engaging in the establishment of who they think they are, what issues are important to them and the moral codes by which they establish 'acceptable' behaviour for youngsters like themselves (Black/Asian/Male/Female/Working class/Middle Class/British) even if this is through a discussion of characters who are not like them in circumstances they are unlikely to experience.

In this way the 'self' can reflect upon its relationship to formal morality but also work out its own ethical stance. In Foucault's work this distinction is important and Barker uses it to focus upon the role of 'ethical reflection' in the social construction of identity:

> Ethics . . . is concerned with the actual practices of subjects in relation to the rules which are recommended to them which they enact with varying degrees of compliance and creativity . . . This more dynamic conception of self suggests a route by which ethics can be seen as the site of a form of self-fashioning activity. (1999:)

Through the two related but contradictory responses to characters (*condemnation* and *explanation*) the audience not only 'slag off' the bad characters for breaking the rules of conventional morality (condemnation) they also come to a more forgiving position which sees behaviour as relative to circumstances as well as some overarching set of absolute rules (explanation). Somewhere between the two they do some important 'identity work' of their own.

Questions

1. *How much time do you spend discussing soaps/reality TV?*

2. *Which characters/storylines excite the most discussion?*

3. *Is there a clear moral agenda in these episodes? What is it?*

4. *Is there much disagreement over such readings?*

5. *Does the social nature of the audience (class, gender, ethnicity) make a difference to the reading?*

6. *Does TV play a part in the formation of identity? Who is in control – them or us?*

The models we have looked at are not supposed to be mutually exclusive but indicate the different perspectives which may be applied to the study of media effects. Depending on circumstances, the effectiveness of a particular message will be affected by the quality of its production, the needs of individual consumers, the social context of its consumption and the cultural circumstances surrounding its transmission. Where the balance between these factors is right, the media have the power to transform people's lives, but when the relationship becomes unbalanced the magic ceases to work.

In concluding his discussion on the effects of the media, McQuail identifies the ways in which the media demonstrate their power:

> That we cannot trace very precise causal connections or make reliable predictions about the future does not nullify this conclusion (about media effects). The question of the power of the mass media is a different one . . . Control over the mass media offers several important possibilities. First, the media can attract and direct attention to problems, solutions or people in ways which can favour those with power and correlatively divert attention from rival individuals or groups. Second, the mass media can confer status and confirm legitimacy. Third, in some circumstances, the media can be a channel for persuasion and mobilisation. Fourth, the mass media can help to bring certain kinds of public into being and maintain them. Fifth, the media are a vehicle for offering psychic rewards and gratifications. They can divert and amuse and they can flatter. In general, mass media are very cost-effective as a means of communication in society; they are also fast, flexible and relatively easy to plan and control.
>
> (McQuail 1977: 90–91)

Summary

➤ The mass media play an ever-increasing part in our modern way of life. People depend on the media for information and for their entertainment.

➤ Technological developments have increased the range and changed the nature of the mass media that are available to people. The diversity of channels and broadcast services available enables consumers virtually to create their own viewing schedules.

➤ While there have always been attempts by governments to control the mass media, recent developments have led to a greater concern about the power of the media. Restrictions on the media include economic, political and legal controls and regulations.

➤ There are a number of theoretical perspectives which explore the relationship between the media and society. These perspectives do not fall conveniently under 'conventional' sociological headings. There is a broad distinction between theories that take a generally optimistic view of the media – that emphasize their ability to provide us with more information and a greater choice of material to read, listen to and view – and those that express concern over the negative consequences of the role of the media – highlighting the danger of the media being used as instruments for manipulation and control.

➤ The extent to which the media affect attitudes and behaviour is contentious. While it is clear that people will be influenced by what they read, see and hear, evidence on whether the media directly determine specific forms of behaviour – whether watching violence causes children to behave violently, for instance – is inconclusive.

➤ There have been various theoretical attempts to explain the relationship between the media and their audience. Early models tended to emphasize the power of the media, and the short-term effects on the individual, while later work has focused on the ability of the audience to interpret the media and has highlighted the longer-term impact of media messages within different cultural contexts.

Links

The media permeates all aspects of modern life and most of the topics and issues covered throughout this textbook will involve a concern with how they are represented by the media.

However, the section on the mass media and control, especially political control, pages 684–686, have particular links to the discussion of power and politics in Chapter 5.

Further reading

Bell, E. and Alden, C. (eds) (2003) *Media Directory 2004*, Guardian Newspapers.
Contains a wealth of data and information. Useful for students and media practitioners.

Briggs, A. and Burke, P. (2005) *A Social History of the Media*, Cambridge: Polity.
Provides a clear overview of the communications media and of the social and cultural contexts within which they have emerged.

Briggs, A. and Cobley, P. (2002) *The Media: An Introduction*, 2nd edn, Harlow: Longman.
This text provides a useful and up-to-date introduction to developments in the media, including some of the less fully researched areas such as comics, advertising and marketing and new technology.

Chippendale, P. and Horrie, C. (1999) *Stick It Up Your Punter: The Rise and Fall of the Sun*, London: Mandarin.
An inside account of the tabloid culture of the *Sun*. Easy to read and very amusing.

Curran, J. and Seaton, J. (1997) *Power Without Responsibility: The Press and Broadcasting in Britain*, London: Routledge.
A detailed account of the history and development of the media in Britain that also provides an introduction to the main theories of the media.

French, K. (1997) *Screen Violence: An Anthology*, London: Bloomsbury.

A reader that covers a variety of perspectives – personal, professional and political – on this contentious topic.

Gauntlett, D. (1995) *Moving Experiences: Understanding Television's Influences and Effects*, London: John Libbey.

An excellent critical review of 'media effects' research.

Glasgow University Media Group (1996) *The Media and Mental Illness*, London: Longman.

An innovative approach to representations of mental illness in the media.

Keane, J. (1991) *The Media and Democracy*, Cambridge: Polity Press.

An important contribution to the debate over the public service nature of the media and the move towards deregulation.

Lull, J. (1995) *Media, Communication and Culture*, Cambridge: Polity Press.

An up-to-date and readable discussion of the relationship between social order and the ideological power of the media.

McQuail, D. (2005) *Mass Communications Theory: An Introduction*, 5th edn, London: Sage.
Now in its fifth edition, the standard text on the sociology of the media. Its coverage of theories of the media is particularly extensive.

Williams, G. (1994) *Britain's Media: How They are Related*, London: CPBF.

This brief introduction is packed with information and ideas about media ownership in Britain. It is available from the Campaign for Press and Broadcasting Freedom (8 Cynthia Street, London N1 9JF).

`http://www.` **Web sites**

www.cpbf. org.uk
A pressure group defending public service broadcasting and the freedom of journalists – it is mainly conceerned with issues of media ownership and political control.

www.cmpa.com
Is the site for the US-based Centre for Media and Public Affairs which conducts research into the news and entertainment media.

www.mediated.co.uk
A free rolling news web site with online subscription database access to news stories and also free text search.

Activities

Activity 1

Neophiliacs and cultural pessimists

In looking at the historical development of the media, some of the range of current technological innovations were introduced and discussed. Such a review is almost bound to be out of date as soon as it is committed to print as technological innovation shows little sign of slowing up. However, here are differing views over the effects of these developments for society. The positive view that improved media technologies will benefit society through increasing customer choice and providing greater opportunities for education and democratic participation is termed by Curran and Seaton (1991) the **neophiliac approach**. Those adopting a **cultural pessimistic** viewpoint believe that a decline in quality and cultural standards inevitably accompanies new forms of media and communication.

Look at the following list of positive statements about change in the modern media from the 'neophiliac' approach. Give an example of each one.

How might a 'cultural pessimist' respond? Again give an example for each row. The first row has been completed as an illustration. You might find the following chapters useful in completing this task: Curran and Seaton (1991: ch. 14); O'Sullivan *et al.* (1994: ch. 8); G. Williams (1994: ch. 1).

▶

Activities (continued)

Neophiliacs	Cultural pessimists
More services offer more choice	More channels = more of the same
End of broadcasting monopoly	
Two-way technology is interactive	
Access to global information/other cultures	
Introduction of new work practices	
End of traditional class divisions	
New educational opportunities	
Political empowerment of individuals	

Activity 2

Life without the media

Have you ever considered what life would be like without the media?

Try it out for one day as an experiment – and don't cheat!

No newspapers, no radio, no magazines and no television (even if you have to record your favourite programmes for future viewing).

Make some notes as to how you feel at different times of the day.

Which media did you miss most and for what reasons?

At the end of the experiment consider the questions asked earlier (p. 659).

How did your life change?

What were the effects on social life and interpersonal communication?

glossary

Active audience A notion used in the study of the media which suggests that the audience has powers of discrimination and uses the media rather than reacts to it. It rejects the simplistic cause–effect model of media influence.

Afterlife A term reflecting belief in life after death in some form. Most religions believe in an afterlife, though the form varies. Examples include heaven and hell in Christianity and Islam and more temporary states such as reincarnation in Hinduism and Buddhism.

Age of majority The age in society at which a child becomes considered an adult in social, legal and/or political terms. The exact age varies across time and culture and the specificities of rights and responsibilities can vary within societies. Some societies have rituals celebrating or marking such 'coming of age'.

Ageing The process of growing old. This is both a physical and a social process, as are the changes associated with old age. **Ageism** refers to prejudice or discrimination on the basis of age.

Agency Being capable of acting within society, being capable of change and action.

Agents of socialisation Institutions that contribute to the development of social norms within individuals; these include family, peers, school, media, political structures etc.

Alienation The condition in which individuals feel detached or estranged from themselves and others and from specific situations, such as their work situation.

Anglican Communion The fellowship of Churches throughout the world sharing a close relationship with the Church of England, the head of which is the Archbishop of Canterbury.

Anomie A situation where an individual or group no longer supports or follows the norms of society: a condition of normlessness (see **norms**).

Anti-racist education Educational policies aimed at eliminating the practice of labelling people according to the colour of their skin or racial identity.

Anti-sexist education Educational policies aimed at challenging male domination of the education system and society in general.

Articulation of modes of production A term most closely associated with the work of Ernesto Laclau in the 1970s. Laclau uses it as a critique of dependency theory. It refers to the notion that there can be several different modes of production operating at the same time across the globe. The dominant mode of production, for example capitalism, is able to articulate – that is to say direct and control – other modes of production for its own ends.

Artificial insemination A process of unnatural conception involving the injection of semen into the womb by artificial means.

Asceticism A doctrine or practice of self-denial and abstinence in which sensual/physical pleasures are denied in order for spiritual fulfilment to occur.

Assimilation This refers to the process by which 'outsiders' adjust culturally to the host country through a relinquishment of social and cultural characteristics and the adoption of the host culture and identity. Originating in the USA, and having some popularity in political debates in 1960s–1970s Britain, the term has more recently been used by critical writers to refer to a form of social control by the powerful over the powerless.

Autonomy The ability to act in a self directed manner; to think, choose and act without guidance from another person or group.

Bahā'īs A religious movement arising out of a Persian Islamic sect in the 1860s. Bahā'īs believe in the oneness of God, the unity of all faiths and the inevitable unification of humankind. Social goals as well as spiritual truth are emphasized.

Bias In sociological research, this refers to the difference between the 'true' value of a characteristic and the value that is found by the research.

Biomedicine Western, or cosmopolitan, medicine founded on principles of modern science.

Birth rate The number of births per thousand females of childbearing age per year. **Fertility** refers to the actual number of live births in a population unit in one year.

Bourgeoisie In a narrow sense, the term used by Marxists to refer to the owners of property in capitalist society. More loosely, it has been used to describe the middle and upper classes, who are both presumed to support the capitalist system.

Branch Davidians A breakaway from a sect which itself broke away from the Seventh Day Adventists, a millenarian movement. A large number of Branch Davidians following the charismatic authority of David Koresh were killed in a siege and subsequent storming of their compound in Waco, Texas, in 1993.

Buddhism A set of traditions and teachings derived from the Buddha about 2,500 years ago. Central teachings include the law of *karma* by which reward or punishment results from good and evil acts. There is much variety within Buddhism and two main historical traditions: Theravada and Mahāyāna.

Bureaucracy A particular form of administration that is characterized by a set of clearly defined rules and a hierarchy and that emphasizes efficiency and impersonality. It is seen as the typical form of large-scale organization in modern societies.

Calvinism The beliefs and teachings following the theology of sixteenth-century Protestant reformer John Calvin. Key aspects of his theology included the sovereignty of God, the centrality of the Bible, the rule of predestination and justification by faith alone.

Capitalism A form of economic organization in which the means of production are privately owned and controlled.

Capitalist world metropolis A concept derived from André Gunder Frank used to describe those countries at the centre of a chain of exploitation that reaches into some of the poorest societies. The capitalist world metropolis exercises its control over societies at the periphery primarily through economic means.

Case study A piece of research that focuses on a single example or case, rather than a larger sample, and examines it in some depth.

Child abuse Maltreatment of a child. Child abuse may involve physical, verbal and/or sexual abuse and it is important to remember that its effects may not necessarily be visible.

Childhood The state of being a child. In physical terms this usually means the time from birth to puberty. Sociologists are also interested in the social, political and legal meanings of childhood and highlight how the meaning and designation of childhood varies across time and culture.

Children's rights The notion and definition of the just and fair treatment of children. These have been formally outlined and ratified by a number of countries following the United Nations Convention on the Rights of the Child in 1989. In practice, however, children's rights continue to be violated in many ways and throughout the world.

Christianity An inclusive term referring to the world religion founded on the life, teachings and work of Jesus of Nazareth, an Israeli Jew. The term 'Christ', meaning anointed one, refers to the belief that Jesus was the Messiah. There are many branches within Christianity, including Eastern or Orthodox Churches, the Roman Catholic Church and those Protestant Churches arising out of the Reformation.

Citizenship Refers to belonging to a collective – either a local unit such as a town or city, or a wider unit such as the state. Citizenship entails both rights and responsibilities.

Civic culture The symbols, norms and attitudes that legitimate a system of political power.

Class A basic type of social stratification. In sociological theorizing, classes have been defined in economic terms, by economic characteristics such as occupation or income. They are used to refer to divisions in society, for instance the dividing of a society into upper, middle and working classes.

Cohabitation The state of living together outside marriage. Cohabitation implies being involved in a sexual relationship. It may apply to both heterosexual and homosexual couples.

Collective conscience The term associated with the work of Durkheim that refers to the moral consensus of society: the beliefs and values that are held by (the majority of) citizens in a particular society.

Communitarianism A political perspective emphasizing a balance between the rights of individuals and their responsibilities to the community. The aim is to remove severe impediments to community relationships, for example, by providing education for parenthood or devolving considerable government power to a local level.

Complementary medicine Non-biomedical healing traditions such as herbalism, acupuncture or aromatherapy founded on principles other than modern science, e.g. humoral balance or energy meridians.

Confucianism Or K'ung Fu-tse. A school of thought following the ideas of the Chinese philosopher Confucius (551–479 BC). Confucius emphasized moral values as the basis of the social and political order, including the notion of respect for the family and the state.

Conjugal Of marriage. Traditionally the notion of 'conjugal rights' referred to the right of sexual intercourse with a spouse.

Content analysis A research technique used to quantify media texts according to predetermined and clearly defined categories. By measuring the amount of space or time devoted to stories, images or symbols, it is possible to make comparative assessments of media content.

Core In development theory, these are the most advance industrialized societies. These societies are already developed and in many ways control the process of development for others at the periphery.

Corporatist state A political system in which some large interest groups have become more powerful than others in the political and economic arena. Decision making is generally by compromise between a representative of labour (unions), capital (employers) and the state.

Correspondence principle Similarities between social relationships in schools and the division of labour at work. Associated with the Marxist-based work of Bowles and Gintis.

Credential inflation The tendency for qualifications to be valued less highly as more people have them. In response to the increasing number of candidates with the necessary qualifications, employers will raise the qualifications required for specific jobs.

Crime Behaviour that breaks the criminal law and that can be followed by criminal proceedings and formal punishment.

Criterion referencing Assessing an individual's educational attainment by checking whether items on a list of criteria have been satisfied.

Critical theory A form of social analysis that originally developed in the first half of the twentieth century (particularly the 1930s and 1940s) based around the writing and theorizing of the Frankfurt Institute for Social Research (known as the Frankfurt School). It draws on the work of Marx but criticizes positivism in Marxism and the social sciences in general. It argues that criticism should be self-critical.

Cross-media ownership The diversification of media corporations into several fields of media production and distribution (e.g. News International has interests in book publishing, newspapers and television as a producer and distributor).

Cultural capital This refers to 'ownership' of the dominant culture, including social and linguistic competences and qualities such as style, manners, aspirations and the perception of chances of success. It is associated with Bourdieu, who claimed that the degree of cultural capital individuals possessed the more successful they would be in the educational system.

Cultural deprivation Exclusion from the usual standards of material and social existence experienced by others who live in the particular culture. It is often used by sociologists to refer to educational deprivation.

Cultural diversity The differences in culture between different groups and societies: what is regarded as normal and acceptable by one culture may be quite unacceptable in another.

Cultural relativism Social and cultural forces affect the conditions under which knowledge is produced. Certain knowledge comes to be regarded as superior because people in power define it as such.

Culture The beliefs, values and attitudes shared by a particular group of people or a particular society.

Culture of poverty The phrase originated with the work of US anthropologist Oscar Lewis, who used it to explain how poor people in Latin America reacted to their situation by producing strategies for survival which endured to form a culture, which in turn became an explanation for their continued poverty. These ideas are now strongly associated with the political right in Britain and the USA and in particular with Charles Murray's writings on the underclass.

Daoism Chinese philosophy and religion based on the writings of Laozi more than 300 years BC. Key themes include harmony with nature, including balancing the powers of *yin* and *yang*.

Dark figure of crime Crimes that are not included in the official crime statistics. This can include crime not known about by the authorities and also crimes that the police may know about but do not record.

Dealignment Although most voters are still strong identifiers with a particular political party, the notion of dealignment suggests that such 'identifiers' have declined as a proportion of all votes (party dealignment) and that social class is no longer a major influence on voting behaviour (class dealignment).

De-industrialization A term used to describe the decline in the employment in, and scale of, the manufacturing and extractive industries.

Democracy This may be simply defined as 'rule by the people', although this ignores power relationships and fundamental assumptions about human rights. Wider definitions would include some sort of recognition of those who are excluded from influence.

Democratization The process of creating a (usually liberal) democratic system. It is sometimes agreed that, for this to happen, society must already have a civic culture. Giddens argues that in many liberal democracies, democratization occurs through making politicians more accountable to the people.

Dependent variable A variable that changes as a result of changes in something else – another variable. It is sometimes the variable that a particular hypothesis tries to explain.

Descriptive An analytical skill through which appropriate labels are applied to things, people, events and ideas that are observed.

De-skilling Associated with Braverman, who thought that within the context of capitalist society skilled work becomes increasingly broken down into a series of simple, and hence more easily managed and controlled, tasks.

Development The process by which societies move from agrarian-based economies and social structures to become complex modern industrial societies.

Deviance In sociology and everyday usage, this refers to behaviour that does not conform to conventional standards of behaviour and that is disapproved of. Deviant behaviour may be criminal but can also include behaviour that does not break the criminal law.

Diagnostic assessment A form of assessment which is likely to include a summative assessment but will go further by providing an indication of what the next stage of the learning process should be (by, for example, identifying special educational needs).

Disciplinary power In Foucault's writing, the exercise of power over a population through monitoring and surveillance.

Discourse theory Associated with Michel Foucault, this attempts to identify how social institutions, behaviours and identities are historically and culturally constructed by a series of discourses (e.g. legal discourses, medical discourses).

Doctrine The official or orthodox teaching of a religion which is believed to have been divinely inspired. Doctrines may be written (scripture) or passed on orally.

Domestic violence Violence within the home, which may take various forms, including verbal, physical and sexual abuse.

Effects model The belief that the media and in particular television can affect the beliefs and behaviour of the audience, usually for the worse.

Elaborated code A complex language code: analytical, abstract and with explicit meanings. It is associated with the work of Bernstein, who contrasted it with a more restricted code which is less analytical and abstract.

Election A mechanism for selecting people to exercise political power.

Elite Any select group with privileged status, often united by common ties of interests and aims.

Elitism The systematic exclusion of the majority from political influence. The elitist government relies on the deference of the masses, created by their socialization into an acceptance of elite domination.

Embourgeoisment The term used to describe the process by which working-class people come to desire and embrace a middle-class lifestyle and outlook.

Empirical sociology Sociology based on research that involves the collection of real data, for instance, from questionnaires or interviews.

Empty shell marriage A marriage where a husband and wife formally remain together but there is no substance to the relationship in the sense of a conjugal relationship.

Epiphenomenon A secondary symptom of something.

Epistemology The theory of knowledge; in sociology it is used to refer to the procedures by which sociological knowledge is acquired.

Equal opportunities An often unspecified ideal of equal chances in education with definitions varying between weak and strong extremes.

Eschatological Pertaining to 'last things'. Eschatological beliefs often refer to the last days before the end of the world.

Essentialism The view that due to natural/biological attributes, all members of a group share certain core attitudes, experiences and behaviours.

Ethics/ethical codes Guidelines relating to correct ways of behaving for individuals or society. All religions develop views about right and wrong, though the nature and degree of prescription varies.

Ethnicity A contested term used to refer to cultural identity that defines the members of a group. Cultural affiliations can be based, for example, around a sense of shared history, religion, language or political identity. It has been introduced by writers as an alternative to the 'race' concept, with 'ethnicity' used to highlight the cultural, as opposed to biological, basis of group membership.

Ethnocentrism The belief that the customs, values and beliefs of the dominant group are superior to those of the 'inferior' group. It has been used, historically, as a justification for political and cultural intervention by the West into less 'civilized' societies (e.g. through the missionary movement).

Ethnography The detailed study, based on observation, of a particular group or culture; the description and evaluation of the study.

Ethnomethodology A theoretical branch of sociology that focuses on the ways in which people construct their social world and how they make sense of their everyday lives. It was developed by Harold Garfinkel as a challenge to the conventional sociological view that the social world is ordered and structured and can be taken for granted.

EU The EU was originally formed in 1957 out of an agreement by Germany, Belgium, France, the Netherlands and Luxembourg to regulate trade between them. The UK joined the EU (or Common Market as it was then known) in the mid-1960s. Membership now stands at 25, the most recent countries to join being Cyprus, the Czech Republic, Estonia, Hungary, Latvia, Malta, Poland, Slovenia and Slovakia in May 2004.

Executive Government and civil service.

Experiment A method of research which involves the systematic and controlled analysis of variables. Typically the subjects of the research are assigned to two different groups: an experimental and a control group. The experimental group is then exposed to an independent variable, the control group is not, and the results are observed and analysed.

External locus of control In psychology, a belief that one's destiny is largely controlled by factors outside, and beyond the control of, the individual, such as powerful others or fate.

Externalizing system In the anthropology of health, a set of beliefs which attribute ill health to factors outside the individual, e.g. evil eye, germs.

False consciousness A Marxist term used to explain the lack of class consciousness and the failure of revolutionary action. It implies the deliberate use of ideology by those in power to disguise their true interest from the working class.

Fascism Generally described as extremely right-wing views because of the assumption that inequalities are biologically determined, although in some cases fascists have been suspicious of free-market capitalism. Fascism promotes common fears and hatreds, the appeal of superiority and domination over others and strong authoritarian leadership.

Feminism A body of thought that suggests that women are disadvantaged in modern society and that advocates gender equality. There are many different strands within contemporary feminism and it is more appropriate to talk about feminisms, rather than feminism.

Feral children Literally wild children: children brought up without any meaningful contact with other human beings.

Feudalism The social and political structure that characterized medieval Europe, based on a system of mutual obligation and dependence between the nobility and peasants.

First World A term referring to the affluent industrialized and developed societies. The USA, Britain, France, the Netherlands, Germany and, more recently others, such as Japan, are examples of First World countries.

Flexibility An imprecise term that refers to a range of changes in working practices – such as part-time work, casual labour, short-term contracts – which allow for the easier management, deployment and control of labour.

Flexible firm A model developed by Atkinson to highlight purported changes to work organization, particularly the breaking down of the workforce into a core and a peripheral group.

Fordism This term is sometimes seen to be synonymous with mass production, but it is also used to describe a socio-economic system developed in many countries in the post-war period.

Formal health-care system The provision of health care by paid professionals.

Fourth World A term that attempts to make a distinction between Third World societies that have the potential to develop and those that appear destined to remain non-industrial and poverty-stricken (see also **super-poor**).

Fragmentation The way in which social groups such as classes lose their cohesiveness and feelings of identity and unity because of differentials in pay and status which divide the group against itself.

Framing (of the curriculum) The extent to which areas of knowledge are linked. It also refers to the power relationships involved in interaction and how much control students and teachers have over the transmission of knowledge.

If, for example, the area of politics is strongly framed, students studying political processes will have little influence on the choice of subject matter and little contact with students in other fields.

Functionalism A theoretical perspective that analyzes social institutions and phenomena in terms of their function (or contribution) to the maintenance of the particular society: for instance, what function does the family play in the maintenance and running of society.

G8 This group of leading industrialized economies comprising the USA, Japan, Germany, France, the UK, Italy, Canada and Russia. The GIO group also includes Belgium, the Netherlands and Sweden.

Gender The socially produced categories of masculinity and femininity. Refers to the social, cultural and psychological characteristics associated with maleness or femaleness in particular cultures and societies.

Genetic engineering The deliberate modification of hereditary features. The notion that this aspect of reproductive technology may be used for social and political purposes has generated much ethical debate.

Globalization Globalization reflects the growing interdependency of world society. It can take place on any number of levels: economically, culturally, politically and militarily.

Government Another name for the executive.

Guest worker A system for the employment of non-native workers within an industrial society. The guest-worker system has been widely used in many European societies, such as Germany, France and Switzerland, in the post-war period. Such workers are accorded few, if any, civil rights.

Health beliefs model A model which accounts for health behaviour in terms of an individual's assessment of the costs and benefits of that behaviour.

Hegemony A term coined by Gramsci to refer to ideological domination of society by a 'ruling class', whose control depends in part on convincing the mass of society that the *status quo* is inevitable or natural.

Heterogeneity When a group or culture is characterized by differences we refer to it as being heterogeneous.

Heterosexual Sexual desire for members of the opposite sex. How heterosexual desire is formed is much debated.

Hidden curriculum Traits of behaviour or attitudes that are learned at school but which are not included within the formal curriculum (see also **paracurriculum**).

Hinduism A collective term for a diverse range of religious beliefs and practices developed over thousands of years in India. Hinduism embraces various scriptures, deities and practices, including the notion of reincarnation or rebirth.

Historical materialism Marx's theory of historical development. Different social structures (at different historical periods) are seen as resulting from the ways in which the production of material goods is organized in different societies.

Homogeneity When a group or culture shares similar characteristics we refer to it as being homogeneous.

Horizontal integration The process by which corporations expand to dominate one aspect of media operations within a particular market (e.g. the takeover of one newspaper by another).

Horizontal segregation This describes the way in which women and men tend to be concentrated in different sectors of the labour market, with women being concentrated in a narrower range of sectors.

Human rights The notion and details pertaining to just and fair treatment of all persons on the basis of their humanity. Increasingly such rights are spelt out in written statements or charters.

Iatrogenesis Ill health or adverse effects caused by medicine itself, e.g. the side-effects of medications.

Ideal type A general, abstract concept that describes a 'pure' type that does not actually exist. It can be used as a means for comparing and evaluating actual social phenomena.

Ideology In strict terms this is simply the science of ideas. However, as it has been developed in the social sciences it refers to a set of beliefs, values and attitudes that are used to explain and/or justify particular forms of social relationship. In Marxist thought it denotes thinking which is unscientific and has the function of obscuring the truth. Writers such as Mannheim suggest that all knowledge is ideological.

Illness iceberg The large number of symptoms of ill health for which people do not seek professional help.

Imam A religious leader within Islam. The term means 'model' or 'example'.

IMF The International Monetary Fund, based in Washington, and the organization that attempts to regulate and control, via international agreements, the world monetary system.

Independent variable A variable that is controlled or manipulated by the researcher so as to observe how it affects other variables.

Industrialization This refers to the transformation of predominantly agricultural societies into societies where manufacturing and the extractive industries are central to the economy.

Infant mortality rate The number of deaths per 1,000 children under 1 year old in a given year.

Infrastructure A Marxist term meaning the economic base or structure of a society. In some texts it is called the substructure or economic base of society. For Marx, all the non-economic aspects and institutions of a society are seen as being determined by its infrastructure.

Institution Any large-scale rule-governed social activity.

Institutionalized racism Used to refer to those instances by which racist attitudes and practices are continuous and integral to the structures of a society; racism, for example, may be institutionalized in the judiciary, the government or the police force. Usually covert in nature, institutionalized racism works to reinforce a society's beliefs about racial characteristics.

Internal locus of control In psychology, a belief that one's destiny is largely controlled by the self.

Internalizing system In the anthropology of health, a set of beliefs which attribute ill health to factors within the individual.

Interview A method of gathering data by asking people a series of questions.

Interviewer bias This can refer to inaccurate or unrepresentative information given to an interviewer by a respondent, either by consciously misleading the interviewer or unconsciously giving inaccurate information. It can also arise from the actions or background of the interviewer: for example, the status of the interviewer may affect the replies given by the respondent.

Islam A term meaning 'submission'. Followers of Islam (Muslims) see their faith as embracing every aspect of life. They believe God (Allah)'s will was revealed to the Prophet Muhammad and is incorporated in the Holy Book (Qur'an). Most of the 700 million Muslims worldwide belong to the moderate Sunni branch. The largest minority group is Shi'ism.

Japanization A broad term which encompasses a range of work and design practices carried out within some Japanese companies, such as the use of teamworking and the just-in-time system.

Jehovah's Witnesses A millenarian movement whose followers emphasize the imminent second coming of Christ and the literal translation of the Bible. Witnessing includes house-to-house preaching, the publication of a newsletter, *The Watchtower* and regular meetings in Kingdom Halls.

Job enrichment This involves an attempt to empower workers by giving them a measure of control, planning and variety within their job in order to counteract the negative consequences of boring and repetitive labour.

Judaism The religion of the Jews, who believe that God delivered their Israelite ancestors out of bondage. There are various branches of Judaism, ranging from the traditional Orthodox strand to more reformed or liberal branches.

Judiciary The legal system.

Kinship This refers to blood relations and the social relationships deriving from these. Anthropologists distinguish between ties based on descent and ties based on marriage (or 'affinity').

Labelling The process by which individuals and/or types of behaviour are categorized by more powerful groups in society. These labels generally have negative connotations and labelling as a theoretical concept has been applied particularly to the study of crime and deviance.

Labour market This refers to the interactions between the buyers and sellers of labour power.

Labour migration A system found primarily in South Africa under the apartheid system, but also in southern states of the USA. Such workers are often employed in low-wage areas of the economy and are forced to return home when demand for their work decreases.

Labour process This involves purposeful human activity in relation to an object of some kind and the tools with which it is carried out.

Lay health beliefs Concepts used by non-professionals to explain health and illness.

Legislature One or more consultative chambers or assemblies for political debate and the scrutiny and passing of legislation.

Legitimation crisis German sociologist Habermas' theory that capitalism is inherently unstable and the state regularly intervenes in the economy to try to maintain stability. Voters see social problems as political rather than economic and therefore question the legitimacy of the state.

Liberal democracy A form of government in states that have regular and free elections for representative institutions of government and have guarantees of individual rights.

Liberalism An ideology that takes freedom (or liberty) to be a fundamental value; it also regards individuals as naturally equal, although natural equality is, for many liberals, compatible with significant material inequality.

Life course A socially defined timetable of events from birth to death. The life course takes into account both cross-cultural and historical variations of an individual's passage through life.

Life expectancy The average length of life.

Life history A method of research that consists of autobiographical material that has usually been obtained from a particular individual by an interview or conversation.

Lone/single parent family A family headed by one parent. These tend to be women, though single parents can also be men.

McDonaldization A term coined by Ritzer, who uses the global fast-food industry as a graphic example of the all-pervasive process of rationalization in contemporary societies.

Managerial revolution A theory put forward by US sociologist James Burnham to support the view that the power of a ruling class had been reduced by the emergence of a managerial class who are trained administrators. The control of the economy is transferred away from the vested interests of the owners and into the hands of people who manage according to rational principles on behalf of all parties.

Marginalization The process by which individuals and groups are excluded from the mainstream of social life. Members of such groups often feel they are not receiving the prestige and/or economic rewards they deserve.

Marriage A cultural and legal relationship between partners which confers legitimacy on their offspring. In many societies marriage is based on the principle of romantic love and partners' choice. In other communities marriages may be arranged by parents and may involve consolidating property and forming family alliances.

Mass Observation An organization founded in Britain in 1936 to conduct social surveys on the population. The results of its surveys produced a detailed picture of British life and social change before and during the Second World War.

Mass production The systematic production of large volumes of standardized products for mass consumption.

Mechanical solidarity A form of social integration based on the similarity between individuals who hold the same beliefs and values and feel the same emotions. Durkheim saw this form of solidarity as typical of traditional societies.

Medicalization The process by which aspects of social life (such childbirth, dying, alcoholism) become seen as medical problems.

Meritocracy A society in which social rewards are allocated not according to ascribed characteristics, but according to merit: talent and effort.

Methodology The theory and analysis of how research should proceed. It includes the rules and practices that guide the gathering of data and the conclusions drawn from it.

Millenarianism This refers to the belief within Christianity in the return of Christ based on the Biblical Book of Revelation. Different Christian groups vary in their interpretation of the meaning and significance of this belief. Social scientists use the term more broadly to refer to any religious group stressing the impending end of the world through transformation.

Missionary movements Missionary activity involves active promotion of a faith or cause and attempts to gain new converts. Not all religions engage in active mission; those that do tend to stress a unique or universal truth and emphasize the importance of spreading their message.

Mode of production An abstract analytical model of the relationship between the relations of production (the relationships between people involved in production) and the means or forces of production (factories, machinery and raw materials involved in the production process). Different forms of society have different modes of production, for example, the feudal mode of production.

Mode of production In the classical Marxism sense a mode of production is an integrated system that links together complex economic, productive and social forces. Marx believed that each mode of production contained the seeds of its own destruction. Thus the slave-based mode of production gave way to the feudal mode of production, which in turn gave way to the capitalist mode of production. This in its turn would give way to the socialist, and eventually the communist, mode of production.

Modernization The process by which societies become developed, moving from agrarian to industrial economies. All Western societies can be said to have undergone a process of modernization in the last 200 years. It is associated with the work of Rostow, who defined five stages of modernization.

Monogamy The state of being married to one person at a time. The increase in divorce has resulted in 'serial monogamy', that is, the remarriage of divorcees.

Moral panic Public concern about issues such as drug abuse, teenage violence or football hooliganism are exaggerated or 'amplified' by the media out of all proportion to their real threat to social order. Public reaction often requires 'folk devils' to be identified as scapegoats.

Morbidity Illness and/or disease.

Mortality rate The number of people per thousand who die in a given year.

Multiculturalism An ideology advocating respect for cultural differences between groups enjoying a common citizenship. The implementation of this ideology would involve, for instance, encouraging groups to retain distinctive languages.

Multicultural education Teaching pupils and students about a wide range of cultures. The assumption is that this will generate a greater degree of tolerance, not only in the individual but also in society as a whole.

Nation A group of people that claim the right to live in a given territory, bounded and organized by a central state, by virtue of a common culture and historical descent.

Nationalism An ideology that claims that the political boundaries of a nation should be those of the cultural boundaries of a people. It insists that the interest of the nation take priority over all other interests.

New Labour The name used increasingly since 1994 to signal the changes that have taken place in the British Labour Party. These changes include the abandonment of Clause 4 of Labour's constitution, which, in theory, had bound the party to a policy of nationalization of industry. New Labour embraces the concepts of enterprise, individual responsibility and the market economy and has been criticized for being a weak version of socialism.

New Right Views within the British Conservative Party which originate in classical liberalism. The state is seen as overloaded by responsibilities as a result of trying to satisfy the ever-increasing demands of various interests. The emphasis is on letting market forces operate naturally.

New social movements Seen (particularly in Europe) as a new style of movement emerging from the protest movements of the 1960s. Critical of established political structures, they are loose, fluid networks with decentralized, open, democratic structures. They emphasize values that are universalistic rather than class-based (e.g. environmentalism, gay rights).

Norm-referencing A form of assessment in which the performance of one individual is ranked in comparison with that of others. Usually the aim of this approach is to ration the number of 'passes' (for example, when selecting pupils at 11+ for a limited number of places in a popular secondary school).

Norms Socially accepted rules or standards of behaviour.

OECD The Organisation for Economic Co-operation and Development. This is a Paris-based organization of industrialized economies which attempts to promote trade and economic co-operation between member states. Membership of the OECD extends further than that of the G7 nations to include countries such as Sweden, Finland, Denmark, Switzerland, Australia and New Zealand.

Official statistics Statistical data produced by governments or government agencies. While providing a great deal of useful data, sociologists have to be aware that they are not produced for sociological research and may reflect official (i.e. governmental) priorities.

Oligarchy A political structure in which an individual (oligarch) or small group (oligarchy) control the decision-making process.

OPEC The Organization of Petroleum Exporting Countries. This organization, made up of major oil-exporting countries, attempts to set the worldwide prices for crude oil. It gained prominence in the 1970s when it increased the cost of oil several-fold. Today it is far less powerful than it was.

Organic solidarity A form of social integration or cohesion that Durkheim felt typified modern, advanced societies. In more complex societies, individuals are increasingly interdependent and this interdependence encourages solidarity.

Paracurriculum This describes all that is taught in schools alongside the formal curriculum. The term acknowledges a common awareness that this part of the curriculum exists (and is therefore not really a 'hidden curriculum').

Paradigm The ideas, assumptions and rules that form a model for analyzing phenomena. The hypothetico-deductive method employed in the natural sciences is a good example.

Paradigm shift A radical change in the theories and concepts used to explain the world.

Participant observation A research method in which researchers observe behaviour and situations in which they are participants. Such participation allows the observer to observe either covertly, in other words without the other participants being aware, or overtly.

Part-time work An increasingly common form of work arrangement where people are employed for fewer hours than in a 'normal' full-time job.

Patriarchy The dominance of men over women in a society or a family system. A key concept in feminist theory.

Pauperization A Marxist term that refers to the belief that capitalism could only survive by driving down wages and increasing the exploitation of the workers. This continual impoverishment of the workers would create the conditions necessary for a social revolution.

Periphery Societies which are underdeveloped and connected to the core developed societies by a chain of exploitation (see also **core**).

Phenomenology A philosophical approach based on the analysis and description of everyday life. Phenomenologists study the ways which people come to understand the world they live in; they emphasize how human beings create social worlds.

Phrenology The now discredited practice of assessing personality traits from head shape.

Pluralism A perspective usually associated with the study of politics or the media which suggests that the institutions of a democratic society are responsive to the diversity of interests in that society.

Pluralism (political) A system of government that aims to embrace a number of sectional interests. Government responses are portrayed as a compromise between a plurality of influences. Power is spread across a wide range of social locations; organizations representing various interests exist because no one interest group is allowed to dominate.

Political economy A Marxist model of the media which emphasizes the influence and power of owners and advertisers in decision making.

Polygamy Having more than one marriage partner at a time. Some religious and cultural communities sanction this type of marriage arrangement. It may involve **polygyny** (one man and two or more wives), **polyandry** (one woman and two or more husbands) or **group marriage** (several husbands and wives).

Positivism A doctrine that science (including the social sciences) can deal only with observable things and that phenomena, in any form, have to be studied in a scientific manner. It does not take account of the individual's interpretation of the situation.

Post-Fordism A conception of socio-economic change which highlights a move away from mass production and mass consumption towards more flexible forms of work and production, often utilizing new technologies, the break-up of mass markets and shifting patterns of consumption.

Post-industrialism A conception of contemporary societies which emphasizes the increasing role of the service industries, the key role of new information technologies and the control, production and manipulation of knowledge.

Postmodernism A theoretical approach or position that emphasizes the uncertain nature of the modern world and the variety of cultural styles and choices in modern societies. It has been applied in a number of disciplines, most notably in literature and the arts. In sociology, postmodernism has been critical of those 'grand' theoretical perspectives that have produced all-encompassing theories based on logical and rational accounts of the development of societies.

Post-structuralism Developed in France in the 1960s and based on the structuralism of linguistics, post-structuralism treats social life in general as 'text' which is open to analysis. It rejects the basic assumption of structuralism that there is a universal principle or structure in the social world.

Power The capacity of individuals, groups and political bodies to ensure that their decisions are enacted and realised.

Prejudice A pre-judged attitude that is unfavourable towards persons assigned to a particular grouping.

Pressure groups Groups aiming to put pressure on decision-making bodies to support their demands. They are smaller and more formally structured than social movements and, unlike political parties, they seek to influence rather than to govern.

Priesthood A priest is a religious leader, usually ordained, who serves the non-ordained or lay people (laity). Within Christianity the priest may fulfil a range of duties including sacraments. Christian traditions have differing views on the nature and meaning of priesthood based on theological interpretation.

Primary groups Term used by Cooley to describe groups based on close, personal relationships and face-to-face interaction between the members.

Privatization Providing formerly state-owned services through privately owned companies.

Professionalization The process by which an occupational group achieves the status of a profession, through gaining a monopoly over its work.

Proletarianization The term used to describe the process by which some white-collar occupations have become de-skilled and poorly paid.

Proletariat The Marxist term for the working classes: the wage earners and property-less in capitalist societies.

Proportional representation There are several versions of PR, all of which aim to make the proportion of seats held by each party reflect the proportion of the electorate voting for that party.

Protestant ethic The Protestant ethic refers to a particular type of Protestantism that believed in an absolute, all-powerful God who had predestined every individual to salvation or damnation and that advocated a puritanical, austere lifestyle. The Protestant ethic thesis is the title given to Weber's argument that there was a link or 'spiritual affinity' between modern capitalism and this form of Protestantism.

Public service broadcasting The notion that broadcasting is too important to be left to market forces and that regulation is needed to ensure the public gets a balanced diet of education, information and entertainment. As a public corporation financed through the licence fee, the BBC is regarded as the best example of public service broadcasting.

Qualitative research Research which produces data that is not based on precise statistical measurement, and that is often expressed in words. This style of research encourages sociological analysis that aims to understand and interpret experiences and phenomena in ways that do not require detailed statistical comparisons. Typical methods of qualitative research include participant observation and unstructured interviews.

Quantitative research Research which produces data that can be expressed statistically – as numbers, percentages, tables and so on – and that can be subjected to statistical testing. Sociologists adopting this style of research emphasize that the data they collect are less open to bias resulting from the interpretation of the researcher. Typical methods of quantitative research include large-scale social surveys and structured interviews.

Questionnaire A method of collecting information in which the respondents complete a formal and standardized form. The questions may be closed or open-ended or a combination of both. Closed questions are more open to statistical testing and analysis.

Race A socially constructed term used to refer to the division of human beings into distinct 'types', recognizable through reference to physical characteristics (e.g. skin colour). While the term is commonplace in its usage, sociologists such as Robert Miles suggest that inverted commas should be placed around the term to highlight the fact that the 'race' term has no scientific validity. Others, such as Michael Banton, argue that the term 'race' has a social relevance, with very real consequences, and should therefore be retained without commas.

Race relations A field of study that gained academic and political popularity during the 1970s and continues to have some significance today. It studies a range of phenomena including the development of racial beliefs, the history of 'relations' between racial groups, and the life chances of the black community today.

Racialism This refers to behaviour based on racist beliefs, also known as *racial discrimination*. Whereas *racism* refers to beliefs or ideologies, racialism is confined to the 'acting out' of these beliefs. Examples of racialism include discrimination against individuals by employers on the basis of an individual's membership of a particular group.

Racism While theorists differ about their usage and application of the concept, a basic definition might see racism as referring to a belief in the existence of distinct racial groups, defined biologically, which are perceived to display genetically determined patterns of social, cultural, political and economic behaviour. These beliefs may just stay as beliefs, or they may be 'acted out'.

Reflexivity In the context of social research this refers to the researchers' examination of their own role and behaviour and their use of this to help make sense of their research. In interpretative sociology it is used more generally to refer to the human ability to reflect on its actions.

Reliability The reliability of research is the extent to which repeated measurements that use the same method produce the same results. Data or information that has been collected is said to be 'reliable' if, when the same research method is used again, the same results are produced.

Representation The symbolic construction of meaning through words or images. It is usually used in combination with the concept of stereotyping to understand how the media shapes audience perceptions of other social groups.

Republican This favours a form of government without a monarch. It also means the supporter of a republican party (which in the USA represents right-wing political views).

Rites of passage Public ceremonies to mark and celebrate the transition of an individual or group to a new social, religious or legal status. Rites of passage include marriage, coming-of-age celebrations (e.g. 18th or 21st birthday parties), and funerals.

Roman Catholicism The Catholic Church claims a line of succession from the earliest Christians and the authority of its leader, the Pope, deriving from St Peter (the first 'Bishop of Rome'). During the Protestant ('protesting') Reformation of the sixteenth century denominations broke away from the Church and establishing their own organization, theology and practices.

Ruling class An ambiguous Marxist term which indicates the political power of the dominant economic class. Marx argued that politics can be explained by economic forces and, consequently, the class which controls the economy is the one which runs society.

Sacred and Profane The sacred refers to that which is set apart, treated with special respect and regarded as holy. It is regarded as distinct from the worldly or profane, which is that belonging to the material world.

Sampling Collecting information from a subgroup of a particular population. Various methods can be used to select a sample, but the aim is essentially the same: to find a sample that will be representative of a wider population or group.

Scientific management This is often associated with the doctrines of FW Taylor and involves the systematic breaking down of tasks into simple operations which can be more easily monitored and controlled. Often referred to as 'Taylorism'.

Secondary groups Formal groups or organizations which are less personal and intimate than primary groups – schools, for instance. Such groups will often provide individuals with their first formal contact with society in general and with the generally accepted standards of behaviour in society.

Self-fulfilling prophecy The theory that pupils and students strive to realize their own self-images and expectations.

Semiotics The process by which meanings can be decoded from media texts. This is sometimes referred to as the 'science of signs'.

Service class Those members of the middle class who are directly responsible for the management of the interests of the capitalist class and most closely associated with it via income, education and lifestyle.

Sex This describes the biological categories of male and female.

Sexual division of labour This describes how the performance of labour, both unpaid domestic labour and paid employment, is shaped by gender. Most commonly it refers to the observation that women have greater responsibility for unpaid domestic labour and child care and that women and men are integrated into the paid labour market on a differential and inequitable basis.

Sexuality This term is used to encompass human sexual desire, pleasure, behaviour and identity.

Shivism Shi'ite Muslims are the largest minority group within Islam, mainly concentrated in Iran, Iraq and the Indian subcontinent. The problem of suffering is a key theme as illustrated in the concept of *Jihad* ('struggle'). One interpretation of this is 'holy war' against those who reject Islam.

Shrine A shrine is a sacred place regarded as having particular power and significance and often associated with key events in a group or society's history and identity.

Sick role The set of norms and expectations which pattern a person's behaviour when ill.

Social capital The cultural and social resources held by an individual or community.

Social control The ways by which behaviour is constrained and guided by society, in particular by social institutions. Such control can be exercised informally (through friends and family, for instance) or formally (perhaps through school rules or the law).

Social mobility The process by which individuals move up or down the social scale. An open society is one characterized by high levels of social mobility.

Social movement A collection of individuals who share a common interest (e.g. environmentalism or women's liberation) and the potential for mass mobilization in order to promote their aims.

Socialization The process by which individuals learn the beliefs, values and behaviour that are accepted in and approved by the society in which they are placed.

Socio-biology A field of study that attempts to characterize human and animal kind by reference to biological characteristics (such as genetic and/or chromosomal composition). While not perceived by sociologists as adequately explaining the complexities of human behaviour, recent (albeit controversial) studies from writers such as Charles Murray suggest a revival in approaches to 'race' which posit a biological basis to explain, for example, different levels of educational attainment among social groups.

Special educational needs Although exceptionally gifted children may be seen as having special educational needs, the term is generally used to refer to educational disadvantages caused by physical or mental disabilities.

Stagflation This can best be described as economic recession combined with high inflation levels in the economy. In the developed world, stagflation was evident during the mid-1970s, partly because of the rise in oil prices that took place at that time. Many developing and Third World societies have faced recent periods of stagflation.

Standard English The use of 'correct' grammatical constructions and pronunciation in written and spoken English. Individuals and groups using alternative forms of English language (e.g. dialects) have often been labelled as deficient or incompetent.

State An entity which claims the exclusive right to coerce people within a particular territory. Many of the state's functions do not, however, appear coercive. The state should not be confused with the government (which is part of the state).

Step-family A family resulting from the remarriage of a parent.

Stigma A discrediting attribute or characteristic usually associated with a person, e.g. a disability or HIV.

Structuralism A theoretical approach that in sociology emphasizes the analysis of social structures rather than individuals. It is derived from (and most usually associated with) the study of language, which is seen as the basic structure in society.

Sub-culture A distinguishable group within a broader culture which has its own beliefs and rules; these differ from those of the broader culture. These beliefs and values are usually exhibited in forms of behaviour that set the sub-culture apart from mainstream society, for example, in a delinquent sub-culture.

Summative assessment A form of assessment aiming to describe an individual's current knowledge and/or ability. This may lead to a grading or some other type of summary or label (e.g. GCSE grades, degree classifications).

Super-poor Commonly used to describe societies that are most economically deprived and disadvantaged. As a concept 'super-poor' can be said to unite not just countries sharing common conditions but disparate groups in several societies. Thus many women in Third World societies can be said to be 'super-poor'.

Superstructure A Marxist term used to refer to all aspects of society apart from the economic: so institutions such as the family, the school and the mass media constitute part of the superstructure of a society.

Survey A systematic method of gathering data through asking people a series of questions, either in an interview or in a questionnaire. The data can then be interpreted by statistical analysis.

Symbolic interactionism An intrepretative perspective, based on the work of social scientists working at the University of Chicago in the 1920s and 1930s, in particular George Herbert Mead. It suggests that social structures are created and maintained in the course of human interaction. In its focus on human interaction, individuals are seen as learning meanings through their interactions with others; these meanings become the basis around which they organize their lives.

Theology The study of the divine or God. Theology is often associated with the study of Christian beliefs and teachings but there are also schools of theology focusing on other religious traditions, such as Islamic or Buddhist theology.

Third way A political perspective that seeks to transcend the traditions of old-style social democracy ('old' Labour policies in Britain) and neoliberalism (the New Right in Britain). It favours a mixed economy and emphasizes citizens' obligations and responsibilities as well as equality and the protection of the vulnerable in society.

Third World The term most often used to describe less affluent non-industrialized societies. Any nation outside the economic orbit or control of either the USA or, until the early 1990s, the Soviet Union, was seen to be a Third World nation.

Tiger economies A term that refers to the economies of Asian nations that appeared to be undergoing dramatic rises in economic and industrial development during the period from the late 1970s onwards, for example, Malaysia.

TNCs Transnational corporations: globally (transnational) operating companies, very large, very wealthy and very powerful. Examples of TNCs include the Anglo-Dutch oil company Shell Oil and the American-owned telephone corporation AT&T.

Totalitarianism A state in which opposition to the dominant political group and its associated states is not allowed.

Totemism A common religion in tribal societies which involves treating the totem (a symbol of a person or the group) with awe and veneration. Within totemism supernatural powers are attributed to objects and creatures and this is reflected in various rituals involving the totem.

Trade unions Organizations that developed to protect the interests of workers against employers.

Tradition A regular social practice that is legitimated and maintained because it is assumed that it has a historical basis.

Transnational corporation Often huge companies that can organize production on an international, rather than a national, basis.

Transvestism A term that describes the behaviour of men who identify as male but choose to dress, on occasion, in 'female' clothing.

Triangulation The use of more than one method of research when carrying out a piece of research. This will enable research to benefit from the strengths of (and avoid any problems with) different methods of research. So it is likely to increase the validity of the research.

Underclass Used by sociologists to describe those at the very bottom of society with little or no regular connection with the labour market and no stake in society. In general usage, the term has moralistic and negative overtones.

Underdevelopment A condition in which certain societies remain in a permanent condition of poverty, lacking the resources, social structures or political systems to allow them to become developed.

Unemployment The condition of having no paid employment.

Unification Church A religious movement founded by and following Sun Myung Moon (hence followers are known as 'Moonies'). In the past Moonies were accused of 'brainwashing' as a method of recruitment and this phenomenon, as well as practices such as mass weddings, have been studied by sociologists of religion.

Urbanization The growth of city living, although it is often used to refer to the phenomenal expansion of new centres of economic activity and mass living in the nineteenth and twentieth centuries.

Utopia An imaginary, ideal state. The term 'utopian' is often associated with an idealism that can never be achieved.

Validity The extent to which a research method measures what it is intended to measure. Although a research method may be reliable, do the data gathered provide a true representation of what the researcher wishes to measure? For instance, is occupation a satisfactory measure for classifying people by social class?

Value-freedom The notion that social research should not be influenced by the researcher's beliefs and ideas. It is particularly associated with the positivist approach in sociology.

Variable A characteristic or behaviour that varies from one individual, group or society to another. For example, age is a variable by which people can be classified according to the number of years they have lived.

Verstehen A German term meaning empathetic or interpretative understanding. It was advocated by Weber as an approach to understanding social behaviour through empathy: through putting ourselves in the position of the individual or group being investigated so as to discover the motives behind our actions.

Vertical integration The process by which a media corporation extends its influence by expanding into areas of operation previously left to other organizations (e.g. the movement of hardware manufacturers into the production of software).

Vertical segregation The way in which within many occupational sectors of the labour market, women are under-represented in the better-paid and more senior positions (i.e. the higher up the occupational ladder, the fewer the women).

Vocationalism Education with the emphasis placed on job-related training.

Wage-labour This is often equated with work in general but it involves a monetary payment in exchange for a certain amount of labour.

White-collar crime Crime committed in the context of a legitimate occupational role. It includes crimes committed by employees 'against' their employers, such as fraud or fiddling, and crimes committed by businesses or corporations, such as the breaking of health and safety legislation. This latter form of white-collar crime is more usually considered as 'corporate' crime.

World systems theory A theoretical model developed by Wallerstein which postulates that movement from a condition of underdeveloped to developed is possible. However, such movement can only come about by the express agreement of those societies who are themselves at the pinnacle of development, those at the core.

WTO World Trade Organization: the organization based in Washington responsible for the enforcement of free and fair trade agreements at a global level.

Xenophobia Fear of strangers. It is generally used to denote negative attitudes towards immigrant groups on account of their cultural differences.

references

Abbot, D. (2001) 'The death of class?', *Sociology Review*, November.

Abbott, P. (1991) 'Feminist perspectives in sociology: the challenge to "mainstream" orthodoxy', in J. Aaron and S. Walby (eds) *Out of the Margins: Women's Studies in the Nineties*, Brighton: Falmer.

—— and Wallace, C. (1990) *An Introduction to Sociology: Feminist Perspectives*, London: Routledge.

—— and —— (1997) *An Introduction to Sociology: Feminist perspectives*, 2nd edn, London: Routledge.

Abdalla, A. (1988) 'Child labour in Egypt: leather tanning in Cairo', in A. Bequele and J. Boyden (eds) *Combating Child Labour*, Geneva: International Labour Organisation.

Abelove, H., Barale, M.A. and Halperin, M. (eds) (1993) *The Lesbian and Gay Studies Reader*, London: Routledge.

Abercrombie, N. and Urry, J. (1983) *Capital, Labour and the Middle Classes*, London: Allen & Unwin.

—— and Warde, A. (eds) (1992) *Social Change in Contemporary Britain*, Cambridge: Polity.

—— and Warde, A. with Soothill, K., Urry, J. and Walby, S. (1994) *Contemporary British Society* 2nd edn, Cambridge: Polity Press.

—— and Warde A. (2000) *Contemporary British Society* (3rd edn), Cambridge: Polity Press.

Abrams, M., Gerard, D. and Timms, N. (eds) (1985) *Values and Social Change in Britain*, London: Macmillan.

Abrams, P. (1968) *The Origins of British Sociology*, Chicago, IL: University of Chicago Press.

Acker, S., Barry, K. and Esseveld, J. (1983) 'Objectivity and truth: problems in doing feminist research', *Women's Studies International Forum* 6(4): 423–35.

Action Aid International (2004) *Power Hungry: Six Reasons to Regulate Global Food Companies*, Johannesburg, South Africa.

Acton, H. (1967) *What Marx Really Said*, London: Macdonald.

Acton, J. (1887) Letter to Bishop Mandell Creighton, 3 April, in J. Button (1995) *The Radicalism Handbook*, London: Cassell.

Adams, C. (1990) *The Sexual Politics of Meat*, Cambridge: Polity.

Adkins, L. (1995) *Gendered Work: Sexuality, Family and the Labour Market*, Milton Keynes: Open University Press.

Aggleton, P. (1987) *Rebels without a Cause? Middle-Class Youth and the Transition from School to Work*, London: Falmer Press.

Ahmad, W. (ed.) (1993) *'Race' and Health in Contemporary Britain*, Milton Keynes: Open University Press.

Albrow, M. (ed.) (1990) *Globalization, Knowledge and Society*, London: Sage.

Alcock, P. *et al.* (2001) *Welfare and Wellbeing: Richard Titmuss's Contribution to Social Policy*, Cambridge: The Polity Press.

Alderman, G. (1983) *The Jewish Community in British Politics*, Oxford: Clarendon Press.

Aldred, C. (1981) *Women at Work*, London: Pan.

Alexander, C. (2004) 'Embodying Violence: 'riots', dis/order and the private lives of 'the Asian gang', in Alexander, C. and Knowles, C. (eds) *Making Race Matters*, Basingstoke: Palgrave.

Alibhai, Y. (1990) 'Still papering over the cracks', *Guardian*, 10 September.

Alibhai-Brown, Y. (2001) *Mixed Feelings: The Complex Lives of Mixed-race Britons*, London: The Women's Press.

Allan, G. and Crow, G. (2001) *Families, Households and Society*, Basingstoke: Palgrave Macmillan.

Allen, J. and Massey, D. (1988) *The Economy in Question*, London: Sage.

——, Braham P. and Lewis, P. (eds) (1992) *Political and Economic Forms of Modernity*, Cambridge: Polity.

Allen, S. and Walkowitz, C. (1987) *Homeworking Myths and Realities*, London: Macmillan.

Almond, G. and Verba, S. (1963) *The Civic Culture*, Boston: Little, Brown.

Althusser, L. (1969 [1965]) *For Marx*, London: Allen Lane.

Althusser, L. (1971) *Lenin and Philosophy and Other Essays*, London: New Left Books.

—— (1972) 'Ideology and ideological state apparatuses', in B. Cosin (ed.) *Educational Structure and Society*, Harmondsworth: Penguin.

Amos, V. and Parmar, P. (1984) 'Challenging imperial feminism', *Feminist Review* 17(July): 3–20.

Andermahr, S., Lovell, T. and Wolkowitz, C. (1997) *A Concise Dictionary of Feminist Thought*, London: Arnold.

Anderson, B. (1983) *Imagined Communities: Reflections on the Origin and Spread of Nationalism*, London: Verso.

Anderson, C. (1974) *Towards a New Sociology*, Homewood, IL: Dorsey.

Anderson, M. (1971) 'Family, household and the industrial revolution', in M. Anderson (ed.) *The Sociology of the Family*, Harmondsworth: Penguin.

Andreski, S. (ed.) (1971) *Herbert Spencer*, London: Nelson.

Ang, I. (1985) *Watching 'Dallas': Soap Opera and the Melodramatic Imagination*, London: Methuen.

—— (1991) *Desperately Seeking the Audience*, London: Routledge.

Annandale, E. (1998) *The Sociology of Health and Medicine: A Critical Introduction*, Cambridge: Polity.

Anthias, F. and Yuval-Davis, N. (1993) *Racialized Boundaries: Race, Nation, Gender, Colour, Class and the Anti-Racist Struggle*, London: Routledge.

Anti-Slavery International (1993) *Britain's Secret Slaves*, London: Anti-Slavery International.

Appadurai, A. (1990) 'Disjuncture and difference in the global cultural economy', *Theory, Culture and Society* 7: 295–310.

Arber, S. and Evandrou, M. (1993) 'Mapping the territory: ageing, independence and the life course', in S. Arber and M. Evandrou (eds) *Ageing, Independence and the Life Course*, London: Jessica Kingsley.

Arber, S. and Ginn, J. (1991) *Gender and Later Life: A Sociological Analysis of Resources and Constraints*, London: Sage.

—— and —— (1992) 'Gender and resources in later life', *Sociology Review* 2(2): 6–10.

—— (1993) 'Class, caring and the life course', in S. Arber and M. Evandrou (eds) *Ageing, Independence and the Life Course*, London: Jessica Kingsley.

Archard, D. (1993) *Children: Rights and Childhood*, London: Routledge.

Archbishop's Commission on Urban Priority Areas (ACUPA) (1985) *Faith in the City*, London: Church of England.

Ariès, P. (1962) *Centuries of Childhood*, London: Jonathan Cape.

—— (1973) *Centuries of Childhood*, Harmondsworth: Penguin.

Armen, J.C. (1974) *Gazelle Boy*, London: Bodley Head.

Armstrong, D. (1983) *Political Anatomy of the Body*, Cambridge: Cambridge University Press.

Armstrong, F., Clarke, M. and Murphy, D. (1995) '". . . some kind of barmpot": young people in care and their experiences of the education system', in P. Potts, F. Armstrong and M. Masterton *Equality and Diversity in Education 1: Learning, Teaching and Managing Schools*, London: Open University/Routledge.

Arnold, M. (1963 [1869]) *Culture and Anarchy*, Cambridge: Cambridge University Press.

Arnot, M. (1986) *Race, Gender and Educational Policy Making*, Module 4, E333, Milton Keynes: Open University Press.

—— (1991) 'Equality and democracy: a decade of struggle over education', *British Journal of Sociology of Education* 12(4).

—— David, M. and Weiner, G. (1997) 'Educational reform, gender equality and school cultures', in B. Cosin and M. Hales (eds) *Families, Education and Social Differences*, London: Open University/Routledge.

Askew, M. and Ross, S. (1988) *Boys Don't Cry: Boys and Sexism in Education*, Milton Keynes: Open University Press.

Assiter, A. (1996) *Enlightened Women: Modernist Feminism in a Postmodern Age*, London: Routledge.

—— and Avedon, C. (1993) *Bad Girls and Dirty Pictures: The Challenge to Reclaim Feminism*, London: Pluto Press.

—— (1996) *Modernist Feminism in a Postmodern Age*, London: Routledge.

Atkinson, J. (1984) 'Flexibility, uncertainty and manpower management', Institute of Management Studies, Report 89, Brighton: Falmer.

Atkinson, P. (1981) *The Clinical Experience: Construction and Reconstruction of Medical Reality*, Farnborough: Gower.

Babb, P. *et al.* (2004) *Focus on Social Inequalities*. London: ONS.

Bachrach, P. (1967) *The Theory of Democratic Elitism*, Boston, MA: Little, Brown.

Back, L. (1997) 'Globalisation, culture and locality', *Sociology Review* 7(2) November.

Baehr, H. and Ryan, M. (1984) *Shut Up and Listen: Women and Local Radio*, London: Comedia.

Bagdikian, B. (1988) *The Media Monopoly*, Boston, MA: Beacon.

Baignent, M., Leigh, R. and Lincoln, H. (1986) *The Messianic Legacy*, London: Corgi.

Balarajan, R. and Raleigh, V.S. (1990) 'Variations in perinatal, neonatal, postneonatal and infant mortality in England and Wales by mother's country of birth, 1982–85', in M. Britton (ed.) *Mortality and Geography, OPCS Series DS No. 9*. London: OPCS.

van Balen, F. and Inhorn, M.C. (2002) Interpreting Infertility: A View from the Social Sciences, in M.C. Inhorn and F. van Balen (eds), *Infertility Around The Globe: New Thinking on Childlessness, Gender and Reproductive Technologies*, Berkeley and Los Angeles, CA: University of California Press.

Ball, S. (1981) *Beachside Comprehensive: A Case Study of Secondary Schooling*, Cambridge: Cambridge University Press.

—— (1991) *Politics and Policy Making in Education*, London: Routledge.

—— (ed.) (2004) *The RoutledgeFalmer Reader in Sociology of Education*, London: RoutledgeFalmer.

Ballard, C., Guibbay, J. and Middleton, C. (eds) (1997) *The Students Comparison to Sociology*, London: Blackwell.

Ballaster, R., Betham, M. and Hebron, S. (1991) *Women's Worlds: Ideology, Feminism and the Women's Magazine*, London: Macmillan.

Banks, O. (1968) *The Sociology of Education*, London: Batsford.

Banton, M. (1977) *The Idea of Race*, London: Tavistock.

—— (1987) *Racial Theories*, Cambridge: Cambridge University Press.

—— (1997) *Ethnic and Racial Consciousness*, 2nd edn, Harlow: Longman.

—— and Harwood, J. (1975) *The Race Concept*, Newton Abbot: David & Charles.

Baran, P. and Sweezy, P. (1966) *Monopoly Capital*, Harmondsworth: Penguin.

Barbalet, J.M. (2001) 'Weber's inaugural lecture and its place in his sociology', *Journal of Classical Sociology* 1:2: 147–70.

Barnes A., Elias R. and Walsh P. (2000*)* *Cocky: The Rise and Fall of Curtis Warren, Britain's Biggest Drug Baron*, London: Milo Books.

Barker, C. (1999) *Television, Globalisation and Cultural Identities*. Milton Keynes: Open University Press.

Barker, E. (1984) *The Making of a Moonie*, Oxford: Blackwell.

—— (1989) *New Religious Movements: A Practical Introduction*, London: HMSO.

Barker, M. (1981) *The New Racism*, London: Junction Books.

—— (1984) *A Haunt of Fears: The Strange History of the British Horror Crimes Campaign*, London: Pluto.

—— and Petley, J. (1997) *Ill Effects: The Media/Violence Debate*, London: Routledge.

Barker, R. (1992) 'Civil disobedience as persuasion: Dworkin and Greenham Common', *Political Studies* 4(2).

Barley, N. (1986) *The Innocent Anthropologist*, Harmondsworth: Penguin.

Barnett, S. (1989) *The Listener Speaks: The Radio Audience and the Future of Radio*, London: John Libbey.

Barrett, M. (1980) *Women's Oppression Today*, London: Verso.

—— and McIntosh, M. (1982) *The Anti-Social Family*, London: Verso.

Barron, P. and Sweezy, P. (1968) *Monopoly Capitalism*, Harmondsworth: Penguin.

Barron, R.D. and Norris, G.M. (1976) 'Sexual divisions and the dual labour market', in L.D. Barker and S. Allen (eds) *Dependence and Exploitation in Work and Marriage*, London: Longman.

Barth, F. (ed.) (1969) *Ethnic Groups and Boundaries: The Social Organization of Culture Difference*, London: Verso.

Barthes, R. (1972) *Mythologies*, London: Jonathan Cape.

Bartky, S.L. (1990) *Femininity and Domination*, London: Routledge.

Barton, L. and Tomlinson, S. (eds) (1981) *Special Education: Policy, Practices and Social Issues*, London: Harper & Row.

Bartos, A. and Hitchens, C. (1995) *International Territory: The UN 1945–95*, London: Verso.

Barzun, J. (1937) *Race: A Study in Superstition*, New York: Harcourt Brace.

Batty, D. (2003) 'Draining the South', *The Guardian*, 11.3.2003.

Baudrillard, J. (1990) *Cool Memories*, London: Verso.

Bauman, Z. (1989) *Modernity and the Holocaust*, Oxford: Polity.

—— (1990) *Thinking Sociologically*, Oxford: Blackwell.

Bauman, Z. (1998) *Globalisation: The Human Consequences*, Cambridge: Polity Press.

—— (2000) *The Individualized Society*, Cambridge: Polity Press.

Baumeister, R. (1986) *Identity: Cultural Change and the Struggle for Self*, Oxford University Press.

Bausinger, H. (1984) 'Media, technology and daily life', *Media, Culture and Society* 6(4).

de Beauvoir, S. (1974) *The Second Sex*, New York: Vintage.

Beck, U. (1992) *Risk Society: Towards a New Modernity*, London: Sage.

Becker, H. (1932) *Systematic Sociology on the Basis of the Bezeitunglehre and Gebidelehre of Leopold von Wiese*, New York: Wiley.

Becker, H.S. (1963) *Outsiders: Studies in the Sociology of Deviance*, New York: Free Press.

—— (1982) 'Problems of inference and proof in participant observation', in R. McCormick, J. Bynner, P. Clift, M. James and L.M. Brown (eds) *Calling Education to Account*, London: Open University Press/Heinemann.

Beckford, J. (1975) *Religious Organization*, The Hague: Mouton.

—— (1985) *Cult Controversies: The Societal Response to the New Religious Movements*, London: Tavistock.

Bedein, D. (2004) 'What are children learning in Palestinian schools?', *Jewish Chronicle*, http://www.jewishtribune.ca/tribune/jt-041021-14.html, 21 October.

Beechey, V. (1978) 'Women and production: a critical analysis of some sociological theories of women's work', in A. Kuhn and A.M. Wolpe (eds) *Feminism and Marginalism: Women and Modes of Production*, London: Routledge.

Bell, D. (1960) *End of Ideology*, Glencoe, ILL: Illinois Free Press.

—— (1973) *The Coming of Post-Industrial Society: A Venture in Social Forecasting*, London: Heinemann.

—— (1988) *The End of Ideology*, Harvard: Harvard University Press.

Bell, D. and Binnie, J. (2000) *The Sexual Citizen: Queer Politics and Beyond*, Cambridge: Polity.

—— and Klein, R. (1996) *Radically Speaking: Feminism Reclaimed*, London: Zed Books.

Bell, E. and Alden, C. (eds) (2003) *Media Directory 2004* Guardian Newspapers Ltd.

Bellah, R. (1967) 'Civil religion in America', *Daedalus* 96: 1–21.

—— (1975) *The Broken Covenant: American Civil Religion in Time of Trial*, New York: Seabury.

Belsey, A. and Chadwick, R. (eds) (1992) *Ethical Issues in Journalism and the Media*, London: Routledge.

Bem, S. (1993) *The Lenses of Gender*, New Haven, CT: Yale University Press.

Beniger, J.R. (1986) *The Control Revolution*, Harvard: Harvard University Press.

Bennett, T. (1982) 'Theories of media, theories of society', in M. Gurevitch, T. Bennett, J. Curran and J. Woollacott (eds) *Culture, Society and the Media*, London: Methuen.

Berelson, B., Lazarsfeld, P. and McPhee, W. (1954) *Voting: A Study of Opinion Formation in a Presidential Campaign*, Chicago, IL: University of Chicago Press.

Berger, A. (1991) *Media Analysis Techniques*, London: Sage.

Berger, P.L. (1967a) *Invitation to Sociology: A Humanistic Perspective*, Harmondsworth: Penguin.

—— (1967b) *The Social Reality of Religion*, Harmondsworth: Penguin.

—— and Luckmann, T. (1963) 'Sociology of religion and sociology of knowledge', *Sociology and Social Research* 47: 417–27.

Bernardes, J. (1997) *Family Studies: An Introduction*, London: Routledge.

Bernstein, B. (1971) 'On the classification and framing of educational knowledge', in M.F.D. Young (ed.) *Knowledge and Control: New Directions for the Sociology of Education*, London: Collier-Macmillan.

—— (1974) 'Sociology and the sociology of education', in J. Rex (ed.) *Approaches to Sociology*, London: Routledge & Kegan Paul.

—— (1975) *Class, Codes and Control*, vol. 3, London: Routledge & Kegan Paul.

Bernstein, P. (1998) *Against the Gods: The Remarkable Story of Risk*, New York: John Wiley and Sons.

Best, S. (2005) *Understanding Social Divisions*. London: Sage.

Beveridge, W. (1942) *Social Insurance and Allied Services*, London: HMSO.

Beynon, H. (1975) *Working for Ford*, London: Allen Lane.

—— and Nichols, T. (1977) *Living with Capitalism*, London: Routledge.

Bhabha, H.K. (1990) 'The third space: interview with Homi Bhabha', in J. Rutherford (ed.) *Identity: Community, Culture, Difference*, London: Routledge.

Bhat, A., Carr-Hill, R. and Ohri, S. (eds) (1988) *Britain's Black Population: A New Perspective*, 2nd edn, Aldershot: Gower.

Bhattacharyya, G., Ison, L., Blair, M. (2003) *Minority Ethnic Attainment and Participation in Education and Training: The Evidence*, Department for Education and Skills: Research Topic Paper RTP01-03.

Bhavnani, R. (1993) 'Talking racism and the editing of women's studies', in D. Richardson and V. Robinson (eds) *Introducing Women's Studies*, London: Macmillan.

—— (1994) *Black Women in the Labour Market: A Research Review*, Organisation Development Centre, City University, Equal Opportunities Commission.

Biggs, S. (1993) *Understanding Ageing: Images, Attitudes and Professional Practice*, Buckingham: Open University Press.

Billig, M. (1995) *Banal Nationalism*, London: Sage.

Billington, R., Strawbridge, S., Greensides, L. and Fitzsimons, A. (1991) *Culture and Society*, London: Macmillan.

Bilton, T., Bonnett, K., Jones, P., Lawson, T., Skinner, D., Stanworth, M., Webster, A. (2002) *Introductory Sociology*, 4th edn, Basingstoke: Palgrave Macmillan.

Birke, L. (1992) 'In pursuit of difference', in G. Kirkup and L. Smith-Keller (eds) *Inventing Women*, Cambridge: Polity.

Black Manifesto (2005) www.blink.org.uk/bm/manifesto

Blackburn, R. and Mann, M. (1981) 'The dual labour market model', in P. Braham, E. Rhodes and M. Pearn (eds) *Discrimination and Disadvantage in Employment: The Experience of Black Workers*, London: Harper & Row.

Blanchard, S. and Morley, D. (1982) *What's This Channel Four?*, London: Comedia.

Blanchet, T. (1996) *Lost Innocence, Stolen Childhoods*, Dhaka: The University Press Limited.

Blau, P.M. (1963) *The Dynamics of Bureaucracy*, Chicago, IL: University of Chicago Press.

Blauner, R. (1972) *Racial Oppression in America*, New York: Harper & Row.

Blaxter M. (1990) *Health and Lifestyles*, London: Routledge.

Block, N. and Dworkin, G. (eds) (1977) *The IQ Controversy*, London: Quartet.

Bloomfield, F. (1983) *The Book of Chinese Belief*, London: Arrow.

Blumler, J.G. and Katz, E. (eds) (1974) *The Uses of Mass Communications*, London: Sage.

Bocock, R. (1986) *Hegemony*, London: Tavistock.

Boff, L. (1987) *Feet-on-the-Ground-Theology*, Maryknoll, NY: Orbis.

Bond, J., Coleman, P. and Peace, S. (1993) *Ageing in Society: An Introduction to Gerontology*, London: Sage.

Bonnet, M. (1993) 'Child labour in Africa', *International Labour Review* 132(3): 371–91.

Booth, C. (1889) *Life and Labour of the People in London*, London: Williams & Norgate.

Borstein, K. (1994) *Gender Outlaw: On Men, Women and the Rest of Us*, London: Routledge.

Boston Women's Health Book Collective (1998) *Our Bodies Our Selves*, 25th Anniversary edn, New York: Touchstone.

Bottomore, T.B. (1963) *Karl Marx: Early Writings*, London: C.A. Watts.

—— (1965) *Classes in Modern Society*, London: Allen & Unwin.

—— (1983) *A Dictionary of Marxist Thought*, Oxford: Blackwell.

Bouquet, T. (1994) 'Computer porn, a degrading menace', *Reader's Digest*, June.

Bourdieu, P. (1997) 'The forms of capital' in Halsey *et al.* (eds) *Education, Culture, Economy, Society*.

—— and Passeron, J.C. (1977) *Reproduction in Education, Society and Culture*, Beverly Hills, CA: Sage.

Bourne, R. (1991) *Lords of Fleet Street*, London: Unwin Hyman.

Bourque, S. and Grossholtz, J. (1984) 'Politics, an unnatural practice: political science looks at female participation', in J. Siltanen and M. Stanworth (eds) *Women in the Public Sphere: A Critique of Sociology and Politics*, London: Hutchinson.

Bowen-Jones, C. (1992) 'Multiple marriage', *Marie Claire* 9 (July).

Bower, T. (1995) *Maxwell the Outsider*, London: Mandarin.

Bowker, G.C. and Star, S.L. (1999) *Sorting Things Out: Classification and its Consequences*, Cambridge, MA: MIT Press.

Bowler, I. (1993) ' "They're not the same as us": midwives' stereotypes of South Asian descent maternity patients, *Sociology of Health and Illness* 15: 157–78.

Bowles, S. and Gintis, H. (1976) *Schooling in Capitalist America: Educational Reform and the Contradictions of Economic Life*, London: Routledge & Kegan Paul.

Bowling, B. and Phillips, C. (2002) *Racism, Crime and Justice*, Harlow: Longman.

Box, S. (1983) *Power, Crime and Mystification*, London: Tavistock.

Boyden, J. (1990) 'A comparative perspective on the globalization of childhood', in A. James and A. Prout (eds) *Constructing and Reconstructing Childhood: Contemporary Issues in the Sociological Study of Childhood*, Basingstoke: Falmer Press.

—— and Ennew, J. (eds) (1997) *Children in Focus: A Manual for Experiential Learning in Participatory Research with Children*, Stockholm: Rädda Barnen.

——, Ling, B. and Myers, W. (1998) *What Works for Working Children*, Stockholm: Rädda Barnen/ UNICEF.

Bradley, H. (1996) *Fractured Identities: Changing Patterns of Inequality*, Cambridge: Polity.

—— Erickson, M., Stephenson, C. and Williams, S. (2000) *Myths at Work*, Cambridge: Polity.

Brah, A. (1994) 'Time, places, and others: discourses of race, nation, and ethnicity', *Sociology Review* August: 806.

Braham, P. (ed.) (1992) *Racism and Anti-Racism: Inequalities, Opportunities and Policies*, London: Sage.

—— and Janes, L. (2002) *Social Differences and Social Divisions*, Oxford: Oxford University Press.

——, Rhodes, E. and Pearn, M. (eds) (1981) *Discrimination and Disadvantage in Employment: The Experience of Black Workers*, London: Harper & Row.

Bramson, L. (1961) *The Political Content of Sociology*, Princeton, NJ: Princeton University Press.

Brannen, J. and Moss, P. (1991) *Managing Mothers: Dual Earner Households after Maternity Leave*, London: Unwin Hyman.

Branston, G. and Stafford, R. (1996) *The Media Student's Book*, London: Routledge.

Braverman, H. (1974) *Labour and Monopoly Capital: The Degradation of Work within the Twentieth Century*, New York: Monthly Review.

Breen, R. and Goldthorpe, J. (1999) 'Class inequality and meritocracy: a critique of Saunders and an alternative analysis', *British Journal of Sociology*, 50: 1–27.

Brent Community Health Council (1981) *Black People and the Health Service*, Brent Community Health Council.

Briault, E.W.H. (1976) 'A distributed system of educational administration: an international viewpoint', *International Review of Education* 22(4): 429–39.

Brierley, P. and Hiscock, V. (eds) (1993) *UK Christian Handbook 1994–5*, London: Christian Research Association.

Brierly, S. (1998) 'Advertising and the new media environment', in Briggs, A. and Cobley, P. (eds).

Briggs, A. (1961) *The Birth of Broadcasting*, Oxford: Oxford University Press.

—— (1967) 'The language of "class" in early-nineteenth-century England', in A. Briggs and J. Saville (eds) *Essays in Labour History*, London: Macmillan.

—— and Cobley, P. (eds) (1998) *The Media: An Introduction*, Harlow: Longman.

Brittan, A. (1989) *Masculinity and Power*, New York: Blackwell.

Brittan, L. (1983) *The Role and Limits of Government*, London: Temple Smith.

Broadbridge, A. (1991) 'Images and goods: women in retailing', in A. Redclift and T. Sinclair (eds) *Working Women: International Perspectives on Labour and Gender Ideology*, London: Routledge.

Broadcasting Standards Council (BSC) (1994) *Radio and Audience Attitudes*, London: BSC.

Broadfoot, P. (1988) 'Educational research: two cultures and three estates', *British Educational Research Journal* 14(1).

Brod, H. and Kaufman, M. (1994) *Theorizing Masculinity*, London: Sage.

Broom, L., Selznick, P. and Darroch, D. (1981) *Sociology*, New York: Harper & Row.

Brown, C. (1992) ' "Same difference": the persistence of racial disadvantage in the British employment market', in P. Braham (ed.) *Racism and Anti-Racism: Inequalities, Opportunities and Policies*, London: Sage.

Brown, P. (1989) 'Education', in P. Brown and R. Sparks, *Beyond Thatcherism: Social Policy, Politics and Society*, Milton Keynes: Open University Press.

—— and Scase, R. (eds) (1991) *Poor Work: Disadvantage and the Division of Labour*, Buckingham: Open University Press.

Brown, R. (1992) *Understanding Industrial Organizations*, London: Routledge.

Brown, R.K. (ed.) (1997) *The Changing Shape of Work*, Basingstoke: Macmillan.

Brownmiller, S. (1976) *Against Our Will: Men, Women and Rape*, Harmondsworth: Penguin.

Bruhn, J.G. and Wolf, S. (1979) *The Roseto Story*, Norman: University of Oklahoma Press.

Bryan, B. Dadzie, S. and Scafe, S. (1985) *The Heart of the Race*, London: Virago.

——, —— and —— (1987) 'Learning to resist: black women and education', in G. Weiner and M. Arnot (eds) *Gender under Scrutiny*, London: Hutchinson.

Bryson, V. (1992) *Feminist Political Theory: An Introduction*, London: Macmillan.

Buckingham, D. (1996) *Moving Images*, Manchester: Manchester University Press.

Buckley, W.F., Jr (1959) *Up from Liberalism*, New York: McDonnell, Oblensky.

Budge, I., Crewe, I., McKay, D. and Newton, K. (1998) *The New British Politics*, Harlow: Longman.

Bunch, C. (1981) 'Not for lesbians only', in The Quest Book Committee, *Building Feminist Theory: Essays from Quest*, London: Longman.

Burawoy, M. (1985) *The Politics of Production*, London: Verso.

Burchill, J. (1985) 'The last sacred cow', *New Society* 20–27 December.

Burnet, D. (1992) 'Freedom of speech, the media and the law', in A. Belsey and R. Chadwick (eds) *Ethical Issues in Journalism and the Media*, London: Routledge.

Burney, E. (1988) *Steps to Racial Equality: Positive Action in a Negative Climate*, London: Runnymede Trust.

Burnham, J. (1945) *The Managerial Revolution*, Harmondsworth: Penguin.

Burns, T. (ed.) (1969) *Industrial Man*, Harmondsworth: Penguin.

—— (1977) *The BBC: Public Institution and Private World*, London: Macmillan.

Burns, T. (1992) *Erving Goffman*, London: Routledge.

Burrows, R. and Loader, B. (eds) (1994) *Towards a Post-Fordist Welfare State?*, London: Routledge.

Burt, C. (1925) *The Young Delinquent*, London: University of London.

Burtonwood, N. (1986) *The Culture Concept of Educational Studies*, Windsor: NFER Nelson.

Bury, M. (1982) 'Chronic illness as biographical disruption', *Sociology of Health and Illness* 4, 167–82.

Busfield, J. (1996) *Men and Madness*, Basingstoke: Macmillan.

Butler, D. and Kavanagh, D. (1997) *The British General Election of 1997*, London: St Martin's Press.

—— and —— (2001) *The British General Election of 2001*, London: Palgrave Macmillan.

—— and Stokes, D. (1974) *Political Change in Britain: The Evolution of Electoral Choice*, 2nd edn, London: Macmillan.

Butler, J. (1990) *Gender Trouble: Feminism and the Subversion of Identity*, London: Routledge.

—— (1993) *Bodies That Matter: On the Discursive Limits of Sex*, London: Routledge.

Butterworth, D. (1993) 'Wanking in cyberspace: the development of computer porn', *Trouble and Strife* 27.

Button, J. (1995) *The Radicalism Handbook*, London: Cassell.

Byrne, D., Williamson, B. and Fletcher, B. (1975) *The Poverty of Education: A Study of the Politics of Opportunity*, Oxford: Martin Robertson.

Byrne, E. (1978) *Women and Education*, London: Tavistock.

CACE (Central Advisory Council for Education) (1954) *Early Leaving*, Gurney-Dixon Report, London: HMSO.

—— (1959) *15 to 18*, Crowther Report, London: HMSO.

—— (1963) *Half our Future*, Newsom Report, London: HMSO.

—— (1967) *Children and their Primary Schools*, Plowden Report, London: HMSO.

Calcutt (1990) *Report of the Committee on Privacy*, London: HMSO.

Callinicos, A. (1990) *Against Postmodernism*, London: St Martin's Press.

—— (1993) *Race and Class*, London: Bookmarks.

—— (2001) *Against the Third Way*. Polity.

—— and Harman, C. (1987) *The Changing Working Class*, London: Bookmarks.

Camera, Dom Helder, *Sentences and Thoughts*, www.domhelder.com

Campbell, C. (1971) *Toward a Sociology of Irreligion*, London: Macmillan.

Cantril, H. (1940) *The Invasion from Mars: A Study in the Psychology of Panic*, Princeton: Princeton University Press.

Carby, H.V. (1982a) 'White women listen! Black feminism and the boundaries of sisterhood', in Centre for Contemporary Cultural Studies, *The Empire Strikes Back*, London: Hutchinson.

—— (1982b) 'Schooling in Babylon', in Centre for Contemporary Cultural Studies, *The Empire Strikes Back*, London: Hutchinson.

Carter, R.T. and Helms, J.E. (1990) 'White racial identity: attitudes and cultural values', in J.E. Helms (ed.) *Black and White Racial Identity: Theory, Research and Practice*. Westport, Conn.: Greenwood Press.

Carvel, J. (2004) 'Agencies defy code on poaching foreign nurses', *The Guardian*, 30.12.2004.

Cashmore, E. (1984) *No Future: Youth and Society*, London: Heinemann.

—— (1994) *. . . and there was Telev!s!on*, London: Routledge.

—— and McLoughlin, E. (eds) (1991) *Out of Order: Policing Black People*, London: Routledge.

—— and Troyna, B. (1990 [1983]) *Introduction to Race Relations*, 2nd edn, London: Falmer.

Castells, M. (1989) *The Information Age: Economy, Society & Culture*, London: Blackwell.

—— (1996) *The Rise of the Network Society*, Oxford: Blackwell.

—— (2000) *The Rise of the Network Society*, 2nd edn, Oxford: Blackwell.

Castles, S. and Kosack, G. (1972) 'The function of labour immigration in Western European capitalism', in P. Braham, E. Rhodes and M. Pearn (eds) (1981) *Discrimination and Disadvantage in Employment: The Experience of Black Workers*, London: Harper & Row.

—— and —— (1973) *Immigrant Workers and Class Structure in Western Europe*, Oxford: Oxford University Press.

Cavadino, M. and Dignan, J. (1993) *The Penal System: An Introduction*, London: Sage.

Cavadino, J. and Dignan, M. (2002) *The Penal System*, 3rd edn, London: Sage.

Centre for Contemporary Cultural Studies (1981) *Unpopular Education: Schooling and Social Democracy in England since 1944*, London: Hutchinson.

—— (1982) *The Empire Strikes Back: Race and Racism in 70s Britain*, London: Hutchinson.

Chadwick, B.A., Bahr, H.M. and Albrecht, A.L. (1984) *Social Science Research Methods*, London: Prentice Hall.

Chambers, J. (2000) *Gender and Globalisation*, Department for International Development, with IDS/BRIDGE, DFID.

Chapkis, W. (1986) *Beauty Secrets*, London: Women's Press.

Chappell, A.L. (1998) 'Still out in the cold: people with learning difficulties and the social model of disability', in T. Shakespeare (ed.) *The Disability Reader*, Social Science Perspectives, London: Cassell.

Charles, N. and Kerr, M. (1988) *Women, Food and Families*, Manchester: Manchester University Press.

Charlesworth, S. (2000) *A Phenomenology of Working Class Experience*. Cambridge: Cambridge University Press.

Charmaz, K. (1983) 'Loss of self: a fundamental form of suffering in the chronically ill', *Sociology of Health and Illness* 5.

Cheal, D. (2002) *Sociology of Family Life*, Basingstoke: Palgrave Macmillan.

Chesney, K. (1991) *The Victorian Underworld*, Harmondsworth: Penguin.

Chippendale, P. and Horrie, C. (1992) *Stick It Up Your Punter: The Rise and Fall of the Sun*, London: Mandarin.

Chomsky, N. (1972) 'The fallacy of Richard Herrnstein's IQ', *Social Policy* May–June.

—— (1989) *Necessary Illusions: Thought Control in Democratic Societies*, Pluto Press.

Chopp, R. (1986) *The Praxis of Suffering: An Interpretation of Liberation and Political Theories*, Maryknoll, NY: Orbis.

Cicourel, A.V. (1976) *The Social Organization of Juvenile Justice*, London: Heinemann.

Clark, E. (1873) *Sex in Education*, London.

Clarke, H., Chandler, J. and Barry, J. (eds) (1994) *Organizations and Identities*, London: Chapman & Hall.

Clarke, J., Critcher, C., and Johnson, R. (eds) (1979) *Working Class Culture Studies in Theory and History*, London: Hutchinson.

Clarke, N. and Riddell, E. (1992) *The Sky Barons*, London: Methuen.

Clay, J. (1839) 'Criminal statistics of Preston', *Journal of the Statistical Society of London* 2.

Cloward, R.A. and Ohlin, L.E. (1961) *Delinquency and Opportunity*, New York: Free Press.

Coard, B. (1971) *How the West Indian Child is Made Educationally Subnormal in the British School System*, London: New Beacon.

Cockburn, C. (1983) *Brothers: Male Dominance and Technological Change*, London: Pluto.

—— (1985) *Machinery of Dominance*, London: Pluto.

—— (1987) *Women, Trade Unions and Political Parties*, Fabian Research Series 349, London: The Fabian Society.

—— (1993) *Gender and Technology in the Making*, London: Sage.

Cockerell, M., Hennessy, P. and Walker, D. (1984) *Sources Close to the Prime Minister*, London: Macmillan.

Coe, T. (1992) *The Key to the Men's Club*, Bristol: IM Books.

Cohen, A.K. (1955) *Delinquent Boys: The Culture of the Gang*, New York: Free Press.

Cohen, R. (1994) *Frontiers of Identity: The British and the Others*, Harlow: Longman Sociology Series.

Cohen, R. and Kennedy, P. (2000) *Global Sociology*, Palgrave, Macmillan.

Cohen, S. (1972) *Folk Devils and Moral Panics: The Creation of the Mods and Rockers*, MacGibbon & Kee: London.

—— and Kennedy, P. (2000) *Global Sociology*, London: Palgrave Macmillan.

Cohn, T. (1988) 'Sambo: a study in name calling', in E. Kelly and T. Cohn, *Racism in Schools: New Research Evidence*, Stoke-on-Trent: Trentham.

Cole, B. (1988) *Princess Smartypants*, London: HarperCollins.

Coleman, C. and Moynihan, J. (1996) *Understanding Crime Data: Haunted by the Dark Figure*, Buckingham: Open University Press.

Coleman, S., Jemphrey, A., Scraton, P. and Skidmore, P. (1990) *Hillsborough and After: The Liverpool Experience*, Edge Hill: Centre for Studies in Crime and Social Justice.

Coleridge, N. (1994) *Paper Tigers: Latest Greatest Newspaper Tycoons and How They Won the World*, London: Mandarin.

Colhoun, H. and Prescott, C. (1996) *Health Survey for England 1994*, London: HMSO.

Collier, R. (1992) 'The new man: fact or fad', *Achilles' Heel* 14: 34–8.

—— (2002) 'The dirty little secret of credential inflation', the Department of Sociology, University of Pennsylvania, *Chronicle of Higher Education*, 27 September.

Collins, R., Garnham, N. and Locksley, G. (1988) *The Economics of Television: The UK Case*, London: Sage.

Collinson, C., Collinson, D. and Knight, C. (1992) *Managing to Discriminate*, London: Routledge.

Connell, R.W. (1987) *Gender and Power*, Cambridge: Polity.

—— (2001) *The Men and the Boys*, University of California Press.

Connolly, P., Smith, A. and Kelly, B. (2002) 'Too young to notice?: the cultural and political awareness of 3–6 year olds in Northern Ireland', Belfast: Northern Ireland Community Relations Council.

Cook, D. (1989) *Rich Law, Poor Law: Different Responses to Tax and Supplementary Benefit Fraud*, Milton Keynes: Open University Press.

Cooper, D. (1972) *The Death of the Family*, Harmondsworth: Penguin.

—— (1998) 'Regard between strangers: diversity, equality and the recognition of public space' *Critical Social Policy* 18: 465–92.

Coppock, V. (1997) 'Families in crisis' in P. Scraton (ed.) *Childhood in Crisis*, London: UCL Press.

Corby, B. (2000) *Child Abuse: Towards a Knowledge Base*, Buckingham: Open University Press.

Coser, L.A. and Rosenberg, B. (1969) *Sociological Theory: A Book of Readings* (3rd edn), London: Macmillan.

Cowie, J., Cowie, S. and Slater, E. (1968) *Delinquency in Girls*, London: Hutchinson.

Cox, O.C. (1970) *Caste, Class and Race*, New York: Monthly Review.

Coyle, J. (1999) 'Exploring the meaning of "Dissatisfaction" with health care: the importance of "Personal Identity Threat"', *Sociology of Health and Illness* 18(1): 17–44.

Craft, M. and Craft, A. (1983) 'The participation of ethnic minority pupils in further and higher education', *Educational Review* 25(1).

Cragg, C. (1992) *Media Education in the Primary School*, London: Routledge.

Craib, I. (1992) *Modern Social Theory*, Hemel Hempstead: Harvester Wheatsheaf.

CRE (Commission for Racial Equality) (1984) *Race and Council Housing in Hackney: A Report of Formal Investigation*, London: CRE.

—— (1987a) *Formal Investigation: Chartered Accountancy Training Contracts*, London: CRE.

—— (1987b) *Employment of Graduates from Ethnic Minorities: A Research Report*, London: CRE.

—— (1988) *Homelessnesss and Discrimination*, London: CRE.

—— (1989) *Racial Discrimination in Liverpool City Council: A Report of Formal Investigation in the Housing Department*, London: CRE.

—— (1990) *Sorry, It's Gone*, London: CRE.

Crewe, I. (1992) Why did Labour lose (yet again)? *Politics Review*, 2(1), No. 1, September 1992.

—— with Norris, P., Denver, D. and Broughton, D. (1992) *British Elections and Parties Yearbook 1992*, Hemel Hempstead: Harvester Wheatsheaf.

Crisell, A. (1988) *Understanding Radio*, London: Methuen.

Crisell, A. (1994) *Understanding Radio*, 2nd edn, London: Routledge.

—— (1997) *An Introductory History of British Broadcasting*, London: Routledge.

—— (1998) 'Public service, commercialism and the paradox of choice', in A. Briggs and P. Cobley (eds). *The Media: An Introduction*, Harlow: Longman.

—— (2002) 'Radio, Commercialism and the Paradox of Choice' in Briggs, A. and Cobley, P. (2002)

—— H. (1992) *White-Collar Crime: Criminal Justice and Criminology*, Buckingham: Open University Press.

—— (1998) *Crime and Society in Britain*, Harlow: Addison Wesley Longman.

Crompton, R. (1989) 'Class theory and gender', *British Journal of Sociology* 40(4): 565–87.

—— (1993) *Class and Stratification*, Cambridge: Polity.

—— and Jones, G. (1984) *White-Collar Proletariat: Deskilling and Gender in Clerical Work*, London: Macmillan.

Crook, S., Pakulshi, J. and Waters, M. (1992) *Postmodernisation Change in Advanced Societies*, London: Sage.

Crowley, H. and Himmelweit, S. (eds) (1992) *Knowing Women*, Buckingham: Open University Press.

Cuff, E.C., Sharrock, W.W. and Francis, D.W. (1990) *Perspectives in Sociology*, 3rd edn, London: Unwin Hyman.

——, —— and —— (1998) *Perspectives in Sociology*, 4th edn, London: Routledge.

Cumberbatch, G. (1998) 'Media effects: the continuing controversy', in Briggs, A. and Cobley P. (eds) (1998) *The Media: An Introduction*, Harlow: Longman.

—— and Howitt, D. (1989) *A Measure of Uncertainty: The Effects of the Mass Media*, London: John Libbey.

Cumming, E. and Henry, W. (1961) *Growing Old: The Process of Disengagement*, New York: Basic Books.

Curran, J. and Gurevitch, M. (eds) (1991) *Mass Media and Society*, London: Edward Arnold.

——, Gurevitch, M. and Woollacott, J. (eds) (1977) *Mass Communication and Society*, London: Edward Arnold/Open University Press.

—— and Seaton, J. (1991) *Power Without Responsibility: The Press and Broadcasting in Britain*, London: Routledge.

—— and Seaton, J. (1997) *Power without Responsibility*, London: Routledge.

Curtice, J. (1994) 'Political Sociology 1945–92', in J. Obelkevich and R. Catterall (eds) (1994) *Understanding Post-War British Society*, London: Routledge.

Curtice, J. and Steed, P.M. (1997) Appendix 2 in Butler and D. Kavanagh (1997) *The British ⌐l Election of 1997*, London: Macmillan.

⌐84) *Ireland: The Propaganda War*,

Dahl, R.A. (1958) '*A Critique of the Ruling Elite Model*', *APSR*, 52.

—— (1961) *Who Governs?*, New Haven, CT: Yale University Press.

Dahrendorf, R. (1959) *Class and Class Conflict in an Industrial Society*, London: Routledge & Kegan Paul.

—— (1992) 'Footnotes to the discussion', in D. Smith (ed.) *Understanding the Underclass*, London: Policy Studies Institute.

Dalley, G. (1996) *Ideologies of Caring*, London: Macmillan.

Dalton, R. and Keuchler, M. (eds) (1990) *Challenging the Political Order: New Social and Political Movements in Western Democracies*, Oxford: Oxford University Press.

Daly, M. (1991) *Beyond God the Father*, London: Women's Press.

—— and Wilson, M. (1988) *Homicide*, New York: Aldine de Gruyter.

Daniel, P. and Ivatts, J. (1998) *Children and Social Policy*, Basingstoke: Macmillan.

Daniel, W.W. (1968) *Racial Discrimination in England*, Harmondsworth: Penguin.

Darwin, C. (1968 [1859]) *On the Origin of Species*, Harmondsworth: Penguin.

Daud, F. (1985) *Minah Karan: The Truth about Malaysian Factory Girls*, Kuala Lumpur: Berita.

David, M. (1993) 'The citizen's voice in education: parents, gender and educational reform', paper presented at International Conference on the Public Sphere, University of Salford, January.

David, T. (1993) *Child Protection and Early Years Teachers*, Buckingham: Open University Press.

Davie, G. (1994) *Religion in Britain since 1945: Believing Without Belonging*, Oxford: Blackwell.

Davies, B. (2002, originally 1998), 'Becoming Male or Female', (from *Frogs, Snails and Feminist Tales*, Sydney: Allen & Unwin) in S. Jackson and S. Scott (eds), *Gender: A Sociological Reader*, London: Routledge.

Davis, K. (1949) *Human Society*, London: Macmillan.

—— (2003) *Dubious Equalities: Cultural Studies on Cosmetic Surgery*, Oxford: Rowman and Littlefield.

—— and Moore, W.E. (1967) 'Some principles of stratification', in R. Bendix and S.M. Lipset (eds) *Class, Status and Power*, 2nd edn, London: Routledge & Kegan Paul.

Dawkins, R. (1976) *The Selfish Gene*, Oxford: Oxford University Press.

—— (1977) 'Sex and the immortal gene', *Vogue*.

Debray, R. (1977) 'Marxism and the national question', interview, *New Left Review* 105: 25–41.

Deem, R. (1978) *Women and Schooling*, London: Routledge & Kegan Paul.

Delbridge, R. (1998) *Life on the Line: The Workplace Experience of Lean Production and the 'Japanese' Model*, Oxford: Oxford University Press.

Delphy, C. (1984), *Close to Home: A Materialist Analysis of Women's Oppression*, London: Hutchinson.

Demaine, J. and Entwistle, H. (1996) *Beyond Communitarianism: Citizenship, Politics and Education*, Basingstoke: Macmillan.

Dennis, N., Henriques, F. and Slaughter, C. (1956) *Coal is our Life*, London: Eyre & Spottiswoode.

Denscombe, M. (ed.) (2002, 1998, 1997, 1995, 1994, 1993, 1992) *Sociology Update*, Leicester: Olympus.

Denver, D. (1989) *Elections and Voting Behaviour in Britain*, London: Philip Allan.

DES (Department of Education and Science) (1965) *The Organization of Secondary Education*, Circular 10/65, London: HMSO.

—— (1988) *Advancing A Levels*, Higginson Report, London: HMSO.

—— (1992) *Statistics of Education: Teachers in Service, England and Wales 1990*, London: HMSO.

Devine, D. (2003) *Children, Power and Schooling: How Childhood is Structured in the Primary School*, Stoke on Trent: Trentham Books.

Devine, F. (1994) ' "Affluent Workers" revisited', *Sociology Review* 3(3): 6–9.

Devine, F. (2004) *Class Practices: How Parents Help Their Children Get Good Jobs*. Cambridge: Cambridge University Press.

Dex, S. (1985) *The Sexual Division of Work*, Hemel Hempstead: Harvester.

DHSS (Department of Health and Social Security) (1988) *Working Together*, London: HMSO.

Di Marco, A.D. and Di Marco, H. (2003), 'Investigating cybersociety: a consideration of the ethical and practical issues surrounding online research in chat rooms', in Yvonne Jewkes (ed.) *Dot.cons: Crime, Deviance and Identity on the Internet*, Devon: Willan.

Dickens, R., Gregg, P. and Wadsworth, J. (2004) *The Labour Market Under New Labour: The State of Working Britain*, London: Palgrave Macmillan.

Dimmock, B. (2004) 'Young people and family life: apocalypse now or business as usual?' in J. Roche, S. Tucker, R. Thomson and R. Flynn (eds) *Youth in Society*, 2nd edn, London: Sage.

Disraeli, B. (1835) *Vindication of the English Constitution*, London.

Dizard, W. (1982) *The Coming Information Age: An Overview of Technology, Economics and Politics*, London: Longman.

Dobash, R.E. and Dobash, R.P. (1992) *Women, Violence and Social Change*, London: Routledge.

DoH (Department of Health) (1999) *Health and Personal Social Services Statistics for England, 1999*, London: TSO.

Donald, R.R. (1992), 'Masculinity and Machismo in Hollywood War Films', in S. Craig (ed.) *Men, Masculinities and the Media*, London: Sage.

Donaldson, F. (1976) *Edward VIII*, London: Futura.

Dostoevsky, F. (1962 [1860]) *The House of the Dead*, London: Dent.

Douglas, J.W.B. (1964) *The Home and the School*, London: MacGibbon & Kee.

Douglas, S. (1995) *Where the Girls Are: Growing Up Female with the Mass Media*, London: Penguin.

Doward, J. and Hinsliff, G. (2004) 'British hostility to Muslims "could trigger riots" ', *Observer*, 30 May.

Dowmunt, A. (ed.) (1994) *Channels of Resistance*, London: British Film Institute.

Dowse, R.E. and Hughes J.A. (1986) *Political Sociology*, 2nd edn, Chichester: Wiley.

Doyal, L. (1995) *What Makes Women Sick: Gender and the Political Economy of Health*, Basingstoke: Macmillan.

—— (ed.) (1998) *Women and Health Services: An Agenda for Change*, Buckingham: Open University Press.

—— and Harris, R. (1986) *Empiricism, Explanation and Rationality*, London: Routledge & Kegan Paul.

——, Hunt, G. and Mellor, G. (1981) 'Your life in their hands: migrant workers in the National Health Service', *Critical Social Policy* 1(2): 54–71.

Doyle, G. (2004) 'Changes in media ownership', *Sociology Review*, February, vol. 13 no. 3.

Drakulic, S. (2004) *They Would Never Hurt A Fly: War Criminals on Trial in the Hague*, London: Abacus.

Draper, A. (1991) 'Liberal studies for life', *Guardian* 13 August.

Drever, F., Whitehead, M. and Roden, M. (1996) 'Current patterns and trends in male mortality by social class (based on occupation)' *Population Trends* 86 (Winter) 15–21.

Drew, D. and Gray, J. (1989) 'The fifth-year examination achievements of black young people in England and Wales', University of Sheffield Research Centre.

—— and —— (1991) 'The black–white gap in examination results: a statistical critique of a decade's research', *New Community* 17(2).

Driver, G. (1980) 'How West Indians do better at school', *New Society* 17 January.

DSS (Department of Social Security) (1994) *Households Below Average Income*, London: HMSO.

Duelli-Klein, R. (1983) 'How to do what we want to do: thoughts about feminist methodology', in G. Bowles and R. Duelli-Klein (eds) *Theories of Women's Studies*, London: Routledge.

Duncombe, J. and Marsden, D. (1998) ' "Stepford wives" and "hollow men"?: Doing emotion work, doing gender and "authenticity" in intimate heterosexual relationships' in G. Bendelow and S.J. Williams (eds) *Emotions and Social Life: Critical Themes and Contemporary Issues*, London: Routledge.

Dunne, G. (1999) 'A passion for "sameness": sexuality and gender accountability', in E. Silva and C. Smart (eds) *The New Family?*, London: Sage.

Dunleavy, P. (1980) *Urban Political Analysis*, London: Macmillan.

Durkheim, E. (1963 [1897]) *Suicide: A Study in Sociology*, London: Routledge & Kegan Paul.

—— (1956 [1903]) *Education and Sociology*, New York: Free Press.

—— (1960 [1893]) *The Division of Labour in Society*, New York: Free Press.

—— (1976 [1912]) *The Elementary Forms of the Religious Life*, trans. J.W. Swain, London: Allen & Unwin.

—— (1964 [1895]) *The Rules of Sociological Method*, New York: The Free Press.

Dworkin, A. (1983) *Pornography: Men Possessing Women*, London: Women's Press.

Dynes, R. (2003) 'Finding order in disorder: continuities in the 9–11 response', *International Journal of Mass Emergencies and Disasters*, 21(3): 9–23.

Easthope, A. (1986) *What's a Man Gotta Do: The Masculine Myth in Popular Culture*, London: Paladin.

Easton, D. (1953) *The Political System: An Inquiry into the State of Political Science*, New York.

Economist (2004) 'What's it worth?', 15.1.04.

Eden, F.M. (1797) *The State of the Poor*, London: Frank Cass.

Edgell, S. (1993) *Class*, London: Routledge.

Edley, N. and Wetherell, M. (1994) *Men in Perspective*, London: Harvester Wheatsheaf.

Edwards, M. (1996) 'New approaches to children and development: introduction and overview', *Journal of International Development* 8(6): 813–27.

Edwards, R. (1979) *Contested Terrain*, London: Heinemann.

—— (1993) *Mature Women Students*, London: Taylor & Francis.

Edwards, V. (1976) *West Indian Language: Attitudes and the School*, London: National Association for Multiracial Education.

—— (1979) *The West Indian Language Issue in British Schools*, London: Routledge & Kegan Paul.

Eggleston, J., Dunn, D. and Anjali, M. (1986) *Education for Some: The Educational and Vocational Experiences of 15–18 Year Old Members of Ethnic Minority Groups*, Stoke-on-Trent: Trentham.

EGRIS (European Group for Integrated Social Research) (2001) 'Misleading trajectories: transition dilemmas of young adults in Europe', *Journal of Youth Studies* 4(1): 101–18.

Ehrenreich, B. (2002) 'Maid to order', in B. Ehrenreich and A.R. Hochschild (eds) *Global Woman: Nannies, Maids and Sex Workers in the New Economy*, London: Granta.

Ehrlich, C. (1976) 'The conditions of feminist research', Research Group One, Report 21, Baltimore, MD.

Eisenstadt, S. (1956) *From Generation to Generation: Age Groups and Social Structure*, New York: Free Press.

Elder, G. (1978) 'Family History and the Life Course', in T. Hareven (ed.) *Transitions: The Family and the Life Course in Historical Perspective*, London: Academic Press.

Elias, N. (1996), *The Germans: Power Struggles and the Development of Habitus in the Nineteenth and Twentieth Centuries*, ed. by M. Schröter; trans. from the German and with a preface by E. Dunning and S. Mennell, Cambridge: Polity Press.

Elliot, F.R. (1986) *The Family: Change or Continuity*, London: Macmillan.

Elliot, L. and Atkinson, D. (1999) *The Age of Insecurity*, London: Verso.

Elliot, P. (1974) 'Uses and gratifications research: a critique and sociological alternative', reprinted in Marris, P. and Thornham, S. (1997) (eds) *Media Studies*. A reader, Edinburgh: Edinburgh University Press.

Elster, J. (1985) *Making Sense of Marx*, Cambridge: Cambridge University Press.

Engels, F. (1958 [1845]) *The Condition of the Working Class in England*, Oxford: Blackwell.

—— (1972 [1884]) *The Origin of the Family, Private Property and the State*, London: Lawrence & Wishart.

—— (1995) 'Health: 1844', in B. Davey, A. Gray and C. Seale (eds) *Health and Disease: A reader*, Buckingham: Open University Press.

EOC (Opportunities Commission) (1995) *New Earnings Survey*, Manchester: EOC.

—— (1998) *EOC Analysis of Labour Force Survey Spring 1997*, London: Office for National Statistics.

Epsom, J. (1978) 'The mobile health clinic: a report on the first year's work', in D. Tuckett and J. Kaufert (eds) *Readings in Medical Sociology*, London: Tavistock.

Etzioni, A. (1993) *The Spirit of Community: The Reinvention of American Society*, New York: Simon & Schuster.

Evans, J. (1995) *Feminist Theory Today: An Introduction to Second Wave Feminism*, London: Sage.

Evans-Pritchard, E.E. (1976) *Witchcraft, Oracles and Magic among the Azande*, Oxford: Oxford University Press.

Ewing, K.D. and Gearty, C.A. (1990) *Freedom under Thatcher: Civil Liberties in Modern Britain*, Oxford: Clarendon.

Ewington, T. (2004) 'Red tops need blue-sky thinking', *Financial Times*, March 9, http://www.humancapital.co.uk/ press_ft_9mar04_print.htm

Eyre, A. (1989) 'After Hillsborough: an ethnographic account of life in Liverpool in the first few weeks', unpublished paper.

—— (1995) 'Religion, politics and development in Malaysia', in R.H. Roberts (ed.) *Religion and the Transformations of Capitalism: Comparative Approaches*, London: Routledge.

Eysenck, H.J. (1971) *Race, Intelligence and Education*, London: Temple Smith.

Fairbrother, H. (1983) 'Who's the brightest of them all?', *Radio Times* 19–25 February: 8–9.

Fanning, D. (2004) 'Caught in the Net', *Macworld*, June.

Fawcett, H. and Pichaud, D. (1984) *The Unequal Struggle*.

Featherstone, M. (1991a) *Consumer Culture and Post Modernism*, London: Sage.

—— (1991b) *Global Culture: Nationalism, Globalization and Modernity*, London: Sage.

—— and Hepworth, M. (1989) 'Ageing and old age: reflections on the postmodern life course', in B. Bytheway, T. Keil, P. Allatt and A. Bryman (eds) *Becoming and Being Old: Sociological Approaches to Later Life*, London: Sage.

Ferguson, M. (1985) *Forever Feminine: Women's Magazines and the Cult of Femininity*, London: Heinemann.

Ferguson, N. (2004) *Empire*, London: Allen Lane.

Festinger, L., Riecken, H.W. and Schachter, S. (1956) *When Prophecy Fails: A Social and Psychological Study of a Modern Group that Predicted the Destruction of the World*, London: Harper & Row.

Feuer, L.S. (ed.) (1969) *Marx and Engels: Basic Writings on Politics and Philosophy*, London: Fontana.

Feuerbach, L. (1957) *The Essence of Christianity*, London and New York: Harper.

Fevre, R. (1984) *Cheap Labour and Racial Discrimination*, Aldershot: Gower.

—— (1992) *The Sociology of Labour Markets*, Hemel Hempstead: Harvester Wheatsheaf.

Field, D. (1992) 'Elderly people in British society', *Sociology Review* April: 16–20.

Field, F. (1989) *Losing Out: The Emergence of Britain's Underclass*, Oxford: Blackwell.

—— and Hankin, P. (1971) *Black Britons*, Oxford: Oxford University Press.

Finch, J. and Groves, D. (1983) *A Labour of Love: Women, Work and Caring*, London: Routledge & Kegan Paul.

Fincham, R. and Rhodes, P.S. (1994) *The Individual, Work and Organization*, Oxford: Oxford University Press.

Fine, M., Weis, L., Powell, L.C. and Wong, L.M. (eds) (1997) *Off White: Readings on Race, Power and Society*, London: Routledge.

Fineman, S. (1987) *Unemployment: Personal and Social Consequences*, London: Tavistock.

Finkelstein, V. (1980) *Know your Own Approach: The Handicapped Person in the Community* (Course Workbook), Milton Keynes: Open University Press.

Fiorenza, E.S. and Copeland, M.S. (eds) (1994) *Violence Against Women*, London: SCM Press.

Firth, R. (1956) *Two Studies of Kinship in London*, London: Athlone.

Fiske, J. (1987) *Television Culture*, London: Routledge.

—— (1989) *Reading the Popular*, London: Unwin Hyman.

—— and Hartley, J. (1978) *Reading Television*, London: Methuen.

Flax, J. (1990) *Thinking Fragments: Psychoanalysis, Feminism and Postmodernism in the Contemporary West*, University of California Press.

Fleming, D. (1993) *Media Teaching*, London: Blackwell.

Fletcher, A. (1999) *Gender, Sex and Subordination in England, 1500–1800*, London: Yale University Press.

Fletcher, R. (1988) *The Abolitionists: The Family and Marriage under Attack*, London: Routledge.

Fletcher, W. (1992) *A Glittering Haze*, London: NTC.

Flew, A. (1984) *Education, Race and Revolution*, Centre for Policy Studies London.

Flude, M. and Ahier, J. (1974) *Educability, Schools and Ideology*, London: Croom Helm.

Fogelson, R.M. (1971) *Violence as Protest: A Study of Riots in Ghettos*, New York: Doubleday.

Foreman, S. and Dallos, R. (1993) 'Domestic violence' in R. Dallos and E. McLaughlin (eds) *Social Problems and the Family*, London: Sage.

Foucault, M. (1965) *Madness and Civilisation*, New York: Random House.

—— (1967) *Madness and Civilisation: A History of Insanity in the Age of Reason*, London: Tavistock.

—— (1976) *The Birth of the Clinic*, London: Tavistock.

—— (1977 [1975]) *Discipline and Punish: The Birth of the Prison*, London: Allen Lane.

—— (1981 [1976]) *The History of Sexuality Volume 1: An Introduction*, Harmondsworth: Penguin.

Fouch, S. (2004) 'Globalisation and health', *Christian Medical Fellowship Files: No. 24*. http://www.cmf.org.uk

Fox, A. (1974) *Beyond Contract: Work, Power and Trust Relations*, London: Faber & Faber.

Francis, M. (1988) 'Issues in the fight against the Education Bill', *Race and Class* 29(3).

Frank, A.G. (1967) *Capitalism and Underdevelopment in Latin America*, New York: Monthly Review.

Frankenburg, R. (1993) *White Women, Race Matters: The Social Construction of Whiteness*, Minneapolis: University of Minnesota Press.

Franklin, B. and Murphy, D. (1991) *What News? The Market, Politics and the Local Press*, London: Routledge.

Franks, S. (1998) *Having None of It: Women, Men and the Future of Work*, London: Granta.

Fraser, R. (ed.) (1968) *Work: Twenty Personal Accounts*, Harmondsworth: Penguin.

Freeman, T. (2003) 'Loving fathers or deadbeat dads: the crisis of fatherhood in popular culture', in S. Earle and G. Letherby (eds) *Gender, Identity and Reproduction: Social Perspectives*, Basingstoke: Palgrave Macmillan.

Freidson, E. (1970) *Profession of Medicine: A Study of the Sociology of Applied Knowledge*, New York: Dodd Mead.

Freire, P. (1972 [1970a]) *Pedagogy of the Oppressed*, Harmondsworth: Penguin.

—— (1976 [1970b]) 'A. few notions about the word "conscientization"', in Schooling and Society Course Team, *Schooling and Capitalism: A Sociological Reader*, Milton Keynes: Open University Press.

Friedan, B. (1963) *The Feminine Mystique*, London: Norton.

Friedman, A.L. (1979) *Industry and Labour: Class Struggle at Work and Monopoly Capitalism*, London: Macmillan.

Friedman, M. (1962) *Capitalism and Freedom*, Harmondsworth: Penguin.

Frith, K.T. and Mueller, B. (2003) *Advertising and Society: Global Issues*, New York: Peter Lang.

Frobel, F., Heinrichs, J. and Dreye, O. (1980) *The New International Division of Labour*, Cambridge: Cambridge University Press.

Fromm, E. (1960) *The Fear of Freedom*, London: Routledge & Kegan Paul.

Fryer, P. (1984) *Staying Power: The History of Black People in Britain*, London: Pluto.

—— (1991) *Black People in the British Empire*, London: Pluto.

Fukuyama, F. (1989) 'The end of history?', *The National Interest* 16: 3–17.

Fuller, M. (1980) 'Black girls in a London comprehensive school', in R. Deem (ed.) *Schooling for Women's Work*, London: Routledge & Kegan Paul. Also in M. Hammersley and P. Woods (eds) (1984) *Life in Schools: The Sociology of Pupil Culture*, Milton Keynes: Open University Press.

Furlong, A. and Cartmel, F. (1997) 'Young People and Social Change' *Sociology Review*.

Furlong, A. and Cartmel, F. (1997) *Young People and Social Change*, Buckingham: Open University Press.

Gainer, B. (1972) *The Alien Invasion: The Origins of the Aliens Act of 1905*, London: Heinemann.

Gaines, J. (1990) 'Introduction: fabricating the female body', in J. Gaines and C. Herzog (eds) *Fabrications: Costume and the Female Body*, London: Routledge.

Galbraith, J.K. (1967) *The New Industrial State*, Harmondsworth: Penguin.

Gallie, D. (2000) *A Globalizing World? Culture, Economy and Politics*, London: Routledge.

—— (ed.) (1989) *Employment in Britain*, Oxford: Blackwell.

——, Marsh, C. and Vogler, V. (1993) *Social Change and the Experience of Unemployment*, Oxford: Oxford University Press.

—— and Paugam, S. (eds) (2000) *Welfare Regimes and the Experience of Unemployment in Europe*, Oxford: Oxford University Press.

Gamman, L. and Marshment, M. (1988) *The Female Gaze*, London: Women's Press.

Gans, H. (1974) *Popular Culture and High Culture*, New York: Basic Books.

Gantley, M., Davies, D.P. and Murcott, A. (1993) 'Sudden infant death syndrome: links with infant care practices', *British Medical Journal* 306: 16–20.

Garaudy, R. (1970) *Marxism in the Twentieth Century*, London: Collins.

Gardner, H. (1983; 1993) *Frames of Mind: The Theory of Multiple Intelligences*, New York: Basic Books (second edition published in Britain by Fontana Press).

Garfinkel, H. (1967) *Studies in Ethnomethodology*, Englewood Cliffs, NJ: Prentice-Hall.

Garland, D. (1990) *Punishment and Modern Society*, Oxford: Clarendon.

Garmarnikov, E., Morgan, D., Purvis, J. and Taylorson, D. (eds) (1983) *Gender, Class and Work*, London: Heinemann.

Garrard, J. (1971) *The English and Immigration 1880–1910*, London: Oxford University Press.

Gates, B. (1995) *The Road Ahead*, Viking.

Gauntlett, D. (1995) *Moving Experiences: Understanding Television's Influences and Effects*, London: John Libbey.

Gehrig, G. (1981) 'The American civil religion debate', *Journal for the Scientific Study of Religion* 20(1): 51–63.

Gelles, R.J. (1997) *Intimate Violence in Families*, London: Sage.

Gellner, E. (1983) *Nations and Nationalism*, Oxford: Basil Blackwell.

—— (1991) 'Nationalism and politics in eastern Europe', *New Left Review* 189: 127–34.

—— (1996) 'Do nations have navels?: The Warwick debate', *Nations and Nationalism*, 2:1: 366–70.

—— (1997) 'Reply to Critics', *New Left Review*, ?: 81–118.

Geraghty, C. (1991) *Women and Soap Operas*, Cambridge: Polity.

Gerbner, G. (1995) 'TV violence and what to do about it, *Gender Race and Class in Media: A Critical Text Reader*, Sage.

Gershunny, J.I. and Miles, I. (1983) *The New Service Economy: The Transformation of Employment in Industrial Relations*, London: Frances Pinter.

Gerth, H.H. and Mills, C.W. (eds) (1991 [1970]) *From Max Weber: Essays in Sociology*, London: Routlege.

Gerzina, G. (1995) *Black England*, London: John Murray.

Geser, H. (2004) *Towards a Sociological Theory of the Mobile Phone*, http://socio.ch/mobile/t_geser1.htm#5 (accessed 5/5/05).

Gibson, C. (1994) *Dissolving Wedlock*, London: Routledge.

Gibson, R. (1995) *The Best of Enemies: Anglo-French relations since the Norman Conquest*, London: Sinclair-Stevenson.

Giddens, A. (1972) *Emile Durkheim: Selected Writings*, Cambridge: Cambridge University Press.

—— (1973) *The Class Structure of the Advanced Societies*, London: Hutchinson.

—— (1984) *The Constitution of Society*, Berkeley: University of California Press.

—— (1986) 'The rich', in M. Williams (ed.) *Society Today*, London: Macmillan.

—— (1989) *Sociology*, Cambridge: Polity Press.

—— (1990) *The Consequences of Modernity*, Cambridge: Polity.

—— (1991) *Modernity and Self-Identity*, Cambridge: Polity Press.

—— (1992a) *The Transformation of Intimacy: Sexualities, Love and Eroticism in Modern Societies*, Stanford, CA: Stanford University Press.

—— (ed.) (1992b) *Human Societies: An Introductory Reader in Sociology*, Cambridge: Polity Press.

—— (1993) 'Dare to care, conserve and repair', *New Statesman and Society*, 29 October.

—— (1994) *Beyond Left and Right: The Future of Radical Politics*, Cambridge: Polity Press.

—— (1996) 'T.H. Marshall, the state and democracy' in M. Bulmer and A.M. Rees (eds) *Citizenship Today: The Contemporary Relevance of T.H. Marshall*, London: University College of London Press.

—— (1997a) *Sociology*, 3rd edn, Cambridge: Polity Press.

—— (ed.) (1997b) *Sociology: Introductory Readings*, Cambridge: Polity Press.

—— (1998) *The Third Way: The Renewal of Social Democracy*, Cambridge: Polity Press.

—— (2001) *Sociology*, 4th edn, Cambridge: Polity.

Gide, A. (1952) *The Journals of André Gide 1889–1949*, trans. J. O'Brien, New York: Knopf.

Gifford (1989) *Loosen the Shackles: First Report of the Liverpool 8 Inquiry into Race Relations in Liverpool*, London: Karia.

Gilbert, A.G. and Gugler, J. (1992) *Cities, Poverty and Development: Urbanization in the Third World*, 2nd edn, Oxford: Oxford University Press.

Gilbert, N. (1993) *Researching Social Life*, London: Sage.

Gilbert, P. (1992) 'The oxygen of publicity: terrorism and reporting restrictions', in A. Belsey and R. Chadwick (eds) *Ethical Issues in Journalism and the Media*, London: Routledge.

Gill, D., Mayor, B. and Blair, M. (1992) *Racism and Education: Structures and Strategies*, London: Sage.

Gill, T. (1990) 'Too high a price for excellence?', *Daily Mail*, 28 July.

Gillies, V. (2000) 'Young people and family life: analysing and comparing disciplinary discourses', *Journal of Youth Studies*, 3(2): 211–28.

Gilroy, P. (1987) *There Ain't No Black in the Union Jack*, London: Hutchinson.

—— (1993a) *The Black Atlantic: Modernity and Double Consciousness*, London: Verso.

—— (1993b) *Small Acts*, London: Serpent's Tail.

Ginn, J. and Arber, S. (1993) 'Ageing and cultural stereotypes of older women' in J. Johnson and R. Slater (eds) *Ageing and Later Life*, London: Sage.

Ginsburg, N. (1992) 'Racism and housing: concepts and reality', in P. Braham (ed.) *Racism and Anti-Racism: Inequalities, Opportunities and Policies*, London: Sage.

Giroux, H. (1992) *Border Crossings: Cultural Workers and the Politics of Education*, London: Routledge.

Gittins, D. (1993) *The Family in Question*, London: Macmillan.

—— (1998) *The Child in Question*, Basingstoke and London: Macmillan Press.

Glasgow University Media Group (1982) *Really Bad News*, London: Writers & Readers.

—— (1985) *War and Peace News*, Milton Keynes: Open University Press.

—— (1996) *The Media and Mental Illness*, London: Longman.

Glasner, P. (1977) *The Sociology of Secularisation*, London: Routledge & Kegan Paul.

Glass, D. (ed.) (1954) *Social Mobility in Britain*. XXXX: RKP.

Glendinning, C. and Millar, J. (1992) *Women and Poverty: Women's Poverty in the 1990s*, Hemel Hempstead: Harvester Wheatsheaf.

Glock, C.Y. and Stark, R. (1968) 'Dimensions of religious commitment', in R. Robertson (ed.) *Sociology of Religion*, Harmondsworth: Penguin.

Glodava, M. and Onizuka, R. (1994) *Mail-order Brides: Women for Sale*, Fort Collins, CO: Alaken.

Glover, D. (1985) '*The sociology of mass media*', Ormskirk: Causeway Press.

Goffman, E. (1963) *Stigma: Notes on the Management of Spoiled Identity*, New York: Prentice Hall.

—— (1968) *Asylums: Essays on the Social Situation of Mental Patients and Other Inmates*, Harmondsworth: Penguin.

—— (1969) *The Presentation of Self in Everyday Life*, Harmondsworth: Penguin.

—— (1971) *Relations in Public*, Harmondsworth: Penguin.

Goldberg, D.V. (1993) *Racist Culture: Philosophy and the Culture of Meaning*, Oxford: Blackwell.

Golding, P. (1974) *The Mass Media*, London: Longman.

—— and Murdock, G. (1991) 'Culture, communications and political economy', in J. Curran and M. Gurevitch (eds) *Mass Media and Society*, London: Edward Arnold.

Goldthorpe, J. (1996) 'Class analysis and the re-orientation of class theory: the case of persisting differentials in educational attainment, *British Journal of Sociology*, 47: 481–505.

—— et al. (1980) *Social Mobility and Class Structure in Modern Britain*, Oxford: Clarendon Press.

Goldthorpe, J.H., Lockwood, D., Bechhofer, F. and Platt, J. (1968) *The Affluent Worker: Industrial Attitudes and Behaviour*, Cambridge: Cambridge University Press.

——, ——, —— and —— (1969) *The Affluent Worker in the Class Structure*, Cambridge: Cambridge University Press.

—— Llewellyn, C. and Payne, C. (1980) *Social Mobility and Class Structure in Modern Britain*, Oxford: Clarendon.

Goode, E. (1997) *Deviant Behaviour*, New York: Prentice Hall.

—— and Ben-Yehuda, N. (1994) *Moral Panics; The Social Construction of Deviance*, Blackwell: Oxford.

Gorbutt, D. (1972) 'The new sociology of education', *Education for Teaching* 89 (autumn).

Gordon, D. (1988) 'The global economy', *New Left Review* 168.

Gordon, P. (1988) 'The New Right, race and education', *Race and Class* 29(3): 95–103.

—— and Newham, A. (1986) *Different World*, London: Runnymede Trust.

Goring, R. (ed.) (1992) *Larousse Dictionary of Beliefs and Religion*, Edinburgh: W & R Chambers.

Gorz, A. (ed.) (1979) *The Division of Labour*, Brighton: Harvester.

—— (1982) *Farewell to the Working Class*, London: Pluto.

Gospel, H. and Wood, S. (eds) (2003) *Representing Workers: Trade Union Recognition and Membership in Britain*, London: Routledge.

Gouldner, A.W. (1954) *Patterns of Industrial Bureaucracy*, New York: Free Press.

—— (1971) *The Coming Crisis of Western Sociology*, London: Heinemann.

—— (1973) 'Anti-minotaur: the myth of a value free society', in A.W. Gouldner (1975) *For Sociology: Renewal and Critique in Sociology Today*, Harmondsworth: Penguin.

—— (1975) *For Sociology: Renewal and Critique in Sociology Today*, Harmondsworth: Penguin.

Grabrucker, M. (1988) *There's a Good Girl: Gender Stereotyping in the First Three Years of Life: A Diary*, London: Women's Press.

Graham, H. (1984a) *Women, Health and the Family*, Brighton: Wheatsheaf.

—— (1984b) 'Surveying through stories', in C. Bell and H. Roberts (eds) *Social Researching*, London: Routledge & Kegan Paul.

—— (1986) *Caring for the Family, Research Reports*, no. 1, London: Health Education Council.

—— (1987) 'Women's smoking and family health', *Social Science and Medicine* 25: 47–56.

Gramsci, A. (1971) *Selections from Prison Notebooks*, London: Lawrence & Wishart.

Grant, D. (1989) *Learning Relations*, London: Routledge.

Graunt, J. (1973 [1662]) *Natural and Political Observations mentioned in the Following Index and made upon Bills of Mortality*, New York: Arno.

Green, A., Wolf, A. and Leney, T. (1999) *Convergence and Divergence in European Education and Training Systems*, Bedford Way Series, London: Institute of Education.

Green, E., Hebron, S. and Woodward, D. (1990) *Women's Leisure, What Leisure?*, London: Macmillan.

Green, T.H. (1988 [1911]) *Works*, ed. R. Nettleship, Oxford: Oxford University Press.

Greenfeld, L. (1992) *Nationalism: Five Roads to Modernity*, Harvard, MA: Harvard University Press.

Grint, K. (1998) *The Sociology of Work*, 2nd edn, Cambridge: Polity.

Grittiths, V. (1988a) 'Stepping out: the importance of dancing for young women', in E. Wimbush, and M. Talbot, (eds) *Relative Freedoms: Women and Leisure*, Milton Keynes: Open University Press.

—— (1988b) 'From "playing out" to "dossing out": young women and leisure', in E. Wimbush and M. Talbot (eds) *Relative Freedoms: Women and Leisure*, Milton Keynes: Open University Press.

Gross, E. (1992) 'What is feminist theory', in H. Crowley and S. Himmelweit (eds) *Knowing Women*, Cambridge: Polity.

Guardian (annually) *Guardian Political Almanac*, London: Fourth Estate.

Gubrium, J. and Wallace, J. (1990) 'Who theorises age', *Ageing and Society*, 10(2): 131–50.

Gunter, B. (1985) *Dimensions of Television Violence*, Aldershot: Gower.

—— and McAleer, J. (1990) *Children and Television: The One Eyed Monster*, London: Routledge.

Gurr, T. (1970), *Why Men Rebel*, New Jersey: Princeton University Press.

Gutierrez, G. (1973) *A Theology of Liberation*, Maryknoll, NY: Orbis.

—— (1990) *The Truth Shall Set You Free*, Maryknoll, NY: Orbis.

—— (2001) *A Theology of Liberation*, London: SCM Press.

Habermas, J. (1971a) *Legitimation Crisis*, London: Heinemann.

—— (1971b) *Knowledge and Human Interests*, J. Shapiro (tr.), Boston: Beacon Press.

—— (1976a) *Legitimation Crisis*, London: Heinemann.

—— (1976b) Adaptation of his Theory of Legitimation Crisis, Open University D209 Unit 23, p. 78 and D102 Unit 15, p. 79, Milton Keynes.

Haines, H. (1988) *Black Radicals and the Civil Rights Mainstream, 1954–1970*, Tennessee: University of Tennessee Press.

Hakim, C. (1979) *Occupational Segregation: A Comparative Study of the Degree and Patterns of Differentiation between Men's and Women's Work in Britain, the United States and Other Countries*, Research Paper 9, London: Department of Employment.

Hall, S. (1977) 'The "political" and the "economic" in Marx's theory of classes', in A. Hunt (ed.) *Class and Class Structure*, London: Lawrence & Wishart.

—— (1982) *Culture and the State*, Milton Keynes: Open University Press.

—— (1992) 'New ethnicities', in J. Donals and A. Rattansi (eds) *Race, Culture and Difference*, London: Sage/Open University Press.

Hall, S. and Jacques, M. (1989) *New Times*, London: Lawrence & Wishart.

—— and Jefferson, T. (1976) *Resistance through Rituals*, London: Hutchinson.

—— Critcher, C., Jefferson, T., Clarke, J. and Roberts, B. (1978) *Policing the Crisis: Mugging, the State and Law and Order*, London: Macmillan.

Hall, S. *et al.* (1979) *Policing the Crisis: Mugging, The State, and Law and Order*, London: Macmillan.

——, Held, D. and McGrew, T. (eds) (1992) *Modernity and its Futures*, Cambridge: Polity.

Halsey, A.H., Floud, J. and Anderson, C.A. (1961) *Education, Economy and Society*, New York: Free Press.

—— Heath, A.F. and Ridge, J.M. (1980) *Origins and Destinations: Family, Class and Education in Modern Britain*, Oxford: Clarendon.

Hammersley, M. (1992) 'Introducing ethnography', *Sociology Review* 2(2): 18–23.

—— and Woods, P. (eds) (1984) *Life in Schools: The Sociology of Pupil Culture*, Milton Keynes: Open University Press.

Hammond, P. (1976) 'The sociology of American civil religion: a biographical essay', *Sociological Analysis* 37(2): 169–82.

Hamnett, C. (2004) 'In both Britain and United States, wealth inequality has increased since the 1970s', *Independent*, 3.8.2004.

Hanmer, J. and Saunders, S. (1984) *Well Founded Fear: A Community Study of Violence to Women*, London: Hutchinson.

Haralambos, M. and Holborn, M. (eds) (1995) *Sociology: Themes and Perspectives*, 4th edn, London: HarperCollins.

Harding, S. (1987) *Feminism and Methodology*, Milton Keynes: Open University Press.

Hardman, C. (2001/1973) 'Can there be an anthropology of children?' *Childhood*, 8(4): 501–17.

Hargreaves, D.H. (1967) *Social Relations in a Secondary School*, London: Routledge & Kegan Paul.

—— (1978) 'Power and the paracurriculum', in C. Richards (ed.) *Power and the Curriculum: Issues in Curriculum Studies*, Driffield: Nafferton.

Hargreaves, I. (1993) *Sharper Vision*, Demos.

Harraway, D. (1991) *Simians, Cyborgs and Women*, London: Free Association Books.

Harris, G. (1988) *The Sociology of Development*, London: Longman.

Harris, N. (1992) 'Codes of conduct for journalists', in A. Belsey and R. Chadwick (eds) *Ethical Issues in Journalism and the Media*, London: Routledge.

Harris, R. (1993) ' "The Child of the Barbarian": rape, race and nationalism in France during the First World War', *Past and Present* 141.

Harrison, T. and Madge, C. (1986 [1939]) *Britain by Mass Observation*, London: Hutchinson.

Hart, A. (1991) *Understanding the Media: A Practical Guide*, London: Routledge.

—— and Wilson, T. (1992) 'The politics of part-time staff', *AUT Bulletin*, January.

Hart, J. (1985) 'Why do women commit less crime?', *New Society* 30 August.

Hart, L. (1997) 'In defence of radical direct action', in J. Purkis and J. Brown *Twenty-First Century Anarchism: Unorthodox Ideas For a New Millennium*, London: Cassell.

Hart, N. (1976) *When Marriage Ends*, London: Tavistock.

Hartmann, H. (1981) 'The unhappy marriage of Marxism and feminism: towards a more progressive union', in L. Sergent (ed.) *Women and Revolution*, New York: Monthly Review.

Harvey, D. (1990) *The Condition of Postmodernity*, London: Blackwell.

Hattersley, R. (1981) Speech 16 July, *Hansard* 18, cols 1407–9.

Hayek, F.A. (1944) *The Road to Serfdom*, Chicago: University of Chicago Press.

—— (1960) *The Constitution of Liberty*, London: Routledge & Kegan Paul.

—— (1967) *Studies in Philosophy, Politics and Economics*, London: Routledge & Kegan Paul.

—— (1976) *The Constitution of Liberty*, London: Routledge & Kegan Paul.

Hayes, D. and Hudson, A. (2001) *The Mood of the Nation*. Basildon: Demos. Available online at www.demos.co.uk

Hearn, G. (1987) *The Gender of Oppression: Men, Masculinity and the Critique of Marxism*, London: Pluto.

Heath, A. (1992) 'The attitudes of the underclass', in D.J. Smith (ed.) *Understanding the Underclass*, London: Policy Studies Institute.

Hebdige, D. (1979) *Subculture: The Meaning of Style*, London: Methuen.

Hecht, T. (1998) *At Home in the Street: Street Children of Northeast Brazil*. Cambridge: Cambridge University Press.

Heery, E. and Salmon, J. (eds) (2000) *The Insecure Workforce*, London: Routledge.

Hegel, G.W.F. and Knox, T.M. (1952 [1821]) *Hegel's Philosophy of Right*, Oxford: Oxford University Press.

Heidensohn, F. (1989) *Crime and Society*, London: Macmillan.

—— (1997) 'Gender and Crime', in M. Maguire, M. Morgan and R. Reiner (eds) *The Oxford Handbook of Criminology*, 2nd edn, Oxford: Oxford University Press.

Held, D. (1999) *Global Transformations: A Reader*, Cambridge: Polity.

Held D. (2000) *A Globalizing World? Culture, Economics and Politics*, London: Routledge.

—— and McGrew, A. (2003) *Globalization/Anti-Globalization*, Cambridge: Polity.

Heidensohn, F. (2002) 'Gender and Crime', in Maguire, M., Morgan, R. and Reiner, R. (eds) *The Oxford Handbook of Criminology*, 3rd edn, Oxford: Oxford University Press.

Helman, C. (1985) *Culture, Health and Illness*, Bristol: Wright.

Henley Centre (1993) *Media Futures* (July), Henley, Oxon.

Hennelly, A. (ed.) (1990) *Liberation Theology: A Documentary History*, Maryknoll, NY: Orbis.

Henry, C. and Hiltel, M. (1977) *Children of the SS*, London: Corgi.

Henwood, M., Rimmer, L. and Wicks, M. (1987) *Inside the Family*, London: Family Policy Studies Centre.

Herder, G. (1969) *Herder on Social and Political Culture*, ed. and trans. by F.M. Barnard, Cambridge: Cambridge University Press.

Hermes, J. (1995) *Reading Women's Magazines*, London: Routledge.

Herrnstein, R. and Murray, C. (1994) *The Bell Curve: Intelligence and the Class Structure*, New York: Free Press.

Herzlich, C. (1973) *Health and Illness*, London: Academic Press.

Hester, S. and Eglin, P. (1992) *A Sociology of Crime*, London: Routledge.

Heywood, C. (2001) *A History of Childhood: Children and Childhood in the West from Medieval to Modern Times*, Cambridge: Polity.

Hibbert, A. and Meager, N. (2003) 'Key indicators of women's position in Britain', *Labour Market Trends*, 111(10), www.statistics.gov.uk

Hill-Collins, P. (1990) *Black Feminist Thought: Knowledge, Consciousness, and the Politics of Empowerment*, London: Unwin Hyman.

Hills, J. (1997) *Income and Wealth: the Latest Evidence*. London: Joseph Rowntree Foundation.

Hilton, R.H. (1969) *The Decline of Serfdom in Medieval England*, London: Macmillan.

Hinnells, J. (1984) *Dictionary of Religions*, Harmondsworth: Penguin.

Hirst, P. and Thompson, G. (eds) (1996) *Globalization in Question: The International Economy and the Possibilities of Governance*, Cambridge: Polity Press.

—— and —— (eds) (1999) *Globalization in Question*, 2nd edn, Cambridge: Polity.

Hite, S. (1981) *The Hite Report on Male Sexuality*, London: Macdonald.

—— (1993) *Women As Revolutionary Agents of Change: The Hite Reports*, London: Sceptre.

Hitler, A. (1969 [1925]) *Mein Kampf*, trans. R. Manheim, London: Hutchinson.

Hobbs, D. (1995) *Bad Business: Professional Crime in Modern Britain*, Oxford: Oxford University Press.

Hobsbawm, E. (1990) *Nations and Nationalism Since 1780*, Cambridge: Cambridge University Press.

—— (1992) 'The crisis of today's ideologies', *New Left Review* I:192: 55–64.

—— (1994) *The Age of Extremes: The Short Twentieth Century, 1914–1991*, London: Michael Joseph.

—— (1998) 'Markets, meltdown and Marx', *Guardian*, 20 October.

—— and Ranger, T. (1983) *The Invention of Tradition*, Cambridge: Cambridge University Press.

Hobson, D. (1982) *Crossroads: The Drama of Soap Opera*, London: Methuen.

Hochschild, A.R. (1983) *The Managed Heart: The Commercialization of Human Feeling*, Berkeley, CA: University of California Press.

—— (1990) *The Second Shift*, London: Piatkus.

Hockey, J. and James, A. (1993) *Growing Up and Growing Old*, London: Sage.

—— and —— (2003) *Social Identities across the Lifecourse*, Basingstoke: Palgrave Macmillan.

Hodge, B. and Tripp, D. (1986) *Children's Television*, Cambridge: Polity.

Holdaway, S. (1996) *The Racialisation of British Policing*, Basingstoke: Palgrave Macmillan.

Hollway, W. (1994) 'Women's power in heterosexual sex' *Women's Studies International Forum* 7: 66–8.

Holland, J. (2005) http://www.thinkingpeace.com/pages/arts2/arts352.html 22/1/05

Holmes, C. (1979) *Anti-Semitism in British Society 1876–1939*, London: Edward Arnold.

—— (1988) *John Bull's Island: Immigration and British Society 1871–1971*, London: Macmillan.

Holmes, E.R. and Holmes, L.D. (1995) *Other Cultures, Elder Years*, London: Sage.

Holt, J. (1969) *How Children Fail*, Harmondsworth: Penguin.

Home Office (1927) *Children as Victims*, London: HMSO.

Honey, J. (1983) *The Language Trap: Race, Class and the 'Standard English' Issue in British Schools*, Kenton, Middlesex.

Honeyford, R. (1984) 'Education and race: an alternative view', *Salisbury Review* winter.

Hood-Williams, J. (1990) 'Patriarchy for children: on the stability of power relations in children's lives,' in L. Chisholm *et al.* (eds) *Childhood, Youth and Social Change: A Comparative Perspective*, London: Falmer Press.

hooks, b (1984) *Feminist Theory: From Margin to Centre*, Boston, MA: South End Press.

—— (1989) *Talking Back: Thinking Feminist, Thinking Black*, Boston, MA: South End Press.

Horkheimer, M. and Adorno, T. (1973, original 1944) *Dialetic of the Enlightenment*, Harmondsworth: Allen Lane.

Hough, M. and Mayhew, P. (1993) *The British Crime Survey*, London: HMSO.

Hovland, C. (1949) *Experiments in Mass Communications*, Princeton, NJ: Princeton University Press.

Howson, A. (2004) *The Body in Society: An Introduction*, Cambridge: Polity.

Hoyles, M. (ed.) (1979) *Changing Childhood*, London: Writer and Reader Publishing Cooperative.

Hughes, J. (1984) 'The concept of class', in R. Anderson and W. Sharrock (eds) *Teaching Papers in Sociology*, London: Longman.

Hughey, M. (1993) *Civil Religion and Moral Order*, Westport, CT: Greenwood.

Hulme, D. (1990) *Sociology and Development: Theories and Practice*, Hemel Hempstead: Harvester Wheatsheaf.

Humm, M. (ed.) (1992) *Feminisms: A Reader*, Hemel Hempstead: Harvester Wheatsheaf.

Humphries, J. and Rubery, J. (eds) (1995) *The Economics of Equal Value*, Manchester: Equal Opportunities Commission.

Hunt P. (1996) *Changing Eating and Exercise Behaviour*, Oxford: Blackwell.

Hunte, J. (1965) *Nigger Hunting in England?*, London: West Indian Standing Conference.

Hutchings, M. (2002) *Towards a Representative Teaching Profession: Gender*, Institute for Public Policy Research report.

Huxley, A. (1932) *Brave New World*, Toronto: Clarke Irwin.

Ignatieff, M. (1994) *Blood and Belonging: Journeys into the New Nationalism*, London: Vintage.

Illich, I. (1975) *Medical Nemesis*, London: Calder & Boyars.

Independent Television Commission (ITC) (1993) *Television: The Public's View*, London: ITC/John Libbey.

Information Technology Advisory Panel (ITAP) (1982a) *Inquiry into Cable Expansion and Broadcasting (Hunt Report)*, London: HMSO.

—— (1982b) *Report on Cable Systems*, London: HMSO.

Inglehart, R. (1977a) *The Silent Revolution: Changing Values and Political Styles among Western Publics*, Princeton, NJ: Princeton University Press.

—— (1997b) *Modernization and Postmodernization: Cultural, Economic and Political Change in 43 Societies*, Princeton: Princeton University Press.

—— (2003) *Human Values and Social Change: Findings from the Values Survey*, Leiden: Brill.

Inkeles, A. (1997) *National Character: A Psycho–Social Perspective*, New Brunswick: Transaction Publishers.

International Federation of Red Cross and Red Crescent Societies (1998) *World Disasters Report 1998*, Oxford: Oxford University Press.

Institute of Economic Affairs (IEA) (1992) *Equal Opportunities: A Feminist Fallacy*, London: IEA.

Institute of Public Policy Research (IPPR) (1993) *Education: A Different Vision*, London: IPPR.

Itzin, C. (1990) *Age and Sexual Divisions: A Study of Opportunity and Identity in Women*, University of Kent: PhD Thesis.

—— (1994) 'A harm-based equality approach to legislating against pornography without censorship', paper presented at Sexualities in Social Context Conference, University of Central Lancashire, Preston, 28–31 March.

Jackson, B. and Marsden, D. (1963) *Education and the Working Class*, London: Routledge & Kegan Paul.

Jackson, D. (1990) *Unmasking Masculinity: A Critical Autobiography*, London: Routledge.

—— and Salisbury, J. (1993) 'The playing fields of masculinity', *Achilles' Heel* 14: 12–15.

Jackson, P. (1968) *Life in Classrooms*, New York: Holt, Rinehart & Winston.

Jackson, S. and Scott, A. (2000) 'Childhood' in G. Payne (ed.) *Social Divisions*, London: Macmillan.

Jacobs, B. (1988) *Racism in Britain*, London: Croom Helm.

Jaggar, A. (1983) *Feminist Politics and Human Nature*, New Jersey: Rowman & Allanheld.

Jagger, G. and Wright, C. (eds) (1999) 'Introduction', *Changing Family Values*, London: Routledge.

James, A. and Prout, A. (1990) *Constructing and Reconstructing Childhood: Contemporary Issues in the Sociological Study of Childhood*, London: Falmer Press.

——, Jenks, C. and Prout, A. (1998) *Theorizing Childhood*, Cambridge: Polity Press.

James, W. (1890) *Principles of Psychology*, London: Henry Holt.

Jamieson, L. (1999) 'Intimacy transformed?: a critical look at the "Pure Relationship"', *Sociology* 33: 3.

Jamrozik, A. and Nocella, L. (1998) *The Sociology of Social Problems*, Cambridge: Cambridge University Press.

Jayaratne, T.E. (1993) 'The value of quantitative methodology for feminist research', in M. Hammersley (ed.) *Social Research Philosophy, Politics and Practice*, London: Sage.

Jeffcoate, R. (1979) *Positive Image toward a Multiracial Curriculum*, London: Chameleon.

Jeffrey, B. and Woods, P. (1998) *Testing Teachers: The Effect of School Inspections on Primary Teachers*, London: Falmer Press.

Jeffrey, R. (1995) 'Normal rubbish: deviant patients in casualty departments', in B. Davey, A. Gray and C. Seale (eds) *Health and Disease: A Reader*, Buckingham: Open University Press.

Jeffreys, S. (1990) *Anticlimax: A Feminist Perspective on the Sexual Revolution*, London: The Women's Press.

—— (1994) *The Lesbian Heresy: A Feminist Perspective on the Lesbian Sexual Revolution*, London: Women's Press.

Jencks, C. (1993) *Culture*, London: Routledge.

Jenkins, J. (1988) *GCSE Religious Studies: Contemporary Moral Issues*, London: Heinemann.

Jenkins, P. (1987) *Mrs Thatcher's Revolution*, London: Jonathan Cape.

Jenkins, S. (1986) *Market for Glory*, London: Faber & Faber.

Jenks, C. (1996) *Childhood*, London: Routledge.

Jensen, A.R. (1969) 'How much can we boost IQ and scholastic achievement?', *Harvard Educational Review* 39(1).

—— (1973) *Educational Differences*, London: Methuen.

Jermier, J.M., Knights, D. and Nord, R.W. (eds) (1994), *Resistance and Power in Organisations*, London: Routledge.

Jewson, N.D. (1976) 'The disappearance of the sick man from medical cosmology', *Sociology* 10(2): 225–44.

Johnson, A.G. (1989) *Human Arrangements: An Introduction to Sociology*, 2nd edn, Orlando, FL: Harcourt Brace Jovanovich.

Johnson, J. and Bytheway, B. (1993) 'Ageism: concept and definition,' in J. Johnson and R. Slater (eds) *Ageing and Later Life*, London: Sage.

Johnson, N. (ed.) (1985) *Marital Violence*, London: Routledge & Kegan Paul.

Johnson, R. (1983) 'Educational politics: the old and the new', in A.M. Wolpe and J. Donald (eds) *Is There Anyone Here from Education?*, London: Pluto.

Johnson, S. (2005) *Everything Bad is Good for You*, London: Allen Lane.

Jones, C. and Mahony, P. (1989) *Learning our Lines*, London: Women's Press.

Jones, J. and Cameron, D. (1984) 'Social class analysis – an embarrassment for epidemiology', *Community Medicine* 6: 37–46.

Jones, N. (1995) *Soundbites and Spindoctors*, London: Cassell.

Jones, P. (1993) *Studying Society: Sociological Theories and Research Practices*, London: Collins.

Jones P. (2003) *Introducing Social Theory*, Cambridge: Polity Press.

Jones, S. (1991) 'We are all cousins under the skin', *Independent*, 12 December.

Jordon, B. (1984) *Invitation to Social Work*, Oxford: Blackwell.

Jowell, R. and Witherspoon, S. (eds) (1985) *British Social Attitudes Survey*, Aldershot: Gower.

—— Brook, L., Prior, G. and Taylor, B. (eds) (1992) *British Social Attitudes Survey*, Ninth Annual Report, Aldershot: Dartmouth.

Jupp, V. and Norris, C. (1993) 'Traditions in documentary analysis', in M. Hammersley (ed.) *Social Research: Philosophy, Politics and Practice*, London: Sage.

Kamin, L. (1977) 'Heredity, intelligence, politics and psychology', in N. Block and G. Dworkin (eds) *The IQ Controversy*, London: Quartet.

Kanter, R.M. (1977) *Men and Women of the Corporation*, New York: Basic Books.

Karabel, J. and Halsey, A.H. (1977) *Power and Ideology in Education*, Oxford: Oxford University Press.

Karn, V., Kemeny, J. and Williams, P. (1983) 'Race and housing in Britain: the rule of major institutions', in N. Glazer and K. Young (eds) *Ethnic Pluralism and Public Policy*, London: Heinemann.

Kasl, S.V. and Cobb, S. (1966) 'Health behaviour, illness behaviour, and sick role behaviour', *Archives of Environmental Health* 12: 246–66.

Katz, E. and Lazarsfeld, P. (1955) *Personal Influence*, London: Free Press.

Katz, J. (1995) 'Advertising and the Construction of Violent White Masculinity' in G. Dines and J.M. Humez (eds) *Gender, Race and Class in the Media: A Text Reader*, Thousandoaks, CA: Sage.

Kavanagh, D. (1992) 'Opinion polls, predictions and politics', *Politics Review* 2(2): 6–14.

Keane, J. (1991) *The Media and Democracy*, Cambridge: Polity.

Keddie, N. (ed.) (1973) *Tinker, Tailor, . . . The Myth of Cultural Deprivation*, Harmondsworth: Penguin.

Kedourie, E. (1960) *Nationalism*, London: Hutchinson.

Kefyalew, F. (1996) 'The reality of child participation in research: experience from a capacity-building programme', *Childhood* 3(2): 203–13.

Kelly, A. (ed.) (1981) *The Missing Half: Girls and Science Education*, Manchester: Manchester University Press.

Kelly, E. (1988) *Surviving Sexual Violence*, Cambridge: Polity.

——, Regan, L. and Burton, S. (1992) 'Defending the indefensible: quantitative methods and feminist research', in H. Hinds, A. Phoenix and J. Stacey (eds) *Working Out New Directions for Women's Studies*, Brighton: Falmer.

Kemshall, H. (2003) *Understanding Risk in Criminal Justice*, Buckingham: Open University Press.

Kennedy, P. (1993) *Preparing for the 21st Century*, London: Random House.

Kent, J. (2000) *Social Perspectives on Pregnancy and Childbirth for Midwives, Nurses and the Caring Professions*, Buckingham: Open University.

Kent, R. (1981) *A History of British Empirical Sociology*, Aldershot: Gower.

Kenway, J. and Willis, S. (1990) *Hearts and Minds: Self-Esteem and the Schooling of Girls*, Northern Territory, Australia: Darwin University Press.

Kern, M. (1989) *30 Second Politics: Political Advertising in the Eighties*, New York: Praeger.

Kerr, C., Dunlop, J.T., Harbison, F.H. and Mayers, C.A. (1962) *Industrialism and Industrial Man*, London: Heinemann.

Kerr, M. (1958) *The People of Ship Street*, London: Routledge & Kegan Paul.

Kettle, M. and Hodges, L. (1982) *Uprising! The Police, the People and the Riots in Britain's Cities*, London: Pan.

Keynes, J.M. (1985 [1936]) *A General Theory of Employment, Interest and Money*, Vol. VII of his *Collected Works*, Basingstoke: Macmillan.

Kiernan, K. (1992) 'The impact of family disruption in childhood on transitions in young adult life', *Population Studies*, 46(3): 51–82.

Kilborn, R. (1992) *Television Soaps*, London: Batsford.

Kimmel, M.S. (1990) *Revolution: A Sociological Interpretation*, Cambridge: Polity.

—— and Messner, M.A. (2004) *Men's Lives*, 6th edn, Boston and New York: Pearson.

King, A. (1993) 'Mystery and imagination: the case of pornography effects studies', in A. Assiter and C. Avendon (eds) *Bad Girls and Dirty Pictures*, London: Pluto.

Kingdom, J. (1991) *Government and Politics in Britain*, Cambridge: Polity.

Kinsey, A.C., Pomeroy, W.B. and Martin, C.E. (1948) *Sexual Behavior in the Human Male*, Philadelphia, PA: W.B. Saunders.

——, ——, —— and Gebhard, P.H. (1953) *Sexual Behavior in the Human Female*, Philadelphia, PA: W.B. Saunders.

Klein, J. (1965) *Samples from English Cultures*, vol. 1, London: Routledge & Kegan Paul.

Klein, N. (2000) *No Logo*, Flamingo: London.

Klein R. and Bell D. (1996) *Radically Speaking: Feminism Reclaimed*, London: Zed Books.

Kleinman, A. (1978) 'Concepts and a model for the comparison of medical systems', *Social Science and Medicine* 12, 2B: 85–93.

Kogan, M. (1975) *Educational Policy Making*, London: Allen & Unwin.

Kohn, M. (1996) *The Race Gallery*, London: Vintage.

Koss, S. (1973) *Fleet Street Radical: A G Gardiner and the Daily News*, London: Allen Lane.

Krippendorf, K. (1980) *Content Analysis: An Introduction to its Methodology*, London: Sage.

Kritzman L. (1988) *Michel Foucault: Politics, Philosophy and Culture: Interviews and Other Writings 1977–1984*, New York: Routledge.

Kuhn, T. (1962) *The Structure of Scientific Revolutions*, Chicago: Chicago University Press.

Kumar, K. (1978) *Prophecy and Progress: The Sociology of Industrial and Post-Industrial Society*, Harmondsworth: Penguin.

—— (1995) *From Post-Industrial to Post-Modern Society*, Oxford: Blackwell.

Labov, W. (1969) 'The logic of non-standard English', in P.P. Giglioli (ed.) (1972) *Language and Social Context*, Harmondsworth: Penguin. Also in N. Keddie (ed.) (1973) *Tinker, Tailor, ... The Myth of Cultural Deprivation*, Harmondsworth: Penguin.

Lacey, C. (1970) *Hightown Grammar: The School as a Social System*, Manchester: Manchester University Press.

Laclau, E. (1977) 'Feudalism and capitalism in Latin America', *New Left Review* 67: 19–38.

Laing, R.D. and Esterson, A. (1970) *Sanity, Madness and the Family*, Harmondsworth: Penguin.

Lambart, A. (1976) 'The sisterhood', in M. Hammersley and P. Woods (eds) *The Process of Schooling*, London: Routledge & Kegan Paul.

Laslett, P. (1972) 'Mean household size in England since the 16th century', in P. Laslett (ed.) *Household and Family in Past Times*, Cambridge: Cambridge University Press.

Lasswell, H. (1948) 'The structure and function of communications in society', in L. Bryson (ed.) *The Communication of Ideas*, London: Harper.

—— (1950) *Politics: Who Gets What, When, How*, Peter Smith Publishers.

Lather, P. (1988) 'Feminist perspectives on empowering research methodology', *Women's Studies International Forum* 11(9): 569–81.

Laungani, P. (2004) 'Changing Patterns of Family Life in India', in J. Roopnarine and U. Gielen (eds) *Families in Global Perspective*, London: Pearson Education.

Lavalette, M. and Cunningham, S. (2002) 'The sociology of childhood,' in B. Goldson, M. Lavalette and J. McKechnie (eds) *Children, Welfare and the State*, London: Sage.

Laver, M. (1997) *Private Desires, Political Action: Invitation to the Politics of Rational Choice*, London: Sage.

Lawson, T. (1986) 'In the shadow of science', *Social Studies Review* 2(2): 36–41.

Laver, M. (1997) *Private Desires, Political Actions: An Invitation to the Politics of Rational Choice*, London: Sage.

Layder, D. (1994) *Understanding Social Theory*, London: Sage.

Layton-Henry, Z. (1989) 'Black electoral participation: an analysis of recent trends', in H. Gouldbourne (ed.) (1990) *Black People and British Politics*, Aldershot: Avebury.

—— and Rich, P. (eds) (1986) *Race, Government and Politics in Britain*, London: Macmillan.

Lazarsfeld, P., Berelson, B. and Gauder, H. (1944) *The People's Choice*, New York: Duell, Sloan & Pearce.

Lea, J. and Young, J. (1984) *What's to be Done About Law and Order?*, Harmondsworth: Penguin.

Leach, E. (1967) *A Runaway World?*, London: BBC Publications.

Leadbetter, C. (1987) 'The divided workforce', *Marxism Today*, April.

Lee, C.H. (1995) *Scotland and the UK*, Manchester: Manchester University Press.

Lee, D. and Newby, H. (1983) *The Problem of Sociology*, London: Hutchinson.

—— and Turner, B.S. (1996) *Conflicts about Class: Debating Inequality in Late Industrialism*, London: Longman.

Lee, J. (1989) 'Social class and schooling', in M. Cole (ed.) *The Social Contexts of Schooling*, London: Falmer.

Leeds Revolutionary Feminists Group (1981) 'Political lesbianism: the case against heterosexuality', in Onlywomen (eds) *Love your Enemy? The Debate between Heterosexual Feminism and Political Lesbianism*, London: Onlywomen Press.

Lees, S. (1986) *Losing Out: Sexuality and Adolescent Girls*, London: Hutchinson.

—— (1993) *Sugar and Spice: Sexuality and Adolescent Girls*, Harmondsworth: Penguin.

Lee-Treweek, G. (1994) 'Bedroom abuse: the hidden work in a nursing home', *Generations Review* 4(1): 2–4.

Leibowitz, L. (1986), 'In the beginning . . . The origins of the sexual division of labour and the development of the first human societies', in S. Coontz and P. Henderson (eds), *Women's Work, Men's Property: The Origins of Gender and Class*, London: Verso.

—— (ed.) (1993) *Social Theory: The Multicultural and Classic Readings*, Oxford: Westview.

Lemert, C. (1997) *Social Things*, Oxford: Rowman and Littlefield.

Lenin, I.V. (1978 [1917]) *Imperialism, the Highest Stage of Capitalism*, London: Progress.

Leonard, D. (1990) 'Persons in their own right: children and sociology in the UK', in L. Chisholm (ed.) *Childhood, Youth and Social Change: A Comparative Perspective*, London: Falmer Press.

Letherby, G. (2003a) *Feminist Research in Theory and Practice*, Buckingham: Open University.

Letherby, G. (2003b) 'I didn't think much of his bedside manner but he was very skilled at his job: medical encounters in relation to "infertility"' in S. Earle and G. Letherby *Gender, Identity and Reproduction: Social Perspectives*, Basingstoke: Palgrave Macmillan.

—— and Marchbank, J. (2003) 'Cyber-chattels: buying brides and babies on the net' in Y. Jewkes (ed.) *Dot.cons: Crime, Deviance and Identity on the Internet*, Devon: Willan.

Levin, J. (1993) *Sociological Snapshots*, Newbury Park, CA: Pine Forge Press.

Levitas, R. (ed.) (1986) *The Ideology of the New Right*, Oxford: Polity.

Levy, S. (2004) 'Google's Two Revolutions', *Newsweek*, December 27–January 3rd issue.

Lewis, G. (1986) 'Concepts of health and illness in a Sepik society', in C. Currer and M. Stacey (eds) *Concepts of Health, Illness and Disease: A Comparative Perspective*, Leamington Spa: Berg.

Lewis, L. (1990) *The Adoring Audience*, London: Unwin Hyman.

Lewis, O. (1966) *La Vida*, New York: Random House.

Lewis, P. and Booth, J. (1989) *The Invisible Medium: Public, Commercial and Community Radio*, London: Macmillan.

Lichter, S., Rotham, S. and Lichter L. (1986) *The Media Elite: America's New Powerbrokers*, Bethesda, MD: Adler & Adler.

Liebert, R.M. and Baron, R.A. (1972) 'Some immediate effects of televised violence on children's behaviour', *Development Psychology* 6: 469–75.

Lijphart, A. (1975) *The Politics of Accommodation: Pluralism and Democracy in the Netherlands*, Berkeley/London: University of California Press.

Lindsey, L. (1990) *Gender Roles: A Sociological Perspective*, London: Sage.

Lion (1988) *The World's Religions: A Lion Handbook*, Oxford: Lion.

Lipsitz, G. (1995) 'The possessiveness investment in whiteness', *American Quarterly*, 47(3), September.

—— (1995) *Life in the Struggle*, Temple University Press.

Littler, C.R. (1982) *The Development of the Labour Process in Capitalist Societies*, London: Heinemann.

Lobo, E. (1978) *Children of Immigrants to Britain*, London: Hodder & Stoughton.

Locke, J. (1956 [1690]) *The Second Treatise on Government*, ed. J. Gough, Oxford: Blackwell.

Lockwood, D. (1989 [1958]) *The Blackcoated Worker*, 2nd edn, Oxford: Oxford University Press.

Lodge, P. and Blackstone, T. (1982) *Educational Policy and Educational Inequality*, Oxford: Martin Robertson.

Lombroso C. (1876) *L'Uomo Delinquente (The Criminal Man)*, Turin: Fratelli Bocca (Milan: Hoepli).

Lombroso, C. and Ferrero, W. (1895) *The Female Offender*, London: T. Fisher Unwin.

Longman Community Information (1995) *Education Yearbook*, London: Longman.

Lord, D.N. (1992) 'Marriage could become irrelevant', *Independent*, 10 February: 2.

Lorenz, K. (1965) *Evolution and Modification of Behaviour*, Chicago, IL: University of Chicago Press.

—— (1973) *Civilised Man's Eight Deadly Sins*, New York: Methuen.

Lovelace, C. (1978) 'British press censorship during the First World War', in G. Boyce (ed.) *Newspaper History: From the Seventeenth Century to the Present Day*, London: Constable.

Lovenduski, J. and Randall, V. (1993) *Feminist Politics*, Oxford: Oxford University Press.

Luckmann, T. (1967) *The Invisible Religion: The Problem of Religion in Modern Society*, New York: Macmillan.

Lukes, S. (1973) *Emile Durkheim, His Life and Work: A Historical and Critical Study*, Harmondsworth: Penguin.

Lull, J. (1991) *China Turned On: Television, Reform and Resistance*, London: Routledge.

—— (1995) *Media, Communication and Culture*, Cambridge: Polity.

—— (2000) *Media Communication Culture: A Global Approach*, 2nd edn, Cambridge: Polity.

Lyndon, N. (1992) *No More Sex War: The Failures of Feminism*, London: Sinclair-Stevenson.

Lynn, R. (1970) 'Comprehensives and quality: the quest for the unattainable', in C.B. Cox and A.E. Dyson (eds) *Black Paper Two: The Critical Survey 1968–70*, London: Critical Quarterly Society.

Lyon, M. (1972) 'Race and ethnicity in pluralistic societies', *New Community* 1: 256–62.

—— (1973) 'Ethnic minority problems: an overview of some recent research', *New Community* 2(4): 329–52.

Lyotard, J. (1985) *The Postmodern Condition*, Minneapolis, MN: University of Minneapolis Press.

Mac an Ghaill, M. (1996) 'Sociology of education, state schooling and social class: beyond critiques of the New Right hegemony', *British Journal of Sociology of Education* 17(2) June: 163–76.

McClelland, D. (1961) *The Achieving Society*, New York: Van Nostrand.

McCrone, D. (2001*) Understanding Scotland: The Sociology of a Nation*, 2nd edn, London: Routledge.

McCulloch, J.R. (1825) *Principles of Political Economy: With a Sketch of the Rise and Progress of Science*, London.

MacDonald, J.F.(1992) *Blacks and White TV*, Nelson-Hall.

MacDonald, I. (2003) *The People's Music*, Pimlico.

—— (1983) *Immigration Law and Practice in the UK*, London: Butterworth.

——, Bhavnani, R., Kahn, L., and John, G. (1990) *Murder in the Playground*, London: Longsight.

McFadden, M.G. (1996) 'Resistance to schooling and educational outcomes: questions of structure and agency', *British Journal of Sociology of Education* 16(3) September: 293–308.

Macfarlane, J.K. (1977) 'Developing a theory of nursing: the relation of theory to practice, education and research', *Journal of Advanced Nursing* 2: 261–70.

McGhee, D. (2005) *Intolerant Britain: Hate, Citizenship and Difference*, Maidenhead: Open University Press.

McGuire, M. (1992) *Religion: The Social Context*, Wadsworth, CA: Belmont.

McIlroy, J. (1995) *Trade Unions in Britain Today*, 2nd edn, Manchester: Manchester University Press.

MacKay, G. (1996) *Senseless Acts of Beauty: Cultures of Resistance Since the 1960s*, London: Verso.

MacInnes, J. (2001) 'The Crisis of Masculinity' in S.M. Whitehead and F.J. Barrett (eds) *The Masculinities Reader*, Cambridge: Polity.

McIntosh, I. (1991) 'Ford at Trafford Park', unpublished PhD thesis, University of Manchester.

—— (1995) 'It was worse than Alcatraz: working for Ford at Trafford Park', *Manchester Regional History Review*, May, 9.

—— and Broderick, J. (1996) 'Neither one thing nor the other: competitive compulsory tendering and Southburch Cleansing Services', *Work, Employment and Society* 10: 2.

McKenzie, J. (1993) *Education as a Political Issue*, Aldershot: Avebury.

McKeown, T. (1979) *The Role of Medicine*, Oxford: Basil Blackwell.

McKie, D. and Bindman, D. (1994) *The Guardian Political Almanac, 1994/5*, London: Fourth Estate.

MacKinnon, C. (1982) 'Feminism, Marxism, method and the state: an agenda for theory', *Signs* 7(3): 515–44.

MacKinnon, C.A. (1989) *Towards a Feminist Theory of the State*, Cambridge, MA: Harvard University Press.

MacKinnon, D., Statham, J. and Hales, M. (1996) *Education in the UK: Facts and Figures*, London: Hodder & Stoughton/Open University.

McLaughlin, E. and Muncie, J. (eds) (1996) *Controlling Crime*, London: Sage.

McLaughlin, J. (1997) 'Feminist Relations with Postmodernism: Reflections on the Positive Aspects of Involvement', *Journal of Gender Studies* 6:1, 5–15.

MacLean, C. (1977) *The Wolf Children*, London: Allen Lane.

McLuhan, M. (1962) *The Guttenberg Galaxy*, Toronto: Toronto University Press.

—— (1964) *Understanding Media*, London: Routledge & Kegan Paul.

—— and Fiore, Q. (1967) *The Medium is the Message*, Harmondsworth: Penguin.

McNeill, P. (1990) *Research Methods*, 2nd edn, London: Routledge.

McQuail, D. (ed.)(1972) *Sociology of Mass Communications*, Harmondsworth: Penguin.

—— (1977) 'The influences and effects of mass media', in Curran, J., Gurevitch, M. and Woollacott, J. (eds).

—— (1994) *Mass Communications Theory: An Introduction*, London: Sage.

—— (2000) *McQuail's Mass Communication Theory*, London: Sage.

——, Blumler, J.G. and Brown, J. (1972) 'The television audience: a revised perspective', in D. McQuail (ed.) (1972).

McRobbie, A. (1982) 'Jackie: an ideology of adolescent femininity', in B. Waites (ed.) *Popular Culture: Past and Present*, Milton Keynes: Open University Press.

—— (1991) 'The politics of feminist research', in A. McRobbie (ed.) *Feminism and Youth Culture*, London: Macmillan.

McRury, I. (2002) 'Advertising and the new media environment' in Briggs and Cobley (2002).

Macionis, J. and Plummer, K. (1998) *Sociology: A Global Introduction*, London: Prentice Hall.

—— and —— (2002) *Sociology: A Global Introduction*, 2nd edn, Harlow: Pearson.

Maguire, M. (2002) 'Crime Statistics; the 'data explosion' and its implications', in Morgan, R. and Reiner, R. (eds) *The Oxford Handbook of Criminology*, 3rd edn, Oxford: Oxford University Press.

Maguire, M.J. and Ashton, D.N. (1981) 'Employers' perceptions and use of educational qualifications', *Educational Analysis* 3(2).

Maguire, M., Morgan, R. and Reiner, R. (eds) (1997) *The Oxford Handbook of Criminology*, 2nd edn, Oxford: Clarendon.

Maidment, S. (1985) 'Domestic violence and the law: the 1976 Act and its aftermath', in N. Johnson (ed.) *Marital Violence*, London: Routledge & Kegan Paul.

Malamuth, N., Addison, A. and Koss, M. (2000) 'Pornography and sexual aggression: are there reliable effects and can we understand them?', *Annual Review of Sex Research* 11: 26–91.

Malik, R. (1995) 'Young "forced into FE to avoid poverty trap"', *Times Educational Supplement*, 21 July.

Malinowski, B, (1926) 'Magic, science and religion', in J. Needham (ed.) *Science, Religion and Reality*, London: Macmillan.

Malson, L. and Itard, J. (1972) *Wolf Children*, London: New Left Books.

Malthus, T.R. (1973) *An Essay on the Principle of Population*, London: Dent.

Mama, A. (1992) 'Black women and the British state: race, class and gender analysis for the 1990s', in P. Braham (ed.) *Racism and Anti-Racism: Inequalities, Opportunities and Policies*, London: Sage.

Mannheim, K. (1952) *Essays in the Sociology of Knowledge*, London: Routledge.

Manning, P. (1992) *Erving Goffman and Modern Sociology*, Cambridge: Polity.

Mao ze Dung (1966) *Quotations from Chairman Mao Tse-Tung*, Beijing.

Marchbank, J. (2000), *Women, Power and Policy: Comparative Studies of Childcare*, London: Routledge.

Marcuse, H. (1964) *One Dimensional Man: Studies in the Ideology of Advanced Industrial Society*, Boston, MA: Beacon.

Marmot, M.G., Rose, G., Shipley, M. and Hamilton, P.J.S. (1978) 'Employment grade and coronary heart disease in British civil servants', *Journal of Epidemiology and Community Health* 32: 244–9.

Marris, P. and Thornham, S. (1997) *Media Studies: A Reader*, Edinburgh: Edinburgh University Press.

Mars, G. (1982) *Cheats at Work: An Anthology of Workplace Crime*, London: Allen & Unwin.

Marsh, I. (ed.) (2002) Theory and Practice in Sociology, London: Prentice Hall.

——, Campbell, R. and Keating, M. (eds) (1998) *Classic and Contemporary Readings in Sociology*, Harlow: Addison Wesley Longman.

Marshall, G., Newby, H., Rose, D. and Vogler, C. (1988) *Social Class in Modern Britain*, London: Hutchinson.

Marshall, T.H. (1992 [1947]) 'Citizenship and social class', in T.H. Marshall and T. Bottomore *Sociology at the Crossroads*, London: Heinemann.

Martin, J. and Roberts, C. (1984) *Women and Employment: A Lifetime Perspective*, London: HMSO.

Martin, K.A. (2002) '"I couldn't ever picture myself having sex . . .": gender differences in sex and sexual subjectivity', in C.L. Williams and A. Stein (eds) *Sexuality and Gender*, Oxford: Blackwell.

Martindale, D. (1960) *The Nature and Types of Sociological Theory*, London: Lowe & Brydon.

Marx, K. (1967 [1867]) *Das Kapital, Volume 1*, London: Lawrence & Wishart.

—— (1969 [1875]) 'Critique of the Gotha Programme', in L.S. Feuer (ed.) *Marx and Engels: Basic Writings on Politics and Philosophy*, London: Fontana.

—— (1970 [1845]) *The German Ideology: Students' Edition*, London: Lawrence & Wishart. Also in (1976) *Collected Works*, vol. 5, London: Lawrence & Wishart.

—— and Engels, F. (1952 [1848]) *The Manifesto of the Communist Party*, Moscow: Progress.

—— and —— (1955) *On Religion*, Moscow: Foreign Languages Publishing House.

—— and —— (1976) *Collected Works*, 10 vols, London: Lawrence & Wishart.

—— and —— (2002) *The Communist Manifesto*, London: Penguin.

Maslow, A.H. (1970) *Motivation and Personality*, 2nd edn, New York: Harper & Row.

Mason, D. (2000) *Race and Ethnicity in Modern Britain*, 2nd edn, Oxford: Oxford University Press.

Mason, H. and Ramsay, T. (1992) *A Parents' A–Z of Education*, London: Chambers.

Mason, T. (1995) *Passion of the People?: Football in South America*, London: Verso.

Massey, D. (1994) *Space, Place and Gender*, Oxford: Polity.

—— and Allen, J. (1988) *Uneven Re-Development: Cities and Regions in Transition*, London: Hodder & Stoughton.

Masterman, L. (1985) *Teaching About Television*, London: Macmillan.

—— (ed.) (1986) *Television Mythologies*, London: Comedia.

Masters, W. and Johnson, V. (1966) *Human Sexual Response*, London: Churchill.

—— and —— (1970) *Human Sexual Inadequacy*, London: Churchill.

Matza, D. (1969) *Becoming Deviant*, London: Prentice-Hall.

Mayall, B. (2002) *Towards a Sociology for Childhood*, Buckingham: Open University Press.

Mayhew, H. (1949) 'Mayhew's London', in P. Quennell (ed.) *Mayhew's London*, London: Pilot.

Maynard, M. (1990) 'The reshaping of sociology? Trends in the study of gender', *Sociology* 24(2): 269–90.

—— and Purvis, J. (eds) (1994) *Researching Women's Lives*, London: Taylor & Francis.

Mays, J.B. (1954) *Growing up in the City*, Liverpool: University of Liverpool Press.

Mead, M. (1935) *Sex and Temperament in Three Primitive Societies*, London: Routledge & Kegan Paul.

Means, R. and Smith, R. (1994) *Community Care: Policy and Practice*, London: Macmillan.

Mediaweek (2000) *Redtops Look to Stop Singing the Blues*, http://www.mediaweek.co.uk (accessed 19/4/05).

Medved, M. (1992) *Hollywood vs America*, New York: HarperCollins.

Meehan, D. (1983) *Ladies of the Evening: Women Characters on Prime Time TV*, Metuchen, NJ: Scarecrow.

Meetham, K. (2001) *Tourism in a Global Society*, Basingstoke: Palgrave Macmillan.

Meighan, R. (1986 [1981]) *A Sociology of Educating*, 2nd edn, London: Cassell.

——, Shelton, I. and Marks, T. (eds) (1979) *Perspectives on Society*, Sunbury on Thames: Thomas Nelson.

Mendelsohn, H. (1966) *Mass Entertainment*, New Haven, CT: College and University Press.

Mennell, S. (1992) *The Sociology of Food and Eating*, London: Sage.

Mental Health Foundation (MHF) (1993) *Mental Illness: The Fundamental Facts*, London: MHF.

Menzies, G. (2002) *1421: The Year China Discovered the World*, London: Bantam Press.

Merton, R.K. (1938) 'Social structure and anomie', *American Sociological Review* 3: 672–82.

—— (1952) 'Bureaucratic structure and personality', in R.K. Merton, *A Reader in Bureaucracy*, New York: Free Press.

Metcalf, M. and Humphries, A. (eds) (1985) *The Sexuality of Men*, London: Pluto.

Meyer, S. (1981) *The Five Dollar Day*, New York: Albany.

Michels, R. (1959) *Political Parties*, New York: Dover Publications.

Miers, M. (2000) *Gender Issues and Nursing Practices*, Basingstoke: Macmillan Press.

Mies, M. (1986) *Patriarchy and Accumulation on a World Scale*, London: Zed.

Mihill, C. (1995) 'Public enemy number one', *Guardian*, 2 May.

Miles, R. (1982) *Racism and Migrant Labour: A Critical Text*, London: Routledge & Kegan Paul.

—— (1987) 'Recent Marxist theories of nationalism and the issue of racism', *British Journal of Sociology* 38(1): 24–43.

—— (1989) *Racism*, London: Routledge.

—— (1990) 'Racism, ideology and disadvantage', *Social Studies Review* 4 (March): 148–51.

—— (1993) *Racism after 'Race Relations'*, London: Routledge.

—— and Phizacklea, A. (1984) *White Man's Country: Racism in British Politics*, London: Pluto.

Miles, S. (1997) 'How to present your sociological education to the labour market', in Ballard, C. *et al. The Student's Companion to Sociology*, London: Blackwell.

Milgram, S. (1974) *Obedience to Authority*, London: Harper & Row.

Miliband, R. (1969) *The State in Capitalist Society*, London: Weidenfeld & Nicolson.

Mill, J.S. (1985 [1859]) *On Liberty*, Harmondsworth: Penguin.

—— (1985 [1848]) *Principles of Political Economy*, Harmondsworth: Penguin.

Miller, A. (1983) *For Your Own Good: The Roots of Violence in Child-Rearing*, London: Virago.

Miller, H. (1970 [1945]) *The Air-Conditioned Nightmare*, New York: New Directions.

Miller, W. (1991) *Media and Voters*, Oxford: Clarendon.

Miller, W.B. (1958) 'Lower-class culture as a generating milieu of gang delinquency', *Journal of Sociological Issues* 14: 5–19.

Millett, K. (1970) *Sexual Politics*, London: Abacus.

Mills, C.W. (1951) *White Collar: The American Middle Classes*, Oxford: Oxford University Press.

—— (1956) *The Power Elite*, Oxford: Oxford University Press.

—— (1970) *The Sociological Imagination*, Harmondsworth: Penguin.

Milner, D. (1983) *Children and Race Ten Years On*, London: Alan Sutton.

Mingo, J. (1983) *The Official Couch Potato Handbook*, London: Capra Press.

——, Armstrong, R. and Dodge, A. (1985) *The Couch Potato Guide to Life*, Avon Books.

Mintz, S. (1974) *Caribbean Transformation*, Chicago, IL: Aldine.

Mirza, H. (1991) *Young, Female and Black*, London: Routledge.

—— (1997) *Black British Feminism: A Reader*, London: Routledge.

Mitchell, G.D. (1968) *A Hundred Years of Sociology*, London: Duckworth.

Modood, T. (2005) *Multicultural Politics Racism, Ethnicity, and Muslims in Britain*, Minneapolis, Hinn: University of Minnesota Press.

——, Berthoud, R. Lakey, J., Nazroo, J. Smith, P., Virdee, S. and Beishon, P. (1997) *Ethnic Minorities in Britain: Diversity and Disadvantage*, London: Policy Studies Institute.

Mohanty, C., Russo, A. and Lourdes, T. (eds) (1991) *Third World Women and the Politics of 'Feminism'*, Bloomington, IN: Indiana University Press.

Moir, A. and Jessel, D. (1989) *Brain Sex: The Real Difference Between the Sexes*, London: Mandarin.

Moore, M. (2003) *Dude Where's My Country?*, London: Penguin.

Moore, S. (1988) *Investigating Deviance*, London: Unwin Hyman.

—— and Rosenthal, D. (1993) *Sexuality in Adolescence*, London: Routledge.

Morgan, D. (1975) *Social Theory and the Family*, London: Routledge & Kegan Paul.

—— (1981) 'Men, masculinity and the process of sociological enquiry', in H. Roberts (ed.) *Doing Feminist Research*, London: Routledge & Kegan Paul.

—— (1991) *Discovering Men*, London: Routledge.

—— (1992) 'Sociology, society and the family', in T. Lawson, J. Scott, H. Westergaard and J. Williams (eds) *Sociology Reviewed*, London: Collins.

—— (1994a) 'The family', in M. Haralambos (ed.) *Developments in Sociology*, vol. 10, Ormskirk: Causeway.

—— (1994b) 'Theater of war: combat, the military and masculinities', in H. Brod and M. Kaufman (eds) *Theorizing Masculinities*, London: Sage.

—— (1994c), 'Family, Gender and Masculinities' in A. Leira (ed.), *Family Sociology and Social Change*, Oslo: Institution for Social Research.

—— (1998) 'Thinking about family life', *Sociology Review* 7(4).

Morgan, M., Calnan, M. and Manning, N. (1983) *Sociological Approaches to Health and Medicine*, London: Routledge.

Morgan, R. (2002) 'Imprisonment: a brief history, the contemporary scene and likely prospects' in Maguire, M., Morgan, R. and Reiner, R. (eds) *The Oxford Handbook of Criminology*, 3rd edn, Oxford: Oxford University Press.

Morison, M. (1986) *Methods in Sociology*, London: Longman.

Morris, D. (1968) *The Naked Ape*, London: Corgi.

—— (1977) *Manwatching: A Field Guide to Human Behaviour*, London: Jonathan Cape.

Morrison, D. and Tumber, H. (1988) *Journalists at War: The Dynamics of News Reporting During the Falklands Conflict*, London: Sage.

Morrow, V. (1994) 'Responsible children?: aspects of children's work and employment outside school in contemporary UK', in B. Mayall (ed.) *Children's Childhoods: Observed and Experienced*, London: Falmer Press.

Mosca, G. (1939) *The Ruling Class*, New York: McGraw-Hill.

Moxnes, K. (2003) 'Children coping with parental divorce: what helps, what hurts?' in A. Jensen and L. McKee (eds) *Children and the Changing Family: Between Transformation and Negotiation*, London: RoutledgeFalmer.

Muggeridge, M. (1978) *Things Past*, London: Collins.

Mullard, C. (1982) 'Multi-racial education in Britain: from assimiliation to cultural pluralism', in J. Tierney (ed.) *Race, Migration and Schooling*, London: Holt.

Muncie, J. and Sparks, R. (eds) (1991) *Imprisonment: European Perspectives*, Hemel Hempstead: Harvester Wheatsheaf.

Murdock, G. (1990) 'Redrawing the map of the communications industries', in M. Ferguson (ed.) *Public Communication*, London: Sage.

—— and McCron, R. (1979) 'The broadcasting and delinquency debate', *Screen Education* 30: 51.

Murphy, L. and Livingstone, J. (1985) 'Racism and the limits of radical feminism', *Race and Class* 4 (spring): 61–70.

Murray, C. (ed.) (1990) *The Emerging British Underclass*, London: IEA Health & Welfare Unit.

Musgrave, P.W. (1965) *The Sociology of Education*, London: Methuen.

Myrdal, G. (1968) *Asian Drama*, New York: Pantheon.

Nairn, T. (1988) *The Enchanted Glass: Britain and its Monarchy*, London: Hutchinson.

Nakane, C. (1973) *Japanese Society*, Harmondsworth: Penguin.

Nathanson, C.A. (1984) 'Sex differences in mortality', *Annual Review of Sociology* 10: 191–213.

National Association of Citizens' Advice Bureaux (NACAB) (1988) *Homelessness: A National Survey of CAB Clients*, London: NACAB.

National Commission on Education (1993) *Learning to Succeed*, London: HMSO.

National Heritage Select Committee (1993) *Privacy and Media Intrusion*, London: HMSO.

National Society for the Prevention of Cruelty to Children (NSPCC) (1989) *Child Abuse Trends in England and Wales 1983–1987*, London: NSPCC.

National Viewers' and Listeners' Association (NVLA) (1994) *A Culture of Cruelty and Violence*, Colchester: NVLA.

Navarro, V. (1983) 'Radicalism, Marxism and medicine', *International Journal of the Health Services* 13: 179–202.

Nayak, A. (2003) ' "Boyz to Men": masculinities, schooling and labour transitions in de-industrial times', *Educational Review*, 55: 2.

Negrine, R. (1998) 'Media institutions in Europe', in Briggs, A. and Cobley, P. (eds).

Neibuhr, H. (1957) *The Social Sources of Denominationalism*, Cleveland, OH: World Publishing.

Nettle, D. (2003) 'Intelligence and class mobility in the British population', *British Journal of Psychology*, 94: 551–61.

Nettleton, S. (1995) *The Sociology of Health and Illness*, Cambridge: Polity Press.

—— and Watson, J. (eds) (1998) *The Body in Everyday Life*, London: Routledge.

New Earnings Survey 1977 (1977) London: Office For National Statistics.

Newburn, T. (1995) *Crime and Criminal Justice Policy*, London: Longman.

—— and Hagell, A. (1995) 'Violence on screen: just child's play', *Sociology Review*, February: 7–10.

—— and Stanko, E. (eds) (1994a) *Just Boys Doing Business: Men, Masculinities and Crime*, London: Routledge.

—— and Stanko, E.A. (1994b) 'When men are victims: the failure of victimology', in T. Newburn and E.A. Stanko (eds), *Just Boys Doing Business?: Men, Masculinities and Crime*, London: Routledge.

Newson, E. (1994) 'Video violence and the protection of children', Child Development Research Unit, University of Nottingham.

Newton, M. (2002) *Savage Girls and Wild Boys: A History of Feral Children*, London: Faber and Faber.

Nichols, T. (1979) 'Social class: official, sociological and Marxist', in J. Irvine, I. Miles and J. Evans (eds) *Demystifying Social Statistics*, London: Pluto.

Nicholson, L. (ed.) (1990) *Feminism/Postmodernism*, London: Routledge.

—— and Fraser, N. (1990) 'Social criticism without philosophy', in L. Nicholson (ed.) *Feminism/Postmodernism*, London: Routledge.

Nilsen, A.P. (1975) *The Cult of the Apron*.

Nisbet, R.A. (1970) *The Sociological Tradition*, London: Heinemann.

Noble, G. (1975) *Children in Front of the Small Screen*, London: Constable.

Nott, J.C. and Gliddon, G.R. (1854) *Types of Mankind*, Philadelphia, PA.

Oakley, A. (1972) *Sex, Gender and Society*, London: Temple Smith.

—— (1974a) *Housewife*, London: Allen Lane.

—— (1974b) *The Sociology of Housework*, Oxford: Martin Robertson.

—— (1980) *Women Confined: Towards a Sociology of Childbirth*, Oxford: Martin Robertson.

—— (1981) 'Interviewing women: a contradiction in terms', in H. Roberts (ed.) *Doing Feminist Research*, London: Routledge & Kegan Paul.

—— and Oakley, R. (1981) 'Sexism in official statistics', in J. Irvine, I. Miles and J. Evans (eds) *Demystifying Social Statistics*, London: Pluto.

O'Brien, M. (1981) *The Politics of Reproduction*, London: Routledge & Kegan Paul.

The Observer (2002) 'Curse or coincidence? The catalogue of 'Scream' killings', June 9.

O'Donnell, K. (1999) 'Lesbian and gay families: legal perspectives', in G. Jagger and C. Wright (eds) *Changing Family Values*, London: Routledge.

O'Donnell, M. (1993) *New Introductory Reader in Sociology*, London: Nelson.

O'Faolain, J. and Martinez, L. (1979) *Not in God's Image*, London: Virago.

Offe, C. (1985) 'New social movements: challenging the boundaries of institutional politics', *Social Research*, 52(4): 817–68.

OHE (Office of Health Economics) (1995) *Compendium of Health Statistics*, 9th edn, London: OHE.

Oldman, D. (1994) 'Childhood as a mode of production', in B. Mayall (ed.) *Children's Childhoods: Observed and Experienced*, London: Falmer Press.

Oliver, M. (1996) *Understanding Disability*, London: Macmillan.

ONS (Office for National Statistics) (annually) *Social Trends*, London: HMSO.

—— (1998a) *Living in Britain: The Results of the 1996 General Household Survey*, London: The Stationery Office.

—— (1998b) *Informal Carers*, London: The Stationery Office.

—— (1998c) *Labour Market Trends*, September.

—— (2001) *Living in Britain 2001*, http://www.statistics.gov.uk, accessed 27 January 2004.

—— (2003a) *Labour Force Survey*, www.statistics.gov.uk

—— (2003b) *Census 2001*, http://www.statistics.gov.uk (accessed 23 December 2003).

—— (2004) *Social Trends 34*, http://www.statistics.gov.uk (accessed 3 February 2004).

Oppenheim, C. (1993) *Poverty: The Facts*, London: Child Poverty Action Group.

Orwell, G. (1968 [1941]) *The Collected Essays of George Orwell, Volume II: My Country Right or Left*, ed. S. Orwell and I. Angus, London: Secker and Warburg.

Osborne, P. and Segal, L. (1994) 'Gender as performance: an interview with Judith Butler', *Radical Philosophy*, 67, Summer.

Osgerby, B. (1997) *Youth Culture in Post – War Britain*, Oxford.

Osheron, S.D. and Amara Singham, L.R. (1981) 'The machine metaphor in medicine', in E.G. Mischler *et al.* (eds) *Social Contexts of Health, Illness and Patient Care*, Cambridge: Cambridge University Press.

O'Sullivan, T., Dutton, B. and Raynor, P. (1994) *Studying the Media: An Introduction*, London: Edward Arnold.

O'Toole, R. (1984) *Religion: Classic Sociological Approaches*, Whitby, Ontario: McGraw-Hill.

Ottoway, A.K.C. (1953) *Education and Society*, London: Routledge & Kegan Paul.

Owen, D. (1991) *Ethnic Minority Women and the Labour Market: Analysis of the 1991 Census*, Centre for Research in Ethnic Relations (CRER), University of Warwick, Equal Opportunities Commission.

Pachman, J. (1981) *The Children's Generation*, Oxford: Blackwell.

Pahl, J. (1989) *Money and Marriage*, London: Macmillan.

Pahl, R.E. (1984) *Divisions of Labour*, Oxford: Blackwell.

—— (ed.) (1988) *On Work*, Oxford; Blackwell.

—— and Wallace, C. (1988) 'Neither angels in marble nor rebels in red: privatization and working-class consciousness', in D. Rose (ed.) *Social Stratification and Economic Change*, London: Hutchinson.

Pakulski, J. and Waters, M. (1996) *The Death of Class*, London: Sage.

Pareto, V.F.D. (1935) *The Mind and Society*, 4 vols, London: Jonathan Cape. Also in P. Bachrach (1967) *The Theory of Democratic Elitism*, Boston, MA: Little, Brown.

Park, R. (1952) *Human Communities: The City and Human Ecology*, New York: Free Press.

Park, R.E., Burgess, E. and Mackenzie, R. (1923) *The City*, Chicago, IL: University of Chicago Press.

Parker-Jenkins, M., Haw, K. and Khan, S. (1997) 'Trying twice as hard to succeed: Perceptions of Muslim women in Britain', *Times Education Supplement*, 24 October.

Parkin, F. (1972) *Class, Inequality and Political Order*, London: Paladin.

Parry, G., Moyser, G. and Day, N. (1989) *Participation and Democracy: Political Activity and Attitudes in Contemporary Britain*, Cambridge: Cambridge University Press.

Parsons, T. (1951) *The Social System*, London: Routledge & Kegan Paul.

—— (1954) 'The kinship system of the contemporary United States', in T. Parsons, *Essays in Sociological Theory*, New York: Free Press.

—— (1959) 'The school class as a social system: some of its functions in American society', *Harvard Educational Review* 29. Also in A.H. Halsey, J. Floud and C.A. Anderson (eds) (1961) *Education, Economy and Society*, New York: Free Press.

—— (1966) *Societies: Evolutionary and Comparative Perspectives*, London: Prentice-Hall.

—— (1971) 'Belief, unbelief and disbelief', in R. Caporale and A. Grumelli (eds) *The Culture of Unbelief*, Berkeley, CA: University of California Press.

—— and Bales, R.F. (1955) *Family, Socialization and Interaction Process*, New York: Free Press.

Parton, N. (1985) *The Politics of Child Abuse*, London: Macmillan.

Partington, G. (1982) Article in *Police*, August.

—— (1986) 'History: re-written to ideological fashion', in D. O'Keeffe (ed.) *The Wayward Curriculum: A Cause for Parents' Concern?*, London: Social Affairs Unit.

Pascall, G. (1995) 'Women on top? Women's careers in the 1990s', *Sociology Review*, February: 2–6.

—— and Cox, P. (1993) 'Education and domesticity', *Gender and Education* 5(1).

Pateman, C. (1987) 'Feminist critiques of the public/private dichotomy', in A. Phillips (ed.) *Feminism and Equality*, Oxford: Blackwell.

Pawson, R. (1989) 'Methodology', in M. Haralambos (ed.) *Developments in Sociology*, vol. 5, Ormskirk: Causeway.

Payne, G. (2000) *Social Divisions*, St Martin's Press.

—— *Social Divisions*, New York: St Martin's Press.

Peach, C. (1972) *West Indian Migration to Britain*, Oxford: Institute of Race Relations.

Peacock (1986) *Report of the Committee on Financing the BBC*, London: HMSO.

Peake, S. and Fisher, P. (eds) (1998) *The Media Guide*, London: Fourth Estate.

Pearson, G. (1983) *Hooligan: A History of Respectable Fears*, London: Macmillan.

Pearson, J. (1972) *The Profession of Violence: The Rise and Fall of the Kray Twins*, London: Weidenfeld & Nicolson.

Pearson, M. (1986) 'Racist notions of ethnicity and culture in health education', in S. Rodmell and A. Watt (eds) *The Politics of Health Education*, London: Routledge & Kegan Paul.

Pelling, H. (1992) *A History of British Trade Unionism*, 5th edn, Basingstoke: Macmillan.

Penelope, J. (1986) 'The lesbian perspective', in J. Allen (ed.) *Lesbian Philosophy: Explorations*, Palo Alto, CA: Institute of Lesbian Studies.

Persell, C.H. (1990) *Understanding Society: An Introduction to Sociology*, 3rd edn, New York: Harper & Row.

Petchesky, R. (1985) *Abortion and Woman's Choice*, New York: Northeastern University Press.

Peters, T.J. and Austin, N. (1985) *A Passion for Excellence*, New York: Random House.

—— and Waterman, R.H. (1982) *In Search of Excellence: Lessons from America's Best Run Companies*, New York: Harper & Row.

Phillips, A. (1987) *Divided Loyalties: Dilemmas of Sex and Class*, London: Virago.

—— (1993) *The Trouble with Boys*, London: Pandora.

—— and Taylor, B. (1980) 'Sex and skill: notes toward a feminist economics', *Feminist Review* 6: 79–83.

Phillips B. and Bowling C (2002) *Race, Crime and Justice*, Harlow: Longman.

Philips, D. (1986) *What Price Equality? Report on the Allocation of GLC Housing in Tower Hamlets*, London: Greater London Council.

Phillipson, C. (1998) *Reconstructing Old Age: New Agendas in Social Theory and Practice*, London: Sage.

Phizacklea, A. (1994), 'A single or segregated market? gendered and racialised divisions', in H. Afshar and M. Maynard (eds), *The Dynamics of 'Race' and Gender*, London: Taylor & Francis.

Phoenix, A. (1991) 'Mothers under twenty: outsider and insider views', in A. Phoenix, A. Woollett and E. Lloyd (eds) *Motherhood: Meanings, Practices and Ideologies*, London: Sage.

Pilcher, J. (1995) *Age and Generation in Modern Britain*, Oxford: Oxford University Press.

——, Williams, J. and Pole, C. (2003) 'Rethinking adulthood: families, transitions and social change', *Sociological Research Online*, 8(4) http://www.socresonline.org.uk/8/4/pilcher.html

Pilger, J. (1994) 'Death for sale', *Guardian*, 12 November.

—— (1997) *Breaking the Mirror*, Central Television.

Pilkington (1962) *Report of the Committee on Broadcasting*, London: HMSO.

Pines, M. (1981) 'The civilising of Genie', *Psychology Today* 15.

Piore, M. (1973) 'On the technological foundation dualism', MIT Working Paper 112a, Manchester, May.

—— and Sabel, C. (1984) *The Second Industrial Divide*, New York: Basic Books.

Plint, T. (1851) *Crime in England: Its Relation, Character and Extent, as Developed from 1801 to 1848*, London: Charles Gilpin.

Plowden (1967) *Children and their Primary Schools*, London: HMSO.

Plummer, K. (1978) 'Men in love: observations on male homosexual couples', in M. Corbin (ed.) *The Couple*, Harmondsworth: Penguin.

Policy Studies Institute (PSI) (1983) *The Police and People in London*, London: PSI.

—— (1994) *Ethnic Minorities and Higher Education: Why are There Different Rates of Entry?*, London: PSI.

Polity (1994) *Polity Reader in Gender Studies*, Cambridge: Polity.

Pollard, C. (1998) 'Keeping the Queen's peace', *Criminal Justice Matters* 31: 14–16.

Pollert, A. (1981) *Girls, Wives, Factory Lives*, London: Macmillan.

—— (1988a) 'The flexible firm: fact or fiction?', *Work, Employment and Society* 2(3): 281–316.

—— (1988b) 'Dismantling flexibility', *Capital and Class* 34: 42–75.

Pollock, L. (1983) *Forgotten Children: Parent–Child Relations 1500–1900*, Cambridge: Cambridge University Press.

Popham, P. (1992) 'Throwing away the key', *Independent Magazine*, 17 October.

Popper, K. (1961) *The Poverty of Historicism*, London: Routledge.

Population Estimates Unit (1997) *Children's Day Care Facilities at 31 March, England*, London: Department of Health, Office for National Statistics.

Postman, N. (1987) *Amusing Ourselves to Death*, London: Methuen.

Potter, D. (1994) 'The present tense', interview, *New Left Review*, I/205: 131–40.

Potter, R.B. and Lloyd-Evans, A. (1998) *The City in the Developing World*, Harlow: Pearson Education.

Poulantzas, N. (1973) 'The problems of the capitalist state', in J. Urry and J. Wakeford (eds) *Power in Britain*, London: Heinemann.

—— (1979) *Class in Contemporary Capitalism*, London: New Left Books.

Powell, E. (1981) Speech to Thurrock Conservative Association, 30 October, reported *Guardian*, 9 November.

Propp, V. (1968) *Morphology of Folk Tales*, Austin, TX: University of Texas Press.

Pryke, S. (1998) 'Nationalism and sexuality: what are the issues?', *Nations and Nationalism* 4:4: 529–46.

Pugh, A. (1990) 'My statistics and feminism: a true story', in L. Stanley (ed.) *Feminist Praxis*, London: Routledge.

Punch, S. (2001a) 'Negotiating autonomy: childhoods in rural Bolivia', in L. Alanen and B. Mayall (eds) *Conceptualising Child–Adult Relations*, London: Routledge Falmer.

—— (2001b) 'Household division of labour: generation, gender, age, birth order and sibling composition', *Work, Employment & Society*, 15(4): 803–23.

—— (2002a) 'Youth transitions and interdependent adult–child relations in rural Bolivia', *Journal of Rural Studies*, 18(2): 123–33.

—— (2002b) 'Research with children: the same or different from research with adults?' *Childhood*, 9(3): 321–41.

Qvortrup, J. (1994) 'Introduction', in J. Qvortrup, M. Bardy, G. Sgritta and H. Wintersberger (eds) *Childhood Matters: Social Theory, Practice and Politics*, Aldershot: Avebury.

Radcliffe-Brown, A.R. (1952) *Structure and Function in Primitive Society*, London: Cohen & West.

Radford, G., Hester, R. and Kelly, L. (eds) (1995) *Women, Violence and Male Power: Feminist Activism, Research and Practice*, Milton Keynes: Open University Press.

Radical Statistics Health Group (RSHG) (1987) *Facing the Figures: What Really is Happening to the National Health Service?*, London: RSHG.

Radway, J. (1984) *Reading the Romance: Women, Patriarchy and Popular Literature*, Chapel Hill, NC: University of North Carolina Press.

Radzinowicz, L. and King, J. (1977) *The Growth of Crime*, London: Hamish Hamilton.

Ramazanoglu, C. (1991a) 'Feminist epistemology and research', in J. Gubbay (ed.) *Teaching Methods of Social Research*, report of a City conference, City University, London, November.

—— (1991b) 'Gender', in M. Haralambos (ed.) *Developments in Sociology*, Ormskirk: Causeway.

—— (1993) *Up Against Foucault: Explorations of Some Tensions Between Foucault and Feminism*, London: Routledge.

Ramdin, R. (1987) *The Making of the Black Working Class in Britain*, Aldershot: Gower.

Rampton (1981) *West Indian Children in Our Schools: Report of the Committee of Inquiry into the Education of Children from Ethnic Minority Groups*, London: HMSO.

Redcliffe Maud (1969) *The Report of the Royal Commission on Local Government in England, 1966/69*, London: HMSO, Cmnd 4040.

Reed, J. (2004) Review of Devine (2004) Sociological Research Online vol. 9(4) 30/11/2004.

Reid, I. (1978) *Sociological Perspectives on School and Education*, Shepton Mallet: Open Books.

—— (1989) *Social Class Differences in Britain*, 3rd edn, London: Fontana.

—— (1998) *Class in Britain*, Cambridge: Polity Press.

Reiner, R. (1992) *The Politics of the Police*, 2nd edn, London: Harvester Wheatsheaf.

Reinharz, S. (1993) 'The principles of feminist research: a matter of debate', in C. Kramarae and D. Spender (eds) *The Knowledge Explosion: Generations of Feminist Scholarship*, Hemel Hempstead: Harvester Wheatsheaf.

Reith, J. (1924) *Broadcast Over Britain*, London: Hodder & Stoughton.

Renan, E. (1990) 'What is the nation?' in H. Bhabha, *Nation as Narration*, London: Routledge (originally published in 1882).

Rex, J. (1970) *Race Relations in Sociological Theory*, London: Weidenfeld & Nicolson.

—— (1973) *Race, Colonialism and the City*, London: Routledge & Kegan Paul.

—— and Mason, D. (eds) (1986) *Theories of Race and Ethnic Relations*, Cambridge: Cambridge University Press.

—— and Moore, R. (1967) *Race, Community and Conflict: A Study of Sparkbrook*, Oxford: Oxford University Press.

—— and Tomlinson, S. (1979) *Colonial Immigrants in a British City: A Class Analysis*, London: Routledge & Kegan Paul.

Rey, P.P. (1976) *Las Avanzas de Classes*, Mexico: Giglo.

Reynolds, P. (1991) *Dance Civet Cat: Child Labour in the Zambezi Valley*, Athens, CH: Ohio University Press.

Ribbens McCarthy, J., Edwards, R. and Gillies, V. (2003) *Making Families: Moral Tales of Parenting and Step-Parenting*, Durham: Sociology Press.

Rich, A. (1977) *Of Woman Born: Motherhood as Experience and Institution*, London: Virago.

—— (1980) 'Compulsory heterosexuality and lesbian existence', *Signs*, 5, Summer, 631–60.

Rich, P.B. (1986) *Race and Empire in British Politics*, Cambridge: Cambridge University Press.

Richardson, D. and Robinson, V. (1993) *Introducing Women's Studies: Feminist Theory and Practice*, London: Macmillan.

Richardson, J. and Lambert, J. (1985) *The Sociology of Race*, Ormskirk: Causeway.

Richardson, R. (1989) *Death, Dissection and the Destitute*, Harmondsworth: Penguin.

Riessman, F. (1962) *The Culturally Deprived Child*, New York: Harper & Row.

Rifkin, J. (2001) *The Age of Access*, New York: Putnam.

Riley, M. (1988) *Power, Politics and Voting Behaviour: An Introduction to the Sociology of Politics*, Hemel Hampstead: Harvester Wheatsheaf.

Ritzer, G. (2003) *Sociological Theory*, 6th edn, New York: McGraw-Hill.

—— (1993) The McDonaldization of Society, London: Sage.

—— (2004) *The McDonaldization of Society*, 3rd edn, Thousand Oaks: California.

Robbins (1963) *Higher Education: Report*, Cmnd 2154, London: HMSO.

Roberts, I., DiGuiseppi, C. and Ward, H. (1998) 'Childhood injuries: extent of the problem, epidemiological trends, and costs', *Injury Prevention* 4 (Supplement): s10–16.

Roberts, K. (2001) *Class in Modern Britain*, London: Palgrave Macmillan.

——, Cook, F.G., Clark, S.C. and Sememeoff, E. (1977) *The Fragmentary Class Structure*, London: Heinemann.

Roberts, R.H. (ed.) (1995) *Religion and the Transformations of Capitalism: Comparative Approaches*, London: Routledge.

Robertson, G. (1998) *The Justice Game*, London: Chatto & Windus.

—— and Nicol, A. (1992) *Media Law: The Rights of Journalists*, Harmondsworth: Penguin.

Robertson, R. (1970) *The Sociological Interpretation of Religion*, Oxford: Blackwell.

Robins, K. and Webster, F. (1986) 'Today's television and tomorrow's world', in L. Masterman (ed.) *Television Mythologies*, London: Comedia.

Robinson, C.J. (1983) *Black Marxism*, London: Zed.

Robinson, M., Butler, I., Scanlan, L., Douglas, G. and Murch, M. (2003) 'Children's experience of their parents' divorce', in A. Jensen and L. McKee (eds) *Children and the Changing Family: Between Transformation and Negotiation*, London: RoutledgeFalmer.

Roche, M. (1995) 'Recent European and American conceptions of democracy and politics and the public sphere' in S. Edgell, S. Walklate and G. Williams (eds) *Debating the Future of the Public Sphere*, Avebury.

Roiphe, K. (1994) *The Morning After: Sex, Fear and Feminism*, London: Hamish Hamilton.

Roman, L.G. (1993) 'White is a color! White defensiveness, postmodernism, and anti-racist pedagogy', in C. McCarthy and W. Crichlow (eds) *Race, Identity, and Representation in Education*, New York: Routledge.

Roper, M. and Tosh, J. (1991) *Manful Assertions*, London: Routledge.

Rose, D. (ed.) (1988) *Social Stratification and Economic Change*, London: Hutchinson.

—— and Gershuny, J. (1995) 'Social surveys and social change', *Sociology Review* 4(4): 11–14.

—— and O'Reilly, K. (eds) (1997) *Constructing Classes*. Swindon: ESRC/ONS.

Rose, E.J.B. (1969) *Colour and Citizenship*, Oxford: Institute of Race Relations/Oxford University Press.

Rosenau, J. (1990) *Turbulence in World Politics*, Hemel Hempstead: Harvester Wheatsheaf.

Rosenthal, R. and Jacobson, L. (1968) *Pygmalion in the Classroom*, New York: Holt, Rinehart & Winston.

Rostow, W.W. (1960) *The Stages of Economic Growth: A Non-Communist Manifesto*, Cambridge: Cambridge University Press.

Rotter, J.B. (1966) 'Generalised expectancies for internal versus external control of reinforcement', *Psychological Monographs* 80(1).

Rousseau, J.J. (1965 [1754]) 'A dissertation on the origin and foundation of the inequality of mankind', in T.B. Bottomore, *Classes in Modern Society*, London: Allen & Unwin.

—— (1968 [1762]) *The Social Contract*, trans. M. Cranston, Harmondsworth: Penguin.

Rowbotham, S. (1982) 'The trouble with patriarchy', in M. Evans (ed.) *The Women Question*, London: Fontana.

Rowntree Foundation (1995) *Income and Wealth*, York.

Rowntree, B.S. (1901) *Poverty: A Study of Town Life*, London: Macmillan.

Roy, D. (1954) 'Efficiency and the fix', *American Journal of Sociology* 60: 255–66.

Rubin, G. (1993) 'Misguided, dangerous and wrong: an analysis of anti-pornography of politics', in A. Assiter and C. Avendon (eds) *Bad Girls and Dirty Pictures*, London: Pluto.

Runciman, W.G. (1990) 'How many classes are there in contemporary society?', *Sociology* 24: 377–96.

Rusche, G. (1980 [1933]) 'Labour market and penal sanctions: thoughts on the sociology of punishment', in T. Platt and P. Takagi (eds) *Punishment and Penal Discipline*, Berkeley, CA: University of California Press.

—— and Kirchheimer, O. (1968 [1939]) *Punishment and Social Structure*, New York.

Russell, D. (1990) *Rape in Marriage*, 2nd edn, Indiana: Indiana University Press.

Rutherford, J. (1990) 'A place called home: identity and the cultural politics of difference', in J. Rutherford (ed.) *Identity: Community, Culture, Difference*, London: Routledge.

Rutter, M., Maughan, B., Mortimore, P. and Ouston, J. (1979) *Fifteen Hundred Hours: Secondary Schools and their Effects on Children*, Shepton Mallet: Open Books.

Sabel, C. (1982) *Work and Politics*, Cambridge: Cambridge University Press.

Saggar, S. (1992) *Race and Politics in Britain*, Hemel Hempstead: Harvester Wheatsheaf.

—— (1997) 'Racial politics', *Parliamentary Affairs*, 50.

Saks, M. (1994) 'The alternatives to medicine' in J. Gabe, D. Kelleher and G. Williams (eds) *Challenging Medicine*, London: Routledge.

Salvage, J. (1985) *The Politics of Nursing*, London: Heinemann Nursing.

—— (1987) *Nurses, Gender and Sexuality*, London: Heinemann Nursing.

Sampson, E.E. (1993) *Celebrating the Other: A Dialogic Account of Human Nature*, Hemel Hempstead: Harvester Wheatsheaf.

Samuel, R. (1982) 'The SDP and the new political class', *New Society*, 22 April.

Saporiti, A. (1994) 'A methodology for making children count', in J. Qvortrup, M. Bardy, G. Sgritta and H. Wintersberger (eds) *Childhood Matters: Social Theory, Practice and Politics*, Aldershot: Avebury.

Saraga, E. (1993) 'The abuse of children' in R. Dallos and E. McLaughlin (eds) *Social Problems and the Family*, London: Sage.

Sarre, P., Philps, D. and Skellington, R. (1989) *Ethnic Minority Housing: Explanations and Policies*, Aldershot: Avebury.

Saunders, P. (1987) *Social Theory and the Urban Question*, London: Unwin Hyman.

—— (1997) 'Social Mobility in Britain: An Empirical Evaluation of Two Competing Explanations', *Sociology*, 31: 261–88.

—— (2002) 'Reflections on the meritocracy debate in Britain: a response to Richard Breen and John Goldthorpe' *British Journal of Sociology* 53, 559–74.

—— and Harris, C. (1994) *Privatization and Popular Capitalism*, Milton Keynes: OUP.

Savage, M., Barlow, J., Dickens, A. and Fielding, T. (1992) *Property, Bureaucracy and Culture: Middle Class Formation in Contemporary Britain*, London: Routledge.

—— and Egerton, M. (1997) 'Social mobility, individual ability and the inheritance of class inequality', *Sociology*, 31: 645–72.

Sayer, A. and Walker, R. (1992) *The New Social Economy*, Oxford: Blackwell.

Scambler, G. and Hopkins, A. (1986) 'Being epileptic: coming to terms with stigma', *Sociology of Health and Illness* 8: 26–43.

Scannell, P. and Cardiff, D. (1987) 'Broadcasting and national unity', in J. Curran, A. Smith and P. Wingate (eds) *Impacts and Influences: Essays on Media Power in the 20th Century*, London: Methuen.

—— and —— (1991) *A Social History of Broadcasting, Volume 1 1922–39*, Oxford: Blackwell.

Scarman (1982) *The Brixton Disorders 10–12 April 1981: Report of an Enquiry by the Rt Hon. Lord Scarman OBE*, Cmnd 8427, London: HMSO.

Scase, R. (1992) *Class*, Milton Keynes: Open University Press.

Schattschneider, E.E. (1969) *The Semi-Sovereign People*, New York: Holt, Rinehart & Winston.

Schiller, H. (1989) *Culture, Inc.: The Corporate Takeover of Public Expression*, Oxford: Oxford University Press.

—— (1993) *Mass Communication and the American Empire*, Boulder: Westview Press.

Schlosser, E. (2002) *Fast Food Nation*, London: Penguin Books.

Scholes, R.J. (1999) 'The "mail-order bride" industry and its impact on US immigration', Appendix Q, INS (Immigration and Naturalization Service) (available at www.ins.usdoj.gov/graphics/aboutins/repsstudies/mobappa.htm).

Schramm, W., Lyle, V. and Parker, E. (1961) *Television in the Lives of our Children*, Stanford, CA: Stanford University Press.

Schudson, M. (1991) 'The sociology of news revisited', in J. Curran and M. Gurevitch (eds) *Mass Media and Society*, London: Edward Arnold.

Schulze, L. (1990) 'On the muscle', in J. Gaines and C. Herzog (eds) *Fabrications: Costume and the Female Body*, London: Routledge.

Schuman, H., Steel, C. and Bobo, L. (1985) *Racial Attitudes in America: Trends and Interpretation*, Cambridge, MA: Harvard University Press.

Schumpeter, J.A. (1976) *Capitalism, Socialism and Democracy*, 5th edn, London: Allen & Unwin.

Scott, A. (1990) *Ideology and the New Social Movement*, London: Unwin Hyman.

Scott, J. (1991) *Who Rules Britain?*, Cambridge: Polity.

—— (1992) *The Upper Classes: Property and Privilege in Britain*, London: Macmillan.

—— (1994) *Poverty and Wealth: Citizenship, Deprivation and Privilege*, London: Longman.

—— (1997) *Corporate Business and Capitalist Classes*, Oxford: Oxford University Press.

Scully, D. (1990) *Understanding Sexual Violence: A Study of Convicted Rapists*, London: Unwin/Hyman.

Seacole, M. (1984[1857]) *The Wonderful Adventures of Mary Seacole in Many Lands*, ed. Z. Alexander and A. Dewjee, New York: Falling Wall Press.

Seager, A. (2004) 'Women close the pay gap', *Guardian* 29.10.04.

Seaton, J. and Pimlott, B. (1987) *The Media in British Politics*, Aldershot: Avebury.

Segal, L. (1994) *Straight Sex: The Politics of Pleasure*, London: Virago.

Seidler, V. (1989) *Rediscovering Masculinity*, London: Routledge.

—— (ed.) (1991) *Men, Sex and Relationships*, London: Routledge.

—— (1994) *Recovering the Self: Morality and Social Theory*, London: Routledge.

Seymour-Ure, C. (1992) *The British Press and Broadcasting since 1945*, Oxford: Blackwell.

Shakespeare, T. (ed.) (1998) *The Disability Reader: Social Science Perspectives*, London: Cassell.

Sharma, U. (1996) 'Using complementary therapies: a challenge to orthodox medicine?' in S. Williams and M. Calnan (eds) *Modern Medicine: Lay Perspectives and Experiences*, London: UCL Press.

Sharpe, S. (1994a [1976]) *Just Like a Girl*, 2nd edn, Harmondsworth: Penguin.

—— (1994b) 'Great expectations', *Everywoman* December.

Shaw, M. (1995) *The Global State and the Politics of Intervention*, London: Centre for Study of Global Governance.

Shawcross, W. (1992) *Murdoch by Shawcross*, London: Chatto & Windus.

Sheeran, Y. (1993) 'The role of women and family structure', *Sociology Review*, April.

Sheppard, D. (1983) *Bias to the Poor*, London: Hodder & Stoughton.

SHIL (Single Homeless in London) and LHU (London Housing Unit) (1989) *Local Authority Policy and Practice on Single Homelessness Among Black and Other Ethnic Minority People*, London: SHIL/LHU.

Shilling, C. (1993) *The Body and Social Theory*, London: Sage.

Shils, E. (1959) 'Mass society and its culture', in N. Jacobs (ed.) *Culture for the Millions? Mass Media in Modern Society*, London: Van Nostrand.

—— and Young, M. (1956) 'The meaning of the coronation', *Sociological Review* 1(2): 63–81.

Showalter, E. (1987) *Female Malady: Women, Madness and English Culture 1830–1980*, London: Virago.

Siltanen, J. and Stansworth, M. (eds) (1984) *Women in the Public Sphere: A Critique of Sociology and Race*, London: Hutchinson.

Silva, E. and Smart, C. (eds) (1999) *The New Family?*, London: Sage.

Simmel, G. (1955) *Conflict and the Web of Group Affiliations*, Glencoe, IL: The Free Press.

Simpson, A. (1981) *Stacking the Decks: A Study of Race, Inequality and Council Housing in Nottingham*, Nottingham Community Relations Council.

Simpson, E.S. (1994) *The Developing World: An Introduction*, 2nd edn, London: Longman.

Sinclair, J. (1974 [1791–9]) *Statistical Account of Scotland drawn up from the Communications of Ministers of the different Parishes*, 21 vols, Edinburgh: William Creech/Witherington & Grant, E.P. Publishing.

Sinclair, M.T. (1991) 'Work, women and skill: economic theories and feminist perspectives', in N. Redclift and M.T. Sinclair (eds) *Working Women: International Perspectives on Labour and gender Ideology*, London: Routledge.

Singh-Raud, H. (1997) 'Educating Sita: the education of British Asian girls', *Times Educational Supplement*, 24 October.

—— (1998) Asian women undergranduates in British universities and the dangers of creedism', *Times Educational Supplement*, 30 October.

Sivanandan, A. (1982) *A Different Hunger: Writings on Black Resistance*, London: Pluto.

—— (1990) *Communities of Resistance*, London: Verso.

Skeggs, B. (1997) *Formations of Class and Gender*, London: Sage.

—— (2003) *Class, Self and Culture*, London: Routledge.

Skellington, R. (1992) *'Race' in Britain Today*, London: Sage.

Sklair, L. (1991) *Sociology and the Global Process*, Hemel Hempstead: Harvester Wheatsheaf.

—— (2001) *The Transnational Capitalist Class*, Oxford; Blackwell.

Skolnick, R. (1969) *The Politics of Protest*, New York: Simon & Schuster.

Skuse, D. (1984) 'Extreme deprivation in early childhood', *Journal of Child Psychology and Psychiatry* 25(4).

Smaje, C. (1995) *Health, Race and Ethnicity: Making Sense of the Evidence*, London: King's Fund Institute.

Smart, C., Neale, B., and Wade, A. (2001) *The Changing Experience of Childhood: Families and Divorce*, Cambridge: Polity.

Smart, N. (1978) *The Phenomenon of Religion*, Oxford: Mowbray.

Smith, A. (1964 [1776]) *An Inquiry in the Nature and Causes of the Wealth of Nations*, vol. II, ed. E. Cannon, London: Methuen.

—— (1991) 'Towards a global culture?' in M. Featherstone (ed.) (1990) *Global Culture: Nationalism, Globalisation and Modernity*, London: Sage.

—— (1999) *Which Equalities Matter?* Polity Press.

Smith, A.D. (1971) *Theories of Nationalism*, London: Duckworth.

—— (1986) *The Ethnic Origin of Nations*, London: Blackwell.

—— (1991) *National Identity*, Harmondsworth: Penguin.

—— (1995) 'The dark side of nationalism: the revival of nationalism in late twentieth-century Europe', in L. Cheles (ed.) *The Far Right in Western and Eastern Europe*, London: Longman.

—— (1998) *Nationalism and Modernism: A Critical Survey of Recent Theories of Nations and Nationalism*, London: Routledge.

Smith, A.M. (1994) *New Right Discourse On Race and Sexuality – Cultural Margins, Britain 1968–1990*, Cambridge: Cambridge University Press.

Smith, B. (1987) *The Everyday World as Problematic: A Feminist Sociology*, Milton Keynes: Open University Press.

Smith, D. (1980) *Overseas Doctors in the National Health Service*, London: Policy Studies Institute.

—— (ed.) (1992) *Understanding the Underclass*, London: Policy Studies Institute.

Smith, D.J. and Gray, J. (1983) *Police and People in London IV: The Police in Action*, London: Policy Studies Institute.

Snow, J. (2004) *Shooting History*, London: Harper Collins.

Snow, L.F. (1974) 'Folk medical beliefs and their implications for care of patients', *Annals of Internal Medicine* 81: 82–96.

Social Affairs Unit (1997) 'The British woman today – a qualitative survey of images in women's magazines', London.

Sokolovsky, J. (ed.) (1990) *The Cultural Context of Aging: Worldwide Perspectives*, New York: Bergin and Garvey.

Solomos, J. (1989) *Race and Racism in Contemporary Britain*, London: Macmillan.

—— and Rackett, T. (1991) 'Policing and urban unrest: problem constitution and policy response', in E. Cashmore and E. McLoughlin (eds) *Out of Order? Policing Black People*, London: Routledge.

Sommerville, J. (1982) *The Rise and Fall of Childhood*, Beverly Hills, CA: Sage.

Sontag, S. (1972) 'The double standard of aging', *Saturday Review of the Society*, 23 September.

de Soto, H. (2000) *The Mystery of Capital*, Harlow: Pearson.

Southern, R.W. (1988) *The Middle Ages*, Harmondsworth: Penguin.

Spencer, C. (1986) *Colin Spencer's Fish Cookbook*, London: Pan.

Spencer, I. (1997) *British Immigration Policy since 1939: The Making of Multinational Britain*, London: Routledge.

Spender, D. (1981) *Men's Studies Modified: The Impact of Feminism on the Academic Disciplines*, Oxford: Pergamon.

—— and Sarah, E. (1980) *Learning to Lose: Sexism and Education*, London: Women's Press.

Sprott, W.J.H. (1954) *The Social Background of Delinquency*, Nottinghan: Nottingham University Press.

Sreberny-Mohammadi (1991) 'The global and the local in international communications', in Curran, J. and Gurevitch, M. (eds) *Mass Media and Society*, London: Edward Arnold.

Stacey, J. (1988) 'Can there be a feminist ethnography?', *Women's Studies International Forum* 11(1): 21–7.

—— (1993) 'Untangling feminist theory', in D. Richardson and V. Robinson (eds) *Introducing Women's Studies*, London: Macmillan.

Stacey, M. (1988) *The Sociology of Health and Healing*, London: Routledge.

Stafford, C. (1995) *The Roads of Chinese Childhood: Learning and Identification in Angang*, Cambridge: Cambridge University Press.

Stanko, E. (1992) 'Wife battering: all in the family', in A. Giddens (ed.) *Human Societies*, Cambridge: Polity.

Stanley, L. (ed.) (1990) *Feminist Praxis: Research, Theory and Epistemology in Feminist Sociology*, London: Routledge.

—— and Wise, S. (1983) *Breaking Out: Feminist Consciousness and Feminist Research*, London: Routledge & Kegan Paul.

—— and —— (1993) *Breaking Out Again: Feminist Ontology and Epistemology*, London: Routledge.

Stanworth, M. (1983) *Gender and Schooling: A Study of Sexual Division in the Classroom*, London: Women's Research and Resources Centre.

—— (1984) 'Women and class analysis: a reply to John Goldthorpe', *Sociology* 18(2): 159–70.

Stark, E. and Flitcraft, A. (1985) 'Women battering, child abuse and social heredity: what is the relationship?', in N. Johnson (ed.) *Marital Violence*, London: Routledge & Kegan Paul.

Statham, J. (1986) *Daughters and Sons: Experiences of Non-Sexist Childraising*, Oxford: Blackwell.

——, Mackinnon, D., Cathcart, H. and Hales, M. (1991) *The Education Fact File: A Handbook of Education Information in the UK*, 2nd edn, London: Hodder & Stoughton.

Stevens, P. and Willis, C. (1979) *Race, Crime and Arrests*, London: HMSO.

Stewart, A., Prandy, K. and Blackburn, R.M. (1980) *Social Stratification and Occupations*, London: Macmillan.

Stewart, J. and Stoker, G. (eds) (1989) *The Future of Local Government*, London: Macmillan.

Stiglit, J. (2002) *Globalization and its Discontents*, New York: W.W. Norton & Co.

Stirk, P.M.R. and Weigall, D. (1995) *An Introduction to Political Ideas*, London: Cassell.

Stolenberg, J. (1990) *Refusing to be a Man*, London: Fontana.

Stone, M. (1981) *The Education of the Black Child in Britain: The Myth of Multiracial Eduction*, London: Fontana.

Strange, S. (1996) *Retreat of the State*, Cambridge: Cambridge University Press.

Stones, R. (2001) 'Mobile phones and the transformation of public space', *Sociology Review*, November, vol. 11, no. 2.

Strauss, A., Fagerhaugh, S., Suczek, B. and Weiner, C. (1997) *Social Organization of Medical Work*, New Brunswick: Transaction Publishers.

Street, J. (1997) ' "Across the universe": the limits of global popular culture', in J. Scott (ed.) *The Limits of Globalization*, London: Routledge.

Strinati, D. (1992) 'Postmodernism and popular culture', *Sociology Review* 1(4): 2–7.

Swann (1985) *Education for All: Report of Committee of Inquiry into the Education of Children from Ethnic Minority Groups*, Cmnd 9453, London: HMSO.

Swingewood, A. (1991) *A Short History of Sociological Thought*, London: Macmillan.

Sydie, R. (1987) *Natural Women, Cultured Men*, Milton Keynes: Open University Press.

Syer, M. (1982) 'Racism, ways of thinking and school', in J. Tierney (ed.) *Race, Migration and Schooling*, London: Holt Education.

Szasz, T. (1961) *The Myth of Mental Illness*, New York: Harper.

Taking Liberties Collective (1989) *Learning the Hard Way: Women's Oppression in Men's Education*, London: Macmillan.

Tanner, D.M. (1978) *The Lesbian Couple*, Lexington, MA: Lexington Books.

Tasker, F. and Golombok, S. (1991) 'Children raised by lesbian mothers: the empirical evidence', *Family Law*: 184–7.

Taylor, F.W. (1967 [1911]) *The Principles of Scientific Management*, New York: W.W. Norton.

Taylor, I., Walton, P. and Young, J. (1973) *The New Criminology*, London: Routledge & Kegan Paul.

——, —— and —— (eds) (1975) *Critical Criminology*, London: Routledge & Kegan Paul.

Taylor, S. (1992) 'Measuring child abuse', *Sociology Review* 1(3): 23–9.

Thane, P. (1982) *The Elderly in Modern Society*, London: Longman.

Thomas, S. (1995) 'Parents' perspectives: towards positive support for disabled children and those experiencing difficulties in learning', in P. Potts, F. Armstrong and M. Masterton (eds) *Equality and Diversity in Education 2: National and International Contexts*, London: Routledge.

Thompson, E.P. (1968) *The Making of the English Working Class*, Harmondsworth: Penguin.

Thompson, H.S. (1967) *Hell's Angels*, Harmondsworth: Penguin.

Thompson, I. (1986) *Religion*, London: Longman.

Thompson, K. and Tunstall, J. (eds) (1971) *Sociological Perspectives*, Harmondsworth: Penguin.

Thompson, M. (1999) *Forging War: The Media in Serbia, Croatia, Bosnia and Hercegovina*, Luton: University of Luton Press.

Thompson, P. (1983) *The Nature of Work*, London: Macmillan.

—— (1989) *The Nature of Work*, 2nd edn, Basingstoke: Macmillan.

—— and McHugh, D. (2003) *Work Organisations* 3rd edn, London: Palgrave Macmillan.

Thorogood, N. (1990) 'Caribbean home remedies and their importance for black women's health care in Britain', in P. Abbott and G. Payne (eds) *New Directions in the Sociology of Health*, Basingstoke: Falmer Press.

Tiefer, L. (1995) *Sex is Not a Natural Act*, Oxford: Westview.

Tierney, J. (1996) *Criminology: Theory and Context*, Harlow: Longman.

Tilly, L. and Scott, J. (1987) *Women, Work and Achievement*, London: Macmillan.

Timperley, C. (1994) 'Bringing home the bacon', *Everywoman* May.

Tinker, A. (1996) *Elderly People in Modern Society*, 4th edn, London: Longman.

Tiratsoo, N., Fielding, S. and Thompson, P. (1995) *"England Arise!": The Labour Party and Popular Politics in 1940s Britain*, Manchester: Manchester University Press.

Tocqueville, de A. (1995) *Democracy in America*, trans. H. Reeve, New York: Amereon House (first published 1838).

Toffler, A. (1970) *Future Shock*, New York: Random House.

—— (1980) *The Third Wave*, London: Collins.

Tomlinson, S. (1983) *Ethnic Minorities in British Schools: A Review of the Literature, 1960–1982*, London: Heinemann.

Tonge, J. (1994) 'The anti-poll tax movement: a pressure movement?', *Politics*, 14(2): 93–9.

Touraine, A. (1971) *The Post-Industrial Society*, New York: Wildwood House.

—— (1985) 'An introduction to the study of social movements', *Social Research* 52(4), Winter.

Townsend, P. (1981) 'The structured dependency of the elderly: creation of social policy in the twentieth century,' *Ageing and Society*, 1: 5–28.

——, Davidson, N. and Whitehead, P. (1988) *Inequalities in Health*, Harmondsworth: Pelican.

Toye, J. (1993) *Dilemmas of Development*, 2nd edn, Oxford: Blackwell.

Toynbee, P. (1983) 'The crime rate', *Guardian*, 10.10.83.

Tran, M. (2003) 'Executive pay', *Guardian*, 28.4.03.

Trenchard, L. and Warren, H. (1984) *Something To Tell You*, London: Gay Teenage Group.

Trigg, R. (1985) *Understanding Social Science*, Oxford: Blackwell.

Troeltsch, E. (1931) *The Social Teaching of the Christian Churches*, London: Allen & Unwin.

Trowler, P. (1988) *Investigating the Media*, London: Collins.

Tuchman, G., Daniels, A. and Benet, J. (1978) *Hearth and Home: Image of Women in the Mass Media*, Oxford: Oxford University Press.

Tumin, M.M. (1967) 'Some principles of stratification: a critical analysis', in R. Bendix and S.M. Lipset (eds) *Class, Status and Power*, 2nd edn, London: Routledge & Kegan Paul.

Tunstall, J. (1962) *The Fishermen*, London: MacGibbon & Kee.

—— (1977) *The Media are American*, London: Constable.

—— and Palmer, M. (eds) (1991) *Media Moguls*, London: Routledge.

Turner B. S. (1997) *The Blackwell Companion to Social Theory*, London: Blackwell.

Turner, E. (1965) *The Young Man's Companion*, London: Hugh Evelyn.

Turner, R. (1961) 'Modes of social ascent through education', in A.H. Halsey, J. Floud and C.A. Anderson (eds) *Education, Economy and Society*, New York: Free Press.

Tutt, N. (1974) *Care or Custody: Community Homes and the Treatment of Delinquency*, London: Dartford Longman & Todd.

Twomey, B. (2002) 'Women in the labour market: results for the spring 2001 LFS', *Labour Market Trends*, 110(3), www.statistics.gov.uk

Udall, A.T. and Sinclair, S. (1982) 'The luxury unemployment thesis: a review of recent evidence', *World Development* 10: 49–62.

UKCC (United Kingdom Central Council for Nursing, Midwifery and Health Visiting) (1986) *Project 2000: A New Preparation for Practice*, London: UKCC.

Unemployment Unit (1995) *Working Brief*, 61, February.

—— (1995) *Working Brief*, 106, September.

UNESCO (1972) *Apartheid*, 2nd edn, Paris: UNESCO.

United Nations (1984) *World Development Report*, Washington, DC: United Nations.

—— (1997) *Human Development Report*, New York: Oxford University Press.

—— (1998) *Human Development Report*, New York: Oxford University Press.

—— (2004) *Human Development Report*, New York: Oxford University Press.

US Bureau of Transportation (2004) *Journal of Transportation and Statistics*, 7:1.

Ussher, J.M. (1997) *Fantasies of Femininity: Reframing the Boundaries of Sex*, London: Penguin.

—— (2000) *Women's Health: Contemporary International Perspectives*, Leicester: The British Psychological Society.

Van Every, J. (1999) 'From modern nuclear family households to postmodern diversity?: the sociological construction of "Families"', in G. Jagger and C. Wright (eds) *Changing Family Values*, London: Routledge.

Van Zoonen, L. (1991) 'Feminist perspectives on the media', in J. Curran and M. Gurevitch (eds) *Mass Media and Society*, London: Edward Arnold.

—— (1994) *Feminist Media Studies*, London: Sage.

Vance, C. (1992) *Pleasure and Danger: Exploring Female Sexuality*, London: Routledge.

de Vaus, D.A. (1986) *Surveys in Social Research*, London: Allen & Unwin.

Veljanovski, C. (1989) *Freedom in Broadcasting*, London: Institute of Economic Affairs.

—— (1991) *The Media in Britain Today*, London: News International.

Victor, C. (1994) *Old Age in Modern Society: A Textbook of Social Gerontology*, 2nd edn, London: Chapman and Hall.

Vincent, J. (2000) 'Age and old age', in G. Payne (ed.) *Social Divisions*, London: Macmillan.

—— (2003) *Old Age*, London: Routledge.

Waddington, D. (1992) *Contemporary Issues in Public Disorder*, London and New York: Routledge.

——, Jones, K. and Critcher, C. (1989) *Flashpoints: Contemporary Issues in Public Disorder*, London: Routledge.

Waddington, P.A.J. (1993) *Calling the Police: The Interpretation of, and Response to, Calls for Assistance from the Public*, Aldershot: Avebury.

Wadsworth, M., Butterfield, W. and Blaney, R. (1971) *Health and Sickness: The Choice of Treatment*, London: Tavistock.

Wagg, S. (1992) 'I blame the parents: childhood and politics in modern Britain', *Sociology Review*, April: 10–15.

Wajcman, J. (1983) *Women in Control*, Milton Keynes: Open University Press.

Waksler, F. (1996) *The Little Trials of Childhood and Children's Strategies for Dealing with Them*, London: Falmer Press.

Walby, S. (1986) *Patriarchy at Work*, Cambridge: Polity.

—— (1990) *Theorizing Patriarchy*, Oxford: Blackwell.

Waldron, I. (1985) 'What do we know about causes of sex differences in mortality? A review of the literature', *Population Bulletin of the United Nations* 18: 59–76.

Walker, A. (1990) 'Blaming the victim', in C. Murray (ed.) *The Emerging British Underclass*, London: IEA Health & Welfare Unit.

——, O'Brien, M. and Traynor, J. (2002) *Living in Britain: Results from the 2001 General Household Survey*, London: TSO.

—— and Walker, C.A. (1987) *The Growing Divide: A Social Audit 1979–87*, London: Child Poverty Action Group.

Walker, N. (1991) *Why Punish?*, Oxford: Oxford University Press.

Wallerstein, E. (1979) *The Capitalist World Economy*, Cambridge: Cambridge University Press.

—— (1983) *Historical Capitalism*, London: Verso.

Wallis, R. (1976) *The Road to Total Freedom: A Sociological Analysis of Scientology*, London: Heinemann.

Walter, N. (1990) *Blasphemy Ancient and Modern*, London: Rationalist Press Association.

Walters, R. (2003) *Deviout Knowledge: Criminology, Politics and Policy*, Cullompton: Willan Publishing.

Ward, C. (1972) *Work*, Harmondsworth: Penguin.

Warnock (1978) *Special Education Needs: Report of the Committee of Enquiry into the Education of Handicapped Children and Young People*, London: HMSO.

Watson, J. (1998) *Golden Arches East: McDonald's in East Asia*, Cambridge: Cambridge University Press.

—— (2000) *Male Bodies: Health, Culture and Identity*, Buckingham: Open University Press.

Webb, C. (1986) *Feminist Practice in Women's Health Care*, Chichester: John Wiley and Sons Ltd.

Weber, E. (1976) *Peasants into Frenchmen*, Stanford, CA: Stanford University Press.

Weber, M. (1949) *The Methodology of the Social Sciences*, New York: Free Press.

—— (1958) *From Max Weber: Essays in Sociology*, trans., ed. and with an introduction by H.H. Gerth and C. Wright Mills, New York: Oxford University Press.

—— (1963 [1920]) *The Sociology of Religion*, Boston, MA: Beacon.

—— (1964 [1922]) *The Theory of Social and Economic Organization*, Oxford: Oxford University Press.

—— (1974 [1902]) *The Protestant Ethic and the Spirit of Capitalism*, London: Unwin.

—— (1991) *The Protestant Ethic and the Spirit of Capitalism*, trans. by T. Parsons; introduction by A. Giddens, London: Harper Collins.

Webster, F. (1995) *Theories of the Information Society*, London: Routledge.

Webster, J. (1996) *Shaping Women's Work: Gender, Employment and Information Technology*, London: Longman.

Weeks, J. (1986) *Sexuality*, London: Tavistock.

—— (1990) *Coming Out*, Aylesbury: Hazell.

—— (1991a) *Between the Acts: Lives of Homosexual Men 1885–1967*, London: Routledge.

—— (1991b) *Against Nature: Essays on History, Sexuality and Identity*, London: Rivers Oram.

—— (2000) *Making Sexual History*, Cambridge: Polity.

Weelock, J. (1990) *Husbands at Home*, London: Routledge.

Weiner, G. (1985) *Just a Bunch of Girls*, Milton Keynes: Open University Press.

Weiss, L. (1990) *Working Class Without Work: High School Students in a De-industrializing Economy*, New York: Routledge.

—— (1998) *State Capacity: Governing the Economy in a Global Era*, Cambridge: Polity.

—— Donovan, C. and Heaphy, B. (1999) 'Everyday experiments: narratives of non-heterosexual relationships', in E. Silva and C. Smart (eds) *The New Family?*, London: Sage.

Welehan, I. (1995) *Modern Feminist Thought: From Second Wave to Post-Feminism*, Edinburgh: Edinburgh University Press.

Wellings, K., Field, J., Johnson, A. and Wadsworth, J. (1994) *Sexual Behaviour in Britain: The National Survey of Sexual Attitudes and Lifestyles of the British Population*, Harmondsworth: Penguin.

Wellman, D. (1977) *Portraits of White Racism*, Cambridge: Cambridge University Press.

Wells, T. (1993) *The World in Your Kitchen*, Oxford: New Internationalist.

Westergaard, J. (1970) 'The rediscovery of the cash nexus', in R. Miliband and J. Saville (eds) *The Socialist Register*, London: Merlin.

—— and Resler, H. (1976) *Class in a Capitalist Society*, Harmondsworth: Penguin.

Westwood, S. (1983) *All Day and Every Day: Factory and Family in the Making of Women's Lives*, London: Pluto.

—— and Bachi, P. (1989) *Enterprising Women: Ethnicity, Economy and Gender*, London: Routledge.

Weymouth, A. and Lamizet, B. (1996) *Markets and Myths: Forces for Change in the European Media*, London: Longman.

Whale, J. (1980) *The Politics of the Media*, London: Fontana.

Whannel, G. and Williams, J. (1993) 'The rise of satellite TV', *Sociology Review* 2(3).

Wheeler, E. and Tan, S.W. (1983) 'Food for equilibrium: the dietary principles and practice of Chinese families in London', in A. Murcott (ed.) *The Sociology of Food*, Aldershot: Gower.

Wheen, F. (1982) 'Having a smashing time', *New Statesman*, 22 October.

Whitaker, B. (1981) *News Ltd*, London: Minority.

Whitehead, S.M. and Barrett, F.J. (eds) (2001), *The Masculinities Reader*, Cambridge: Polity.

Whiteside, N. (1991) *Bad Times*, London: Faber & Faber.

WHO (World Health Organization) (1978) *Report of the International Conference on Primary Health Care, Alma Ata 1978*, Geneva: WHO.

—— (1980) *International Classification of Impairments, Disabilities and Handicaps*, Geneva: WHO.

Wilkinson, R. (1996) *Unhealthy Societies*, London: Routledge.

Wilkinson, S. and Kitzinger, C. (1994) 'Towards a feminist approach to breast cancer', in S. Wilkinson and C. Kitzinger (eds), *Women and Health: Feminist Perspectives*, London: Taylor and Francis.

Williams, G. (1994) *Britain's Media: How They are Related*, London: Campaign for Press and Broadcasting Freedom.

Williams, K., Cutler, T., Williams, J. and Haslam, C. (1987) 'The end of mass production?', *Economy and Society* 16(3): 405–39.

Williams, M. (1986) *Society Today*, London: Macmillan.

Williams, R. (1958) *Culture and Society: 1780–1850*, Harmondsworth: Penguin.

—— (1974) *Television, Technology and Cultural Form*, London: Fontana.

—— (1983) *Towards 2000*, Harmondsworth: Penguin.

Williamson, J. (1978) *Decoding Advertisements*, London: Marion Boyars.

Willis, P. (1977) *Learning to Labour: Why Working-Class Kids Get Working-Class Jobs*, Farnborough: Saxon House.

Willmott, P. (1988) 'Urban kinship past and present', *Social Studies Review*, November: 44–6.

Wilson, A. (1986) 'The family', in P. McNeill and C. Townley (eds) *Fundamentals of Sociology*, Cheltenham: Stanley Thornes.

Wilson, B. (1963) 'A typology of sects in a dynamic and comparative perspective', *Archives de Sociologie de Religion* 16: 49–63.

—— (1969) *Religion in Secular Society*, Harmondsworth: Penguin.

—— (1982) *Religion in Sociological Perspective*, Oxford: Oxford University Press.

—— and Dobbelaere, K. (1994) *A Time to Chant: The Soka Gakkai Buddhists in Britain*, Oxford: Blackwell.

Wilson, C., Letherby, G., Brown, G. and Bailey, N. (2002) 'The baby brigade: teenage mothers and sexuality', *Journal of the Association of Research on Mothering* 4:1.

Wilson, E. (1986) *Adorned in Dreams: Fashion and Modernity*, London: Virago.

—— (1989) *The Myth of British Monarchy*, London: Journeyman.

—— and Rodgerson, G. (1991) *Pornography and Feminism*, London: Lawrence & Wishart.

Wilson, G. (2000) *Understanding Old Age: Critical and Global Perspectives*, London: Sage.

Wilson, M. (1967) 'Nyakyusa age villages' in R. Cohen and J. Middleton (eds) *Comparative Political Systems*, Garden City, [KS]: Natural History Press.

Wilton, T. (1992) *Antibody Politic: AIDS and Society*, Cheltenham: New Clarion Press.

—— (1993) 'Queer subjects: lesbians, heterosexual women and the academy', in M. Kennedy, C. Lubelska and V. Walsh (eds) *Making Connections*, London: Taylor & Francis.

—— (1995) *Lesbian Studies: Setting an Agenda*, London: Routledge.

Winship, J. (1986) *Inside Women's Magazines*, London: Pandora.

Witte, R. (1996) *Racial Violence and the State: A Comparative Analysis of Britain, France, and the Netherlands*, Harlow: Longman.

Wolf, N. (1991) *The Beauty Myth*, London: Vintage.

Wollstonecraft, M. (1982[1792]) *Vindication of the Rights of Woman*, Harmondsworth: Penguin.

Wolpe, H. (1980) 'Capitalism and cheap labour power in South Africa: from segregation to apartheid', in H. Wolpe (ed.) *The Articulation of Modes of Production*, London: Routledge & Kegan Paul.

Wood, S. (ed.) (1982) *The Degradation of Work?*, London: Hutchinson.

—— (ed.) (1989) *The Transformation of Work?*, London: Unwin Hyman.

Woodhead, M. (1999) 'Combating child labour: listen to what the children say', *Childhood*, 6(1): 27–49.

Woodhouse, A. (1989) *Fantastic Women*, London: Macmillan.

Woodward, K. (2003) 'Representations of motherhood' in S. Earle and G. Letherby, *Gender, Identity and Reproduction: Social Perspectives*, Basingstoke: Palgrave Macmillan.

Woolf, R. (1969) 'Beyond tolerance', in R. Woolf, B. Moore and H. Marcuse, *A Critique of Pure Tolerance*, London: Jonathan Cape.

World Bank (2002) *Heavily Indebted Poor Countries (HIPC) Initiative: Status of Implementation*, Vol. 1, Washington: World Bank.

Worsley, P. (1964) *The Third World*, London: Weidenfeld & Nicolson.

—— (1987) *The New Introductory Sociology*, Harmondsworth: Penguin.

—— (ed.) (1991) *The New Modern Sociology Readings*, Harmondsworth: Penguin.

Wrench, J. and Modood, T. (2000) *The Effectiveness of Employment Equality Policies in Relation to Immigrants and Ethnic Minorities in the UK*, ILO Report: http://www.ilo.org.

Wright, C.R. (1960) 'Functional analysis and mass communication revisited', *Public Opinion Quarterly* 24: 606–20.

Wright, E.O. (1985) *Classes*, London: Verso.

Wright, P. (1987) *Spycatcher: The Candid Autobiography of a Senior Intelligence Officer*, New York: Viking.

Wright Mills, C. (1959) *The Sociological Imagination*, London: Oxford University Press.

Wyn, J. and Dwyer, P. (1999) 'New directions in research on youth in transition,' *Journal of Youth Studies*, 2(1): 5–21.

—— and White, R. (1997) *Rethinking Youth*, London: Sage.

Wynne, D. (1990) 'Leisure, lifestyle and the construction of social position', *Leisure Studies* 9: 21–34.

Yaffe, M. and Nelson, E. (1982) *The Influence of Pornography on Behaviour*, London: Academic.

Yinger, J.M. (1946) *Religion in the Struggle for Power*, Durham, NC: Duke University Press.

Young, J. (1992) 'The rising demand for law and order and our Maginot lines of defence against crime', in N. Abercrombie and A. Warde (eds) *Social Change in Contemporary Britain*, Cambridge: Polity.

—— and Mathews, R. (eds) (1992) *Rethinking Criminology: The Realist Debate*, London: Sage.

Young, M. and Willmott, P. (1962 [1957]) *Family and Kinship in East London*, Harmondsworth: Penguin.

—— and —— (1975) *The Symmetrical Family*, Harmondsworth: Penguin.

Young, M.F.D. (ed.) (1971) *Knowledge and Control: New Directions in the Sociology of Education*, London: Collier-Macmillan.

Zakaria, R. (1988) *The Struggle within Islam: The Conflict between Religion and Politics*, Harmondsworth: Penguin.

Zeitlin, M. (1989) *The Large Corporation and Contemporary Classes*, Cambridge: Polity.

Zimbardo, P. (1972) 'Pathology of imprisonment', *Society* 9: 4–8.

Zola, I. (1972) 'Medicine as an instrument of social control', *Sociological Review* 20: 487–504.

—— (1973) 'Pathways to the doctor: from person to patient', *Social Science and Medicine* 7: 677–89.

Zukin, S. (1991) *Landscapes of Power*, Berkeley, CA: University of California Press.

index